The New Encyclopedia of Home Designs

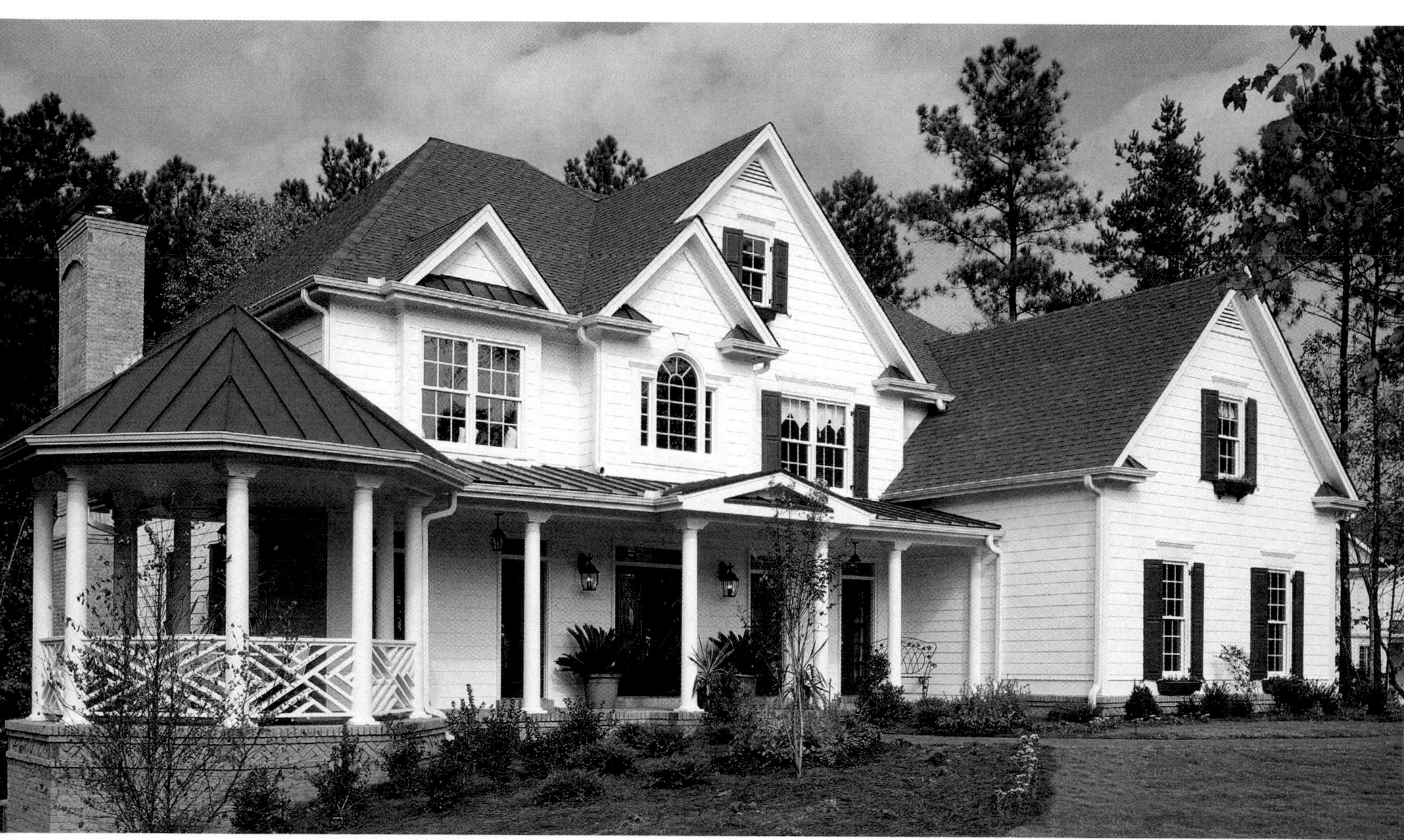

600 House Plans

Published by Hanley Wood
One Thomas Circle, NW, Suite 600
Washington, DC 20005

Distribution Center
29333 Lorie Lane
Wixom, Michigan 48393

The New Encyclopedia of Home Designs

hanley wood

Group Publisher, Andrew Schultz
Associate Publisher, Editorial Development, Jennifer Pearce
Managing Editor, Hannah McCann
Senior Editor, Nate Ewell
Associate Editor, Simon Hyoun
Senior Plan Merchandiser, Nicole Phipps
Plan Merchandiser, Hillary Huff
Proofreader/Copywriter, Dyana Weis
Graphic Artist, Joong Min
Plan Data Team Leader, Susan Jasmin
Production Manager, Brenda McClary

Vice President, Retail Sales, Scott Hill
National Sales Manager, Bruce Holmes
Director, Plan Products, Matt Higgins

Most Hanley Wood titles are available at quantity discounts with bulk purchases for educational, business, or sales promotional use. For information, please contact Bruce Holmes at bholmes@hanleywood.com.

BIG DESIGNS, INC.
President, Creative Director, Anthony D'Elia
Vice President, Business Manager, Megan D'Elia
Vice President, Design Director, Chris Bonavita
Editorial Director, John Roach
Assistant Editor, Carrie Atkinson
Senior Art Director, Stephen Reinfurt
Production Director, David Barbella
Photo Editor, Christine DiVuolo
Art Director, Jacque Young
Graphic Designer, Frank Augugliaro
Graphic Designer, Billy Doremus
Graphic Designer, Tim Vienckowski
Assistant Production Manager, Rich Fuentes

PHOTO CREDITS
Front Cover: Design HPK1700563 on page 480. Photo provided by Frank Betz Associates, Inc.
Back Cover, Top Left: Design HPK1700201 on page 180. Photo by Bob Greenspan.
Back Cover, Bottom Left: Design HPK1700225 on page 199. Photo courtesy of Islands of Beaufort—Beaufort, South Carolina.
Back Cover, Right: Design HPK1700216 on page 191. Photo by Ron & Donna Kolb—Exposure Unlimited.

10 9 8 7 6 5 4 3 2 1

Printed in the United States of America

Library of Congress Control Number: 2005927716

ISBN-13: 978-1-93113-148-3
ISBN-10: 1-931131-48-1

106

contents

hanley wood
Passageway

ONLINE EXTRA

Go to: www.hanleywoodbooks.com/newencyclopedia for access to the Hanley Wood Passageway, your passage to bonus home plans, bonus articles, online ordering, and more!

Features of this site include:

- A dynamic link that lets you search and view bonus home plans
- Online-related feature articles
- Built-in tools to save and view your favorite home plans
- A dynamic web link that allows you to order your home plan online
- Contact details for the Hanley Wood Home Plan Hotline
- Free subscriptions for Hanley Wood Home Plan e-news

Home-Building Reference Guide

How to get the most out of your home plan

Building a home is a complicated process. There's no way to wave a magic wand and make a brand-new home appear—but it doesn't have to be difficult. In fact, armed with the right information, building your new home could be one of the most exciting and rewarding projects you'll ever undertake. Providing that information is the goal of this reference guide.

Turn to this guide for helpful advice on everything from selecting a home plan to working with your builder. We've tried to cover topics that owners and builders have told us are important to them—including ways to make your new home more affordable and efficient, and how to find trustworthy professionals.

What's Not Covered

This book assumes that you already know about the significant cost advantage of building a home from predrawn plans versus an original plan drawn from scratch by an architect. The difference in price is accounted for by the amount of work that the architect must put into an original design—not an unreasonable choice for buyers who have a highly defined sense of aesthetic and want an artist's touch upon every square foot of their new home, or who are interested in progressive building methods. Of course, such attention from an architect will carry a hefty price—typically 10-15% of the value of the home. What most people don't realize, however, is that predrawn plans

Start with a plan—like this 2,400-square-foot colonial, design HPK1700225. See more on page 199.

PHOTO COURTESY OF: WILLIAM E. POOLE DESIGNS, INC. - ISLANDS OF BEAUFORT, BEAUFORT, SC

can be customized after purchase by a hired architect or home designer, which gives you all the benefits of a custom home for much lower cost. We'll talk more in-depth about customizing predrawn plans later in the book.

This guide also assumes that you will be working with a qualified builder who will be with you from the beginning—evaluating your plan and providing an estimate—to the end of the process, ensuring that the home meets building codes and, most importantly, your approval at final walk-through. This book does not provide a how-to for residential construction or for acting as your own contractor.

Will your new home need a full formal dining room? Or is this space better used as a family room?

Assess Your Needs

With so many options available—this book alone contains 600 unique plans!—picking the right one can be a daunting task. How can you best determine what type of home you want? In trying to balance your needs and desires, we've put together a few questions to consider as you begin narrowing your search.

Where will I build my new home? What's the climate of the region? If you're planning on building your new home in a region that typically gets a lot of snow, then choose a plan that is suited to colder climates. A Mediterranean-style house would not be appropriate in Minnesota or Maine. You should consider a design with a steeper-pitched roof, such as a Victorian, Cape Cod, or Colonial. Likewise, if your new home will be built in warmer climates, you may consider a Southern-style home with large, wraparound porches or sunrooms, which can take advantage of the temperate outdoors.

What style homes are prevalent in my new neighborhood? While it's not necessary to have your home replicate all the other homes in your neighborhood, it should seek to complement them. A Pueblo Revival ranch home on the beach in New Jersey would look a bit out of place. Let the homes of your neighbors serve as your guide.

How much time will I spend outdoors? Do I need a porch, patio, or deck? If you and your family love spending time outside—either eating a meal or just visiting with each other—then plan your space accordingly. There are all kinds of options for you to consider when choosing a home plan. Many Mediterranean home plans call for verandas or lanais, and porches are a common feature on farmhouses and Victorian plans.

Do I prefer one or two levels? Does anyone in my family mind climbing stairs? Perhaps climbing stairs doesn't bother you now, but will it in the future? If you're

THE **BIG** STEPS

There are countless little steps in the home-building process, but there are some big ones to get you started. We'll help with advice for each of these stages on the following pages.

FIND A PLAN
Building your dream home begins with finding the right plan for you and your family.

FIND A LOT
In many cases you'll have a lot before you shop for a plan. Either way, as they always tell you in real estate, location is everything.

FIND FINANCING
Home-building financing has some crucial differences from a conventional mortgage, so you should learn as much as you can about the process before you begin.

FIND A BUILDER
The most important player in your home-building adventure, a builder you trust can be the key to success.

MARK SAMU

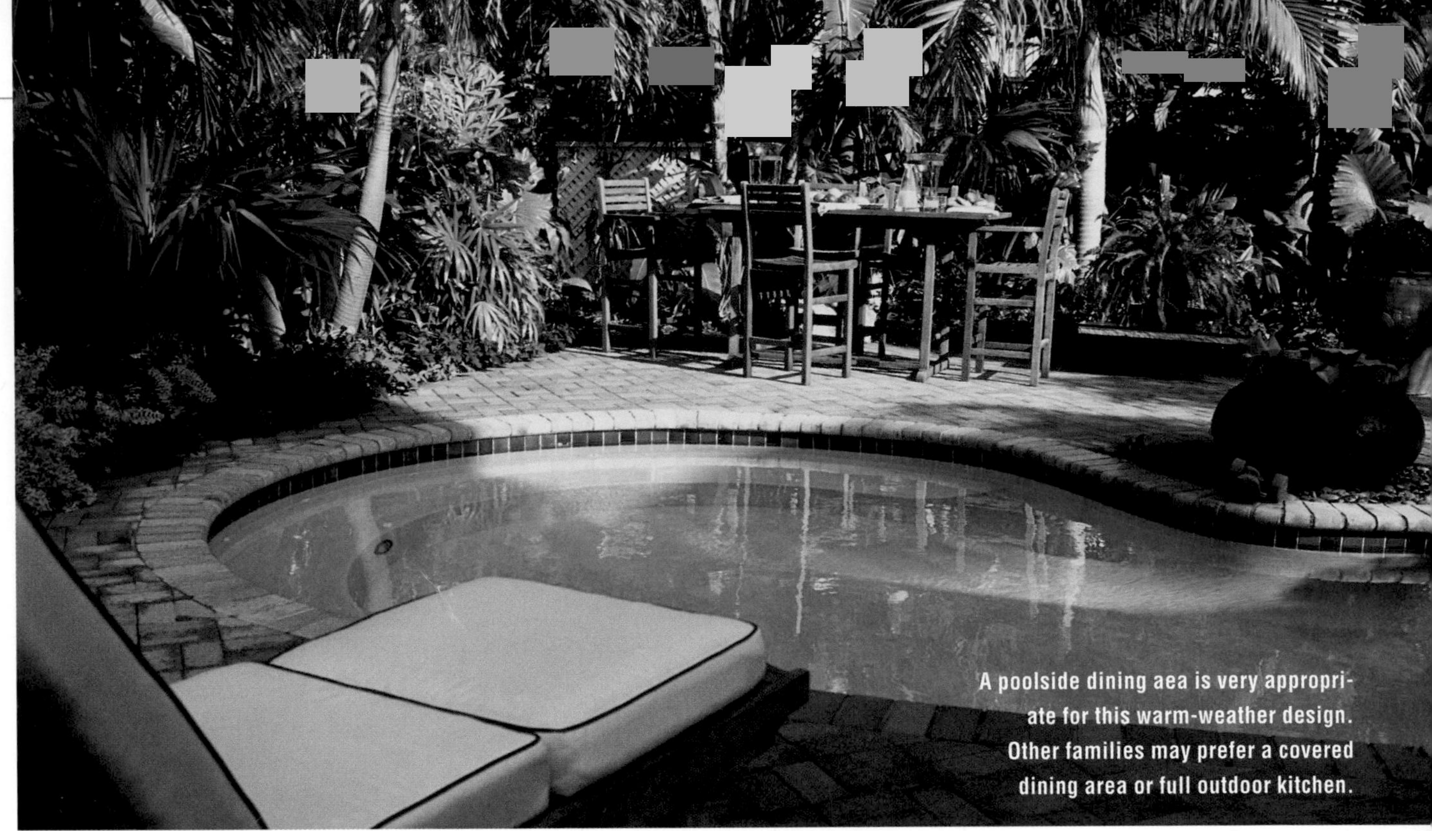

A poolside dining aea is very appropriate for this warm-weather design. Other families may prefer a covered dining area or full outdoor kitchen.

spending the time and money to build your dream home, chances are you're planning on staying in it for a while. You'll save money down the road if you consider now what features you'll want in your home in the long run. If you want to avoid stairs altogether, consider building a ranch-style home. If you love the style of more traditional multilevel homes, like Colonial or Victorian, but don't want to deal with the stairs on a daily basis, consider plans with master suites on the first floor. A plan with a bedroom and full bath on the home's first level may be just right for households with elderly parents.

When entertaining, will my guests prefer more formal, separate rooms or more open, casual spaces? Depending on how often you entertain at home—and what sort of entertaining you typically do—you'll want your home plan to reflect those interests. If you prefer more traditional, formal affairs, you'll want to choose a plan with both a formal dining room and living room, which are especially common in Victorian, Colonial, and Federalist plans. Perhaps more casual gatherings are the norm in your home. If so, you'll likely want an open floor plan, where the great room adjoins the kitchen and guests can easily mingle with the host or hostess.

What is my family's favorite vacation spot? Are there design elements from another region or country that I'd like to recreate in my new home? Take inspiration from your favorite travel destination. What is it about that spot that you like so much? Do you prefer southern France or the Swiss Alps? New England or the Southwest? Perhaps there's a way to bring a bit of that place you love so much into your home—by seeking plans that feature architectural elements from another region. Again, you'll want to consider what your neighbors' homes look like before building a Southwestern home in a town full of Cape Cods. But wouldn't it be great to come home to a place every day that reminds you of a special town or country many miles away?

Will there be children in the home? Raising kids plays a huge role in choosing the type and size of home you build. Aside from the obvious question of how many bedrooms and baths you'll need to include, you must consider other factors, too. Will you want to include a game room? Or perhaps an island snack bar in the kitchen? And, if you have young children, you may not want a master suite on the opposite end of the home from the other bedrooms.

Will I need a home office? Whether you telecommute on a regular basis or just have the occasional assignment to finish up at home, you'll need to determine how important it is to include space for a home office or study. If you only need the computer to check your e-mail, setting it up in the kitchen or the family room may work just fine. But if you need a space that will be quiet and minimize distractions, plan ahead. The home plan you like might not specifically call for an office or study, but if it has an extra bedroom or bonus room, either could be converted to accommodate your needs.

What kinds of extra features—such as storage spaces or fireplaces—should be included? Regardless of the style of home you want or the location where you plan to build, coming up with a list of special features to include is an important step. Perhaps you have visions of a fireplace or cathedral ceilings adorning your great room, or ample storage spaces throughout the house.

TONY GIAMMARINO

Choose A Plan

Once you have a working set of assumptions about the type of home you want to build—two-story versus one-story, traditional rather than contemporary, an outdoor porch or maybe a sunroom—start refining your criteria by browsing home plans. However, putting those ideas together and considering the hundreds of other details that will make your home perfect can be daunting.

Work from Experience

One way to help further define what you would like to have in your new home is to list the pluses and minuses of homes you've lived in before. You already know what you liked about those houses, so put it down on paper to help sort out your criteria and draw more conclusions.

While browsing the home plans sections in this book, keep the following in mind. The facade, shown in the rendering of the home plan, may be flexible. Today's siding materials often make it possible to choose a home plan showing horizontal wood siding that can be built with brick siding.

Top It Off

Selecting a roof type is a major decision and will go hand-in-hand with the style of home you choose. While flat roofs are fine in warm, mild climates, they simply won't hold up in snow country. In many areas, there are specific roofing codes to accommodate snow loads and high winds. If you suspect this may be the case in your building area, familiarize yourself with the code before you choose a plan.

You also will face decisions about foundation choices. Some plans are designed with a specific foundation (basement, crawlspace, slab, or pier) but, once again, can be converted by a qualified professional.

Remember that floor plans represented in this book and in other publications are simplified versions of the fully detailed blueprints that will be used in construction of the home. In fact, when you have narrowed your choices to a handful of designs, it may be a good idea to buy a set of study plans (a single set of the full working drawings) for the designs you are considering. Working blueprints will show all elevations and levels for the home, including a finished basement if it is part of the design.

Rooms should be clearly defined as bedrooms, bathrooms, living areas, utility areas, and bonus spaces. Closets, cabinets and other built-ins, windows and doors (interior and exterior), stairways, and other pertinent features should be distinctly marked. The plan's overall width and depth (at its widest and deepest points) should be indicated somewhere near the floor plans.

COMMON **TERMS**

BALUSTRADE:
An entire railing system for a porch or stairs including a top rail and its balusters, and sometimes a bottom rail.

BAY WINDOW:
A bumped-out window, usually with three glass panels, two of which are at an angle to the middle panel. A variation called a box or a box-bay window puts the two glass panels at right angles to the middle panel.

DORMER:
A structure projecting from a sloping roof most commonly accommodating a window or louver.

FACADE:
One of the exterior walls (usually the front) of a home.

FENESTRATION:
The arrangement and design of windows in a building.

GABLE:
The upper, triangular area of a home, beneath the area where two roof planes meet.

HIPPED ROOF:
A roof that rises from all four sides of a building.

NICHE:
A recess in a wall—often used for displaying art treasures.

PALLADIAN WINDOW:
A stylized window consisting of one large central panel of glass, two narrower side panels, and a half-round piece crowning the center panel.

Plan For Your Site

Sloping lots, wetlands acreage, and narrow-width sites are all buildable sites—if you have the right home plan. Sloping lots, for example, can even offer advantages, from the cost of the land to the fact that they generally offer great views and cool breezes.

Tough lots can be tamed by a hillside plan designed to fit a slope to the front, back, or side, as needed by the lot. You might consider a plan with a drive-under garage or a finished basement that makes perfect use of a sloping lot.

Wetlands or other areas prone to swampy ground or high water, even for part of the year, may be accommodated by building a home with a pier foundation. These foundations raise the main body of the home up and away from soggy sites. In dry seasons, the area formed by the piers under the house provides great storage for a boat or other seaside perks.

If your lot is unusually narrow, there are hundreds of plans available with a slender footprint—some as little as 25 feet in width that have great livability. Another option is choosing a plan that is fairly wide (but not very deep) and turning it to fit the lot. With some plans, it may be possible to adapt them to a narrow lot by tucking the garage to the rear, thus narrowing the footprint.

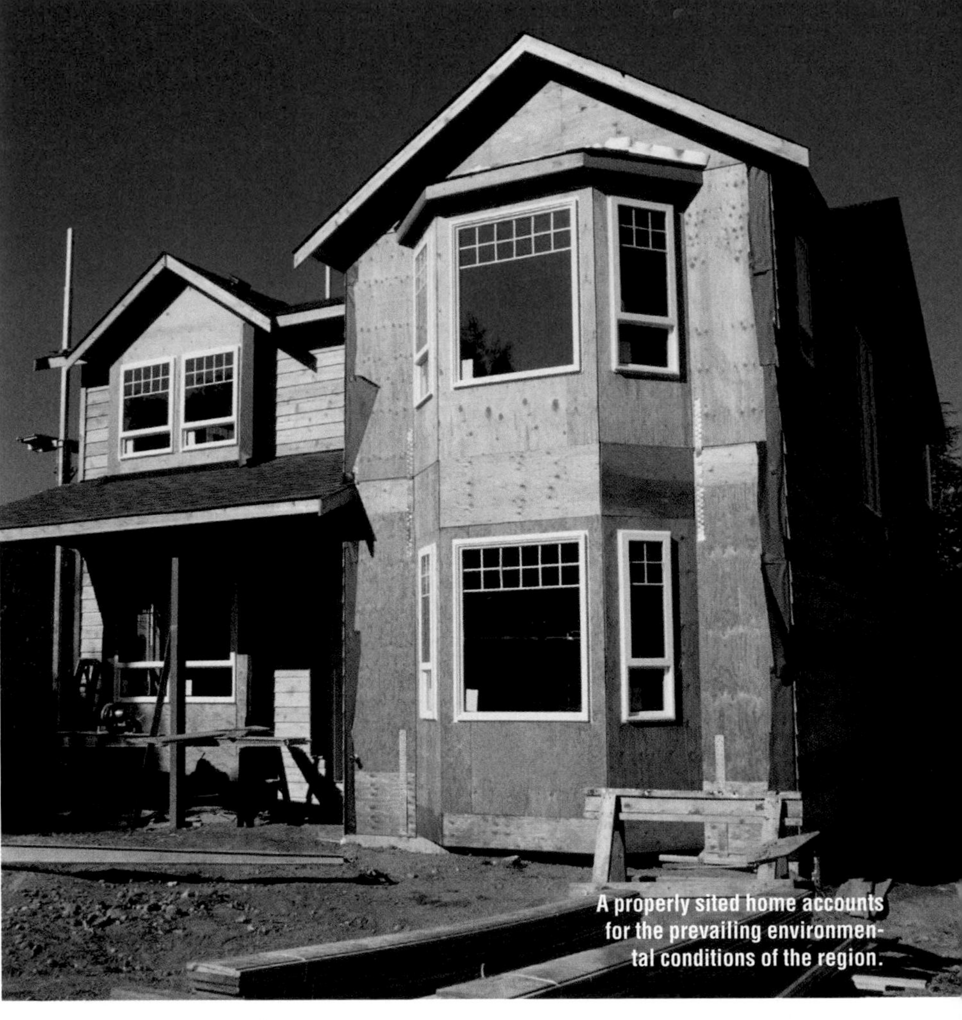

A properly sited home accounts for the prevailing environmental conditions of the region.

GETTY IMAGES

Set Your Site

Proper "siting" of a home means situating it on your lot to take full advantage of (or protect your home from) sun exposure and prevailing winds, while also maximizing great views and ease of access.

Home siting takes into account grade changes on the lot, available views, orientation to the sun, prevailing winds, and existing vegetation. Your builder should be able to help you with a site plan for placing your home optimally on your lot. Some local building departments require such a document before they will approve plans and issue permits. If your plan doesn't completely meet site requirements, the builder may be able to suggest modifications that will make it more workable.

A big part of correct siting involves considering the specific climatic conditions in your building area. Correctly orienting your home on the building site will keep your home comfortable, while saving on heating and cooling bills. In hot climates, for example, locate the living areas in your home on the north or east side of the plan, reserving the south and west sides for non-living space, such as garages or storage areas.

Homes built in temperate climates should emphasize sun exposure in the cool months and shade in the summer, while reducing the impact of winter wind and increasing the flow of summer breezes. Here living areas should be on the south and west sides of the home, with non-living areas on the northeast.

Cold climates require that homes be arranged to gather the most sun exposure. That's why living areas are best placed on the south and west sides of the home, reserving the northeast side for non-living spaces. Choose a plan with a steeply pitched roof that can be placed on the windward side of the lot to deflect winter winds. If possible, minimize windows on the north side of the home and protect against wind intrusion with courtyard walls or recessed entries on the windward side.

TEN **MONEY-SAVING** IDEAS

1. Look for a so-called "problem lot"—a hillside, narrow, or in-fill property. These might not sell as quickly or for as high of a price, but the right plan and a capable contractor can make them perfect for your new home.

2. Buy low-maintenance building materials like vinyl siding and metal roofing. Even if they are slightly more expensive at installation, they will pay for themselves in the long run.

3. Collect salvaged materials from demolition sites. Old barnwood, used bricks, and distinctive wood doors can add character to a home without exorbitant cost.

4. Splurge only on those things that you truly cannot live without. But don't skimp on structural components or windows, since those will add to the safety and energy-efficiency of your home for years to come.

5. Don't overbuild for your neighborhood. A home that is bigger and better than any other in its area will not command a fair price at resale.

6. Monitor construction allowances as the home is being built. This ensures that you are getting what you asked for (and are paying for).

7. Try to avoid site-preparation charges like hauling in-fill dirt, grading, clearing trees, or blasting rocks. Choose the best site you can afford and pick a plan that fits that site or can be modified to better suit it.

8. Avoid change orders—the changes in materials or blueprints that invariably occur in the midst of the building process. Not only do change orders cost more money, they add considerable time and frustration to the building process.

9. If you really want ceramic tile or hardwood flooring but it's beyond the budget, consider vinyl flooring. Vinyl makes a good underlayment, and the tile or wood can be installed right on top of it at a later date.

10. Do you really need a three-car garage? If you only have two vehicles but were counting on the extra bay for storage space, consider other areas of the home that will work just as well—attic space, space under a stairwell, or a spare bedroom. Or put up a garden shed, which is cheaper than building a huge garage and often more convenient.

Mortgage Information

Finding the money to build a new home differs from taking out a conventional mortgage on an existing home To build a home, you essentially need three loans: one for the land, one for the construction phase, and one for the permanent financing of the home after it is built.

But the process is not nearly as difficult to navigate as it may seem, as many lenders combine these three loans into two or even one loan. Here is some basic information about the process to get you started:

Buying land: Most lenders are cautious about lending money on raw land because it can often be difficult to resell in case of default. Those that will lend may want a large down payment—20 percent or more—with a high interest rate. It might be best to pay cash, if you can.

GETTY IMAGES

Building the home: In order to build, you'll need a construction loan, which isn't offered by all lenders. Those that do will require blueprints and specifications, appropriate permits, and a licensed, bonded contractor before they will consider lending for construction. This type of loan allows the contractor to make draws on the total amount of money as each phase of construction is completed. The lender may want to inspect the property to ensure that the work has been done.

Permanent financing: Once the home is completed, construction financing ends—which means that loan must be paid off. Usually this happens with a permanent loan, the same way any real property is refinanced.

When each of these three loans is accomplished separately, there are three closings and all of the attendant closing costs, legal fees, and taxes. Combination financing, which ties together all or at least two of the loans, minimizes these costs and paperwork.

One unique approach is a rollover loan, which allows money for the purchase of land, construction of the home, and permanent financing all in one package. You need to qualify only once and pay only one set of closing costs. Or you may be able to tie only the construction and permanent loans together, if you've already purchased the land or intend to pay cash for it. In some cases, you may be able to use the equity in the land as a down payment for a construction-to-permanent loan.

Every lender is different in their approach to construction-to-permanent loans. To get the best rates and the most appropriate lending plan, shop around and compare.

MORTGAGE TERMS

ADJUSTABLE-RATE MORTGAGE (ARM):
This loan type allows the lender to adjust the interest rate during the term of the loan. Usually changes are based on market conditions and determined by an index. Most have a rate change and lifetime cap.

ANNUAL PERCENTAGE RATE (APR):
A standard format developed by the federal government to provide an effective interest rate for comparison shopping of loans. Some closing costs are factored into the APR. Actual monthly payments are based on the periodic interest rate, not the APR.

APPRAISED VALUE:
This is the property's fair-market value, based on an appraiser's knowledge and an analysis of the property, which takes into account home values in the area.

ASSESSED VALUE:
The valuation is determined by a public tax assessor for taxation purposes.

BALLOON MORTGAGE:
This is a short-term fixed-rate loan with smaller payments for a certain period of time and one large payment for the entire balance due at the end of the loan term.

CONVENTIONAL MORTGAGE:
A mortgage that is not insured or guaranteed by a government agency.

CONVERTIBLE ARM:
An adjustable-rate mortgage (ARM) that allows a borrower to convert their mortgage to a fixed-rate loan for the remainder of the loan term if certain conditions are met.

ESCROW:
Funds paid by one party to another to hold until a specific date when the funds are released to a designated individual.

FIXED-RATE MORTGAGE:
A mortgage in which the monthly principal and interest payments remain the same throughout the life of the loan. The most common mortgage terms are 30 and 15 years.

INITIAL INTEREST RATE:
The original, starting interest rate at the time of closing. This rate can change in the future in an adjustable-rate mortgage.

P&I:
This is the monthly principal and interest payment required when repaying a mortgage in accordance with its terms.

Find a Builder

Ordering take-out may be as easy as picking up the phone book, but getting what you want from your builder requires a little more homework. The challenge now: find a builder who will embrace your vision of a great home and help make it a reality.

1 Ask for referrals from everyone you know—friends, acquaintances, business associates, etc. Learn about their experiences, and ask to see the builder's work. Ask whether the house was completed on time, came in on budget, and met all their needs.

2 Contact professional associations like the local builders' association or the Chamber of Commerce. Talk to people who keep tabs on the building industry, and who are qualified to give you names of trustworthy, reliable builders. Local lumberyard managers and building supply outlets can also provide advice, including which builders may have had trouble with payments or materials. Call the Better Business Bureau, which can tell you if complaints were filed on any builders you are considering (although it is not at liberty to tell you whether those complaints were resolved).

3 Visit neighborhoods you like, or new developments, and ask people who are tending their gardens or washing their cars about their experiences. Find out if they are happy with their new homes, and whether or not they would enthusiastically recommend their builder. New homeowners are generally thrilled to share the excitement of building a new home with others. Model homes offer good opportunities to judge workmanship and the quality of materials and products that the builder deems appropriate.

4 Evaluate the level of on-site supervision provided by the builder. "A

BRAND X PICTURES

TIPS FOR **WORKING WITH** YOUR BUILDER

- **Ask questions.** If there's any part of the process that you don't understand, ask. Make sure that you choose a contractor who you feel comfortable turning to for answers—and make sure they feel comfortable with answering your questions along the way.
- **Get references.** Don't hire a person or service to work on your home without checking with references first. A few quick phone calls could save you headaches down the road.
- **Sign on the dotted line.** Have a clear, signed agreement before any work is done on your home.
- **Plan ahead and stay organized.** Knowing what you want ahead of time will help keep the process moving and save you money—change orders are the biggest reason for cost increases. Keeping all the information organized will help you navigate the process as well.
- **Stand your ground.** Don't be a pushover for architects who want more than you can afford, or builders who want to eliminate items from your wish list. If it's something you want, stick with your convictions.

builder should be able to guarantee an end product, and the people he hires should conduct themselves properly and be well-trained," says Dan Giddings, a New York-based builder. "A good builder will know how to manage his people whether or not he spends all day on site. Ultimately, he should be held accountable for any problems, and most importantly, he should be instantly accessible should problems or delays arise."

5 Once you've compiled a list of several builders, be sure each one is a member of a professional organization. Narrow the list to five candidates, and request an interview with each one at their office.

Ask for a sample copy of a contract. Find out how long they have been in business, and ask for a list of clients you can contact to arrange for a tour of their homes. Always ask to see the completed work. Tell them your needs, your time frame, and your budget. Discuss warranties and ask for bank references to ensure that your builder is in good financial standing.

Try to determine not only whether each builder is a good match for you, but whether you are a good match for them. If the builder regularly constructs million-dollar homes, and you want to spend $200,000, you may be better off with someone else. Pay special attention to your comfort level during the meeting—do you feel as if you can communicate easily and successfully convey your wants and concerns to the builder?

6 Ask for a written estimate from the top three candidates. You'll need to compare bids on an apples-to-apples basis, so give them copies of your plans and materials list. Expect some builders to charge fees to prepare an estimate (which will probably be waived if they are awarded the project). The process takes time; do not be surprised if your bids are not ready for several weeks.

7 Analyze the completed bids not only in terms of final cost, but also for attention to detail and thorough preparation. And remember: don't select the lowest bidder unless you are sure he is capable of delivering a high-quality product, on time. After all, you'll be counting on this builder to make your dreams come true.

Finishing Touches

We hope this reference guide has given you a better sense of the basics of the home-building process. But before you start digging into the collection of plans in this book, there are still a few more topics to consider.

Customization

If you find a design that would be perfect with a few alterations, consider the option of customizing (also called "modifying") the plan. Hiring a professional to customize predrawn home plan is an affordable way to personalize the existing design without paying for the full services of an architect.

The modifications made to the home plan are categorized as either major or minor changes. Major modifications typically refer to a room addition or roofline change; minor ones usually involve adding windows or moving doors. The sidebar at right offers some general ideas about cost (beyond the initial cost to purchase the plan) of modification. For a more detailed estimate, we suggest a phone consultation with a residential designer or architect regarding your specific requests.

The typical savings over the cost of hiring a custom home architect are considerable and worth analyzing. Reflect on the following example. Hanley Wood offers a consultation with one of our designers for a nominal fee of $50 for prospective customers. (If you decide to use the customization service, the $50 consultation fee will be applied to the total cost of the modifications.) The designer then works with you on a one-on-one basis to flesh out your ideas, then asks you to complete a

ANDERSON

Customizing a predrawn plan to your specifications gives you a chance to create perfect personalized spaces.

checklist that reflects your final customization request. Based on the checklist, he or she makes the appropriate changes to the plan you have purchased (or intend to purchase, if it is a plan available through Hanley Wood) and charges you a fee for the modification (or gives you an estimate for the changes to be made). A detailed cost estimate will be sent out within 48 hours or two business days of receipt of your custom changes. After you review and approve the estimate, return a signed copy and the customization specialists will complete the plan.

The average price for modifying a plan in this way is about $1,250, depending entirely on the complexity of the changes requested. The average cost of a reproducible set of blueprints for a home in this book is $1,200. Doing the math, the total bill for a reproducible set of your made-to-order home plans comes to about $2,750. By contrast, the market rate of a custom-designed home plan drawn from

L^P CORPORATION

AVERAGE **COST** OF **MODIFICATIONS** TO **PLANS**

Modification	Cost
Adding or removing living space (square footage)	Quote required
Adding or removing a garage	$400–$680
Changing a garage from front entry to side loading	Starting at $300
Adding a screened porch	$280–$600
Adding a bonus room in the attic	$450–$780
Changing a full basement to crawlspace or vice versa	Starting at $220
Changing a full basement to slab or vice versa	Starting at $260
Changing exterior building material	Starting at $200
Changing roof lines	$360–$630
Adjusting ceiling height	$280–$500
Adding, moving, or removing an exterior opening	$55 per opening
Adding or removing a fireplace	$90–$200
Modifying a nonbearing wall or room	$55 per room
Changing exterior walls from 2"x4" to 2"x6"	Starting at $200
Redesigning a bathroom or kitchen	$120–$280
Reverse plan right reading	Quote required
Adapting plans for local building code requirements	Quote required
Engineering stamping only	$450 / any state
Adjust plan for handicapped accessibility	Quote required
Interactive illustrations (choices of exterior materials)	Quote required
Metric conversion of home plan	$400

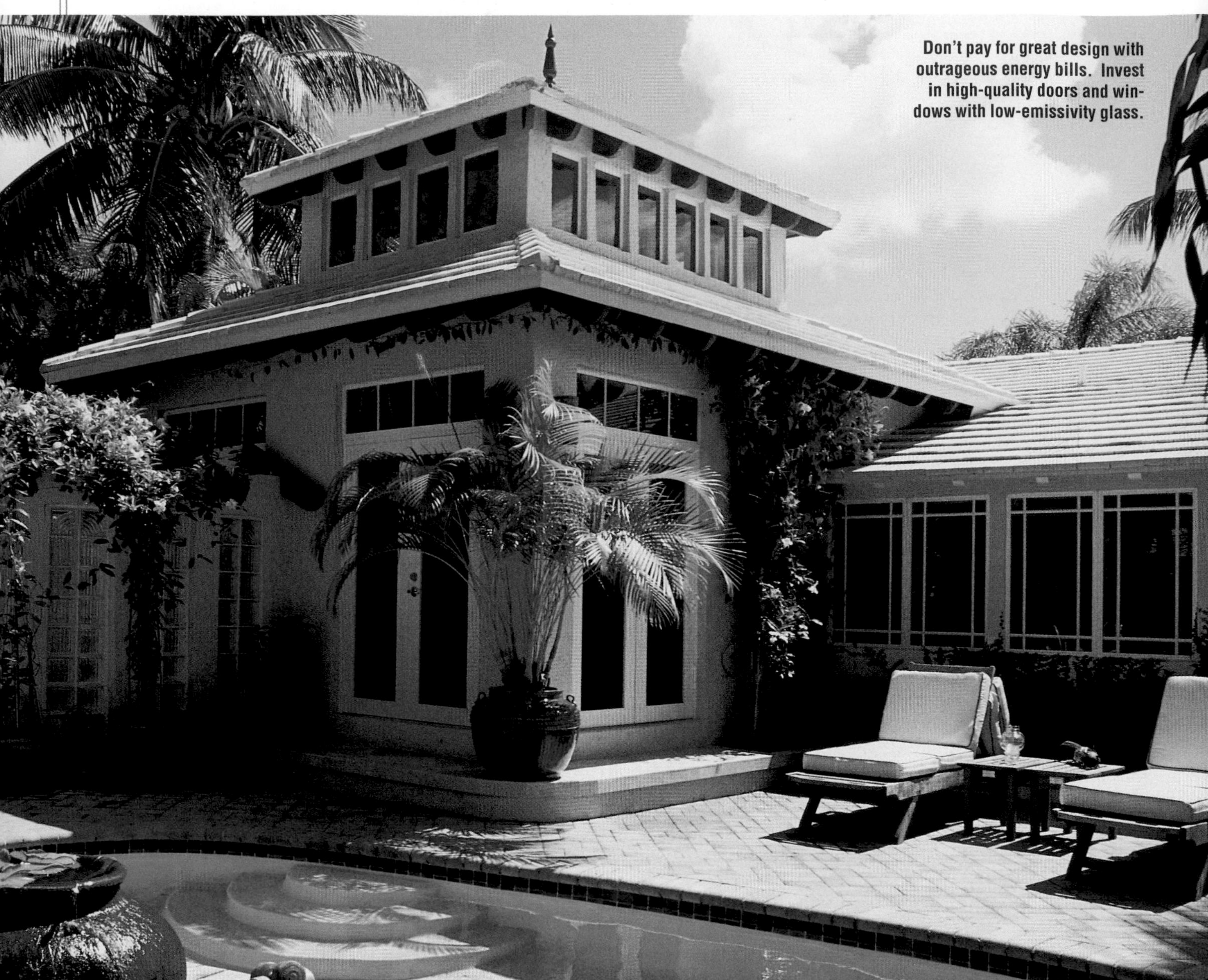

Don't pay for great design with outrageous energy bills. Invest in high-quality doors and windows with low-emissivity glass.

TONY GIAMMARINO

scratch by an architect is 10-20 percent of the total value of the home—that's $25,000-$50,000 for a $250,000 home. To find out more about Hanley Wood's modification services, turn to page 516 of this book.

Energy Efficiency and Smart Design

Chances are, as you plan your new home, your mind is filled with plans and possibilities: gables, dormers, wraparound porches, elegant foyers, and a grand master bath. With all that in mind, who could blame you if air ducts and insulation weren't at the top of your to-do list?

On the other hand, what if incorporating these, and other, energy-efficient design elements into your new home could save hundreds, perhaps thousands, of dollars per year? It's true. It has never been easier, or more advantageous, to design an energy-efficient home. What's more, the time and effort you invest now will pay you back in a home that offers greater comfort, lower maintenance, and higher resale value—and a more eco-friendly structure.

Evaluate the building site to take advantage of climate and seasonal changes. Is the home positioned on the lot to take maximum advantage of natural sunlight, cooling breezes, and temperature changes?

Consider surrounding topography: Nestling the home among sheltering hills, existing vegetation, and surrounding shade trees may create a natural buffer zone, as well as keep heating and cooling costs down.

Insulate the foundation: To prevent energy loss, your home's foundation should be as well insulated as your living spaces. Using thermal mass materials, like concrete, brick, or packed earth, will keep your home warmer in the winter and cooler in the summer.

Head upstairs: If you're planning a two-story home, consider locating bedrooms on the first level and living areas on the second. Aesthetically, you'll benefit by more light, better views, and varied ceiling heights. Plus, downstairs sleeping areas will naturally remain comfortably cooler.

The Thermal Envelope

A home's "thermal envelope" shields the living space from the outdoors. The tighter the envelope, or "seal," the more efficiently your home will operate and the greater your energy savings. The overall design, building techniques, and quality of construction of your home will determine how tightly it is sealed from the elements. Specific areas to address with your builder include:

Air leakage: Takes place when air enters or leaves the home through gaps between framing materials, plumbing and wiring holes, or around improperly installed doors and windows. Ask your contractor what steps are taken to minimize air loss. Also, consider having a "blower" test conducted by a third party on your finished home to find possible leaks before you sign off.

Air ducts: A typical home loses 20 to 30 percent of the air forced through its ventilation system. The culprit: ill-fitting ducts that allow air to escape, causing costly losses of heat and air conditioning. To optimize your system's efficiency, ensure that your builder has properly sealed and insulated all ducts and joints, especially those routed through attics and basements, where temperatures may vary widely from the home's living spaces.

Thermal insulation: The type and amount of insulation required in new homes varies by climate. Thermal insulation is assigned an 'R-value' based upon its ability to resist heat; the higher the number, the greater the

WATER, INC

CONSERVE **AND** SAVE

With the greater demand for energy efficiency throughout the marketplace, the selection of energy-efficient products is better than ever. In addition to the typical big-ticket items, like furnaces and refrigerators, Energy Star® offers suggestions on other products like:

LIGHT
The right bulbs can significantly reduce energy bills and time spent changing them. Smart lighting systems also can be controlled from afar, or feature automatic shutoff.

TOILETS AND FAUCETS
Low-flow toilets and faucets can save water and energy.

HOME ELECTRONICS
Home audio systems, televisions, and even cordless phones can be designed to save energy.

OFFICE EQUIPMENT
Those always-on items like computer monitors and printers can offer vast energy savings.

material's ability to keep your home warmer in the winter and cooler in the summer. Check with local utility companies and professional home-building associations to find your area's recommended R-value. Keep in mind that living spaces should be separated from attics, basements, and garages by insulated barriers.

Windows: When selecting windows, look for double-glazed or double-paned units that offer twice the insulation of single-paned models. Also, shop for windows with a transparent low-emissivity (low-e) coating on the glass, which helps to reduce heat loss. Manufacturers have made the job easier by assigning windows a rating for purposes of comparison. The National Fenestration Rating Council assigns each encased window manufactured in the U.S. a "U-factor." In this case, the lower the U-factor, the better the insulating ability of the window. Once installed, your builder should weatherstrip all windows to eliminate air leaks.

Heating and Cooling Systems

Installing the correct-sized heating and cooling equipment in your home will guarantee comfort as well as savings. For maximum efficiency, forced-air furnace and air-conditioning units should be tailored to the square footage of your home. Once again, manufacturers have assigned ratings that meet industry standards for performance and efficiency. Look for furnaces with an Annual Fuel Utilization Efficiency (AFUE) rating of at least 80 percent and central air-conditioning units with a Seasonal Energy Efficiency Rating (SEER) of at least 12. Regardless of the system you choose, you'll want to make sure your builder installs an energy-saving programmable thermostat to regulate your indoor climate. One more tip: To keep your equipment running in top form, mark your calendar to change air filters at least twice a year once you've moved into your new home.

Water

Talk to your contractor about installing your hot-water heater off the kitchen or laundry room, rather than in an unheated basement. Not only will you minimize the distance that the water travels to point of use, but locating the tank in a warmer area of the home means it will take less energy to heat it. Also, by simply installing low-flow faucets, showerheads, and toilets, your household can easily save hundreds of gallons of water per year. In the near future, watch for instant hot-water heaters to make their way to the U.S. residential market. Already popular in Europe, these fuel-efficient systems eliminate holding tanks by instantly heating water as it travels through the pipes.

Appliances

To select the best appliances for your home, start by taking a look at your family's needs and matching those with the many models available. For example, buying a refrigerator that's too large can waste energy and money; on the other hand, one that's too small for your family adds up to extra trips to the market. Next, look for appliances that carry the Energy Star® label. This program, developed by the Environmental Protection Agency, is your best guide to selecting major appliances that use less energy and cost less to operate than similar models in the same category. How much can you save? A typical household that does approximately 400 loads of laundry per year would save 7,000 gallons of water, as well as the energy it takes to heat it, by choosing an Energy Star®-qualified washer

Lighting

Use dimmer switches and motion-detector sensors on household lights to extend bulb life and automatically turn lights out when that area of the home is not in use. Use compact fluorescent light bulbs in place of traditional incandescent lights. Though these bulbs cost up to $15 apiece, you can expect an extended bulb life of up to 10 times longer than incandescent bulbs. ■

WATER WORKS, MAYTAG

Homes Under 1,500 Square Feet

Arched transoms set off by keystones add the final details to the traditional exterior of this home. See plan HPK1700058 on page 62.

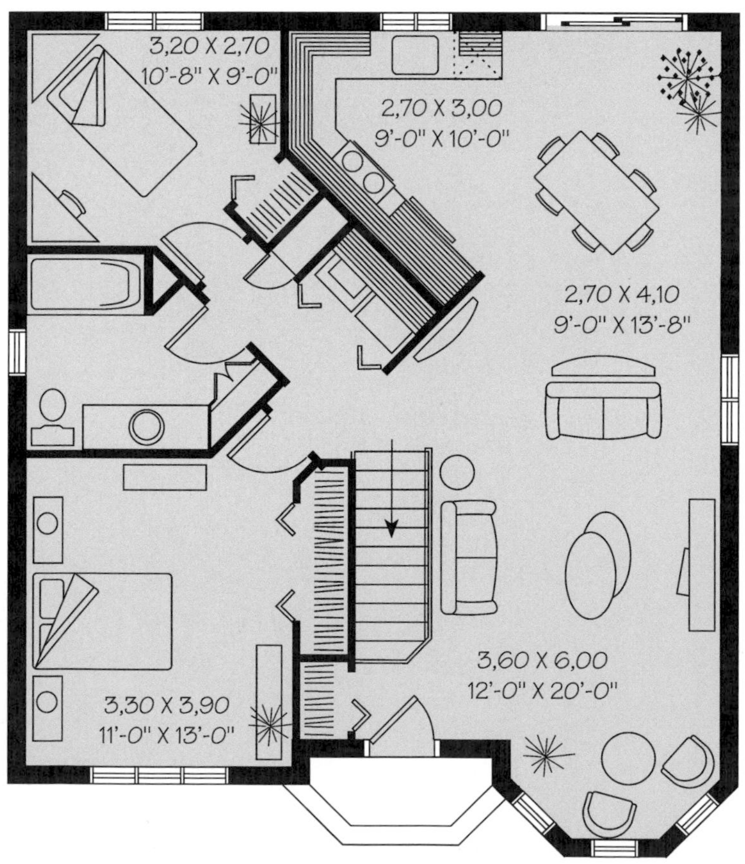

plan # HPK1700001

Style: Country Cottage

Square Footage: 972

Bedrooms: 2

Bathrooms: 1

Width: 30' - 0"

Depth: 35' - 0"

Foundation: Unfinished Basement

eplans.com

Eye-catching exterior details distinguish this small Victorian design. Inside, natural light flows through the living area from the turret's windows, where there's a sitting bay. The living room and dining room make one open space, which is helpful for entertaining. A sliding door in the dining room leads to the backyard. An angled kitchen provides plenty of workspace. The master bedroom and a second bedroom share a full bath.

plan # HPK1700002

Style: Country Cottage
Square Footage: 996
Bedrooms: 3
Bathrooms: 1
Width: 24' - 4"
Depth: 43' - 8"
Foundation: Crawlspace

eplans.com

EDITOR'S PICK

This budget-friendly, low-maintenance plan takes a direct approach to functional design that first-time owners will love. The mudroom/laundry room and galley-style kitchen handle even big chores with ease. But check out also the formal dining room and family room—great for relaxing and having friends over. We also love the home's versatility: convert one of the bedrooms into an office or den. Or better yet, customize the plan to include a full master suite and add a half bath for guests.

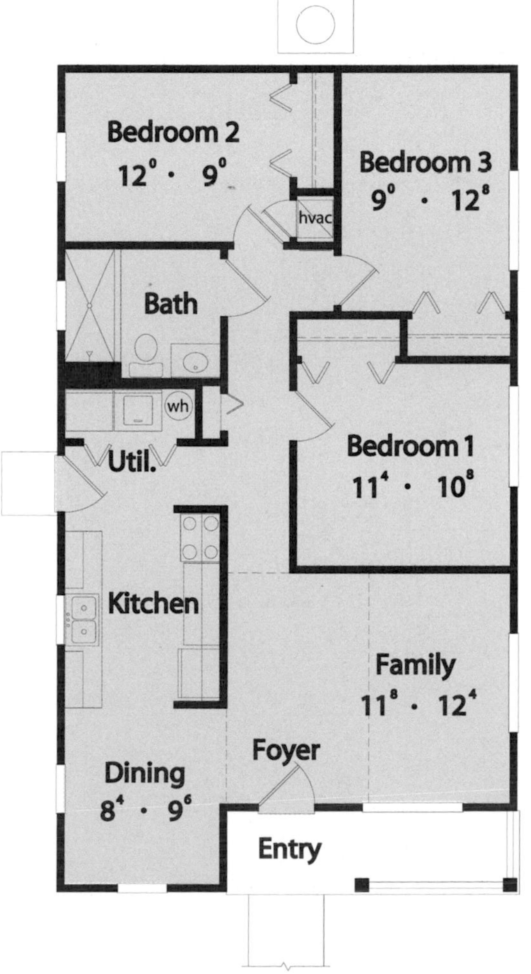

plan# HPK1700003
Style: Country Cottage
Square Footage: 1,080
Bedrooms: 3
Bathrooms: 2
Width: 50' - 0"
Depth: 36' - 0"
Foundation: Crawlspace, Unfinished Walkout Basement
eplans.com

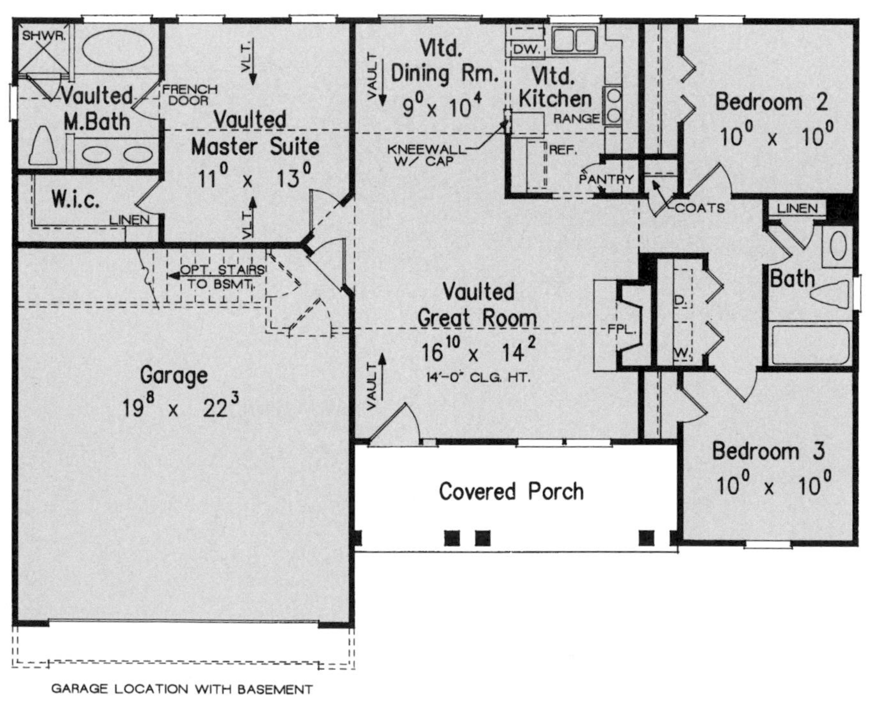

This traditional design is perfect for those who want all their living space on one level. A covered porch welcomes guests and ushers them into the vaulted great room where a fireplace warms the room. An open dining space sits across from the efficient kitchen for easy serving and clean-up. Two family bedrooms are split to the right of the plan. A full hall bath sits between the bedrooms and is convenient for guests. On the left, the master suite enjoys privacy, a walk-in closet, and a full bath with dual vanities.

plan# HPK1700004

Style: Farmhouse
Square Footage: 1,092
Bedrooms: 3
Bathrooms: 1
Width: 46' - 0"
Depth: 32' - 0"
Foundation: Crawlspace, Slab

eplans.com

Perfect for a cabin on the lake or a nice lot in the woods, this home features a covered porch and rear deck. Take advantage of the great room fireplace on chilly evenings. A large vaulted kitchen includes a dining space and deck access. Three bedrooms provide closet space and share a full hall bath.

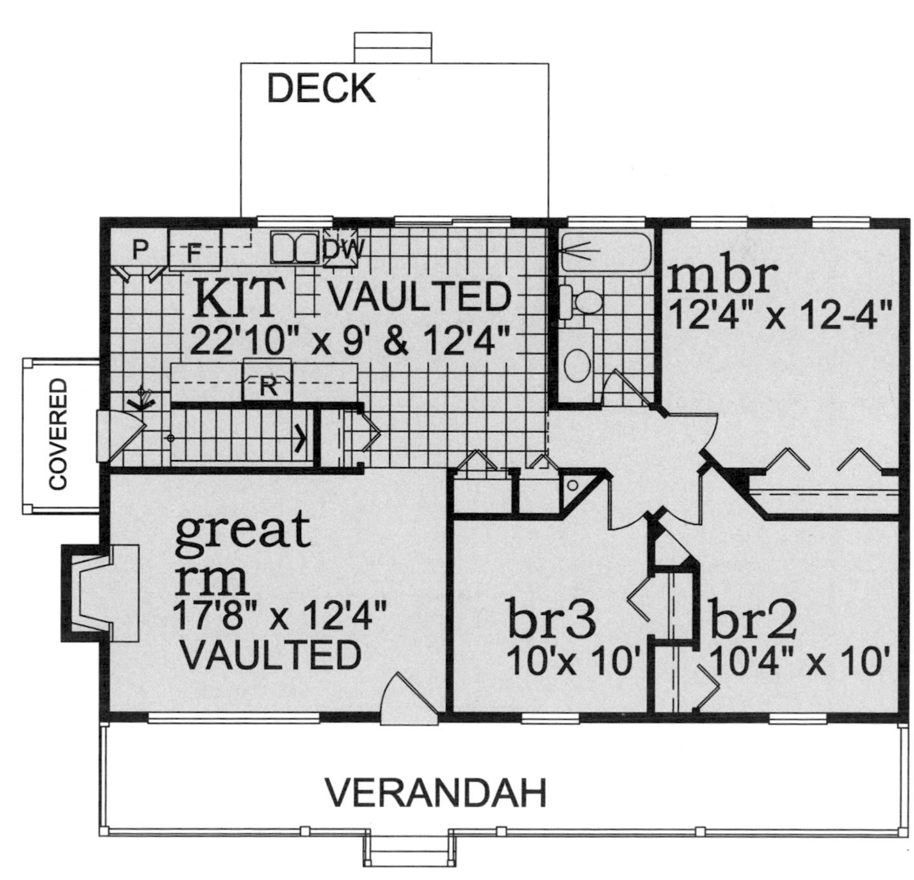

plan# HPK1700005

Style: Country Cottage
Square Footage: 1,118
Bedrooms: 2
Bathrooms: 2
Width: 44' - 4"
Depth: 47' - 4"
Foundation: Slab

eplans.com

Compact and perfect for starters or empty-nesters, this is a wonderful single-level home. The beautiful facade is supplemented by a stylish and practical covered porch. Just to the left of the entry is a roomy kitchen with bright windows and convenient storage. The octagonal dining room shares a three-sided fireplace with the living room. A covered patio to the rear enhances outdoor living. A fine master suite enjoys a grand bath and is complemented by a secondary bedroom and full bath.

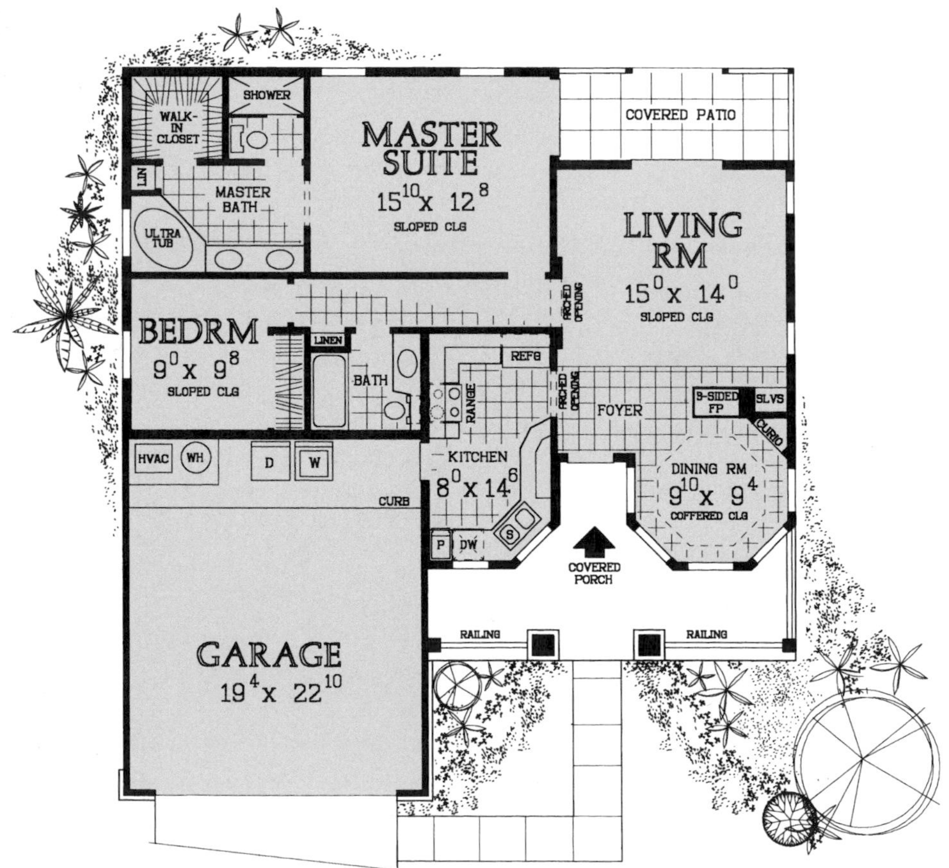

plan # HPK1700006

Style: Traditional

Square Footage: 1,140

Bedrooms: 3

Bathrooms: 2

Width: 44' - 0"

Depth: 27' - 0"

Foundation: Unfinished Basement

eplans.com

This stellar single-story symmetrical home offers plenty of living space for any family. The front porch and rear deck make outdoor entertaining delightful. The living and dining rooms are open and spacious for family gatherings. A well-organized kitchen with an abundance of cabinetry and a built-in pantry completes the functional plan. Three bedrooms reside on the left side of the plan.

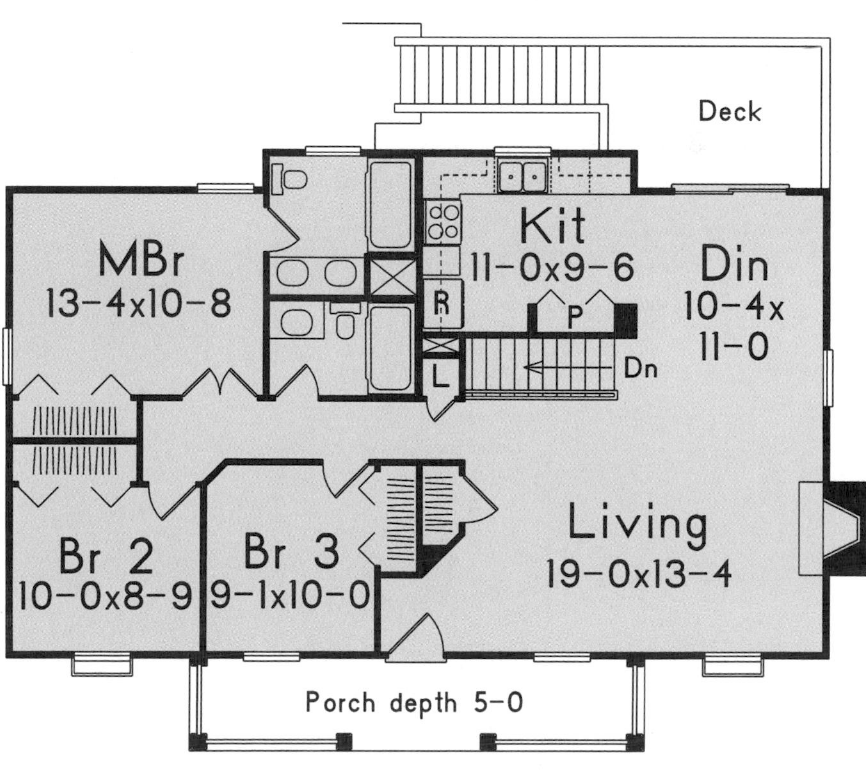

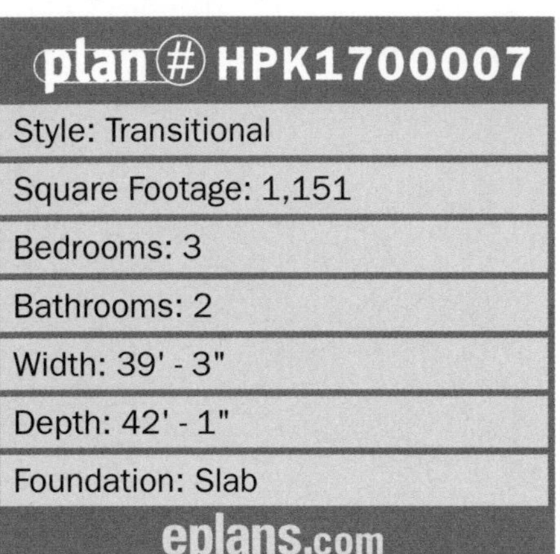

plan# HPK1700007

Style: Transitional

Square Footage: 1,151

Bedrooms: 3

Bathrooms: 2

Width: 39' - 3"

Depth: 42' - 1"

Foundation: Slab

eplans.com

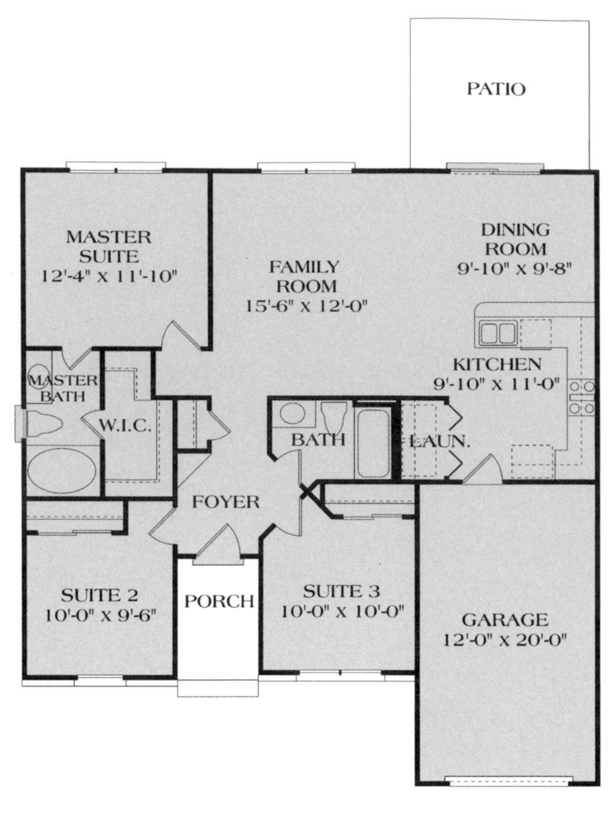

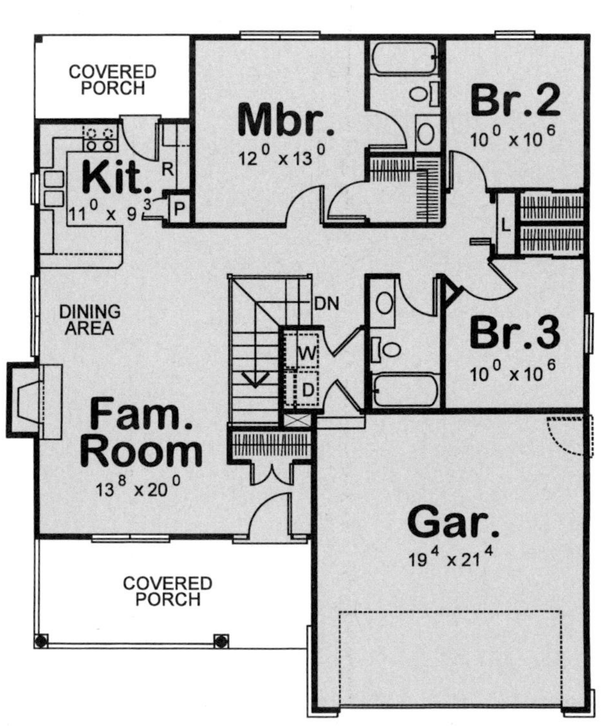

plan# HPK1700008

Style: Craftsman

Square Footage: 1,195

Bedrooms: 3

Bathrooms: 2

Width: 40' - 0"

Depth: 48' - 8"

eplans.com

plan# HPK1700009

Style: Traditional
Square Footage: 1,204
Bedrooms: 3
Bathrooms: 2
Width: 43' - 1"
Depth: 47' - 1"
Foundation: Slab

eplans.com

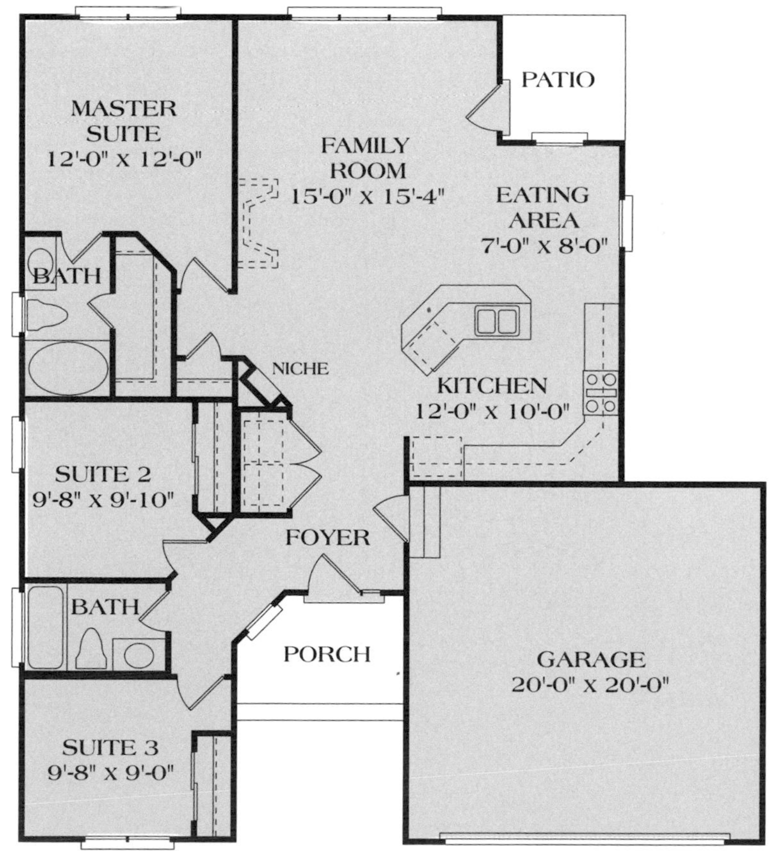

A welcoming porch leads to an entry that features a sidelight and transom. Inside, the foyer carries guests past a utility closet and niche to the island kitchen with a snack bar. The kitchen opens to the eating area and the family room (with an optional fireplace) accessible to the rear patio. The secluded master suite provides privacy and features a master bath and walk-in closet. Suites 2 and 3 are separated from the living area and share a full hall bath. The well-placed garage entrance opens to the foyer.

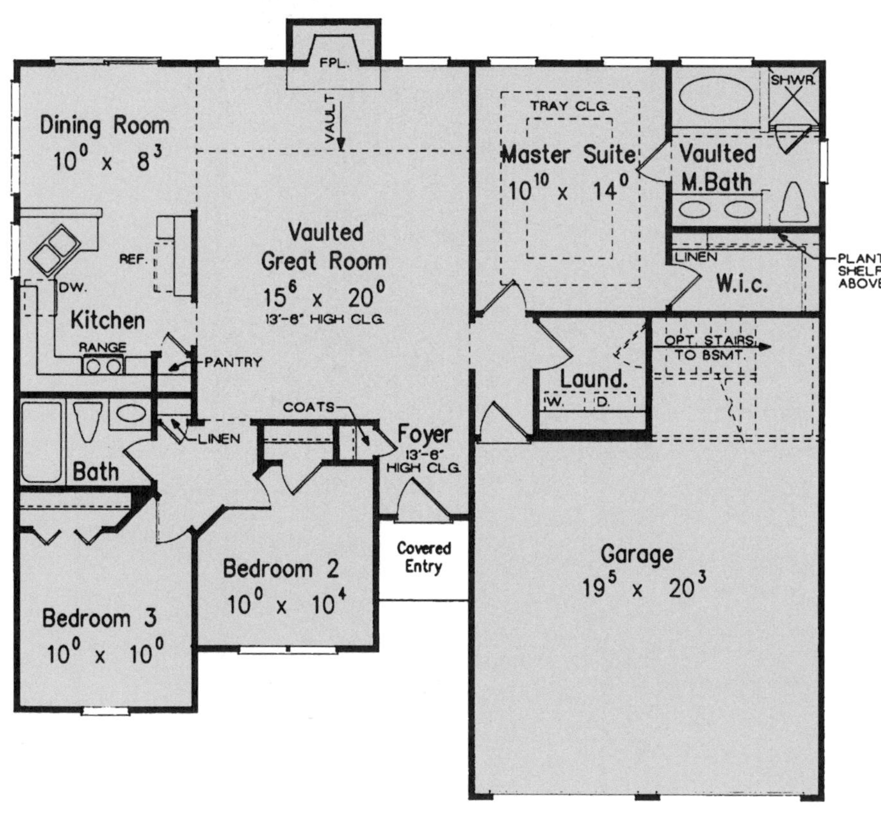

plan # HPK1700010

Style: Country Cottage

Square Footage: 1,232

Bedrooms: 3

Bathrooms: 2

Width: 46' - 0"

Depth: 44' - 4"

Foundation: Unfinished Walkout Basement, Crawlspace, Slab

eplans.com

Gabled rooflines, shutters, and siding—all elements of a fine facade. The foyer opens directly to the vaulted great room, where a fireplace waits to warm cool winter evenings. Nearby, the efficient kitchen easily accesses the dining room. Two secondary bedrooms share a full hall bath. The deluxe master suite offers a vaulted bath and a spacious walk-in closet. A laundry room is located in between the master suite and the two-car garage.

plan# HPK1700011

Style: Tidewater
Square Footage: 1,288
Bedrooms: 2
Bathrooms: 2
Width: 32' - 4"
Depth: 60' - 0"
Foundation: Crawlspace

eplans.com

Welcome home to casual, unstuffy living with this comfortable Tidewater design. The heart of this home is the great room, where a put-your-feet-up atmosphere prevails, and the dusky hues of sunset can mingle with the sounds of ocean breakers. An efficiently designed kitchen opens to a dining room that accesses the rear porch. French doors open the master suite to a private area of the covered porch, where sunlight and sea breezes mingle with a spirit of bon vivant.

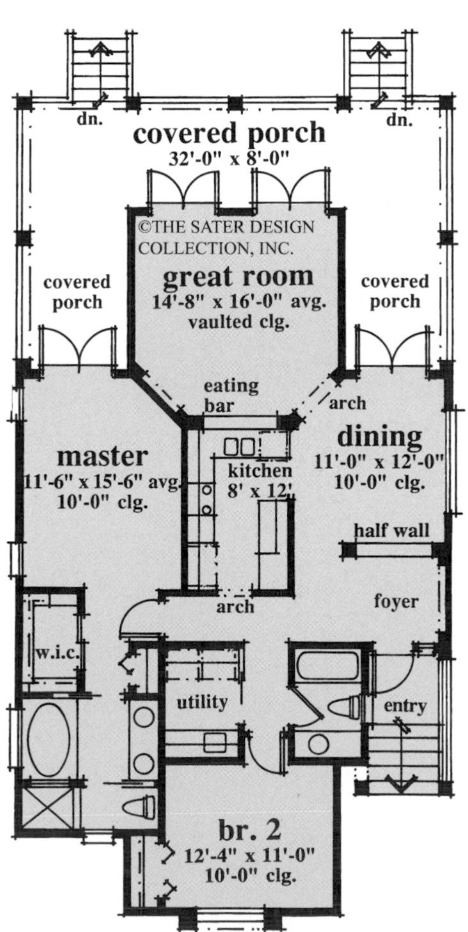

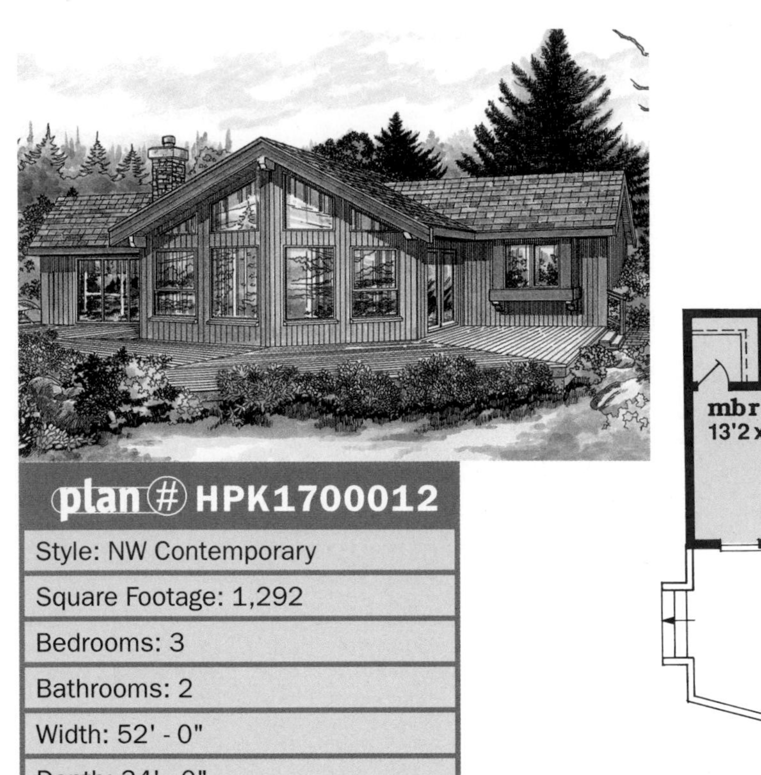

plan # HPK1700012

Style: NW Contemporary

Square Footage: 1,292

Bedrooms: 3

Bathrooms: 2

Width: 52' - 0"

Depth: 34' - 0"

Foundation: Crawlspace

eplans.com

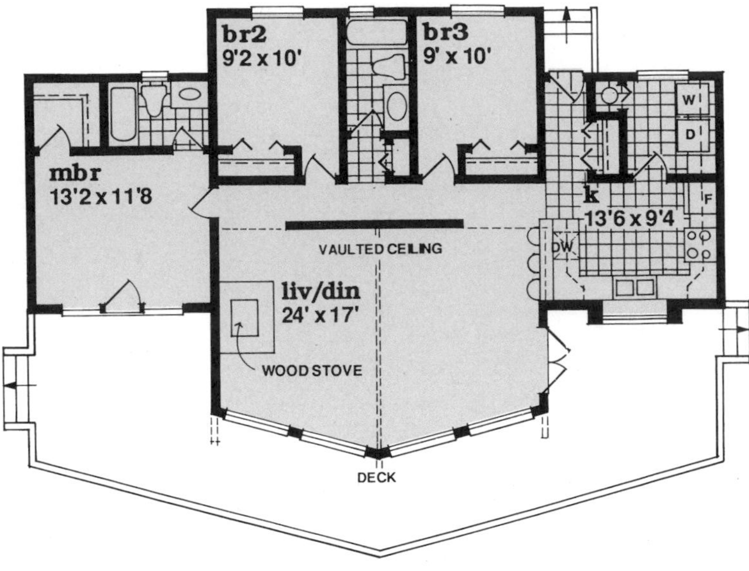

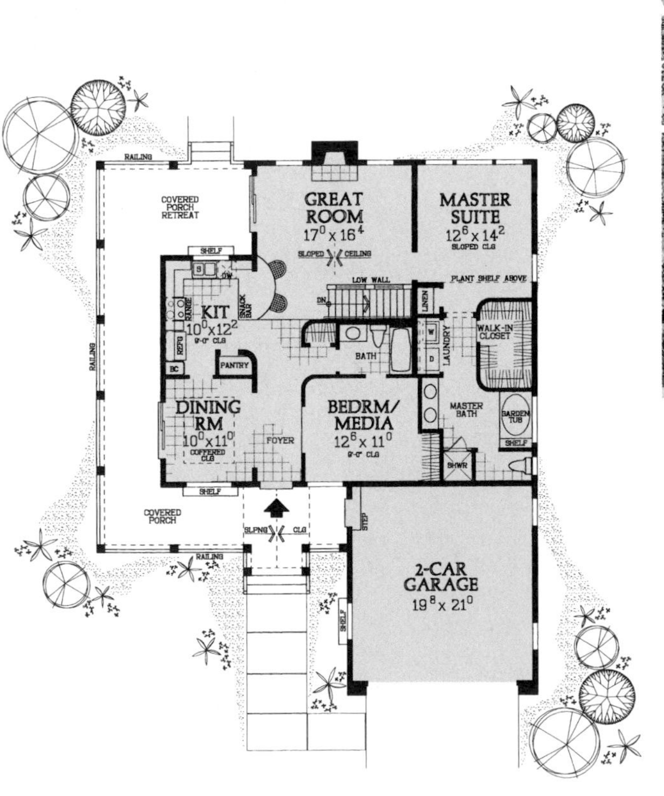

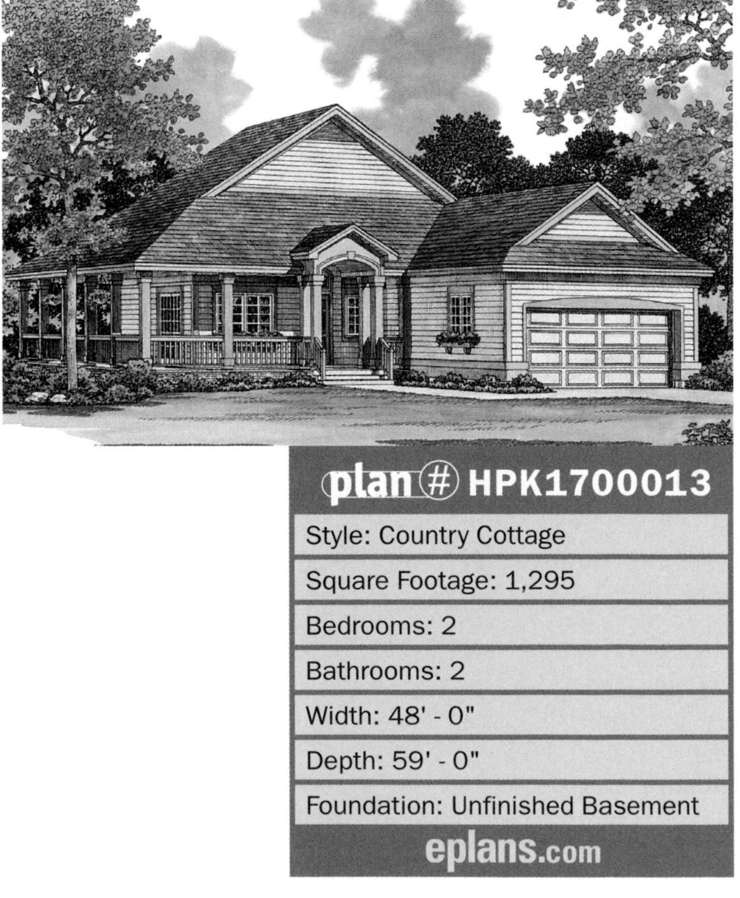

plan # HPK1700013

Style: Country Cottage

Square Footage: 1,295

Bedrooms: 2

Bathrooms: 2

Width: 48' - 0"

Depth: 59' - 0"

Foundation: Unfinished Basement

eplans.com

plan# HPK1700014

Style: Ranch
Square Footage: 1,298
Bedrooms: 3
Bathrooms: 2
Width: 70' - 0"
Depth: 36' - 0"
Foundation: Crawlspace, Unfinished Basement

eplans.com

A front veranda, cedar lattice, and solid stone chimney enhance the appeal of this one-story country-style home. The open plan begins with the great room, which includes a fireplace and a plant ledge over the wall separating the living space from the country kitchen. The U-shaped kitchen provides an island work counter and sliding glass doors to the rear deck and a screened porch. The master suite also has a wall closet and a private bath with window seat.

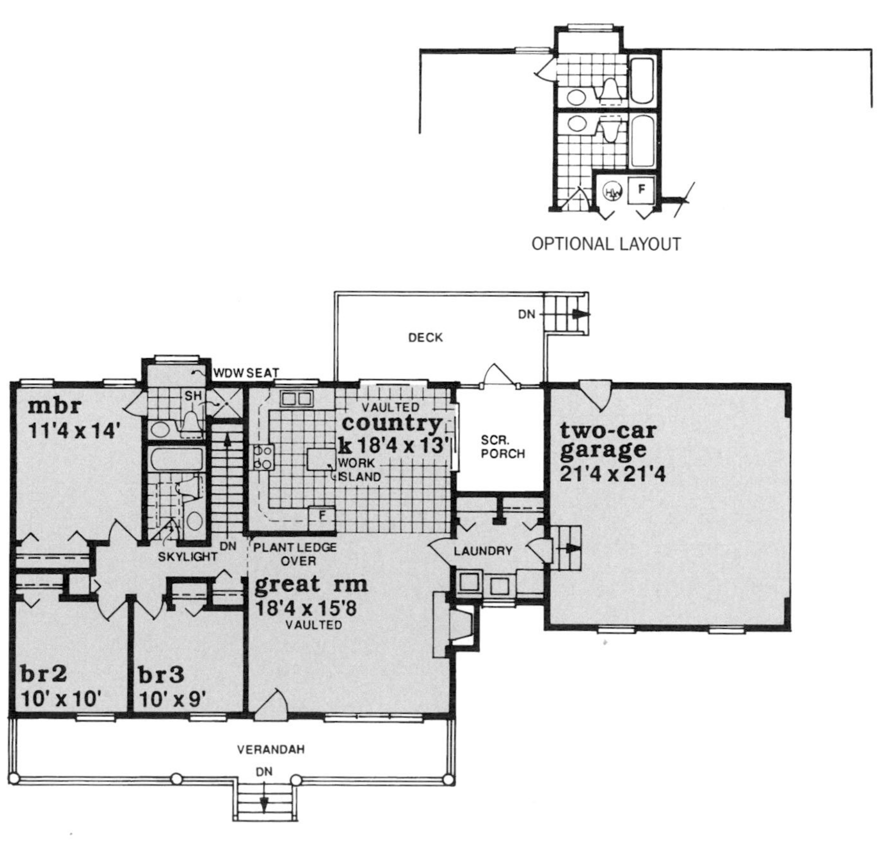

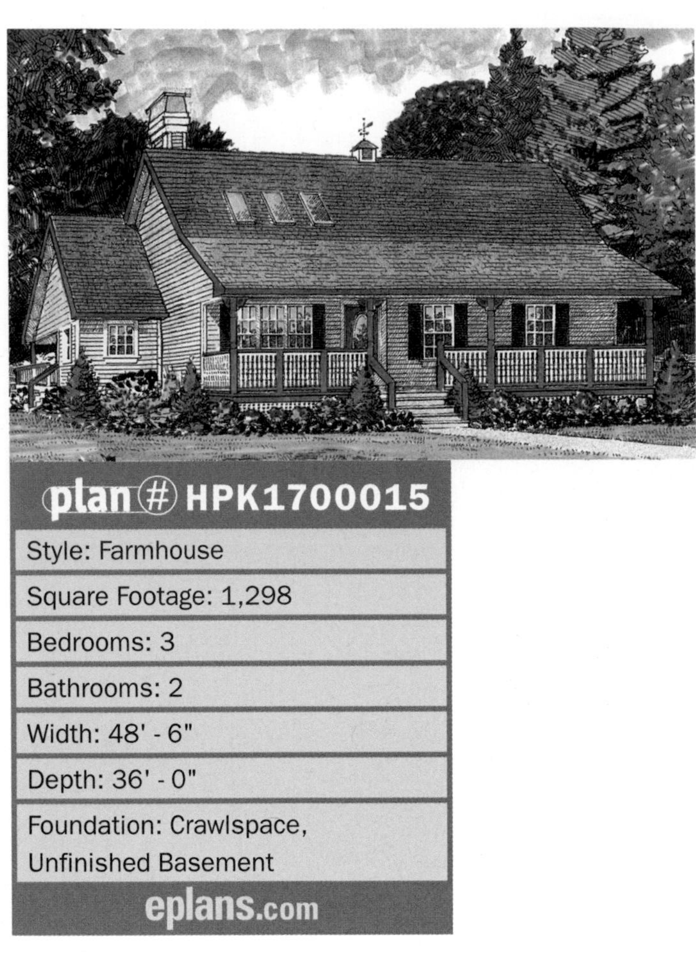

plan# HPK1700015

Style: Farmhouse
Square Footage: 1,298
Bedrooms: 3
Bathrooms: 2
Width: 48' - 6"
Depth: 36' - 0"
Foundation: Crawlspace, Unfinished Basement

eplans.com

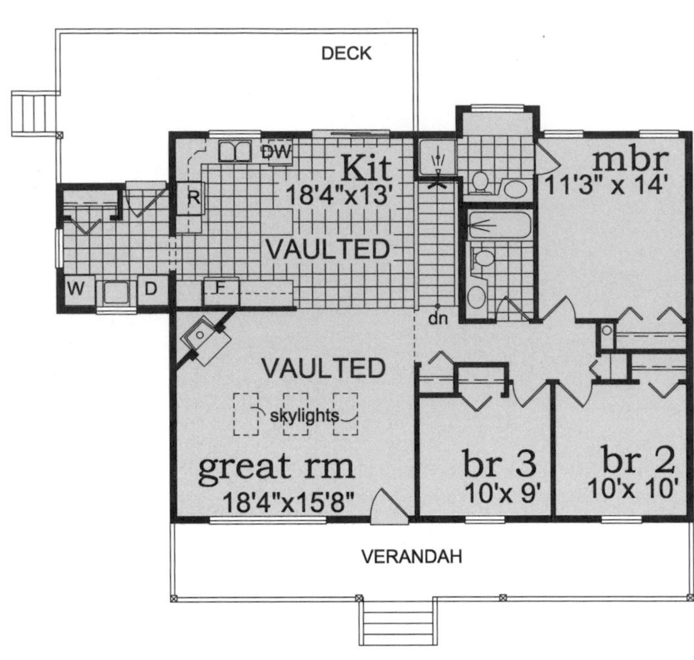

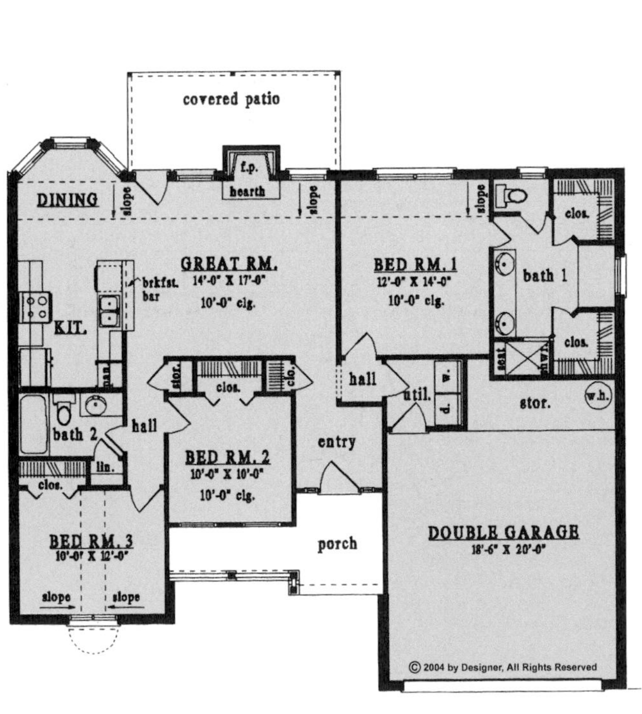

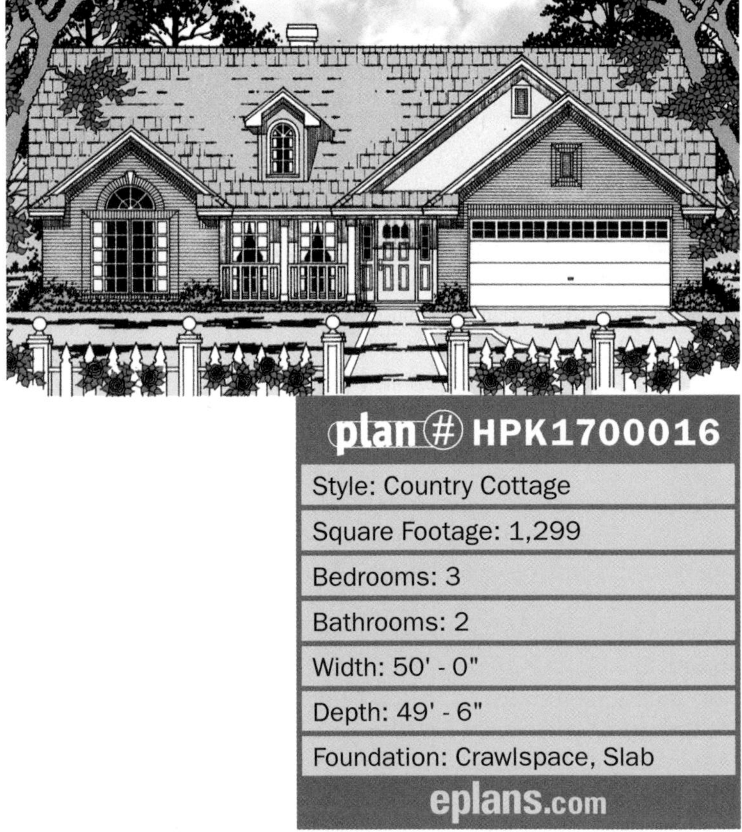

plan# HPK1700016

Style: Country Cottage
Square Footage: 1,299
Bedrooms: 3
Bathrooms: 2
Width: 50' - 0"
Depth: 49' - 6"
Foundation: Crawlspace, Slab

eplans.com

plan# HPK1700017

Style: Bungalow
Square Footage: 1,344
Bedrooms: 3
Bathrooms: 2
Width: 48' - 0"
Depth: 34' - 0"
Foundation: Unfinished Basement

eplans.com

DESIGN NOTE

Even this old-fashioned country porch is a relatively modern example of an architectural feature that dates back to Renaissance Italy and Ancient Greece. European settlers brought the porch to North America, where later innovations in home building and the people's desire to connect with the exceptional beauty of the land established the porch as a quintessentially American place of leisure in the home. Today, porches are a home's intermediary to the outside and a signature feature of many architectural styles. They are both where homeowners welcome visitors and the home's own greeting to the neighborhood.

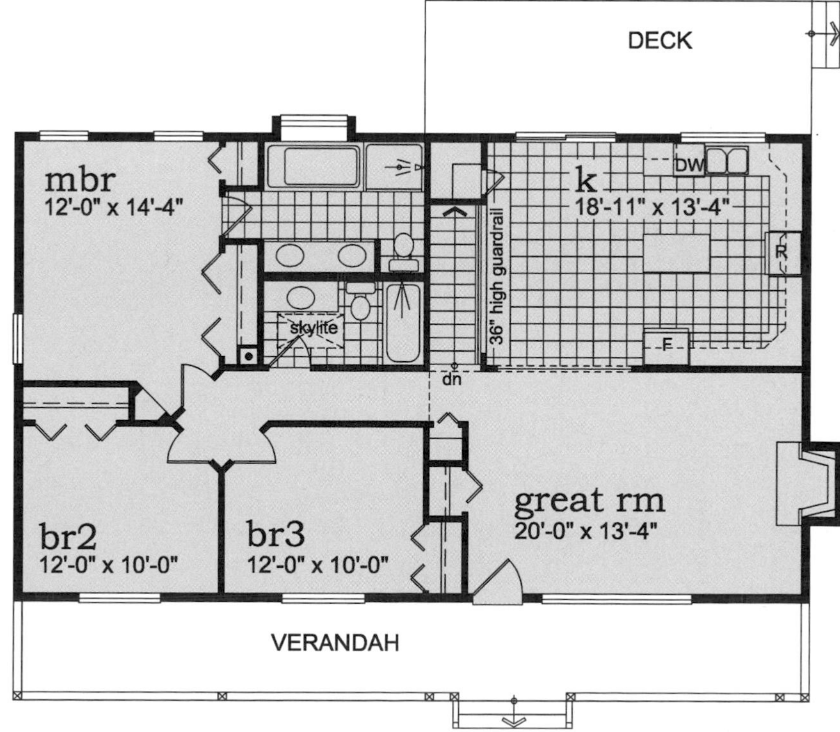

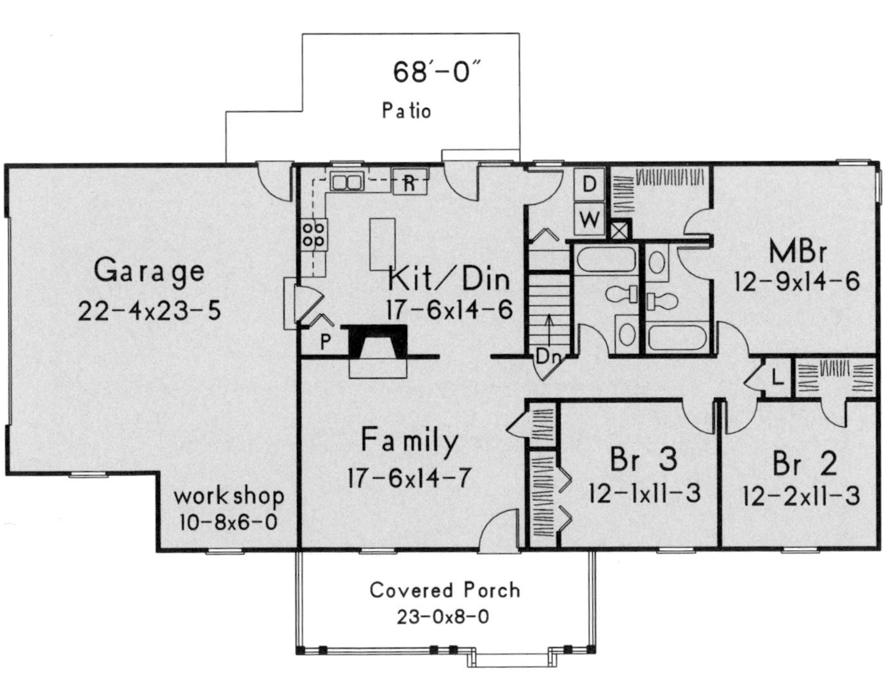

plan# HPK1700018

Style: Traditional
Square Footage: 1,360
Bedrooms: 3
Bathrooms: 2
Width: 68' - 0"
Depth: 30' - 0"
Foundation: Crawlspace, Slab, Unfinished Basement

eplans.com

This ranch-style home offers a comfortable atmosphere. The center highlight of this plan may well be the kitchen/dining area with a work island and plenty of preparation and eating space. A large walk-in closet and private bath make the master bedroom that much more enjoyable. The laundry room is adjacent to the kitchen for easy access. The garage includes a convenient workshop.

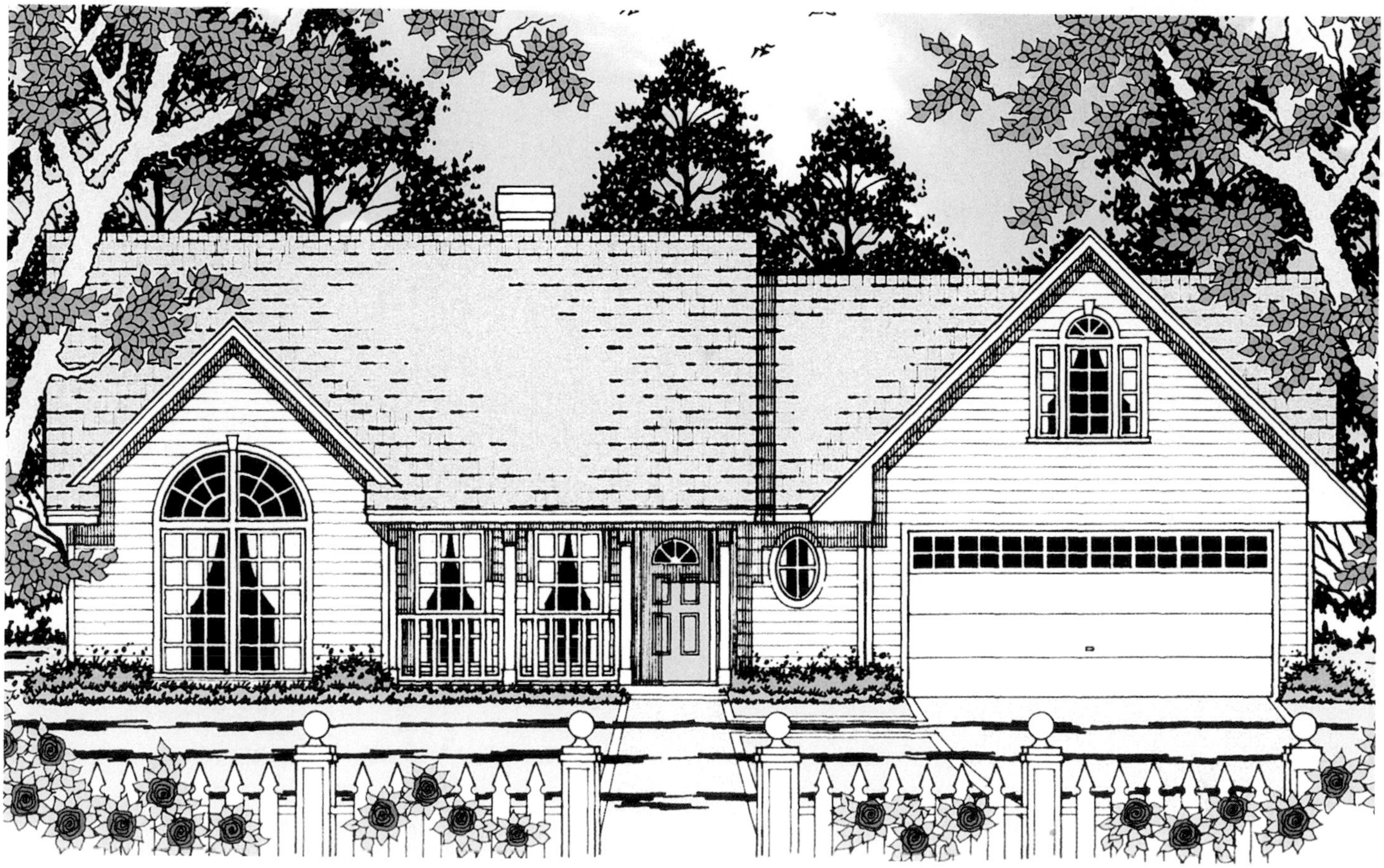

plan # HPK1700019

Style: Farmhouse
Square Footage: 1,360
Bonus Space: 312 sq. ft.
Bedrooms: 3
Bathrooms: 2
Width: 54' - 8"
Depth: 44' - 8"
Foundation: Slab, Crawlspace

eplans.com

A front porch with beautiful wood columns and wood rail lead to the front door of this lovely country home. The entry opens into a large great room, dining room, and kitchen. The kitchen features a wraparound breakfast bar. A covered patio invites the possibility of alfresco meals. The master suite has a raised ceiling and a bath with double walk-in closets. A two-car garage completes this plan.

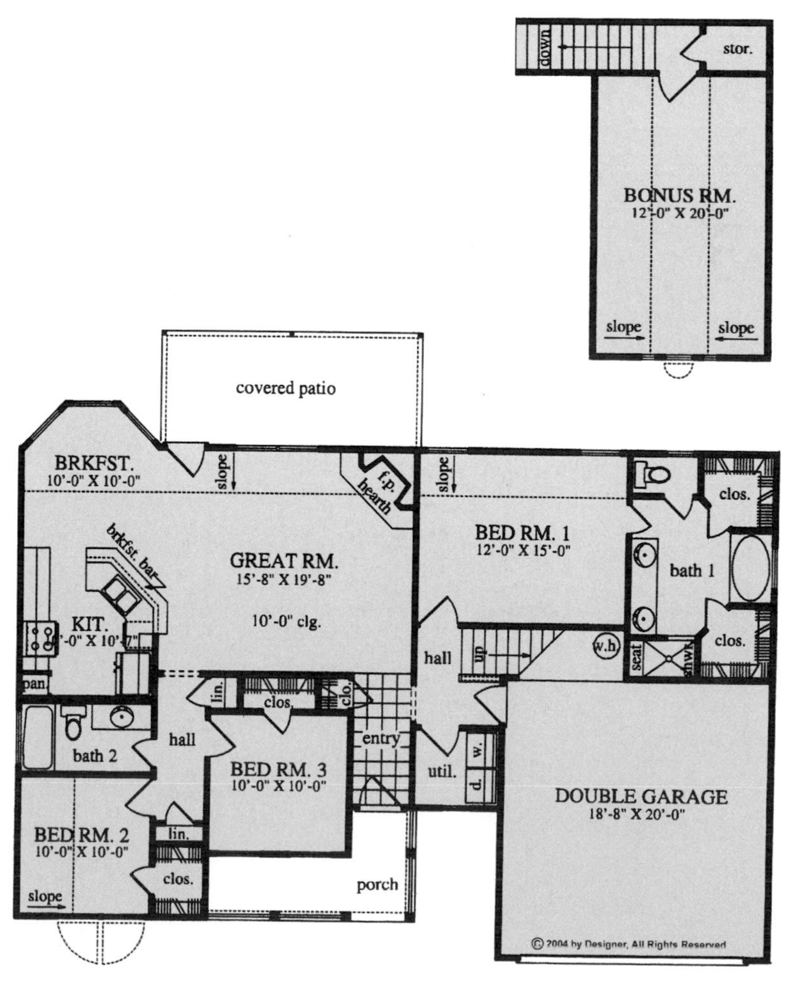

plan # HPK1700020

Style: Traditional
Square Footage: 1,360
Bedrooms: 3
Bathrooms: 2
Width: 40' - 0"
Depth: 49' - 10"
Foundation: Slab

eplans.com

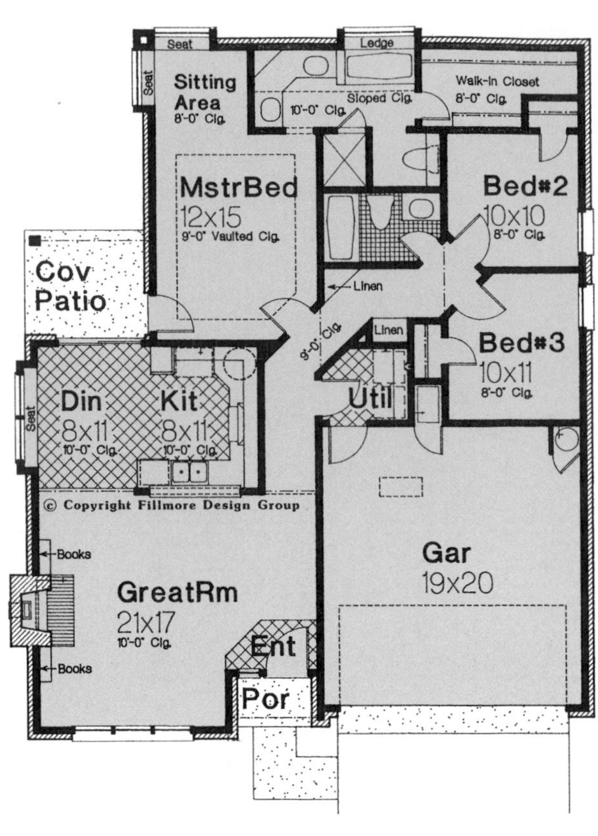

plan # HPK1700021

Style: Country Cottage
Square Footage: 1,370
Bedrooms: 3
Bathrooms: 1
Width: 58' - 0"
Depth: 36' - 0"
Foundation: Unfinished Basement

eplans.com

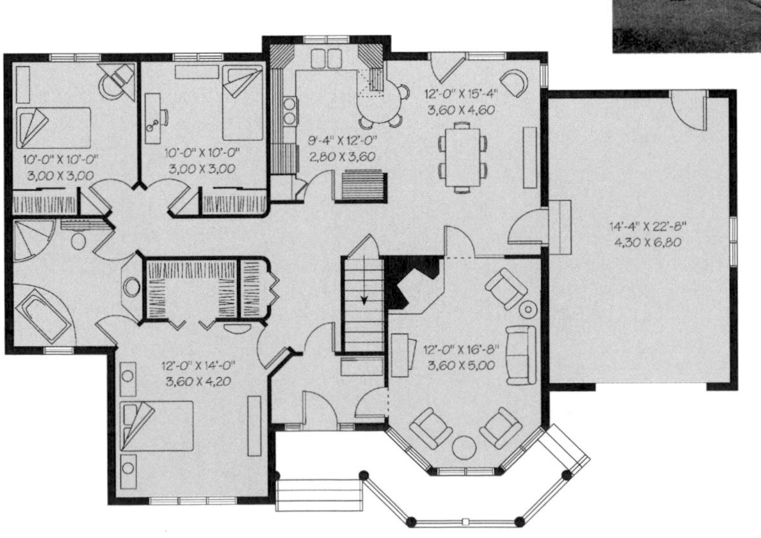

plan# HPK1700022

Style: Garage
Square Footage: 1,370
Bedrooms: 1
Bathrooms: 1
Width: 52' - 0"
Depth: 34' - 0"
Foundation: Crawlspace

eplans.com

This design will house two members of the family fleet and includes a comfortable apartment—great for servant's quarters or tenants. Rustic country accents enhance the siding and stone exterior. This superb design includes a spacious floor plan with a bay window in the living room and skylit kitchen. Adding to the charm of this lovely one-bedroom design are the covered porch and central fireplace. A two-car garage occupies the left half of this design and includes a separate outdoor entrance.

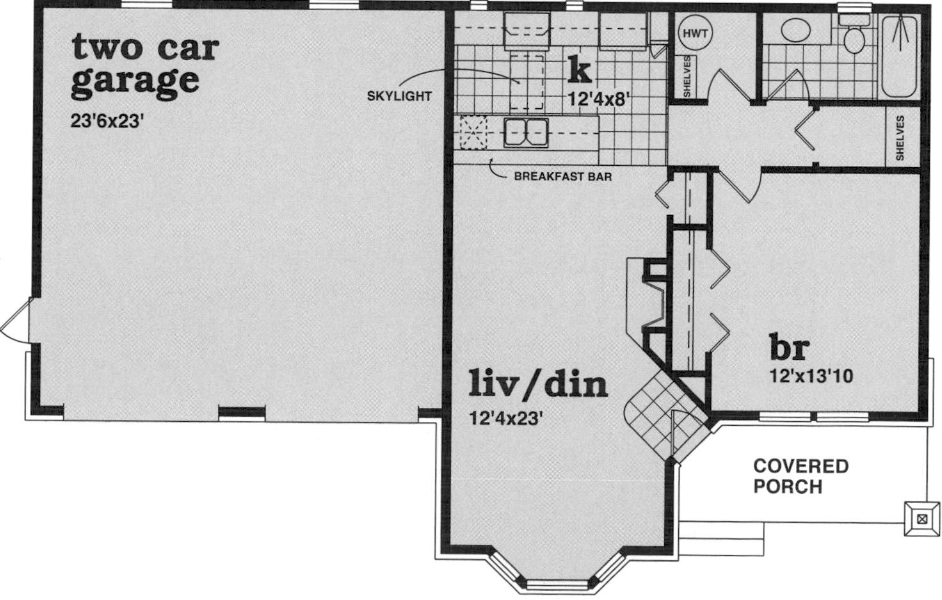

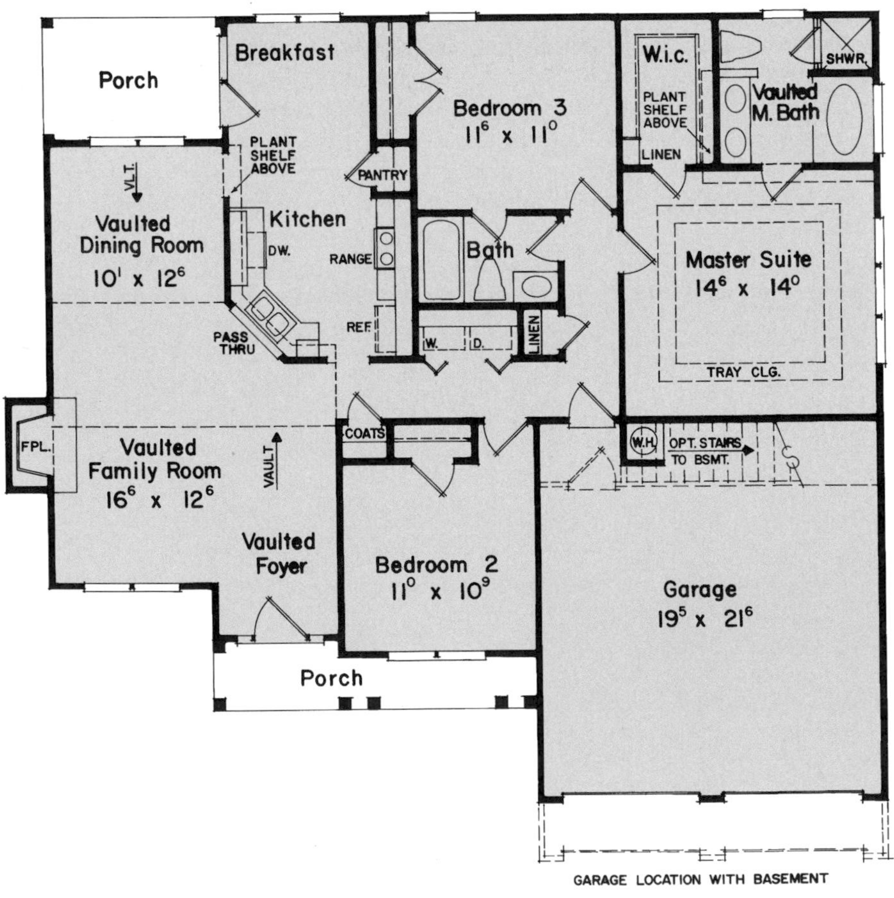

plan# HPK1700023
Style: Country Cottage
Square Footage: 1,373
Bedrooms: 3
Bathrooms: 2
Width: 50' - 4"
Depth: 45' - 0"
Foundation: Unfinished Walkout Basement, Crawlspace
eplans.com

A steep gable roofline punctuated with dormer windows and a columned front porch give a traditional welcome to this family home. A vaulted ceiling tops the family and dining rooms, which are nicely accented with a fireplace and bright windows. An amenity-filled kitchen opens to the breakfast room. The master suite has a refined tray ceiling and a vaulted bath. Two family bedrooms, a laundry center, and a full bath—with private access from Bedroom 3—complete this stylish plan.

plan # HPK1700024

Style: Traditional
Square Footage: 1,376
Bedrooms: 3
Bathrooms: 2
Width: 40' - 0"
Depth: 59' - 10"
Foundation: Slab

eplans.com

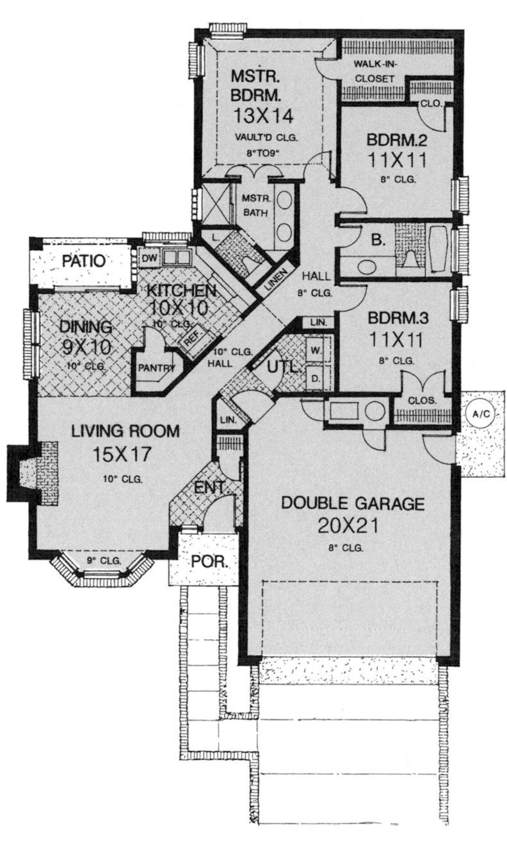

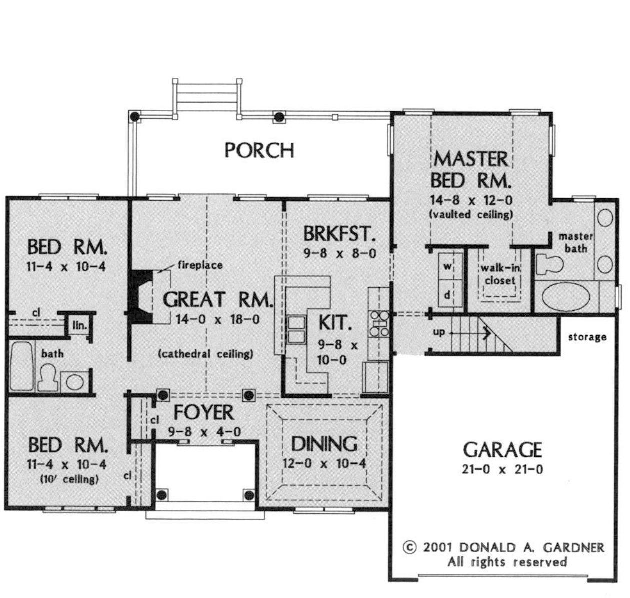

© 2001 Donald A. Gardner, Inc.

down
attic storage
BONUS RM.
13-4 x 21-0
attic storage

plan # HPK1700025

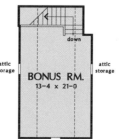

Style: Traditional
Square Footage: 1,377
Bonus Space: 322 sq. ft.
Bedrooms: 3
Bathrooms: 2
Width: 57' - 8"
Depth: 44' - 0"

eplans.com

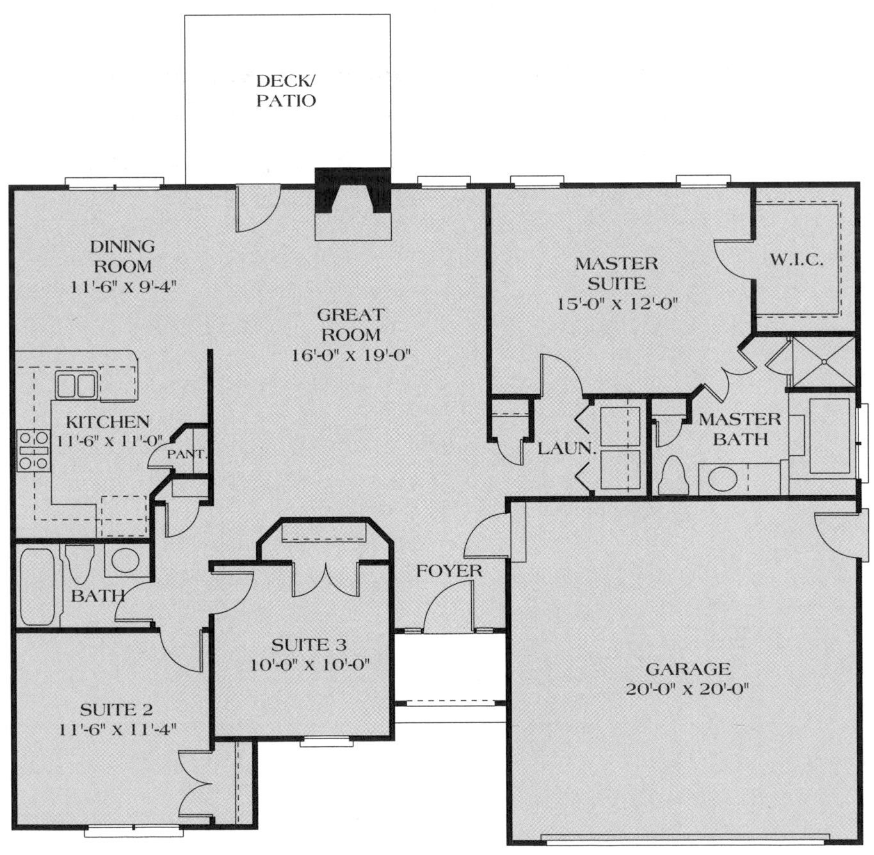

plan # HPK1700026

Style: Colonial

Square Footage: 1,383

Bedrooms: 3

Bathrooms: 2

Width: 50' - 0"

Depth: 49' - 0"

Foundation: Crawlspace, Slab

eplans.com

Shuttered windows, an arched portico, and elegant, wooden entrance greet visitors to this Early American. You can enter the foyer via the garage or front stoop. From this vantage, the great room and dining room create the appearance of one large room. A laundry and master suite are on the right-hand side, with a huge walk-in closet located in the bedroom. To the left of the great room lie the kitchen with walk-in pantry, dining room, and deck access. Two family bedrooms are located at the other end, sharing a bath and separated from the kitchen.

plan # HPK1700027
Style: Farmhouse
Square Footage: 1,389
Bedrooms: 3
Bathrooms: 2
Width: 44' - 8"
Depth: 54' - 6"
Foundation: Slab
eplans.com

Two exteriors, one floor plan—what more could you ask? Simple rooflines and an inviting porch enhance the floor plan. A formal living room has a warming fireplace and a delightful bay window. The U-shaped kitchen shares a snack bar with the bayed family room. Note the sliding glass doors to the rear yard here. Three bedrooms include two family bedrooms served by a full bath and a lovely master suite with its own private bath.

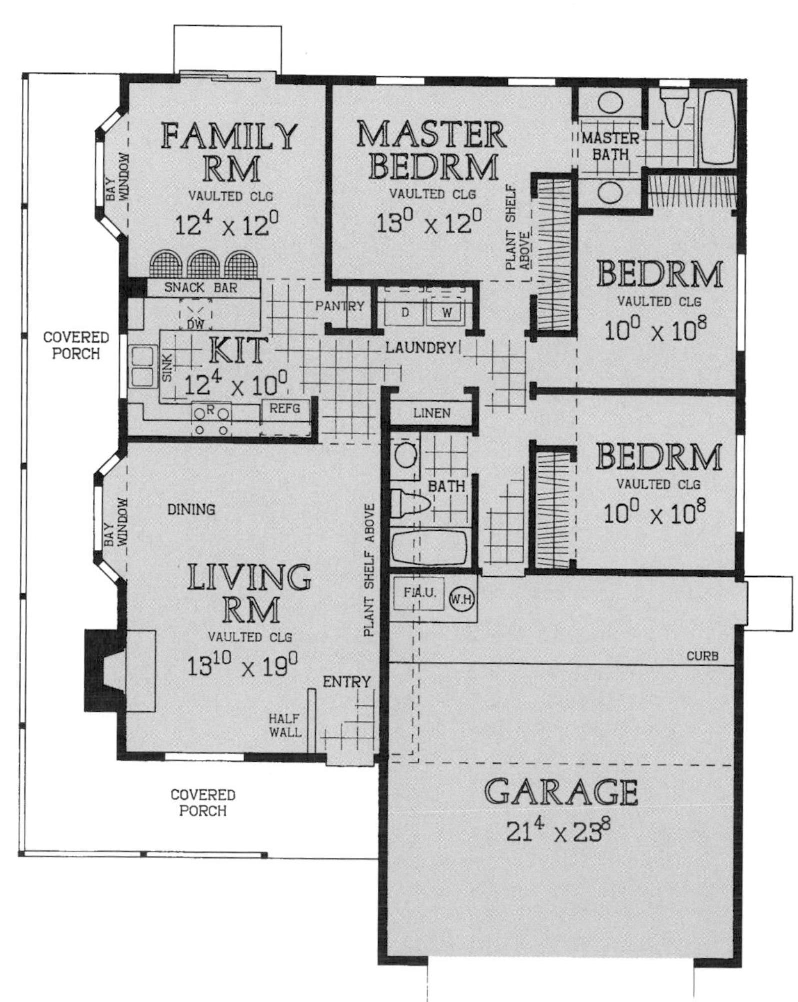

plan# HPK1700028

Style: Country Cottage

Square Footage: 1,390

Bedrooms: 3

Bathrooms: 2

Width: 50' - 0"

Depth: 55' - 8"

Foundation: Unfinished Walkout Basement

eplans.com

Stone and siding, a front porch, and multiple gables decorate the exterior of this charming one-floor plan. An open design creates a feeling of spaciousness throughout, allowing for the enjoyment of formal and casual spaces. Defined by decorative columns, each room is separate, yet accessible to the others. Traffic flows easily from room to room. Guests are comfortably accommodated in two additional rooms on the second floor. Other options include a kitchen that can accommodate a small dining area or be designed to offer more cabinets and a larger great room. The gas fireplace can be located in the corner or on the rear wall. The master bedroom enjoys a raised-center ceiling and a private bath. This delightful home is designed with an unfinished walk-out basement that can be decorated to provide additional living space.

plan # HPK1700029

Style: Bungalow
Square Footage: 1,392
Bedrooms: 3
Bathrooms: 2
Width: 44' - 0"
Depth: 52' - 6"
Foundation: Unfinished Basement, Crawlspace

eplans.com

SMART TIP

The built-in media center and fireplace combination is a great space-saving detail in this small design. Take advantage of similar space-reclaiming features, such as the dine-in kitchen and combination mudroom/laundry area. If room allows, upgrade to a full-sized deck that could be accessed from the bedrooms—great for parties as well as for private enjoyment.

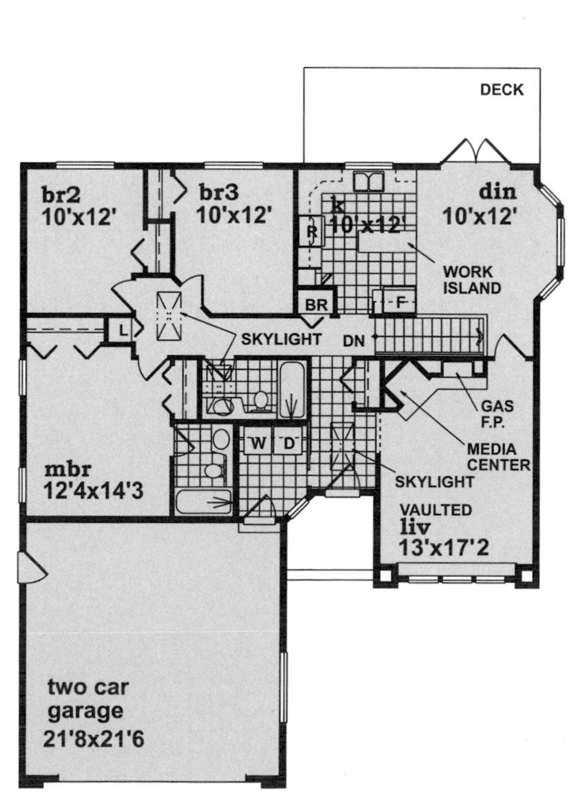

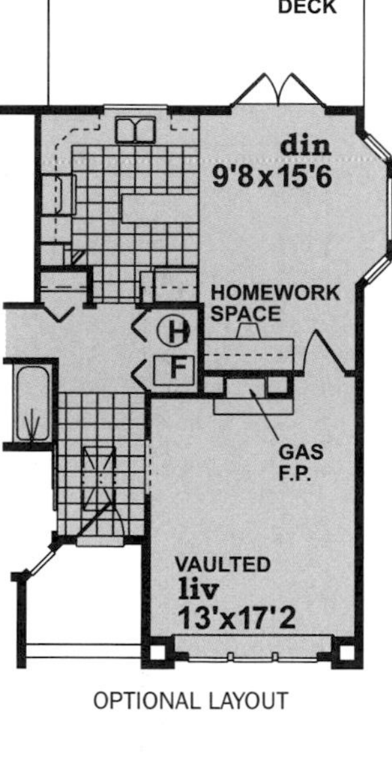

OPTIONAL LAYOUT

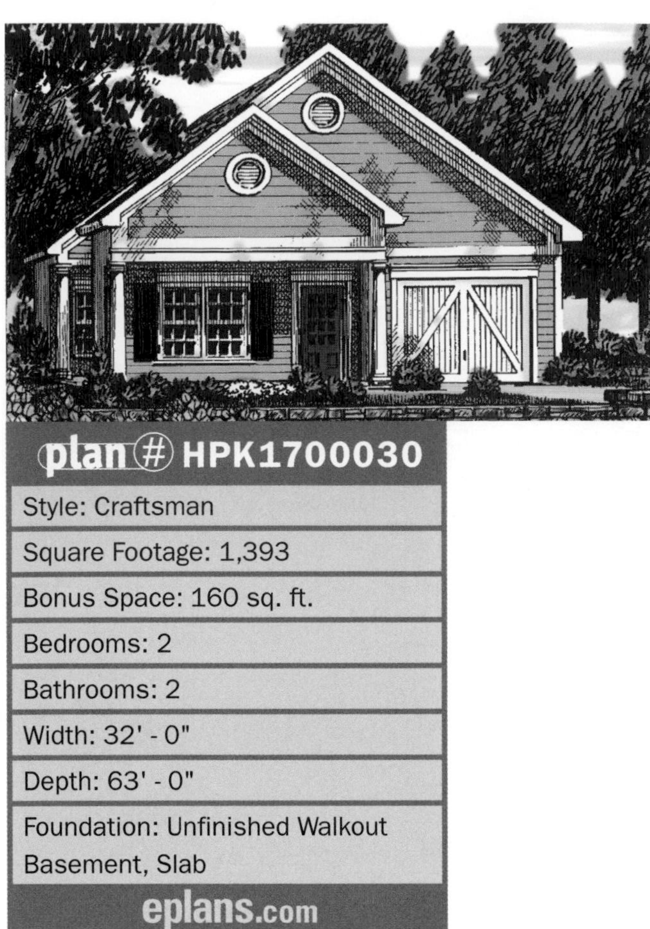

plan# HPK1700030

Style: Craftsman

Square Footage: 1,393

Bonus Space: 160 sq. ft.

Bedrooms: 2

Bathrooms: 2

Width: 32' - 0"

Depth: 63' - 0"

Foundation: Unfinished Walkout Basement, Slab

eplans.com

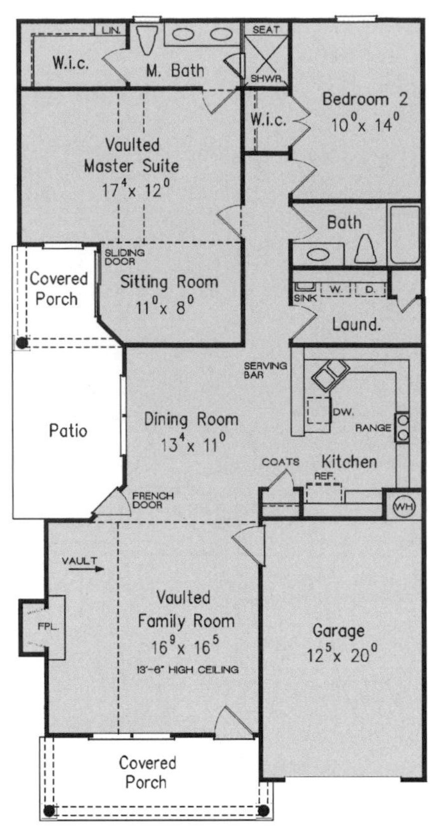

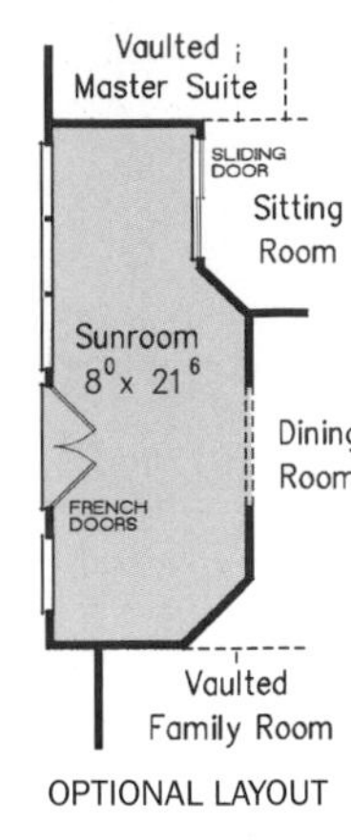

OPTIONAL LAYOUT

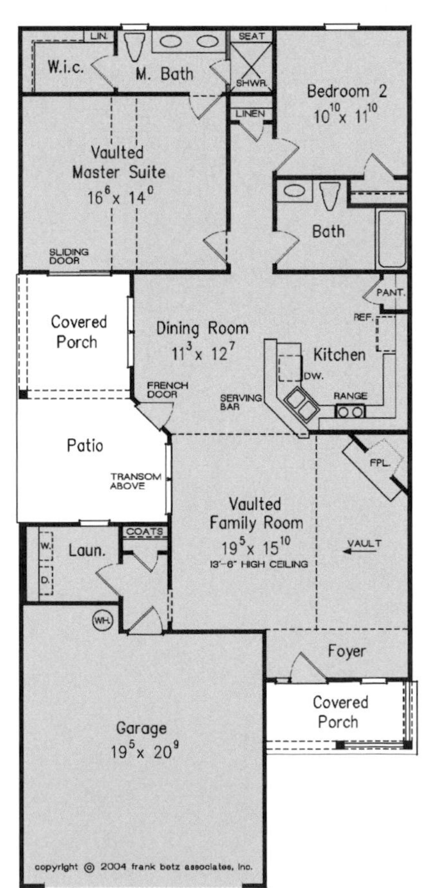

Vaulted Master Suite
SLIDING DOOR
FRENCH DOORS
Dining Room
Sunroom
11⁹x 20⁰
Vaulted Family Room
W.
D.
Laun.
COATS

OPTIONAL LAYOUT

plan# HPK1700031

Style: Bungalow

Square Footage: 1,393

Bonus Space: 206 sq. ft.

Bedrooms: 2

Bathrooms: 2

Width: 32' - 0"

Depth: 70' - 0"

Foundation: Crawlspace, Unfinished Walkout Basement

eplans.com

plan# HPK1700032

Style: Transitional
Square Footage: 1,395
Bedrooms: 3
Bathrooms: 2
Width: 44' - 11"
Depth: 50' - 1"
Foundation: Slab
eplans.com

Quaint cottage style graces the exterior of this lovely home. The three bedrooms are made up of two familiy suites that share a hall bath, and a master bedroom on the opposite side of the home. The master suite includes a private bath with two linen closets, a garden tub, and a walk-in closet. A family room with a fireplace is open to a dining area, which overlooks the rear patio deck. The kitchen accesses a laundry room conveniently connected to the garage.

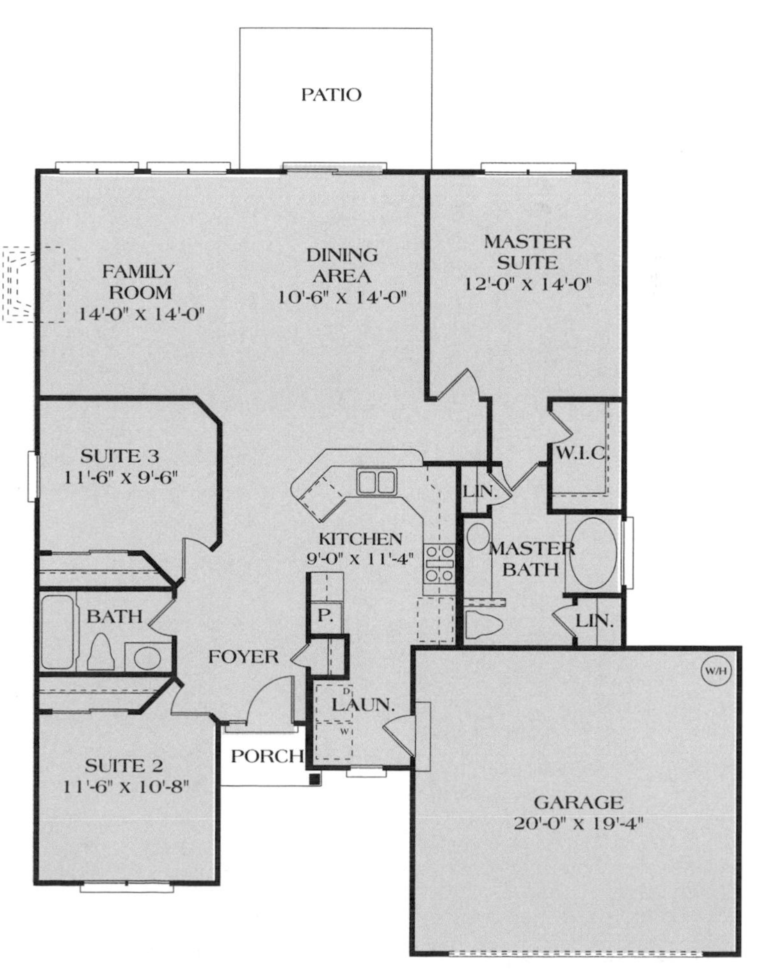

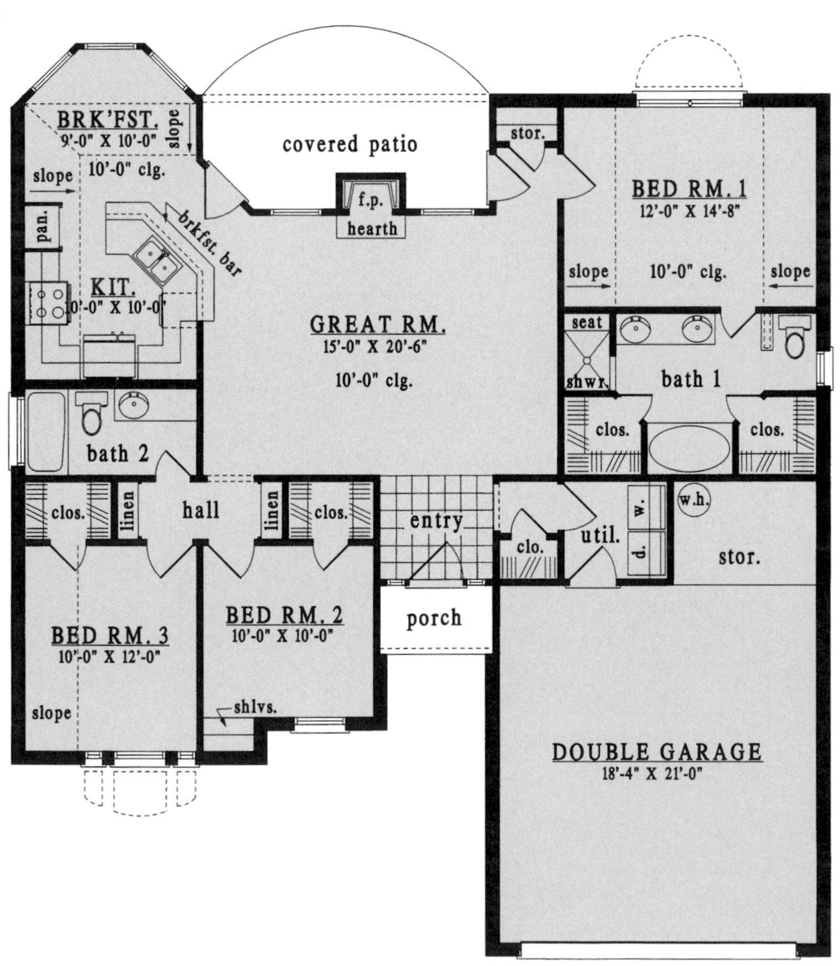

plan # HPK1700033

Style: Traditional
Square Footage: 1,399
Bedrooms: 3
Bathrooms: 2
Width: 47' - 4"
Depth: 50' - 1"
Foundation: Crawlspace, Slab

eplans.com

Bedroom 3 has an incredible arched window, extending all the way to the ceiling, on this charmer. Also note the attractive, fanlight transom above the entrance. With all of your needs situated on one floor, you'll be amazed at how much elegant living this interior accommodates. The great room features a cozy fireplace and two different exits to the exquisite covered patio. The master bedroom features a sloped ceiling and gracious bay window. Discover an oversized tub in the bath for long soaks, surrounded by His and Hers closets. The breakfast alcove faces a snack bar in the kitchen and offers a view of the patio.

plan# HPK1700034

Style: Vacation

Square Footage: 1,404

Bonus Space: 256 sq. ft.

Bedrooms: 2

Bathrooms: 2

Width: 54' - 7"

Depth: 46' - 6"

Foundation: Crawlspace

eplans.com

This rustic Craftsman-style cottage provides an open interior with good flow to the outdoors. The front covered porch invites casual gatherings; inside, the dining area is set for both everyday and formal occasions. Meal preparations are a breeze with a cooktop/snack-bar island in the kitchen. A centered fireplace in the great room shares its warmth with the dining room. A rear hall leads to the master bedroom and a secondary bedroom; upstairs, a loft has space for computers.

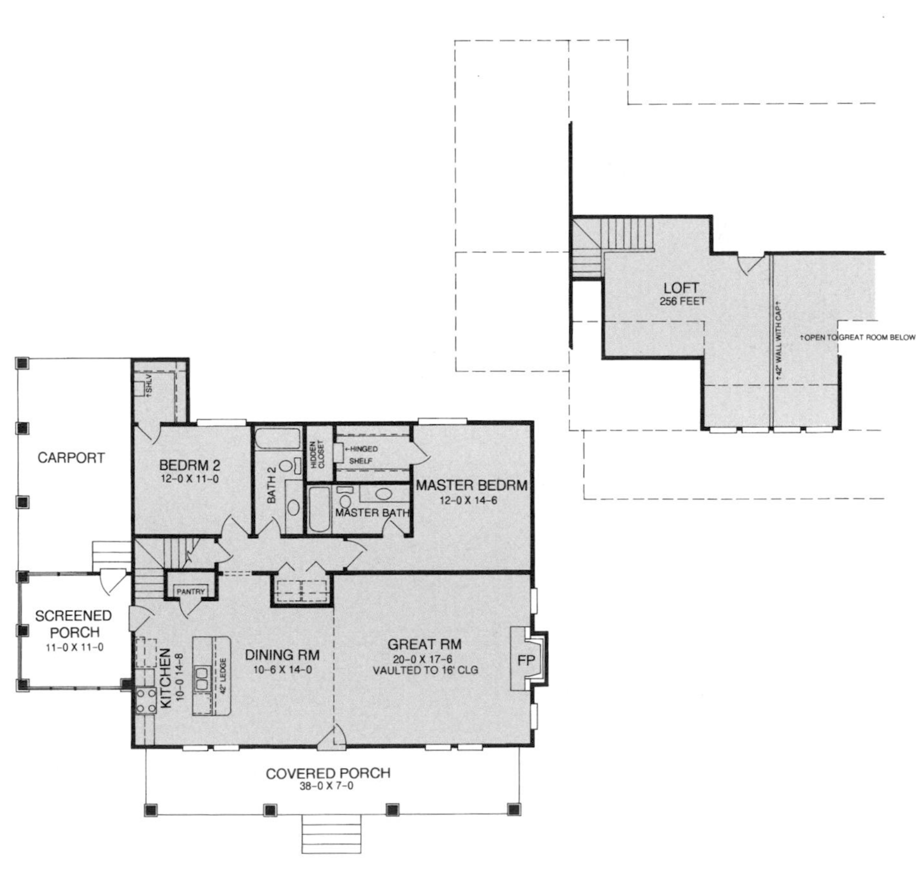

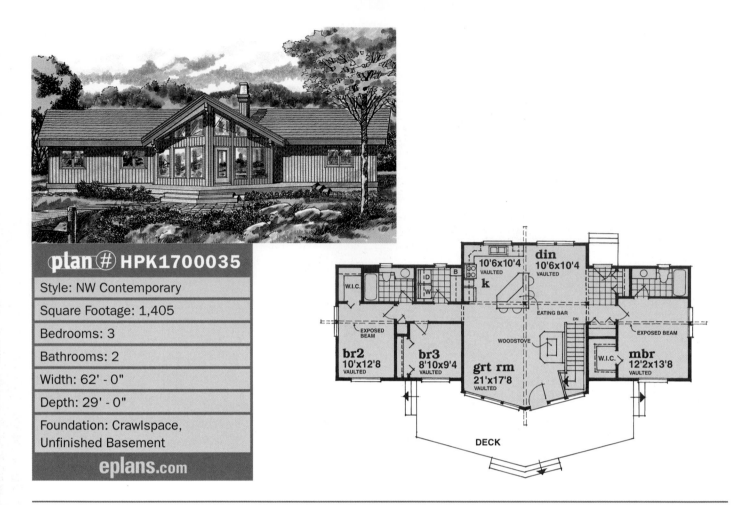

plan# HPK1700035

Style: NW Contemporary
Square Footage: 1,405
Bedrooms: 3
Bathrooms: 2
Width: 62' - 0"
Depth: 29' - 0"
Foundation: Crawlspace, Unfinished Basement

eplans.com

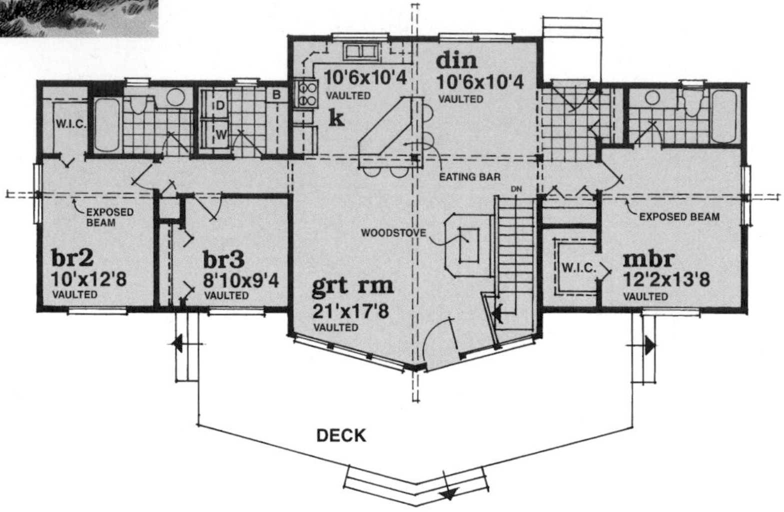

W.I.C.
B
D
W
10'6x10'4
VAULTED
k
din
10'6x10'4
VAULTED
EATING BAR
DN
EXPOSED BEAM
EXPOSED BEAM
WOODSTOVE
br2
10'x12'8
VAULTED
br3
8'10x9'4
VAULTED
grt rm
21'x17'8
VAULTED
W.I.C.
mbr
12'2x13'8
VAULTED
DECK

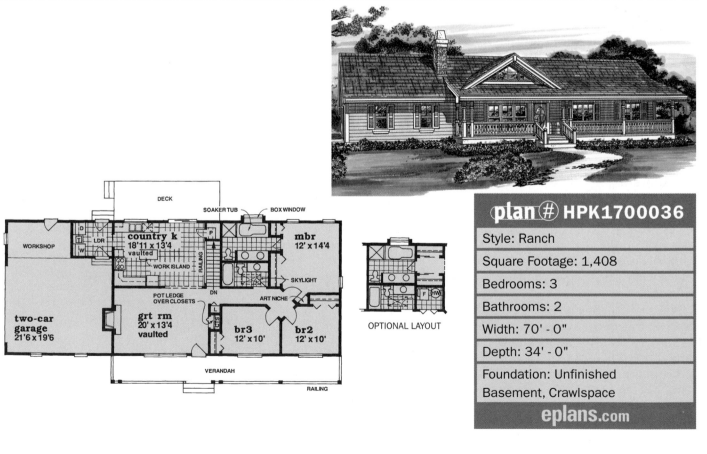

plan# HPK1700036

Style: Ranch
Square Footage: 1,408
Bedrooms: 3
Bathrooms: 2
Width: 70' - 0"
Depth: 34' - 0"
Foundation: Unfinished Basement, Crawlspace

eplans.com

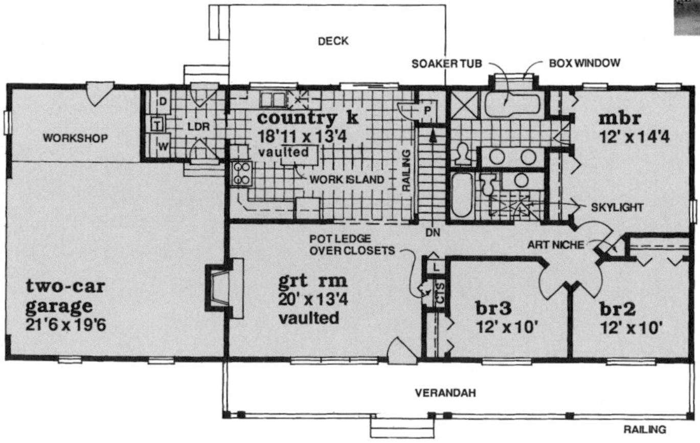

DECK
SOAKER TUB
BOX WINDOW
WORKSHOP
D
T
W
LDR
country k
18'11 x 13'4
vaulted
P
mbr
12' x 14'4
WORK ISLAND
RAILING
SKYLIGHT
DN
POT LEDGE OVER CLOSETS
ART NICHE
two-car garage
21'6 x 19'6
grt rm
20' x 13'4
vaulted
L
C/S
br3
12' x 10'
br2
12' x 10'
VERANDAH
RAILING

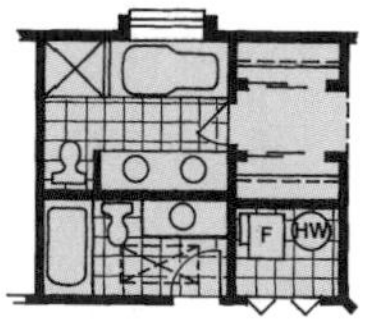

F
HW
OPTIONAL LAYOUT

plan# HPK1700037

Style: Traditional

Square Footage: 1,416

Bedrooms: 3

Bathrooms: 2

Width: 49' - 0"

Depth: 58' - 0"

eplans.com

A front walk leads to the porch, alongside the front-loading garage (with workshop area), in this great first-time home. Enter through an arched ceiling into the formal living room, where a cozy fireplace beneath a sloped-ceiling awaits. The kitchen and dining room are just to the left; the kitchen features a curving snack bar, suitable for accommodating hungry neighborhood pals. To the right of the main entry lies the master suite, with mammoth walk-in closet (large enough for its own window!) and dual vanities. The living room also lets off onto a rear screened porch—which, in turn, offers access to the exterior. The dining room offers views to the porch, living room, and kitchen, creating an expansive effect. The kitchen accesses the pantry and laundry room, simplifying housework. Bedrooms 2 and 3 exist to the left of the plan, through the dining room, with shared bath and separate closets.

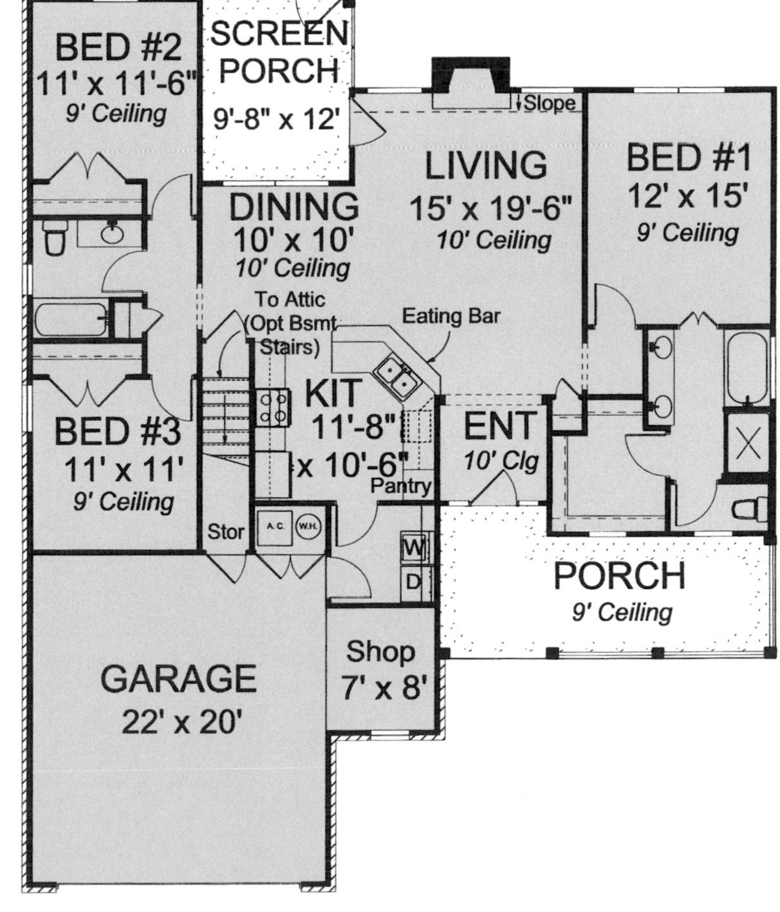

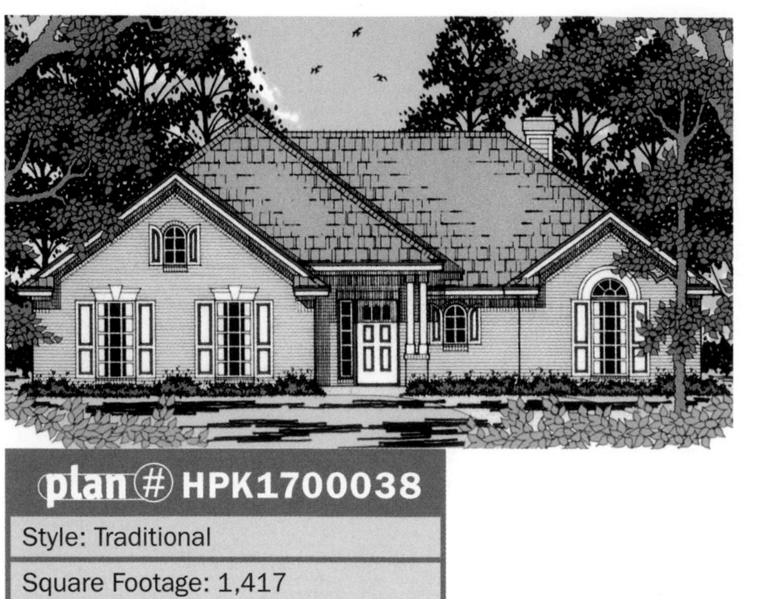

plan# HPK1700038

Style: Traditional

Square Footage: 1,417

Bedrooms: 3

Bathrooms: 2

Foundation: Slab, Crawlspace

eplans.com

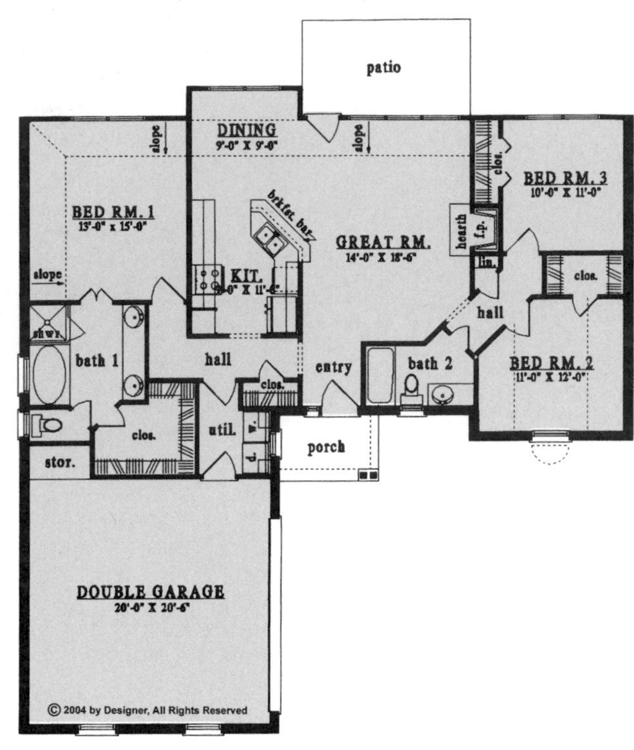

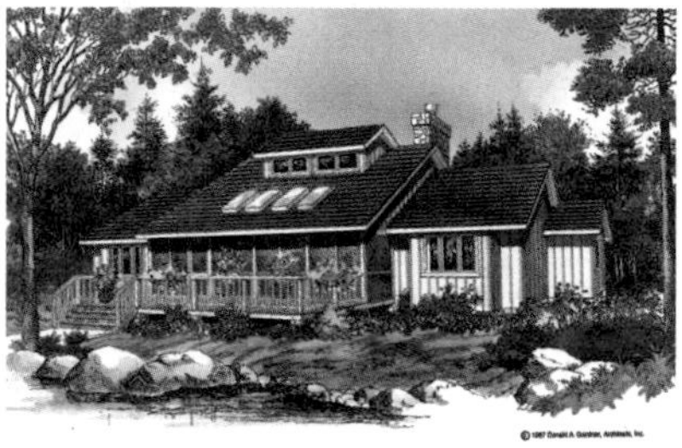

patio
DINING
9'-0" X 9'-0"
slope
BED RM. 1
13'-0" x 15'-0"
brkfst. bar
GREAT RM.
14'-0" X 18'-6"
hearth
f.p.
clos.
BED RM. 3
10'-0" X 11'-0"
lin.
clos.
KIT.
hall
bath 1
hall
clos.
entry
bath 2
BED RM. 2
11'-0" X 12'-0"
clos.
util.
porch
stor.
DOUBLE GARAGE
20'-0" X 20'-6"
© 2004 by Designer, All Rights Reserved

REAR EXTERIOR

© 1987 Donald A. Gardner, Architects, Inc.

down
hot tub
DECK
29-8 x 9-0
skylights
SCREENED PORCH
29-0 x 10-0
cl
lin.
BED RM.
10-8 x 11-0
clerestory above
KIT.
8-10 x 11-8
MASTER BED RM.
13-4 x 17-0
walk in closet
bath
fireplace
BED RM.
10-8 x 11-0
GREAT RM.
20-0 x 21-6
(cathedral ceiling)
cl
master bath
tub
pd. rm.
FOYER
dry
wash
© 1987 Donald A. Gardner Architects, Inc.
PORCH
27-6 x 6-0
down

plan# HPK1700039

Style: Key West Style

Square Footage: 1,426

Bedrooms: 3

Bathrooms: 2½

Width: 67' - 6"

Depth: 36' - 8"

eplans.com

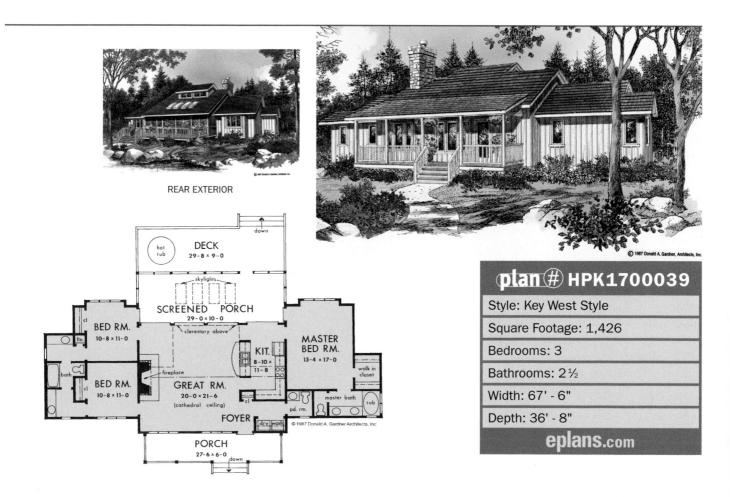

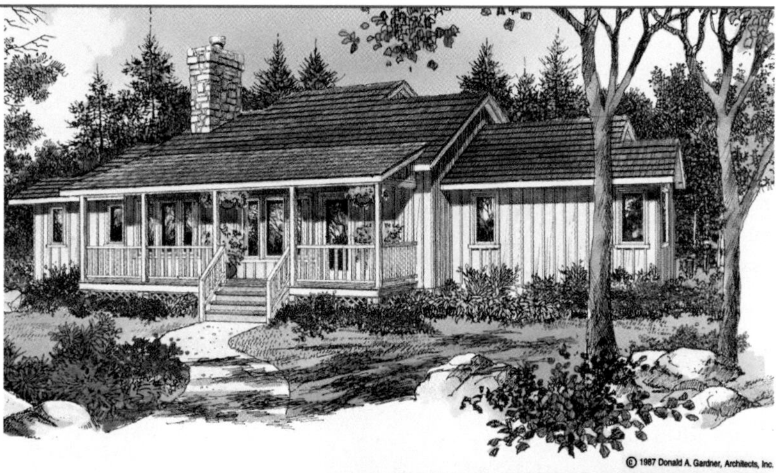

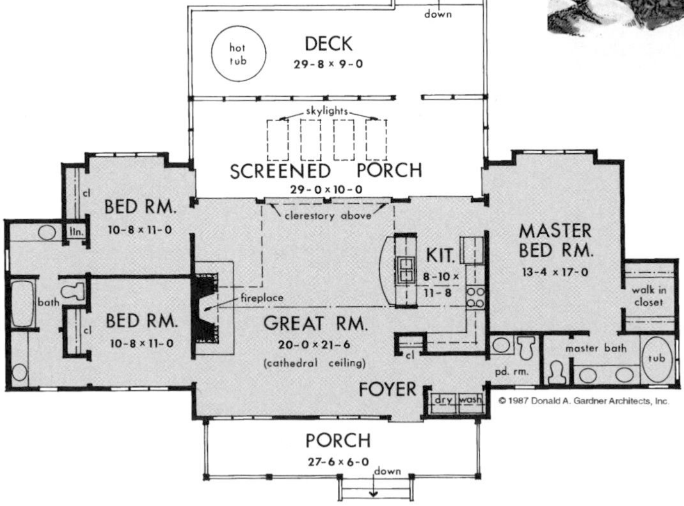

plan# HPK1700040

Style: Country Cottage
Square Footage: 1,429
Bedrooms: 3
Bathrooms: 2
Width: 49' - 0"
Depth: 53' - 0"
Foundation: Slab, Unfinished Walkout Basement, Crawlspace

eplans.com

This home's gracious exterior is indicative of the elegant yet extremely livable floor plan inside. Volume ceilings that crown the family living areas combine with an open floor plan to give the modest square footage a more spacious feel. The formal dining room is set off from the foyer and vaulted family room with stately columns. The spacious family room has a corner fireplace, rear-yard door, and serving bar from the open galley kitchen. A bay-windowed breakfast nook flanks the kitchen on one end, and a laundry center and wet bar/serving pantry leads to the dining room on the other. The split-bedroom plan allows the amenity-rich master suite maximum privacy. A pocket door off the family room leads to the hall housing the two family bedrooms and a full bath.

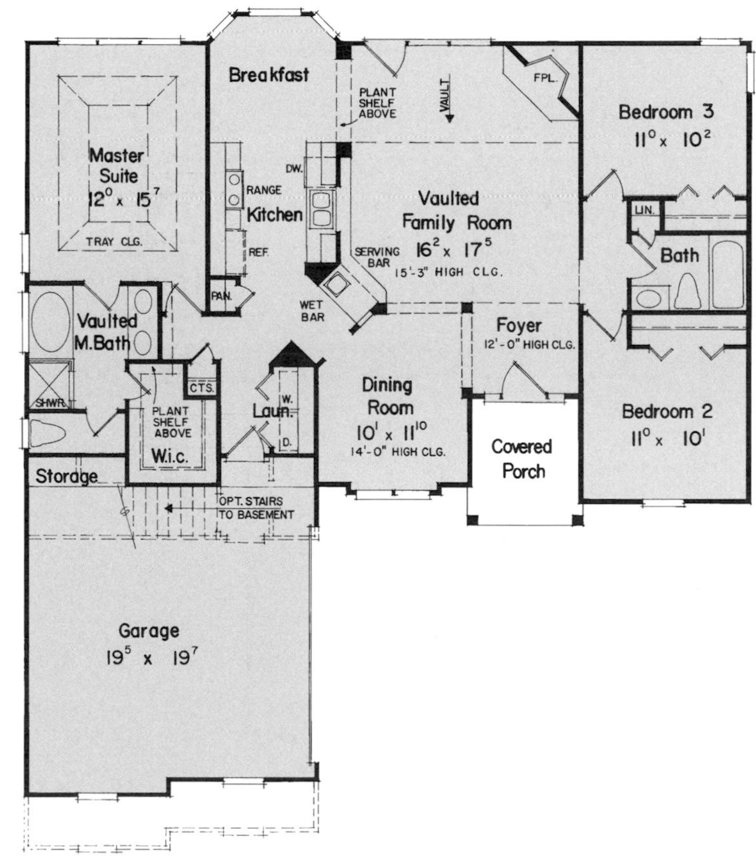

plan# HPK1700041

Style: Bungalow

Square Footage: 1,444

Bedrooms: 3

Bathrooms: 2

Width: 49' - 6"

Depth: 52' - 4"

Foundation: Unfinished Basement

eplans.com

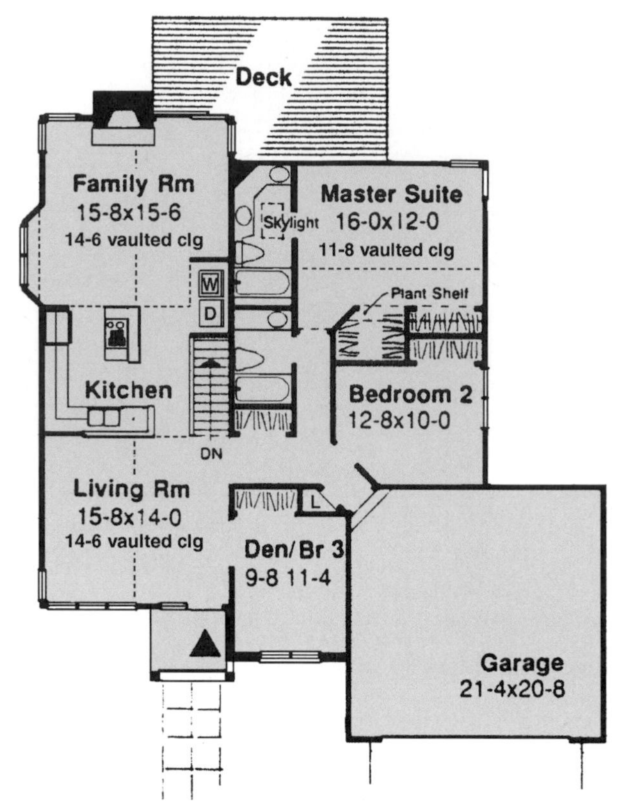

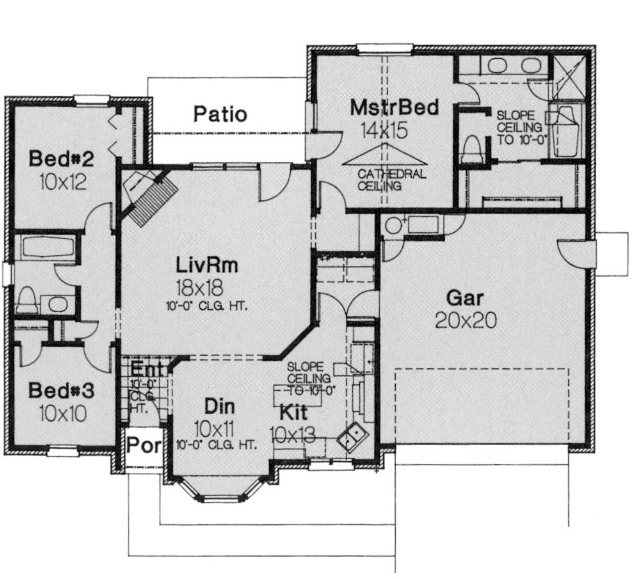

plan# HPK1700042

Style: Traditional

Square Footage: 1,452

Bedrooms: 3

Bathrooms: 2

Width: 55' - 0"

Depth: 40' - 10"

Foundation: Slab

eplans.com

plan# HPK1700043

Style: Farmhouse
Square Footage: 1,455
Bedrooms: 3
Bathrooms: 2
Width: 50' - 6"
Depth: 38' - 0"
Foundation: Crawlspace, Unfinished Basement

eplans.com

This country home invites the outdoors in with a triple skylight above the great room, a front porch, and a large rear deck. An open kitchen with a small island flows right into the vaulted dining area. The master suite features a private bath and walk-in closet. Two secondary bedrooms share a hall bath. The laundry room doubles as a mud room for inclement weather.

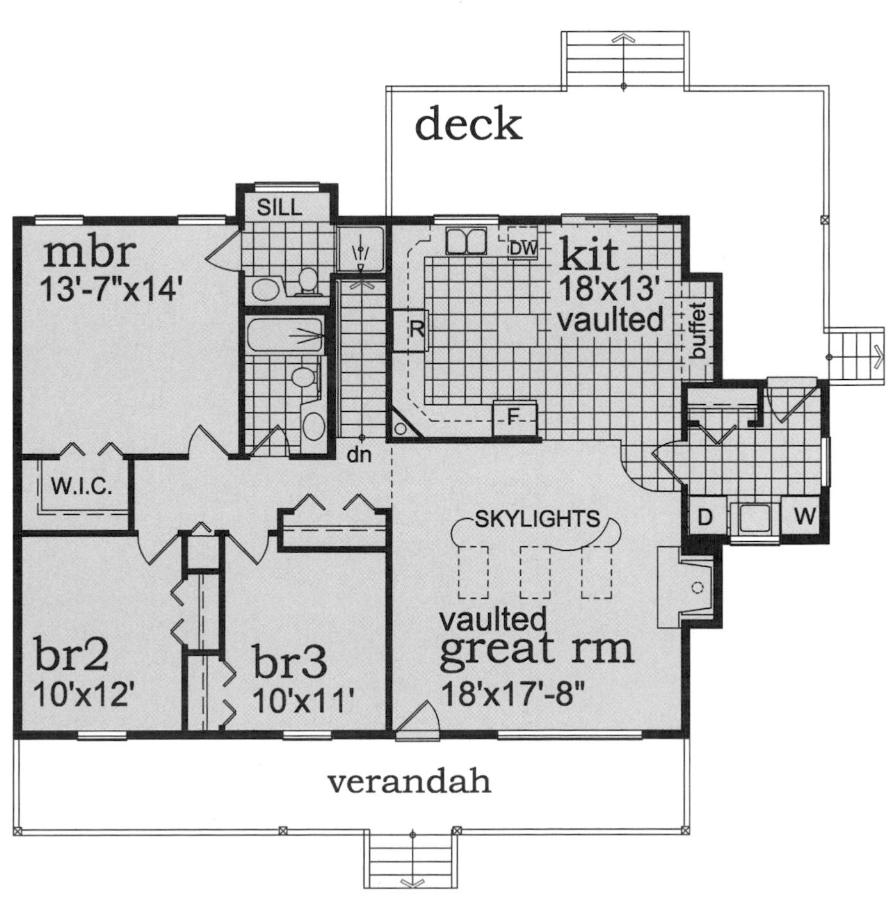

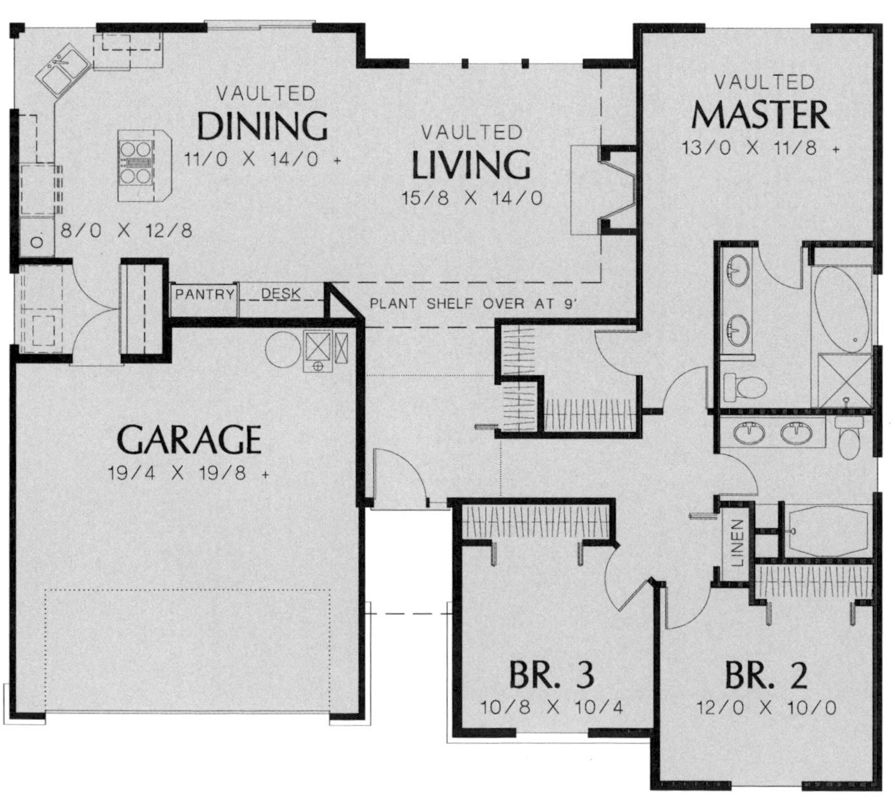

plan# HPK1700044

Style: Country Cottage

Square Footage: 1,467

Bedrooms: 3

Bathrooms: 2

Width: 49' - 0"

Depth: 43' - 0"

Foundation: Crawlspace

eplans.com

This charming traditional design boasts a cozy, compact floor plan. Vaulted ceilings add spaciousness to the dining area, living room, and master bedroom. The kitchen is open to the dining room and includes an island cooktop and corner sink. A service entry leads to the two-car garage and holds the laundry alcove and a storage closet. The master suite is as gracious as those found in much larger homes, with a walk-in closet and a bath with a spa tub, separate shower, and double sinks.

plan# HPK1700045

Style: Craftsman
Square Footage: 1,472
Bedrooms: 2
Bathrooms: 2
Width: 32' - 0"
Depth: 63' - 0"
Foundation: Crawlspace, Unfinished Walkout Basement

eplans.com

This narrow-lot plan still manages to feel balanced and coordinated by incorporating great height and flow-through. The vaulted ceilings in the master bedroom and bath and in the family room keep spaces bright and airy. The functional kitchen, dining room, and patio span the width of the plan for ease of use. A full bath attends the second bedroom, located near the foyer for use also as a powder room. The separate laundry room and pantry near the garage is a welcome accomodation that shows sensible planning.

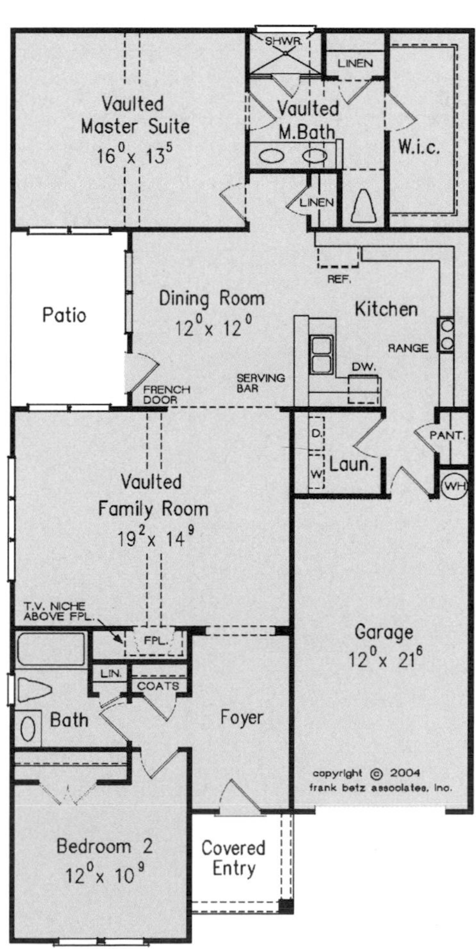

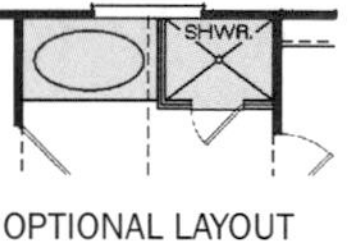

OPTIONAL LAYOUT

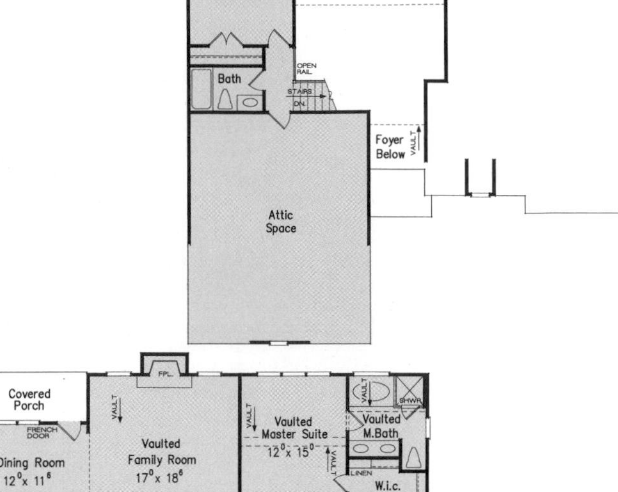

plan# HPK1700046

Style: Country Cottage
Square Footage: 1,477
Bonus Space: 283 sq. ft.
Bedrooms: 3
Bathrooms: 2
Width: 51' - 0"
Depth: 51' - 4"
Foundation: Crawlspace, Unfinished Walkout Basement

eplans.com

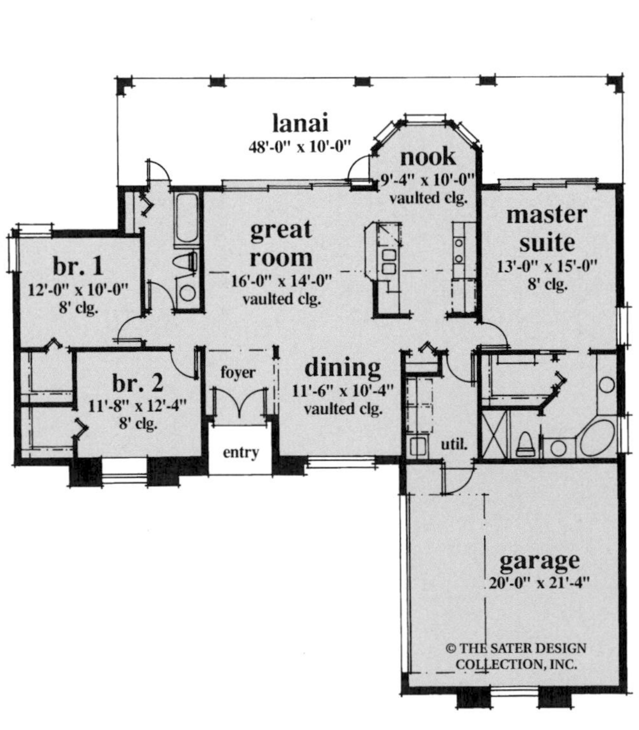

plan# HPK1700047

Style: Floridian
Square Footage: 1,487
Bedrooms: 3
Bathrooms: 2
Width: 58' - 0"
Depth: 58' - 0"
Foundation: Slab

eplans.com

plan# HPK1700048

Style: Craftsman
Square Footage: 1,488
Bonus Space: 375 sq. ft.
Bedrooms: 3
Bathrooms: 2
Width: 51' - 10"
Depth: 58' - 0"

eplans.com

EDITOR'S PICK

We love how this small home doesn't skimp on style or comfort. Check out the great cathedral ceiling in the great room and tastefully rustic exterior. Decorative ceilings also adorn the dining room and the master bedroom. The large walk-in attends the master bath, complete with a well-situated whirlpool. Finish the bonus space as a media room or library and you'll have built yourself a family home that pleases all.

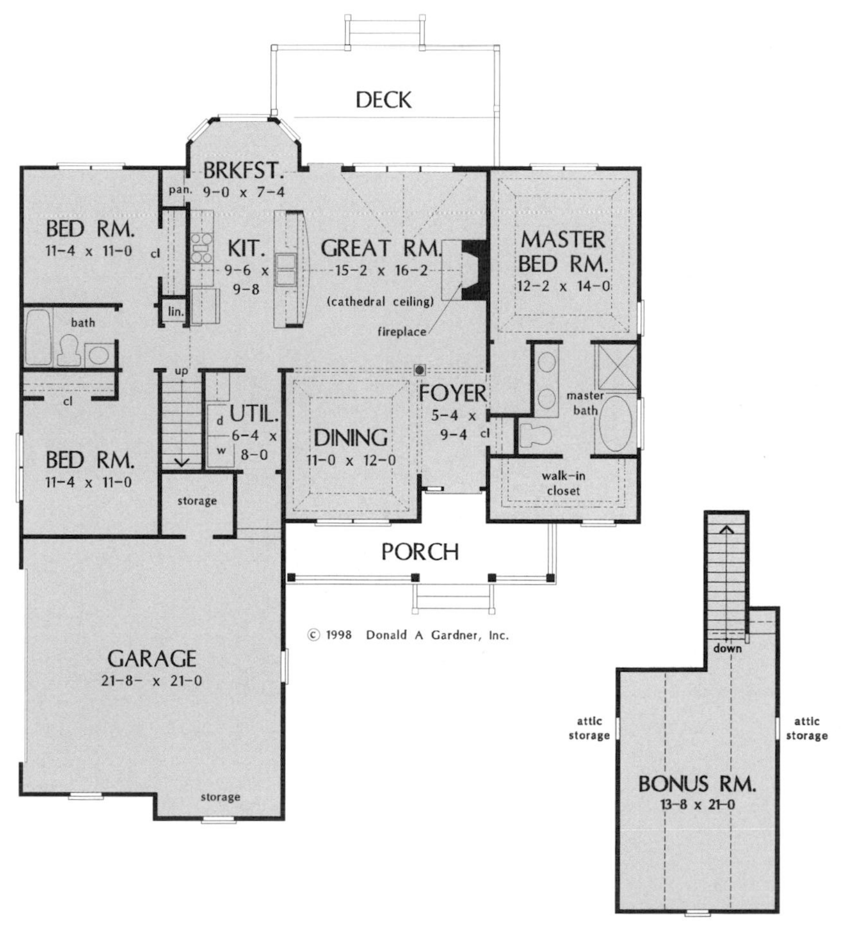

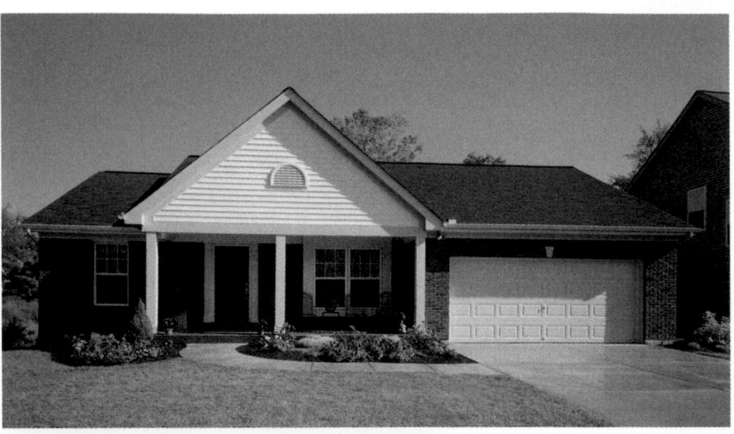

RON & DONNA KOLB-EXPOSURES UNLIMITED

Deck
DN.
24" DESK
36"
Bath
Master Bedroom 12'-0" x 17'-0"
Laun.
Bedroom 11'-4" x 12'-0"
Dining 12'-3" x 13'-11"
SLOPE CEIL.
FLOOR MATERIAL CHANGE
Kitchen 9'-2" x 13'-11"
8'-1" CEIL. HGT. (TYP.)
WALK-IN CLOSET
DN.
Bath
Great Room 18'-0" x 15'-4"
Den/ Bedroom 10'-0" x 11'-9"
Foyer
SLOPE CEIL.
FLOOR MATERIAL CHANGE
Garage 20'-0" x 20'-10"
Porch

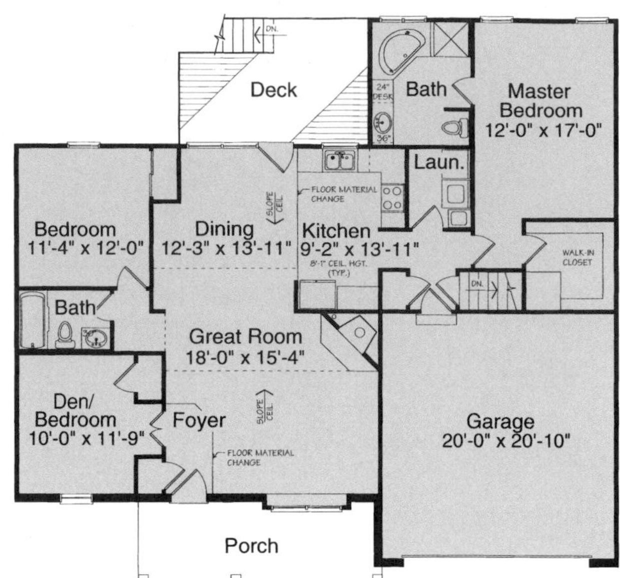

plan # HPK1700049

Style: Traditional

Square Footage: 1,488

Bedrooms: 3

Bathrooms: 2

Width: 51' - 8"

Depth: 47' - 0"

Foundation: Unfinished Basement

eplans.com

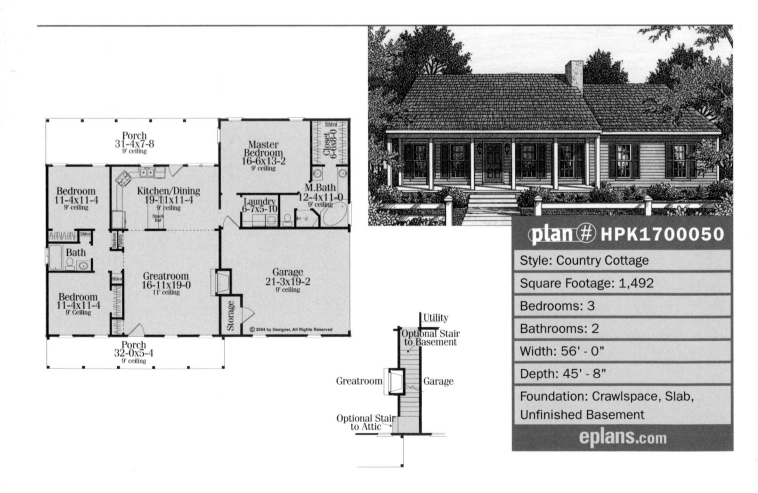

Porch 31-4x7-8 9' ceiling
Master Bedroom 16-6x13-2 9' ceiling
Shlvs
Closet 6-6x8-0
Bedroom 11-4x11-4 9' ceiling
Kitchen/Dining 19-11x11-4 9' ceiling
Snack Bar
M.Bath 12-4x11-0 9' ceiling
Laundry 6-7x5-10
Shlvs
Shelves
Pantry
Bath
Shlvs
Greatroom 16-11x19-0 11' ceiling
Garage 21-3x19-2 9' ceiling
Bedroom 11-4x11-4 9' Ceiling
Storage
© 2004 by Designer, All Rights Reserved
Porch 32-0x5-4 9' ceiling

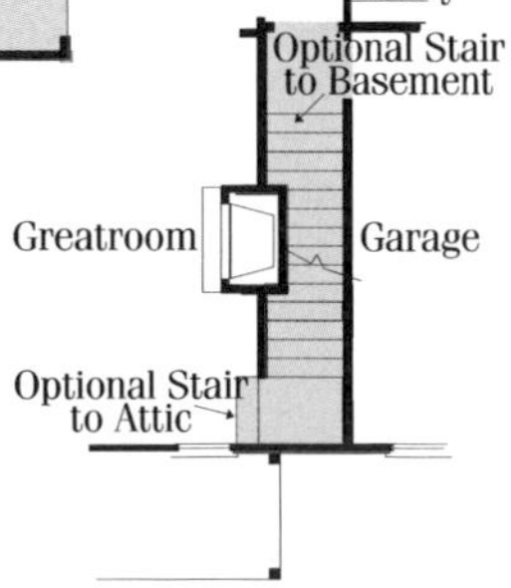

Utility
Optional Stair to Basement
Greatroom
Garage
Optional Stair to Attic

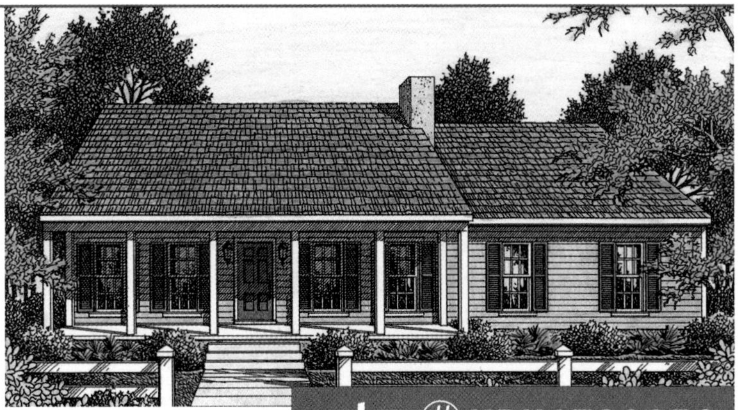

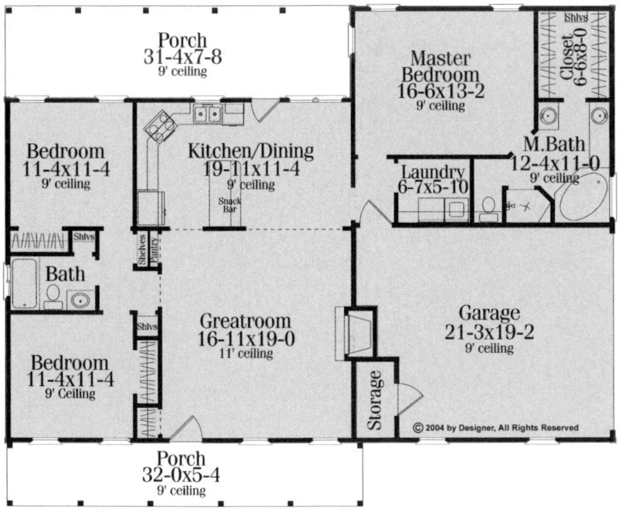

plan # HPK1700050

Style: Country Cottage

Square Footage: 1,492

Bedrooms: 3

Bathrooms: 2

Width: 56' - 0"

Depth: 45' - 8"

Foundation: Crawlspace, Slab, Unfinished Basement

eplans.com

plan # HPK1700051

Style: NW Contemporary

Square Footage: 1,495

Bedrooms: 3

Bathrooms: 2

Width: 58' - 6"

Depth: 33' - 0"

Foundation: Crawlspace

eplans.com

This three-bedroom cottage has just the right rustic mix of vertical wood siding and stone accents. High vaulted ceilings are featured throughout the living room and master bedroom. The living room also has a fireplace and full-height windows overlooking the deck. The dining room has double-door access to the deck. A convenient kitchen includes a U-shaped work area with storage space.

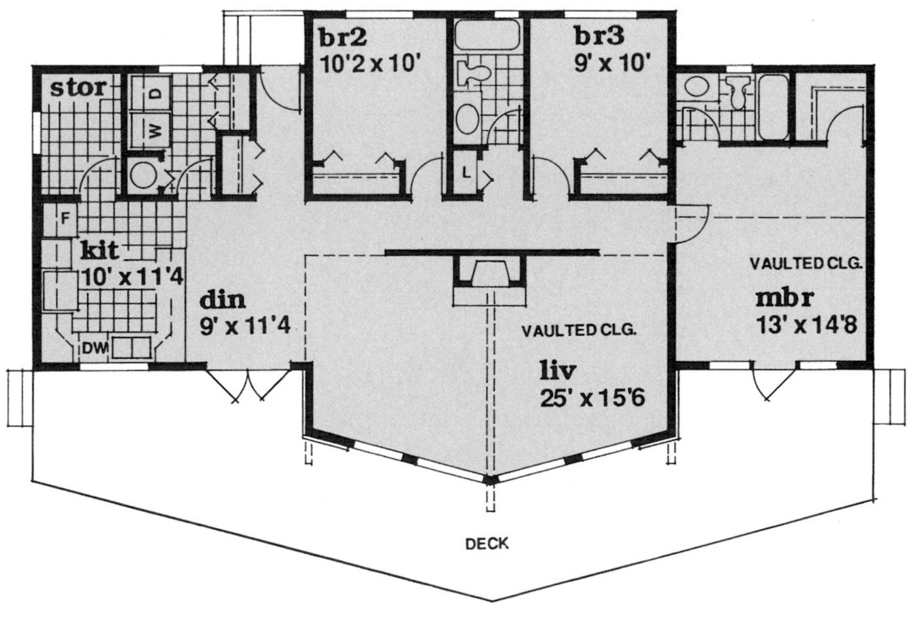

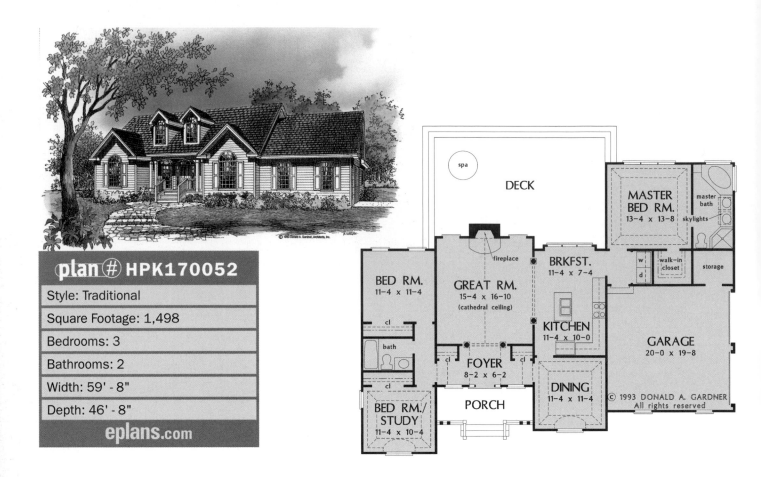

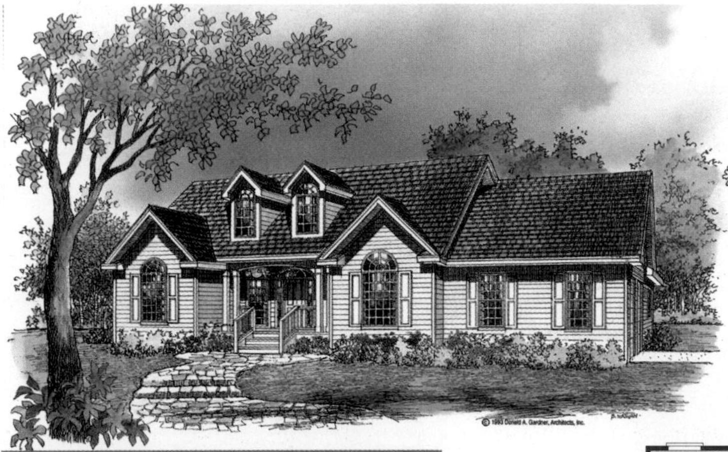

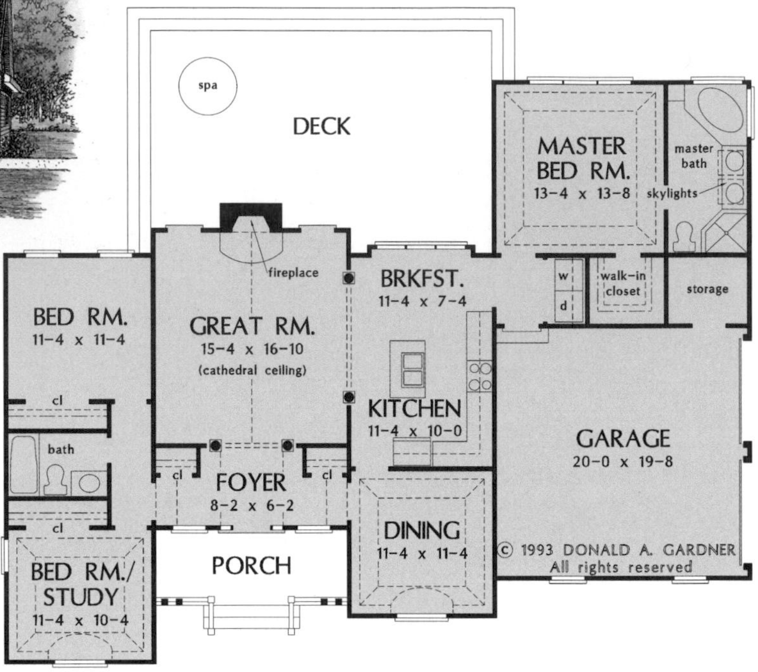

spa
DECK
MASTER BED RM.
13-4 x 13-8
master bath
skylights
fireplace
BRKFST.
11-4 x 7-4
w
d
walk-in closet
storage
BED RM.
11-4 x 11-4
GREAT RM.
15-4 x 16-10
(cathedral ceiling)
KITCHEN
11-4 x 10-0
GARAGE
20-0 x 19-8
cl
bath
cl
FOYER
8-2 x 6-2
cl
cl
DINING
11-4 x 11-4
© 1993 DONALD A. GARDNER
All rights reserved
BED RM./ STUDY
11-4 x 10-4
PORCH

plan# HPK170052

Style: Traditional
Square Footage: 1,498
Bedrooms: 3
Bathrooms: 2
Width: 59' - 8"
Depth: 46' - 8"

eplans.com

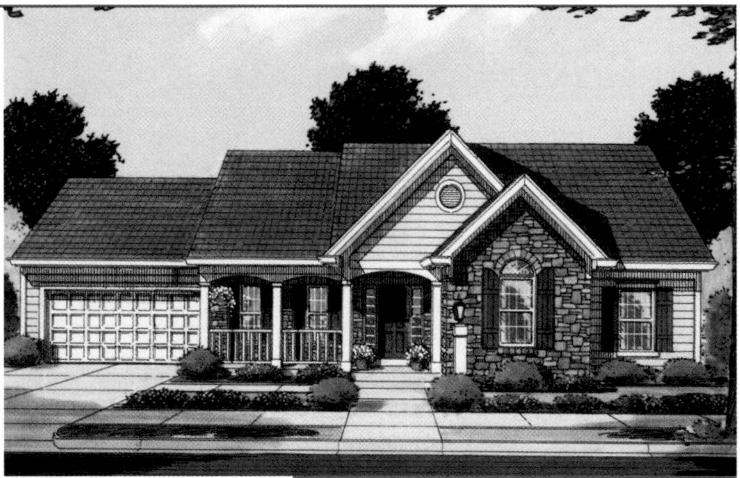

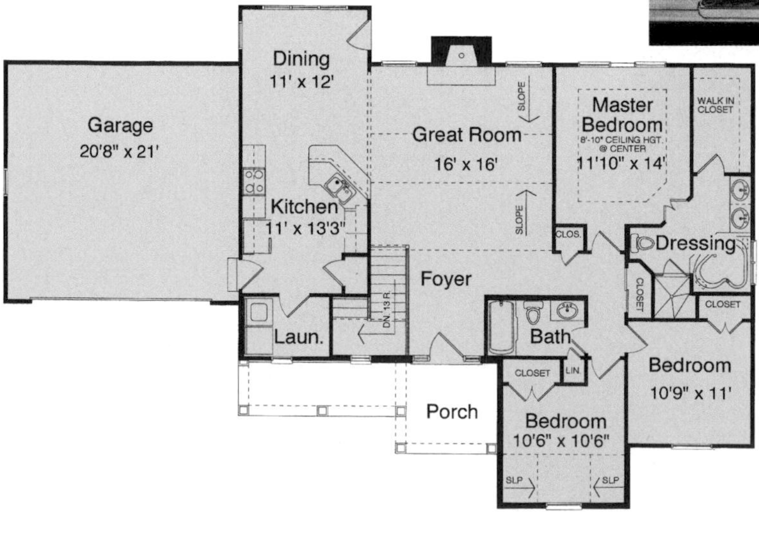

Dining
11' x 12'
Garage
20'8" x 21'
Great Room
16' x 16'
SLOPE
SLOPE
Master Bedroom
8'-10" CEILING HGT. @ CENTER
11'10" x 14'
WALK IN CLOSET
Kitchen
11' x 13'3"
CLOS.
Dressing
Foyer
DN 13R
CLOSET
CLOSET
Laun.
Bath
LIN.
CLOSET
Bedroom
10'9" x 11'
Porch
Bedroom
10'6" x 10'6"
SLP
SLP

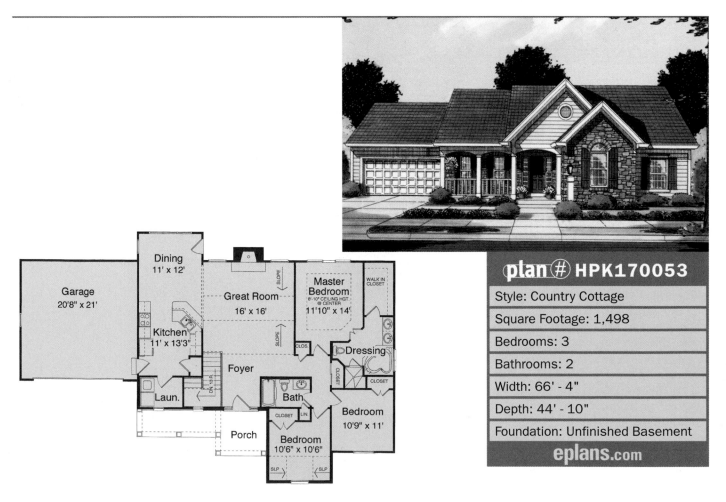

plan# HPK170053

Style: Country Cottage
Square Footage: 1,498
Bedrooms: 3
Bathrooms: 2
Width: 66' - 4"
Depth: 44' - 10"
Foundation: Unfinished Basement

eplans.com

plan# HPK1700054

Style: Farmhouse

First Floor: 1,036 sq. ft.

Second Floor: 273 sq. ft.

Total: 1,309 sq. ft.

Bedrooms: 2

Bathrooms: 2

Width: 39' - 0"

Depth: 38' - 0"

Foundation: Crawlspace

eplans.com

This charming farmhouse design will be economical to build and a pleasure to occupy. Like most vacation homes, this design features an open plan. The large living area includes a living room, a dining room, and a massive stone fireplace. A partition separates the kitchen from the living room. The first floor also holds a bedroom, a full bath, and a laundry room. Upstairs, a spacious sleeping loft overlooks the living room. Don't miss the large front porch—this will be a favorite spot for relaxing.

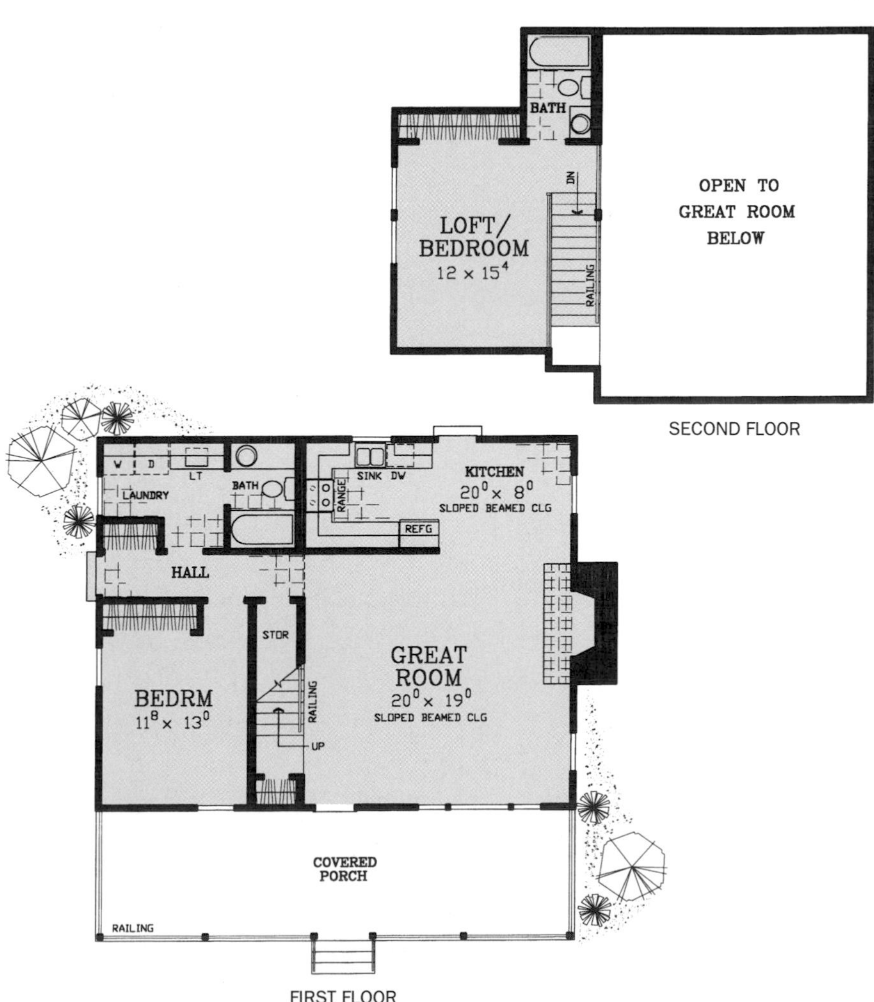

SECOND FLOOR

FIRST FLOOR

plan # HPK170055

Style: Key West Style

First Floor: 1,002 sq. ft.

Second Floor: 336 sq. ft.

Total: 1,338 sq. ft.

Bedrooms: 3

Bathrooms: 2

Width: 36' - 8"

Depth: 44' - 8"

eplans.com

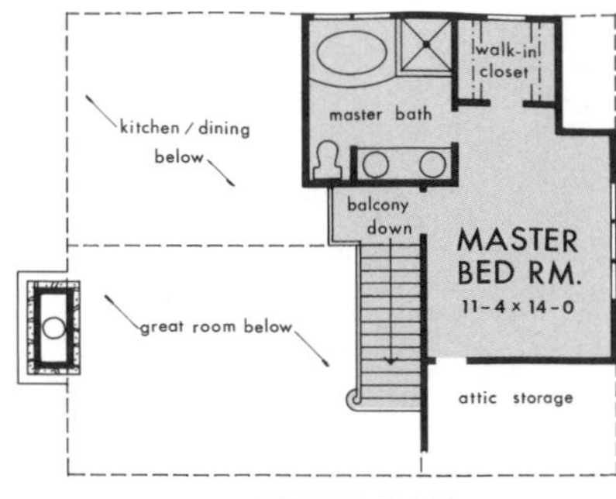

SECOND FLOOR

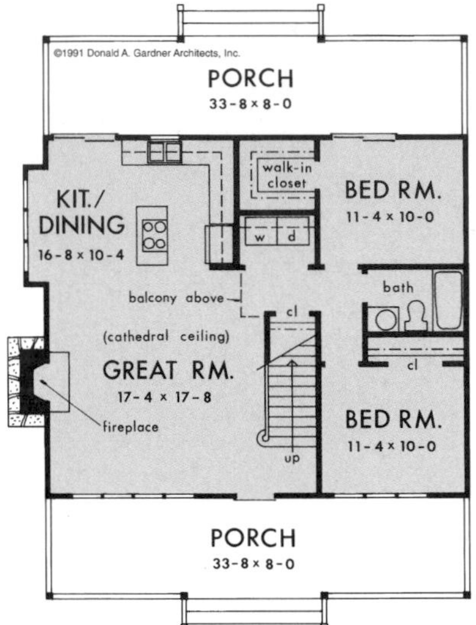

FIRST FLOOR

REAR EXTERIOR

SECOND FLOOR

FIRST FLOOR

plan # HPK170056

Style: Country Cottage

First Floor: 792 sq. ft.

Second Floor: 573 sq. ft.

Total: 1,365 sq. ft.

Bedrooms: 3

Bathrooms: 2

Width: 42' - 0"

Depth: 32' - 0"

Foundation: Crawlspace, Unfinished Basement

eplans.com

plan # HPK1700057

Style: Craftsman
First Floor: 636 sq. ft.
Second Floor: 830 sq. ft.
Total: 1,466 sq. ft.
Bedrooms: 3
Bathrooms: 2½
Width: 28' - 0"
Depth: 43' - 6"
Foundation: Crawlspace

eplans.com

Traditional and Craftsman elements shape the exterior of this lovely family home. The two-story foyer leads down the hall to a great room with a warming fireplace. The U-shaped kitchen includes a window sink and is open to the breakfast nook. A powder room is located near the garage. Upstairs, the master suite provides a private bath and walk-in closet. The two family bedrooms share a full hall bath across from the second-floor laundry room. Linen closets are available in the hall and inside the full hall bath

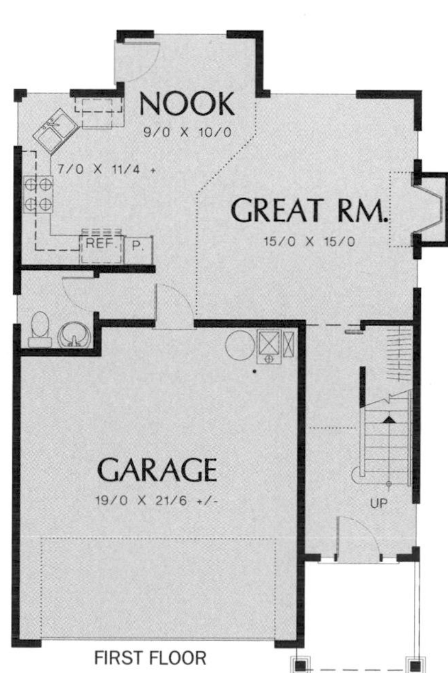

FIRST FLOOR

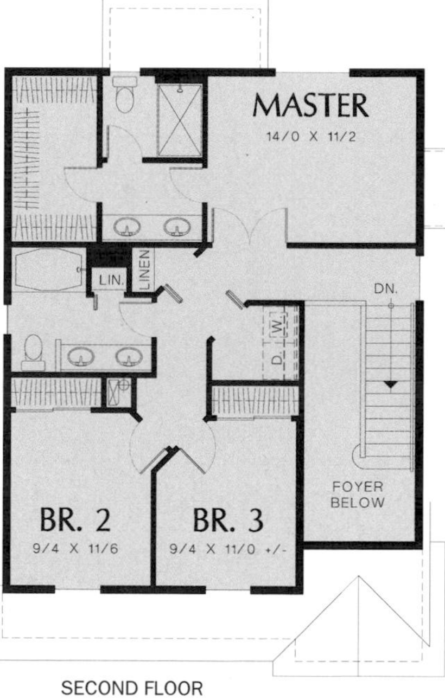

SECOND FLOOR

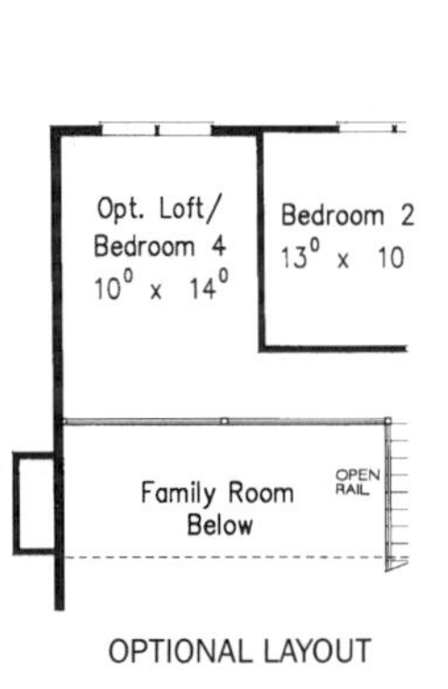

OPTIONAL LAYOUT

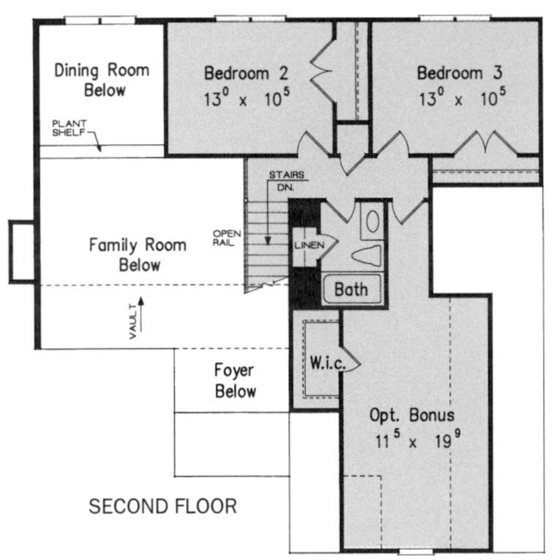

SECOND FLOOR

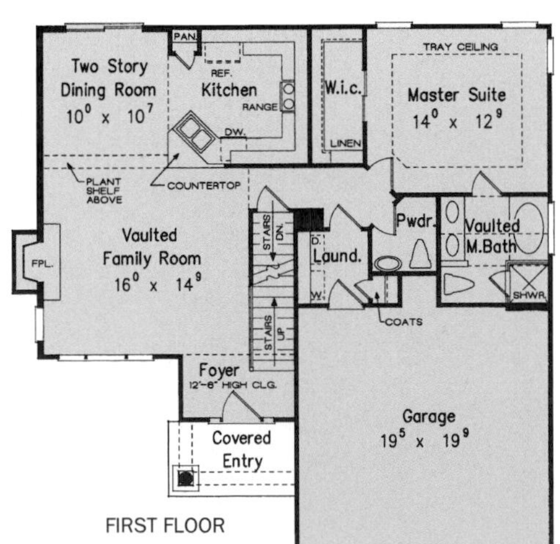

FIRST FLOOR

plan# HPK1700058

Style: Country Cottage
First Floor: 1,001 sq. ft.
Second Floor: 466 sq. ft.
Total: 1,467 sq. ft.
Bonus Space: 292 sq. ft.
Bedrooms: 3
Bathrooms: 2½
Width: 42' - 0"
Depth: 42' - 0"
Foundation: Crawlspace, Unfinished Walkout Basement, Slab

eplans.com

Arched transoms set off by keystones add the final details to the traditional exterior of this home. The foyer opens to a vaulted family room, which enjoys a warm fireplace and leads to a two-story dining area with built-in plant shelves and to a U-shaped kitchen with an angled countertop and spacious pantry. Down the hall, the abundant master suite boasts a tray ceiling and can be found in its own secluded area. Upstairs, two additional bedrooms are found sharing a full bath—note both bedrooms enjoy French doors. An optional bonus room with a walk-in closet is included in this plan.

plan# HPK1700060

Style: NW Contemporary
Square Footage: 1,484
Bedrooms: 3
Bathrooms: 2
Width: 38' - 0"
Depth: 70' - 0"
Foundation: Crawlspace

eplans.com

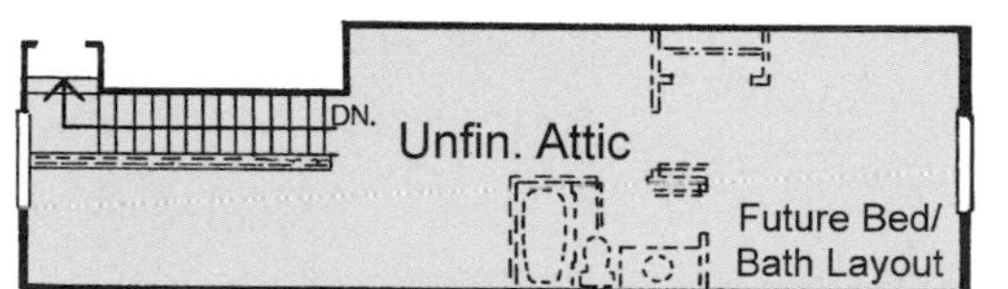

Ideal for narrow lots, this fine bungalow is full of amenities. The entry is just off a covered front porch and leads to a living room complete with a fireplace. The formal dining room is nearby and works well with the L-shaped kitchen. The breakfast nook opens onto a rear patio. Sleeping quaters consist of a master suite with a walk-in closet and private bath, as well as two family bedrooms sharing a full bath. An unfinished attic waits future development; a two-car garage easily shelters the family vehicles.

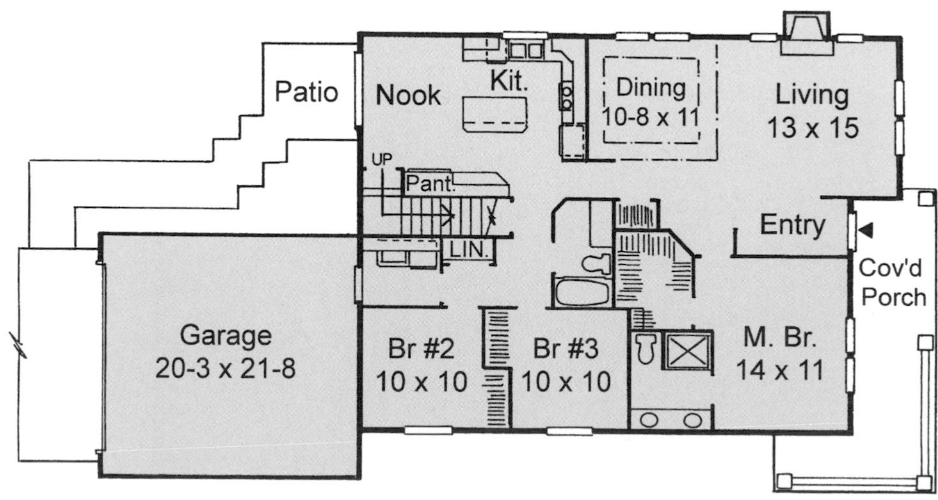

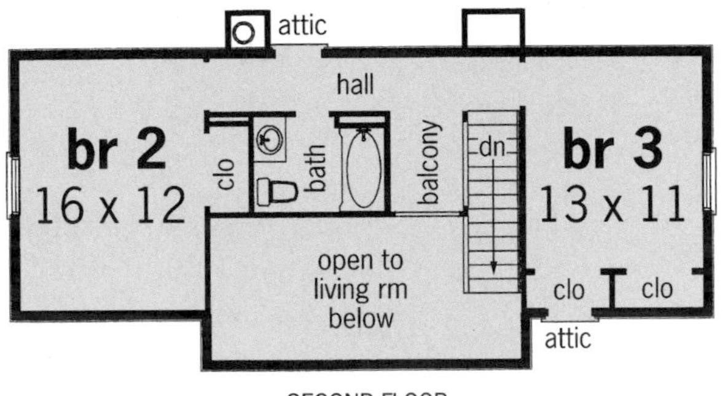

SECOND FLOOR

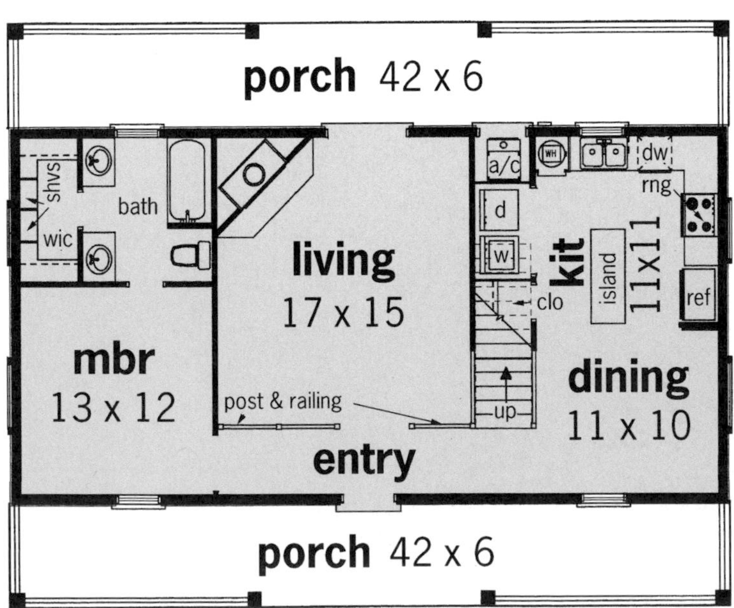

FIRST FLOOR

plan# HPK1700059

Style: Traditional

First Floor: 924 sq. ft.

Second Floor: 561 sq. ft.

Total: 1,485 sq. ft.

Bedrooms: 3

Bathrooms: 2

Width: 42' - 0"

Depth: 34' - 0"

Foundation: Crawlspace, Slab, Unfinished Basement

eplans.com

Efficient elegance is found within these four walls. The covered porch announces the entry, which opens to the living room with its volume ceiling and second-floor balcony overlook. The master suite is secluded on the left for privacy. Here the master bath offers twin vanities and a walk-in closet. The U-shaped kitchen enjoys an island work station. The sunny dining area is situated for ease of service. The second floor holds the two family bedrooms and a shared, full bath.

plan# HPK1700061

Style: Tudor
First Floor: 1,061 sq. ft.
Second Floor: 430 sq. ft.
Total: 1,491 sq. ft.
Bedrooms: 3
Bathrooms: 2½
Width: 40' - 4"
Depth: 36' - 0"
Foundation: Unfinished Walkout Basement

eplans.com

This country cottage boasts a wide covered porch that offers room to sit and enjoy the sunrise. Inside, the vaulted family room provides a warming fireplace. The kitchen features a snack bar and a pantry and opens to the dining area. A tray ceiling in the master bedroom adds depth, and the master bath includes a tub, separate shower, linen closet, and walk-in closet. The powder room sits near the laundry room. Bedrooms 2 and 3 are on the second floor and share a full hall bath and a linen closet.

FIRST FLOOR

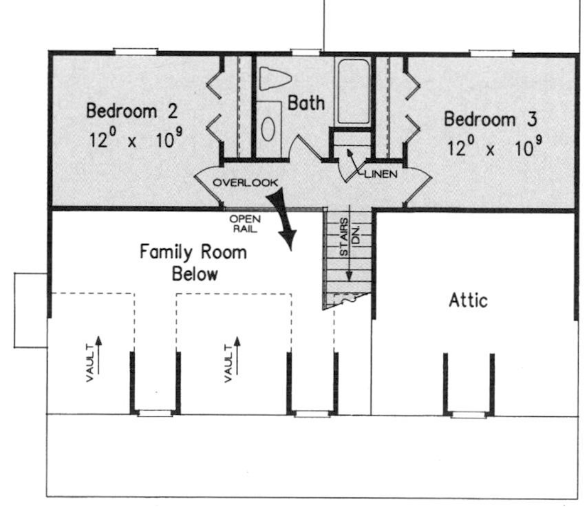

SECOND FLOOR

plan# HPK170062

Style: Vacation
First Floor: 1,042 sq. ft.
Second Floor: 456 sq. ft.
Total: 1,498 sq. ft.
Bedrooms: 3
Bathrooms: 2
Width: 36' - 0"
Depth: 35' - 8"
Foundation: Crawlspace, Unfinished Basement

eplans.com

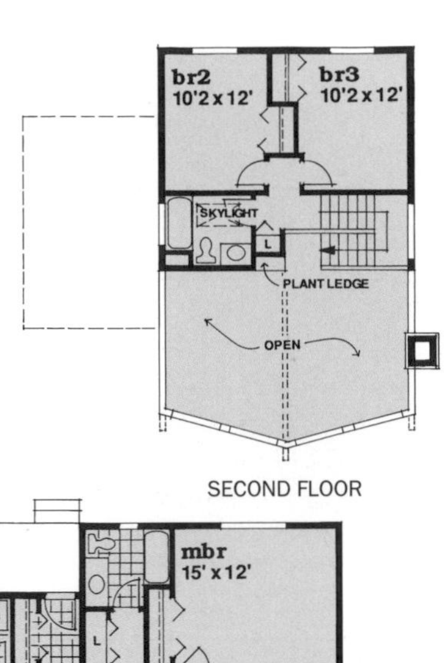

SECOND FLOOR

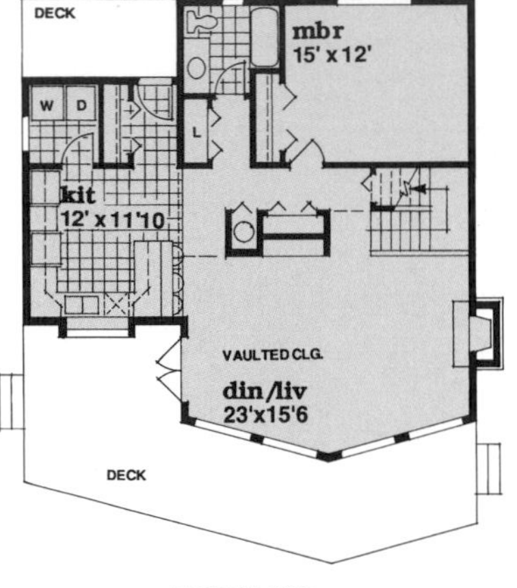

FIRST FLOOR

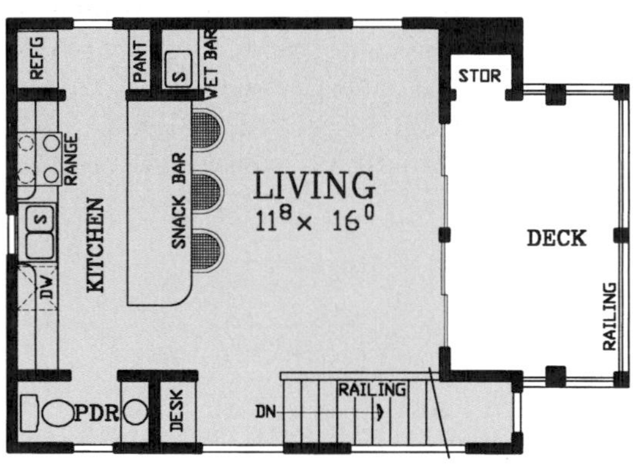

SECOND FLOOR

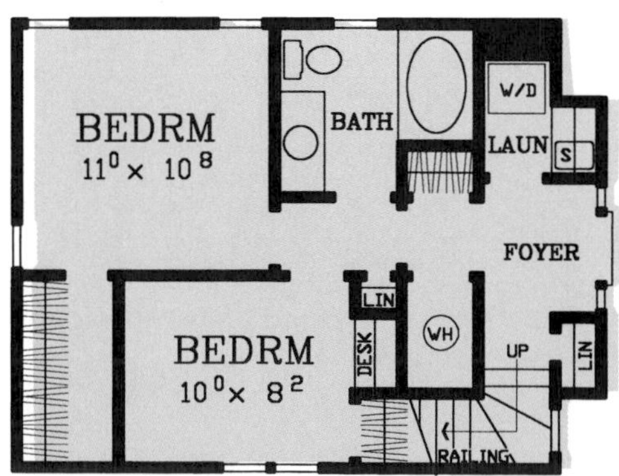

FIRST FLOOR

plan# HPK170063

Style: Bungalow
First Floor: 507 sq. ft.
Second Floor: 438 sq. ft.
Total: 945 sq. ft.
Bedrooms: 2
Bathrooms: 1½
Width: 20' - 0"
Depth: 26' - 0"
Foundation: Crawlspace

eplans.com

plan# HPK1700064

Style: Farmhouse
First Floor: 96 sq. ft.
Second Floor: 896 sq. ft.
Total: 992 sq. ft.
Bedrooms: 2
Bathrooms: 1½
Width: 28' - 0"
Depth: 32' - 0"
Foundation: Slab

eplans.com

Garage space is topped by a lodging area perfect for guests, in-laws, or visiting college-aged children. With plenty of room for your car and some toys—like ATVs, a golf cart, a second car, kids bikes—or just as extra storage space, the garage is ideal. Upstairs houses two bedrooms, each with a private balcony, and a full bath. An eat-in kitchen is fully equipped and ready for meal preparation. The family room provides space for friends and family to gather. A laundry room rounds out the plan.

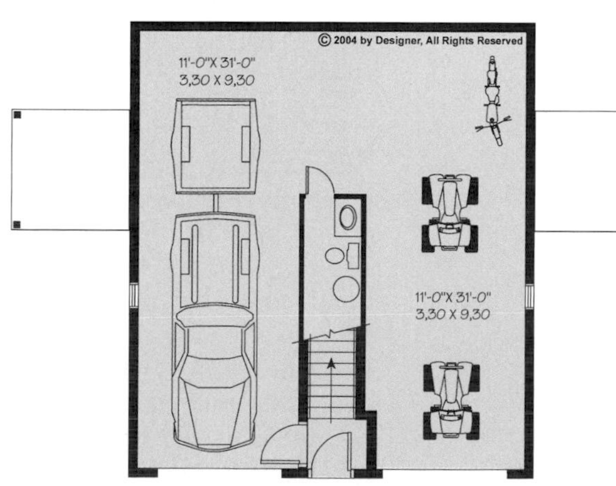

FIRST FLOOR

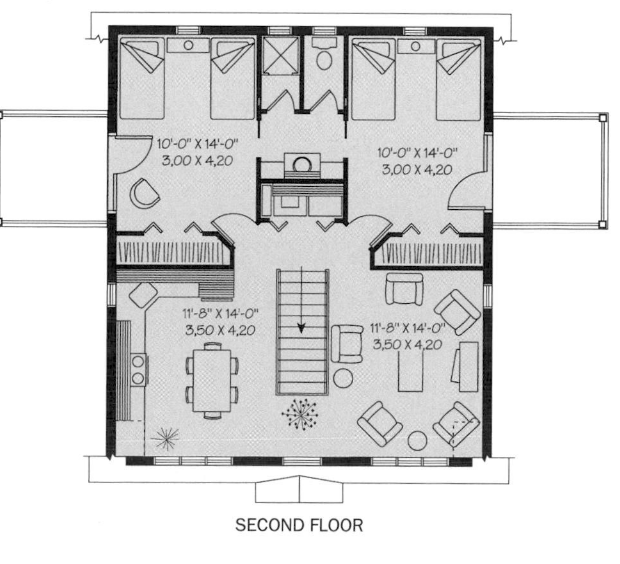

SECOND FLOOR

plan# HPK1700065

Style: Country Cottage
First Floor: 672 sq. ft.
Second Floor: 401 sq. ft.
Total: 1,073 sq. ft.
Bedrooms: 3
Bathrooms: 1½
Width: 24' - 0"
Depth: 36' - 0"
Foundation: Crawlspace, Unfinished Basement

eplans.com

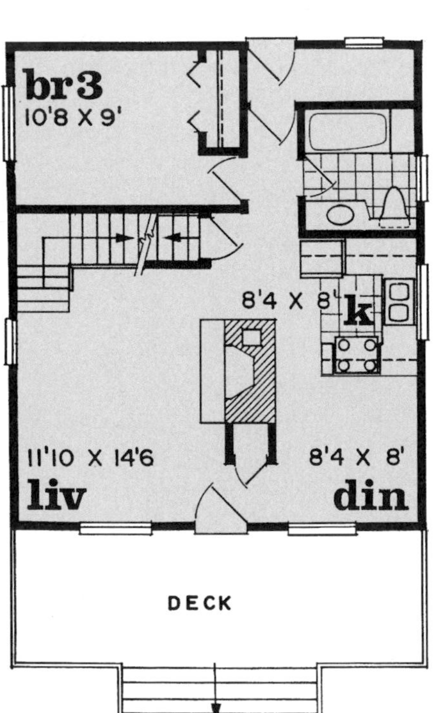

FIRST FLOOR

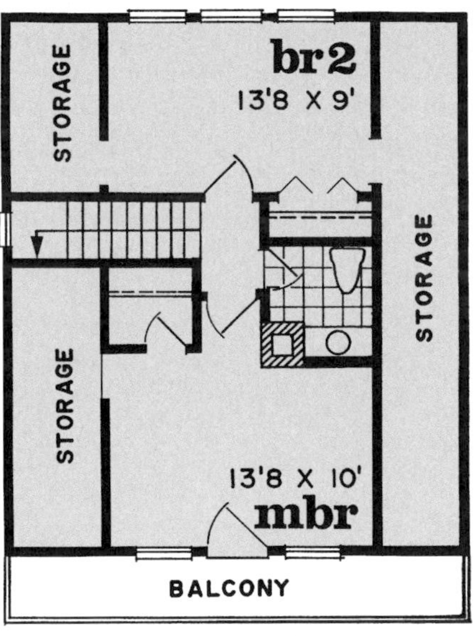

SECOND FLOOR

DESIGN NOTE

While not a true A-frame design—which would have no sidewalls or wall-roof junctions—this home invokes a modern folk spirit that vacationers will appreciate. The no-frills interior is dominated by the first-floor living room and dining area, which open from the kitchen. The central fireplace is another thematic, as well as practical, element. Upstairs storage areas take advantage of spaces created by the steeply gabled roof.

plan# HPK1700066

Style: Country Cottage

First Floor: 728 sq. ft.

Second Floor: 420 sq. ft.

Total: 1,148 sq. ft.

Bedrooms: 1

Bathrooms: 1½

Width: 28' - 0"

Depth: 26' - 0"

Foundation: Unfinished Basement

eplans.com

This stunning contemporary cottage has a heart of gold, with plenty of windows to bring in a wealth of natural light. Open planning allows the first-floor living and dining room to share the wide views of the outdoors. Glass doors frame the fireplace and open to the deck. A second-floor mezzanine enjoys an overlook to the living area and leads to a generous master suite with a walk-in closet, private bath, and a sitting area.

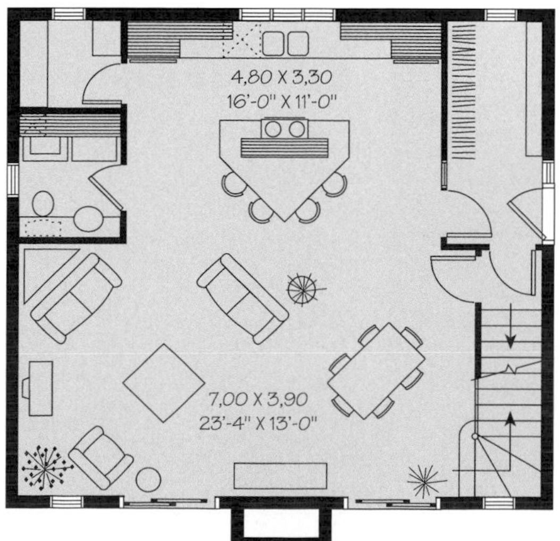

FIRST FLOOR

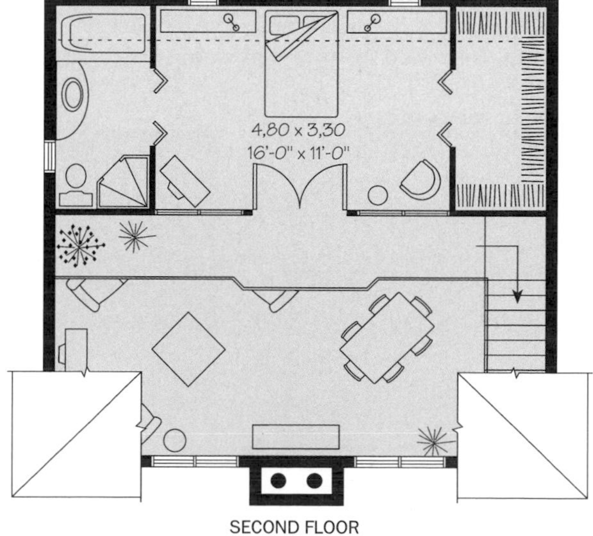

SECOND FLOOR

A triangular deck off the living areas of this vacation home provides the perfect spot for barbeques and relaxation by the lake. Two sets of windows are symmetrically placed on either side of the chimney, which is also flanked by sliding glass doors to the deck. The first floor is devoted to living spaces which are open to each other, making entertaining a breeze. The island in the kitchen is the perfect place for casual vacation-style meals. There is a dining area adjacent to the family room—both topped by cathedral ceilings—for more formal occasions. A powder room rounds out this level. The second floor is solely devoted to the master suite. Double French doors provide the grand entrance to this lavish retreat. To the left of the sleeping area is an expansive walk-in closet, large enough to please any clothes horse. To the right is the master bath, complete with a corner shower and separate tub.

plan# HPK1700067

Style: Contemporary
First Floor: 728 sq. ft.
Second Floor: 420 sq. ft.
Total: 1,148 sq. ft.
Bedrooms: 1
Bathrooms: 1½
Width: 28' - 0"
Depth: 26' - 0"
Foundation: Unfinished Basement

eplans.com

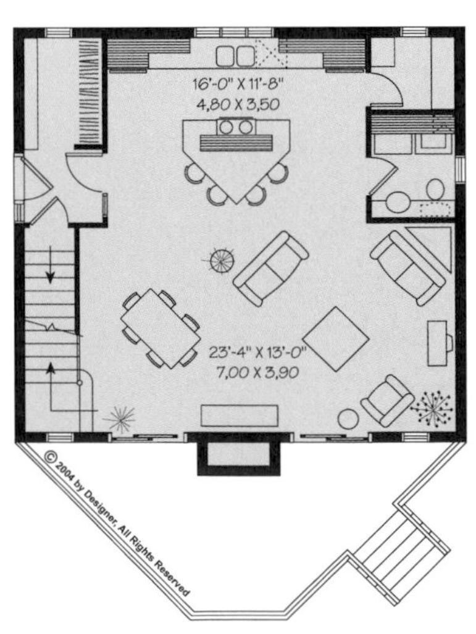

FIRST FLOOR

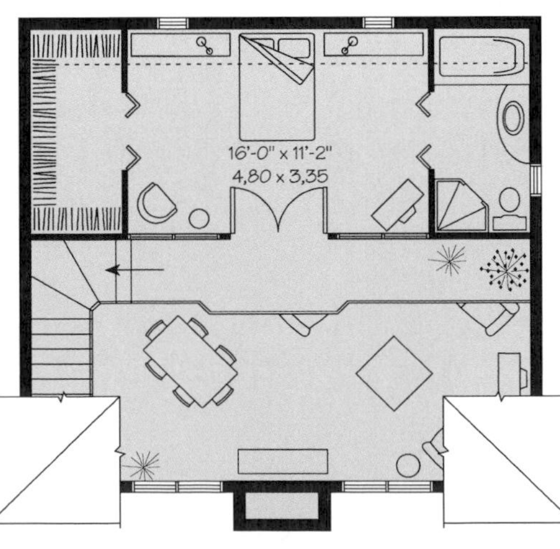

SECOND FLOOR

plan # HPK1700068

Style: Resort Lifestyles
First Floor: 630 sq. ft.
Second Floor: 546 sq. ft.
Total: 1,176 sq. ft.
Bedrooms: 2
Bathrooms: 1½
Width: 26' - 8"
Depth: 24' - 0"
Foundation: Unfinished Basement

eplans.com

This lovely country cottage features a cozy wraparound covered porch, extending outdoor living for seasonal occasions. Double doors open into a spacious living area that extends into the dining room and kitchen. A casual snack bar adds counter space for the kids. A door near the kitchen accesses the backyard. A mud room and powder/utility room are located on the left side of the house, completing the first floor. Upstairs, two family bedrooms share a full hall bath.

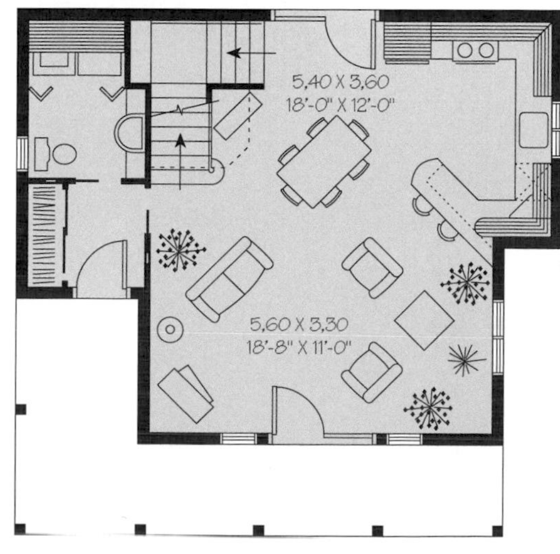

FIRST FLOOR

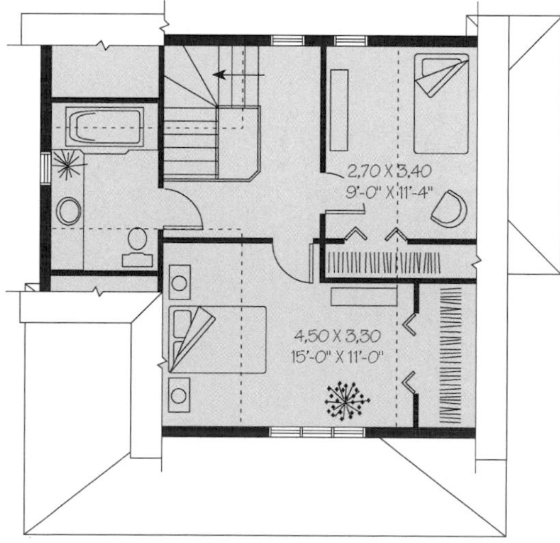

SECOND FLOOR

Large windows, a covered porch, and an upper balcony make this home perfect for waterfront living. Inside, find a very comfortable plan including a family room, a dining room with French-door access to the patio, and an L-shaped kitchen with a breakfast area. A convenient powder room and laundry facilities are also on this floor. Upstairs are the two bedrooms that share a full bath with a separate tub and shower. The larger bedroom has French doors opening to the balcony.

plan # HPK1700069

- Style: Cape Cod
- First Floor: 691 sq. ft.
- Second Floor: 555 sq. ft.
- Total: 1,246 sq. ft.
- Bedrooms: 2
- Bathrooms: 1½
- Width: 28' - 0"
- Depth: 40' - 0"
- Foundation: Unfinished Basement

eplans.com

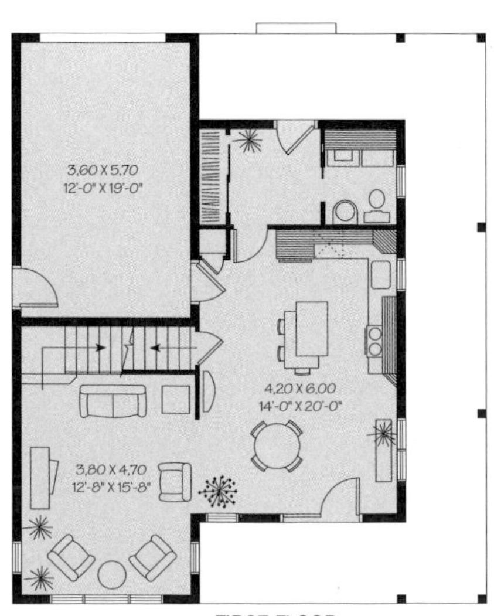

FIRST FLOOR

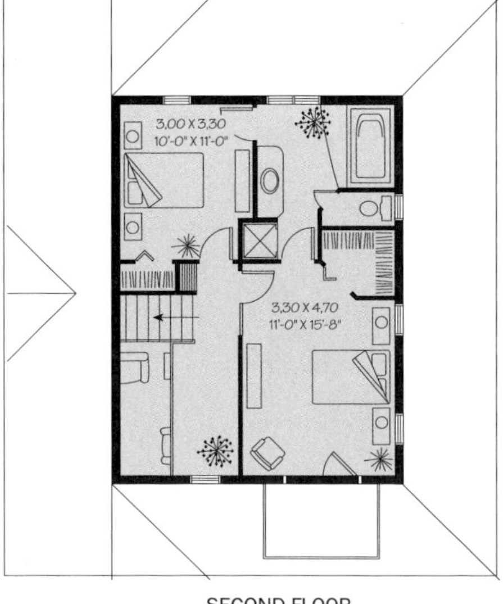

SECOND FLOOR

plan # HPK1700070

Style: Garage
First Floor: 770 sq. ft.
Second Floor: 497 sq. ft.
Total: 1,267 sq. ft.
Bedrooms: 1
Bathrooms: 1
Width: 47' - 6"
Depth: 22' - 0"
Foundation: Slab

eplans.com

A portico-style entry is a warm welcome to this detached three-car garage, styled to complement many of the neighborhood designs. Bonus space above offers 497 square feet of additional living area or a recreation room. With a morning kitchen, full bath, vaulted ceiling, and three dormered windows, Option A may be developed as a comfortable guest suite or a charming artist's studio. The entry vestibule provides ample storage space as well as a wrapping stair to the bonus level.

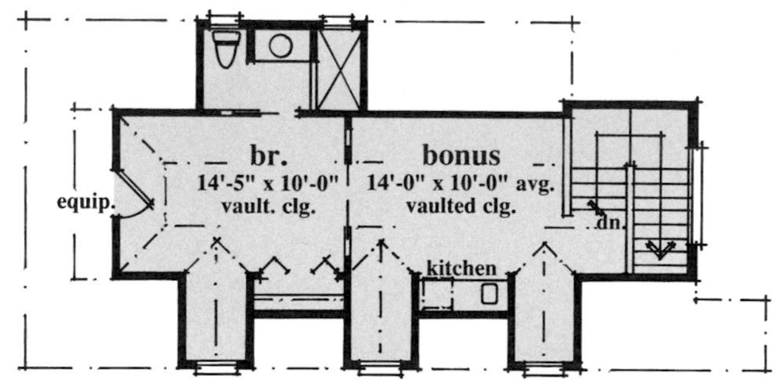

SECOND FLOOR

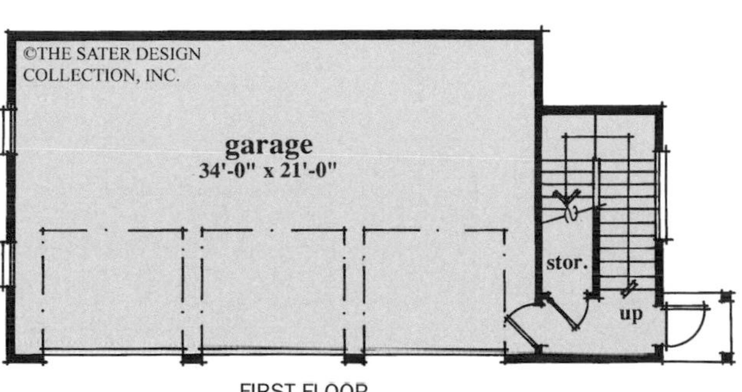

FIRST FLOOR

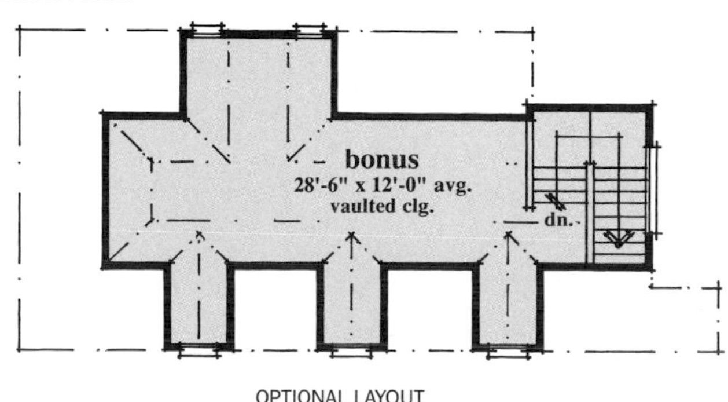

OPTIONAL LAYOUT

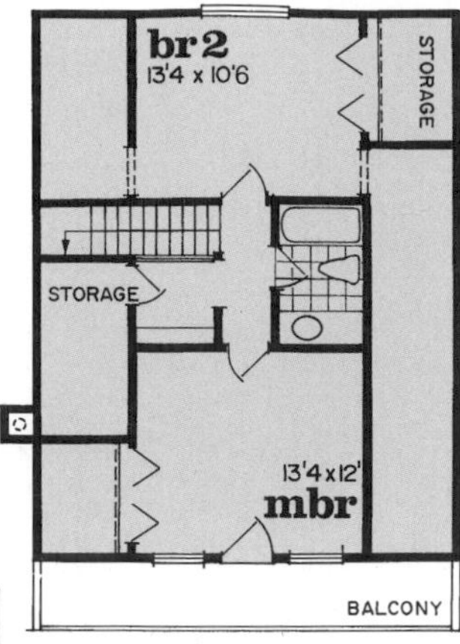

SECOND FLOOR

plan# HPK170071

Style: Vacation
First Floor: 725 sq. ft.
Second Floor: 561 sq. ft.
Total: 1,286 sq. ft.
Bedrooms: 3
Bathrooms: 2
Width: 25' - 0"
Depth: 36' - 6"
Foundation: Crawlspace

eplans.com

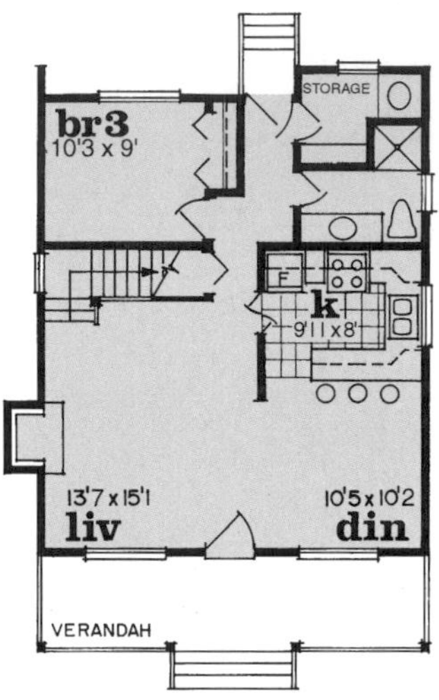

FIRST FLOOR

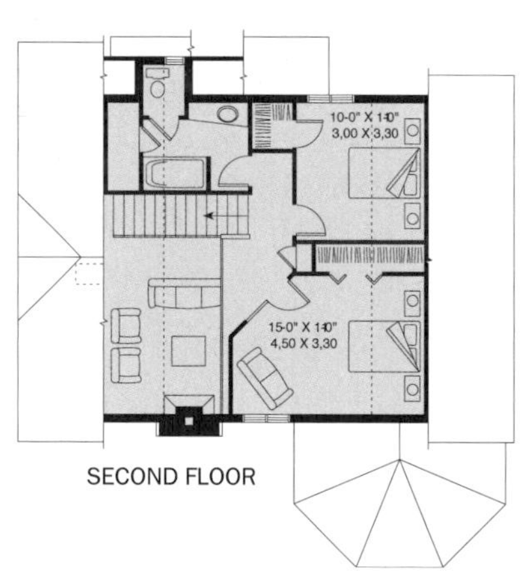

SECOND FLOOR

PHOTOGRAPHY BY DRUMMOND DESIGNS, INC.

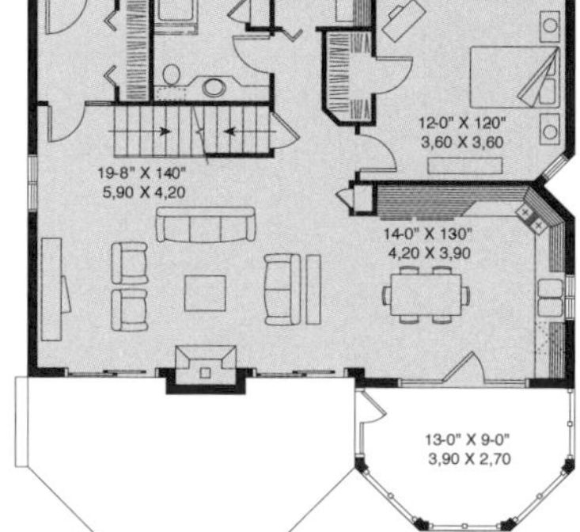

FIRST FLOOR

plan# HPK170072

Style: Cape Cod
First Floor: 958 sq. ft.
Second Floor: 510 sq. ft.
Total: 1,468 sq. ft.
Bedrooms: 3
Bathrooms: 2
Width: 35' - 0"
Depth: 29' - 8"
Foundation: Unfinished Basement

eplans.com

plan# HPK1700073

Style: Farmhouse
First Floor: 716 sq. ft.
Second Floor: 754 sq. ft.
Total: 1,470 sq. ft.
Bedrooms: 3
Bathrooms: 2½
Width: 45' - 4"
Depth: 38' - 0"

eplans.com

This compact traditional home offers an attractive exterior and a comfortable floor plan. The front door opens directly to the family room, which includes a fireplace and a built-in entertainment center. Just beyond, the kitchen features a walk-in pantry and adjoins a sunlit dining bay with access to the backyard. A two-car garage completes the first floor. Upstairs, three bedrooms are conveniently close to the laundry area. The master suite and Bedroom 2 provide walk-in closets.

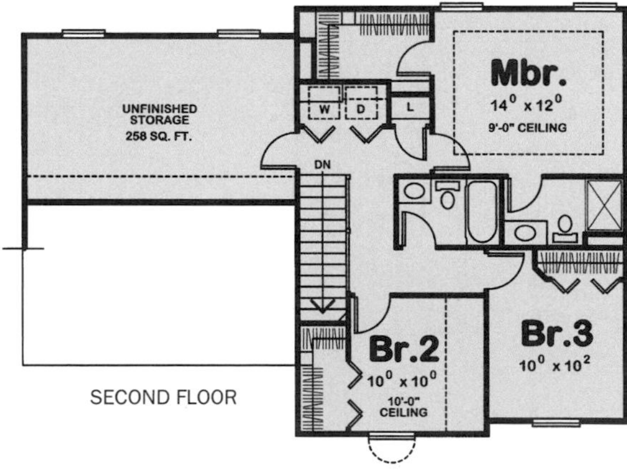

SECOND FLOOR

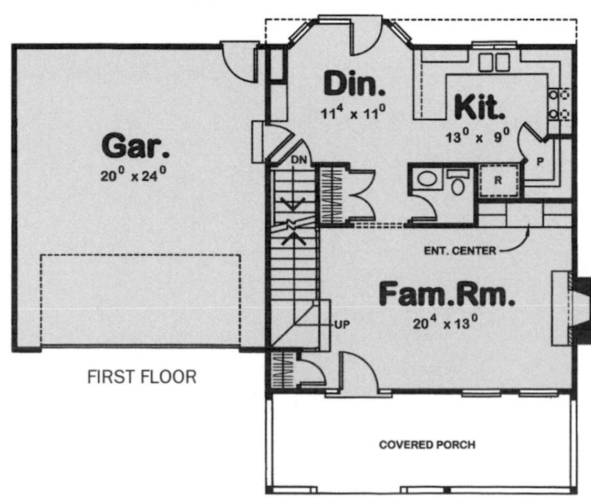

FIRST FLOOR

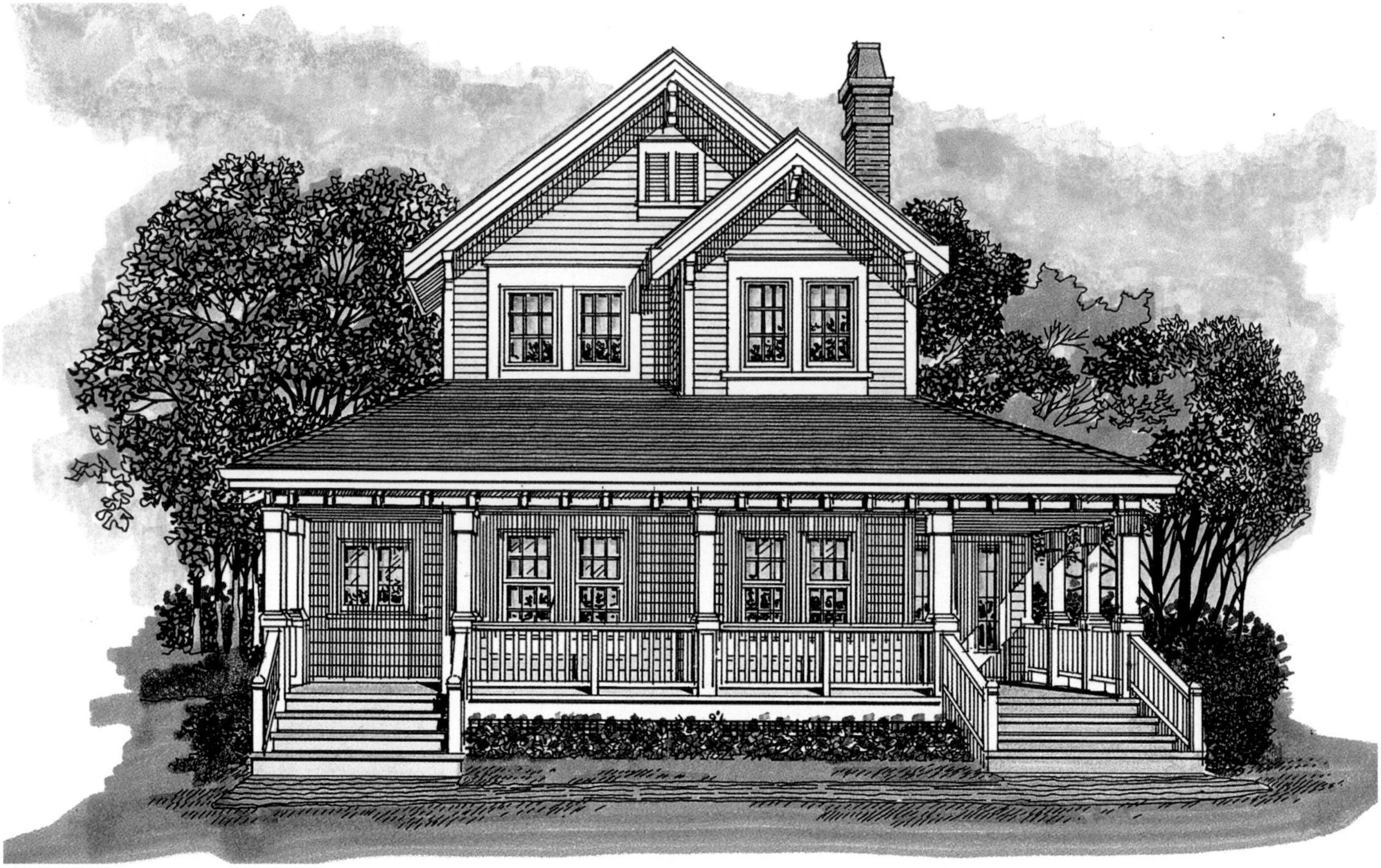

What an appealing plan! Its rustic character is defined by cedar lattice, covered columned porches, exposed rafters, and multi-pane, double hung windows. The great room/dining room combination is reached through double doors off the veranda and features a fireplace towering two stories to the lofty ceiling. A U-shaped kitchen contains an angled snack counter that serves this area and loads of space for a breakfast table—or use the handy side porch for alfresco dining. To the rear resides the master bedroom with a full bath and double doors to the veranda. An additional half-bath sits just beyond the laundry room. Upstairs, two family bedrooms and a full bath finish the plan.

plan# HPK1700074
Style: Country Cottage
First Floor: 995 sq. ft.
Second Floor: 484 sq. ft.
Total: 1,479 sq. ft.
Bedrooms: 3
Bathrooms: 2½
Width: 38' - 0"
Depth: 44' - 0"
Foundation: Crawlspace, Unfinished Basement
eplans.com

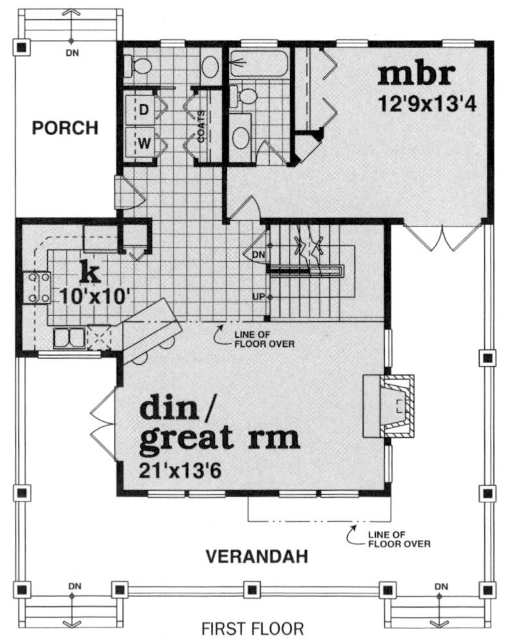

FIRST FLOOR

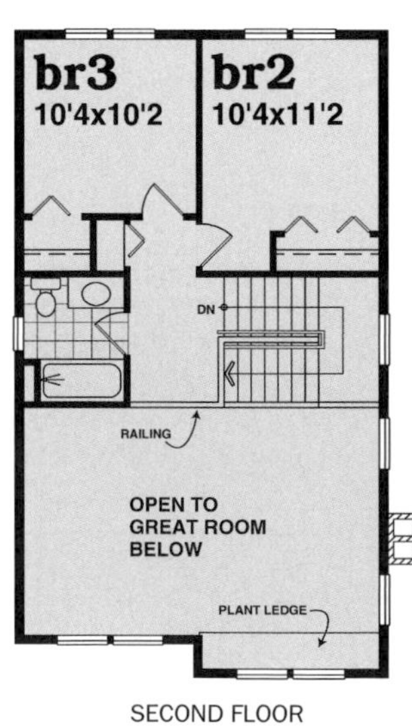

SECOND FLOOR

plan # HPK1700075

Style: Contemporary
First Floor: 1,024 sq. ft.
Second Floor: 456 sq. ft.
Total: 1,480 sq. ft.
Bedrooms: 2
Bathrooms: 2
Width: 32' - 0"
Depth: 40' - 0"
Foundation: Unfinished Basement

eplans.com

A conservative and charming traditional plan delivers easy living and awaits a personal touch. The two-story great room and dining area handles family gatherings, apart from the master bedroom at the top of the plan. The second bedroom resides upstairs, along with a reading room or media room. Full baths accompany both bedrooms. A classic front porch frames the entryway and brings interest to the cross-gabled design. A small mudroom/utility space receives traffic from the rear entry.

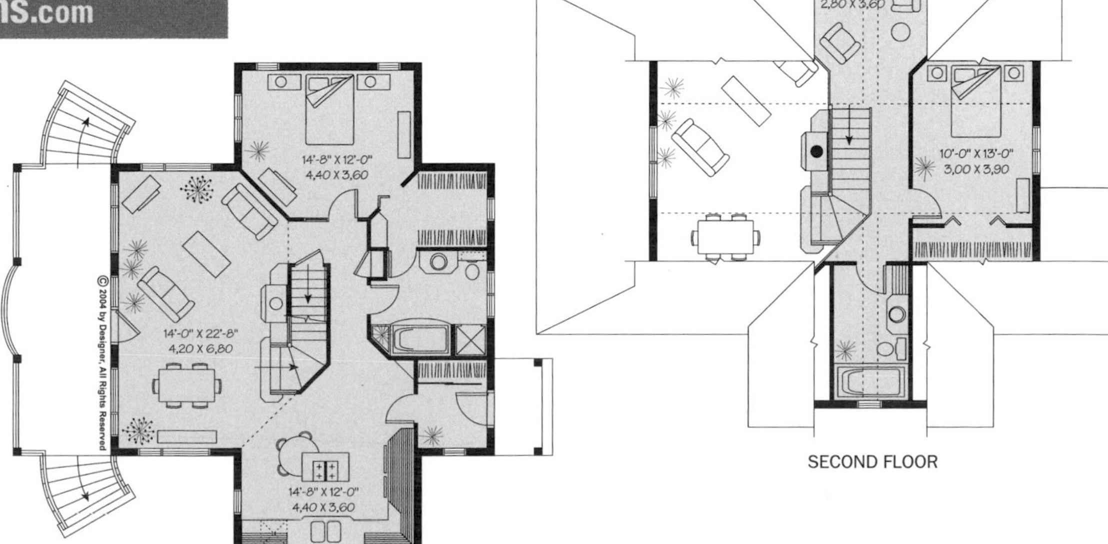

FIRST FLOOR

SECOND FLOOR

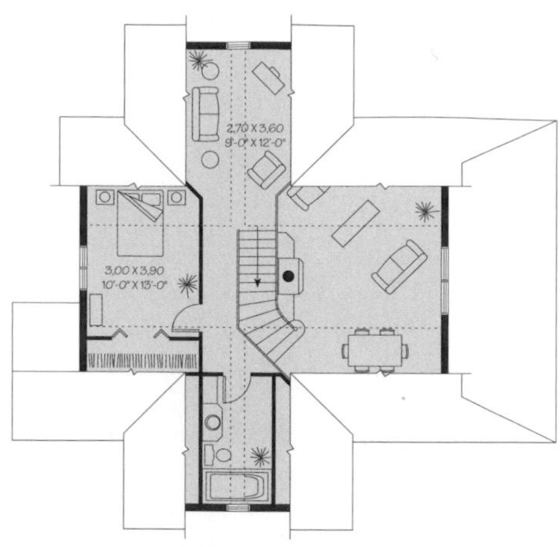

SECOND FLOOR

plan# HPK170076

Style: Cape Cod

First Floor: 1,024 sq. ft.

Second Floor: 456 sq. ft.

Total: 1,480 sq. ft.

Bedrooms: 2

Bathrooms: 2

Width: 32' - 0"

Depth: 40' - 0"

Foundation: Finished Walkout Basement

eplans.com

FIRST FLOOR

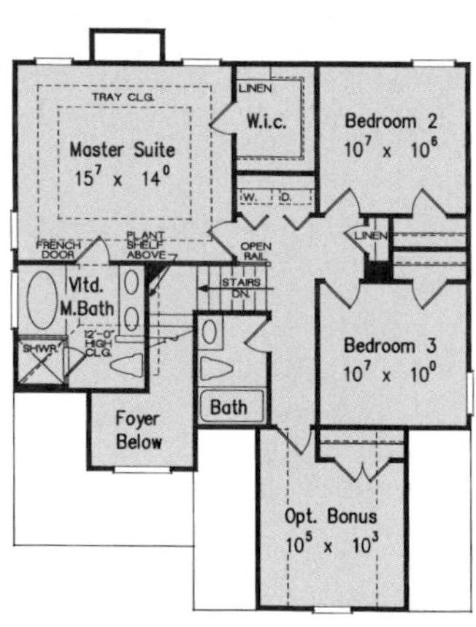

SECOND FLOOR

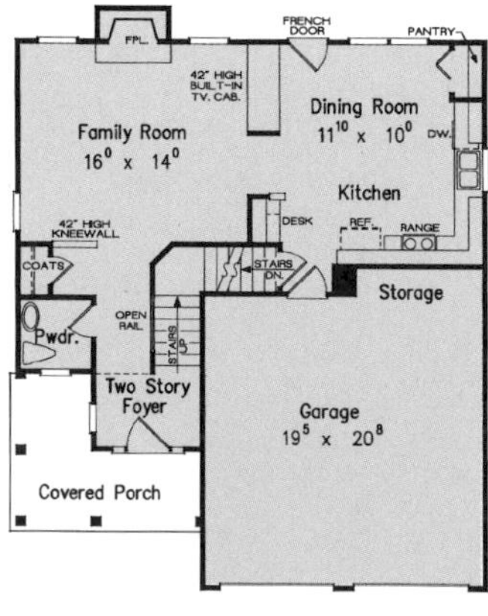

FIRST FLOOR

plan# HPK170077

Style: Country Cottage

First Floor: 696 sq. ft.

Second Floor: 786 sq. ft.

Total: 1,482 sq. ft.

Bonus Space: 141 sq. ft.

Bedrooms: 3

Bathrooms: 2½

Width: 33' - 0"

Depth: 41' - 4"

Foundation: Slab, Crawlspace, Unfinished Walkout Basement

eplans.com

plan# HPK1700078
Style: Contemporary
First Floor: 908 sq. ft.
Second Floor: 576 sq. ft.
Total: 1,484 sq. ft.
Bedrooms: 3
Bathrooms: 2
Width: 26' - 0"
Depth: 48' - 0"
Foundation: Unfinished Basement
eplans.com

SMART TIP

Note how this home has been designed to combine outdoor living with cooking and dining. The sunroom at the bottom of the plan is conveniently situated to handle overflow from the main dining area. The result is a small plan that can handle a crowd of guests with aplomb. Convert the first-floor bedroom into a recreation area and your home will be the life of the party.

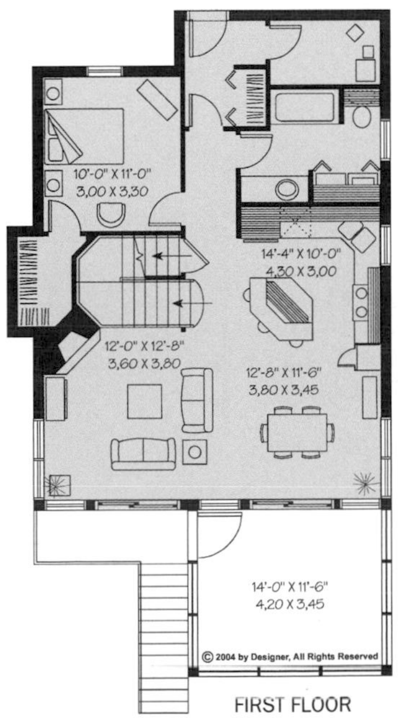

FIRST FLOOR

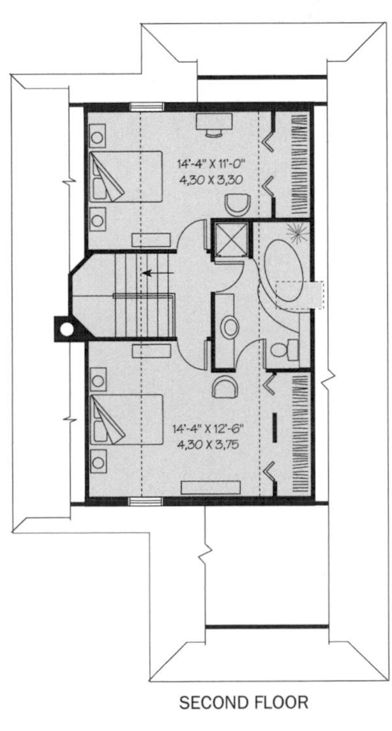

SECOND FLOOR

For an in-fill lot, a lake site, or seaside retreat, this plan offers three floors of living and a very narrow footprint to make it conform to your needs. A high-pitched roofline accommodates an enchanting dormer window, and a covered porch screens the setback entry. The lower floor at garage level holds a bedroom with full bath and laundry alcove. Built-ins include a desk and drawers along one wall. Outdoor access leads to convenient storage for lawn equipment and other essentials. The main level upstairs holds a vaulted living room with built-in media center, and L-shaped booth seating for dining, an island kitchen with double-door pantry and display shelves, and the master suite. An outdoor deck lies just beyond the living area. A cozy vaulted study loft is graced by a huge built-in bookshelf.

plan# HPK1700079
Style: Craftsman
First Floor: 436 sq. ft.
Second Floor: 792 sq. ft.
Third Floor: 202 sq. ft.
Total: 1,430 sq. ft.
Bedrooms: 2
Bathrooms: 2
Width: 16' - 0"
Depth: 54' - 0"
Foundation: Crawlspace
eplans.com

FIRST FLOOR

SECOND FLOOR

OPTIONAL LAYOUT

plan# HPK1700080

Style: Country Cottage
Main Level: 1,273 sq. ft.
Lower Level: 47 sq. ft.
Total: 1,320 sq. ft.
Bedrooms: 3
Bathrooms: 2
Width: 48' - 0"
Depth: 35' - 4"
Foundation: Unfinished Walkout Basement

eplans.com

This traditional move-up home will accustom owners to the taste of luxury living. A spacious great room featuring a fireplace and vaulted ceiling anchors the center of the plan, as well as providing a thoughtful amount of distance between the master suite and kitchen. The suite comprises a spacious bedroom accompanied by a gorgeous bath with dual vanities and compartmented toilet. Built-in plant shelves bring a soft touch to the room. The U-shaped kitchen and nearby pantry are naturally lit and fully functional. Finally, two bedrooms with closets share a full bath.

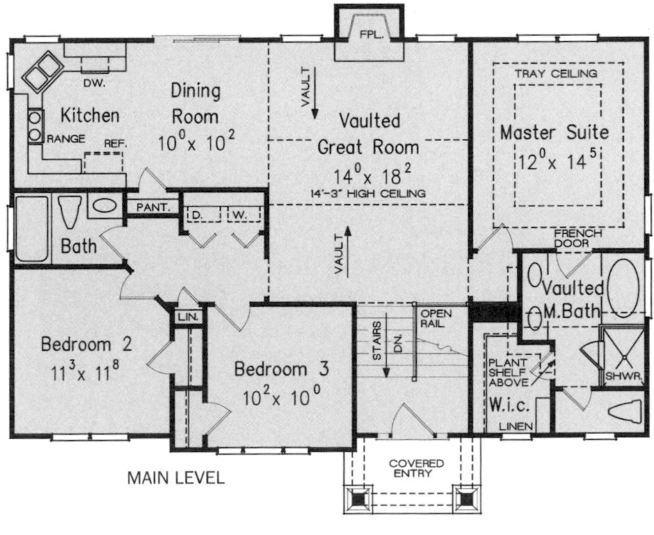

MAIN LEVEL

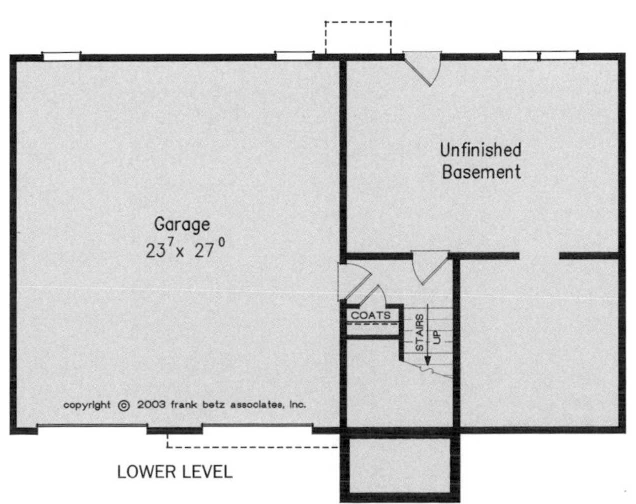

LOWER LEVEL

plan# HPK1700081

Style: Traditional

Square Footage: 1,363

Lower Level: 669 sq. ft.

Bedrooms: 3

Bathrooms: 2

Width: 44' - 0"

Depth: 43' - 0"

Foundation: Unfinished Basement

eplans.com

A columned, covered entry charms the exterior of this three-bedroom, split-entry home. Inside, a one-and-a-half-story foyer boasts a dual staircase—one up to the main-floor living area and the other down to the basement. The living area includes a gas fireplace and windows on all walls, ensuring natural light. The adjacent dining room with a buffet alcove exits through a sliding glass door to the rear patio. The roomy kitchen has a raised snack bar, built-in pantry, and access to a bayed eating area surrounded by windows. A skylight brightens the hall to the three bedrooms. Look for His and Hers closets and a private bath in the master suite. Future expansion is reserved for space on the lower level.

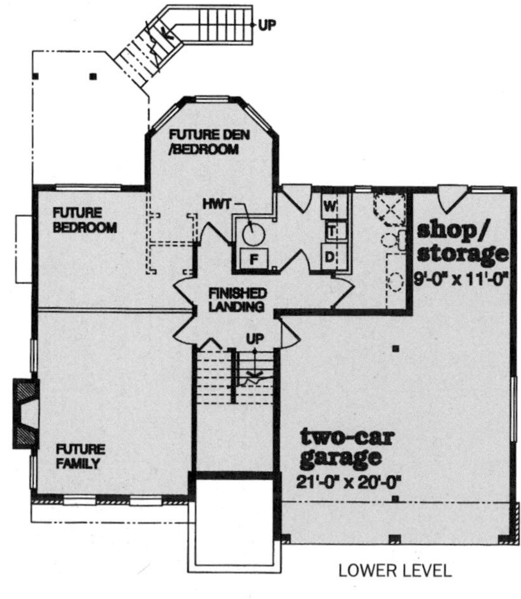

LOWER LEVEL

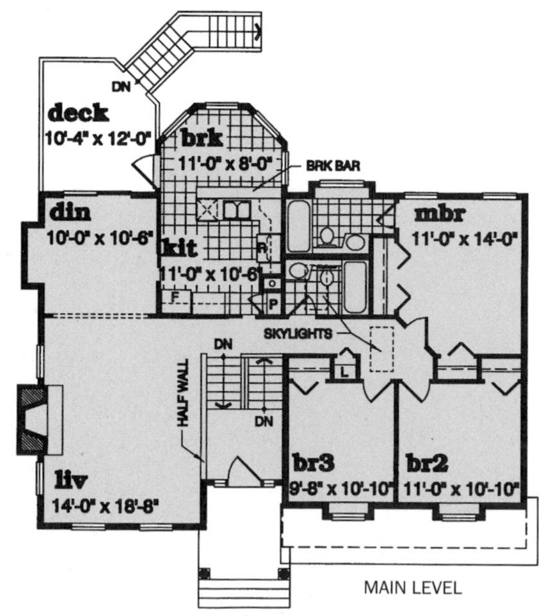

MAIN LEVEL

Homes From 1,500 to 1,999 Square Feet

A traditional neighborhood look is accented by stone and decorative arches on this stylish new design. See plan HPK1700135 on page 127.

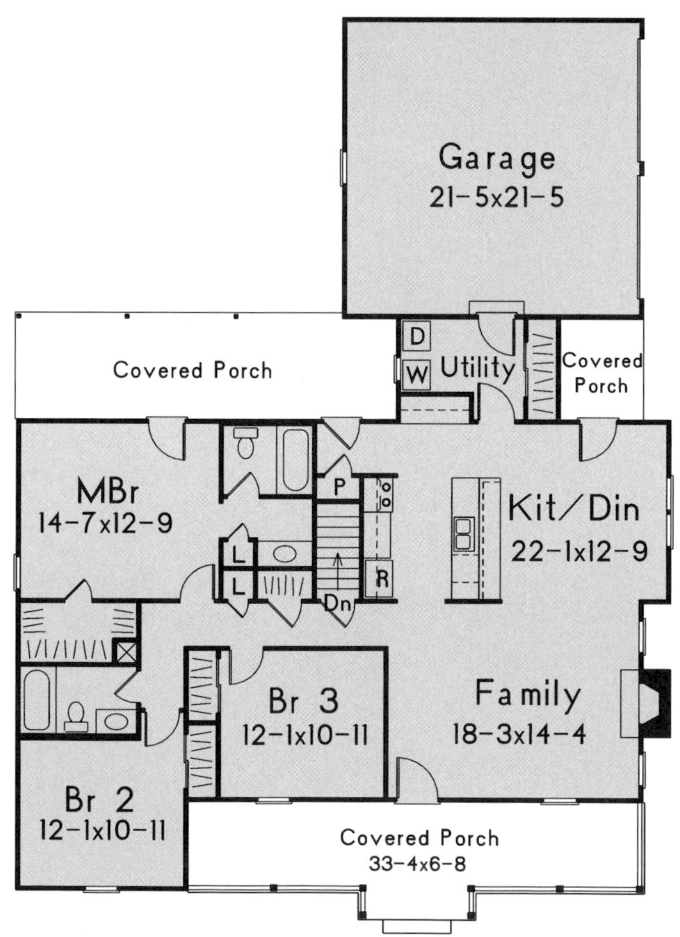

plan# HPK1700082

Style: Traditional

Square Footage: 1,501

Bedrooms: 3

Bathrooms: 2

Width: 48' - 0"

Depth: 57' - 4"

Foundation: Crawlspace, Slab, Unfinished Basement

eplans.com

This ranch-style home provides an inviting front covered porch with rustic accents. Inside, the family room provides a lovely fireplace and is open to a kitchen/dining area that accesses a rear covered porch. Nearby, a utility room leads into the two-car garage. The master bedroom provides spacious views of the rear property and privately accesses the rear covered porch. This bedroom also features a walk-in closet and a full bath with linen storage. Bedrooms 2 and 3 share a full hall bath.

plan# HPK1700083

Style: Traditional
Square Footage: 1,517
Bonus Space: 287 sq. ft.
Bedrooms: 3
Bathrooms: 2
Width: 61' - 4"
Depth: 48' - 6"

eplans.com

The foyer opens to a spacious great room with a fireplace and a cathedral ceiling in this lovely traditional home. Sliding doors open to a rear deck from the great room, posing a warm welcome to enjoy the outdoors. The U-shaped kitchen features an angled peninsula counter with a cooktop. A private hall leads to the family sleeping quarters, which includes two bedrooms and a full bath with a double-bowl lavatory. Sizable bonus space above the garage provides a skylight.

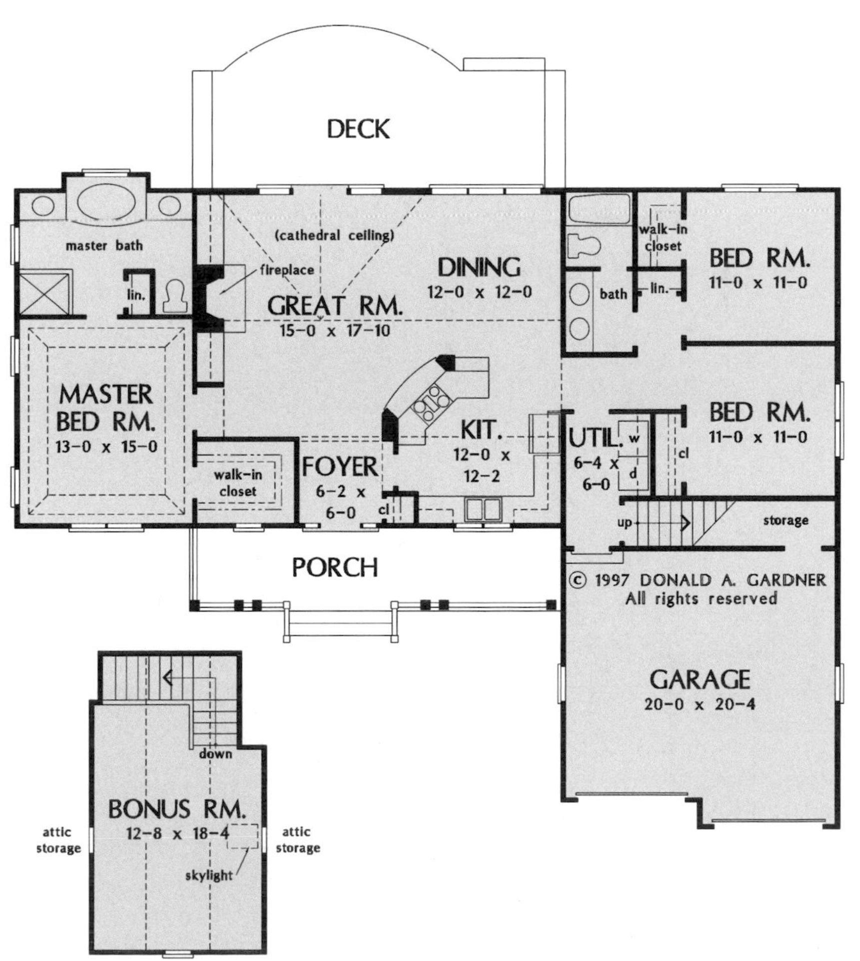

PHOTO BY: JANNIS VANN

plan# HPK1700084

Style: Traditional

Square Footage: 1,869

Bedrooms: 3

Bathrooms: 2

Width: 54' - 0"

Depth: 60' - 6"

Foundation: Unfinished Walkout Basement, Slab, Crawlspace

eplans.com

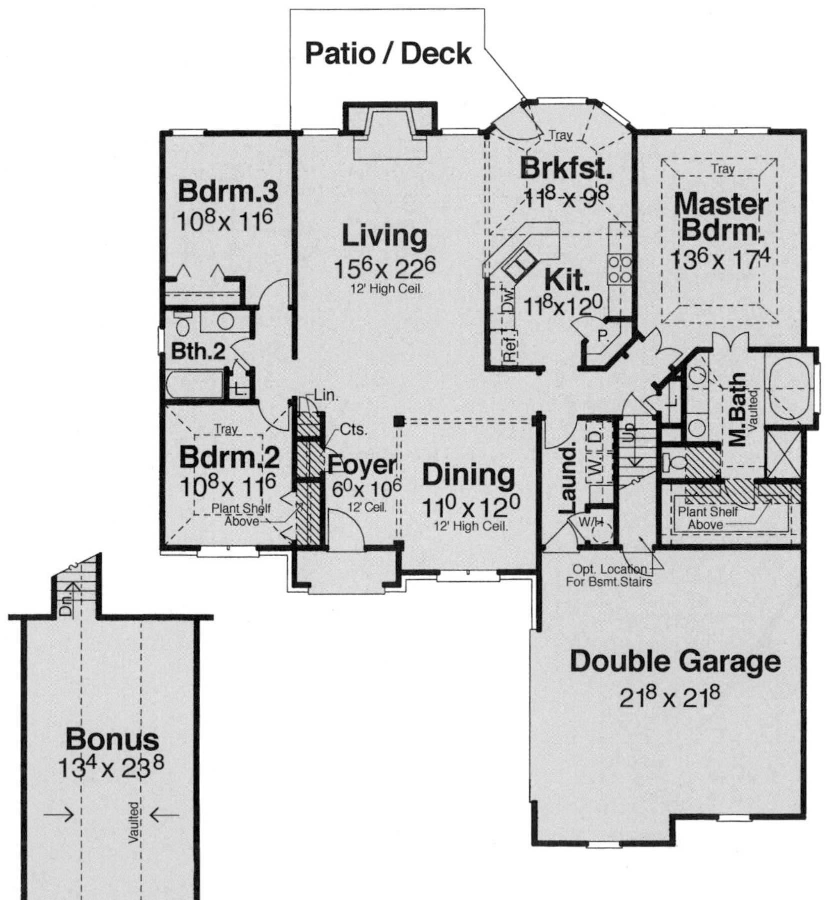

This quaint design is picture perfect for any neighborhood setting. Inside, a foyer opens to the formal dining room. The living room is warmed by a fireplace. The kitchen easily serves the bayed breakfast nook, which accesses the rear patio/deck. The master bedroom is located to the right side of the plan and features an elegant master bath with a walk-in closet. A laundry room accesses the two-car garage. Bedrooms 2 and 3 share a hall bath. Upstairs, the bonus room is great for a private home office, guest suite, or attic space.

plan# HPK1700085

Style: Country Cottage
Square Footage: 1,580
Bedrooms: 3
Bathrooms: 2½
Width: 50' - 0"
Depth: 48' - 0"
Foundation: Crawlspace

eplans.com

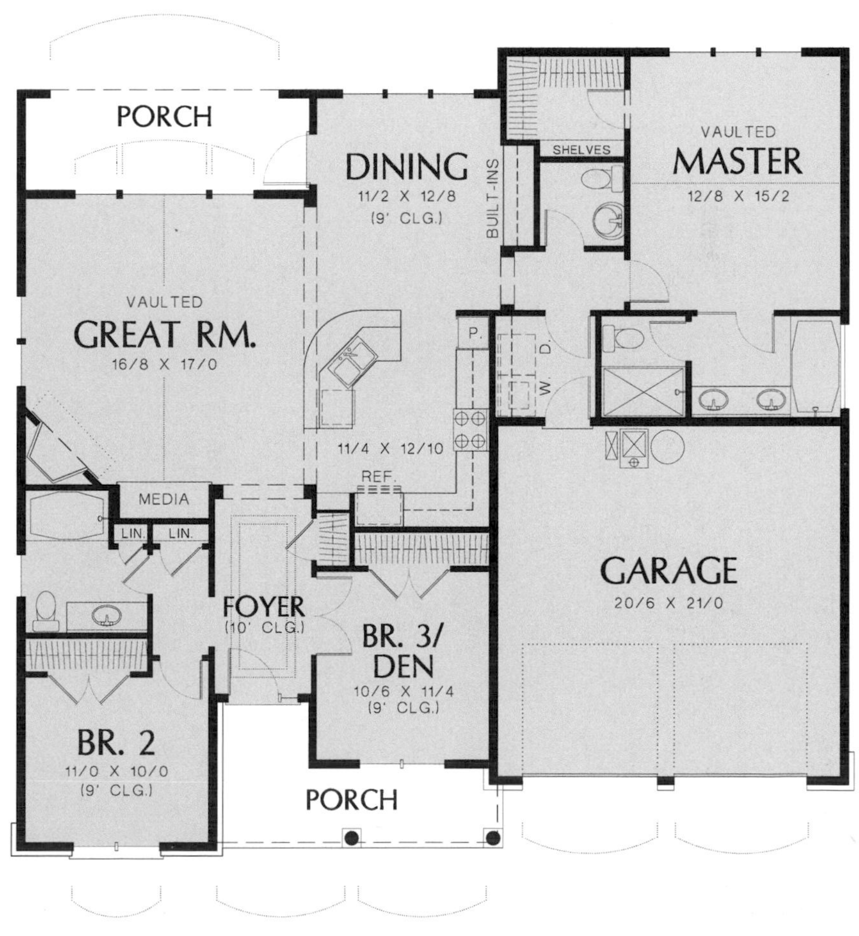

This charming one-story plan features a facade that is accented by a stone pediment and a shed-dormer window. Inside, elegant touches grace the efficient floor plan. Vaulted ceilings adorn the great room and master bedroom, and a 10-foot tray ceiling highlights the foyer. One of the front bedrooms makes a perfect den; another accesses a full hall bath with a linen closet. The great room, which opens to the porch, includes a fireplace and a media niche. The dining room offers outdoor access and built-ins for ultimate convenience.

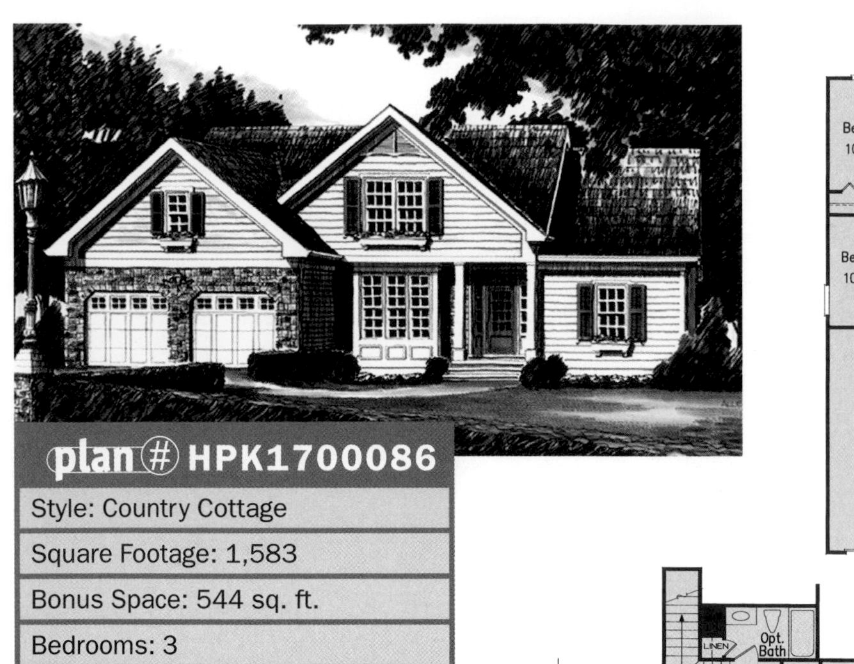

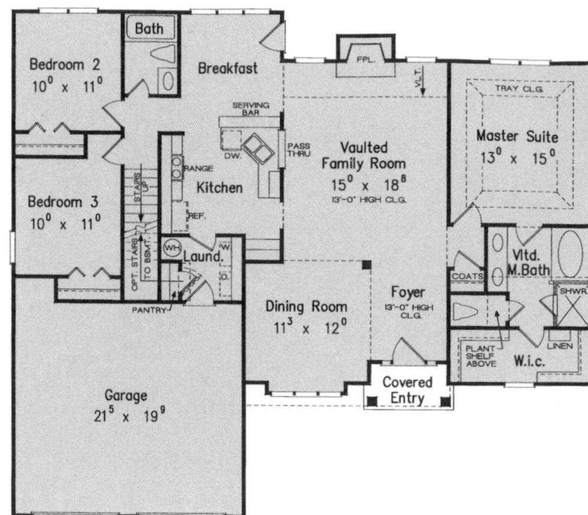

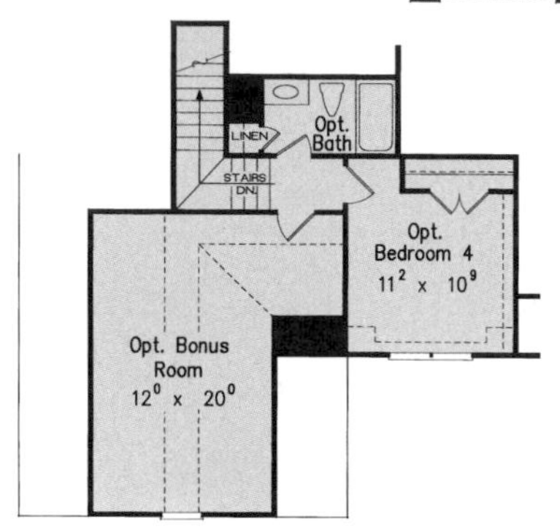

plan# HPK1700086

Style: Country Cottage
Square Footage: 1,583
Bonus Space: 544 sq. ft.
Bedrooms: 3
Bathrooms: 2
Width: 54' - 0"
Depth: 47' - 0"
Foundation: Crawlspace, Unfinished Walkout Basement, Slab

eplans.com

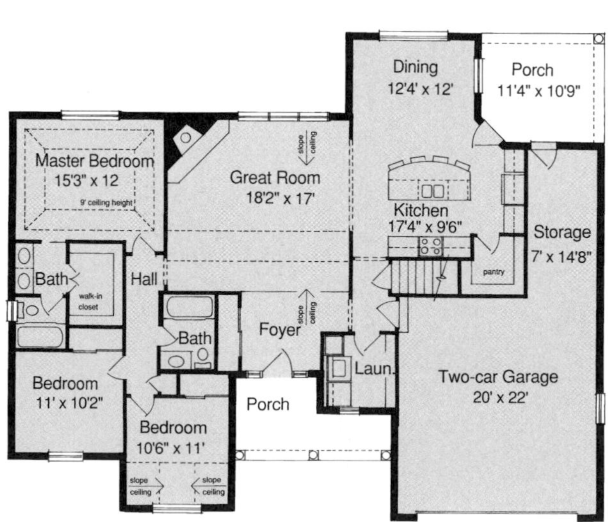

plan# HPK1700087

Style: Transitional
Square Footage: 1,593
Bedrooms: 3
Bathrooms: 2
Width: 60' - 0"
Depth: 48' - 10"
Foundation: Unfinished Basement

eplans.com

plan # HPK1700088

Style: European Cottage

Square Footage: 1,595

Bonus Space: 312 sq. ft.

Bedrooms: 3

Bathrooms: 2

Width: 49' - 0"

Depth: 60' - 0"

eplans.com

Varying rooflines and strong brick columns leading to the entrance provide bold first impressions to visitors of this home. Come inside to find a practical and inviting floor plan filled with thoughtful touches. Secluded to the far left of the plan are two bedrooms which share a full bath; the master suite is tucked away in the back right corner of the plan with an enormous walk-in closet and master bath. Living spaces are open to each other, with the kitchen easily serving the nook and living room—adorned with a lovely plant ledge—and a dining room nearby. Venture upstairs to the optional game room and finish it at your leisure.

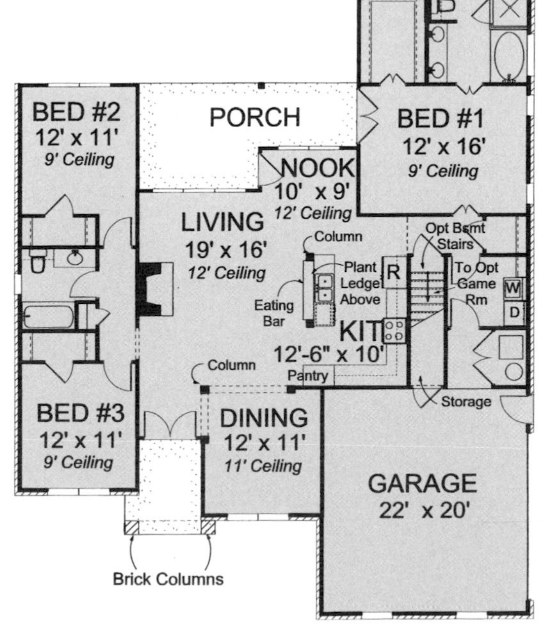

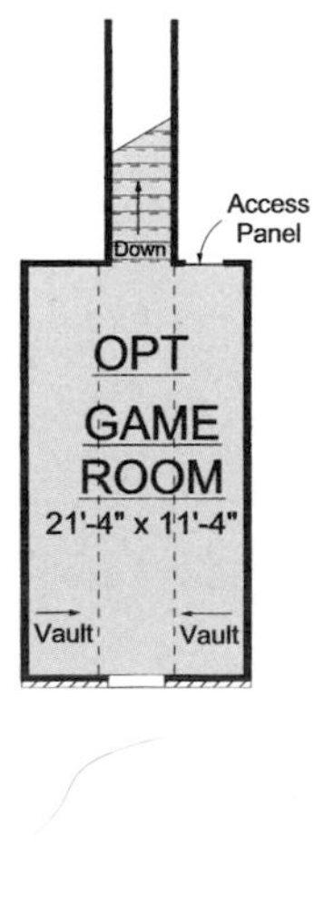

plan# HPK1700089

Style: European Cottage
Square Footage: 1,612
Bedrooms: 2
Bathrooms: 2
Width: 42' - 0"
Depth: 67' - 4"
Foundation: Slab, Unfinished Basement

eplans.com

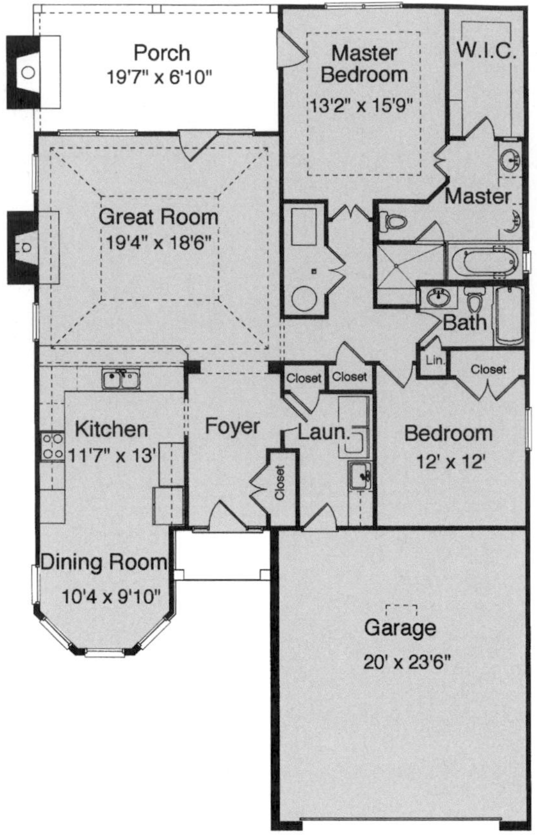

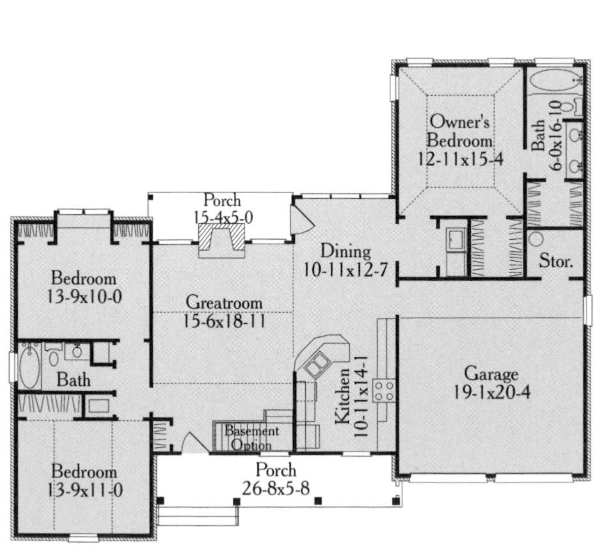

plan# HPK1700090

Style: Traditional
Square Footage: 1,643
Bedrooms: 3
Bathrooms: 2
Width: 62' - 2"
Depth: 51' - 4"
Foundation: Crawlspace, Slab, Unfinished Basement

eplans.com

plan# HPK1700091

Style: Traditional

Square Footage: 1,675

Bedrooms: 3

Bathrooms: 2

Width: 57' - 5"

Depth: 59' - 6"

Foundation: Slab, Crawlspace, Unfinished Basement

eplans.com

A fine brick presentation, this home boasts brick quoins, keystone lintels, muntin windows, and a covered porch entryway. Sleeping quarters flank either end of the general living areas. On the right side of the plan are two family bedrooms, which share a full bath. On the left side, a vaulted master suite resides, complete with a garden tub and His and Hers sinks and walk-in closets. In the center of the plan is a large living room with a fireplace, a bayed nook with rear-deck access, a dining room with a pillared entrance, and a large kitchen. Storage space is provided just off the garage.

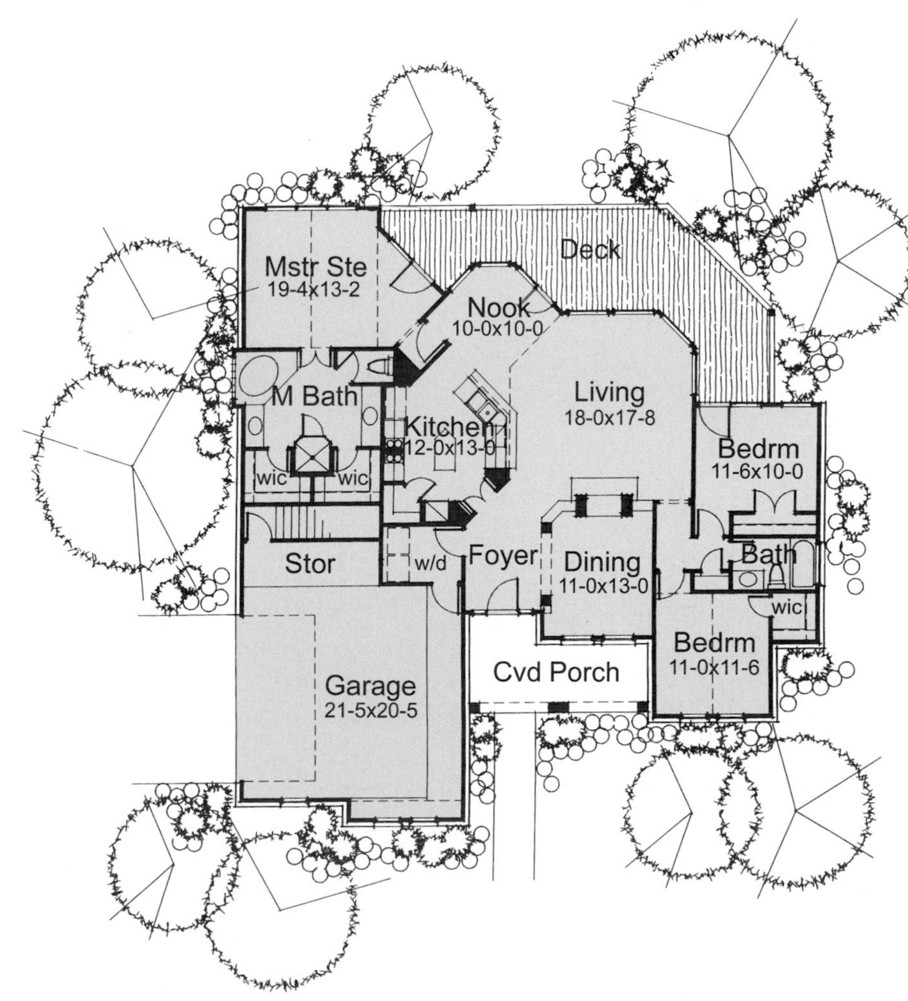

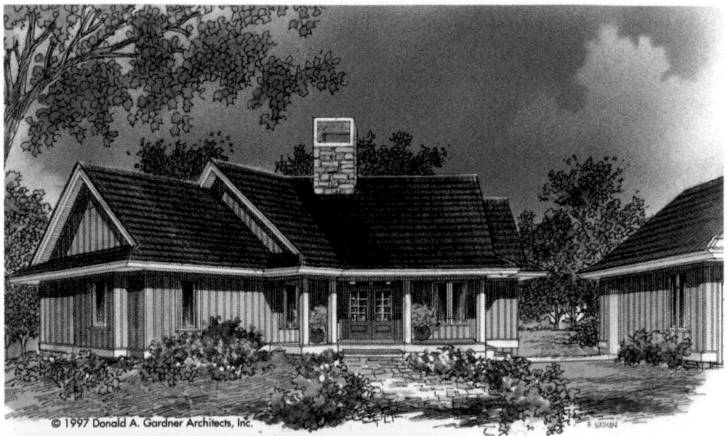

© 1997 Donald A. Gardner Architects, Inc.

plan# HPK1700092

Style: Contemporary

Square Footage: 1,680

Bedrooms: 3

Bathrooms: 2

Width: 62' - 8"

Depth: 59' - 10"

eplans.com

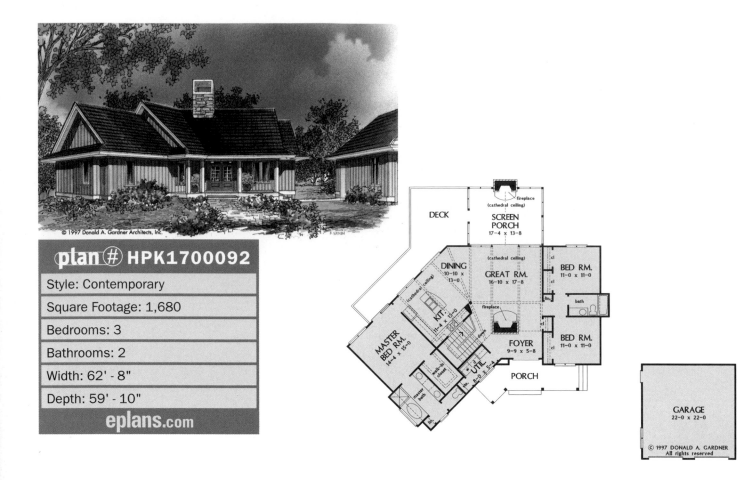

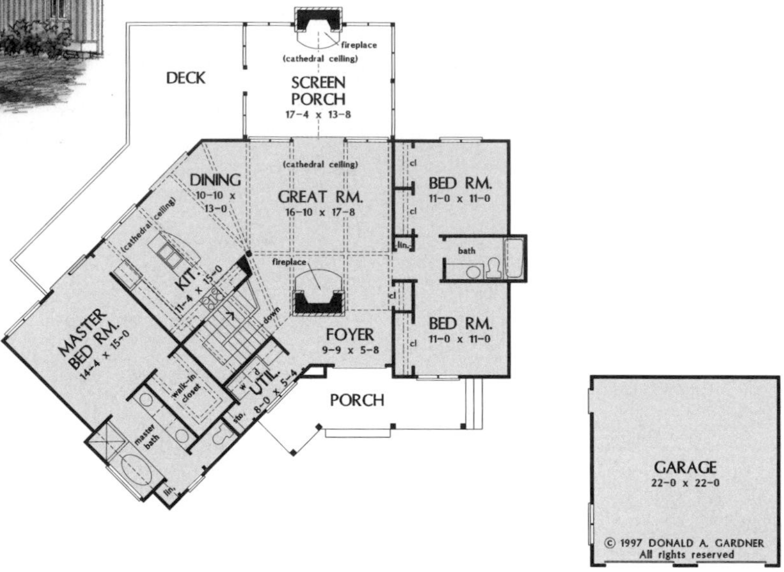

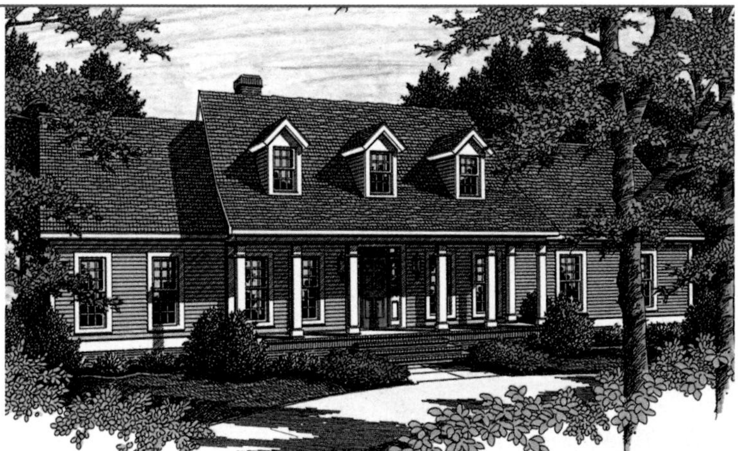

DECK
SCREEN PORCH 17-4 x 13-8 (cathedral ceiling) fireplace
DINING 10-10 x 13-0
GREAT RM. 16-10 x 17-8 (cathedral ceiling)
BED RM. 11-0 x 11-0
bath
KIT. 11-4 x 13-0 (cathedral ceiling)
fireplace
MASTER BED RM. 14-4 x 15-0
FOYER 9-9 x 5-8
BED RM. 11-0 x 11-0
walk-in closet
UTIL. 6-0 x 5-4
master bath
PORCH
GARAGE 22-0 x 22-0

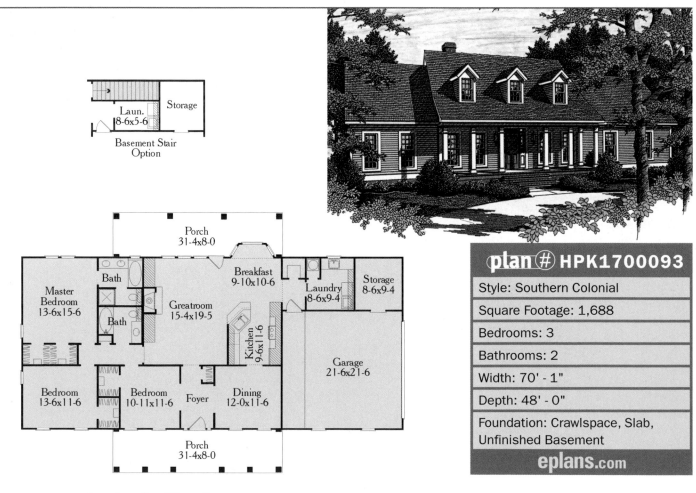

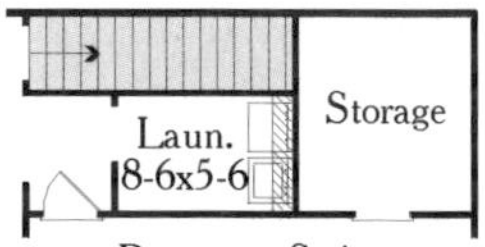

Laun. 8-6x5-6
Storage
Basement Stair Option

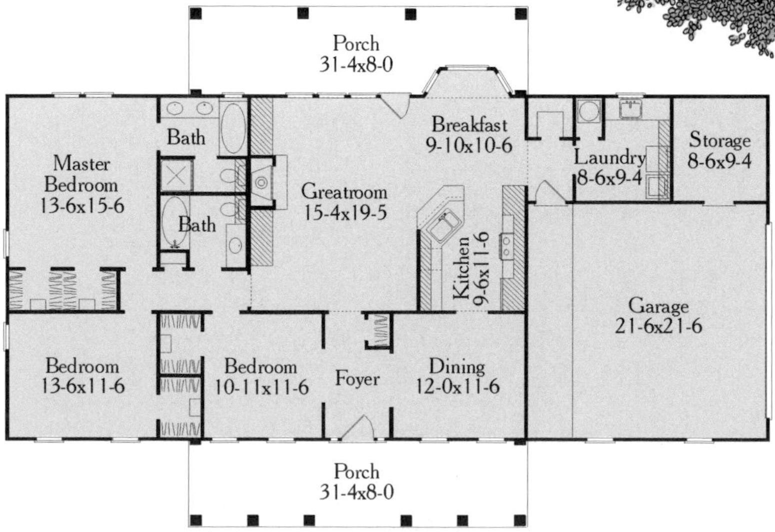

Porch 31-4x8-0
Breakfast 9-10x10-6
Bath
Master Bedroom 13-6x15-6
Greatroom 15-4x19-5
Laundry 8-6x9-4
Storage 8-6x9-4
Bath
Kitchen 9-6x11-6
Garage 21-6x21-6
Bedroom 13-6x11-6
Bedroom 10-11x11-6
Foyer
Dining 12-0x11-6
Porch 31-4x8-0

plan# HPK1700093

Style: Southern Colonial

Square Footage: 1,688

Bedrooms: 3

Bathrooms: 2

Width: 70' - 1"

Depth: 48' - 0"

Foundation: Crawlspace, Slab, Unfinished Basement

eplans.com

plan# HPK1700094

Style: Traditional
Square Footage: 1,721
Bedrooms: 3
Bathrooms: 2
Width: 83' - 0"
Depth: 42' - 0"
Foundation: Unfinished Walkout Basement

eplans.com

This home offers a beautifully textured facade. Keystones and lintels highlight the beauty of the windows. The vaulted great room and dining room are immersed in light from the atrium window wall. The breakfast bay opens to the covered porch in the backyard. A curved counter connects the kitchen to the great room. Three bedrooms, including a deluxe master suite, share the right side of the plan. All enjoy large windows of their own. The garage is designed for two cars, plus space for a motorcycle or yard tractor.

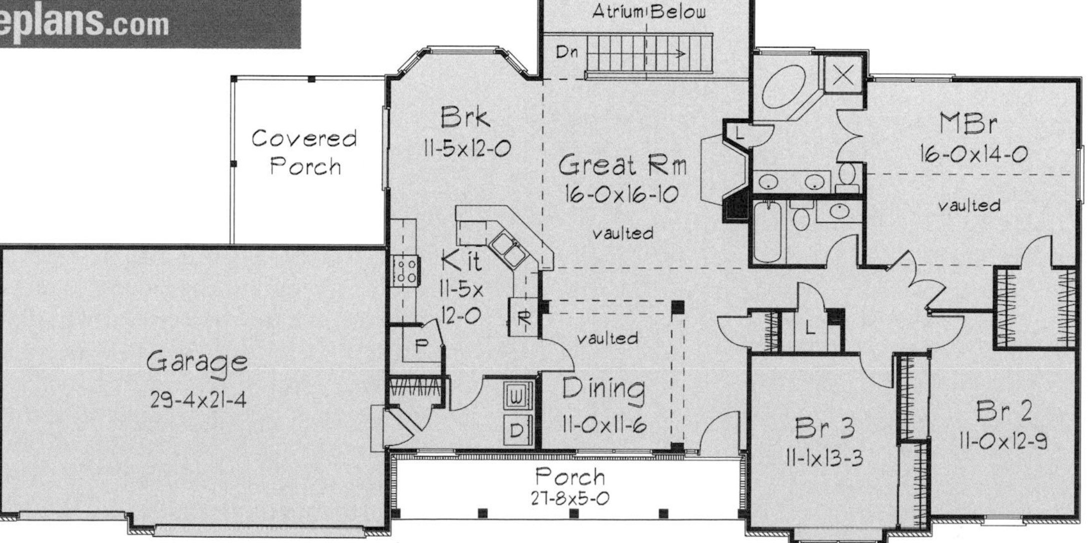

plan# HPK1700095

Style: Craftsman

Square Footage: 1,724

Bonus Space: 375 sq. ft.

Bedrooms: 3

Bathrooms: 2

Width: 53' - 6"

Depth: 58' - 6"

Foundation: Crawlspace, Unfinished Walkout Basement, Slab

eplans.com

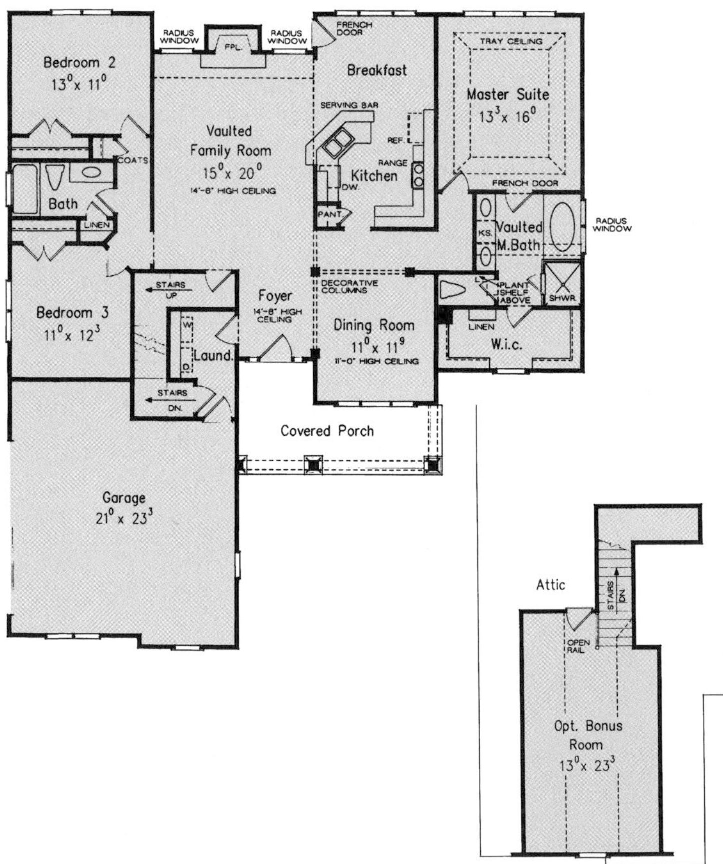

EDITOR'S PICK

Here's a one-story plan has all the comforts and necessities for down-home family living. The vaulted family room, along with the adjoining country-style kitchen and breakfast nook, is at the center of the plan. The extended hearth fireplace flanked by radius windows will make this a cozy focus for family get-togethers. Defined by decorative columns, the dining room is another welcoming spot for entertaining. But let's not forget about the owners: A resplendent master suite assumes the entire right wing, finding privacy from the bedrooms located on the other side of the plan. Built-in plant shelves in the master bath create a spa-like environment that'll be waiting for you at the end of every workday.

plan# HPK1700096

Style: Traditional
Square Footage: 1,733
Bedrooms: 3
Bathrooms: 2½
Width: 55' - 6"
Depth: 57' - 6"
Foundation: Walkout Basement

eplans.com

Delightfully different, this brick one-story home has everything for the active family. The foyer opens to a formal dining room, accented with four columns, and a great room with a fireplace and French doors to the rear deck. The efficient kitchen has an attached light-filled breakfast nook. The master bath features a tray ceiling, His and Hers walk-in closets, a double-sink vanity, and a huge garden tub. The two-car garage is accessed through the laundry room.

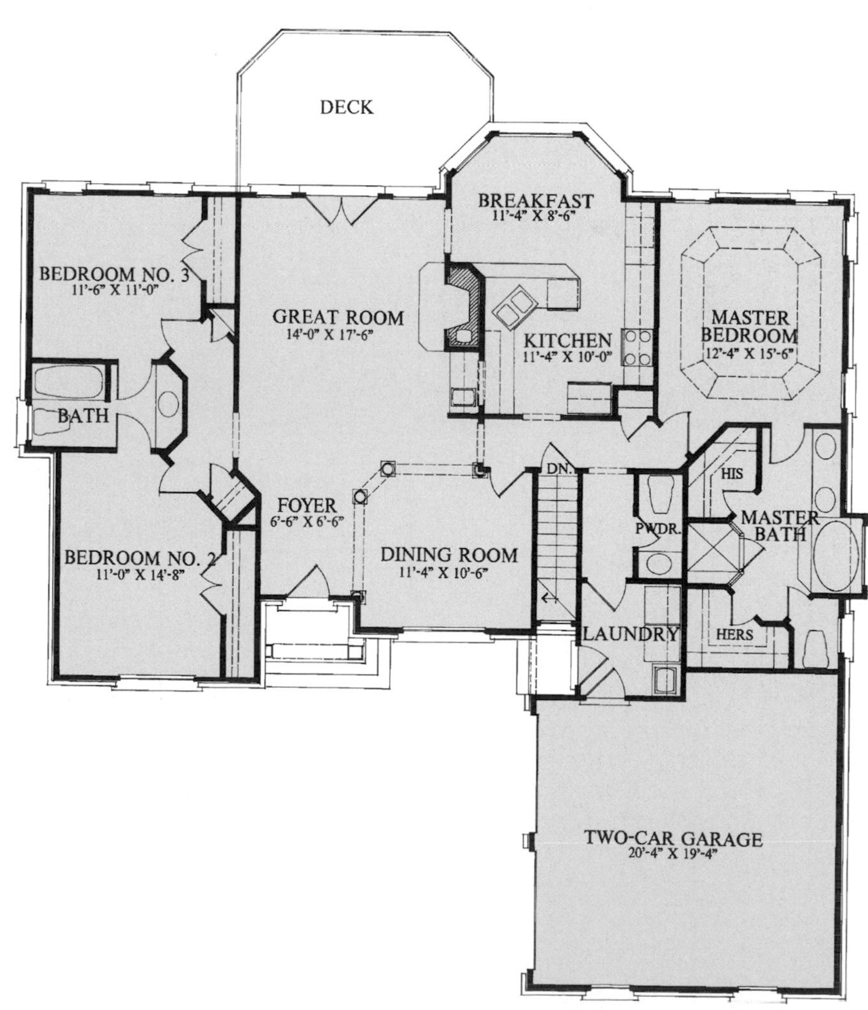

plan# HPK1700097

Style: Traditional

Square Footage: 1,746

Bedrooms: 3

Bathrooms: 2

Width: 58' - 0"

Depth: 59' - 4"

Foundation: Slab

eplans.com

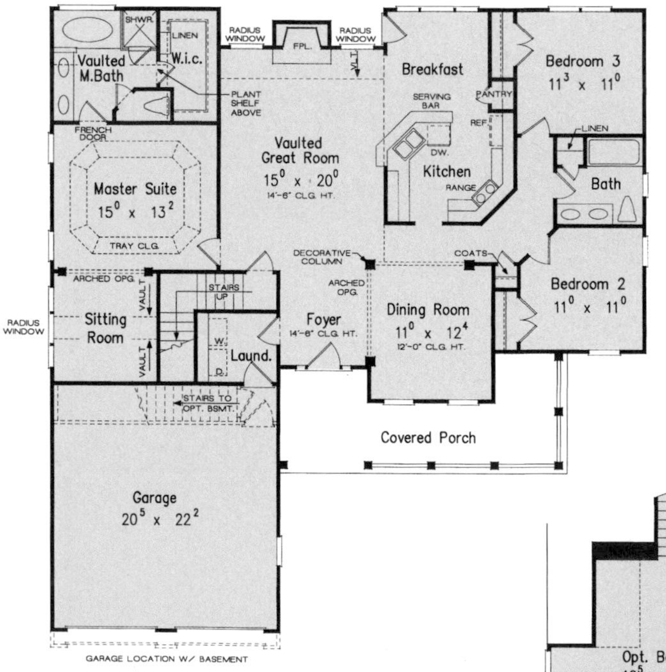

Vaulted M.Bath · W.i.c. · Master Suite $15^0 \times 13^2$ · Tray Clg. · Vaulted Great Room $15^0 \times 20^0$ 14'-6" CLG. HT. · Breakfast · Kitchen · Bedroom 3 $11^3 \times 11^0$ · Bath · Bedroom 2 $11^0 \times 11^0$ · Sitting Room · Foyer 14'-6" CLG. HT. · Laund. · Dining Room $11^0 \times 12^4$ 12'-0" CLG. HT. · Covered Porch · Garage $20^5 \times 22^2$ · Garage Location w/ Basement

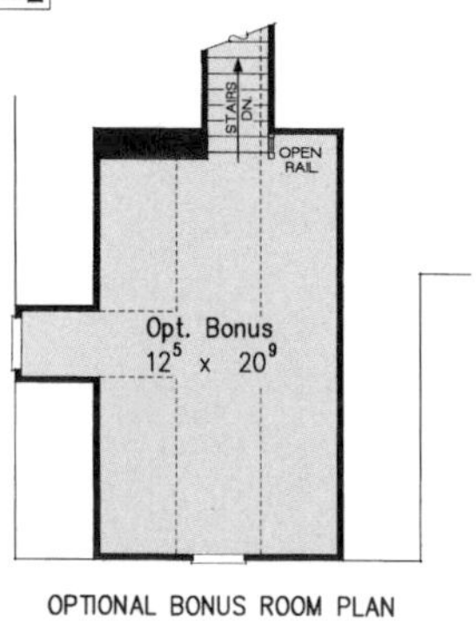

Opt. Bonus $12^5 \times 20^9$

OPTIONAL BONUS ROOM PLAN

plan# HPK1700098

Style: Country Cottage

Square Footage: 1,749

Bonus Space: 308 sq. ft.

Bedrooms: 3

Bathrooms: 2

Width: 54' - 0"

Depth: 56' - 6"

Foundation: Crawlspace, Unfinished Walkout Basement

eplans.com

plan # HPK1700099

Style: Traditional
Square Footage: 1,755
Bedrooms: 3
Bathrooms: 2
Width: 78' - 6"
Depth: 47' - 7"
Foundation: Unfinished Basement

eplans.com

A sunburst window set within a brick exterior and multigabled roof lends a vibrant aura to this three-bedroom home. The slope-ceilinged great room features a fireplace with French doors at each side. The nearby bay-windowed dining room accesses the rear porch—a perfect place for a barbecue grill. Conveniently placed near the garage for fast unloading, the U-shaped kitchen is sure to please. The master suite enjoys a walk-in closet and a luxurious bath including a separate shower, whirlpool tub, and twin-sink vanity. The two family bedrooms benefit from front-facing windows and share a full bath.

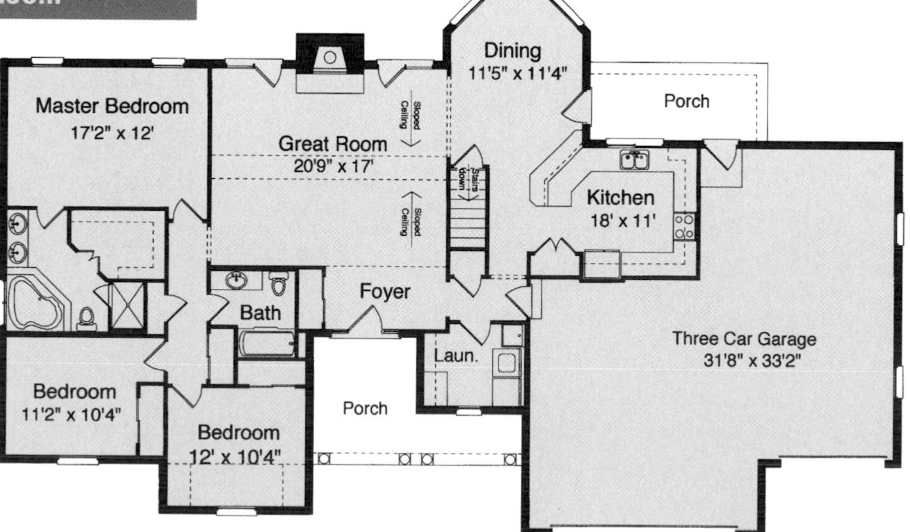

plan# HPK1700100

Style: Craftsman
Square Footage: 1,759
Bedrooms: 3
Bathrooms: 2
Width: 82' - 10"
Depth: 47' - 5"
Foundation: Unfinished Basement

eplans.com

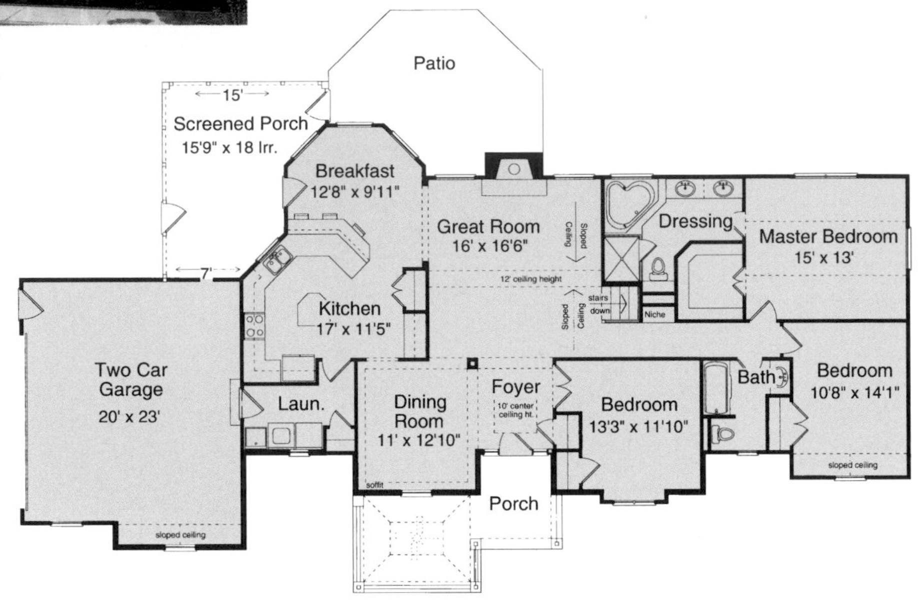

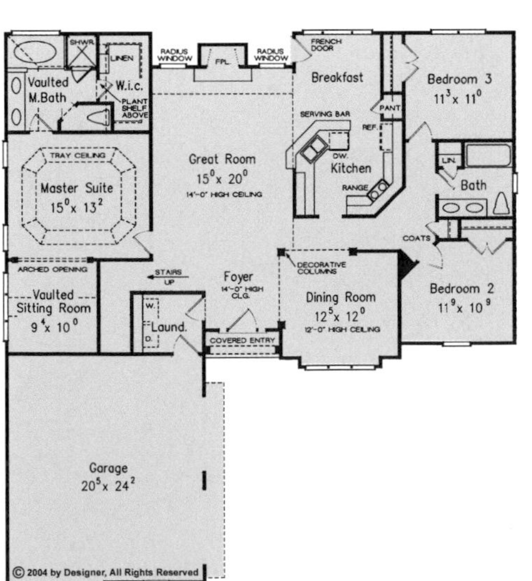

plan# HPK1700101

Style: Georgian
Square Footage: 1,768
Bonus Space: 354 sq. ft.
Bedrooms: 3
Bathrooms: 2
Width: 54' - 0"
Depth: 59' - 6"
Foundation: Slab, Unfinished Walkout Basement, Crawlspace

eplans.com

plan# HPK1700102

Style: Country Cottage
Square Footage: 1,792
Bonus Space: 255 sq. ft.
Bedrooms: 3
Bathrooms: 2
Width: 50' - 0"
Depth: 62' - 6"
Foundation: Crawlspace, Unfinished Walkout Basement

eplans.com

The country charm of this Cape Cod-style home belies the elegance inside. The beautiful foyer, accented by columns that define the formal dining room, leads to the family room. Here, the vaulted space is warm and cozy, courtesy of an extended-hearth fireplace. The kitchen is open and welcoming with angled counters that offer plenty of workspace. The laundry is conveniently located near the garage entrance. In the master suite, the star is the vaulted compartmented bath. Two additional bedrooms—both with ample closets and one with a raised ceiling—complete the plan. An optional upstairs addition includes a fourth bedroom and a full bath.

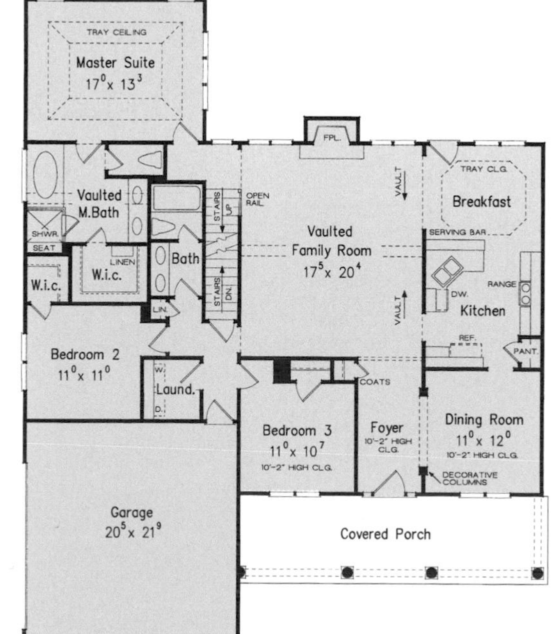

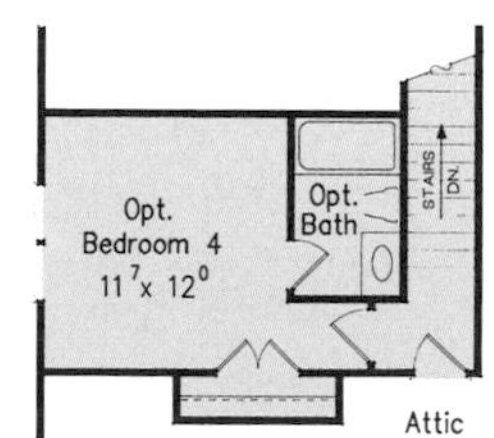

plan# HPK1700103

Style: Traditional
Square Footage: 1,812
Bonus Space: 210 sq. ft.
Bedrooms: 3
Bathrooms: 2
Width: 46' - 0"
Depth: 65' - 0"

eplans.com

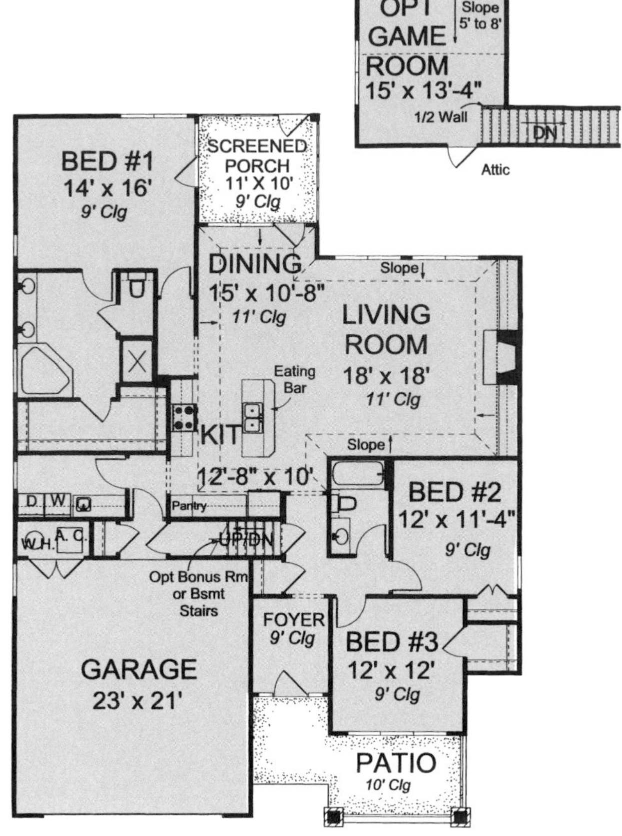

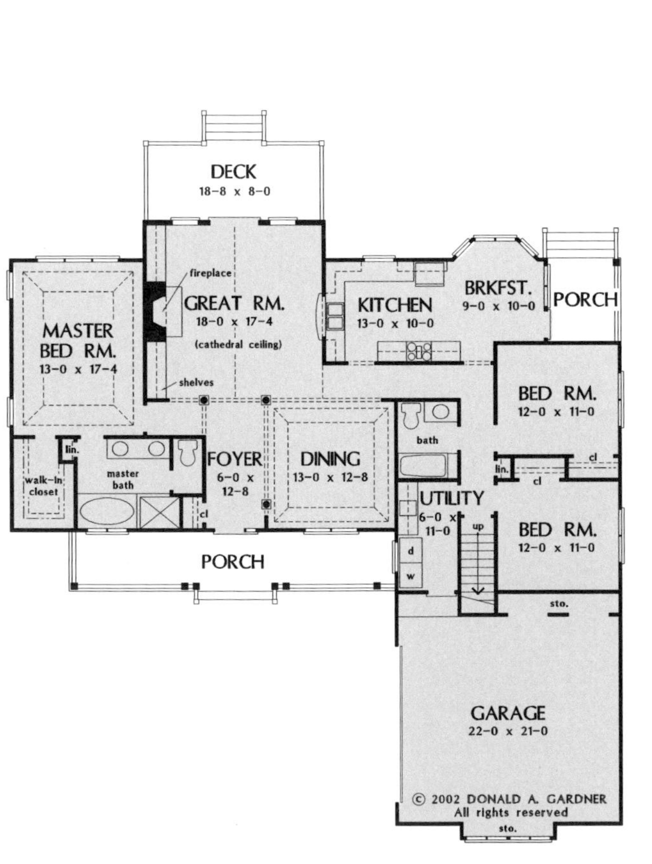

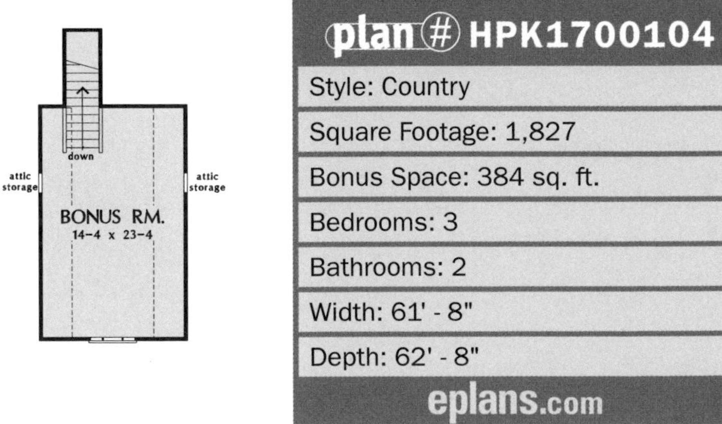

plan# HPK1700104

Style: Country
Square Footage: 1,827
Bonus Space: 384 sq. ft.
Bedrooms: 3
Bathrooms: 2
Width: 61' - 8"
Depth: 62' - 8"

eplans.com

FOR MORE DETAILED INFORMATION, PLEASE CHECK THE FLOOR PLANS CAREFULLY.

plan# HPK1700105

Style: Farmhouse
Square Footage: 1,830
Bedrooms: 3
Bathrooms: 2
Width: 75' - 0"
Depth: 43' - 5"
Foundation: Unfinished Basement

eplans.com

This charming one-story traditional home greets visitors with a covered porch. A uniquely shaped galley-style kitchen shares a snack bar with the spacious gathering room where a fireplace is the focal point. The dining room furnishes sliding glass doors to the rear terrace, as does the master bedroom. This bedroom area also includes a luxury bath with a whirlpool tub and separate dressing room. Two additional bedrooms, one that could double as a study, are located at the front of the home. The two-car garage features a large storage area and can be reached through the service entrance or from the rear terrace.

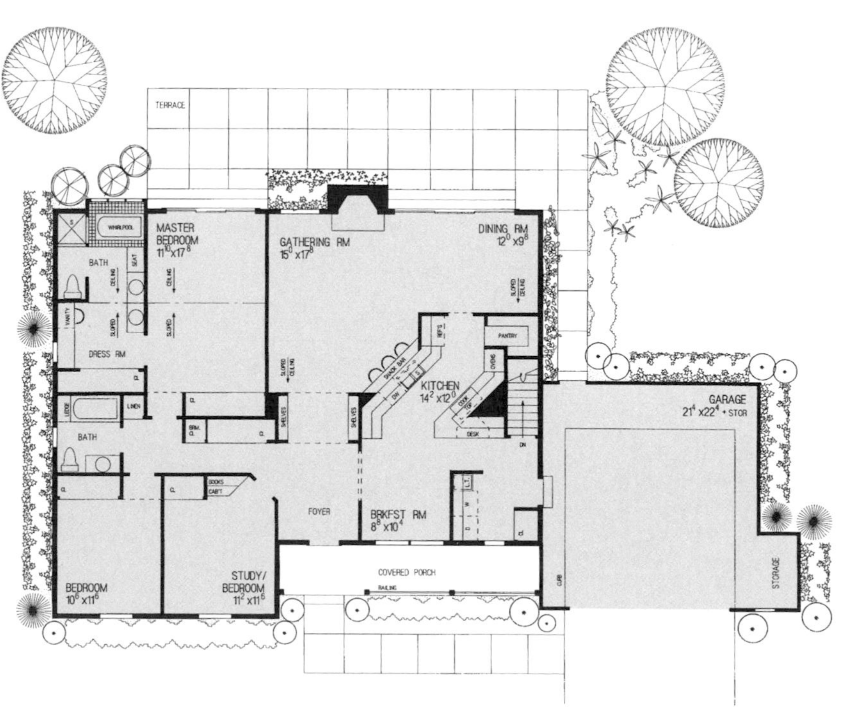

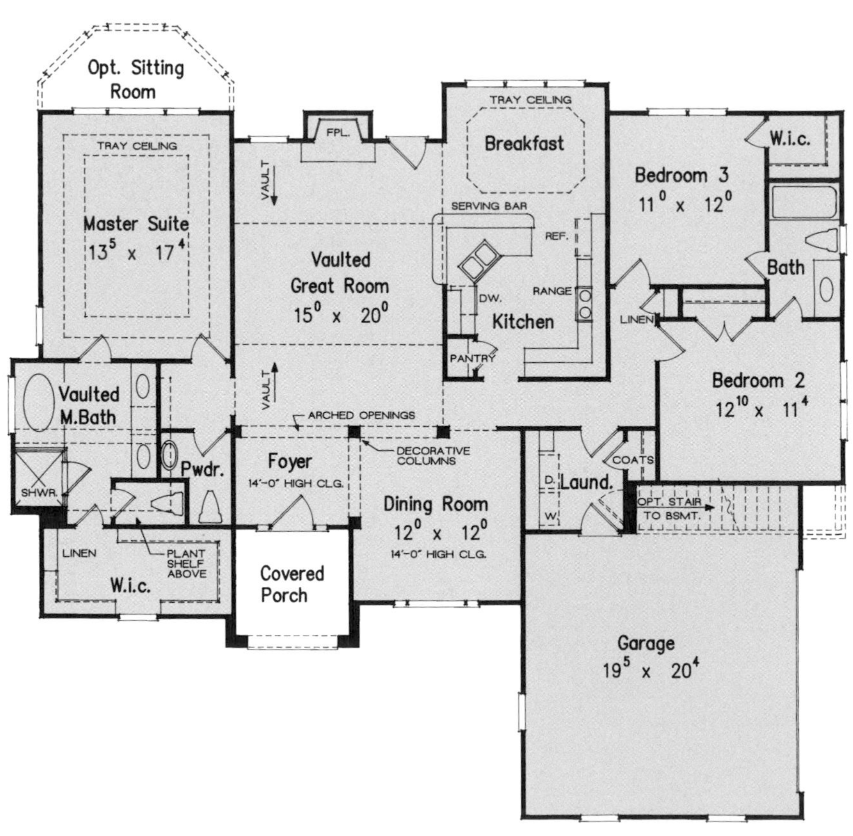

plan# HPK1700106

Style: Country Cottage

Square Footage: 1,832

Bonus Space: 68 sq. ft.

Bedrooms: 3

Bathrooms: 2½

Width: 59' - 6"

Depth: 52' - 6"

Foundation: Crawlspace, Slab, Unfinished Walkout Basement

eplans.com

This compact one-story has plenty of living in it. The master suite features an optional sun-washed sitting area with views to the rear of the home. A vaulted great room with fireplace conveniently accesses the kitchen via a serving bar. Meals can also be taken in the cozy breakfast area. For formal occasions the dining room creates opulence with its decorative columns. Two family bedrooms flank the right of the home with a shared bath, linen storage, and easy access to laundry facilities.

plan # HPK1700107

Style: Traditional
Square Footage: 1,836
Bedrooms: 3
Bathrooms: 2
Width: 65' - 8"
Depth: 55' - 0"
Foundation: Crawlspace, Slab, Unfinished Basement

eplans.com

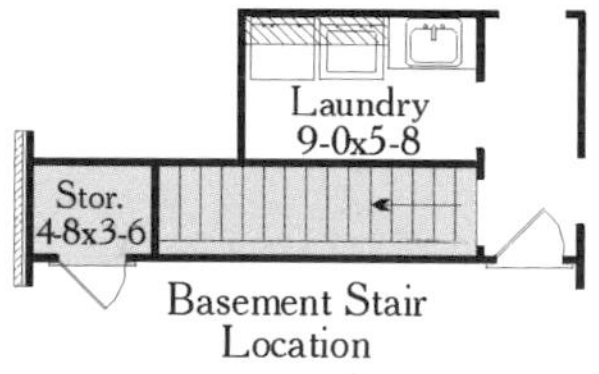

SMART TIP

Take heed of recent trends in home organization to make your next laundry room and storage areas work smarter. Families with children should consider turning the laundry room into a fully-loaded "landing zone" for incoming household traffic, complete with lockers, shelves, and plenty of bins for gear. Similarly, don't relegate storage areas to dark, musty closets overrun with boxes. Customize the space to accommodate your family's favorite hobbies and activities. Even the small storage space adjacent to the garage can become a modest art studio, reading room, or wine cellar.

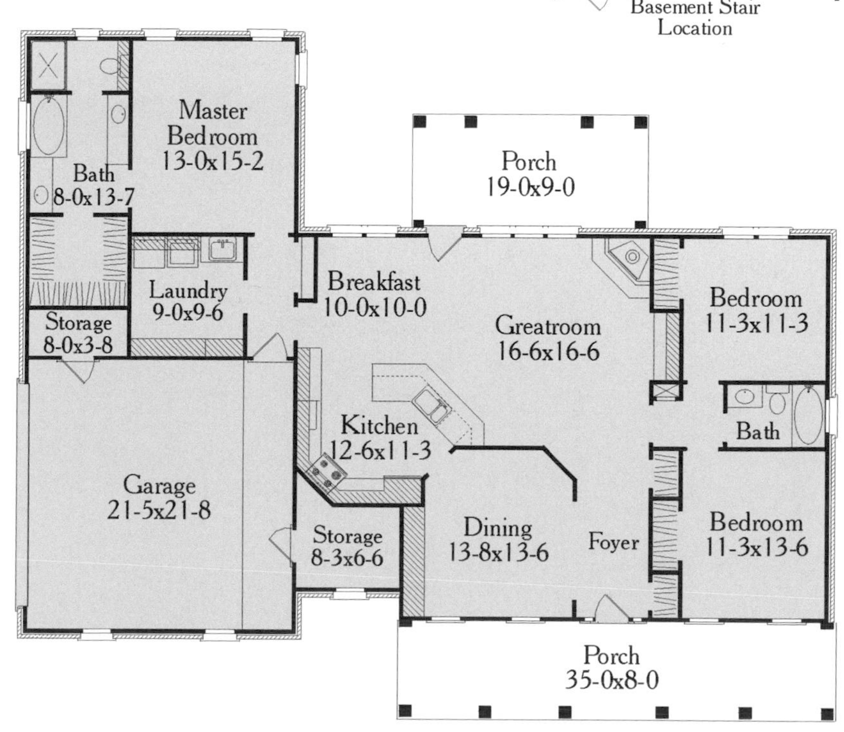

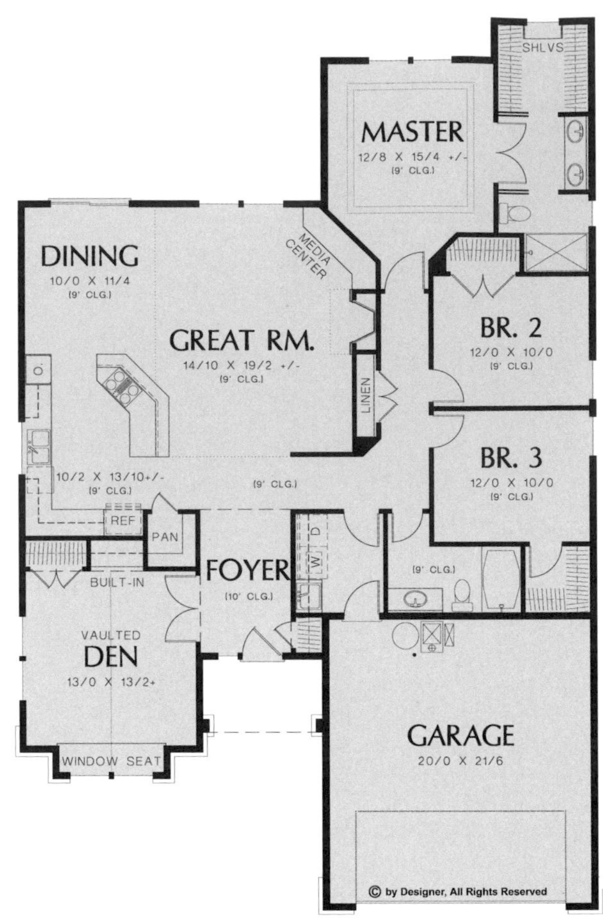

plan # HPK1700108

Style: Craftsman
Square Footage: 1,850
Bedrooms: 3
Bathrooms: 2
Width: 44' - 0"
Depth: 68' - 0"
Foundation: Crawlspace

eplans.com

plan # HPK1700109

Style: Farmhouse
Square Footage: 1,864
Bonus Space: 420 sq. ft.
Bedrooms: 3
Bathrooms: 2 ½
Width: 71' - 0"
Depth: 56' - 4"

eplans.com

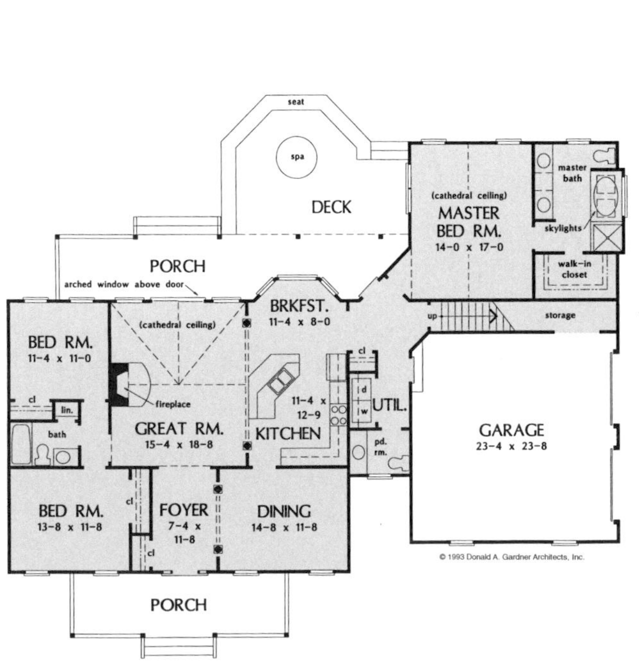

plan # HPK1700110
Style: Traditional
Square Footage: 1,869
Bonus Space: 336 sq. ft.
Bedrooms: 3
Bathrooms: 2
Width: 54' - 0"
Depth: 60' - 6"
Foundation: Unfinished Walkout Basement, Crawlspace, Slab
eplans.com

A rustic exterior of shingles, siding, and stone provides a sweet country look. Inside, the foyer is flanked by a dining room and family bedrooms. Bedrooms 2 and 3 share a full hall bath. The master suite, located on the opposite side of the home for privacy, boasts a tray ceiling and a pampering bath with an oversized tub. The kitchen opens to a breakfast room that accesses the rear sun deck. The enormous living room is warmed by a central fireplace. The laundry room and double-car garage complete this plan.

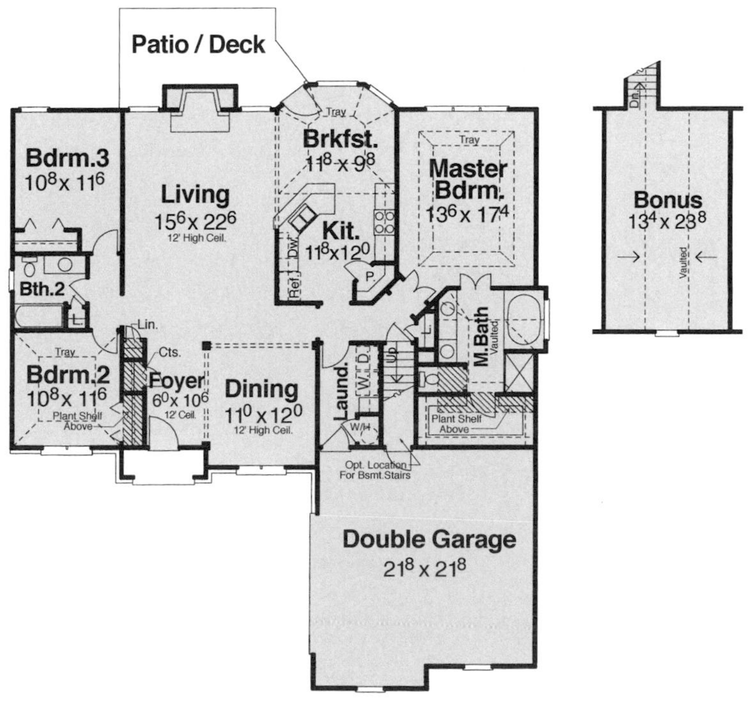

REAR EXTERIOR

plan# HPK1700111

- Style: Country Cottage
- Square Footage: 1,879
- Bonus Space: 360 sq. ft.
- Bedrooms: 3
- Bathrooms: 2
- Width: 66' - 4"
- Depth: 55' - 2"

eplans.com

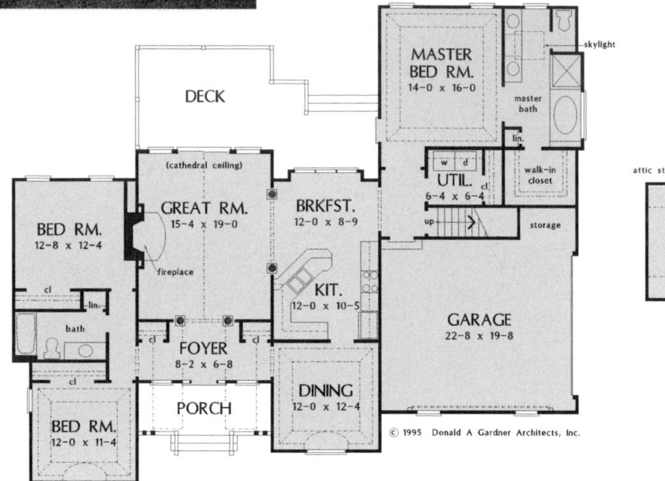

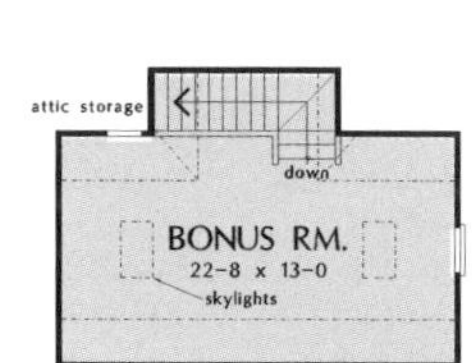

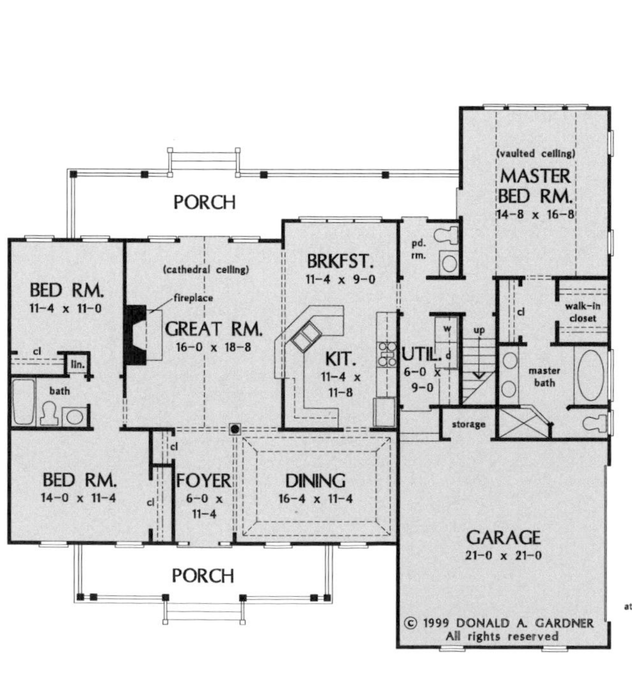

plan# HPK1700112

- Style: Country
- Square Footage: 1,882
- Bonus Space: 363 sq. ft.
- Bedrooms: 3
- Bathrooms: 2½
- Width: 61' - 4"
- Depth: 55' - 0"

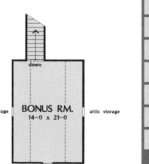

eplans.com

plan # HPK1700113

Style: Santa Fe
Square Footage: 1,883
Bedrooms: 3
Bathrooms: 2
Width: 66' - 2"
Depth: 59' - 8"

eplans.com

Home on the range—where luxury and livability go hand-in-hand. Rustic details like heavy shutters and beams accent the facade of this Santa Fe classic. Enter the front covered porch to the spacious foyer, which opens at a unique angle to the windowed formal dining room to the right. At the center of the home is the hearth-warmed great room, which flows right into the island serving-bar kitchen and bayed breakfast nook—both feature 11-foot ceilings. The left wing of the plan is taken up by the sleeping quarters, including two family bedrooms—each with its own walk-in closet—and a deluxe master suite. The suite boasts another curved wall of windows, a walk-in closet, twin-vanity bath, and rear-porch access.

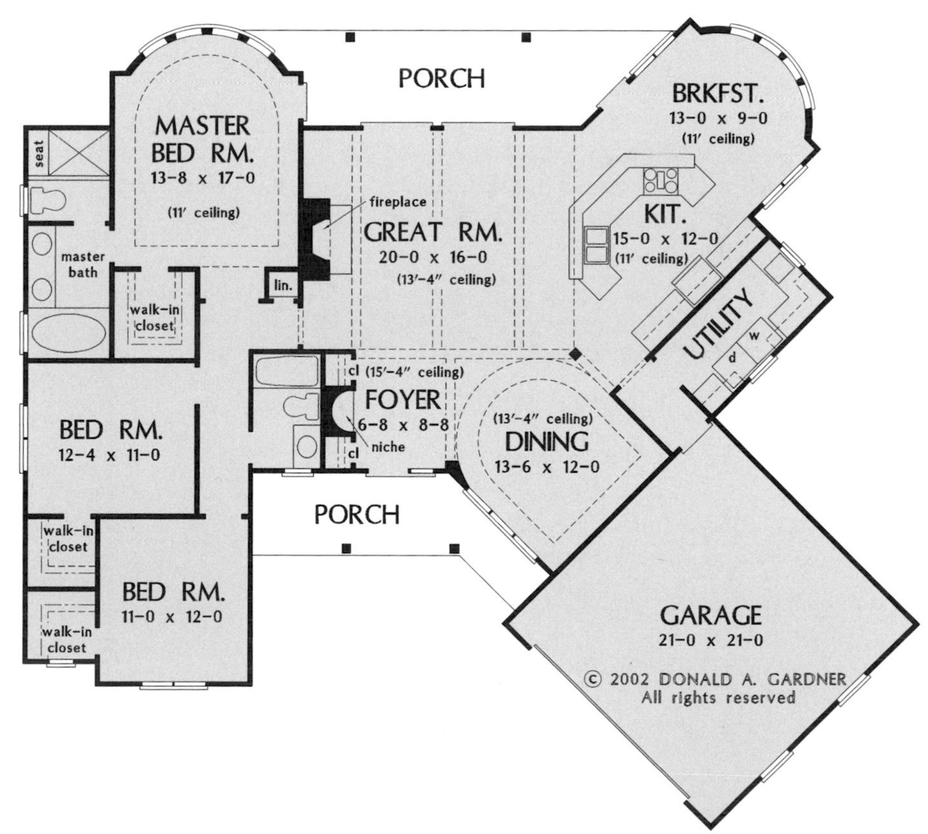

Giddyup! Santa Fe style at its best brings you back to the days of open skies and covered wagons. Rich with history on the outside, this plan's interior has all the up-to-date amenities that today's families require. The arched loggia entry opens to a soaring foyer, flanked on the right by a formal dining room. To the left is a bedroom that could easily become a study. Straight ahead, the hearth-warmed great room enjoys sliding-glass-door access to the rear loggia. Another bedroom is tucked in the back left corner, convenient to a full hall bath. On the other side of the great room, a roomy kitchen opens to a breakfast nook with a curved wall of windows. Secluded to the back is the luxurious master suite, featuring a 10-foot ceiling and spectacular private bath. The two-car garage opens to a utility room with a handy linen closet.

plan# HPK1700114

- Style: Santa Fe
- Square Footage: 1,895
- Bedrooms: 3
- Bathrooms: 2
- Width: 65' - 10"
- Depth: 59' - 9"

eplans.com

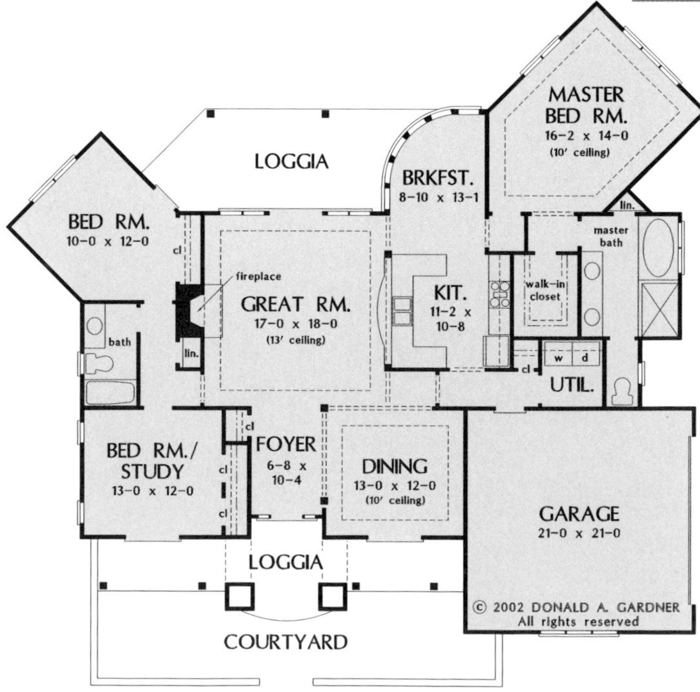

plan# HPK1700115

Style: Country Cottage
Square Footage: 1,895
Bedrooms: 3
Bathrooms: 2
Width: 66' - 0"
Depth: 69' - 0"
Foundation: Unfinished Basement

eplans.com

A brick exterior with quoins, arched windows and wood trim creates a rich, solid look to this delightful one-level home. An open great room and dining room are topped with a sloped ceiling that reaches a 12-foot height. The great room is decorated by a gas fireplace, and offers a view to the rear yard. A large kitchen with snack bar, and the breakfast area open generously to the great room for a continuous traffic flow. The screened-in porch offers a great outdoor living space. The luxurious master suite enjoys a whirlpool tub, double bowl vanity, and shower enclosure. Stairs off the foyer lead to an unfinished basement.

plan# HPK1700116

Style: Traditional

Square Footage: 1,895

Bedrooms: 3

Bathrooms: 2½

Width: 72' - 0"

Depth: 42' - 8"

Foundation: Unfinished Basement

eplans.com

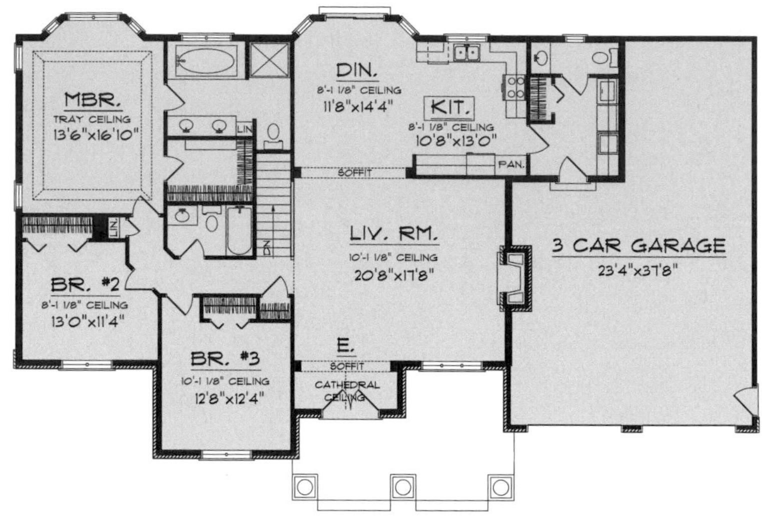

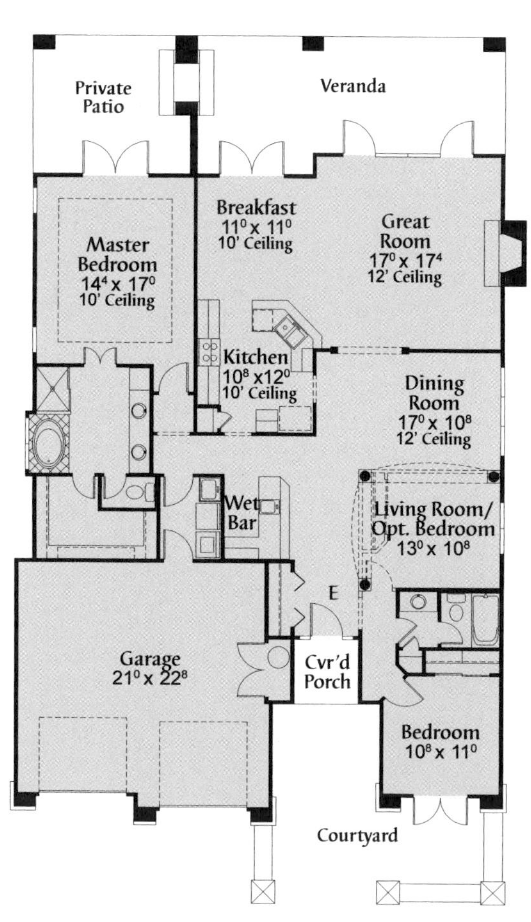

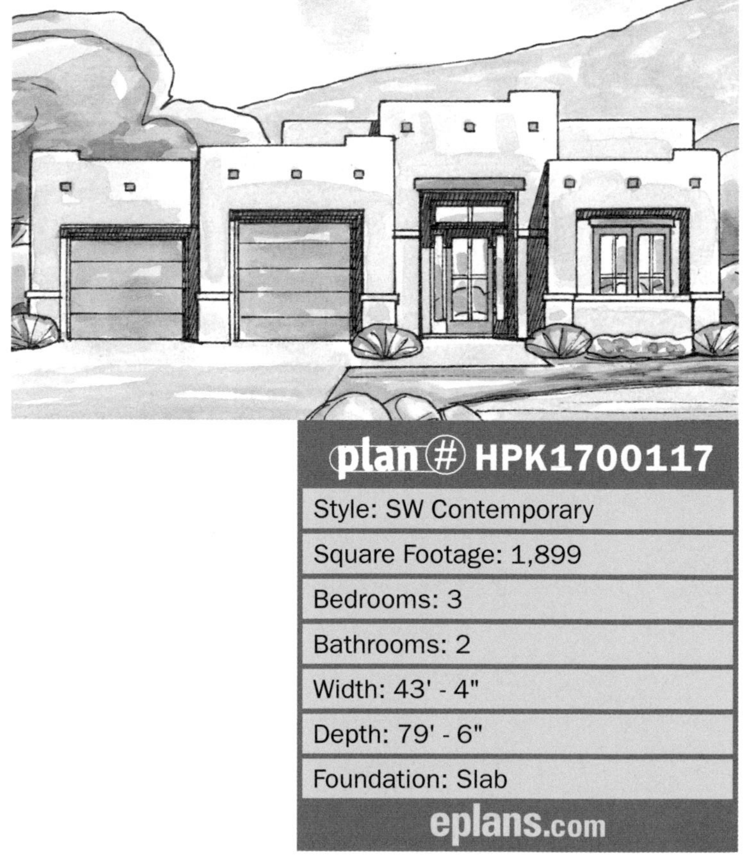

plan# HPK1700117

Style: SW Contemporary

Square Footage: 1,899

Bedrooms: 3

Bathrooms: 2

Width: 43' - 4"

Depth: 79' - 6"

Foundation: Slab

eplans.com

plan # HPK1700118
Style: Traditional
Square Footage: 1,932
Bedrooms: 4
Bathrooms: 3
Width: 63' - 0"
Depth: 45' - 0"
Foundation: Unfinished Walkout Basement, Crawlspace
eplans.com

Special architectural aspects turn this quaint home into much more than just another one-story ranch design. A central great room acts as the hub of the plan and is graced by a fireplace flanked on either side by windows. It is separated from the kitchen by a convenient serving bar. Formal dining is accomplished to the front of the plan in a room with a tray ceiling. Casual dining takes place in the breakfast room with its full wall of glass. Two bedrooms to the left share a full bath. The master suite and one additional bedroom are to the right.

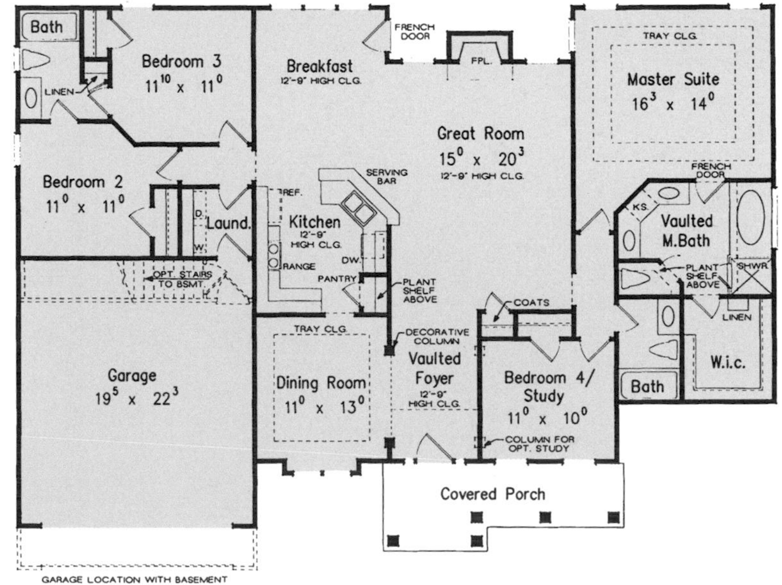

Traditional in every sense of the word, you can't go wrong with this charming country cottage. The foyer opens on the right to a columned dining room, and ahead to the family room. Here, a raised ceiling and bright radius windows expand the space, and a warming fireplace lends a cozy touch. A sunny bayed breakfast nook flows into the angled kitchen for easy casual meals. Down the hall, two bedrooms share a full bath, tucked behind the two-car garage to protect the bedrooms from street noise. The master suite is indulgent, pampering homeowners with a bayed sitting area, tray ceiling, vaulted spa bath, and an oversized walk-in closet. A fourth bedroom and bonus space are available to grow as your family does.

plan # HPK1700119

Style: Country Cottage

Square Footage: 1,933

Bonus Space: 519 sq. ft.

Bedrooms: 3

Bathrooms: 2½

Width: 62' - 0"

Depth: 50' - 0"

Foundation: Crawlspace, Unfinished Walkout Basement

eplans.com

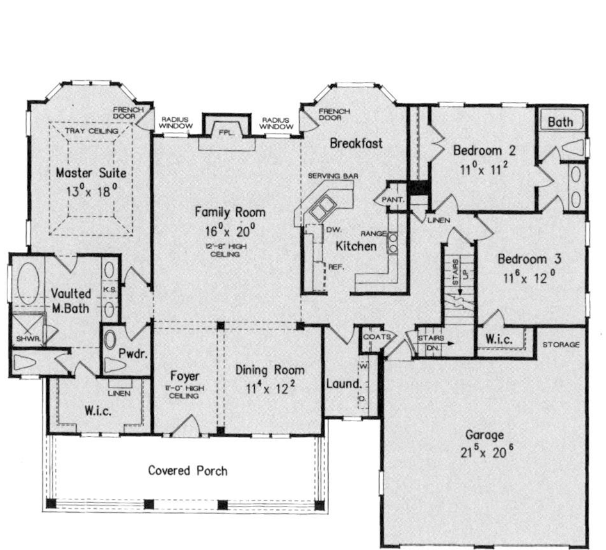

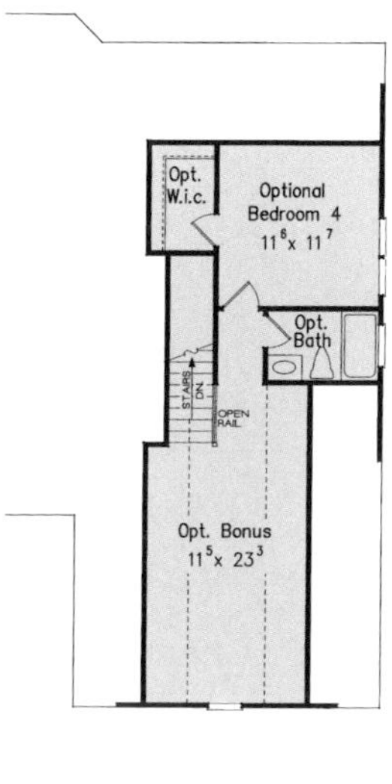

plan# HPK1700120

Style: Santa Fe

Square Footage: 1,934

Bedrooms: 3

Bathrooms: 2½

Width: 61' - 6"

Depth: 67' - 4"

Foundation: Slab

eplans.com

DESIGN NOTE

Fans of the Pueblo Revival style will delight in the many signature features present in this plan: exposed roof beams, stucco exterior, rounded edges, and a welcoming courtyard. The present-day examples of the style, such as those prevalent around Arizona and New Mexico, draw on historical precedents from Spanish Colonial architecture and Native American pueblos. Note also how the style takes cues from its natural environment by implementing outdoor rooms, gardens, and earth-toned materials.

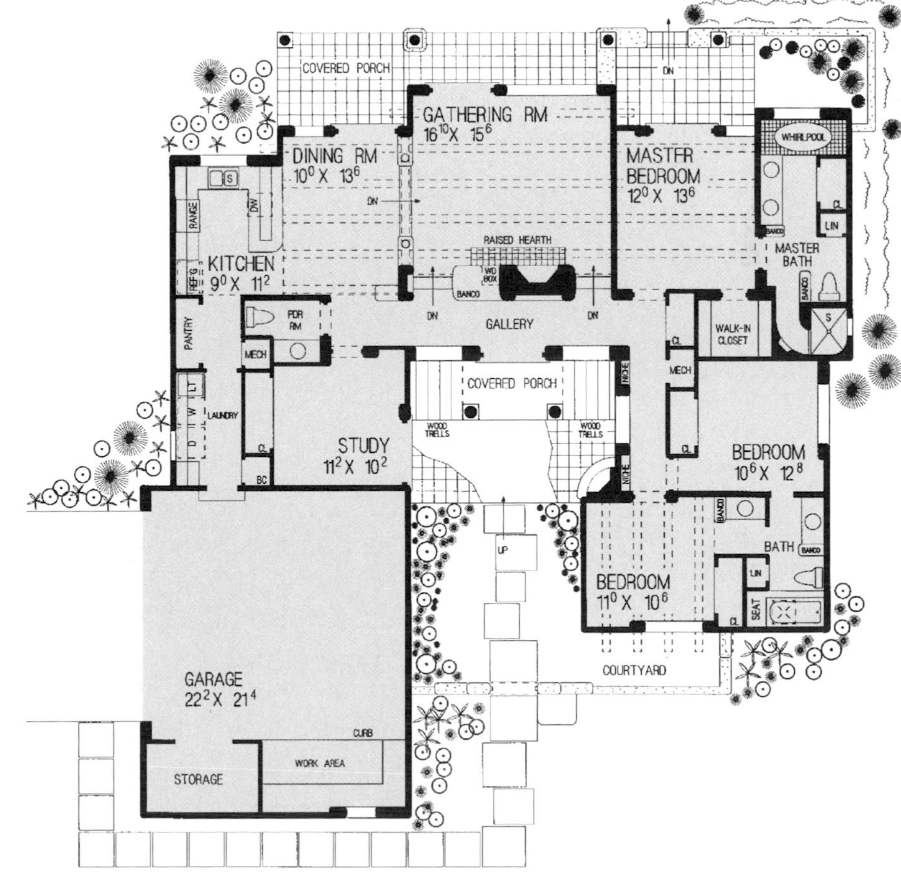

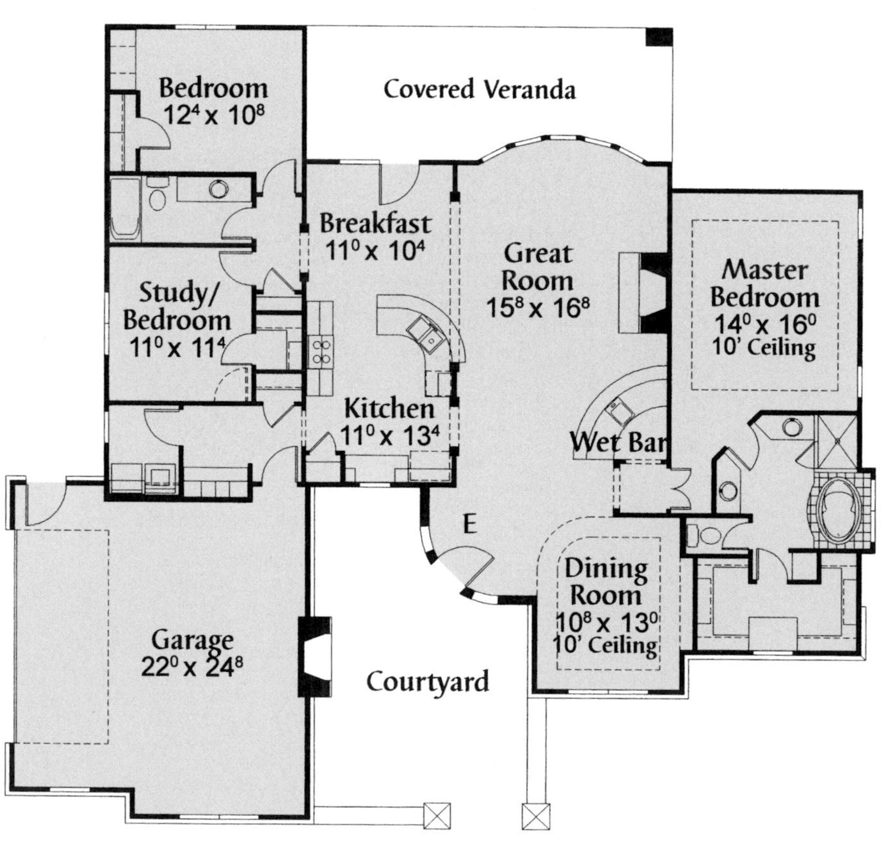

plan# HPK1700121
Style: SW Contemporary
Square Footage: 1,950
Bedrooms: 3
Bathrooms: 2
Width: 65' - 4"
Depth: 60' - 0"
Foundation: Slab
eplans.com

Clean lines and plenty of windows add style to this contemporary Pueblo design. A fireplace makes the expansive entry courtyard even more welcoming. Inside, another fireplace, a wet bar, and a curved wall of windows enhance the great room. The kitchen easily serves the formal dining room and the breakfast area, which opens to a covered rear veranda. A split-bedroom plan places the master suite, with its indulgent dual-vanity bath and walk-in closet, to the right of the plan; two family bedrooms sit to the left of the plan.

plan# HPK1700122

Style: European Cottage
Square Footage: 1,964
Bedrooms: 3
Bathrooms: 2
Width: 38' - 10"
Depth: 90' - 1"
Foundation: Slab

eplans.com

This narrow-lot plan has all the appeal and romance of a European cottage. The front porch welcomes you to a charming set of double doors. Two family bedrooms, a hall bath, a laundry room, and the two-car garage with storage are located at the front of the plan. The island kitchen easily serves the dining room, which accesses a private garden and the casual breakfast room. The spacious family room offers a warming fireplace, built-ins, and back-porch access. The plan is completed by thc master suite, which features a private bath and walk-in closet.

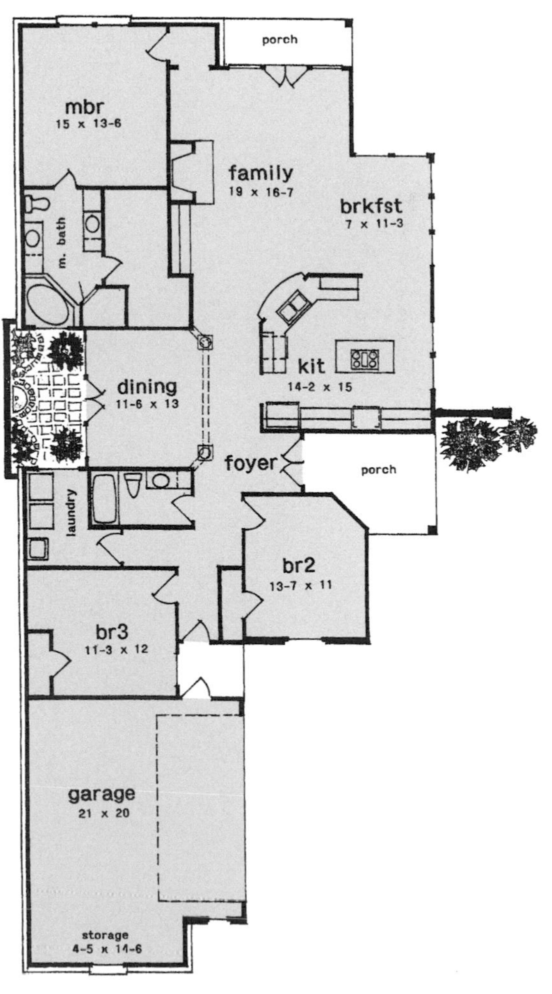

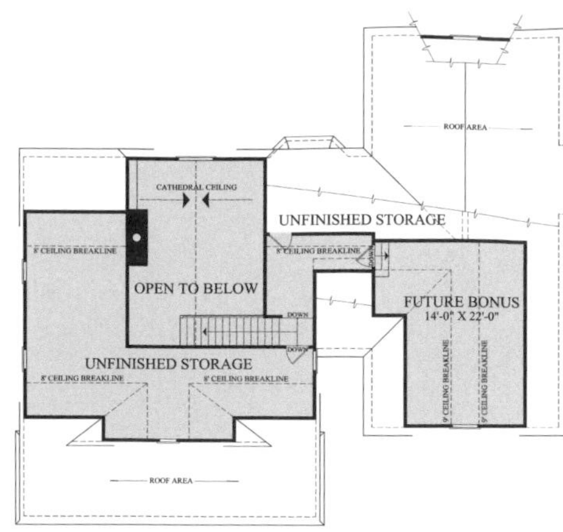

plan# HPK1700123

Style: Country Cottage

Square Footage: 1,973

Bonus Space: 368 sq. ft.

Bedrooms: 3

Bathrooms: 2

Width: 64' - 10"

Depth: 58' - 2"

Foundation: Crawlspace, Unfinished Basement

eplans.com

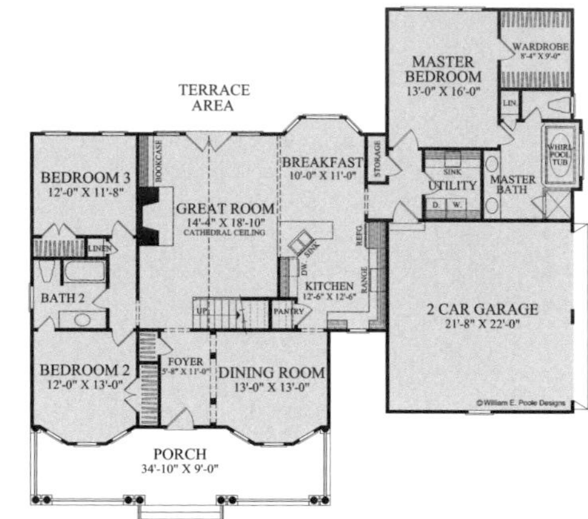

REAR EXTERIOR

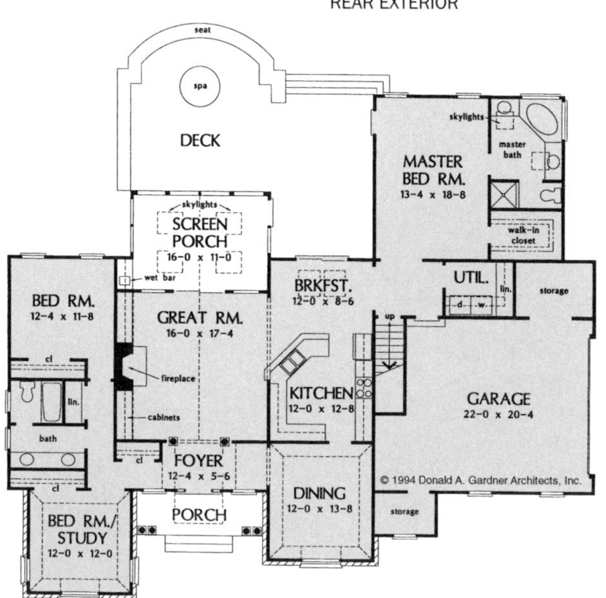

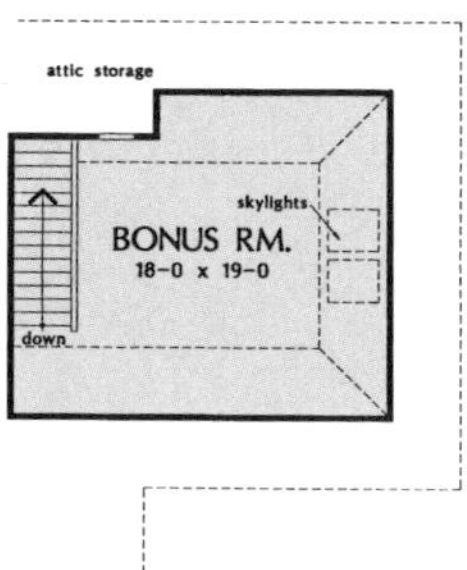

plan# HPK1700124

Style: Traditional

Square Footage: 1,977

Bonus Space: 430 sq. ft.

Bedrooms: 3

Bathrooms: 2

Width: 69' - 8"

Depth: 59' - 6"

eplans.com

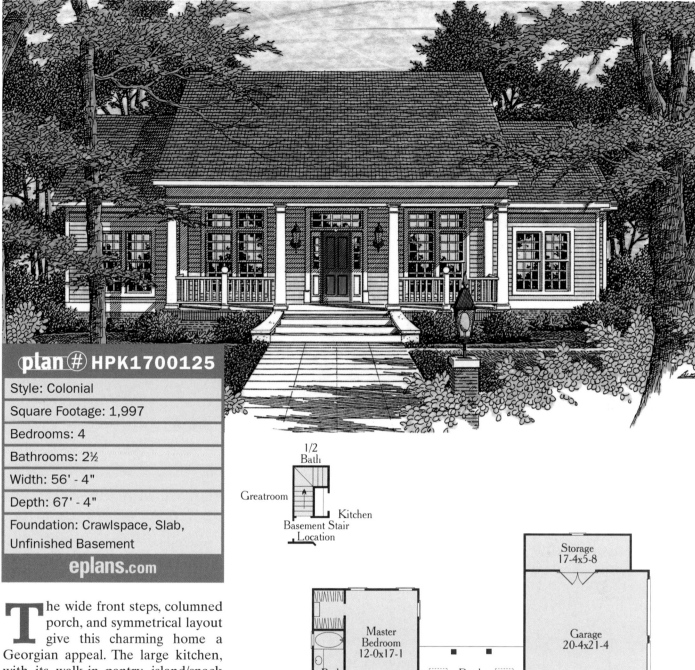

plan# HPK1700125

Style: Colonial
Square Footage: 1,997
Bedrooms: 4
Bathrooms: 2½
Width: 56' - 4"
Depth: 67' - 4"
Foundation: Crawlspace, Slab, Unfinished Basement

eplans.com

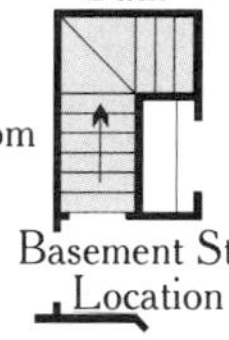

The wide front steps, columned porch, and symmetrical layout give this charming home a Georgian appeal. The large kitchen, with its walk-in pantry, island/snack bar, and breakfast nook, will gratify any cook. The central great room offers radiant French doors on both sides of the fireplace. Outside those doors is a comfortable covered porch with two skylights. To the left of the great room reside four bedrooms—three secondary bedrooms and a master bedroom. The master bedroom enjoys a walk-in closet, twin-vanity sinks, a separate shower and tub, and private access to the rear porch.

1/2 Bath
Greatroom
Kitchen
Basement Stair Location

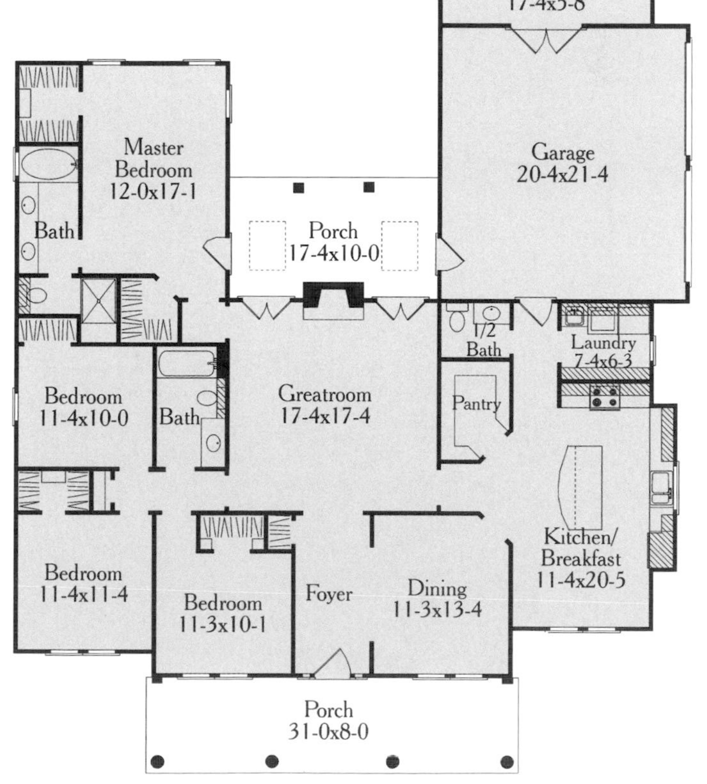

This adorable abode could serve as a vacation cottage, guest house, starter home, or in-law quarters. The side-gabled design allows for a front porch with a "down-South" feel. Despite the small size, this home is packed with all the necessities. The first-floor master suite has a large bathroom and a walk-in closet. An open, functional floor plan includes a powder room, a kitchen/breakfast nook area, and a family room with a corner fireplace. Upstairs, two additional bedrooms share a bath. One could be used as a home office.

plan# HPK1700126

Style: Country Cottage
First Floor: 1,050 sq. ft.
Second Floor: 458 sq. ft.
Total: 1,508 sq. ft.
Bedrooms: 3
Bathrooms: 2½
Width: 35' - 6"
Depth: 39' - 9"
Foundation: Pier (same as Piling)

eplans.com

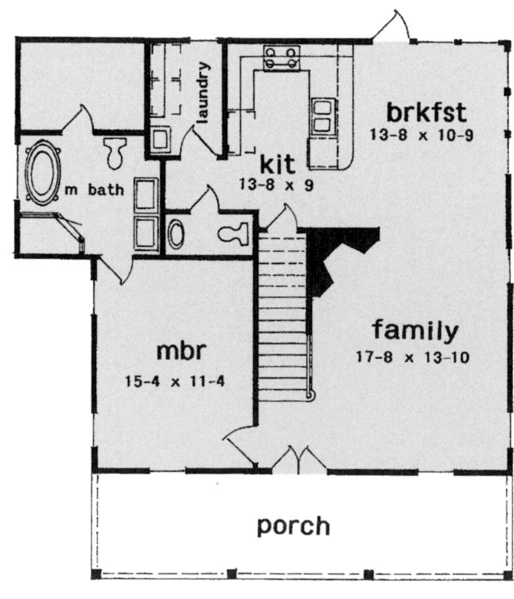

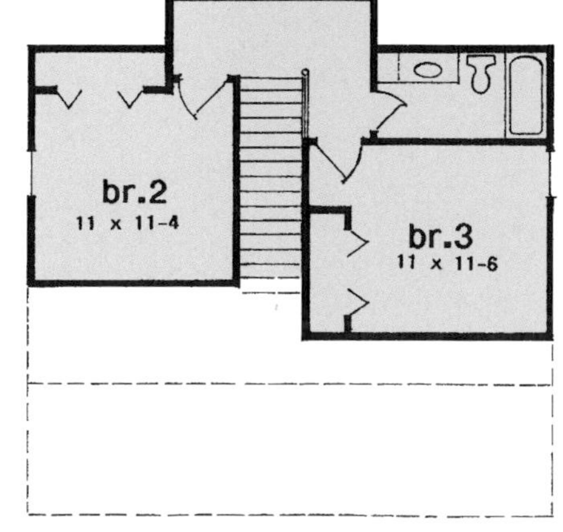

plan # HPK1700601

Style: Country Cottage
First Floor: 1,050 sq. ft.
Second Floor: 533 sq. ft.
Total: 1,583 sq. ft.
Bedrooms: 3
Bathrooms: 2
Width: 42' - 0"
Depth: 38' - 0"
Foundation: Crawlspace, Unfinished Basement

eplans.com

What a combinationa charming turn-of-the-century exterior with a contemporary interior! A wraparound railed porch and rear deck expand the living space to outdoor entertaining. Vaulted ceilings throughout the great room and dining room add spaciousness; a fireplace warms the area. An open kitchen plan includes a preparation island, breakfast bar, and window over the sink. The master suite is on the first floor for privacy and convenience. It boasts a roomy walk-in closet and private bath with a garden whirlpool tub, separate shower, and dual vanities. Two vaulted family bedrooms on the second floor share a full bath. Note the loft area and extra storage space.

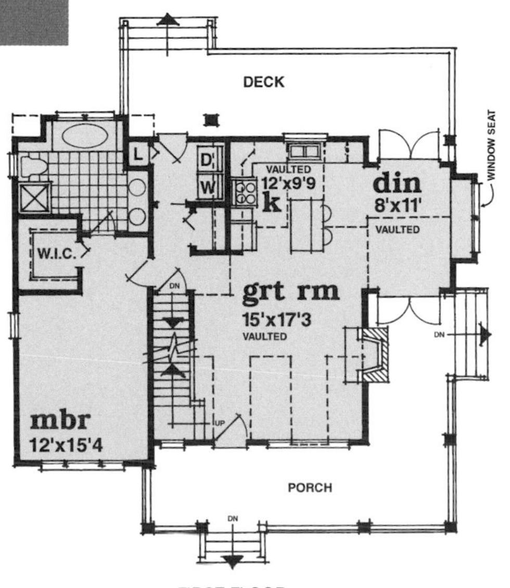

FIRST FLOOR

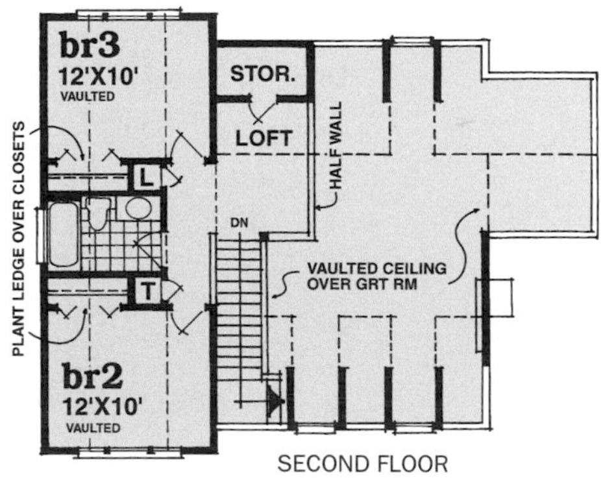

SECOND FLOOR

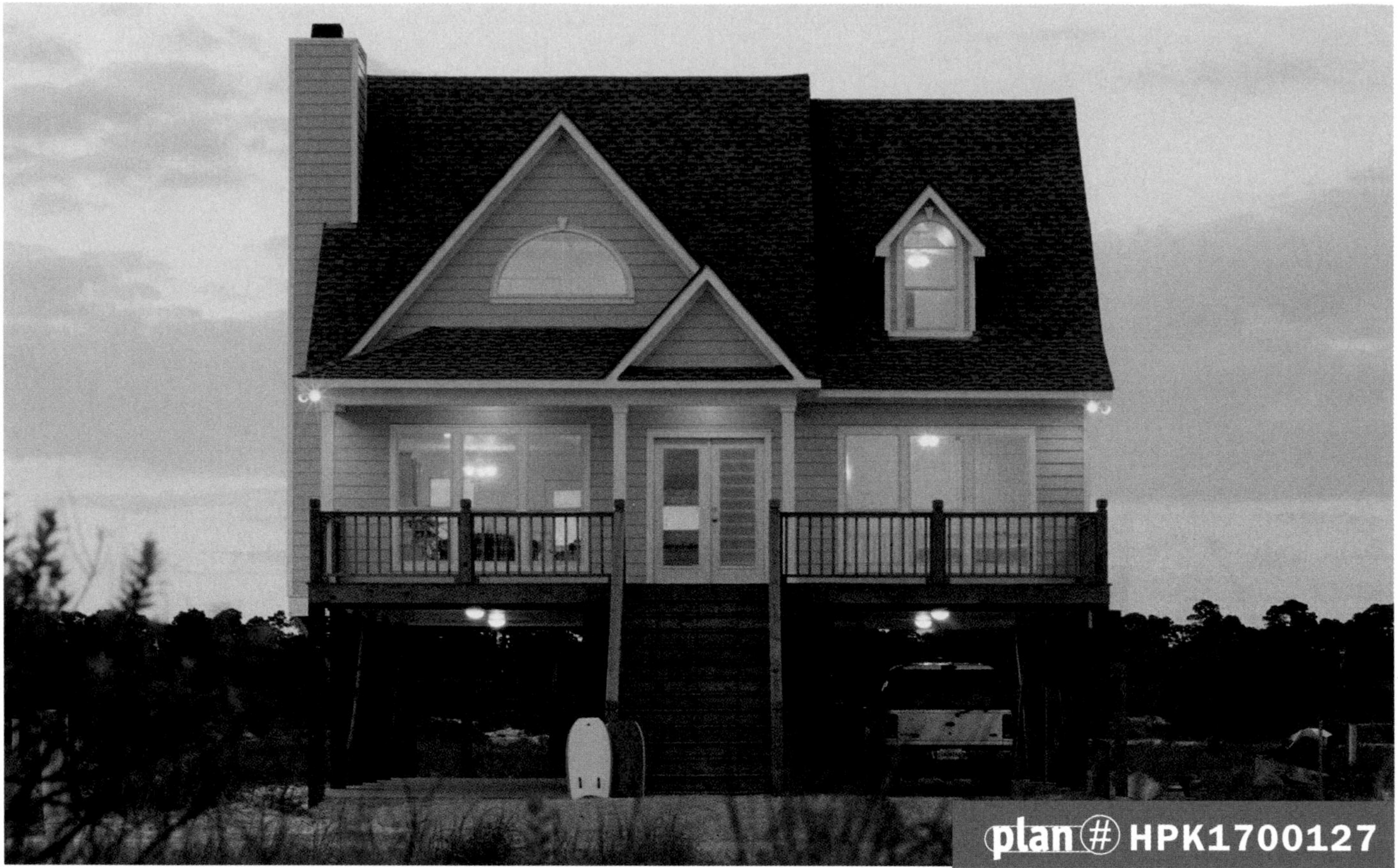

PHOTOS BY CHRIS A. LITTLE OF ATLANTA (PHOTOGRAPHER)

plan# HPK1700127

Style: Seaside
First Floor: 1,122 sq. ft.
Second Floor: 528 sq. ft.
Total: 1,650 sq. ft.
Bedrooms: 4
Bathrooms: 2
Width: 34' - 0"
Depth: 52' - 5"
Foundation: Pier (same as Piling)

eplans.com

FIRST FLOOR

SECOND FLOOR

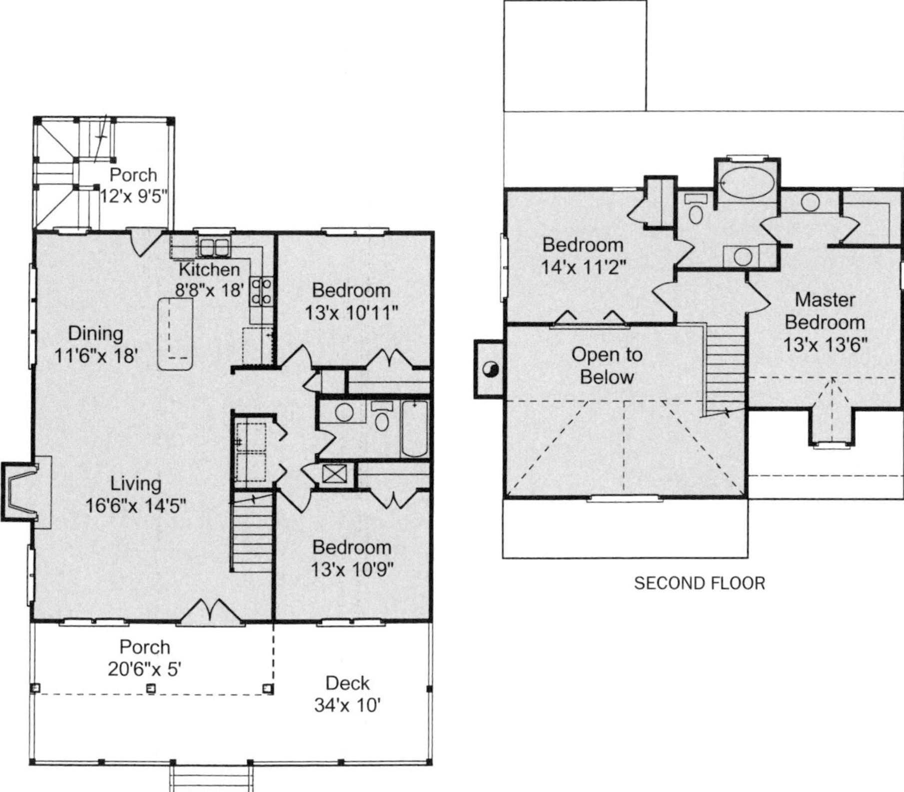

This lovely seaside vacation home is perfect for seasonal family getaways or for the family that lives coastal year round. The spacious front deck is great for private sunbathing or outdoor barbecues, providing breathtaking ocean views. The two-story living room is warmed by a fireplace on breezy beach nights, and the island kitchen overlooks the open dining area nearby. Two first-floor family bedrooms share a hall bath. Upstairs, the master bedroom features a walk-in closet, dressing area with a vanity, and access to a whirlpool tub shared with an additional family bedroom.

plan # HPK1700128

Style: Country Cottage
First Floor: 1,179 sq. ft.
Second Floor: 479 sq. ft.
Total: 1,658 sq. ft.
Bonus Space: 338 sq. ft.
Bedrooms: 3
Bathrooms: 2½
Width: 41' - 6"
Depth: 54' - 4"
Foundation: Slab, Unfinished Walkout Basement, Crawlspace

eplans.com

With vaulted ceilings in the dining room and the great room, a tray ceiling in the master suite, and a sunlit two-story foyer, this inviting design offers a wealth of light and space. The counter-filled kitchen opens to a large breakfast area with backyard access. The master suite is complete with a walk-in closet and pampering bath. Upstairs, two secondary bedrooms share a hall bath and access to an optional bonus room. Note the storage space in the two-car garage.

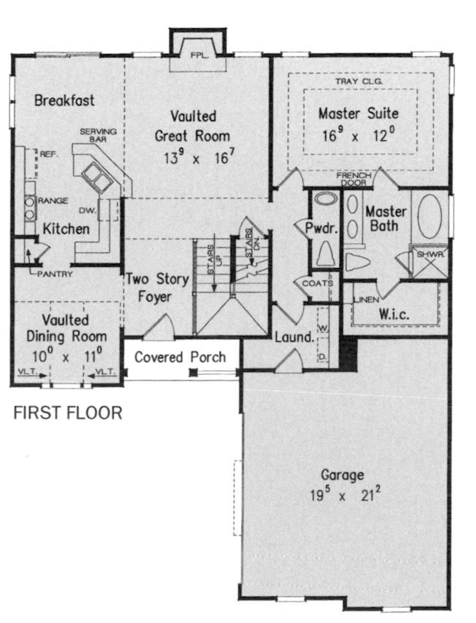

FIRST FLOOR

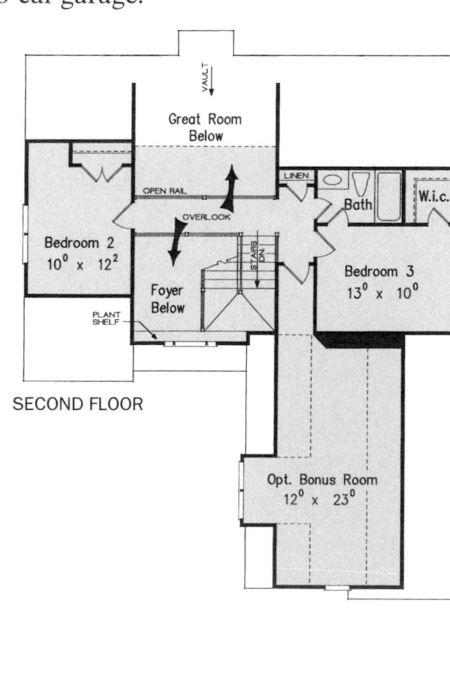

SECOND FLOOR

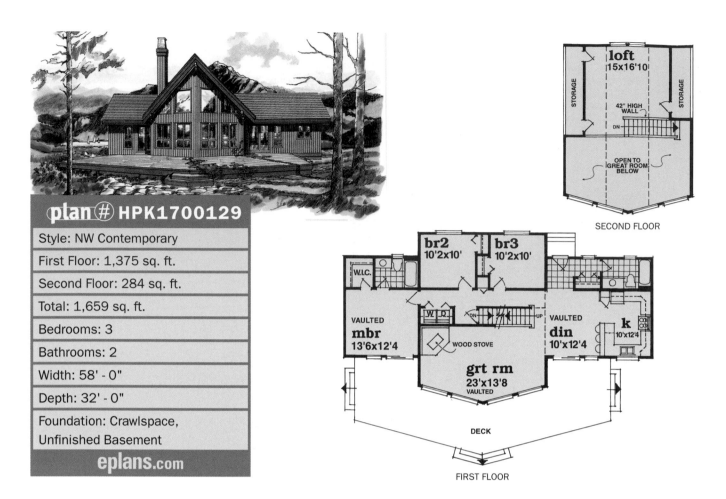

plan# HPK1700129

Style: NW Contemporary

First Floor: 1,375 sq. ft.

Second Floor: 284 sq. ft.

Total: 1,659 sq. ft.

Bedrooms: 3

Bathrooms: 2

Width: 58' - 0"

Depth: 32' - 0"

Foundation: Crawlspace, Unfinished Basement

eplans.com

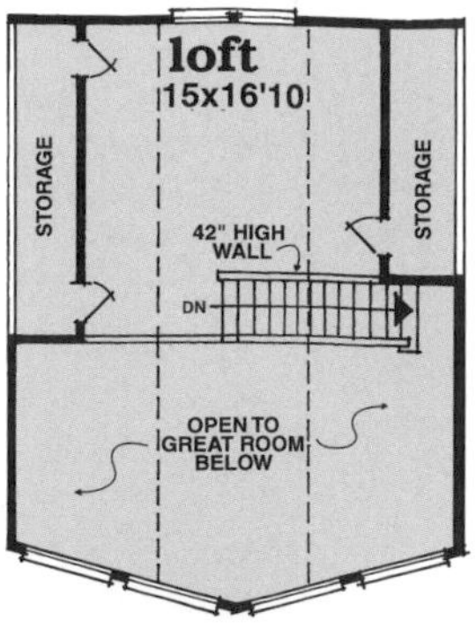

loft 15x16'10
STORAGE
STORAGE
42" HIGH WALL
DN
OPEN TO GREAT ROOM BELOW

SECOND FLOOR

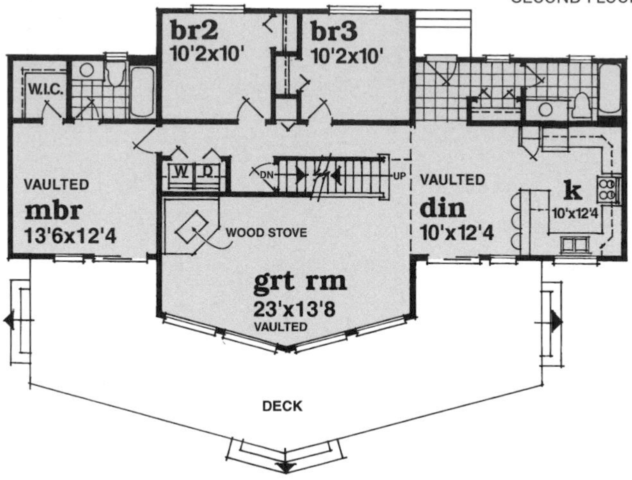

br2 10'2x10'
br3 10'2x10'
W.I.C.
VAULTED mbr 13'6x12'4
W D
DN
UP
WOOD STOVE
VAULTED din 10'x12'4
k 10'x12'4
grt rm 23'x13'8 VAULTED
DECK

FIRST FLOOR

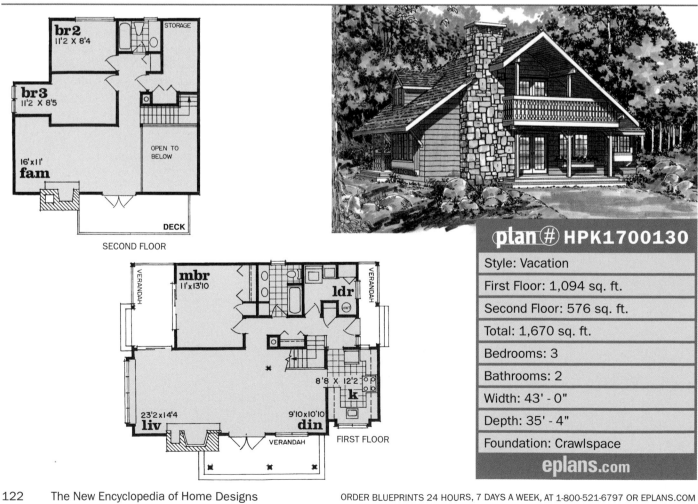

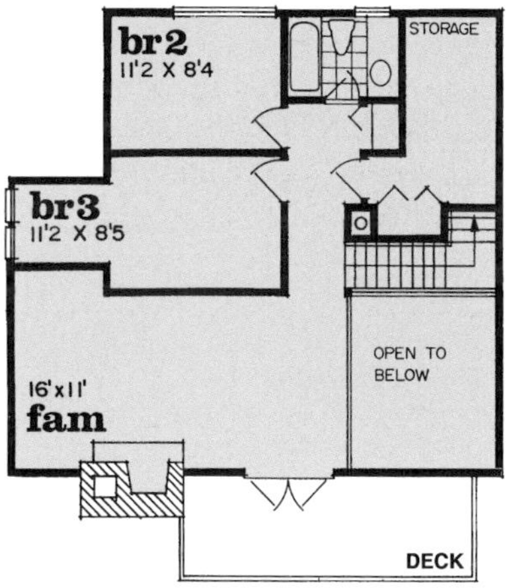

br2 11'2 X 8'4
STORAGE
br3 11'2 X 8'5
OPEN TO BELOW
16'x11' fam
DECK

SECOND FLOOR

mbr 11'x13'10
VERANDAH
VERANDAH
ldr
HWT
8'8 X 12'2 k
23'2x14'4 liv
9'10x10'10 din
VERANDAH

FIRST FLOOR

plan# HPK1700130

Style: Vacation

First Floor: 1,094 sq. ft.

Second Floor: 576 sq. ft.

Total: 1,670 sq. ft.

Bedrooms: 3

Bathrooms: 2

Width: 43' - 0"

Depth: 35' - 4"

Foundation: Crawlspace

eplans.com

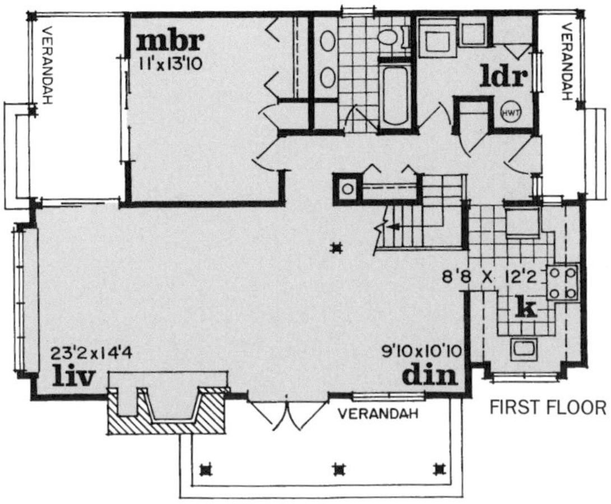

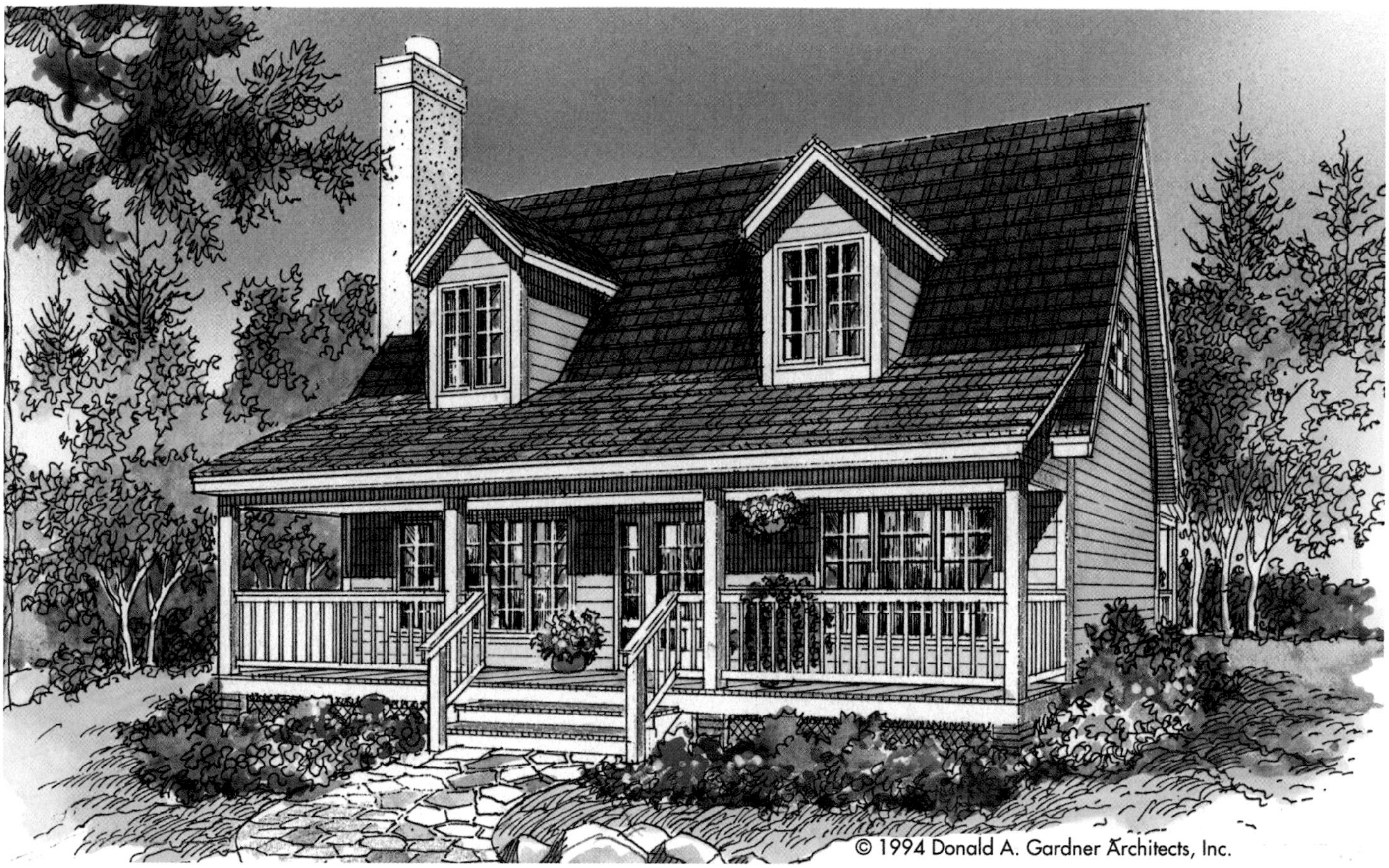

plan# HPK1700131

- Style: Farmhouse
- First Floor: 1,100 sq. ft.
- Second Floor: 584 sq. ft.
- Total: 1,684 sq. ft.
- Bedrooms: 3
- Bathrooms: 2
- Width: 36' - 8"
- Depth: 45' - 0"

eplans.com

A relaxing country image projects from the front and rear covered porches of this rustic three-bedroom home. Open planning extends to the great room, the dining room, and the efficient kitchen. A shared cathedral ceiling creates an impressive space. Completing the first floor are two family bedrooms, a full bath, and a handy utility area. The second floor contains the master suite featuring a spacious walk-in closet and a master bath with a whirlpool tub and a separate corner shower. A generous loft/study overlooks the great room below.

SECOND FLOOR

FIRST FLOOR

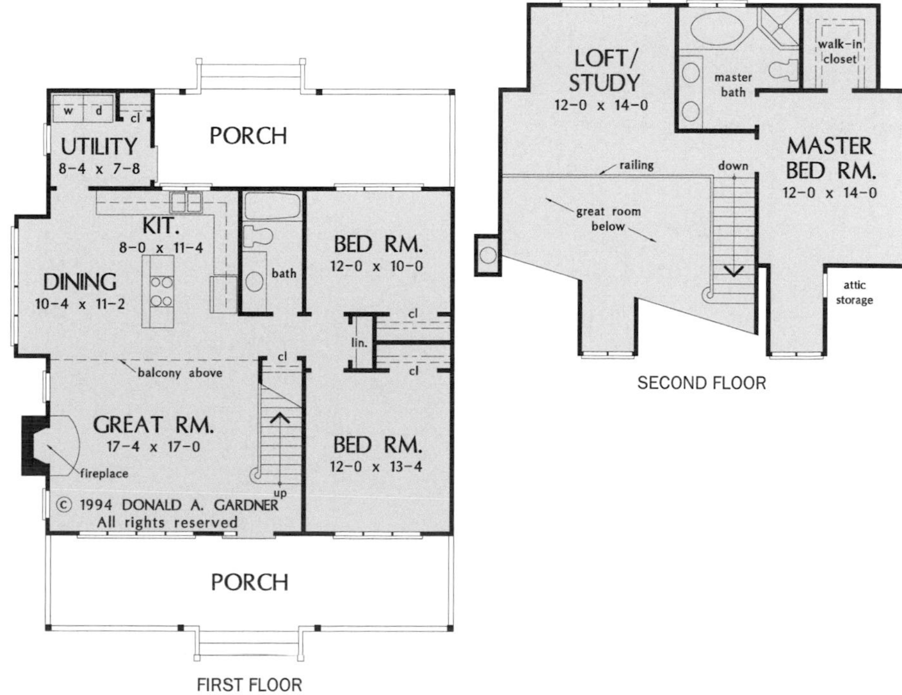

If there's a narrow-lot home that provides a lot of living for its square footage, this is it. While a front-entry garage provides convenience, a spacious patio encourages outdoor relaxation. With a central hall dividing the common rooms from the sleeping quarters, the floor plan marries openness with privacy. Both the foyer and great room have two-story ceilings, which expand visual space; a bay window with a seat extends the breakfast nook. The dining room is topped by a cathedral ceiling. In the master suite, a tray ceiling crowns the bedroom. The master bath includes a double vanity, garden tub, shower with seat, and a compartmented toilet.

plan# HPK1700132

Style: Traditional

First Floor: 1,408 sq. ft.

Second Floor: 476 sq. ft.

Total: 1,884 sq. ft.

Bedrooms: 3

Bathrooms: 2½

Width: 41' - 8"

Depth: 56' - 4"

eplans.com

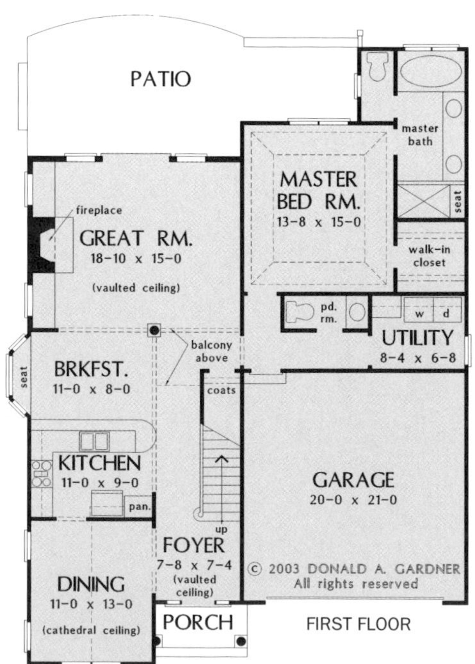

FIRST FLOOR

SECOND FLOOR

plan# HPK1700133

Style: Country
First Floor: 1,437 sq. ft.
Second Floor: 531 sq. ft.
Total: 1,968 sq. ft.
Bedrooms: 3
Bathrooms: 2½
Width: 51' - 4"
Depth: 41' - 6"

eplans.com

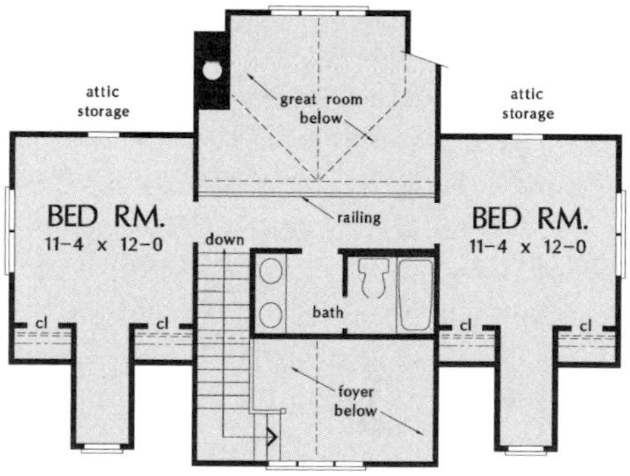

attic storage
great room below
attic storage
BED RM. 11-4 x 12-0
railing
BED RM. 11-4 x 12-0
down
bath
cl
foyer below

SECOND FLOOR

This sophisticated country home is economical and cozy, yet it has all the amenities of a larger plan. From the wraparound porch to the vaulted great room, this floor plan provides space for family togetherness, as well as personal privacy. The secluded master suite contains two spacious walk-in closets, double lavatories, and a garden tub. Another incredible feature is the large master shower. Upstairs, a full bath and impressive balcony view separate the two bedrooms. Bay windows highlight the breakfast nook and dining room; the central dormer floods the foyer with light. Other special features include the kitchen's angled countertop, complementing an open floor plan in the family areas.

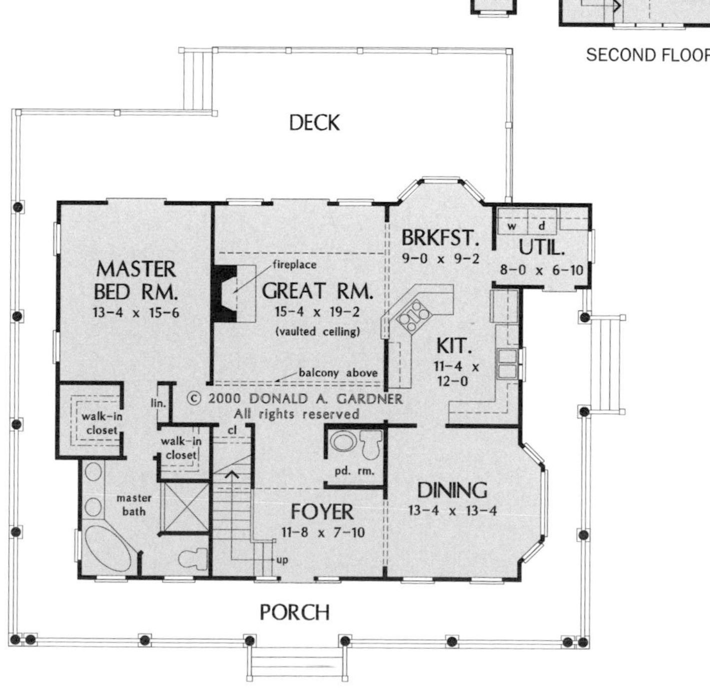

FIRST FLOOR

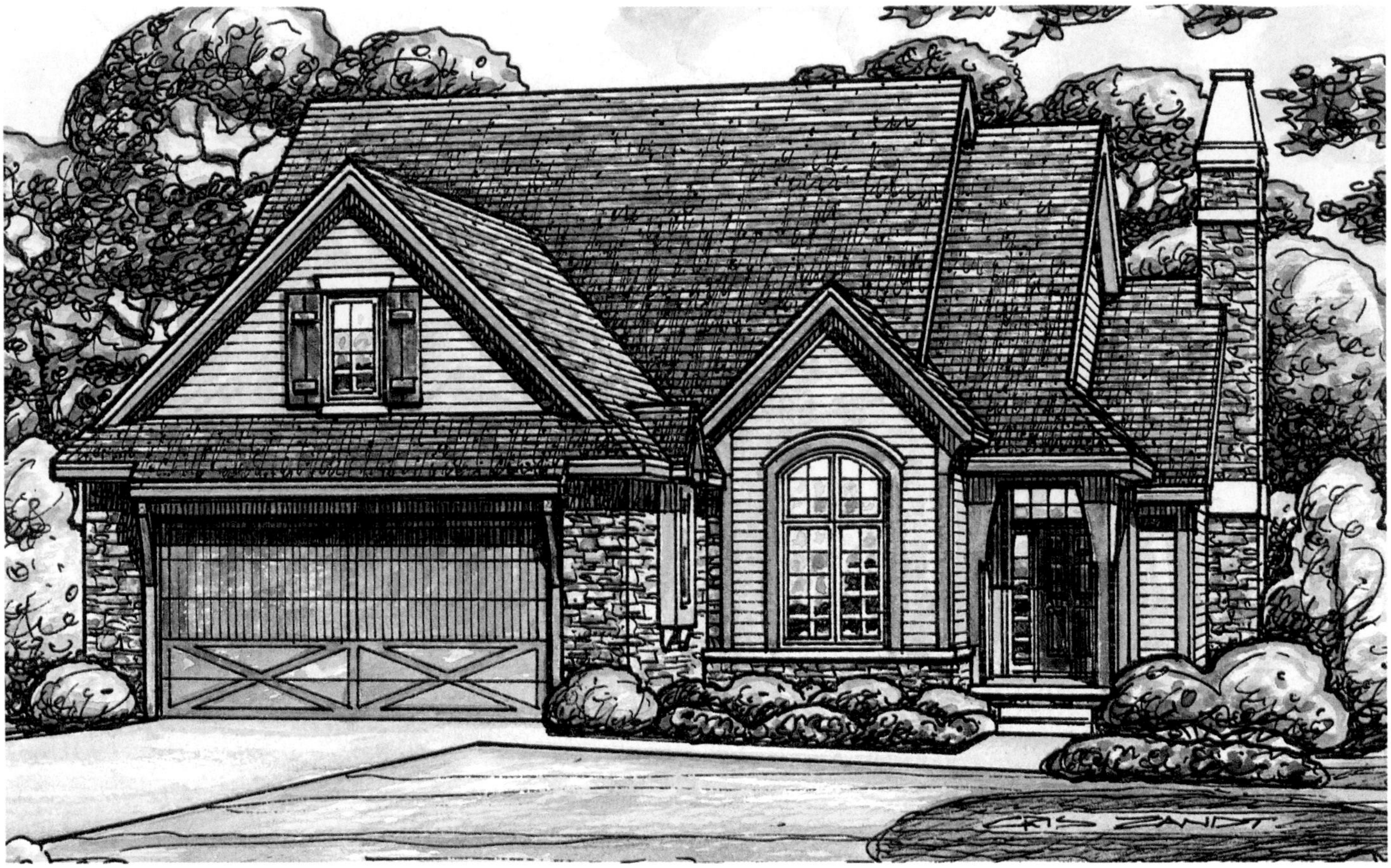

Euro-French, Country traditional sums up this exquisite hideaway. A complex roof line sits astride rustic exteriors and a chimney sure to charm! Cathedral-style ceilings adorn the main level. Enter your home and be greeted by a fireplace in the foyer on your immediate right, and a den on the left. Continue straight ahead to the great room, where you can view your enclosed deck and access your kitchen with accompanying eating area. A master suite with walk-in closet is to the right of the kitchen. A second bathroom and garage are accessed through the kitchen as well. Upstairs you will find plenty to do, including an office with built-in desk, and an extra kitchen!

plan# HPK1700134
Style: Traditional
First Floor: 1,619 sq. ft.
Second Floor: 372 sq. ft.
Total: 1,991 sq. ft.
Bonus Space: 82 sq. ft.
Bedrooms: 3
Bathrooms: 3
Width: 46' - 8"
Depth: 70' - 8"
eplans.com

BASEMENT

FIRST FLOOR

SECOND FLOOR

OPTIONAL LAYOUT

OPTIONAL LAYOUT

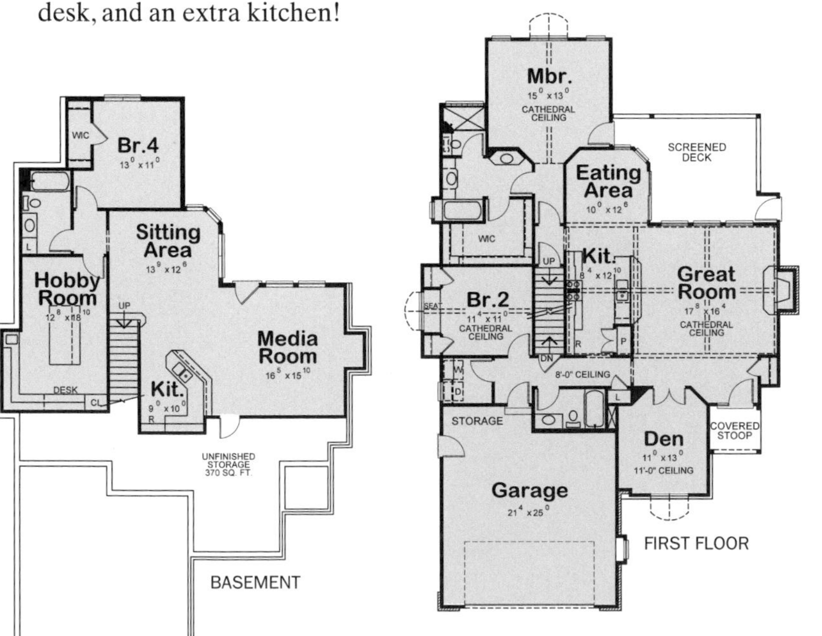

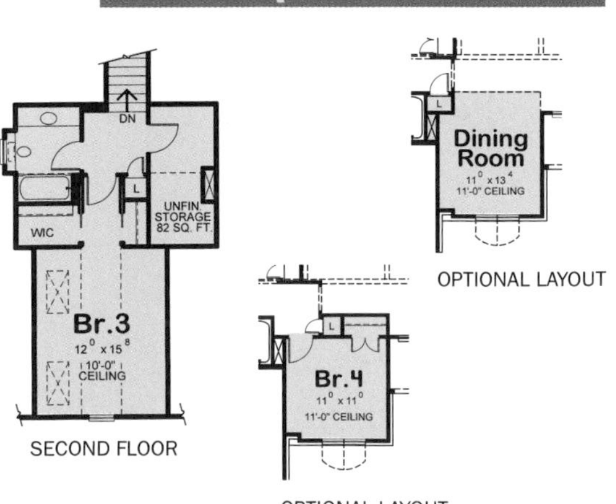

plan# HPK1700135
Style: Traditional
First Floor: 716 sq. ft.
Second Floor: 784 sq. ft.
Total: 1,500 sq. ft.
Bedrooms: 3
Bathrooms: 2½
Width: 36' - 0"
Depth: 44' - 0"
Foundation: Crawlspace
eplans.com

A traditional neighborhood look is accented by stone and decorative arches on this stylish new design. Simplicity is the hallmark of this plan, giving the interior great flow and openness. The foyer, with a coat closet, leads directly into the two-story great room with abundant natural light and a warming fireplace. The island kitchen and dining area are to the left and enjoy rear-porch access. Upstairs, a vaulted master suite with a private bath joins two additional bedrooms to complete the plan.

FIRST FLOOR

SECOND FLOOR

plan# HPK1700136

Style: Traditional

First Floor: 767 sq. ft.

Second Floor: 738 sq. ft.

Total: 1,505 sq. ft.

Bedrooms: 3

Bathrooms: 2½

Width: 47' - 10"

Depth: 36' - 0"

Foundation: Unfinished Walkout Basement, Slab, Crawlspace

eplans.com

A clear focus on family living is the hallmark of this traditional two-story plan. A columned porch leads to an open foyer and family room complete with a fireplace. A dining room with a sliding glass door is thoughtfully placed between the family room and kitchen. A bayed breakfast nook works well with the roomy kitchen. On the second level a large master suite features a tray ceiling, detailed bath, and a space-efficient, walk-in closet. Two family bedrooms, a hall bath, and convenient laundry center round out the plan.

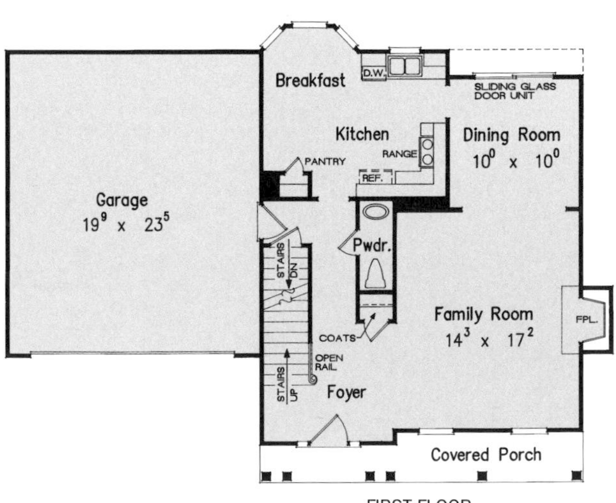

FIRST FLOOR

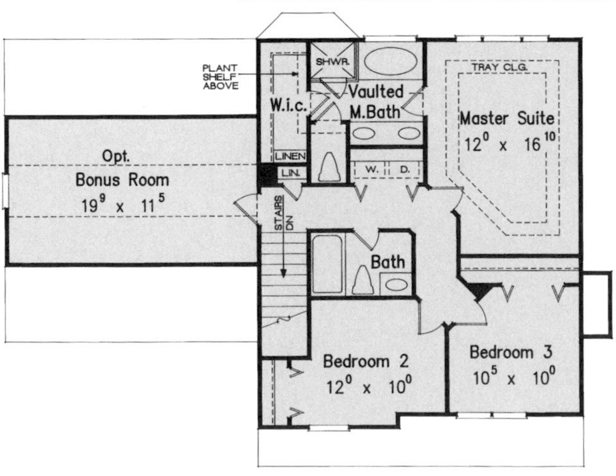

SECOND FLOOR

plan # HPK1700137

Style: Victorian
First Floor: 805 sq. ft.
Second Floor: 779 sq. ft.
Total: 1,584 sq. ft.
Bedrooms: 3
Bathrooms: 1½
Width: 25' - 0"
Depth: 36' - 0"
Foundation: Unfinished Basement

eplans.com

The charming front porch and the two-story turret welcome guests to this lovely home. The turret houses the living room on the first floor and the master suite on the second floor. The dining room is open to the living room and provides a box-bay window. The L-shaped kitchen features a breakfast room accessible to the backyard. A curved staircase next to the powder room leads upstairs to three bedrooms and a bath. Each family bedroom contains a walk-in closet.

FIRST FLOOR

SECOND FLOOR

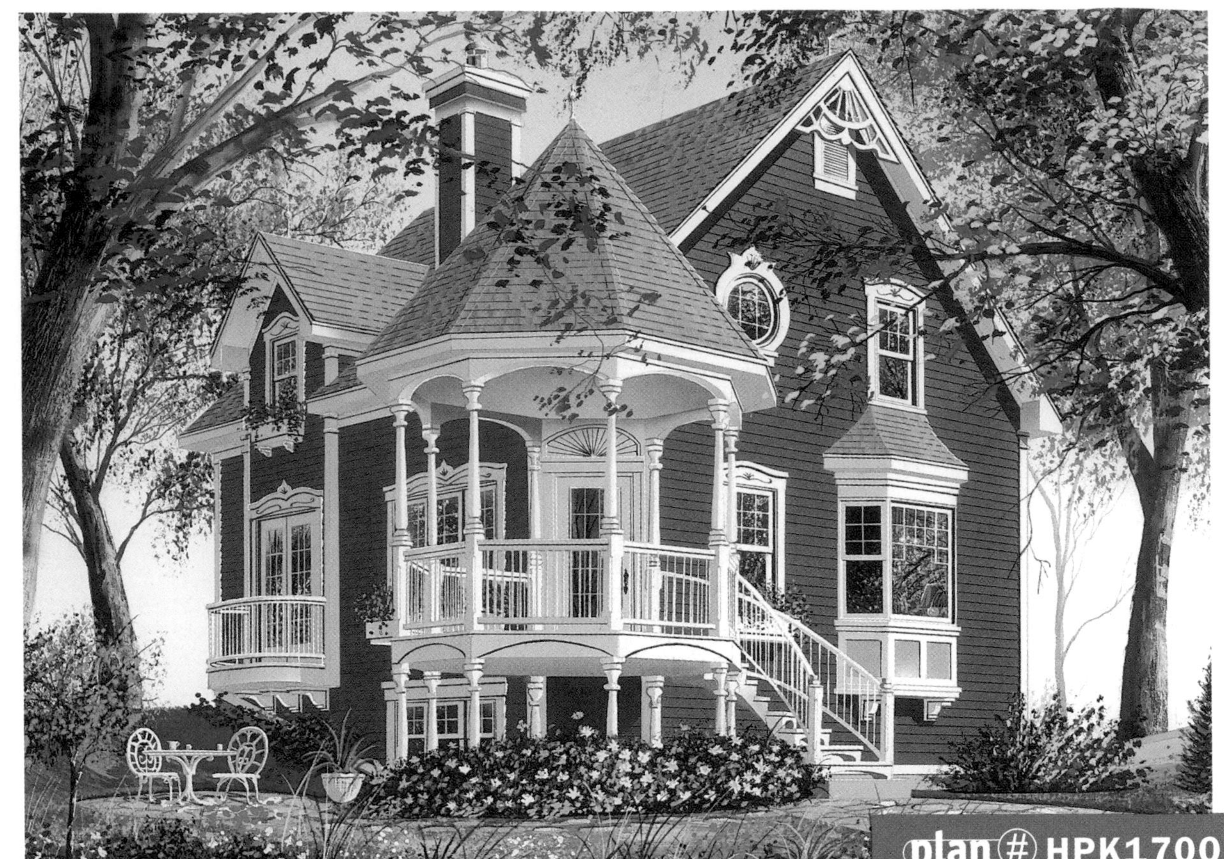

plan# HPK1700138

Style: Victorian
First Floor: 840 sq. ft.
Second Floor: 757 sq. ft.
Total: 1,597 sq. ft.
Bedrooms: 3
Bathrooms: 3
Width: 26' - 0"
Depth: 32' - 0"
Foundation: Unfinished Basement

eplans.com

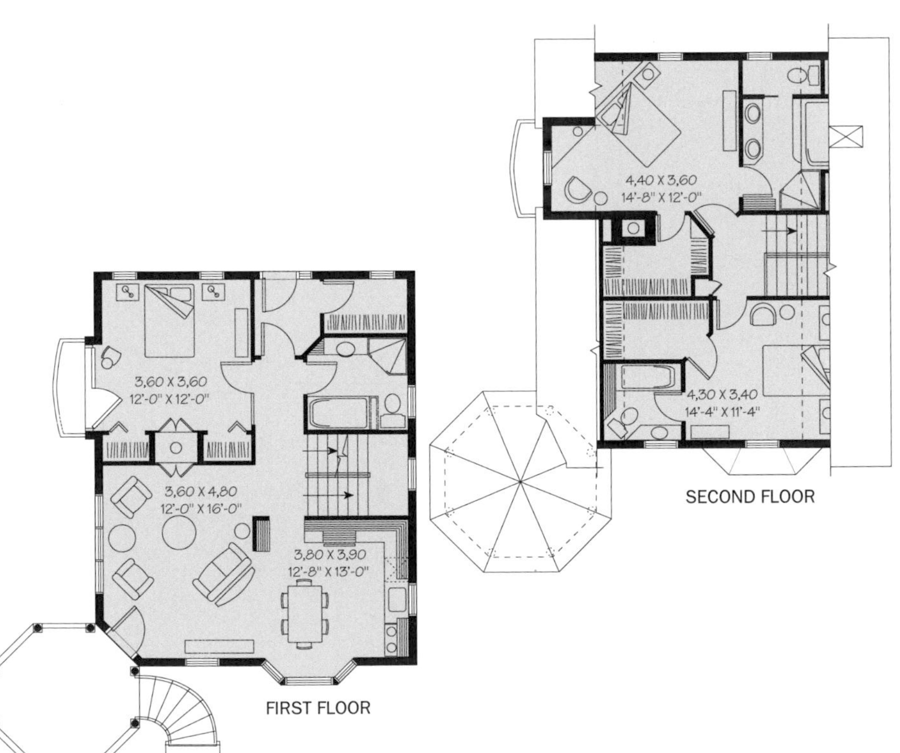

The amazing turret/gazebo porch on this classy home has an authentic Victorian flavor. Exceptional details accent this classic view. The bedroom on the first level offers a protruding balcony, which adds appeal both inside and outside. The entrance leads to the living room, located just left of the dining area and L-shaped kitchen. The master suite features a walk-in closet and a private bath with dual sinks. Two more family bedrooms are located on the second level.

plan# HPK1700139
Style: Country Cottage
First Floor: 872 sq. ft.
Second Floor: 734 sq. ft.
Total: 1,606 sq. ft.
Bedrooms: 3
Bathrooms: 3
Width: 40' - 0"
Depth: 29' - 6"
Foundation: Crawlspace
eplans.com

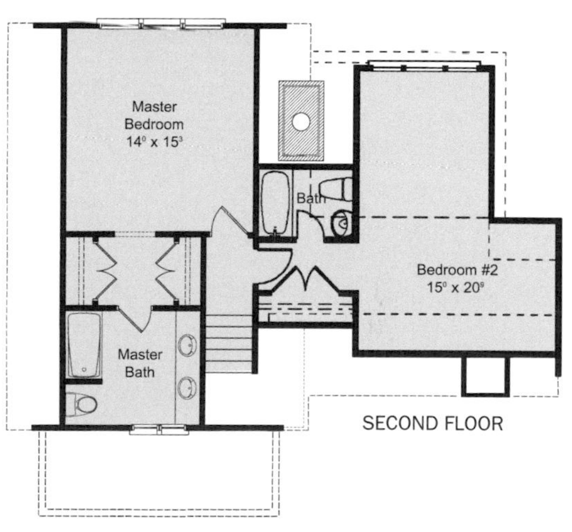

SECOND FLOOR

DESIGN NOTE

Decorative trusses, steeply pitched gables, and a cross-gable roof all point to this home's Victorian influence. Siding that recreates wooden shingles or boards reference the style's history. But the interior is decidedly modern. There is no formal dining room or parlor, and the kitchen encourages a casual relationship with the living room. The upstairs master suite makes significant allowances for contemporary amenities.

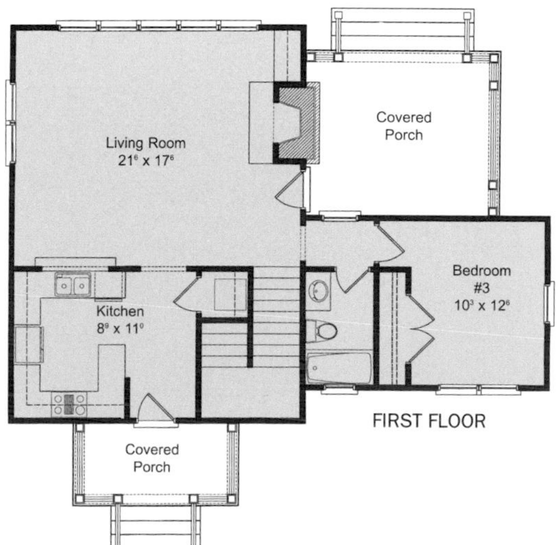

FIRST FLOOR

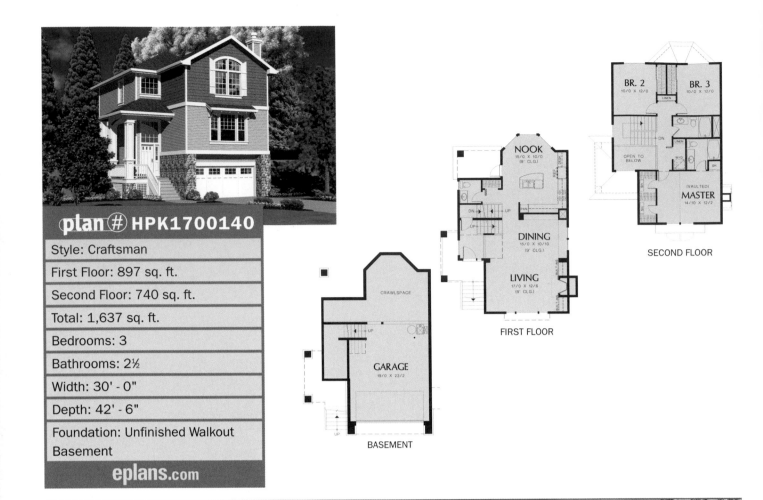

plan# HPK1700140

Style: Craftsman
First Floor: 897 sq. ft.
Second Floor: 740 sq. ft.
Total: 1,637 sq. ft.
Bedrooms: 3
Bathrooms: 2½
Width: 30' - 0"
Depth: 42' - 6"
Foundation: Unfinished Walkout Basement

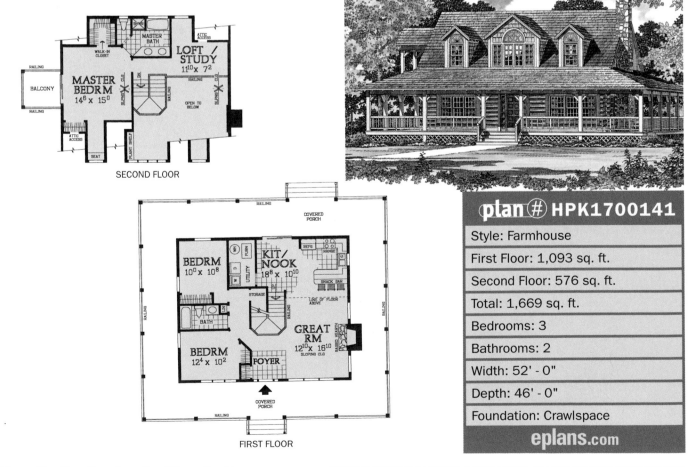

eplans.com

SECOND FLOOR

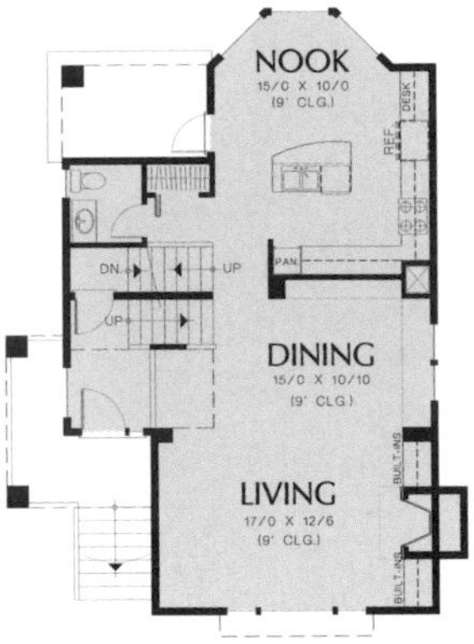

FIRST FLOOR

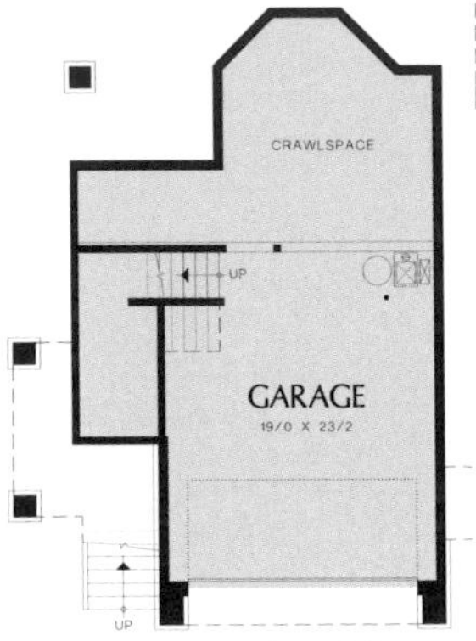

BASEMENT

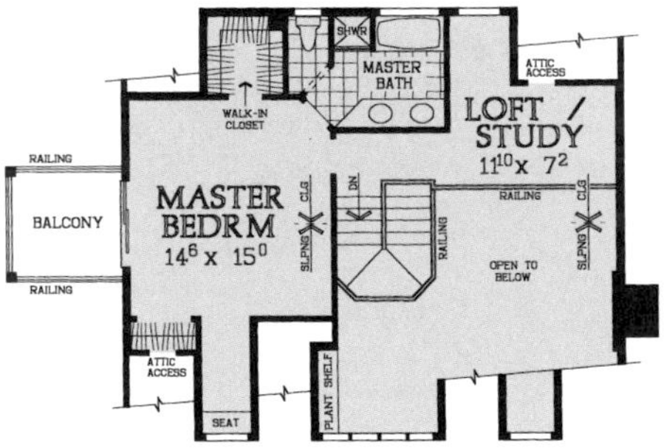

SECOND FLOOR

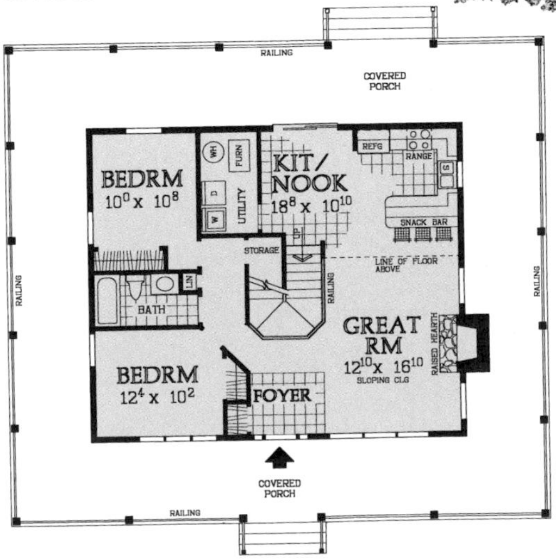

FIRST FLOOR

plan# HPK1700141

Style: Farmhouse
First Floor: 1,093 sq. ft.
Second Floor: 576 sq. ft.
Total: 1,669 sq. ft.
Bedrooms: 3
Bathrooms: 2
Width: 52' - 0"
Depth: 46' - 0"
Foundation: Crawlspace

eplans.com

plan# HPK1700142

Style: Traditional
First Floor: 906 sq. ft.
Second Floor: 798 sq. ft.
Total: 1,704 sq. ft.
Bedrooms: 3
Bathrooms: 2½
Width: 29' - 8"
Depth: 33' - 10"
Foundation: Unfinished Basement

eplans.com

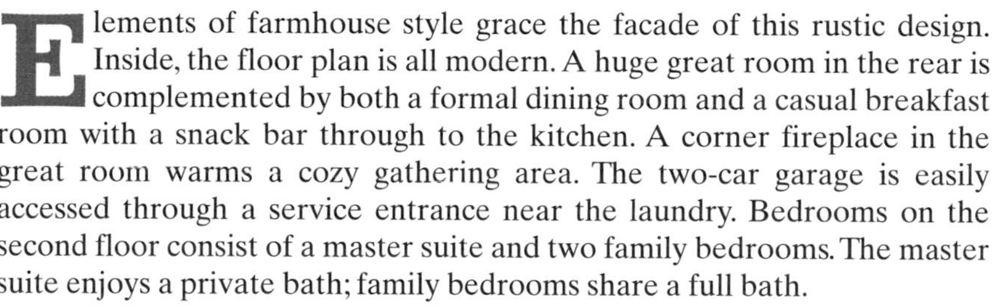

Elements of farmhouse style grace the facade of this rustic design. Inside, the floor plan is all modern. A huge great room in the rear is complemented by both a formal dining room and a casual breakfast room with a snack bar through to the kitchen. A corner fireplace in the great room warms a cozy gathering area. The two-car garage is easily accessed through a service entrance near the laundry. Bedrooms on the second floor consist of a master suite and two family bedrooms. The master suite enjoys a private bath; family bedrooms share a full bath.

SECOND FLOOR

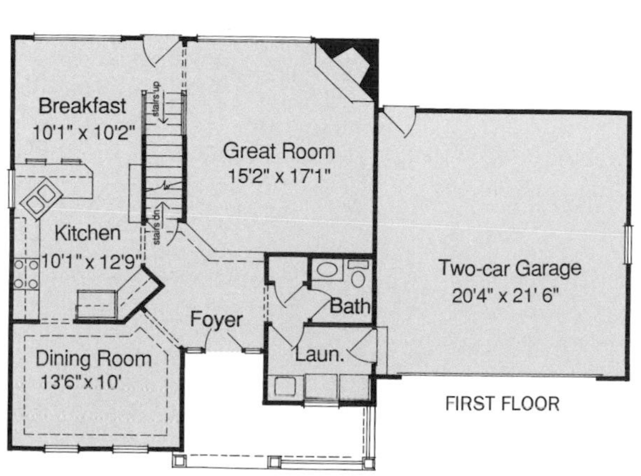

FIRST FLOOR

plan# HPK1700143

Style: European Cottage

First Floor: 939 sq. ft.

Second Floor: 788 sq. ft.

Total: 1,727 sq. ft.

Bonus Space: 210 sq. ft.

Bedrooms: 3

Bathrooms: 2½

Width: 34' - 0"

Depth: 52' - 0"

Foundation: Unfinished Walkout Basement

eplans.com

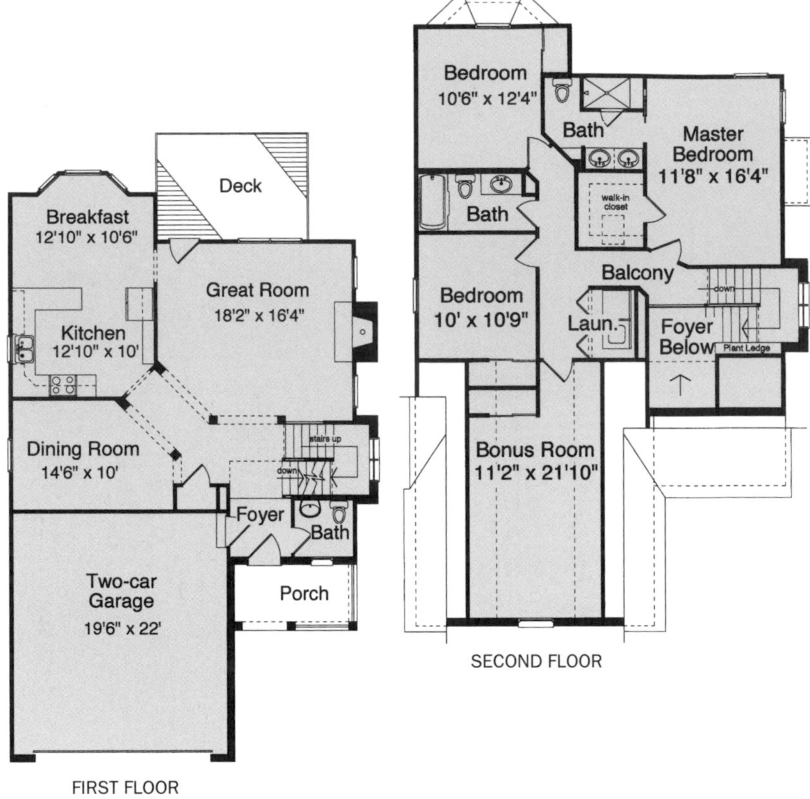

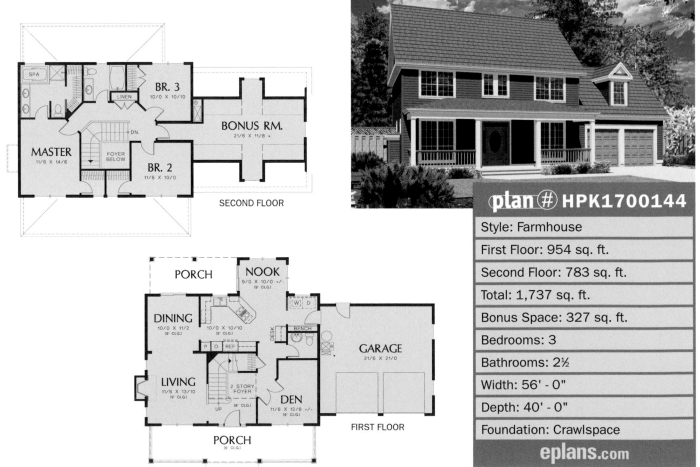

SPA
BR. 3
10/0 X 10/10
LINEN
BONUS RM.
21/6 X 11/8 +
DN.
MASTER
11/6 X 14/6
FOYER
BELOW
BR. 2
11/6 X 10/0
SECOND FLOOR

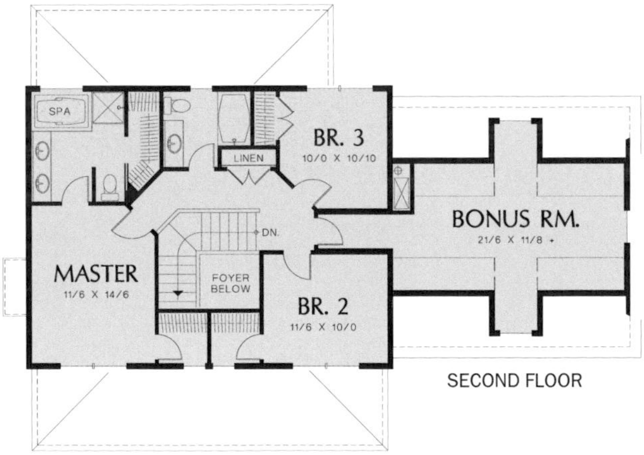

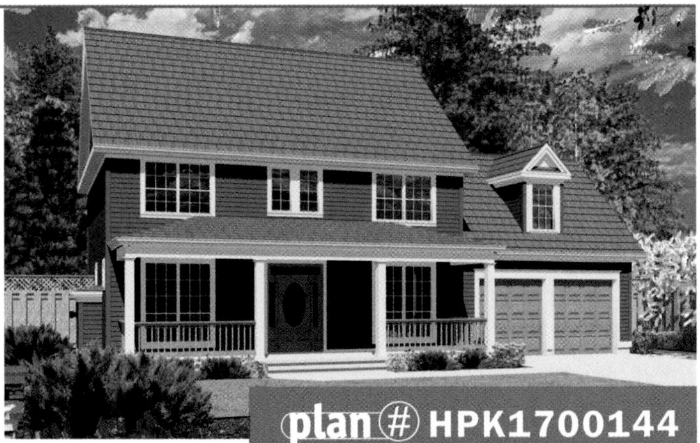

PORCH
NOOK
9/0 X 10/0 +/-
[9' CLG.]
W D
DINING
10/0 X 11/2
[9' CLG.]
10/0 X 10/10
[9' CLG.]
DESK
BENCH
P O REF
GARAGE
21/6 X 21/0
LIVING
11/6 X 13/10
[9' CLG.]
2 STORY
FOYER
UP
[9' CLG.]
DEN
11/6 X 12/6 +/-
[9' CLG.]
PORCH
[9' CLG.]
FIRST FLOOR

plan# HPK1700144

Style: Farmhouse

First Floor: 954 sq. ft.

Second Floor: 783 sq. ft.

Total: 1,737 sq. ft.

Bonus Space: 327 sq. ft.

Bedrooms: 3

Bathrooms: 2½

Width: 56' - 0"

Depth: 40' - 0"

Foundation: Crawlspace

eplans.com

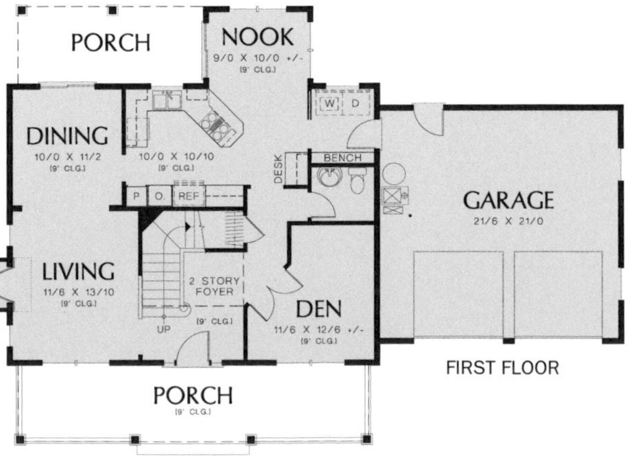

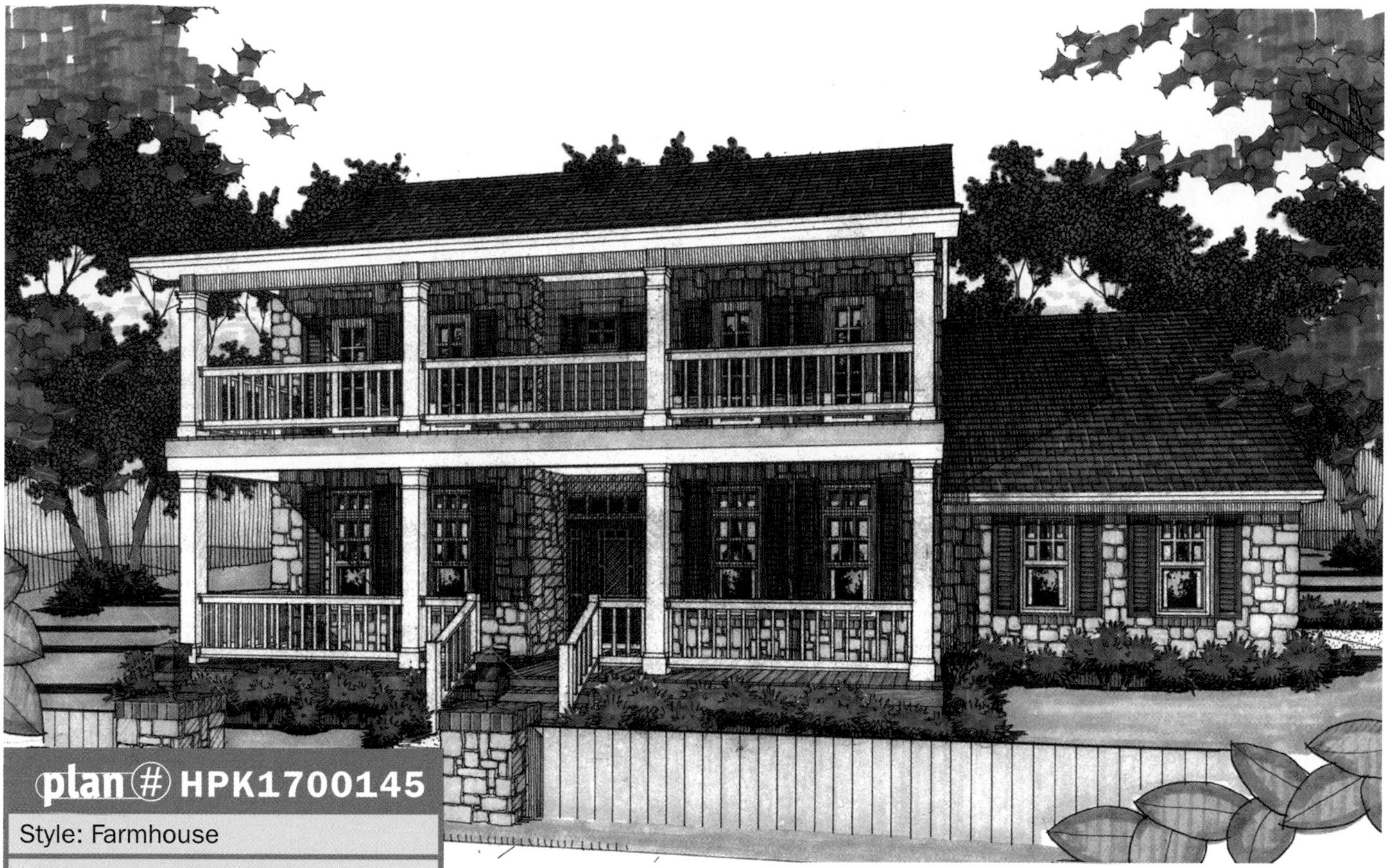

plan# HPK1700145

Style: Farmhouse	
First Floor: 1,320 sq. ft.	
Second Floor: 433 sq. ft.	
Total: 1,753 sq. ft.	
Bonus Space: 209 sq. ft.	
Bedrooms: 3	
Bathrooms: 2½	
Width: 51' - 11"	
Depth: 50' - 0"	
Foundation: Crawlspace, Slab, Unfinished Basement	

eplans.com

Truly a sight to behold, this home borrows elements from the Colonial styling of the South. Flagstone enhances the facade, while a two-story porch brings out the uniqueness of the design. Enter through the foyer to find a dining room, hearth-warmed great room, and kitchen/nook area; the nook opens to a rear porch. The right side of the plan is home to the master suite with a full bath. Upstairs, two additional bedrooms, a full bath, a covered porch, and a balcony open to the great room below can be found.

SECOND FLOOR

FIRST FLOOR

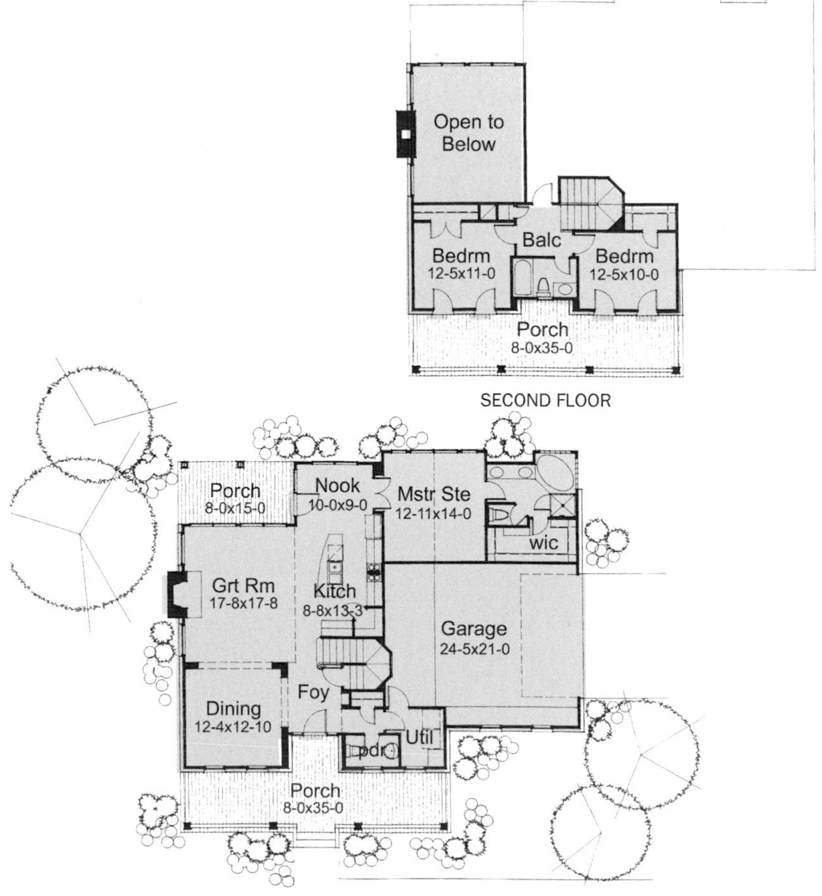

Incorporating Old World style and elements, this house combines stone and stucco with gable peaks and arched windows for a stunning European facade. The grand portico leads to an open floor plan, which is equally impressive. Built-in cabinetry, French doors, and a fireplace enhance the great room; an angled counter separates the kitchen from the breakfast nook. The first-floor master suite is located in the quiet zone with no rooms above it. Upstairs, a balcony overlooks the great room. The bonus room features convenient second-floor access and shares a full bath with two upstairs bathrooms.

plan# HPK1700146

- Style: Traditional
- First Floor: 1,345 sq. ft.
- Second Floor: 452 sq. ft.
- Total: 1,797 sq. ft.
- Bonus Space: 349 sq. ft.
- Bedrooms: 3
- Bathrooms: 2½
- Width: 63' - 0"
- Depth: 40' - 0"

eplans.com

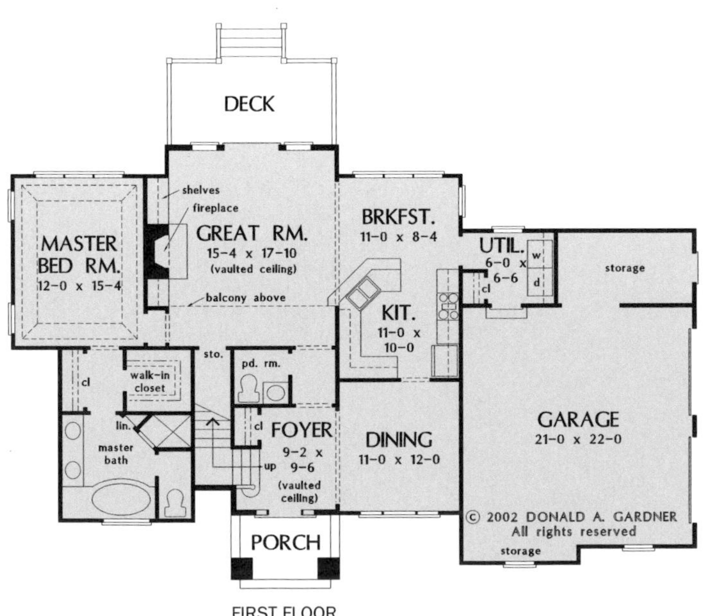

FIRST FLOOR

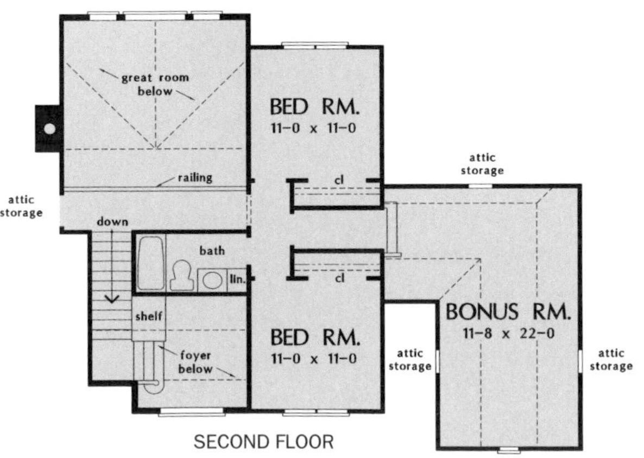

SECOND FLOOR

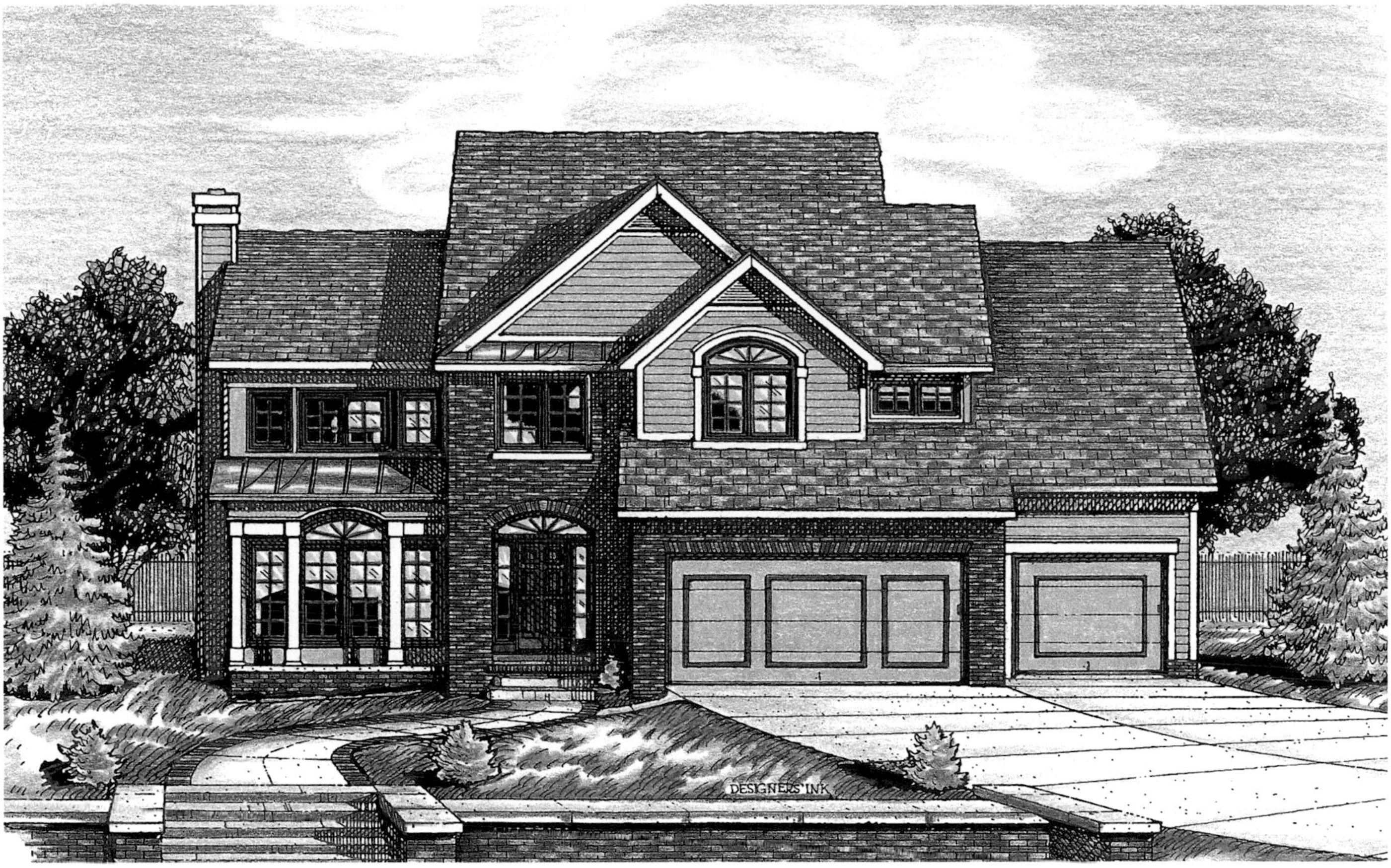

plan# HPK1700147
Style: Traditional
First Floor: 837 sq. ft.
Second Floor: 977 sq. ft.
Total: 1,814 sq. ft.
Bedrooms: 4
Bathrooms: 2½
Width: 58' - 4"
Depth: 41' - 4"
eplans.com

This traditional design features a garden room with twin skylights, a sloped ceiling, and two walls of windows. The kitchen provides plenty of counter space and easily serves the formal dining room, which opens through double doors to the garden room. A balcony overlooks the great room, which is warmed by a fireplace. All four bedrooms including the master suite with its full bath and plentiful storage space, are on the upper level.

SECOND FLOOR

FIRST FLOOR

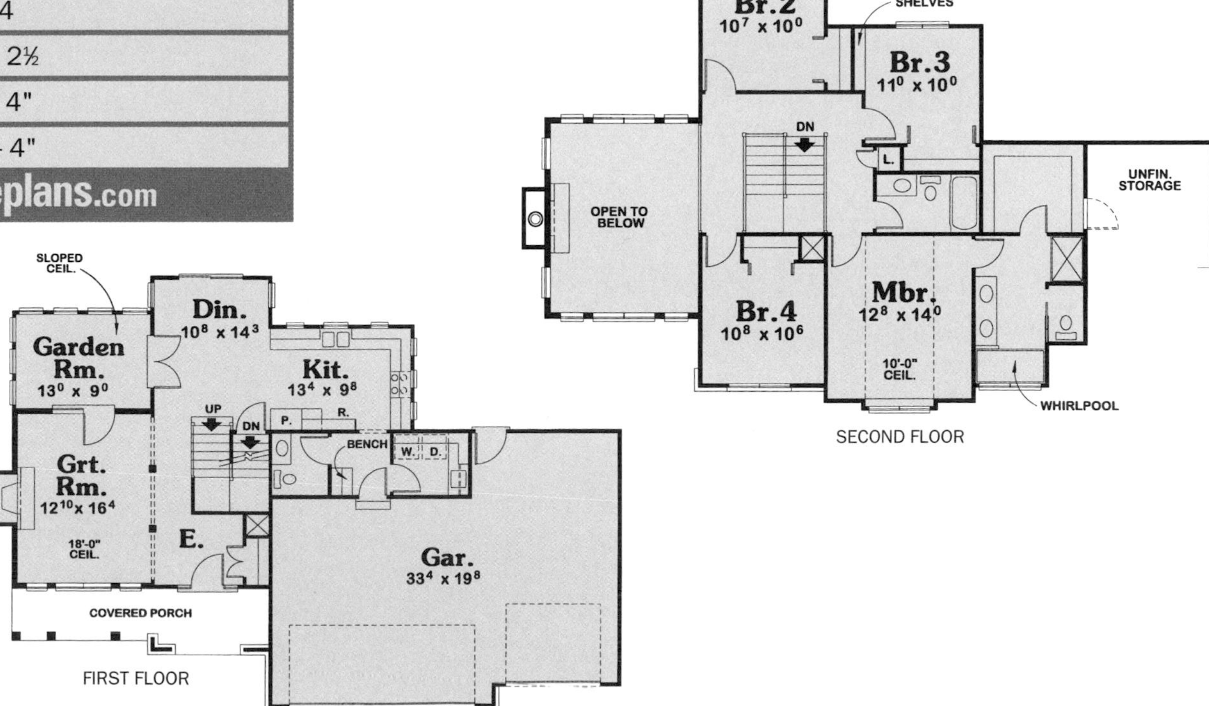

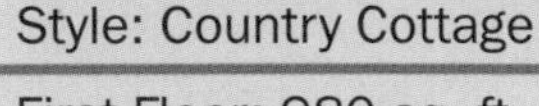

HPK1700148

Style: Country Cottage
First Floor: 980 sq. ft.
Second Floor: 858 sq. ft.
Total: 1,838 sq. ft.
Bedrooms: 3
Bathrooms: 2½
Width: 49' - 8"
Depth: 32' - 0"
Foundation: Unfinished Basement

eplans.com

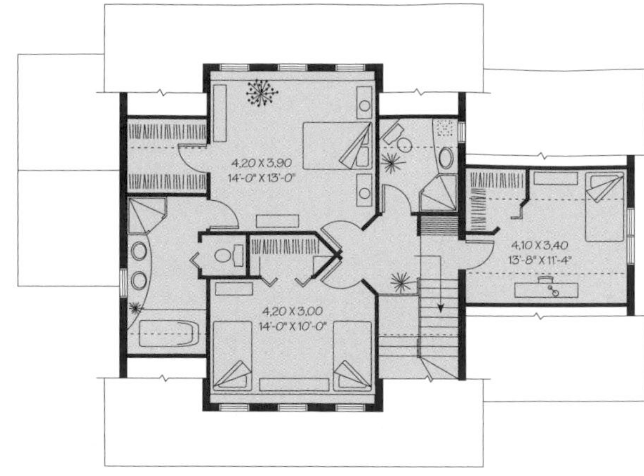

SECOND FLOOR

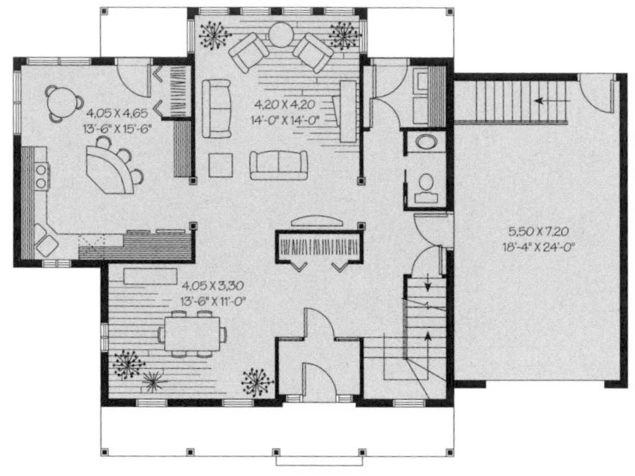

FIRST FLOOR

SECOND FLOOR

plan# HPK1700149

Style: Country Cottage
First Floor: 846 sq. ft.
Second Floor: 998 sq. ft.
Total: 1,844 sq. ft.
Bedrooms: 3
Bathrooms: 2½
Width: 49' - 4"
Depth: 38' - 0"
Foundation: Crawlspace, Unfinished Walkout Basement

eplans.com

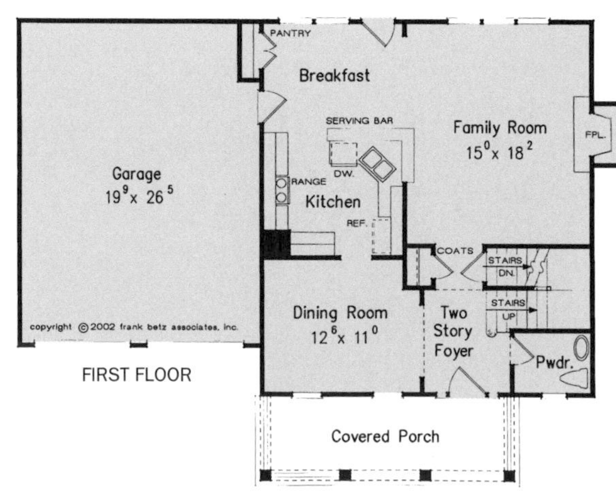

FIRST FLOOR

plan# HPK1700150
Style: Tidewater
First Floor: 1,342 sq. ft.
Second Floor: 511 sq. ft.
Total: 1,853 sq. ft.
Bedrooms: 3
Bathrooms: 2½
Width: 44' - 0"
Depth: 40' - 0"
Foundation: Island Basement
eplans.com

Detailed fretwork complements a standing-seam roof on this tropical cottage. An arch-top transom provides an absolutely perfect highlight to the classic clapboard facade. An unrestrained floor plan offers cool digs for kicking back and a sensational retreat for guests—whether the occasion is formal or casual. French doors open to a rear porch from the great room letting in fresh air and the sights and sounds of the great outdoors. Inside, the master bedroom leads to a dressing space with linen storage and a walk-in closet. The lavish bath includes a garden tub, oversized shower, and a wraparound vanity with two sinks. Two secondary bedrooms on the upper level share a spacious loft that overlooks the great room. One of the bedrooms opens to a private deck.

SECOND FLOOR

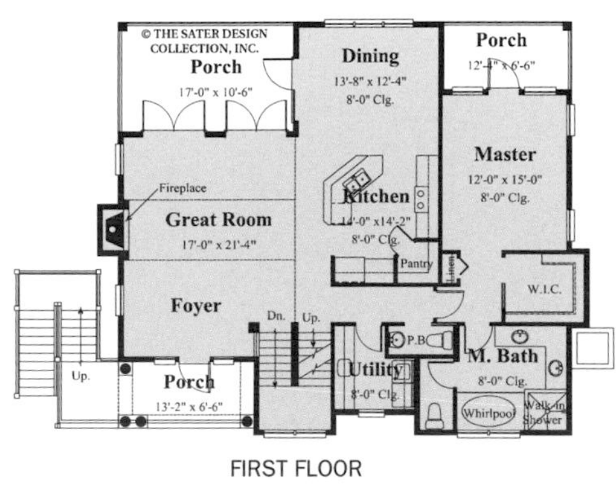

FIRST FLOOR

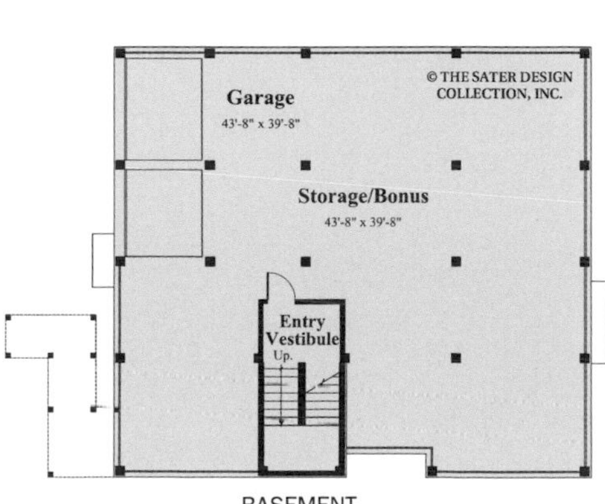

BASEMENT

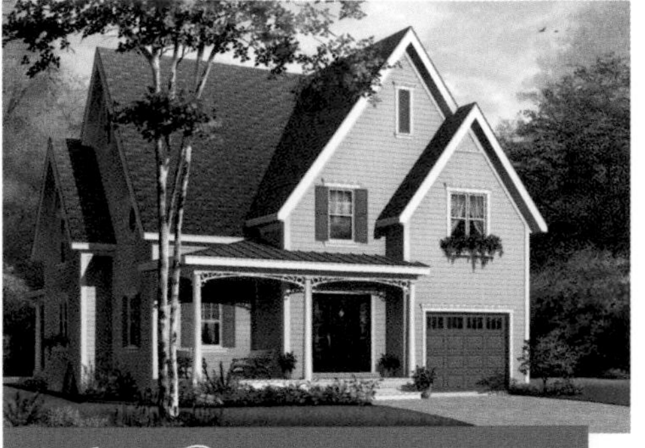

plan# HPK1700151

Style: Farmhouse	
First Floor: 908 sq. ft.	
Second Floor: 967 sq. ft.	
Total: 1,875 sq. ft.	
Bonus Space: 213 sq. ft.	
Bedrooms: 3	
Bathrooms: 2	
Width: 36' - 0"	
Depth: 40' - 0"	
Foundation: Unfinished Basement	

eplans.com

12'-8" X 12'-8"
3,80 X 3,80
22'-0" X 16'-0"
6,60 X 4,80
12'-0" X 22'-0"
3,60 X 6,60

FIRST FLOOR

15'-0" X 12'-8"
4,50 X 3,80
14'-0" X 10'-0"
4,20 X 3,00
11'-0" X 11'-4"
3,30 X 3,40
9'-4" X 8'-0"
2,80 X 2,40
12'-4" X 15'-8"
3,70 X 4,70

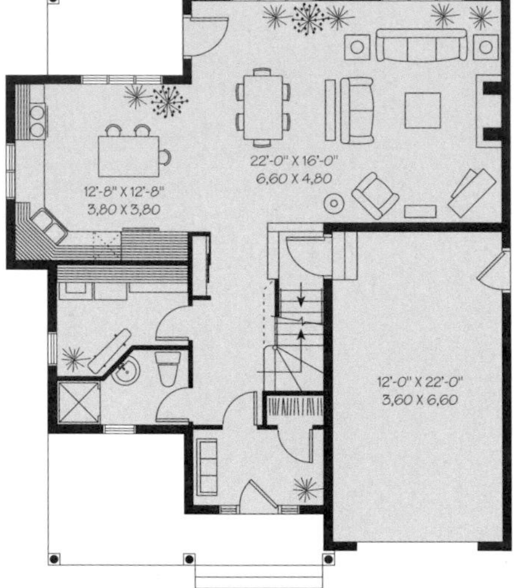

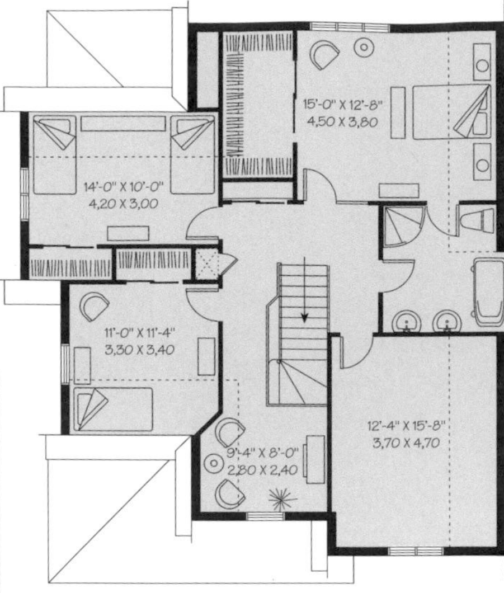

SECOND FLOOR

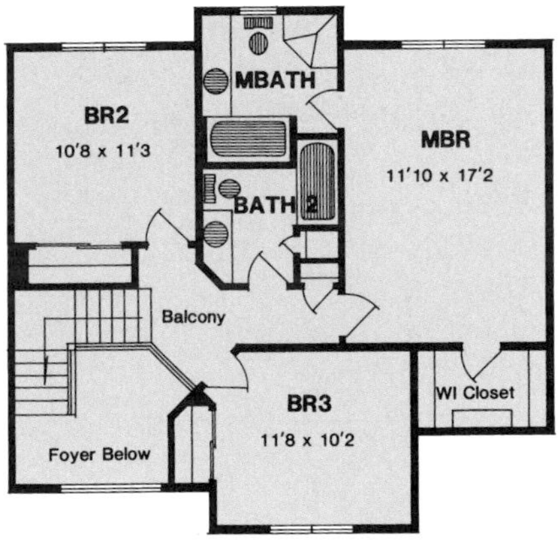

BR2
10'8 x 11'3
MBATH
MBR
11'10 x 17'2
BATH 2
Balcony
BR3
11'8 x 10'2
WI Closet
Foyer Below

SECOND FLOOR

JOHN GIERSCH, PHOTOGRAPHER

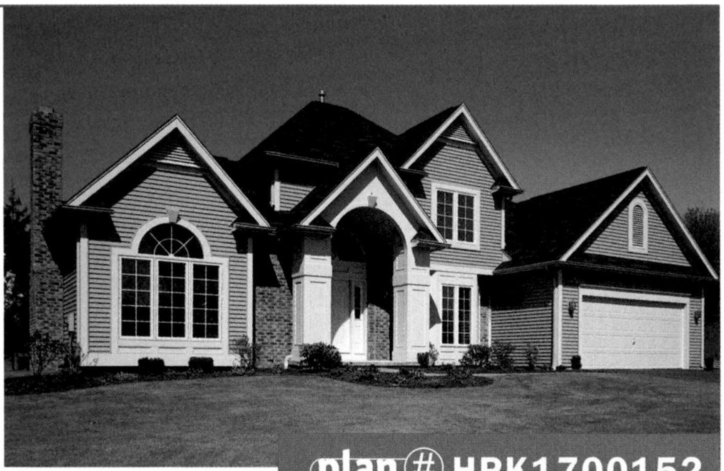

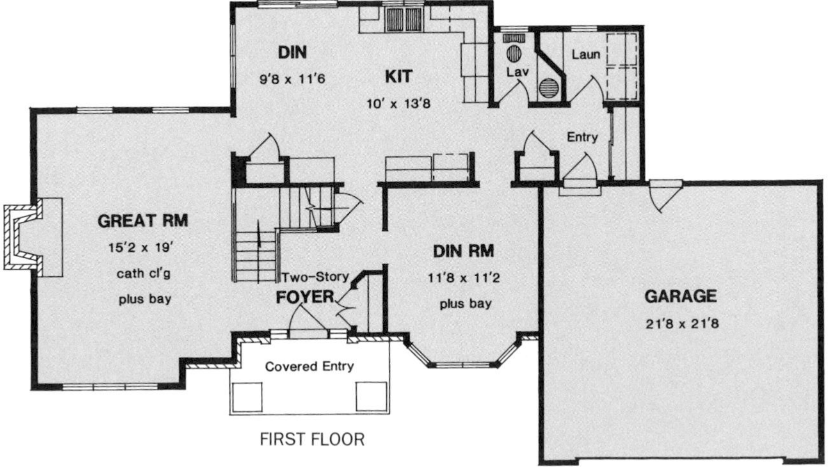

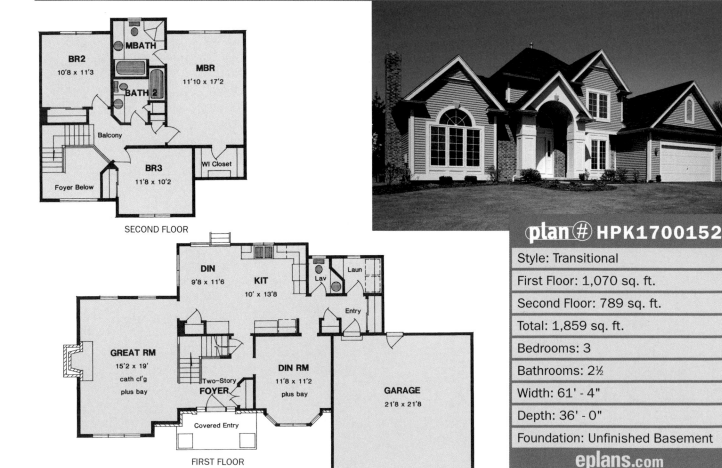

plan# HPK1700152

Style: Transitional	
First Floor: 1,070 sq. ft.	
Second Floor: 789 sq. ft.	
Total: 1,859 sq. ft.	
Bedrooms: 3	
Bathrooms: 2½	
Width: 61' - 4"	
Depth: 36' - 0"	
Foundation: Unfinished Basement	

eplans.com

DIN
9'8 x 11'6
KIT
10' x 13'8
Lav
Laun
Entry
GREAT RM
15'2 x 19'
cath cl'g
plus bay
Two-Story
FOYER
DIN RM
11'8 x 11'2
plus bay
GARAGE
21'8 x 21'8
Covered Entry

FIRST FLOOR

plan# HPK1700153

Style: Southern Colonial
First Floor: 1,103 sq. ft.
Second Floor: 759 sq. ft.
Total: 1,862 sq. ft.
Bonus Space: 342 sq. ft.
Bedrooms: 4
Bathrooms: 3
Width: 50' - 4"
Depth: 35' - 0"
Foundation: Crawlspace, Unfinished Walkout Basement, Slab

eplans.com

This charming country home speaks well of an American vernacular style, with classic clapboard siding, shutters, and sash windows—all dressed up for 21st-Century living. A flex room on the first floor can be a study, playroom, or fourth bedroom. The casual living space enjoys a fireplace, wide views of the rear property, and a French door to the outside. Upstairs, the master suite features a vaulted bath with separate shower, dual vanity, and walk-in closet with linen storage.

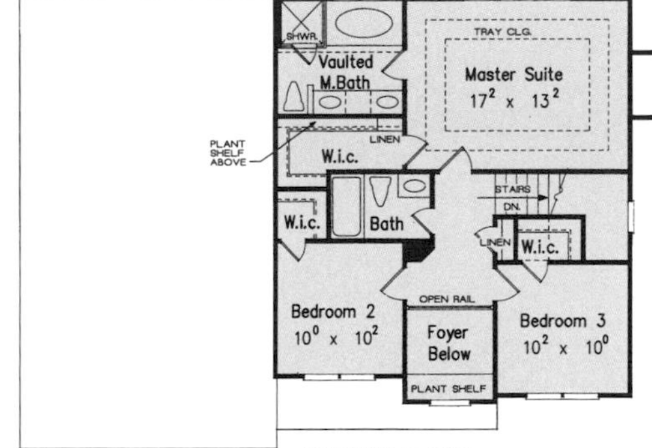

SECOND FLOOR

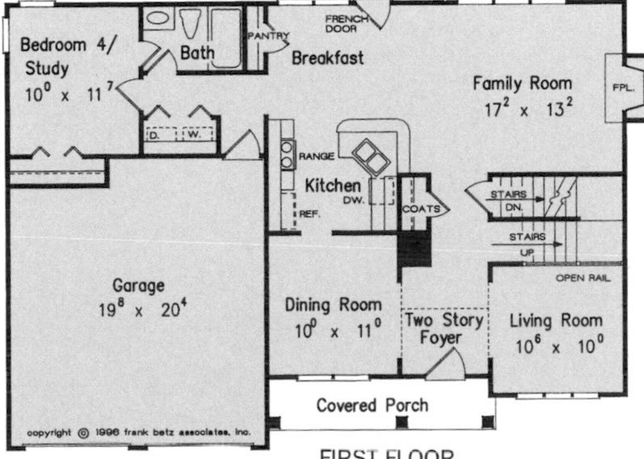

FIRST FLOOR

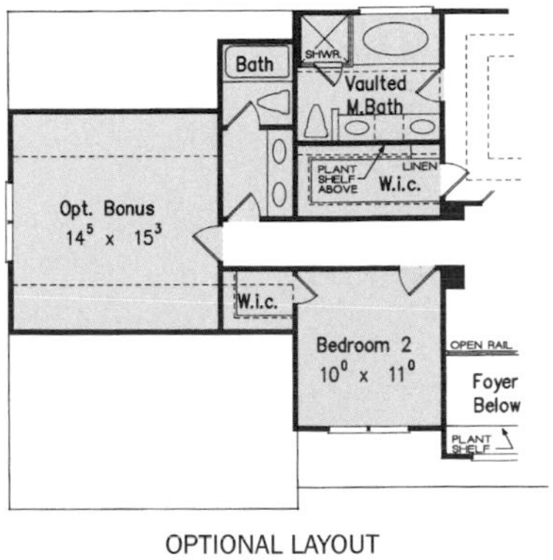

OPTIONAL LAYOUT

plan# HPK1700154

Style: Tidewater
First Floor: 1,314 sq. ft.
Second Floor: 552 sq. ft.
Total: 1,866 sq. ft.
Bonus Space: 398 sq. ft.
Bedrooms: 3
Bathrooms: 2½
Width: 44' - 2"
Depth: 62' - 0"
Foundation: Crawlspace

eplans.com

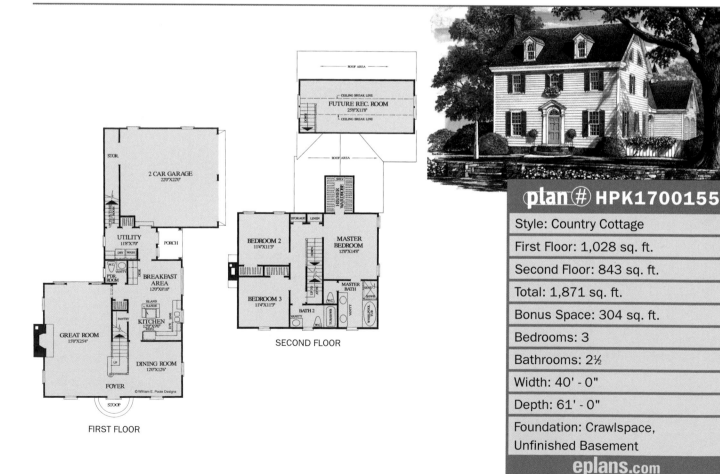

FIRST FLOOR

SECOND FLOOR

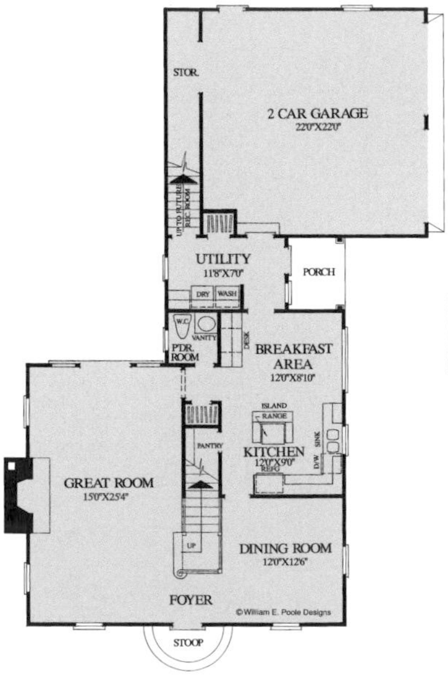

FIRST FLOOR

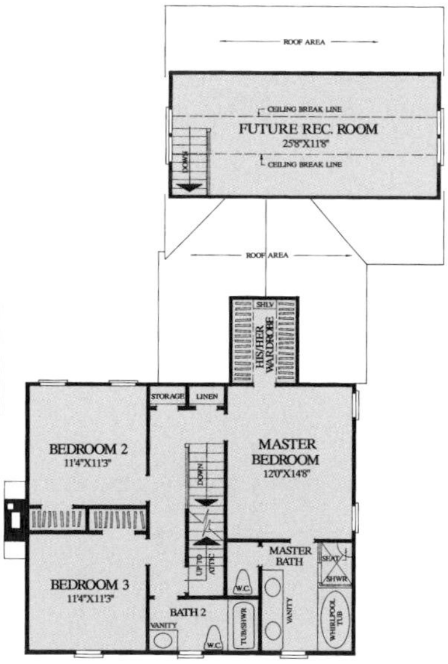

SECOND FLOOR

plan# HPK1700155

Style: Country Cottage
First Floor: 1,028 sq. ft.
Second Floor: 843 sq. ft.
Total: 1,871 sq. ft.
Bonus Space: 304 sq. ft.
Bedrooms: 3
Bathrooms: 2½
Width: 40' - 0"
Depth: 61' - 0"
Foundation: Crawlspace, Unfinished Basement

eplans.com

plan# HPK1700156

Style: Country Cottage
First Floor: 1,407 sq. ft.
Second Floor: 472 sq. ft.
Total: 1,879 sq. ft.
Bonus Space: 321 sq. ft.
Bedrooms: 3
Bathrooms: 2½
Width: 48' - 0"
Depth: 53' - 10"
Foundation: Crawlspace, Unfinished Walkout Basement

eplans.com

SMART TIP

What is bonus space? First of all, it's square footage that's not calculated in the price of the blueprints. More importantly, it's an opportunity to fine-tune your home to suit your family's needs. Larger families may want to turn the space into another bedroom or a second suite. Other options include a recreation room, library, art studio, exercise room, media room, or one heck of a storage closet.

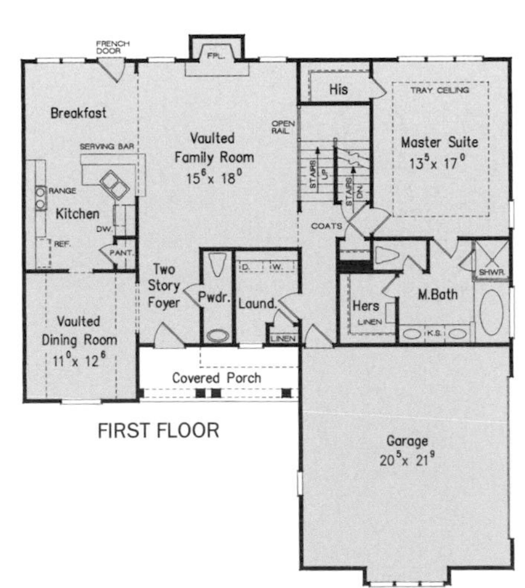

FIRST FLOOR

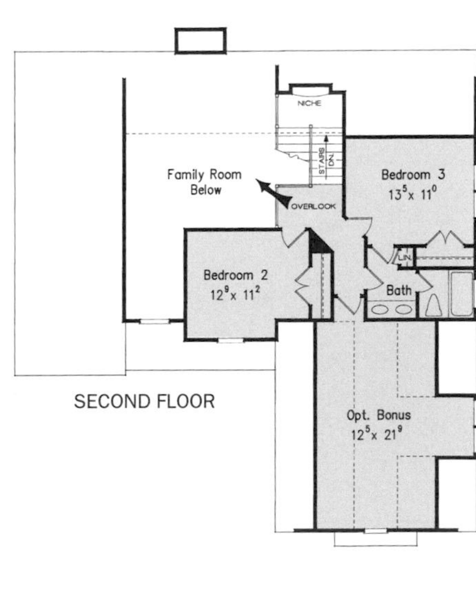

SECOND FLOOR

A brick one-story garage with a flowerbox window lends this two-story home a cottage feel. Inside, efficient use of space and flexibility adds to the appeal. A formal dining room opens from the two-story foyer, and leads to a cleverly designed kitchen. A serving bar connects the kitchen and breakfast nook. The hearth-warmed family room is just steps away. Four bedrooms—three family bedrooms and a roomy master suite—fill the second level. Note the option of turning Bedroom 4 into a sitting area for the master suite.

plan # HPK1700157

Style: Country Cottage

First Floor: 947 sq. ft.

Second Floor: 981 sq. ft.

Total: 1,928 sq. ft.

Bedrooms: 4

Bathrooms: 2½

Width: 41' - 0"

Depth: 39' - 4"

Foundation: Crawlspace, Unfinished Walkout Basement

eplans.com

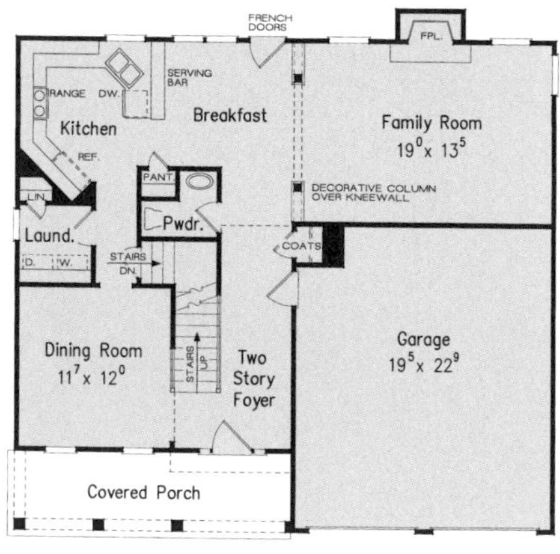

FIRST FLOOR

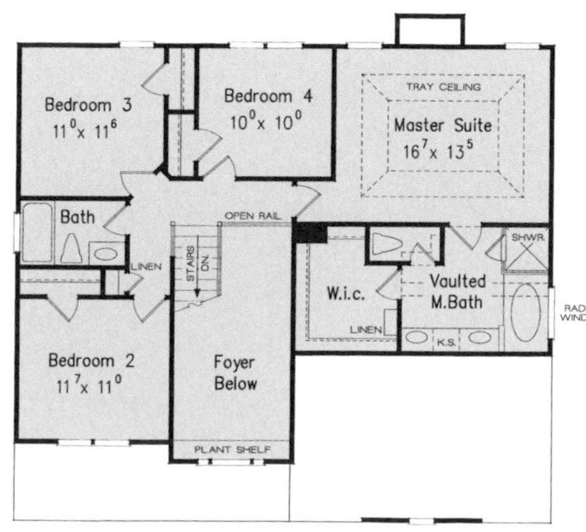

SECOND FLOOR

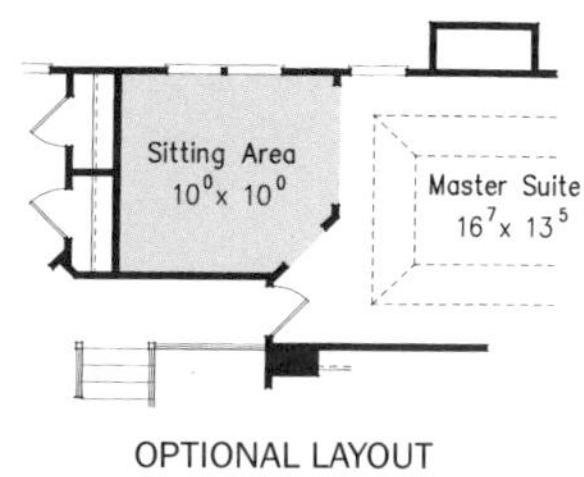

OPTIONAL LAYOUT

plan# HPK1700158

Style: Traditional
First Floor: 911 sq. ft.
Second Floor: 1,029 sq. ft.
Total: 1,940 sq. ft.
Bedrooms: 3
Bathrooms: 2½
Width: 20' - 10"
Depth: 75' - 10"
Foundation: Crawlspace

eplans.com

With irresistible charm and quiet curb appeal, this enchanting cottage conceals a sophisticated interior that's prepared for busy lifestyles. Built-in cabinetry in the great room frames a massive fireplace, which warms the area and complements the natural views. An open kitchen provides an island with a double sink and snack counter. Planned events are easily served in the formal dining room with French doors that lead to the veranda. On the upper level, a central hall with linen storage connects the sleeping quarters. The master suite boasts a walk-in closet and a roomy bath with a dual-sink vanity. Each of two secondary bedrooms has plenty of wardrobe space. Bedroom 3 leads out to the upper-level deck.

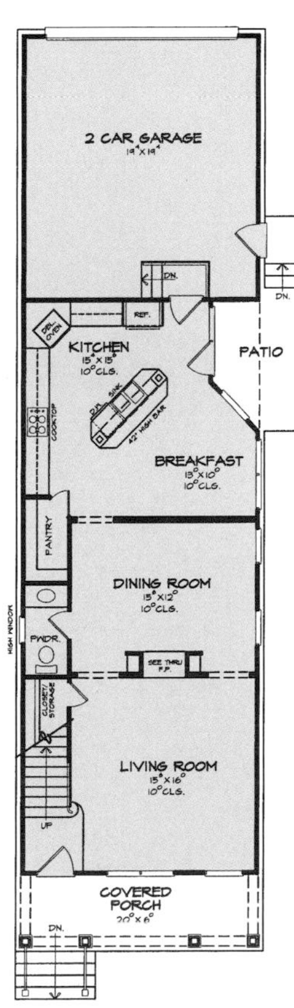

FIRST FLOOR

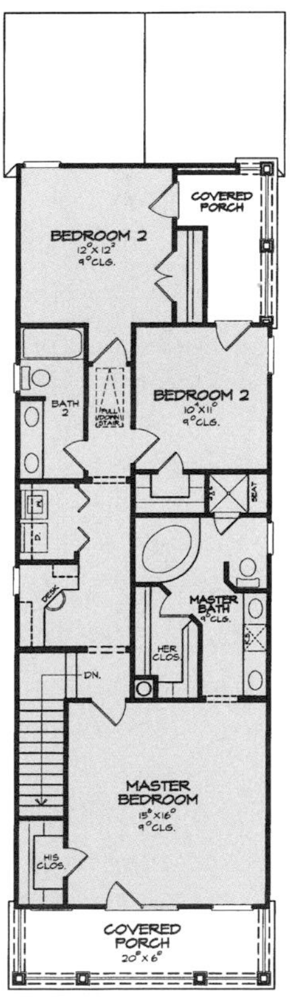

SECOND FLOOR

SECOND FLOOR

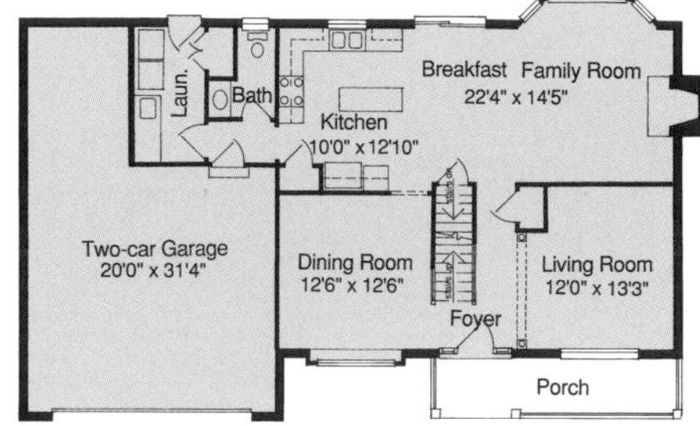

FIRST FLOOR

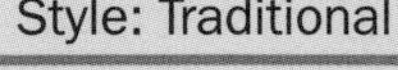

plan# HPK1700159

Style: Traditional

First Floor: 1,113 sq. ft.

Second Floor: 835 sq. ft.

Total: 1,948 sq. ft.

Bedrooms: 3

Bathrooms: 2½

Width: 54' - 0"

Depth: 34' - 8"

Foundation: Unfinished Basement

eplans.com

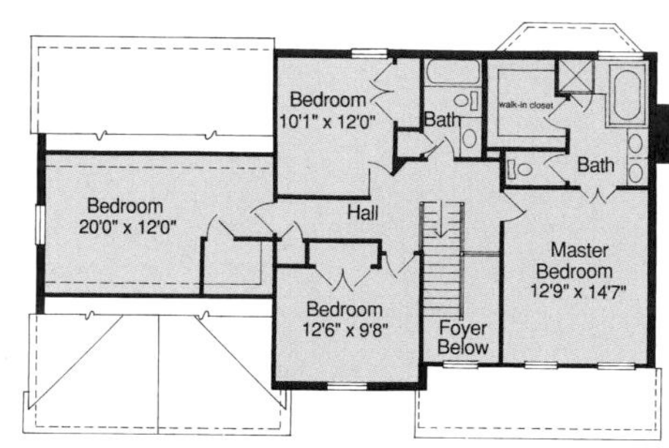

OPTIONAL LAYOUT

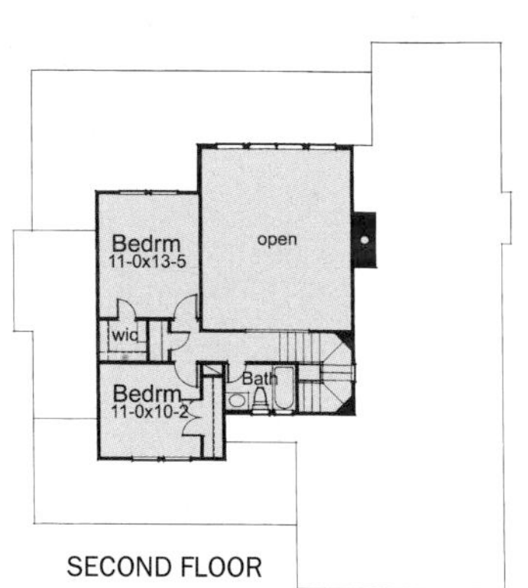

SECOND FLOOR

FIRST FLOOR

plan# HPK1700160

Style: Country

First Floor: 1,510 sq. ft.

Second Floor: 442 sq. ft.

Total: 1,952 sq. ft.

Bedrooms: 3

Bathrooms: 2½

Width: 54' - 7"

Depth: 60' - 3"

Foundation: Slab, Unfinished Basement, Crawlspace

eplans.com

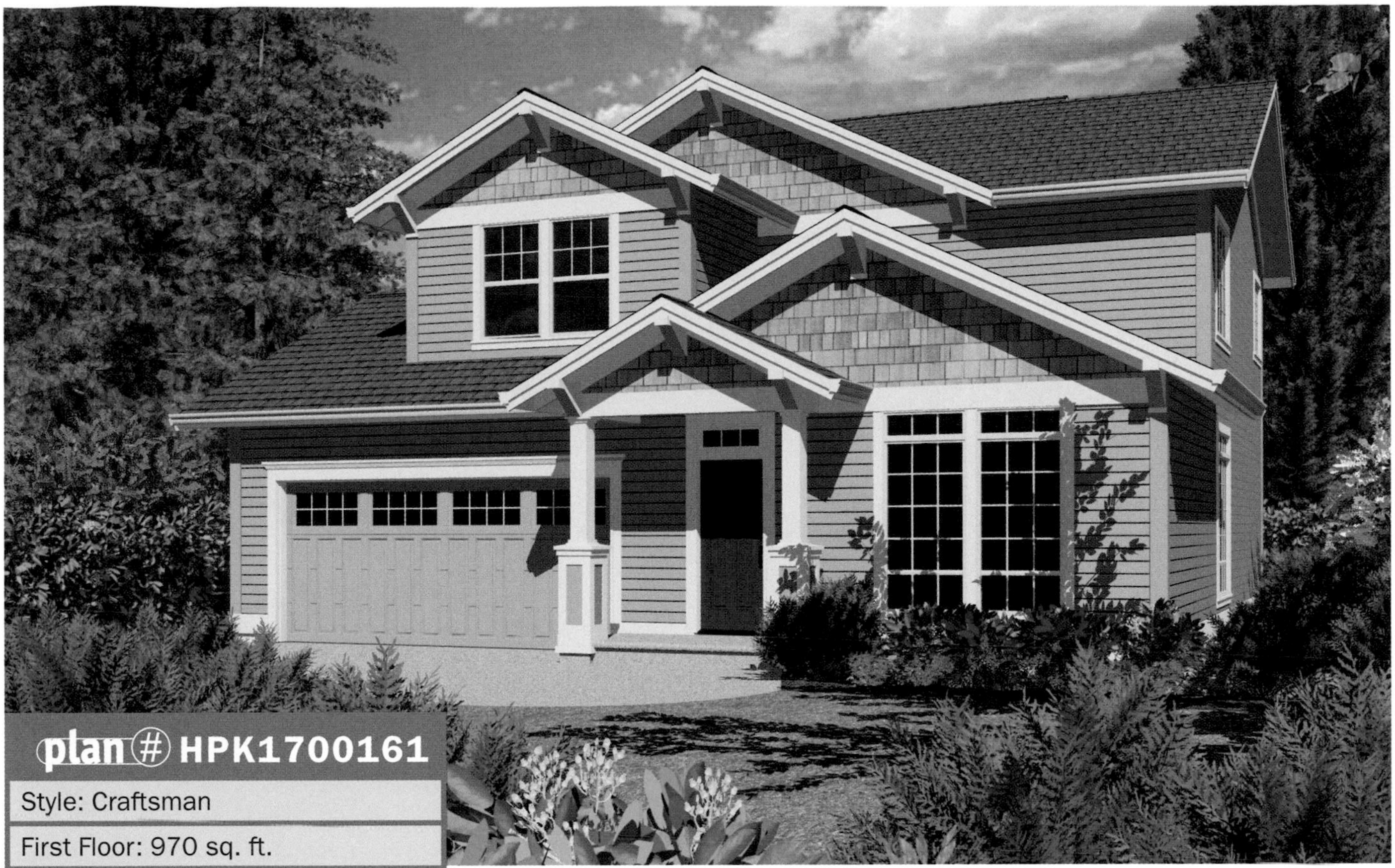

plan# HPK1700161

Style: Craftsman
First Floor: 970 sq. ft.
Second Floor: 988 sq. ft.
Total: 1,958 sq. ft.
Bedrooms: 3
Bathrooms: 2½
Width: 40' - 0"
Depth: 43' - 0"
Foundation: Crawlspace

eplans.com

A sensible floor plan, with living spaces on the first floor and bedrooms on the second floor, is the highlight of this Craftsman home. Elegance reigns in the formal living room, with a vaulted ceiling and columned entry; this room is open to the dining room, which is brightened by natural light from two tall windows. Ideal for informal gatherings, the family room boasts a fireplace flanked by built-in shelves. The efficient kitchen includes a central island and double sink, and the nearby nook features easy access to the outdoors through sliding glass doors. The master suite includes a lavish bath with a corner spa tub and compartmented toilet; two additional bedrooms, one with a walk-in closet, share a full bath.

SECOND FLOOR

FIRST FLOOR

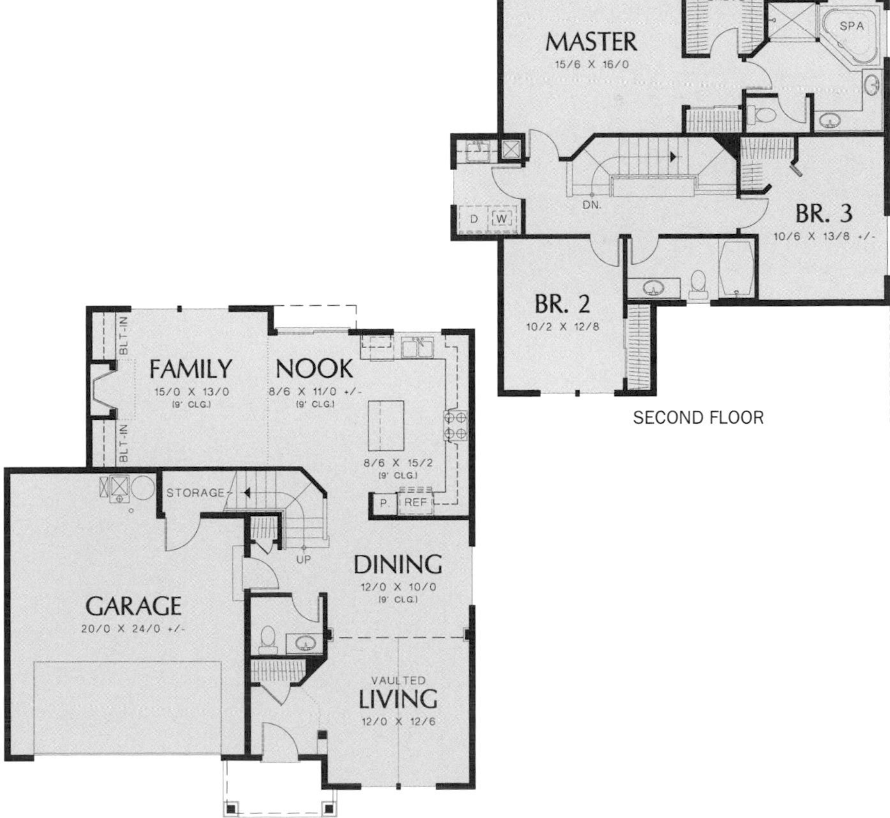

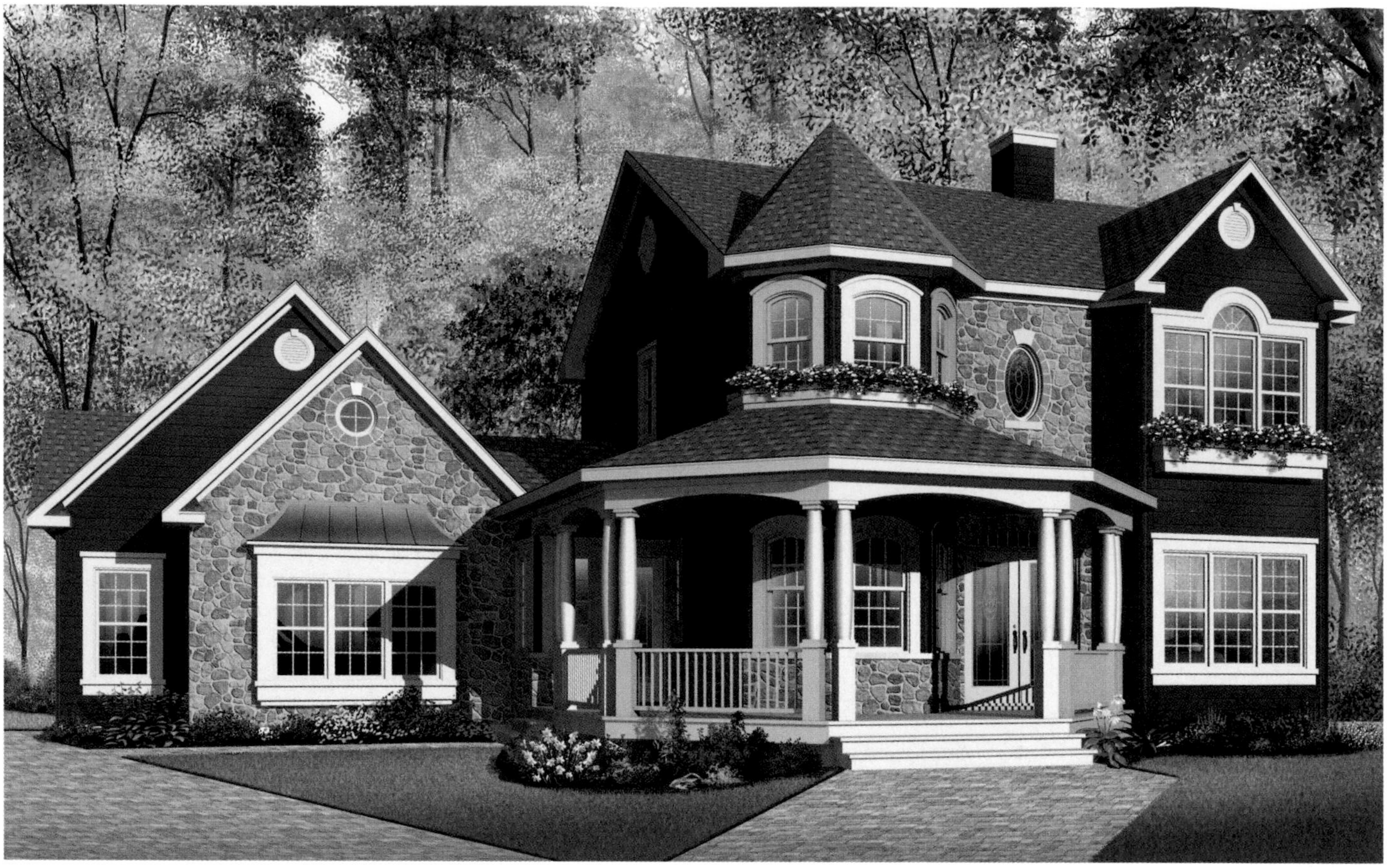

Contemporary on the outside, this plan won't let you down once you're inside. A superior layout places bedrooms, a laundry room, and full baths on the second floor and living spaces on the main level. Bedrooms include the master suite with an enormous walk-in closet leading to the master bath—complete with dual-sink vanities, separate tub and shower, and a compartmented toilet. The media room brings the family together for movie night. An L-shaped kitchen has plenty of cabinet and counter space, ensuring that feeding the family around the island or in the breakfast nook will be a breeze. The dining area and adjacent family room facilitate spending cozy time with everyone.

plan# HPK1700162

Style: Contemporary
First Floor: 1,044 sq. ft.
Second Floor: 892 sq. ft.
Total: 1,936 sq. ft.
Bonus Space: 289 sq. ft.
Bedrooms: 3
Bathrooms: 2½
Width: 58' - 0"
Depth: 43' - 6"
Foundation: Unfinished Basement

eplans.com

FIRST FLOOR

SECOND FLOOR

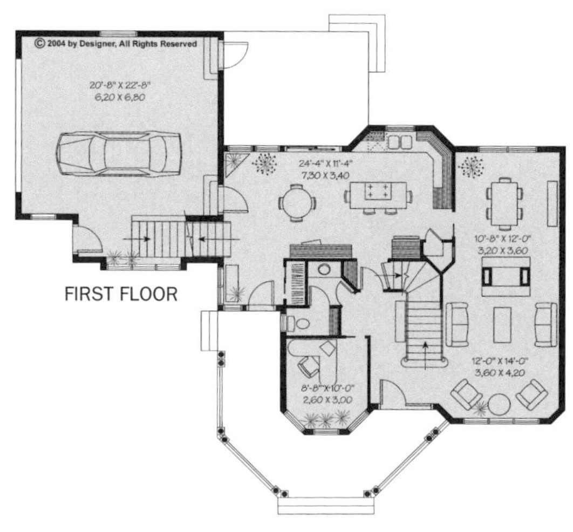

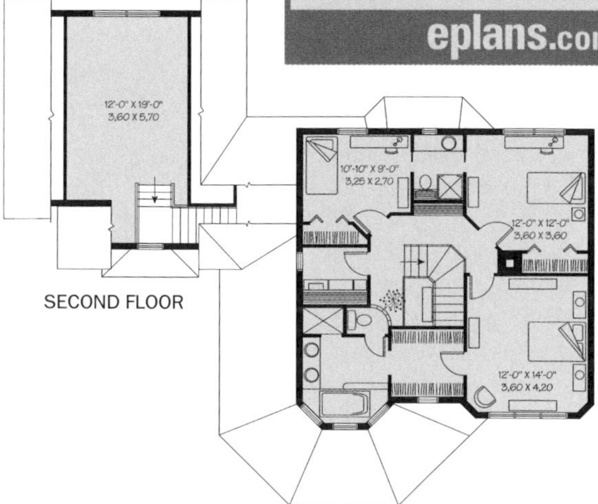

plan# HPK1700163

Style: Craftsman
First Floor: 1,060 sq. ft.
Second Floor: 914 sq. ft.
Total: 1,974 sq. ft.
Bedrooms: 3
Bathrooms: 3
Width: 32' - 0"
Depth: 35' - 0"
Foundation: Crawlspace

eplans.com

This charming Craftsman design offers a second-story master bedroom with four windows under the gabled dormer. The covered front porch displays column and pier supports. The hearth-warmed gathering room opens to the dining room on the right, where the adjoining kitchen offers enough space for an optional breakfast booth. A home office/guest suite is found in the rear. The second floor holds the lavish master suite and a second bedroom suite with its own private bath.

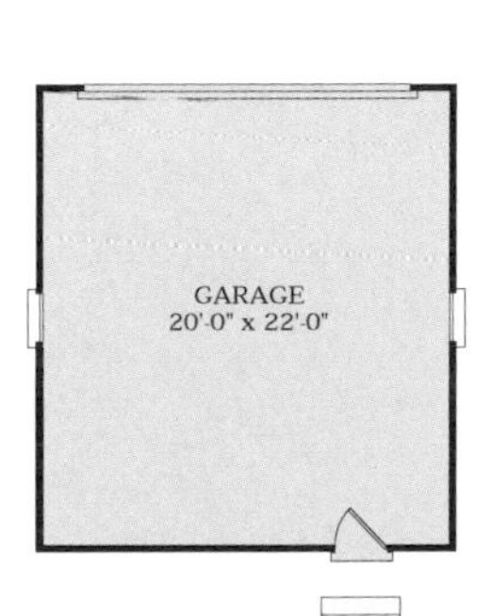

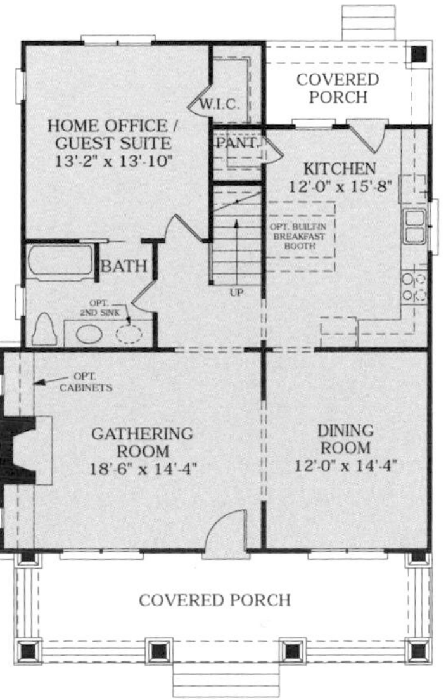

FIRST FLOOR

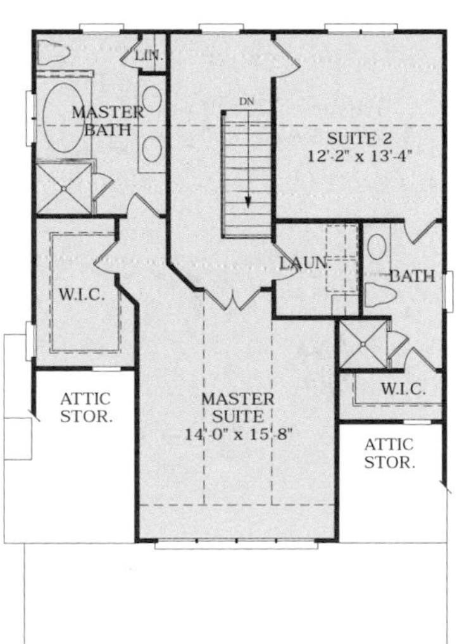

SECOND FLOOR

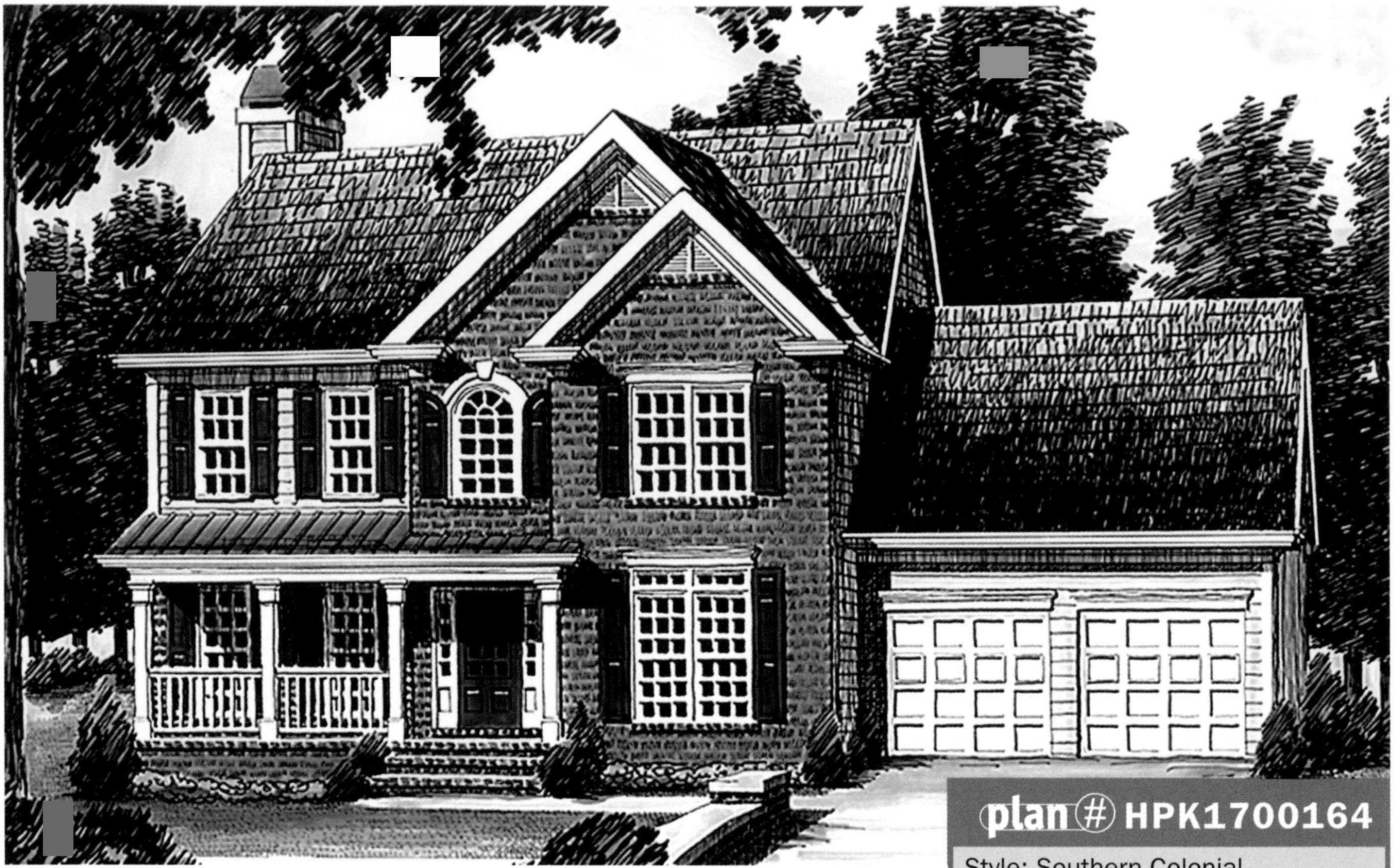

plan# HPK1700164

Style: Southern Colonial

First Floor: 1,071 sq. ft.

Second Floor: 924 sq. ft.

Total: 1,995 sq. ft.

Bonus Space: 280 sq. ft.

Bedrooms: 3

Bathrooms: 2½

Width: 55' - 10"

Depth: 38' - 6"

Foundation: Crawlspace, Unfinished Walkout Basement, Slab

eplans.com

SHWR.
LINEN
W.i.c.
Vltd. M.Bath
PLANT SHELF ABOVE
Bedroom 3
11⁰ x 11⁶
W.i.c.
Bath
FRENCH DOOR
TRAY CLG.
Master Suite
12⁹ x 17⁰
STAIRS DN.
OPEN RAIL
Opt. Bonus
17⁵ x 13⁵
LINEN
Foyer Below
Bedroom 2
13⁰ x 11⁰

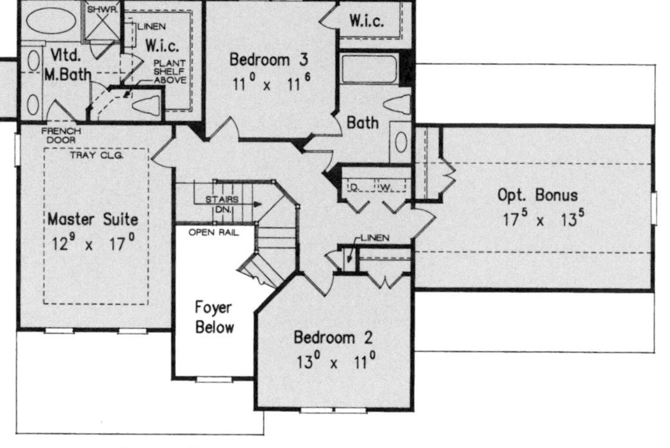

SECOND FLOOR

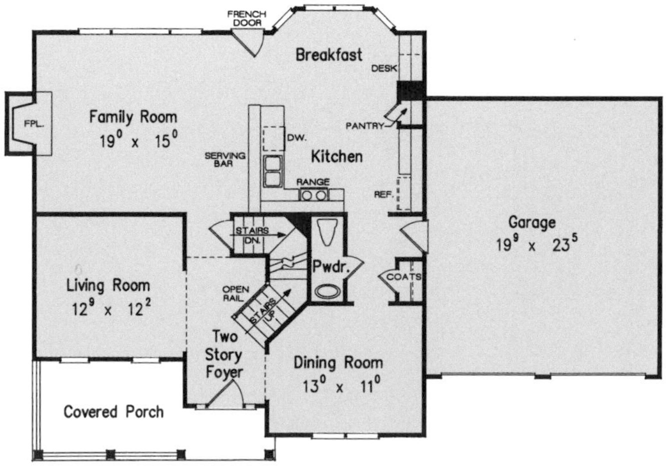

FRENCH DOOR
Breakfast
DESK
FPL.
Family Room
19⁰ x 15⁰
PANTRY
DW.
SERVING BAR
Kitchen
RANGE
REF.
Garage
19⁹ x 23⁵
STAIRS DN.
Pwdr.
COATS
Living Room
12⁹ x 12²
OPEN RAIL
STAIRS UP
Two Story Foyer
Dining Room
13⁰ x 11⁰
Covered Porch

FIRST FLOOR

Move-up buyers can enjoy all the luxuries of this two-story home highlighted by an angled staircase separating the dining room from casual living areas. A private powder room is tucked away behind the dining room—convenient for formal dinner parties. A bay window and built-in desk in the breakfast area are just a few of the plan's amenities. The sleeping zone occupies the second floor—away from everyday activities—and includes a master suite and two secondary bedrooms.

plan# HPK1700165

Style: Transitional
First Floor: 1,530 sq. ft.
Second Floor: 469 sq. ft.
Total: 1,999 sq. ft.
Bedrooms: 3
Bathrooms: 2½
Width: 59' - 6"
Depth: 53' - 0"
Foundation: Unfinished Basement, Slab, Crawlspace

eplans.com

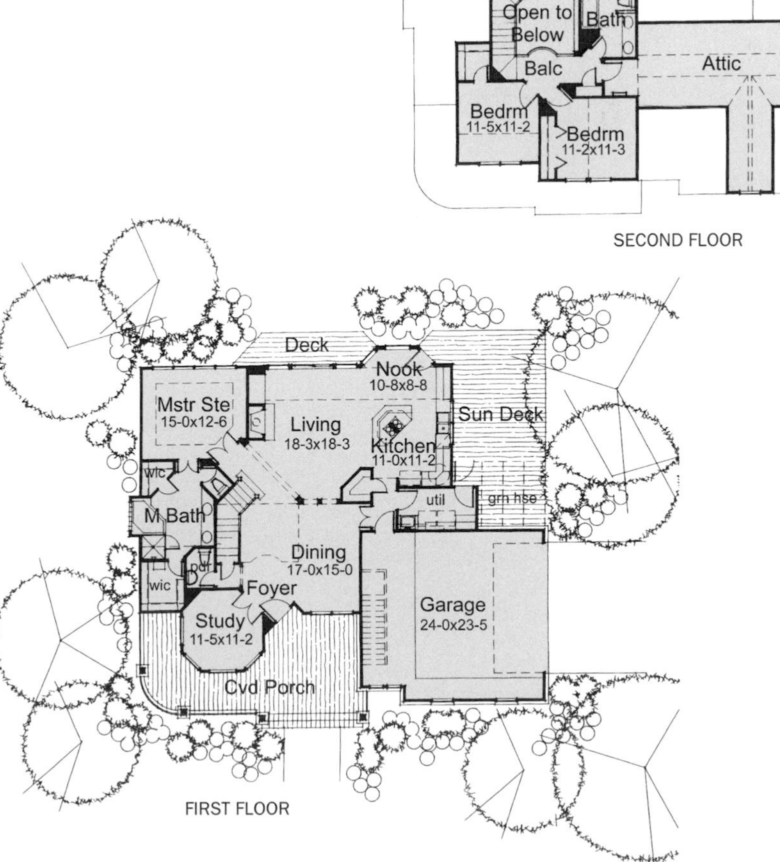

Stone porch supports and wide pillars lend a Craftsman look to this design. A truly elegant floor plan awaits within—an octagonal home office is just to the left of the entry, and a formal dining room sits to the right. The central living room offers a fireplace and a wall of windows that overlooks the deck; the nearby island kitchen includes a walk-in pantry and adjoins the breakfast bay. Access the greenhouse from the expansive side deck. Double doors open to the master bedroom, which provides a private bath with an angled soaking tub; two family bedrooms are found upstairs, where a balcony overlooks the two-story living room.

plan# HPK1700166
Style: Adam Style
First Floor: 774 sq. ft.
Second Floor: 754 sq. ft.
Third Floor: 260 sq. ft.
Total: 1,788 sq. ft.
Bedrooms: 2
Bathrooms: 2½
Width: 20' - 0"
Depth: 40' - 0"
Foundation: Unfinished Basement
eplans.com

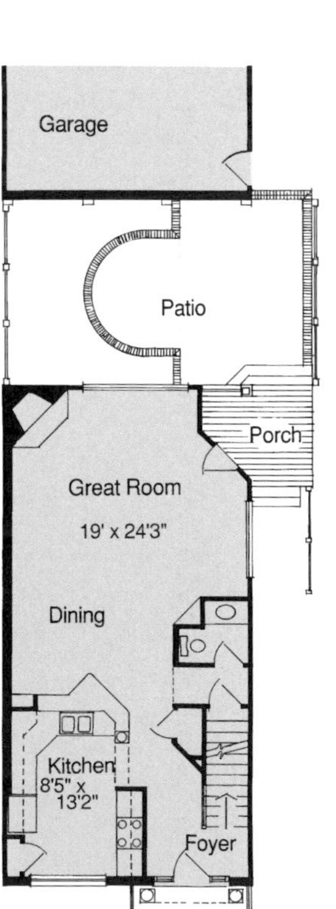

FIRST FLOOR

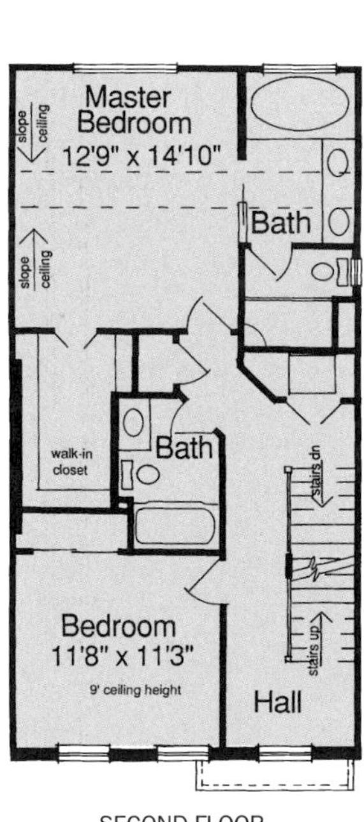

SECOND FLOOR

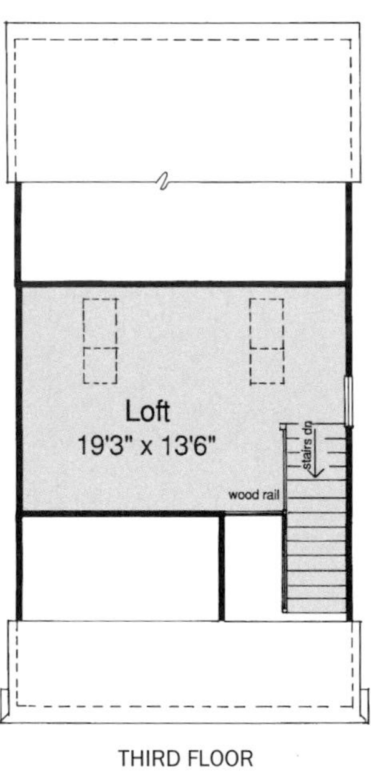

THIRD FLOOR

The luxury of detached housing, combined with the convenience and sophistication of city living, serves as the primary focus of this home. Provocative touches, such as a corner fireplace in the great room, a generous open floor plan, third-floor loft, and an expansive master suite, highlight the Neo-Traditional design. The warmth of the fireplace, windows across the rear (overlooking a courtyard), and angled rear entry are alluring touches. With an expansive rear patio and porch, emphasis is placed on a balance of indoor-outdoor living.

plan# HPK1700167

Style: Country Cottage
Total: 1,509 sq. ft.
Bedrooms: 3
Bathrooms: 2
Width: 49' - 0"
Depth: 34' - 4"
Foundation: Unfinished Walkout Basement

eplans.com

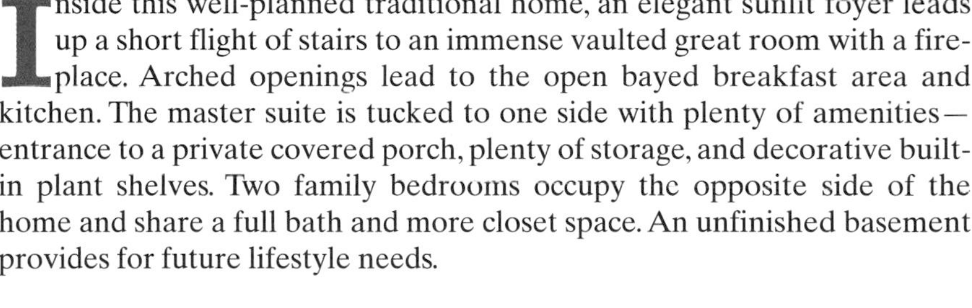

Inside this well-planned traditional home, an elegant sunlit foyer leads up a short flight of stairs to an immense vaulted great room with a fireplace. Arched openings lead to the open bayed breakfast area and kitchen. The master suite is tucked to one side with plenty of amenities—entrance to a private covered porch, plenty of storage, and decorative built-in plant shelves. Two family bedrooms occupy the opposite side of the home and share a full bath and more closet space. An unfinished basement provides for future lifestyle needs.

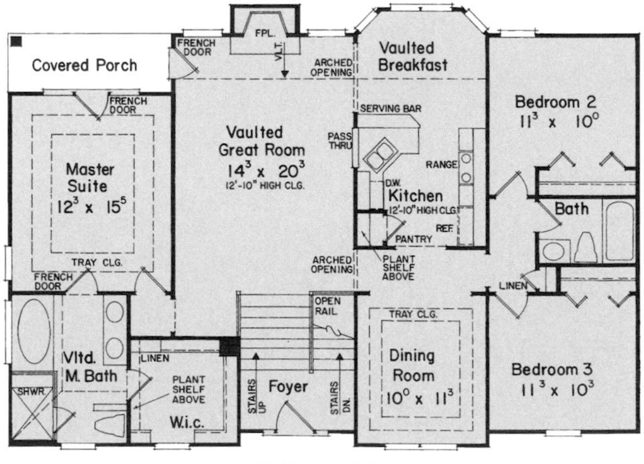

SECOND FLOOR

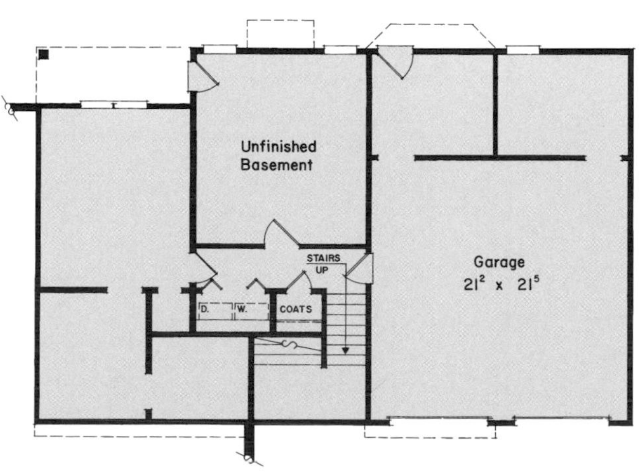

FIRST FLOOR

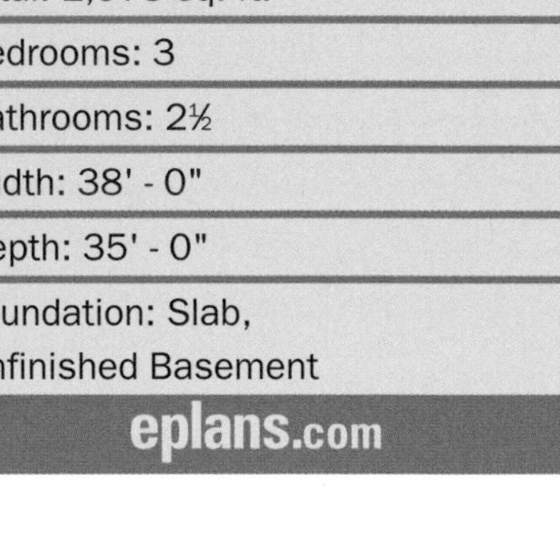

plan# HPK1700168

Style: Craftsman
Main Level: 1,106 sq. ft.
Upper Level: 872 sq. ft.
Total: 1,978 sq. ft.
Bedrooms: 3
Bathrooms: 2½
Width: 38' - 0"
Depth: 35' - 0"
Foundation: Slab, Unfinished Basement

eplans.com

Though this home gives the impression of the Northwest, it will be the winner of any neighborhood. From the foyer, the two-story living room is just a couple of steps up and features a through-fireplace. The U-shaped kitchen has a cooktop work island, an adjacent nook, and easy access to the formal dining room. A spacious family room shares the fireplace with the living room, is enhanced by built-ins, and also offers a quiet deck for stargazing. The upstairs consists of two family bedrooms sharing a full bath and a vaulted master suite complete with a walk-in closet and sumptuous bath. A two-car, drive-under garage has plenty of room for storage.

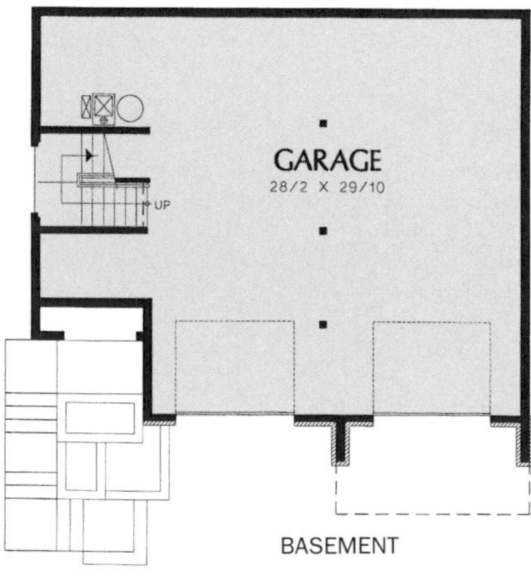

BASEMENT

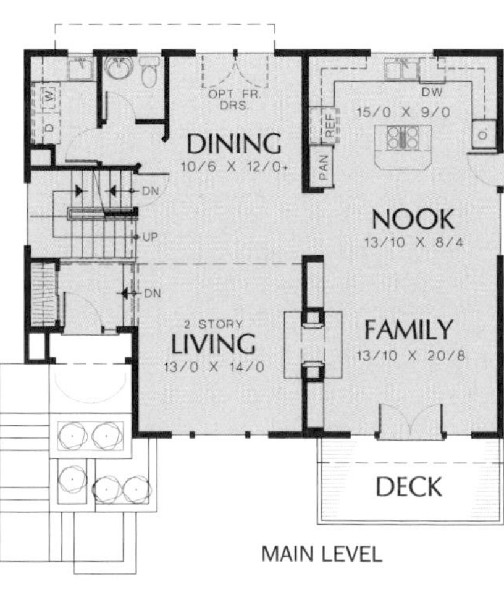

MAIN LEVEL

UPPER LEVEL

plan # HPK1700169

Style: Traditional
Square Footage: 816 / 816
Bedrooms: 2 / 2
Bathrooms: 1 / 1
Width: 48' - 0"
Depth: 34' - 0"
Foundation: Unfinished Basement

eplans.com

This attractive duplex home offers comfortable livability with a convenient one-story elevation. The floor plan is perfect for couples just starting out. A small covered porch welcomes you inside to a casual or formal living room. Here, the room is open to a dining area located close to the kitchen. A storage pantry in the kitchen allows for additional space. The larger family bedroom directly accesses the full bath, while the second bedroom uses the hall entrance to the bath. The second bedroom is also the perfect size for a home office or nursery. This home is designed with a basement foundation.

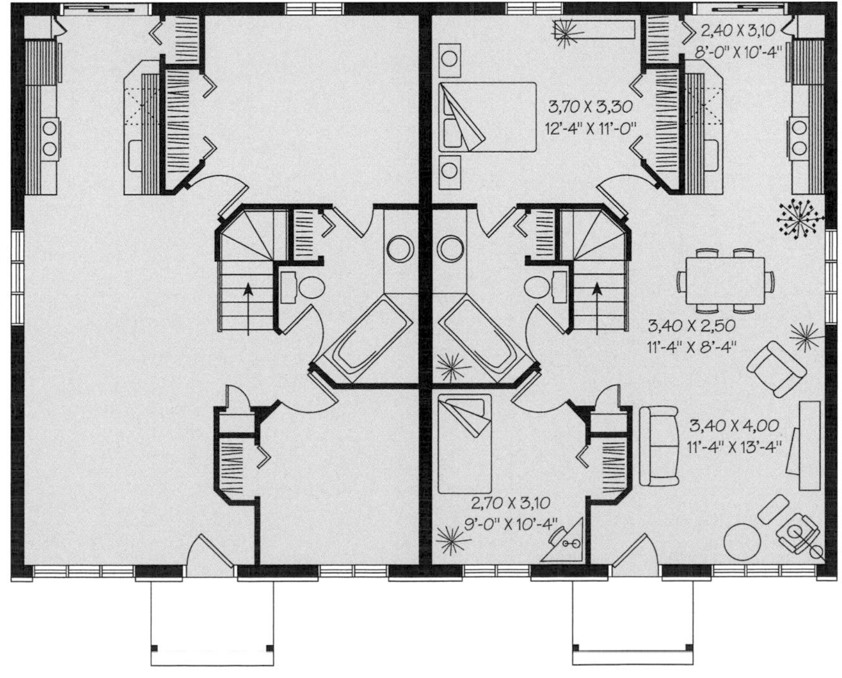

plan# HPK1700170

Style: Mediterranean
Total: 996 sq. ft.
Bedrooms: 2
Bathrooms: 2
Width: 60' - 0"
Depth: 55' - 0"
Foundation: Unfinished Basement

eplans.com

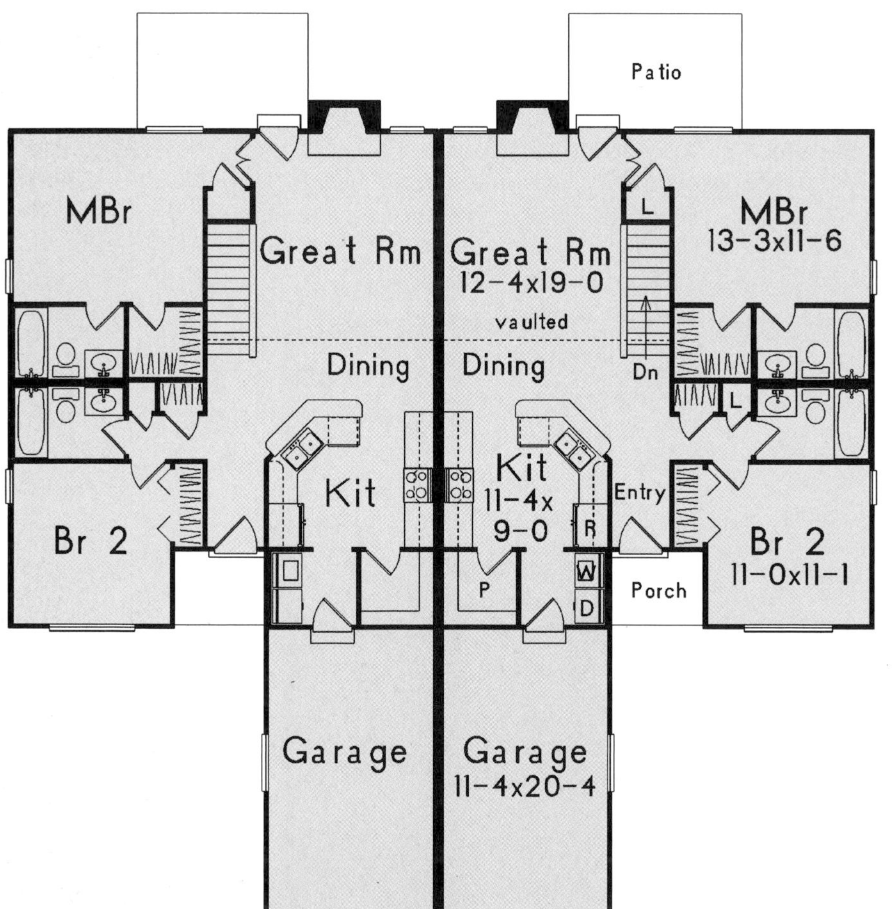

Perfectly suited to warmer climates, this beautiful stucco duplex features stunning European and Mediterranean accents. Enter one of the units through the front porch or the single-car garage. The kitchen provides a walk-in pantry, space for a washer and dryer, and a combined dining/great room with a vaulted ceiling warmed by a fireplace. Access the rear patio for outdoor grilling. The master suite features a linen closet, private bath and walk-in closet. The second family bedroom is located near the full hall bath. Designed for the young or growing family, this charming duplex home is both economical and stylish for any neighborhood setting.

Homes From 2,000 to 2,499 Square Feet

The rebirth of a style—this design salutes the look of Early America. See plan HPK1700238 on page 211.

EDITOR'S PICK

Here's a solid home for the mid-sized family. For family nights, a spacious island kitchen, nook, and rear deck work well with the great room in the center of the plan, as does the 532-square-foot recreation room downstairs. For private times, five bedrooms—including a commodious master suite, with ample closet space—help keep things peaceful and quiet. The three-car garage is a must-have.

plan# HPK1700171
Style: Traditional
Square Footage: 2,003
Bedrooms: 3
Bathrooms: 2½
Width: 63' - 8"
Depth: 66' - 0"
Foundation: Unfinished Walkout Basement
eplans.com

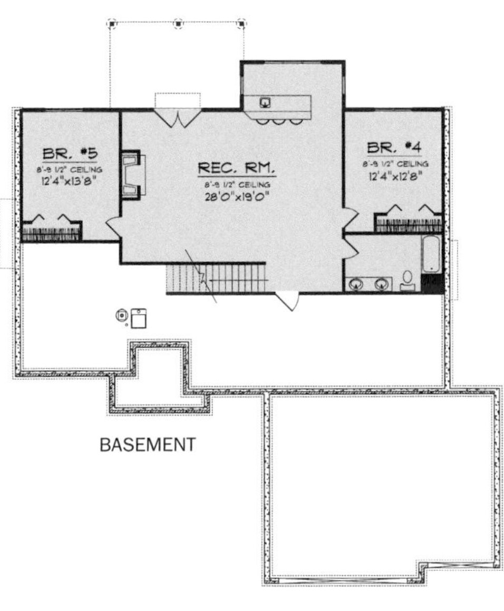

BASEMENT

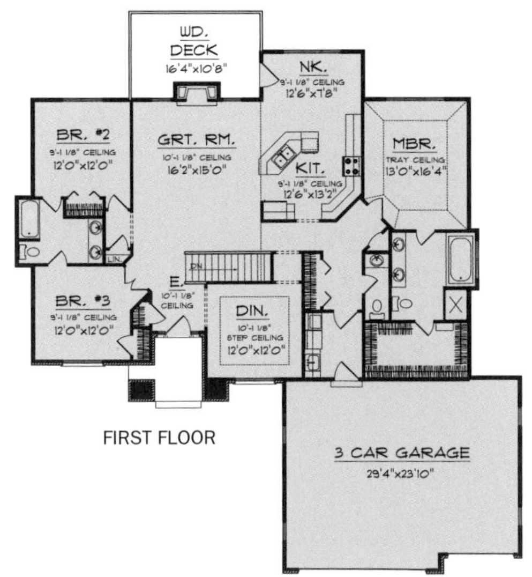

FIRST FLOOR

plan# HPK1700172

Style: European Cottage
Square Footage: 2,007
Bedrooms: 3
Bathrooms: 2½
Width: 40' - 0"
Depth: 94' - 10"
Foundation: Slab

eplans.com

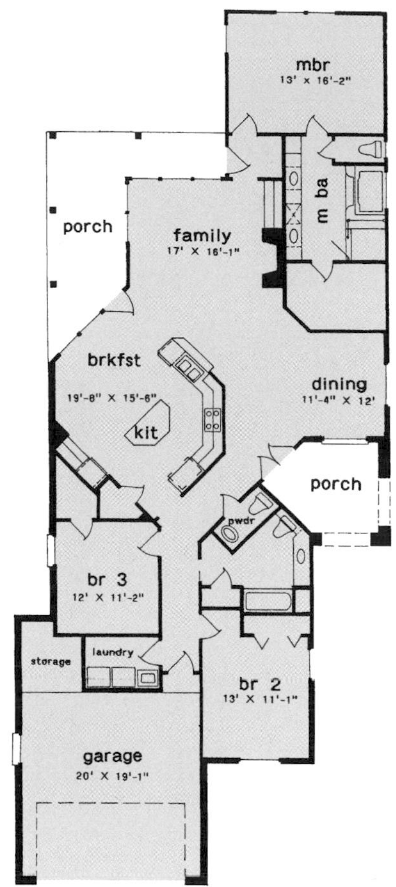

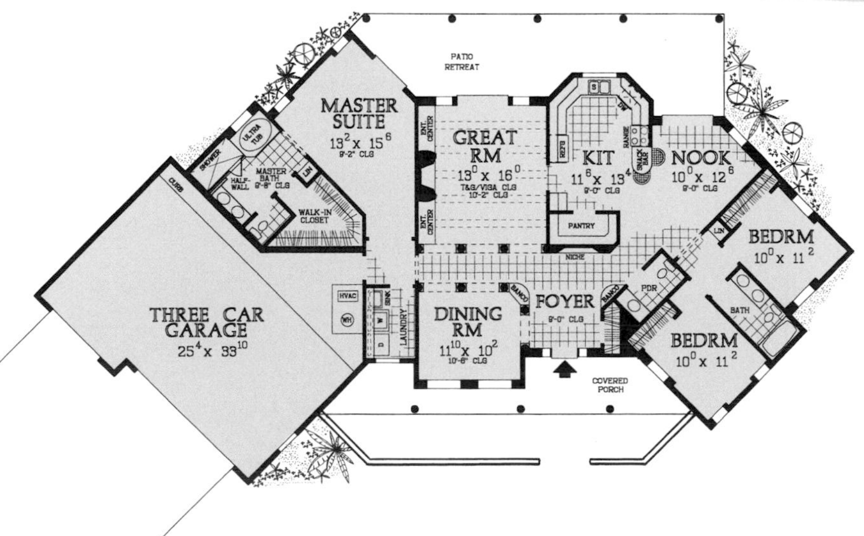

plan# HPK1700173

Style: SW Contemporary
Square Footage: 2,015
Bedrooms: 3
Bathrooms: 2½
Width: 96' - 5"
Depth: 54' - 9"
Foundation: Slab

eplans.com

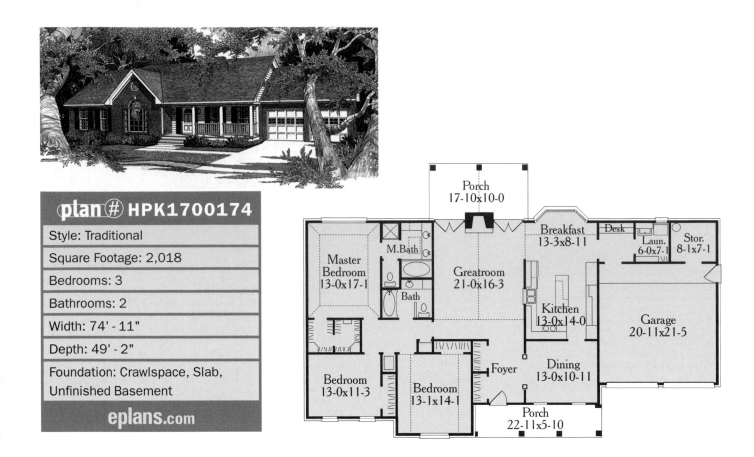

plan# HPK1700174

Style: Traditional
Square Footage: 2,018
Bedrooms: 3
Bathrooms: 2
Width: 74' - 11"
Depth: 49' - 2"
Foundation: Crawlspace, Slab, Unfinished Basement

eplans.com

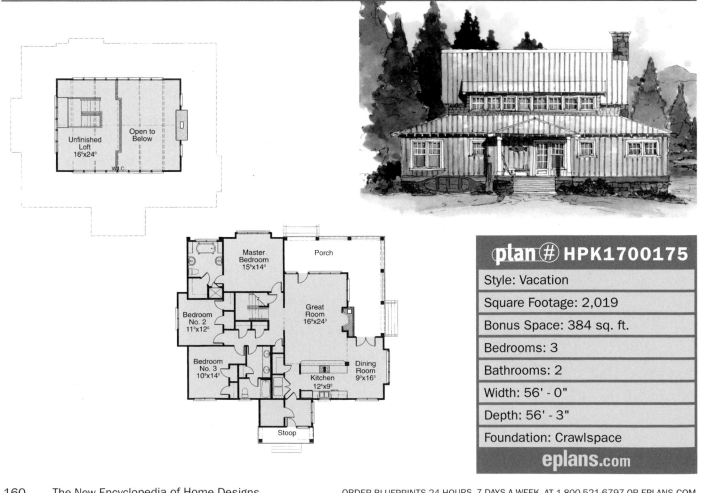

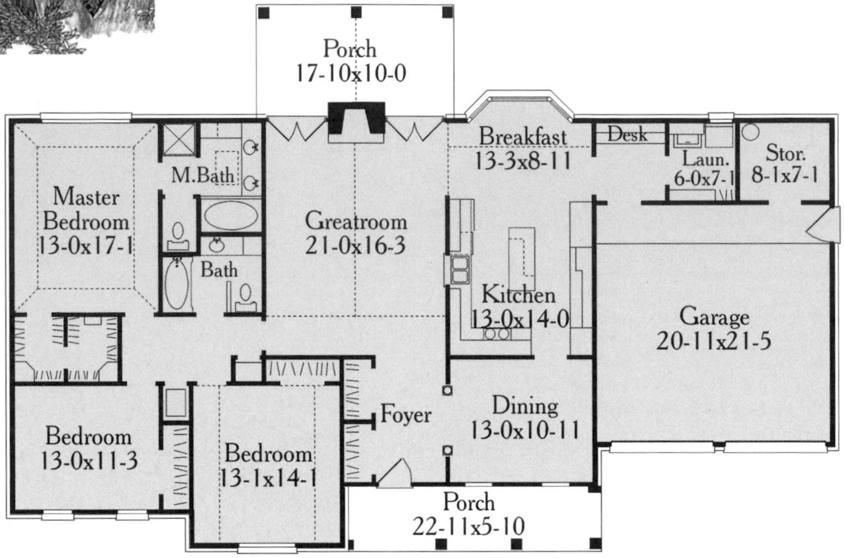

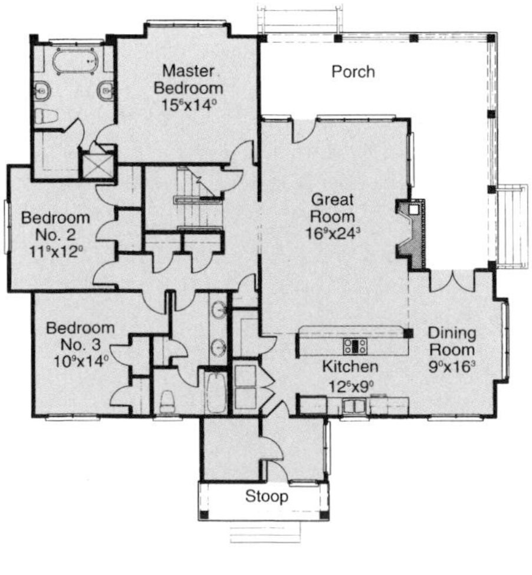

Porch 17-10x10-0
Master Bedroom 13-0x17-1
M.Bath
Bath
Greatroom 21-0x16-3
Breakfast 13-3x8-11
Desk
Laun. 6-0x7-1
Stor. 8-1x7-1
Kitchen 13-0x14-0
Garage 20-11x21-5
Foyer
Dining 13-0x10-11
Bedroom 13-0x11-3
Bedroom 13-1x14-1
Porch 22-11x5-10

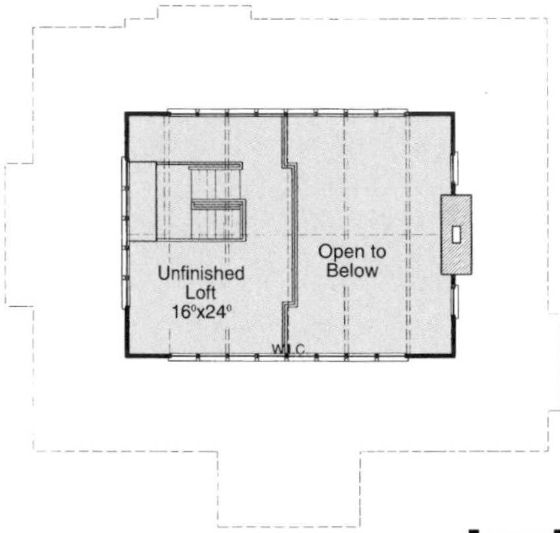

Unfinished Loft 16⁶x24⁰
Open to Below
W.I.C.

Master Bedroom 15⁶x14⁰
Porch
Bedroom No. 2 11⁶x12⁰
Great Room 16⁶x24³
Bedroom No. 3 10⁶x14⁰
Kitchen 12⁶x9⁰
Dining Room 9⁰x16³
Stoop

plan# HPK1700175

Style: Vacation
Square Footage: 2,019
Bonus Space: 384 sq. ft.
Bedrooms: 3
Bathrooms: 2
Width: 56' - 0"
Depth: 56' - 3"
Foundation: Crawlspace

eplans.com

plan# HPK1700176

Style: Traditional
Square Footage: 2,034
Bedrooms: 3
Bathrooms: 2
Width: 75' - 0"
Depth: 47' - 5"
Foundation: Unfinished Basement

eplans.com

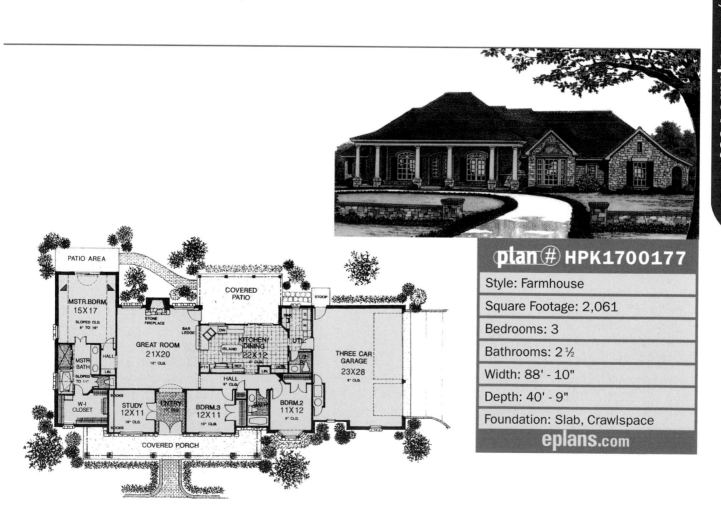

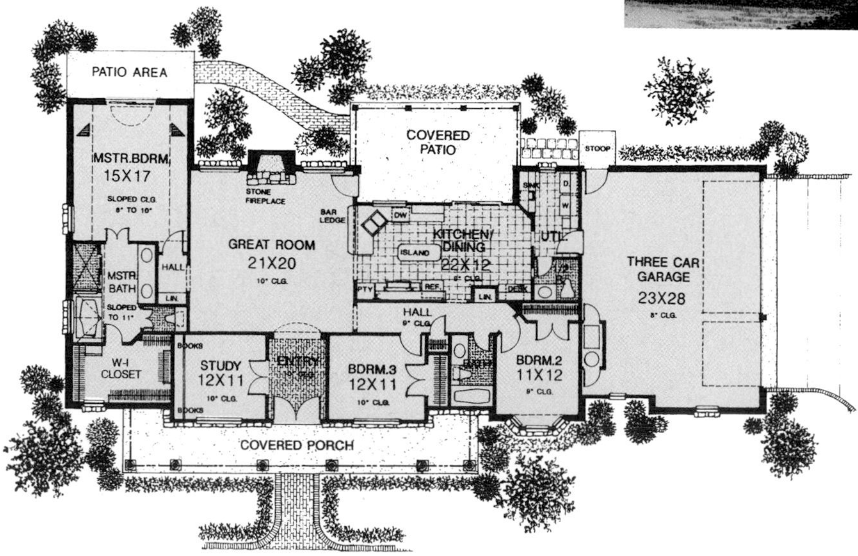

plan# HPK1700177

Style: Farmhouse
Square Footage: 2,061
Bedrooms: 3
Bathrooms: 2½
Width: 88' - 10"
Depth: 40' - 9"
Foundation: Slab, Crawlspace

eplans.com

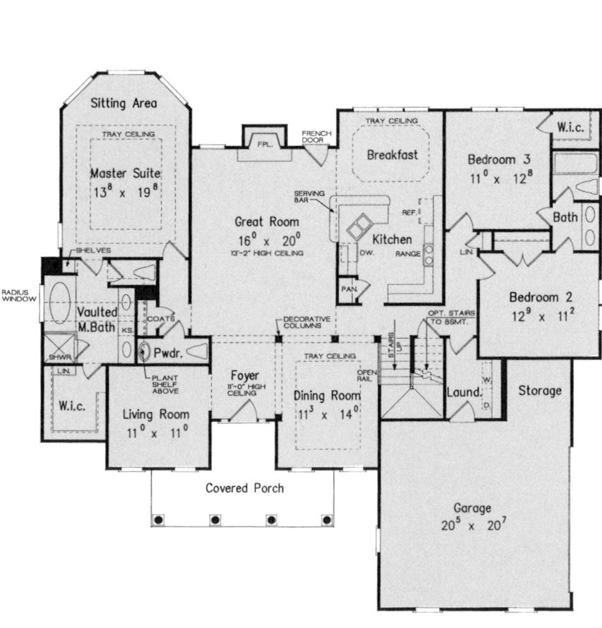

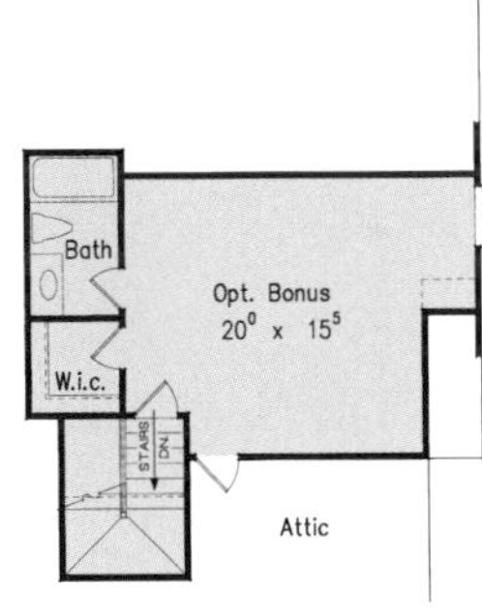

plan # HPK1700178

Style: Country Cottage
Square Footage: 2,072
Bonus Space: 372 sq. ft.
Bedrooms: 3
Bathrooms: 2 ½
Width: 61' - 0"
Depth: 58' - 6"
Foundation: Crawlspace, Unfinished Walkout Basement

eplans.com

Horizontal siding and a columned porch indicate country flavor in this fine three-bedroom home. Inside, the foyer is flanked by a formal living room and dining room; directly ahead, the great room—with a fireplace—opens to the breakfast room and kitchen. Two family bedrooms share a full bath, and the private master suite is full of amenities. Upstairs, an optional fourth bedroom provides plenty of future expansion opportunities.

plan# HPK1700179

Style: Farmhouse
Square Footage: 2,076
Bedrooms: 3
Bathrooms: 2
Width: 64' - 8"
Depth: 54' - 7"
Foundation: Unfinished Basement

eplans.com

Multipane windows, mock shutters, and a covered front porch exhibit the charm of this home's facade. Inside, the foyer is flanked by a spacious, efficient kitchen to the right and a large, convenient laundry room to the left. The living room features a warming fireplace. To the right of the living room is the formal dining room; both rooms share a snack bar and direct access to the kitchen. Sleeping quarters are split, with two family bedrooms and a full bath on the right side of the plan and the deluxe master suite on the left. The private master bath offers such luxuries as a walk-in closet, a twin-sink vanity, a garden tub, and a separate shower.

A charming country cottage adds curb appeal to any neighborhood. The island kitchen easily serves the adjoining lodge room and the breakfast room offers a bayed view of the backyard and access to a rear porch. The master bathroom is equipped with a dual-sink vanity, garden tub, walk-in closet, private toilet, and shower. Two additional bedrooms each have a full bath. The basement is available for future expansion.

plan# HPK1700180

Style: Country Cottage

Square Footage: 2,086

Bedrooms: 3

Bathrooms: 3

Width: 57' - 6"

Depth: 46' - 6"

Foundation: Unfinished Basement

eplans.com

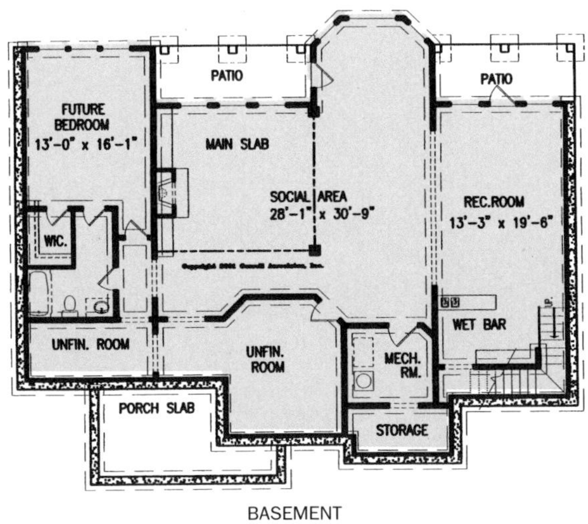

BASEMENT

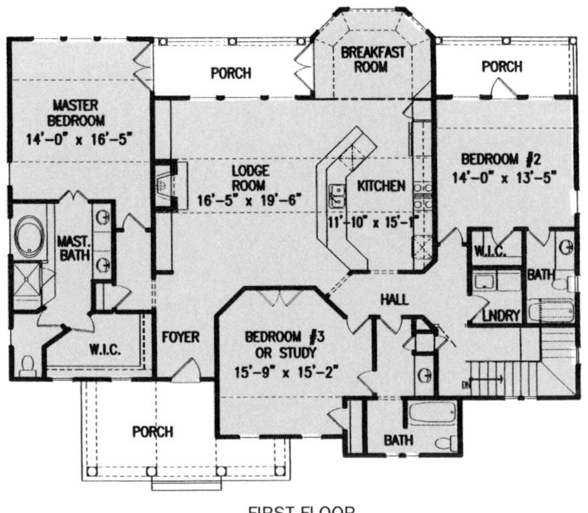

FIRST FLOOR

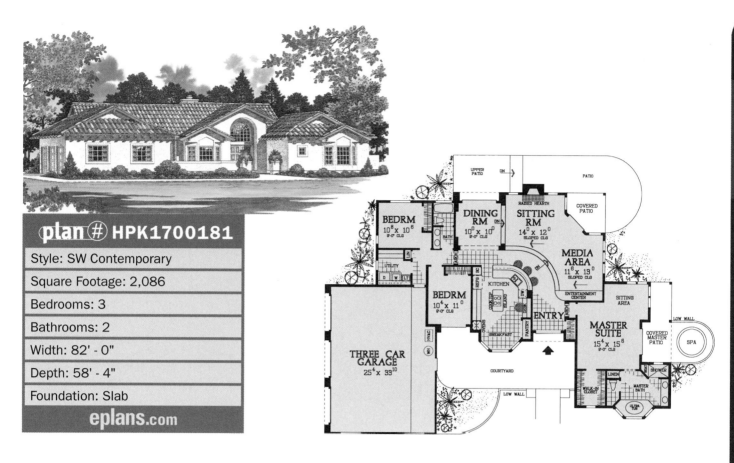

plan# HPK1700181

Style: SW Contemporary
Square Footage: 2,086
Bedrooms: 3
Bathrooms: 2
Width: 82' - 0"
Depth: 58' - 4"
Foundation: Slab

eplans.com

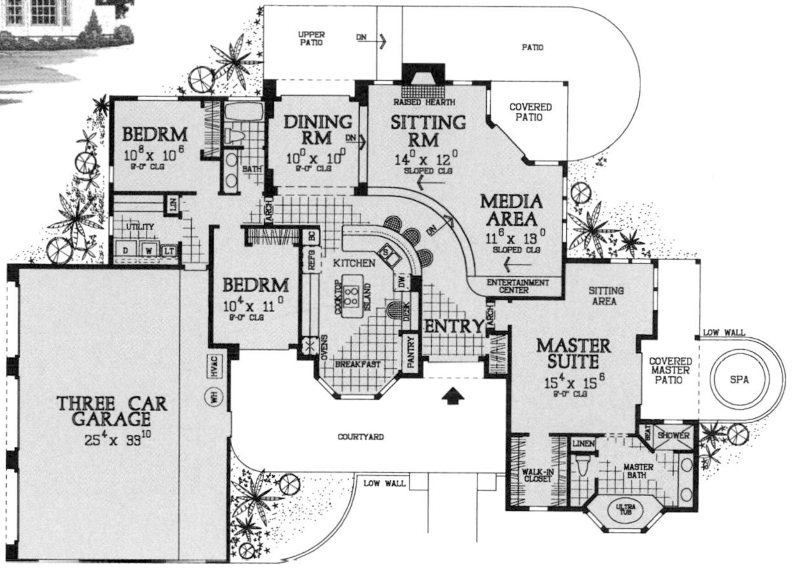

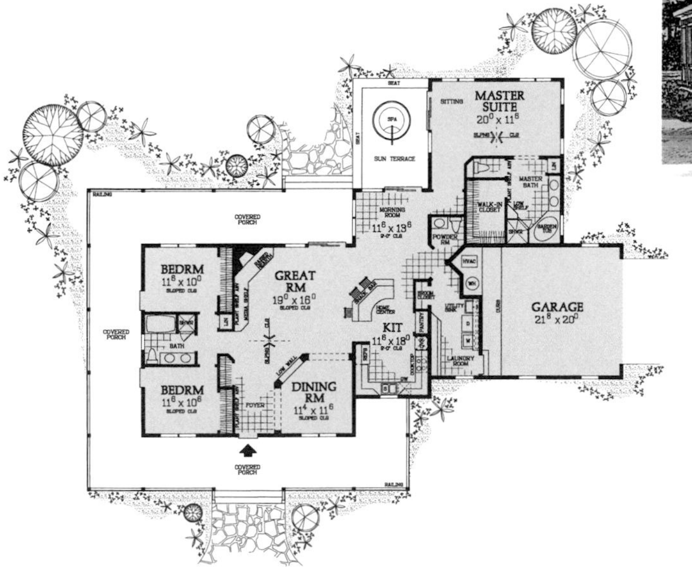

plan# HPK1700182

Style: Farmhouse
Square Footage: 2,090
Bedrooms: 3
Bathrooms: 2½
Width: 84' - 6"
Depth: 64' - 0"
Foundation: Crawlspace

eplans.com

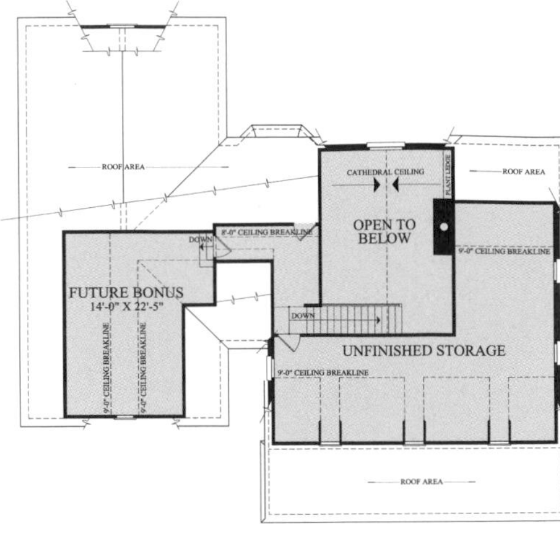

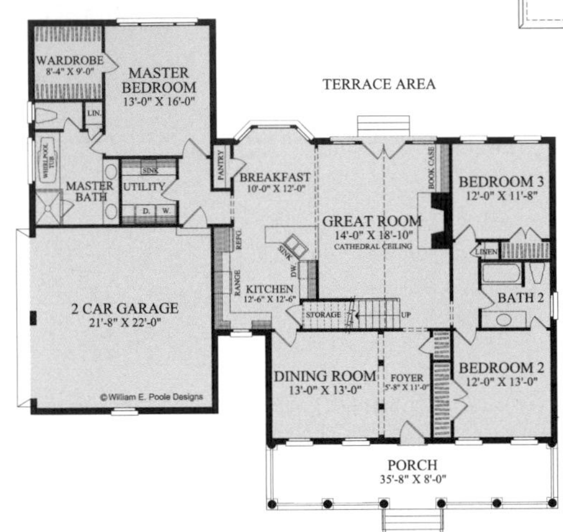

plan# HPK1700183

Style: Country Cottage
Square Footage: 2,096
Bonus Space: 374 sq. ft.
Bedrooms: 3
Bathrooms: 2
Width: 64' - 8"
Depth: 60' - 0"
Foundation: Crawlspace, Unfinished Basement

eplans.com

plan# HPK1700184

Style: Traditional
Square Footage: 2,097
Bedrooms: 3
Bathrooms: 2
Width: 68' - 0"
Depth: 68' - 0"
Foundation: Unfinished Basement

eplans.com

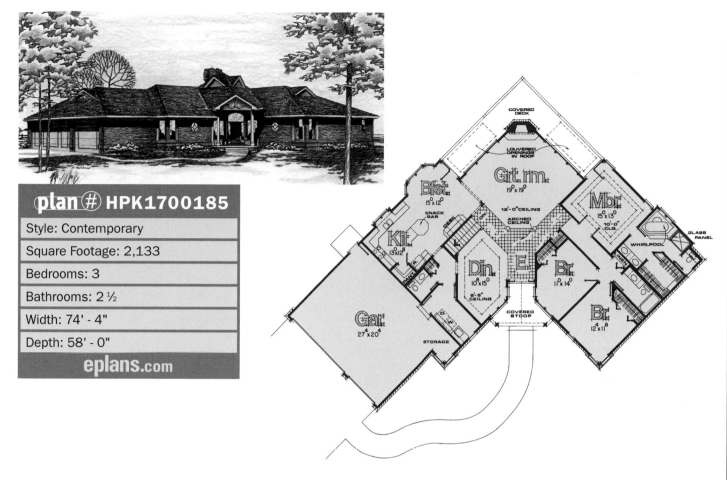

plan# HPK1700185

Style: Contemporary
Square Footage: 2,133
Bedrooms: 3
Bathrooms: 2 ½
Width: 74' - 4"
Depth: 58' - 0"

eplans.com

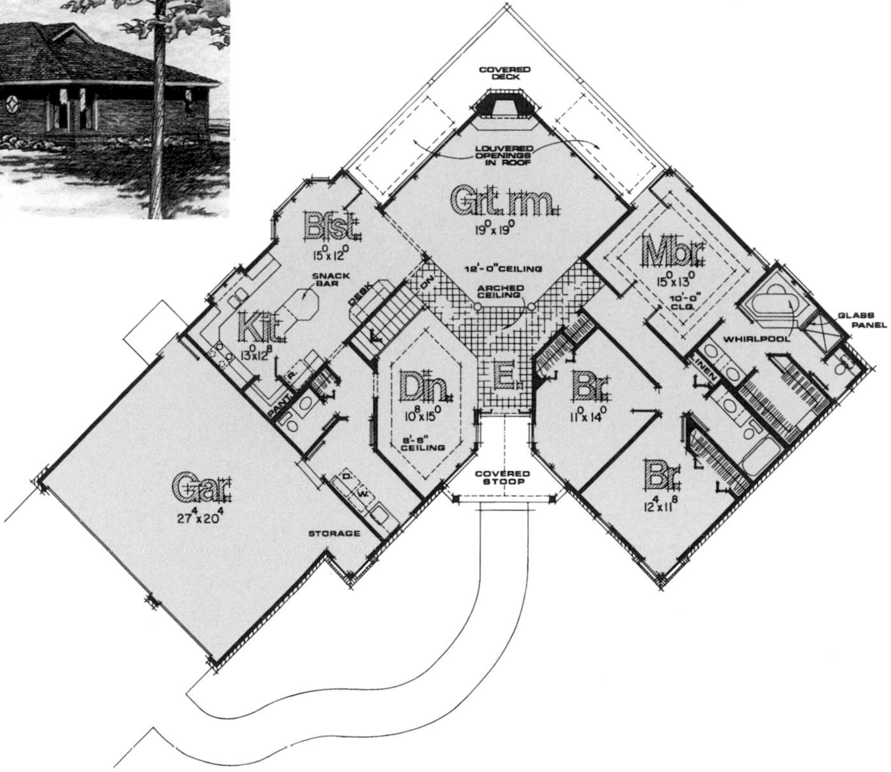

plan# HPK1700186

Style: French
Square Footage: 2,150
Bedrooms: 3
Bathrooms: 2 ½
Width: 64' - 0"
Depth: 60' - 4"
Foundation: Walkout Basement

eplans.com

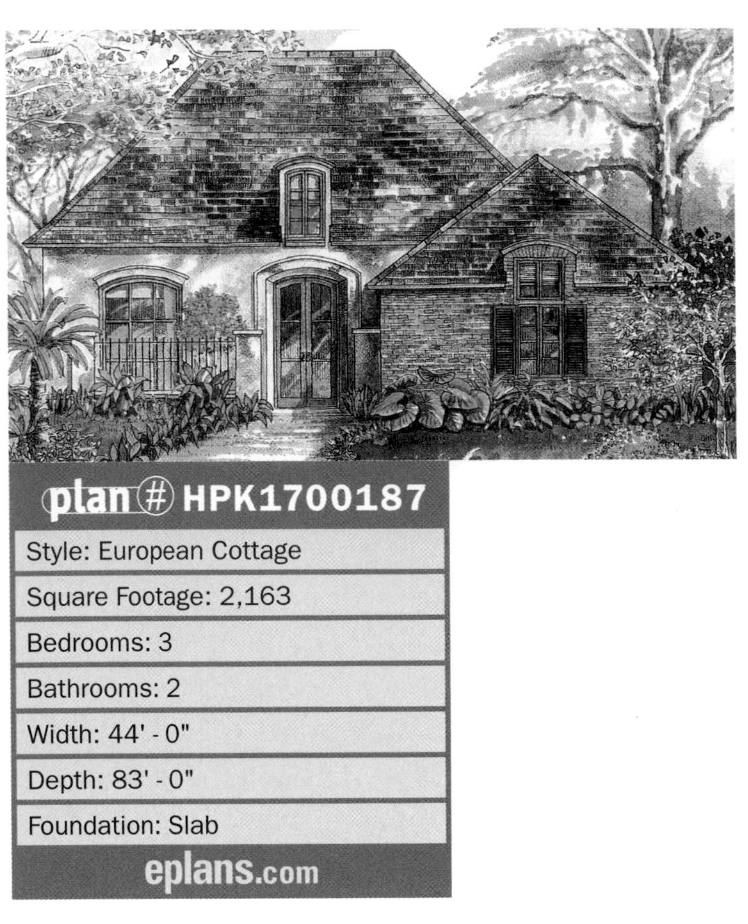

plan# HPK1700187

Style: European Cottage

Square Footage: 2,163

Bedrooms: 3

Bathrooms: 2

Width: 44' - 0"

Depth: 83' - 0"

Foundation: Slab

eplans.com

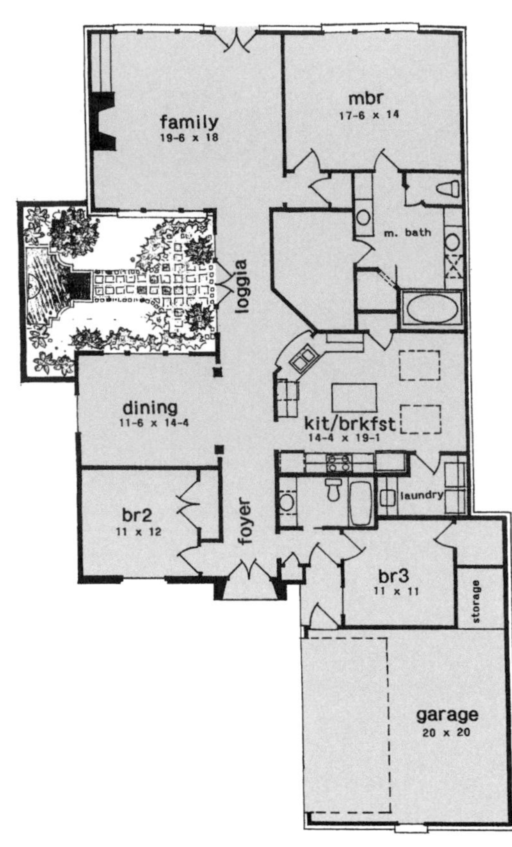

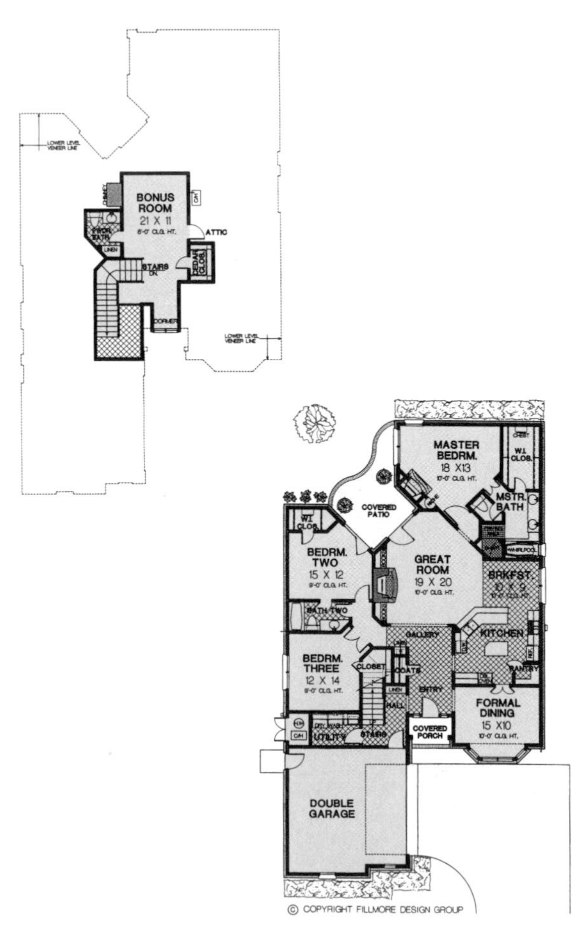

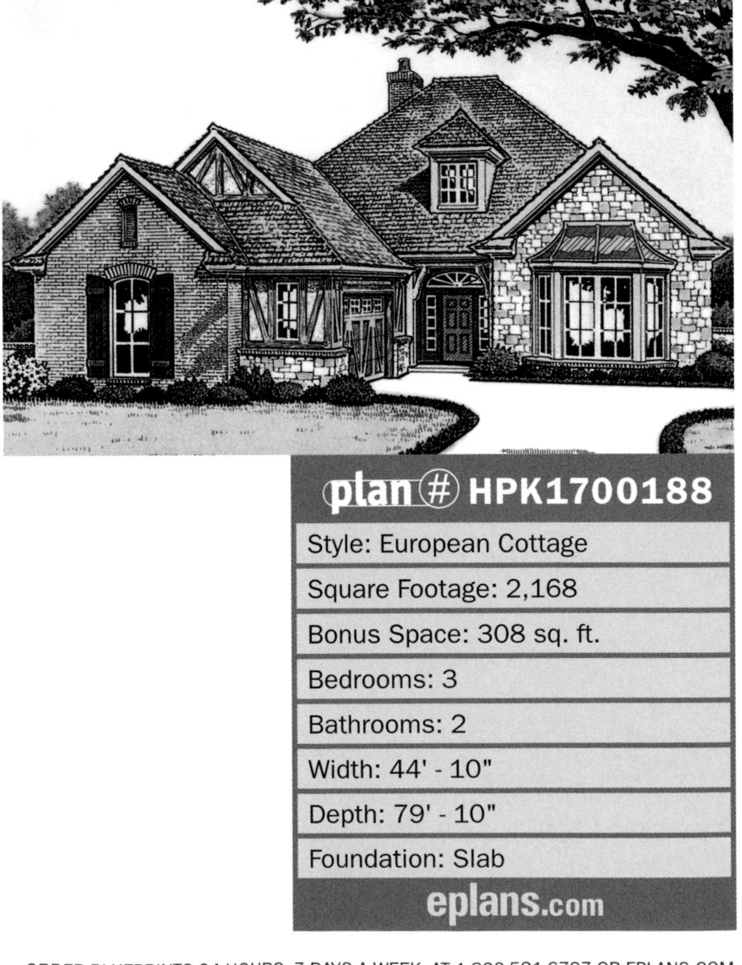

plan# HPK1700188

Style: European Cottage

Square Footage: 2,168

Bonus Space: 308 sq. ft.

Bedrooms: 3

Bathrooms: 2

Width: 44' - 10"

Depth: 79' - 10"

Foundation: Slab

eplans.com

plan# HPK1700189

Style: Country Cottage
Square Footage: 2,170
Bedrooms: 4
Bathrooms: 3
Width: 62' - 0"
Depth: 61' - 6"
Foundation: Walkout Basement

eplans.com

This classic cottage boasts a stone-and-wood exterior with a welcoming arch-top entry that leads to a columned foyer. An extended-hearth fireplace is the focal point of the family room, and a nearby sunroom with covered porch access opens up the living area to the outdoors. The gourmet island kitchen opens through double doors from the living area; the breakfast area looks out to a porch. Sleeping quarters include a master wing with a spacious, angled bath, and a sitting room or den that has its own full bath—perfect for a guest suite. On the opposite side of the plan, two family bedrooms share a full bath.

REAR EXTERIOR

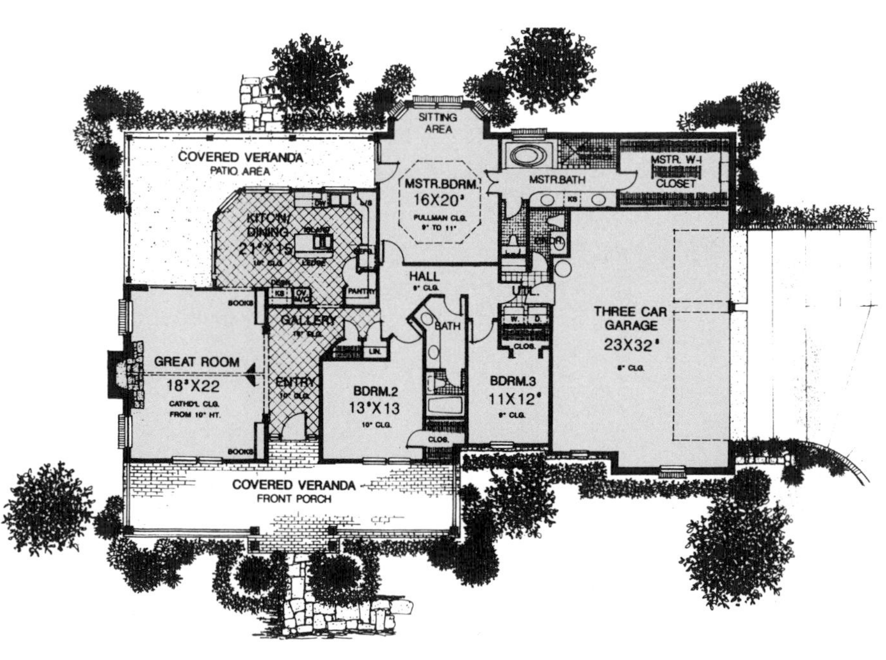

plan# HPK1700190

Style: Farmhouse

Square Footage: 2,172

Bedrooms: 3

Bathrooms: 2

Width: 79' - 0"

Depth: 47' - 0"

Foundation: Crawlspace, Slab

eplans.com

EDITOR'S PICK

We love the way this smartly dressed home caters to empty-nesters. First, the side-loading garage, mix of exterior materials, and country styling distinguish the home from curbside. Second, the single-level plan provides an extraordinary master suite that comprises more than a third of the home's total square footage, and refined transitional spaces, such as the extended foyer and hallways. Finally, outdoor living spaces at the front and back of the plan recommend relaxation and fun for you and the occasional guest.

plan# HPK1700191

Style: European Cottage
Square Footage: 2,191
Bedrooms: 3
Bathrooms: 2 ½
Width: 62' - 10"
Depth: 73' - 6"
Foundation: Slab

eplans.com

The exterior of this beautiful brick-and-stucco home is a lovely Early American rendition; inside, this plan is modern and sophisticated, designed for today's family. The entry presents a study and a dining room on either side of the foyer. The great room warms with an extended-hearth fireplace and lets in lots of natural light through three sets of French doors. An exposed-beam ceiling adds a touch of vintage elegance. The U-shaped island kitchen opens to a nook set in a deep bay. Two family bedrooms share a full bath with dual vanities. On the far left, the master suite revels in a tray ceiling, veranda access, twin walk-in closets, and a luxurious bath with a walk-in shower and whirlpool tub. Don't miss the ample storage space and utility room off the two-car, side-loading garage.

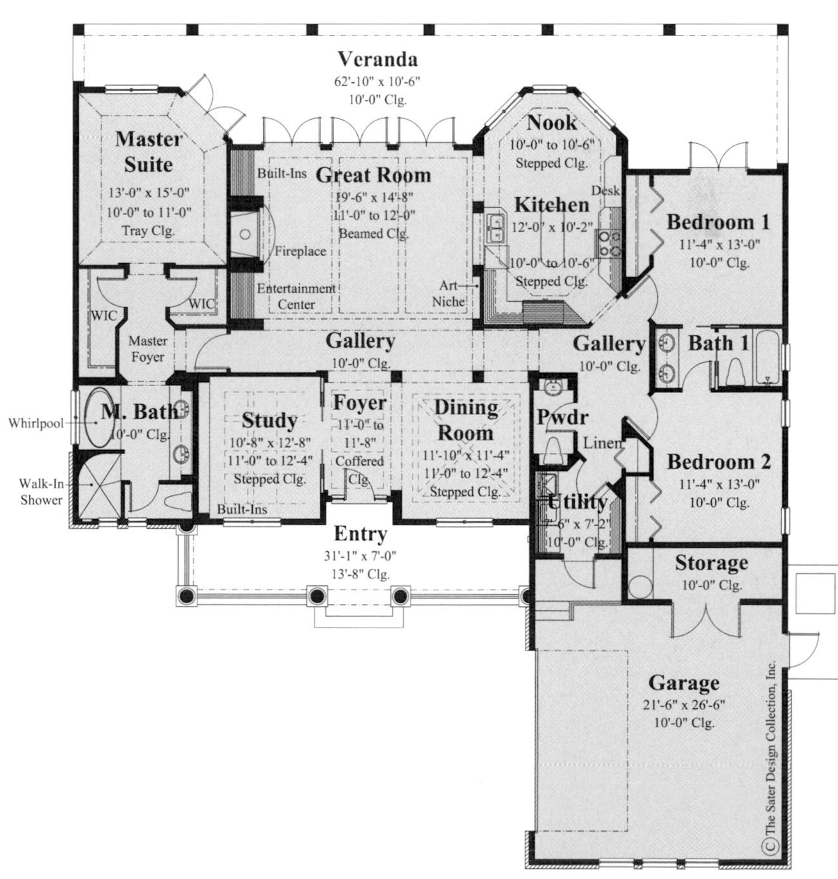

plan# HPK1700192

Style: Contemporary
Square Footage: 2,226
Bedrooms: 3
Bathrooms: 2½
Width: 103' - 1"
Depth: 71' - 11"
Foundation: Slab

eplans.com

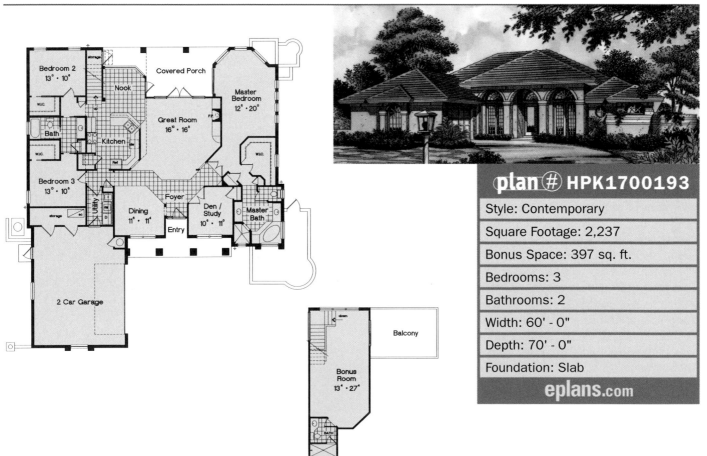

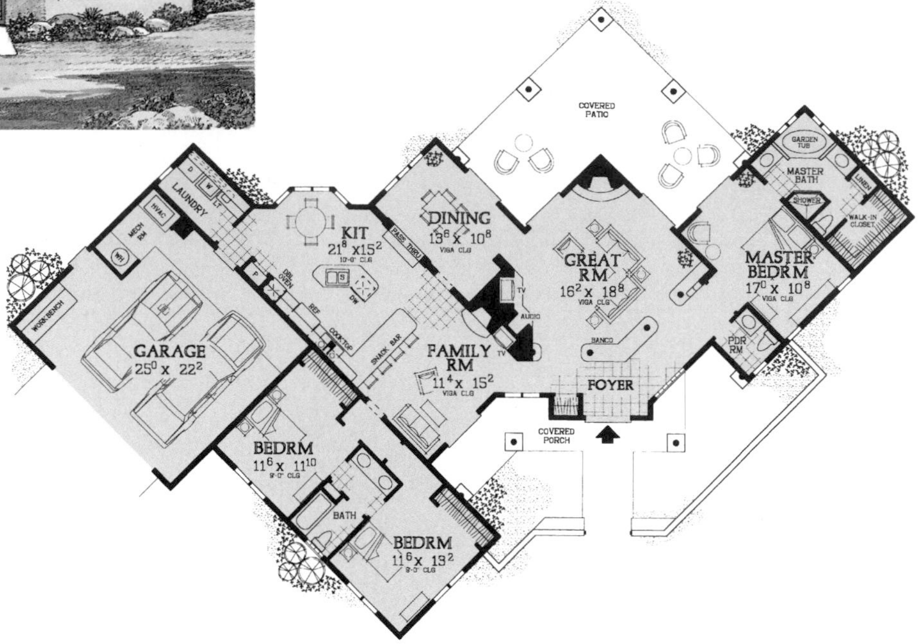

plan# HPK1700193

Style: Contemporary
Square Footage: 2,237
Bonus Space: 397 sq. ft.
Bedrooms: 3
Bathrooms: 2
Width: 60' - 0"
Depth: 70' - 0"
Foundation: Slab

eplans.com

plan# HPK1700194

Style: Mediterranean
Square Footage: 2,259
Bedrooms: 4
Bathrooms: 3
Width: 59' - 8"
Depth: 54' - 4"
Foundation: Slab

eplans.com

This 2,200+ square foot house offers four bedrooms, three full baths, and ample space for living and entertaining. Bring the outdoors in with access to the lanai from the great room, fourth bedroom, and breakfast area. The large, gourmet kitchen offers a snack bar—ideal for casual meals. Retreat to the master suite after a hard day to relax in a spacious bath with huge corner shower, dual sinks, and corner garden tub.

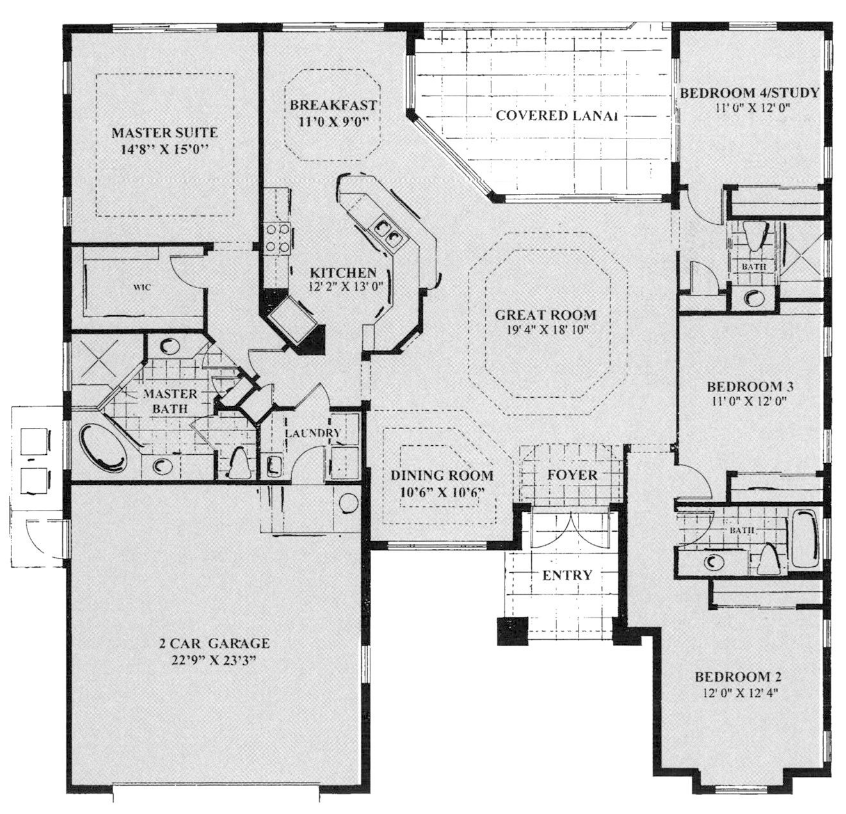

Basement Stair
Location

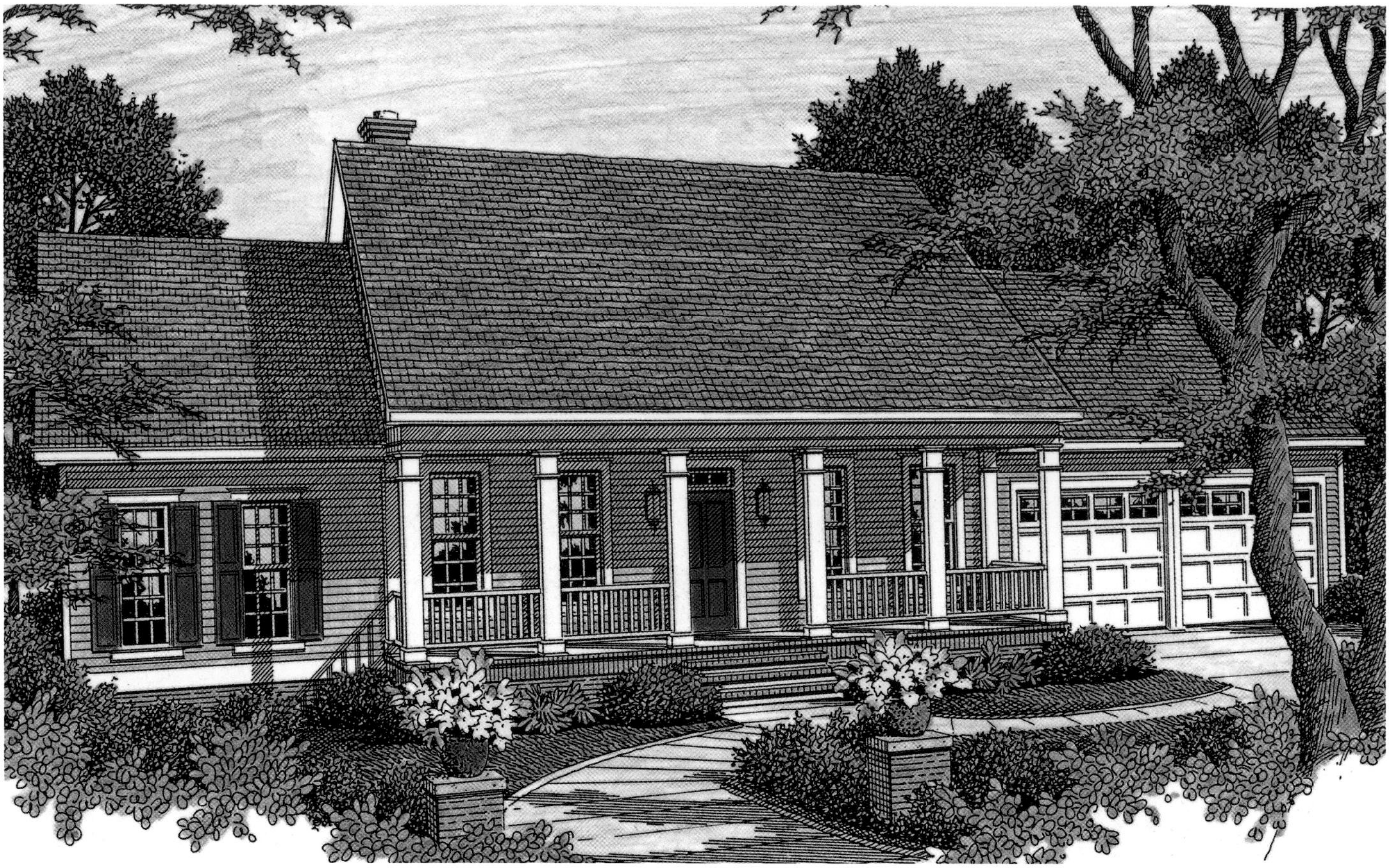

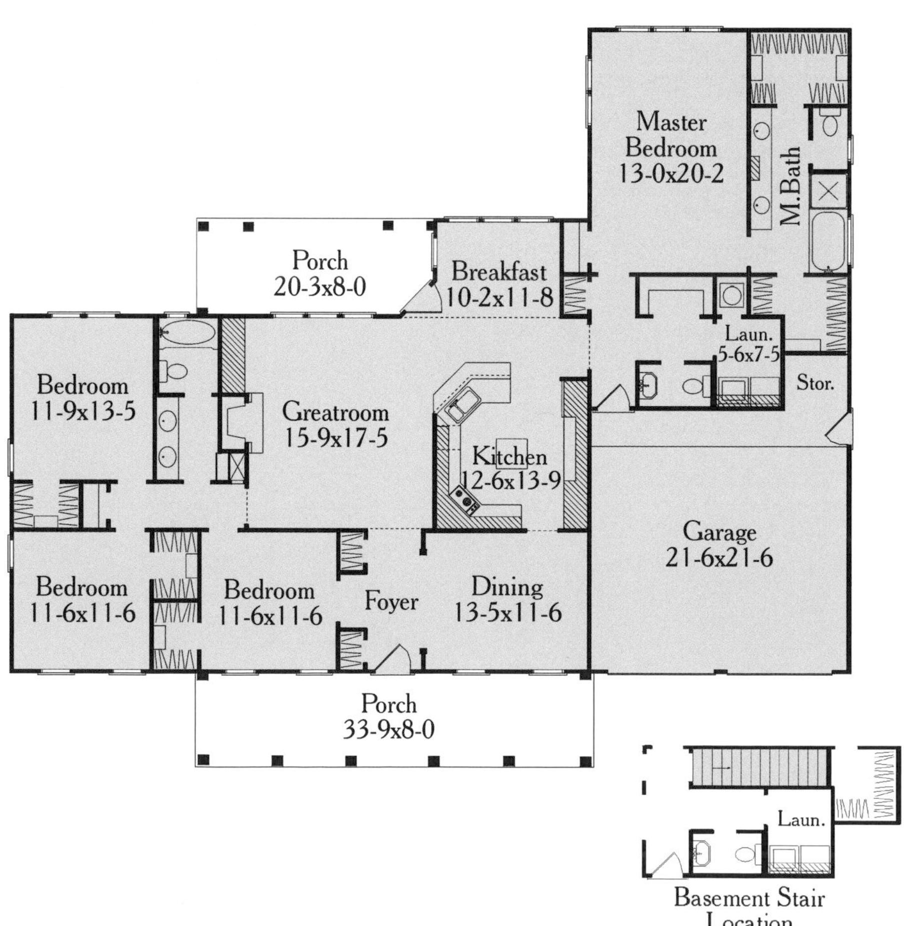

plan # HPK1700195
Style: Country Cottage
Square Footage: 2,267
Bedrooms: 4
Bathrooms: 2 ½
Width: 71' - 2"
Depth: 62' - 0"
Foundation: Unfinished Basement, Crawlspace, Slab
eplans.com

Six columns and a steeply pitched roof lend elegance to this four-bedroom home. To the right of the foyer, the dining area sits conveniently near the efficient island kitchen that enjoys plenty of work space. Natural light will flood the breakfast nook through a ribbon of windows facing the rear yard. Escape to the relaxing master bedroom, with its luxurious bath set between His and Hers walk-in closets. The great room is complete with a warming fireplace and built-ins. Three family bedrooms enjoy private walk-in closets and share a fully appointed bath.

plan# HPK1700196

- Style: Traditional
- Square Footage: 2,275
- Bonus Space: 407 sq. ft.
- Bedrooms: 3
- Bathrooms: 2 ½
- Width: 59' - 4"
- Depth: 69' - 0"
- Foundation: Crawlspace, Unfinished Walkout Basement

eplans.com

Inside this charming cottage you'll find a spacious, open floor plan that is perfect for entertaining. Fireplaces in the family room and keeping room combine to warm the adjoining kitchen and breakfast area. The practical design is ideal for family interaction. French doors lead to a covered porch, an option for outdoor dining or socializing. The master suite features tray ceilings and French-door entry into the master bath. Once inside, the master bath boasts a dual sink vanity, a garden tub, a compartmented shower and toilet, and a large walk-in closet. Two additional family bedrooms share a full bath. Upstairs houses a bonus room with a full bath and a walk-in closet. Two window seats make this a quiet retreat for a visiting guest.

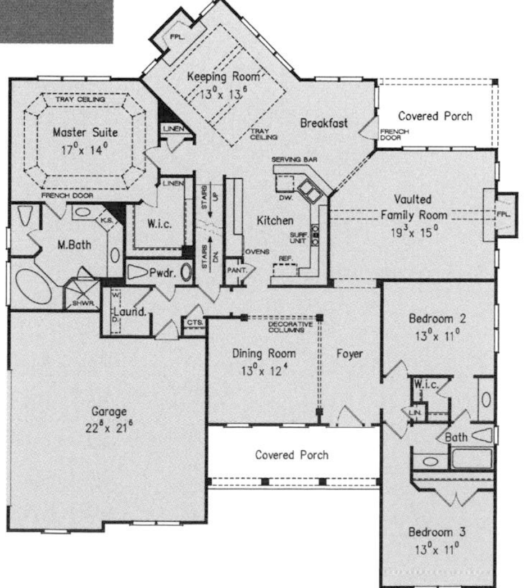

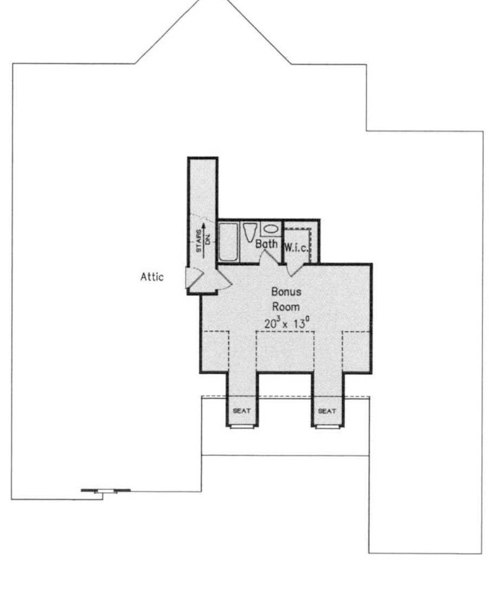

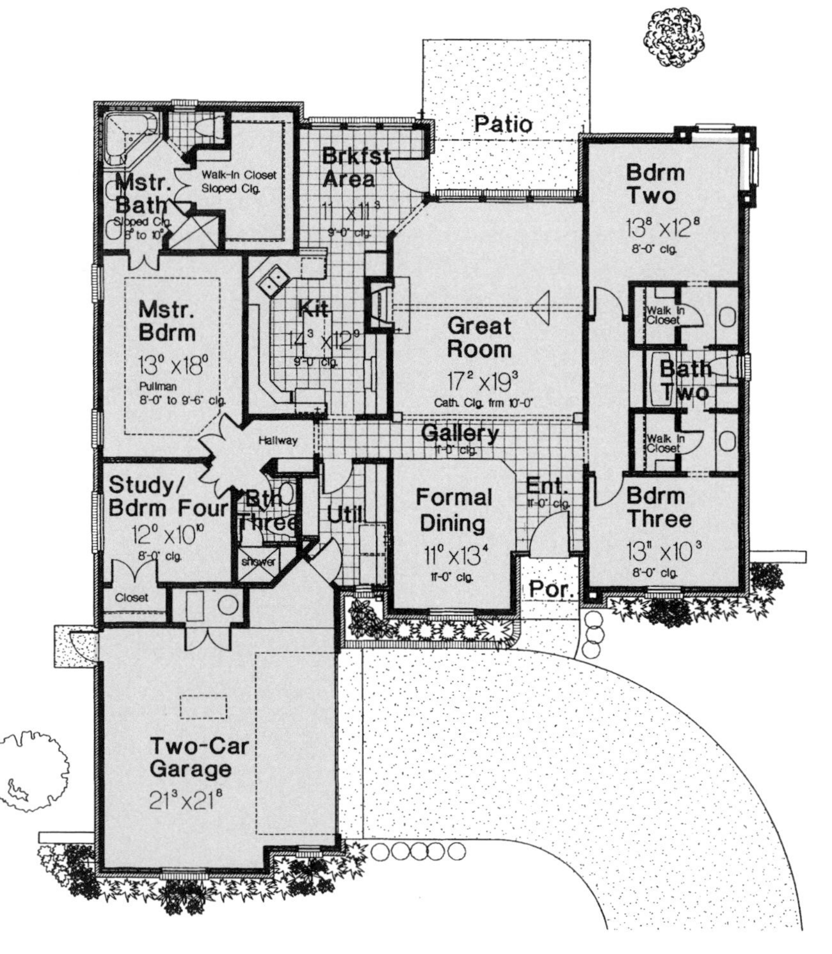

plan# HPK1700197

- Style: European Cottage
- Square Footage: 2,288
- Bedrooms: 4
- Bathrooms: 3
- Width: 57' - 5"
- Depth: 57' - 10"
- Foundation: Slab

eplans.com

Steeply pitched gables on this home's facade bring to mind quaint country churches, but this home takes quaint and pushes it to comfortable luxury. The formal dining room sits across the tiled gallery from the spacious great room. Plenty of natural light filters in from the wall of windows in the great room. To the right, two family bedrooms share a Jack-and-Jill bath and feature walk-in closets. A large kitchen, breakfast area, and utility room serve both casual and formal areas. The master suite enjoys a roomy bath and walk-in closet. An extra bedroom or study is just down the hall, close to a full bath.

plan# HPK1700198
Style: International
Square Footage: 2,293
Bonus Space: 509 sq. ft.
Bedrooms: 3
Bathrooms: 2
Width: 51' - 0"
Depth: 79' - 4"
Foundation: Slab
eplans.com

Multiple rooflines, shutters, and a charming vaulted entry lend interest and depth to the exterior of this well-designed three-bedroom home. Inside, double doors to the left open to a cozy den. The dining room, open to the family room and foyer, features a stunning ceiling design. A fireplace and patio access and view adorn the family room. Two family bedrooms share a double-sink bathroom to the right, and the master bedroom resides to the left. Note the private patio access, two walk-in closets, and luxurious bath that ensure a restful retreat for the homeowner.

REAR EXTERIOR

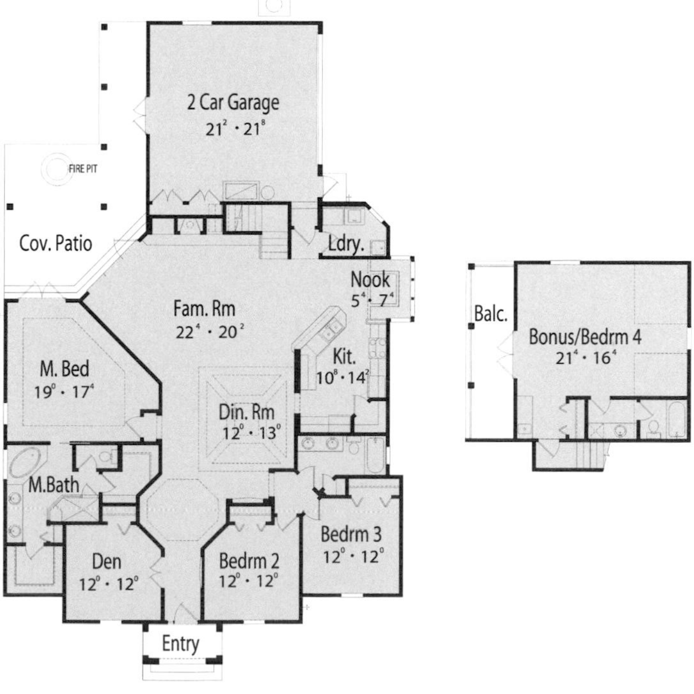

plan # HPK1700199

Style: Traditional

Square Footage: 2,311

Bedrooms: 3

Bathrooms: 2½

Width: 64' - 0"

Depth: 57' - 2"

eplans.com

Interesting details on the front porch add to the appeal of this ranch home. The great room is highlighted by a pass-through wet bar/buffet and sits just across the hall from the formal dining room. A well-planned kitchen features a walk-in pantry and L-shaped island snack bar. The bedrooms are found in a cluster to the right of the home: a master suite, and two family bedrooms sharing a full bath. The master suite has a shower with glass-block detailing, a whirlpool tub, and dual vanities. A three-car garage attaches to the main house via a service entrance.

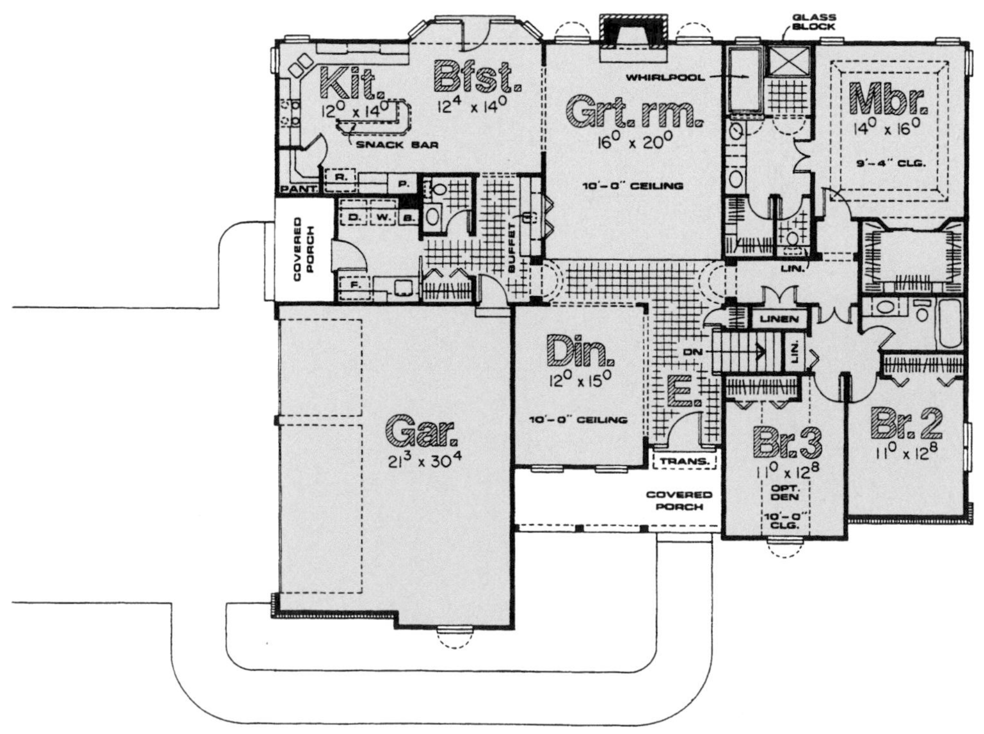

plan# HPK1700200

Style: Country Cottage

Square Footage: 2,322

Bedrooms: 3

Bathrooms: 2½

Width: 62' - 0"

Depth: 61' - 0"

Foundation: Crawlspace, Slab, Unfinished Walkout Basement

eplans.com

An eclectic mix of building materials—stone, stucco, and siding—sings in tune with the European charm of this one-story home. Within, decorative columns set off the formal dining room and the foyer from the vaulted family room; the formal living room is quietly tucked behind French doors. The gourmet kitchen provides an angled snack bar and a sunny breakfast room. Two family bedrooms each have a walk-in closet and private access to a shared bath. The master suite holds an elegant tray ceiling, a bay sitting area, and a lush bath.

COURTYARD
COVERED PORCH
BEDROOM
11⁰ X 11⁰
BATH
BEDROOM
10⁶ X 11⁶
BRKFST
9⁸ x 11⁰
KITCHEN
10⁶ X 14⁰
FAMILY RM
11⁰ X 10⁴
DINING RM
11⁴ x 9⁰
3 CAR GARAGE
29⁶ x 21⁶
SKYLIGHT
FOYER
ENTRY COURTYARD
LIVING RM
12⁰ X 17⁰
STUDY
11² X 11⁰
MASTER BEDROOM
14⁰ X 13⁰
WALK-IN CLOSET
MASTER BATH

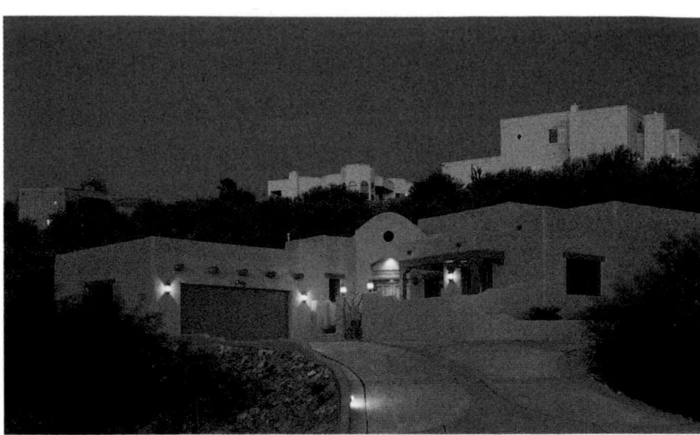

plan# HPK1700201

Style: Santa Fe
Square Footage: 2,350
Bedrooms: 3
Bathrooms: 2½
Width: 92' - 7"
Depth: 79' - 0"
Foundation: Slab

eplans.com

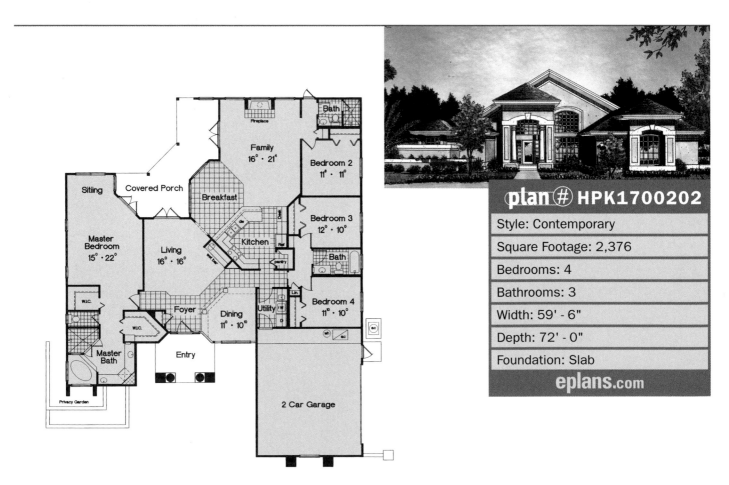

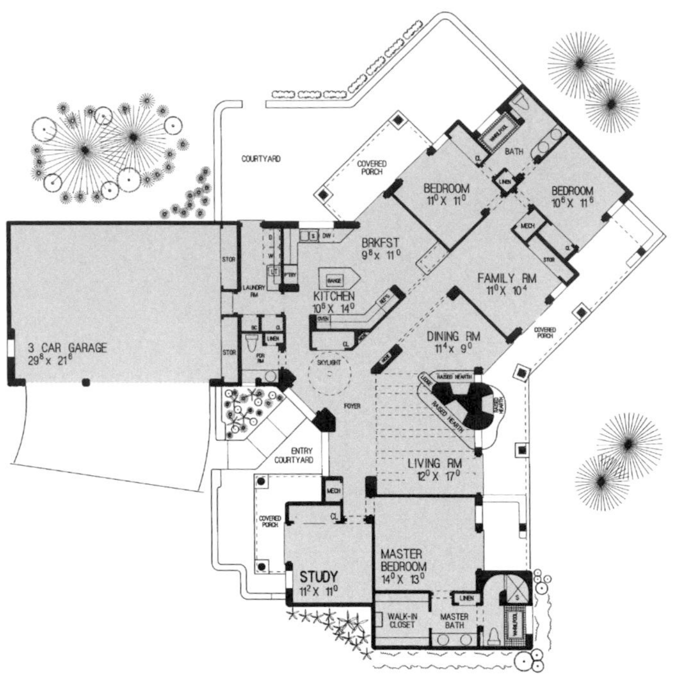

Bath
Fireplace
Family
16° · 21⁴
Bedroom 2
11⁶ · 11°
Sitiing
Covered Porch
Breakfast
Bedroom 3
12° · 10°
Master Bedroom
15° · 22°
Living
16° · 16°
Kitchen
Bath
W.I.C.
Foyer
Dining
11° · 10¹⁰
Utility
Bedroom 4
11¹⁰ · 10°
W.I.C.
Master Bath
Entry
Privacy Garden
2 Car Garage

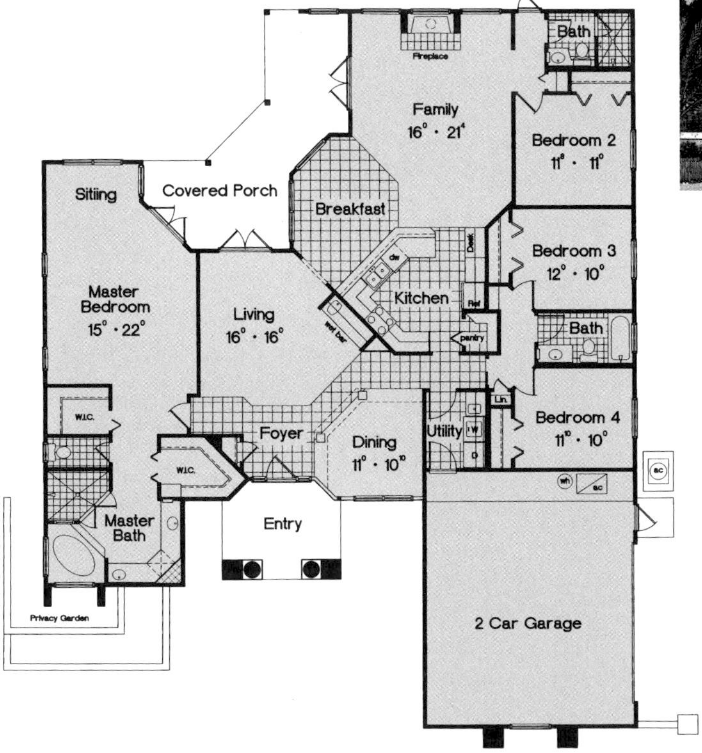

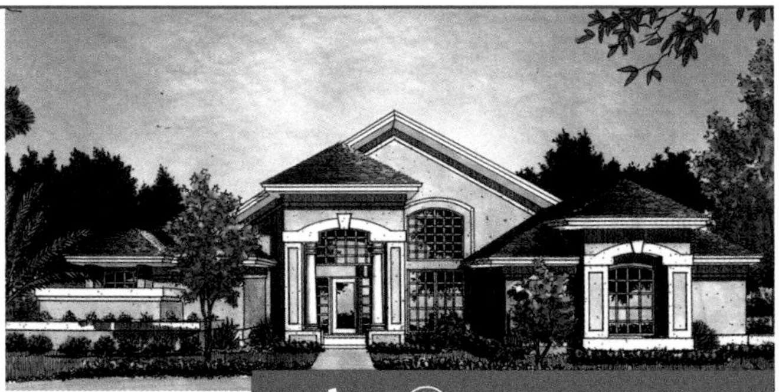

plan# HPK1700202

Style: Contemporary
Square Footage: 2,376
Bedrooms: 4
Bathrooms: 3
Width: 59' - 6"
Depth: 72' - 0"
Foundation: Slab

eplans.com

© The Sater Design Collection, Inc.

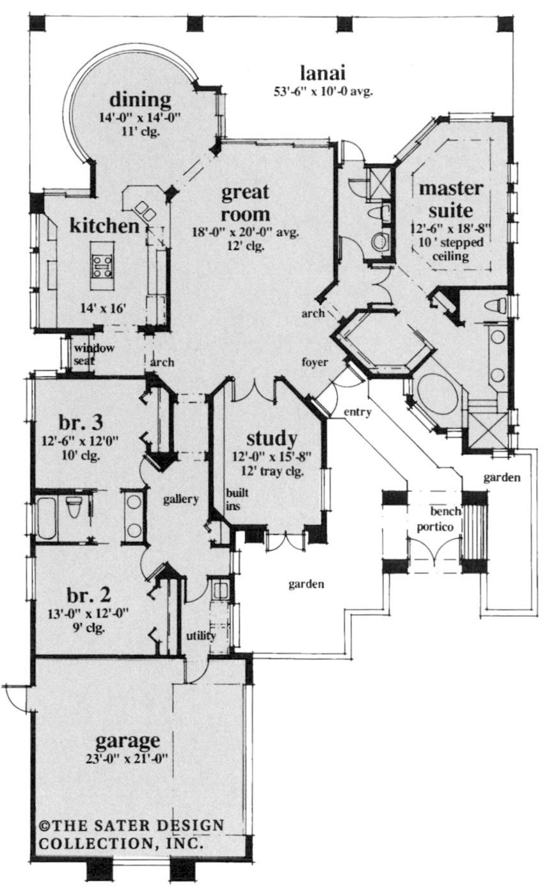

plan # HPK1700203

Style: Contemporary
Square Footage: 2,387
Bedrooms: 3
Bathrooms: 3
Width: 53' - 6"
Depth: 94' - 6"
Foundation: Slab

eplans.com

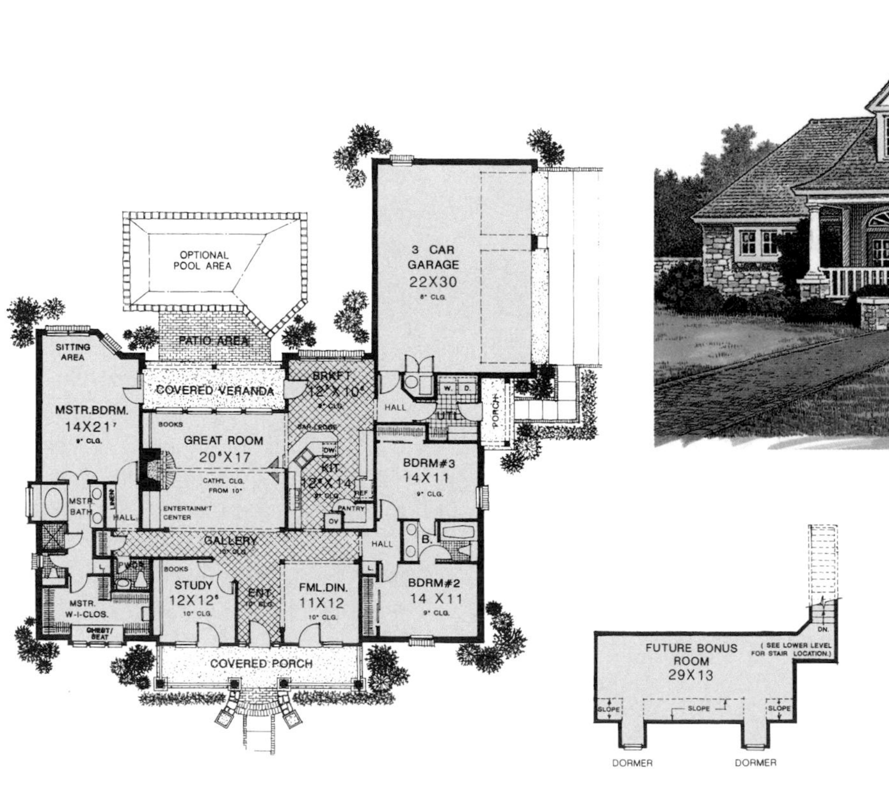

plan # HPK1700204

Style: Craftsman
Square Footage: 2,387
Bonus Space: 377 sq. ft.
Bedrooms: 3
Bathrooms: 2½
Width: 69' - 6"
Depth: 68' - 11"
Foundation: Slab, Crawlspace

eplans.com

plan# HPK1700205

Style: European Cottage

Square Footage: 2,388

Bedrooms: 3

Bathrooms: 2½

Width: 63' - 0"

Depth: 60' - 0"

Foundation: Crawlspace, Unfinished Walkout Basement, Slab

eplans.com

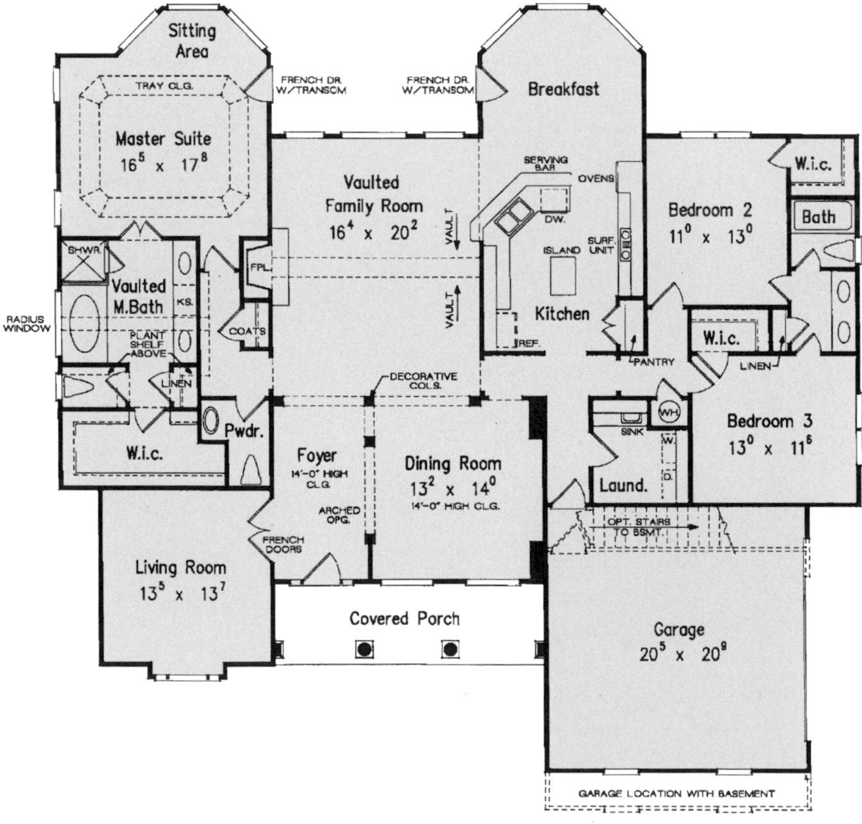

Quoins, arched lintels, and twin pedimented dormers lend this house a sweet country feel. Columns and a vaulted ceiling make the interior elegant. French doors lead to a living room found at the left of the entrance, and decorative columns adorn the elegant dining room. The spacious family room is enhanced by the vaulted ceiling and cozy fireplace. Two lovely bay windows embellish the rear of the house. The island kitchen features a roomy pantry, a serving bar, and a breakfast area with a French door that opens to the outside through a transom. The master suite boasts a tray ceiling, sitting area, a deluxe bath with built-in plant shelves, a radius window, dual vanities, and a large walk-in closet.

plan# HPK1700206

Style: Country Cottage
Square Footage: 2,400
Bonus Space: 845 sq. ft.
Bedrooms: 3
Bathrooms: 2½
Width: 61' - 0"
Depth: 70' - 6"
Foundation: Unfinished Walkout Basement, Crawlspace

eplans.com

Decorative columns can be found throughout, beginning with the covered front porch. Once inside, the foyer opens to the dining room on the right, and the family room straight ahead. Enhanced by a coffered ceiling and built-in cabinets, a fireplace warms the space. A bay window view of the backyard extends private living space to the outdoors. Entry to the vaulted master suite reveals a walk-in closet, roomy bath with dual-sink vanities, separate shower and tub, and a private toilet. A serving bar in the kitchen allows for casual meals and easy interaction between the breakfast area and family room. Two additional family bedrooms share a full bath. Upstairs, a fourth bedroom and full bath, possible guest quarters, and a bonus room complete the plan.

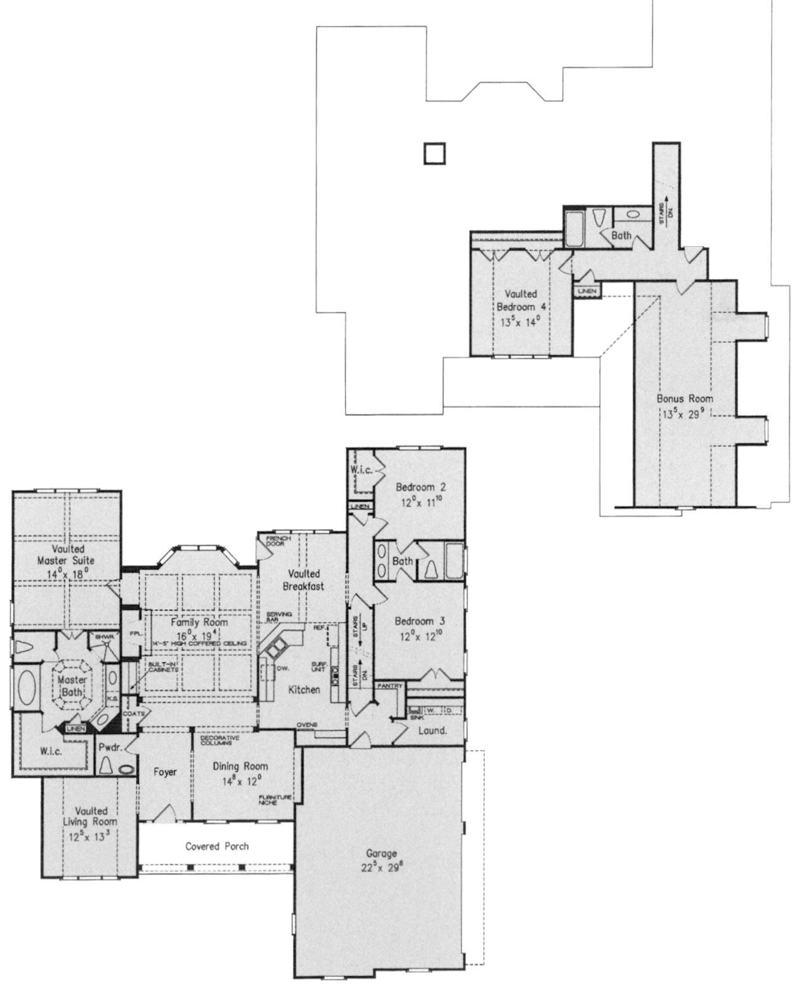

plan # HPK1700207

- Style: Country Cottage
- Square Footage: 2,403
- Bonus Space: 285 sq. ft.
- Bedrooms: 3
- Bathrooms: 2½
- Width: 60' - 0"
- Depth: 67' - 0"
- Foundation: Crawlspace, Slab, Unfinished Walkout Basement

eplans.com

Asymmetrical gables, pediments, and tall, arch-top windows accent a European-style exterior; inside, an unrestrained floor plan expresses its independence. A spider-beam ceiling and a centered fireplace framed by shelves redraw the open space of the family room to cozy dimensions. The vaulted breakfast nook enjoys a radius window and a French door that leads outside. Split sleeping quarters lend privacy to the luxurious master suite.

plan# HPK1700208
Style: NW Contemporary
Square Footage: 2,412
Bedrooms: 3
Bathrooms: 2½
Width: 60' - 0"
Depth: 59' - 0"
Foundation: Slab
eplans.com

This gorgeous design would easily accommodate a sloping lot. With windows and glass panels to take in the view, this design would make an exquisite seaside resort. A grand great room sets the tone inside, with an elegant tray ceiling and French doors to a private front balcony. The formal dining room is off the center of the plan for quiet elegance and is served by a nearby gourmet kitchen. Three steps up from the foyer, the sleeping level includes a spacious master suite with a sizable private bath. The two additional bedrooms access a shared bath with two vanities.

FIRST FLOOR

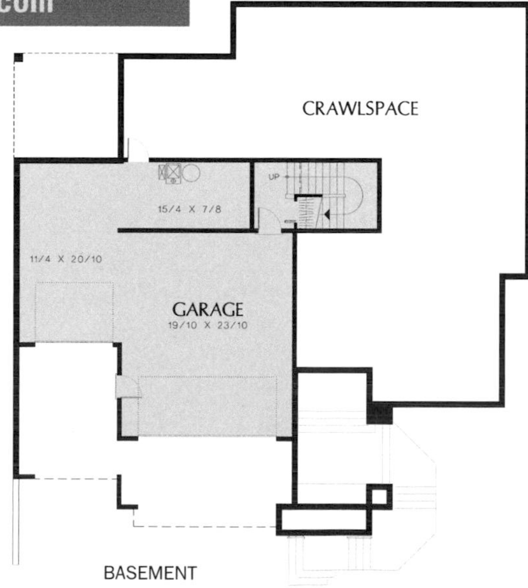

BASEMENT

plan# HPK1700209

Style: Traditional
Square Footage: 2,452
Bedrooms: 3
Bathrooms: 2½
Width: 70' - 8"
Depth: 70' - 0"
Foundation: Unfinished Basement

eplans.com

The large front window highlights the elegance of this home's exterior. The windows pour natural light into the cheery and spacious home office, which includes a private entrance, guest bath, two closets, and vaulted ceiling. The delightful great room features a vaulted ceiling, a fireplace, extra storage closets, and patio doors to the sun deck. An extra-large kitchen contains a walk-in pantry, cooktop island, and bay window. The vaulted master suite includes transomed windows, a walk-in closet, and a luxurious bath.

plan# HPK1700210
Style: Farmhouse
Square Footage: 2,454
Bonus Space: 256 sq. ft.
Bedrooms: 3
Bathrooms: 2
Width: 80' - 6"
Depth: 66' - 6"
Foundation: Crawlspace
eplans.com

DESIGN NOTE

The mix of traditional and European elements in the exterior of this home—the hipped roof, the symmetrical entryway, the arched windows—hints at the style of living you'll find inside. The sprawling one-story plan incorporates an extended foyer and hallway that runs the width of the home and brings natural light to the central spaces. Similarly, the great room and study look to the rear of the plan, where more windows and French doors open brightly to the porch. The combined effect is a sunny, outdoor spirit at the center of the home and great views wherever you turn.

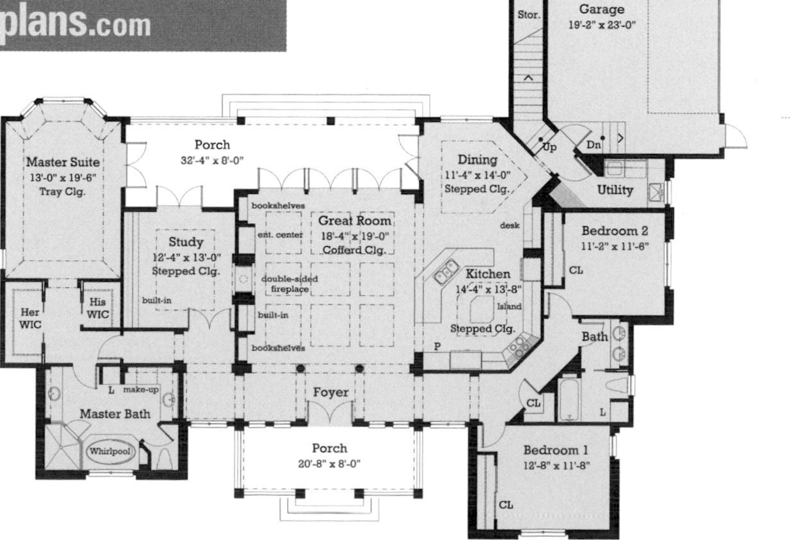

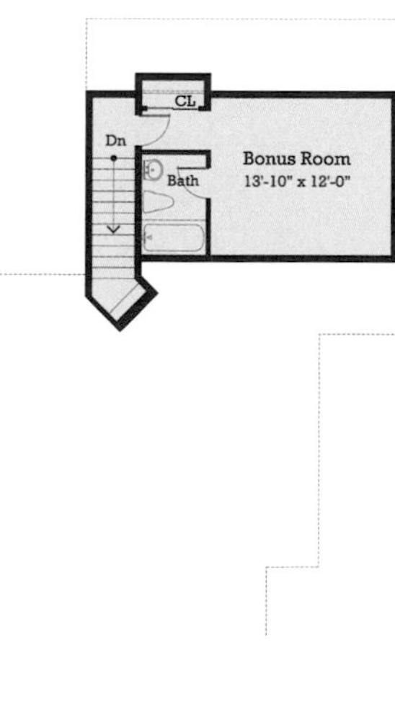

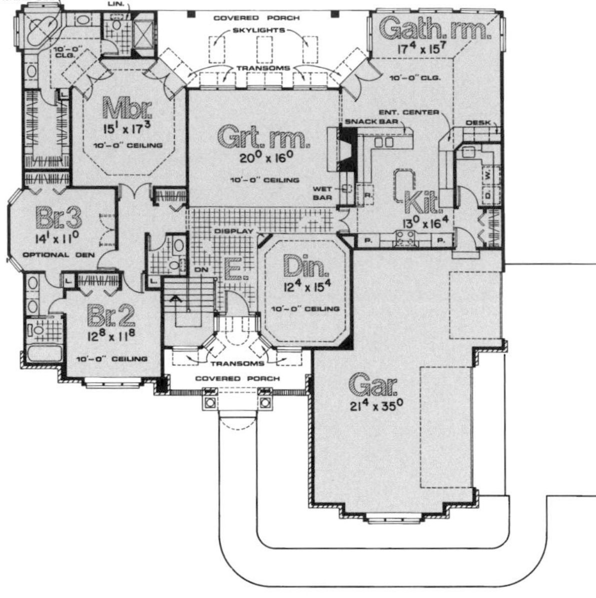

plan# HPK1700211
Style: Traditional
Square Footage: 2,456
Bedrooms: 3
Bathrooms: 2½
Width: 66' - 0"
Depth: 68' - 0"
eplans.com

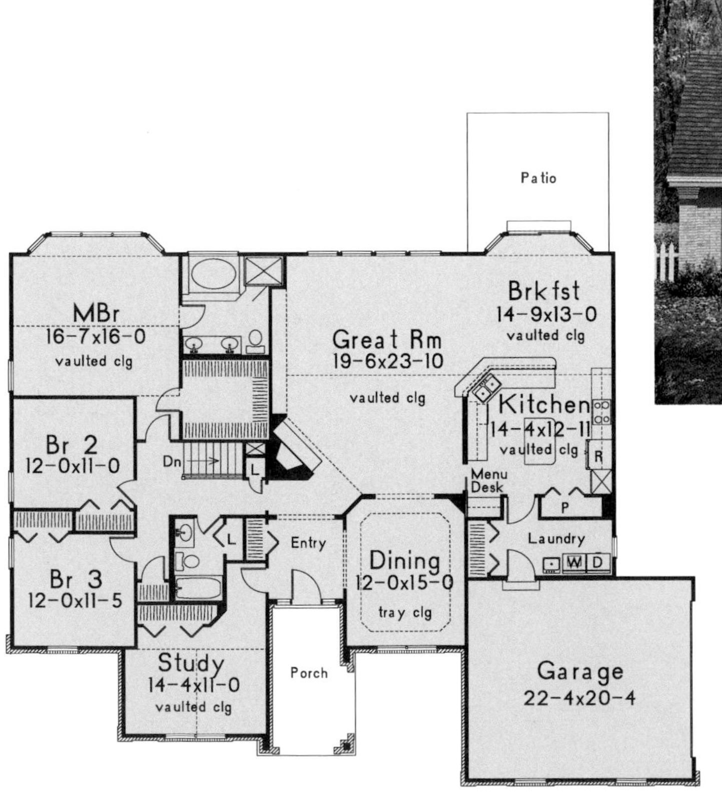

plan# HPK1700212
Style: Traditional
Square Footage: 2,483
Bedrooms: 3
Bathrooms: 2
Width: 69' - 0"
Depth: 53' - 8"
Foundation: Unfinished Basement
eplans.com

plan# HPK1700213

Style: Bungalow
Square Footage: 2,489
Bedrooms: 3
Bathrooms: 2½
Width: 68' - 3"
Depth: 62' - 0"
Foundation: Walkout Basement

eplans.com

This fine bungalow, with its multiple gables, rafter tails, and pillared front porch, will be the envy of any neighborhood. A beam-ceilinged great room is further enhanced by a through-fireplace and French doors to the rear terrace. The U-shaped kitchen features a cooktop island with a snack bar and offers a beam-ceilinged breakfast/keeping room that shares the through-fireplace with the great room. Two secondary bedrooms share a full bath; the master suite is designed to pamper. Here, the homeowner will be pleased with a walk-in closet, a separate shower, and access to the terrace. The two-car garage has a side entrance and will easily shelter the family fleet.

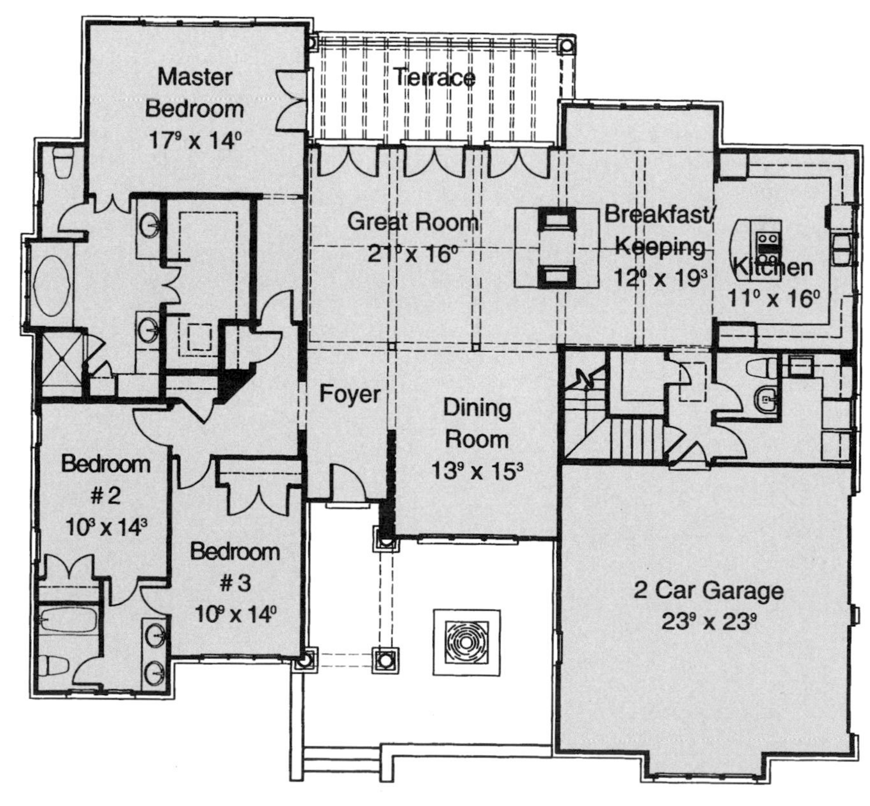

European details bring charm and a bit of joie de vivre to this traditional home, and a thoughtful floor plan warms up to a myriad of lifestyles. Comfortable living space includes a vaulted family room with a centered fireplace that complements the formal dining room, which offers a tray ceiling. A sizable gourmet kitchen contains a walk-in pantry and a center cooktop island counter and overlooks the breakfast area, which opens to a secluded covered porch through a French door. The master suite features a tray ceiling and a private sitting room, bright with windows and a warming hearth.

plan# HPK1700214
Style: Country Cottage
Square Footage: 2,491
Bonus Space: 588 sq. ft.
Bedrooms: 3
Bathrooms: 2½
Width: 64' - 0"
Depth: 72' - 4"
Foundation: Crawlspace, Slab, Unfinished Walkout Basement
eplans.com

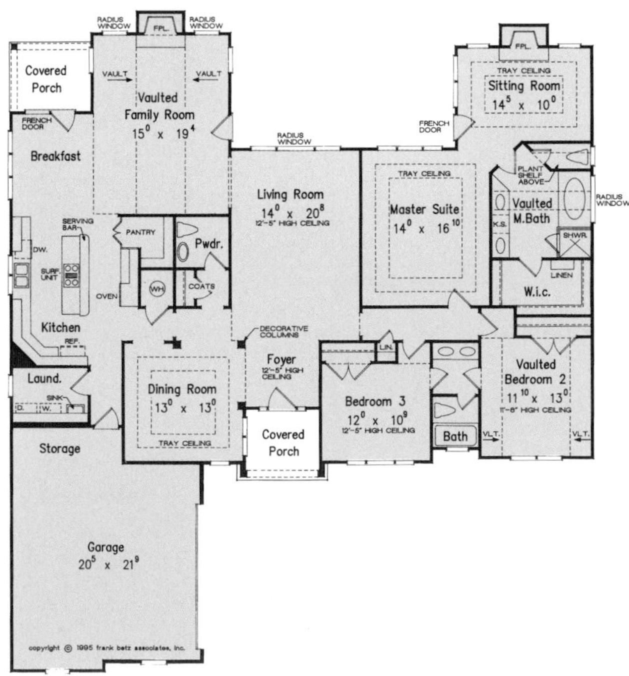

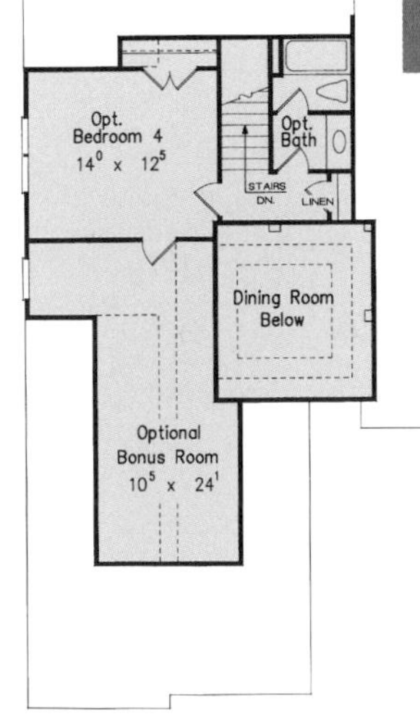

plan # HPK1700215

Style: Farmhouse
First Floor: 1,383 sq. ft.
Second Floor: 703 sq. ft.
Total: 2,086 sq. ft.
Bonus Space: 342 sq. ft.
Bedrooms: 4
Bathrooms: 3½
Width: 49' - 0"
Depth: 50' - 0"

eplans.com

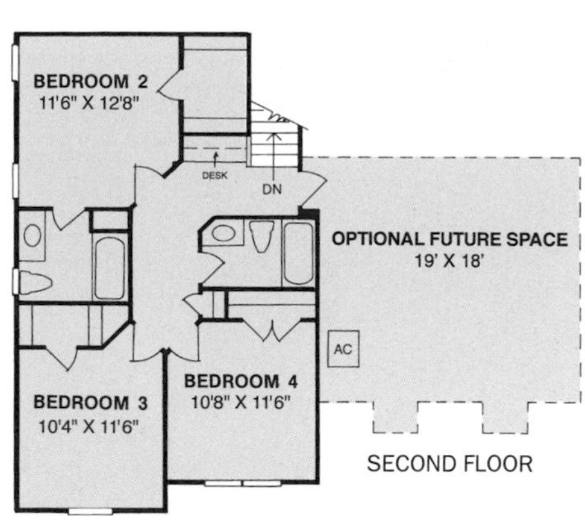

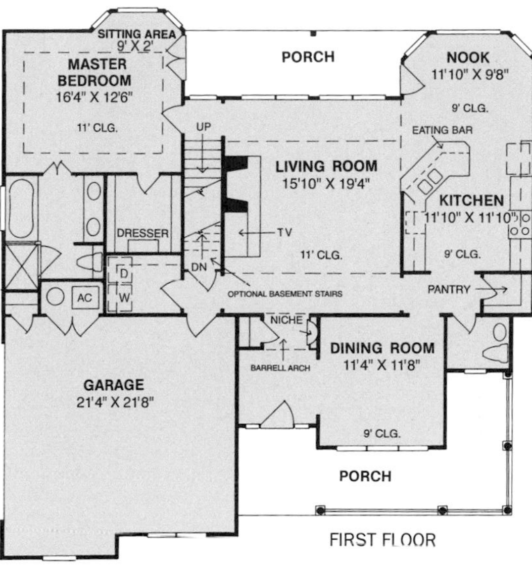

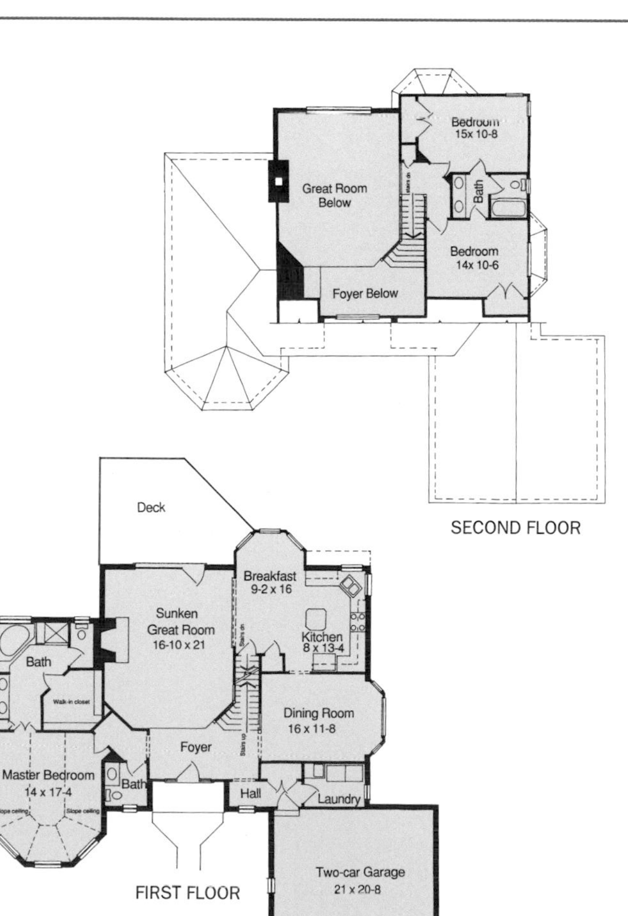

plan # HPK1700216

Style: Cape Cod
First Floor: 1,626 sq. ft.
Second Floor: 475 sq. ft.
Total: 2,101 sq. ft.
Bedrooms: 3
Bathrooms: 2½
Width: 59' - 0"
Depth: 60' - 8"
Foundation: Unfinished Basement

eplans.com

plan# HPK1700217

Style: Country Cottage
First Floor: 1,581 sq. ft.
Second Floor: 534 sq. ft.
Total: 2,115 sq. ft.
Bonus Space: 250 sq. ft.
Bedrooms: 3
Bathrooms: 2½
Width: 53' - 0"
Depth: 43' - 4"
Foundation: Crawlspace, Unfinished Walkout Basement

eplans.com

Behind the gables and arched windows of this fine traditional home lies a great floor plan. The two-story foyer leads past a formal dining room defined by decorative pillars to a vaulted family room with a fireplace. The L-shaped kitchen is open to the sunny breakfast nook and provides access to the rear property. The lavish master suite is separated from the two upper-level bedrooms. Optional bonus space on the second floor invites the possibility of a recreation room, exercise room, or media room.

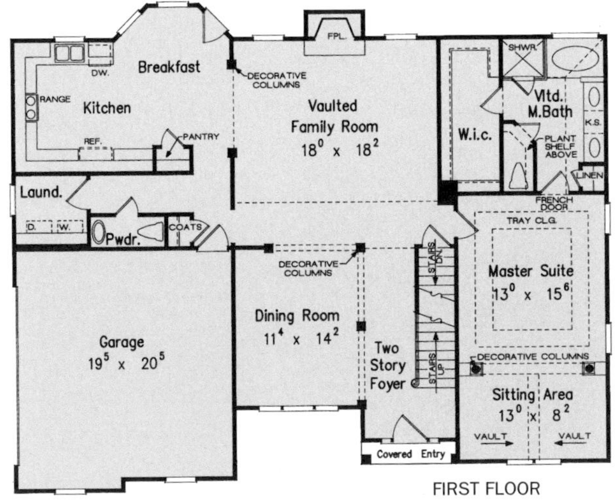

FIRST FLOOR

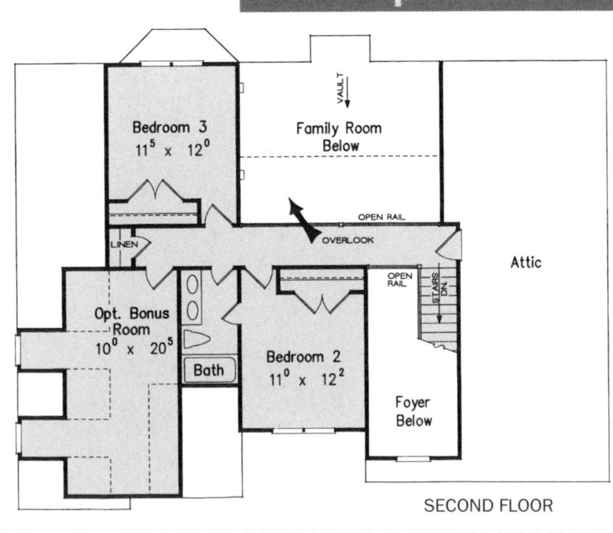

SECOND FLOOR

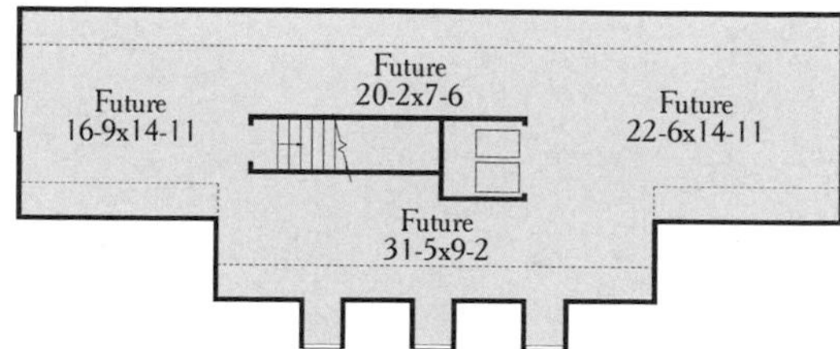

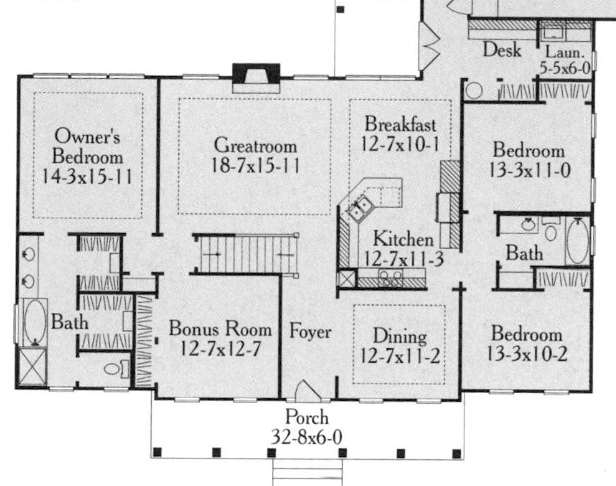

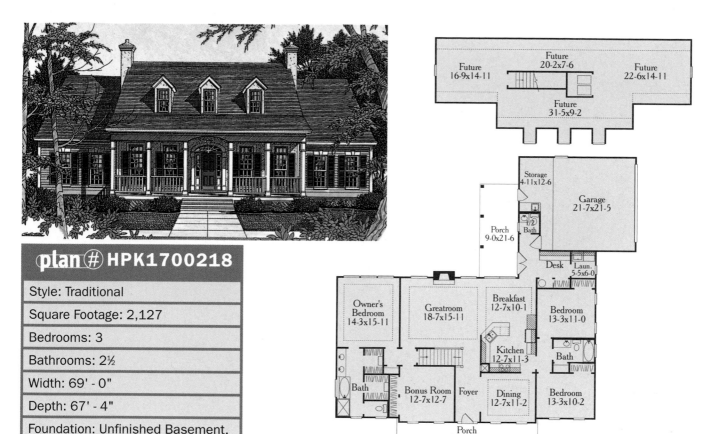

plan # HPK1700218

Style: Traditional
Square Footage: 2,127
Bedrooms: 3
Bathrooms: 2½
Width: 69' - 0"
Depth: 67' - 4"
Foundation: Unfinished Basement, Slab, Crawlspace

eplans.com

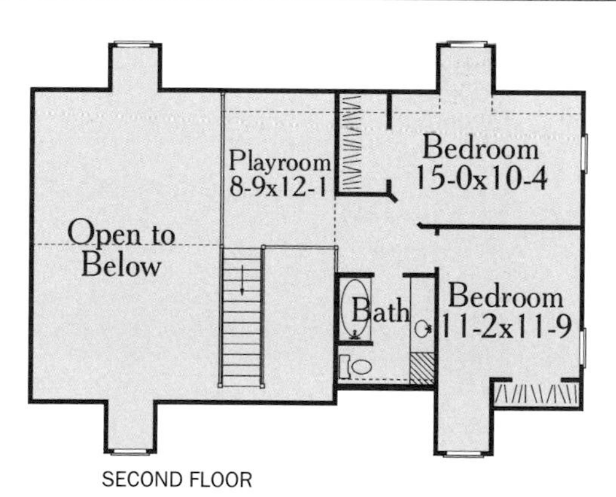

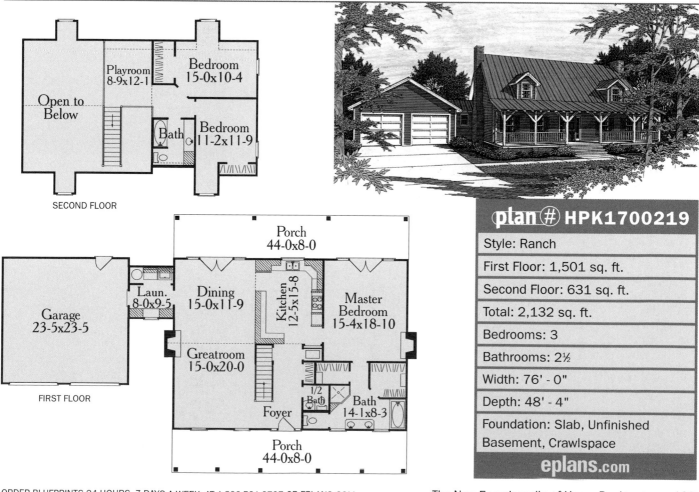

SECOND FLOOR

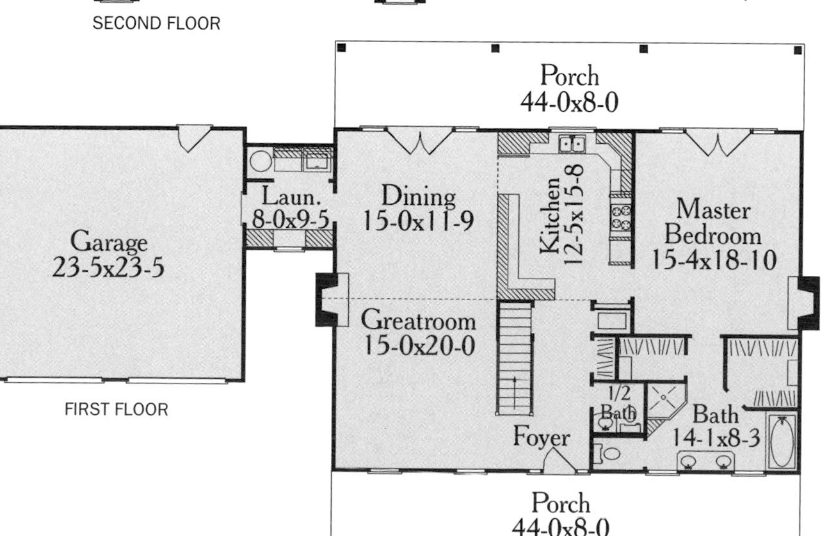

FIRST FLOOR

plan # HPK1700219

Style: Ranch
First Floor: 1,501 sq. ft.
Second Floor: 631 sq. ft.
Total: 2,132 sq. ft.
Bedrooms: 3
Bathrooms: 2½
Width: 76' - 0"
Depth: 48' - 4"
Foundation: Slab, Unfinished Basement, Crawlspace

eplans.com

plan# HPK1700220
Style: Country Cottage
First Floor: 1,561 sq. ft.
Second Floor: 578 sq. ft.
Total: 2,139 sq. ft.
Bonus Space: 284 sq. ft.
Bedrooms: 3
Bathrooms: 2½
Width: 50' - 0"
Depth: 57' - 0"
Foundation: Crawlspace, Finished Walkout Basement
eplans.com

Nostalgic and earthy, this Craftsman design has an attractive floor plan and thoughtful amenties. A column-lined covered porch is the perfect welcome to guests. A large vaulted family room, enhanced by a fireplace, opens to the spacious island kitchen and roomy breakfast area. The private master suite is embellished with a vaulted ceiling, walk-in closet, and vaulted super bath with French-door entry. With family in mind, two secondary bedrooms—each with a walk-in closet—share a computer workstation or loft area. A bonus room can be used as bedroom or home office.

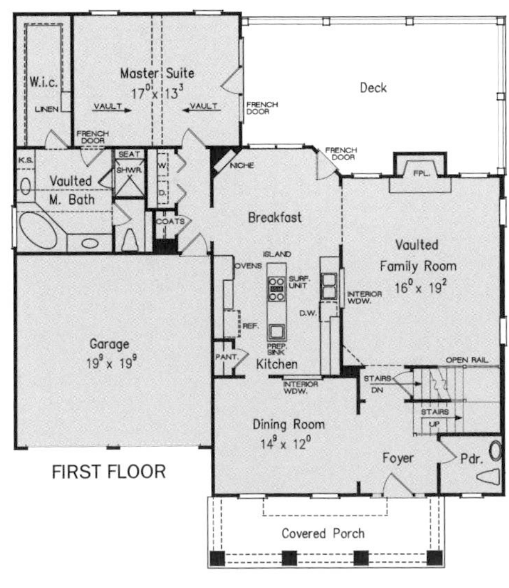

FIRST FLOOR

Optional Bonus Room 14⁹ x 11⁹
Bedroom 3 13⁰ x 12⁴
Family Room Below
Bath
Bedroom 2 12³ x 11⁶

SECOND FLOOR

plan # HPK1700221

Style: Country Cottage
First Floor: 1,688 sq. ft.
Second Floor: 558 sq. ft.
Total: 2,246 sq. ft.
Bonus Space: 269 sq. ft.
Bedrooms: 4
Bathrooms: 3
Width: 54' - 0"
Depth: 48' - 0"
Foundation: Crawlspace, Slab, Unfinished Walkout Basement

eplans.com

Graceful details combine with a covered entryway to welcome friends and family to come on in. The canted bay sitting area in the master suite provides sunny respite and quiet solitude. To be the center of attention, invite everyone to party in the vaulted great room, which spills over into the big, airy kitchen. Guests can make use of the optional study/bedroom. Upstairs, secondary bedrooms share a full bath and a balcony overlook. A spacious central hall leads to a bonus room that provides wardrobe space.

SECOND FLOOR

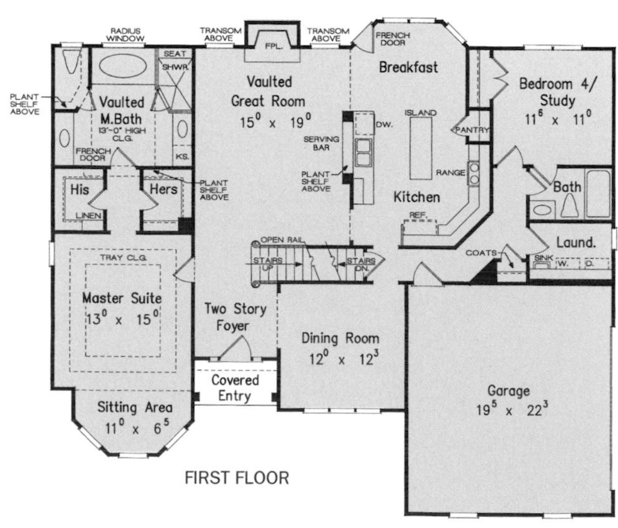

FIRST FLOOR

REAR EXTERIOR

With three dormers and a welcoming front door accented by sidelights and a sunburst, this country cottage is sure to please. The dining room, immediately to the right from the foyer, is defined by decorative columns. In the great room, a volume ceiling heightens the space and showcases a fireplace and built-in bookshelves. The kitchen has plenty of work space and flows into the bayed breakfast nook. A considerate split-bedroom design places the plush master suite to the far left and two family bedrooms to the far right. A fourth bedroom and future space upstairs allow room to grow.

plan# HPK1700222
Style: Country Cottage
First Floor: 1,981 sq. ft.
Second Floor: 291 sq. ft.
Total: 2,272 sq. ft.
Bonus Space: 412 sq. ft.
Bedrooms: 4
Bathrooms: 3½
Width: 58' - 0"
Depth: 53' - 0"
Foundation: Crawlspace
eplans.com

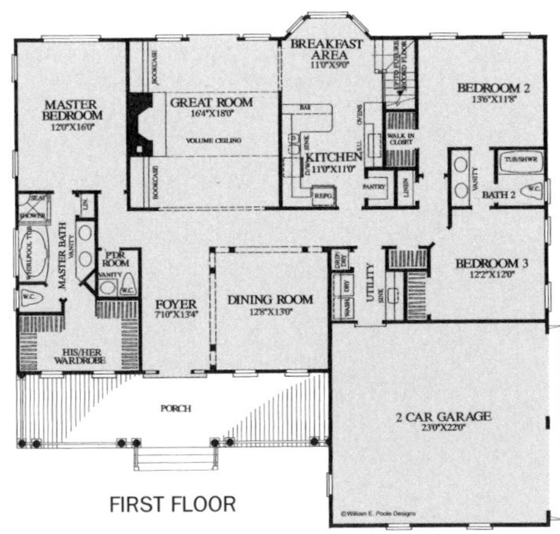

FIRST FLOOR

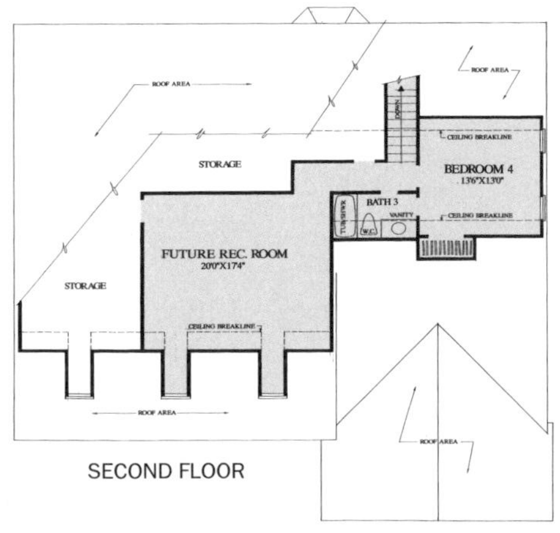

SECOND FLOOR

plan# HPK1700223

Style: Craftsman
First Floor: 1,761 sq. ft.
Second Floor: 577 sq. ft.
Total: 2,338 sq. ft.
Bonus Space: 305 sq. ft.
Bedrooms: 4
Bathrooms: 3
Width: 56' - 0"
Depth: 48' - 0"
Foundation: Crawlspace, Unfinished Walkout Basement

eplans.com

Craftsman-style pillars lend a country look to this Cape Cod-style home. An elegant entry opens to the vaulted family room, where a fireplace warms and bright windows illuminate. The kitchen is designed for the true chef, with step-saving orientation and a serving bar to the vaulted breakfast nook. A bedroom nearby is ideal for a home office or live-in help. The master suite is on the left, pampering with a vaulted bath and enormous walk-in closet. Two bedrooms upstairs share a full bath and an optional bonus room.

SECOND FLOOR

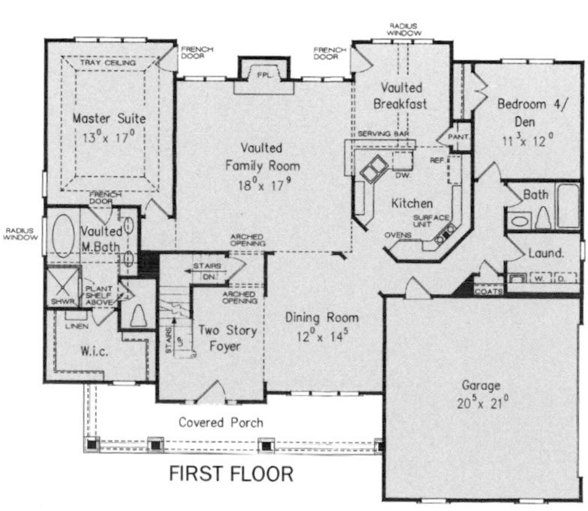

FIRST FLOOR

CHRIS A. LITTLE

plan# HPK1700224

Style: Traditional
First Floor: 2,348 sq. ft.
Second Floor: 80 sq. ft.
Total: 2,428 sq. ft.
Bonus Space: 860 sq. ft.
Bedrooms: 3
Bathrooms: 2½
Width: 70' - 10"
Depth: 65' - 4"
Foundation: Crawlspace, Slab, Unfinished Basement
eplans.com

Traditional charm complements a contemporary interior. The foyer allows direct access to the central great room and the formal dining room. The great room enjoys a large warming fireplace; high ceilings increase the spacious feeling. A casual breakfast area is adjacent to the amenity-filled kitchen. The opposite side of the plan is dedicated to sleeping chambers. The opulent master suite includes an enormous private bath with His and Hers walk-in closets, dual vanities, and a separate shower. Two family bedrooms that share a full bath occupy the remainder of the sleeping wing.

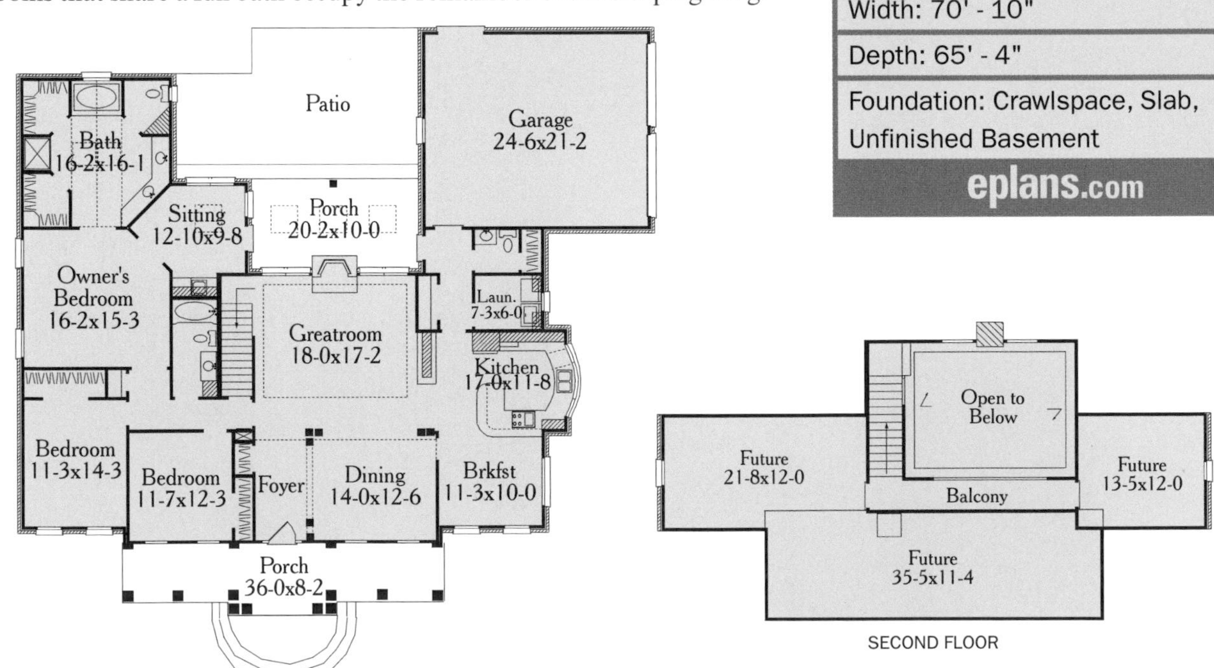

FIRST FLOOR

SECOND FLOOR

plan# HPK1700225

Style: Country Cottage
First Floor: 1,704 sq. ft.
Second Floor: 734 sq. ft.
Total: 2,438 sq. ft.
Bonus Space: 479 sq. ft.
Bedrooms: 3
Bathrooms: 3½
Width: 50' - 0"
Depth: 82' - 6"
Foundation: Crawlspace

eplans.com

DESIGN NOTE

The eye-catching side-gabled roof and flared eaves suggest a variation of the Colonial style that arose with the Dutch settlements in the American northeast during the mid-18th Century. The three dormer windows shown prominently in this design are also true to the style, although the wide porch and railing are more Southern-inspired. The designer, in concern for preserving the historical look of the home, has smartly placed the garage at the rear of the plan.

FIRST FLOOR

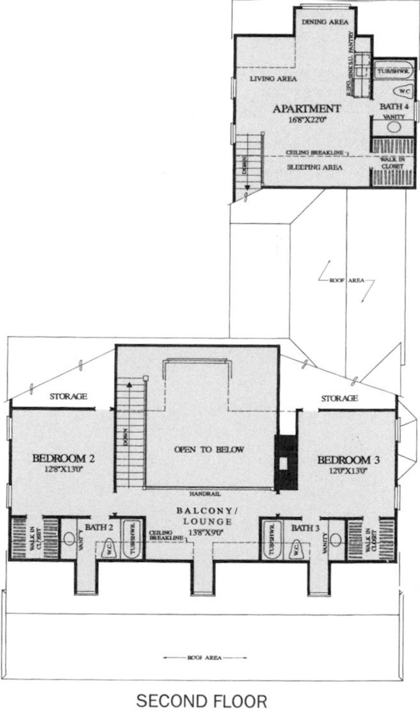

SECOND FLOOR

plan# HPK1700226

Style: Traditional
First Floor: 1,720 sq. ft.
Second Floor: 724 sq. ft.
Total: 2,444 sq. ft.
Bonus Space: 212 sq. ft.
Bedrooms: 4
Bathrooms: 3
Width: 58' - 0"
Depth: 47' - 0"
Foundation: Crawlspace, Unfinished Walkout Basement
eplans.com

Columns announce the front covered porch and entry of this comfortable home. An open arrangement of the interior allows vistas that extend from the two-story foyer to the rear property. A fireplace and two sets of radius windows define the vaulted great room, which allows passage to the casual breakfast area. The well-organized kitchen offers a serving bar, planning desk, and an ample pantry. To the rear of the plan, a flex room offers the possibility of a guest suite or home office. The master suite offers a compartmented bath, separate vanities, and a walk-in closet. Upstairs, two secondary bedrooms share a gallery hall that ends in a computer nook.

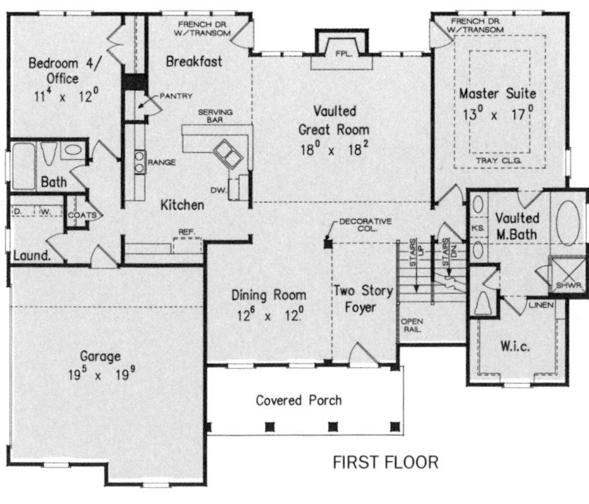

FIRST FLOOR

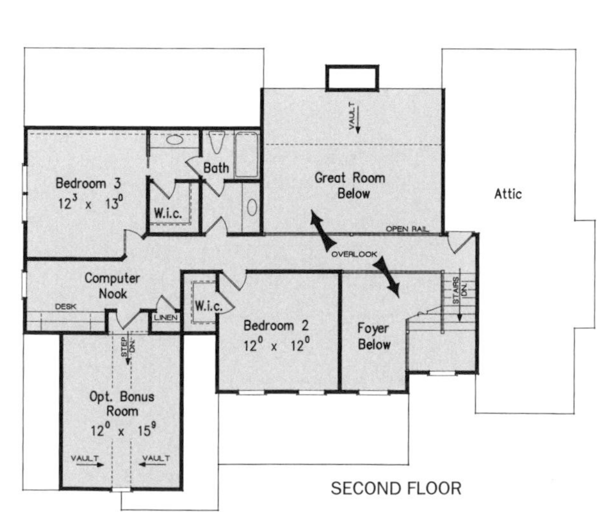

SECOND FLOOR

plan# HPK1700227

Style: Colonial

First Floor: 1,056 sq. ft.

Second Floor: 967 sq. ft.

Total: 2,023 sq. ft.

Bonus Space: 291 sq. ft.

Bedrooms: 3

Bathrooms: 2 ½

Width: 45' - 0"

Depth: 40' - 0"

Foundation: Crawlspace

eplans.com

This charming Early American features fenestration characterized by arched windows and brick facade. A compact, but generous floor plan situates all of the needs of a modern household on two floors. The formal living and dining rooms are connected by a prestigious pillared archway, to the left of the foyer. The kitchen/breakfast nook are partitioned behind the dining room, but easily accessible. The modern kitchen features a wraparound preparation island, built-in desk for recipe storage and retrieval, and walk-in pantry. A rear patio can be accessed from the nook. A family room adjoins the nook on the left, with fireplace and view of the rear property. Back through the foyer to the front of the house is a powder room for freshening, laundry room, and interior garage access. Upstairs are the bedrooms (two family and the master suite) and an unfinished bonus room.

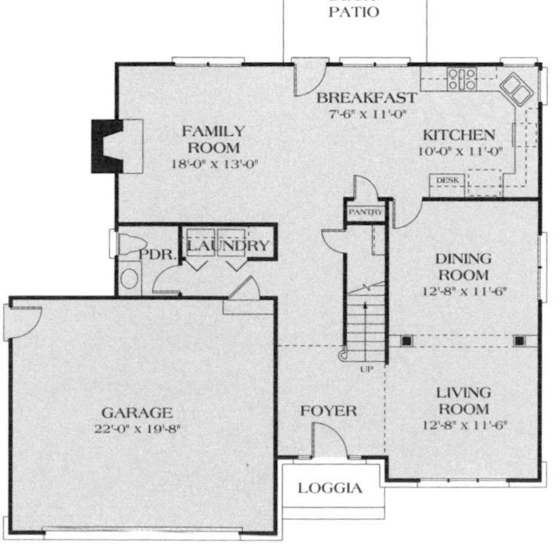

FIRST FLOOR

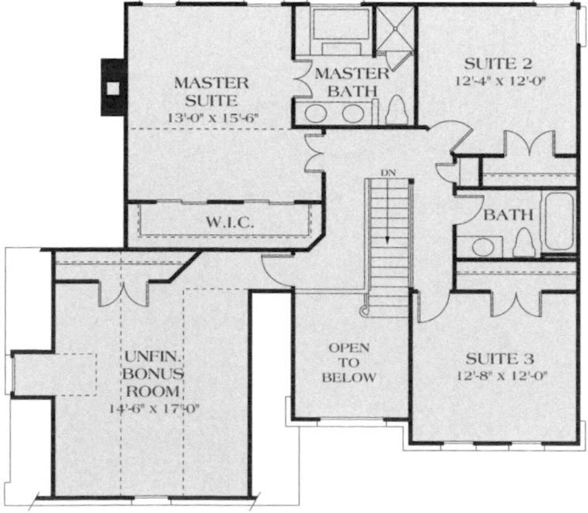

SECOND FLOOR

Perfect for waterfront property, this home boasts windows everywhere. Inside, open planning can be found in the living room, which offers a corner fireplace for cool evenings and blends beautifully into the dining and kitchen areas. All areas enjoy window views. A laundry room is conveniently nestled between the kitchen and the two-car garage. The master suite features a walk-through closet and sumptuous bath. Upstairs, three uniquely shaped bedrooms share a full bath.

plan# HPK1700228
Style: Contemporary
First Floor: 1,347 sq. ft.
Second Floor: 690 sq. ft.
Total: 2,037 sq. ft.
Bedrooms: 4
Bathrooms: 2
Width: 55' - 0"
Depth: 41' - 0"
Foundation: Unfinished Basement
eplans.com

SECOND FLOOR

FIRST FLOOR

REAR EXTERIOR

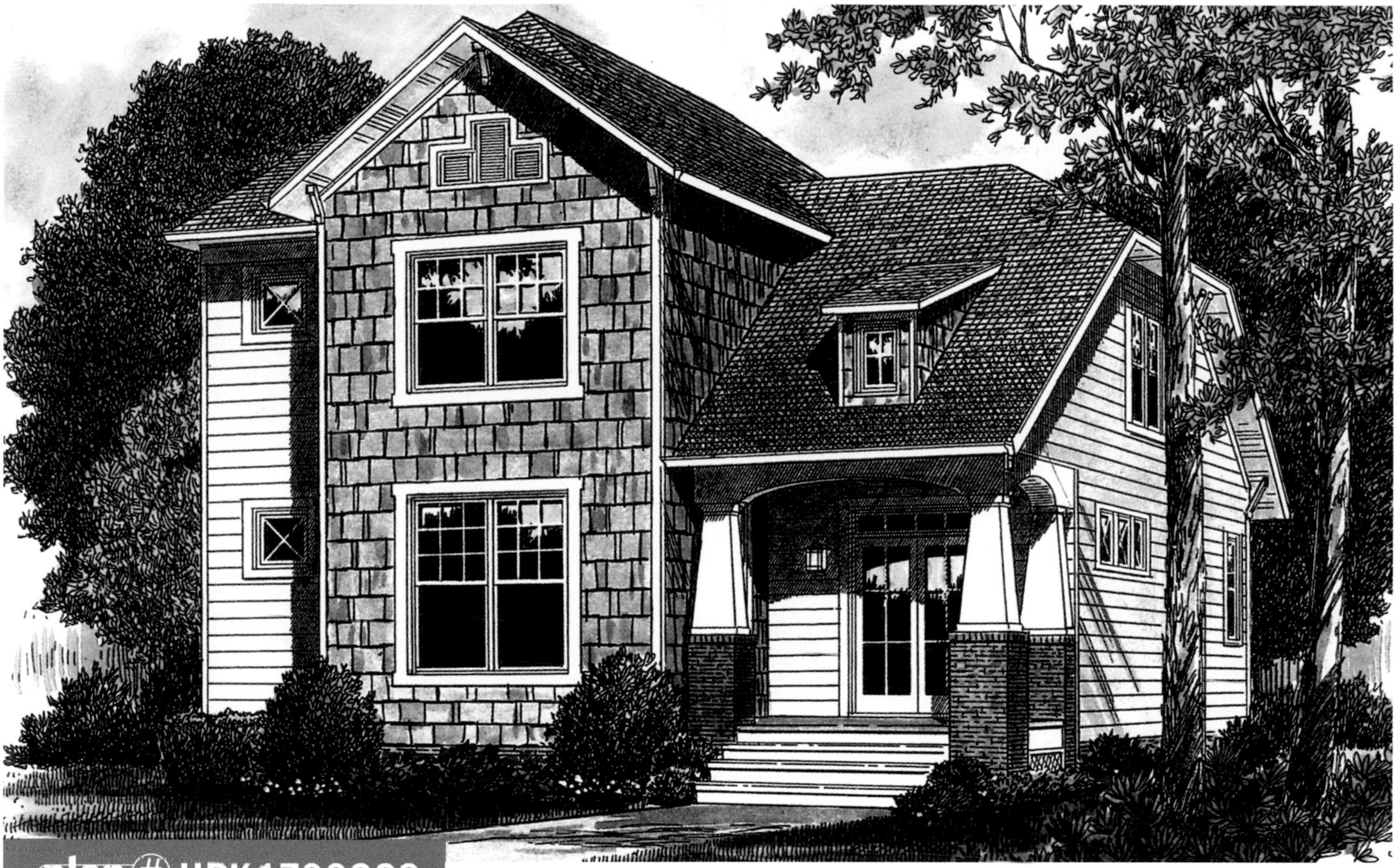

plan# HPK1700229

Style: Craftsman

First Floor: 1,392 sq. ft.

Second Floor: 708 sq. ft.

Total: 2,100 sq. ft.

Bedrooms: 3

Bathrooms: 2½

Width: 32' - 0"

Depth: 55' - 0"

Foundation: Crawlspace

eplans.com

Craftsman stylings grace this two-story traditional home, designed for a narrow lot. Shingles and siding present a warm welcome; the front porch opens to the dining room and the gathering room, allowing great entertainment options. The kitchen connects to the living areas with a snack bar and works hard with an island and lots of counter space. The master suite is on this level and delights in a very private bath. Two bedrooms on the upper level have private vanities and a shared bath. Extra storage or bonus space is available for future development.

FIRST FLOOR

SECOND FLOOR

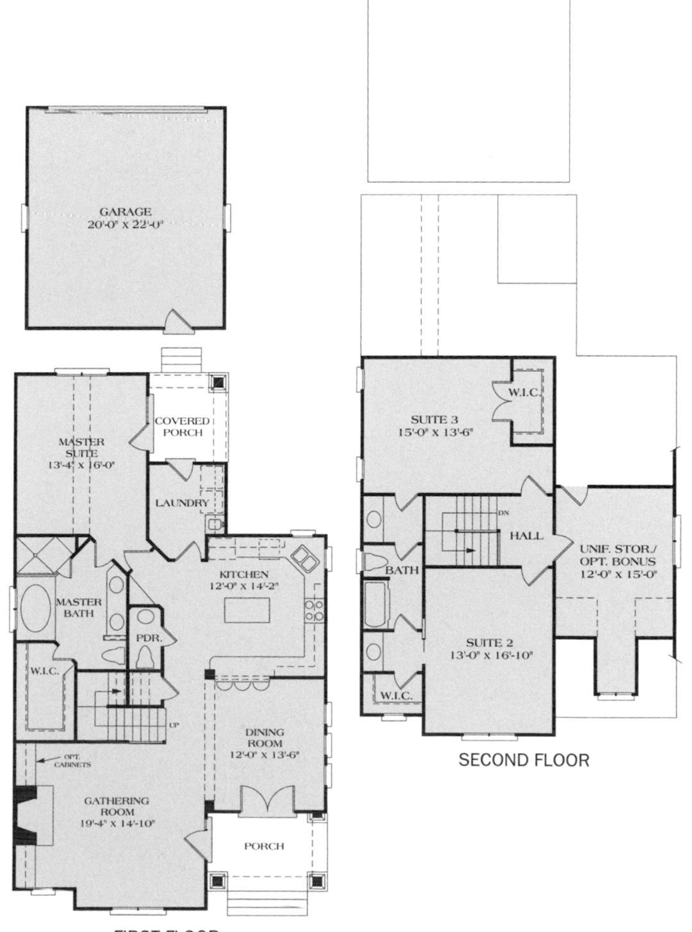

SECOND FLOOR

FIRST FLOOR

plan# HPK1700230

Style: Farmhouse

First Floor: 1,082 sq. ft.

Second Floor: 1,021 sq. ft.

Total: 2,103 sq. ft.

Bedrooms: 4

Bathrooms: 2½

Width: 50' - 0"

Depth: 40' - 0"

eplans.com

A covered porch invites you into this country-style home. Handsome bookcases frame the fireplace in the spacious family room. Double doors off the entry provide the family room with added privacy. The kitchen features an island, a lazy Susan, and easy access to a walk-in laundry. The master bedroom features a boxed ceiling and separate entries to a walk-in closet and a pampering bath. The upstairs hall bath is compartmented, allowing maximum usage for today's busy family.

plan# HPK1700231

Style:	Craftsman
First Floor:	1,561 sq. ft.
Second Floor:	578 sq. ft.
Total:	2,139 sq. ft.
Bonus Space:	238 sq. ft.
Bedrooms:	3
Bathrooms:	2½
Width:	50' - 0"
Depth:	56' - 6"
Foundation:	Crawlspace, Unfinished Walkout Basement, Slab

eplans.com

Come home to this delightful bungalow, created with you in mind. From the covered front porch, the foyer opens to the dining room on the left and vaulted family room ahead. An elongated island in the well-planned kitchen makes meal preparation a joy. A sunny breakfast nook is perfect for casual pursuits. Tucked to the rear, the master suite enjoys ultimate privacy and a luxurious break from the world with a vaulted bath and garden tub. Secondary bedrooms share a full bath upstairs; a bonus room is ready to expand as your needs change.

FIRST FLOOR

SECOND FLOOR

plan# HPK1700232

- Style: Country Cottage
- First Floor: 1,142 sq. ft.
- Second Floor: 1,004 sq. ft.
- Total: 2,146 sq. ft.
- Bonus Space: 156 sq. ft.
- Bedrooms: 4
- Bathrooms: 3
- Width: 52' - 4"
- Depth: 38' - 6"
- Foundation: Crawlspace, Slab, Unfinished Walkout Basement

eplans.com

This gracious four-bedroom home adds siding, gables, and shutters to a very livable floor plan. Three bedrooms and a bedroom/study, along with three full baths, provide plenty of room for family and guests. A tray ceiling adorns the elegant master bedroom, while a vaulted master bath adds to the spaciousness of this private retreat—note the radius window and built-in shelf. The two-story family room sits near the gourmet kitchen featuring a serving bar and bayed breakfast area. An optional bonus room is available upstairs for future expansion.

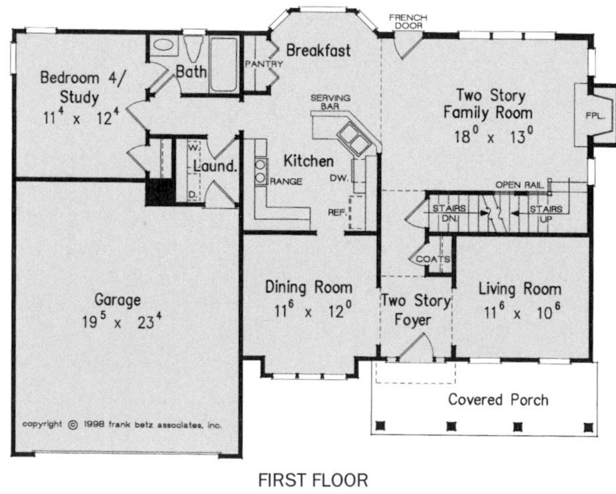

FIRST FLOOR

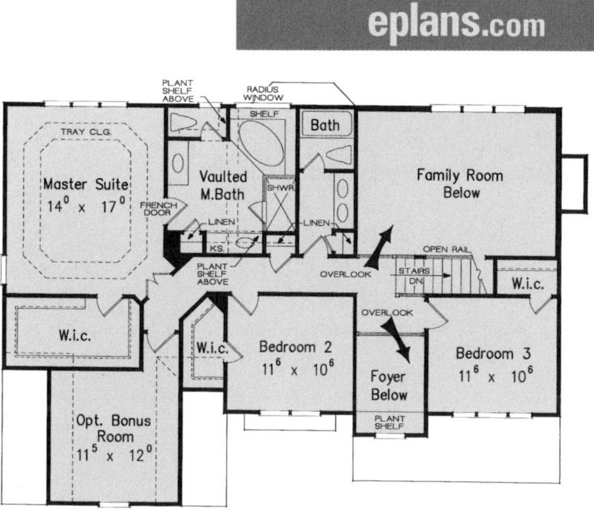

SECOND FLOOR

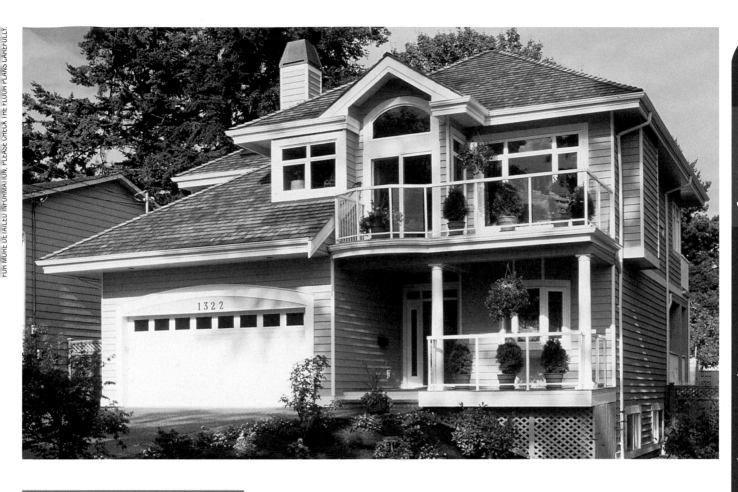

plan# HPK1700233

Style: Traditional
First Floor: 832 sq. ft.
Second Floor: 1,331 sq. ft.
Total: 2,163 sq. ft.
Bedrooms: 3
Bathrooms: 2½
Width: 37' - 6"
Depth: 48' - 4"
Foundation: Unfinished Basement

eplans.com

This home offers two stories, with a twist! The living spaces are on the second floor and include a living/dining room combination with a deck and fireplace. The family room also has a fireplace, plus a built-in entertainment center, and is open to the skylit kitchen. The master bedroom is also on this level and features a private bath. Family bedrooms, a full bath, and a cozy den reside on the first level.

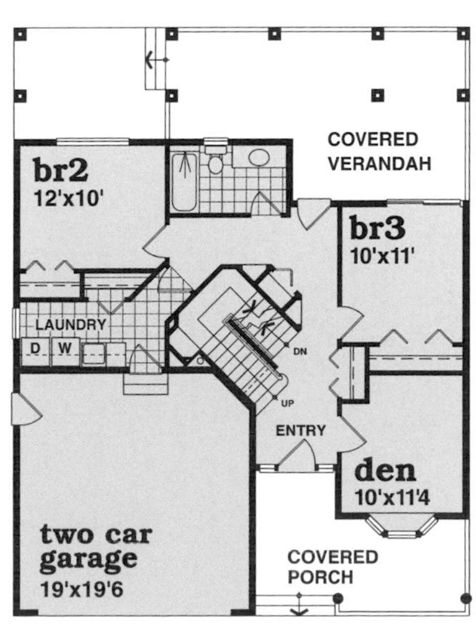

FIRST FLOOR

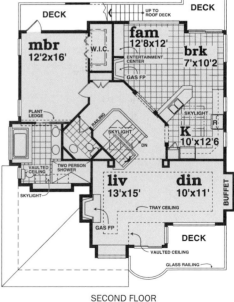

SECOND FLOOR

PHOTO COURTESY OF CAPPELL ASSOCIATES, INC.

This absolutely appealing Craftsman home dresses up any neighborhood. A deep porch anchored by heavy pilasters is an inviting spot for friends and family. The entry gallery introduces a layout that is open, and defines spaces with decorative columns and wall breaks. The dining area looks out onto the front yard and enjoys a view of the fireplace in the gathering room. The island kitchen provides plenty of counter and cabinet space. A sunroom doubles as a breakfast area and has front porch access. Two family bedrooms share a full bath on the second floor. The master suite features a large walk-in closet and resplendent bath. An optional bonus room completes this space.

plan# HPK1700234
Style: Craftsman
First Floor: 1,106 sq. ft.
Second Floor: 1,057 sq. ft.
Total: 2,163 sq. ft.
Bonus Space: 200 sq. ft.
Bedrooms: 3
Bathrooms: 2½
Width: 37' - 6"
Depth: 54' - 0"
Foundation: Slab
eplans.com

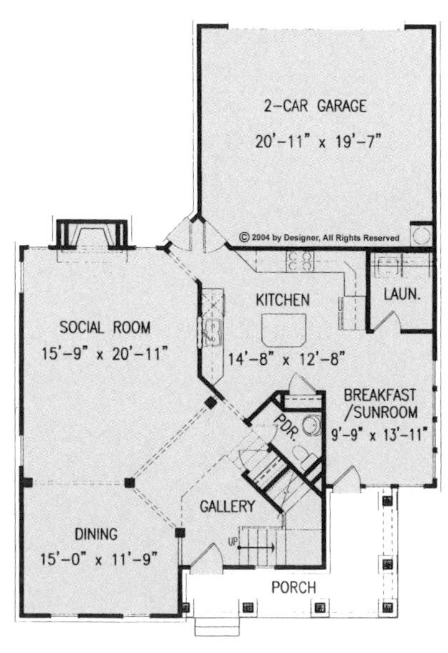

FIRST FLOOR

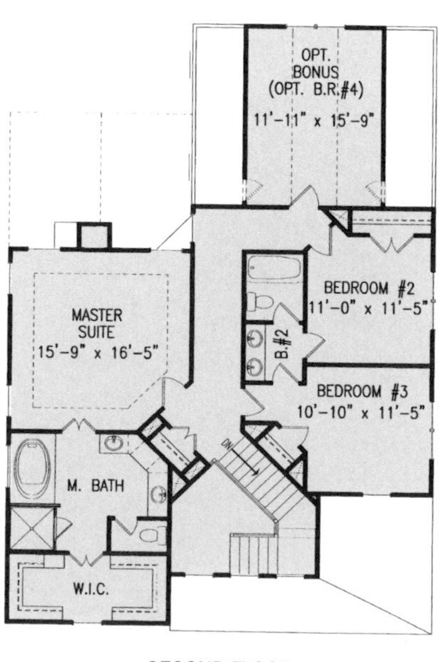

SECOND FLOOR

plan# HPK1700235

Style: Traditional
First Floor: 1,580 sq. ft.
Second Floor: 595 sq. ft.
Total: 2,175 sq. ft.
Bedrooms: 3
Bathrooms: 2½
Width: 50' - 2"
Depth: 70' - 11"
Foundation: Walkout Basement

eplans.com

This home is a true Southern original. Inside, the spacious foyer leads directly to a large vaulted great room with its handsome fireplace. The dining room just off the foyer features a dramatic vaulted ceiling. The spacious kitchen offers both storage and large work areas opening up to the breakfast room. At the rear of the home you will find the master suite with its garden bath, His and Hers vanities, and an oversize closet. The second floor provides two additional bedrooms with a shared bath and a balcony overlook to the foyer below.

FIRST FLOOR

SECOND FLOOR

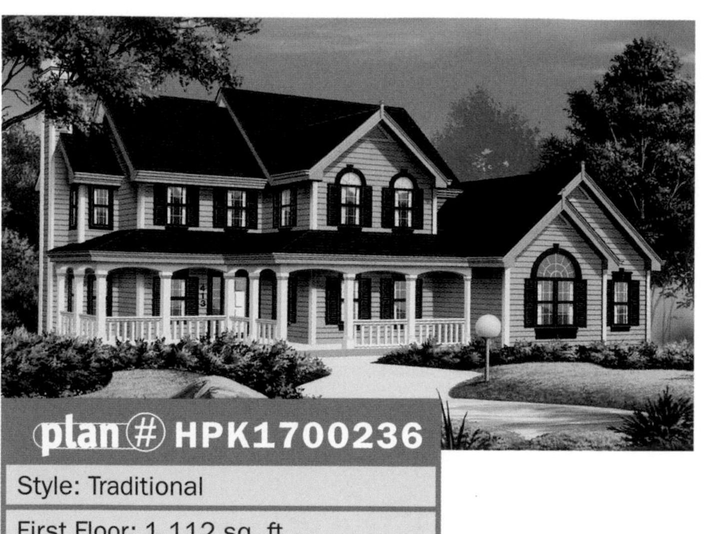

plan# HPK1700236

Style: Traditional

First Floor: 1,112 sq. ft.

Second Floor: 1,070 sq. ft.

Total: 2,182 sq. ft.

Bedrooms: 3

Bathrooms: 3½

Width: 57' - 0"

Depth: 48' - 8"

Foundation: Unfinished Basement

eplans.com

SECOND FLOOR

FIRST FLOOR

SECOND FLOOR

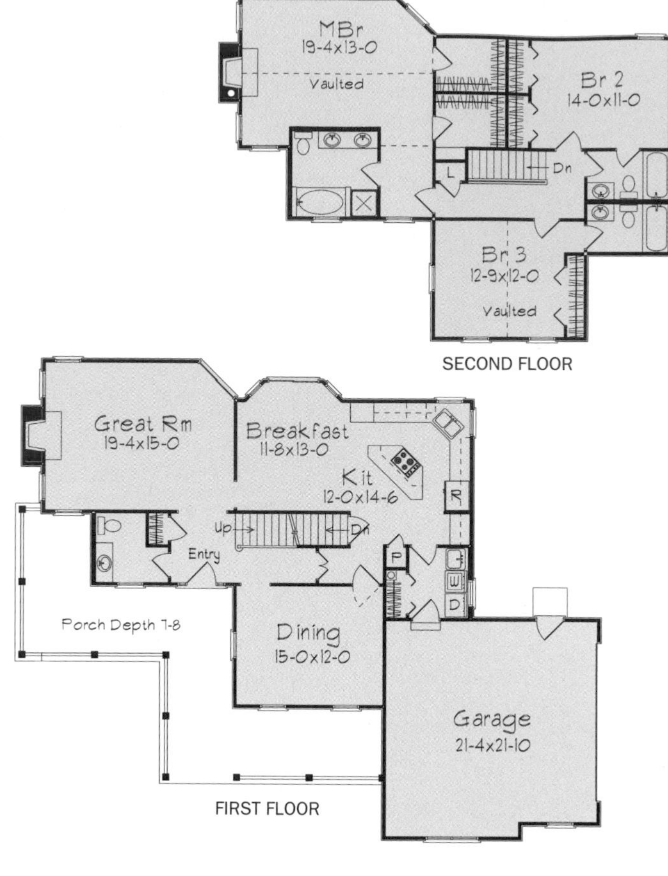

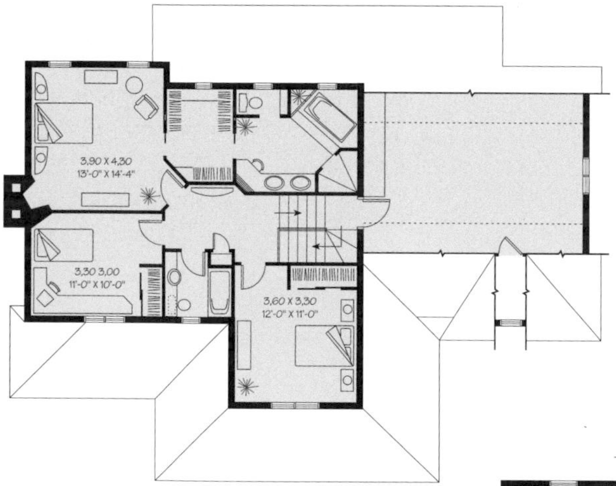

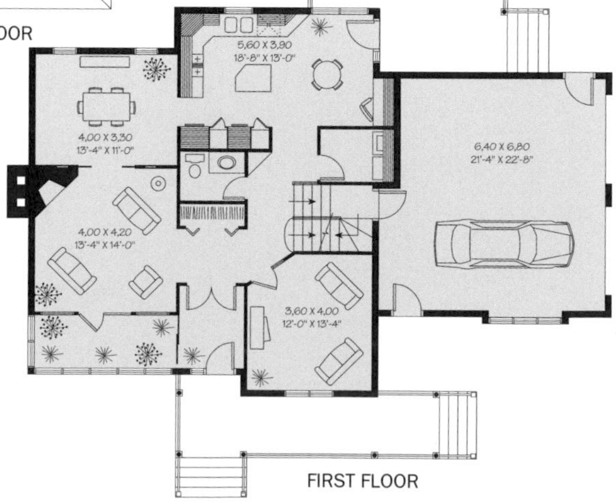

FIRST FLOOR

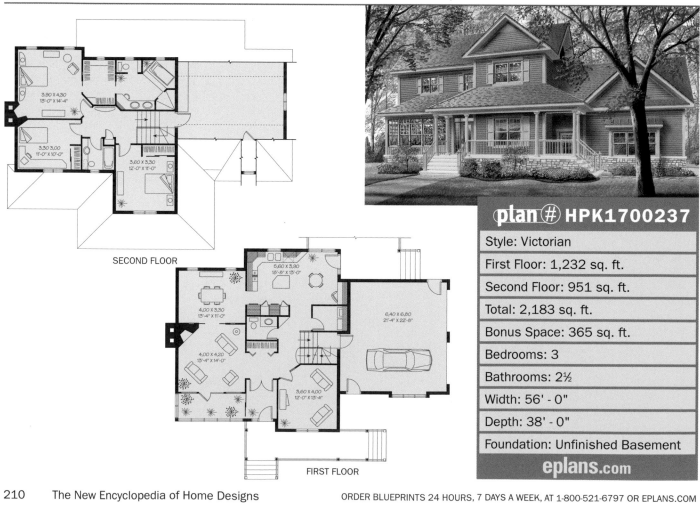

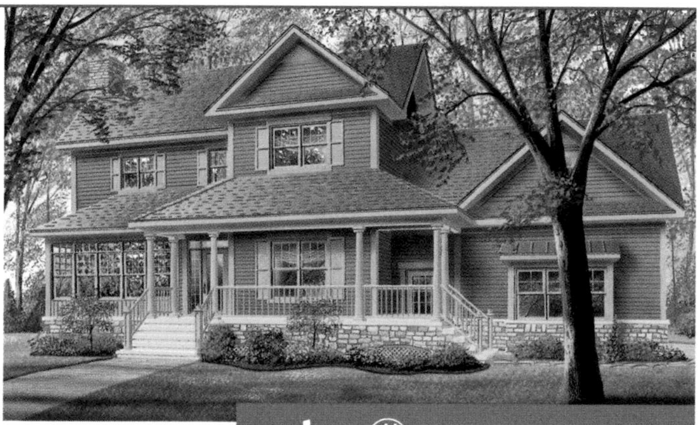

plan# HPK1700237

Style: Victorian

First Floor: 1,232 sq. ft.

Second Floor: 951 sq. ft.

Total: 2,183 sq. ft.

Bonus Space: 365 sq. ft.

Bedrooms: 3

Bathrooms: 2½

Width: 56' - 0"

Depth: 38' - 0"

Foundation: Unfinished Basement

eplans.com

plan# HPK1700238

Style: Georgian
First Floor: 1,209 sq. ft.
Second Floor: 1,005 sq. ft.
Total: 2,214 sq. ft.
Bonus Space: 366 sq. ft.
Bedrooms: 3
Bathrooms: 2½
Width: 65' - 4"
Depth: 40' - 4"
Foundation: Crawlspace

eplans.com

The rebirth of a style—this design salutes the look of Early America. From the porch, step into the two-story foyer, and either venture to the left towards the living room and dining room, or to the right where the family room sits. A central fireplace in the family room warms the island kitchen. The open design allows unrestricted interaction. Upstairs, the master suite boasts a roomy bath with a dual-sink vanity, a whirlpool tub, a private toilet, a separate shower, and His and Hers walk-in closets. Two additional family bedrooms share a full bath. Future expansion space completes this level.

SECOND FLOOR

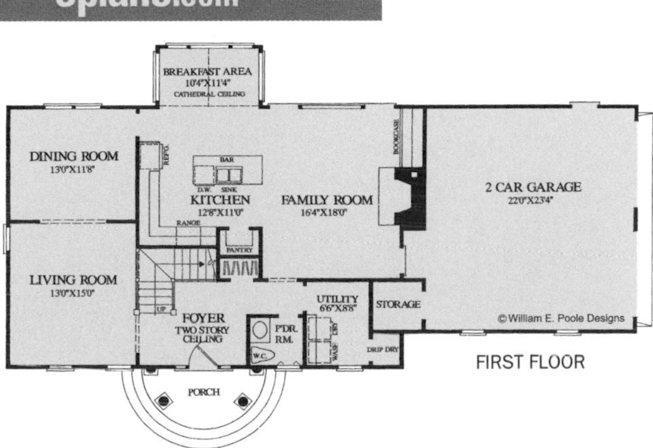

FIRST FLOOR

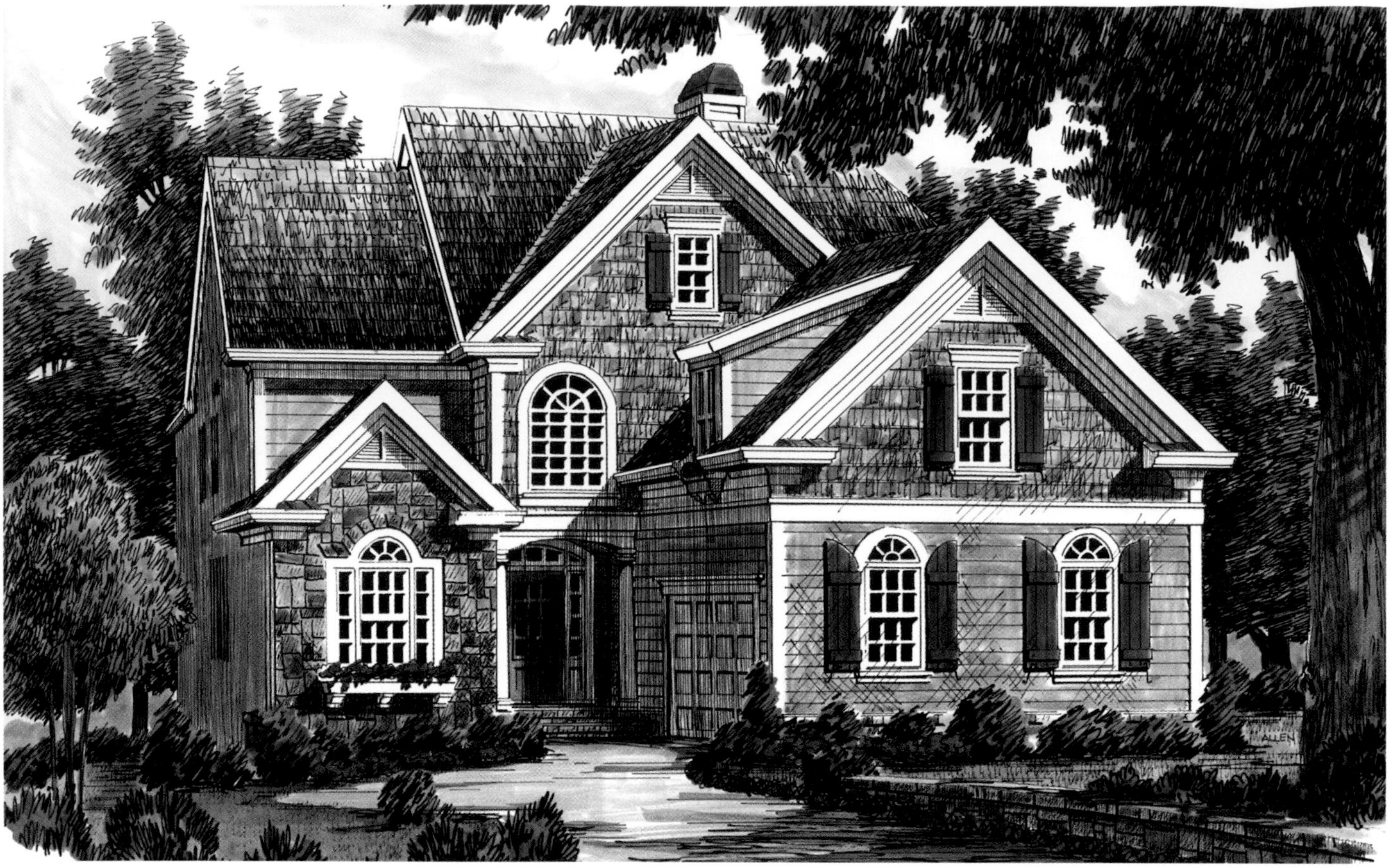

Shingles and stone decorate the exterior of this charming design. Inside, decorative columns separate the living and dining rooms. The kitchen includes a pantry and a work island; the breakfast nook is conveniently nearby. Built-in cabinets flank the fireplace in the two-story family room. One family bedroom resides on the first floor, while the master suite and a second family bedroom are upstairs. An optional bonus room completes the second floor.

plan# HPK1700239

Style: Country Cottage

First Floor: 1,293 sq. ft.

Second Floor: 922 sq. ft.

Total: 2,215 sq. ft.

Bonus Space: 235 sq. ft.

Bedrooms: 3

Bathrooms: 3

Width: 40' - 0"

Depth: 57' - 0"

Foundation: Crawlspace, Unfinished Walkout Basement

eplans.com

FIRST FLOOR

SECOND FLOOR

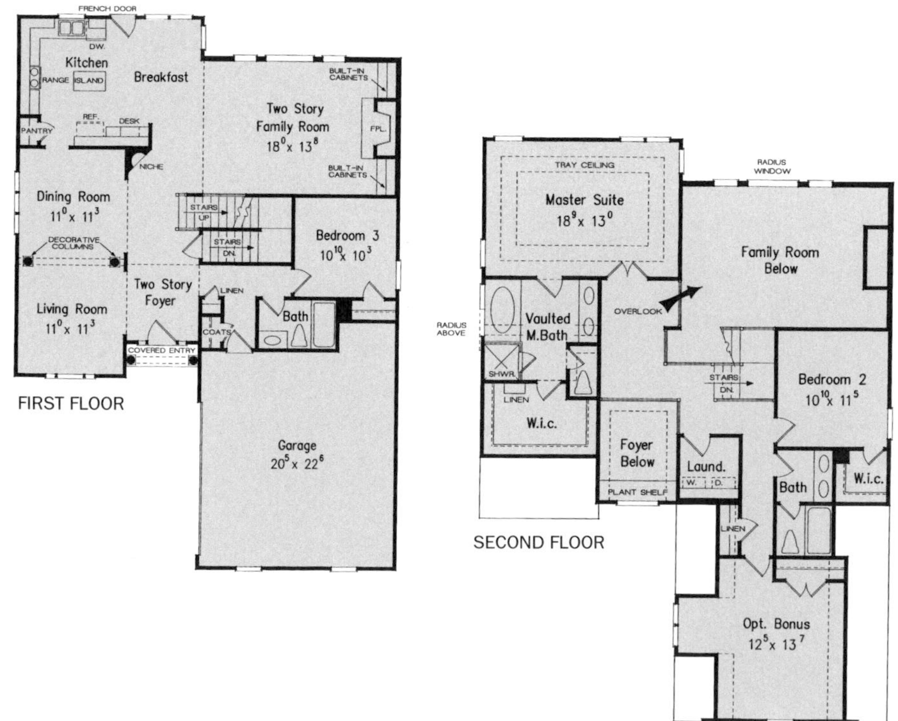

plan # HPK1700240

Style: Adam Style
First Floor: 1,369 sq. ft.
Second Floor: 856 sq. ft.
Total: 2,225 sq. ft.
Bedrooms: 4
Bathrooms: 2½
Width: 36' - 2"
Depth: 71' - 6"
Foundation: Slab

eplans.com

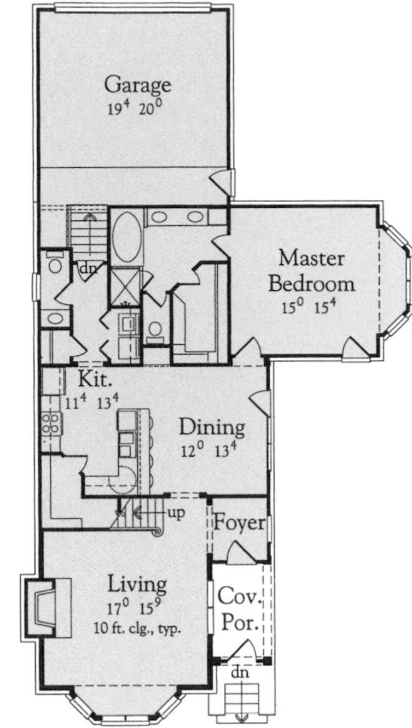

FIRST FLOOR

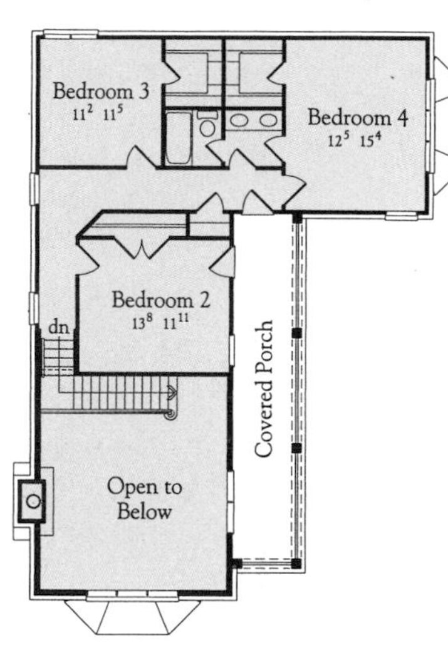

SECOND FLOOR

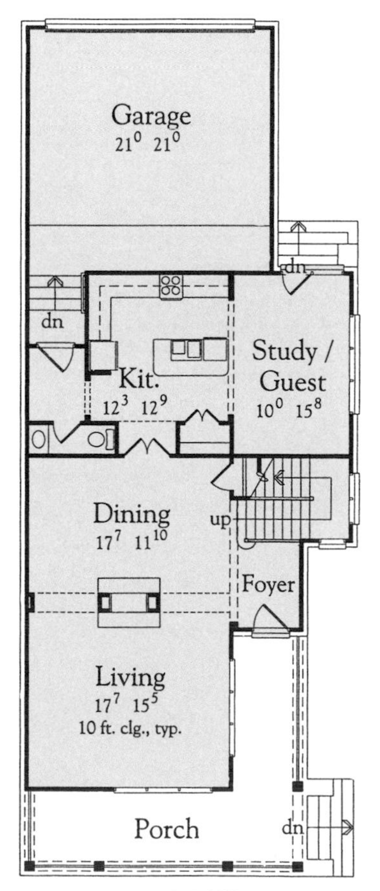

FIRST FLOOR

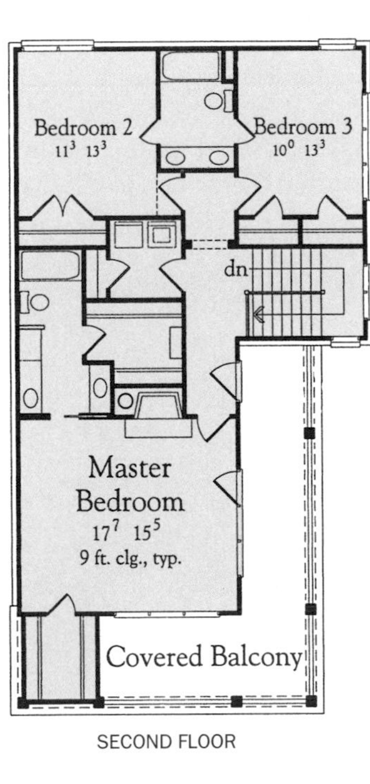

SECOND FLOOR

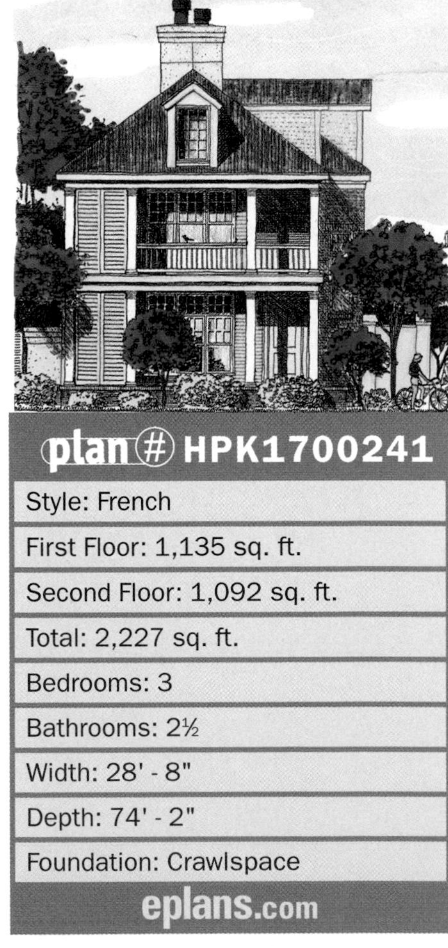

plan # HPK1700241

Style: French
First Floor: 1,135 sq. ft.
Second Floor: 1,092 sq. ft.
Total: 2,227 sq. ft.
Bedrooms: 3
Bathrooms: 2½
Width: 28' - 8"
Depth: 74' - 2"
Foundation: Crawlspace

eplans.com

SMART TIP

The Victorian-style tower and porch bring a lot of visual interest to the exterior of this home. The interior uses the polygonal shapes created by the towers and bay windows to provide cozy dining and other gathering spaces. Sleeping quarters on the second floor also avoid flat walls. As in a true Victorian home, the spirit of the design tends away from regularity of layout and toward interesting asymmetries—which owners can draw inspiration from when designing the interior.

plan# HPK1700242
Style: Contemporary
First Floor: 1,371 sq. ft.
Second Floor: 894 sq. ft.
Total: 2,265 sq. ft.
Bonus Space: 339 sq. ft.
Bedrooms: 4
Bathrooms: 3½
Width: 58' - 0"
Depth: 58' - 4"
Foundation: Unfinished Basement
eplans.com

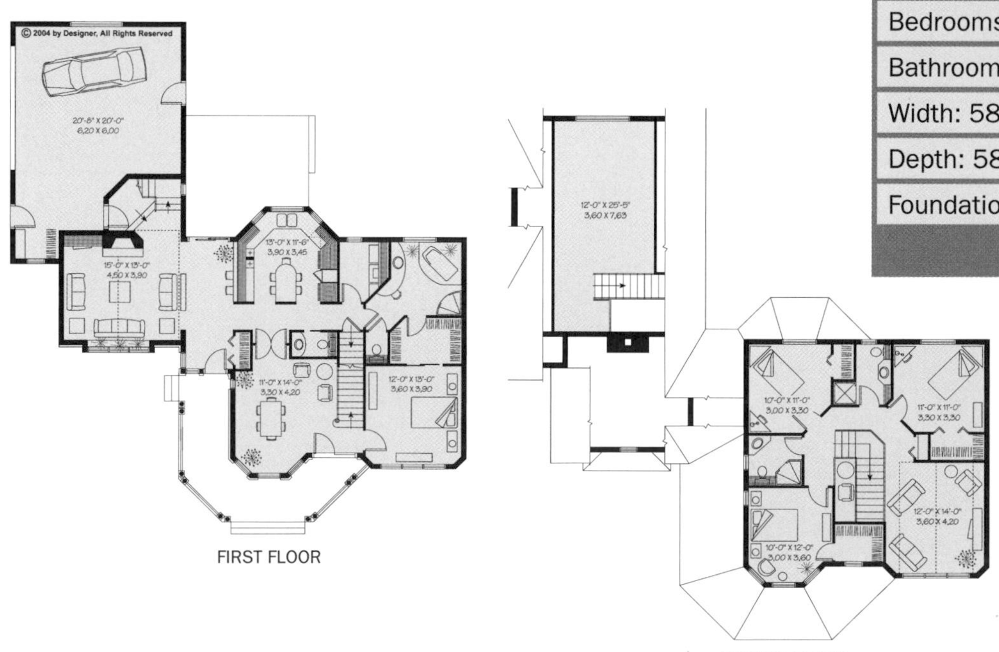

FIRST FLOOR

SECOND FLOOR

plan# HPK1700243

Style: Country Cottage

First Floor: 1,290 sq. ft.

Second Floor: 985 sq. ft.

Total: 2,275 sq. ft.

Bonus Space: 186 sq. ft.

Bedrooms: 4

Bathrooms: 3

Width: 45' - 0"

Depth: 43' - 4"

Foundation: Crawlspace, Unfinished Walkout Basement, Slab

eplans.com

This casually elegant European Country-style home offers more than just a slice of everything you've always wanted: it is designed with room to grow. Formal living and dining rooms are defined by decorative columns and open from a two-story foyer, which leads to open family space. A two-story family room offers a fireplace and shares a French door to the rear property with the breakfast room. A gallery hall with a balcony overlook connects two sleeping wings upstairs. The master suite boasts a vaulted bath, and the family hall leads to bonus space.

SECOND FLOOR

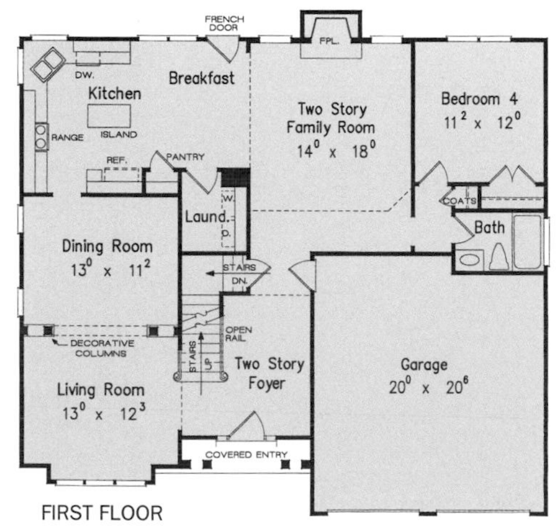

FIRST FLOOR

plan# HPK1700244

Style: Farmhouse

First Floor: 1,778 sq. ft.

Second Floor: 498 sq. ft.

Total: 2,276 sq. ft.

Bonus Space: 315 sq. ft.

Bedrooms: 4

Bathrooms: 3

Width: 54' - 8"

Depth: 53' - 2"

eplans.com

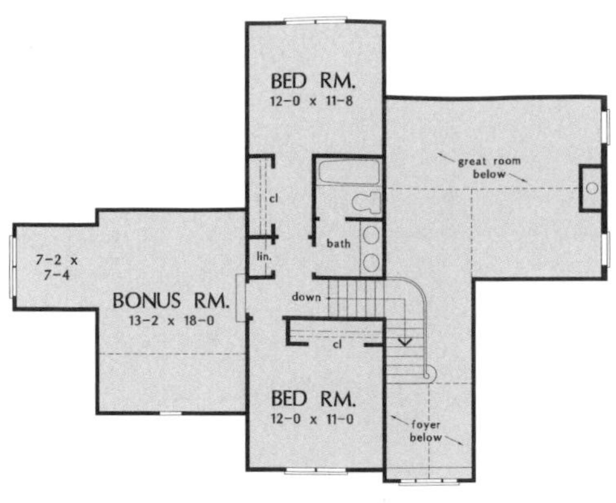

SECOND FLOOR

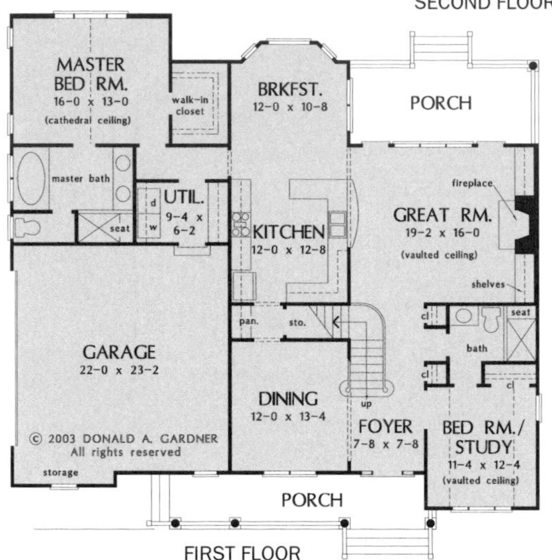

FIRST FLOOR

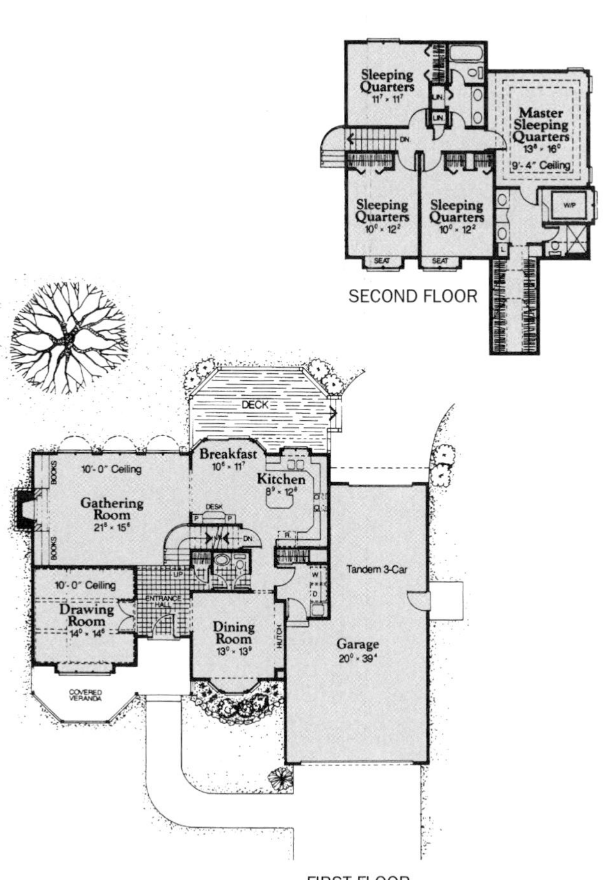

SECOND FLOOR

FIRST FLOOR

plan# HPK1700245

Style: Victorian

First Floor: 1,249 sq. ft.

Second Floor: 1,075 sq. ft.

Total: 2,324 sq. ft.

Bedrooms: 4

Bathrooms: 2½

Width: 56' - 0"

Depth: 46' - 0"

eplans.com

plan# HPK1700246

Style: Bungalow

First Floor: 1,205 sq. ft.

Second Floor: 1,123 sq. ft.

Total: 2,328 sq. ft.

Bedrooms: 4

Bathrooms: 2½

Width: 57' - 2"

Depth: 58' - 7"

Foundation: Unfinished Basement, Crawlspace

eplans.com

With Craftsman details and modern amenities, this design offers an attractive layout. The long foyer opens to the dining and living rooms, which enjoy a flowing space. To the rear, a family room features a corner fireplace and access to the rear grounds. The breakfast nook sports French doors, which liven up the nearby island kitchen with natural light. Upstairs, the master bedroom is luxurious with a spa tub, shower, dual-basin vanity, compartmented toilet, and walk-in closet. Three family bedrooms share a full hall bath.

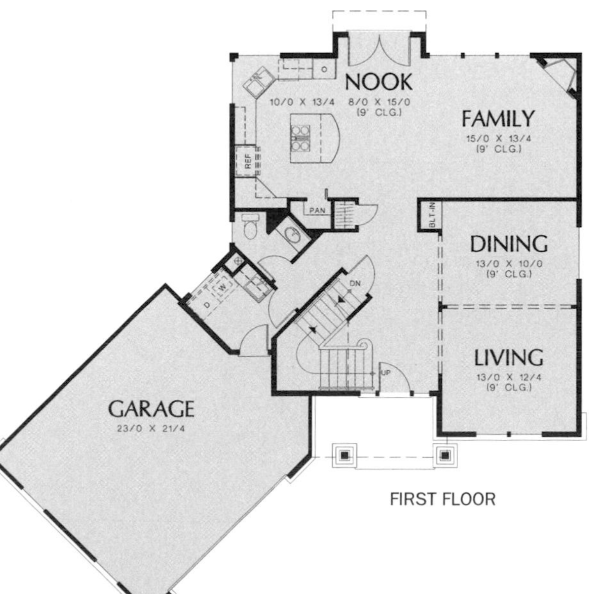

FIRST FLOOR

SECOND FLOOR

plan# HPK1700247

Style: Traditional
First Floor: 1,563 sq. ft.
Second Floor: 772 sq. ft.
Total: 2,335 sq. ft.
Bedrooms: 3
Bathrooms: 2½
Width: 45' - 0"
Depth: 55' - 8"
Foundation: Crawlspace

eplans.com

Graceful, elegant living takes place in this charming cottage, which showcases a stone-and-stucco facade. Inside, the formal dining room features a columned entrance and a tray ceiling; nearby, the kitchen boasts a central island and a bay window. The expansive gathering room includes a fireplace and opens to the covered rear veranda, which extends to a side deck. The master suite, also with a tray ceiling, offers a walk-in closet and lavish private bath. Upstairs, two family bedrooms—both with walk-in closets—share a full bath and the captain's quarters, which opens to a deck.

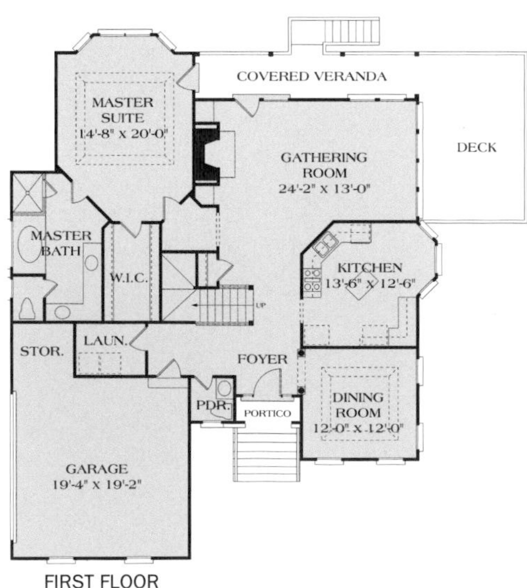

FIRST FLOOR

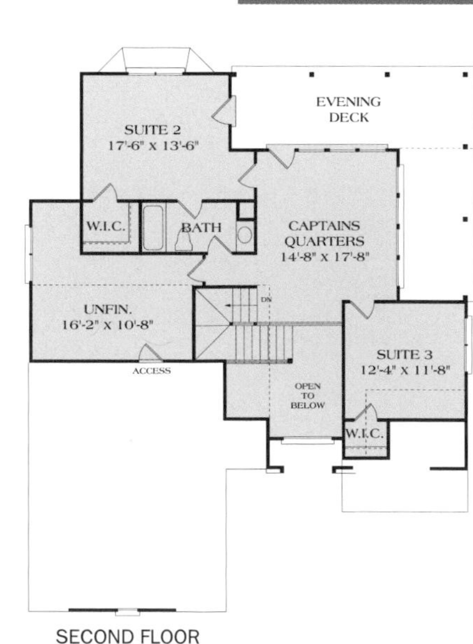

SECOND FLOOR

plan # HPK1700248

Style: Southern Colonial
First Floor: 1,237 sq. ft.
Second Floor: 1,098 sq. ft.
Total: 2,335 sq. ft.
Bedrooms: 3
Bathrooms: 2½
Width: 29' - 4"
Depth: 73' - 0"
Foundation: Slab

eplans.com

The curb appeal of this home can be found in the dazzling details: a bay window, twin sconces illuminating a columned porch, a pretty portico, and classic shutters. The foyer opens to the formal living and dining rooms, subtly defined by a central fireplace. The gourmet kitchen overlooks a spacious family/breakfast area, which leads outdoors. The second floor includes a lavish master suite with a spa-style tub and a private covered balcony. The secondary sleeping area is connected by a gallery hall and a stair landing.

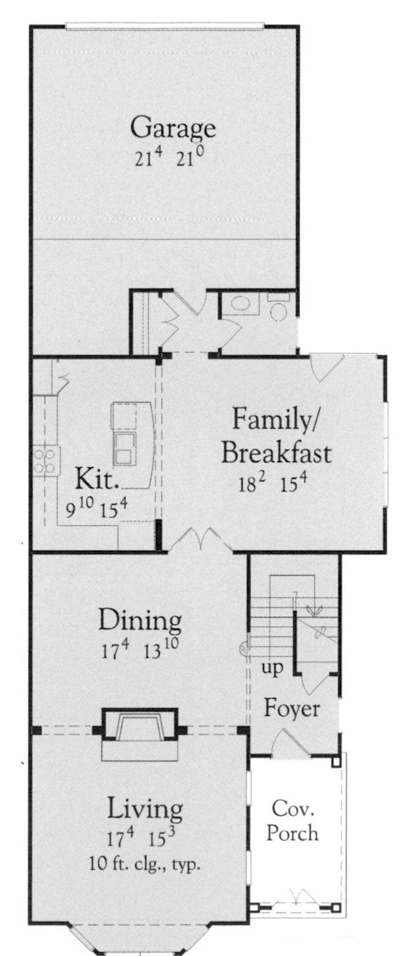

FIRST FLOOR

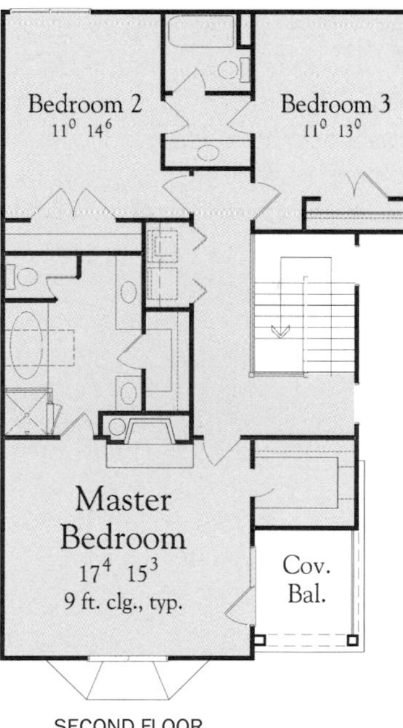

SECOND FLOOR

plan# HPK1700249

Style: Traditional

First Floor: 1,208 sq. ft.

Second Floor: 1,137 sq. ft.

Total: 2,345 sq. ft.

Bedrooms: 3

Bathrooms: 3

Width: 38' - 6"

Depth: 51' - 4"

Foundation: Crawlspace, Unfinished Walkout Basement

eplans.com

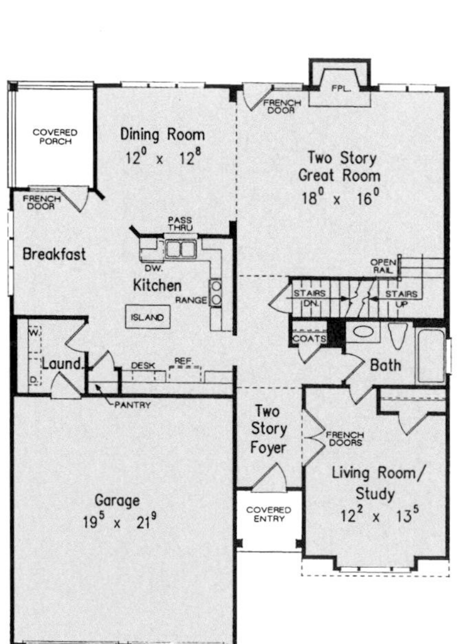

FIRST FLOOR

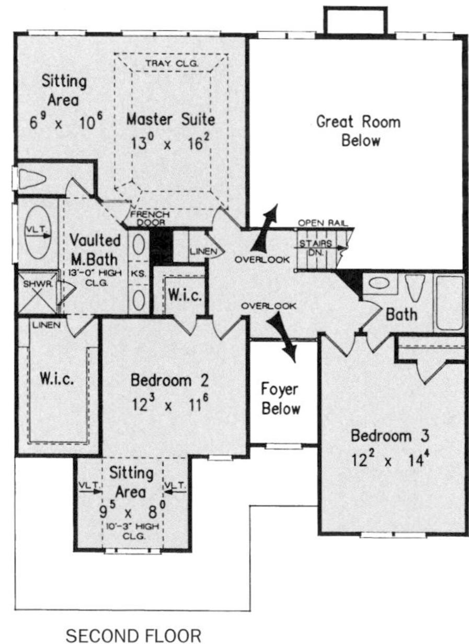

SECOND FLOOR

A hipped roof, siding, and stone accents bring a Neoclassical element to this traditional family home. Inside, the two-story great room is inviting, with a fireplace and lots of natural light. The living room/study is entered through French doors and is set in a box-bay window. A country kitchen serves the dining room and breakfast area with ease; covered-porch access beckons outdoor meals. The second-floor master suite enjoys a sitting area and a vaulted bath with a garden tub. Two bedrooms, one with a sitting area and a walk-in closet, share a full bath.

plan# HPK1700250

Style: Country Cottage
First Floor: 1,279 sq. ft.
Second Floor: 1,071 sq. ft.
Total: 2,350 sq. ft.
Bedrooms: 4
Bathrooms: 3
Width: 50' - 0"
Depth: 42' - 6"
Foundation: Crawlspace, Unfinished Walkout Basement

eplans.com

Rustic details complement brick and siding on the exterior of this home. The interior features vaulted living and family rooms and a convenient kitchen separating the dining and breakfast rooms. The living room provides a fireplace flanked by radius windows, and a French door in the breakfast room opens to the rear property. A bedroom to the back could be used as a study. Second-floor bedrooms include a master suite with a sitting area.

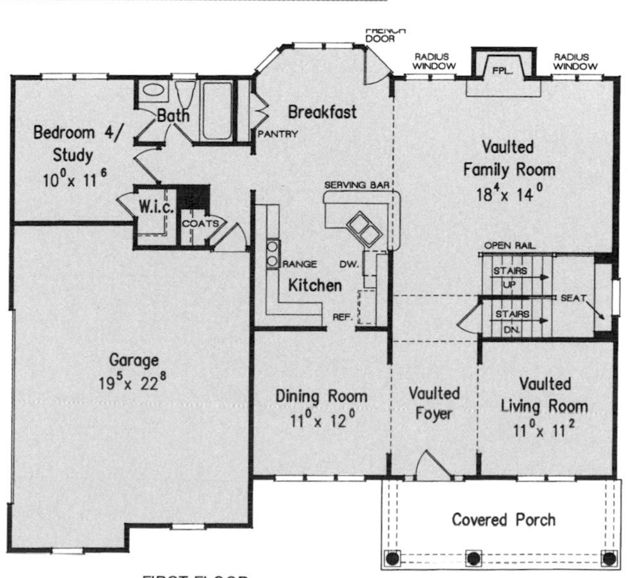

FIRST FLOOR

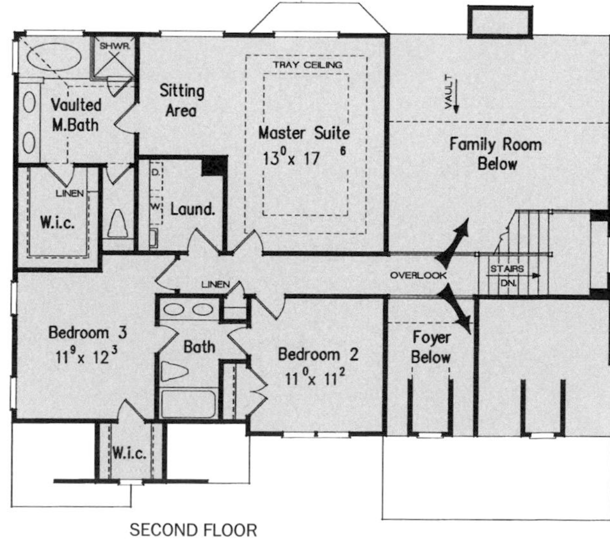

SECOND FLOOR

plan# HPK1700251
Style: Country Cottage
First Floor: 1,803 sq. ft.
Second Floor: 548 sq. ft.
Total: 2,351 sq. ft.
Bonus Space: 277 sq. ft.
Bedrooms: 4
Bathrooms: 3
Width: 55' - 0"
Depth: 48' - 0"
Foundation: Crawlspace, Unfinished Walkout Basement, Slab
eplans.com

This Early American home will delight with brick and siding, a flower-box window, and lots of natural light. The two-story foyer leads to the vaulted great room, perfect for entertaining with a fireplace and serving bar from the island kitchen. The bayed breakfast nook is a lovely morning treat. A first-floor bedroom would make a fine guest room or study. The entire left side of the home is devoted to the master suite, stunning with a vaulted sitting room and pampering bath brightened by a radius window. Two upstairs bedrooms share bonus space and a full bath.

REAR EXTERIOR

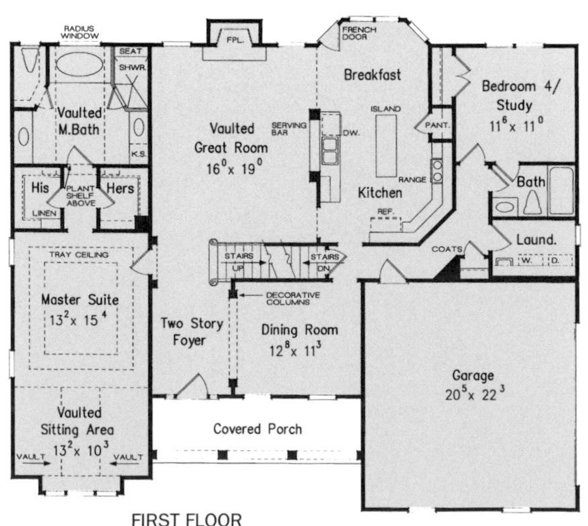

FIRST FLOOR

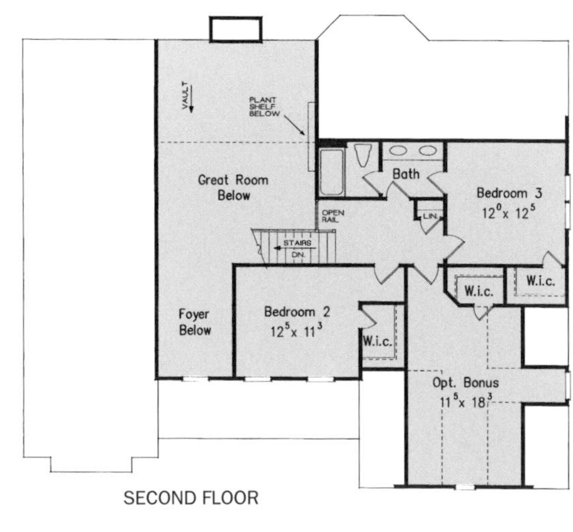

SECOND FLOOR

plan# HPK1700252

Style: Contemporary
First Floor: 1,279 sq. ft.
Second Floor: 1,114 sq. ft.
Total: 2,393 sq. ft.
Bonus Space: 337 sq. ft.
Bedrooms: 4
Bathrooms: 2
Width: 68' - 0"
Depth: 36' - 0"
Foundation: Slab

eplans.com

Covered porches in the front and rear of this contemporary design serve to facilitate a smooth indoor/outdoor relationship. First-floor living spaces are wide open—you'll never miss a word of conversation if you're cooking in the kitchen and serving friends and family in hearth-warmed family room or informal dining area nearby. Also on this level are the laundry room and a full bath. Venture upstairs to find four family bedrooms, each with a spacious closet, and another full bath. Dual sinks in this bathroom help ease the chaos of morning/bedtime rituals.

REAR EXTERIOR

FIRST FLOOR

SECOND FLOOR

plan# HPK1700253

Style: Cape Cod
First Floor: 1,186 sq. ft.
Second Floor: 1,210 sq. ft.
Total: 2,396 sq. ft.
Bedrooms: 4
Bathrooms: 2½
Width: 50' - 0"
Depth: 47' - 6"
Foundation: Crawlspace, Unfinished Walkout Basement

eplans.com

SECOND FLOOR

FIRST FLOOR

Brick and shake create a weathered look for this Colonial home, complemented by a pediment entry; use recycled materials for a more vintage appeal. A two-story foyer is graced with French doors to the living room/study. A two-story family room is enhanced by radius windows and a warming fireplace. The serving-bar kitchen is conveniently central to the bayed breakfast nook and formal dining room. Upstairs, three family bedrooms (one lit by dormer windows) share a full bath. The master suite resides in luxury with a sumptuous private bath that includes a vaulted ceiling and corner tub.

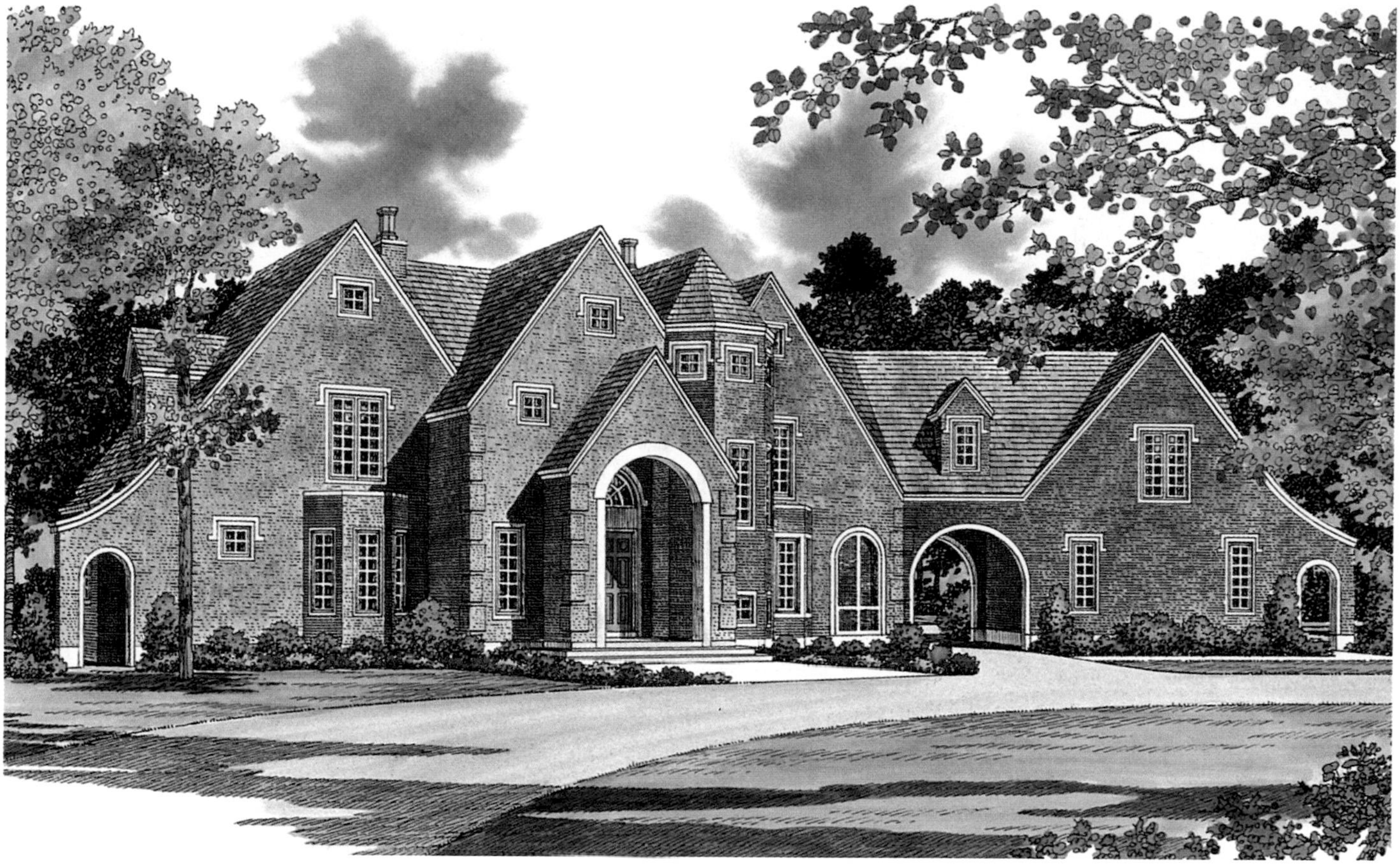

plan # HPK1700254

- Style: French
- First Floor: 1,566 sq. ft.
- Second Floor: 837 sq. ft.
- Total: 2,403 sq. ft.
- Bedrooms: 5
- Bathrooms: 4½
- Width: 116' - 3"
- Depth: 55' - 1"
- Foundation: Unfinished Basement

eplans.com

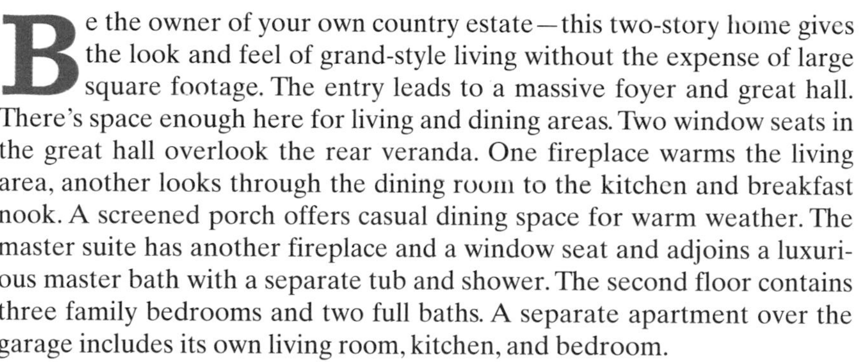

Be the owner of your own country estate—this two-story home gives the look and feel of grand-style living without the expense of large square footage. The entry leads to a massive foyer and great hall. There's space enough here for living and dining areas. Two window seats in the great hall overlook the rear veranda. One fireplace warms the living area, another looks through the dining room to the kitchen and breakfast nook. A screened porch offers casual dining space for warm weather. The master suite has another fireplace and a window seat and adjoins a luxurious master bath with a separate tub and shower. The second floor contains three family bedrooms and two full baths. A separate apartment over the garage includes its own living room, kitchen, and bedroom.

SECOND FLOOR

FIRST FLOOR

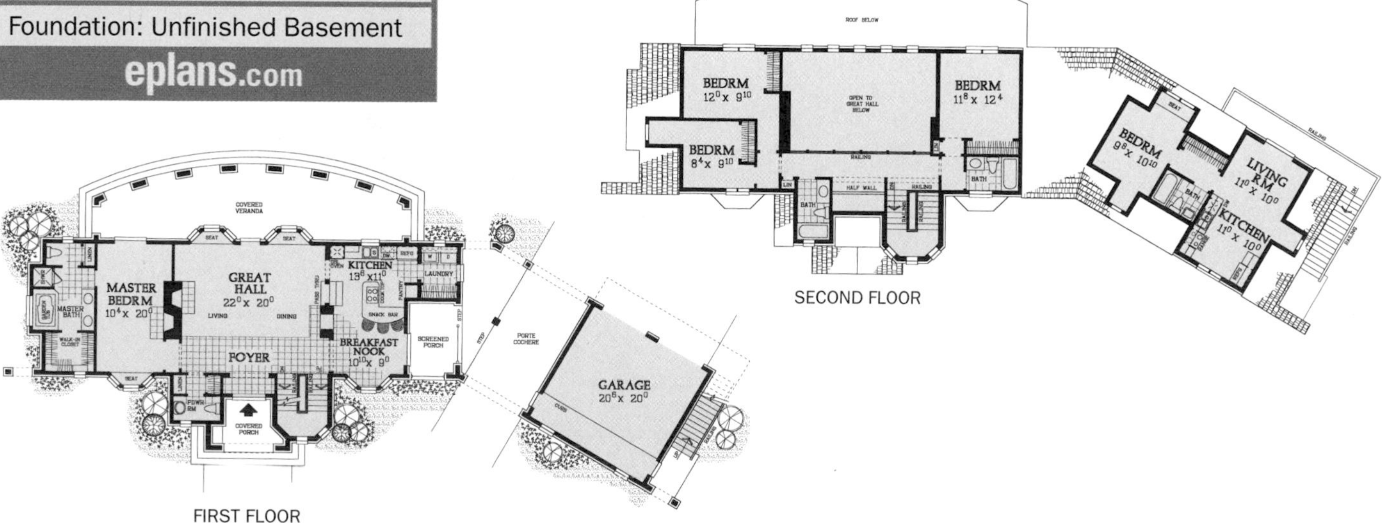

plan# HPK1700255

Style: Georgian
First Floor: 1,327 sq. ft.
Second Floor: 1,099 sq. ft.
Total: 2,426 sq. ft.
Bonus Space: 290 sq. ft.
Bedrooms: 4
Bathrooms: 3
Width: 54' - 4"
Depth: 42' - 10"
Foundation: Crawlspace, Unfinished Walkout Basement
eplans.com

A Southern classic, this lovely home will become a treasured place to call your own. The entry makes a grand impression; double doors open to the foyer where French doors reveal a study. To the right, the dining room is designed for entertaining, with easy access to the angled serving-bar kitchen. A bayed breakfast nook leads into the hearth-warmed family room. Tucked to the rear, a bedroom with a full bath makes an ideal guest room. The master suite is upstairs and enjoys a private vaulted spa bath. Two additional bedrooms reside on this level and join a full bath and an optional bonus room, perfect as a kid's retreat, home gym, or crafts room.

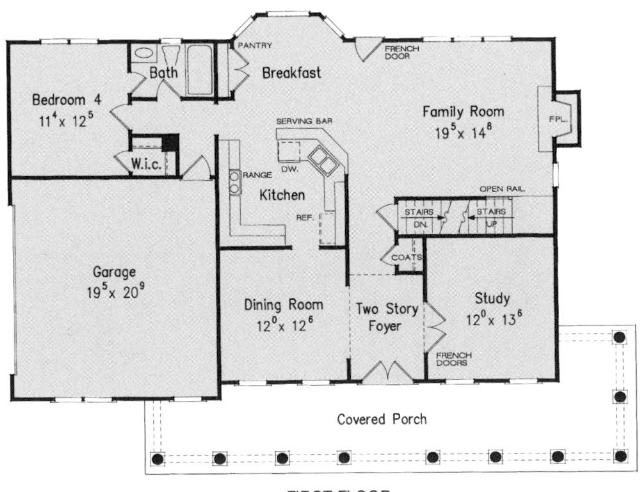

FIRST FLOOR

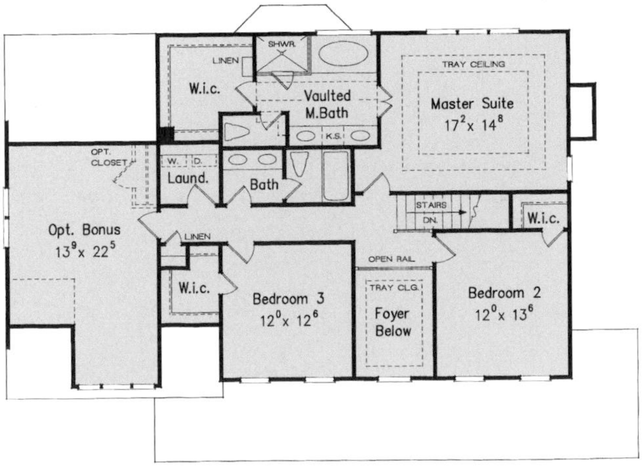

LINEN
SHWR.
W.i.c.
TRAY CEILING
Vaulted M.Bath
Master Suite
17^2x 14^8
K.S.
OPT. CLOSET
W. D.
Laund.
Bath
STAIRS DN.
W.i.c.
Opt. Bonus
13^9x 22^5
LINEN
OPEN RAIL
W.i.c.
Bedroom 3
12^0x 12^6
TRAY CLG.
Foyer Below
Bedroom 2
12^0x 13^6

SECOND FLOOR

plan# HPK1700256

Style: Farmhouse
First Floor: 1,160 sq. ft.
Second Floor: 1,316 sq. ft.
Total: 2,476 sq. ft.
Bedrooms: 4
Bathrooms: 2½
Width: 52' - 0"
Depth: 44' - 0"
Foundation: Unfinished Walkout Basement

eplans.com

Brick detailing, shingles, and siding come together to create a refined exterior on this country farmhouse. The foyer is flanked by a dining room and a living room. At the rear of the house is the two-story family room, which is graced with a central fireplace and rear-door access to a sun deck. The kitchen blends into the breakfast area and is provided with backyard views. Storage space, a powder room, and a computer station complete the first floor of this plan. The sleeping quarters upstairs include a lavish master suite—with a full bath and sitting area—three vaulted family bedrooms, another full bath, and a laundry area.

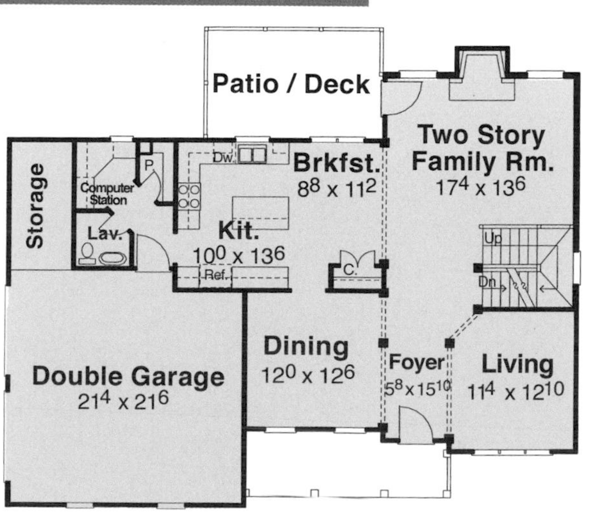

FIRST FLOOR

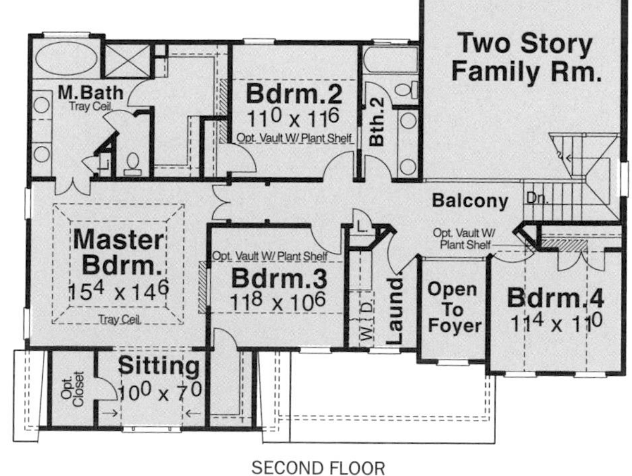

SECOND FLOOR

PHOTO COURTESY OF GABRELL ASSOCIATES, INC.

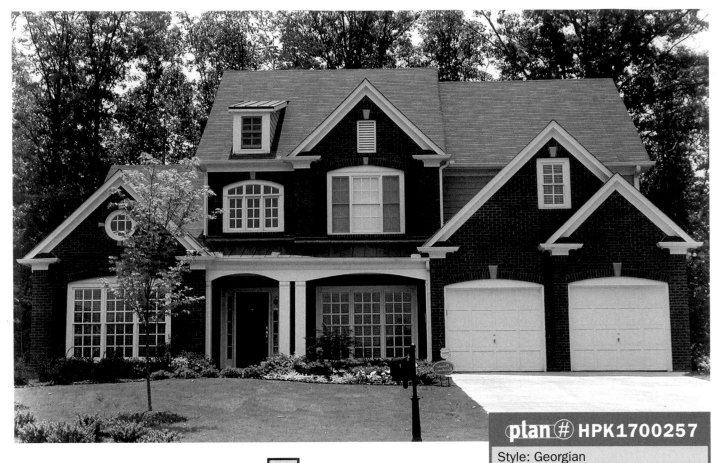

plan# HPK1700257
Style: Georgian
First Floor: 1,773 sq. ft.
Second Floor: 709 sq. ft.
Total: 2,482 sq. ft.
Bedrooms: 4
Bathrooms: 2½
Width: 54' - 0"
Depth: 47' - 6"
Foundation: Slab, Unfinished Walkout Basement
eplans.com

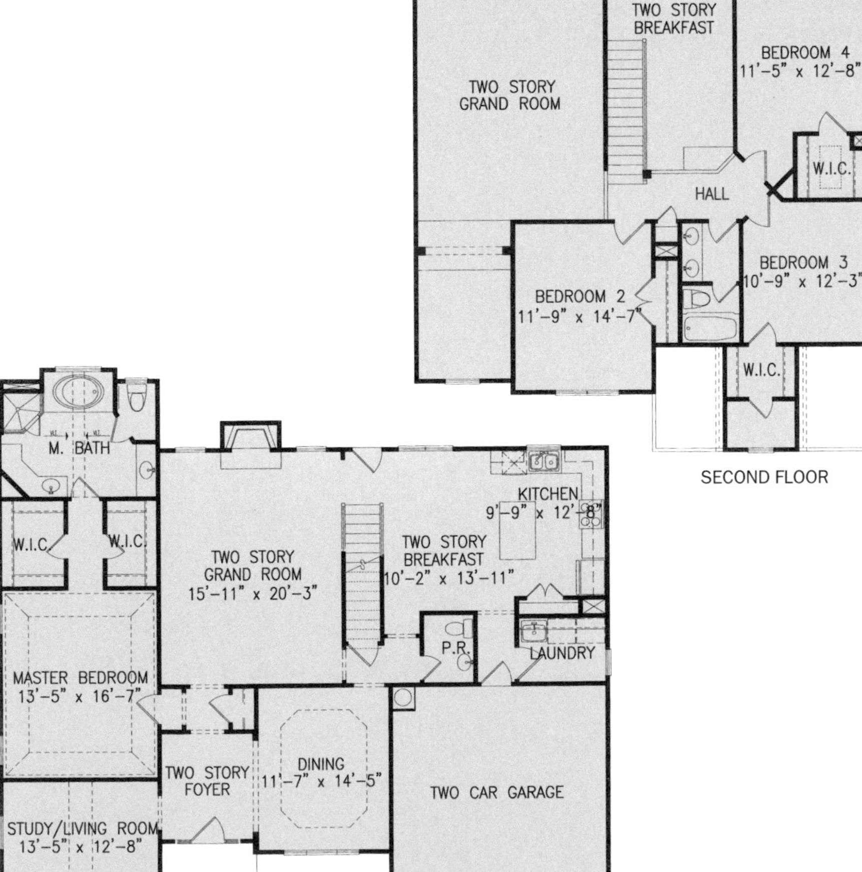

SECOND FLOOR

FIRST FLOOR

This two-story traditional home offers space for everyone. A handsome brick exterior, keystone arches, and an attractive shed dormer provide tons of curb appeal. The foyer is flanked by a study and the dining room. To the rear are the more casual spaces. The grand room features two-story ceilings, a fireplace, and is within steps of the island kitchen and breakfast room. The first-floor master suite is convenient as well as secluded, and offers walk-in closets, a full bath, and tray ceiling. Upstairs, three roomy secondary bedrooms—two with walk-in closets—share a full bath.

plan# HPK1700258
Style: Traditional
First Floor: 1,754 sq. ft.
Second Floor: 744 sq. ft.
Total: 2,498 sq. ft.
Bedrooms: 4
Bathrooms: 2½
Width: 69' - 0"
Depth: 52' - 8"
Foundation: Unfinished Basement
eplans.com

EDITOR'S PICK

The expressive French roof is just one feature we like about this home. How about the two-story foyer and spacious breakfast nook? Or the dual-facing fireplace that both separates and unifies spaces at the center of the plan? Owners will delight in the sumptuous master suite, which includes a great walk-in closet. Meanwhile, the rest of the family resides upstairs, in three bedrooms and a shared bath. Finally, a mudroom/laundry near the garage handles heavy chores with grace.

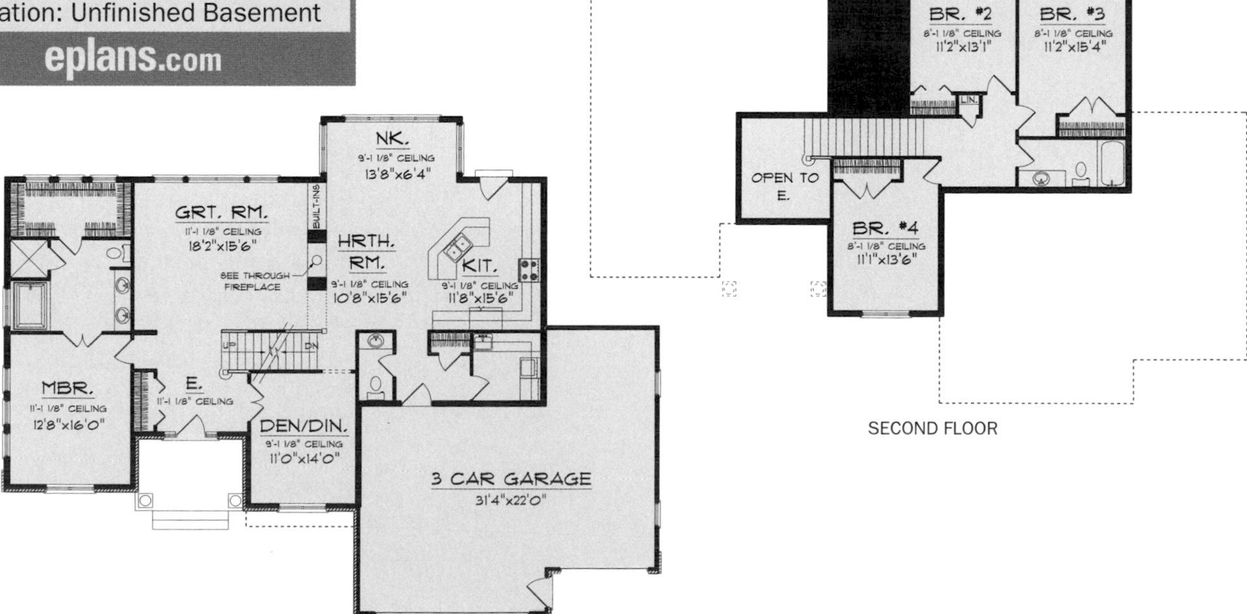

FIRST FLOOR

SECOND FLOOR

plan# HPK1700259
Style: Traditional
First Floor: 1,178 sq. ft.
Second Floor: 1,321 sq. ft.
Total: 2,499 sq. ft.
Bedrooms: 4
Bathrooms: 2½
Width: 50' - 0"
Depth: 44' - 0"
eplans.com

SECOND FLOOR

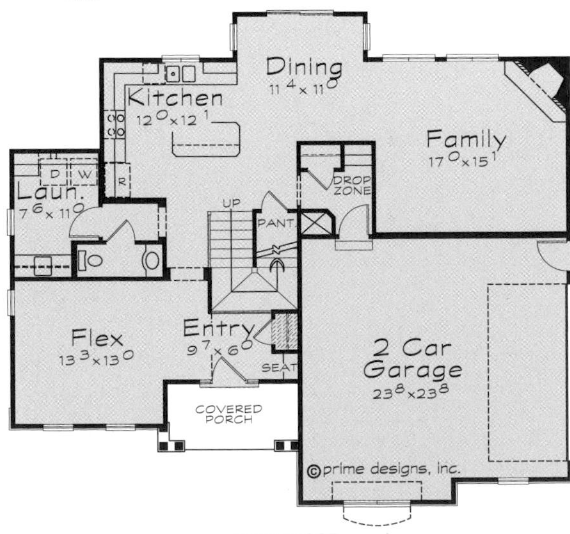

FIRST FLOOR

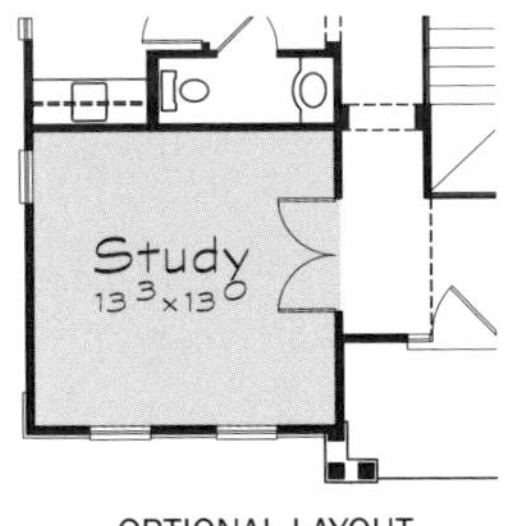

OPTIONAL LAYOUT

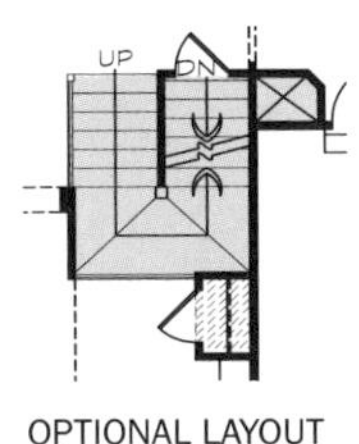

OPTIONAL LAYOUT

A stone masonry facade and arched windows grace the exterior of this house, with Palladian glass dappling the sunlight on the inside. A flexible room on the main floor provides a possibility of five bedrooms in all. Laundry and bath are located behind the flex room, with kitchen, formal dining room, and family room forming one large area. A pantry and drop zone are secreted in the center of this level. Upstairs reside the remaining bedrooms (look at all of the walk-in closet space!), two more baths, linen closet, and perspective to the entry way below. The inhabitant of the master suite will live like royalty amidst its spaciousness.

Homes From 2,500 to 2,999 Square Feet

With elements of country style, this unique Colonial-inspired home presents a rustic attitude blended with the delicate features that make this design one of a kind. See plan HPK1700306 on page 270.

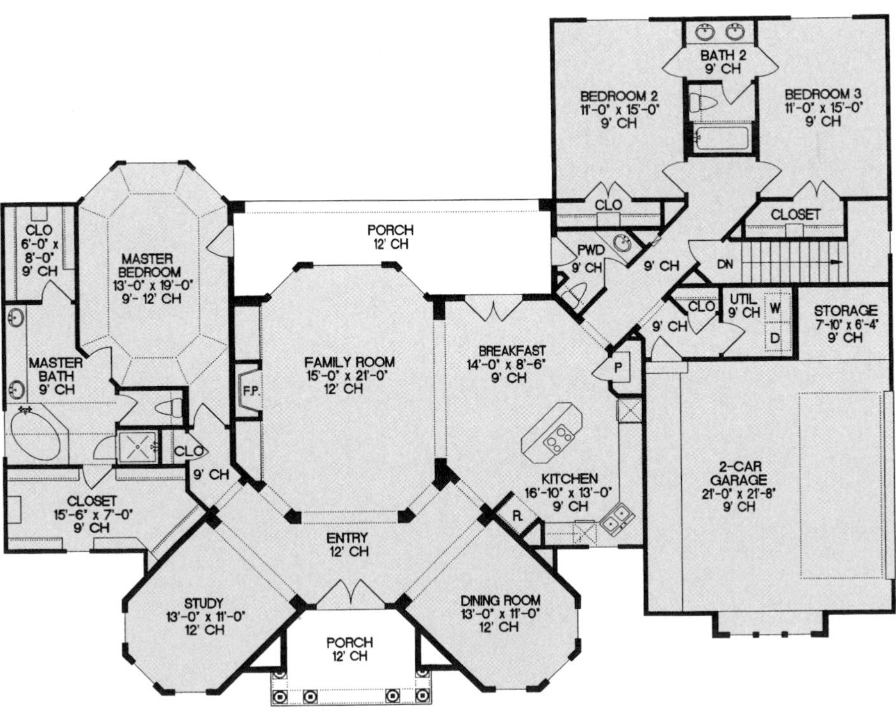

plan# HPK1700260

Style: Traditional
Square Footage: 2,517
Bedrooms: 3
Bathrooms: 2½
Width: 77' - 0"
Depth: 59' - 0"

eplans.com

This European stucco home is a well-designed one-story villa. Turrets top identical bayed rooms that are enclosed behind double doors just off the entry. The formal dining room and study are situated in the window-filled turrets. The family room is a spacious entertaining area with a fireplace and built-ins. An efficient kitchen is uniquely designed with its island and angular shape. The split-bedroom floor plan places the master suite away from the two family bedrooms.

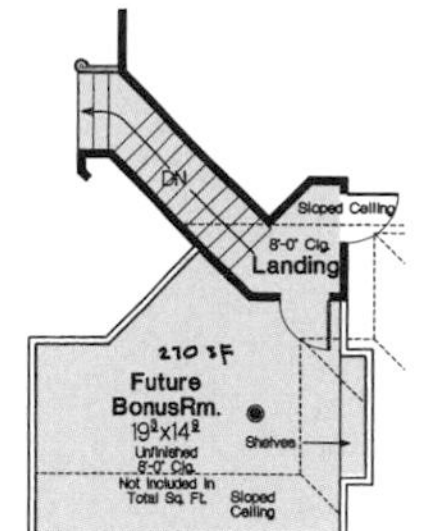

plan # HPK1700261

Style: European Cottage
Square Footage: 2,530
Bonus Space: 270 sq. ft.
Bedrooms: 3
Bathrooms: 2½
Width: 83' - 10"
Depth: 51' - 10"
Foundation: Slab

eplans.com

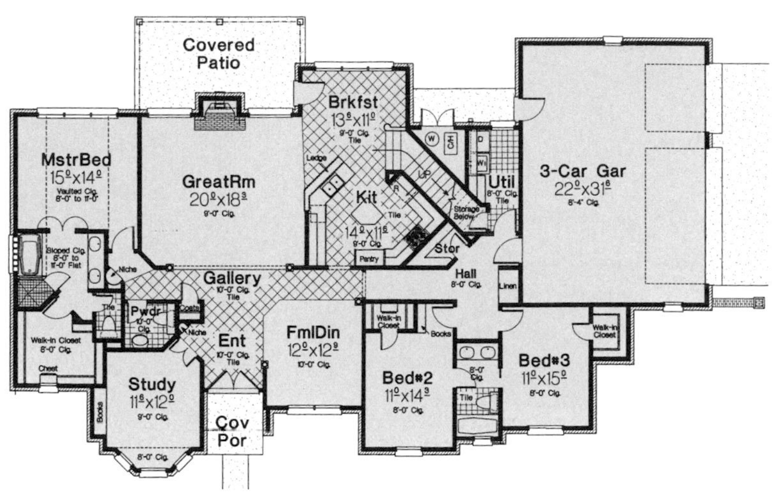

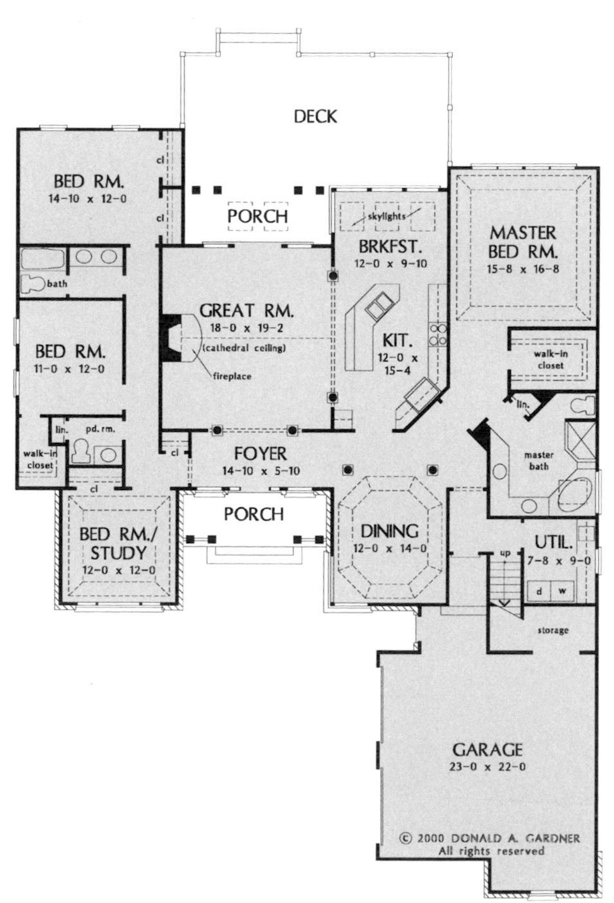

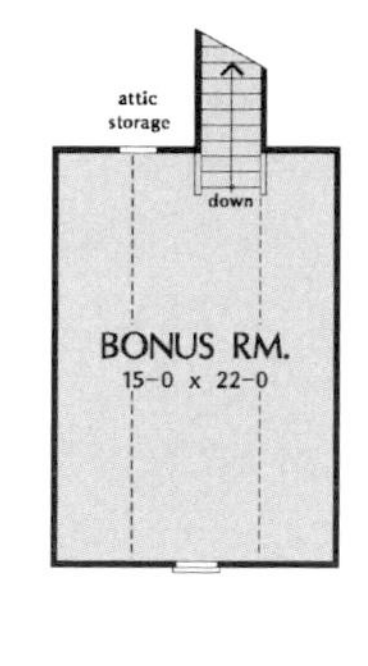

plan # HPK1700262

Style: Traditional
Square Footage: 2,544
Bonus Space: 394 sq. ft.
Bedrooms: 4
Bathrooms: 2½
Width: 62' - 8"
Depth: 82' - 1"

eplans.com

plan# HPK1700263

Style: Traditional

Square Footage: 2,586

Bedrooms: 3

Bathrooms: 2½

Width: 72' - 8"

Depth: 64' - 8"

eplans.com

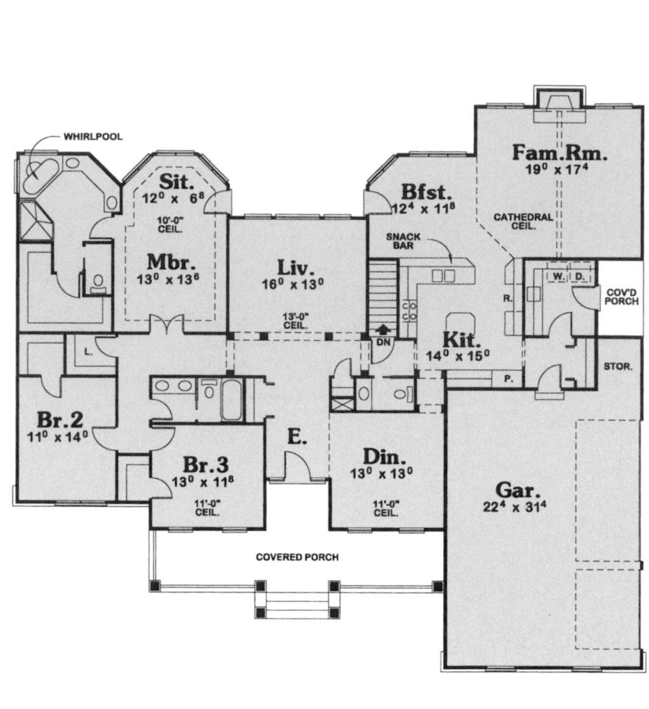

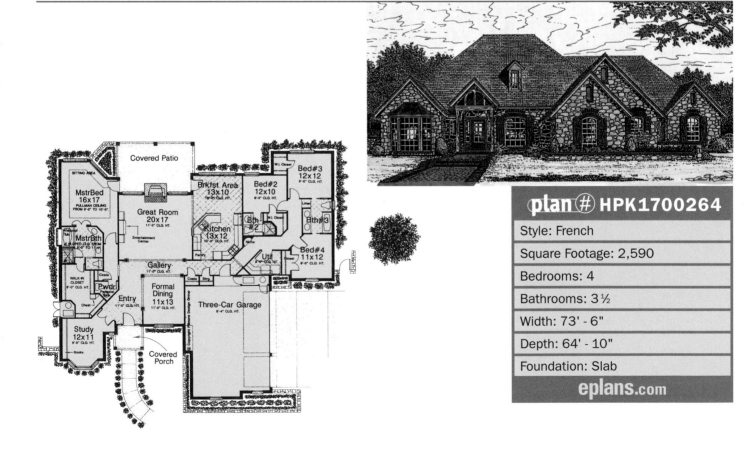

plan# HPK1700264

Style: French

Square Footage: 2,590

Bedrooms: 4

Bathrooms: 3½

Width: 73' - 6"

Depth: 64' - 10"

Foundation: Slab

eplans.com

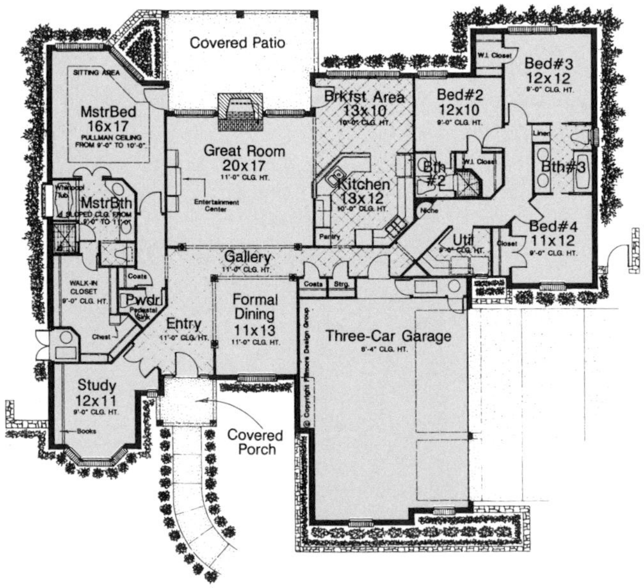

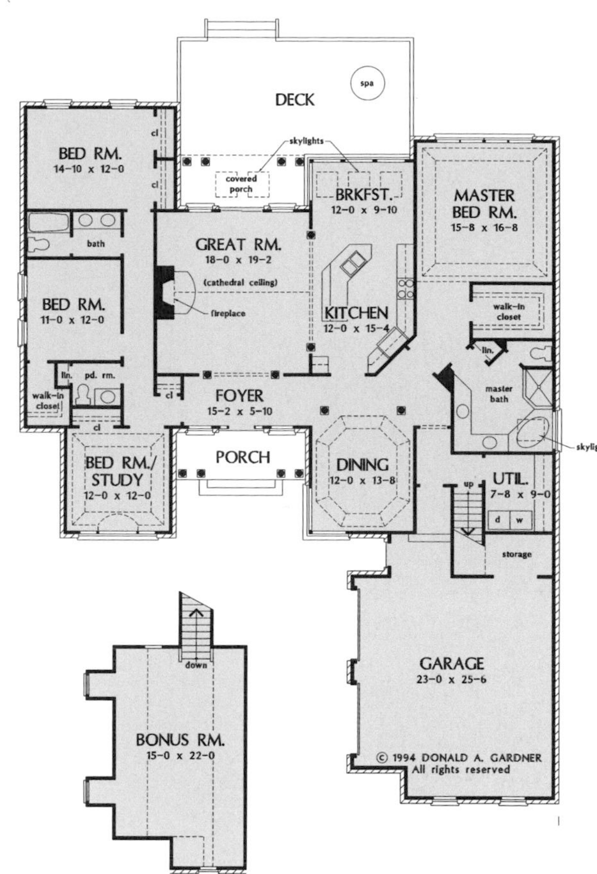

plan# HPK1700265

Style: Traditional
Square Footage: 2,625
Bonus Space: 447 sq. ft.
Bedrooms: 4
Bathrooms: 2½
Width: 63' - 1"
Depth: 90' - 2"

eplans.com

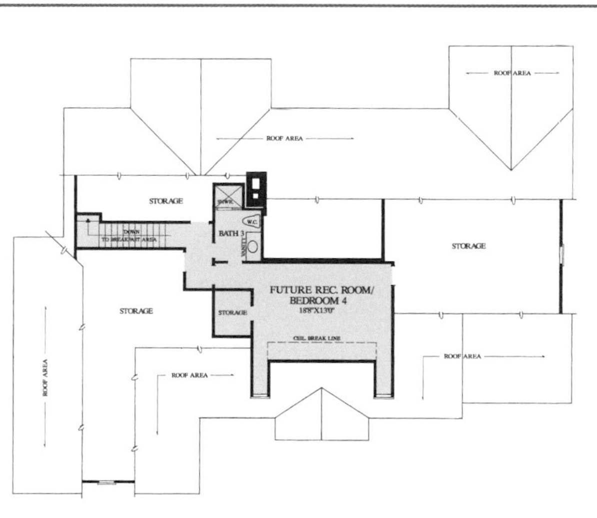

plan# HPK1700266

Style: Colonial
Square Footage: 2,639
Bonus Space: 396 sq. ft.
Bedrooms: 3
Bathrooms: 2½
Width: 73' - 8"
Depth: 58' - 6"
Foundation: Crawlspace

eplans.com

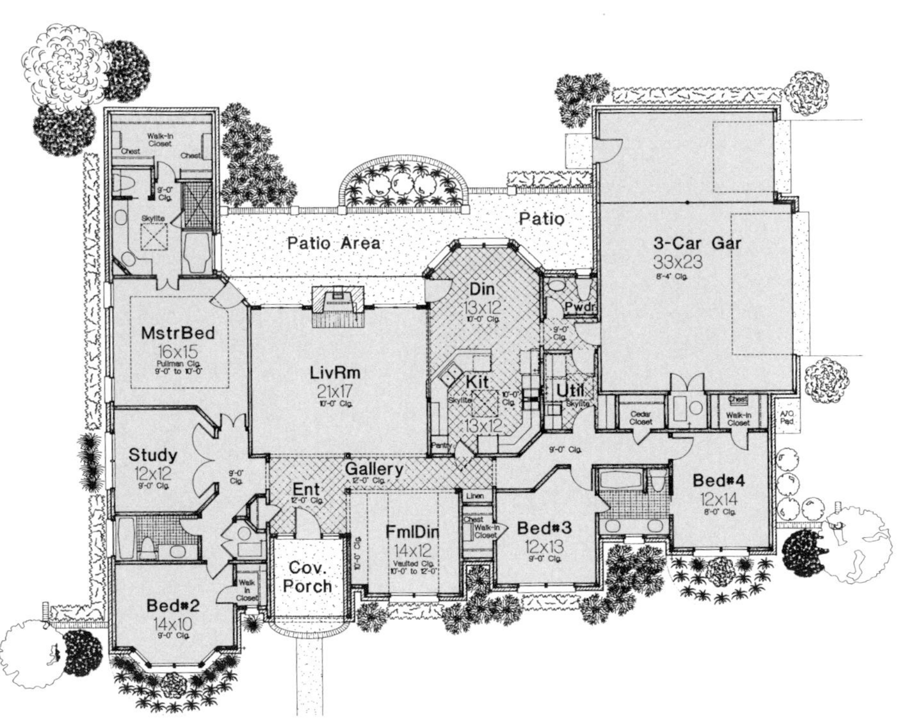

plan # HPK1700267

Style: Traditional

Square Footage: 2,696

Bedrooms: 4

Bathrooms: 3½

Width: 80' - 0"

Depth: 64' - 1"

Foundation: Slab

eplans.com

A brick archway covers the front porch of this European-style home, creating a truly grand entrance. Situated beyond the entry, the living room takes center stage with a fireplace flanked by tall windows. To the right is a bayed eating area and an efficient kitchen. Steps away is the formal dining room. Skillful planning creates flexibility for the master suite. If you wish, use Bedroom 2 as a secondary bedroom or guest room, with the adjacent study accessible to everyone. Or, if you prefer, combine the master suite with the study and use it as a private retreat with Bedroom 2 as a nursery, creating a wing that provides complete privacy. Completing this clever plan are two family bedrooms, a powder room, and a utility room.

plan # HPK1700268

Style: Country Cottage
Square Footage: 2,777
Bonus Space: 424 sq. ft.
Bedrooms: 3
Bathrooms: 2 ½
Width: 75' - 6"
Depth: 60' - 2"
Foundation: Crawlspace, Unfinished Basement

eplans.com

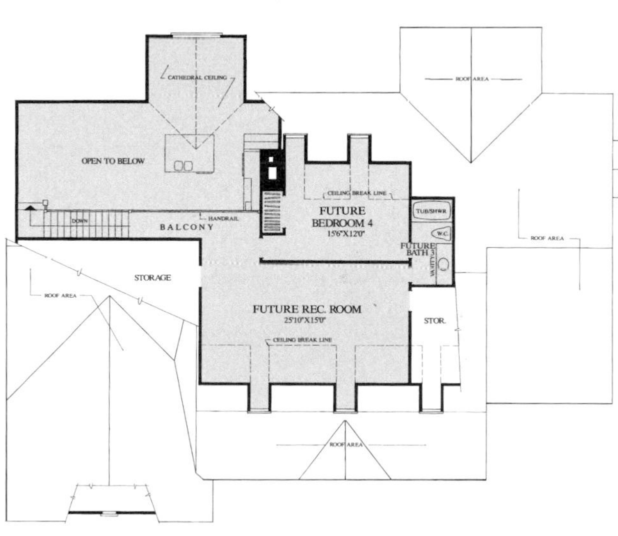

This home is an absolute dream when it comes to living space! Whether formal or casual, there's a room for every occasion. The foyer opens to the formal dining room on the left; straight ahead lies the magnificent hearth-warmed living room. The island kitchen opens not only to a breakfast nook, but to a huge family/sunroom surrounded by two walls of windows! The right wing of the plan holds the sleeping quarters—two family bedrooms sharing a bath, and a majestic master suite. The second floor holds an abundance of expandable space.

OSCAR THOMPSON PHOTOGRAPHY

plan# HPK1700269

Style: Floridian
Square Footage: 2,794
Bedrooms: 3
Bathrooms: 3
Width: 70' - 0"
Depth: 98' - 0"
Foundation: Slab

eplans.com

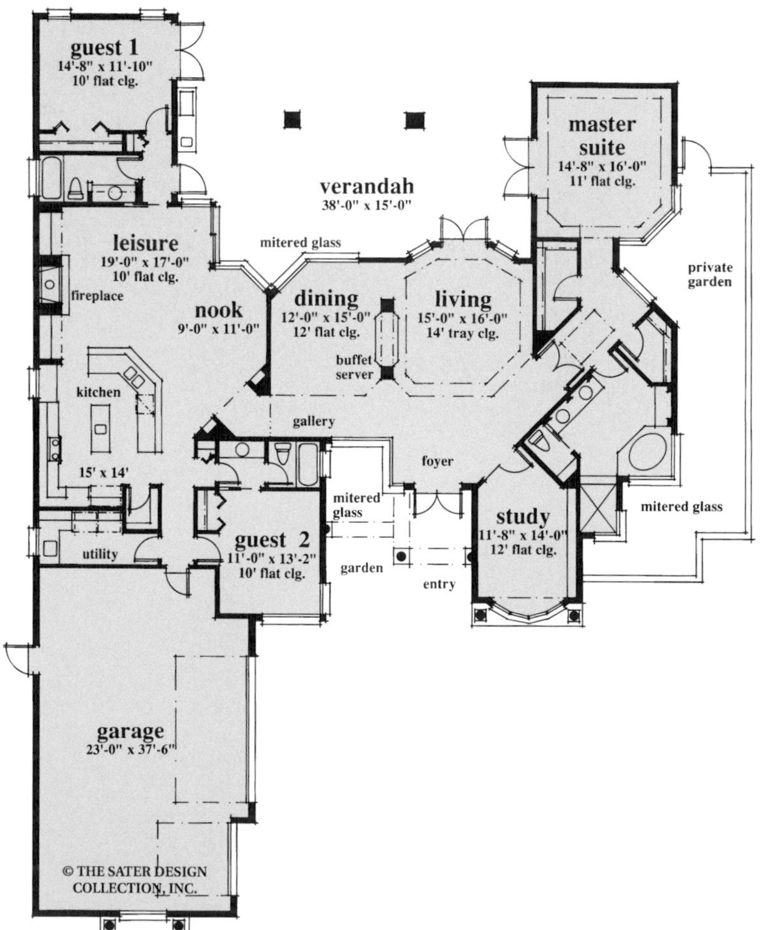

Classic columns, circle-head windows, and a bay-windowed study give this stucco home a wonderful street presence. The foyer leads to the formal living and dining areas. An arched buffet server separates these rooms and contributes an open feeling. The kitchen, nook, and leisure room are grouped for informal living. A desk/message center in the island kitchen, art niches in the nook, and a fireplace with an entertainment center and shelves add custom touches. Two secondary suites have guest baths and offer full privacy from the master wing. The master suite hosts a private garden area; the bath features a walk-in shower that overlooks the garden and a water closet room with space for books or a television. Large His and Hers walk-in closets complete these private quarters.

plan# HPK1700270

Style: European Cottage
Square Footage: 2,816
Bonus Space: 290 sq. ft.
Bedrooms: 4
Bathrooms: 3½ + ½
Width: 94' - 0"
Depth: 70' - 5"
Foundation: Slab

eplans.com

Though designed as a grand estate, this home retains the warmth of a country manor with intimate details on the inside and out. A one-of-a-kind drive court leads to private parking and ends in a two-car garage; a separate guest house is replete with angled walls and sculptured ceilings. A continuous vault follows from the family room through the kitchen and nook. The vault soars even higher in the bonus room with a sundeck upstairs. Two exquisitely appointed family bedrooms with window seats and walk-in closets share a full bath. The master suite has pampering details such as a juice bar and media wall, walk-in closets, and covered patio access.

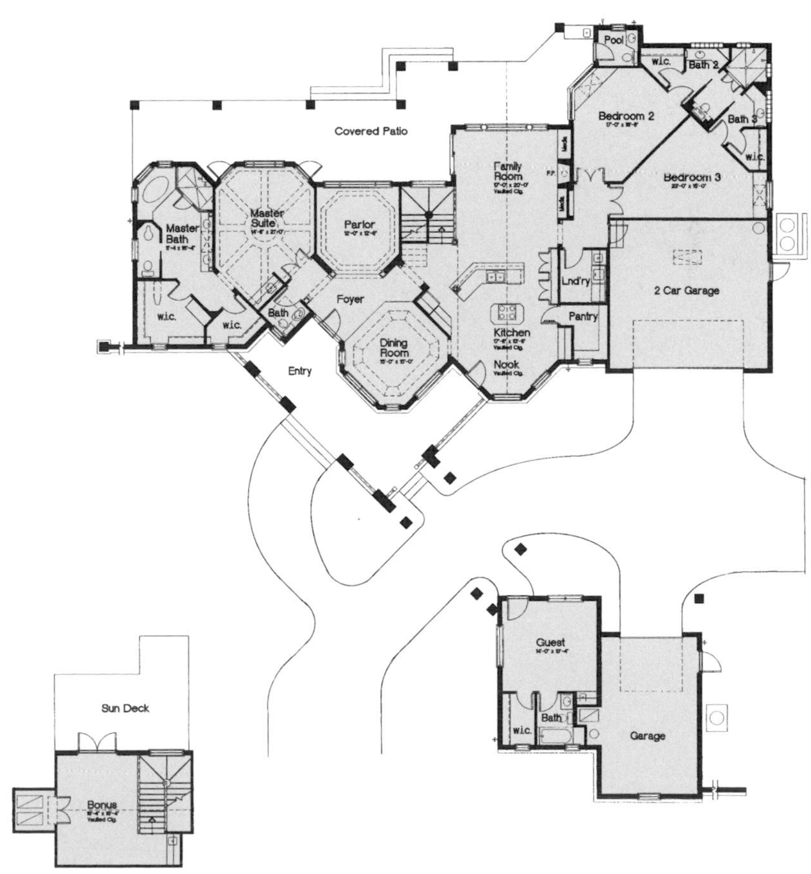

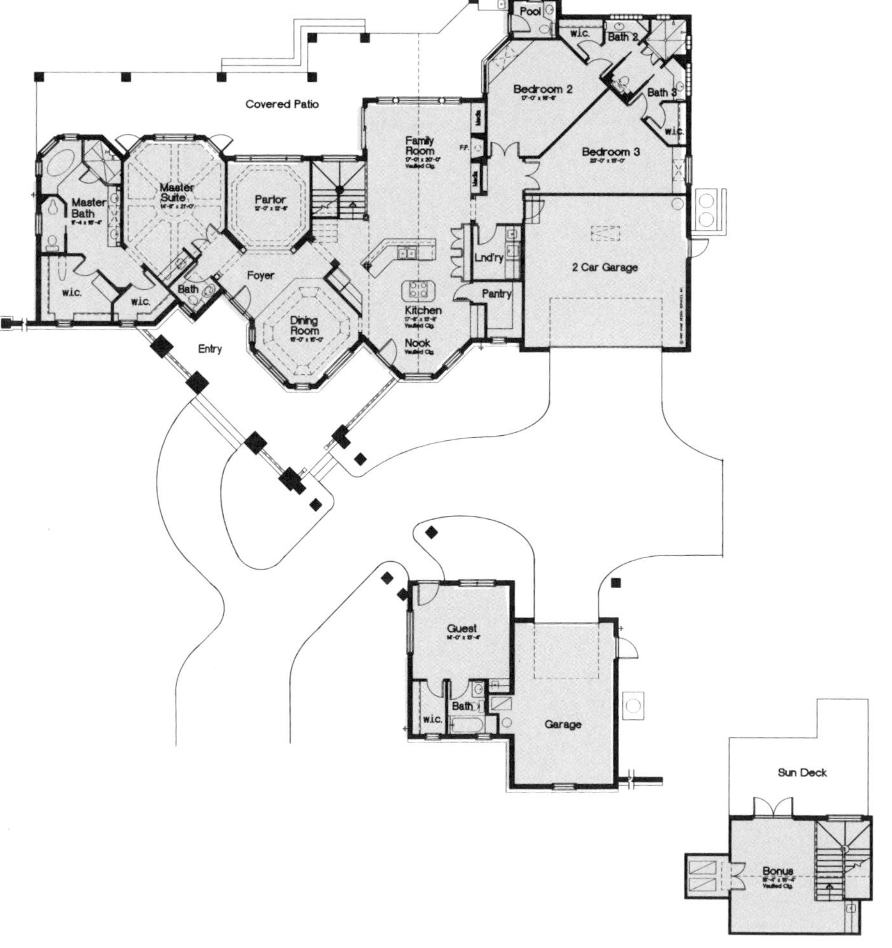

plan # HPK1700271

Style: European Cottage
Square Footage: 2,816
Bonus Space: 290 sq. ft.
Bedrooms: 3
Bathrooms: 3 ½
Width: 94' - 0"
Depth: 114' - 0"
Foundation: Slab

eplans.com

A striking front-facing pediment, bold columns, and varying rooflines set this design apart from the rest. An angled entry leads to the foyer, flanked on one side by the dining room with a tray ceiling and on the other by a lavish master suite. This suite is enhanced with a private bath, two large walk-in closets, a garden tub, a compartmented toilet and bidet, and access to the covered patio. The parlor also enjoys rear-yard views. The vaulted ceilings provide a sense of spaciousness from the breakfast nook and kitchen to the family room. A laundry room and roomy pantry are accessible from the kitchen area. Two family bedrooms reside on the right side of the plan; each has its own full bath and both are built at interesting angles. An upstairs, vaulted bonus room includes French doors opening to a second-floor sundeck.

plan# HPK1700272

Style: Craftsman

Square Footage: 2,818

Bedrooms: 4

Bathrooms: 3

Width: 70' - 0"

Depth: 69' - 10"

eplans.com

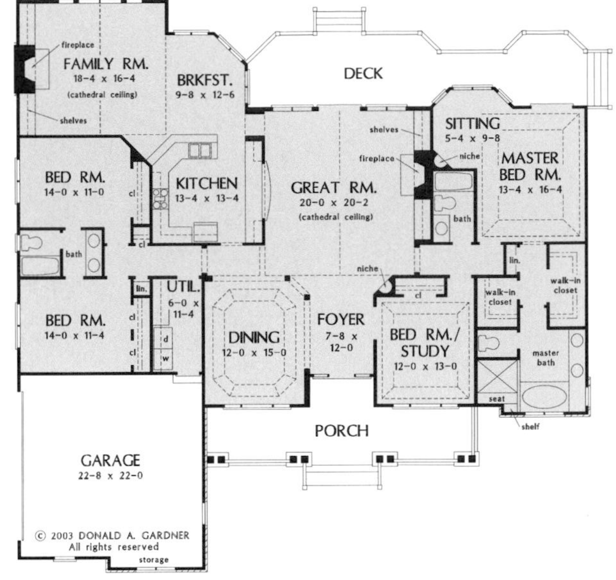

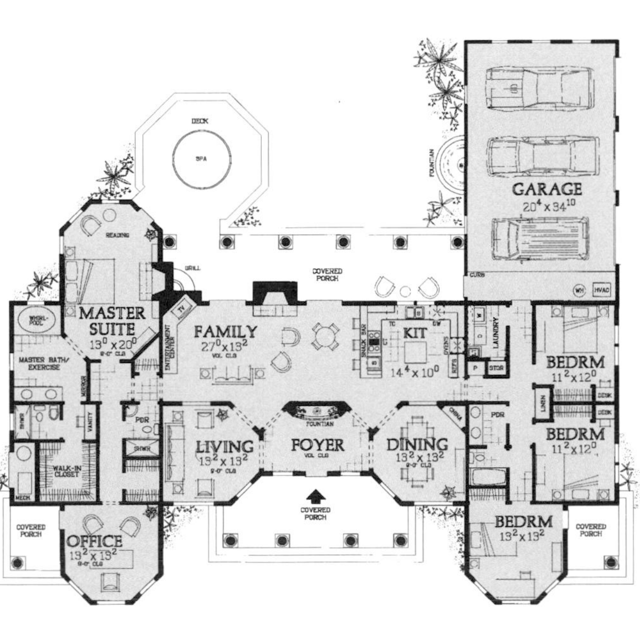

plan# HPK1700273

Style: Mediterranean

Square Footage: 2,831 sq. ft.

Bedrooms: 4

Bathrooms: 3

Width: 84' - 0"

Depth: 77' - 0"

Foundation: Slab

eplans.com

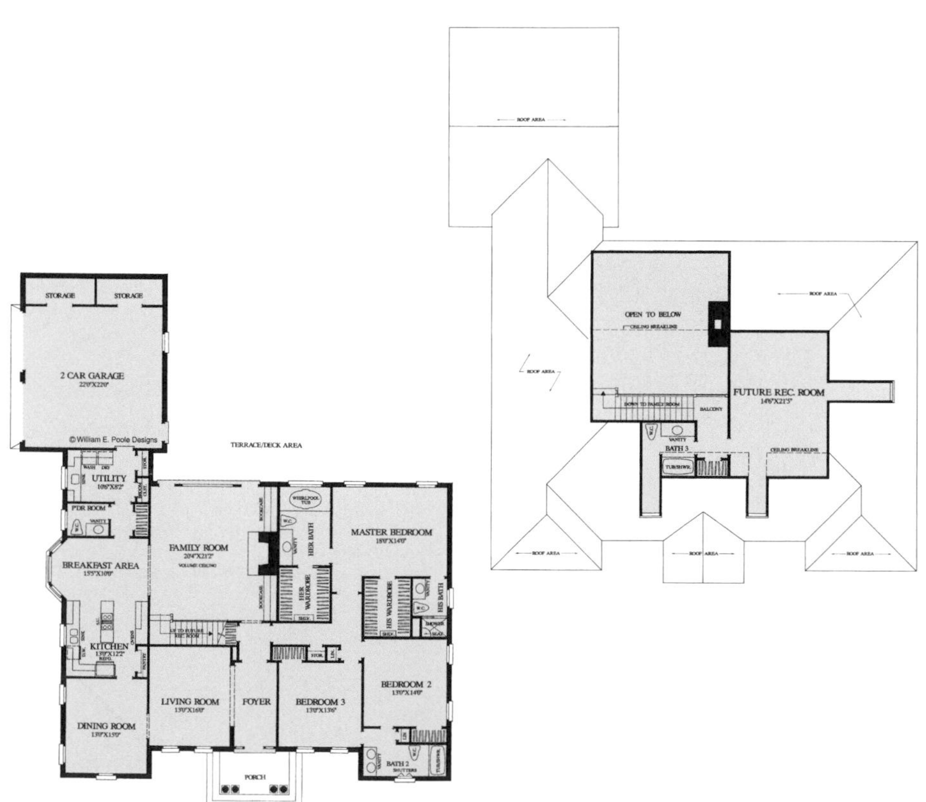

plan # HPK1700274

Style: Georgian
Square Footage: 2,869
Bedrooms: 3
Bathrooms: 3½
Width: 68' - 6"
Depth: 79' - 8"
Foundation: Crawlspace

eplans.com

Here is a beautiful example of Classical Revival architecture complete with shuttered, jack-arch windows and a column-supported pediment over the entry. Inside, the foyer opens to the living room and leads to the family room at the rear. Here, a panoramic view is complemented by an impressive fireplace framed by built-ins. To the left, the efficient island kitchen is situated between the sunny breakfast nook and the formal dining room. The right side of the plan holds two bedrooms and the lavish master suite.

plan# HPK1700275
Style: Contemporary
Square Footage: 2,907
Bedrooms: 3
Bathrooms: 2½
Width: 65' - 0"
Depth: 84' - 0"
Foundation: Slab
eplans.com

Stunning windows and walls of glass enhance the exterior of this contemporary home and provide natural light and wide views to the open interior. The central living room leads to the covered lanai and brings in a wealth of sunlight. Casual living space features a built-in entertainment center and glass doors to the lanai. The gourmet kitchen serves a formal dining room, which has a tray ceiling. The master wing has a walk-in wardrobe, whirlpool tub, two lavatories and access to a private garden.

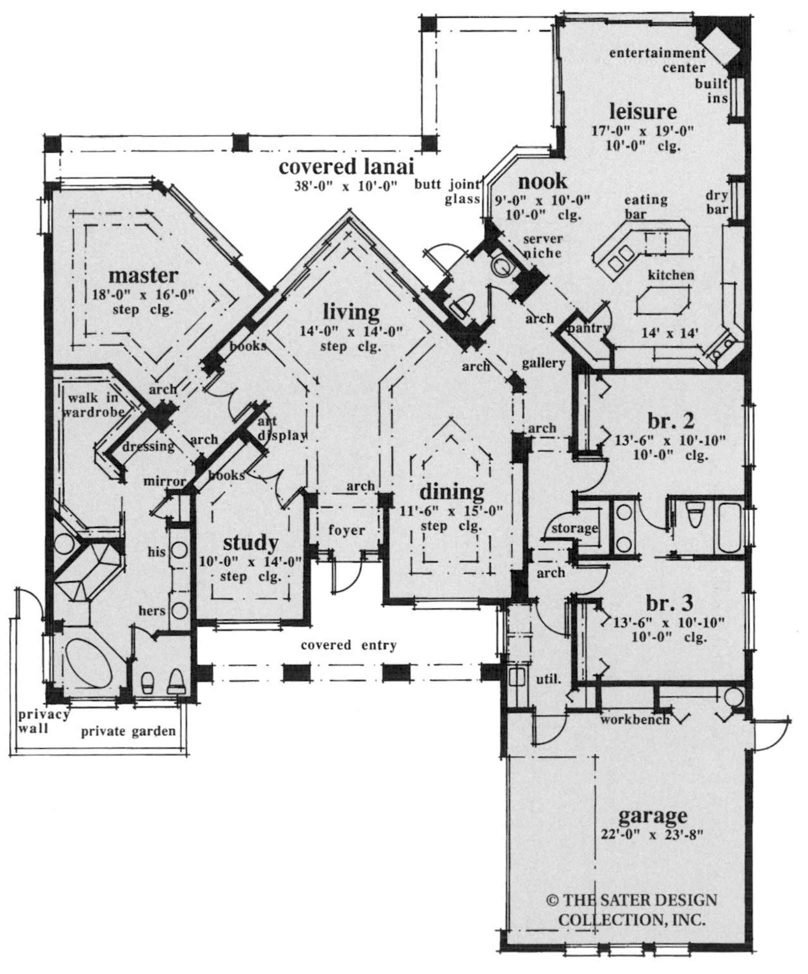

plan# HPK1700276

Style: Plantation
Square Footage: 2,946
Bedrooms: 4
Bathrooms: 3
Width: 94' - 1"
Depth: 67' - 4"
Foundation: Slab

eplans.com

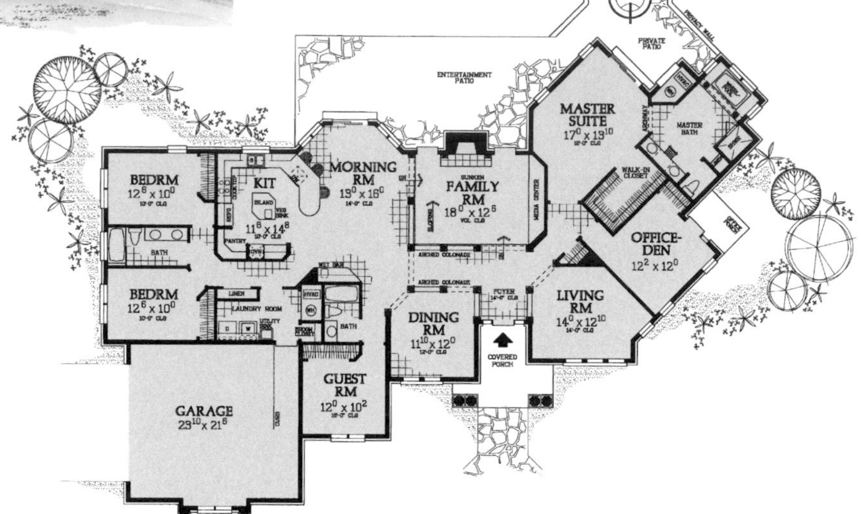

plan# HPK1700277

Style: Transitional
Square Footage: 2,962
Bedrooms: 4
Bathrooms: 3
Width: 70' - 0"
Depth: 76' - 0"
Foundation: Slab

eplans.com

plan# HPK1700278

Style: Traditional
Square Footage: 2,990
Bedrooms: 4
Bathrooms: 3½
Width: 80' - 0"
Depth: 68' - 0"
Foundation: Slab

eplans.com

A brick exterior, cast-stone trim, and corner quoins make up this attractive single-living-area design. The entry introduces a formal dining room to the right and a living room with a wall of windows to the left. The hearth-warmed family room opens to the kitchen/dinette, both with 10-foot ceilings. A large bay window enhances the dinette with a full glass door to the covered patio. A large master suite with vaulted ceilings features a bayed sitting area, a luxurious bath with double sinks, and an oversize walk-in closet.

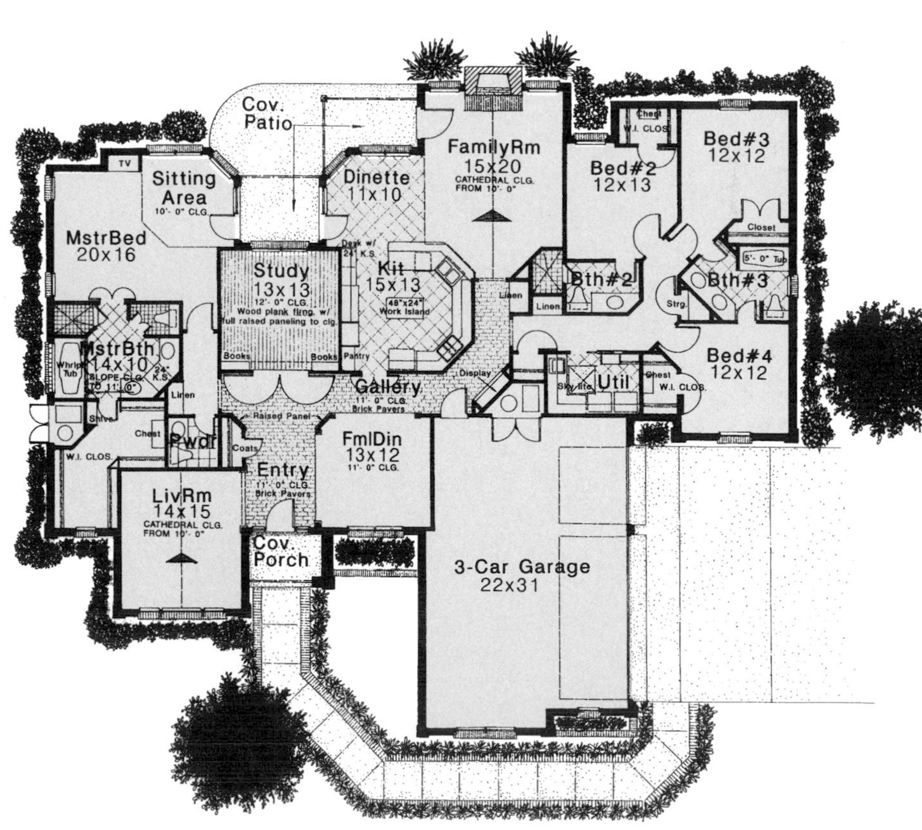

This design exemplifies country living with its front and rear porches, large country kitchen, and a welcoming facade. The foyer is flanked by the formal living room on the left and a coat closet on the right. It leads to the spacious great room complete with vaulted ceiling, a built-in entertainment center, and a fireplace. The master suite dominates the right side of the plan boasting a whirlpool tub, dual vanities, a separate shower, and a huge walk-in closet. Upstairs, there are two additional family bedrooms, each with a full bath. A bonus room offers flexible space with limitless possibilities. A two-car garage completes this plan.

plan # HPK1700279

Style: Country Cottage

First Floor: 1,892 sq. ft.

Second Floor: 608 sq. ft.

Total: 2,500 sq. ft.

Bonus Space: 370 sq. ft.

Bedrooms: 3

Bathrooms: 3½

Width: 61' - 4"

Depth: 82' - 6"

Foundation: Crawlspace

eplans.com

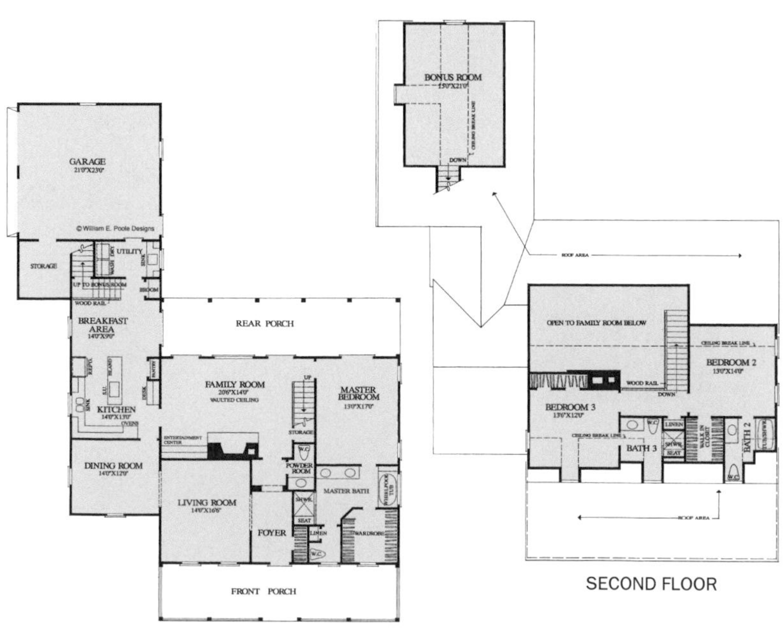

FIRST FLOOR

SECOND FLOOR

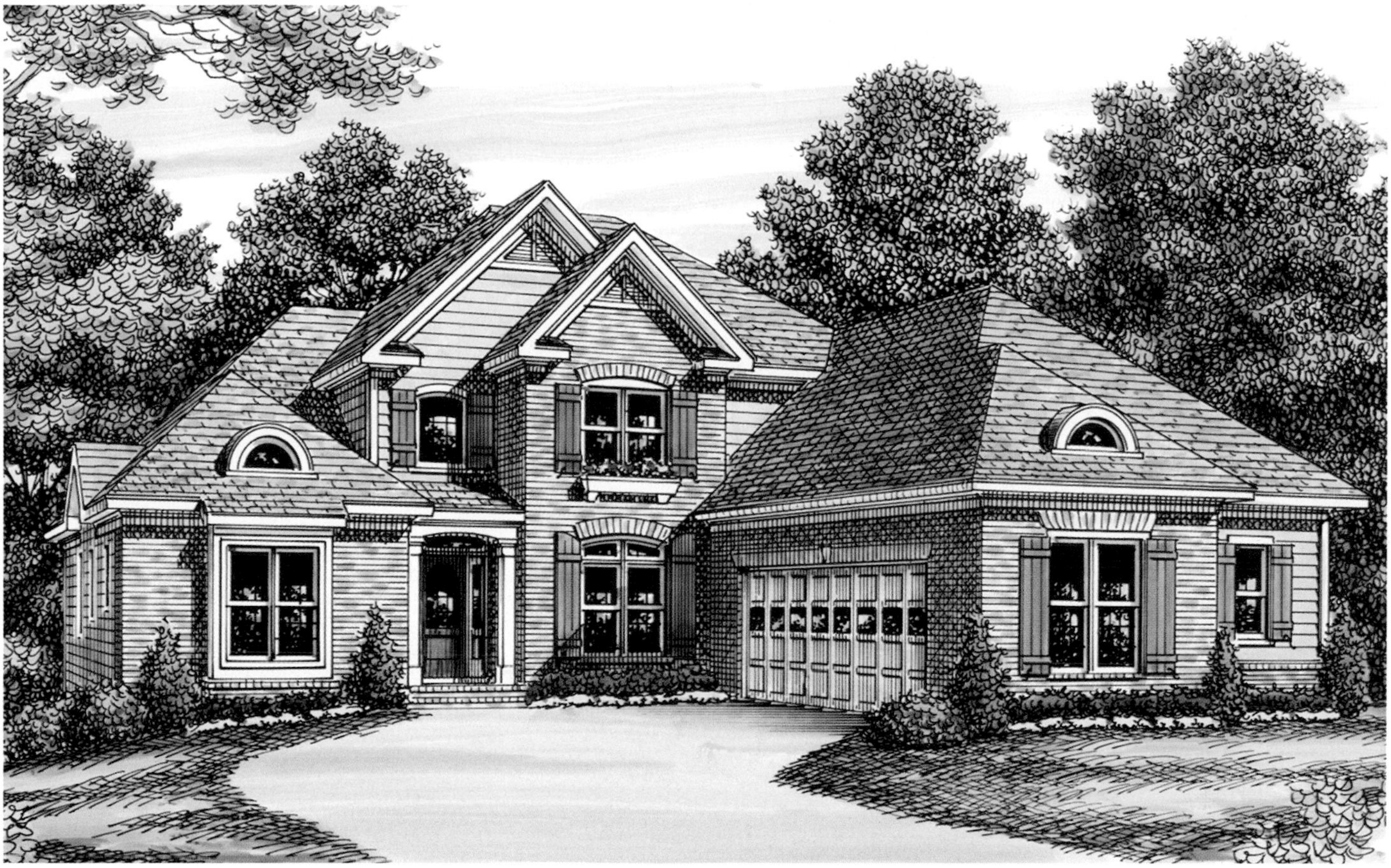

plan# HPK1700280

Style: Traditional
First Floor: 1,946 sq. ft.
Second Floor: 562 sq. ft.
Total: 2,508 sq. ft.
Bonus Space: 366 sq. ft.
Bedrooms: 4
Bathrooms: 3½
Width: 54' - 0"
Depth: 63' - 4"
Foundation: Crawlspace, Unfinished Walkout Basement

eplans.com

The hipped roof, gable accents, and side-entry garage make this a striking home. The vaulted family room features a central fireplace for maximum comfort. The kitchen is open to the breakfast area and the vaulted keeping room. The master suite features a tray ceiling and a vaulted bath with an oval tub under a radius window. Two family bedrooms and an optional bonus room are located on the second level.

SECOND FLOOR

FIRST FLOOR

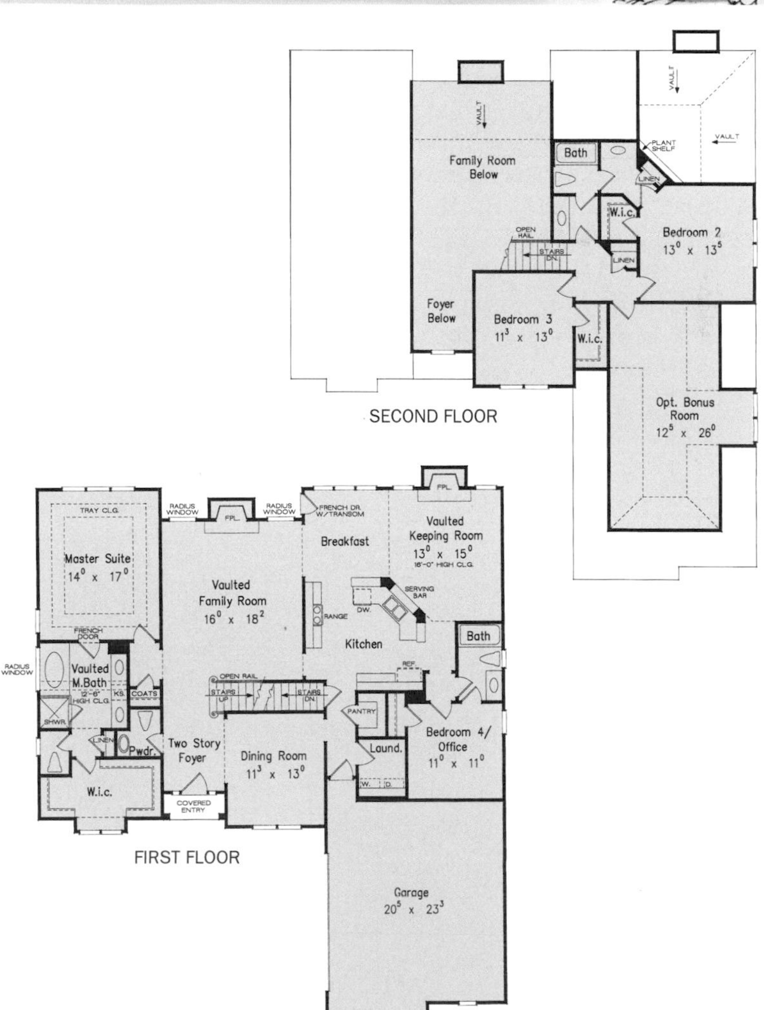

plan# HPK1700281

Style: Farmhouse

First Floor: 1,977 sq. ft.

Second Floor: 585 sq. ft.

Total: 2,562 sq. ft.

Bedrooms: 3

Bathrooms: 3

Width: 80' - 0"

Depth: 60' - 0"

eplans.com

A traditional country farmhouse with modern conveniences. Regenerate your spirit at the end of a long day as you relax on your front porch under a two-story arch. Alternatively, enjoy a more private seclusion at the rear, or in the study/library. Better yet, work from home in your custom office! Linger over coffee and a muffin in the breakfast nook, or plan elaborate meals and parties in the formal dining and living rooms. Locate this dream home off of the beaten path, or adjacent to a busy sidewalk. A three-car garage, three bedrooms, and flexible den or fourth bedroom provide ample room for teenagers (with an optional game room and their own shared bath upstairs).

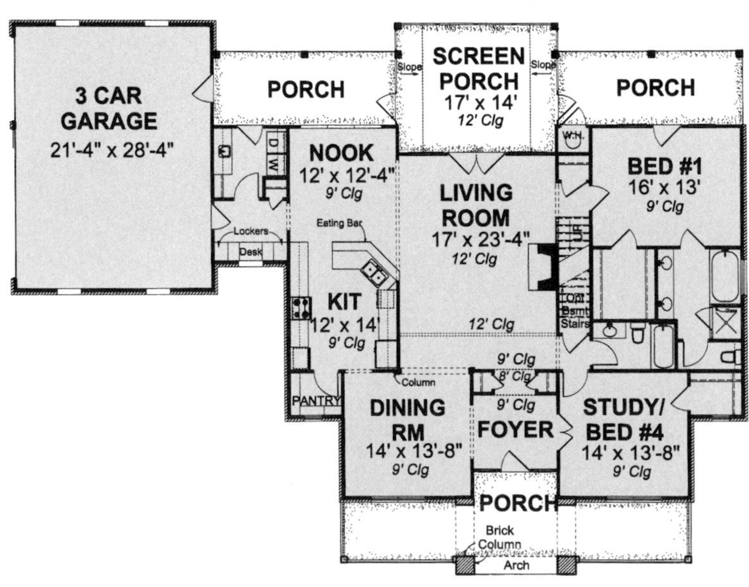

FIRST FLOOR

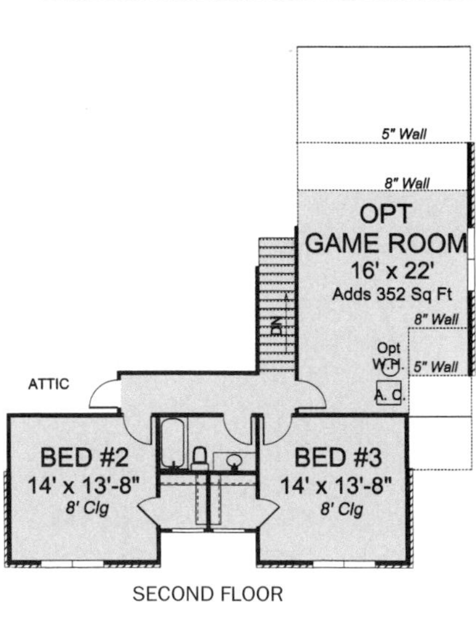

SECOND FLOOR

plan # HPK1700282

Style: Country Cottage
First Floor: 1,694 sq. ft.
Second Floor: 874 sq. ft.
Total: 2,568 sq. ft.
Bonus Space: 440 sq. ft.
Bedrooms: 3
Bathrooms: 3 ½
Width: 74' - 2"
Depth: 46' - 8"
Foundation: Unfinished Basement, Crawlspace

eplans.com

A welcoming front porch lined by graceful columns introduces this fine farmhouse. Inside, the foyer leads through an elegant arch to the spacious great room, which features a fireplace and built-ins. The formal dining room and sunny breakfast room flank a highly efficient kitchen—complete with a pantry and a serving bar. Located on the first floor for privacy, the master suite is filled with pampering amenities. Upstairs, two large bedrooms have private baths and walk-in closets.

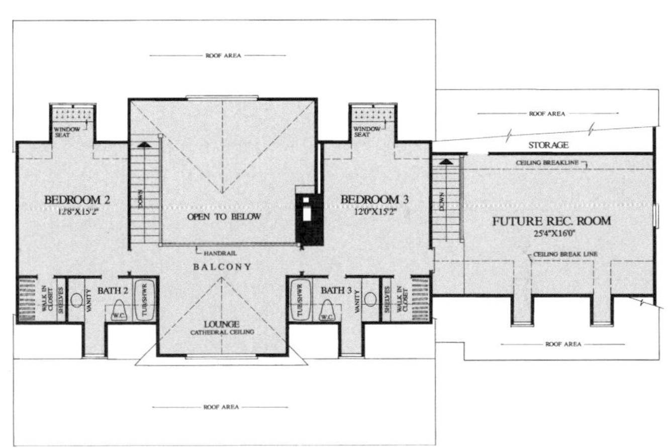

SECOND FLOOR

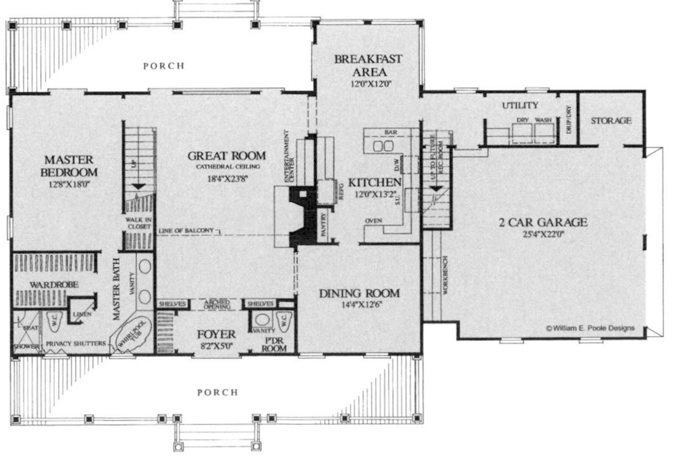

FIRST FLOOR

plan# HPK1700283

Style: Country Cottage
First Floor: 1,755 sq. ft.
Second Floor: 864 sq. ft.
Total: 2,619 sq. ft.
Bedrooms: 4
Bathrooms: 3 ½
Width: 56' - 0"
Depth: 53' - 0"
Foundation: Crawlspace, Unfinished Walkout Basement, Slab
eplans.com

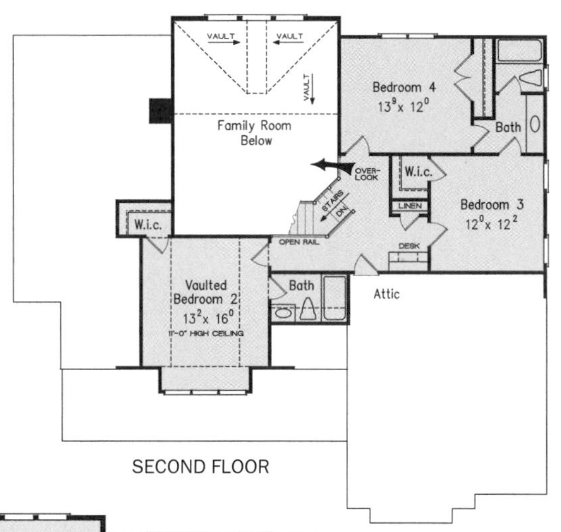

SECOND FLOOR

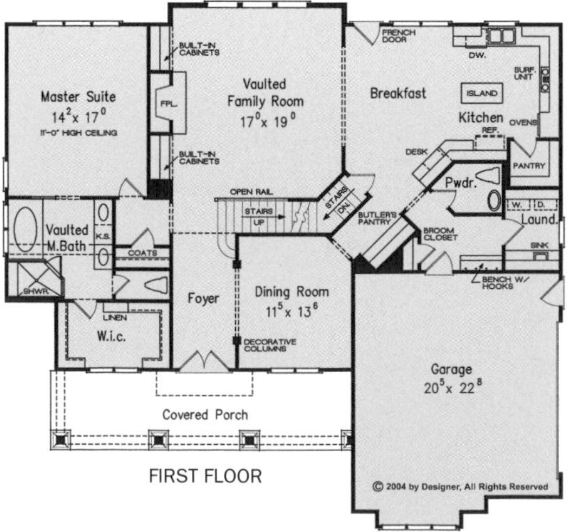

FIRST FLOOR

Open-face gables, broad white trim, and double-hung window sashes create appeal on this cottage's exterior. Inside, a comfortable and modern design of the great room caters to the active family requiring more functional than formal space. The island kitchen will be a favorite hangout. A formal dining room is perfect for entertaining and hosting holiday meals. A first-floor master suite inlcudes an amenity-filled bath and imperial-sized walk-in closet. Upstairs, three secondary bedrooms share two full baths.

plan # HPK1700284

Style: Traditional
First Floor: 2,087 sq. ft.
Second Floor: 552 sq. ft.
Total: 2,639 sq. ft.
Bedrooms: 4
Bathrooms: 3 ½
Width: 68' - 7"
Depth: 57' - 4"

eplans.com

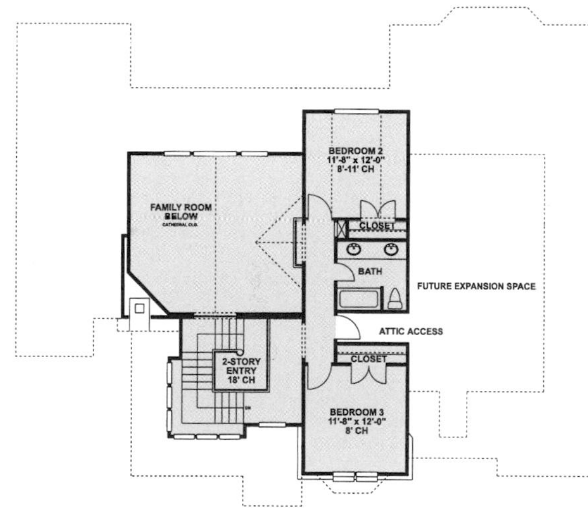

SECOND FLOOR

A fairytale palace on an affordable scale—this European-style home is an impressive addition to any neighborhood. Leading past the grand staircase, the entry opens to the stylish family room with its dazzling view. The angled, island kitchen makes entertaining a breeze with its proximity to the formal dining room, the family room, and the sunny breakfast room. A private guest room lies on the right with a bay window and private bath. The sumptuous master suite sits on the far left with a stunning private bath and generous walk-in closet. Additionally, two family bedrooms share a full bath on the second floor.

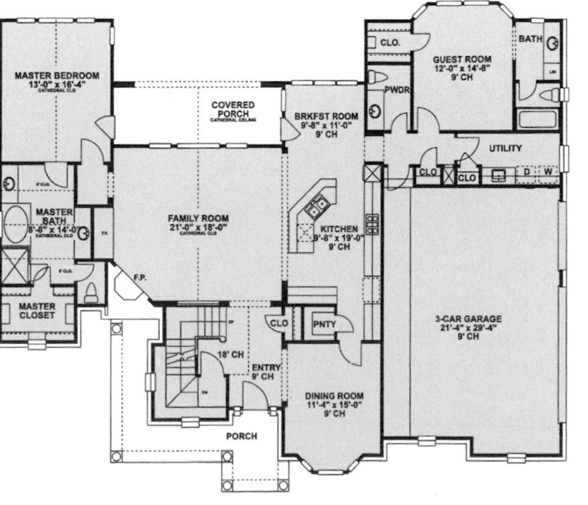

FIRST FLOOR

plan# HPK1700285

Style: Country Cottage
First Floor: 1,845 sq. ft.
Second Floor: 799 sq. ft.
Total: 2,644 sq. ft.
Bedrooms: 4
Bathrooms: 3
Width: 61' - 0"
Depth: 57' - 4"
Foundation: Crawlspace, Unfinished Walkout Basement, Slab

eplans.com

SECOND FLOOR

FIRST FLOOR

Centered windows on front-facing gables perch atop a Craftsman-style porch, creating a delightful neighborhood home. The uncluttered layout takes full advantage of the casual living areas. A vaulted family room features a fireplace with sidelights, and an uninterrupted perspective of the breakfast space and island kitchen. Enjoy alfresco dining on the screened porch. The first-floor master suite is enhanced by a tray ceiling and super bath. Across the hall, a home office gazes upon the front yard. Additional bedrooms are placed on the second level, each sporting a walk-in closet, and having access to the vaulted loft area.

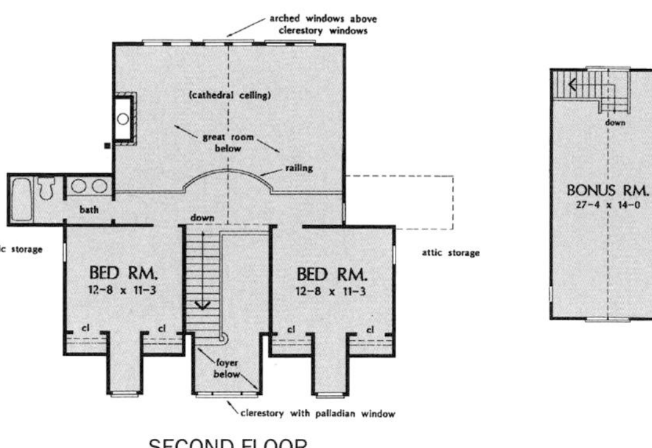

SECOND FLOOR

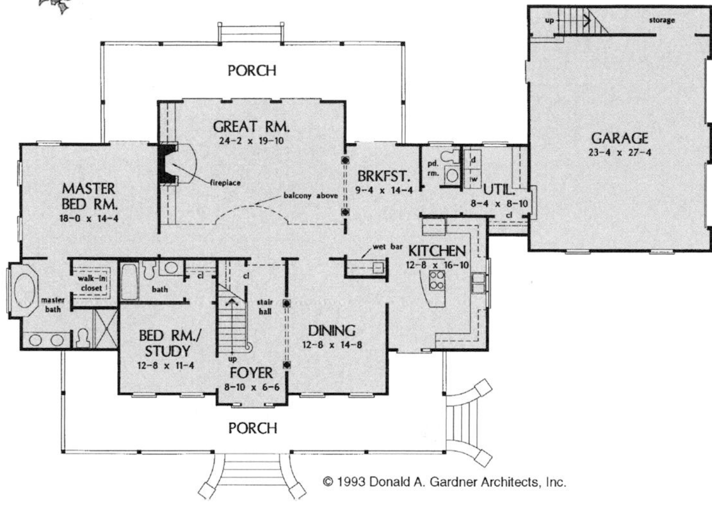

FIRST FLOOR

plan # HPK1700286

Style: Farmhouse

First Floor: 2,064 sq. ft.

Second Floor: 594 sq. ft.

Total: 2,658 sq. ft.

Bonus Space: 483 sq. ft.

Bedrooms: 4

Bathrooms: 3 ½

Width: 92' - 0"

Depth: 57' - 8"

eplans.com

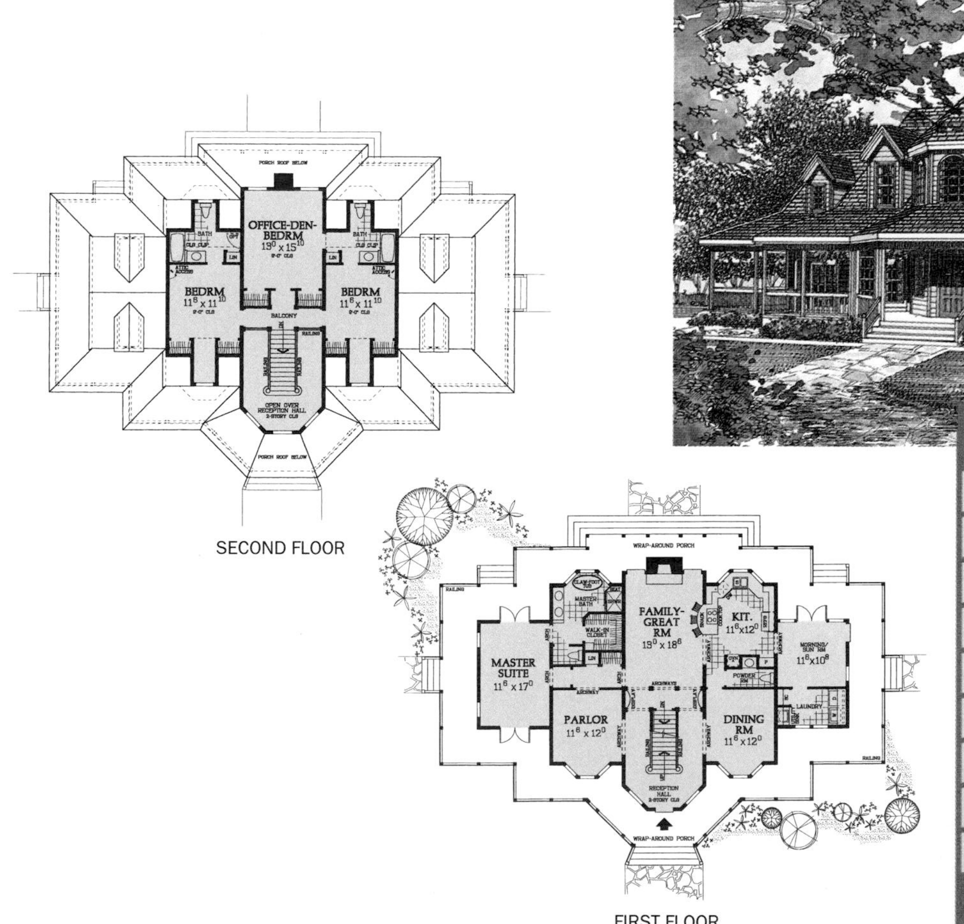

SECOND FLOOR

FIRST FLOOR

plan # HPK1700287

Style: Country Cottage

First Floor: 1,752 sq. ft.

Second Floor: 906 sq. ft.

Total: 2,658 sq. ft.

Bedrooms: 4

Bathrooms: 3 ½

Width: 74' - 0"

Depth: 51' - 7"

Foundation: Unfinished Basement

eplans.com

Stone and siding add color and texture to the exterior of this lovely period home. A covered porch introduces a front entry that leads directly into the living room, and through to the rear of the home. The open floor plan includes a great room with fireplace, dining area, and large kitchen with island and seating. A wall of windows across the rear of the home offers a view to the outdoors, and conveys natural light to the interior. Sliding doors from the great room lead to a deck that spans the width of the home. Split stairs lead to a second floor, where the master bedroom enjoys angled walls, a large walk-in closet, a garden bath with whirlpool tub, a double bowl vanity, a shower enclosure, and a view of the rear property. The simple lines remain true to the arts and crafts style.

plan# HPK1700288

- Style: Craftsman
- First Floor: 1,160 sq. ft.
- Second Floor: 1,531 sq. ft.
- Total: 2,691 sq. ft.
- Bedrooms: 3
- Bathrooms: 2½
- Width: 37' - 8"
- Depth: 53' - 0"
- Foundation: Finished Walkout Basement

eplans.com

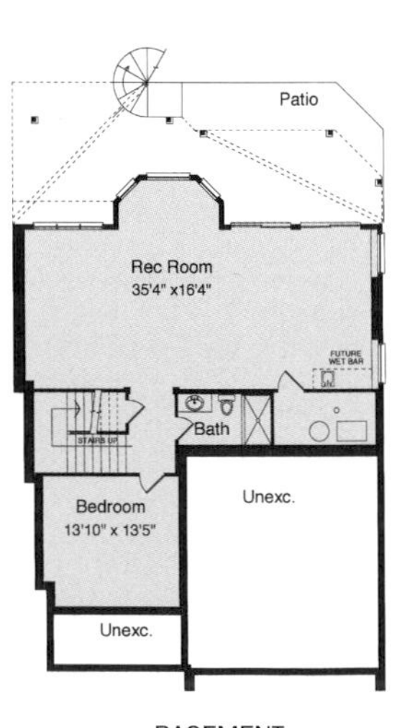

BASEMENT

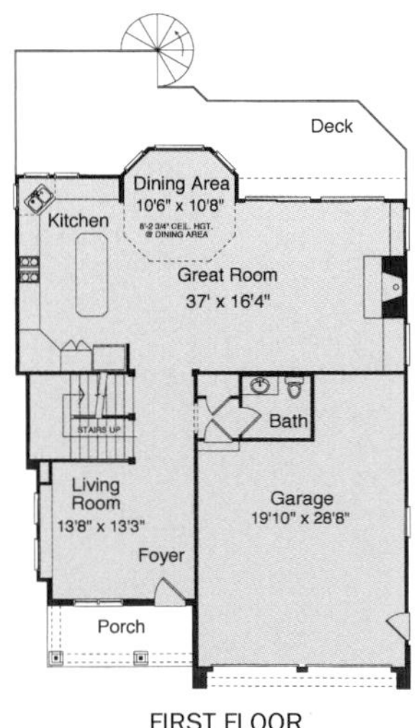

FIRST FLOOR

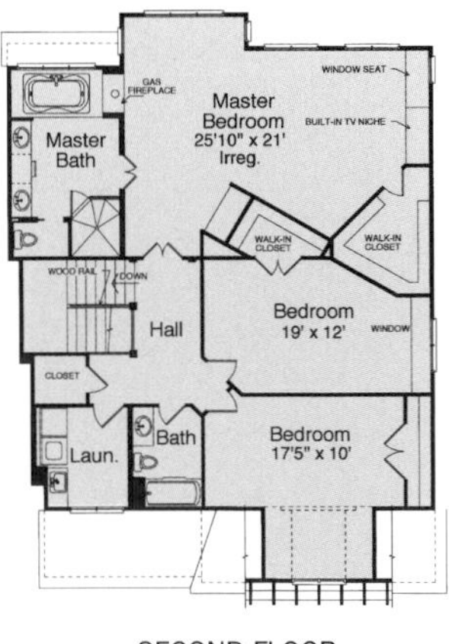

SECOND FLOOR

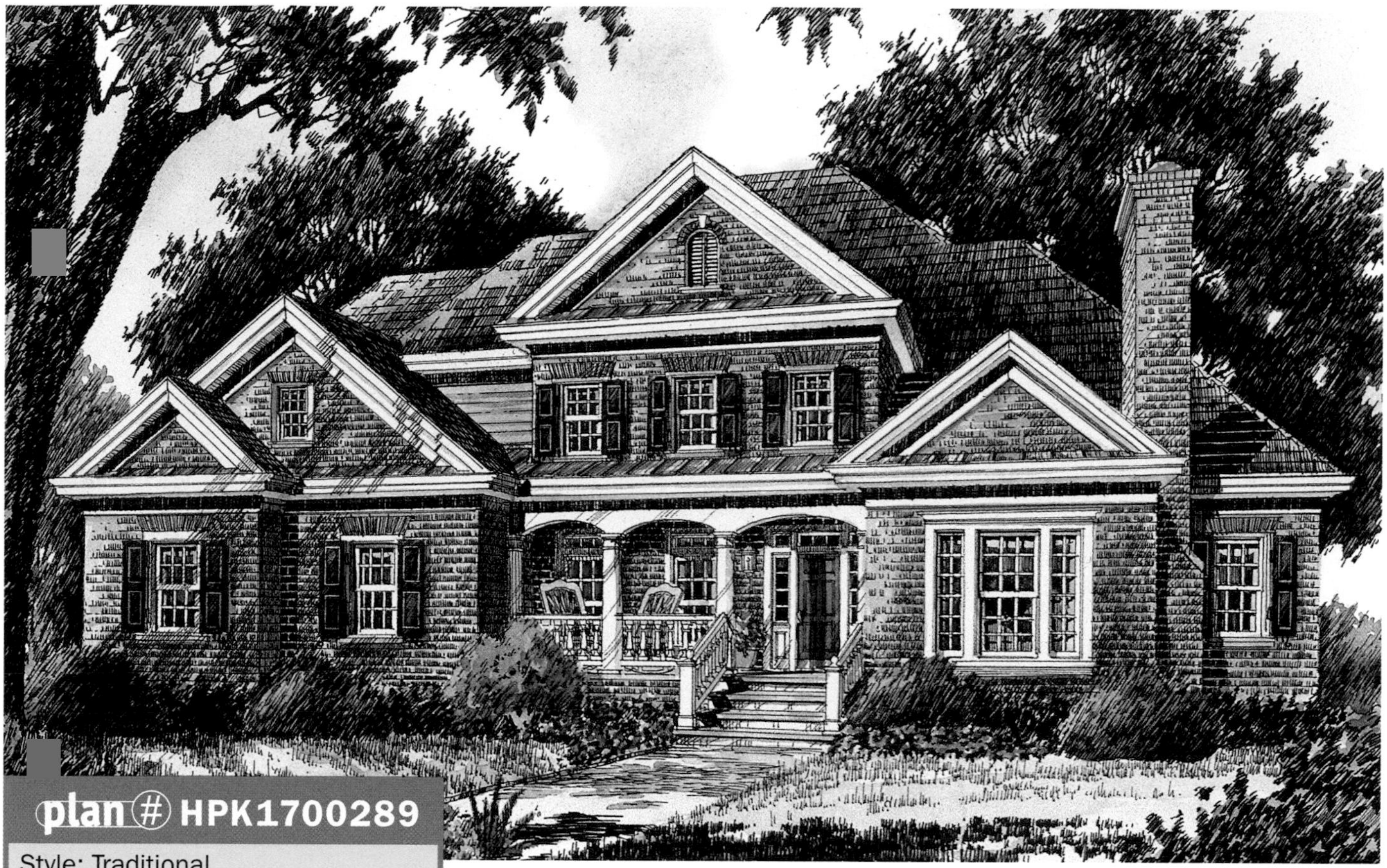

plan# HPK1700289

Style: Traditional
First Floor: 1,932 sq. ft.
Second Floor: 807 sq. ft.
Total: 2,739 sq. ft.
Bedrooms: 4
Bathrooms: 2 ½
Width: 63' - 0"
Depth: 51' - 6"
Foundation: Walkout Basement
eplans.com

This sensational country Colonial exterior is set off by a cozy covered porch, just right for enjoying cool evenings outside. A two-story foyer opens to a quiet study with a centered fireplace and to the formal dining room with views to the front property. The gourmet kitchen features an island cooktop counter and a charming bayed breakfast nook. The great room soars two stories high but is made cozy with an extended-hearth fireplace. Two walk-in closets, a garden tub, and a separate shower highlight the master bath; a coffered ceiling decorates the master bedroom. Three family bedrooms, each with a walk-in closet, share a full bath upstairs.

SECOND FLOOR

FIRST FLOOR

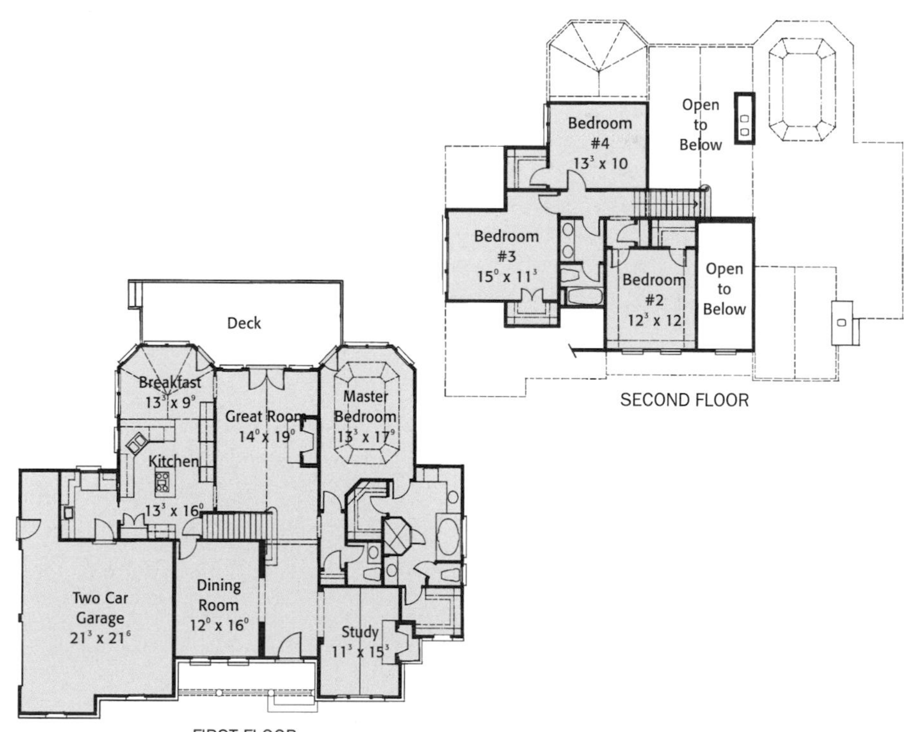

plan# HPK1700290

Style: Georgian
First Floor: 1,465 sq. ft.
Second Floor: 1,332 sq. ft.
Total: 2,797 sq. ft.
Bedrooms: 3
Bathrooms: 2½
Width: 49' - 0"
Depth: 75' - 0"
Foundation: Finished Walkout Basement

eplans.com

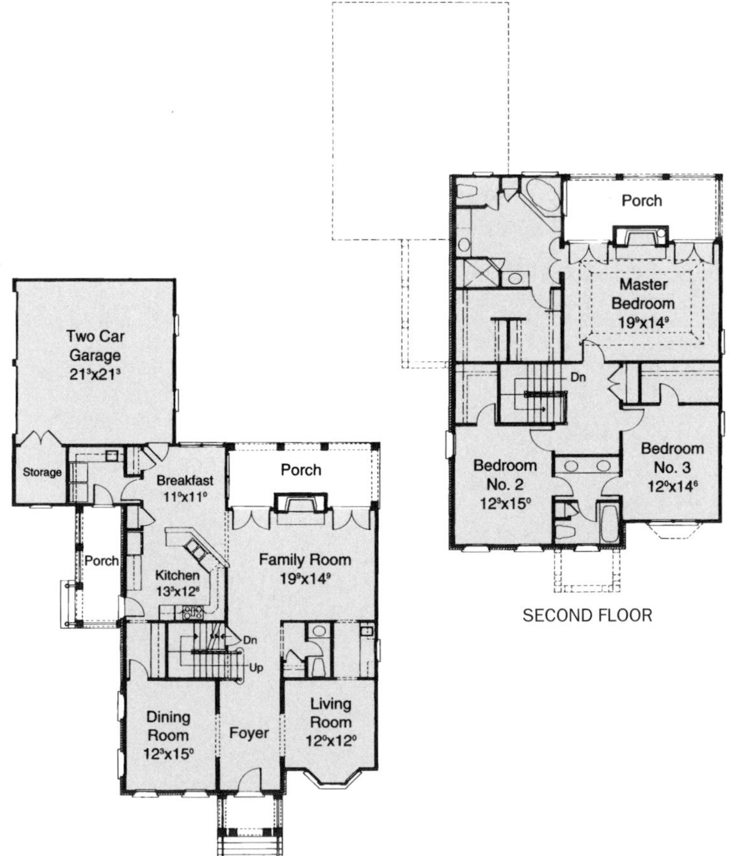

FIRST FLOOR

SECOND FLOOR

Brick, horizontal siding, and a columned porch add elements of style to this graceful Georgian Revival design. Formal rooms flank the foyer, which leads to casual living space with a fireplace and French doors to the rear porch. A convenient butler,s pantry eases service to the dining room from the well-planned kitchen. Angled counter space allows an overlook to the breakfast room. Upstairs, a rambling master suite has its own hearth and two sets of French doors that lead out to a private porch. The homeowner's bath features a split walk-in closet, an angled shower, a whirlpool tub, and a compartmented bath. Each of two family bedrooms enjoys private access to a shared bath.

plan# HPK1700291

Style: Country Cottage
First Floor: 1,639 sq. ft.
Second Floor: 1,158 sq. ft.
Total: 2,797 sq. ft.
Bedrooms: 4
Bathrooms: 3
Width: 80' - 0"
Depth: 44' - 0"
Foundation: Crawlspace, Unfinished Basement

eplans.com

This grand farmhouse design is anything but ordinary. Its lovely details—a Palladian window, a covered veranda, and shutters—put it a cut above the rest. The interior features classic floor planning with a vaulted center-hall foyer and staircase to the second floor. Formal areas—a living room and a dining room—reside on the right; a cozy den and the large family room are on the left. A full bath sits near the den so that it can double as guest space. Four bedrooms on the second floor include a luxurious master suite.

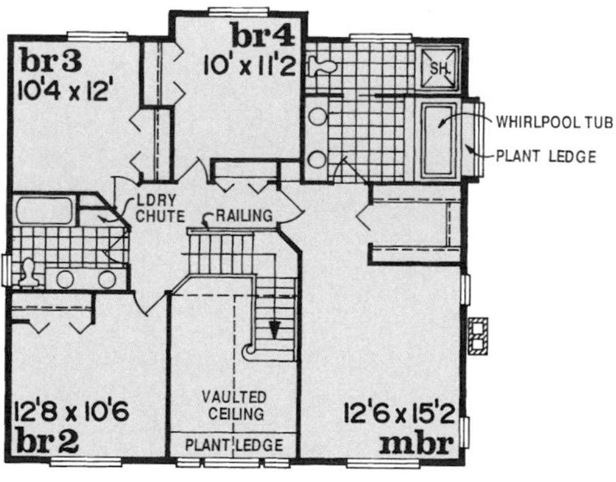

SECOND FLOOR

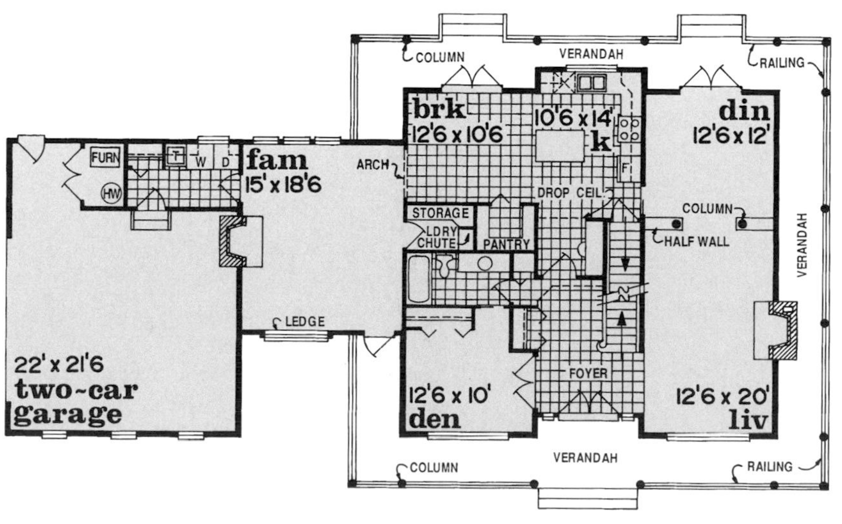

FIRST FLOOR

PHOTO COURTESY OF WILLIAM E. POOLE DESIGNS, INC. PHOTO BY STEVE RIGGS

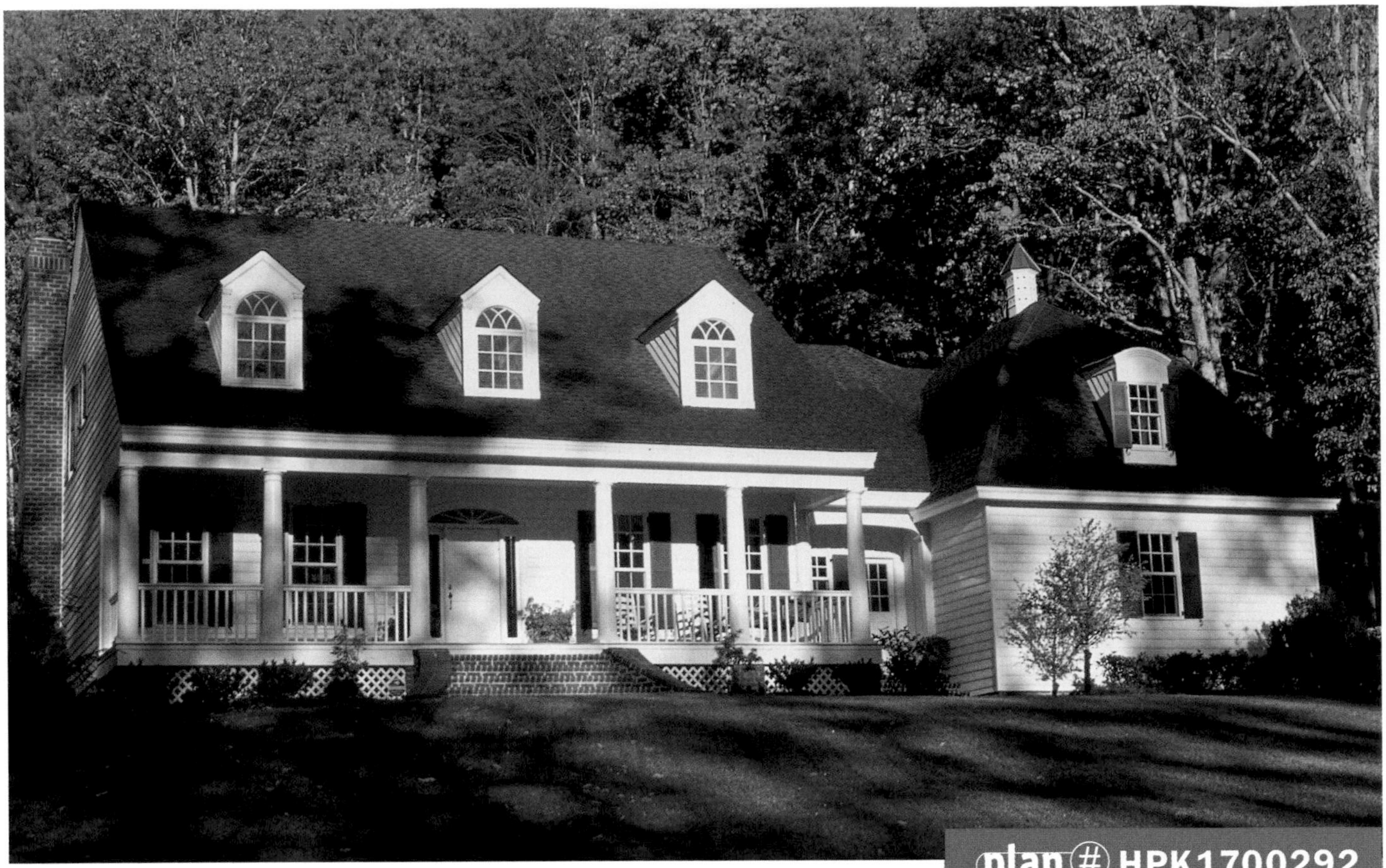

plan# HPK1700292

Style: Country Cottage	
First Floor: 1,927 sq. ft.	
Second Floor: 879 sq. ft.	
Total: 2,806 sq. ft.	
Bonus Space: 459 sq. ft.	
Bedrooms: 4	
Bathrooms: 3 ½	
Width: 71' - 0"	
Depth: 53' - 0"	
Foundation: Crawlspace	

eplans.com

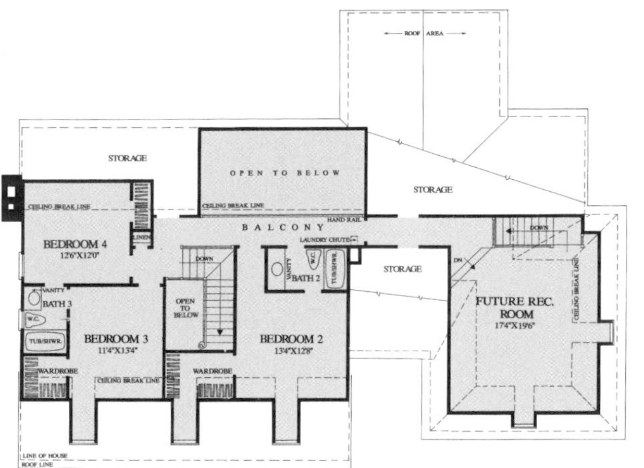

SECOND FLOOR

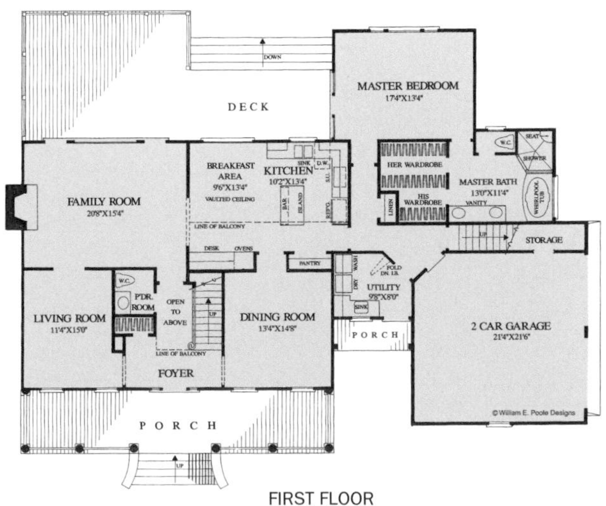

FIRST FLOOR

This charming Southern plantation home packs quite a punch in 2,800 square feet! The elegant foyer is flanked by the formal dining room and the living room. To the rear, the family room enjoys a fireplace and expansive view of the outdoors. An archway leads to the breakfast area and on to the island kitchen. The luxurious master suite is tucked away for privacy behind the two-car garage. Three additional bedrooms rest on the second floor where they share two full baths. Space above the garage is available for future development.

plan# HPK1700293

Style: Country Cottage
First Floor: 2,247 sq. ft.
Second Floor: 637 sq. ft.
Total: 2,884 sq. ft.
Bonus Space: 235 sq. ft.
Bedrooms: 4
Bathrooms: 4
Width: 64' - 0"
Depth: 55' - 2"
Foundation: Crawlspace, Unfinished Walkout Basement

eplans.com

This astonishing traditional home looks great with its gables, muntin windows, keystone lintels, and turret-style bay. Inside, the heart of the home is the vaulted family room with a fireplace. The kitchen conveniently connects to the dining room, breakfast room, and garage. The master bath leads into a walk-in closet. The home office or nursery near the hall bath is illuminated by a bayed wall of windows and could become an additional family bedroom. Family bedrooms upstairs share a loft that overlooks the family room.

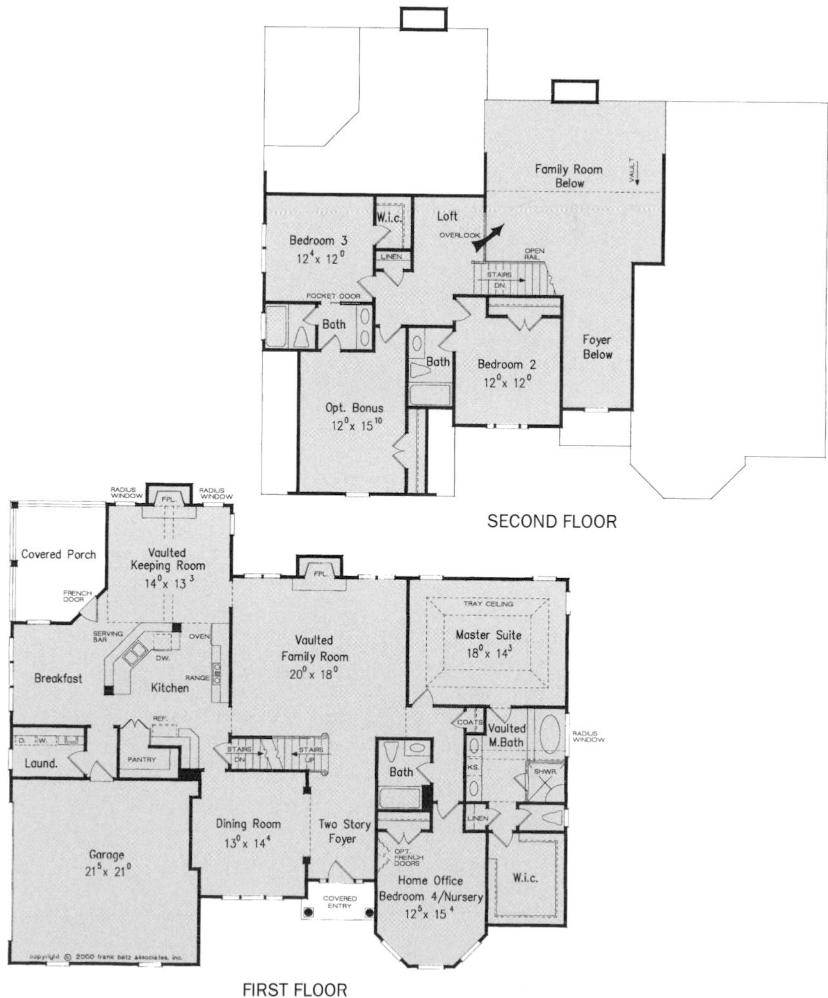

SECOND FLOOR

FIRST FLOOR

© William E. Poole Designs, Inc.

plan# HPK1700294

Style: Farmhouse

First Floor: 1,913 sq. ft.

Second Floor: 997 sq. ft.

Total: 2,910 sq. ft.

Bonus Space: 377 sq. ft.

Bedrooms: 4

Bathrooms: 3 ½

Width: 63' - 0"

Depth: 59' - 4"

Foundation: Crawlspace, Unfinished Basement

eplans.com

REAR EXTERIOR

FIRST FLOOR

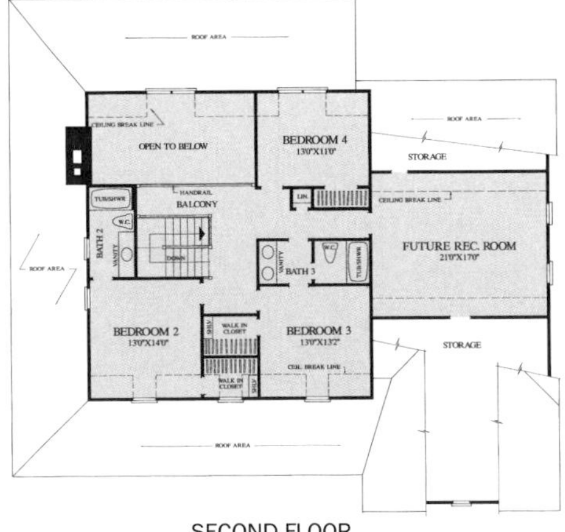

SECOND FLOOR

This enchanting farmhouse brings the past to life with plenty of modern amenities. An open-flow kitchen/breakfast area and family room combination is the heart of the home, opening up to the screened porch and enjoying the warmth of a fireplace. For more formal occasions, the foyer is flanked by a living room on the left and a dining room on the right. An elegant master bedroom, complete with a super-size walk-in closet, is tucked away quietly behind the garage. Three more bedrooms reside upstairs, along with two full baths and a future recreation room.

plan# HPK1700295

Style: European Cottage
First Floor: 1,867 sq. ft.
Second Floor: 1,090 sq. ft.
Total: 2,957 sq. ft.
Bonus Space: 424 sq. ft.
Bedrooms: 4
Bathrooms: 3 ½
Width: 51' - 4"
Depth: 68' - 4"
Foundation: Crawlspace

eplans.com

Muntin windows, keystone lintels and steeply pitched rooflines mark this home's exterior with grace and style. A dining room situated to the right of the foyer is linked to the kitchen through a convenient door. The kitchen boasts a pantry and a nearby breakfast room, which looks to the rear property. The gathering room is enhanced with a fireplace and French doors to the backyard. The master suite, located on the first-floor for privacy, includes many amenities a homeowner would love, including a garden tub, separate bath and compartmented toilet. Three suites reside upstairs, as do two full baths, an unfinished recreation room and a balcony that looks to the foyer below.

REAR EXTERIOR

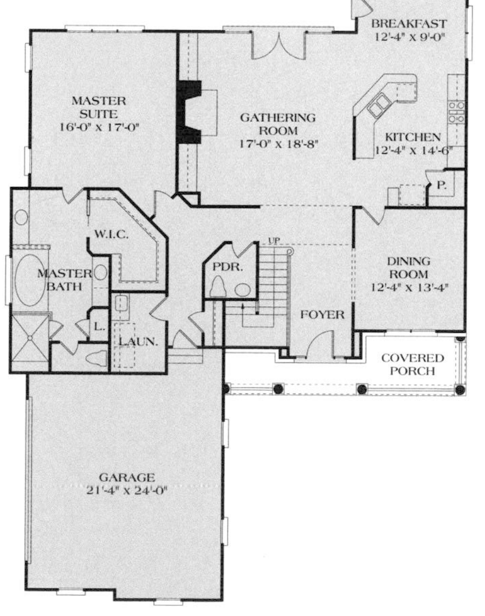

FIRST FLOOR

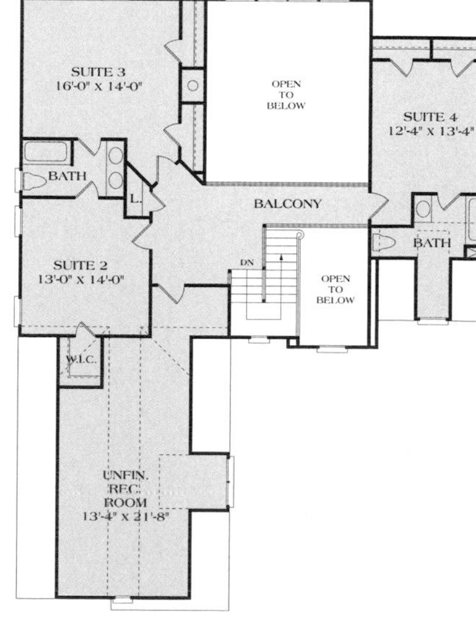

SECOND FLOOR

plan# HPK1700296

Style: Country Cottage

First Floor: 1,614 sq. ft.

Second Floor: 892 sq. ft.

Total: 2,506 sq. ft.

Bonus Space: 341 sq. ft.

Bedrooms: 4

Bathrooms: 2½

Width: 71' - 10"

Depth: 50' - 0"

eplans.com

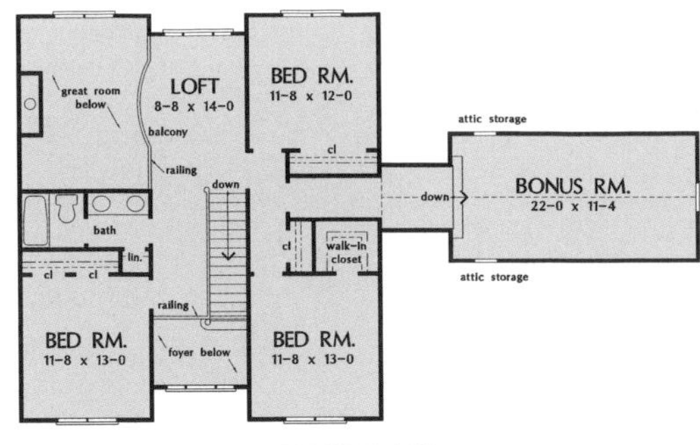

SECOND FLOOR

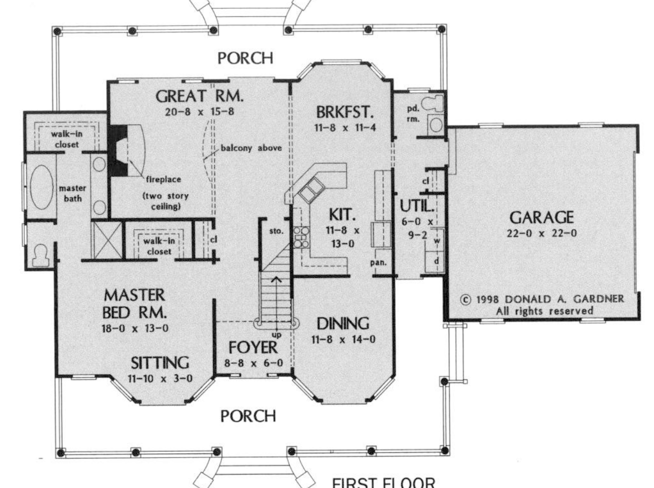

FIRST FLOOR

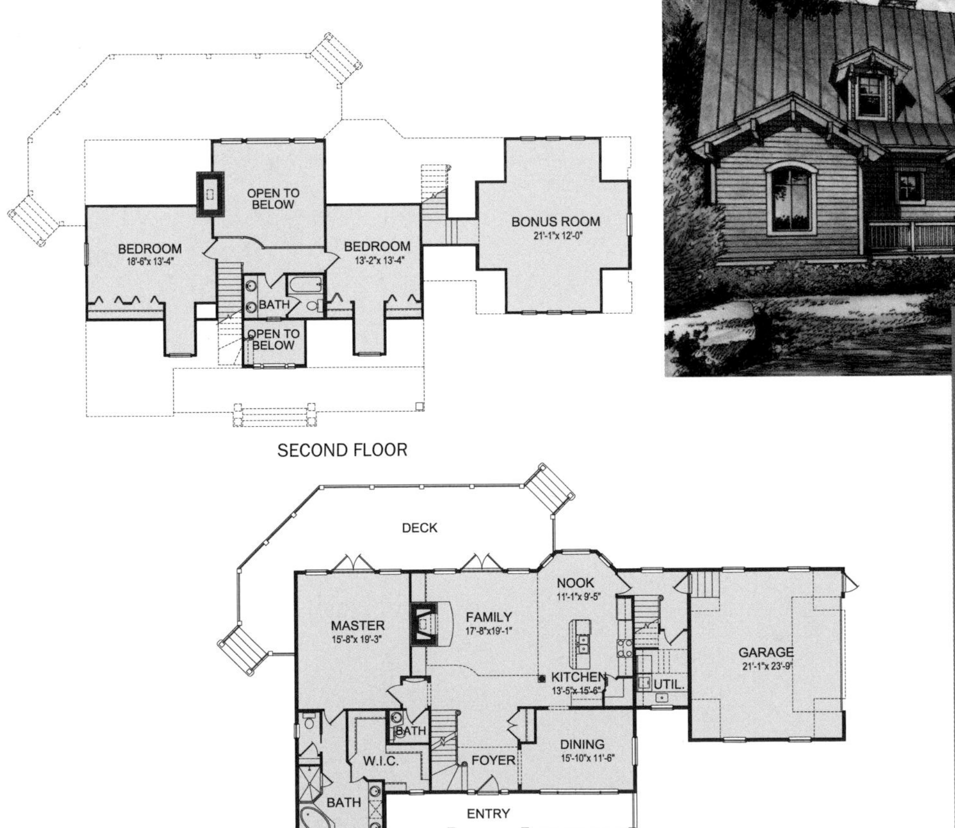

FIRST FLOOR

plan# HPK1700297

Style: Craftsman

First Floor: 1,799 sq. ft.

Second Floor: 709 sq. ft.

Total: 2,508 sq. ft.

Bonus Space: 384 sq. ft.

Bedrooms: 3

Bathrooms: 2½

Width: 77' - 4"

Depth: 41' - 4"

Foundation: Unfinished Walkout Basement

eplans.com

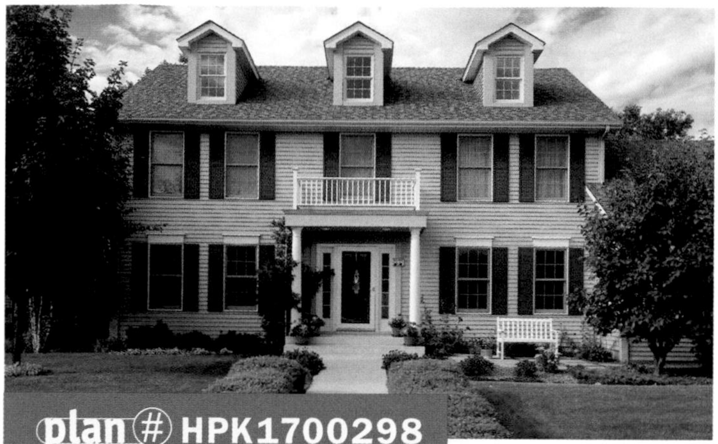

plan# HPK1700298

Style: Colonial
First Floor: 1,368 sq. ft.
Second Floor: 1,140 sq. ft.
Total: 2,508 sq. ft.
Bedrooms: 4
Bathrooms: 2½
Width: 62' - 0"
Depth: 48' - 0"
Foundation: Unfinished Basement

eplans.com

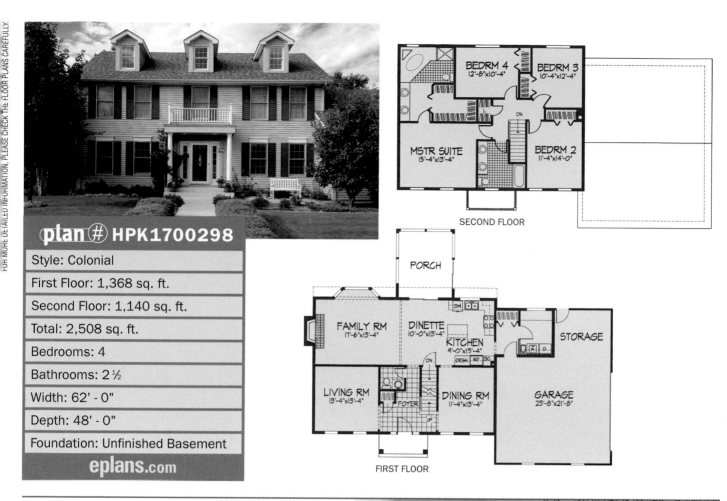

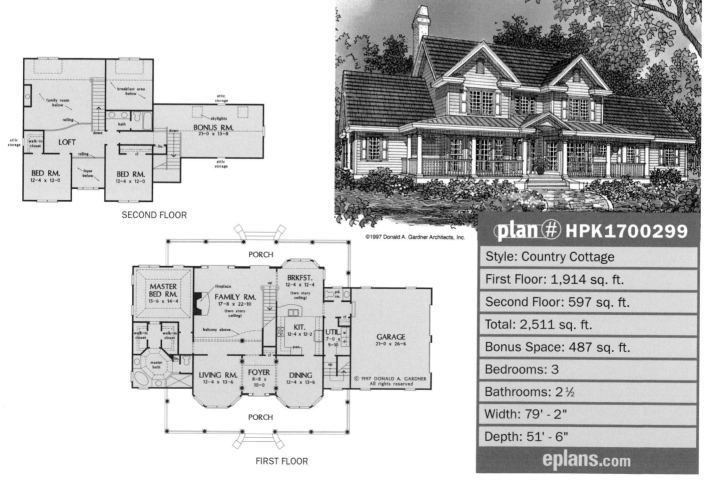

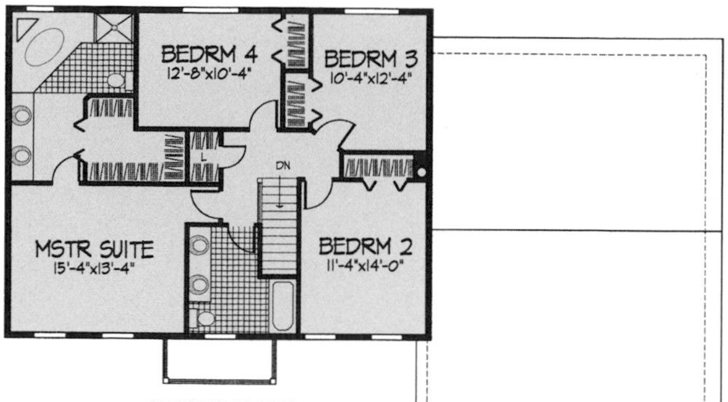

BEDRM 4 12'-8"x10'-4"
BEDRM 3 10'-4"x12'-4"
DN
MSTR SUITE 15'-4"x13'-4"
BEDRM 2 11'-4"x14'-0"

SECOND FLOOR

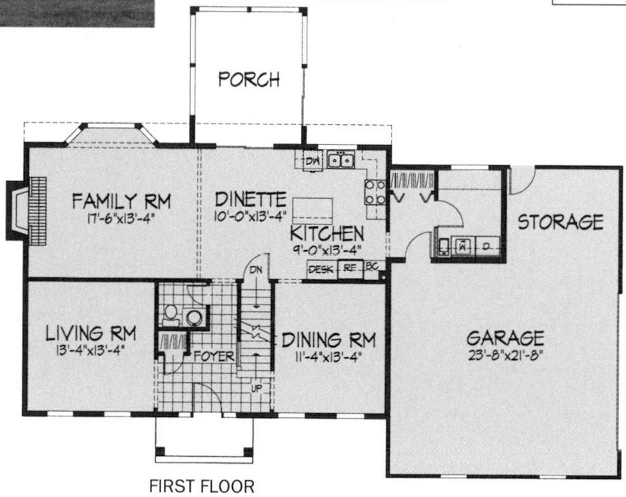

PORCH
FAMILY RM 17'-6"x13'-4"
DINETTE 10'-0"x13'-4"
KITCHEN 9'-0"x13'-4"
DESK RF BC
DN
STORAGE
LIVING RM 13'-4"x13'-4"
FOYER
UP
DINING RM 11'-4"x13'-4"
GARAGE 23'-8"x21'-8"

FIRST FLOOR

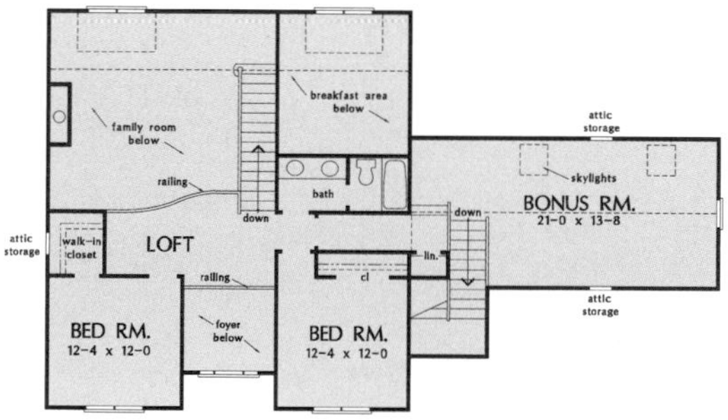

---

family room below
breakfast area below
railing
bath
down
attic storage
skylights
BONUS RM. 21-0 x 13-8
attic storage
walk-in closet
LOFT
railing
cl
lin.
attic storage
BED RM. 12-4 x 12-0
foyer below
BED RM. 12-4 x 12-0

SECOND FLOOR

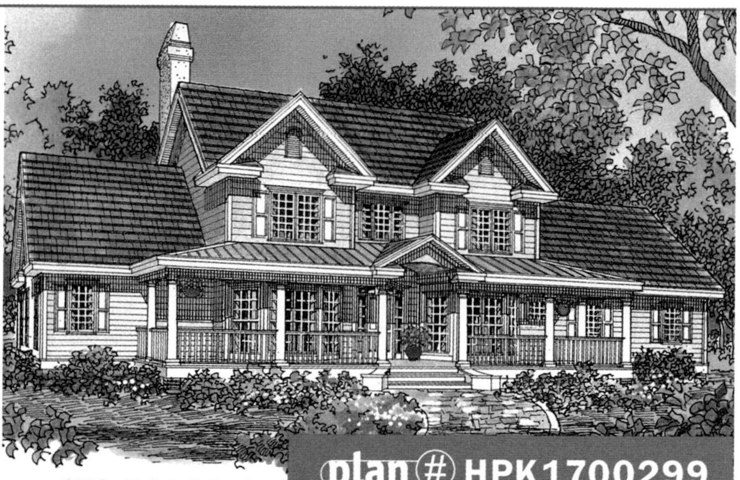

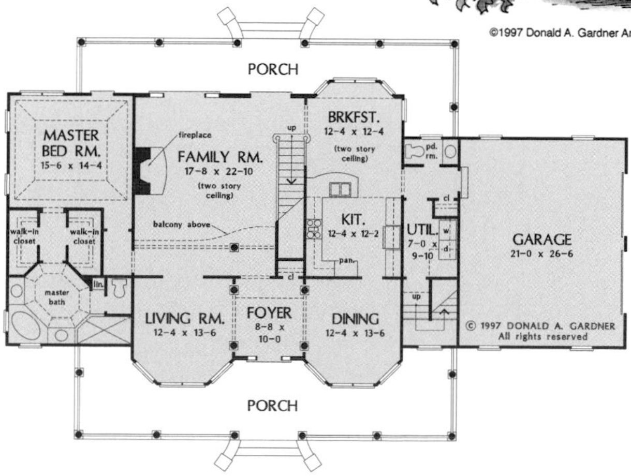

PORCH
MASTER BED RM. 15-6 x 14-4
fireplace
FAMILY RM. 17-8 x 22-10 (two story ceiling)
up
BRKFST. 12-4 x 12-4 (two story ceiling)
pd. rm.
balcony above
KIT. 12-4 x 12-2
pan.
UTIL. 7-0 x 9-10
GARAGE 21-0 x 26-6
walk-in closet
walk-in closet
master bath
lin.
cl
LIVING RM. 12-4 x 13-6
FOYER 8-8 x 10-0
DINING 12-4 x 13-6
up

PORCH

FIRST FLOOR

plan# HPK1700299

Style: Country Cottage
First Floor: 1,914 sq. ft.
Second Floor: 597 sq. ft.
Total: 2,511 sq. ft.
Bonus Space: 487 sq. ft.
Bedrooms: 3
Bathrooms: 2½
Width: 79' - 2"
Depth: 51' - 6"

eplans.com

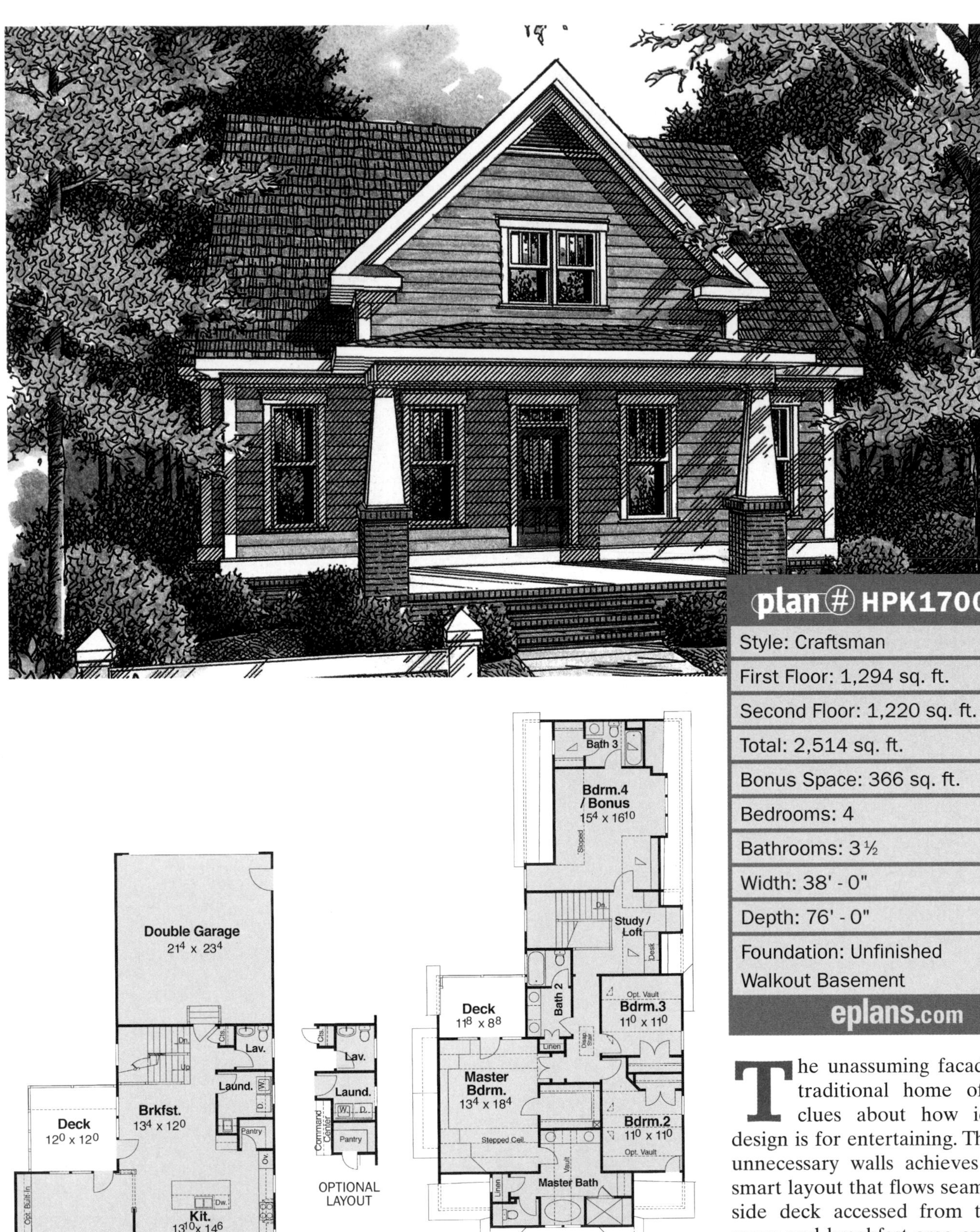

plan# HPK1700300

Style: Craftsman

First Floor: 1,294 sq. ft.

Second Floor: 1,220 sq. ft.

Total: 2,514 sq. ft.

Bonus Space: 366 sq. ft.

Bedrooms: 4

Bathrooms: 3 ½

Width: 38' - 0"

Depth: 76' - 0"

Foundation: Unfinished Walkout Basement

eplans.com

The unassuming facade of this traditional home offers few clues about how ideal this design is for entertaining. The lack of unnecessary walls achieves a clean, smart layout that flows seamlessly. A side deck accessed from the living room and breakfast area extends the gathering outside. Upstairs houses all of the family bedrooms, including the master suite, enhanced by a spacious private deck. Two additional family bedrooms share a full bath. A fourth bedroom boasts a full bath and could be used as a recreation/exercise/guest room. The central study/loft area is perfect for a family computer.

plan# HPK1700301

Style: Farmhouse
First Floor: 1,464 sq. ft.
Second Floor: 1,054 sq. ft.
Total: 2,518 sq. ft.
Bonus Space: 332 sq. ft.
Bedrooms: 4
Bathrooms: 3
Width: 59' - 0"
Depth: 51' - 6"
Foundation: Crawlspace

eplans.com

Country Victoriana embellishes this beautiful home. Perfect for a corner lot, this home begs for porch swings and lemonade. Inside, extra-high ceilings expand the space as a thoughtful floor plan invites family and friends. The two-story great room enjoys a warming fireplace and wonderful rear views. The country kitchen has a preparation island and easily serves the sunny bayed nook and the formal dining room. To the far left, a bedroom serves as a perfect guest room; to the far right, a turret houses a private den. Upstairs, two bedrooms (one in a turret) share a full bath and ample bonus space. The master suite opens through French doors to reveal a grand bedroom and a sumptuous bath with a bumped-out spa tub.

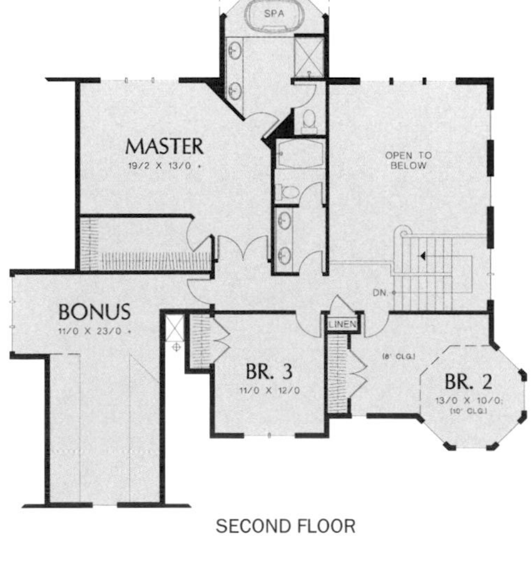

SECOND FLOOR

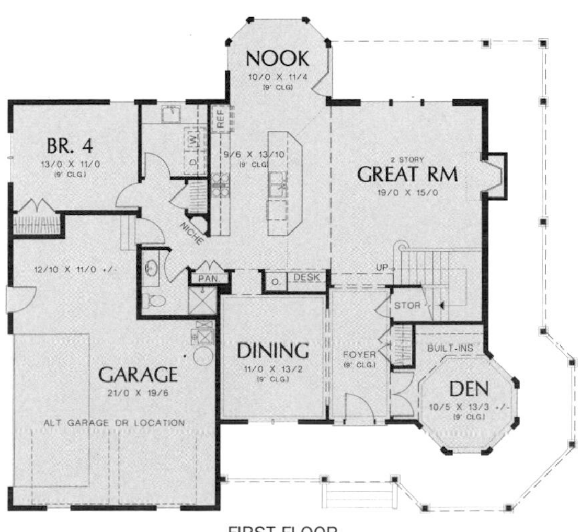

FIRST FLOOR

© William E. Poole Designs, Inc.

Come home to comfort in this country classic! A covered porch, pedimented dormers, and a delightful weather vane atop the garage denote downhome charm, while family life reigns within. Enjoy the fireplace in the soaring two-story great room, which opens to a sunny bayed breakfast nook. The adjacent kitchen, with its curved counter, leads to the formal dining room at the front of the plan. The master suite, complete with an enormous private bath and walk-in closet, is convenient to the utility room, which features a roomy closet. Upstairs, two bedrooms share a bath and a computer workstation; a fourth bedroom has its own bath. A balcony overlook gazes down on the first floor.

plan# HPK1700302
Style: Country Cottage
First Floor: 1,598 sq. ft.
Second Floor: 932 sq. ft.
Total: 2,530 sq. ft.
Bonus Space: 415 sq. ft.
Bedrooms: 4
Bathrooms: 3½
Width: 55' - 8"
Depth: 61' - 0"
Foundation: Crawlspace, Unfinished Basement
eplans.com

plan# HPK1700303

Style: Country Cottage
First Floor: 1,266 sq. ft.
Second Floor: 1,292 sq. ft.
Total: 2,558 sq. ft.
Bedrooms: 4
Bathrooms: 2½
Width: 54' - 0"
Depth: 44' - 0"

eplans.com

This classic American two-story home borrows details from farmhouse, Craftsman and Colonial styles to create a beautiful facade. The covered front porch is a lovely introduction to both formal and informal living spaces on the interior. The living room features a see-through fireplace to the family room and is complemented by a formal dining room with hutch space. The U-shaped island kitchen and bayed breakfast nook combine to form an open area for casual dining. A stairway to the second level boasts twin accesses—in the foyer and in the family room. Sleeping quarters on the second floor include three family bedrooms with a shared bath and walk-in closets. The master bedroom has a private bath with a whirlpool tub.

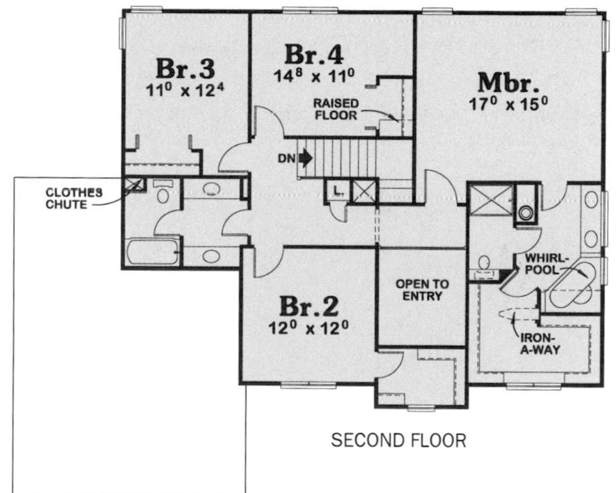

SECOND FLOOR

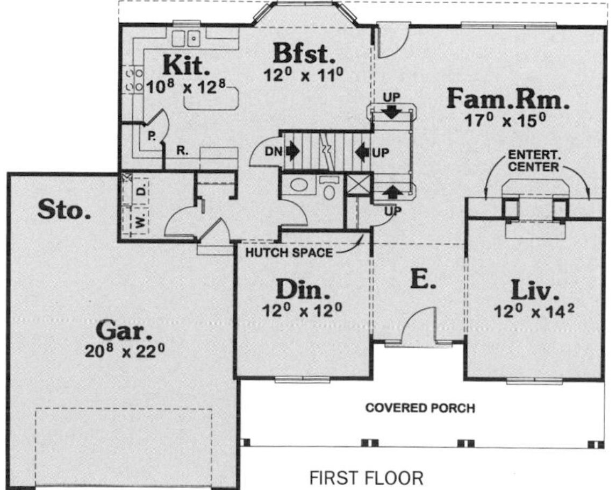

FIRST FLOOR

SECOND FLOOR

FIRST FLOOR

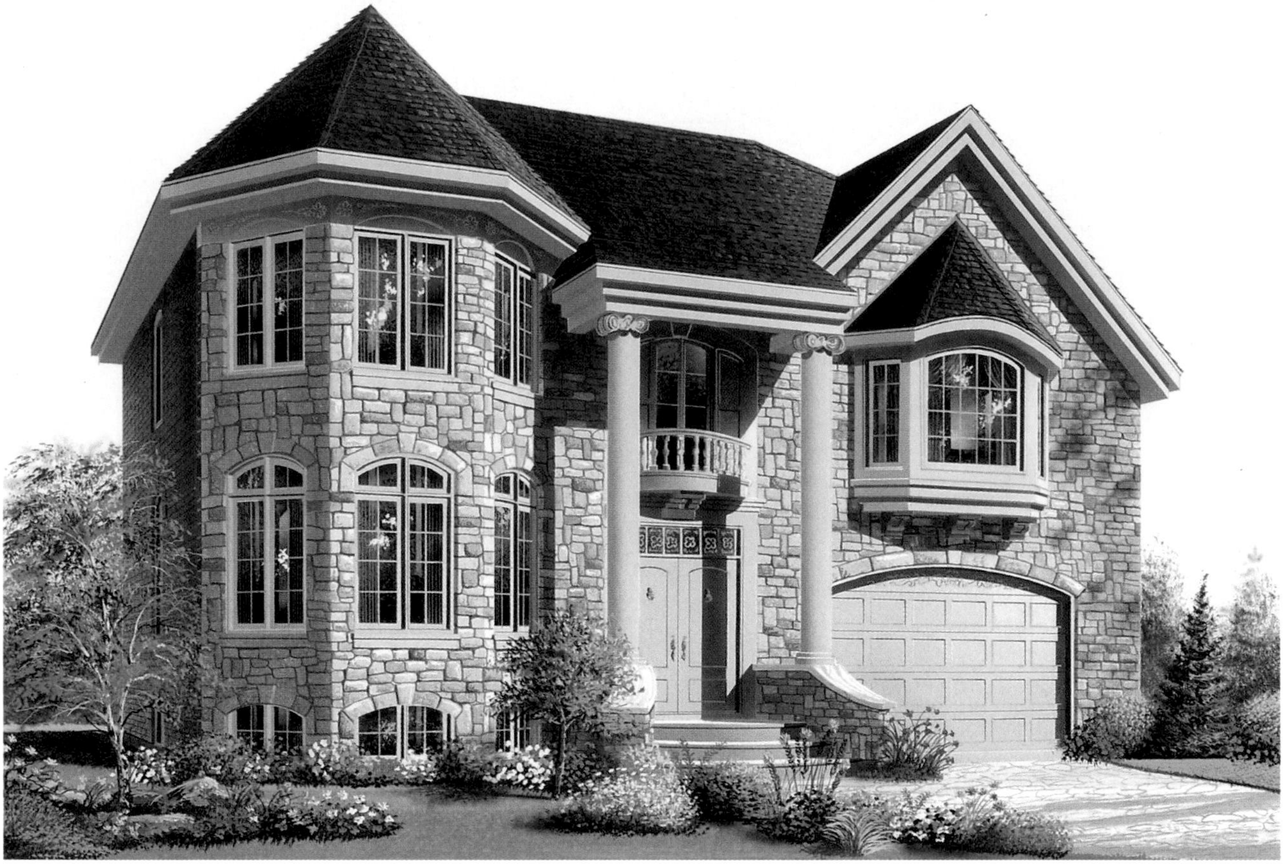

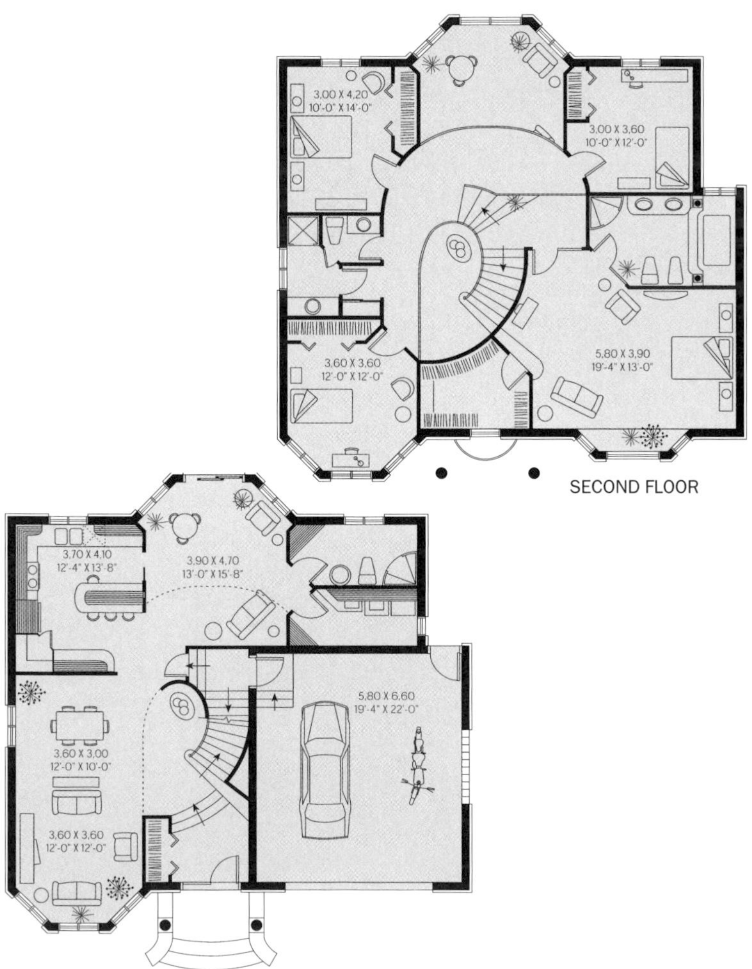

plan# HPK1700304
Style: European Cottage
First Floor: 1,152 sq. ft.
Second Floor: 1,434 sq. ft.
Total: 2,586 sq. ft.
Bedrooms: 4
Bathrooms: 3
Width: 44' - 0"
Depth: 44' - 0"
Foundation: Unfinished Basement
eplans.com

Tall, robust columns flank the impressive two-story entry of this European-style home. Views can be had in the living room—in the turret—and with the open dining area just steps away, entertaining will be a splendid affair. The kitchen features a breakfast bar and adjoining sun room. Upstairs, the master suite is enhanced by a large sitting area, bumped-out bay window, and a relaxing bath. Three family bedrooms and a full bath complete this level.

plan# HPK1700305

Style: Farmhouse
First Floor: 1,322 sq. ft.
Second Floor: 1,272 sq. ft.
Total: 2,594 sq. ft.
Bonus Space: 80 sq. ft.
Bedrooms: 4
Bathrooms: 2½
Width: 56' - 0"
Depth: 48' - 0"

eplans.com

This home has all the comfort you've been looking for! An inviting wraparound porch and sunny breakfast room are just the beginning of this plan's many great features. A sunken family room with a fireplace serves everyday casual gatherings, and the more formal living and dining rooms are reserved for special entertaining situations. The kitchen has a central island with a snack bar and is located most conveniently for serving and cleaning up. Upstairs are four bedrooms, one a lovely master suite with French doors to the private bath and a whirlpool tub with a dramatic bay window. Dual vanities in the shared bath easily serve the three family bedrooms.

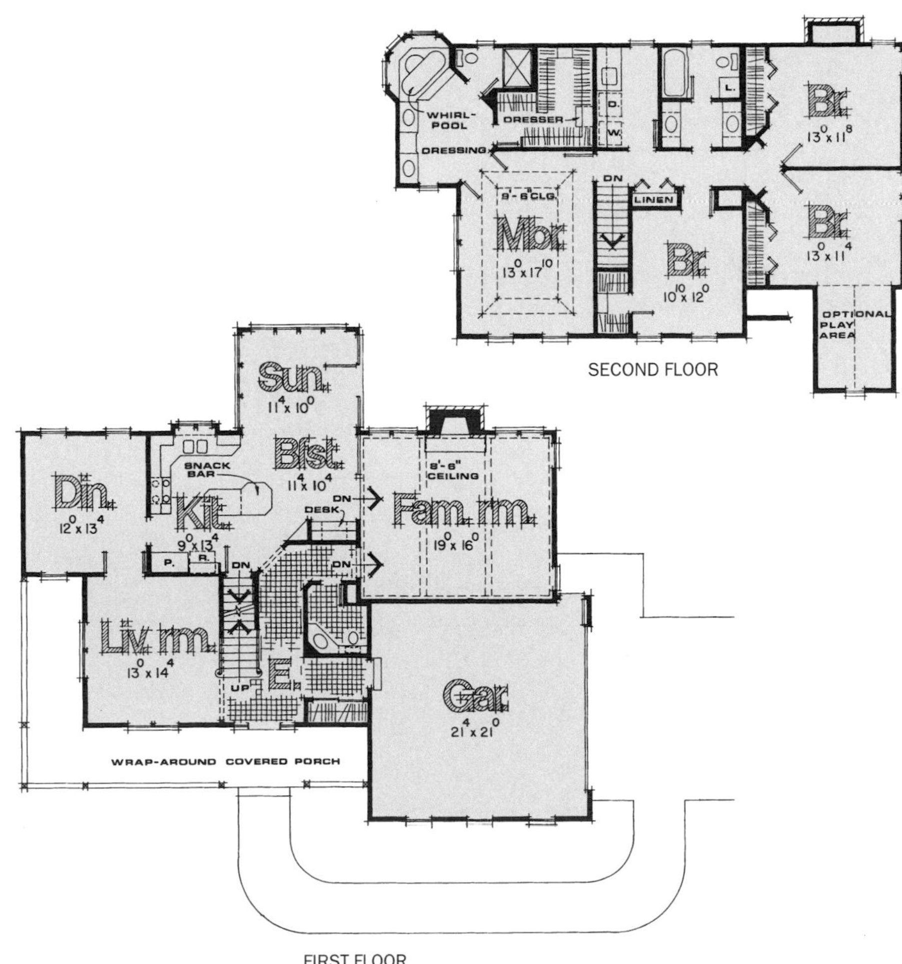

SECOND FLOOR

FIRST FLOOR

plan# HPK1700306

Style: Colonial
First Floor: 1,809 sq. ft.
Second Floor: 785 sq. ft.
Total: 2,594 sq. ft.
Bonus Space: 353 sq. ft.
Bedrooms: 5
Bathrooms: 4
Width: 72' - 7"
Depth: 51' - 5"
Foundation: Crawlspace, Unfinished Walkout Basement, Slab

eplans.com

With elements of country style, this unique Colonial-inspired home presents a rustic attitude blended with the delicate features that make this design one of a kind. Upon entry, a second-story arched window lights the foyer. Straight ahead, the family room soars with a two-story vault balanced by a cozy fireplace. A pass-through from the island kitchen keeps conversation going as the family chef whips up delectable feasts for the formal dining room or bayed breakfast nook. A bedroom at the rear provides plenty of privacy for guests, or as a home office. The master suite takes up the entire right wing, hosting a bayed sitting area and marvelous vaulted bath. Upstairs, three bedrooms access a versatile bonus room, limited only by your imagination.

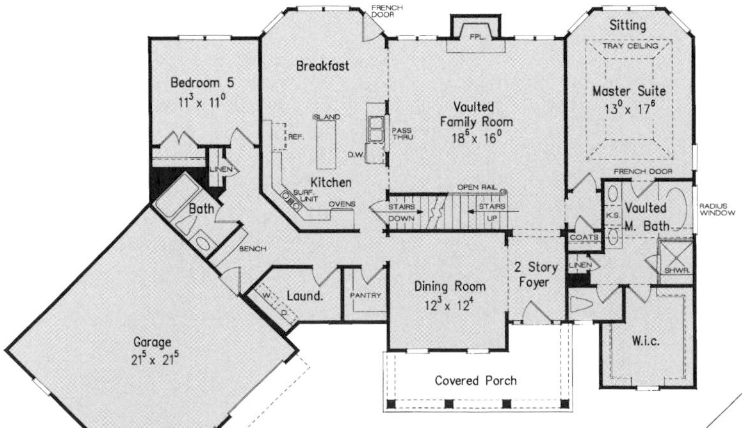

FIRST FLOOR

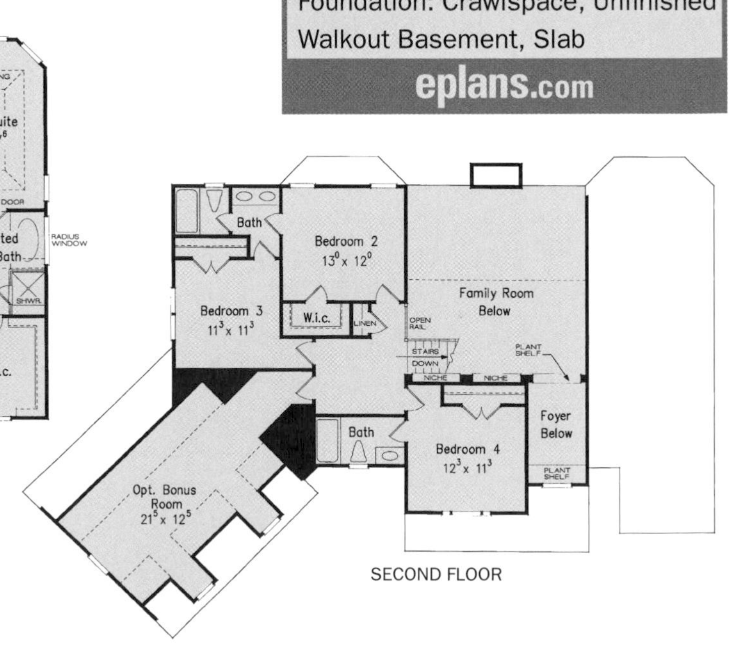

SECOND FLOOR

plan# HPK1700307

Style: Traditional
First Floor: 1,142 sq. ft.
Second Floor: 1,463 sq. ft.
Total: 2,605 sq. ft.
Bedrooms: 3
Bathrooms: 2½
Width: 50' - 0"
Depth: 42' - 0"
Foundation: Crawlspace

eplans.com

A touch of European styling dresses the facade of this comfortable two-story home. Stone detailing at the main level and around the entryway complements board-and-batten siding above. Beyond the foyer lies open living space with a great room, dining room, and kitchen. Decorative columns define the areas, and help to visually separate them, while still providing a sense of space. The great room rises a full two stories, and is graced by a hearth and media center. The dining room features a wall of windows on one side, and sliding glass doors (to the rear yard) on the other. A tucked-away nook at the back of the plan serves well as a home office or den. On the upper level is a vaulted master suite with bath. Bedroom 3 shares a full bath with Bedroom 2. Shop space in the two-car garage will appeal to the family handyperson.

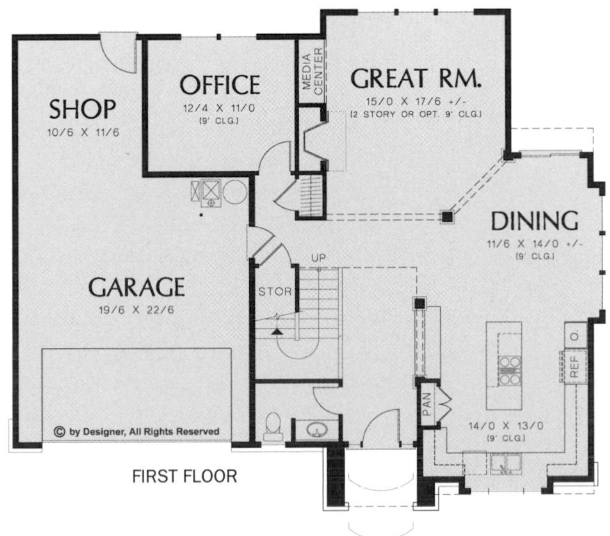

FIRST FLOOR

SECOND FLOOR

PHOTO COURTESY OF STUDER RESIDENTIAL DESIGNS, INC. BUILDER: GOFFMAN DEVELOPMENT, SPRINGBORO, OHIO

plan# HPK1700308

Style: European Cottage	
First Floor: 1,953 sq. ft.	
Second Floor: 652 sq. ft.	
Total: 2,605 sq. ft.	
Bedrooms: 2	
Bathrooms: 3	
Width: 50' - 0"	
Depth: 75' - 0"	
Foundation: Unfinished Basement, Slab	

eplans.com

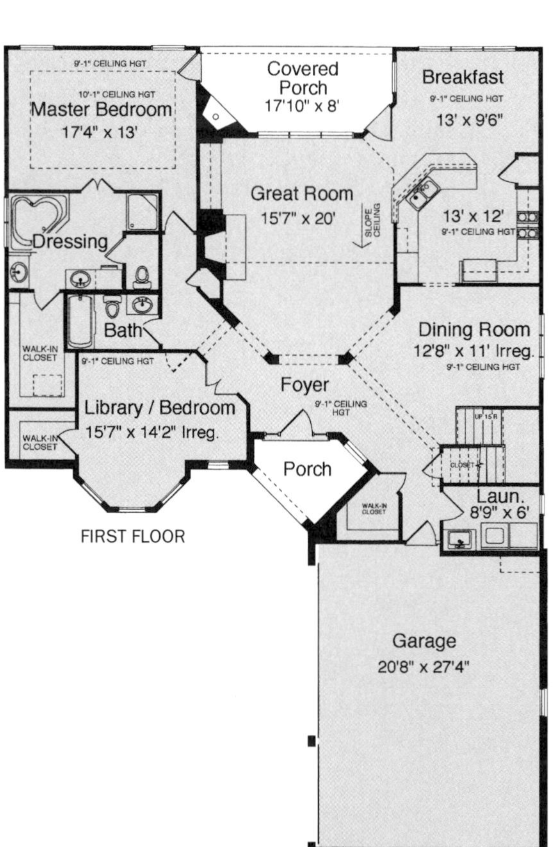

FIRST FLOOR

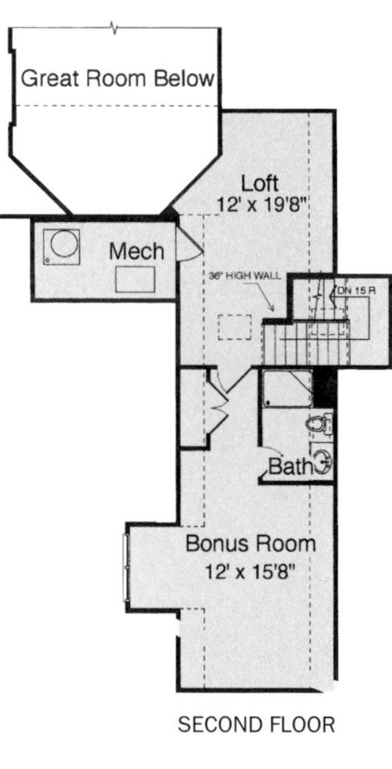

SECOND FLOOR

Angled walls and open areas create loveable living spaces at the heart of the home. The full-service kitchen provides an oven cabinet and bar-style seating for casual meals. The master bedroom features a stepped ceiling, luxury bath, and exclusive access to the rear porch. The porch is equally inviting, with a wood burning fireplace for warm gatherings. The home can be built as a one- or two-story design; the latter features a second-floor loft that overlooks the great room. Drawings include a slab foundation or an eight- or nine-foot basement foundation.

plan # HPK1700309

Style: Craftsman
First Floor: 1,216 sq. ft.
Second Floor: 1,390 sq. ft.
Total: 2,606 sq. ft.
Bedrooms: 4
Bathrooms: 2½
Width: 50' - 0"
Depth: 42' - 0"
Foundation: Crawlspace

eplans.com

Little things mean a lot—and here, the details add up to a marvelous plan. Exterior elements lend curb appeal to the two-story layout. Stone accents, lap siding, and a dormer window highlight the attention in the exterior planning. Both formal and casual dining spaces are included, and flank an open kitchen that overlooks the great room. At the back of the plan, near a service entry to the double garage, are a laundry room and half bath. Sleeping quarters are upstairs, and include three family bedrooms and a master suite. A spa tub, separate shower, dual sinks, and a walk-in closet highlight the master bath. Family bedrooms share a full bath with double sinks.

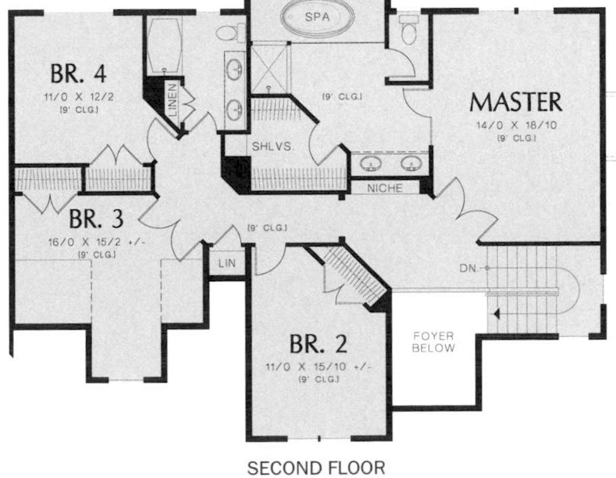

SECOND FLOOR

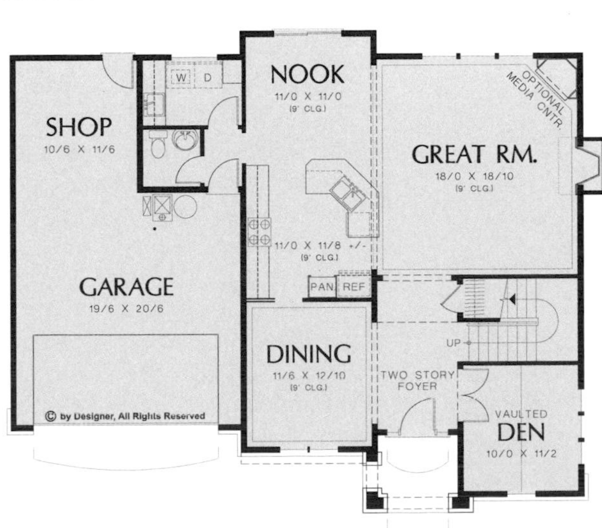

FIRST FLOOR

plan# HPK1700310

Style: Traditional
First Floor: 1,333 sq. ft.
Second Floor: 1,280 sq. ft.
Total: 2,613 sq. ft.
Bonus Space: 294 sq. ft.
Bedrooms: 4
Bathrooms: 3½
Width: 58' - 0"
Depth: 44' - 4"

eplans.com

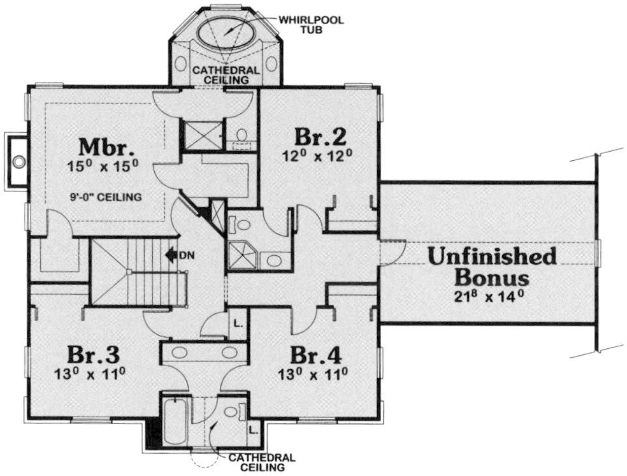

WHIRLPOOL TUB
CATHEDRAL CEILING
Mbr. 15^{0} x 15^{0}
9'-0" CEILING
Br.2 12^{0} x 12^{0}
DN
Unfinished Bonus 21^{8} x 14^{0}
L.
Br.3 13^{0} x 11^{0}
Br.4 13^{0} x 11^{0}
L
CATHEDRAL CEILING

SECOND FLOOR

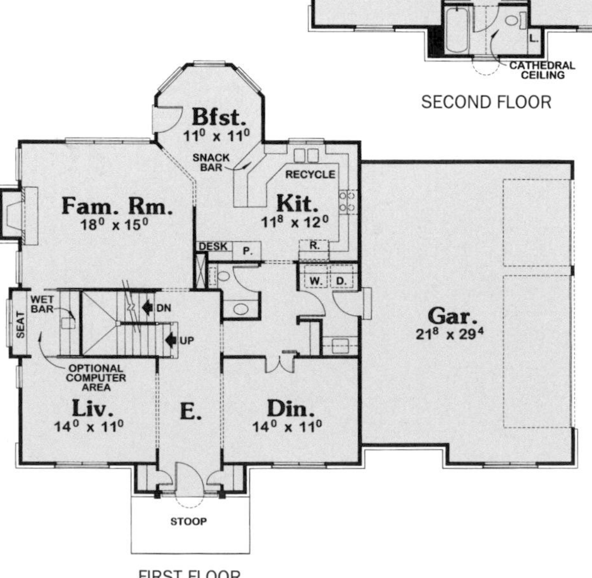

FIRST FLOOR

Classic lines define the statuesque look of this four-bedroom home. The formal rooms flank the foyer and provide views to the front. An angled snack bar in the kitchen serves the breakfast area that is bathed in natural light. Connecting the spacious family room and living room is a wet bar that has the option of being used as a computer den. Upstairs, Bedrooms 3 and 4 share a bath, and Bedroom 2 offers a private bath, making it a fine guest suite. The master bedroom is sure to please with His and Hers walk-in closets, a whirlpool tub, and a tray ceiling. Completing this level is a large bonus room available for future expansion.

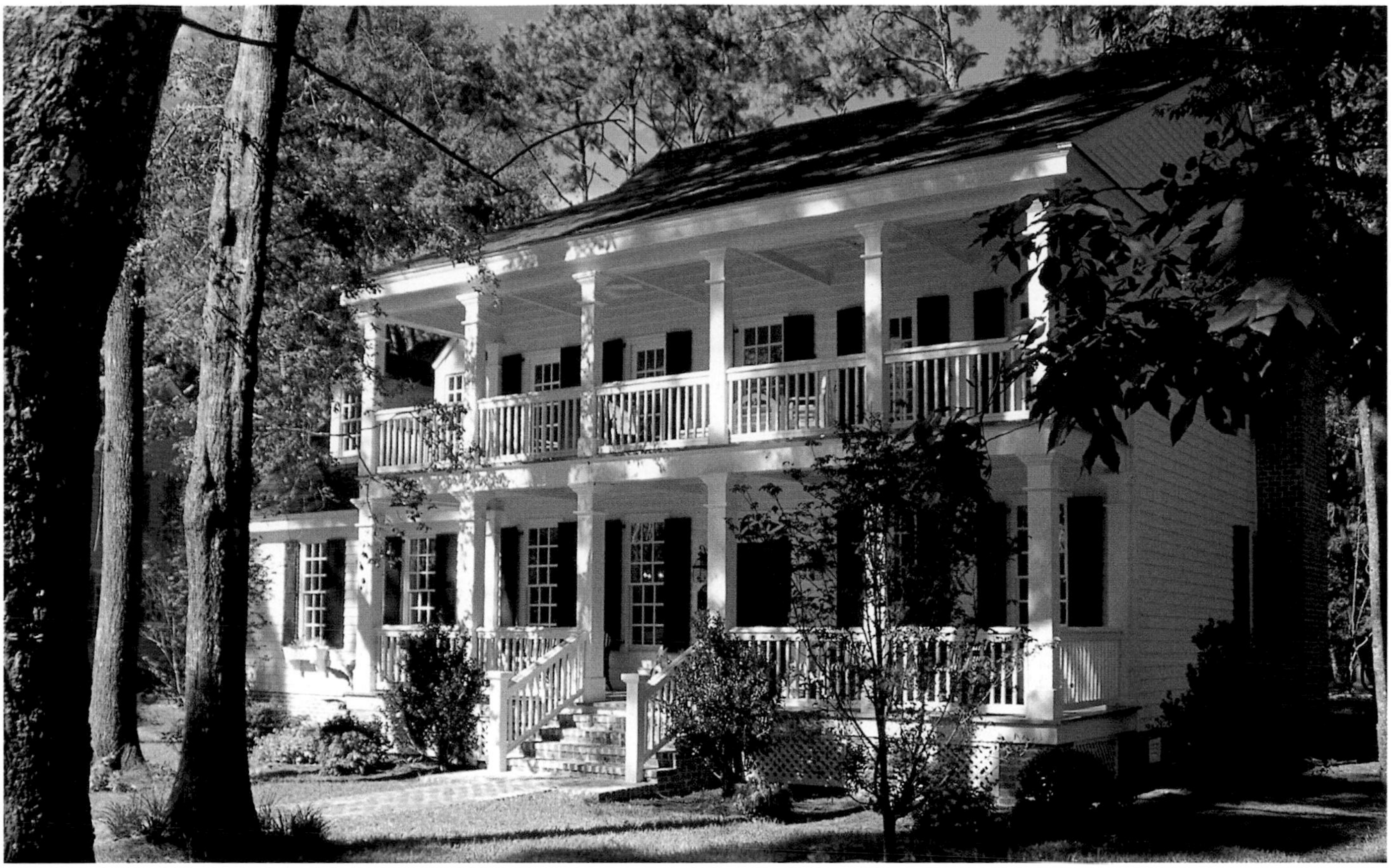

plan# HPK1700311

Style:	Southern Colonial
First Floor:	1,273 sq. ft.
Second Floor:	1,358 sq. ft.
Total:	2,631 sq. ft.
Bedrooms:	4
Bathrooms:	3½
Width:	54' - 10"
Depth:	48' - 6"
Foundation:	Crawlspace

eplans.com

This two-story home suits the needs of each household member. Family gatherings won't be crowded in the spacious family room, which is adjacent to the kitchen and the breakfast area. Just beyond the foyer, the dining and living rooms view the front yard. The master suite features its own full bath with dual vanities, a whirlpool tub, and separate shower. Three family bedrooms—one with a walk-in closet—and two full hall baths are available upstairs. Extra storage space is found in the two-car garage.

SECOND FLOOR

FIRST FLOOR

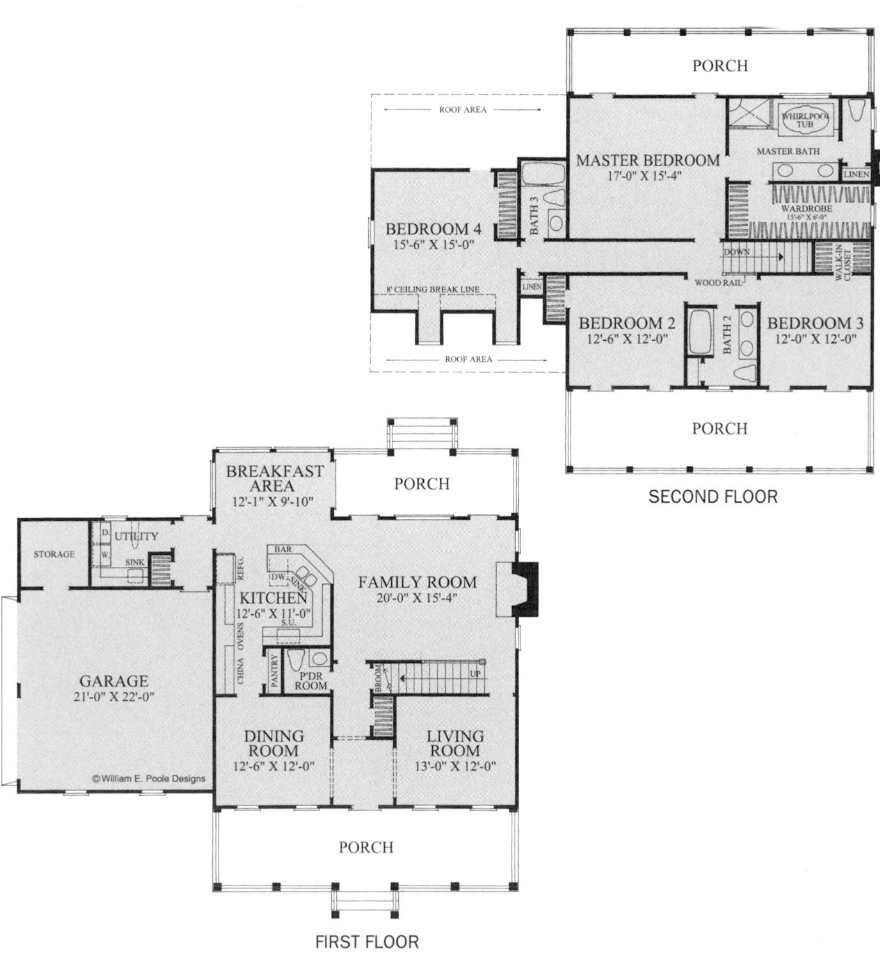

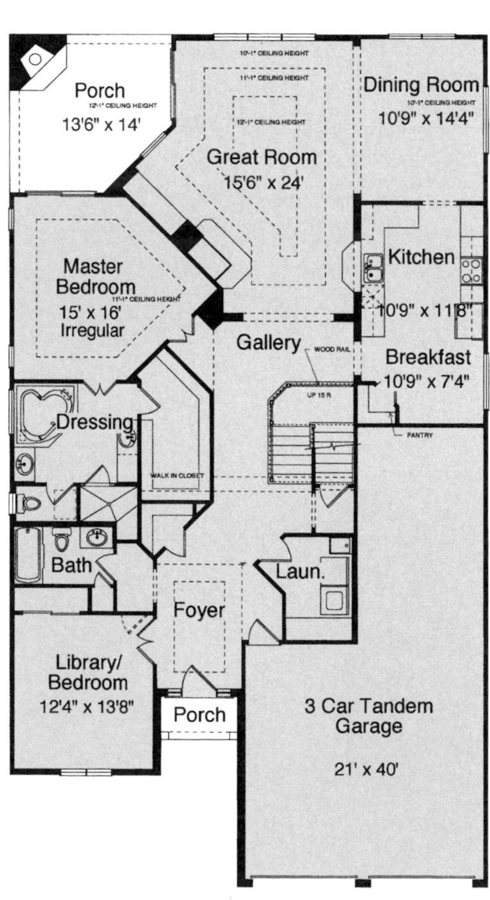

FIRST FLOOR

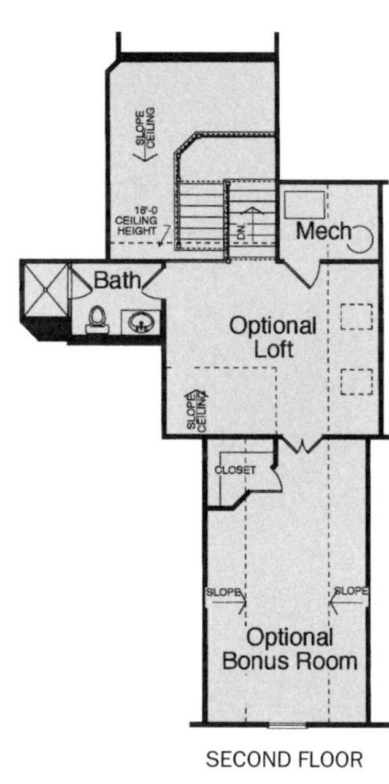

SECOND FLOOR

plan# HPK1700312

Style: Country Cottage
First Floor: 2,037 sq. ft.
Second Floor: 596 sq. ft.
Total: 2,633 sq. ft.
Bedrooms: 2
Bathrooms: 2
Width: 42' - 0"
Depth: 75' - 0"
Foundation: Unfinished Basement, Slab

eplans.com

This beautiful home offers angles and varied ceiling heights throughout. The great room showcases these elements, and enjoys access to the covered porch and a view to the rear yard. Interior and exterior fireplaces provide a cozy atmosphere. Enjoyment of the great room expands into the formal dining area. The master bedroom suite offers a luxurious bath and access to the covered porch. Split stairs overlook the gallery, and lead to the second floor loft, full bath, and bonus room.

plan# HPK1700313

Style: Traditional
First Floor: 1,844 sq. ft.
Second Floor: 794 sq. ft.
Total: 2,638 sq. ft.
Bedrooms: 4
Bathrooms: 3½
Width: 65' - 6"
Depth: 56' - 10"

eplans.com

This engaging home is inspired by French eclectic architecture with striking style. A formal entry presents the dining room on the left, defined by stately columns. French doors open to the study, a quiet place for contemplation. Continue to the two-story family room, lit by tall windows and warmed by a fireplace. Rear-veranda access near the kitchen and breakfast nook encourages alfresco dining. Sloped ceilings in the master suite are emphasized by a Palladian window; a private bath will pamper and soothe. Upstairs, three bedrooms are generously appointed. Optional attic space provides plenty of room for storage.

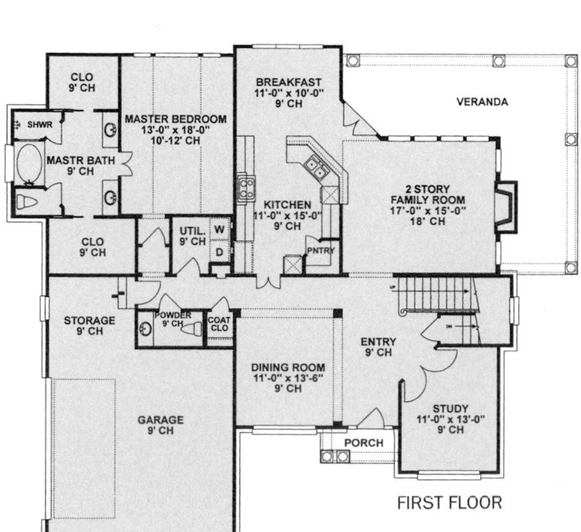

FIRST FLOOR

SECOND FLOOR

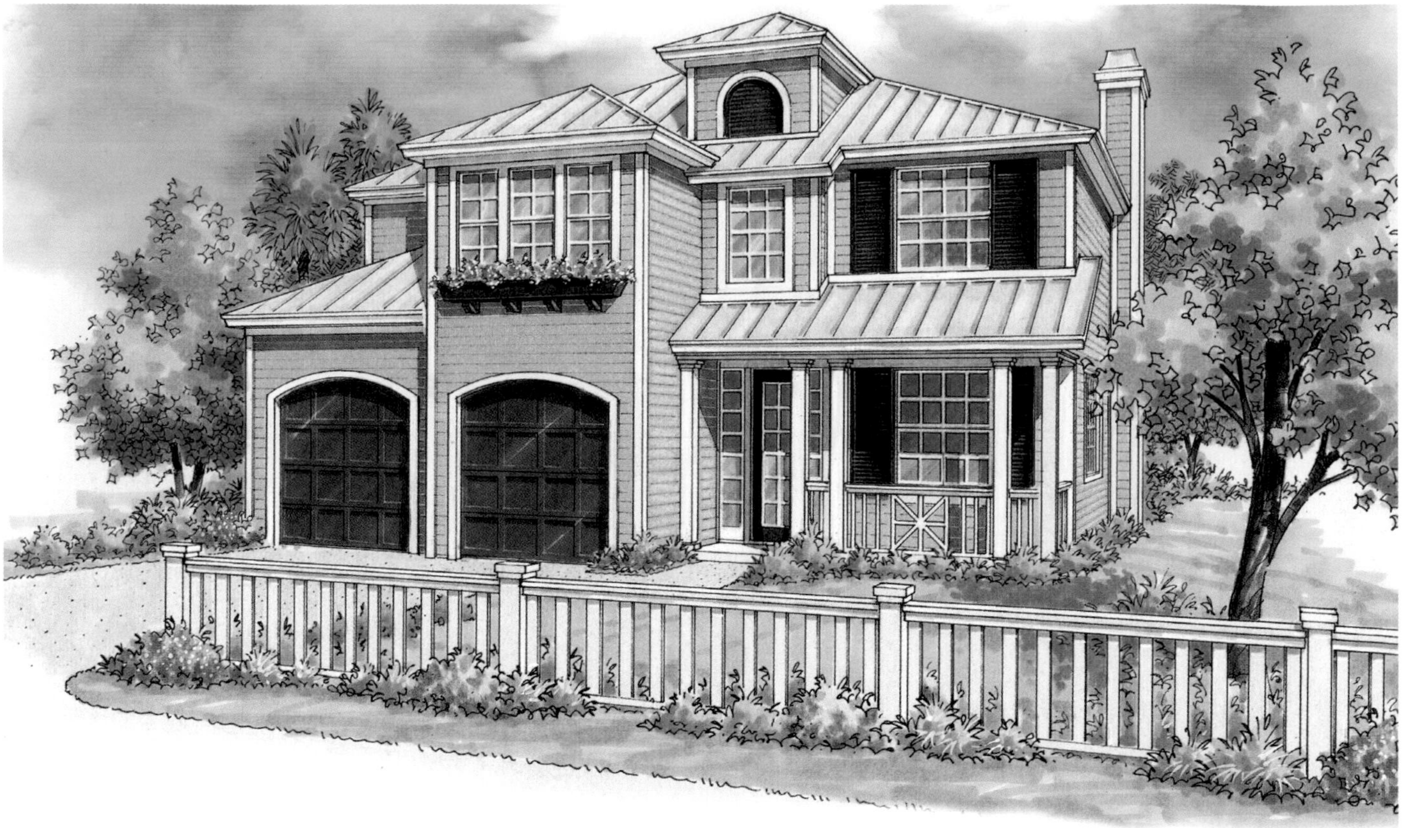

© The Sater Design Collection, Inc.

Clapboard siding and a standing-seam roof set off this cottage elevation—a comfortable seaside retreat with an easygoing style. A central turret anchors a series of varied gables and rooflines, evoking the charm of Caribbean style. Square columns and a spare balustrade define the perimeter of a spacious entry porch, which leads to a gallery-style foyer. Pocket doors seclude a forward study featuring a step ceiling and views of the front property. An open arrangement of the formal rooms progresses into the plan without restrictions, bounded only by wide views of the outdoors. Retreating glass doors permit the living and dining spaces to extend to the veranda. Upstairs, the master suite adjoins a spare room that could serve as a study, and leads out to a rear deck.

plan # HPK1700314
Style: Country Cottage
First Floor: 1,554 sq. ft.
Second Floor: 1,130 sq. ft.
Total: 2,684 sq. ft.
Bedrooms: 4
Bathrooms: 2½
Width: 40' - 0"
Depth: 67' - 0"
Foundation: Slab
eplans.com

FIRST FLOOR

SECOND FLOOR

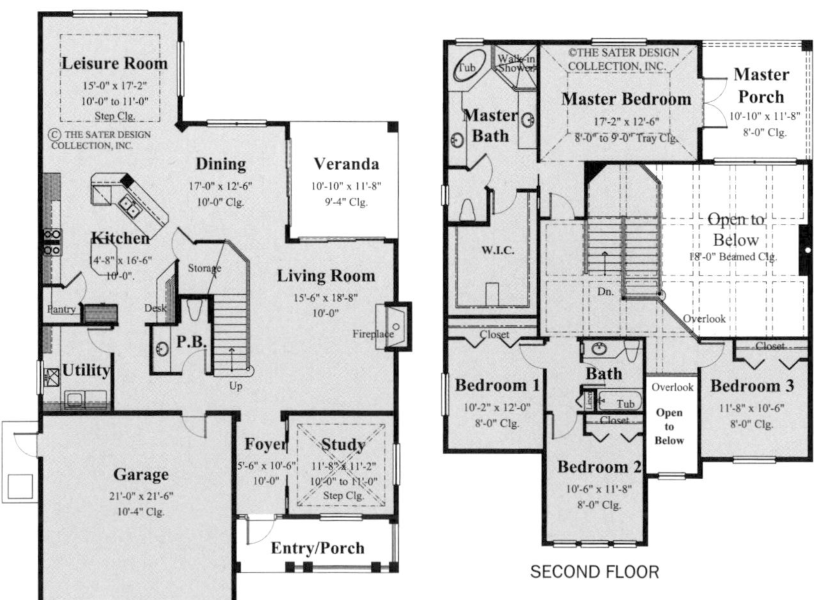

plan# HPK1700315
Style: NE Colonial
First Floor: 1,930 sq. ft.
Second Floor: 755 sq. ft.
Total: 2,685 sq. ft.
Bonus Space: 488 sq. ft.
Bedrooms: 3
Bathrooms: 3½
Width: 46' - 6"
Depth: 71' - 0"
Foundation: Walkout Basement
eplans.com

This home boasts a townhouse silhouette with a country-style facade—ideal for a narrow lot. Massive columns anchor a full porch to the New England-style elevation. Inside, the formal dining room opens from the two-story foyer. The island kitchen offers plenty of space for cooking and overlooks the casual breakfast room. The family room features a fireplace and accesses the rear porch. The master bedroom also offers access to the rear porch and provides a private bath and walk-in closet. A two-car garage completes the first floor. Two additional bedrooms upstairs offer walk-in closets and share a bath between them. The bonus room can be converted to a fourth bedroom or a study.

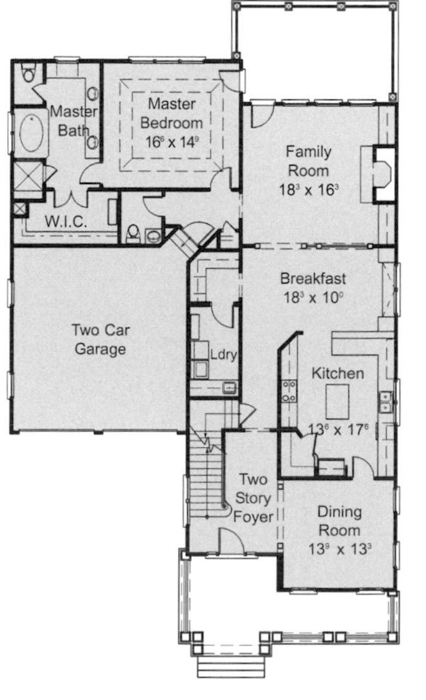

FIRST FLOOR

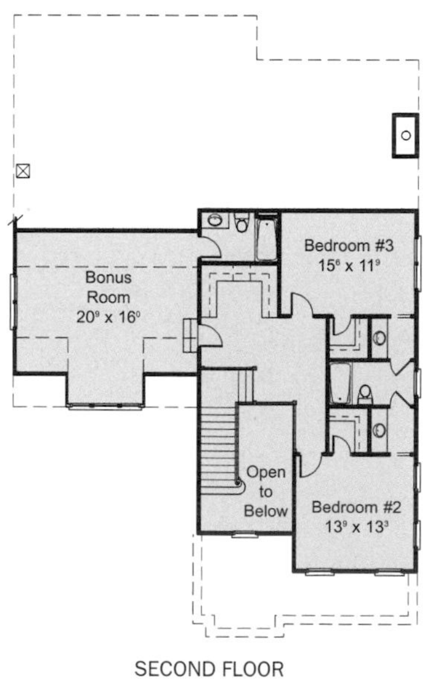

SECOND FLOOR

plan# HPK1700316

Style: Country Cottage
First Floor: 1,315 sq. ft.
Second Floor: 1,380 sq. ft.
Total: 2,695 sq. ft.
Bedrooms: 5
Bathrooms: 3
Width: 50' - 0"
Depth: 44' - 0"
Foundation: Unfinished Walkout Basement

eplans.com

This plan says "welcome home," as Craftsman details make a warm entry. The view from the front door to the family room's two-story fireplace wall is amazing. The garage entry brings you past a home office, which can easily be used as a guest bedroom. The expansive kitchen/breakfast area also features a command center—perfect for the family computer. A staircase leads to the second-floor balcony where three bedrooms share a bath. The master suite features a window seat on the back wall, dramatized by a stepped ceiling and large windows overlooking the back yard. An oversized master closet even has extra storage space that could be cedar-lined for those out-of-season clothes. The second-floor laundry and computer desk complete this well-appointed design.

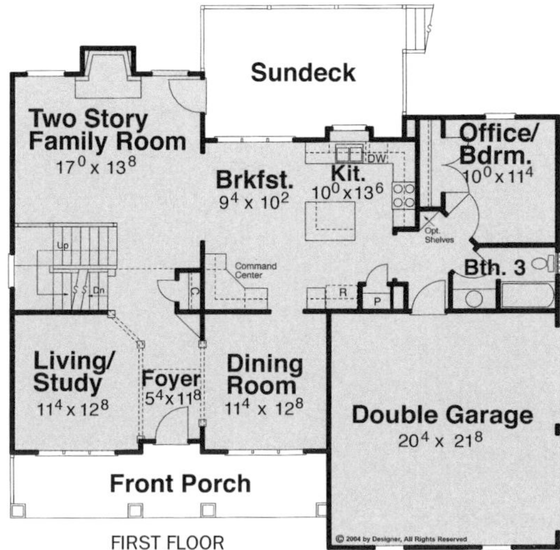

FIRST FLOOR

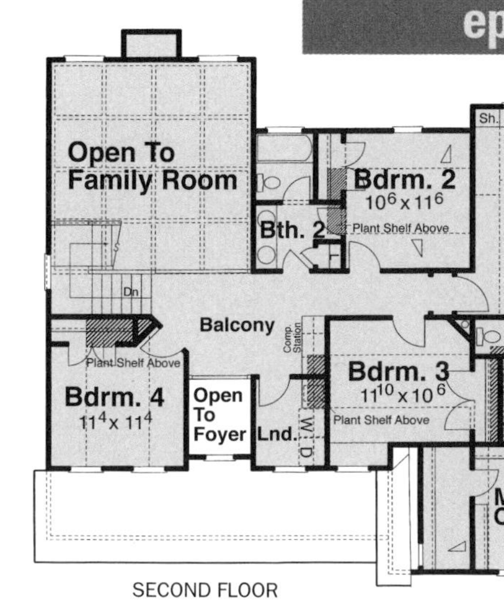

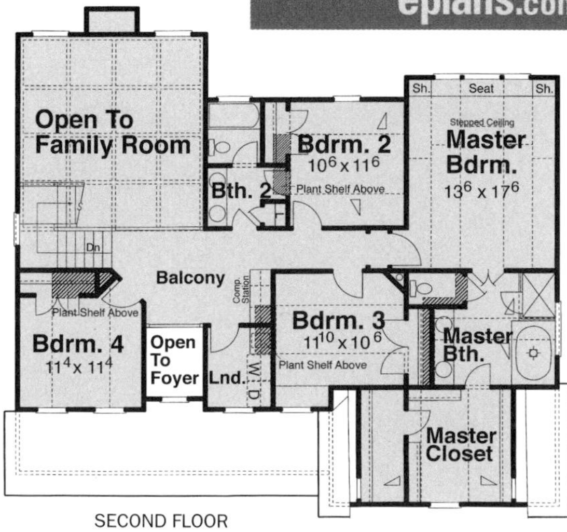

SECOND FLOOR

plan # HPK1700317

Style: Traditional
First Floor: 1,369 sq. ft.
Second Floor: 1,336 sq. ft.
Total: 2,705 sq. ft.
Bedrooms: 4
Bathrooms: 2½
Width: 49' - 0"
Depth: 46' - 4"

eplans.com

This spacious four-bedroom home offers a Craftsman-style facade with shingled gables and column and pier porch supports. A convenient butler's pantry is situated between the dining room and the hearth room. In the far left corner of the first floor, the family room offers a see-through fireplace and a built-in entertainment center. The master suite, three additional bedrooms, and a full bath join a computer loft on the second floor.

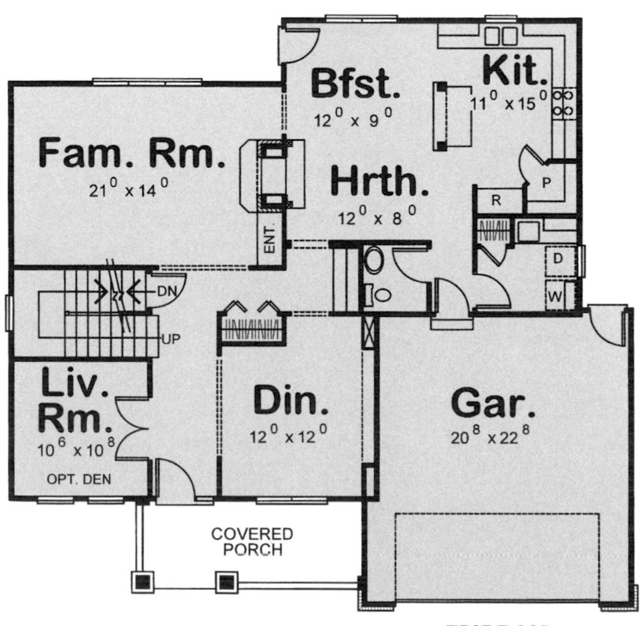

FIRST FLOOR

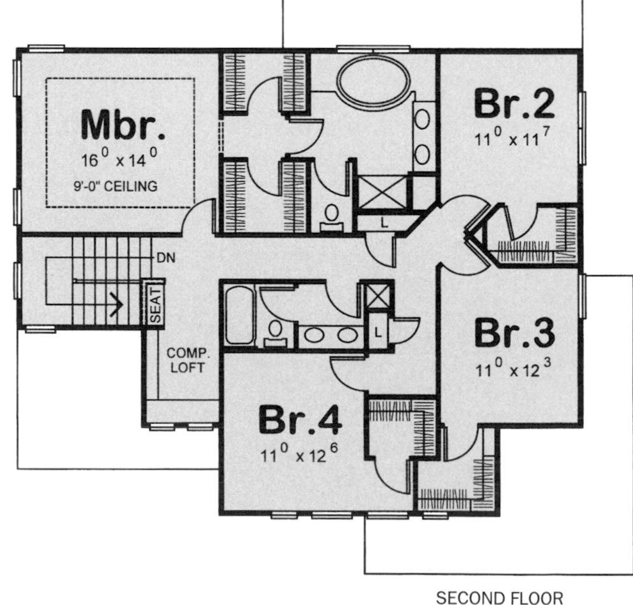

SECOND FLOOR

plan# HPK1700318

Style: European Cottage
First Floor: 1,763 sq. ft.
Second Floor: 947 sq. ft.
Total: 2,710 sq. ft.
Bedrooms: 3
Bathrooms: 2½
Width: 50' - 0"
Depth: 75' - 4"
Foundation: Walkout Basement

eplans.com

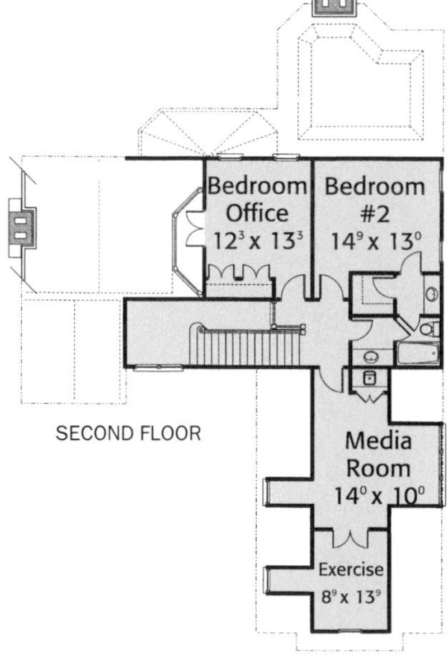

SECOND FLOOR

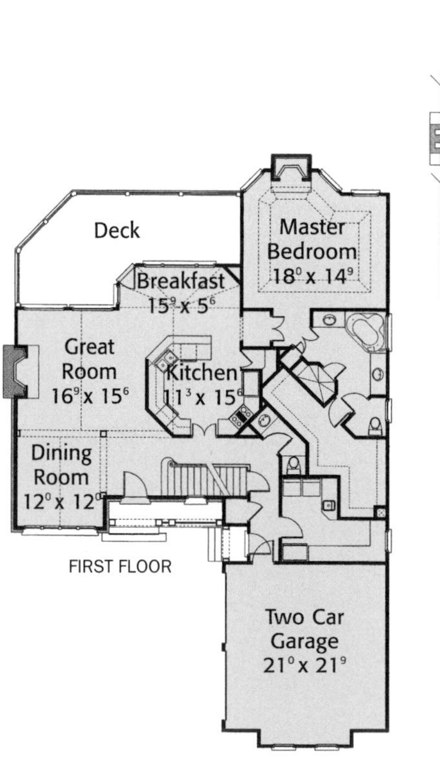

FIRST FLOOR

A special feature of this classy home is the second-floor media room and adjoining exercise area. Convenient to two upstairs bedrooms and a full bath, the media room is a great place for family computers and a fax machine. On the main level, a gourmet kitchen provides a snack counter and a walk-in pantry. Double doors open to a gallery hall that leads to the formal dining room—an enchanting retreat for chandelier-lit evenings—that provides a breathtaking view of the front yard. A classic great room is warmed by a cozy fireplace and brightened by a wall of windows. The outdoor living area is spacious enough for grand events. The master suite is brightened by sweeping views of the backyard and a romantic fireplace just for two.

plan# HPK1700319

Style: Transitional

First Floor: 1,814 sq. ft.

Second Floor: 923 sq. ft.

Total: 2,737 sq. ft.

Bedrooms: 4

Bathrooms: 2½

Width: 50' - 0"

Depth: 54' - 0"

Foundation: Crawlspace

eplans.com

The foyer of this modern stucco home is flanked by a den and formal dining room and leads directly to the dramatic two-story great room. The angled kitchen adjoins the sunny breakfast nook and serves the formal dining room with ease. The master suite boasts a tray ceiling and private bath with a corner tub, separate shower, walk-in closet and dual sinks. Upstairs, three additional family bedrooms share one full bath.

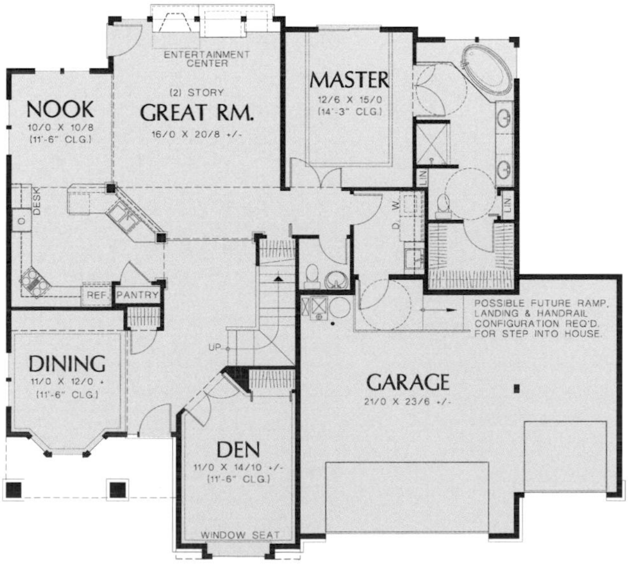

FIRST FLOOR

SECOND FLOOR

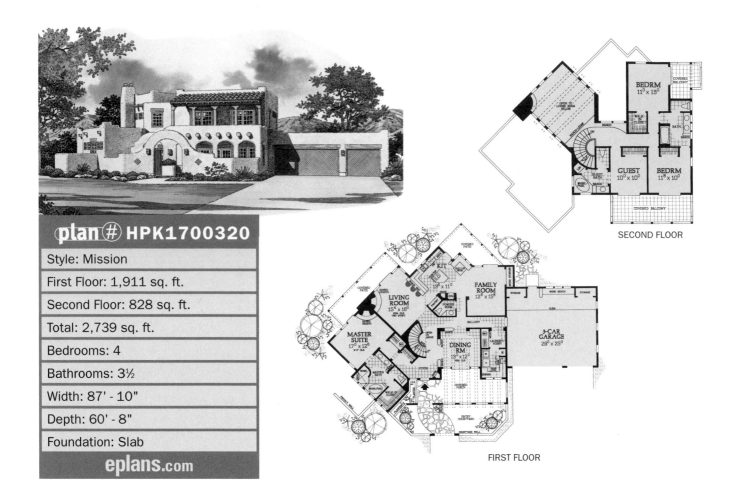

SECOND FLOOR

FIRST FLOOR

plan# HPK1700320

Style: Mission

First Floor: 1,911 sq. ft.

Second Floor: 828 sq. ft.

Total: 2,739 sq. ft.

Bedrooms: 4

Bathrooms: 3½

Width: 87' - 10"

Depth: 60' - 8"

Foundation: Slab

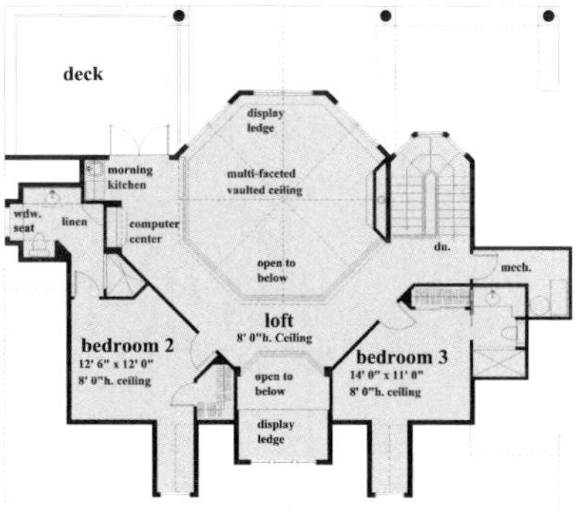

eplans.com

SECOND FLOOR

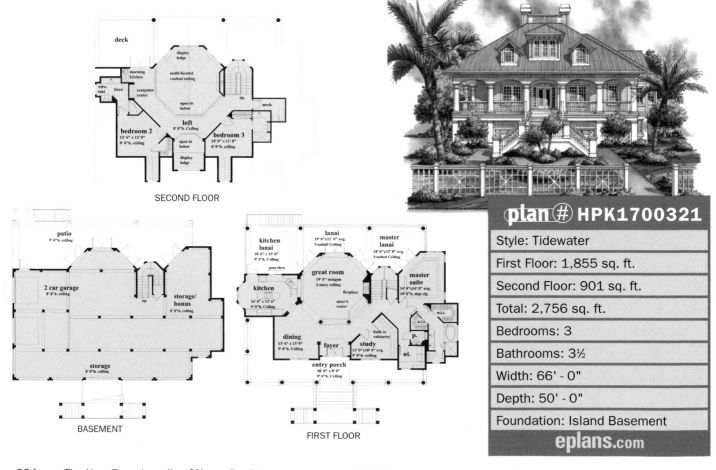

BASEMENT

FIRST FLOOR

plan# HPK1700321

Style: Tidewater

First Floor: 1,855 sq. ft.

Second Floor: 901 sq. ft.

Total: 2,756 sq. ft.

Bedrooms: 3

Bathrooms: 3½

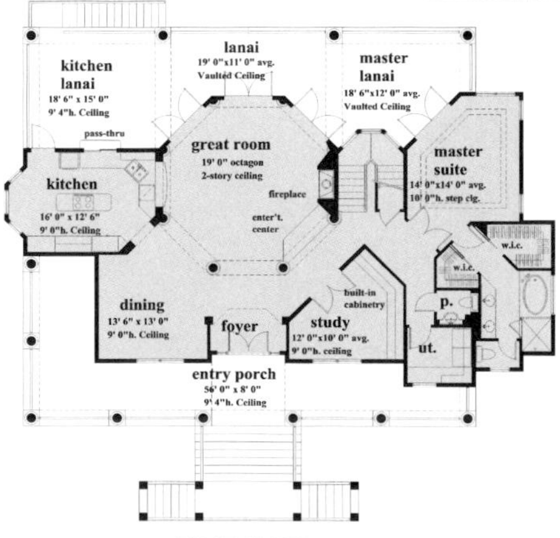

Width: 66' - 0"

Depth: 50' - 0"

Foundation: Island Basement

eplans.com

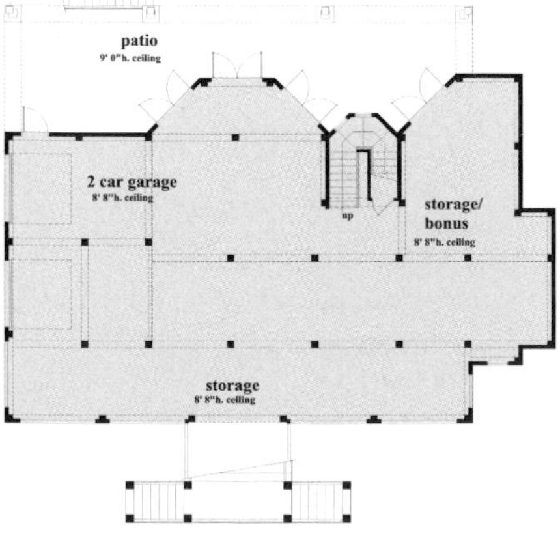

plan# HPK1700322

Style: Country Cottage
First Floor: 1,805 sq. ft.
Second Floor: 952 sq. ft.
Total: 2,757 sq. ft.
Bonus Space: 475 sq. ft.
Bedrooms: 4
Bathrooms: 3½
Width: 48' - 10"
Depth: 64' - 10"
Foundation: Crawlspace, Unfinished Basement

eplans.com

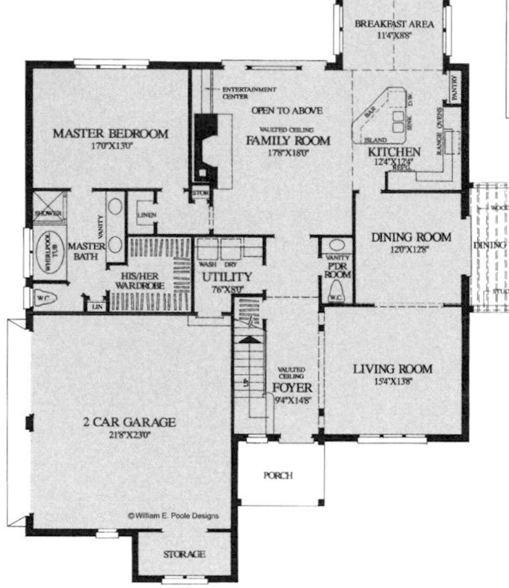

FIRST FLOOR

SECOND FLOOR

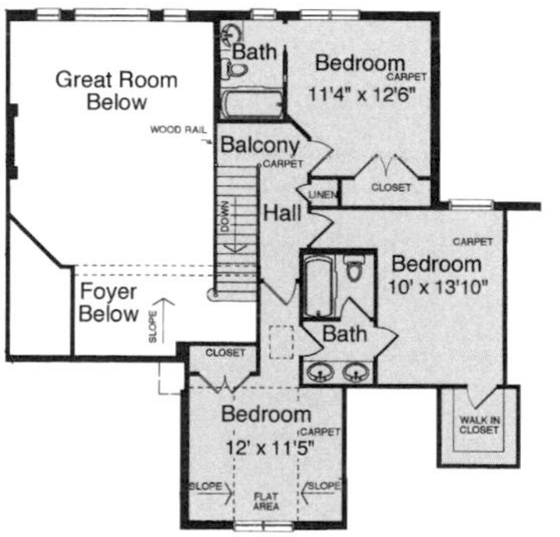

SECOND FLOOR

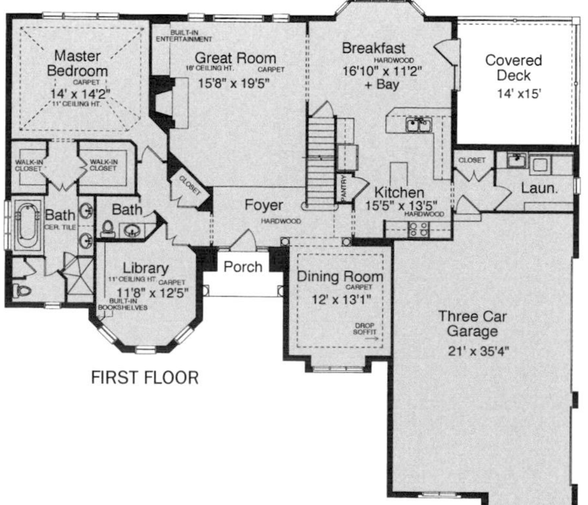

FIRST FLOOR

plan# HPK1700323

Style: Transitional
First Floor: 2,007 sq. ft.
Second Floor: 752 sq. ft.
Total: 2,759 sq. ft.
Bedrooms: 4
Bathrooms: 3½
Width: 67' - 4"
Depth: 59' - 6"
Foundation: Unfinished Walkout Basement

eplans.com

plan# HPK1700324

Style: Southern Colonial

First Floor: 1,364 sq. ft.

Second Floor: 1,398 sq. ft.

Total: 2,762 sq. ft.

Bedrooms: 5

Bathrooms: 4

Width: 51' - 0"

Depth: 45' - 4"

Foundation: Crawlspace, Unfinished Walkout Basement

eplans.com

This sturdy Southern Colonial home is perfect for a large family that likes to stretch out—and it's great for entertaining, too. Upstairs, four bedrooms, including a ravishing master suite, provide ample sleeping quarters. A laundry is conveniently located on this level. Downstairs, a den that could serve as a guest bedroom enjoys hall access to a full bath. Nearby is a study. The two-story family room opens one way to the formal dining area, and the other way to the casual eating area and kitchen, outfitted with a time-saving island counter.

FPL.
FRENCH DOOR
Two Story Family Room 18^0 x 17^0
Bedroom 5/ Den 11^5 x 12^2
Breakfast
Kitchen
DW.
ISLAND
SURF. UNIT
OVENS
REF.
PANT.
STAIRS UP
STAIRS DN.
Bath
COATS
STORAGE
Dining Room 11^0 x 14^0
Garage 20^5 x 22^0
Study 11^5 x 12^{10}
Two Story Foyer
Covered Porch

FIRST FLOOR

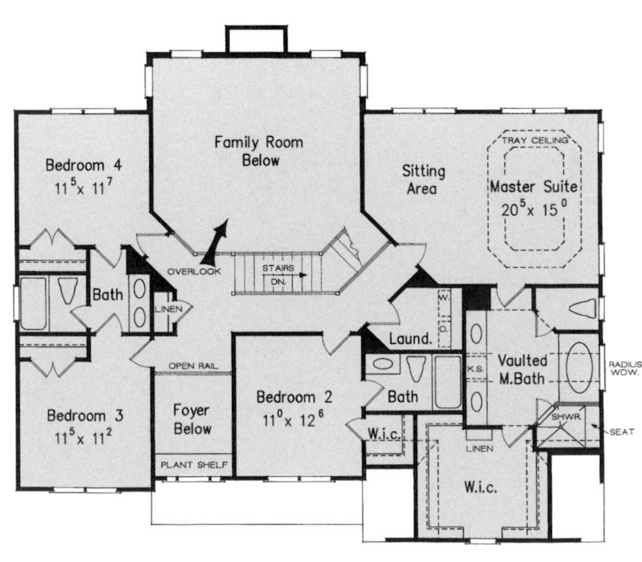

SECOND FLOOR

plan# HPK1700325

Style: Prairie
First Floor: 1,198 sq. ft.
Second Floor: 1,570 sq. ft.
Total: 2,768 sq. ft.
Bedrooms: 4
Bathrooms: 3½
Width: 38' - 0"
Depth: 75' - 0"
Foundation: Crawlspace

eplans.com

EDITOR'S PICK

At a width of 38 feet, this home is a good fit for an urban in-fill lot. The open, first-floor layout offers easy interaction between gathering rooms. Access to a rear deck from the living room and breakfast area makes outdoor dining an attractive possibility. The sleeping quarters are housed upstairs, including the master suite and three additional family bedrooms. Bedroom 4 boasts a private, full bath, a linen storage closet, and the command center control panel for the home automation system. (Turn to the ordering pages at the back of the book to find out more about home automation.) The second floor laundry room is an added convenience.

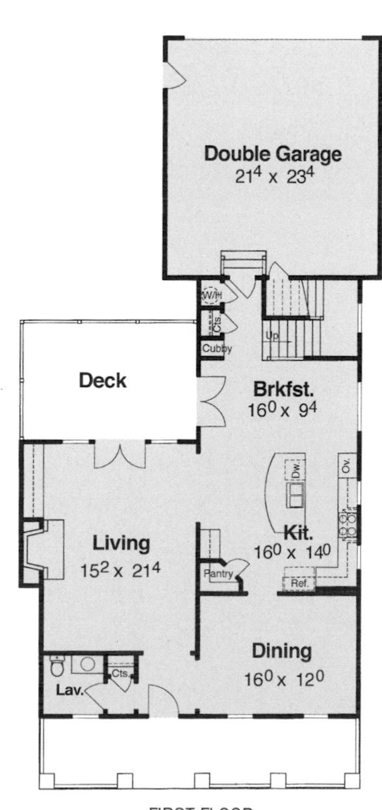

FIRST FLOOR

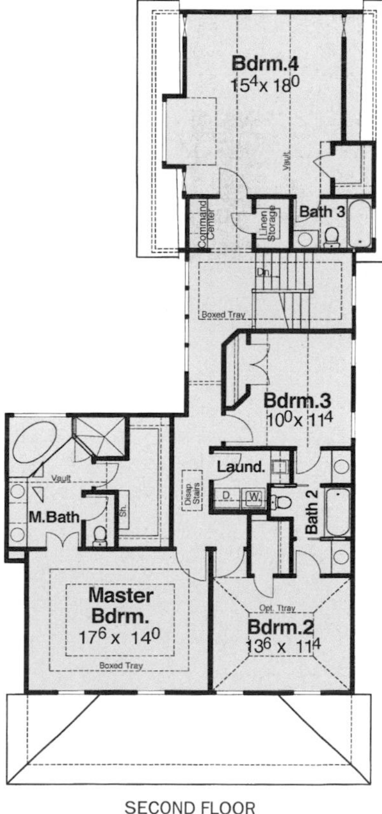

SECOND FLOOR

plan# HPK1700326

Style: Gothic Revival

First Floor: 2,023 sq. ft.

Second Floor: 749 sq. ft.

Total: 2,772 sq. ft.

Bonus Space: 242 sq. ft.

Bedrooms: 4

Bathrooms: 3½

Width: 77' - 2"

Depth: 57' - 11"

Foundation: Slab, Unfinished Basement

eplans.com

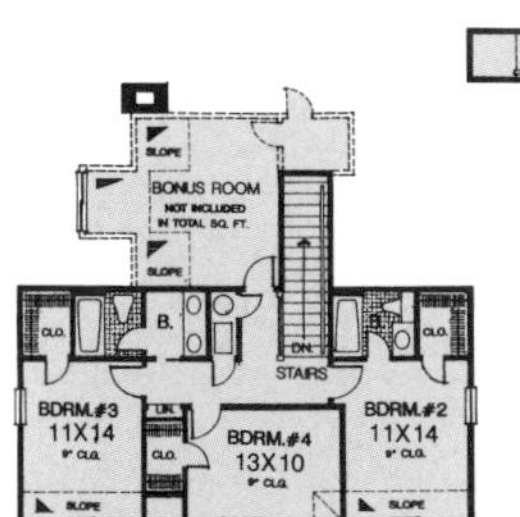

SECOND FLOOR

FIRST FLOOR

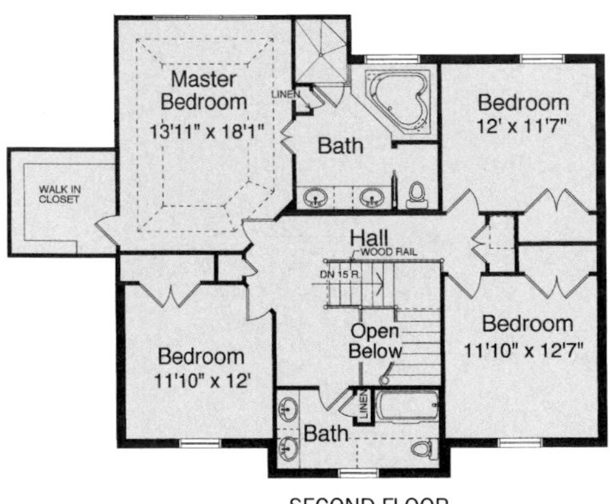

SECOND FLOOR

plan# HPK1700327

Style: Traditional

First Floor: 1,498 sq. ft.

Second Floor: 1,275 sq. ft.

Total: 2,773 sq. ft.

Bedrooms: 4

Bathrooms: 2½

Width: 63' - 0"

Depth: 41' - 2"

Foundation: Unfinished Basement

eplans.com

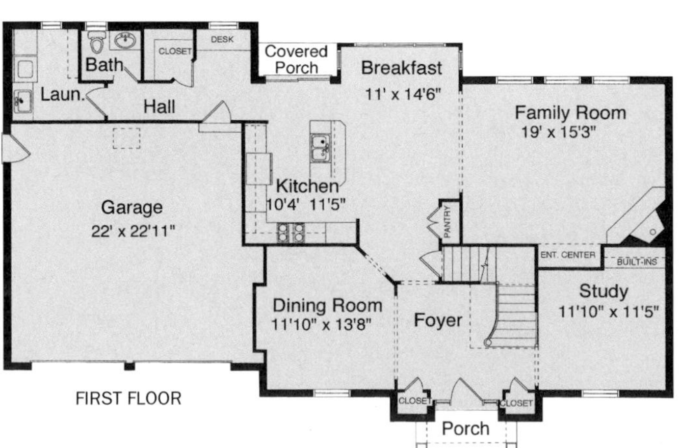

FIRST FLOOR

plan # HPK1700328

Style: Colonial
First Floor: 1,816 sq. ft.
Second Floor: 968 sq. ft.
Total: 2,784 sq. ft.
Bonus Space: 402 sq. ft.
Bedrooms: 4
Bathrooms: 3 ½
Width: 54' - 6"
Depth: 52' - 8"
Foundation: Crawlspace

eplans.com

STORAGE
OPEN TO BELOW
BEDROOM 4
13'0"X11'0"
BALCONY
FUTURE REC. ROOM
21'0"X20'4"
BATH 3
BATH 1
STORAGE
BEDROOM 2
12'0"X11'6"
OPEN TO BELOW
BEDROOM 3
12'0"X13'0"
ROOF AREA

SECOND FLOOR

FIRST FLOOR

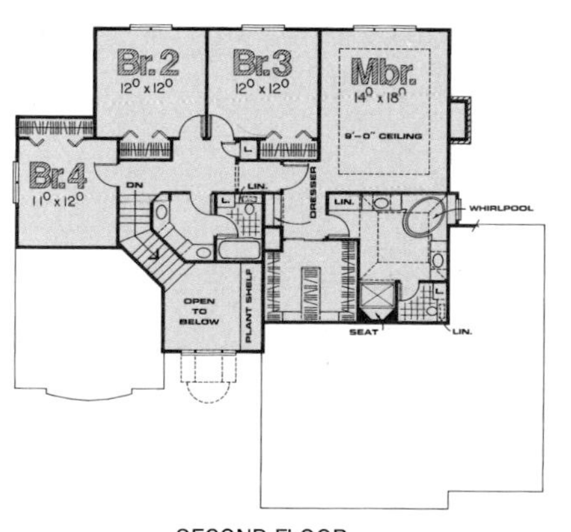

SECOND FLOOR

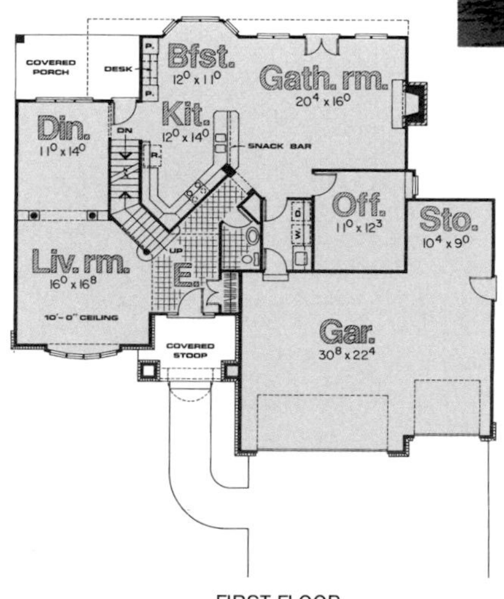

FIRST FLOOR

plan # HPK1700329

Style: Contemporary
First Floor: 1,526 sq. ft.
Second Floor: 1,281 sq. ft.
Total: 2,807 sq. ft.
Bedrooms: 4
Bathrooms: 2 ½
Width: 59' - 8"
Depth: 54' - 0"

eplans.com

plan# HPK1700330

Style: European Cottage
First Floor: 2,230 sq. ft.
Second Floor: 601 sq. ft.
Total: 2,831 sq. ft.
Bedrooms: 2
Bathrooms: 3
Width: 50' - 0"
Depth: 70' - 4"
Foundation: Unfinished Basement, Slab

eplans.com

Although it might appear petite from the outside, this plan proves to be the perfect size for a couple. The first floor master suite is a blend of practicality and lavishness. The library adjacent to the master suite is an ideal location for a home office. The family bedroom on this level—with bay window, for great views and plenty of sun—can serve as a guest suite, or prestigious accommodations for an in-law. The open layout allows the design to flow without the use of unnecessary walls. An eating bar in the spacious kitchen cleverly serves the adjoining dining and great rooms. Access to the rear patio—equipped with an outdoor fireplace—from the dining room, welcomes alfresco meals and entertaining. With the majority of the living space on the first floor, a bonus room and full bath on the second floor is great for additional guests or visiting children.

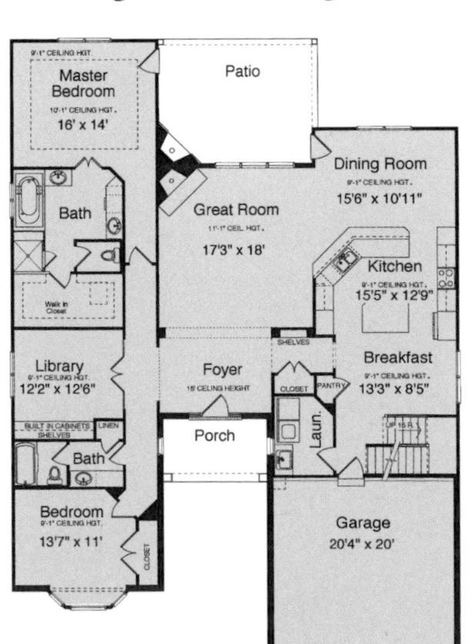

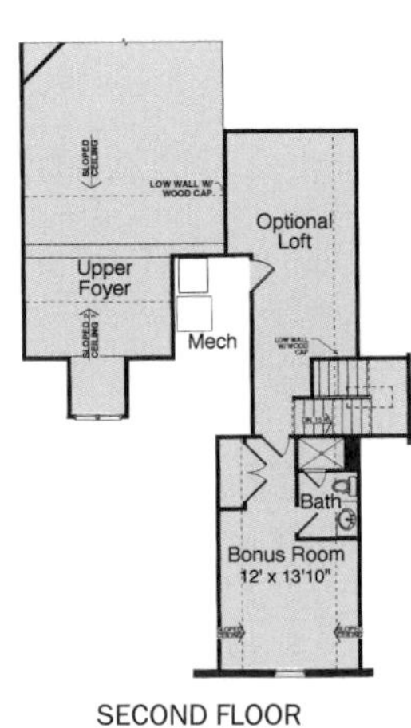

SECOND FLOOR

FIRST FLOOR

plan# HPK1700331

Style: Country Cottage
First Floor: 1,921 sq. ft.
Second Floor: 921 sq. ft.
Total: 2,842 sq. ft.
Bonus Space: 454 sq. ft.
Bedrooms: 4
Bathrooms: 3½
Width: 62' - 2"
Depth: 71' - 0"
Foundation: Crawlspace, Unfinished Basement

eplans.com

A porch wraps around two sides and joins a screened porch in the rear, giving this country-style plan a true down-home appeal. The great room, which soars two stories high, enjoys a fireplace and two entries to the screened porch. It also opens easily into the breakfast alcove and is conveniently tied to the kitchen by an angled counter. A formal dining room is just to the right of the foyer. The luxurious master suite pampers with a walk-in closet, twin-sink vanity, garden tub, and step-up shower. Upstairs, three bedrooms share two baths and a loft study. Ample room is available to add a recreation room. A side-loading garage offers lots of room for storage.

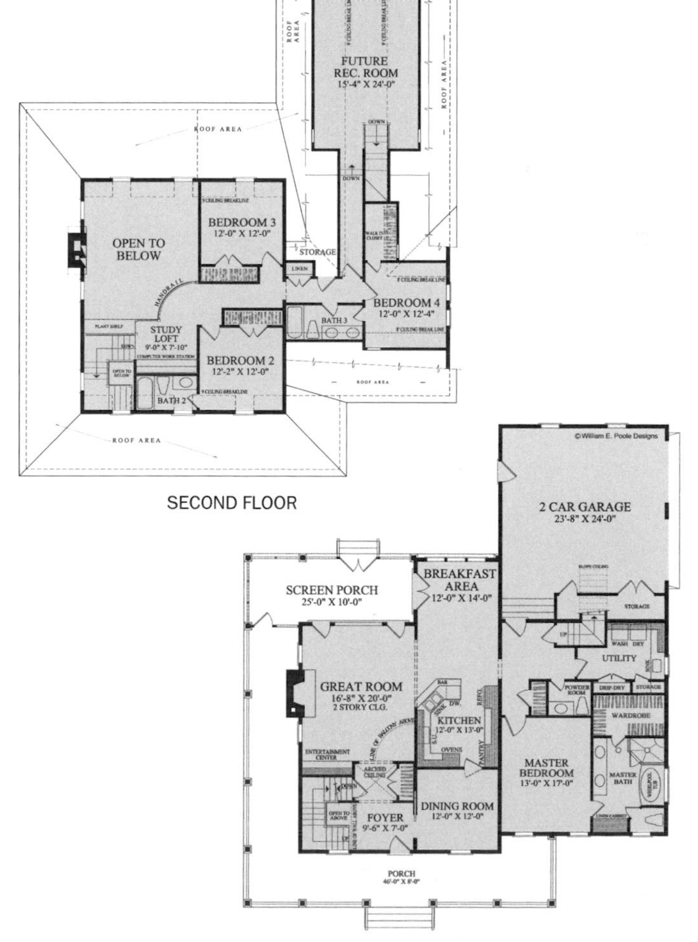

SECOND FLOOR

FIRST FLOOR

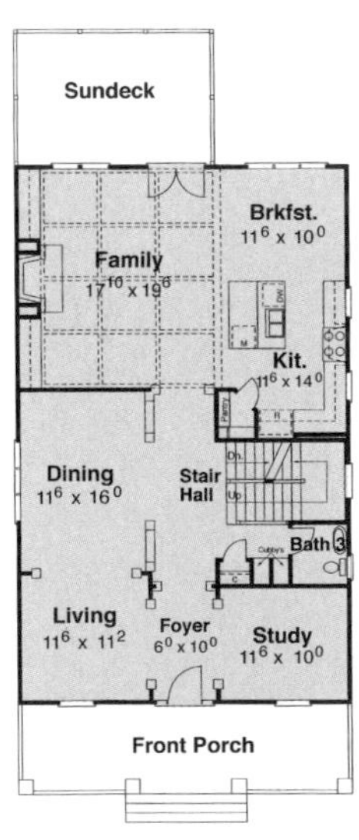

FIRST FLOOR

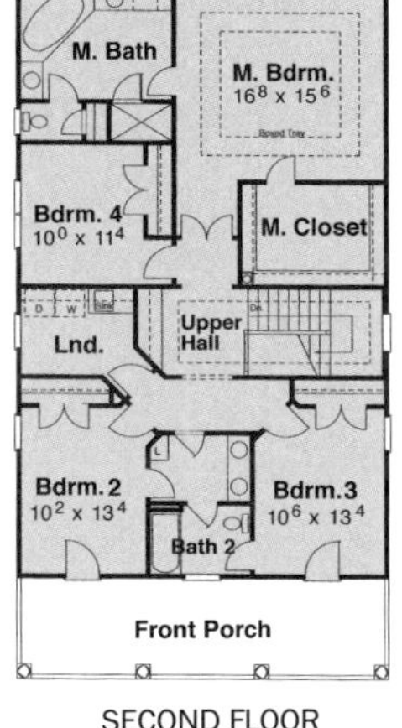

SECOND FLOOR

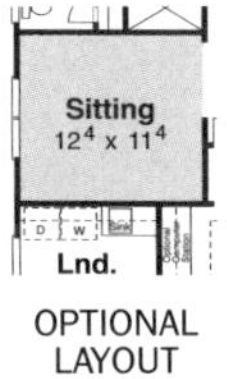

OPTIONAL LAYOUT

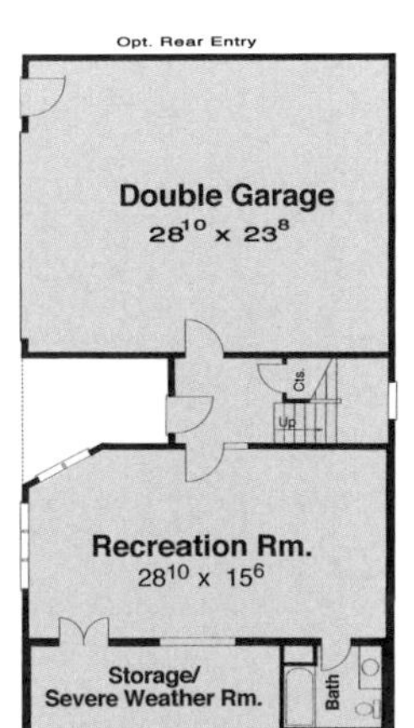

BASEMENT

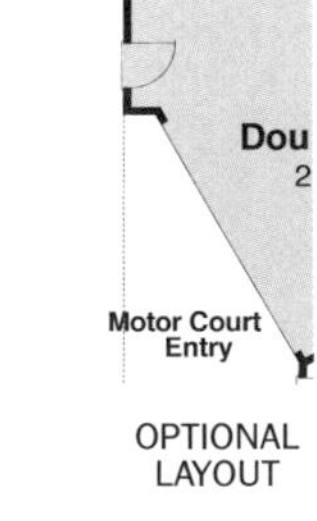

OPTIONAL LAYOUT

plan# HPK1700332

Style: Prairie
First Floor: 1,440 sq. ft.
Second Floor: 1,440 sq. ft.
Total: 2,880 sq. ft.
Bonus Space: 140 sq. ft.
Bedrooms: 4
Bathrooms: 2½
Width: 30' - 0"
Depth: 56' - 0"
Foundation: Unfinished Basement

eplans.com

The impressive exterior gives way to an interior without boundaries. The lack of unnecessary walls creates a feeling of spaciousness. Access to the sundeck from the family room extends the living space, encouraging entertaining. The second floor houses the master suite and three additional family bedrooms. Bedrooms 2 and 3 enjoy private access to a front-facing covered porch. A second-floor laundry room is an added convenience. The finished basement, boasting a sizable recreation room, completes this plan.

plan# HPK1700333

Style: Farmhouse
First Floor: 2,151 sq. ft.
Second Floor: 738 sq. ft.
Total: 2,889 sq. ft.
Bonus Space: 534 sq. ft.
Bedrooms: 3
Bathrooms: 2½
Width: 99' - 0"
Depth: 56' - 0"
Foundation: Crawlspace

eplans.com

REAR EXTERIOR

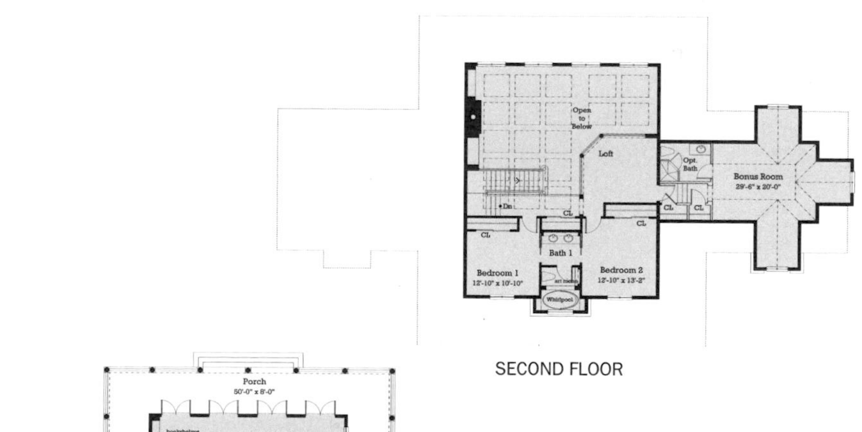

SECOND FLOOR

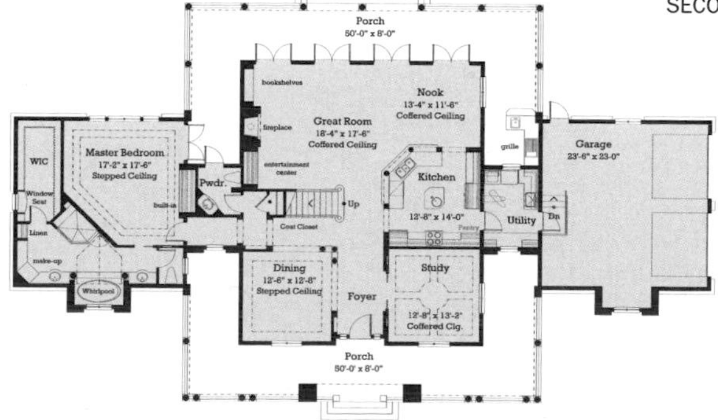

FIRST FLOOR

A wide, welcoming porch and plenty of stone accents highlight the facade of this charming symmetrical design. Inside, coffered ceilings enhance the study, great room, and breakfast nook; the dining room and master suite both boast stepped ceilings. From the great room, four sets of French doors open to a wraparound rear porch with a grilling area. The master bedroom, also with porch access, includes built-in shelves, a walk-in closet with a window seat, and a luxurious bath with a whirlpool tub. On the second floor, two family bedrooms share a full bath with a whirlpool tub; a loft area and a bonus room offer extra space.

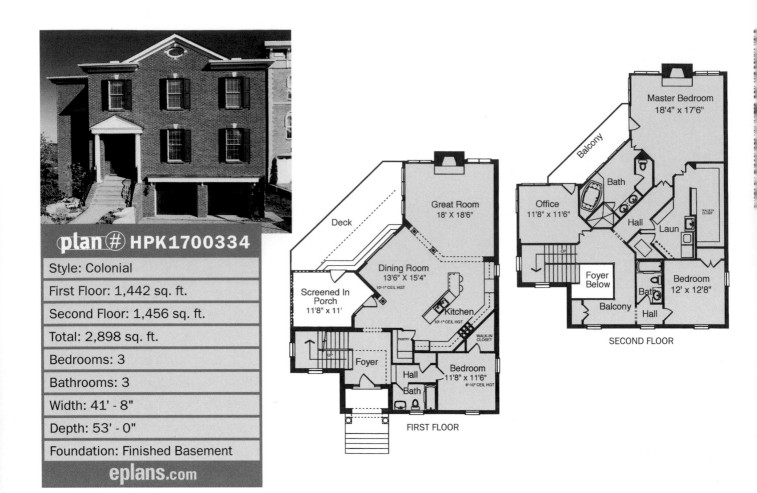

plan# HPK1700334

Style: Colonial

First Floor: 1,442 sq. ft.

Second Floor: 1,456 sq. ft.

Total: 2,898 sq. ft.

Bedrooms: 3

Bathrooms: 3

Width: 41' - 8"

Depth: 53' - 0"

Foundation: Finished Basement

eplans.com

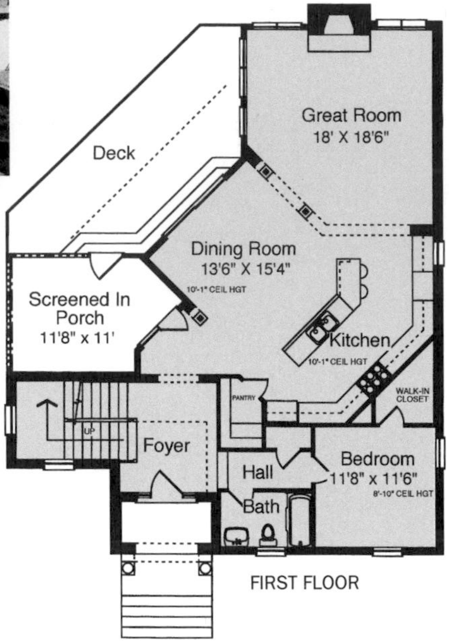

FIRST FLOOR

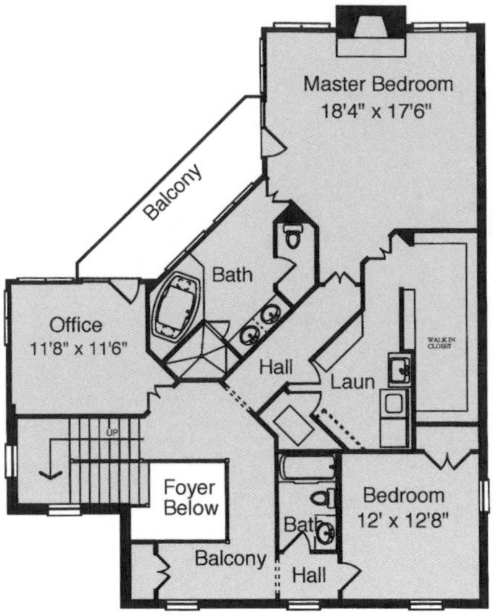

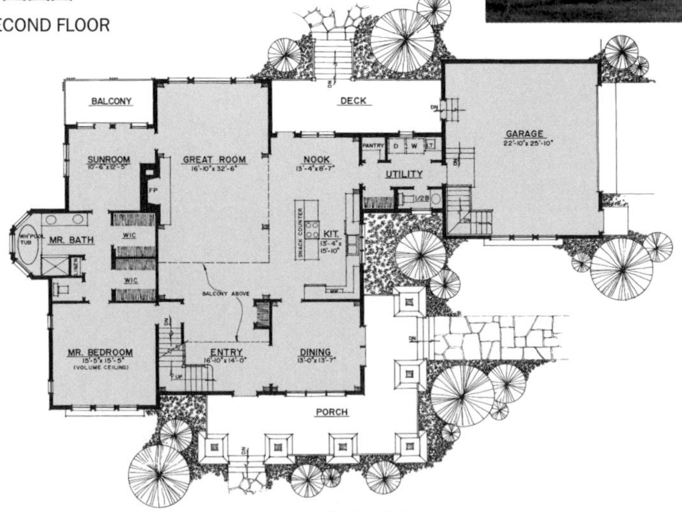

SECOND FLOOR

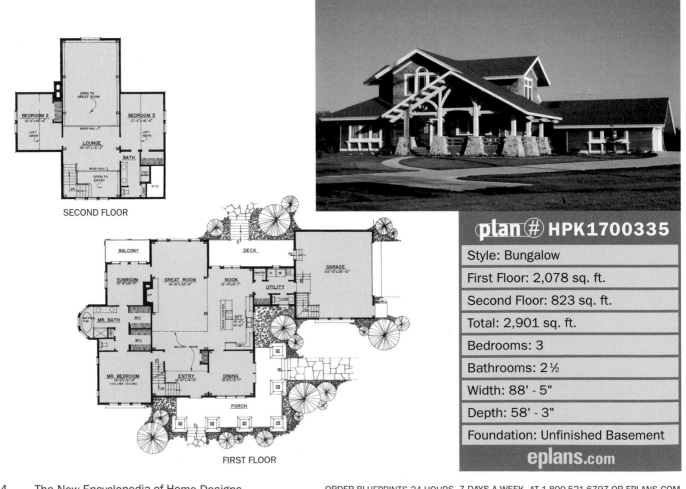

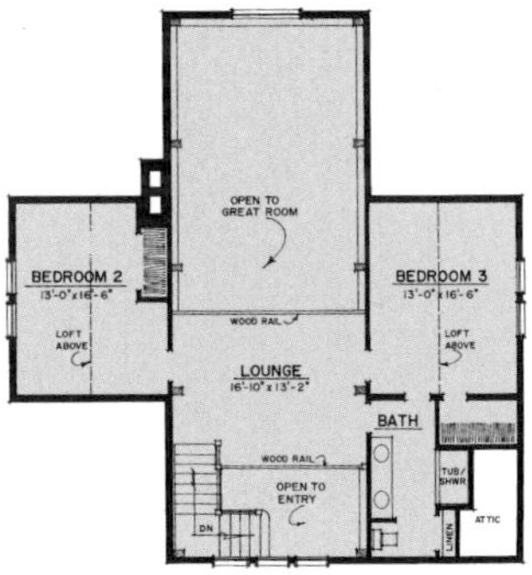

plan# HPK1700335

Style: Bungalow

First Floor: 2,078 sq. ft.

Second Floor: 823 sq. ft.

Total: 2,901 sq. ft.

Bedrooms: 3

Bathrooms: 2½

Width: 88' - 5"

Depth: 58' - 3"

Foundation: Unfinished Basement

eplans.com

SECOND FLOOR

FIRST FLOOR

plan# HPK1700336

Style: Country Cottage
First Floor: 1,475 sq. ft.
Second Floor: 1,460 sq. ft.
Total: 2,935 sq. ft.
Bedrooms: 4
Bathrooms: 3½
Width: 57' - 6"
Depth: 46' - 6"
Foundation: Walkout Basement

eplans.com

SITTING
MASTER BEDROOM 16'-0" X 13'-0"
OPEN TO BELOW
BEDROOM NO. 2 12'-0" X 11'-4"
BALCONY
BATH
MASTER BATH
BATH
OPEN TO BELOW
BEDROOM NO. 3 12'-0" X 11'-4"
W.I.C.
BEDROOM NO. 4 11'-2" X 12'-0"
SECRET ROOM

SECOND FLOOR

FIRST FLOOR

FIRST FLOOR

SECOND FLOOR

OPTIONAL LAYOUT

plan# HPK1700337

Style: Craftsman
First Floor: 1,659 sq. ft.
Second Floor: 1,290 sq. ft.
Total: 2,949 sq. ft.
Bonus Space: 463 sq. ft.
Bedrooms: 4
Bathrooms: 3½
Width: 43' - 4"
Depth: 82' - 0"
Foundation: Unfinished Walkout Basement

eplans.com

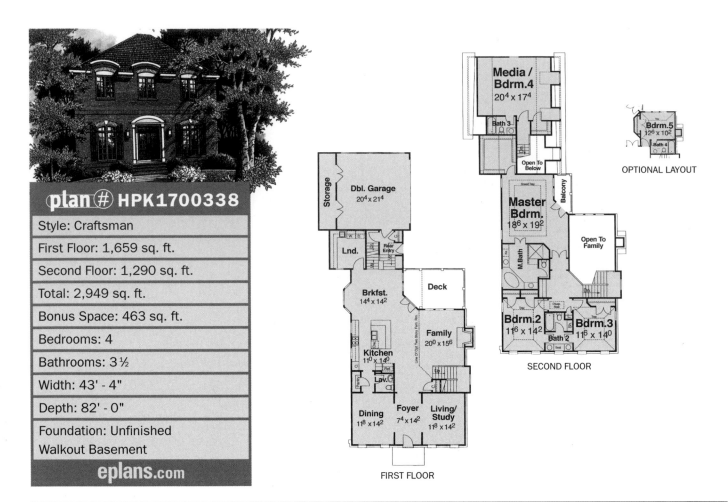

plan# HPK1700338

Style: Craftsman
First Floor: 1,659 sq. ft.
Second Floor: 1,290 sq. ft.
Total: 2,949 sq. ft.
Bonus Space: 463 sq. ft.
Bedrooms: 4
Bathrooms: 3½
Width: 43' - 4"
Depth: 82' - 0"
Foundation: Unfinished Walkout Basement

eplans.com

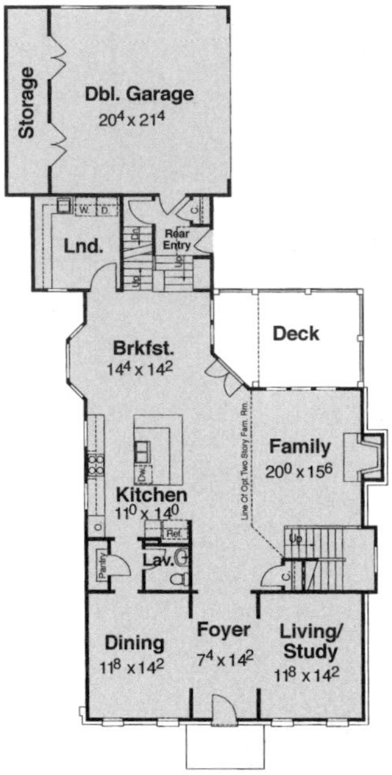

FIRST FLOOR

SECOND FLOOR

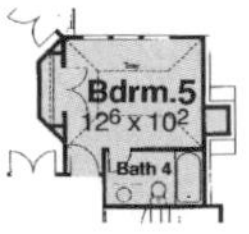

OPTIONAL LAYOUT

SECOND FLOOR

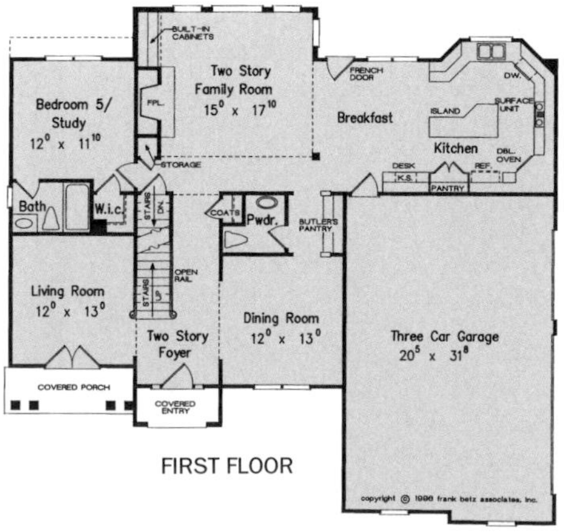

FIRST FLOOR

plan# HPK1700339

Style: Southern Colonial
First Floor: 1,463 sq. ft.
Second Floor: 1,490 sq. ft.
Total: 2,953 sq. ft.
Bedrooms: 5
Bathrooms: 4½
Width: 54' - 0"
Depth: 51' - 6"
Foundation: Crawlspace, Unfinished Walkout Basement, Slab

eplans.com

plan# HPK1700340

Style: Craftsman
First Floor: 1,440 sq. ft.
Second Floor: 1,514 sq. ft.
Total: 2,954 sq. ft.
Bedrooms: 4
Bathrooms: 3½
Width: 30' - 0"
Depth: 68' - 0"
Foundation: Unfinished Walkout Basement

eplans.com

A stylish Craftsman at just under 3,000 square feet, this home features an open layout ideal for entertaining. Rooms are distinguished by columns, eliminating the use of unnecessary walls. At the rear of the home, the expansive family room, warmed by a fireplace, faces the adjoining breakfast area and kitchen. Access to the sundeck makes alfresco meals an option. A walk-in pantry is an added bonus. The second floor houses the family bedrooms, including the lavish master suite, two bedrooms separated by a Jack-and-Jill bath, and a fourth bedroom with a private, full bath. The second floor laundry room is smart and convenient. A centrally located, optional computer station is perfect for a family computer. A sizable recreation room on the basement level completes this plan.

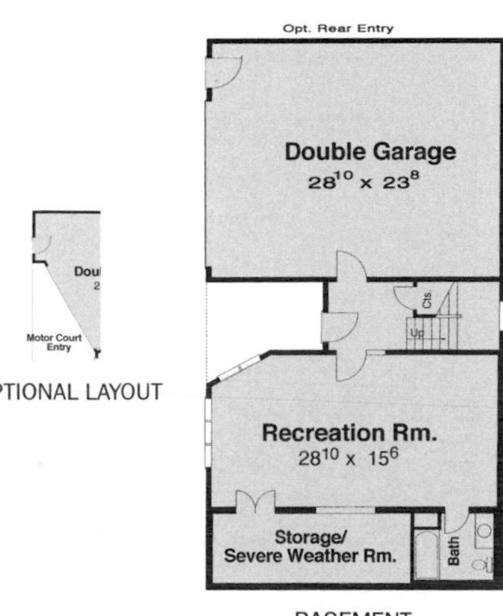

OPTIONAL LAYOUT

BASEMENT

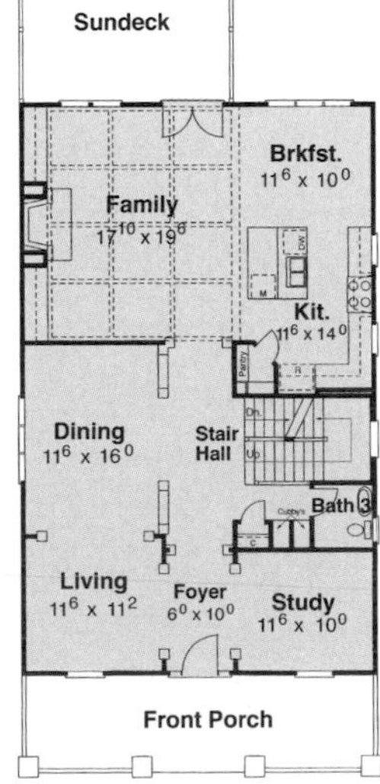

FIRST FLOOR

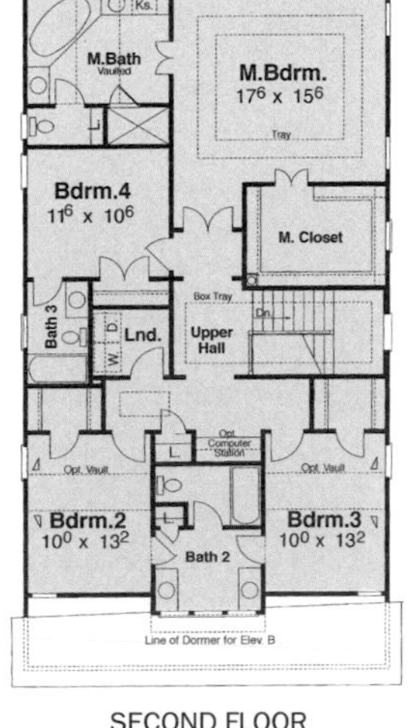

SECOND FLOOR

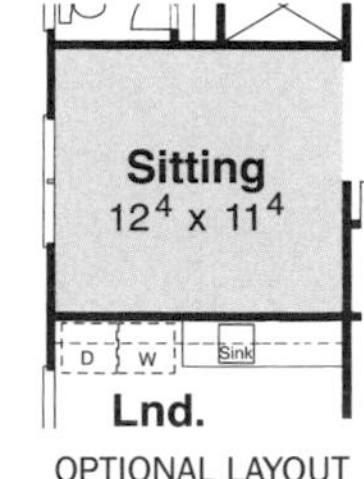

OPTIONAL LAYOUT

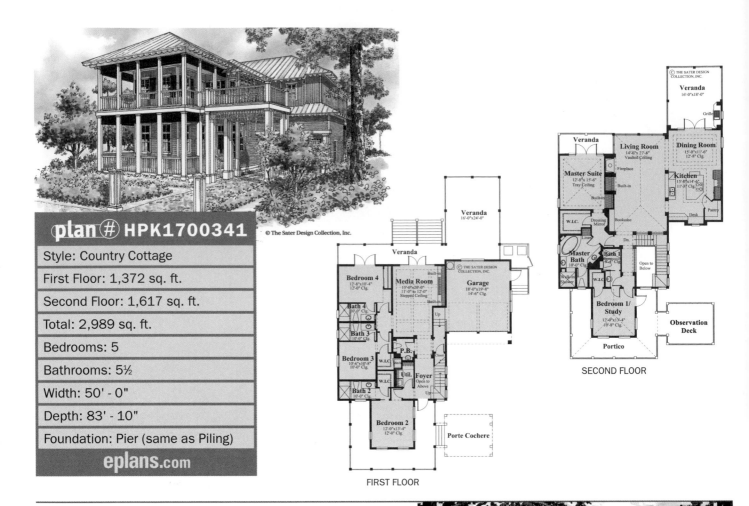

© The Sater Design Collection, Inc.

plan# HPK1700341

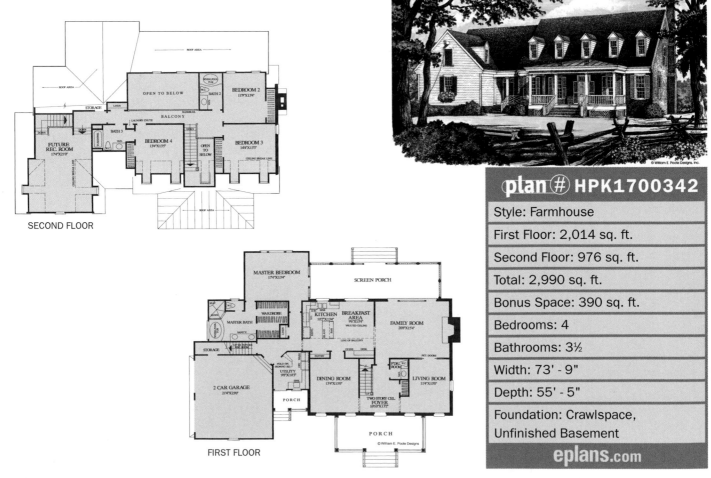

Style: Country Cottage

First Floor: 1,372 sq. ft.

Second Floor: 1,617 sq. ft.

Total: 2,989 sq. ft.

Bedrooms: 5

Bathrooms: 5½

Width: 50' - 0"

Depth: 83' - 10"

Foundation: Pier (same as Piling)

eplans.com

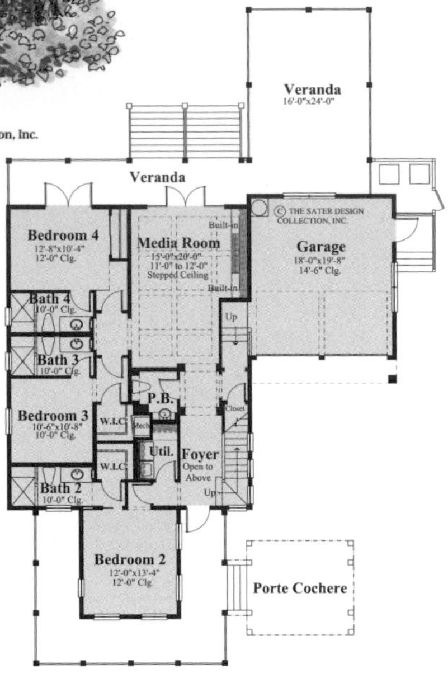

FIRST FLOOR

SECOND FLOOR

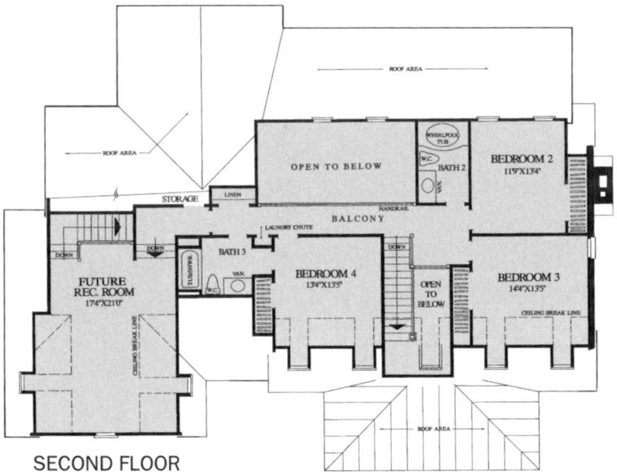

© William E. Poole Designs, Inc.

plan# HPK1700342

Style: Farmhouse

First Floor: 2,014 sq. ft.

Second Floor: 976 sq. ft.

Total: 2,990 sq. ft.

Bonus Space: 390 sq. ft.

Bedrooms: 4

Bathrooms: 3½

Width: 73' - 9"

Depth: 55' - 5"

Foundation: Crawlspace, Unfinished Basement

eplans.com

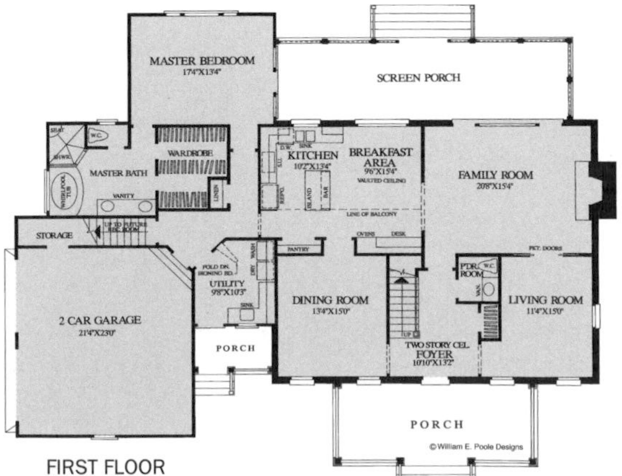

SECOND FLOOR

FIRST FLOOR

© 1999 Donald A. Gardner, Inc.

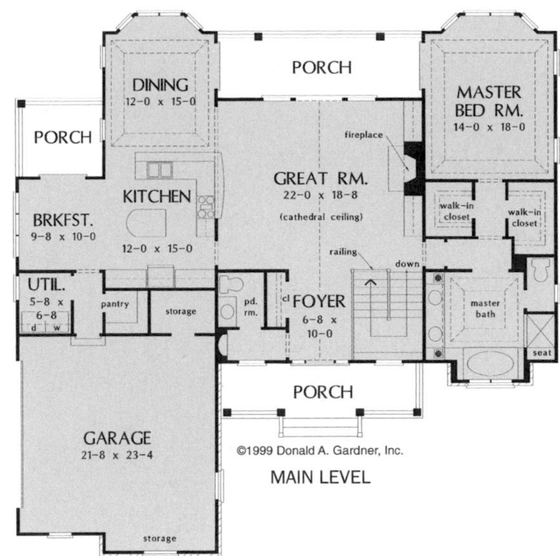

plan# HPK1700343

Style: Traditional
Main Level: 1,725 sq. ft.
Lower Level: 1,090 sq. ft.
Total: 2,815 sq. ft.
Bedrooms: 3
Bathrooms: 3½
Width: 59' - 0"
Depth: 59' - 4"

eplans.com

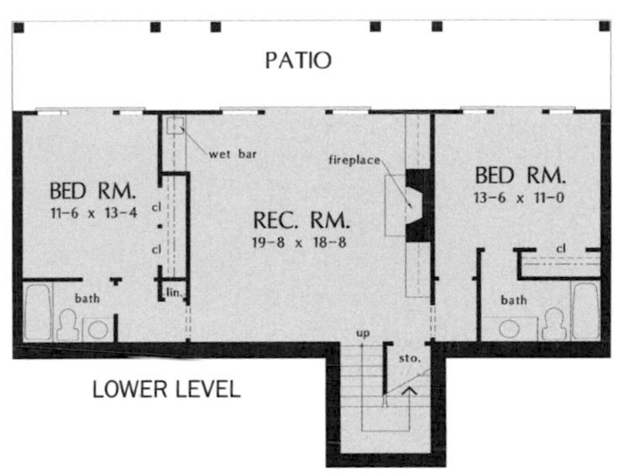

© 1999 Donald A. Gardner, Inc.

plan# HPK1700344

Style: European Cottage
Main Level: 1,901 sq. ft.
Lower Level: 1,075 sq. ft.
Total: 2,976 sq. ft.
Bedrooms: 4
Bathrooms: 3
Width: 64' - 0"
Depth: 62' - 4"

eplans.com

A country front covered porch welcomes you inside to a charming and traditional duplex home. Just inside, a powder room and hall closet flank the foyer. The U-shaped kitchen overlooks the dining area and two-story great room, featuring a fireplace. The first-floor master suite enjoys His and Hers walk-in closets and a private bath. A laundry room connecting to the garage completes the first floor. Upstairs, Bedrooms 2 and 3 share a full hall bath and a balcony hall overlooking the great room and kitchen below.

plan# HPK1700345

- Style: Traditional
- First Floor: 960 sq. ft.
- Second Floor: 533 sq. ft.
- Total: 1,493 sq. ft.
- Bedrooms: 3
- Bathrooms: 2½
- Width: 64' - 0"
- Depth: 50' - 8"
- Foundation: Unfinished Basement

eplans.com

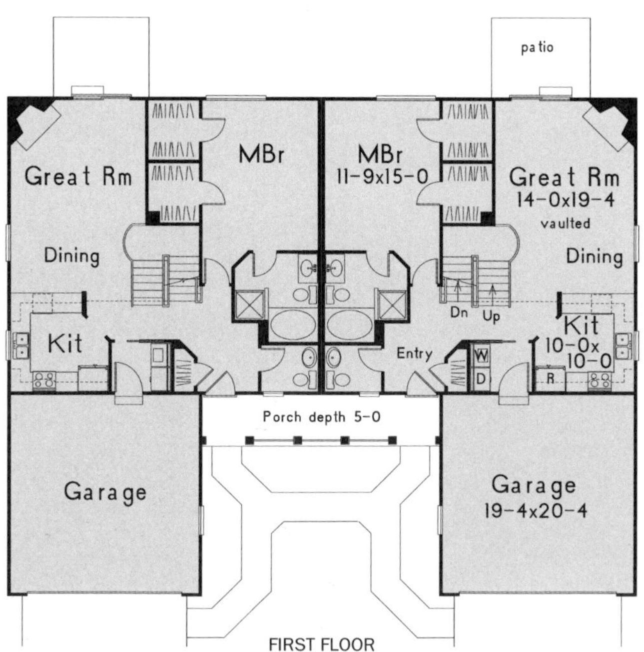

FIRST FLOOR

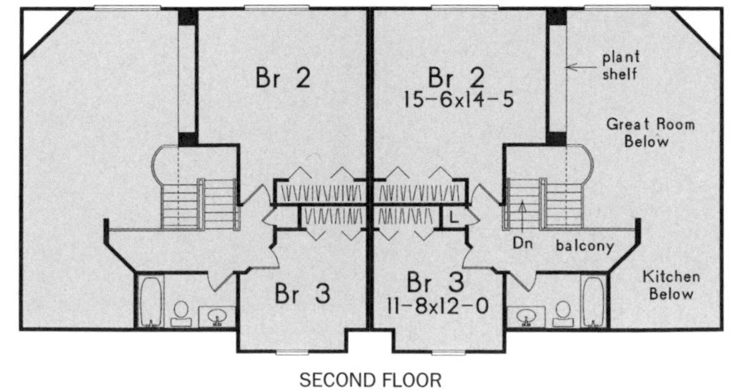

SECOND FLOOR

Homes From 3,000 to 3,499 Square Feet

This distinctive stucco home is reminiscent of early Mission-style architecture. See plan HPK1700356 on page 310.

plan# HPK1700346

Style: French

Square Footage: 3,032 sq. ft.

Bedrooms: 3

Bathrooms: 3

Width: 73' - 0"

Depth: 87' - 8"

Foundation: Slab

eplans.com

This country estate is bedecked with all the details that pronounce its French origins. They include the study, family room, and keeping room. Dine in one of two areas—the formal dining room or the casual breakfast room. A large porch to the rear can be reached through the breakfast room or the master suite's sitting area. All three bedrooms in the plan have walk-in closets. Bedrooms 2 and 3 share a full bath that includes private vanities.

plan # HPK1700347

Style: Tidewater
Square Footage: 3,074
Bedrooms: 3
Bathrooms: 3½
Width: 77' - 0"
Depth: 66' - 8"
Foundation: Island Basement

eplans.com

The individual charm and natural beauty of this sensational home reside in its pure symmetry and perfect blend of past and future. A steeply pitched roof caps a collection of Prairie-style windows and elegant columns. The portico leads to a midlevel foyer, which rises to the grand salon. A wide-open leisure room hosts a corner fireplace that's ultra cozy. The master wing sprawls from the front portico to the rear covered porch, rich with luxury amenities and plenty of secluded space.

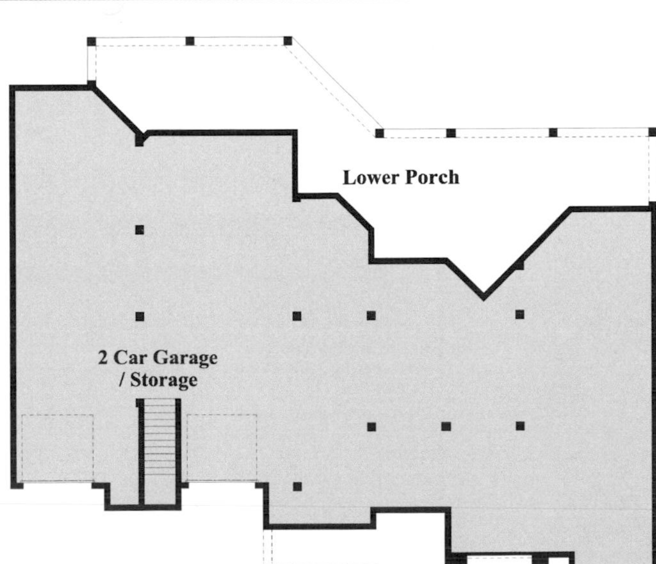

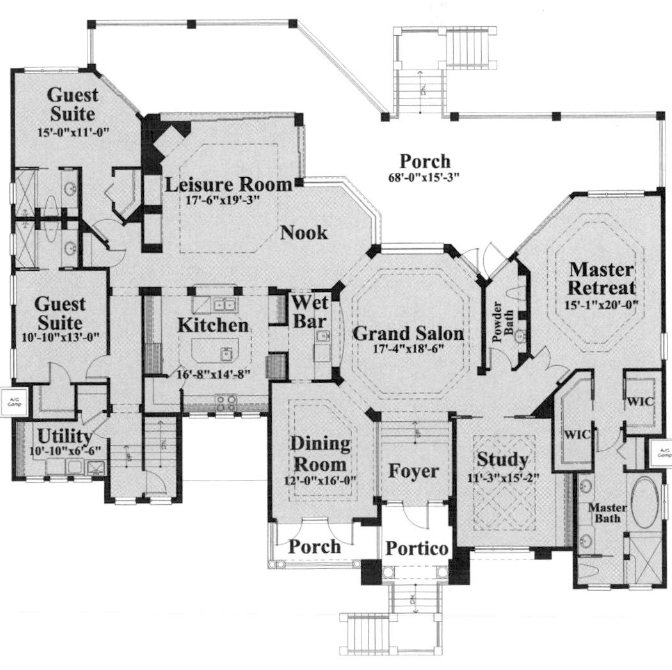

plan# HPK1700348

Style:	Traditional
Square Footage:	3,084
Bedrooms:	3
Bathrooms:	2½
Width:	73' - 9"
Depth:	79' - 3"
Foundation:	Slab, Unfinished Basement, Crawlspace

eplans.com

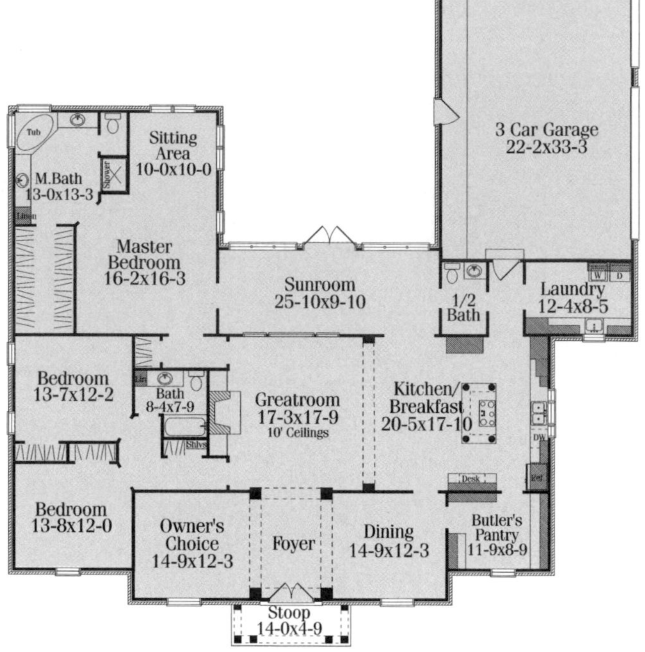

REAR EXTERIOR

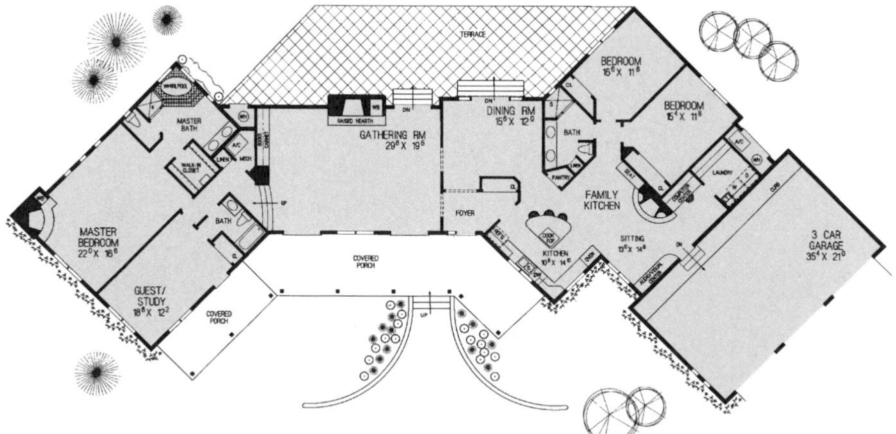

plan# HPK1700349

Style:	Santa Fe
Square Footage:	3,144
Bedrooms:	4
Bathrooms:	3
Width:	139' - 10"
Depth:	63' - 8"
Foundation:	Slab

eplans.com

plan# HPK1700350

Style: SW Contemporary

Square Footage: 3,163

Bedrooms: 4

Bathrooms: 3½

Width: 75' - 2"

Depth: 68' - 8"

Foundation: Slab

eplans.com

An open courtyard takes center stage in this home, providing a happy marriage of indoor/outdoor relationships. Art collectors will appreciate the gallery that enhances the entry and showcases their favorite works. The centrally located great room supplies the nucleus for formal and informal entertaining. A raised-hearth fireplace flanked by built-in media centers adds a special touch. The master suite provides a private retreat where you may relax—try the sitting room or retire to the private bath for a pampering soak in the corner whirlpool tub.

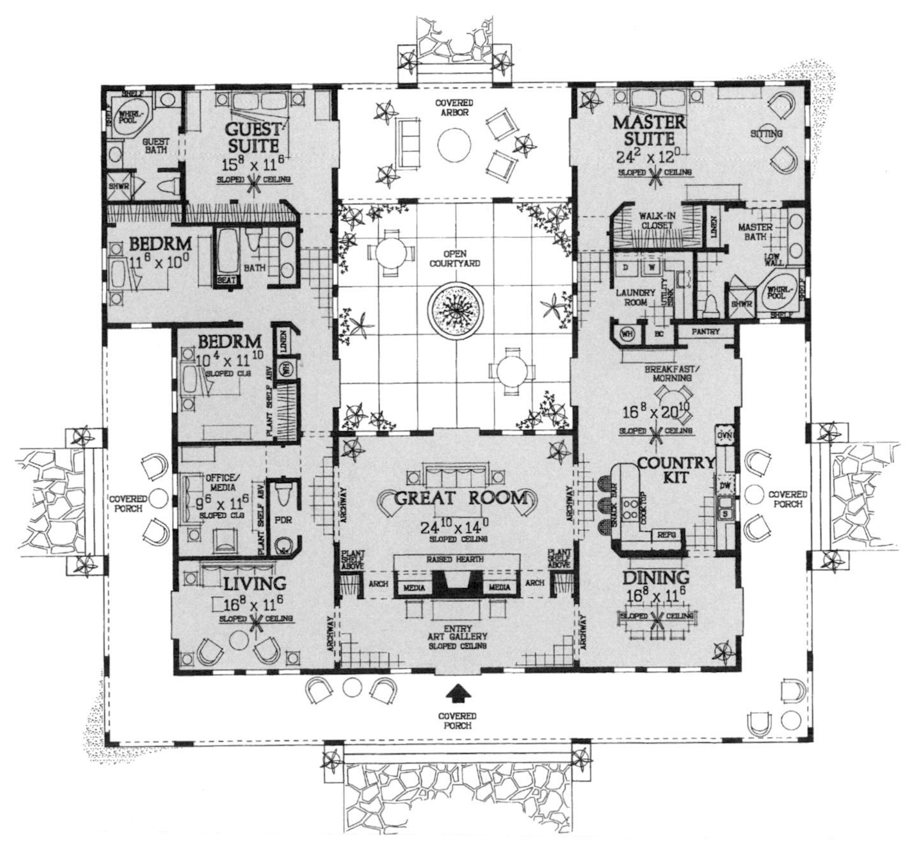

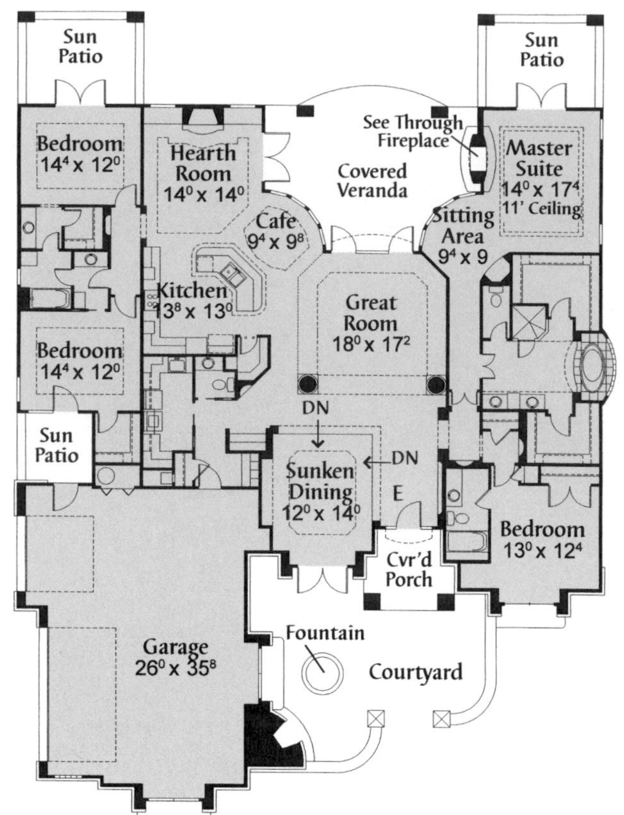

plan # HPK1700351
Style: SW Contemporary
Square Footage: 3,231
Bedrooms: 4
Bathrooms: 3½
Width: 72' - 2"
Depth: 96' - 8"
Foundation: Slab
eplans.com

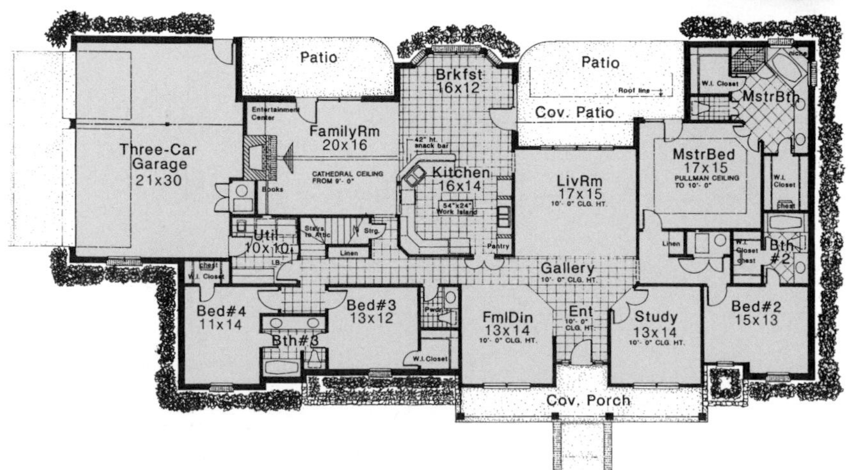

plan # HPK1700352
Style: Traditional
Square Footage: 3,270
Bedrooms: 4
Bathrooms: 3½
Width: 101' - 0"
Depth: 48' - 1"
Foundation: Crawlspace, Slab
eplans.com

plan# HPK1700353
Style: Italianate
Square Footage: 3,271
Bedrooms: 4
Bathrooms: 3½
Width: 74' - 8"
Depth: 118' - 0"
Foundation: Slab
eplans.com

An arched portico and low-pitched tile roof are distinctive features of this European manor. The floor plan calls for luxury at every turn: coffered and tray ceilings in the living room and dining room, and an immense leisure room beside a gourmet island kitchen. The master suite and accompanying bath dominate the left side of the plan, enjoying quiet evenings and private access to the lanai and garden. Two more bedrooms occupy the right side of the plan. A guest suite and bath are located at a comfortable distance in the rear.

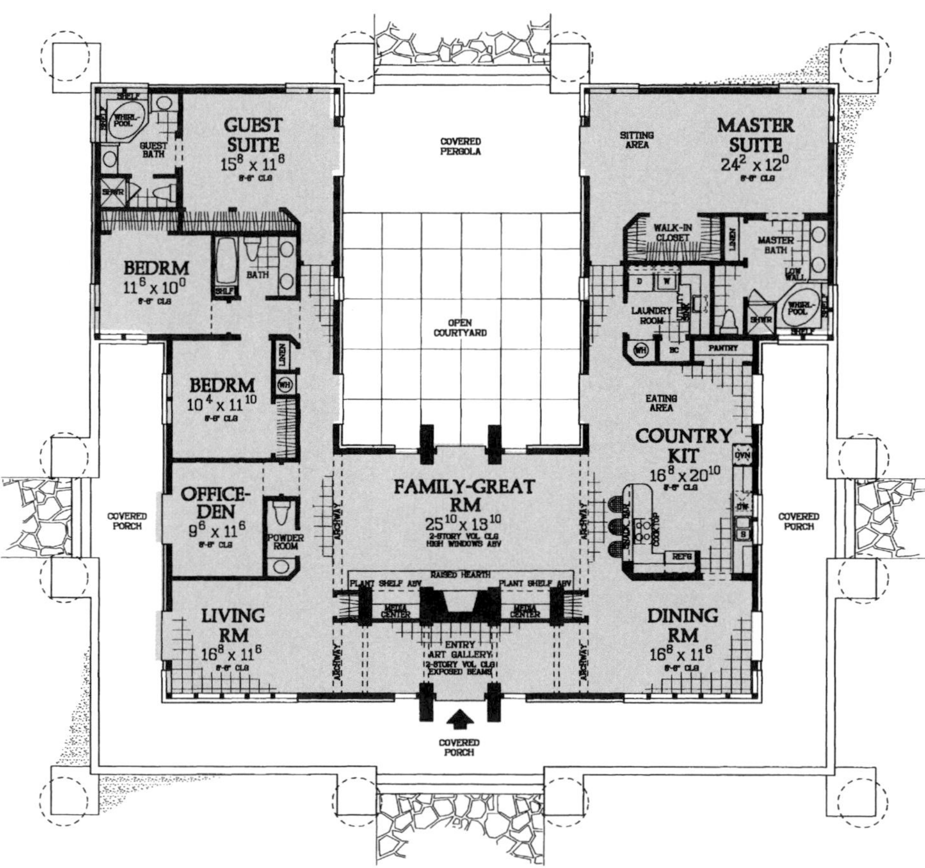

plan # HPK1700354

Style: Craftsman
Square Footage: 3,278
Bedrooms: 4
Bathrooms: 3½
Width: 75' - 10"
Depth: 69' - 4"
Foundation: Crawlspace

eplans.com

Form follows function as dual gallery halls lead from formal areas to split sleeping quarters in this Prairie adaptation. At the heart of the plan, the grand-scale great room offers a raised-hearth fireplace framed by built-in cabinetry and plant shelves. Open planning combines the country kitchen with an informal dining space and adds an island counter with a snack bar. A lavish master suite harbors a sitting area with private access to the covered pergola. The secondary sleeping wing includes a spacious guest suite. A fifth bedroom or home office offers its own door to the wraparound porch.

plan# HPK1700355

Style: Contemporary
Square Footage: 3,312
Bedrooms: 3
Bathrooms: 3½
Width: 90' - 11"
Depth: 81' - 3"

eplans.com

A French facade exposes a floor plan with luxury. The oval entry is an appropriate beginning to the formal living room and open dining room, private study, and gallery hall. The kitchen features an island for the household gourmet and is located conveniently to the dining room, breakfast bay, and family room. The master suite is a secluded paradise of amenities. Included are an oversized walk-in closet, His and Hers vanities, separate shower and tub, compartmented toilet, and another walk-in closet. At the far left of the plan, two secondary bedrooms share a full bath and both feature walk-in closets.

REAR EXTERIOR

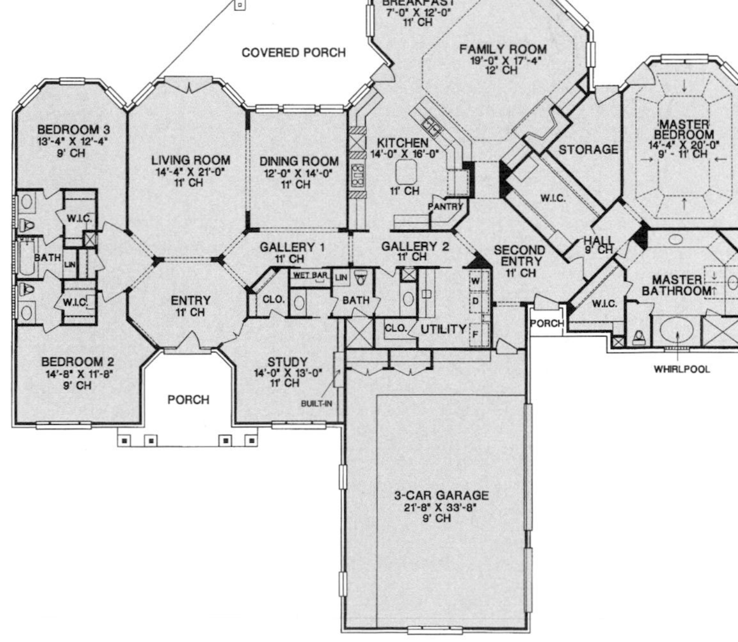

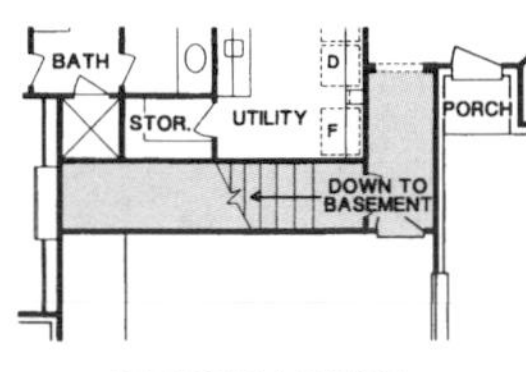

OPTIONAL LAYOUT

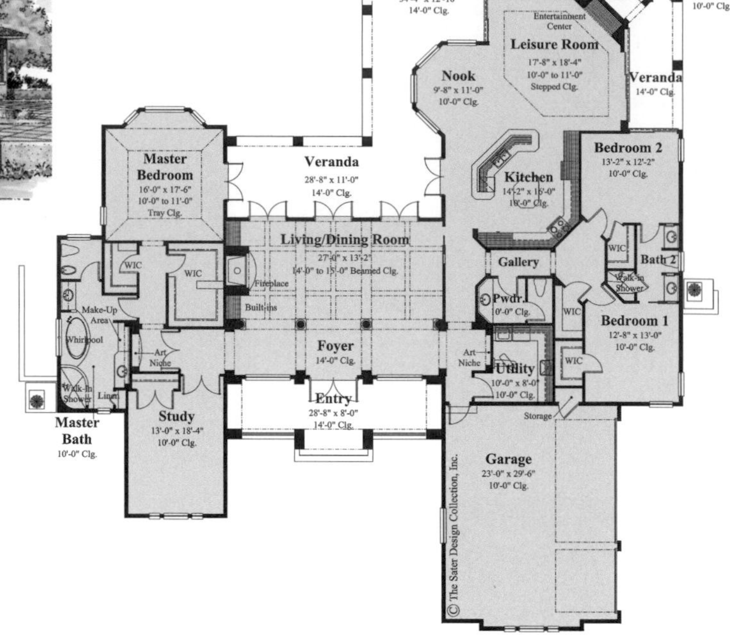

plan# HPK1700356

Style: Mission
Square Footage: 3,343
Bedrooms: 3
Bathrooms: 2½ + ½
Width: 84' - 0"
Depth: 92' - 0"
Foundation: Slab

eplans.com

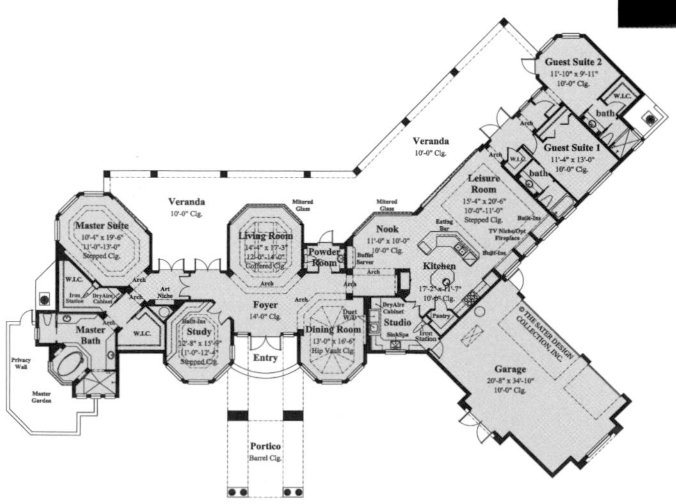

plan# HPK1700357

Style: Mediterranean
Square Footage: 3,398
Bedrooms: 3
Bathrooms: 3½
Width: 121' - 5"
Depth: 96' - 2"
Foundation: Slab

eplans.com

plan# HPK1700358

Style: Mediterranean
Square Footage: 3,424
Bonus Space: 507 sq. ft.
Bedrooms: 5
Bathrooms: 4
Width: 82' - 4"
Depth: 83' - 8"
Foundation: Slab

eplans.com

This lovely five-bedroom home exudes the beauty and warmth of a Mediterranean villa. The foyer views explode in all directions with the dominant use of octagonal shapes throughout. Double doors lead to the master wing, which abounds with niches. The sitting area of the master bedroom has a commanding view of the rear gardens. A bedroom just off the master suite is perfect for a guest room or office. The formal living and dining rooms share expansive glass walls and marble or tile pathways. The mitered glass wall of the breakfast nook can be viewed from the huge island kitchen. Two secondary bedrooms share the convenience of a Pullman-style bath. An additional rear bedroom completes this design.

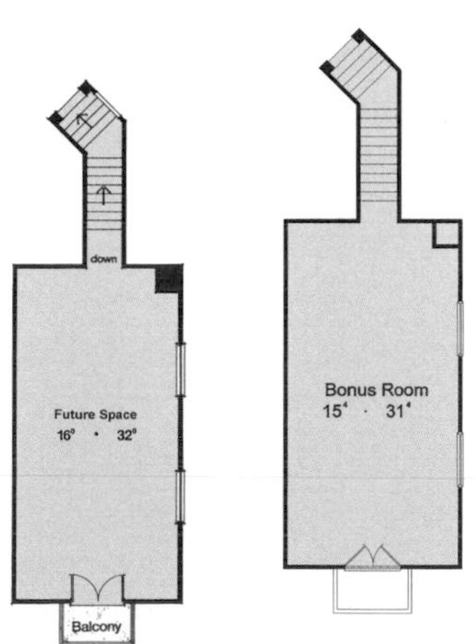

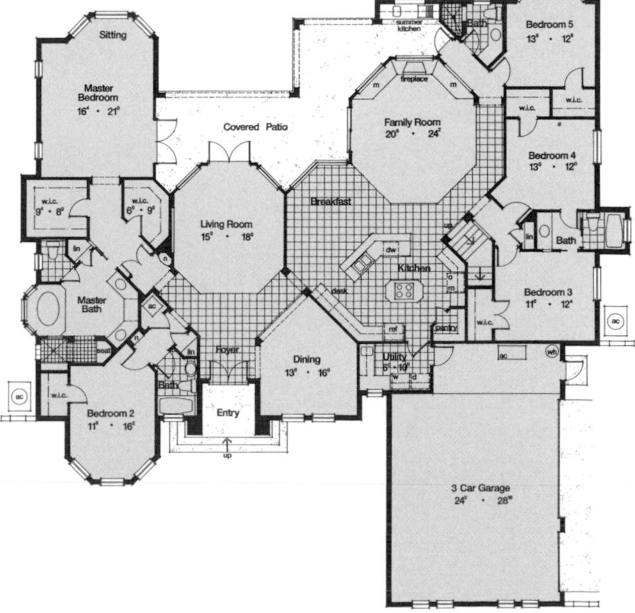

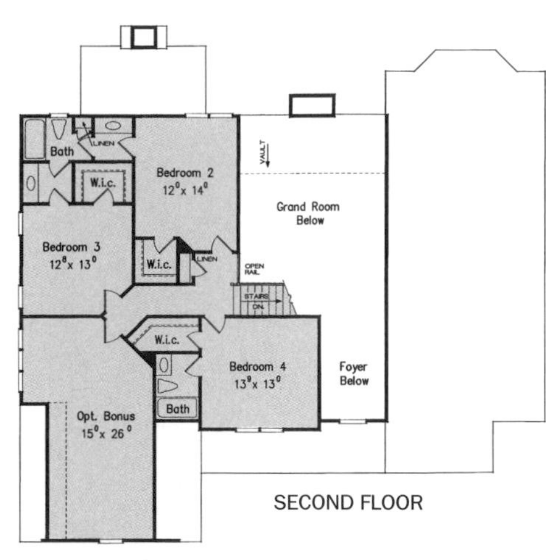

SECOND FLOOR

plan# HPK1700359

Style: French
First Floor: 2,146 sq. ft.
Second Floor: 878 sq. ft.
Total: 3,024 sq. ft.
Bonus Space: 341 sq. ft.
Bedrooms: 4
Bathrooms: 3½
Width: 61' - 0"
Depth: 60' - 4"
Foundation: Crawlspace, Unfinished Walkout Basement

eplans.com

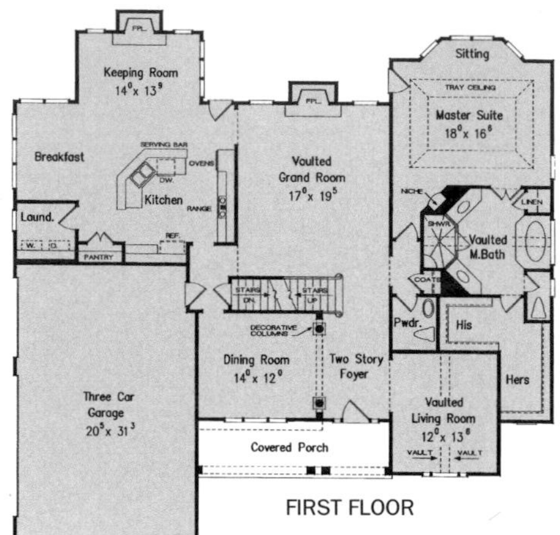

FIRST FLOOR

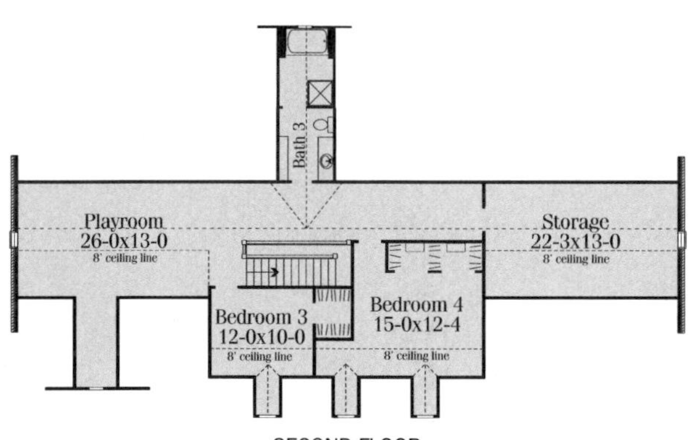

SECOND FLOOR

plan# HPK1700360

Style: Country Cottage
First Floor: 1,888 sq. ft.
Second Floor: 1,154 sq. ft.
Total: 3,042 sq. ft.
Bedrooms: 4
Bathrooms: 3
Width: 78' - 6"
Depth: 48' - 6"
Foundation: Crawlspace, Slab, Unfinished Basement

eplans.com

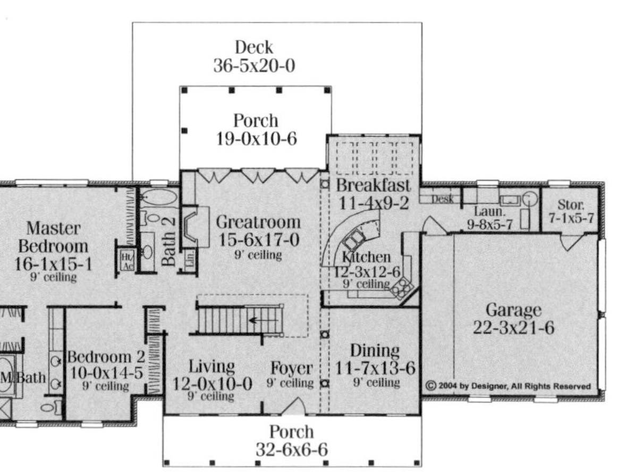

FIRST FLOOR

plan# HPK1700361

Style: European Cottage
First Floor: 1,982 sq. ft.
Second Floor: 1,071 sq. ft.
Total: 3,053 sq. ft.
Bedrooms: 3
Bathrooms: 3½
Width: 48' - 4"
Depth: 69' - 6"
Foundation: Crawlspace

eplans.com

REAR EXTERIOR

A unique collection of windows really draws attention to this European-style home. The private and luxurious master suite is hidden behind the circular staircase of the foyer. A turret in the master bedroom and a bow window in the private bath will fill this suite with an abundance of natural light. A fireplace in the two-story gathering room and another in the keeping room add warmth and charm. Two bedrooms, two baths, and a study complete the second level, which has a balcony overlooking the two-story dining room.

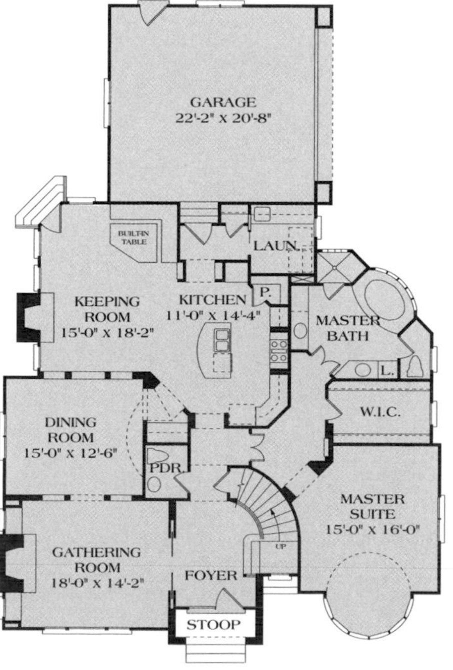

FIRST FLOOR

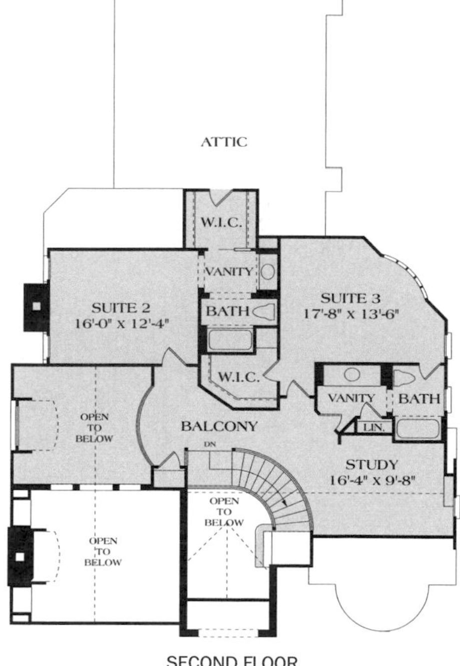

SECOND FLOOR

plan# HPK1700362

Style: European Cottage
First Floor: 2,144 sq. ft.
Second Floor: 920 sq. ft.
Total: 3,064 sq. ft.
Bonus Space: 212 sq. ft.
Bedrooms: 4
Bathrooms: 3½
Width: 59' - 0"
Depth: 79' - 3"
Foundation: Crawlspace, Slab

eplans.com

Fieldstone, stucco, and brick give this cottage harmony in variety. The foyer opens to a private study with bay windows and fireplace. The formal dining room is just down the hall and opens through column accents to the living room. The kitchen serves both the formal and casual spaces. The family room is as cozy with a fireplace and rear-window display. The master suite is really a work of luxury and features His and Hers walk-in closet entrances, vanities, and compartmented toilet. The second level houses three additional bedrooms, two full baths, and bonus space.

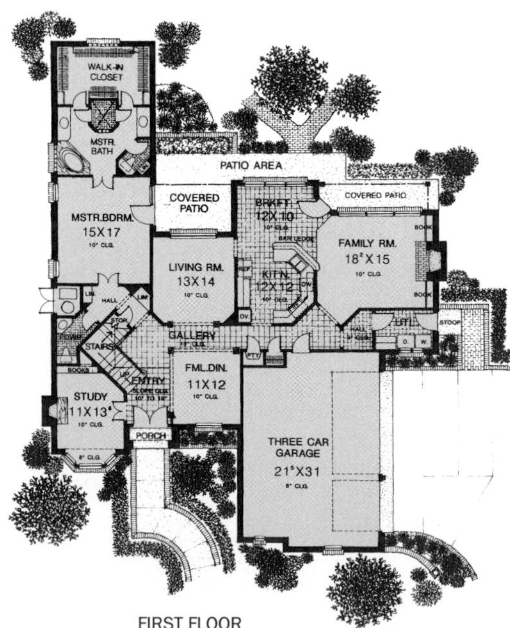

FIRST FLOOR

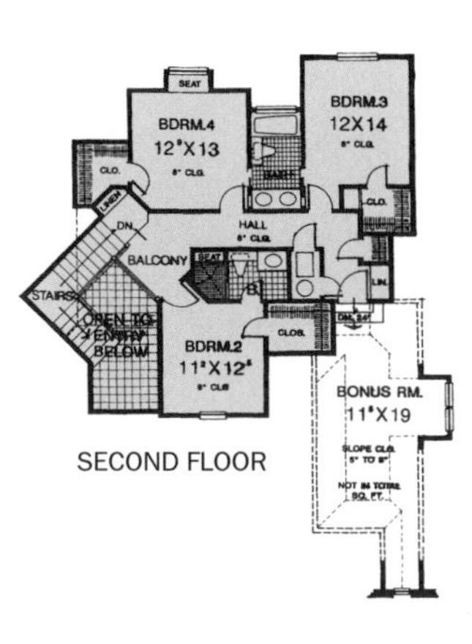

SECOND FLOOR

plan # HPK1700363

Style: Contemporary
First Floor: 2,465 sq. ft.
Second Floor: 617 sq. ft.
Total: 3,082 sq. ft.
Bedrooms: 3
Bathrooms: 2½ + ½
Width: 120' - 10"
Depth: 52' - 4"
Foundation: Unfinished Basement

eplans.com

This New England Colonial design delivers beautiful proportions and great livability on one and a half levels. The main area of the house, the first floor, holds a living room, a library, a family room, a dining room, and a gourmet kitchen. The master bedroom, also on this floor, features a sumptuous master bath with a whirlpool tub and a sloped ceiling. A long rear terrace stretches the full width of the house. Two bedrooms on the second floor share a full bath; each offers a built-in desk.

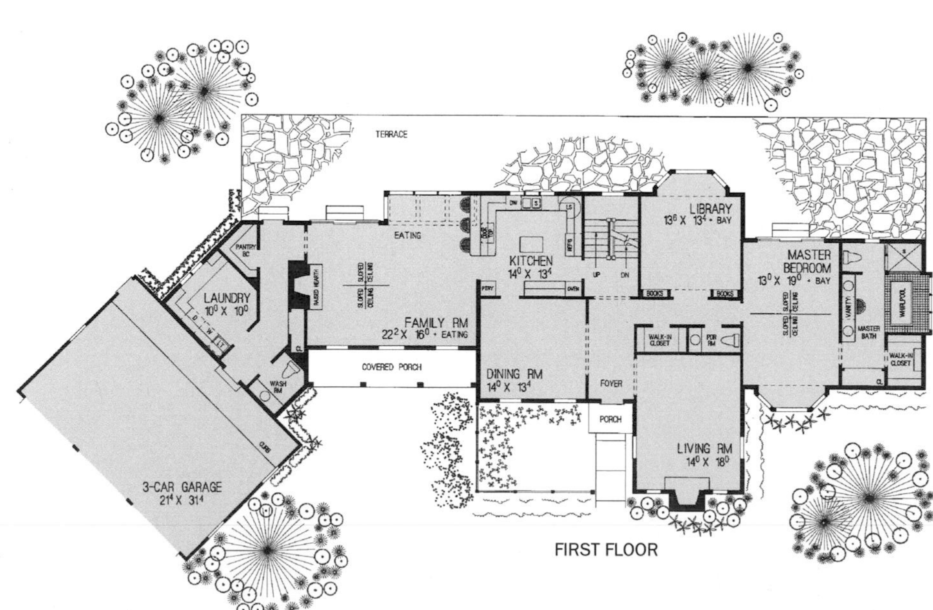

FIRST FLOOR

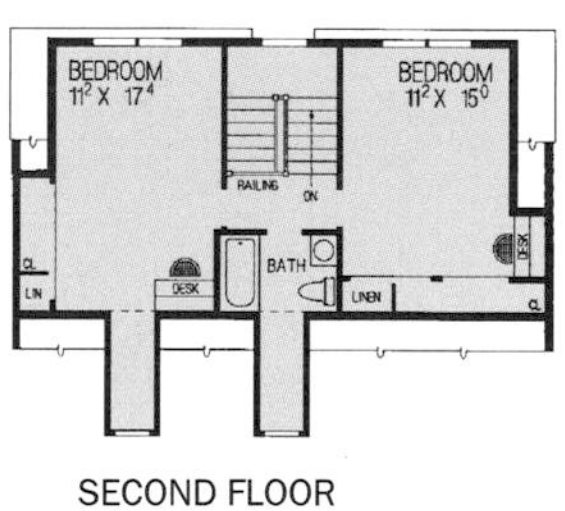

SECOND FLOOR

plan# HPK1700364

Style: Traditional

First Floor: 2,082 sq. ft.

Second Floor: 1,013 sq. ft.

Total: 3,095 sq. ft.

Bedrooms: 4

Bathrooms: 3½

Width: 70' - 6"

Depth: 57' - 10"

Foundation: Slab, Unfinished Basement, Crawlspace

eplans.com

Traditional stylings create an exterior reaming with curb appeal. Just over 3,000 square feet, the interior layout makes efficient use of every inch. The great room, breakfast area, and kitchen are centrally located and act as a common area that separates the family bedrooms on the first floor. To the left, two bedrooms share a full bath, and to the right, the master suite sits at the rear of the home. The second floor houses a fourth bedroom and full bath, ideal for a teenager or a guest. The gameroom amd media room, also on this level, are perfect for entertaining family and friends.

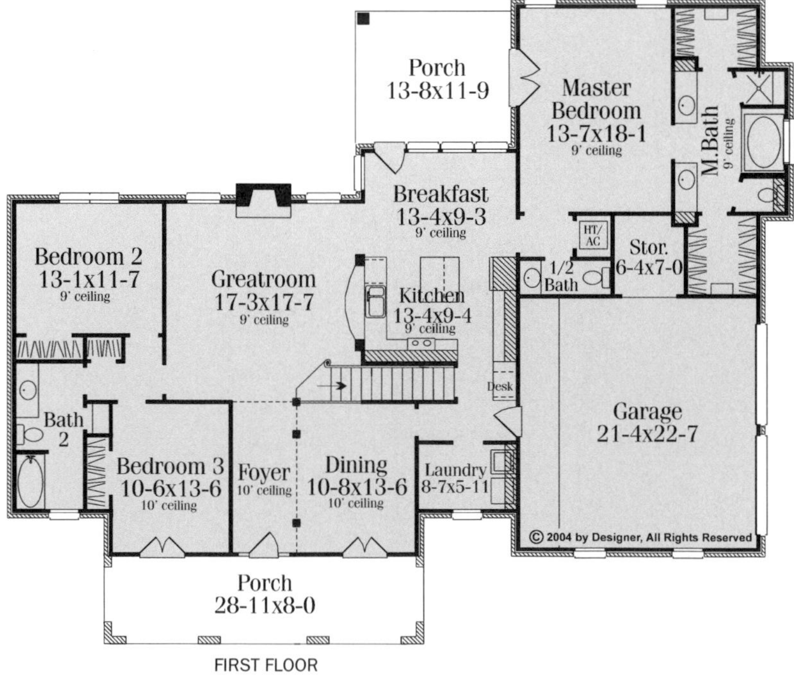

FIRST FLOOR

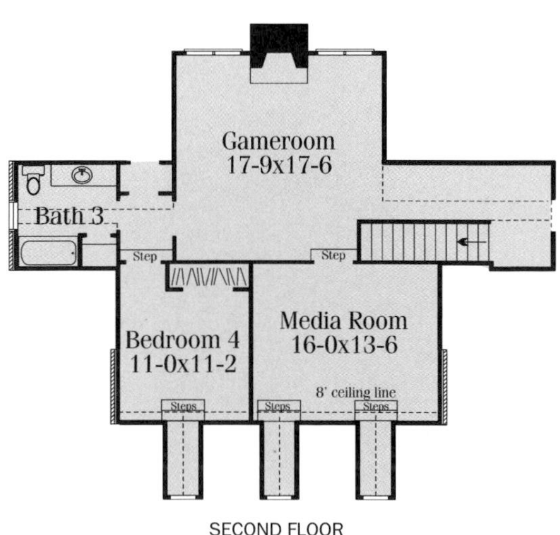

SECOND FLOOR

plan# HPK1700365

Style: Country Cottage
First Floor: 2,142 sq. ft.
Second Floor: 960 sq. ft.
Total: 3,102 sq. ft.
Bonus Space: 327 sq. ft.
Bedrooms: 4
Bathrooms: 3½
Width: 75' - 8"
Depth: 53' - 0"
Foundation: Crawlspace

eplans.com

Imagine driving up to this cottage beauty at the end of a long week. The long wraparound porch, hipped rooflines, and shuttered windows will transport you. Inside, the foyer is flanked by a living room on the left and a formal dining room on the right. Across the gallery hall, the hearth-warmed family room will surely become the hub of the home. To the right, the spacious kitchen boasts a worktop island counter, ample pantry space, and a breakfast area. A short hallway opens to the utility room and the two-car garage. The master suite takes up the entire left wing of the home, enjoying an elegant private bath and a walk-in closet that goes on and on. Upstairs three more bedrooms reside, sharing two full baths. Expandable future space awaits on the right

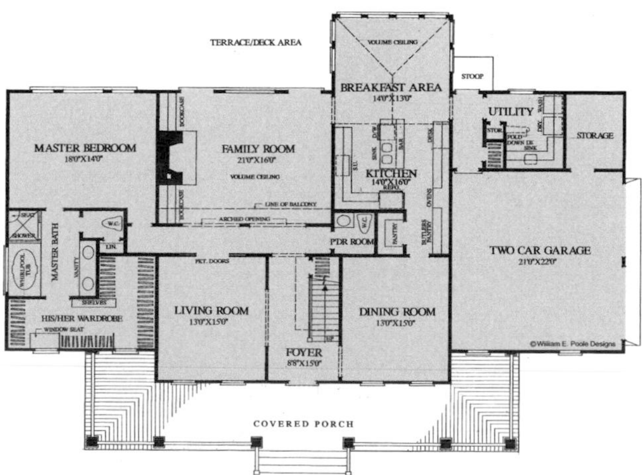

FIRST FLOOR

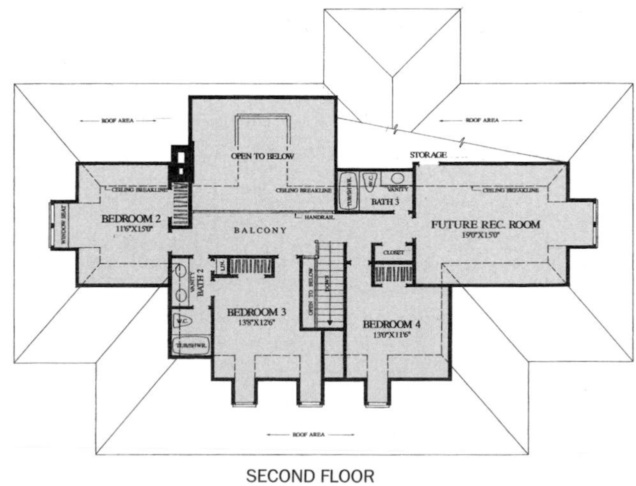

SECOND FLOOR

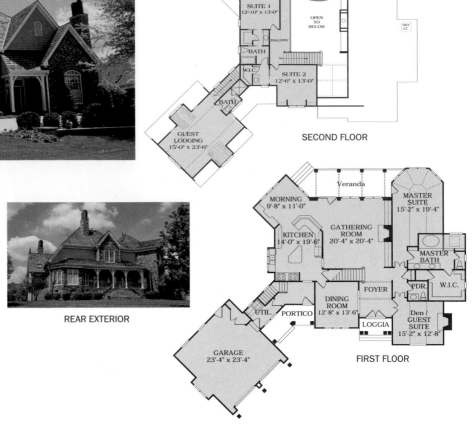

plan# HPK1700366

- Style: French Country
- First Floor: 2,390 sq. ft.
- Second Floor: 765 sq. ft.
- Total: 3,155 sq. ft.
- Bonus Space: 433 sq. ft.
- Bedrooms: 4
- Bathrooms: 3½
- Width: 87' - 11"
- Depth: 75' - 2"
- Foundation: Crawlspace

eplans.com

SUITE 1 12'-10" x 13'-0"
LIBRARY LOFT
OPEN TO BELOW
BALCONY
BATH
W.I.C.
SUITE 2 12'-6" x 13'-0"
BATH
GUEST LODGING 15'-0" x 23'-6"
SKY LT.

SECOND FLOOR

REAR EXTERIOR

FIRST FLOOR

PHOTO COURTESY OF LIVING CONCEPTS

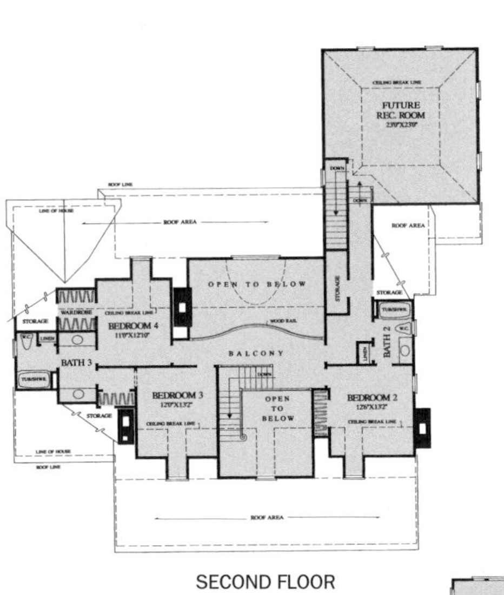

SECOND FLOOR

plan# HPK1700367

- Style: Colonial
- First Floor: 2,200 sq. ft.
- Second Floor: 1,001 sq. ft.
- Total: 3,201 sq. ft.
- Bonus Space: 674 sq. ft.
- Bedrooms: 4
- Bathrooms: 3½
- Width: 70' - 4"
- Depth: 74' - 4"
- Foundation: Crawlspace

eplans.com

2 CAR GARAGE
COVERED PORCH
PORCH
MASTER BEDROOM
BREAKFAST AREA
FAMILY ROOM
UTILITY
MASTER BATH
KITCHEN
LIVING ROOM/ LIBRARY
DINING ROOM
FOYER
PORCH
© William E. Poole Designs

FIRST FLOOR

plan# HPK1700368

Style: Country Cottage
First Floor: 2,293 sq. ft.
Second Floor: 992 sq. ft.
Total: 3,285 sq. ft.
Bonus Space: 131 sq. ft.
Bedrooms: 4
Bathrooms: 3½
Width: 71' - 0"
Depth: 62' - 0"
Foundation: Crawlspace, Unfinished Walkout Basement

eplans.com

A combination of stone, siding, and multiple rooflines creates a cottage feel to this large home. Inside, the grand room and keeping room feature fireplaces and vaulted ceilings—the grand room adds built-in cabinets and windows with transoms. A sumptuous master suite enjoys a sitting room, a tray ceiling, and a lavish private bath featuring a shower with a built-in seat. The gourmet kitchen enjoys an island countertop, a serving bar, and a walk-in pantry that accesses the three-car garage. Three additional bedrooms are found upstairs with two full baths—Bedrooms 3 and 4 each include large walk-in closets.

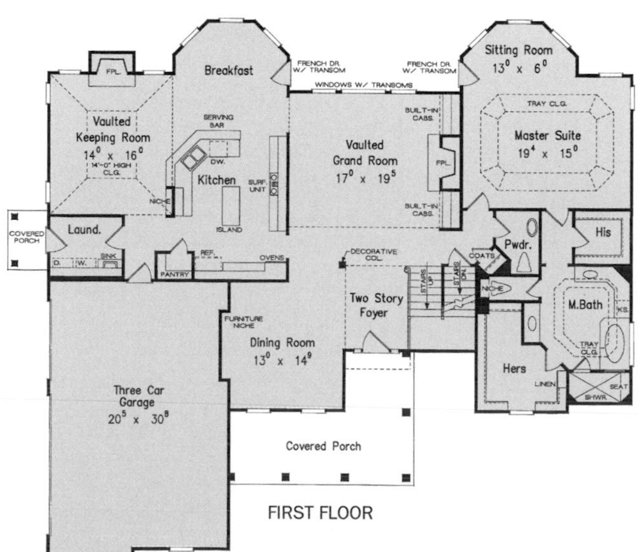

FIRST FLOOR

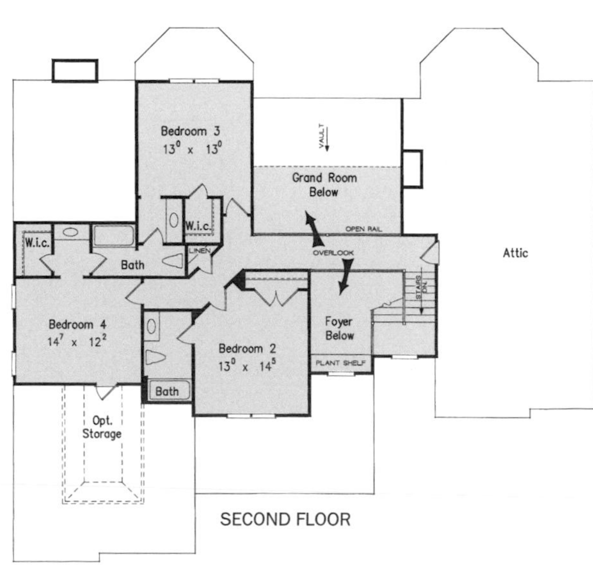

SECOND FLOOR

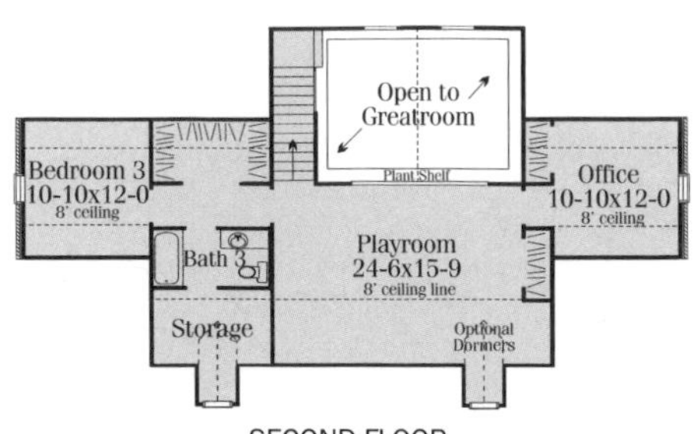

SECOND FLOOR

plan# HPK1700369

Style: Traditional

First Floor: 2,348 sq. ft.

Second Floor: 957 sq. ft.

Total: 3,305 sq. ft.

Bedrooms: 3

Bathrooms: 3½

Width: 70' - 10"

Depth: 65' - 4"

Foundation: Slab, Unfinished Basement, Crawlspace

eplans.com

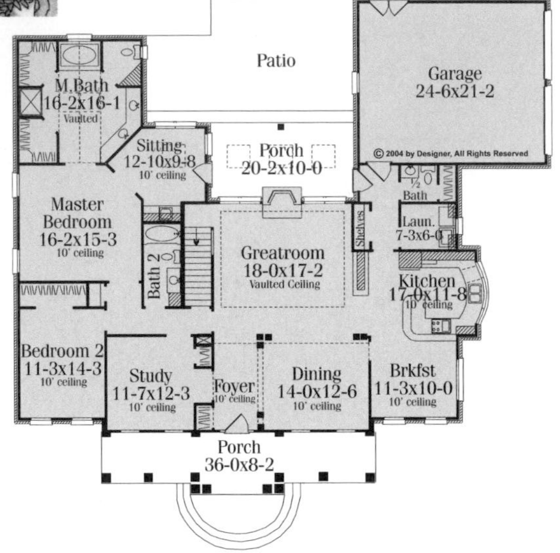

FIRST FLOOR

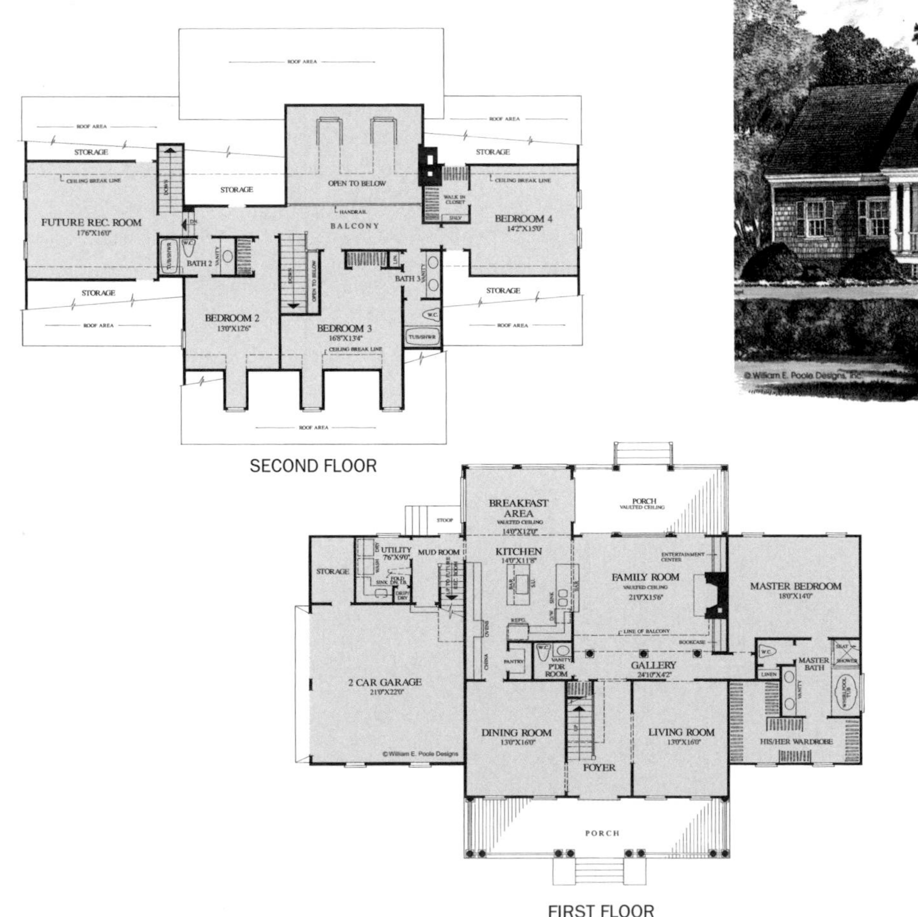

SECOND FLOOR

FIRST FLOOR

plan# HPK1700370

Style: Farmhouse

First Floor: 2,191 sq. ft.

Second Floor: 1,220 sq. ft.

Total: 3,411 sq. ft.

Bonus Space: 280 sq. ft.

Bedrooms: 4

Bathrooms: 3½

Width: 75' - 8"

Depth: 54' - 4"

Foundation: Crawlspace, Unfinished Basement

eplans.com

plan # HPK1700371

Style: Farmhouse

Square Footage: 3,439

Bonus Space: 514 sq. ft.

Bedrooms: 4

Bathrooms: 3½

Width: 100' - 0"

Depth: 67' - 11"

Foundation: Crawlspace, Slab, Unfinished Basement

eplans.com

This gigantic country farmhouse is accented by exterior features that really stand out—a steep roof gable, shuttered muntin windows, stone siding, and the double-columned, covered front porch. Inside, the entry is flanked by the study/Bedroom 2 and the dining room. Across the tiled gallery, the great room provides an impressive fireplace and overlooks the rear veranda. The island kitchen opens to a bayed breakfast room. The right side of the home includes a utility room and a three-car garage, and two family bedrooms that share a bath. The master wing of the home enjoys a bayed sitting area, a sumptuous bath, and an enormous walk-in closet. The second-floor bonus room is cooled by a ceiling fan and is perfect for a guest suite.

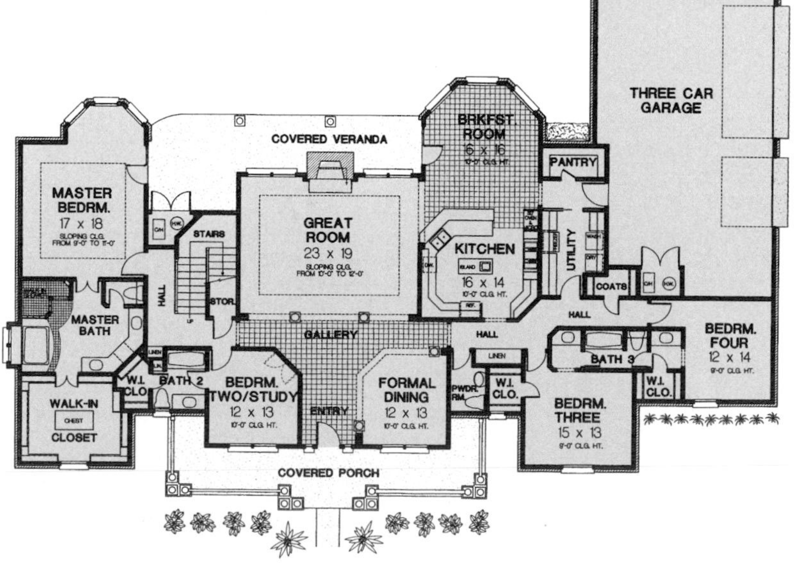

FIRST FLOOR

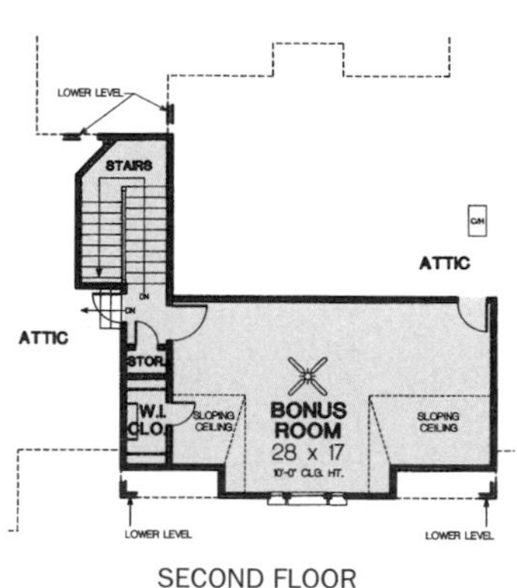

SECOND FLOOR

SECOND FLOOR

plan# HPK1700372

Style: Traditional
First Floor: 2,454 sq. ft.
Second Floor: 986 sq. ft.
Total: 3,440 sq. ft.
Bedrooms: 4
Bathrooms: 3½
Width: 73' - 4"
Depth: 59' - 4"

eplans.com

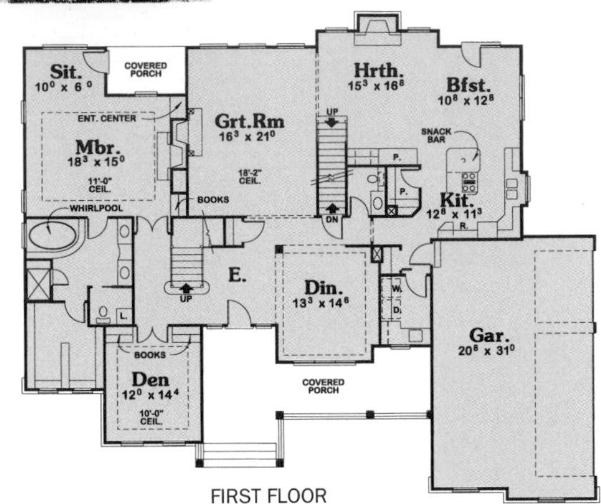

FIRST FLOOR

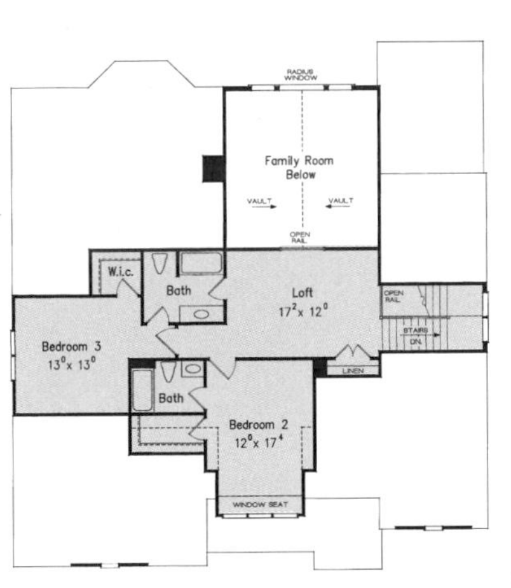

SECOND FLOOR

plan# HPK1700373

Style: Country Cottage
First Floor: 2,123 sq. ft.
Second Floor: 878 sq. ft.
Total: 3,001 sq. ft.
Bedrooms: 4
Bathrooms: 4
Width: 54' - 0"
Depth: 59' - 6"
Foundation: Crawlspace, Slab, Unfinished Walkout Basement

eplans.com

FIRST FLOOR

plan# HPK1700374

Style: Farmhouse
First Floor: 1,771 sq. ft.
Second Floor: 1,235 sq. ft.
Total: 3,006 sq. ft.
Bedrooms: 4
Bathrooms: 3½
Width: 61' - 4"
Depth: 54' - 0"
Foundation: Crawlspace, Slab, Unfinished Walkout Basement

eplans.com

SMART TIP

Take note of the "future space" designed for the second floor of this home. Like a bonus space, this is a room that gives owners the option of leaving it unfinished at time of initial construction. When the need arises—for example, if a child in the family grows old enough to handle a full suite, or if an elderly member joins the household—the space can be finalized to accommodate the growing family.

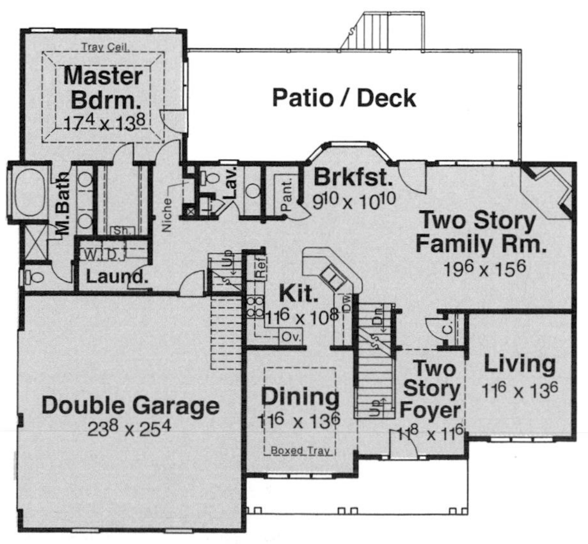

FIRST FLOOR

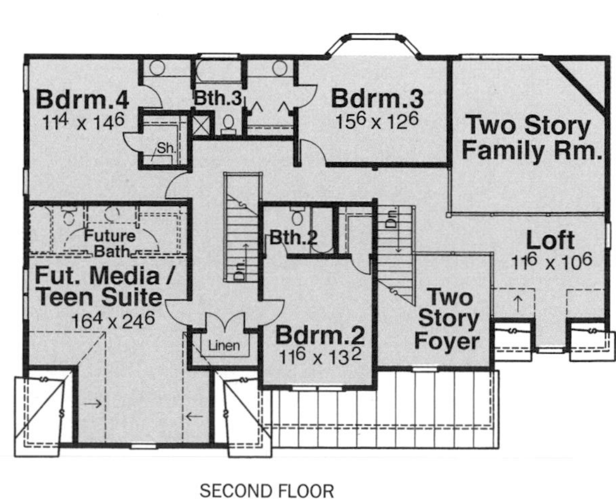

SECOND FLOOR

PHOTO COURTESY OF STEPHEN FULLER, INC.

SECOND FLOOR

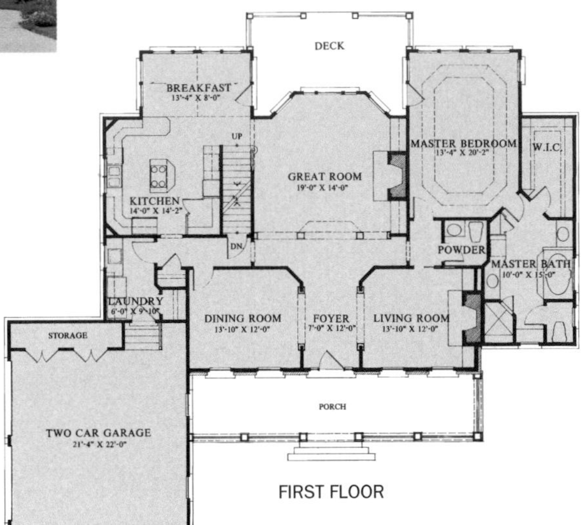

FIRST FLOOR

plan# HPK1700375

Style: Georgian
First Floor: 2,081 sq. ft.
Second Floor: 940 sq. ft.
Total: 3,021 sq. ft.
Bedrooms: 4
Bathrooms: 3½
Width: 69' - 9"
Depth: 65' - 0"
Foundation: Walkout Basement

eplans.com

plan# HPK1700376

Style: Traditional
First Floor: 1,479 sq. ft.
Second Floor: 1,554 sq. ft.
Total: 3,033 sq. ft.
Bedrooms: 4
Bathrooms: 3½
Width: 61' - 0"
Depth: 45' - 0"
Foundation: Unfinished Basement

eplans.com

plan# HPK1700377

Style: Mediterranean

First Floor: 2,114 sq. ft.

Second Floor: 924 sq. ft.

Total: 3,038 sq. ft.

Bedrooms: 3

Bathrooms: 4

Width: 60' - 0"

Depth: 62' - 8"

Foundation: Slab

eplans.com

A Mediterranean dream—amenities abound throughout this three-bedroom home. With large rooms and spacious outdoor living areas, this home is great for entertaining. A summer kitchen on the covered lanai and a full pool bath invite the possibility of warm weather fun. The lavish master suite sits to the right of the first floor, equipped with a sitting area, His & Hers walk-in closets, and a dual-sink vanity. Upstairs houses two additional family bedrooms—both with full baths—a loft area, and a large study. A three-car garage completes this plan.

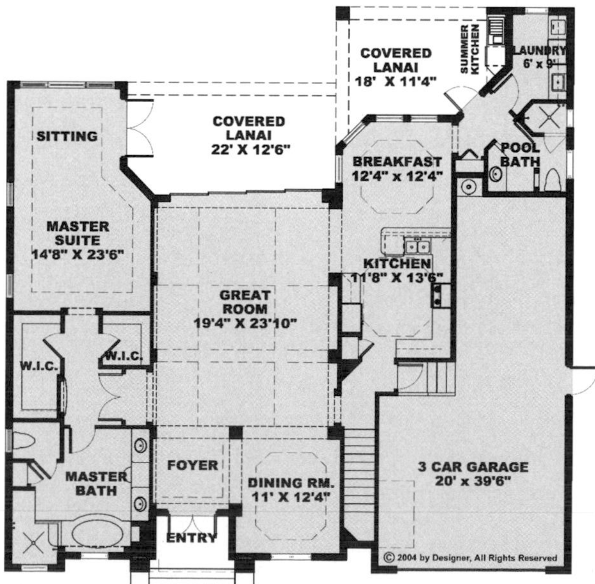

FIRST FLOOR

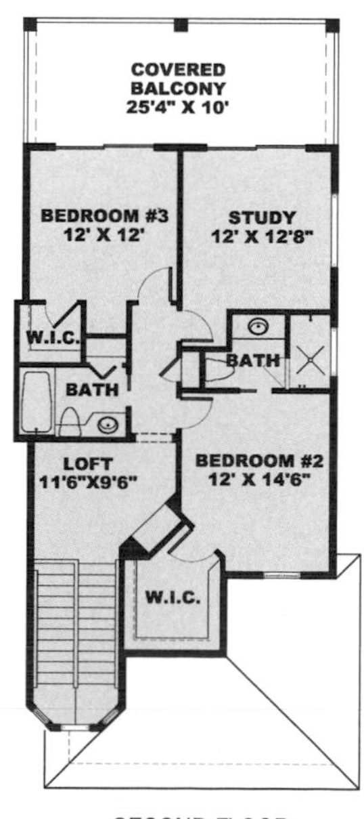

SECOND FLOOR

PHOTO COURTESY OF LIVING CONCEPTS

plan# HPK1700378

Style: Chateau Style

First Floor: 2,149 sq. ft.

Second Floor: 897 sq. ft.

Total: 3,046 sq. ft.

Bonus Space: 521 sq. ft.

Bedrooms: 3

Bathrooms: 3½

Width: 49' - 10"

Depth: 74' - 10"

Foundation: Crawlspace

eplans.com

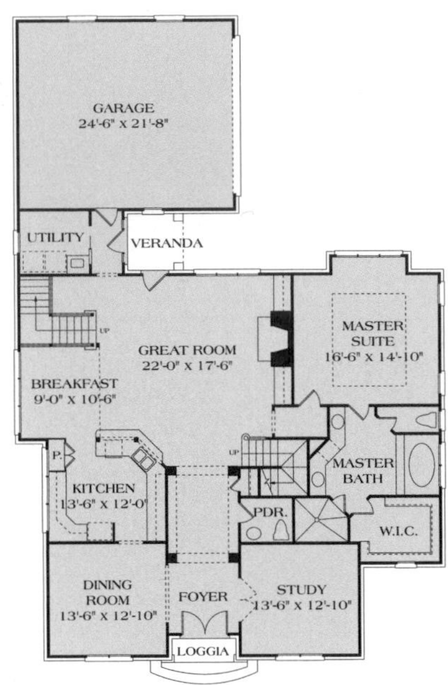

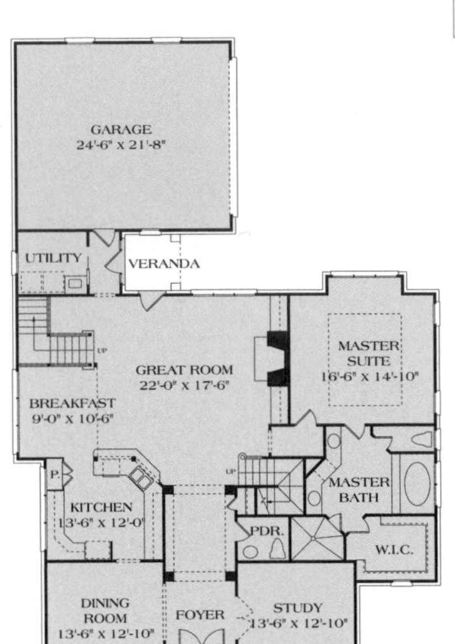

FIRST FLOOR

SECOND FLOOR

plan# HPK1700379

Style: Mediterranean

First Floor: 1,899 sq. ft.

Second Floor: 1,152 sq. ft.

Total: 3,051 sq. ft.

Bedrooms: 4

Bathrooms: 3½

Width: 67' - 8"

Depth: 59' - 8"

Foundation: Slab

eplans.com

SECOND FLOOR

FIRST FLOOR

plan# HPK1700380

Style: Farmhouse
First Floor: 1,555 sq. ft.
Second Floor: 1,523 sq. ft.
Total: 3,078 sq. ft.
Bedrooms: 5
Bathrooms: 4
Width: 54' - 0"
Depth: 44' - 8"
Foundation: Slab, Unfinished Walkout Basement

eplans.com

The main attraction of this home is found upstairs, in the form of an extravagant master suite. Featuring a tray ceiling, sitting area with bayed fireplace, angled bath with oversized tub, and a maze of a walk-in closet, you will never want to come out. As you emerge from the master suite enjoy views of the grand room and foyer below. The fourth bedroom has a private bath, and bedroom #3 enjoys its own walk-in closet. You'll be certain to want to add the optional sunroom located off the breakfast nook. The foyer is flanked by a formal dining room, with tray ceiling, on the right, and a living room, through an elegant archway, to the left. The left-hand rear corner houses a study also suitable for a guest suite.

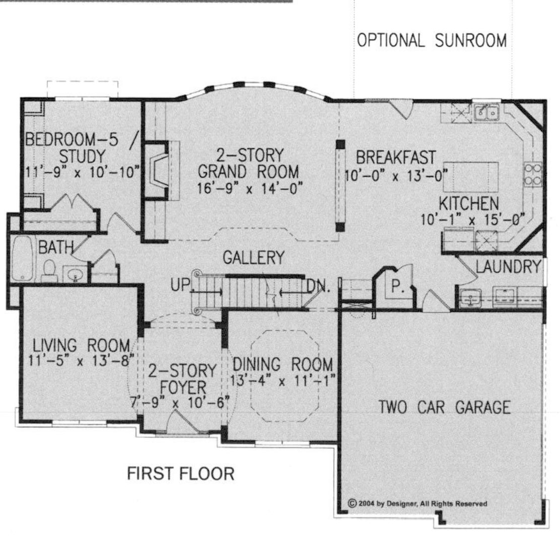

FIRST FLOOR

SECOND FLOOR

plan# HPK1700381

Style: Colonial
First Floor: 1,559 sq. ft.
Second Floor: 1,534 sq. ft.
Total: 3,093 sq. ft.
Bedrooms: 4
Bathrooms: 4
Width: 51' - 0"
Depth: 46' - 0"
Foundation: Unfinished Basement

eplans.com

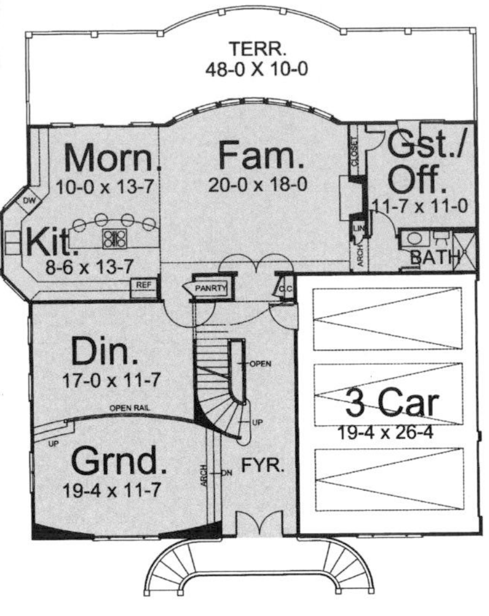

FIRST FLOOR

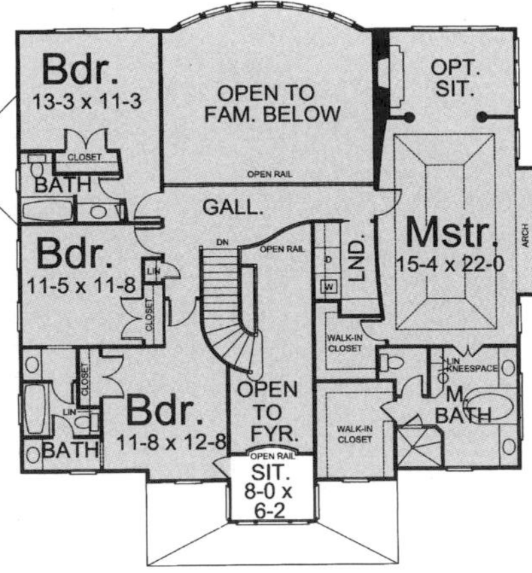

SECOND FLOOR

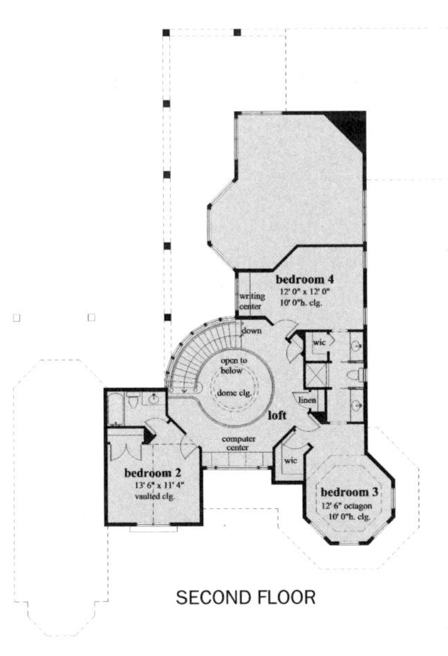

SECOND FLOOR

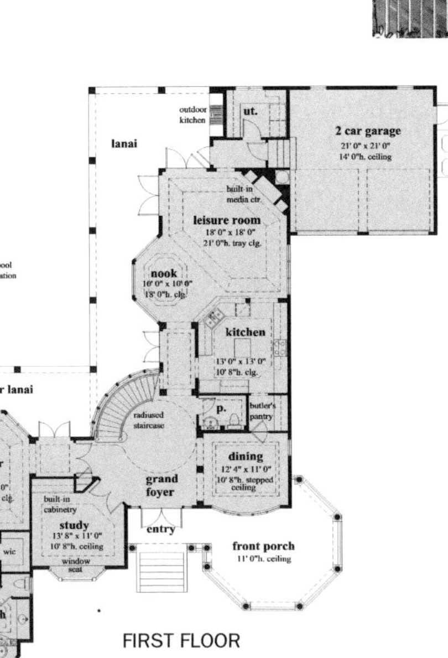

FIRST FLOOR

plan# HPK1700382

Style: Tidewater
First Floor: 2,083 sq. ft.
Second Floor: 1,013 sq. ft.
Total: 3,096 sq. ft.
Bedrooms: 4
Bathrooms: 3½
Width: 74' - 0"
Depth: 88' - 0"
Foundation: Crawlspace

eplans.com

plan# HPK1700383

Style: Tidewater

First Floor: 2,146 sq. ft.

Second Floor: 952 sq. ft.

Total: 3,098 sq. ft.

Bedrooms: 3

Bathrooms: 3½

Width: 52' - 0"

Depth: 65' - 4"

Foundation: Island Basement

eplans.com

Outdoor spaces such as the inviting wraparound porch and the rear veranda are the living areas of this cottage. French doors, a fireplace, and built-in cabinets adorn the great room. A private hall leads to the first-floor master suite. The upper level boasts a catwalk that overlooks the great room and the foyer. A secluded master wing enjoys a bumped-out window, a stunning tray ceiling, and two walk-in closets. The island kitchen conveniently accesses the nook, dining area, and the wet bar.

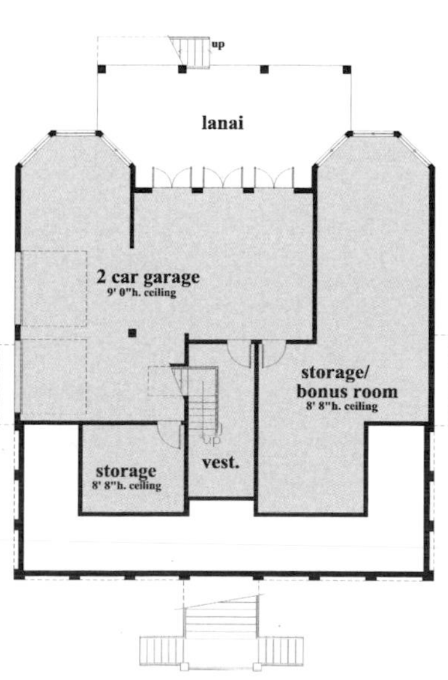

BASEMENT

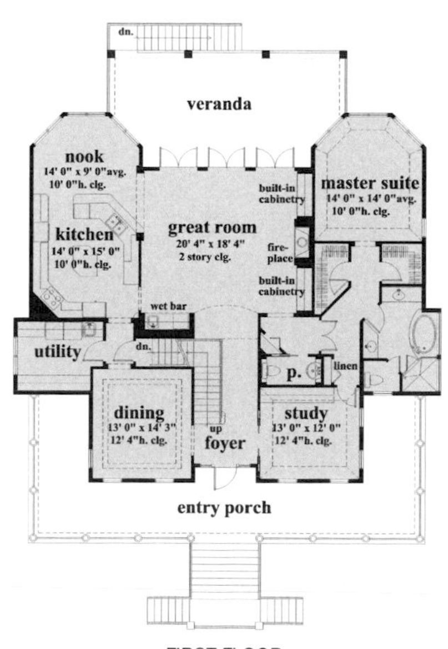

FIRST FLOOR

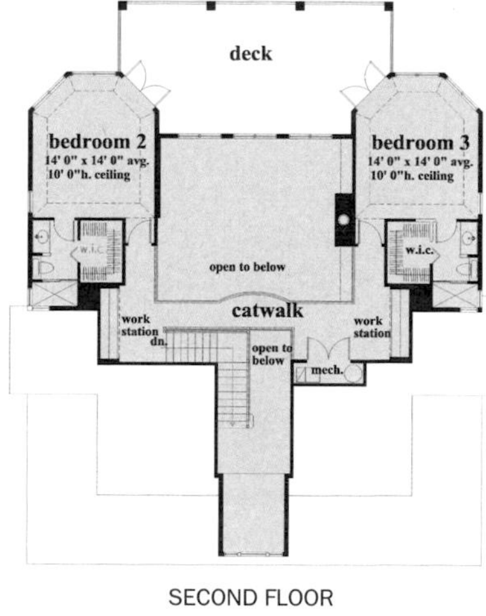

SECOND FLOOR

plan# HPK1700384

Style: Georgian

First Floor: 1,455 sq. ft.

Second Floor: 1,649 sq. ft.

Total: 3,104 sq. ft.

Bedrooms: 4

Bathrooms: 3½

Width: 54' - 4"

Depth: 46' - 0"

Foundation: Walkout Basement

eplans.com

QUOTE ONE®

SECOND FLOOR

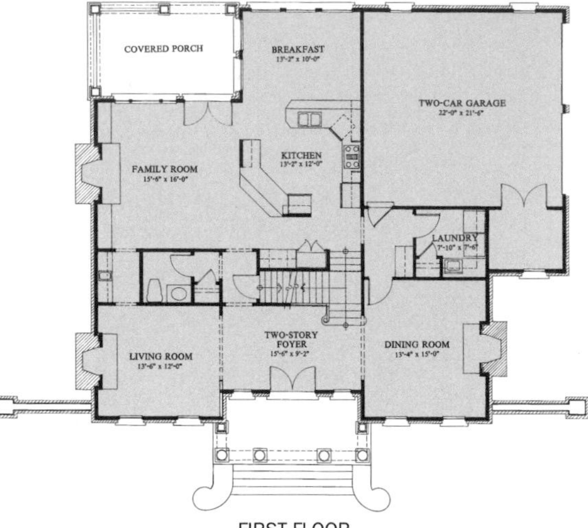

FIRST FLOOR

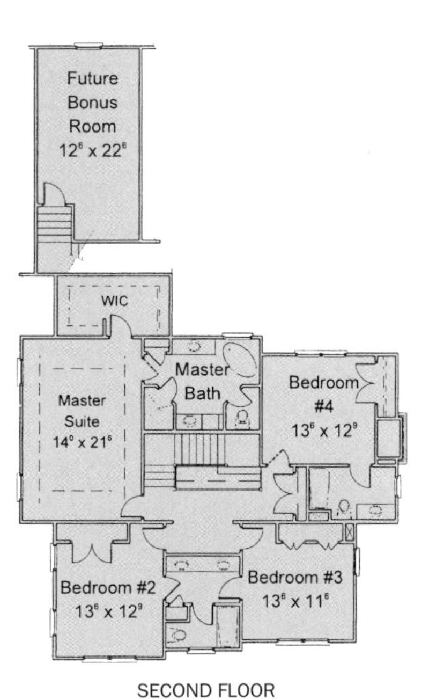

SECOND FLOOR

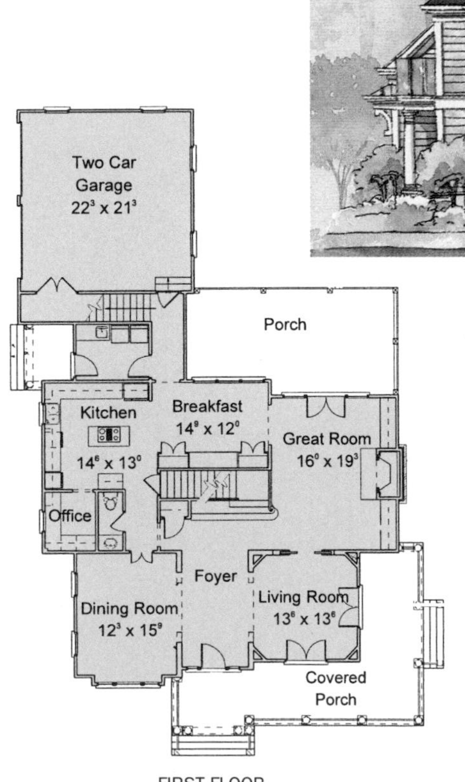

FIRST FLOOR

plan# HPK1700385

Style: Farmhouse

First Floor: 1,652 sq. ft.

Second Floor: 1,460 sq. ft.

Total: 3,112 sq. ft.

Bonus Space: 256 sq. ft.

Bedrooms: 4

Bathrooms: 3½

Width: 48' - 0"

Depth: 78' - 4"

Foundation: Walkout Basement

eplans.com

plan# HPK1700386

Style: Farmhouse
First Floor: 1,578 sq. ft.
Second Floor: 1,543 sq. ft.
Total: 3,121 sq. ft.
Bedrooms: 5
Bathrooms: 4
Width: 53' - 0"
Depth: 40' - 0"
Foundation: Unfinished Walkout Basement

eplans.com

The stone facade of this country home leaves a lasting first impression. A two-story foyer, flanked by formal living and dining areas, leads to the grand room at the heart of the home. The adjoining kitchen and breakfast nook encourage family interaction during meal preparation. Upstairs houses the spacious master suite, equipped with a sitting area, a roomy bath, an exercise room, and His and Hers walk-in closets. Three additional family bedrooms and two full baths complete the second floor. A fifth bedroom on the first floor can serve as a guest/in-law suite.

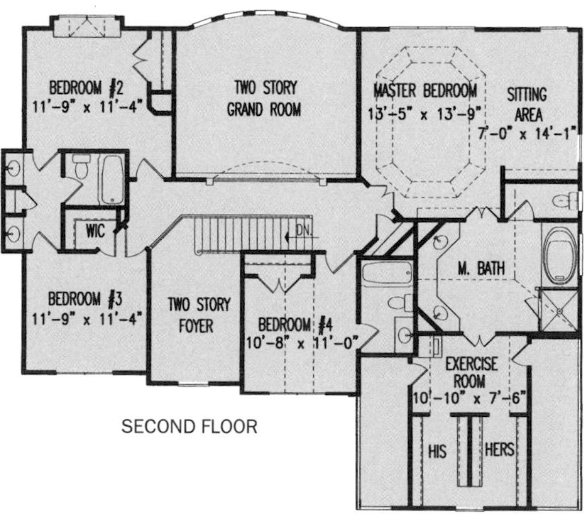

SECOND FLOOR

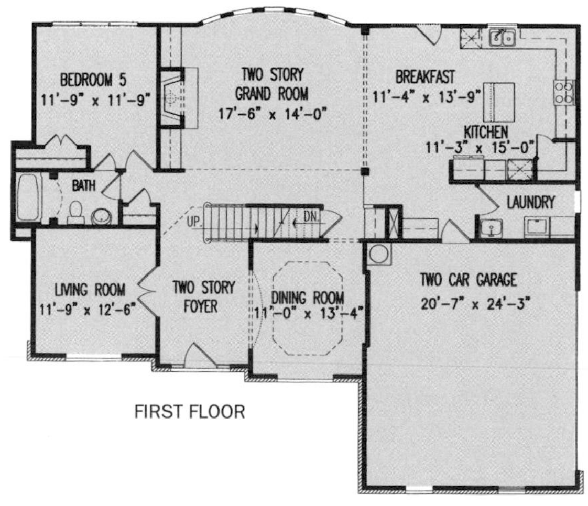

FIRST FLOOR

plan# HPK1700387

Style: Contemporary
First Floor: 2,394 sq. ft.
Second Floor: 730 sq. ft.
Total: 3,124 sq. ft.
Bonus Space: 450 sq. ft.
Bedrooms: 4
Bathrooms: 4½
Width: 67' - 0"
Depth: 93' - 2"
Foundation: Finished Walkout Basement

eplans.com

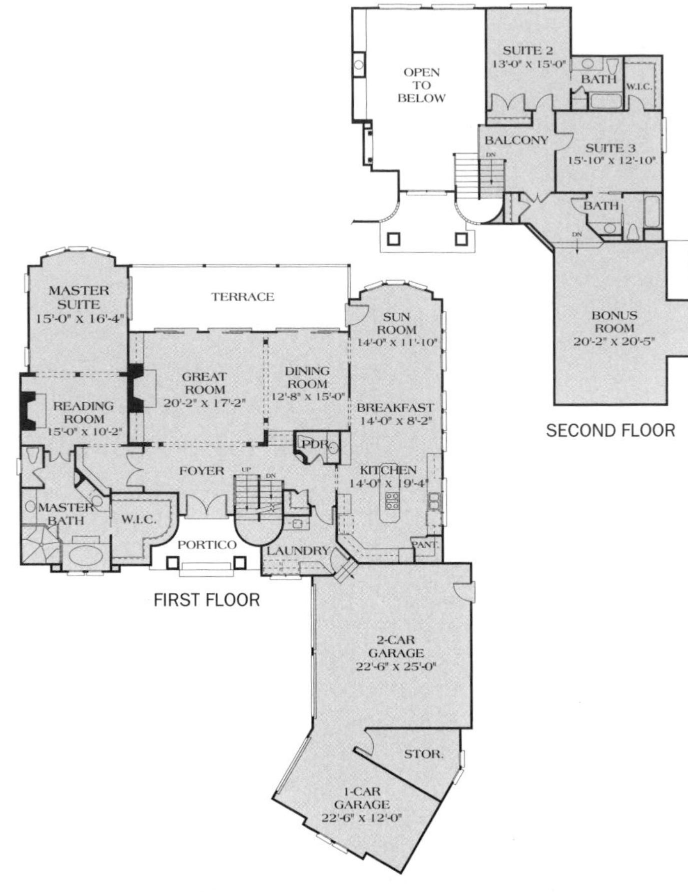

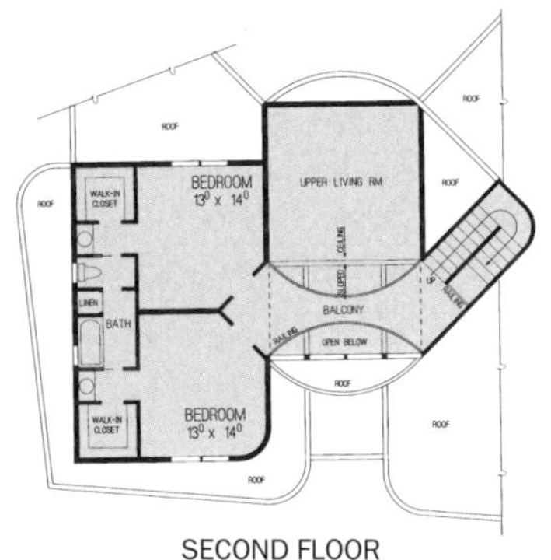

SECOND FLOOR

REAR EXTERIOR

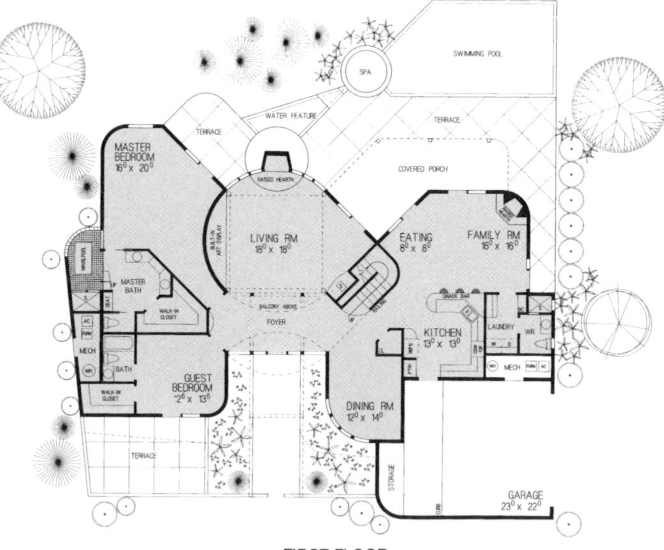

FIRST FLOOR

plan# HPK1700388

Style: SW Contemporary
First Floor: 2,422 sq. ft.
Second Floor: 714 sq. ft.
Total: 3,136 sq. ft.
Bedrooms: 4
Bathrooms: 4
Width: 77' - 6"
Depth: 62' - 0"
Foundation: Slab

eplans.com

plan# HPK1700389

Style: Victorian
First Floor: 2,041 sq. ft.
Second Floor: 1,098 sq. ft.
Total: 3,139 sq. ft.
Bonus Space: 385 sq. ft.
Bedrooms: 4
Bathrooms: 3½
Width: 76' - 6"
Depth: 62' - 2"
Foundation: Slab

eplans.com

The turret and the circular covered porch of this Victorian home make a great impression. The foyer carries you past a library and dining room to the hearth-warmed family room. A spacious kitchen with an island acts as a passageway to the nook and dining area. The master bedroom is located on the first floor and offers its own French doors to the rear covered porch. The master bath is designed to cater to both His and Her needs with two walk-in closets, separate vanities, a garden tub, and separate shower. The second-floor balcony looks to the family room below.

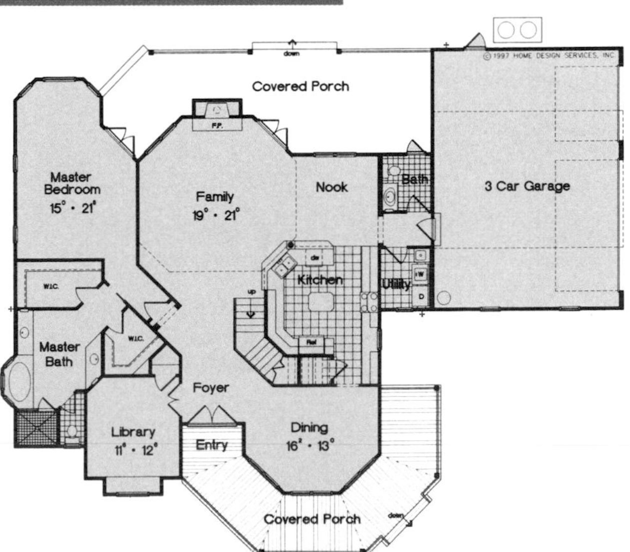

FIRST FLOOR

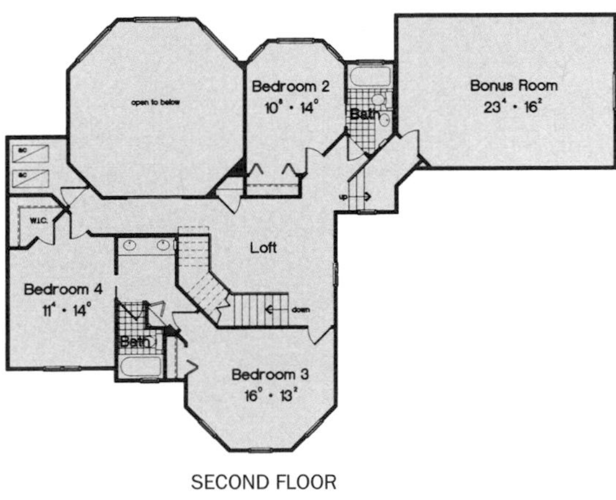

SECOND FLOOR

plan# HPK1700390

Style: European Cottage
First Floor: 2,237 sq. ft.
Second Floor: 931 sq. ft.
Total: 3,168 sq. ft.
Bonus Space: 304 sq. ft.
Bedrooms: 4
Bathrooms: 3½
Width: 68' - 0"
Depth: 55' - 6"
Foundation: Slab

eplans.com

This majestic estate has palatial inspiration, with a plan any modern family will love. A hardwood entry leads to brick flooring in the kitchen and breakfast nook, for vintage appeal. The family room and vaulted living room warm heart and soul with extended-hearth fireplaces. For a quiet retreat, the study opens with French doors from the hall and leads out to the walled lanai courtyard through another set of French doors. The vaulted master suite is impressive, with a bay window, a sumptuous bath, and His and Hers walk-in closets. Upstairs, three ample bedrooms will access the future playroom.

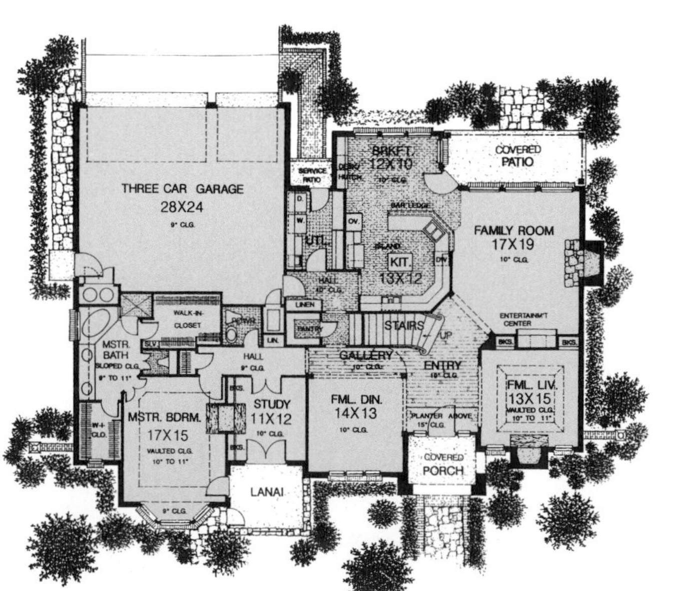

FIRST FLOOR

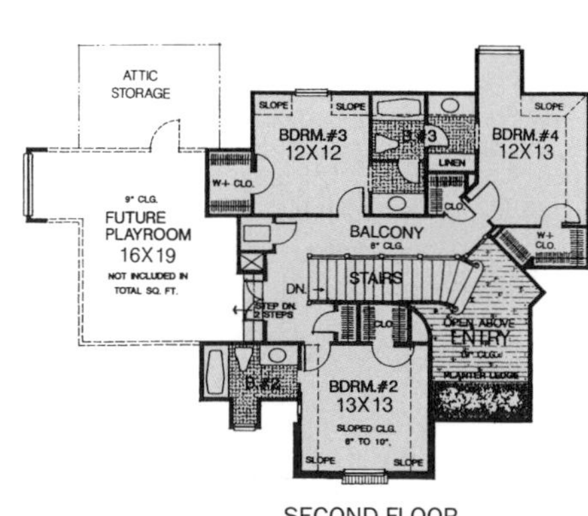

SECOND FLOOR

plan# HPK1700391

Style: Tidewater
First Floor: 1,595 sq. ft.
Second Floor: 1,600 sq. ft.
Total: 3,195 sq. ft.
Bedrooms: 5
Bathrooms: 4
Width: 54' - 0"
Depth: 43' - 0"
Foundation: Unfinished Walkout Basement, Slab

eplans.com

EDITOR'S PICK

We love this home for its good manners: a substantial, two-story foyer pairs with two-story grand room, creating a gallery overlook that separates the upstairs bedrooms from the master suite. Decorative ceiling treatments in the foyer, dining room, and suite are further refinements. The downstairs guest room is a full suite—a considerate touch for visiting friends. Of course, the exterior is refined: a stone-covered entrance, decorative porch anchors and shutters, and nested gables establish a stately curbside presence.

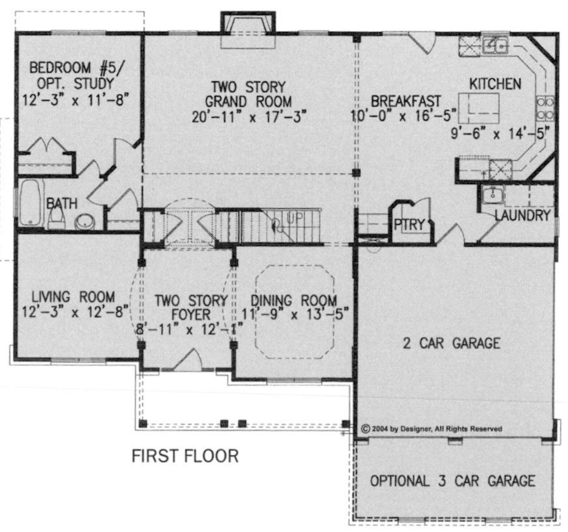

FIRST FLOOR

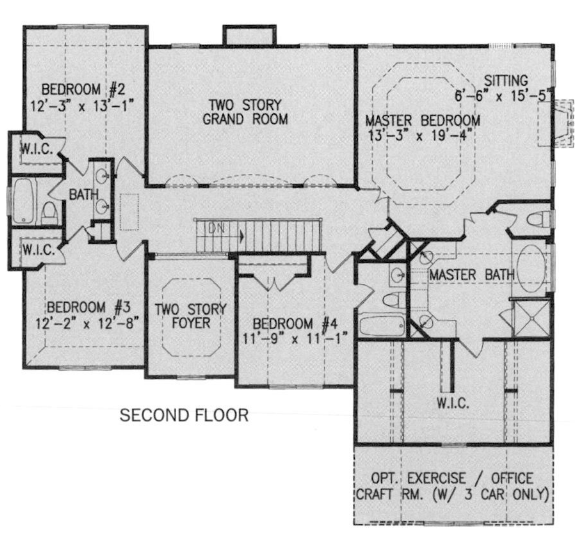

SECOND FLOOR

SECOND FLOOR

plan# HPK1700392

Style: Traditional
First Floor: 2,193 sq. ft.
Second Floor: 1,004 sq. ft.
Total: 3,197 sq. ft.
Bedrooms: 4
Bathrooms: 4½
Width: 67' - 0"
Depth: 74' - 4"
Foundation: Crawlspace

eplans.com

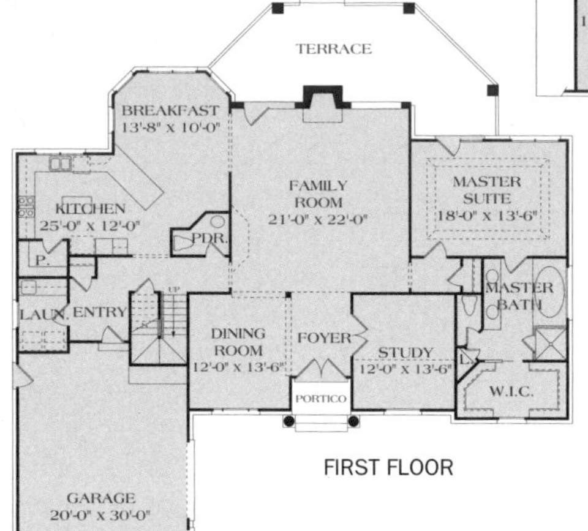

FIRST FLOOR

SECOND FLOOR

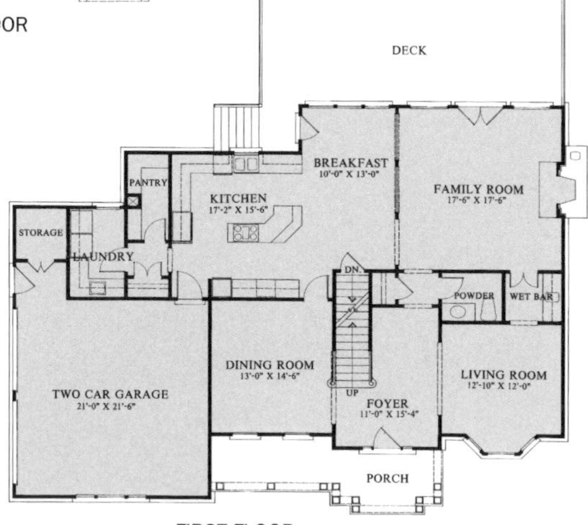

FIRST FLOOR

plan# HPK1700393

Style: Farmhouse
First Floor: 1,570 sq. ft.
Second Floor: 1,630 sq. ft.
Total: 3,200 sq. ft.
Bedrooms: 4
Bathrooms: 3½
Width: 59' - 10"
Depth: 43' - 4"
Foundation: Walkout Basement

eplans.com

plan# HPK1700394

Style: Prairie
First Floor: 2,531 sq. ft.
Second Floor: 669 sq. ft.
Total: 3,200 sq. ft.
Bedrooms: 4
Bathrooms: 3½ + ½
Width: 82' - 4"
Depth: 72' - 0"
Foundation: Slab

eplans.com

This exquisite brick-and-stucco contemporary home takes its cue from the tradition of Frank Lloyd Wright. The formal living and dining areas combine to provide a spectacular view of the rear grounds. "Unique" best describes the private master suite, highlighted by a multitude of amenities. The family living area encompasses the left portion of the plan, featuring a spacious family room with a corner fireplace, access to the covered patio from the breakfast area, and a step-saving kitchen. Bedroom 2 connects to a private bath. Upstairs, two bedrooms share a balcony, a sitting room, and a full bath.

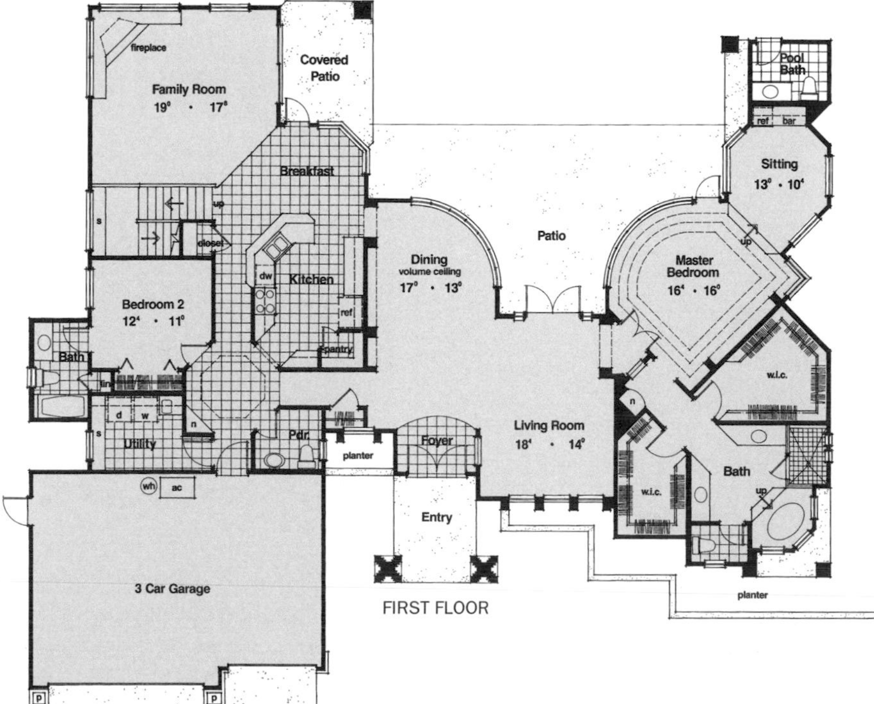

FIRST FLOOR

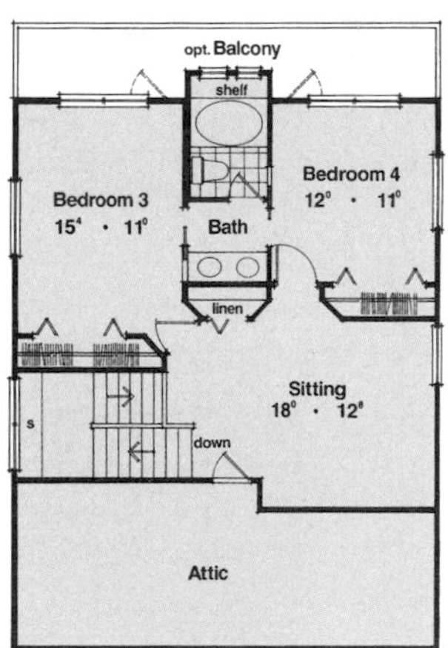

SECOND FLOOR

SECOND FLOOR

plan# HPK1700395

Style: Georgian
First Floor: 1,554 sq. ft.
Second Floor: 1,648 sq. ft.
Total: 3,202 sq. ft.
Bedrooms: 4
Bathrooms: 3½
Width: 60' - 0"
Depth: 43' - 0"
Foundation: Walkout Basement

eplans.com

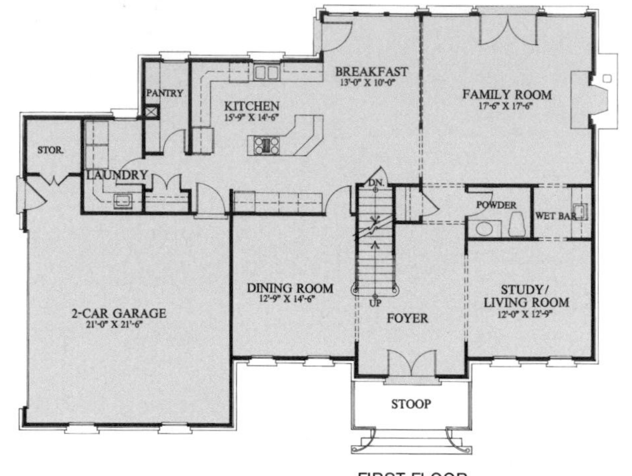

FIRST FLOOR

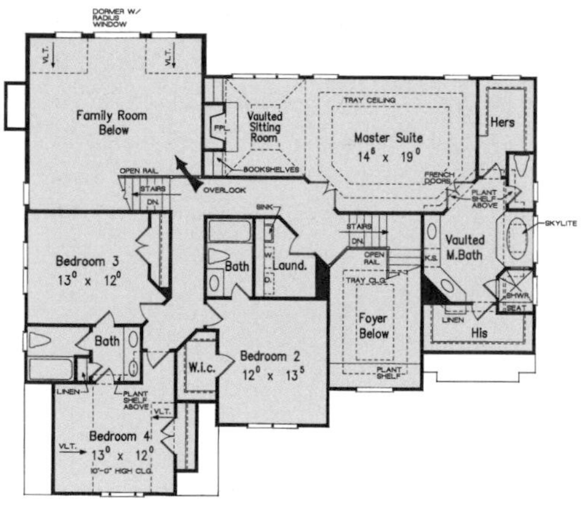

plan# HPK1700396

Style: European Cottage
First Floor: 1,583 sq. ft.
Second Floor: 1,632 sq. ft.
Total: 3,215 sq. ft.
Bedrooms: 5
Bathrooms: 4½
Width: 58' - 4"
Depth: 50' - 0"
Foundation: Crawlspace, Unfinished Walkout Basement

eplans.com

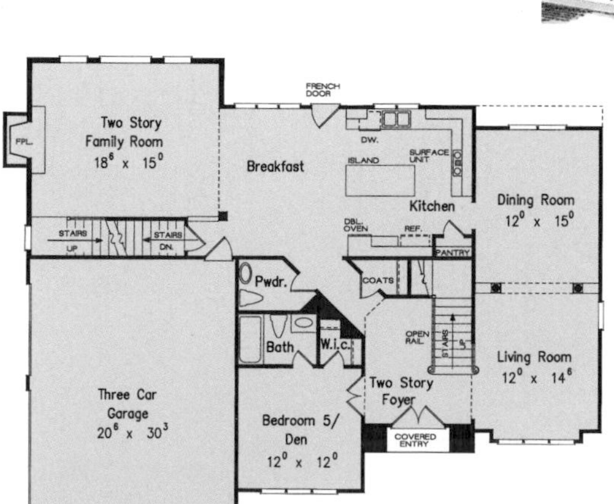

FIRST FLOOR

plan# HPK1700397

Style: Southern Colonial
First Floor: 1,665 sq. ft.
Second Floor: 1,554 sq. ft.
Total: 3,219 sq. ft.
Bedrooms: 5
Bathrooms: 4
Width: 58' - 6"
Depth: 44' - 10"
Foundation: Crawlspace, Unfinished Walkout Basement

eplans.com

This stately transitional home focuses on family living. The formal living areas are traditionally placed flanking the two-story foyer. The two-story family room has a lovely fireplace and windows to the rear yard. The remarkable kitchen features wraparound counters, a breakfast nook, and a cooktop island/serving bar. A bedroom and full bath would make a comfortable guest suite or a quiet den. A balcony hall leads to two bedrooms that share a bath; a third bedroom has its own bath and walk-in closet. The master suite is designed with a tray ceiling and a sitting room with a through-fireplace to the vaulted bath.

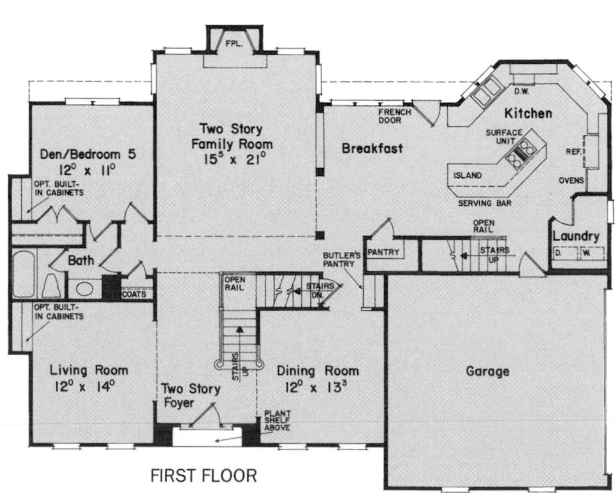

FIRST FLOOR

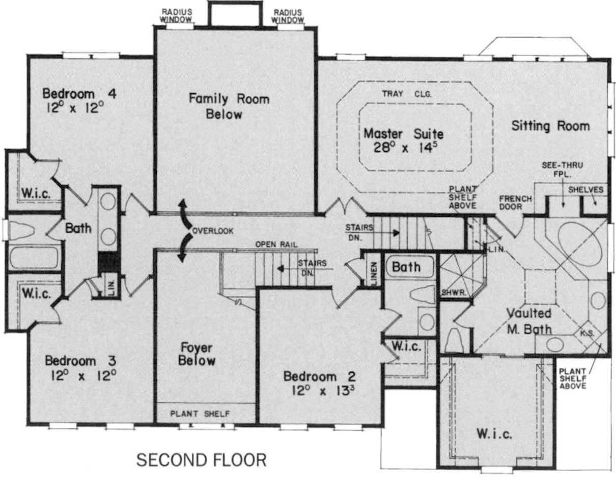

SECOND FLOOR

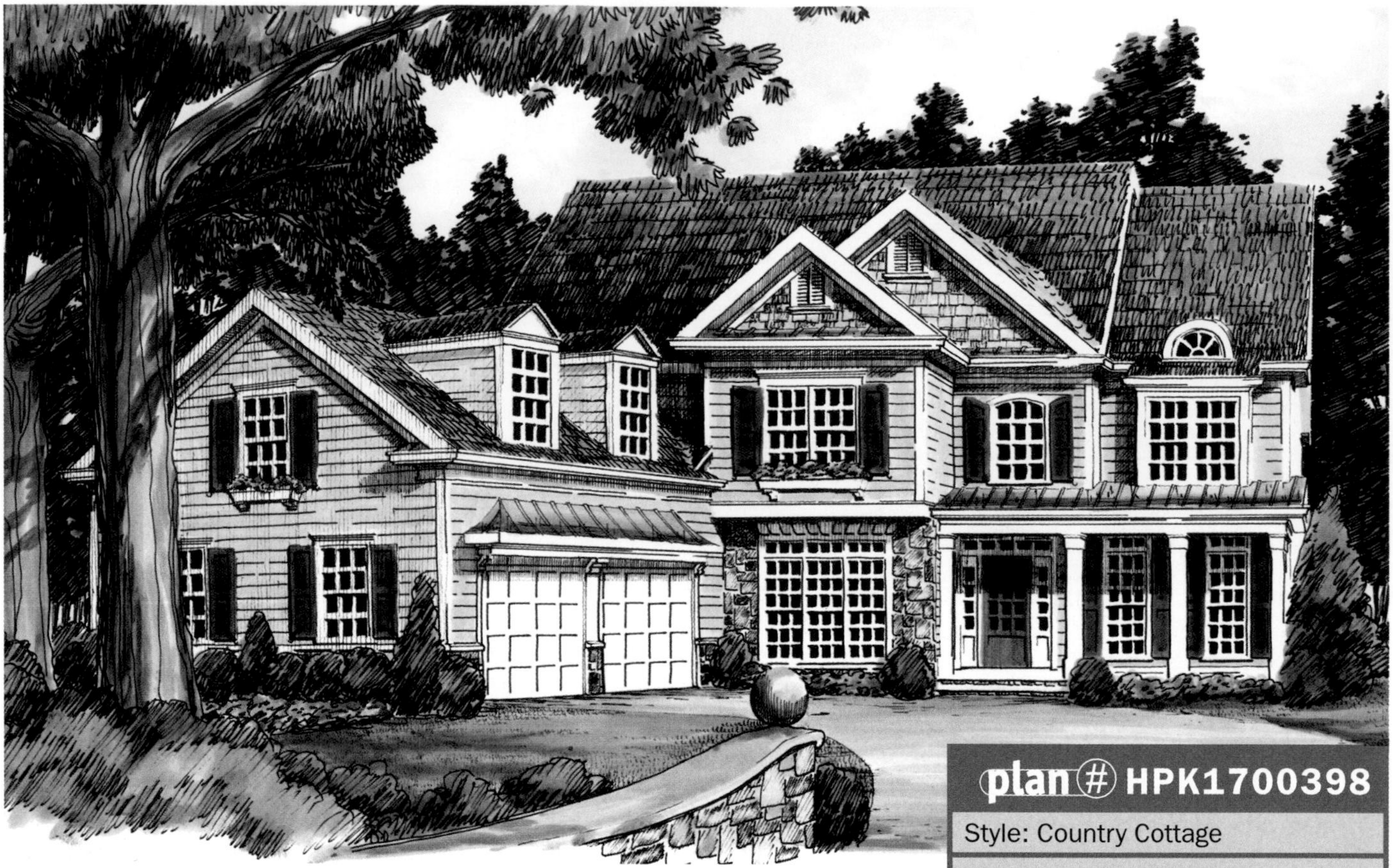

plan# HPK1700398

Style: Country Cottage
First Floor: 1,570 sq. ft.
Second Floor: 1,650 sq. ft.
Total: 3,220 sq. ft.
Bedrooms: 5
Bathrooms: 4
Width: 55' - 6"
Depth: 60' - 0"
Foundation: Crawlspace, Unfinished Walkout Basement

eplans.com

FIRST FLOOR

SECOND FLOOR

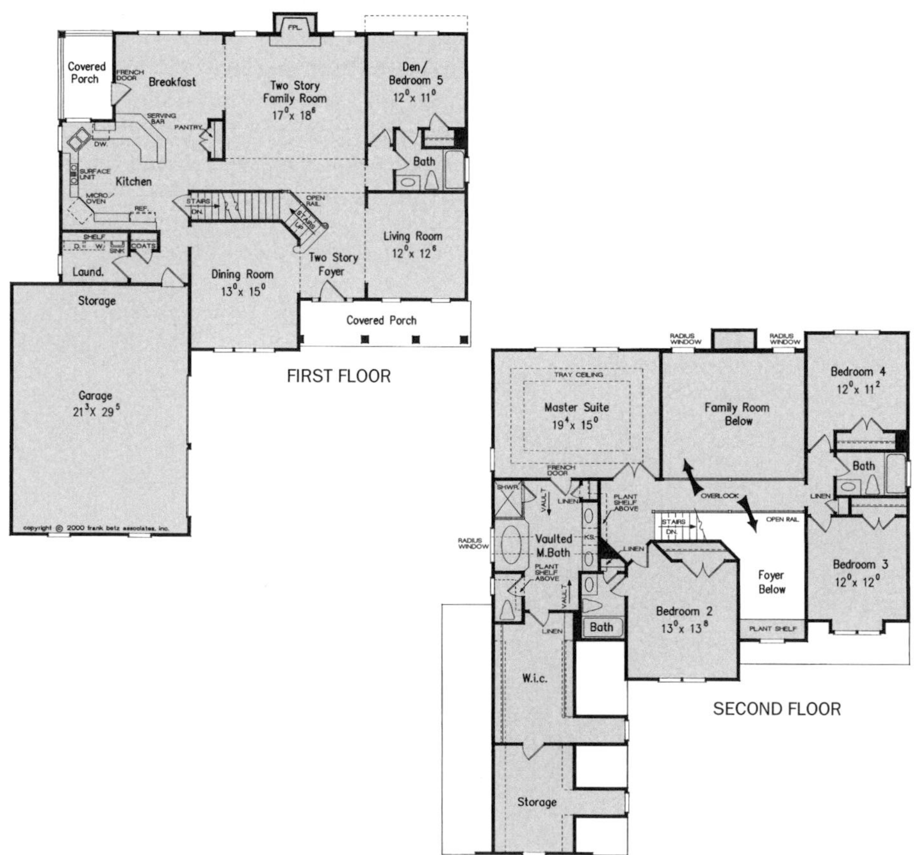

A side-loading garage and stunning country details make this home perfect for a corner lot. Formal rooms at the front of the plan border the two-story foyer. The two-story family room is an inviting gathering place. A C-shaped serving-bar kitchen is well-planned and ready to serve the breakfast nook and dining room. A quiet den with a semi-private bath completes this level. On the second floor, two bedrooms (one with a lovely box-bay window) share a full bath. An additional bedroom has a private bath. The master suite will amaze, with a splendid bath and vast walk-in closet. Extra storage space is an added asset.

plan # HPK1700399

Style: Country Cottage
First Floor: 2,284 sq. ft.
Second Floor: 940 sq. ft.
Total: 3,224 sq. ft.
Bonus Space: 545 sq. ft.
Bedrooms: 4
Bathrooms: 3½
Width: 55' - 0"
Depth: 85' - 0"
Foundation: Crawlspace, Unfinished Walkout Basement

eplans.com

Traditional styling makes this home a great addition to an established neighborhood. Spacious rooms cater to every family member starting with the cook. The kitchen sports an island, plenty of counter and cabinet space, an adjoining laundry room and breakfast area, and a wet bar that connects to the family room. Beyond the breakfast area, the vaulted keeping room is a perfect spot to keep an eye on the kids or to entertain friends while whipping up lunch in the kitchen. A gorgeous master suite features a sitting bay, twin walk-in closets, and a super bath. Upstairs, three family bedrooms, two baths, and plenty of closets complete this level. A large bonus space above the garage can be completed later.

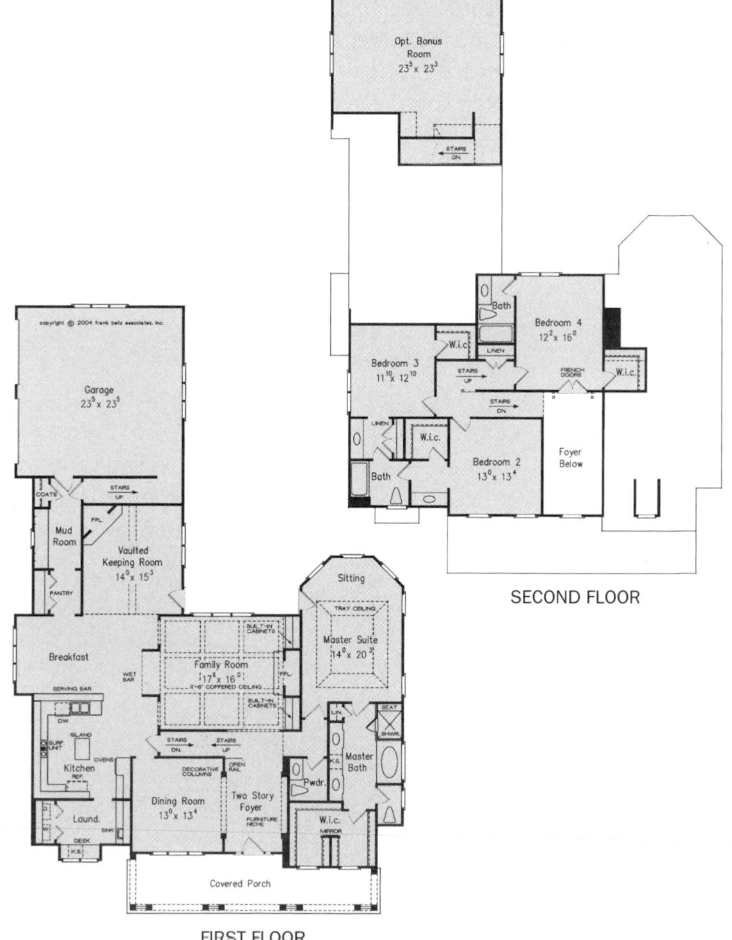

FIRST FLOOR

SECOND FLOOR

A stucco facade with detailed embellishments, and a full-height, arched loggia with hipped gable strikes a distinctive and stylish tone for this transitional-inspired design. Arched, multipaned windows proliferate, providing charm and an airy feel for the interior. This plan bursts with a cornucopia of amenities: a sunroom, guest-suite/library, enormous master suite, a foyer with lots of openings, functional kitchen with generous breakfast nook, a terrace accessible by the great and dining rooms, and a laundry, powder room, built-in bar, and pantry downstairs. Two family bedrooms with shared bath and a bonus room, plus an interior balcony, are all upstairs.

plan# HPK1700400

Style: Transitional
First Floor: 2,517 sq. ft.
Second Floor: 722 sq. ft.
Total: 3,239 sq. ft.
Bonus Space: 400 sq. ft.
Bedrooms: 4
Bathrooms: 2½
Width: 72' - 10"
Depth: 71' - 9"
Foundation: Finished Walkout Basement

eplans.com

BASEMENT

REAR EXTERIOR

FIRST FLOOR

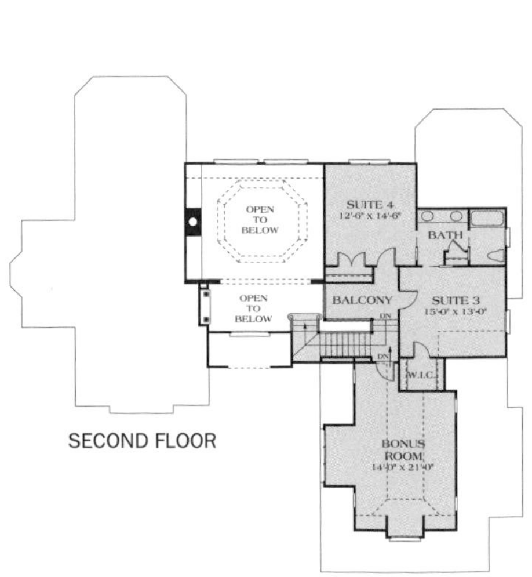

SECOND FLOOR

plan# HPK1700401

Style: Farmhouse
First Floor: 2,642 sq. ft.
Second Floor: 603 sq. ft.
Total: 3,245 sq. ft.
Bonus Space: 255 sq. ft.
Bedrooms: 4
Bathrooms: 3½
Width: 80' - 0"
Depth: 61' - 0"
Foundation: Crawlspace

eplans.com

In this four-bedroom design, the casual areas are free-flowing, open, and soaring, and the formal areas are secluded and well defined. The two-story foyer with a clerestory window leads to a quiet parlor with a vaulted ceiling and a Palladian window. The formal dining room opens from the foyer through decorative columns and is served by a spacious gourmet kitchen. The family room, defined by columns, has an angled corner hearth and is open to the kitchen and breakfast nook. The master suite is full of interesting angles, from the triangular bedroom and multi-angled walk-in closet to the corner tub in the sumptuous master bath. A nearby den has its own bathroom and could serve as a guest room. Upstairs, two additional bedrooms share a full bath and a balcony hall.

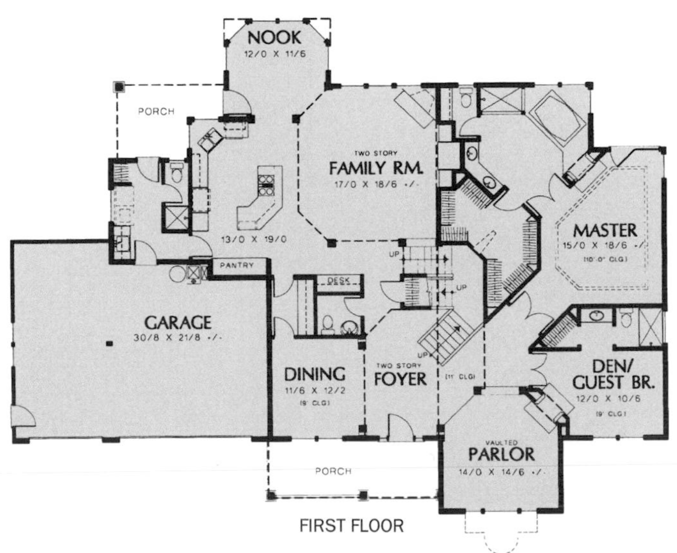

FIRST FLOOR

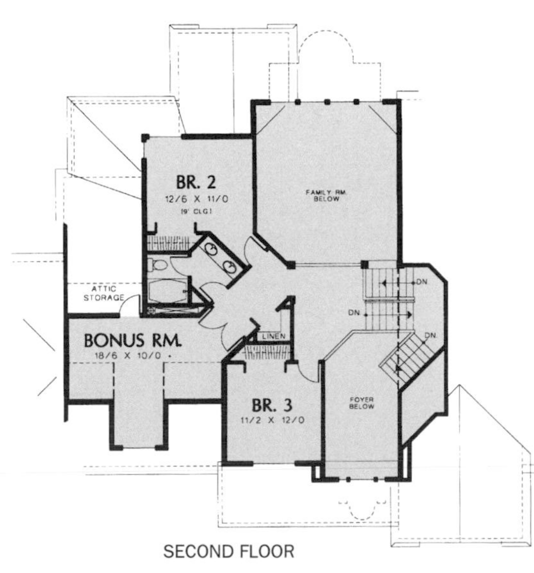

SECOND FLOOR

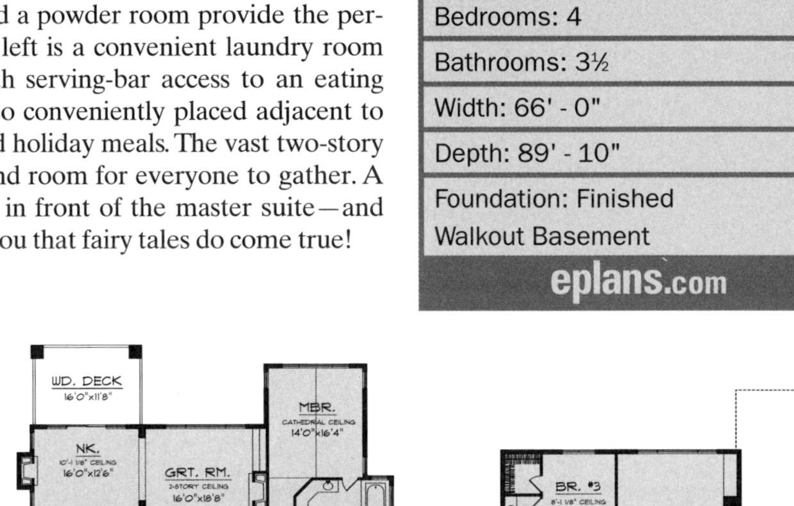

plan# HPK1700402

- Style: Traditional
- First Floor: 2,274 sq. ft.
- Second Floor: 972 sq. ft.
- Total: 3,246 sq. ft.
- Bedrooms: 4
- Bathrooms: 3½
- Width: 66' - 0"
- Depth: 89' - 10"
- Foundation: Finished Walkout Basement

eplans.com

Looking for a fairy-tale home to raise your family and astound your friends? Look no further than this little slice of heaven. The three-car garage and array of rooflines create a look that everyone will enjoy. Inside, four bedrooms, three full baths, and a powder room provide the perfect setting for a loving family. To the far left is a convenient laundry room which gives way to an island kitchen with serving-bar access to an eating nook. The more formal dining room is also conveniently placed adjacent to the kitchen for seemless dinner parties and holiday meals. The vast two-story great room includes a glowing fireplace and room for everyone to gather. A den with built-in bookshelves sits nestled in front of the master suite—and one look at the master bath will convince you that fairy tales do come true!

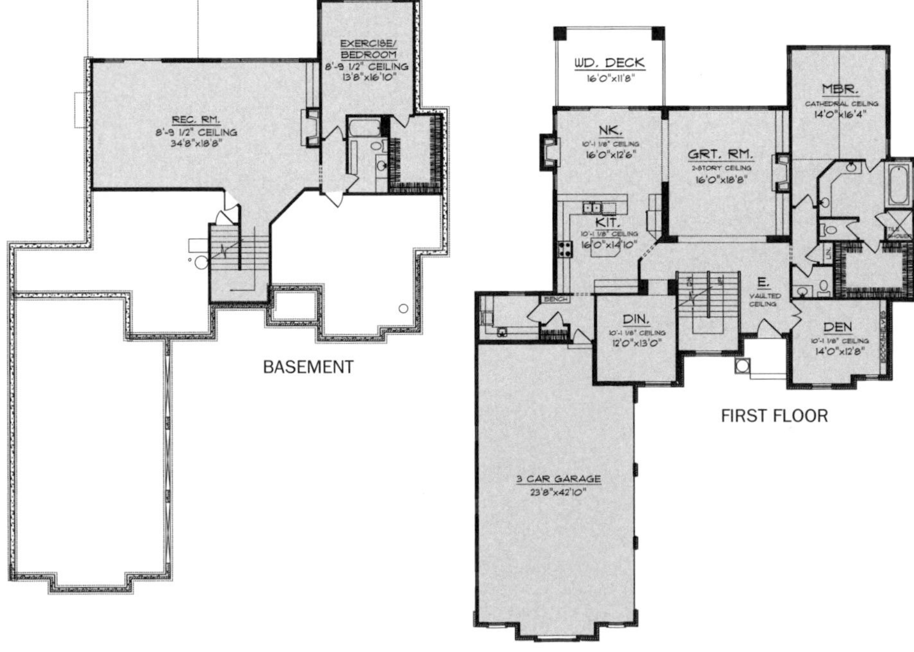

BASEMENT

FIRST FLOOR

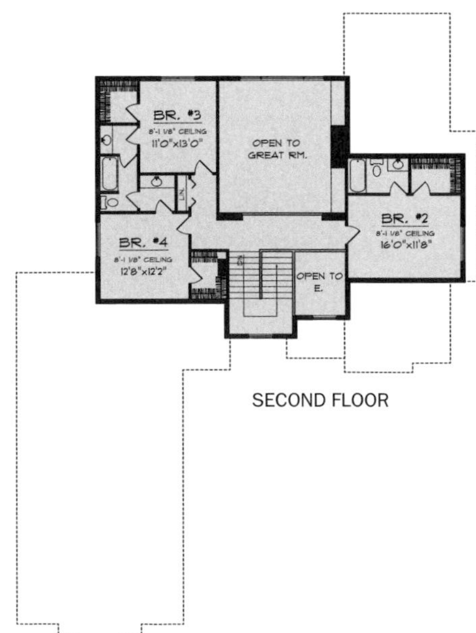

SECOND FLOOR

plan# HPK1700403

Style: Tidewater
First Floor: 1,649 sq. ft.
Second Floor: 1,604 sq. ft.
Total: 3,253 sq. ft.
Bedrooms: 4
Bathrooms: 3½
Width: 69' - 6"
Depth: 53' - 8"
Foundation: Unfinished Walkout Basement, Slab

eplans.com

This classic Colonial home beautifully embodies old and new. Inside, the large grand room is the heart of the home. With access to a rear covered porch and deck, it welcomes outdoor living. Upstairs, the master suite, enhanced by a tray ceiling, features a sitting area, dual-sink vanity, garden tub, private toilet, separate shower, and walk-in closet. Three family bedrooms, two full baths, and a study loft complete this floor.

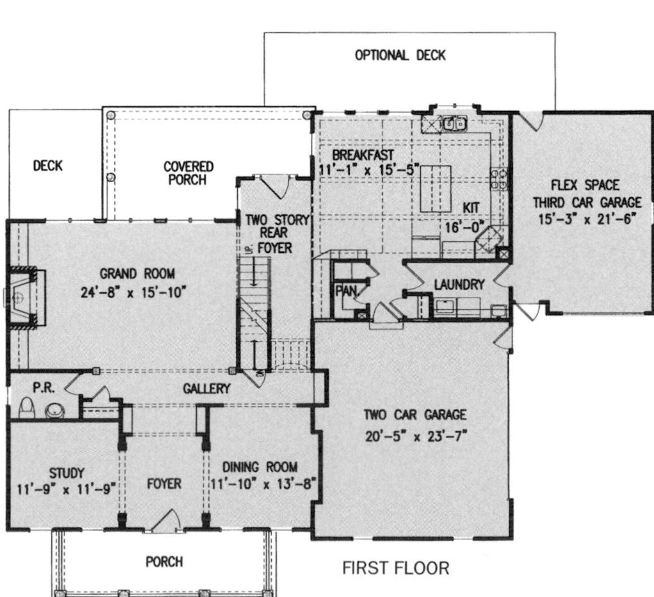

FIRST FLOOR

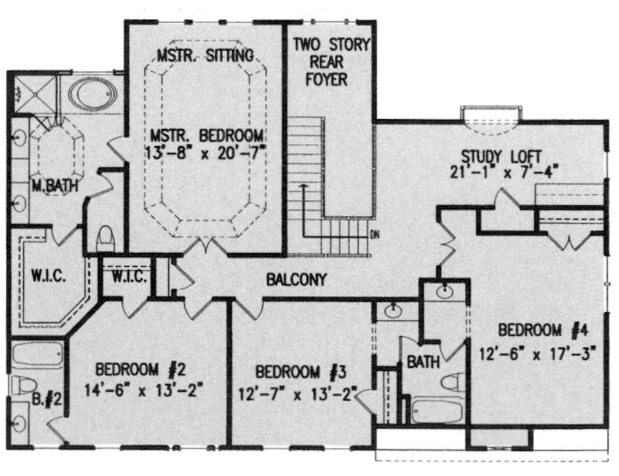

SECOND FLOOR

PHOTO COURTESY OF GARRELL ASSOCIATES, INC.

plan# HPK1700404

Style: Farmhouse
First Floor: 1,670 sq. ft.
Second Floor: 1,590 sq. ft.
Total: 3,260 sq. ft.
Bedrooms: 5
Bathrooms: 4
Width: 53' - 4"
Depth: 50' - 0"
Foundation: Slab, Unfinished Walkout Basement

eplans.com

A brick facade, multigabled roof, and front porch usher you into a magnificent two-story foyer with arched entries on either side to the living room or formal dining room. Straight ahead is the two-story grand room with fireplace and conjunction with three other rooms. A wraparound kitchen opens to the breakfast and keeping room via a handy island, suitable for preparation and serving. A handy laundry room is also in the vicinity, as is access to the garage. Upstairs, an oversized master suite with sitting area and enormous walk-in closet constitutes a major portion of the floor. You can view the grand room or the foyer from the balcony, which connects bedrooms four and five with the other side of the second floor. You also have an optional exercise and craft room.

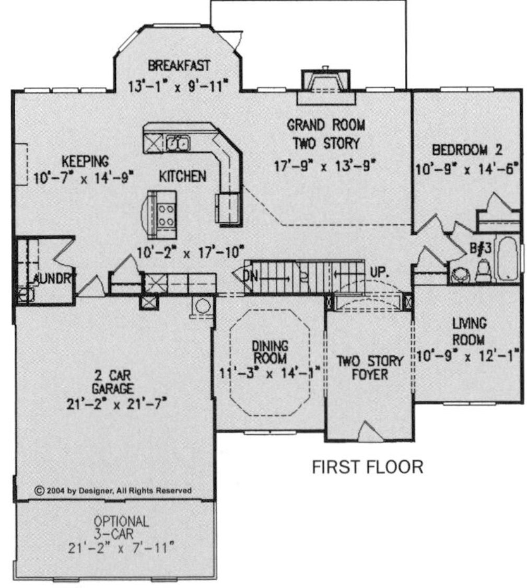

FIRST FLOOR

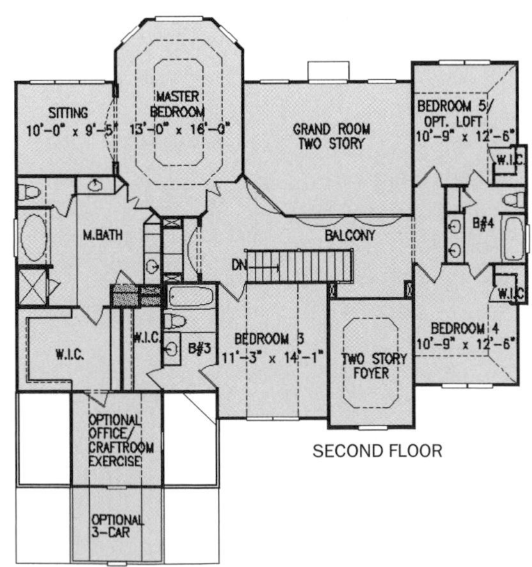

SECOND FLOOR

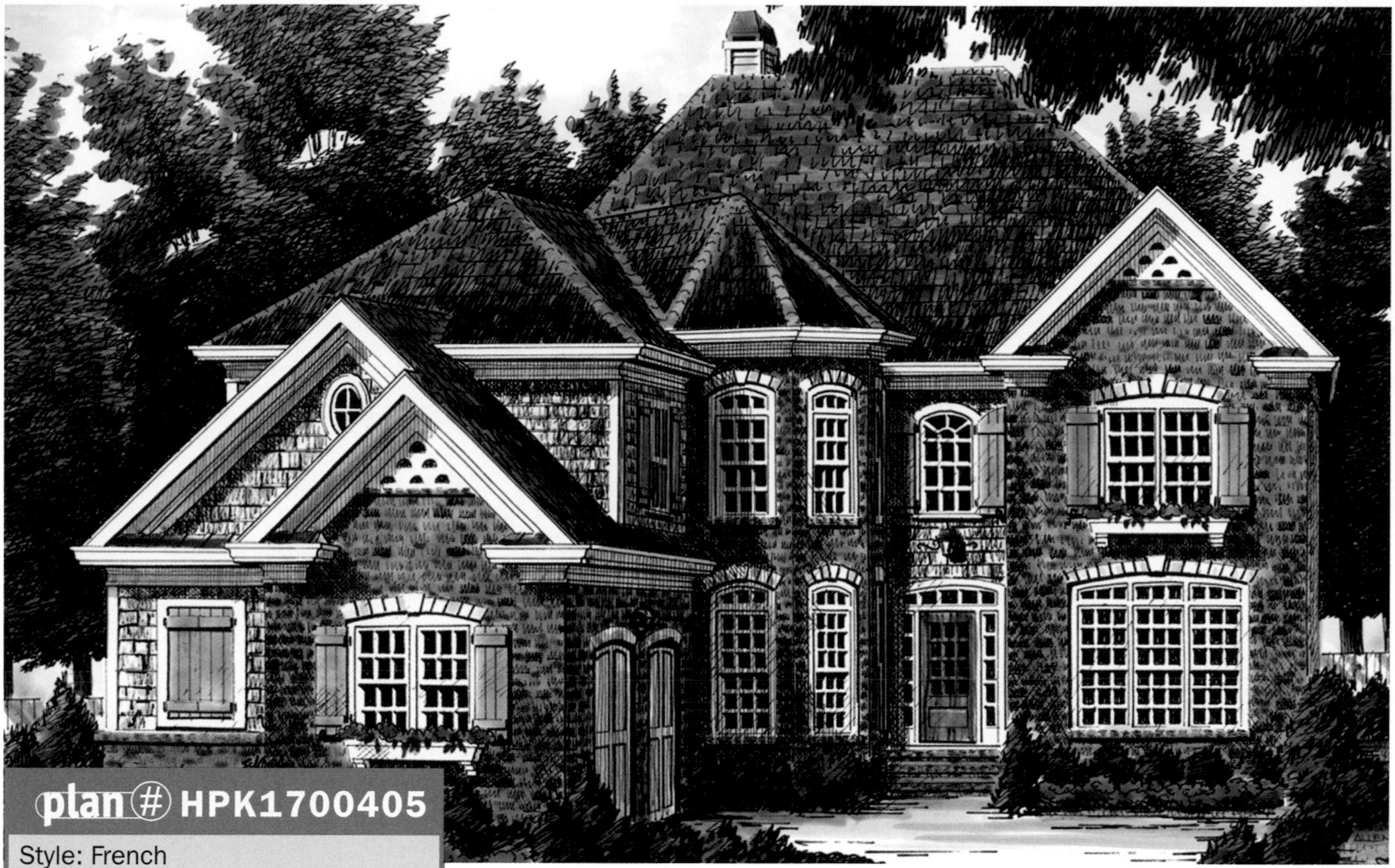

plan# HPK1700405

Style: French
First Floor: 1,685 sq. ft.
Second Floor: 1,596 sq. ft.
Total: 3,281 sq. ft.
Bedrooms: 5
Bathrooms: 4½
Width: 51' - 0"
Depth: 66' - 10"
Foundation: Crawlspace, Unfinished Walkout Basement

eplans.com

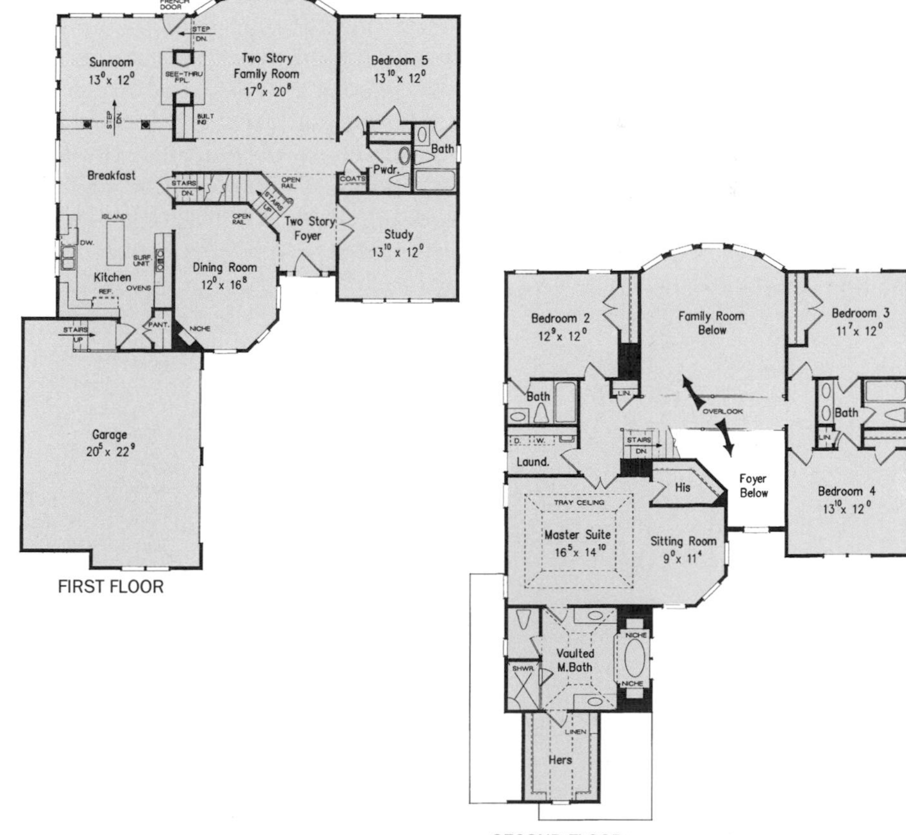

Strong lines lead the eye upwards toward this home's varied roofline. The formal dining room enjoys views from the two-story turret. The breakfast room opens to a glorious sun room with access to the rear property. The two-story family room enjoys a curved wall of windows and a double-sided fireplace. At the right of the plan, a study and powder room share space with a comfortable guest suite. Upstairs, three family bedrooms with ample closet space share two baths. The sumptuous master suite boasts a sitting room, vaulted bath, and His and Hers walk-in closets.

FIRST FLOOR

SECOND FLOOR

plan# HPK1700406

Style: Georgian
First Floor: 1,679 sq. ft.
Second Floor: 1,605 sq. ft.
Total: 3,284 sq. ft.
Bedrooms: 5
Bathrooms: 4
Width: 57' - 0"
Depth: 45' - 4"
Foundation: Crawlspace, Unfinished Walkout Basement

eplans.com

This stately Georgian home combines varied rooflines, a grand pediment entry, and eye-catching brick to create a place your family will delight in for generations. Inside, an intriguing floor plan directs traffic for increased flow and maximizes natural light. The foyer opens on the right to a formal dining room with a box-bay window and reveals a study on the left. An expansive kitchen features an island and a serving bar that views the bayed breakfast nook. Stunning vistas grace the two-story family room, courtesy of a rear bowed window wall. A see-through fireplace is shared with the sun room. Three upstairs bedrooms are generously appointed. The master suite is a romantic retreat with a bayed sitting area and sumptuous bath with a window seat.

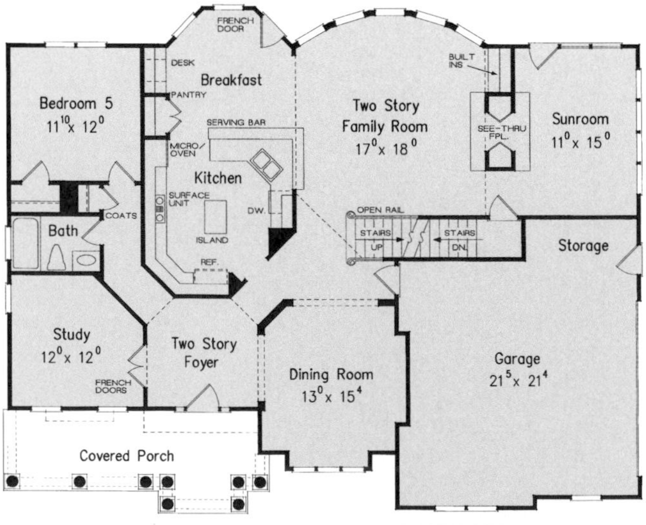

FRENCH DOOR
DESK
Breakfast
PANTRY
Bedroom 5
11^{10}x 12^{0}
SERVING BAR
Two Story
Family Room
17^{0}x 18^{0}
BUILT INS
SEE-THRU FPL.
Sunroom
11^{0}x 15^{0}
MICRO/ OVEN
Kitchen
SURFACE UNIT
DW.
ISLAND
REF.
COATS
Bath
OPEN RAIL
STAIRS UP
STAIRS DN.
Storage
Study
12^{0}x 12^{0}
FRENCH DOORS
Two Story
Foyer
Dining Room
13^{0}x 15^{4}
Garage
21^{5}x 21^{4}
Covered Porch

FIRST FLOOR

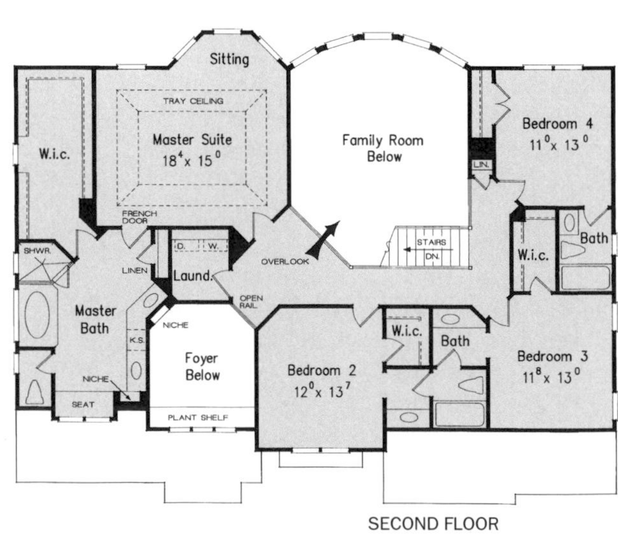

SECOND FLOOR

plan# HPK1700407

Style: Transitional
First Floor: 1,820 sq. ft.
Second Floor: 1,473 sq. ft.
Total: 3,293 sq. ft.
Bonus Space: 308 sq. ft.
Bedrooms: 4
Bathrooms: 4
Width: 61' - 9"
Depth: 48' - 10"
Foundation: Crawlspace

eplans.com

A stucco facade with a grand structure and ornamented detailing are on display here. Arched windows, symmetrical quoins, and a covered, columned porch interact appealingly. The interior floor plan takes advantage of every modern convenience to create the ideal home. The foyer is surrounded by a study, kitchen with pantry and breakfast area, laundry, dining room, and living room. The dining and living rooms are built as one open area, separated by an archway. An optional butler's pantry is provided for, opposite the laundry, perfect for entertaining and formal occasions. The study has an attached bath and can easily be designated as a fifth bedroom. The left of the first floor features the family room, with fireplace and double door access to the deck, and access to one of the two staircases to the second level and the garage. An opulent master suite with tray ceiling is found upstairs, along with three bedrooms and an optional room.

plan# HPK1700408

Style: Norman

First Floor: 2,188 sq. ft.

Second Floor: 1,110 sq. ft.

Total: 3,298 sq. ft.

Bedrooms: 4

Bathrooms: 3½

Width: 69' - 0"

Depth: 64' - 8"

Foundation: Slab

eplans.com

This European-style brick-and-stucco home showcases an arched entry and presents a commanding presence from the curb. Inside, the living room, the dining room, and the family room are located at the rear of the home to provide wide-open views of the rear grounds beyond. A colonnade with connecting arches defines the space for a living room with a fireplace and the dining room. The spacious master suite features a relaxing sitting area, His and Hers closets, and an extravagant bath. Take special note of the private His and Hers bathrooms. On the second floor, three bedrooms, two baths, and a game room complete the home.

FIRST FLOOR

SECOND FLOOR

© The Sater Design Collection, Inc.

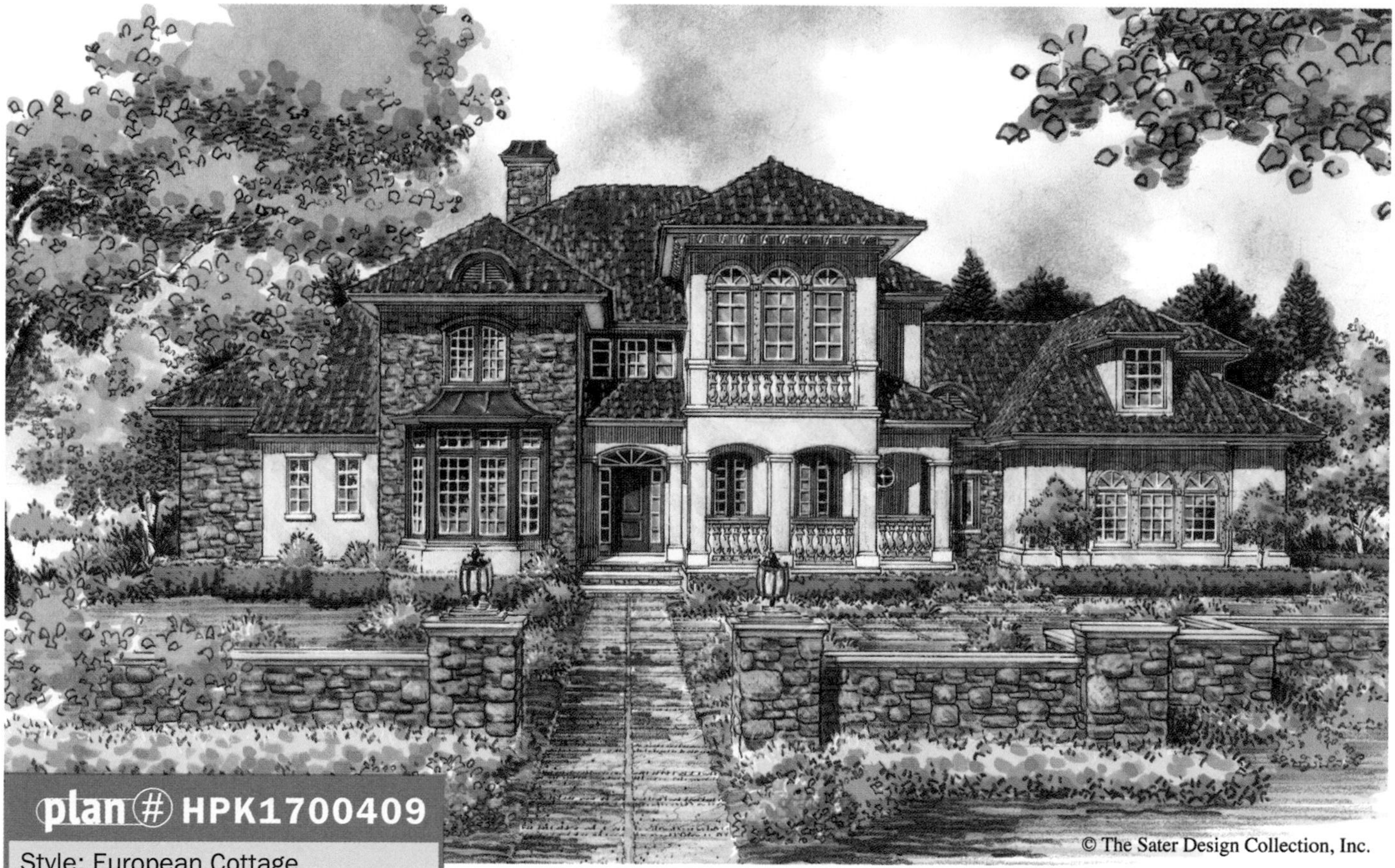

plan # HPK1700409

Style: European Cottage
First Floor: 2,219 sq. ft.
Second Floor: 1,085 sq. ft.
Total: 3,304 sq. ft.
Bonus Space: 404 sq. ft.
Bedrooms: 4
Bathrooms: 3½
Width: 91' - 0"
Depth: 52' - 8"
Foundation: Slab

eplans.com

This home features two levels of pampering luxury filled with the most up-to-date amenities. Touches of Mediterranean detail add to the striking facade. A wrapping front porch welcomes you inside to a formal dining room and two-story great room warmed by a fireplace. Double doors from the master suite, great room, and breakfast nook access the rear veranda. The first-floor master suite enjoys a luxury bath, roomy walk-in closet, and close access to the front-facing office/study. Three additional bedrooms reside upstairs. The bonus room above the garage is great for an apartment or storage space.

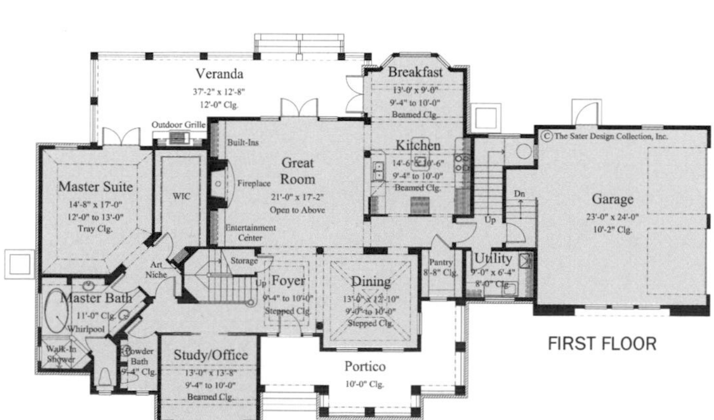

FIRST FLOOR

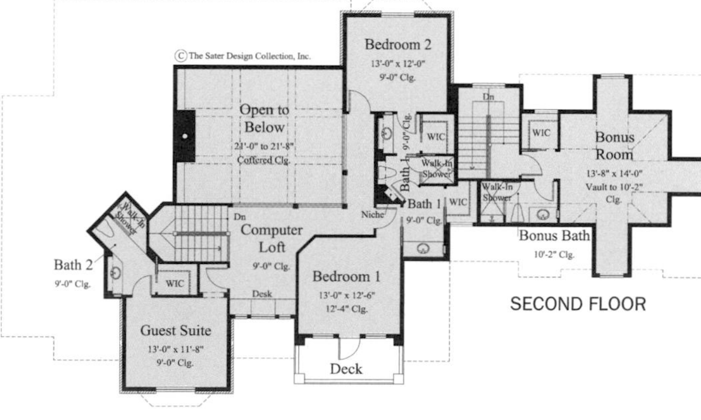

SECOND FLOOR

plan# HPK1700410

Style: French

First Floor: 2,352 sq. ft.

Second Floor: 952 sq. ft.

Total: 3,304 sq. ft.

Bedrooms: 5

Bathrooms: 4

Width: 61' - 0"

Depth: 66' - 8"

Foundation: Slab, Unfinished Walkout Basement

eplans.com

Five gables top this traditional home's exterior. A formal entry is flanked by a vaulted living room and a dining room with tray ceiling. If you need a larger entertainment space, the two-story grand room fills the bill. A fireplace with built-ins provides the focal point and is enjoyed from the breakfast bay and the kitchen. A guest bedroom sits just behind the kitchen. Fine appointments in the master suite create a luxurious place in which to de-stress. Four secondary bedrooms share two full baths and an entertainment loft with media built-ins. Unfinished bonus space can be used for storage.

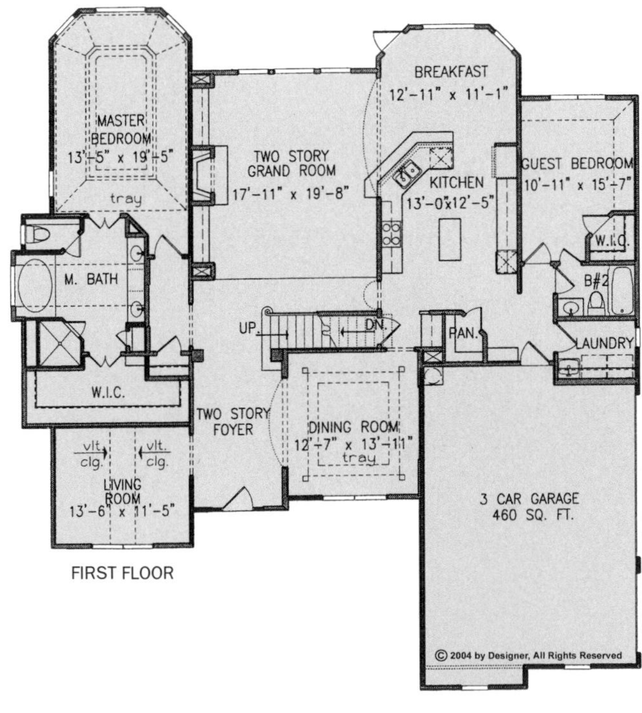

FIRST FLOOR

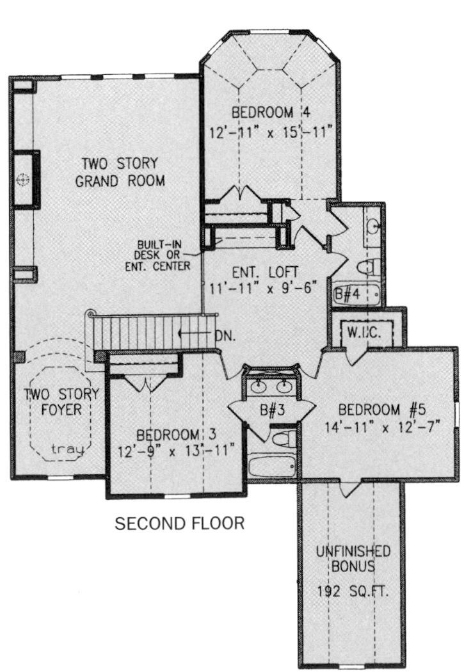

SECOND FLOOR

plan# HPK1700411

Style: Chateau Style

First Floor: 1,710 sq. ft.

Second Floor: 1,607 sq. ft.

Total: 3,317 sq. ft.

Bedrooms: 5

Bathrooms: 4

Width: 54' - 6"

Depth: 44' - 10"

Foundation: Unfinished Walkout Basement

eplans.com

The main attraction on this exterior is an old-fashioned turret, lending a conical shape to the outside of the first floor living room and upper level third bedroom. From the windows, you'll feel like royalty surveying your domain. The two-story grand room is located off the gallery, at the center of the plan. The breakfast area and kitchen are open to the right, with the laundry and access to the double garage conveniently nearby. All of the bedrooms feature ornate vaulted ceilings, except for the master suite, with a tray ceiling and enormous walk-in closet.

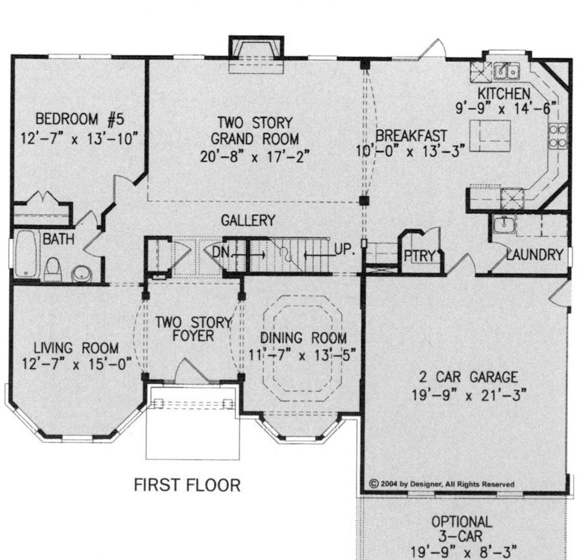

FIRST FLOOR

SECOND FLOOR

plan# HPK1700412

Style: Traditional
First Floor: 2,326 sq. ft.
Second Floor: 994 sq. ft.
Total: 3,320 sq. ft.
Bedrooms: 4
Bathrooms: 3½
Width: 58' - 6"
Depth: 62' - 0"
Foundation: Crawlspace, Unfinished Walkout Basement

eplans.com

This beautiful brick facade is enhanced by large windows, keystone arches, and charming flower boxes. Inside, the two-story foyer presents a stunning design. The living room lies to the left, brightened by a box-bay window. Viewing a decorative niche, the columned dining room flows into a vaulted great room, which hosts tall radius windows and a fireplace framed by bookshelves. The angled kitchen's serving bar accesses the grand breakfast nook and vaulted keeping room. Secluded for privacy, the master suite revels in a bayed sitting area, vaulted spa bath, and His and Hers walk-in closets. Upstairs, three bedrooms (one with a private bath) share a loft and computer station.

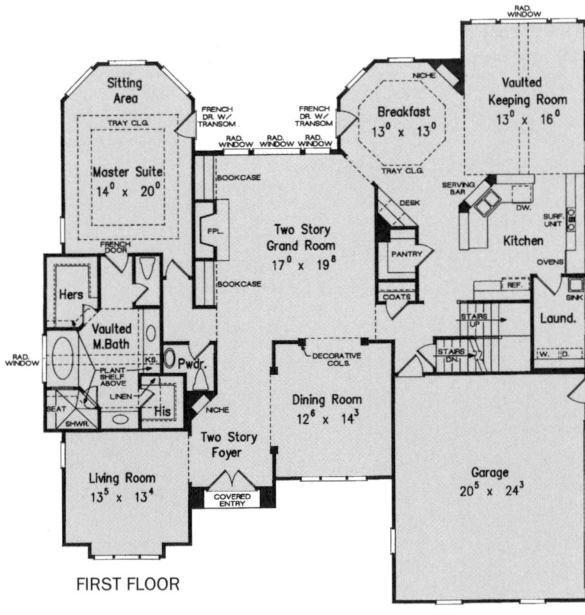

FIRST FLOOR

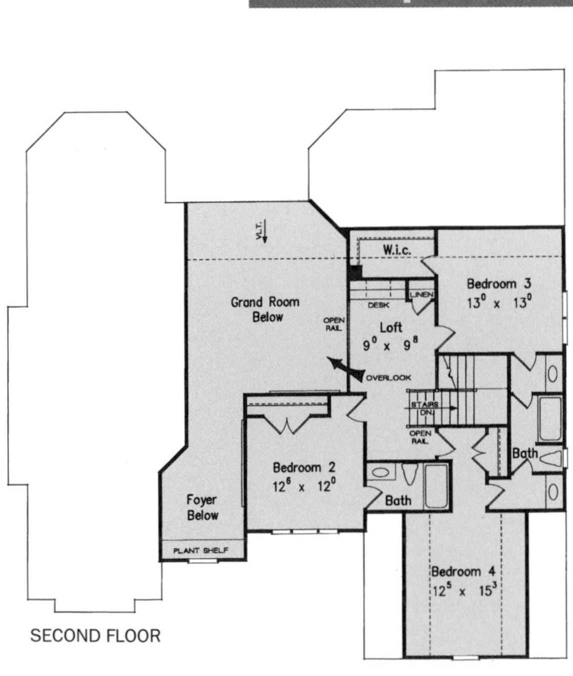

SECOND FLOOR

plan# HPK1700413

Style: Traditional
First Floor: 2,292 sq. ft.
Second Floor: 1,028 sq. ft.
Total: 3,320 sq. ft.
Bedrooms: 5
Bathrooms: 3½ + ½
Width: 68' - 0"
Depth: 56' - 6"
Foundation: Unfinished Basement

eplans.com

This majestic brick home fits new traditional neighborhoods perfectly, with an inviting front porch and a side-loading garage. Formal and flex rooms accommodate modern lifestyles and allow space for surfing online or even a home office. The foyer opens to the dining room and a study—or make it a guest bedroom. The gourmet kitchen boasts an island counter and opens to an old-fashioned keeping room that features a fireplace. The breakfast room offers a bay window to let the sunlight in and opens to an expansive deck. The master suite sports a tray ceiling and a bath that provides more than just a touch of luxury. Upstairs, two family bedrooms share a full bath; a guest bedroom features a private bath.

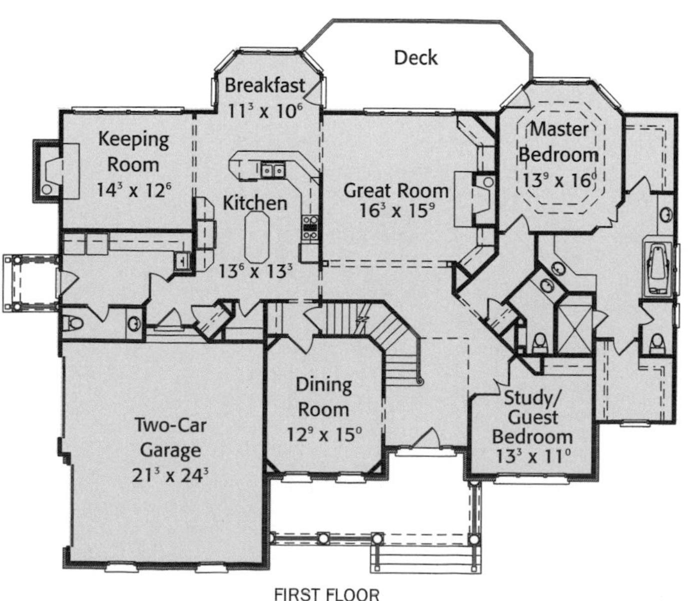

FIRST FLOOR

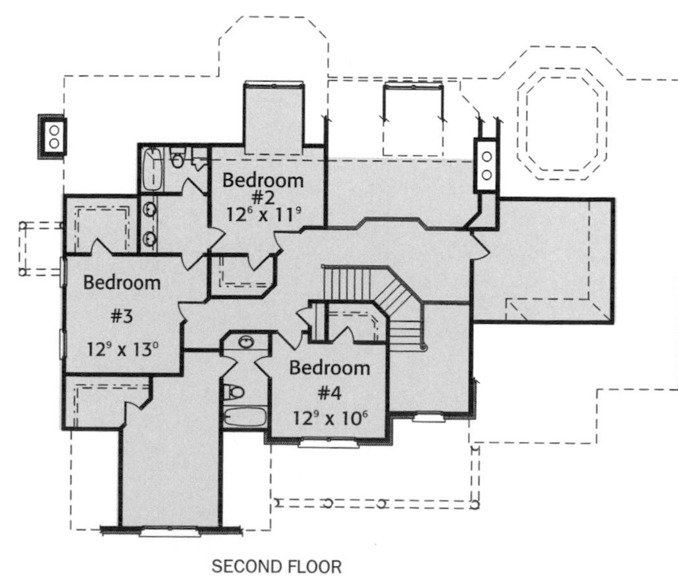

SECOND FLOOR

plan # HPK1700414

Style: Country Cottage
First Floor: 2,438 sq. ft.
Second Floor: 882 sq. ft.
Total: 3,320 sq. ft.
Bonus Space: 230 sq. ft.
Bedrooms: 4
Bathrooms: 4½
Width: 70' - 0"
Depth: 63' - 2"
Foundation: Slab, Unfinished Basement

eplans.com

Wonderful rooflines top a brick exterior with cedar and stone accents and lots of English Country charm. The two-story entry reveals a graceful curving staircase and opens to the formal living and dining rooms. Fireplaces are found in the living room as well as the great room, which also boasts built-in bookcases and access to the rear patio. The kitchen and breakfast room add to the informal area and include a snack bar. A private patio is part of the master suite, which also offers a lavish bath, a large walk-in closet, and a nearby study. Three family bedrooms and a bonus room complete the second floor.

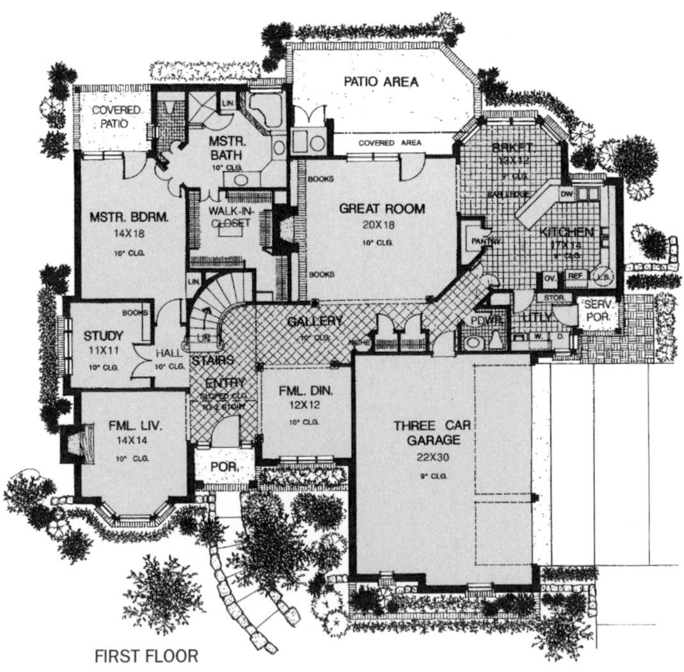

FIRST FLOOR

SECOND FLOOR

plan# HPK1700415

Style: SW Contemporary
First Floor: 2,401 sq. ft.
Second Floor: 927 sq. ft.
Total: 3,328 sq. ft.
Bedrooms: 4
Bathrooms: 3
Width: 104' - 9"
Depth: 62' - 5"
Foundation: Slab

eplans.com

Honored traditions are echoed throughout this warm and inviting Santa Fe home. A large, two-story gathering room with a beehive fireplace provides a soothing atmosphere for entertaining or quiet interludes. A gallery leads to the kitchen and breakfast area where abundant counter space and a work island will please the fussiest of cooks. A nearby laundry room provides entry to the three-car garage. On the right side of the plan, the master suite offers a private study, a fireplace, and a luxurious bath with dual lavatories, a whirlpool tub, and a curved shower. On the second floor, a reading loft with built-in bookshelves complements three family bedrooms.

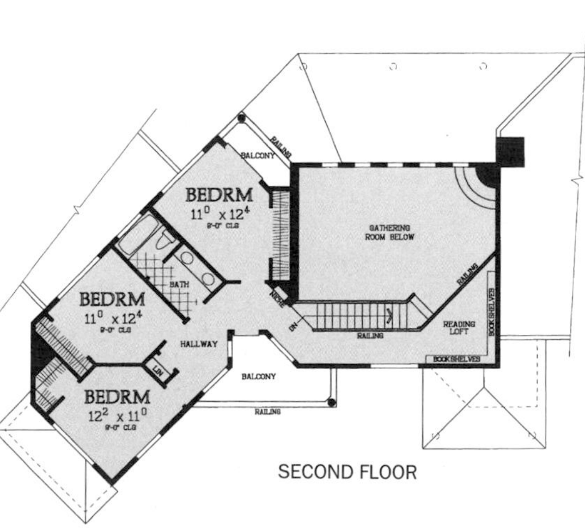

SECOND FLOOR

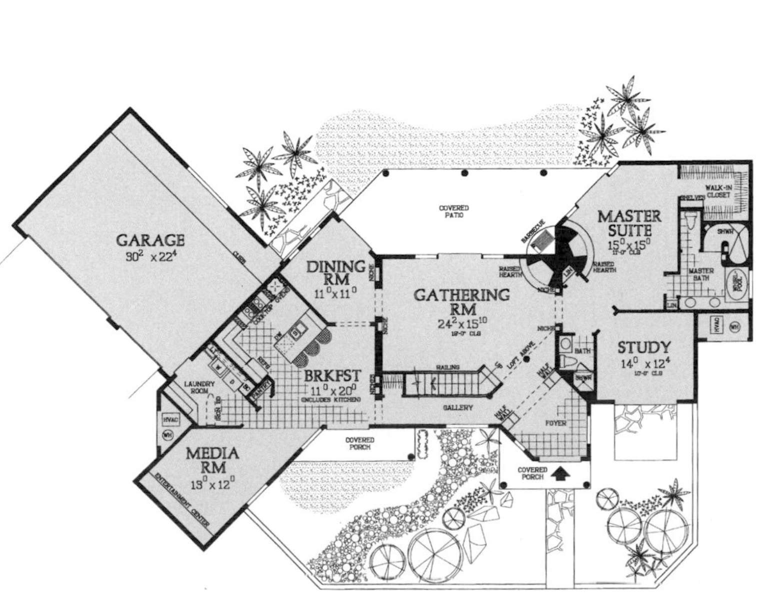

FIRST FLOOR

The elegant symmetry of this four-bedroom Southern traditional plan makes it a joy to own. Six columns frame the covered porch, and two chimneys add interest to the exterior roofline. The two-story foyer opens to the right to a formal living room with a built-in wet bar and a fireplace. A massive family room with a cathedral ceiling leads outside to a large covered patio or to the breakfast room and kitchen. A side-entry three-car garage provides room for a golf cart and separate workshop area. The first-floor master bedroom features vaulted ceilings, a secluded covered patio, and a plant ledge in the master bath. The three bedrooms upstairs share two baths.

plan # HPK1700416

- Style: Federal
- First Floor: 2,432 sq. ft.
- Second Floor: 903 sq. ft.
- Total: 3,335 sq. ft.
- Bedrooms: 4
- Bathrooms: 3½
- Width: 90' - 0"
- Depth: 53' - 10"
- Foundation: Crawlspace, Slab, Unfinished Basement

eplans.com

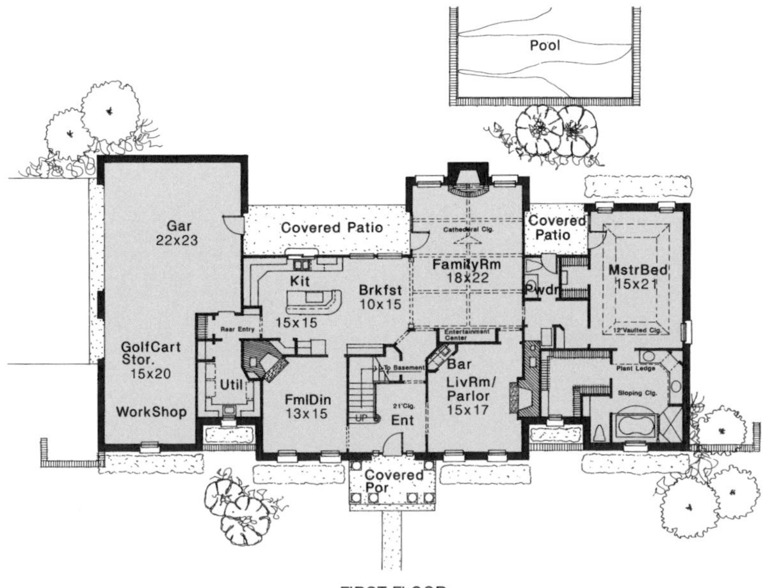

FIRST FLOOR

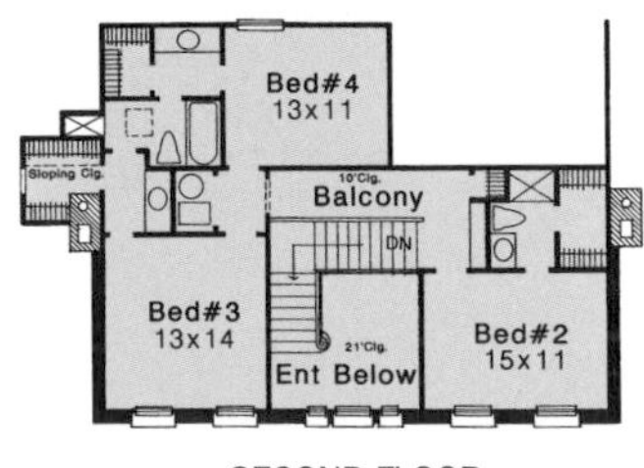

SECOND FLOOR

plan# HPK1700417

Style: Colonial
First Floor: 2,144 sq. ft.
Second Floor: 1,253 sq. ft.
Total: 3,397 sq. ft.
Bedrooms: 3
Bathrooms: 3½
Width: 64' - 11"
Depth: 76' - 7"

eplans.com

This two-story beauty is rich in luxurious style. A dramatic entrance welcomes you to the foyer, where a stunning curved staircase greets you. A turret-style dining room is flooded with light from the bayed windows. Across the gallery, the living room features a through-fireplace to the family room. The island kitchen is open to the breakfast room, which accesses the rear porch and the family room equipped with built-ins. The first-floor master bedroom offers a bath with a whirlpool tub, two walk-in closets, and a dressing room. Two additional bedrooms, a study, and a game room with sundeck access all reside on the second floor.

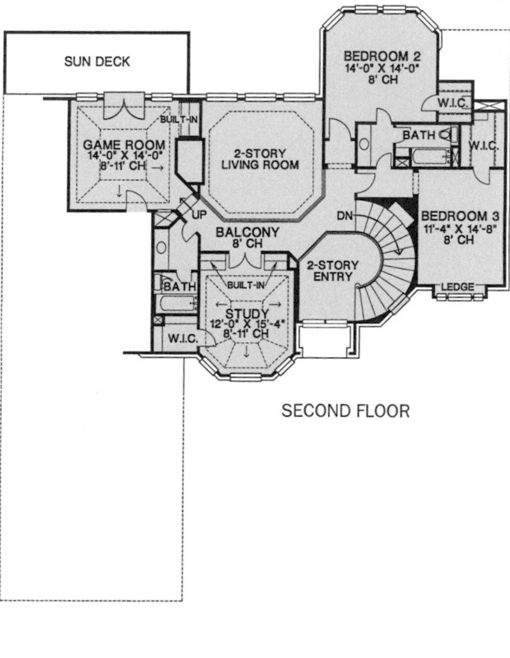

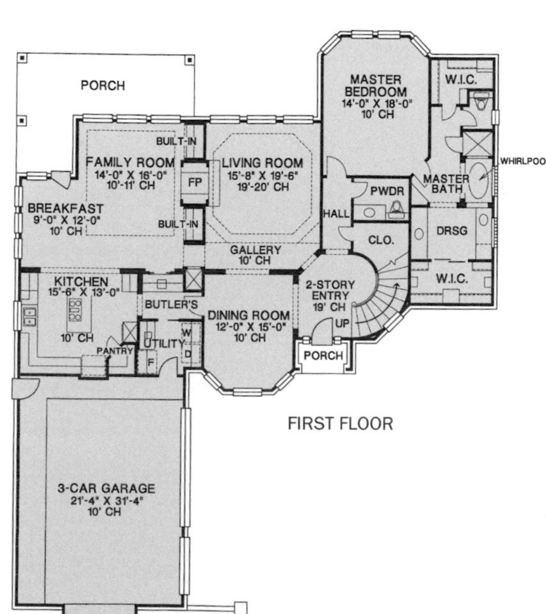

plan# HPK1700418

Style: French

First Floor: 2,216 sq. ft.

Second Floor: 1,192 sq. ft.

Total: 3,408 sq. ft.

Bonus Space: 458 sq. ft.

Bedrooms: 4

Bathrooms: 3½

Width: 67' - 10"

Depth: 56' - 10"

Foundation: Crawlspace

eplans.com

SECOND FLOOR

FIRST FLOOR

REAR EXTERIOR

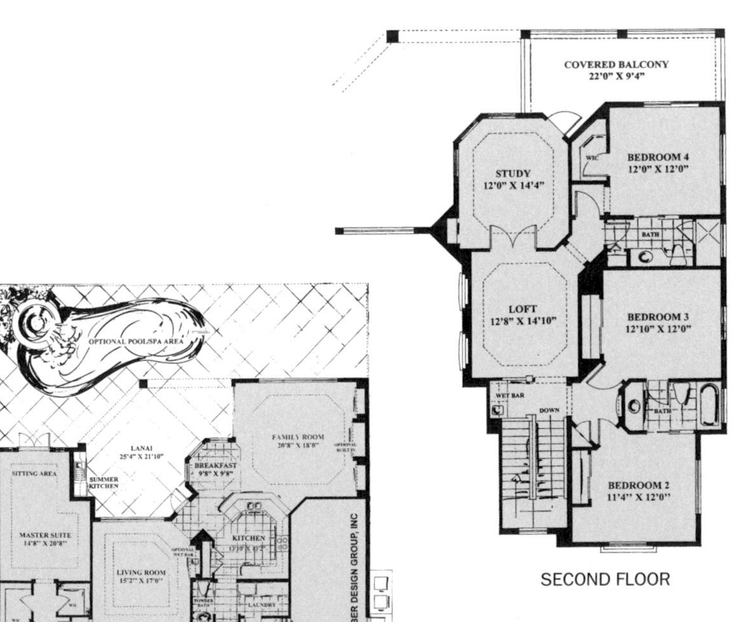

SECOND FLOOR

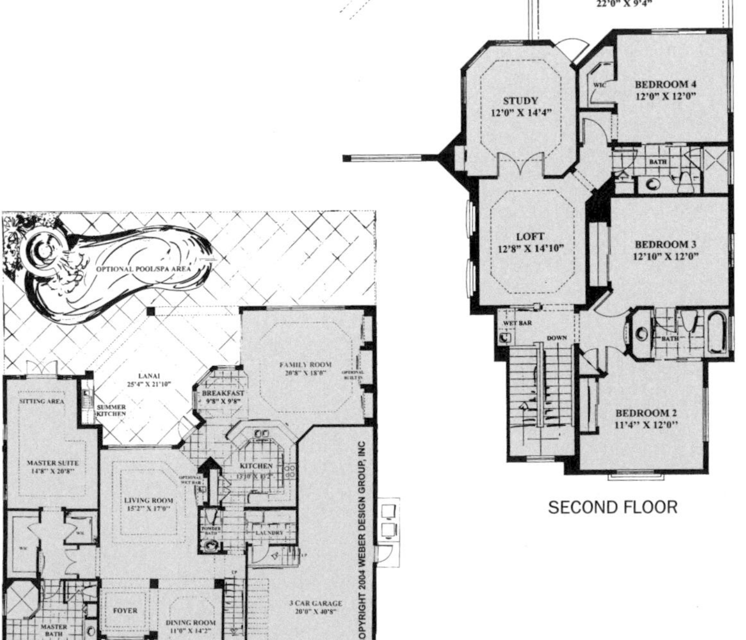

FIRST FLOOR

plan# HPK1700419

Style: Mediterranean

First Floor: 2,207 sq. ft.

Second Floor: 1,223 sq. ft.

Total: 3,430 sq. ft.

Bedrooms: 4

Bathrooms: 3½

Width: 60' - 0"

Depth: 75' - 0"

Foundation: Slab

eplans.com

plan # HPK1700420

Style: French
First Floor: 2,384 sq. ft.
Second Floor: 1,050 sq. ft.
Total: 3,434 sq. ft.
Bonus Space: 228 sq. ft.
Bedrooms: 4
Bathrooms: 3½
Width: 65' - 8"
Depth: 57' - 0"
Foundation: Crawlspace, Unfinished Walkout Basement

eplans.com

The covered front porch of this stucco home opens to a two-story foyer and one of two staircases. Arched openings lead into both the formal dining room and the vaulted living room. The efficient kitchen features a walk-in pantry, built-in desk, work island, and separate snack bar. Ncarby, the large breakfast area opens to the family room. Lavish in its amenities, the master suite offers a separate, vaulted sitting room with a fireplace, among other luxuries. Three bedrooms, along with optional bonus space and attic storage, are found on the second floor.

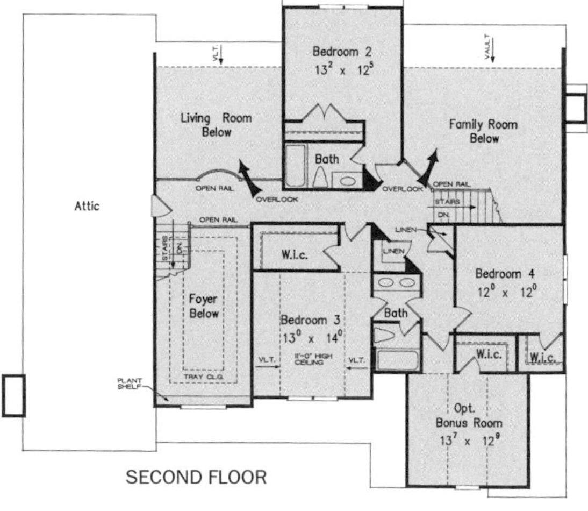

SECOND FLOOR

FIRST FLOOR

plan# HPK1700421

- Style: Farmhouse
- First Floor: 2,347 sq. ft.
- Second Floor: 1,087 sq. ft.
- Total: 3,434 sq. ft.
- Bedrooms: 4
- Bathrooms: 2½
- Width: 93' - 6"
- Depth: 61' - 0"
- Foundation: Unfinished Basement

eplans.com

Dutch-gable rooflines and a gabled wraparound porch provide an extra measure of farmhouse style. The foyer opens on the left to the study or guest bedroom that leads to the master suite. To the right is the formal dining room; the massive great room is in the center. The kitchen combines with the great room, the breakfast nook, and the dining room for entertaining options. The master suite includes access to the covered patio, a spacious walk-in closet, and a full bath with a whirlpool tub.

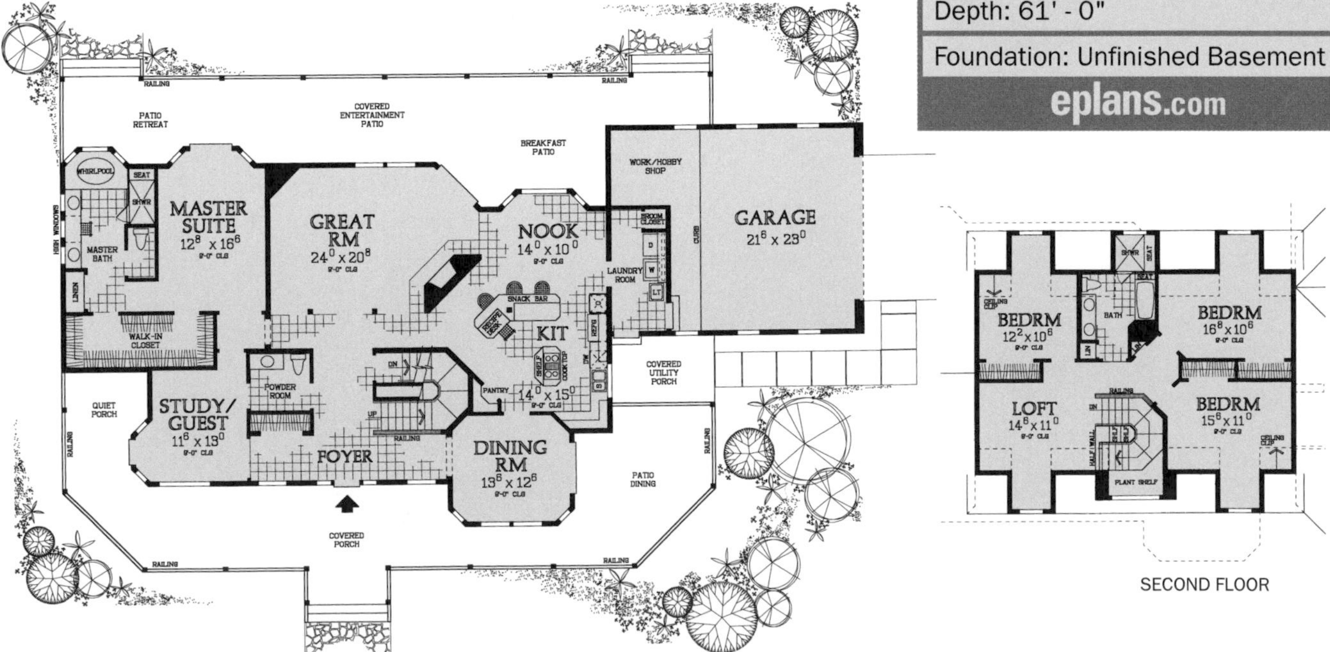

FIRST FLOOR

SECOND FLOOR

plan# HPK1700422

Style: French

First Floor: 2,479 sq. ft.

Second Floor: 956 sq. ft.

Total: 3,435 sq. ft.

Bedrooms: 4

Bathrooms: 3½

Width: 67' - 6"

Depth: 75' - 6"

Foundation: Unfinished Walkout Basement

eplans.com

Rich with Old World elements, this English Country manor steps sweetly into the future with great rooms and splendid outdoor spaces. Varied window treatments define this elegant facade, enhanced by a massive stone turret. A leaded-glass paneled door with sidelights leads to a gallery-style foyer. Grand interior vistas are provided by a soaring triple window capped with an arch-top transom. The living arca leads to the breakfast bay and gourmet kitchen. This culinary paradise features a food-preparation island and a peninsula snack counter. Double doors open to a quiet library with a turret-style bay window. The master retreat boasts views of the secluded side property.

FIRST FLOOR

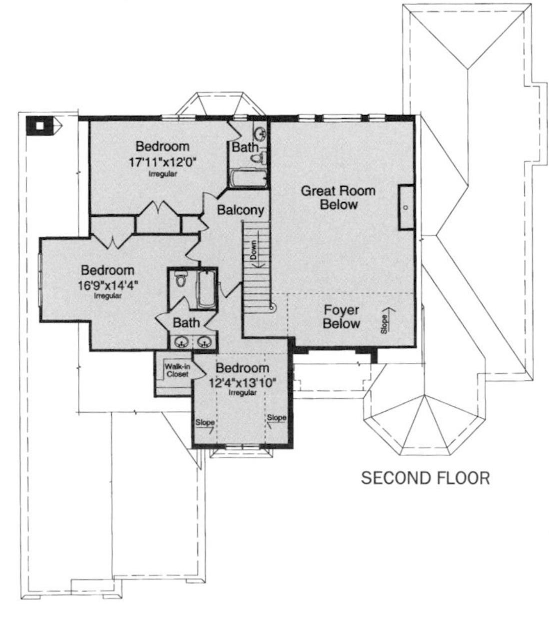

SECOND FLOOR

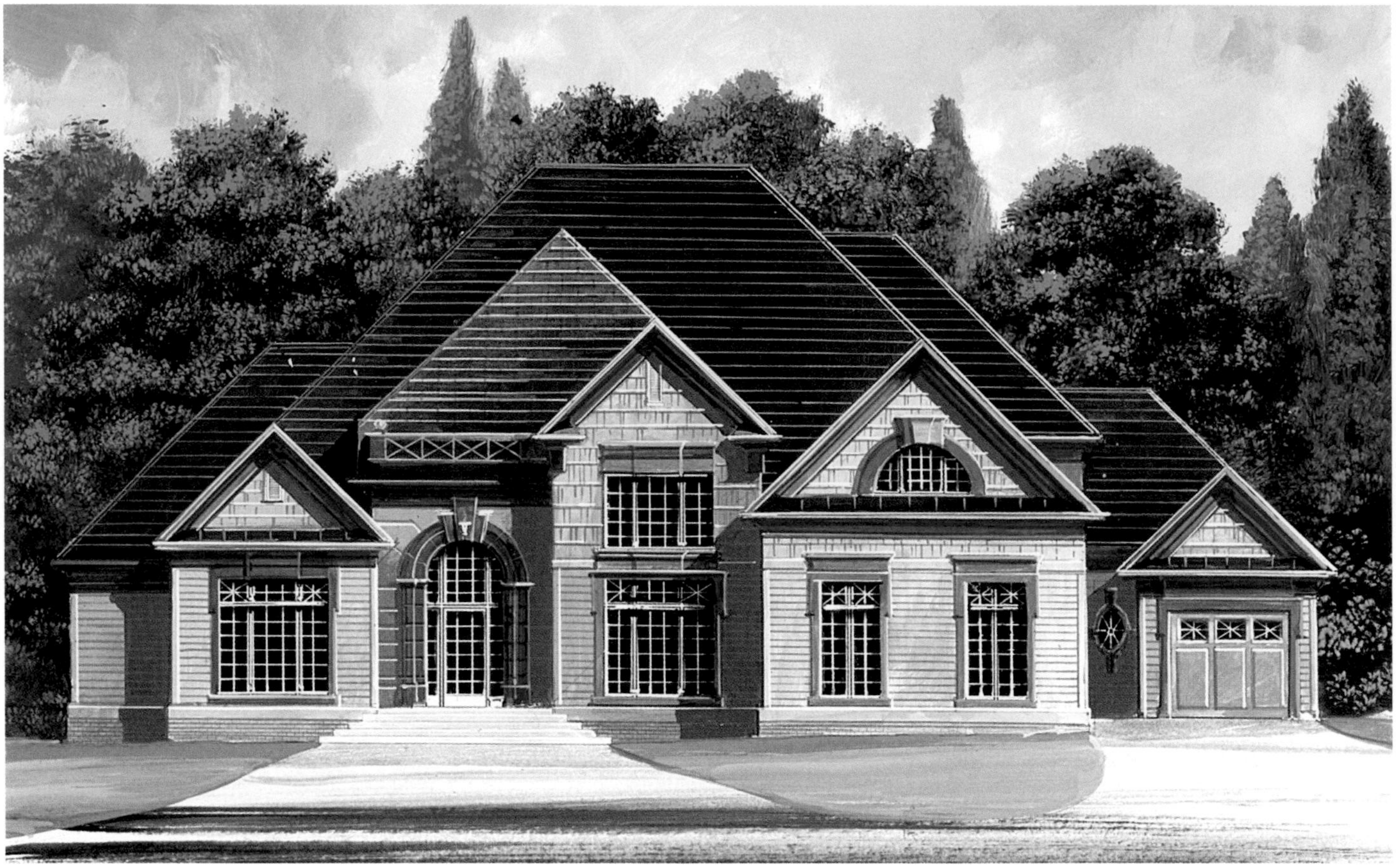

Multiple gables and tall windows adorn the front of the design. Inside, the foyer receives a voluptuous stairway and opens to the parlor. Toward the back of the plan, an airy and well-lit great room features a large fireplace. To the right, a keeping room and breakast nook attend an island kitchen. In addition to the smart layout, a built-in pantry will please the family cook. Much of the first floor has been reserved for the luxurious master suite and bath. The design takes advantage of corner angles to tuck away the bath, shower, vanities, and compartmented toilet. Upstairs, three bedrooms share two full baths. A fourth space has been reserved for a study, which opens onto a balcony.

plan # HPK1700423

Style: Traditional

First Floor: 2,299 sq. ft.

Second Floor: 1,137 sq. ft.

Total: 3,436 sq. ft.

Bedrooms: 4

Bathrooms: 3½

Width: 85' - 0"

Depth: 48' - 0"

Foundation: Unfinished Basement

eplans.com

FIRST FLOOR

SECOND FLOOR

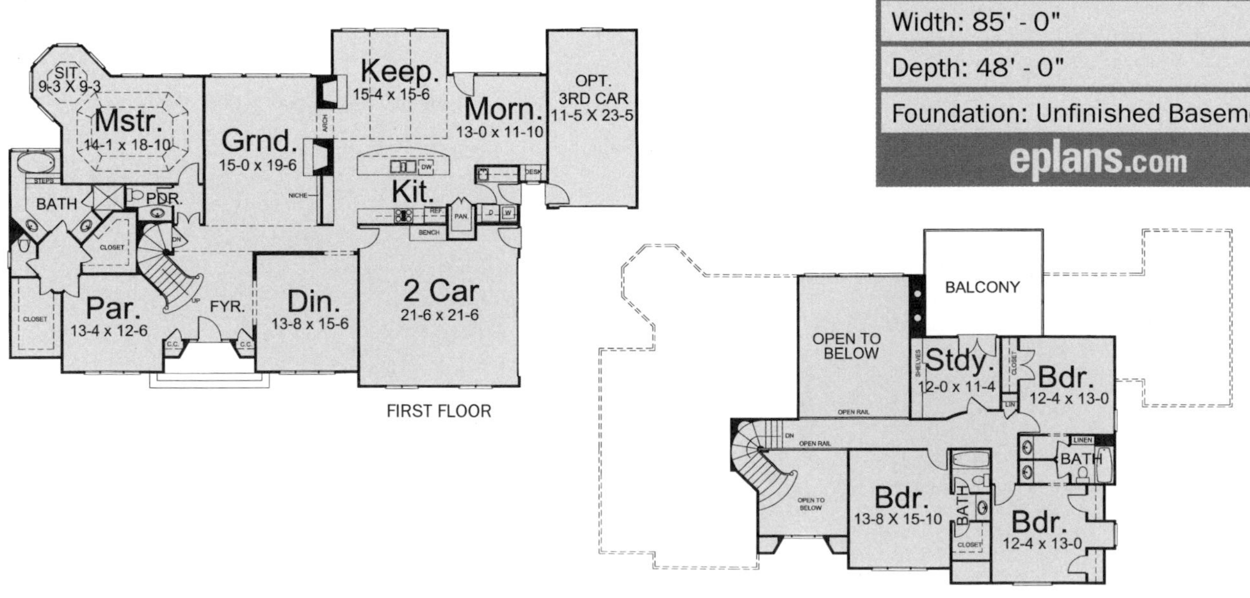

plan # HPK1700424

Style: Traditional
First Floor: 1,998 sq. ft.
Second Floor: 1,442 sq. ft.
Total: 3,440 sq. ft.
Bedrooms: 4
Bathrooms: 4
Width: 61' - 8"
Depth: 51' - 2"
Foundation: Finished Walkout Basement

eplans.com

A full-height portico with an enormous, multipaned window on the second floor, and a glass door and a Palladian window fronting the living room are all handsomely set in a stucco facade. An impressive entrance is formed by the convergence of the living room, dining room, staircase, and front hallway leading to the gathering room, with a view beyond to the fireplace and rear deck. The gathering room shares space with the kitchen and breakfast area, which also contains a convenient butler's pantry. The laundry and access to the garage are located off of the kitchen area. The master suite takes up much of the floor plan upstairs, with two family bedrooms and attic space. A living basement provides for a recreation room, powder room, covered patio, and unfinished storage area.

SECOND FLOOR

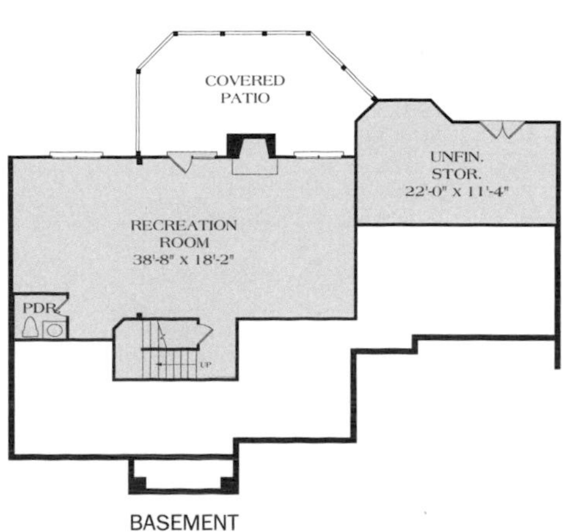

BASEMENT

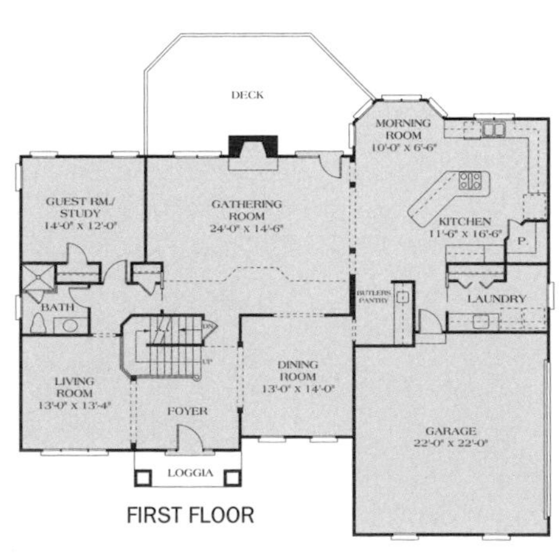

FIRST FLOOR

plan# HPK1700425

Style: Federal

First Floor: 2,558 sq. ft.

Second Floor: 884 sq. ft.

Total: 3,442 sq. ft.

Bedrooms: 4

Bathrooms: 3½

Width: 73' - 1"

Depth: 64' - 3"

Foundation: Unfinished Walkout Basement

eplans.com

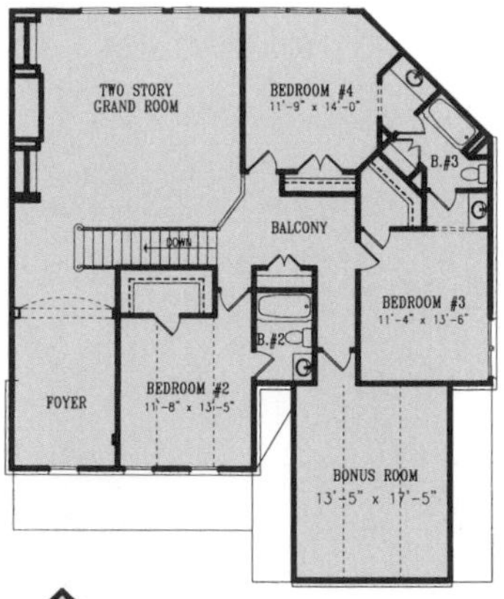

SECOND FLOOR

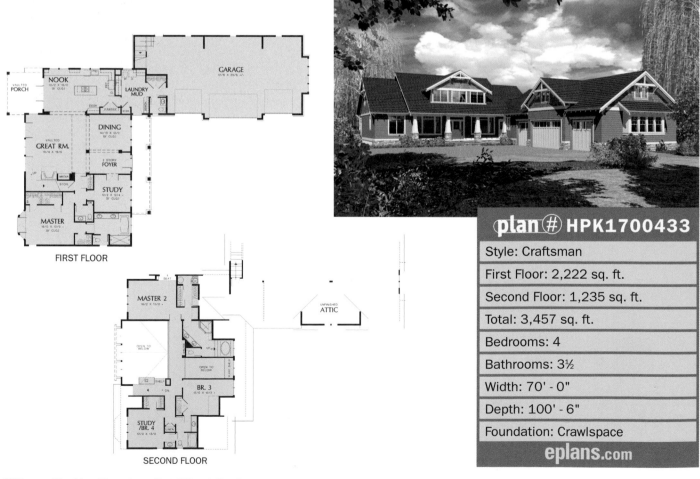

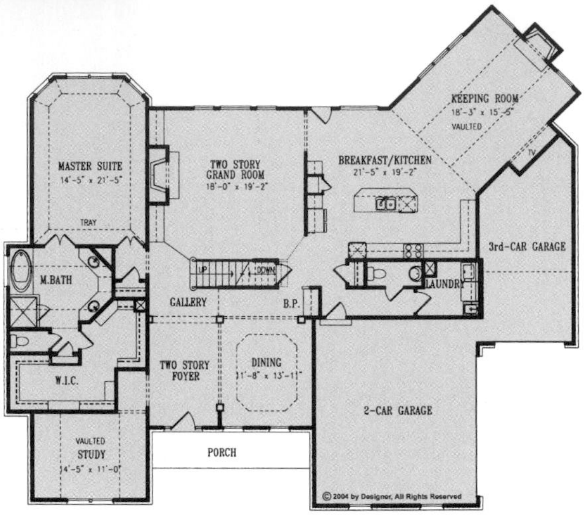

FIRST FLOOR

FIRST FLOOR

SECOND FLOOR

plan# HPK1700433

Style: Craftsman

First Floor: 2,222 sq. ft.

Second Floor: 1,235 sq. ft.

Total: 3,457 sq. ft.

Bedrooms: 4

Bathrooms: 3½

Width: 70' - 0"

Depth: 100' - 6"

Foundation: Crawlspace

eplans.com

plan# HPK1700434

Style: French
First Floor: 1,920 sq. ft.
Second Floor: 1,552 sq. ft.
Total: 3,472 sq. ft.
Bonus Space: 252 sq. ft.
Bedrooms: 3
Bathrooms: 4
Width: 72' - 0"
Depth: 55' - 0"
Foundation: Crawlspace

eplans.com

This stucco exterior with shutters and keystone lintels over the entry and windows lends a fresh European charm to this four-bedroom home. A great area for formal entertaining, the two-story living room pleases with its columns, large windows and fireplace. A wet bar furthers the ambience here. Double doors open to a terrace. Informal living takes off in the breakfast nook, kitchen and family room. The upstairs master suite enjoys lots of privacy and a luxurious bath with twin-vanity sinks, a walk-in closet, spa tub and separate shower. The second-floor stairway is exquisite, with three flights joining into one landing and space for plants.

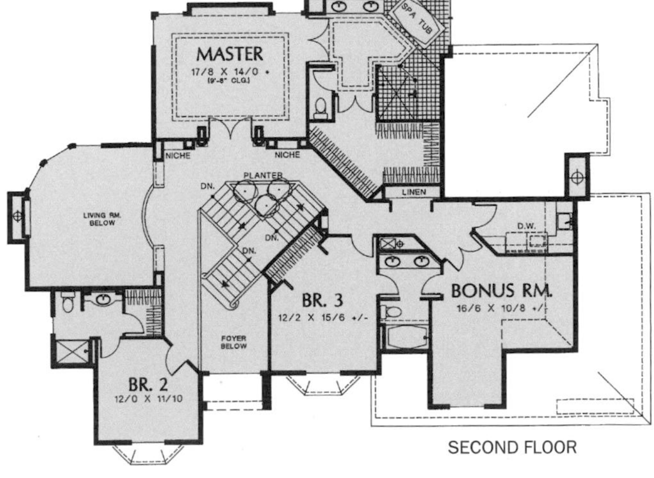

SECOND FLOOR

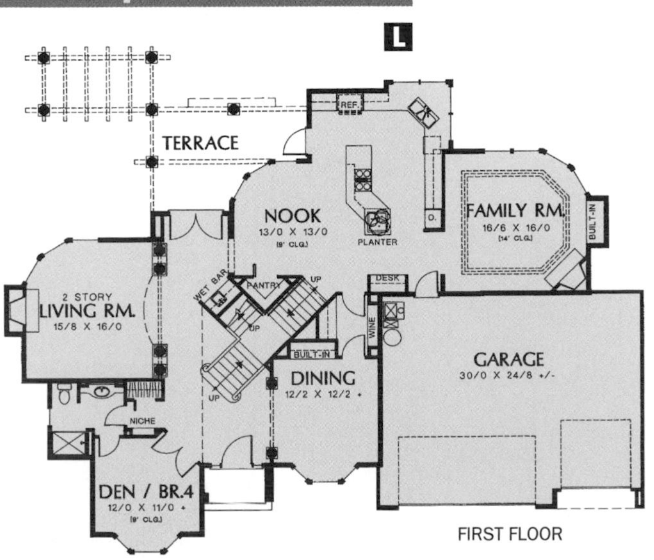

FIRST FLOOR

plan# HPK1700426

Style: Traditional
First Floor: 2,302 sq. ft.
Second Floor: 1,177 sq. ft.
Total: 3,479 sq. ft.
Bedrooms: 4
Bathrooms: 2½
Width: 70' - 0"
Depth: 51' - 0"
Foundation: Walkout Basement
eplans.com

Classic quoins set off a stately pediment on this noble brick exterior. The heart of this home is the great room, which offers a focal-point fireplace and a private door to the rear deck. The formal living room opens from the foyer and features its own hearth. A corner master suite boasts a lavish bath with a spa tub, as well as a bay window and a door to the rear deck. Upstairs, three additional bedrooms enjoy a balcony hall with overlooks to the foyer and to the great room, and share a full bath. This home is designed with a basement foundation.

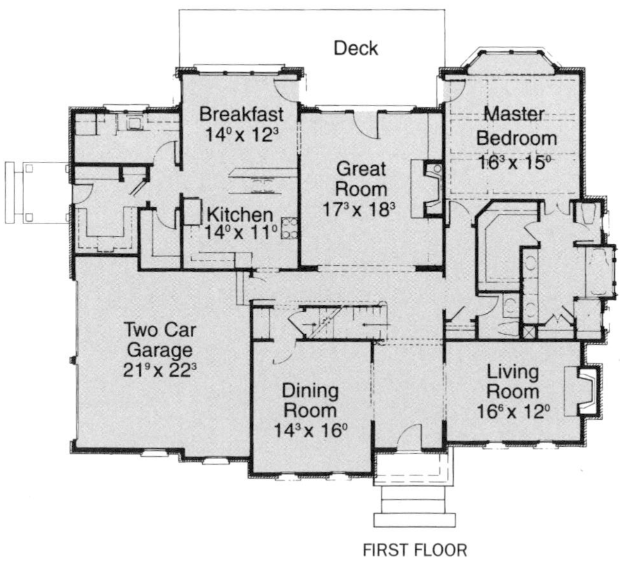

FIRST FLOOR

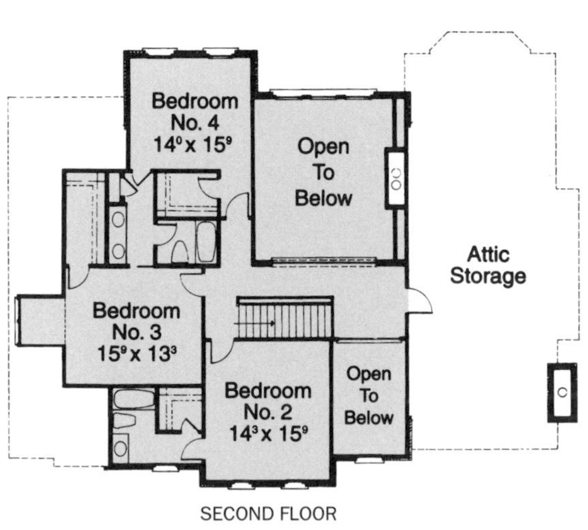

SECOND FLOOR

plan# HPK1700427
Style: Traditional
First Floor: 2,514 sq. ft.
Second Floor: 975 sq. ft.
Total: 3,489 sq. ft.
Bedrooms: 4
Bathrooms: 3½
Width: 74' - 8"
Depth: 64' - 8"
Foundation: Unfinished Basement
eplans.com

You are sure to fall in love with what this traditional French Country two-story design has to offer. The great room hosts a fireplace surrounded by built-in cabinets, a two-story ceiling, and striking arched windows. The study will provide you with a corner of the house to yourself with a view out the front and side. The master bedroom enjoys plenty of space and walk-in closets. The master bathroom features a welcoming arch over the bathtub and large shower.

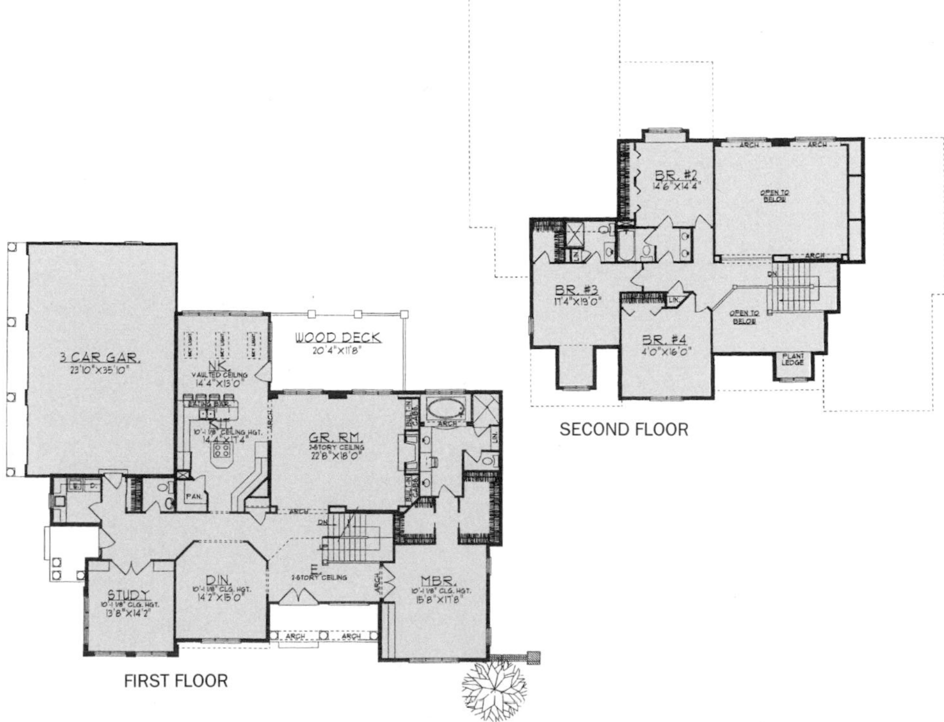

SECOND FLOOR

FIRST FLOOR

While speaking clearly of the past, the inside of this Victorian home coincides with the open, flowing interiors of today. Dine in the elegant dining room with its tray ceiling, or move through the double French doors between the formal living room and informal family room to sense the livability of this charming home. The kitchen boasts a large pantry and a corner sink with a window. The lovely master suite resides upstairs. The raised sitting area off the master bedroom provides the owner with a miniretreat for reading and relaxing. The second floor also includes two large bedrooms and a library/music room.

plan# HPK1700428

Style: Victorian
First Floor: 1,329 sq. ft.
Second Floor: 1,917 sq. ft.
Third Floor: 189 sq. ft.
Total: 3,435 sq. ft.
Bedrooms: 3
Bathrooms: 2½
Width: 40' - 4"
Depth: 62' - 0"
Foundation: Slab

eplans.com

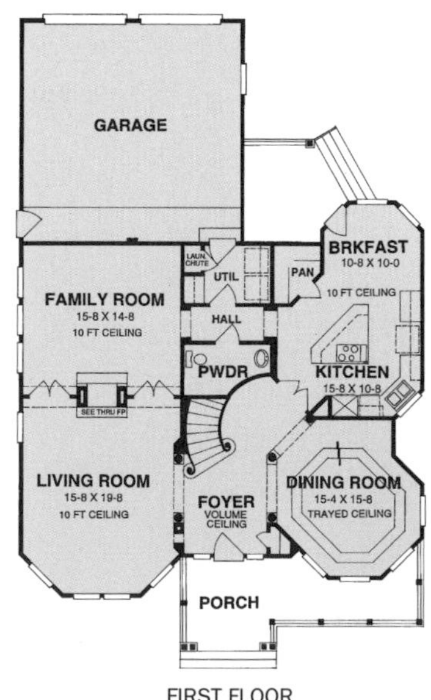

FIRST FLOOR

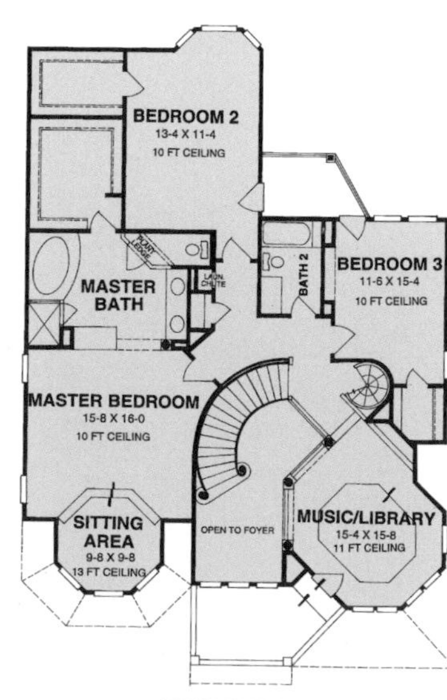

SECOND FLOOR

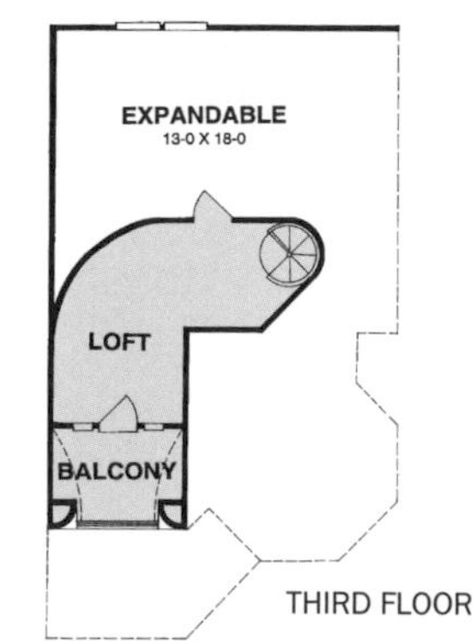

THIRD FLOOR

plan# HPK1700429

Style: Bungalow
Main Level: 2,160 sq. ft.
Lower Level: 919 sq. ft.
Total: 3,079 sq. ft.
Bedrooms: 3
Bathrooms: 2½
Width: 68' - 3"
Depth: 60' - 11"
Foundation: Finished Basement

eplans.com

An eye-catching shed dormer is both lovely and functional, bringing light into the foyer. A mud room is the perfect casual entry off the garage, right next to the main-level laundry and optional third-car garage. The open kitchen works with the keeping, breakfast, and grand rooms. A study—or living room—and formal dining room flank the foyer for entertaining guests.

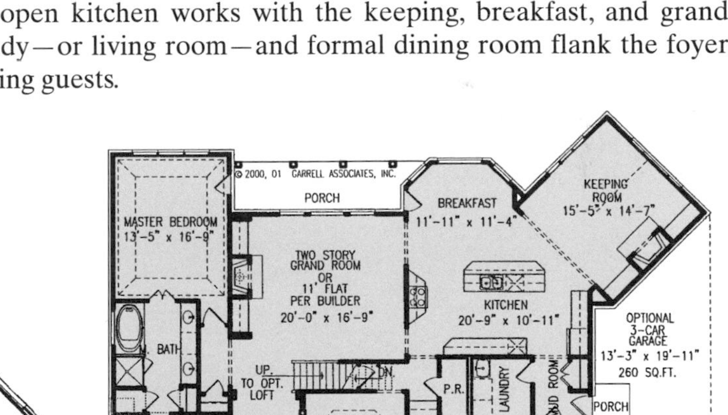

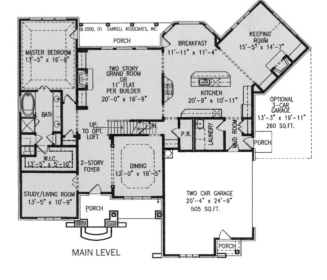

MAIN LEVEL

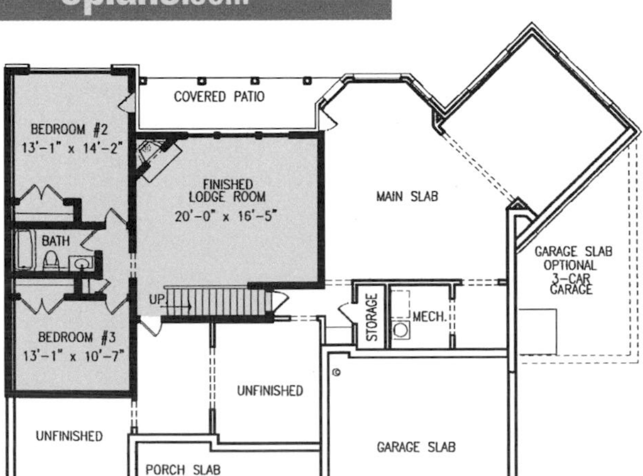

LOWER LEVEL

plan# HPK1700430

Style: Craftsman
Main Level: 2,170 sq. ft.
Lower Level: 1,076 sq. ft.
Total: 3,246 sq. ft.
Bedrooms: 3
Bathrooms: 2½
Width: 74' - 0"
Depth: 54' - 0"
Foundation: Slab, Finished Walkout Basement

eplans.com

Perfect for a sloping lot, this Craftsman design boasts two levels of living space. Plenty of special amenities—vaulted ceilings in the living, dining, and family rooms, as well as in the master bedroom; built-ins in the family room and den; a large island cooktop in the kitchen; and an expansive rear deck—make this plan stand out. All three of the bedrooms—a main-level master suite and two lower-level bedrooms—include walk-in closets. Also on the lower level, find a recreation room with built-ins and a fireplace.

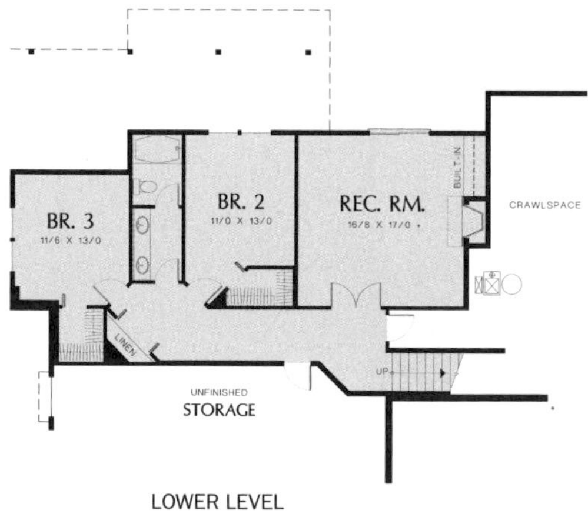

LOWER LEVEL

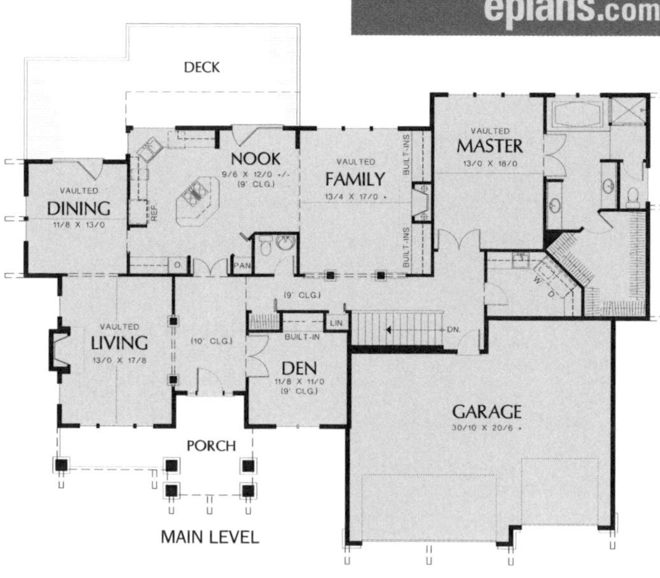

MAIN LEVEL

plan # HPK1700431

Style: Bungalow

Main Level: 1,920 sq. ft.

Lower Level: 1,400 sq. ft.

Total: 3,320 sq. ft.

Bedrooms: 3

Bathrooms: 2½

Width: 69' - 8"

Depth: 56' - 4"

Foundation: Finished Walkout Basement

eplans.com

Elegant hipped and gabled rooflines dress up this country bungalow design. A copper-topped bay window enhances the roomy first-floor study just off the foyer. A full bath with compartmented toilet, separate shower and tub, and a walk-in closet outfit the nearby master suite. Modern convenience places the spacious kitchen, dining bay, hearth room, and great room within a few steps of each other. A beautiful see-through fireplace defines the space between the hearth and great rooms. A lower level opens to the rear property to take advantage of a sloped lot. Two family bedrooms, full bath, large family room, adjoining game room, and plenty of storage complete this level.

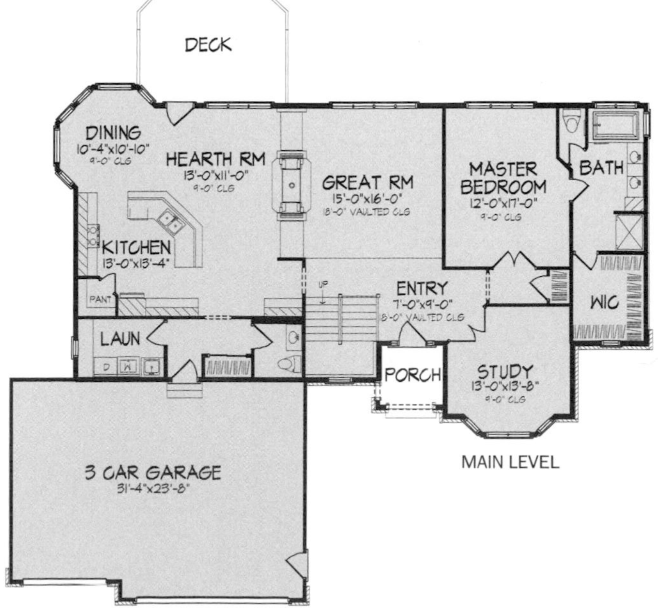

MAIN LEVEL

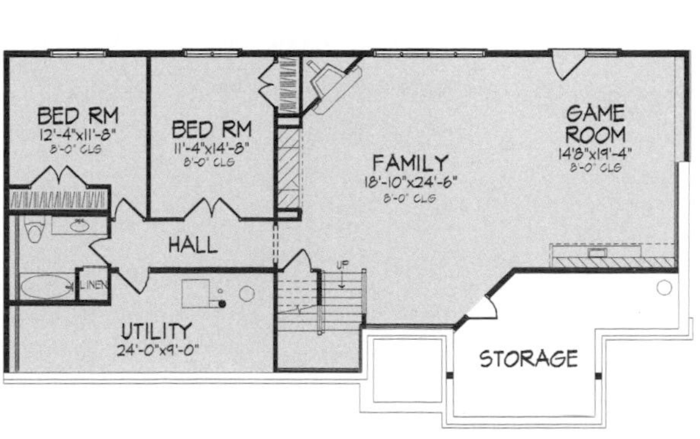

LOWER LEVEL

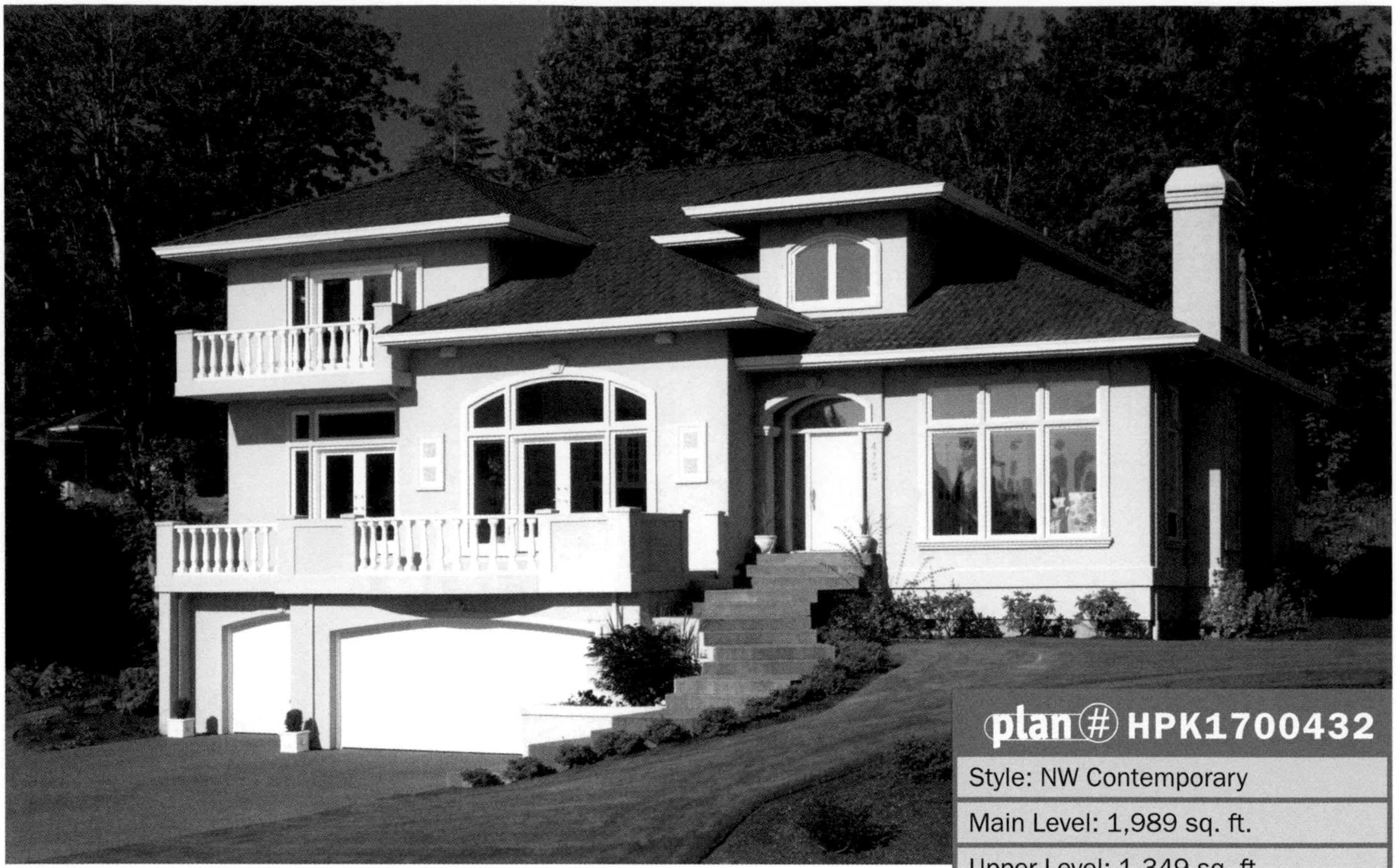

plan# HPK1700432

- Style: NW Contemporary
- Main Level: 1,989 sq. ft.
- Upper Level: 1,349 sq. ft.
- Second Level: 1,349 sq. ft.
- Lower Level: 105 sq. ft.
- Total: 3,443 sq. ft.
- Bonus Space: 487 sq. ft.
- Bedrooms: 3
- Bathrooms: 2½
- Width: 63' - 0"
- Depth: 48' - 0"
- Foundation: Finished Walkout Basement

eplans.com

Dramatic balconies and spectacular window treatments enhance this stunning luxury home. Inside, a through-fireplace warms the formal living room and a restful den. Both living spaces open to a balcony that invites quiet reflection on starry nights. The banquet-sized dining room is easily served from the adjacent kitchen. Here, space is shared with an eating nook that provides access to the rear grounds and a family room with a corner fireplace—perfect for casual gatherings. The upper level contains two family bedrooms and a luxurious master suite that enjoys its own private balcony. The basement accommodates a shop and a bonus room for future development.

MAIN LEVEL

LOWER LEVEL

UPPER LEVEL

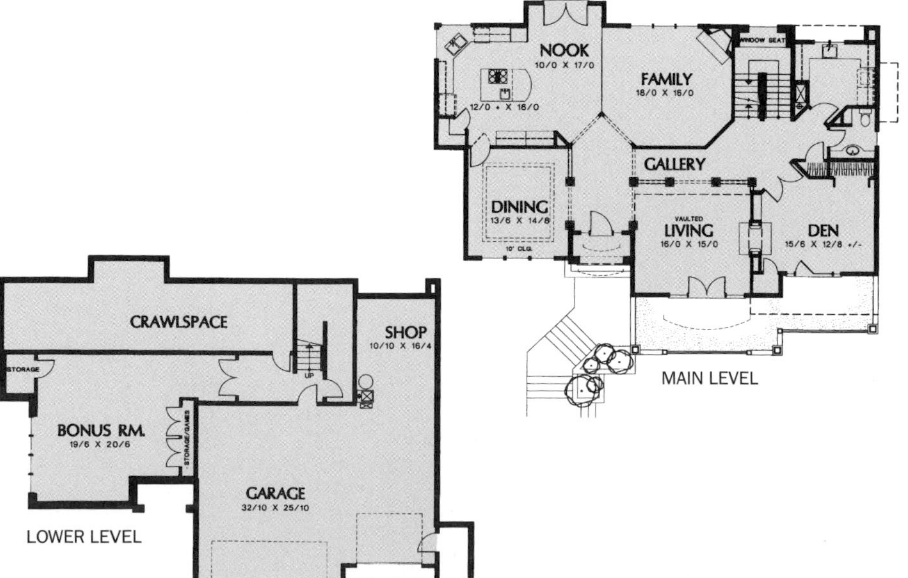

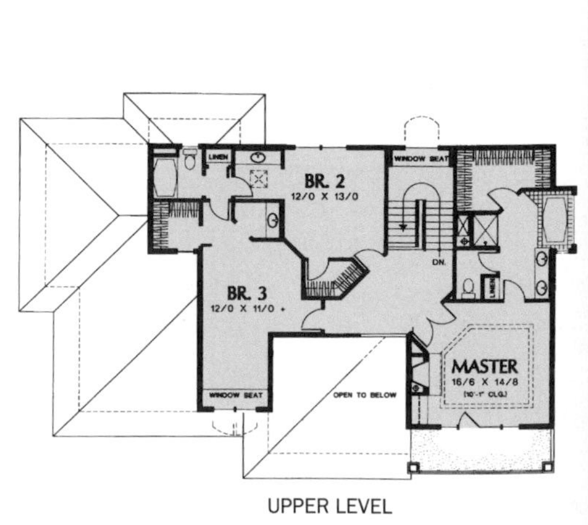

Homes From 3,500 to 3,999 Square Feet

This cottage-style home looks as if it was nestled in the French countryside. The combination of brick, stone, and rough cedar, and multiple chimneys add to the charm of the facade. See plan HPK1700461 on page 394.

plan# HPK1700435
Style: Traditional
Square Footage: 3,504
Bedrooms: 4
Bathrooms: 3½
Width: 93' - 4"
Depth: 61' - 7"
Foundation: Slab
eplans.com

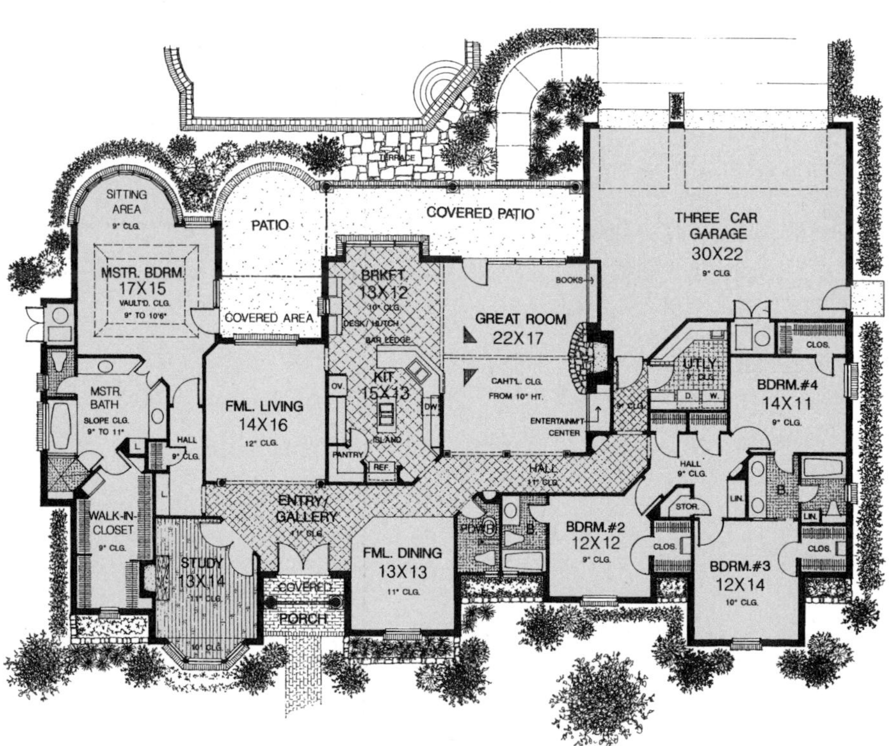

This sprawling one-story charmer offers lots of space for luxurious living and refined entertaining. Formal living and dining rooms, a magnificent great room with an inviting fireplace, and two rear patios will make all your guests feel relaxed. A delightful kitchen with a sunlit breakfast nook, a study, and four bedrooms—one a dream-come-true master suite—will win the heart of your family. A large utility and laundry room is off the rear-loading three-car garage.

plan# HPK1700436

Style: Contemporary
Square Footage: 3,556
Bedrooms: 4
Bathrooms: 3½
Width: 85' - 0"
Depth: 85' - 0"
Foundation: Slab

eplans.com

A beautiful curved portico provides a majestic entrance to this one-story home. To the left of the foyer is a den/bedroom with a private bath, ideal for use as a guest suite. The exquisite master suite features a see-through fireplace and an exercise area with a wet bar. The family wing is geared for casual living with a powder room/patio bath, a huge island kitchen with a walk-in pantry, a glass-walled breakfast nook, and a grand family room with a fireplace and media wall. Two family bedrooms share a private bath.

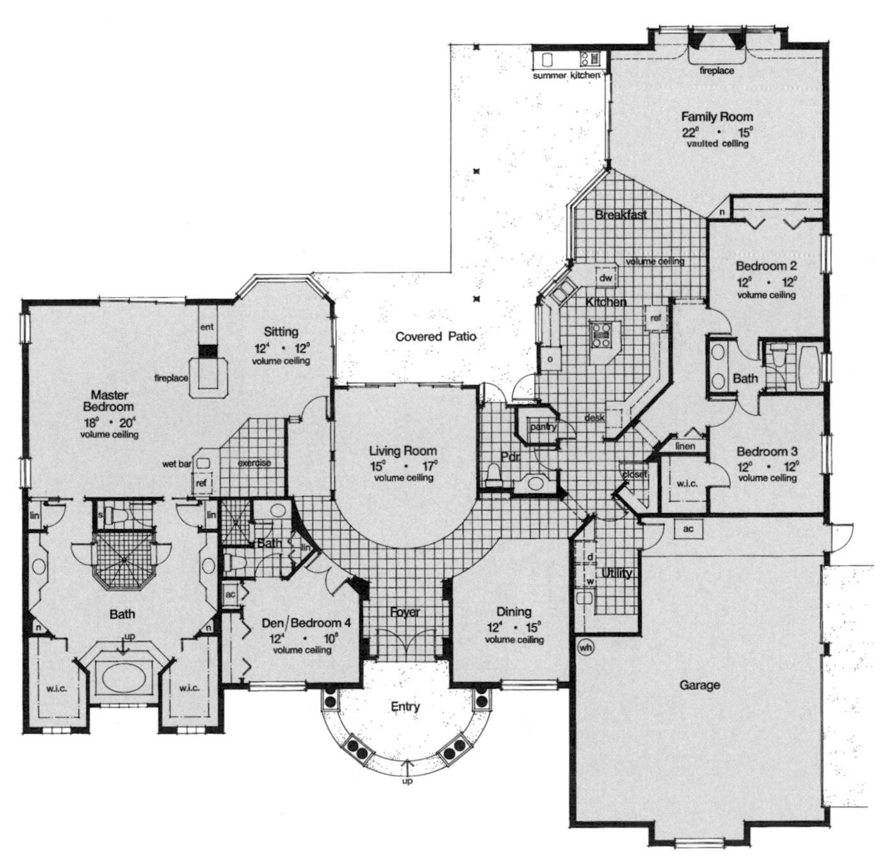

plan # HPK1700437

Style: Mediterranean
Square Footage: 3,566
Bedrooms: 3
Bathrooms: 2½
Width: 88' - 0"
Depth: 70' - 8"
Foundation: Unfinished Walkout Basement

eplans.com

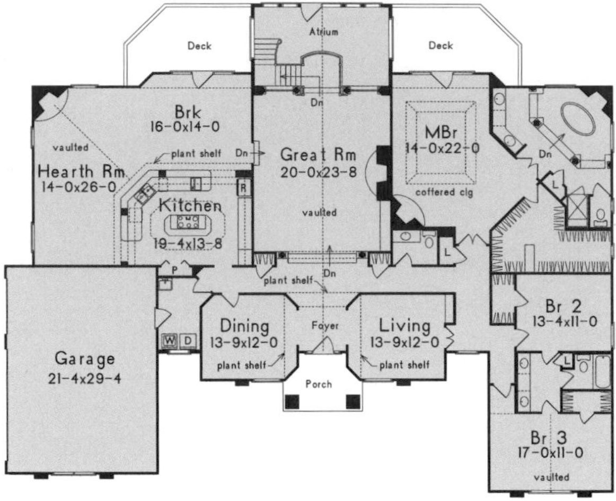

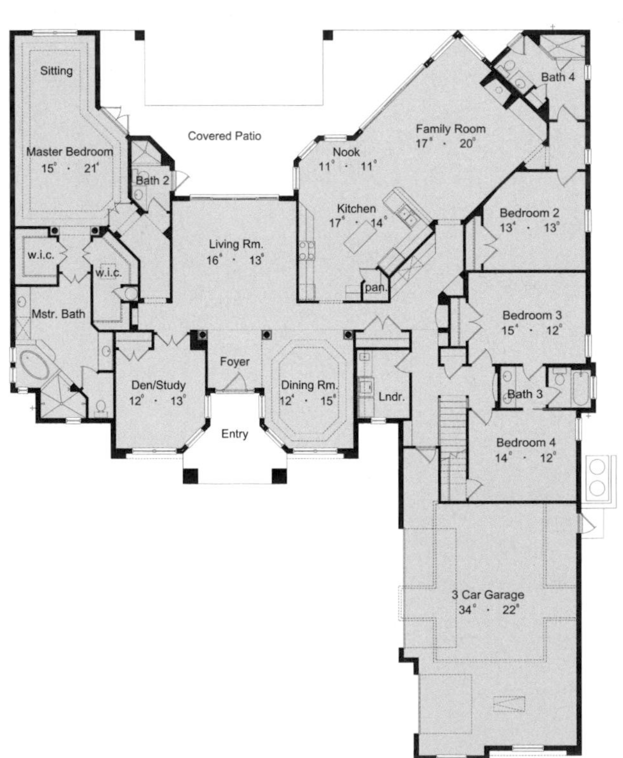

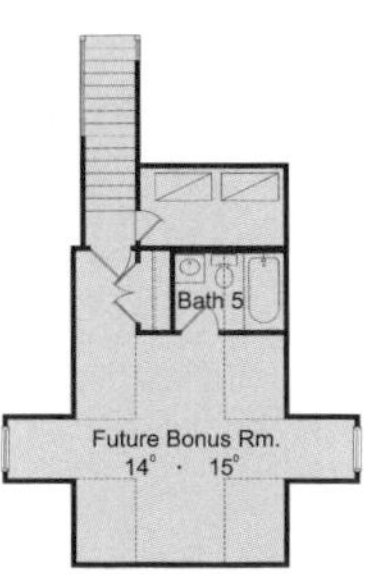

plan # HPK1700438

Style: Italianate
Square Footage: 3,589
Bonus Space: 430 sq. ft.
Bedrooms: 4
Bathrooms: 4
Width: 76' - 0"
Depth: 98' - 0"
Foundation: Slab

eplans.com

plan# HPK1700439

Style: Craftsman
Square Footage: 3,615
Basement: 2,803 sq. ft.
Bedrooms: 2
Bathrooms: 2½
Width: 98' - 0"
Depth: 94' - 0"
Foundation: Finished Basement

eplans.com

A combination of stone, siding, and multiple rooflines creates a cottage feel to this large home. Inside, the master suite opens from a short hallway and enjoys a private fireplace, access to the rear covered porch, a spacious walk-in closet, compartmented toilet, separate shower, garden tub, and dual vanitics. The gourmet kitchen enjoys an island cooktop, snack bar, access to the covered porch, and conveniently serves the adjoining dining room and lodge room. Two additional family bedrooms share a full bath in the basement and a guest suite is located upstairs near the front door.

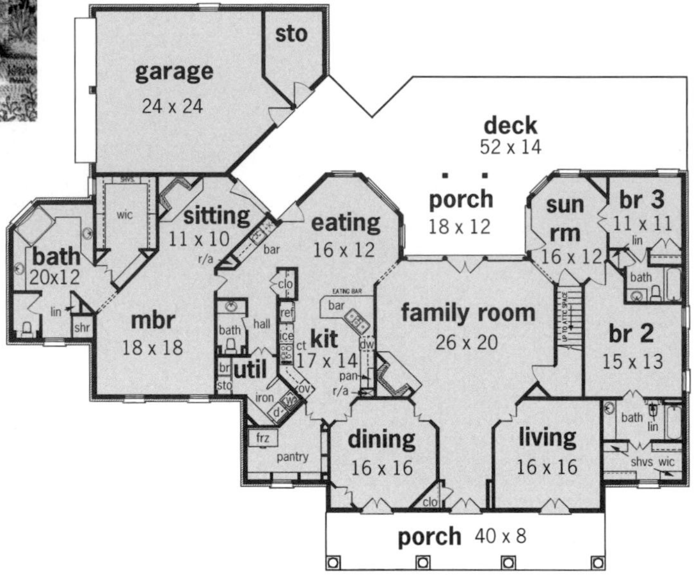

plan# HPK1700440

Style: Southern Colonial
Square Footage: 3,623
Bedrooms: 3
Bathrooms: 3½
Width: 98' - 0"
Depth: 80' - 0"
Foundation: Crawlspace, Slab

eplans.com

REAR EXTERIOR

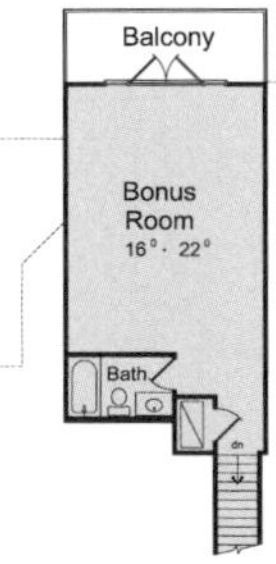

plan# HPK1700441

Style: French
Square Footage: 3,723
Bonus Space: 390 sq. ft.
Bedrooms: 5
Bathrooms: 4
Width: 82' - 4"
Depth: 89' - 0"
Foundation: Slab

eplans.com

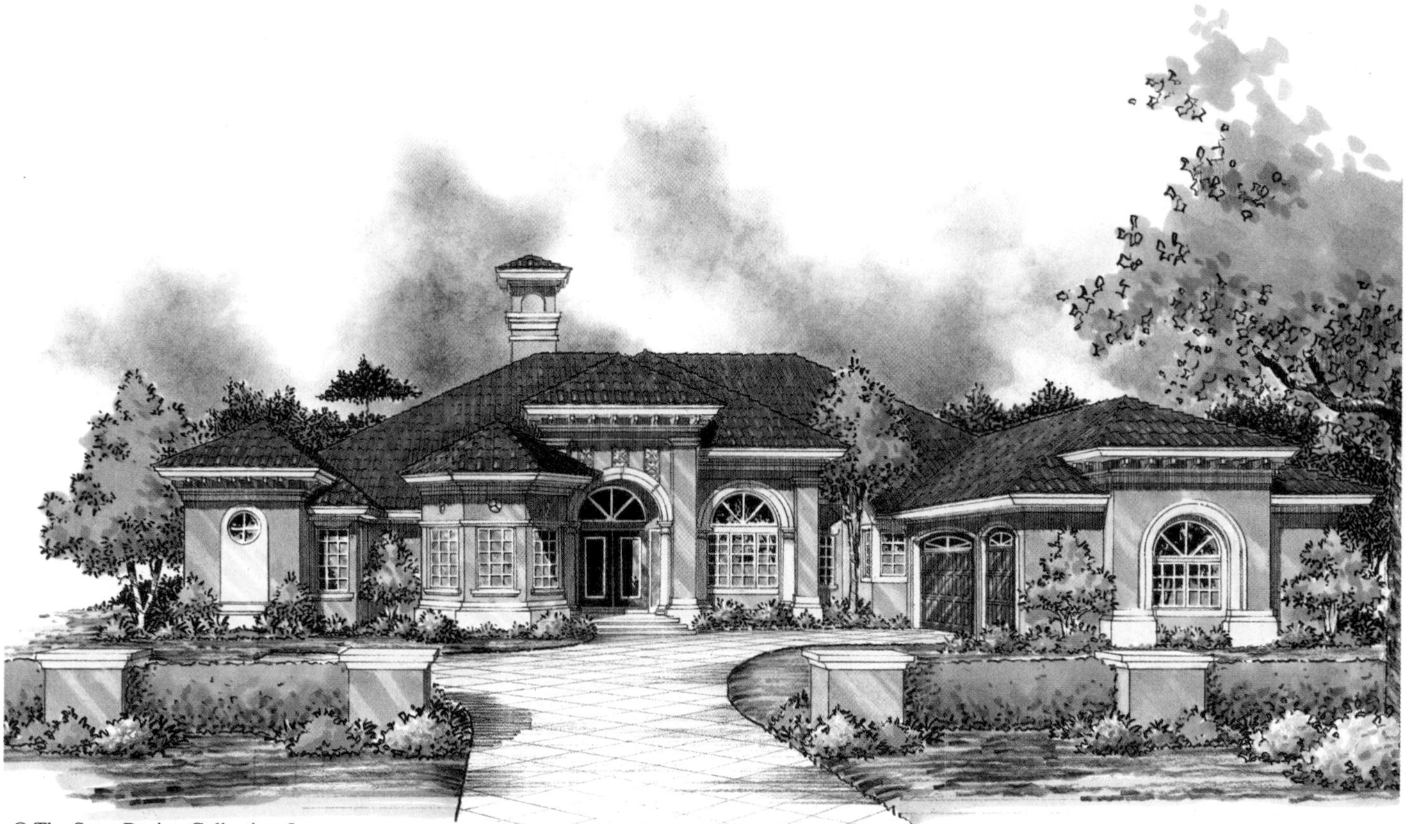

plan# HPK1700442

Style: Italianate
Square Footage: 3,743
Bedrooms: 4
Bathrooms: 3½
Width: 80' - 0"
Depth: 103' - 8"
Foundation: Slab

eplans.com

With California style and Mediterranean good looks, this striking stucco manor is sure to delight. The portico and foyer open to reveal a smart plan with convenience and flexibility in mind. The columned living room has a warming fireplace and access to the rear property. In the gourmet kitchen, an open design with an island and walk-in pantry will please any chef. From here, the elegant dining room and sunny nook are easily served. The leisure room is separated from the game room by a built-in entertainment center. The game area can also be finished off as a bedroom. To the rear, a guest room is perfect for frequent visitors or as an in-law suite. The master suite features a bright sitting area, oversized walk-in closets, and a pampering bath with a whirlpool tub. Extra features not to be missed: the outdoor grill, game-room storage, and gallery window seat.

OPTIONAL LAYOUT

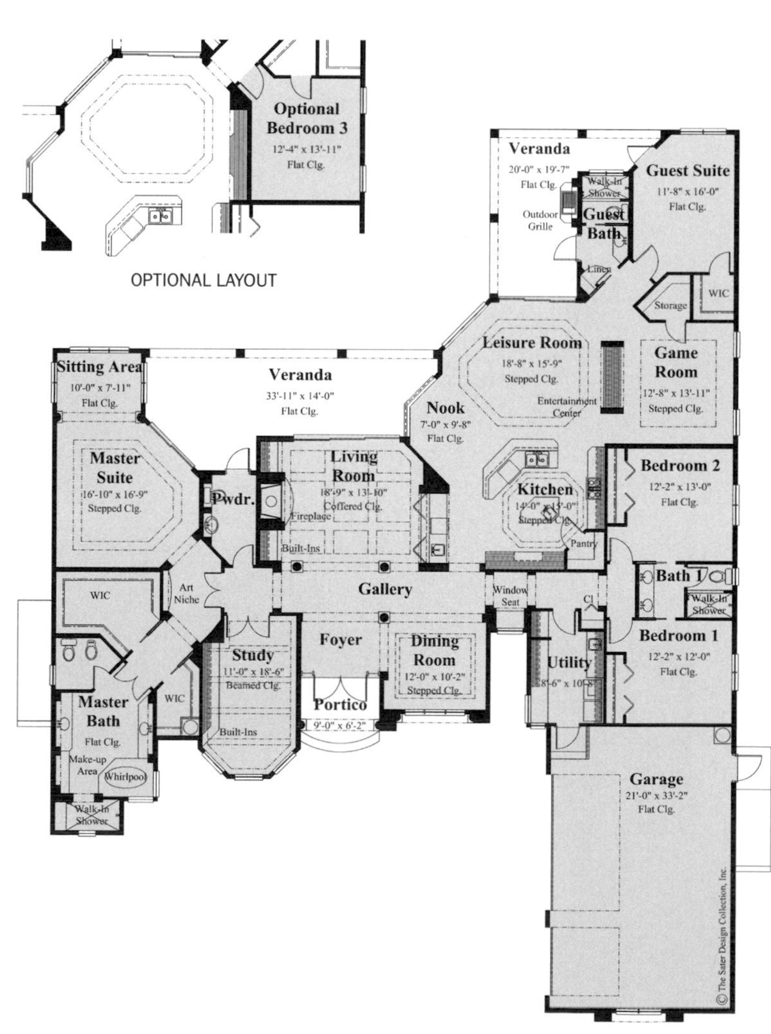

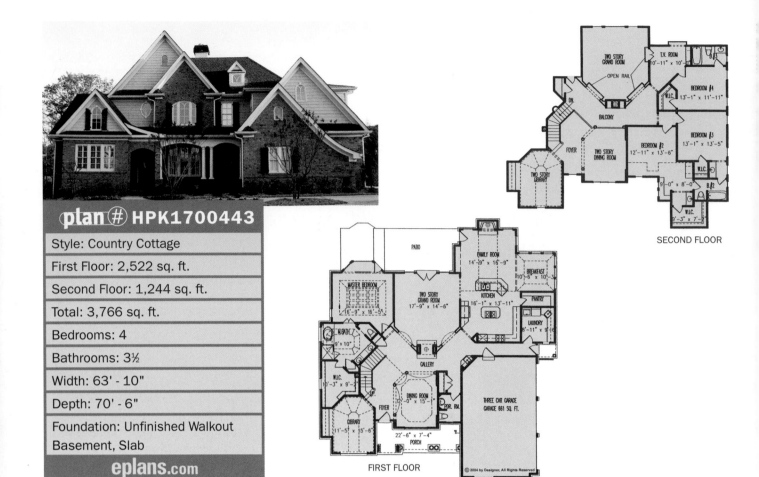

plan# HPK1700443

Style: Country Cottage

First Floor: 2,522 sq. ft.

Second Floor: 1,244 sq. ft.

Total: 3,766 sq. ft.

Bedrooms: 4

Bathrooms: 3½

Width: 63' - 10"

Depth: 70' - 6"

Foundation: Unfinished Walkout Basement, Slab

eplans.com

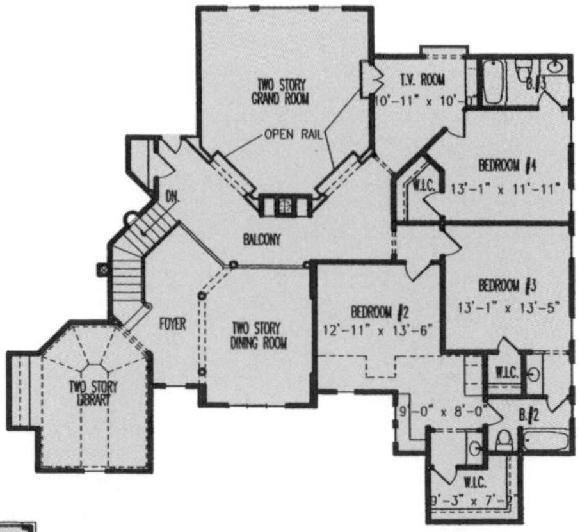

SECOND FLOOR

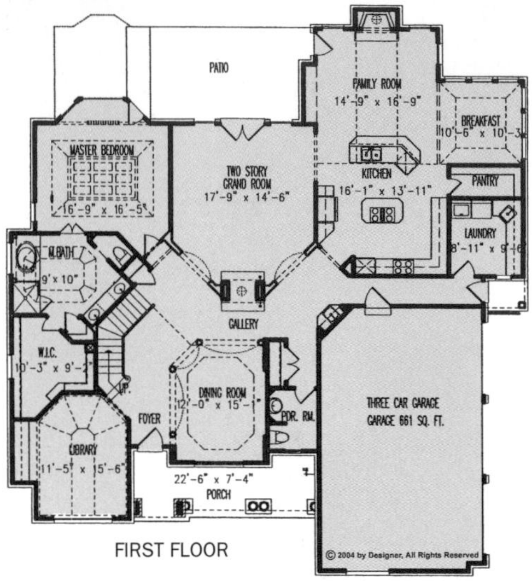

FIRST FLOOR

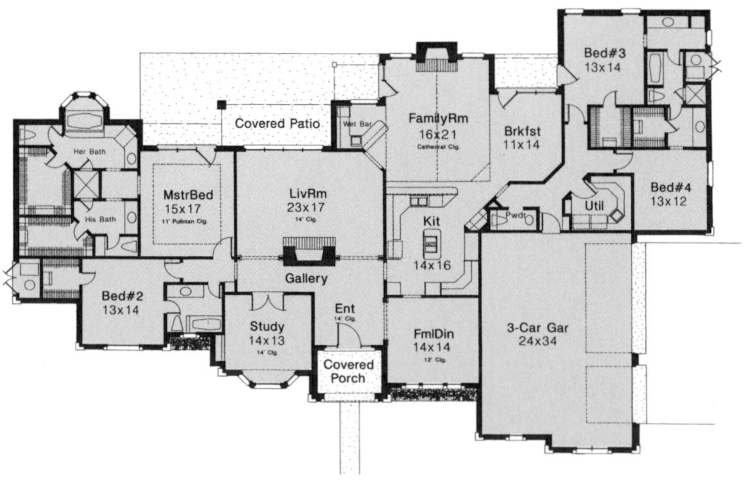

plan# HPK1700444

Style: Traditional

Square Footage: 3,818

Bedrooms: 4

Bathrooms: 3½

Width: 107' - 4"

Depth: 68' - 7"

Foundation: Slab

eplans.com

plan# HPK1700445

Style: Neoclassic

Square Footage: 3,828

Bonus Space: 1,018 sq. ft.

Bedrooms: 3

Bathrooms: 3½ + ½

Width: 80' - 6"

Depth: 70' - 8"

Foundation: Crawlspace

eplans.com

This Neoclassical home has plenty to offer! The elegant entrance is flanked by a formal dining room on the left and a beam-ceilinged study—complete with a fireplace—on the right. An angled kitchen is sure to please with a work island, plenty of counter and cabinet space, and a snack counter that it shares with the sunny breakfast room. A family room with a second fireplace is nearby. The lavish master suite features many amenities, including a huge walk-in closet, a three-sided fireplace, and a lavish bath. Two secondary bedrooms have private baths. Finish the second-floor bonus space to create an office, a play room, and a full bath. A three-car garage easily shelters the family fleet.

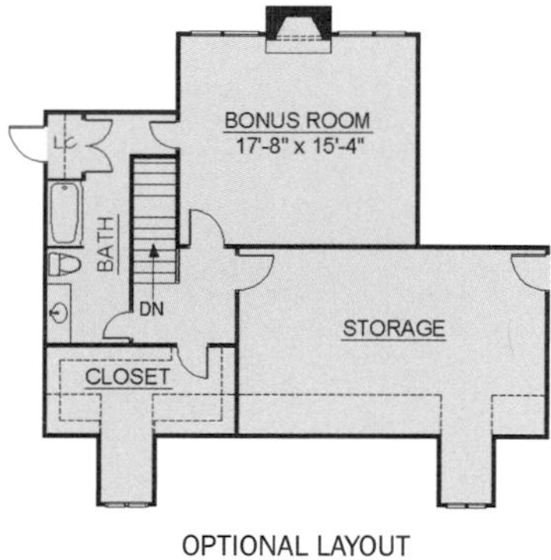

OPTIONAL LAYOUT

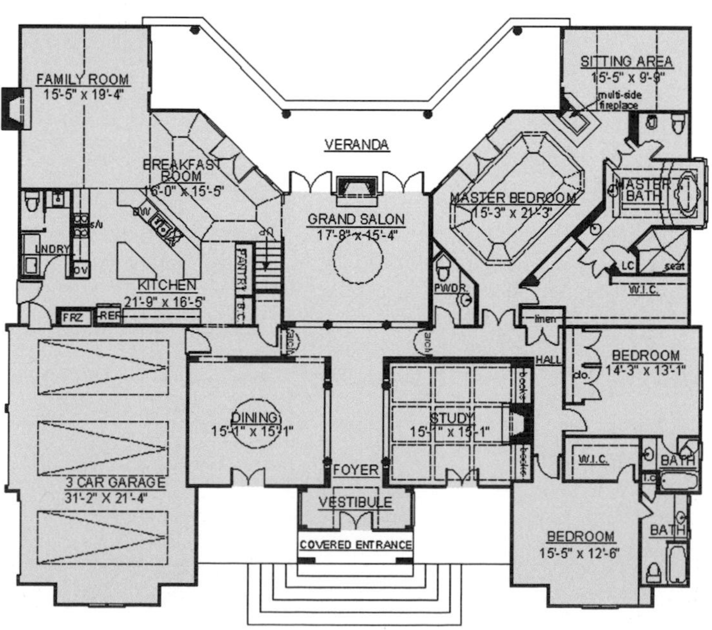

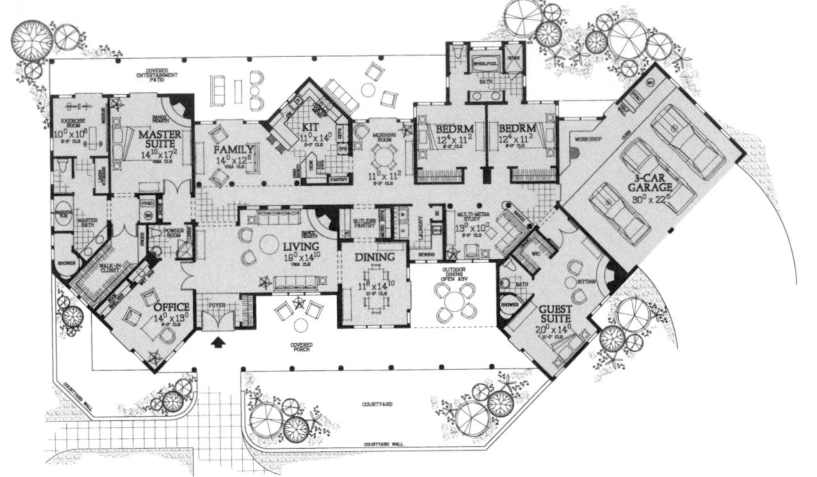

plan# HPK1700446

Style: SW Contemporary

Square Footage: 3,838

Bedrooms: 4

Bathrooms: 3½

Width: 127' - 6"

Depth: 60' - 10"

Foundation: Slab

eplans.com

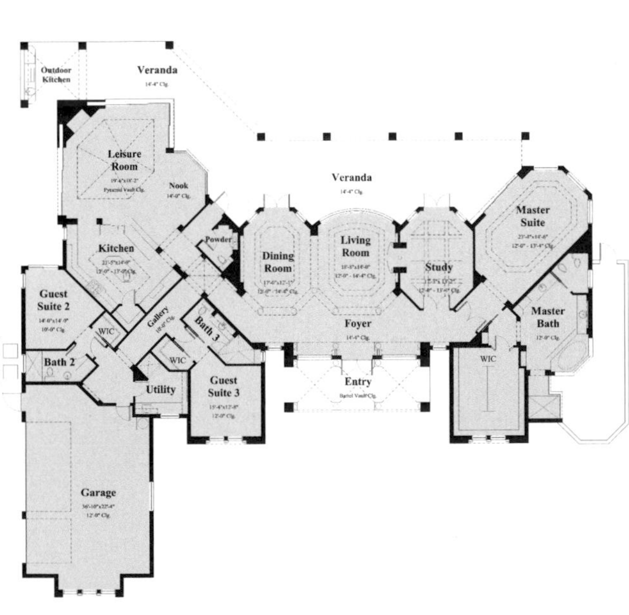

plan# HPK1700447

Style: Mediterranean

Square Footage: 3,877

Bedrooms: 3

Bathrooms: 3½

Width: 102' - 4"

Depth: 98' - 10"

Foundation: Slab

eplans.com

plan # HPK1700448

Style: Farmhouse
Square Footage: 3,886
Bonus Space: 444 sq. ft.
Bedrooms: 4
Bathrooms: 3½
Width: 77' - 4"
Depth: 99' - 0"
Foundation: Slab

eplans.com

Rustic elegance is the theme of this country marvel. An inviting country covered porch wraps around the front. To the right of the foyer, a quaint music room is open to the vaulted gathering room. Through three double doors, a pampering parlor awaits. The central splendor of this design is the family pool and indulging spa. To the right of the pool room, the master suite is secluded for privacy and includes a luxury-style master bath. Next to the master bedroom, a private theater is a quiet and relaxing retreat. A fireside library creates a romantic allure and is an appropriate addition to this heavenly plan.

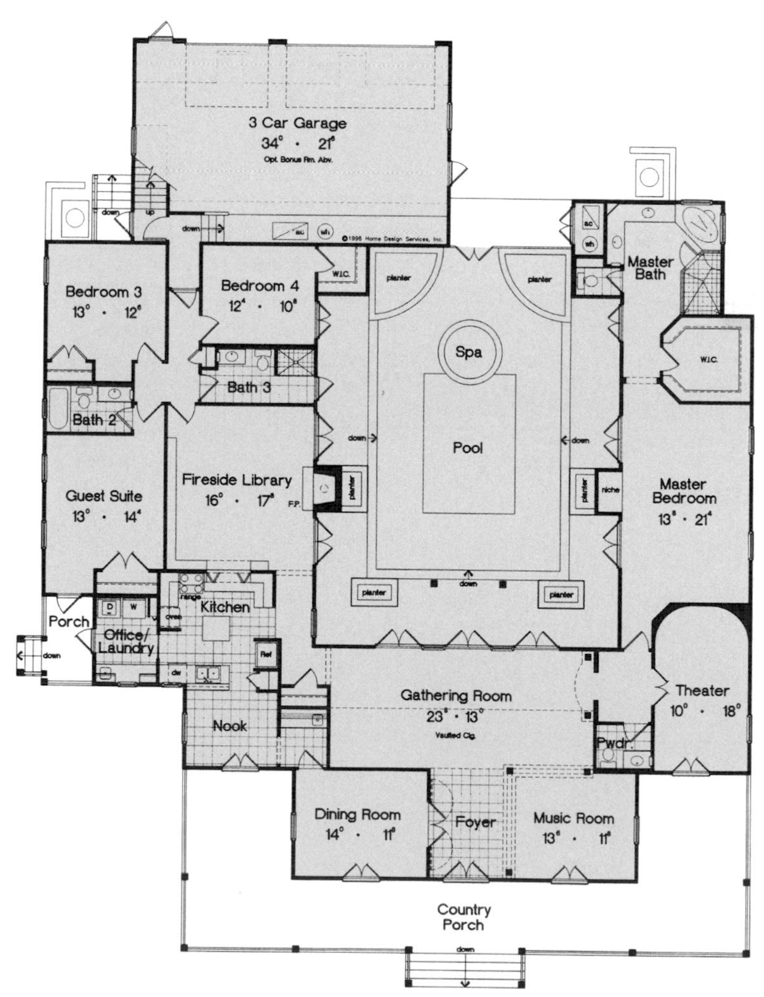

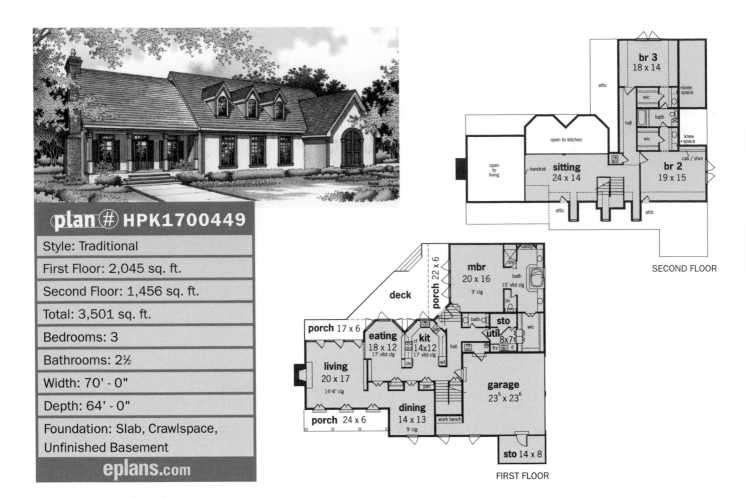

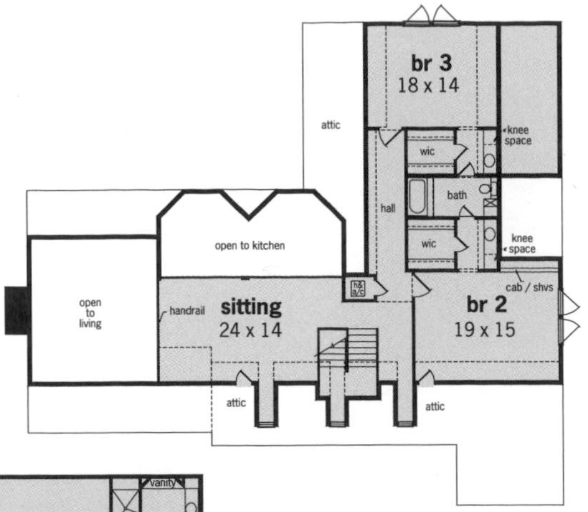

plan# HPK1700449

Style: Traditional

First Floor: 2,045 sq. ft.

Second Floor: 1,456 sq. ft.

Total: 3,501 sq. ft.

Bedrooms: 3

Bathrooms: 2½

Width: 70' - 0"

Depth: 64' - 0"

Foundation: Slab, Crawlspace, Unfinished Basement

eplans.com

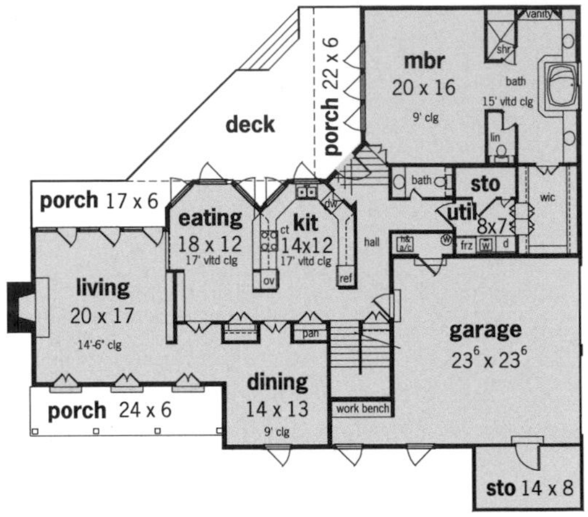

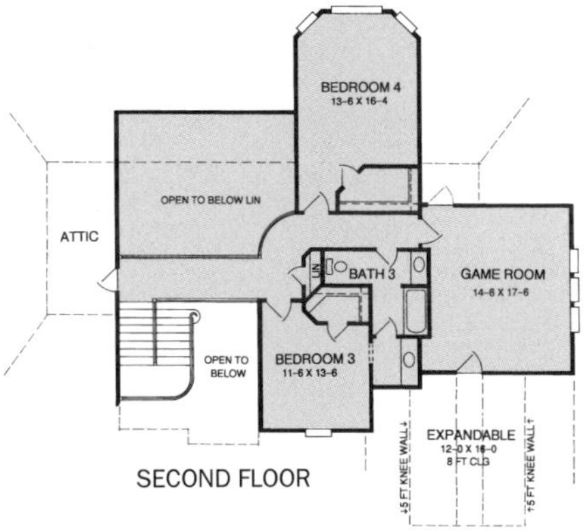

SECOND FLOOR

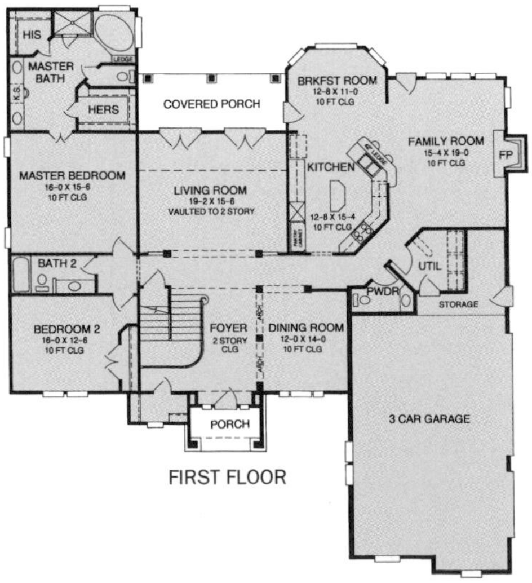

FIRST FLOOR

plan# HPK1700450

Style: European Cottage

First Floor: 2,518 sq. ft.

Second Floor: 1,013 sq. ft.

Total: 3,531 sq. ft.

Bonus Space: 192 sq. ft.

Bedrooms: 4

Bathrooms: 3½

Width: 67' - 8"

Depth: 74' - 2"

Foundation: Unfinished Basement, Crawlspace, Slab

eplans.com

SECOND FLOOR

FIRST FLOOR

plan # HPK1700451
Style: Traditional
First Floor: 2,200 sq. ft.
Second Floor: 1,338 sq. ft.
Total: 3,538 sq. ft.
Bedrooms: 4
Bathrooms: 3½
Width: 83' - 5"
Depth: 68' - 11"
eplans.com

Contemporary and stylish, this home design is a modern achievement of luxury, function, and appeal. A stunning winding staircase is appreciated from the foyer. Enjoy the privacy of the turreted study just beyond the stairs. Enough room for the largest dinner parties; the bay windows enhance the formal dining hall. More windows really open up the spacious great room. Take in the landscape and enjoy breakfast or cooking a new recipe from the unobstructed kitchen. The secluded first-floor master suite caters to every need and the bath will relieve the day's stress. The second floor is dedicated to three family bedrooms, a game room with kitchenette, and unfinished bonus space.

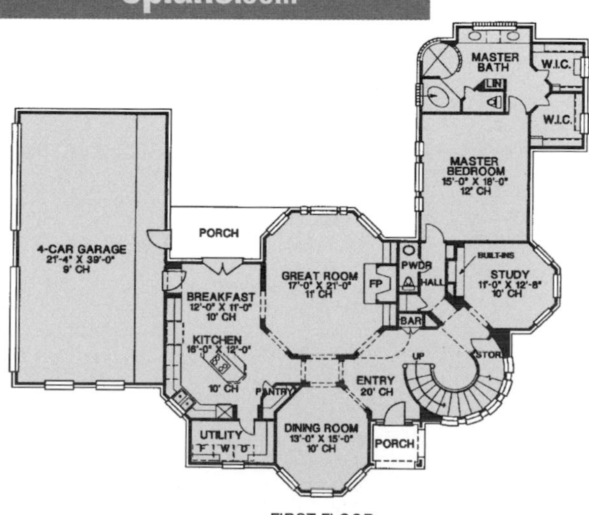

FIRST FLOOR

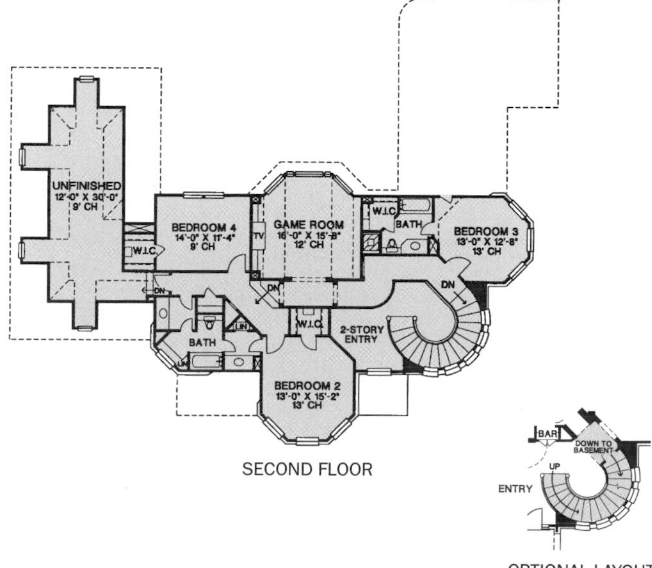

SECOND FLOOR

OPTIONAL LAYOUT

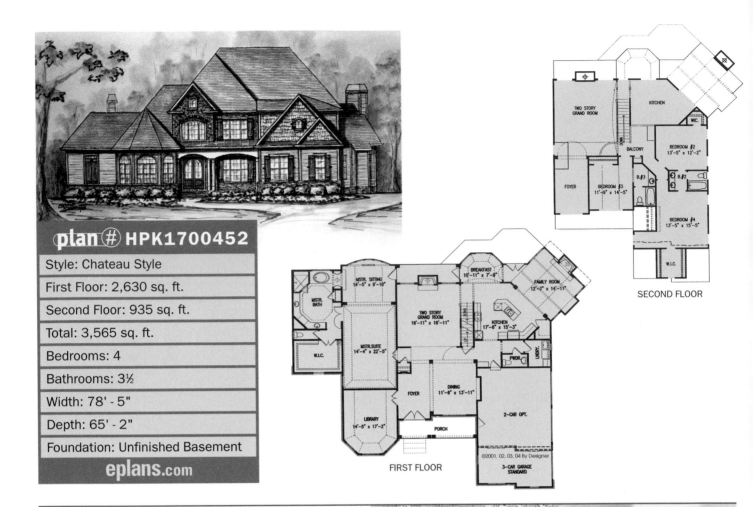

plan# HPK1700452

Style: Chateau Style

First Floor: 2,630 sq. ft.

Second Floor: 935 sq. ft.

Total: 3,565 sq. ft.

Bedrooms: 4

Bathrooms: 3½

Width: 78' - 5"

Depth: 65' - 2"

Foundation: Unfinished Basement

eplans.com

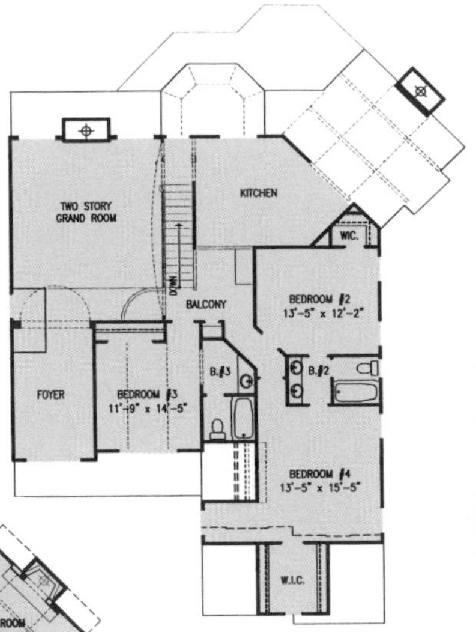

SECOND FLOOR

FIRST FLOOR

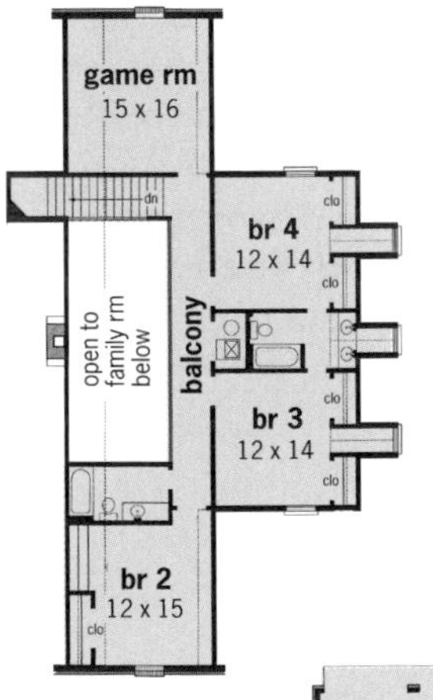

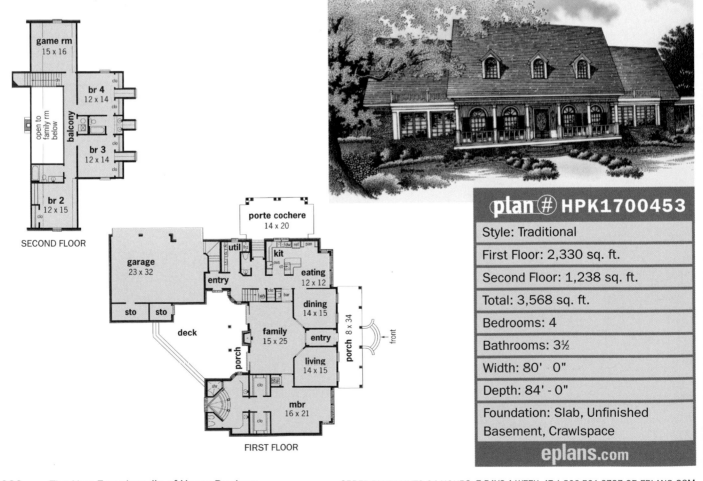

SECOND FLOOR

FIRST FLOOR

plan# HPK1700453

Style: Traditional

First Floor: 2,330 sq. ft.

Second Floor: 1,238 sq. ft.

Total: 3,568 sq. ft.

Bedrooms: 4

Bathrooms: 3½

Width: 80' 0"

Depth: 84' - 0"

Foundation: Slab, Unfinished Basement, Crawlspace

eplans.com

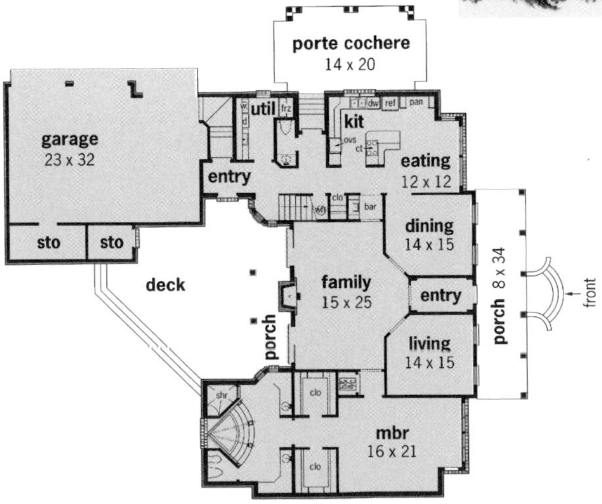

plan # HPK1700454

Style: Traditional
First Floor: 2,496 sq. ft.
Second Floor: 1,090 sq. ft.
Total: 3,586 sq. ft.
Bonus Space: 265 sq. ft.
Bedrooms: 4
Bathrooms: 3½
Width: 76' - 0"
Depth: 60' - 0"
Foundation: Slab, Unfinished Basement

eplans.com

Soaring stone and brick gables combine to grace the exterior of this French country home, enhancing its European appeal. Inside, the two-story entry opens to a columned dining room on the right, through double doors to a study on the left, and straight ahead—an elegant, curving staircase and a gracious living room. The uniquely designed master suite contains a large walk-in closet and a luxurious master bath filled with amenities. An open floor plan brings the casual living areas together, connecting the island kitchen, octagonal breakfast room and family room. Passage to the rear covered patio is supplied by the breakfast room as well as the family room. The second floor offers three family bedrooms—one with its own bath—and a full bath with separate dressing areas.

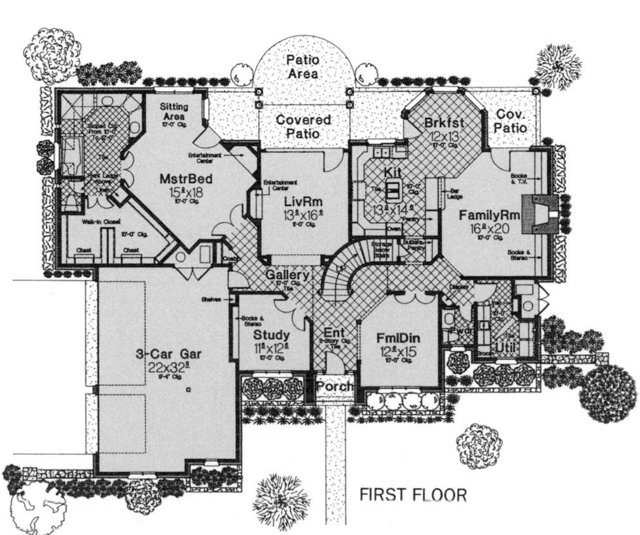

FIRST FLOOR

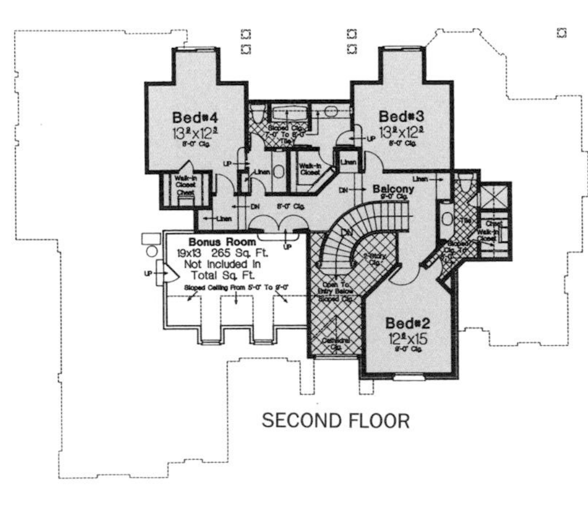

SECOND FLOOR

REAR EXTERIOR

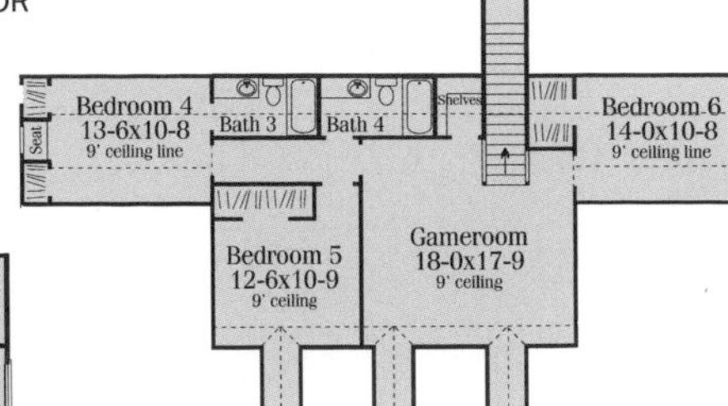

SECOND FLOOR

plan# HPK1700456

Style: Country Cottage

First Floor: 2,465 sq. ft.

Second Floor: 1,128 sq. ft.

Total: 3,593 sq. ft.

Bedrooms: 6

Bathrooms: 4½

Width: 65' - 1"

Depth: 73' - 7"

Foundation: Slab, Unfinished Basement, Crawlspace

eplans.com

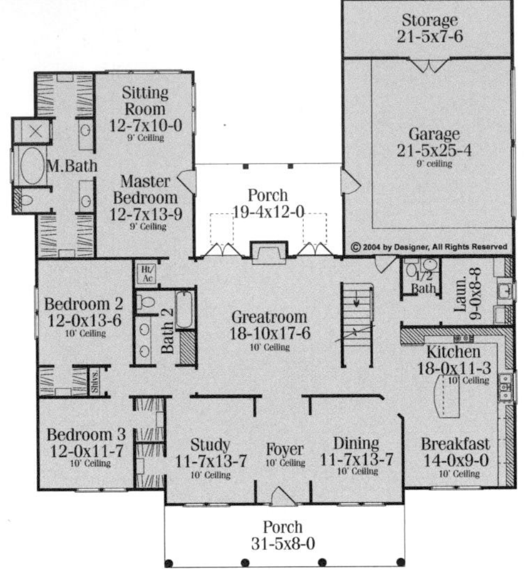

FIRST FLOOR

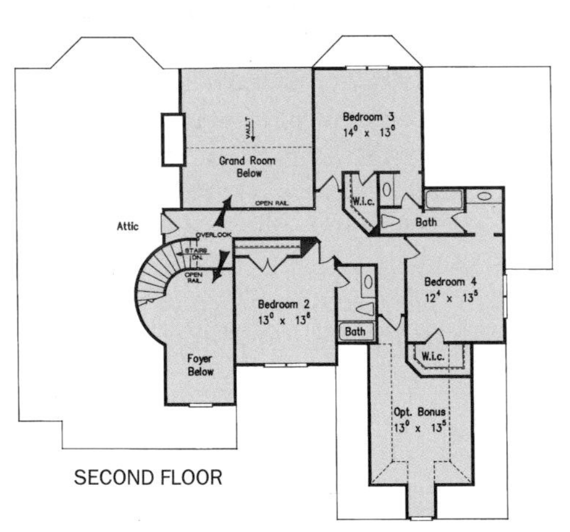

SECOND FLOOR

Sitting Area
Tray Clg.
Master Suite
18⁹ x 19⁰
Vaulted Grand Room
17⁰ x 21⁴
Breakfast
Vaulted Keeping Room
16⁰ x 15⁰
Kitchen
His
Pwdr.
Laund.
M.Bath
Dining Room
13¹⁰ x 15⁷
Two Story Foyer
Three Car Garage
21⁵ x 31⁵
Hers
Den/Office
13⁰ x 12⁰
Covered Entry

FIRST FLOOR

plan# HPK1700437

Style: Traditional

First Floor: 2,602

Second Floor: 1,016

Square Footage: 3,587

Bedrooms: 4

Bathrooms: 3½

Width: 93' - 11"

Depth: 72' - 3"

eplans.com

plan # HPK1700457

Style: Traditional
First Floor: 2,603 sq. ft.
Second Floor: 1,020 sq. ft.
Total: 3,623 sq. ft.
Bedrooms: 4
Bathrooms: 4½
Width: 76' - 8"
Depth: 68' - 0"

Perhaps the most notable characteristic of this traditional house is its masterful use of space. The glorious great room, open dining room, and handsome den serve as the heart of the home. A cozy hearth room with a fireplace rounds out the kitchen and breakfast area. The master bedroom opens up to a private sitting room with a fireplace. Three family bedrooms occupy thc sccond floor, each with private baths. Other special features include a four-car garage, a corner whirlpool tub in the master bath, a walk-in pantry and snack bar in the kitchen, and transom windows in the dining room.

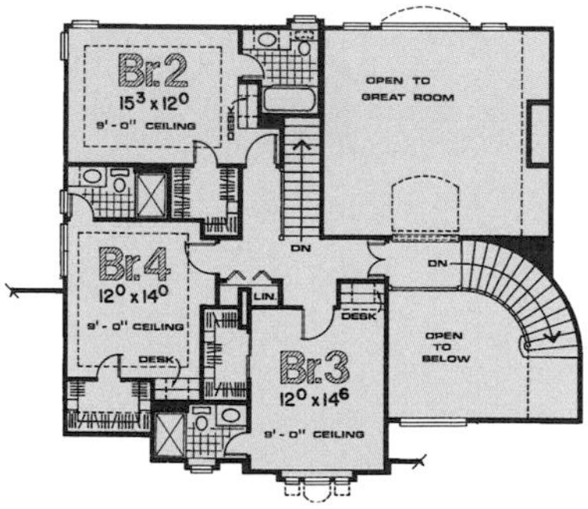

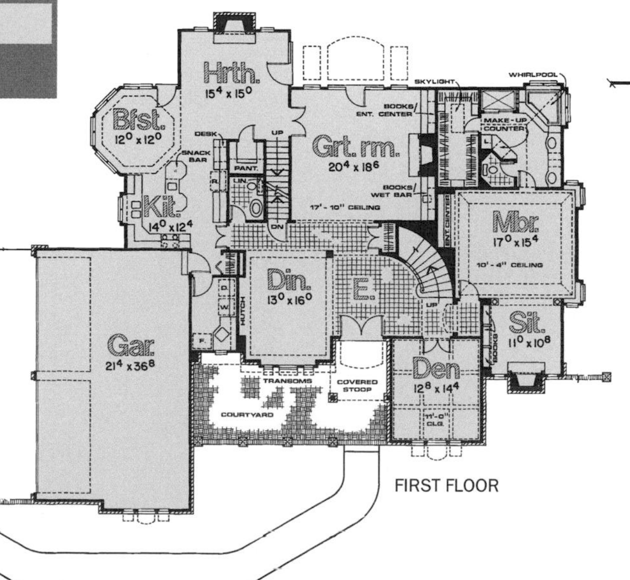

FIRST FLOOR

SECOND FLOOR

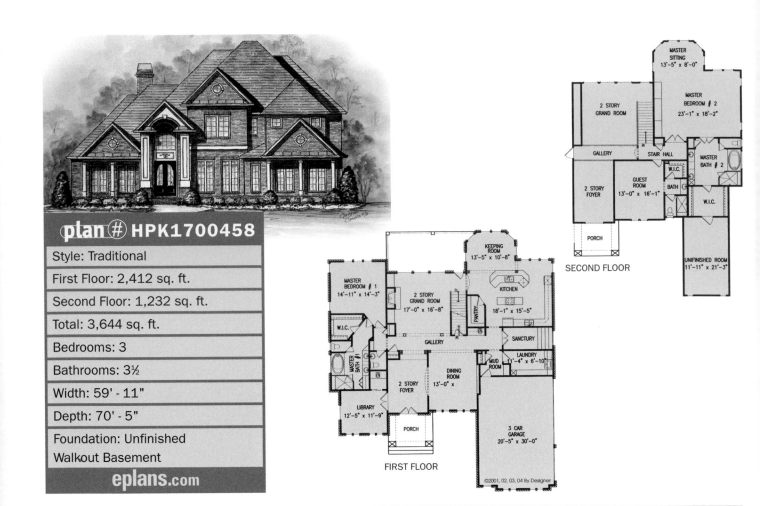

plan# HPK1700458

- Style: Traditional
- First Floor: 2,412 sq. ft.
- Second Floor: 1,232 sq. ft.
- Total: 3,644 sq. ft.
- Bedrooms: 3
- Bathrooms: 3½
- Width: 59' - 11"
- Depth: 70' - 5"
- Foundation: Unfinished Walkout Basement

eplans.com

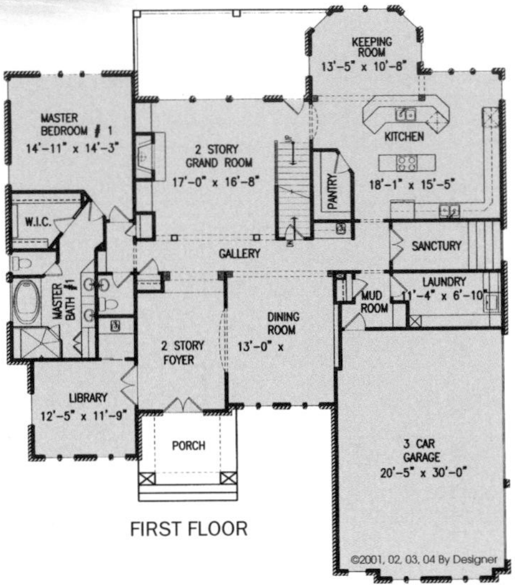

FIRST FLOOR

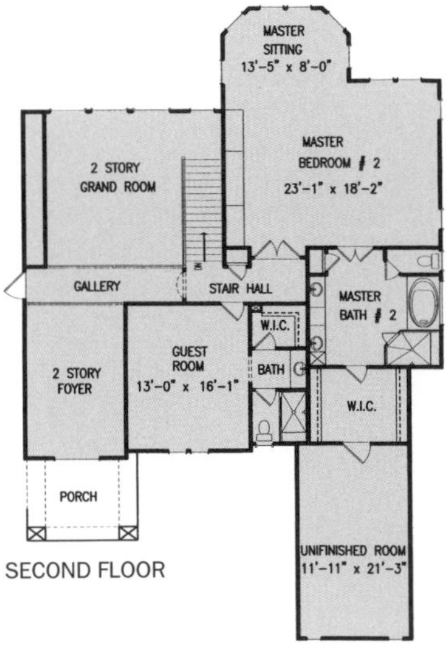

SECOND FLOOR

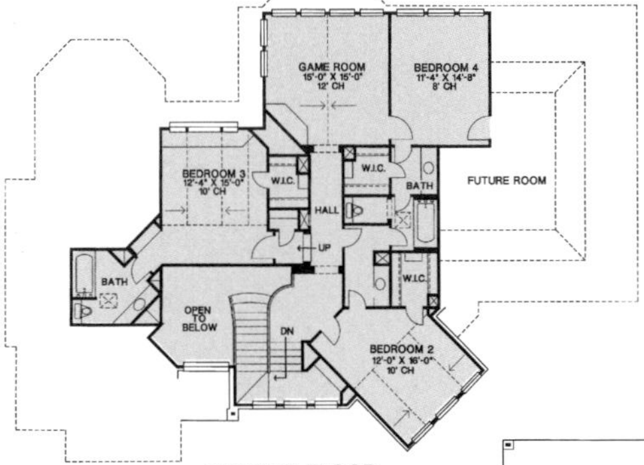

SECOND FLOOR

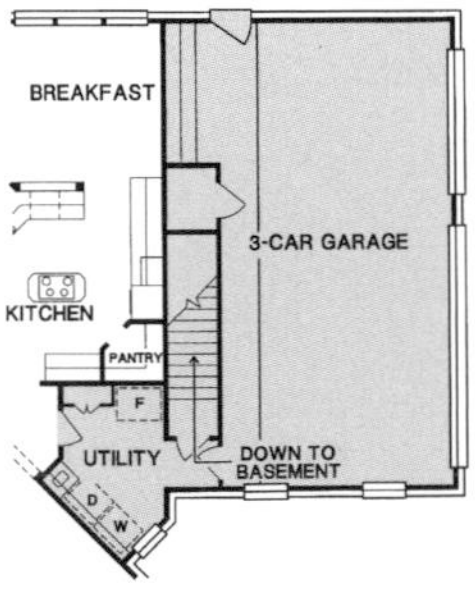

OPTIONAL LAYOUT

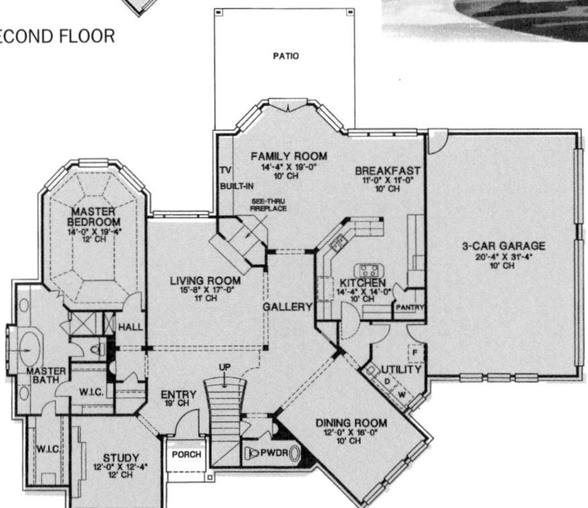

FIRST FLOOR

plan# HPK1700459

- Style: Traditional
- First Floor: 2,362 sq. ft.
- Second Floor: 1,319 sq. ft.
- Total: 3,681 sq. ft.
- Bedrooms: 4
- Bathrooms: 3½
- Width: 77' - 11"
- Depth: 64' - 11"

eplans.com

plan # HPK1700460

Style: Traditional
First Floor: 2,617 sq. ft.
Second Floor: 1,072 sq. ft.
Total: 3,689 sq. ft.
Bedrooms: 4
Bathrooms: 4 ½
Width: 83' - 5"
Depth: 73' - 4"

eplans.com

A spectacular volume entry with a curving staircase opens through columns to the formal areas of this home. The sunken living room contains a fireplace, a wet bar, and a bowed window; the front-facing dining room offers a built-in hutch. The family room, with bookcases surrounding a fireplace, is open to a bayed breakfast nook, and both are easily served from the nearby kitchen. Placed away from the living area of the home, the den provides a quiet retreat. The master suite on the first floor contains an elegant bath and a huge walk-in closet. Second-floor bedrooms also include walk-in closets and private baths.

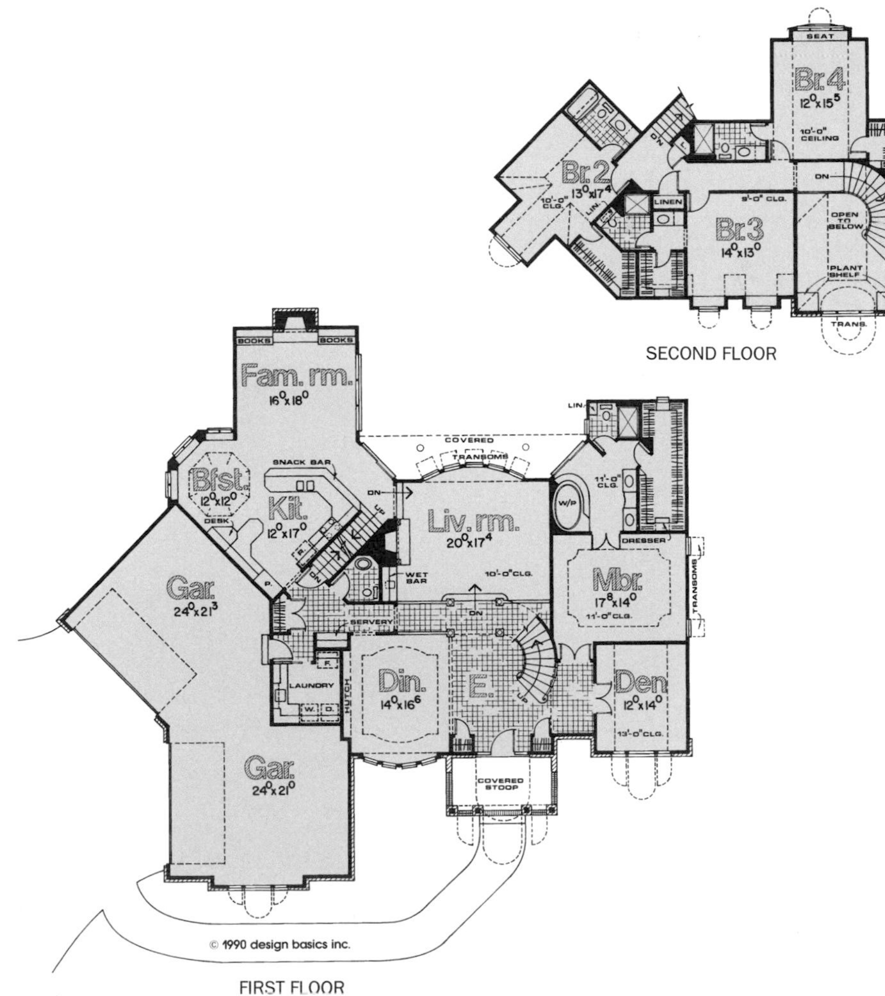

FIRST FLOOR

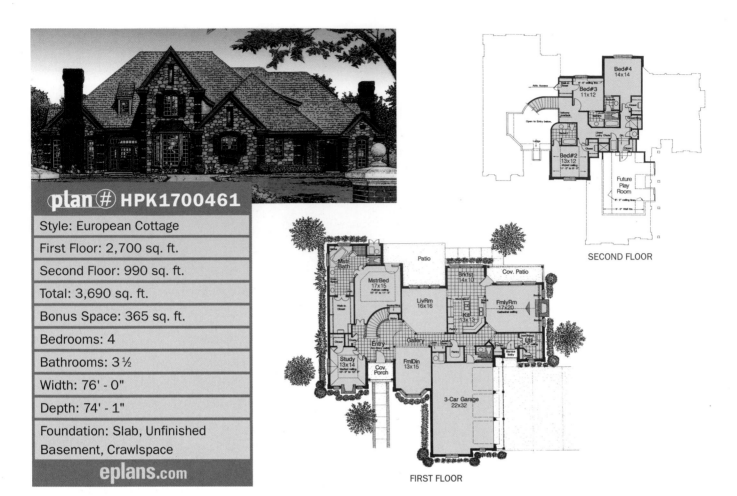

plan# HPK1700461

Style: European Cottage
First Floor: 2,700 sq. ft.
Second Floor: 990 sq. ft.
Total: 3,690 sq. ft.
Bonus Space: 365 sq. ft.
Bedrooms: 4
Bathrooms: 3½
Width: 76' - 0"
Depth: 74' - 1"
Foundation: Slab, Unfinished Basement, Crawlspace

eplans.com

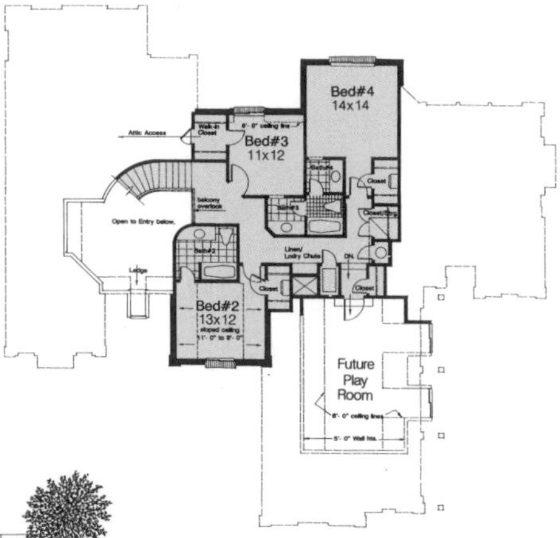

SECOND FLOOR

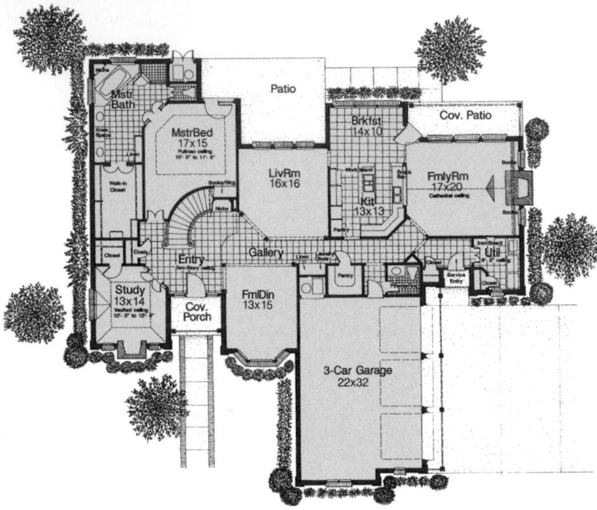

FIRST FLOOR

SECOND FLOOR

FIRST FLOOR

REAR EXTERIOR

plan# HPK1700462

Style: Contemporary
First Floor: 3,067 sq. ft.
Second Floor: 648 sq. ft.
Total: 3,715 sq. ft.
Bedrooms: 3
Bathrooms: 2½ + ½
Width: 97' - 0"
Depth: 102' - 8"
Foundation: Unfinished Basement

eplans.com

plan# HPK1700463

Style: Traditional
First Floor: 2,591 sq. ft.
Second Floor: 1,174 sq. ft.
Total: 3,765 sq. ft.
Bedrooms: 4
Bathrooms: 4 ½
Width: 64' - 4"
Depth: 79' - 4"
Foundation: Crawlspace, Slab, Unfinished Basement

eplans.com

A traditional and symmetrical style informs this exterior, centered around a pleasing front porch with columned arches and three dormers on top. A hushed study and formal dining room adjoin the foyer, leading to the centralized great room. You'll immediately notice the twin sets of French doors at the opposite end, which afford access to the rear porch. The left side of the great room abuts a master suite and family bedroom with adjoining full bath. The master bedrooms holds a cozy and intimate window seat in the left wall. The right of the plan accommodates the kitchen and breakfast nook, laundry and garage, and staircase to the upper level. Two bedrooms with private baths and a game room are upstairs, completing everything you need for classic living with a contemporary beat.

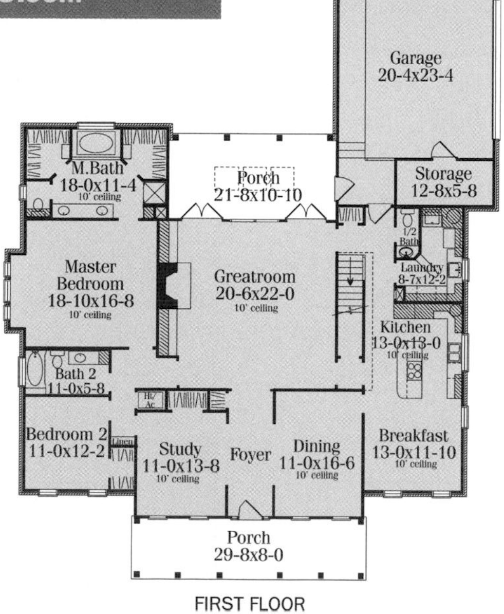

FIRST FLOOR

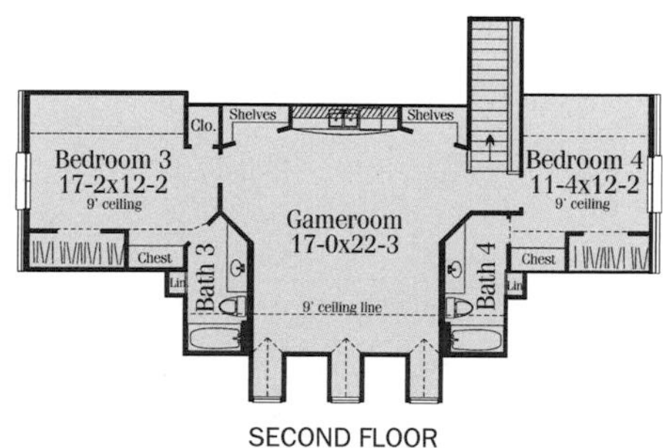

SECOND FLOOR

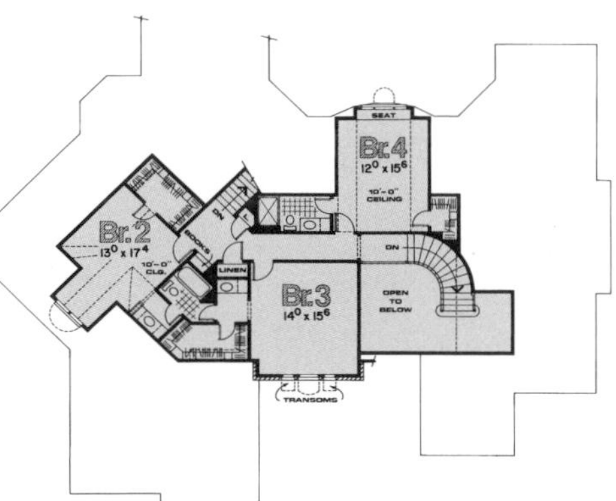

SECOND FLOOR

plan# HPK1700464

Style: Traditional
First Floor: 2,813 sq. ft.
Second Floor: 1,091 sq. ft.
Total: 3,904 sq. ft.
Bedrooms: 4
Bathrooms: 3 ½
Width: 85' - 5"
Depth: 74' - 8"

eplans.com

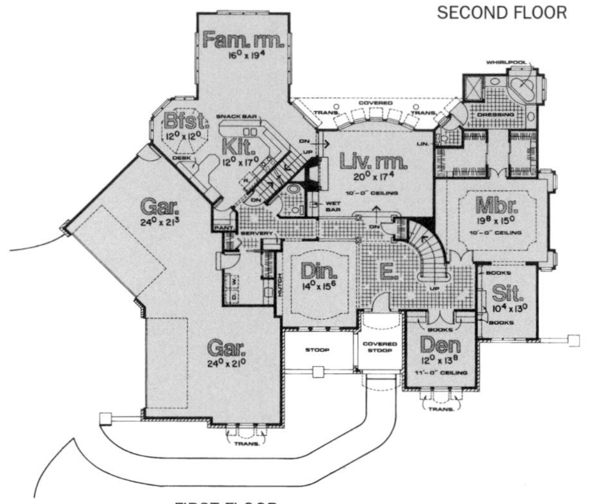

FIRST FLOOR

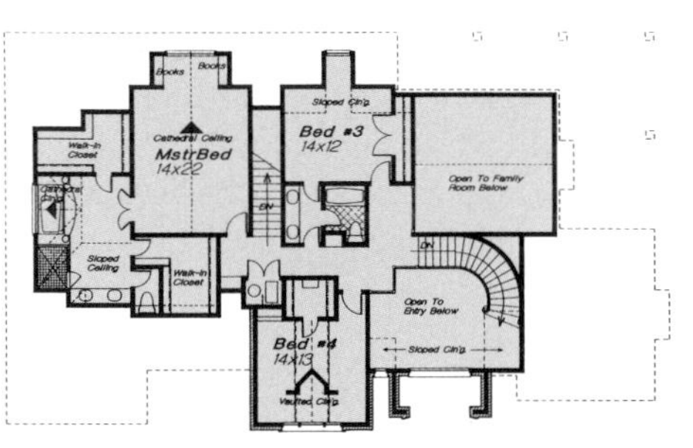

SECOND FLOOR

plan# HPK1700465

Style: Traditional
First Floor: 2,506 sq. ft.
Second Floor: 1,415 sq. ft.
Total: 3,921 sq. ft.
Bedrooms: 4
Bathrooms: 3 ½
Width: 80' - 5"
Depth: 50' - 4"
Foundation: Slab, Unfinished Basement

eplans.com

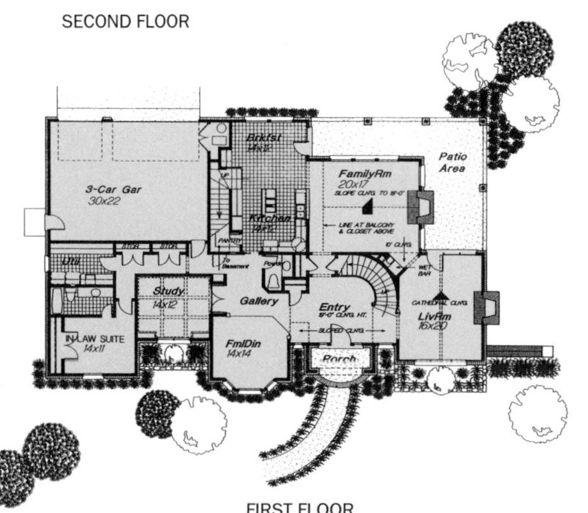

FIRST FLOOR

plan# HPK1700466
Style: Traditional
First Floor: 2,227 sq. ft.
Second Floor: 1,278 sq. ft.
Total: 3,505 sq. ft.
Bedrooms: 4
Bathrooms: 4 ½
Width: 80' - 0"
Depth: 63' - 0"
Foundation: Slab
eplans.com

EDITOR'S PICK

What's great about this design is how effortlessly it strikes the chord of elegance and exuberance. A grand portico that leads to a generous foyer and is flanked by a study and formal dining room attends visitors with a graceful air. But venture on to the spirited great room, kitchen, and nook, and you'll find the home's fun-loving attitude. The rear of the plan encourages outdoor living, providing a cookout kitchen and covered veranda. Finally, find the home's restful spaces on the upper level, including a fully attentive guest suite.

REAR EXTERIOR

FIRST FLOOR

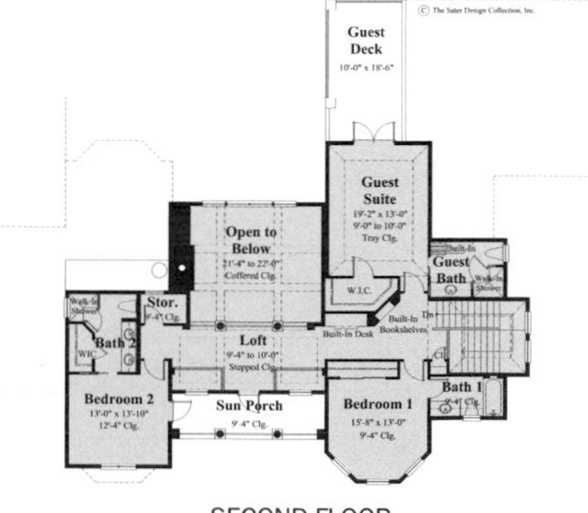

SECOND FLOOR

plan# HPK1700467

- Style: Traditional
- First Floor: 2,658 sq. ft.
- Second Floor: 854 sq. ft.
- Total: 3,512 sq. ft.
- Bonus Space: 150 sq. ft.
- Bedrooms: 4
- Bathrooms: 3½
- Width: 86' - 0"
- Depth: 58' - 1"
- Foundation: Unfinished Basement, Crawlspace, Slab

eplans.com

SECOND FLOOR

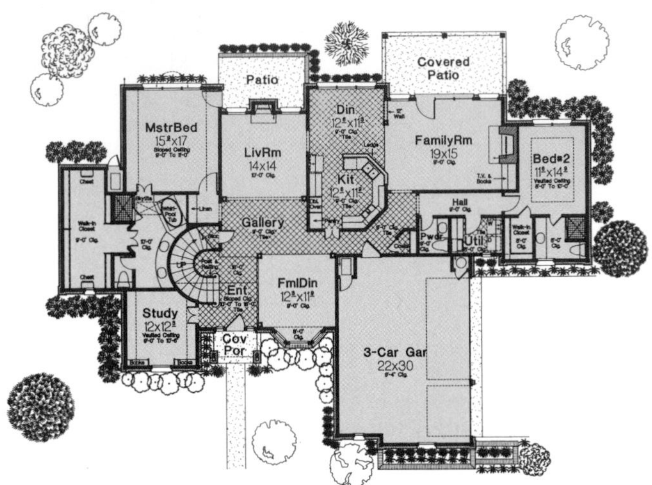

FIRST FLOOR

SECOND FLOOR

plan# HPK1700468

- Style: Farmhouse
- First Floor: 2,589 sq. ft.
- Second Floor: 981 sq. ft.
- Total: 3,570 sq. ft.
- Bedrooms: 4
- Bathrooms: 3½
- Width: 70' - 8"
- Depth: 61' - 10"
- Foundation: Crawlspace

eplans.com

FIRST FLOOR

plan# HPK1700469

Style: Country Cottage
First Floor: 2,660 sq. ft.
Second Floor: 914 sq. ft.
Total: 3,574 sq. ft.
Bedrooms: 3
Bathrooms: 4 ½
Width: 114' - 8"
Depth: 75' - 10"
Foundation: Crawlspace

eplans.com

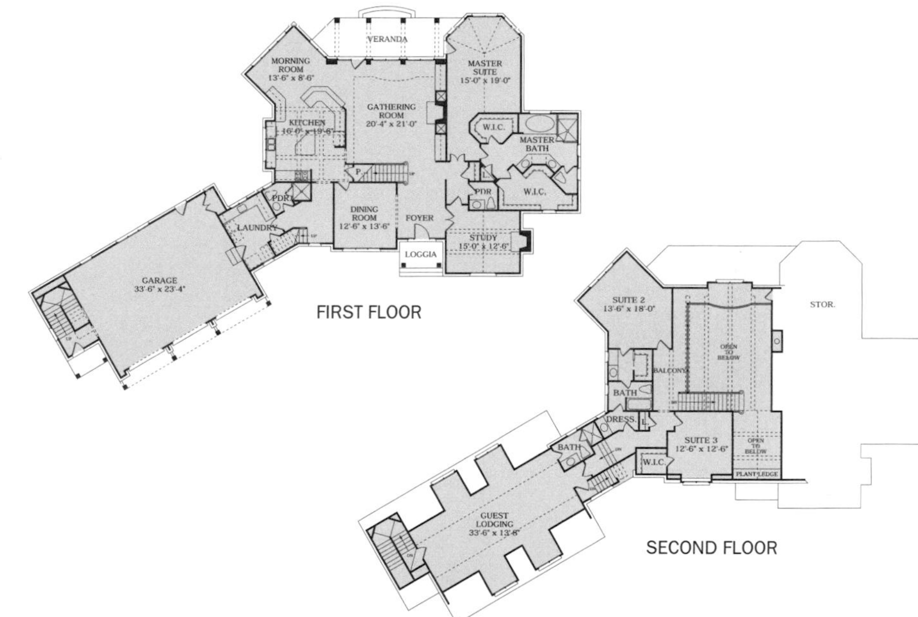

FIRST FLOOR

SECOND FLOOR

Gently curved arches and dormers contrast with the straight lines of gables and wooden columns on this French-style stone exterior. Small-pane windows are enhanced by shutters; tall chimneys and a cupola add height. Inside, a spacious gathering room with an impressive fireplace opens to a cheery morning room. The kitchen is a delight, with a beam ceiling, triangular work island, walk-in pantry, and angular counter with a snack bar. The nearby laundry room includes a sink, a work area, and plenty of room for storage. The first-floor master suite boasts a bay-windowed sitting nook, a deluxe bath, and a handy study.

REAR EXTERIOR

plan# HPK1700470

Style: Country Cottage
First Floor: 2,225 sq. ft.
Second Floor: 1,360 sq. ft.
Total: 3,585 sq. ft.
Bonus Space: 277 sq. ft.
Bedrooms: 4
Bathrooms: 3 ½
Width: 68' - 10"
Depth: 60' - 0"
Foundation: Crawlspace, Unfinished Walkout Basement

eplans.com

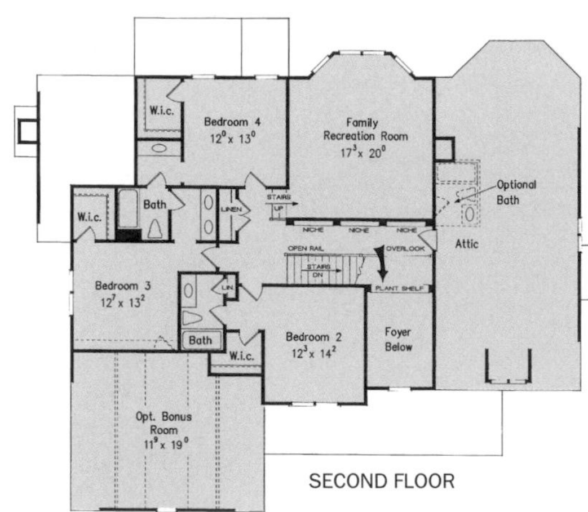

SECOND FLOOR

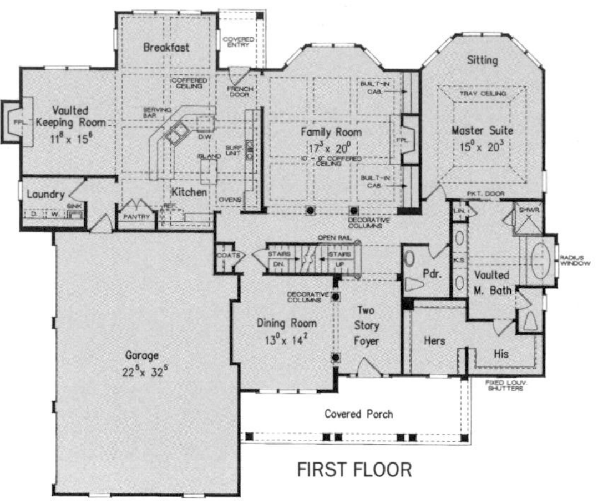

FIRST FLOOR

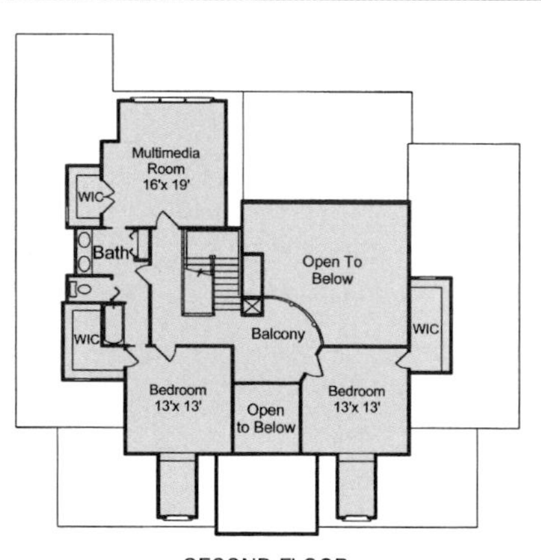

SECOND FLOOR

plan# HPK1700471

Style: Country Cottage
First Floor: 2,390 sq. ft.
Second Floor: 1,200 sq. ft.
Total: 3,590 sq. ft.
Bedrooms: 4
Bathrooms: 3
Width: 61' - 0"
Depth: 64' - 4"
Foundation: Pier (same as Piling)

eplans.com

Wood Deck 36'7"x 10'
Master Bath
Master Bedroom 15'8"x 16'3"
Covered Porch 20'x 13'
Breakfast 12'8"x 13'2"
WIC
Living 20'x 18'
Bath
Kitchen 12'8"x 13'2"
Bedroom 12'8"x 13'
Study 13'x 13'
Foyer
Dining 12'10"x 13'
Utility
Porch 51'x 8'

FIRST FLOOR

REAR EXTERIOR

plan # HPK1700472

Style: French
First Floor: 2,528 sq. ft.
Second Floor: 1,067 sq. ft.
Total: 3,595 sq. ft.
Bedrooms: 4
Bathrooms: 3½+½
Width: 69' - 2"
Depth: 73' - 10"
Foundation: Slab

eplans.com

Fine brick detailing and graceful gables enhance the elegance of this home. Upon entering, one steps into a two-story foyer showcasing a graceful curved staircase and the dining room. Situated with views to the side and rear of the home, the great room is designed with an offset perfect for a grand piano or game table. The kitchen and breakfast room are centrally located and open to the patio. The master suite features a sitting area and luxury bath, and the second floor's three bedrooms, two baths and a game room complete the roomy accommodations.

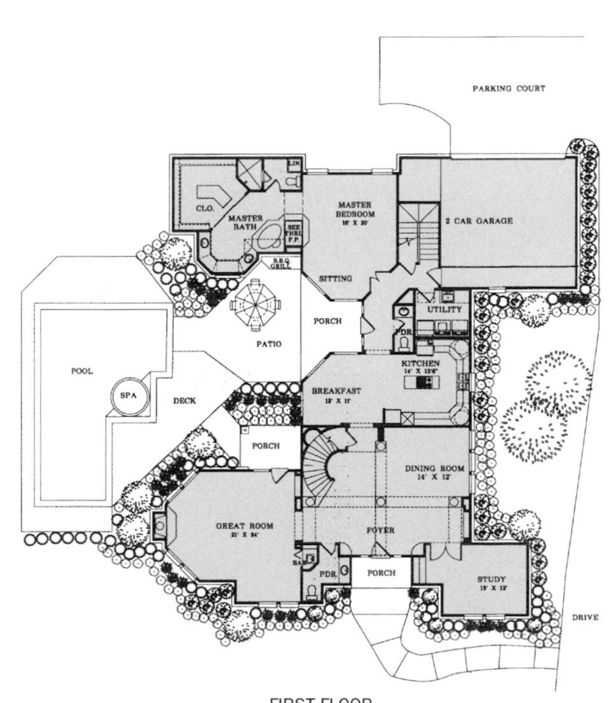

FIRST FLOOR

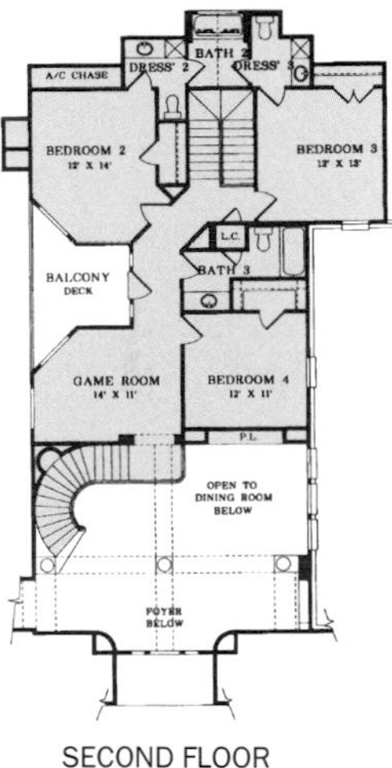

SECOND FLOOR

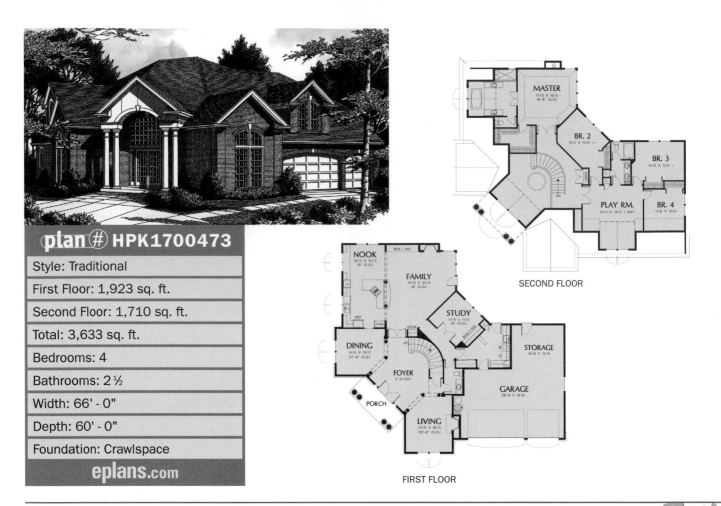

SECOND FLOOR

FIRST FLOOR

plan# HPK1700473

Style: Traditional

First Floor: 1,923 sq. ft.

Second Floor: 1,710 sq. ft.

Total: 3,633 sq. ft.

Bedrooms: 4

Bathrooms: 2½

Width: 66' - 0"

Depth: 60' - 0"

Foundation: Crawlspace

eplans.com

SECOND FLOOR

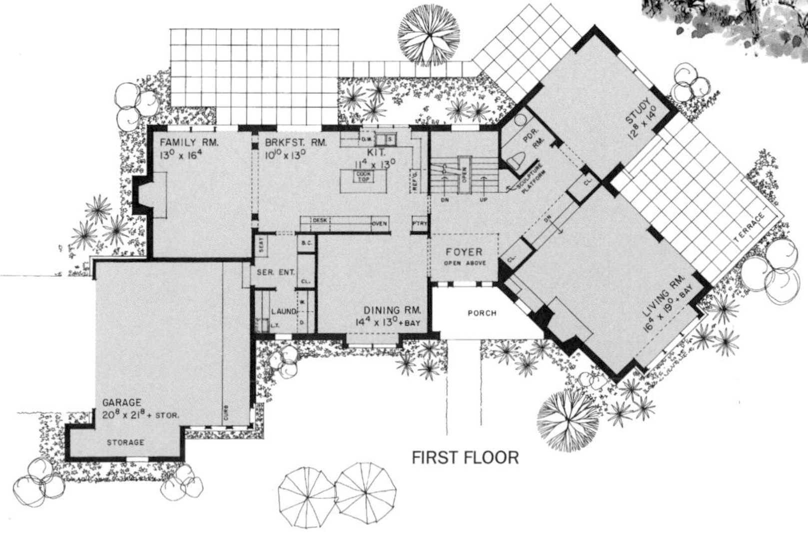

FIRST FLOOR

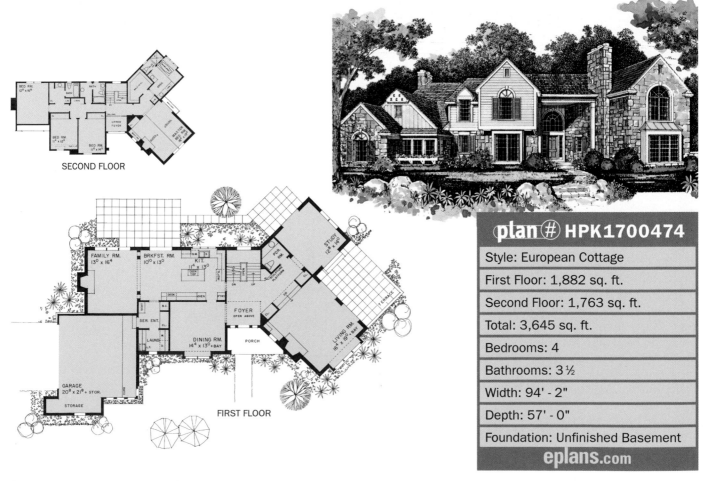

plan# HPK1700474

Style: European Cottage

First Floor: 1,882 sq. ft.

Second Floor: 1,763 sq. ft.

Total: 3,645 sq. ft.

Bedrooms: 4

Bathrooms: 3½

Width: 94' - 2"

Depth: 57' - 0"

Foundation: Unfinished Basement

eplans.com

plan# HPK1700475

Style: European Cottage
First Floor: 2,654 sq. ft.
Second Floor: 1,013 sq. ft.
Total: 3,667 sq. ft.
Bedrooms: 4
Bathrooms: 3½
Width: 75' - 4"
Depth: 74' - 2"
Foundation: Crawlspace, Slab, Unfinished Basement

eplans.com

European accents shape the exterior of this striking family home. Inside, the foyer is open to the dining room on the right and the living room straight ahead. Here, two sets of double doors open to the rear covered porch. Casual areas of the home include a family room warmed by a fireplace and an island kitchen opening to a bayed breakfast room. The first-floor master retreat is a luxurious perk, which offers a bayed sitting area, a whirlpool bath, and large His and Hers walk-in closets. Bedroom 2— with its close proximity to the master suite— is perfect for a nursery or home office. Upstairs, Bedrooms 3 and 4 boast walk-in closets and share a bath. Future space is available just off the game room.

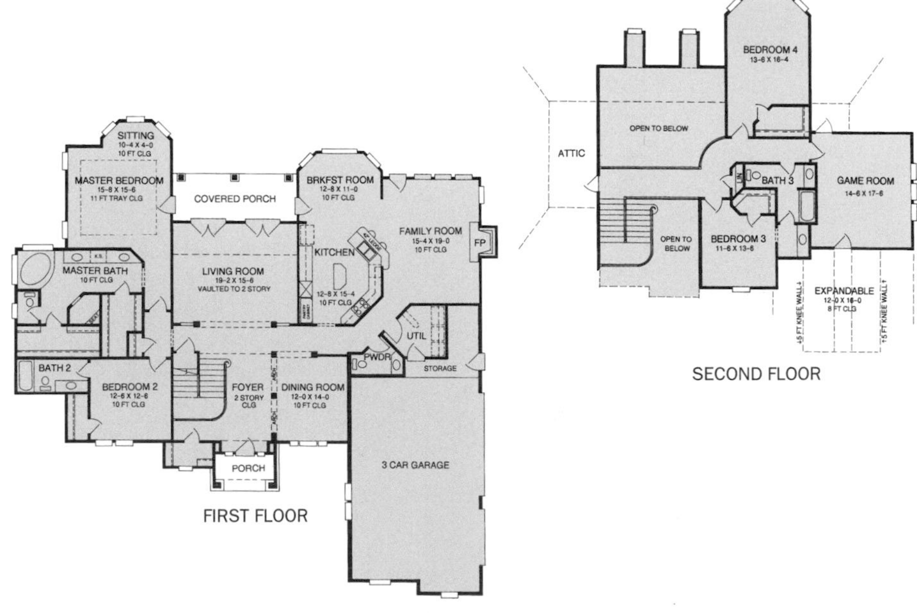

FIRST FLOOR

SECOND FLOOR

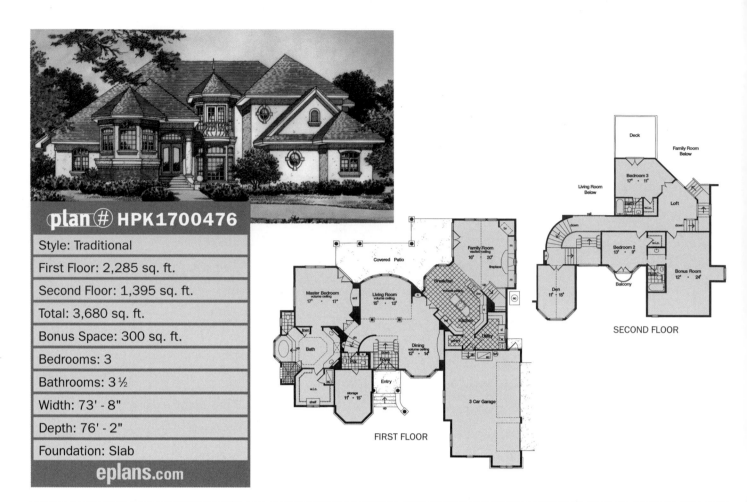

plan# HPK1700476

Style: Traditional

First Floor: 2,285 sq. ft.

Second Floor: 1,395 sq. ft.

Total: 3,680 sq. ft.

Bonus Space: 300 sq. ft.

Bedrooms: 3

Bathrooms: 3 ½

Width: 73' - 8"

Depth: 76' - 2"

Foundation: Slab

eplans.com

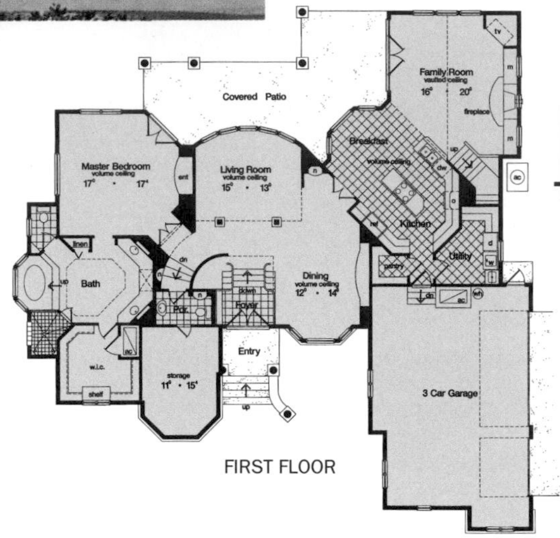

FIRST FLOOR

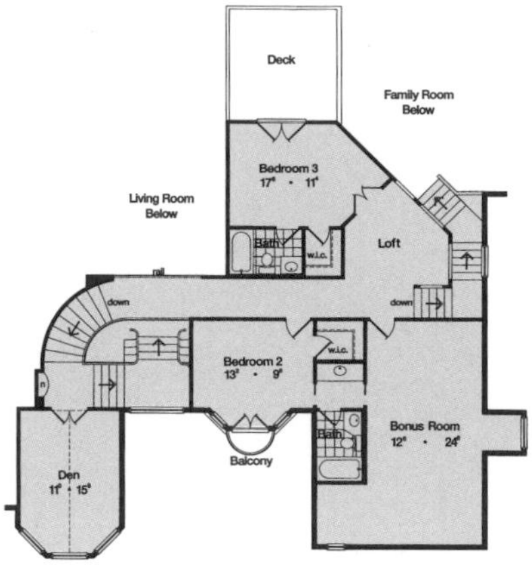

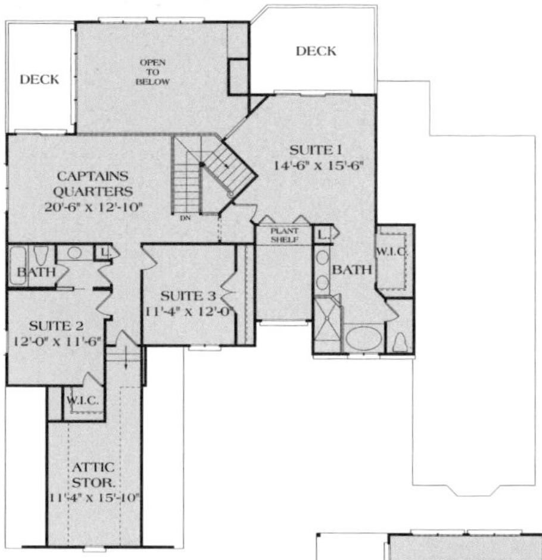

SECOND FLOOR

plan# HPK1700477

Style: Traditional

First Floor: 2,345 sq. ft.

Second Floor: 1,336 sq. ft.

Total: 3,681 sq. ft.

Bedrooms: 4

Bathrooms: 3 ½

Width: 65' - 0"

Depth: 66' - 0"

Foundation: Crawlspace

eplans.com

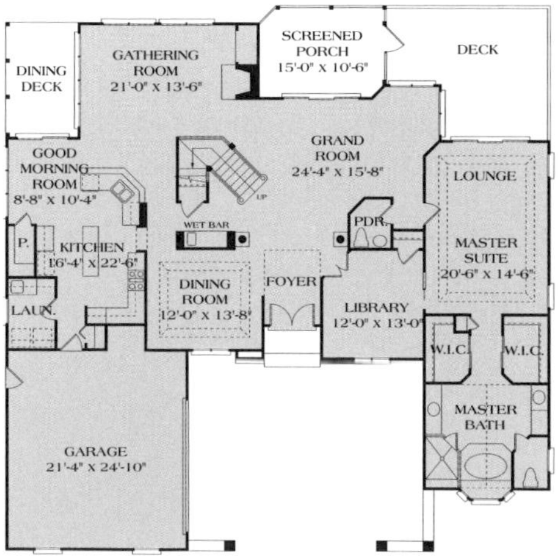

SECOND FLOOR

FIRST FLOOR

plan# HPK1700478

Style: European Cottage

First Floor: 2,657 sq. ft.

Second Floor: 1,026 sq. ft.

Total: 3,683 sq. ft.

Bonus Space: 308 sq. ft.

Bedrooms: 4

Bathrooms: 3½

Width: 75' - 8"

Depth: 74' - 2"

Foundation: Unfinished Basement, Crawlspace, Slab

eplans.com

This breathtaking Mediterranean manor looks great from the curb, but it is the interior that will steal your heart. The entry is lit by twin two-story Palladian windows for subtle drama. On the right, the dining room is defined by columns. The living room makes an elegant impression with a vaulted ceiling and French doors to the rear porch. The kitchen is nearby and sports a "boomerang" counter and a central island. A breakfast bay creates a cheerful place for casual meals. The family room is warmed by a fireplace and brightened by a rear wall of windows. The master suite is in the left wing, decadent with a bayed sitting area, porch access, and an indulgent spa bath. A nearby bedroom makes a great guest suite or home office. Upstairs, two lovely bedrooms share a full bath and a game room.

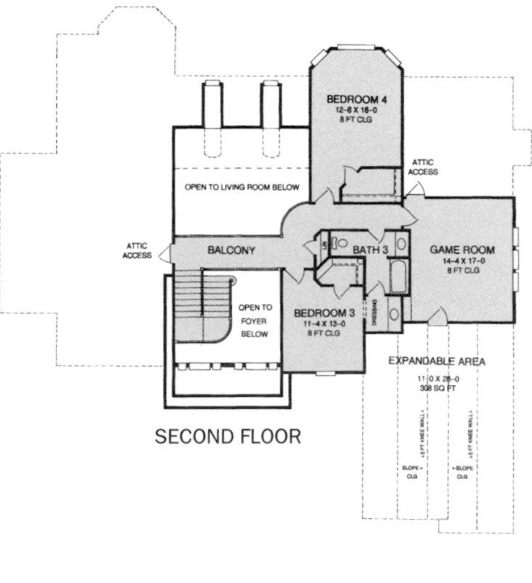

SECOND FLOOR

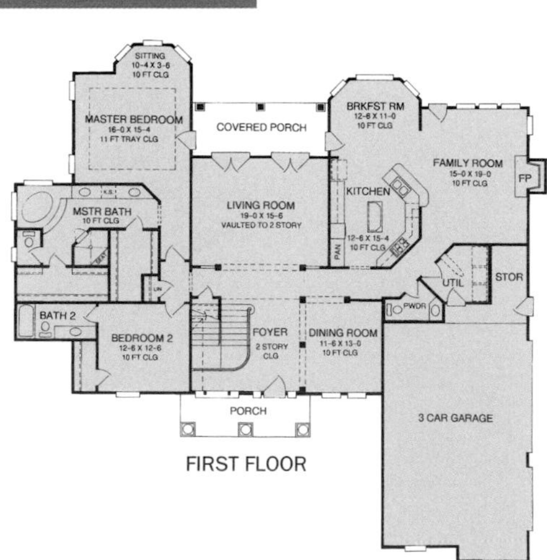

FIRST FLOOR

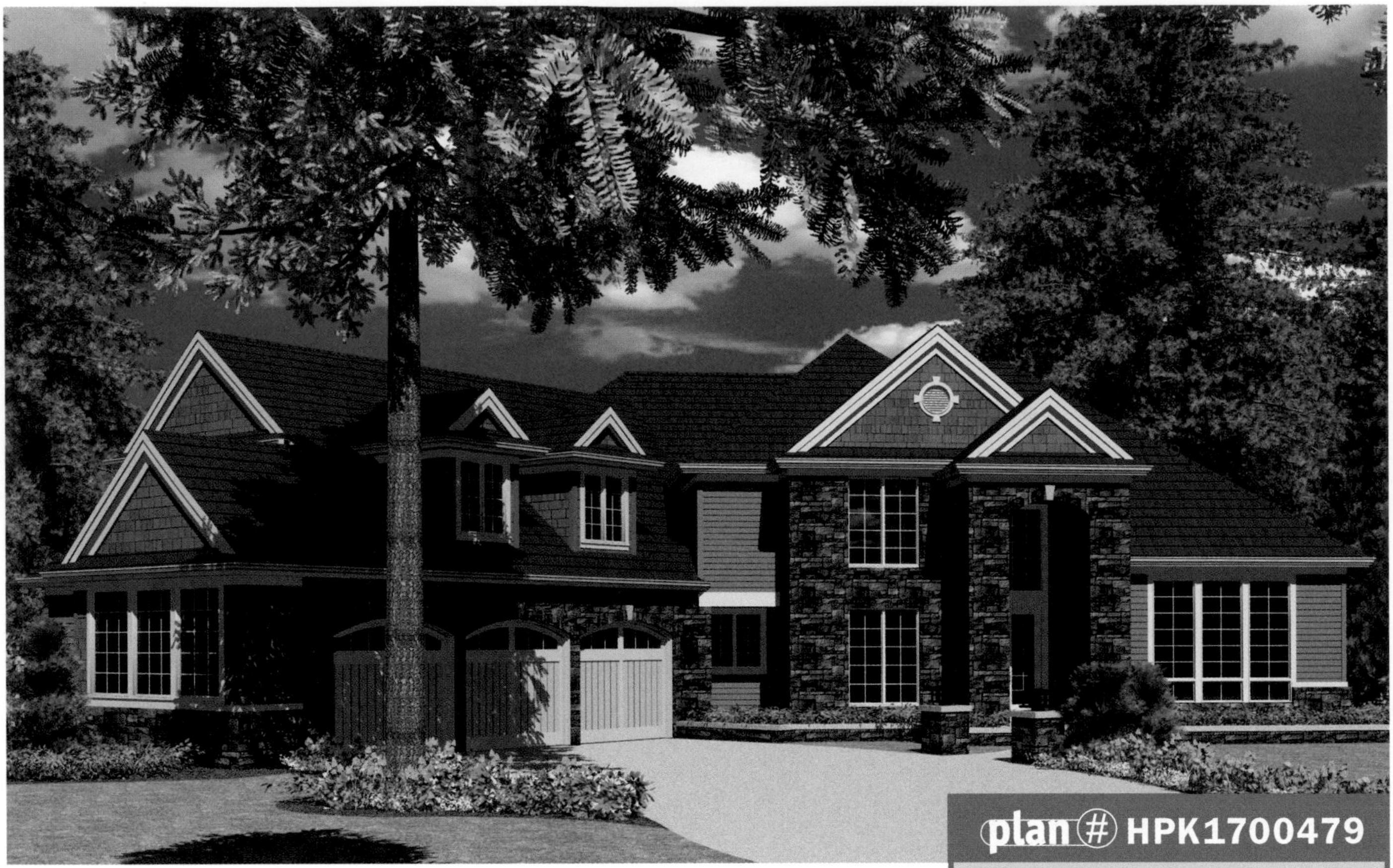

plan# HPK1700479

Style: NW Contemporary

First Floor: 2,148 sq. ft.

Second Floor: 1,541 sq. ft.

Total: 3,689 sq. ft.

Bonus Space: 383 sq. ft.

Bedrooms: 4

Bathrooms: 4

Width: 85' - 5"

Depth: 73' - 0"

Foundation: Crawlspace

eplans.com

SECOND FLOOR

FIRST FLOOR

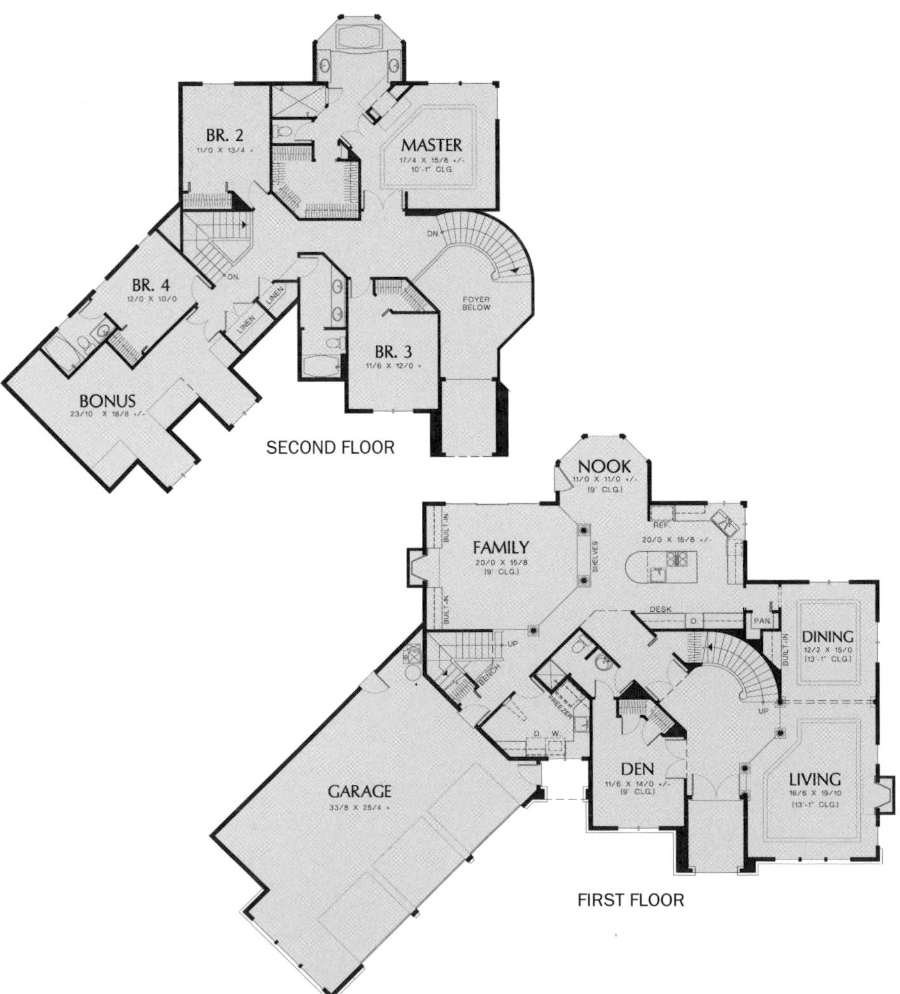

Impressive stone-faced columns frame the entry and give way to a two-story foyer encircled by a curving stairway. The columned living room includes a fireplace. A large island kitchen bridges the formal and family areas of the home, and a sunny breakfast nook provides a place to enjoy the morning together. The first floor is completed by a den or guest room with an adjoining bath, a utility room, and a back stair to the three family bedrooms and large bonus room above the three-car garage. Also upstairs is an elegant master suite, with a walk-in closet and a soaking tub.

plan# HPK1700480

Style: European Cottage
First Floor: 2,772 sq. ft.
Second Floor: 933 sq. ft.
Total: 3,705 sq. ft.
Bedrooms: 4
Bathrooms: 4 ½
Width: 74' - 8"
Depth: 61' - 10"
Foundation: Crawlspace, Slab

eplans.com

A truly grand entry—absolutely stunning on a corner lot—sets the eclectic yet elegant tone of this four-bedroom home. The foyer opens to a dramatic circular stair, then on to the two-story great room that's framed by a second-story balcony. An elegant dining room is set to the side, distinguished by a span of arches. The gourmet kitchen features wrapping counters, a cooktop island, and a breakfast room. A front study and a secondary bedroom are nice accompaniments to the expansive master suite. A through-fireplace, a spa-style bath, and a huge walk-in closet highlight this area. Upstairs, a loft opens to two balconies overlooking the porch and leads to two family bedrooms and a game room.

FIRST FLOOR

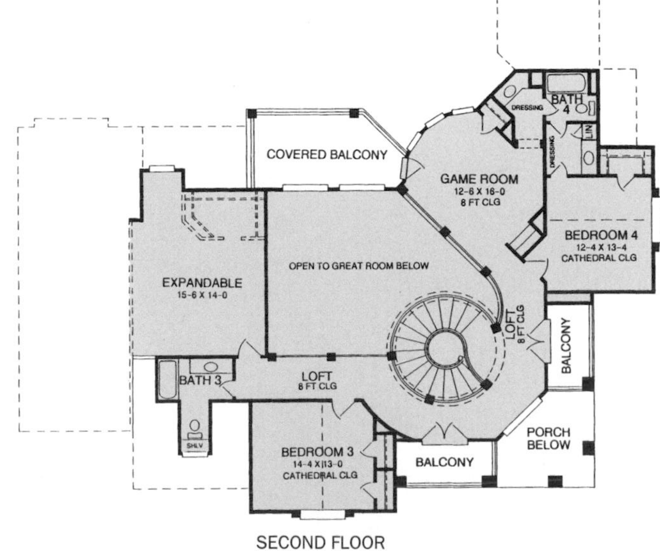

SECOND FLOOR

plan # HPK1700481

Style: Farmhouse

First Floor: 2,442 sq. ft.

Second Floor: 1,286 sq. ft.

Total: 3,728 sq. ft.

Bonus Space: 681 sq. ft.

Bedrooms: 4

Bathrooms: 3½ + ½

Width: 84' - 8"

Depth: 60' - 0"

Foundation: Crawlspace

eplans.com

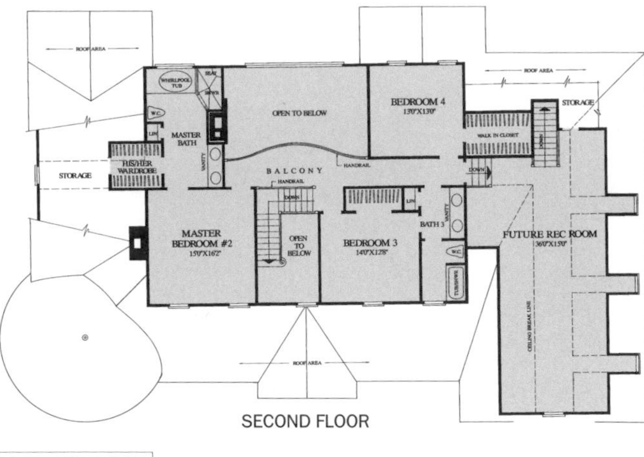

SECOND FLOOR

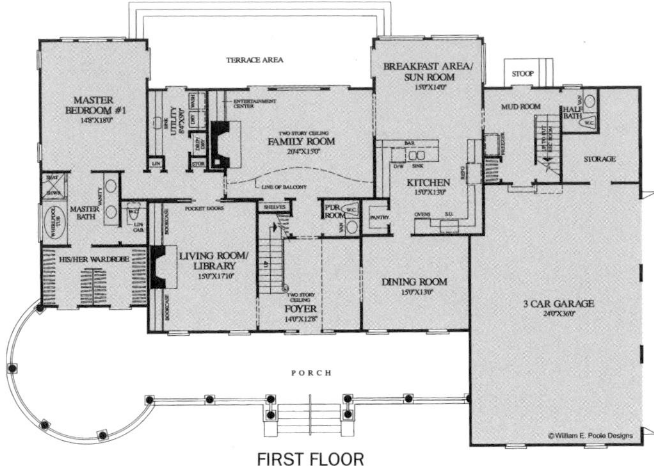

FIRST FLOOR

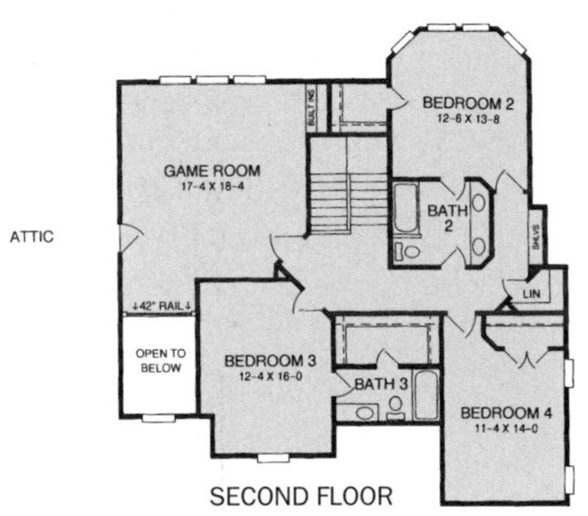

SECOND FLOOR

FIRST FLOOR

plan # HPK1700482

Style: European Cottage

First Floor: 2,369 sq. ft.

Second Floor: 1,363 sq. ft.

Total: 3,732 sq. ft.

Bedrooms: 4

Bathrooms: 3½

Width: 71' - 10"

Depth: 75' - 6"

Foundation: Crawlspace, Slab

eplans.com

plan# HPK1700483

Style: Mediterranean
First Floor: 2,733 sq. ft.
Second Floor: 1,003 sq. ft.
Total: 3,736 sq. ft.
Bedrooms: 4
Bathrooms: 4½
Width: 74' - 8"
Depth: 76' - 3"
Foundation: Crawlspace

eplans.com

A stunning octagonal front porch distinguishes this Mediterranean-style villa. The second-story dormer above the porch draws the eye and accents the entry to this lovely home. The home is designed to capture rear views perfect for a golf course or lakeside site. Through arched openings flanked by columns, the adjoining living room and dining room open off the two-story foyer. A see-through fireplace separates the two rooms. The gourmet kitchen, family room and breakfast room flow together. The owners suite provides access to a private screened porch. A curved staircase leads to a balcony hall and two bedrooms, each with a private bath.

FIRST FLOOR

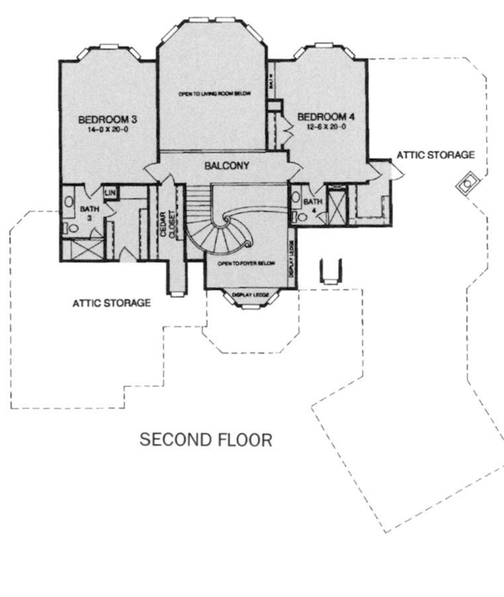

SECOND FLOOR

SECOND FLOOR

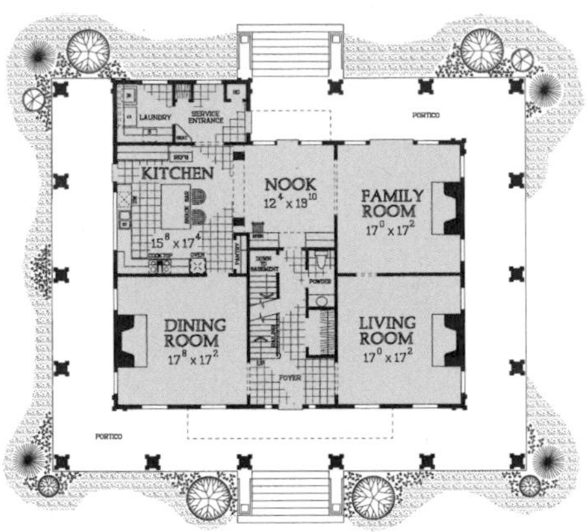

FIRST FLOOR

plan# HPK1700484

Style: Colonial

First Floor: 1,877 sq. ft.

Second Floor: 1,877 sq. ft.

Total: 3,754 sq. ft.

Bedrooms: 4

Bathrooms: 3½

Width: 65' - 0"

Depth: 53' - 0"

Foundation: Unfinished Basement

eplans.com

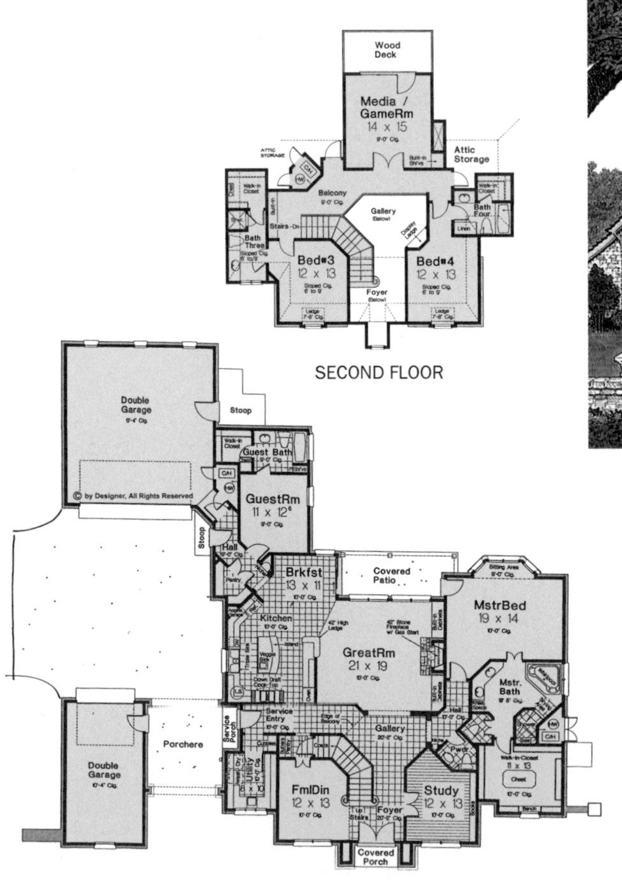

SECOND FLOOR

FIRST FLOOR

plan# HPK1700485

Style: European Cottage

First Floor: 2,742 sq. ft.

Second Floor: 1,027 sq. ft.

Total: 3,769 sq. ft.

Bedrooms: 4

Bathrooms: 4½

Width: 82' - 4"

Depth: 85' - 4"

Foundation: Slab, Unfinished Basement

eplans.com

plan# HPK1700486

Style: Country Cottage
First Floor: 1,901 sq. ft.
Second Floor: 1,874 sq. ft.
Total: 3,775 sq. ft.
Bedrooms: 4
Bathrooms: 3½
Width: 50' - 0"
Depth: 70' - 0"
Foundation: Pier (same as Piling)

eplans.com

SMART TIP

This revised French Colonial design takes great advantage of the L-shaped floor plan by establishing a wrapping porch at the front of the home. The porch also mitigates the amount of natural light entering the home, such as in the living room. For the look of an authentic New Orleans urban home, consider having the builder use wrought-iron balcony railings and windows without decorative pediments.

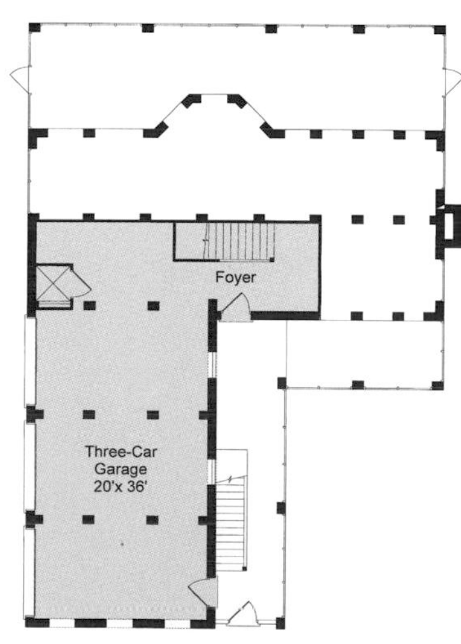

BASEMENT

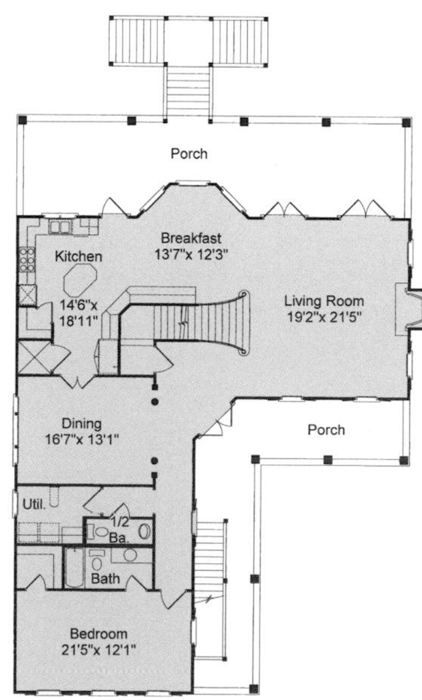

FIRST FLOOR

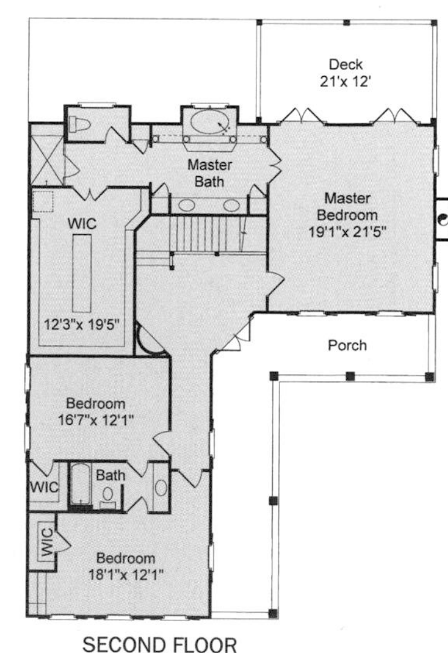

SECOND FLOOR

plan# HPK1700487
Style: French
First Floor: 1,807 sq. ft.
Second Floor: 1,970 sq. ft.
Total: 3,777 sq. ft.
Bedrooms: 4
Bathrooms: 3½
Width: 57' - 4"
Depth: 53' - 6"
Foundation: Unfinished Walkout Basement
eplans.com

For sheer magnificence, this chateau-style mansion is unbeatable. Guests will be enchanted, both by the pillared entry and the inside splendor. The two-story grand room, with an extended-hearth fireplace, is well designed for unforgettable soirees. A front dining room and living room (or make it a library) radiate a gracious welcome. The kitchen can easily serve gourmet dinners and informal family meals. It opens to an exquisite breakfast bay with five windows and to a keeping room with a fireplace. All four bedrooms are situated upstairs, and the posh master suite enjoys His and Hers walk-in closets and vanities. The laundry is conveniently located on this floor.

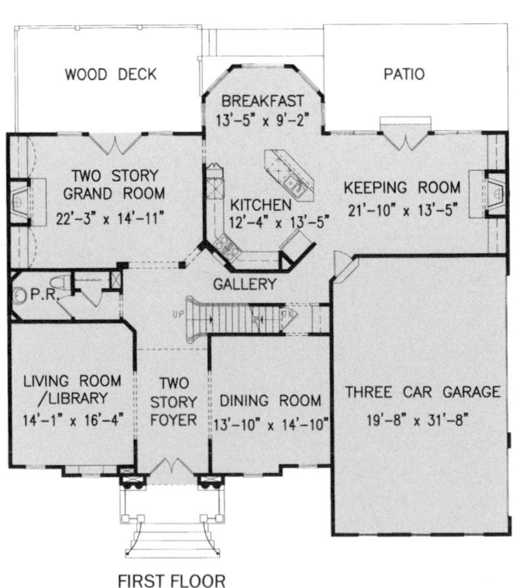

FIRST FLOOR

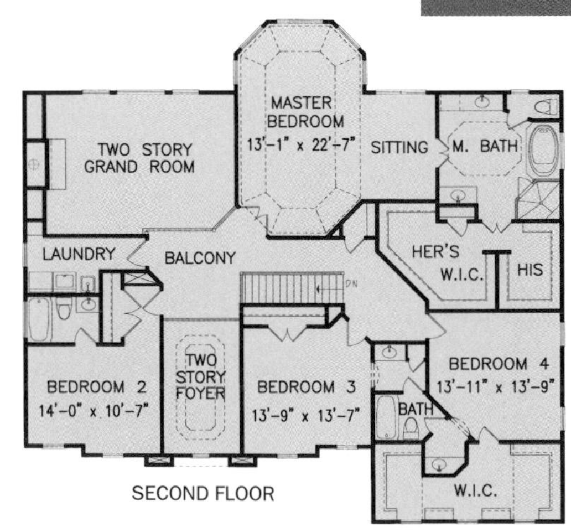

SECOND FLOOR

plan# HPK1700488

Style: Chateau Style
First Floor: 2,814 sq. ft.
Second Floor: 979 sq. ft.
Total: 3,793 sq. ft.
Bedrooms: 4
Bathrooms: 3½
Width: 98' - 0"
Depth: 45' - 10"
Foundation: Slab, Unfinished Basement

eplans.com

A covered, columned porch and symmetrically placed windows welcome you to this elegant brick home. The formal living room offers built-in bookshelves and one of two fireplaces, the other being found in the spacious family room. A gallery running between these rooms leads to the sumptuous master suite, which includes a sitting area, a private covered patio, and a bath with two walk-in closets, dual vanities, a large shower, and a garden tub. The step-saving kitchen features a work island and a snack bar. The breakfast and family rooms offer doors to the large covered veranda. Upstairs you'll find three bedrooms and attic storage space. The three-car garage even has room for a golf cart.

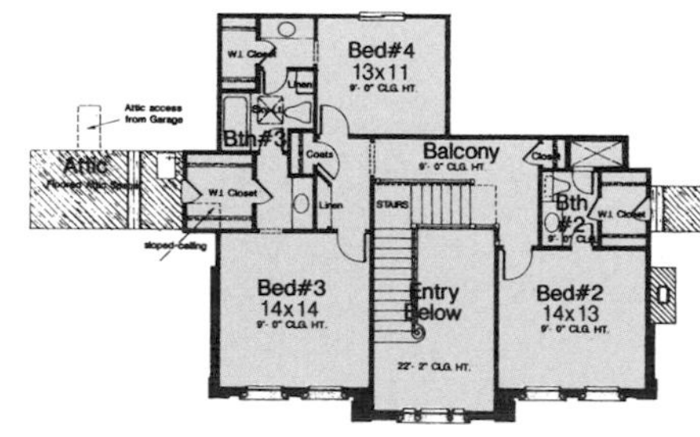

SECOND FLOOR

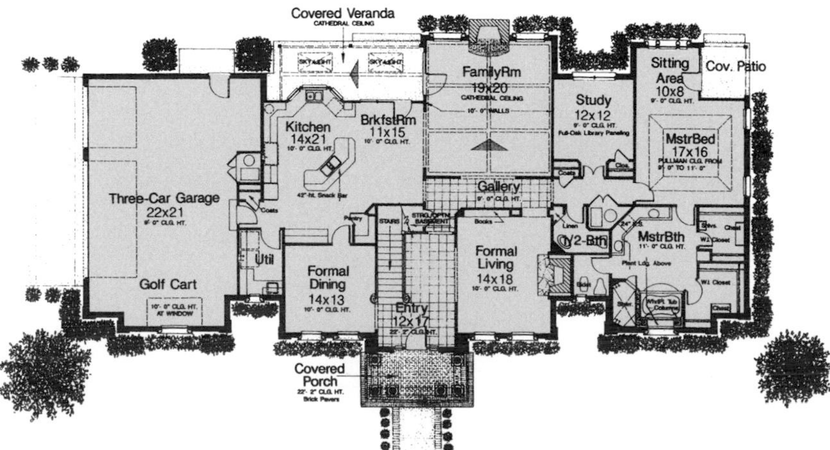

FIRST FLOOR

plan # HPK1700489

Style: Norman
First Floor: 2,520 sq. ft.
Second Floor: 1,305 sq. ft.
Total: 3,825 sq. ft.
Bedrooms: 4
Bathrooms: 3½
Width: 73' - 8"
Depth: 58' - 6"
Foundation: Slab

eplans.com

Distinctive touches to this elegant European-style home make an inviting first impression. The two-story foyer is graced by a lovely staircase and a balcony overlook from the upstairs. To the right is the formal dining room; to the left, a study. The great room directly leads to the two-story double bay windows that introduce the kitchen and keeping room. A huge walk-in pantry and adjacent butler's pantry connect the dining room to the kitchen. A marvelous owners suite features a sitting room and pampering bath. Upstairs, three bedrooms and two full baths complete the plan.

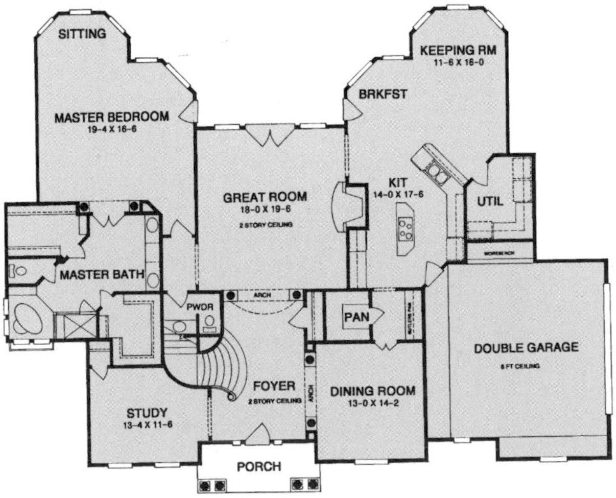

SITTING
MASTER BEDROOM 19-4 X 16-6
MASTER BATH
KEEPING RM 11-6 X 16-0
BRKFST
GREAT ROOM 18-0 X 19-6
KIT 14-0 X 17-6
UTIL
PAN
PWDR
FOYER
DINING ROOM 13-0 X 14-2
DOUBLE GARAGE
STUDY 13-4 X 11-6
PORCH

FIRST FLOOR

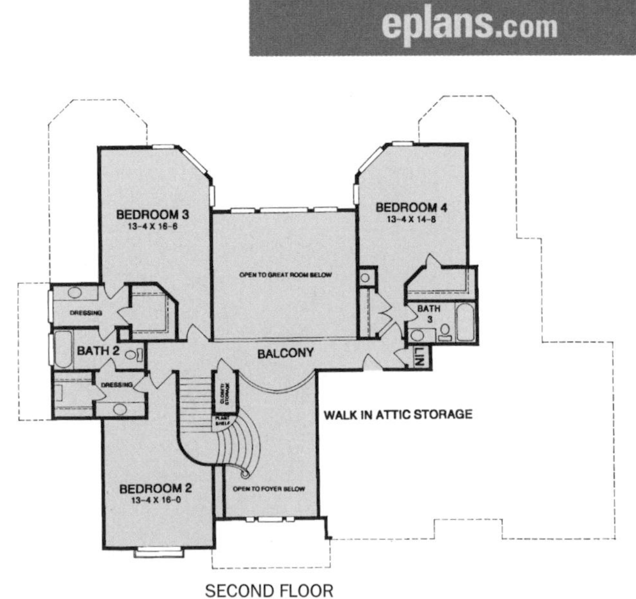

SECOND FLOOR

plan # HPK1700490

Style: European Cottage
First Floor: 1,634 sq. ft.
Second Floor: 2,207 sq. ft.
Total: 3,841 sq. ft.
Bedrooms: 4
Bathrooms: 3½
Width: 64' - 0"
Depth: 50' - 0"
Foundation: Crawlspace

eplans.com

The stone and siding exterior lends a stately appeal to this 3,800 square foot, four bedroom home. The first floor is dedicated to amenity-filled common living spaces that flow easily for an efficient layout. The great room sits at the heart of the home with a central fireplace, built-in bookshelves, and a built-in media center. The expansive, gourmet kitchen conveniently serves the adjacent dining room. Upstairs, the master suite is a homeowner's dream complete with an enormous walk-in closet, a private fireplace, and a spa tub. Three additional family bedrooms are housed on this level; bedroom #4 boasts a full bath and bedrooms #2 and #3 are separated by a Jack-and-Jill bath. The media room is equipped with a snack bar, perfect for entertaining. A second-floor laundry room is an added bonus.

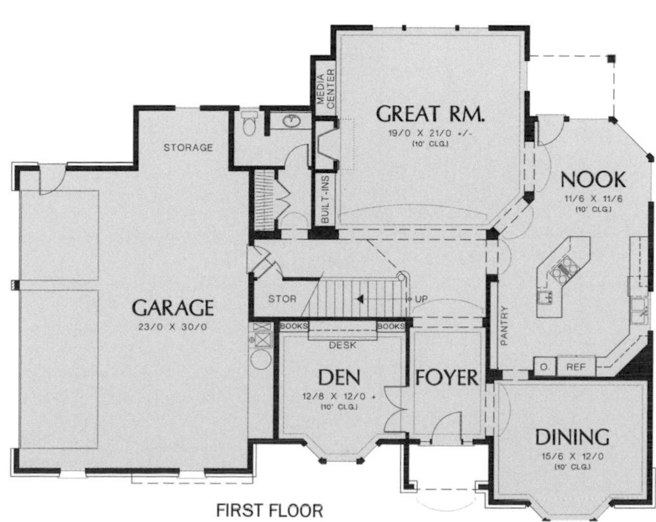

FIRST FLOOR

SECOND FLOOR

plan# HPK1700491

Style: European Cottage

First Floor: 1,992 sq. ft.

Second Floor: 1,851 sq. ft.

Total: 3,843 sq. ft.

Bedrooms: 5

Bathrooms: 4½

Width: 66' - 4"

Depth: 53' - 0"

Foundation: Crawlspace, Unfinished Walkout Basement

eplans.com

SECOND FLOOR

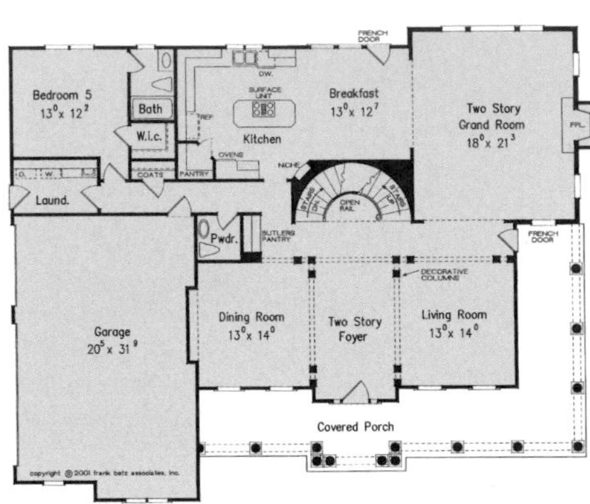

FIRST FLOOR

plan# HPK1700492

Style: Traditional

First Floor: 2,306 sq. ft.

Second Floor: 1,544 sq. ft.

Total: 3,850 sq. ft.

Bedrooms: 5

Bathrooms: 3½

Width: 80' - 8"

Depth: 51' - 8"

Foundation: Unfinished Basement

eplans.com

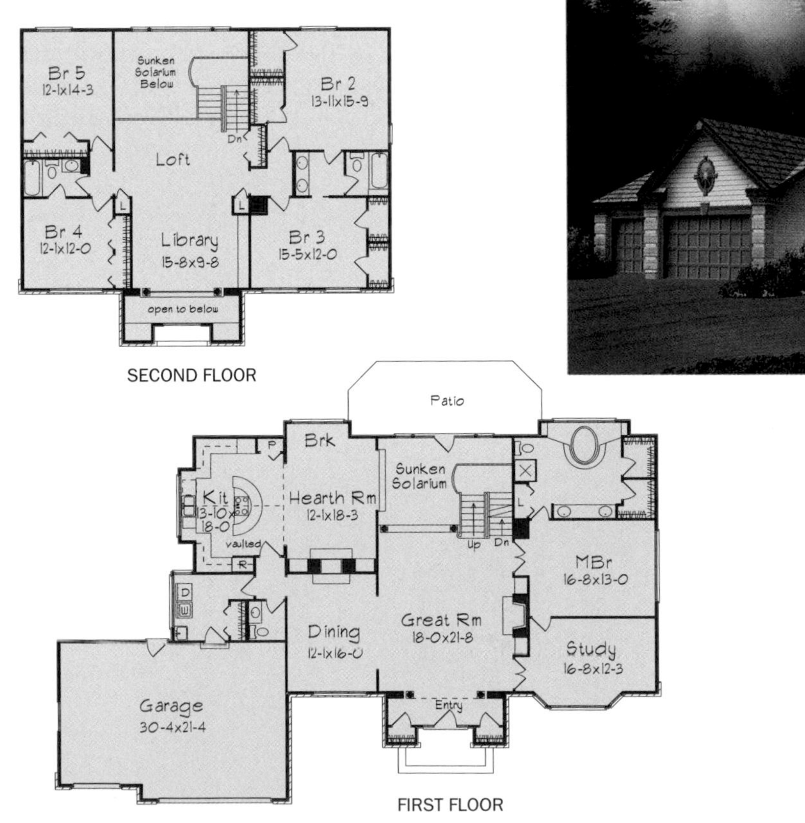

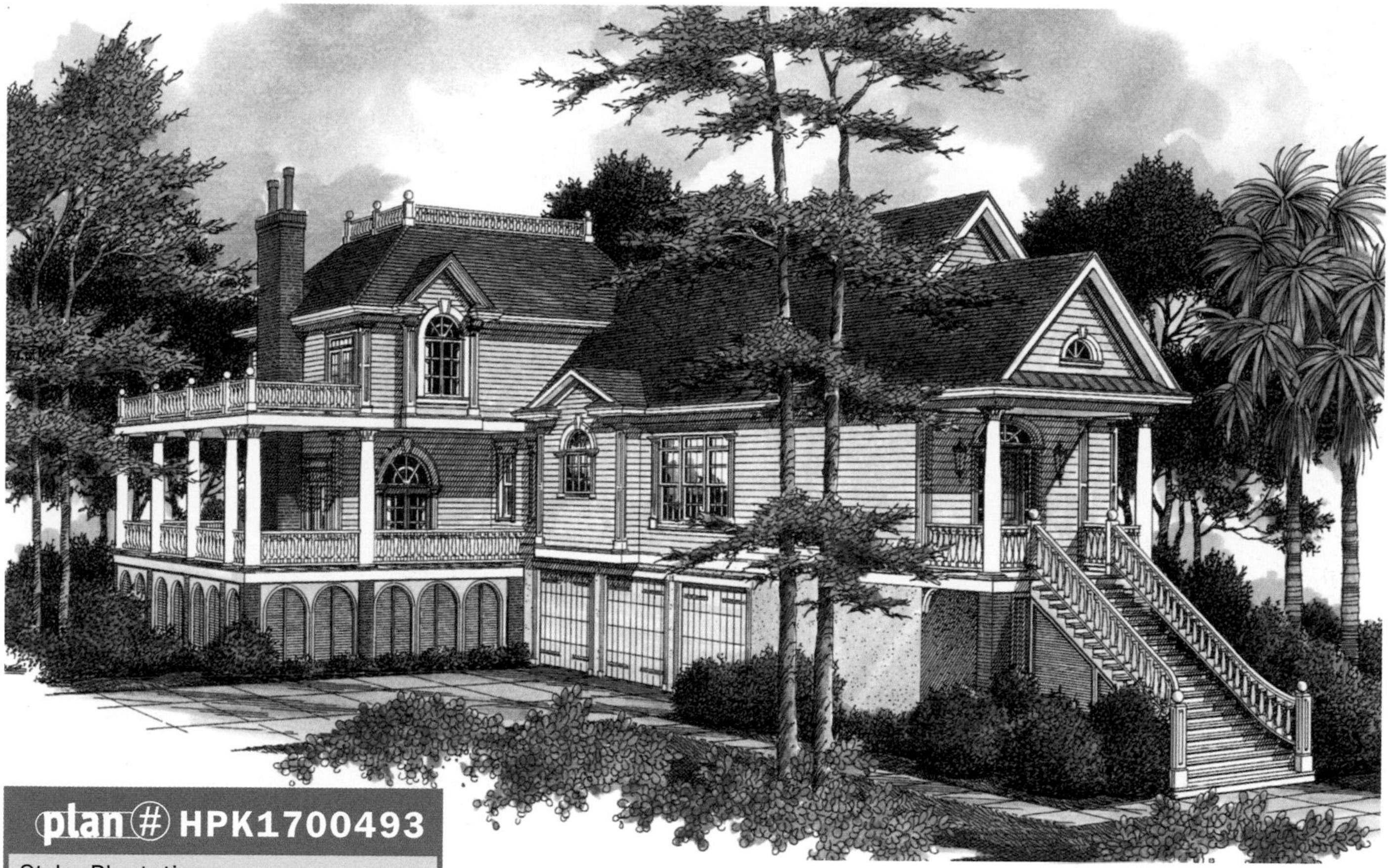

plan # HPK1700493

Style: Plantation
First Floor: 2,578 sq. ft.
Second Floor: 1,277 sq. ft.
Total: 3,855 sq. ft.
Bedrooms: 4
Bathrooms: 4
Width: 53' - 6"
Depth: 97' - 0"
Foundation: Pier (same as Piling)

eplans.com

This charming Charleston design is full of surprises! Perfect for a narrow footprint, the raised foundation is ideal for a waterfront location. An entry porch introduces a winding staircase. To the right is a living room/library that functions as a formal entertaining space. A large hearth and two sets of French doors to the covered porch enhance the great room. The master suite is positioned for privacy and includes great amenities that work to relax the homeowners. Upstairs, three family bedrooms, two full baths, an open media room, and a future game room create a fantastic casual family space.

BASEMENT

FIRST FLOOR

SECOND FLOOR

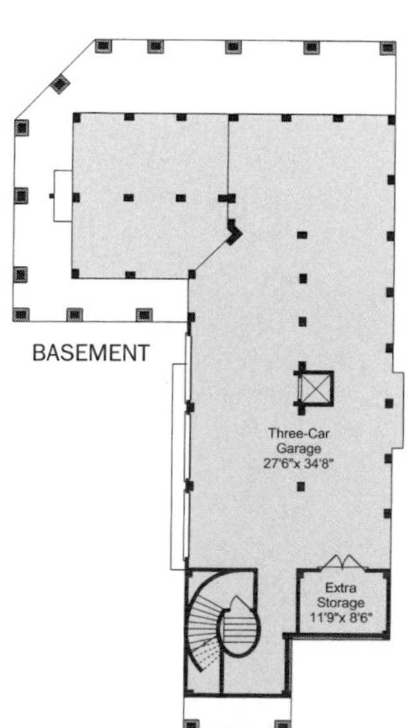

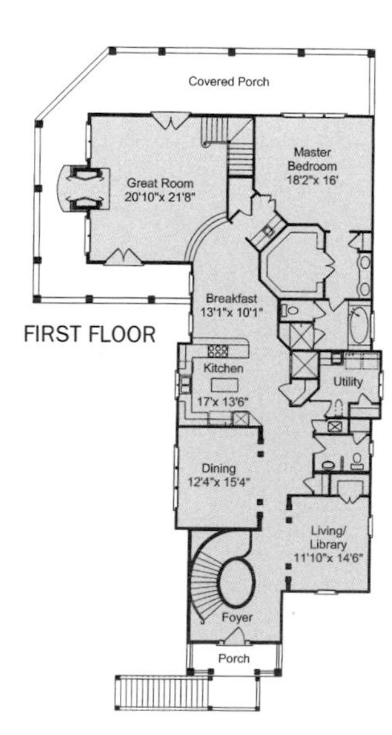

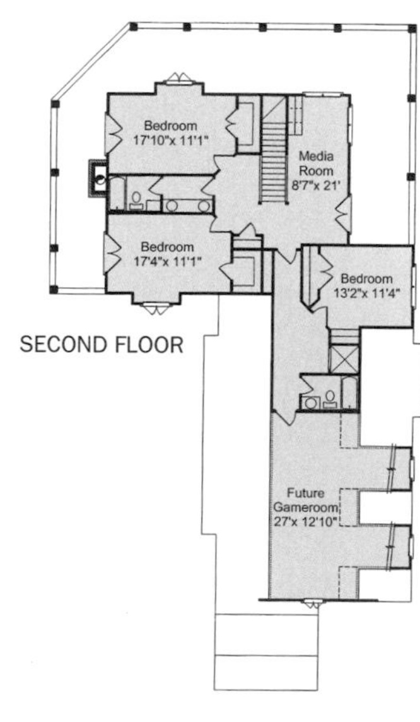

plan# HPK1700494

Style: Farmhouse

First Floor: 2,853 sq. ft.

Second Floor: 1,002 sq. ft.

Total: 3,855 sq. ft.

Bedrooms: 4

Bathrooms: 5

Width: 79' - 4"

Depth: 64' - 8"

Foundation: Slab

eplans.com

This home has it all, from its rich country elevation with a wraparound front porch to its large family floor plan and amenities. Upon entering the foyer, you have a direct view through the living room to the covered patio beyond. To the right is the large family dining room and to the left is a quiet den/study with built-ins. The master suite enjoys two walk-in closets, a lavish bath and private access to the rear covered patio. The island kitchen provides easy access to the dining room, laundry, garage and storage pantry. A second bedroom on the first floor features its own bath and can act as a guest room or mother-in-law suite. Two additional bedrooms and baths on the second floor reside adjacent to a large game room.

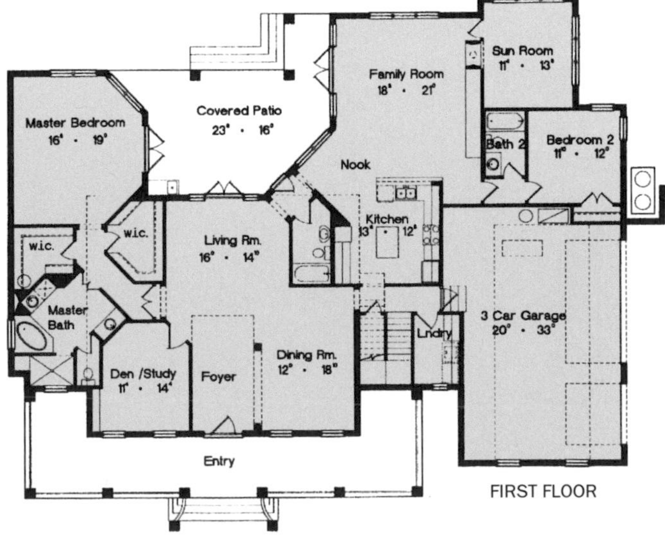

FIRST FLOOR

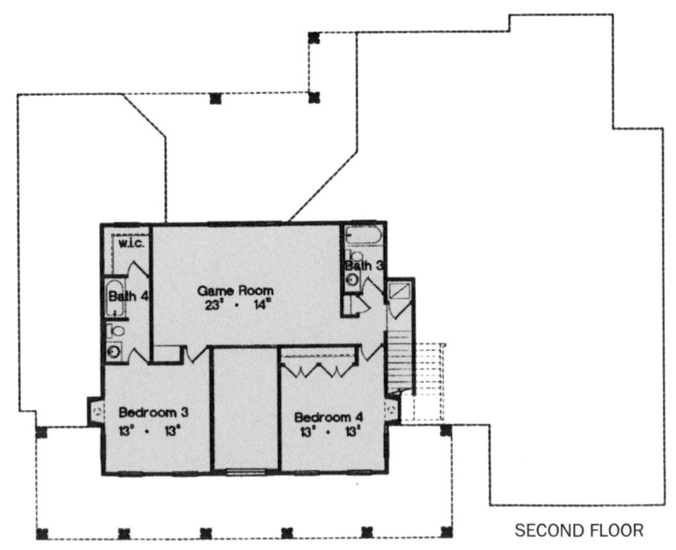

SECOND FLOOR

plan # HPK1700495
Style: Traditional
First Floor: 2,474 sq. ft.
Second Floor: 1,389 sq. ft.
Total: 3,863 sq. ft.
Bedrooms: 4
Bathrooms: 3½
Width: 75' - 1"
Depth: 80' - 3"
eplans.com

This breathtaking estate home takes its cue from European architecture, with bold turrets and bright Palladian windows. Inside, this exceptional floor plan begins with a grand entry that soars with a 19-foot ceiling. Privacy in the formal areas is guaranteed with discreet pocket doors between the hearth-warmed living room and bayed dining room. A butler's pantry makes an elegant passage to the island-cooktop kitchen, where an elongated serving bar and sunny breakfast nook make casual meals fun and easy. In the rear left wing, the bayed master suite celebrates light and luxury. A vaulted bath with a whirlpool tub joins dual walk-in closets for a retreat that will indulge. Upstairs, three generously appointed bedrooms access a game room with a sun deck. A study resides midway between the two levels for a dramatic presentation.

REAR EXTERIOR

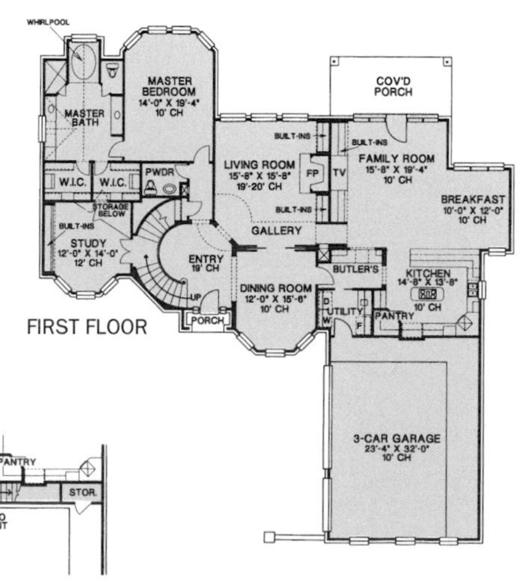

FIRST FLOOR

OPTIONAL LAYOUT

SECOND FLOOR

plan# HPK1700496

Style: European Cottage
First Floor: 3,030 sq. ft.
Second Floor: 848 sq. ft.
Total: 3,878 sq. ft.
Bonus Space: 320 sq. ft.
Bedrooms: 4
Bathrooms: 4½
Width: 88' - 0"
Depth: 72' - 1"
Foundation: Slab

eplans.com

SECOND FLOOR

FIRST FLOOR

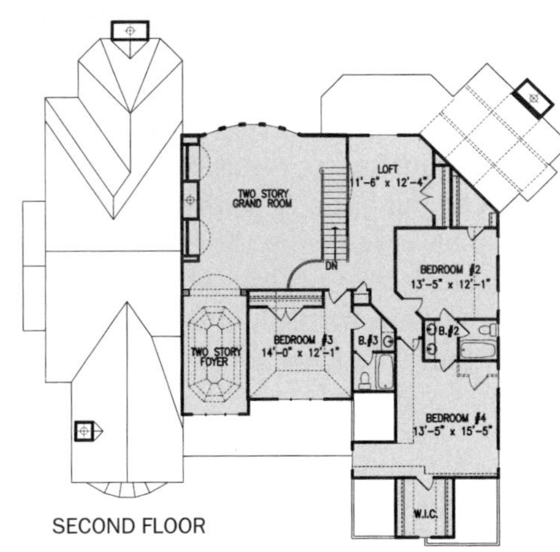

SECOND FLOOR

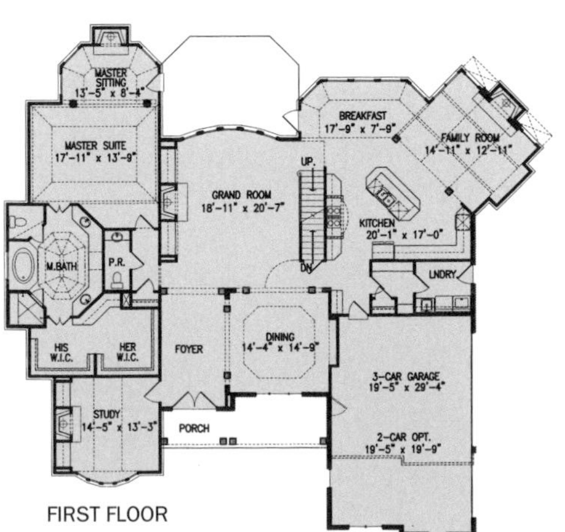

FIRST FLOOR

plan# HPK1700497

Style: Traditional
First Floor: 2,729 sq. ft.
Second Floor: 1,157 sq. ft.
Total: 3,886 sq. ft.
Bedrooms: 4
Bathrooms: 3½
Width: 64' - 6"
Depth: 70' - 11"
Foundation: Slab, Unfinished Walkout Basement

eplans.com

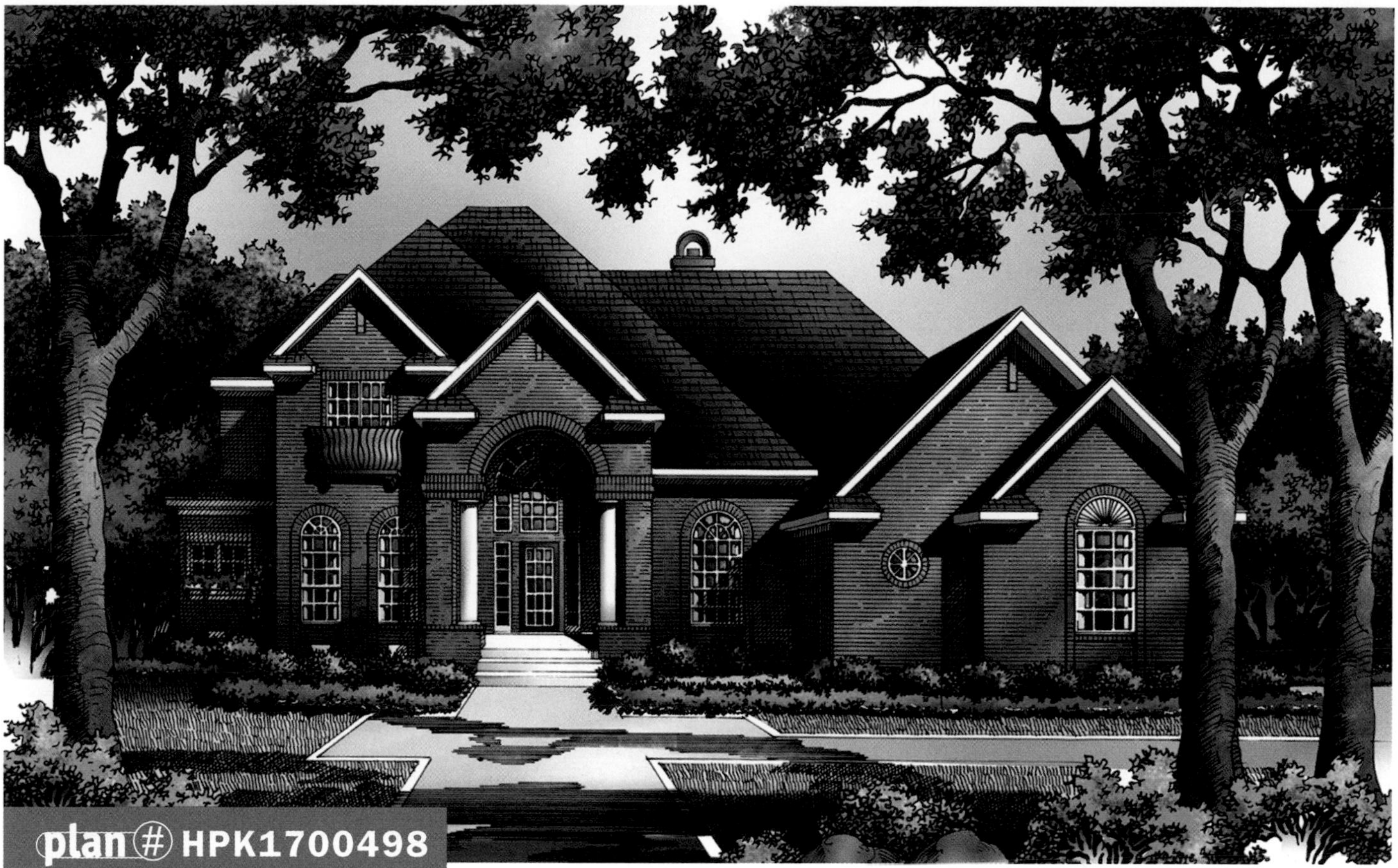

plan# HPK1700498

Style: European Cottage
First Floor: 2,319 sq. ft.
Second Floor: 1,570 sq. ft.
Total: 3,889 sq. ft.
Bedrooms: 4
Bathrooms: 3½
Width: 72' - 0"
Depth: 58' - 0"
Foundation: Crawlspace

eplans.com

Fine brick detailing, multiple arches and gables, and a grand entry give this four-bedroom home plenty of charm. The graceful, window-filled entry leads to a foyer flanked by a formal dining room and a study perfect for a home office. The great room, directly ahead, offers a fireplace and access to outside. A butler's pantry is located between the kitchen and dining room. The master suite is on the first floor. On the second floor three family bedrooms, each with a walk-in closet, share two baths and a game room.

SECOND FLOOR

FIRST FLOOR

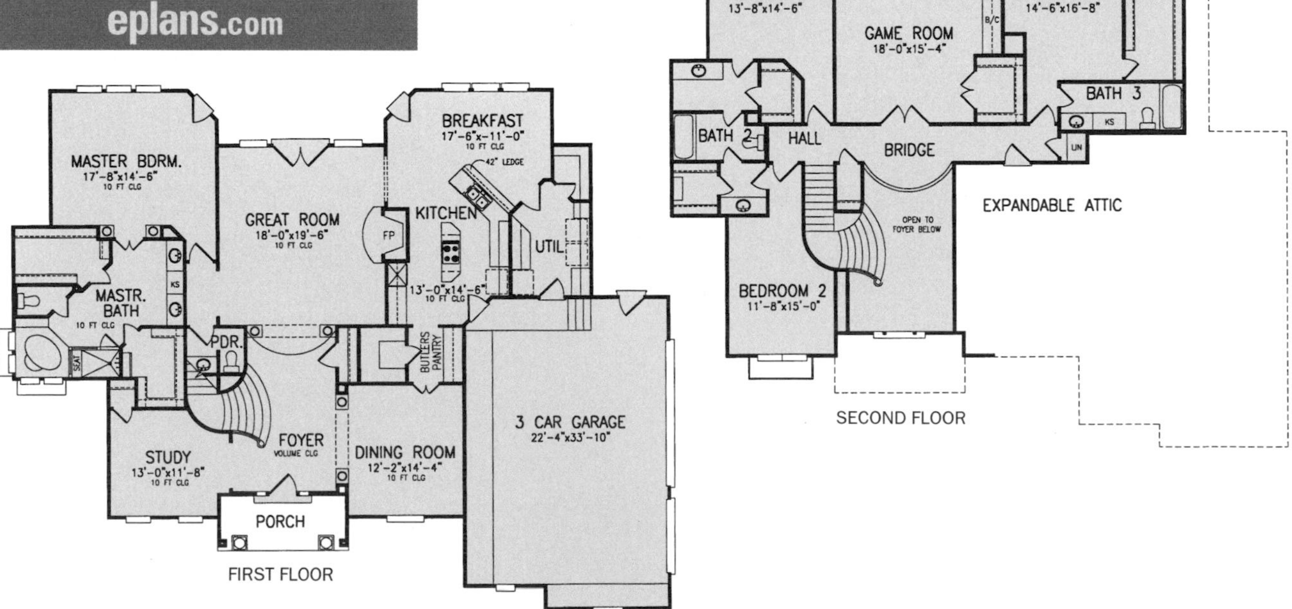

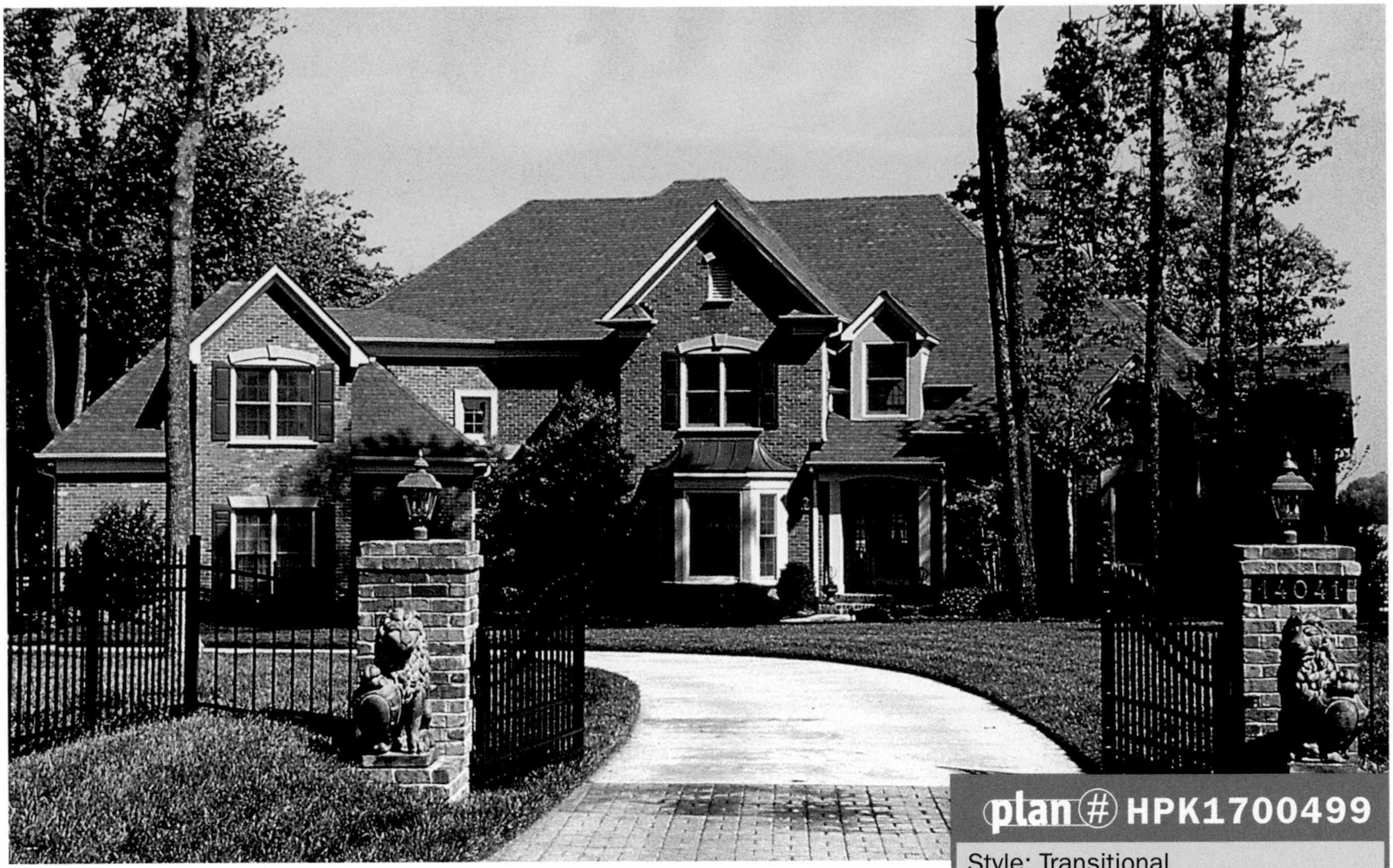

plan# HPK1700499

Style: Transitional	
First Floor: 2,346 sq. ft.	
Second Floor: 1,554 sq. ft.	
Total: 3,900 sq. ft.	
Bonus Space: 455 sq. ft.	
Bedrooms: 3	
Bathrooms: 3½	
Width: 97' - 4"	
Depth: 58' - 6"	
Foundation: Crawlspace	

eplans.com

This plan is definitely the house of sun. A complex roofline sits astride a brick facade, with bay and dormer windows dappling this sweeping exterior. Inside, you'll be in awe of the corner master suite on the main level, which provides plenty of views through the windows, and private outdoor access, not to mention its own spectacular bath. The great room has more of those views in store, plus a pair of stunning French doors. A sun room allows access to a small patio and to the garage.

FIRST FLOOR

SECOND FLOOR

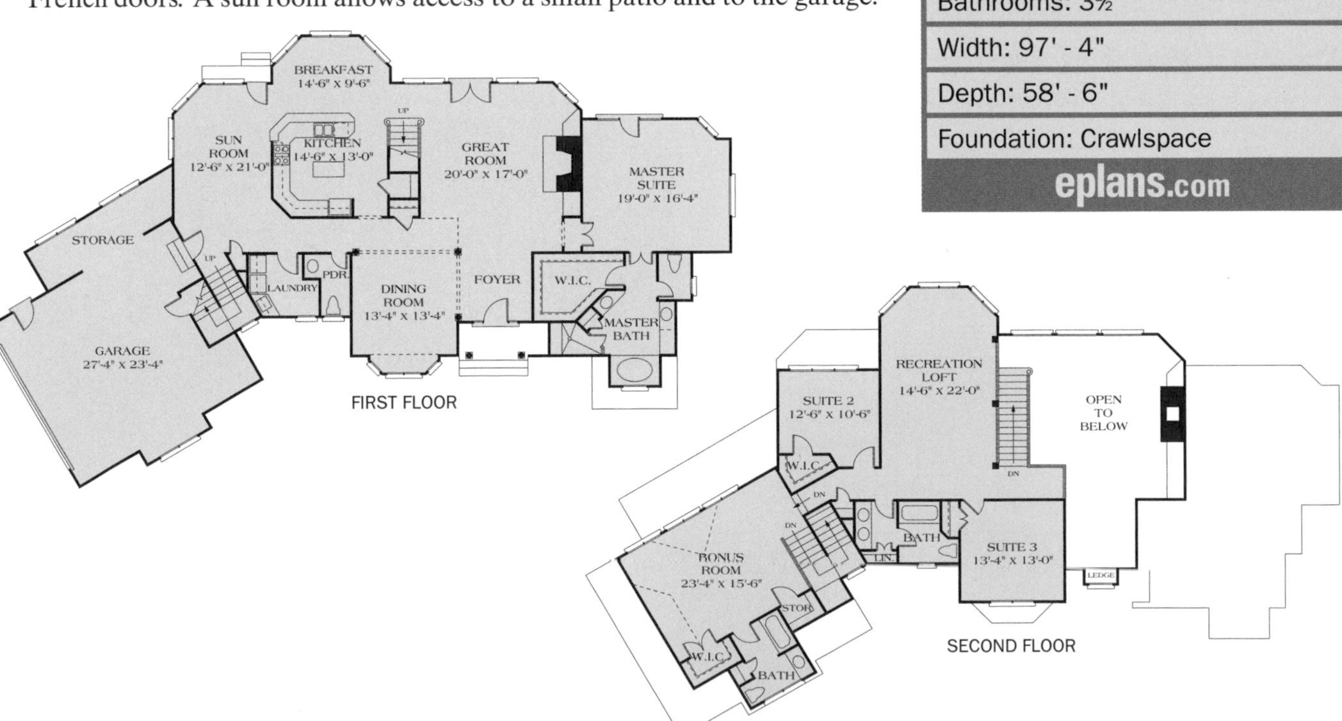

plan# HPK1700500

- Style: French Country
- First Floor: 1,805 sq. ft.
- Second Floor: 2,096 sq. ft.
- Total: 3,901 sq. ft.
- Basement: 1,414 sq. ft.
- Bedrooms: 5
- Bathrooms: 4½
- Width: 62' - 2"
- Depth: 54' - 0"
- Foundation: Finished Walkout Basement

eplans.com

The stone and stucco facade, arches atop the portico, dormers, and arched windows lend this home a distinctly European flavor. A practical floor plan is revealed inside, with living areas on the main level, bedrooms upstairs, and fun and games in the basement. The island kitchen is a dream, with miles of prep space and close proximity to a cozy breakfast area. The family room and rec room each offer gorgeous fireplaces. Guests staying in the lower-level bedroom know they're in for a good time with the billiards room and bar nearby. A huge garage and plenty of storage inside round out the practicality of this design.

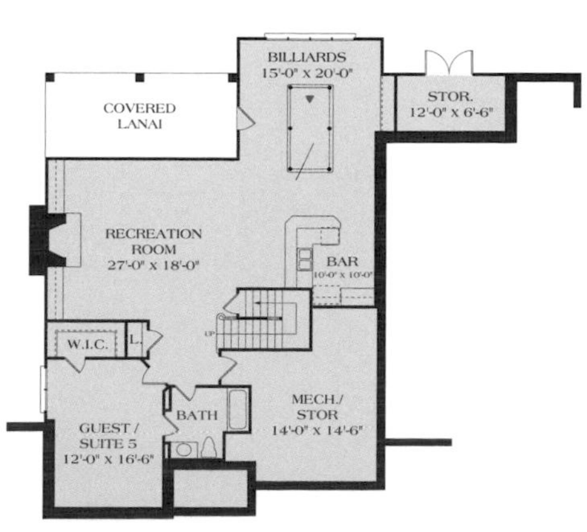

BASEMENT

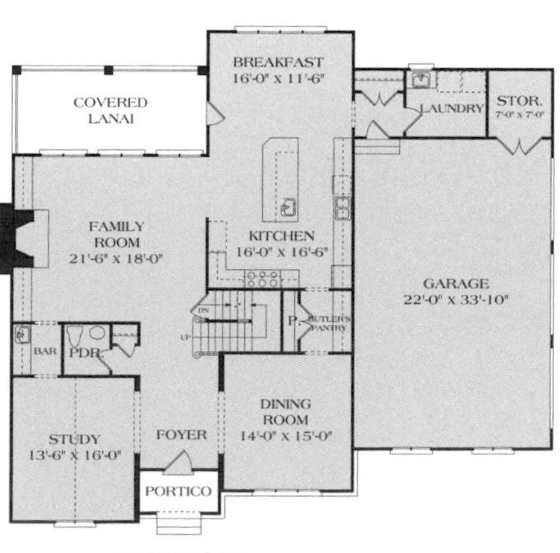

FIRST FLOOR

SECOND FLOOR

plan# HPK1700501

Style: European Cottage
First Floor: 2,788 sq. ft.
Second Floor: 1,116 sq. ft.
Total: 3,904 sq. ft.
Bedrooms: 4
Bathrooms: 3½
Width: 68' - 10"
Depth: 76' - 4"
Foundation: Crawlspace, Slab, Unfinished Basement

eplans.com

Straight from the hills of the French countryside, this whimsical estate features every amenity on your wish list with the style and grace you've been searching for. Enter through French doors to a two-story foyer; on the left, a dining room is defined by columns. The living room is ahead, adorned with columns and leading into a gallery with rear-property access. The master suite is entered via the gallery and delights in a bayed sitting area, lavish whirlpool bath, and two generous walk-in closets. Living areas on the opposite side of the home include a kitchen with a unique serving island and a sunlit family room with a fireplace. The upper level hosts two bedrooms, a game room, and a full bath. A balcony overlook to the living room is an elegant touch.

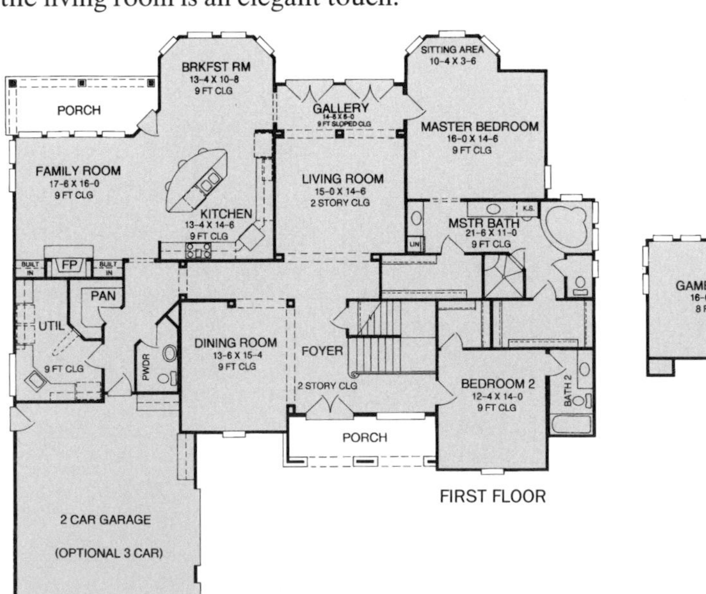

FIRST FLOOR

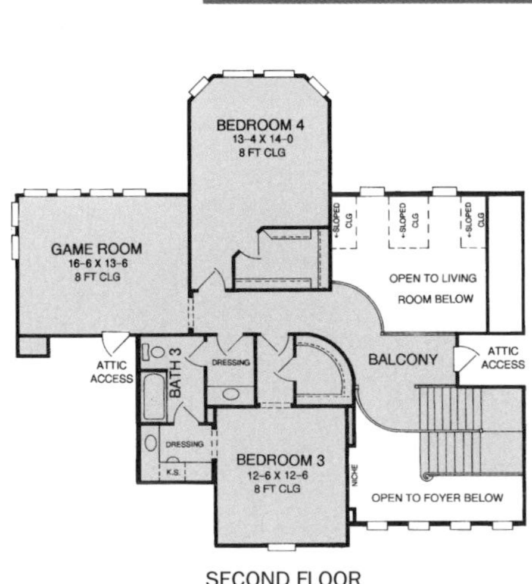

SECOND FLOOR

plan# HPK1700502

Style: European Cottage
First Floor: 2,612 sq. ft.
Second Floor: 1,300 sq. ft.
Total: 3,912 sq. ft.
Bonus Space: 330 sq. ft.
Bedrooms: 4
Bathrooms: 3½
Width: 95' - 6"
Depth: 64' - 0"
Foundation: Unfinished Basement

eplans.com

Lovely stucco columns and a copper standing-seam roof highlight this stone-and-brick facade. An elegant New World interior starts with a sensational winding staircase, a carved handrail, and honey-hued hardwood floor. An open, two-story formal dining room enjoys front-property views and leads to the gourmet kitchen through the butler's pantry, announced by an archway. Beyond the foyer, tall windows brighten the two-story family room and bring in a sense of the outdoors; a fireplace makes the space cozy and warm. The center food-prep island counter overlooks a breakfast niche that offers wide views through walls of windows and access to the rear porch.

REAR EXTERIOR

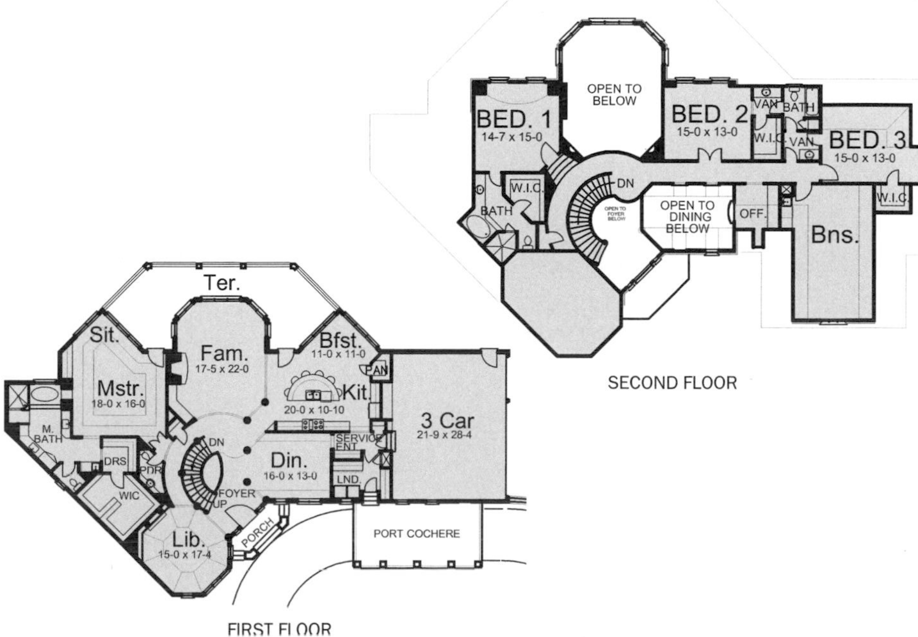

SECOND FLOOR

FIRST FLOOR

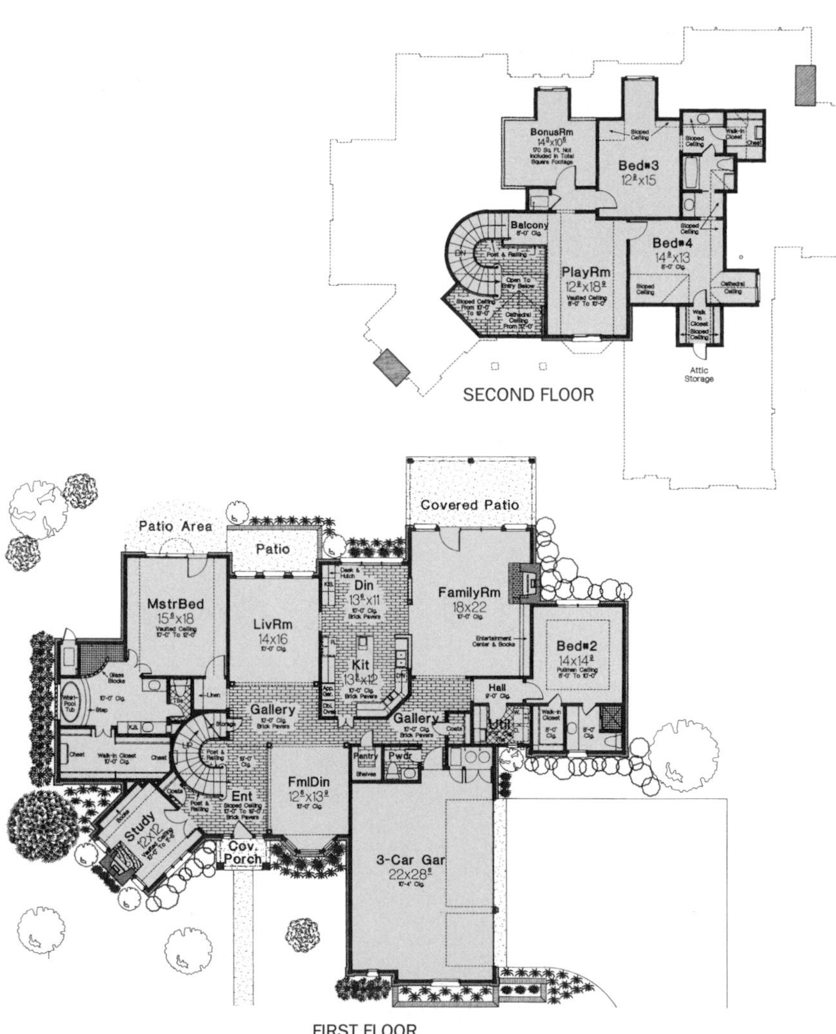

plan# HPK1700503

- Style: Country Cottage
- First Floor: 2,985 sq. ft.
- Second Floor: 938 sq. ft.
- Total: 3,923 sq. ft.
- Bedrooms: 4
- Bathrooms: 3½
- Width: 86' - 0"
- Depth: 68' - 6"
- Foundation: Slab, Unfinished Basement

eplans.com

This French country design, decorated with brick and stone, begins with a cedar-beamed entry. Fireplaces enhance the study and the family room, and the living room and family room both open to patios. The island kitchen works well with both the formal bayed dining room as well as the casual dining area to the back of the home. A secluded bedroom with a private bath can serve as a guest suite. The first-floor master suite is designed to pamper, with a huge walk-in closet, a lavish bath and private access to the backyard. Upstairs, find two family bedrooms, a playroom and bonus space.

plan# HPK1700504

Style: Traditional
First Floor: 2,751 sq. ft.
Second Floor: 1,185 sq. ft.
Total: 3,936 sq. ft.
Bedrooms: 4
Bathrooms: 3½
Width: 79' - 0"
Depth: 66' - 4"
Foundation: Slab, Unfinished Basement

eplans.com

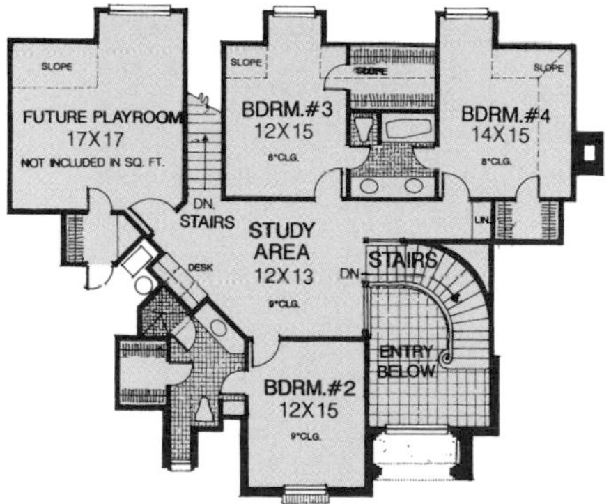

SECOND FLOOR

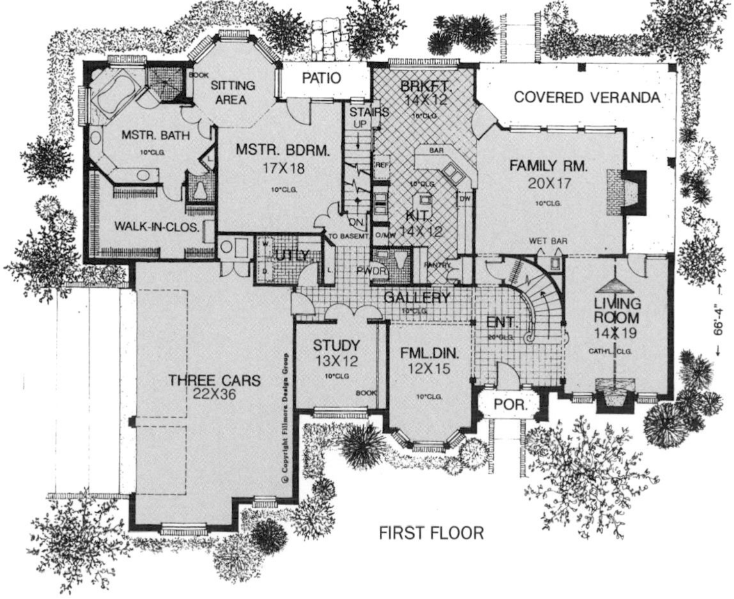

FIRST FLOOR

A grand brick facade, this home boasts muntin windows, multi-level rooflines, cut-brick jack arches, and a beautifully arched entry. A cathedral-ceilinged living room, complete with fireplace, and a family dining room flank the 20-foot-high entry. Relax in the family room, mix a drink from the wet bar, and look out through multiple windows to the covered veranda. A luxurious master suite includes a windowed sitting area looking over the rear view, private patio, full bath boasting a 10-foot ceiling, and a spacious walk-in closet On the second level, the three high-ceilinged bedrooms share two full baths and a study area with a built-in desk.

© The Sater Design Collection, Inc.

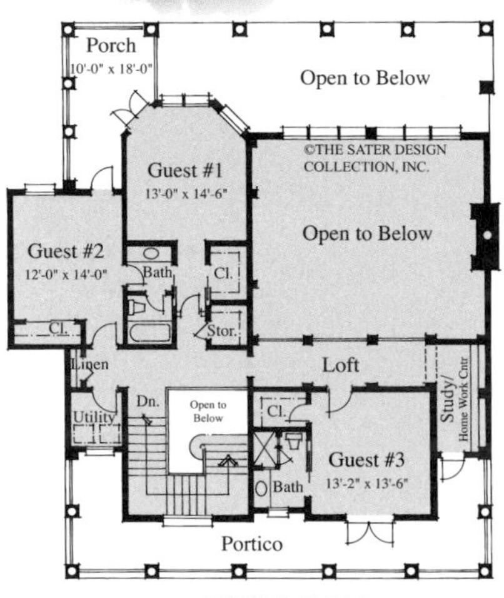

SECOND FLOOR

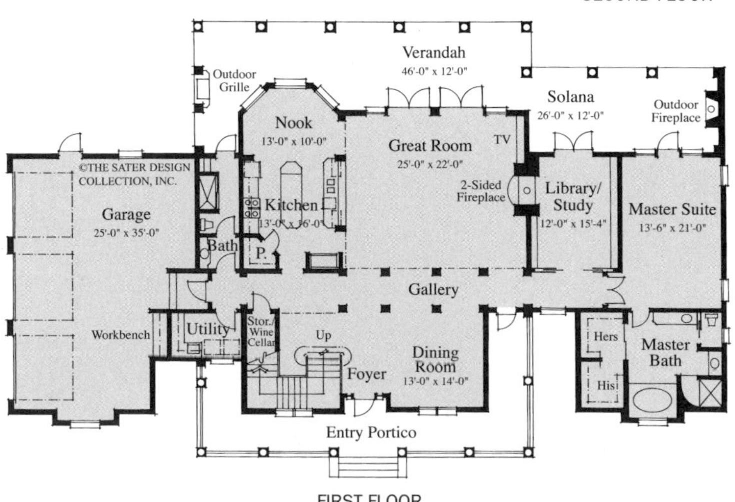

FIRST FLOOR

plan # HPK1700505

Style: Country Cottage

First Floor: 2,705 sq. ft.

Second Floor: 1,241 sq. ft.

Total: 3,946 sq. ft.

Bedrooms: 4

Bathrooms: 4

Width: 98' - 0"

Depth: 60' - 0"

Foundation: Crawlspace, Slab

eplans.com

Tall, stately columns wrap around the full front porch on this wonderful Southern Colonial home. The foyer features a gallery colonnade that separates the formal dining space from the great room. A two-sided fireplace is shared between the great room and private library just off the sumptuous master retreat. The gourmet kitchen works in tandem with the breakfast nook and both have excellent views of the amazing rear porch. Upstairs, three generously sized bedrooms—two with access to a private porch—share a study, laundry room, and two bathrooms.

plan# HPK1700506

Style: Georgian

First Floor: 2,767 sq. ft.

Second Floor: 1,179 sq. ft.

Total: 3,946 sq. ft.

Bonus Space: 591 sq. ft.

Bedrooms: 4

Bathrooms: 3½ + ½

Width: 79' - 11"

Depth: 80' - 6"

Foundation: Crawlspace

eplans.com

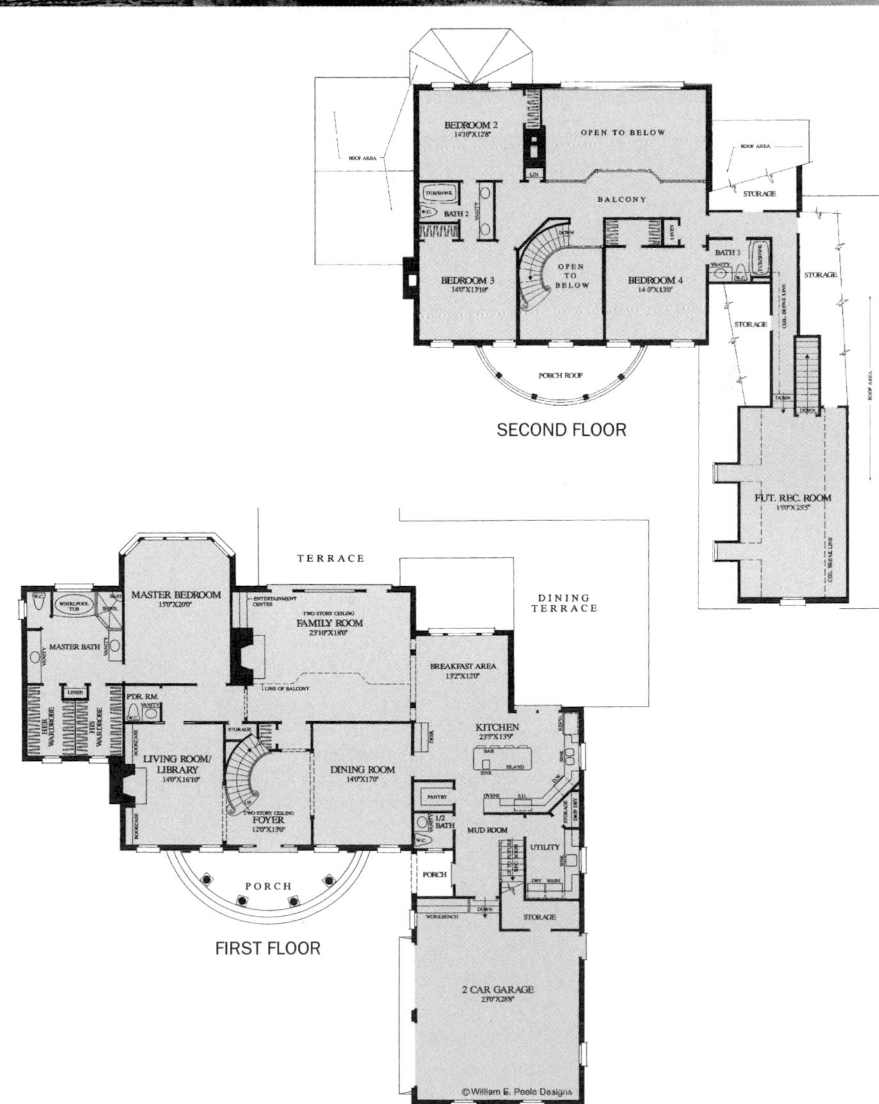

DESIGN NOTE

The five-ranked windows on the main facade and semi-circular entryway recall the Adam house, which was the dominant residential style in the new United States during the late 18th and early 19th Centuries. The style favors decorative door treatments, such as the elliptical fanlight and sidelights on this home, and Palladian windows, such as on the second floor. Decorative cornices under the eaves are also historical elements.

plan# HPK1700507

Style: Prairie
First Floor: 3,097 sq. ft.
Second Floor: 873 sq. ft.
Total: 3,970 sq. ft.
Bedrooms: 3
Bathrooms: 4
Width: 78' - 0"
Depth: 75' - 4"
Foundation: Slab

eplans.com

REAR EXTERIOR

Activity Space 20 10 · 15 4
Bath
Office 11 4 · 13'
Study Niche 9 6 · 7 11
Mech.

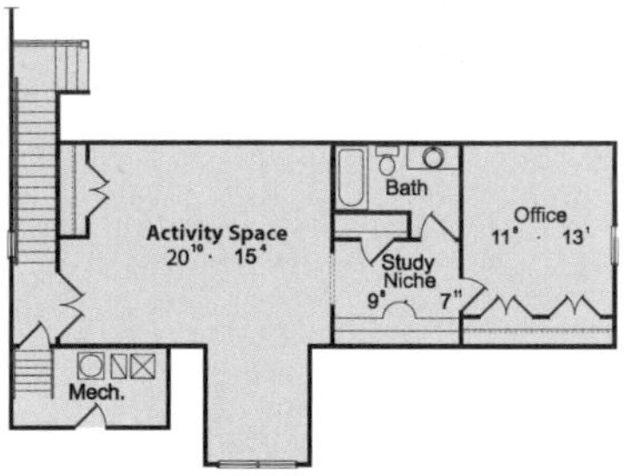

SECOND FLOOR

FIRST FLOOR

Dentils accent the hipped roof, and white double columns outline the entry of this lovely three-bedroom home. Formal entertaining will be enjoyed at the front of the plan, in either the dining room or den. Tucked out of sight from the living room, yet close to the dining area, the island kitchen features acres of counter space and a convenient utility room. The breakfast nook sits open to the family room, sharing the spacious views and warming fireplace of this relaxing informal zone. A wonderful master suite fills the right side of the plan with luxury elements, such as a sitting room, large walk-in closet, and soaking tub. Two family bedrooms to the left of the plan share a full bath.

plan# HPK1700508

- Style: European Cottage
- First Floor: 2,834 sq. ft.
- Second Floor: 1,143 sq. ft.
- Total: 3,977 sq. ft.
- Bedrooms: 4
- Bathrooms: 3½
- Width: 85' - 0"
- Depth: 76' - 8"
- Foundation: Slab

eplans.com

Mediterranean accents enhance the facade of this contemporary estate home. Two fanciful turret bays add a sense of grandeur to the exterior. Double doors open inside to a grand two-story foyer. A two-sided fireplace warms the study and living room, with a two-story coffered ceiling. To the right, the master suite includes a private bath, two walk-in closets, and double-door access to the sweeping rear veranda. Casual areas of the home include the gourmet island kitchen, breakfast nook, and leisure room warmed by a fireplace. A spiral staircase leads upstairs, where a second-floor balcony separates two family bedrooms from the luxurious guest suite.

SECOND FLOOR

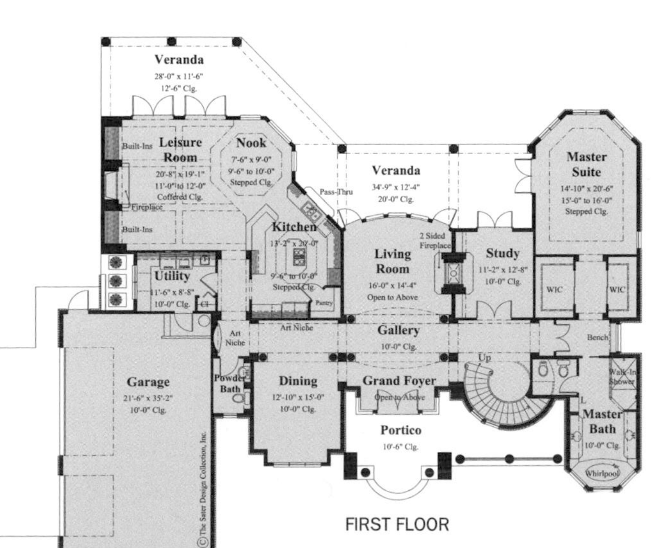

FIRST FLOOR

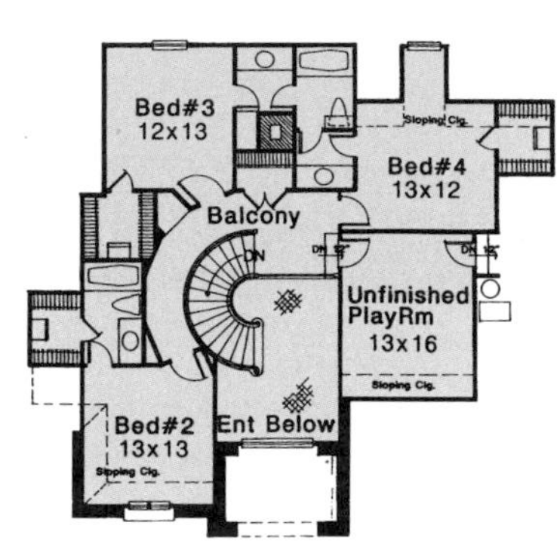

SECOND FLOOR

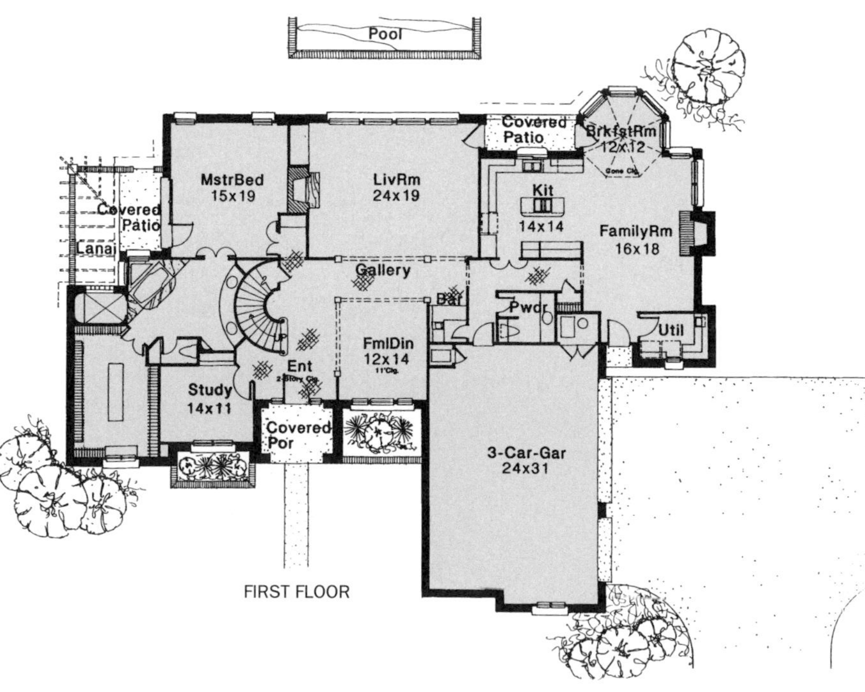

FIRST FLOOR

plan# HPK1700509
Style: Traditional
First Floor: 2,997 sq. ft.
Second Floor: 983 sq. ft.
Total: 3,980 sq. ft.
Bedrooms: 4
Bathrooms: 3½
Width: 89' - 4"
Depth: 71' - 0"
Foundation: Slab, Unfinished Basement, Crawlspace
eplans.com

The distinctive covered entry to this stunning manor leads to a gracious entry with impressive two-story semi-circular fanlights. The entry leads to a study, formal dining, formal living room and master suite. The numerous amenities in the kitchen include an island workstation and built-in pantry. The breakfast room features a cone ceiling. The luxurious master bath, secluded in its own wing, is complete with a covered patio. The master bedroom also contains a huge walk-in closet. Upstairs are three bedrooms, two baths and a future playroom.

plan# HPK1700510

Style: Country Cottage
First Floor: 2,591 sq. ft.
Second Floor: 1,399 sq. ft.
Total: 3,990 sq. ft.
Bedrooms: 4
Bathrooms: 3½
Width: 61' - 4"
Depth: 75' - 0"
Foundation: Slab

eplans.com

A dramatic front stairway announces visitors and welcomes all onto a cozy covered porch. The foyer introduces the living room on the right and the dining area on the left. Straight ahead, the family room boasts a fireplace. The kitchen is set between the breakfast room and a petite outdoor porch—perfect for grilling. Secluded on the first floor for privacy, the master suite includes two luxuriously-sized walk-in closets, private access to the rear deck, and a master bath with access to another porch out front. Upstairs, dormers enhance sunlight in two family bedrooms that share a full bath between them. A third bedroom uses the hall bath.

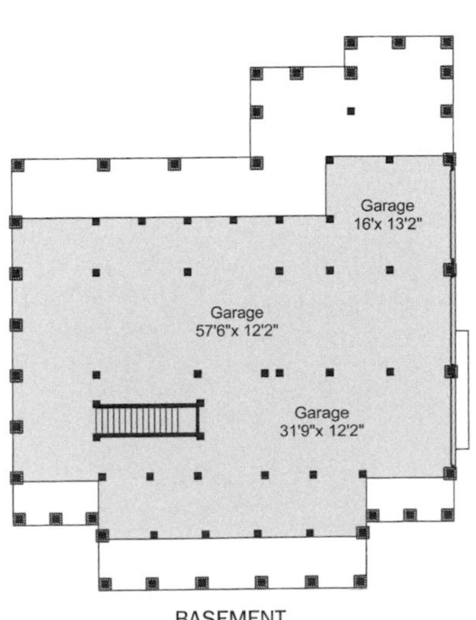

BASEMENT

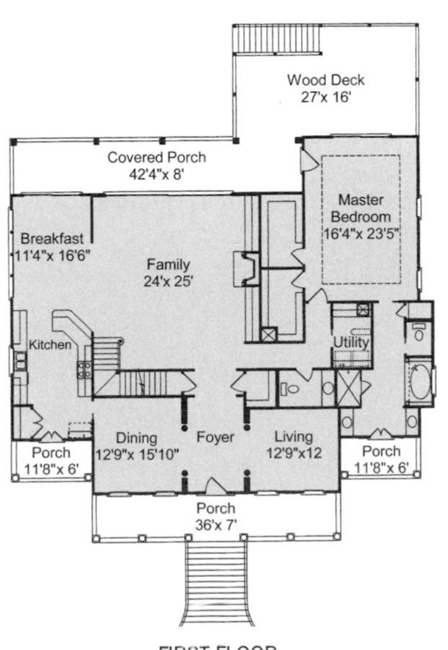

FIRST FLOOR

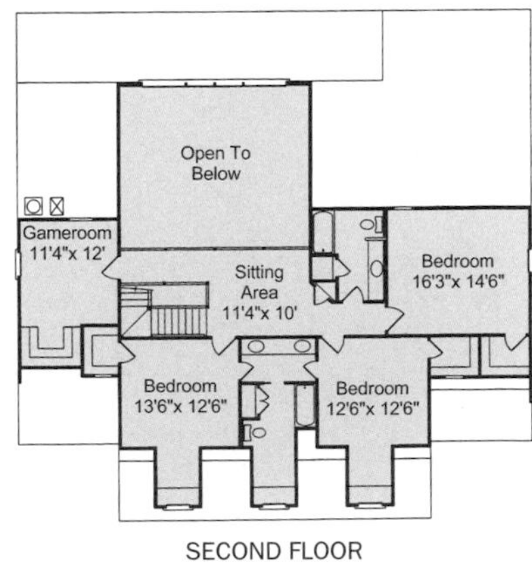

SECOND FLOOR

plan# HPK1700511
Style: Victorian
First Floor: 1,538 sq. ft.
Second Floor: 1,526 sq. ft.
Third Floor: 658 sq. ft.
Total: 3,722 sq. ft.
Bedrooms: 5
Bathrooms: 3½
Width: 67' - 0"
Depth: 66' - 0"
Foundation: Unfinished Basement
eplans.com

This charming Victorian home is reminiscent of a time when letter writing was an art and the scent of lavender hung lightly in the air. However, the floor plan moves quickly into the present with a contemporary flair. A veranda wraps around the living room, providing entrance from each side. The hub of the first floor is a kitchen that serves the dining room, the family room, and the living room with equal ease. Located on the second floor are two family bedrooms, a full bath, and an opulent master suite. Amenities in this suite include a fireplace, a bay-windowed sitting room, a pampering master bath, and a private sundeck. The third floor holds two bedrooms—one a possible study—and a full bath.

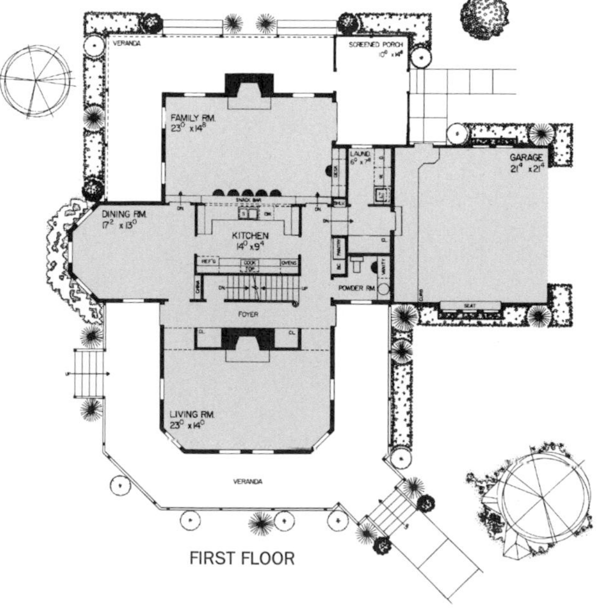

FIRST FLOOR

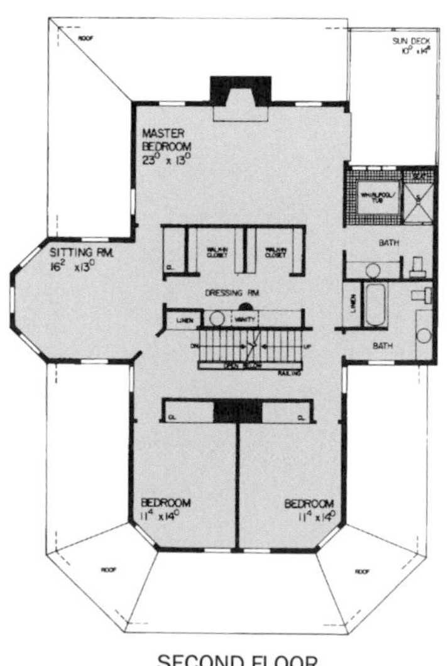

SECOND FLOOR

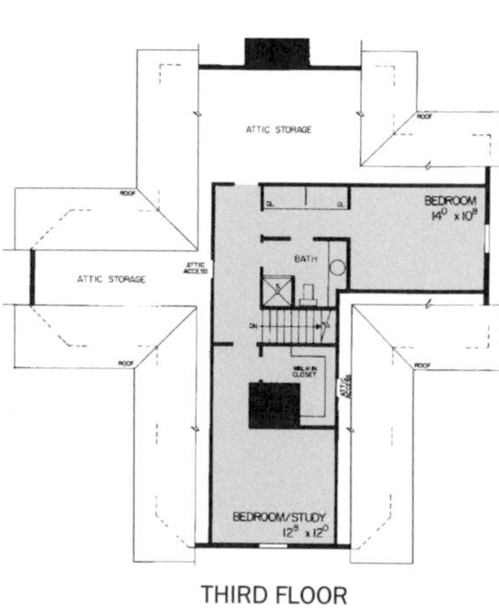

THIRD FLOOR

plan# HPK1700512

Style: Craftsman
Main Level: 2,172 sq. ft.
Lower Level: 1,813 sq. ft.
Total: 3,985 sq. ft.
Bedrooms: 4
Bathrooms: 3½
Width: 75' - 0"
Depth: 49' - 0"
Foundation: Finished Walkout Basement

eplans.com

With the Craftsman stylings of a mountain lodge, this rustic four-bedroom home is full of surprises. The foyer opens to the right to the great room, warmed by a stone hearth. A corner media center is convenient for entertaining. The dining room, with a furniture alcove, opens to the side terrace, inviting meals alfresco. An angled kitchen provides lots of room to move. The master suite is expansive, with French doors, a private bath, and spa tub. On the lower level, two bedrooms share a bath; a third enjoys a private suite. The games room includes a fireplace, media center, wet bar, and wine cellar. Don't miss the storage capacity and work area in the garage.

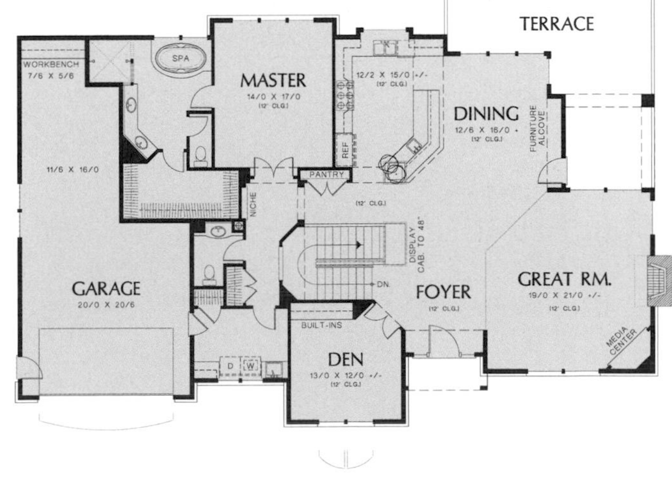

MAIN LEVEL

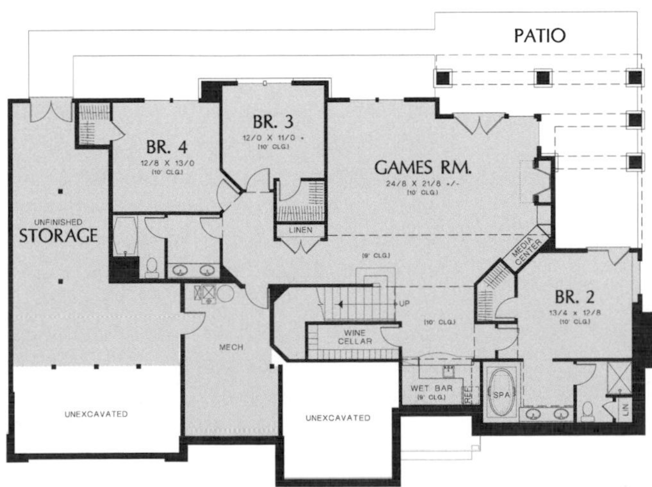

LOWER LEVEL

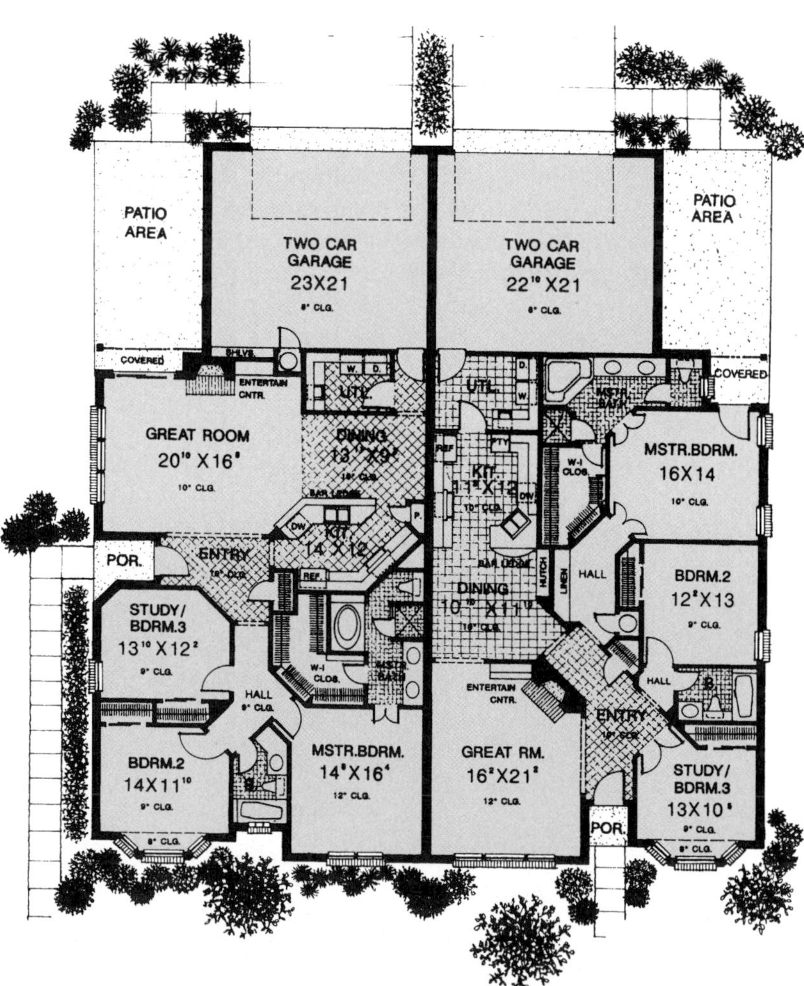

plan# HPK1700513

Style: Traditional

Square Footage: 1,775 / 1,770

Bedrooms: 3 / 3

Bathrooms: 2 / 2

Width: 68' - 10"

Depth: 75' - 3"

Foundation: Slab

eplans.com

This stylish duplex offers a traditional silhouette with elegant French touches. Two layouts with slightly different floor plans are provided for two small families. Enter one unit from the front and the second unit from the side—lending a little more privacy to each family. Each unit offers a great room with a fireplace, a kitchen and dining area, a laundry room and three family bedrooms. Each master bedroom features a private bath and a walk-in closet, while the additional two bedrooms share a hall bath. The third bedroom in each option can convert to a study. A two-car garage and outdoor patio complete each unit.

Homes 4,000 Square Feet and Over

This captivating luxury home puts a contemporary spin on Old World style. Stucco provides a wonderful complement to multiple arched windows on the exterior. See plan HPK1700539 on page 458.

plan# HPK1700514

Style: Farmhouse

Square Footage: 4,038

Bedrooms: 4

Bathrooms: 4½

Width: 98' - 0"

Depth: 90' - 0"

Foundation: Unfinished Basement, Crawlspace, Slab

eplans.com

Reminiscent of the old Newport mansions, this luxury house has volume ceilings, a glamorous master suite with a hearth-warmed sitting area, a glassed-in sunroom, a home office, three porches with a deck, and a gourmet kitchen with a pantry. Graceful French doors are used for all the entrances and in the formal living and dining rooms. The magnificent kitchen boasts a large pantry. A centrally positioned family room is graced with a large fireplace and is accessed by the rear porch, living room, and dining room.

plan# HPK1700515

Style: Traditional
Square Footage: 4,658
Bonus Space: 1,008 sq. ft.
Bedrooms: 3
Bathrooms: 2½
Width: 68' - 1"
Depth: 66' - 0"
Foundation: Crawlspace, Slab, Unfinished Basement

eplans.com

Stately white columns adorn an arched portico in between red brick and dark-colored shingles and shutters on this all-American. The foyer contains a 13-foot ceiling and provides direct access to the formal dining room on the left. A handy double coat closet follows, and then the living room, with a wonderful vaulted ceiling. A fireplace with accompanying view across the rear porch is immediately apparent. The master suite and built-in bookcase and linen closet are to the right. The kitchen connects to the living room via a curved preparation island, restaurant-style. A convenient pantry stands immediately to the left. Breakfast is served in the nook, alongside the porch window. A half bath and access to the garage are found here. A utility area and two bedrooms with shared bath are off of the other end of the kitchen, along with an optional staircase.

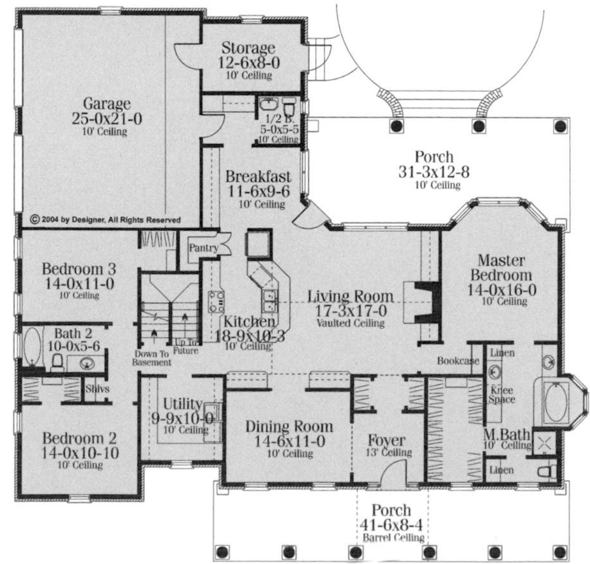

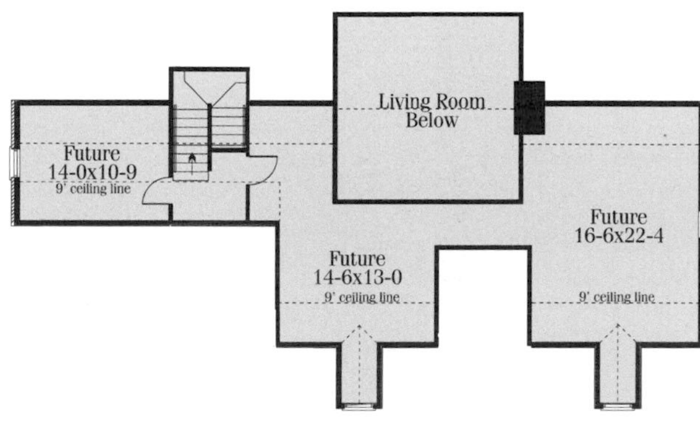

plan# HPK1700516

Style: Neoclassic	
First Floor: 3,489 sq. ft.	
Second Floor: 607 sq. ft.	
Total: 4,096 sq. ft.	
Bedrooms: 4	
Bathrooms: 3½	
Width: 82' - 0"	
Depth: 100' - 0"	
Foundation: Slab	

eplans.com

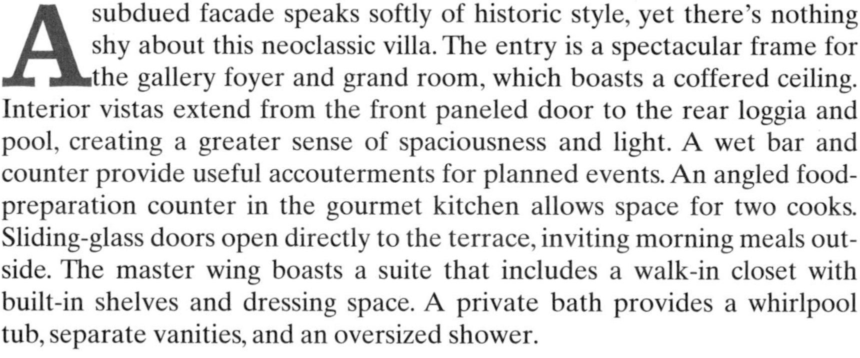

A subdued facade speaks softly of historic style, yet there's nothing shy about this neoclassic villa. The entry is a spectacular frame for the gallery foyer and grand room, which boasts a coffered ceiling. Interior vistas extend from the front paneled door to the rear loggia and pool, creating a greater sense of spaciousness and light. A wet bar and counter provide useful accouterments for planned events. An angled food-preparation counter in the gourmet kitchen allows space for two cooks. Sliding-glass doors open directly to the terrace, inviting morning meals outside. The master wing boasts a suite that includes a walk-in closet with built-in shelves and dressing space. A private bath provides a whirlpool tub, separate vanities, and an oversized shower.

REAR EXTERIOR

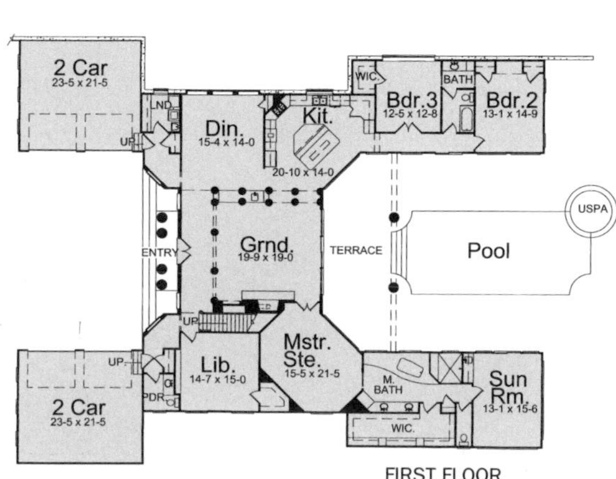

FIRST FLOOR

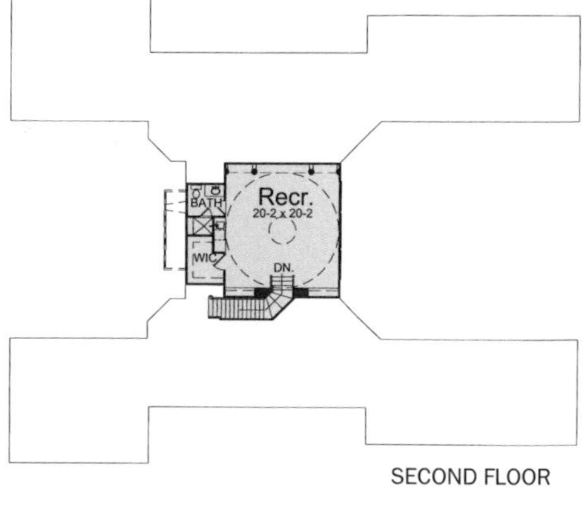

SECOND FLOOR

plan# HPK1700517

Style: Farmhouse
First Floor: 3,166 sq. ft.
Second Floor: 950 sq. ft.
Total: 4,116 sq. ft.
Bedrooms: 5
Bathrooms: 4
Width: 154' - 0"
Depth: 94' - 8"
Foundation: Slab

eplans.com

REAR EXTERIOR

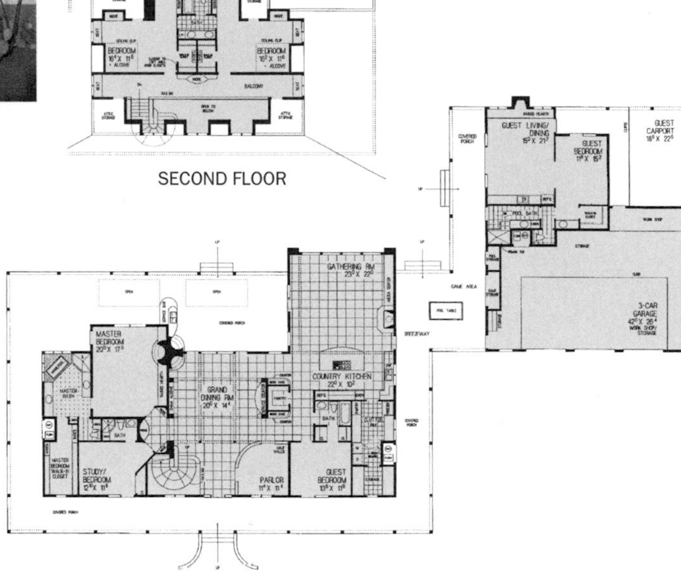

SECOND FLOOR

FIRST FLOOR

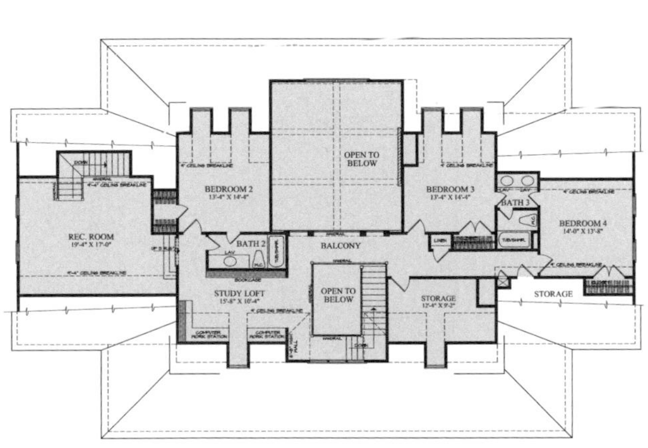

SECOND FLOOR

FIRST FLOOR

plan# HPK1700518

Style: Country Cottage
First Floor: 2,891 sq. ft.
Second Floor: 1,336 sq. ft.
Total: 4,227 sq. ft.
Bonus Space: 380 sq. ft.
Bedrooms: 4
Bathrooms: 3½ + ½
Width: 90' - 8"
Depth: 56' - 4"
Foundation: Crawlspace, Unfinished Basement

eplans.com

plan# HPK1700519

Style: Norman
First Floor: 3,072 sq. ft.
Second Floor: 1,406 sq. ft.
Total: 4,478 sq. ft.
Bedrooms: 5
Bathrooms: 4½
Width: 75' - 5"
Depth: 73' - 11"
Foundation: Unfinished Walkout Basement

eplans.com

EDITOR'S PICK

A stone and brick facade brings just the right amount of the Old World to the facade. Inside, decorative columns distinguish common living spaces within the open layout. Fireplaces provide warmth and ambiance to the grand room and library, as well as in the old-fashioned keeping room. A fourth fireplace in the master suite is nestled near a private entrance to the rear deck, which runs the width of the back of the plan. Count four more bedrooms, three more full baths, a powder room, laundry room, and office—and you end up with a please-all home that'll look great in any neighborhood.

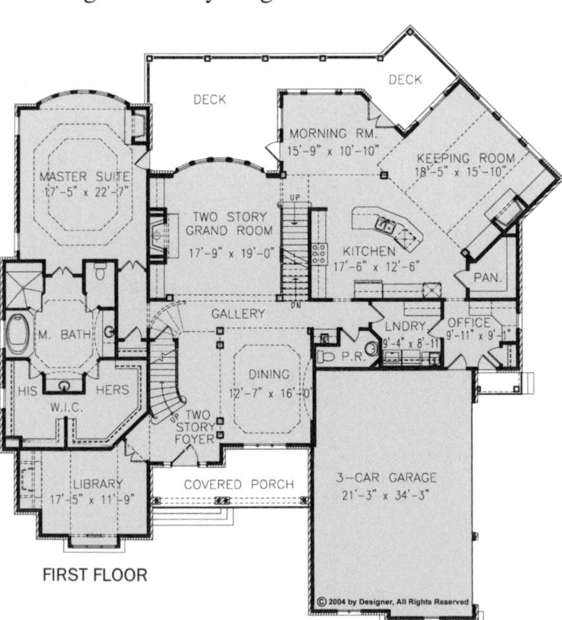

FIRST FLOOR

SECOND FLOOR

plan# HPK1700520

Style: Southern Colonial
First Floor: 2,998 sq. ft.
Second Floor: 1,556 sq. ft.
Total: 4,554 sq. ft.
Bonus Space: 741 sq. ft.
Bedrooms: 4
Bathrooms: 4½
Width: 75' - 6"
Depth: 91' - 2"
Foundation: Crawlspace

eplans.com

The paired double-end chimneys, reminiscent of the Georgian style of architecture, set this design apart from the rest. The covered entry opens to the columned foyer with the dining room on the left and the living room on the right, each enjoying the warmth and charm of a fireplace. Beyond the grand staircase, the family room delights with a third fireplace and a window wall that opens to the terrace. The expansive kitchen and breakfast area sit on the far left; the master suite is secluded on the the right with its pampering private bath. The second floor holds three additional bedrooms (including a second master bedroom), three full baths, a computer room, and the future recreation room.

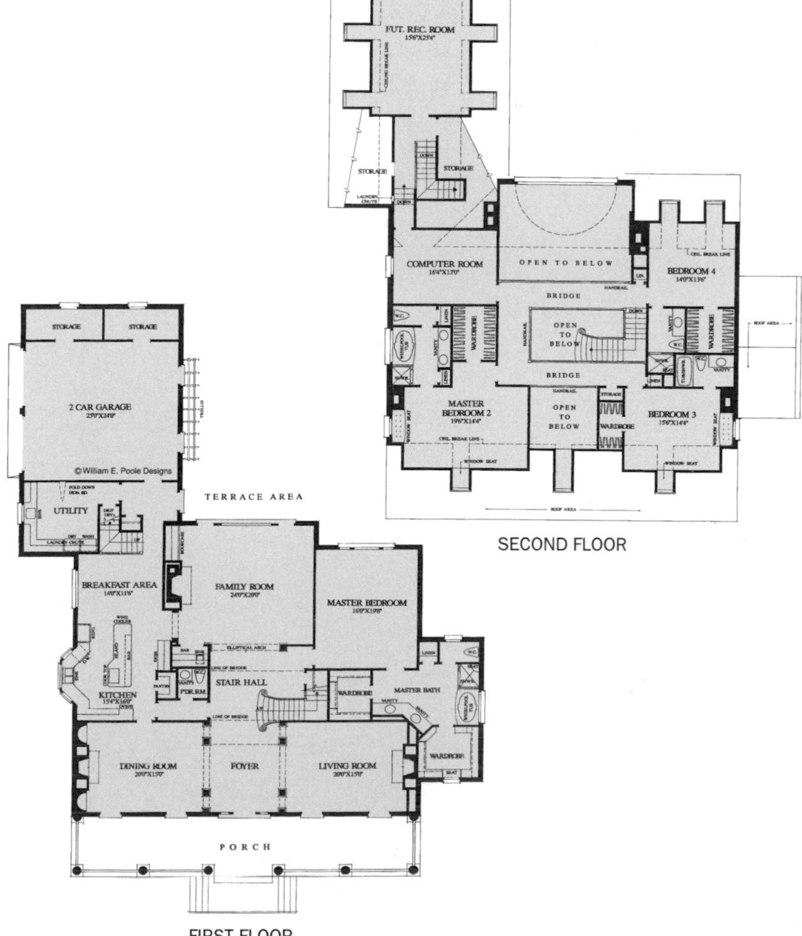

SECOND FLOOR

FIRST FLOOR

plan# HPK1700521

Style: Italianate
First Floor: 3,933 sq. ft.
Second Floor: 719 sq. ft.
Total: 4,652 sq. ft.
Bedrooms: 4
Bathrooms: 4½
Width: 89' - 8"
Depth: 104' - 11"
Foundation: Slab

eplans.com

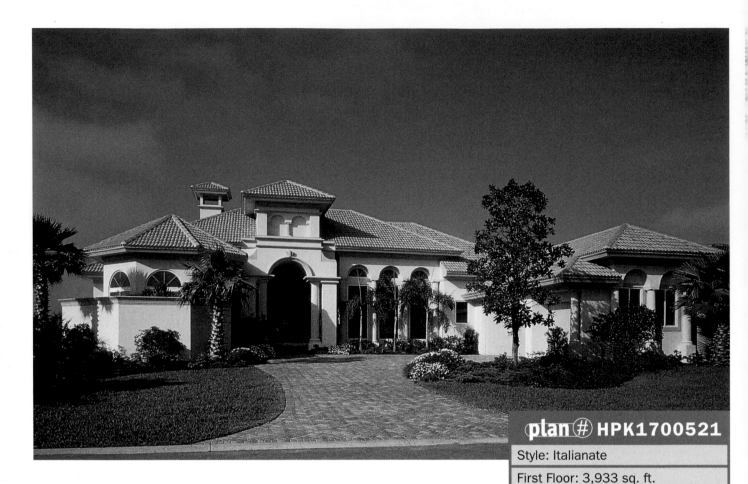

Beautiful and spacious, the artful disposition of this luxurious villa owns a distinctly Mediterranean flavor. Dramatic and inspiring, the vaulted entry is set off by a dashing arch framed by columns, a barrel ceiling, and double doors that open to an expansive interior. The octagonal living room provides a fireplace and opens through two sets of lovely doors to the rear lanai. The master wing is a sumptuous retreat with double doors that open from a private vaulted foyer. One of the spacious guest suites can easily convert to personal quarters for a live-in relative. Another guest suite boasts a full bath, a bay window, and a walk-in closet. An upper-level loft leads to a third guest suite.

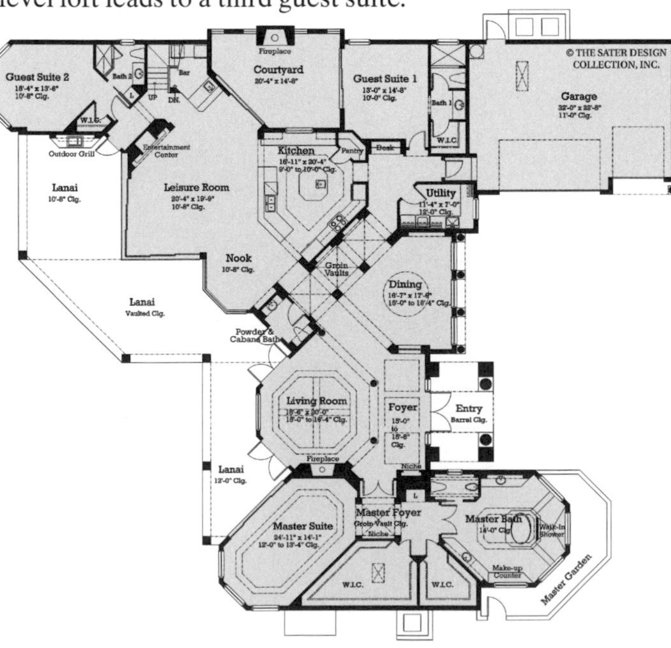

FIRST FLOOR

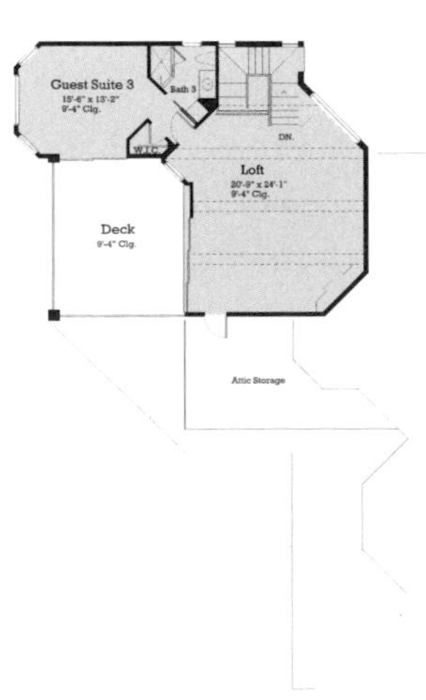

SECOND FLOOR

plan# HPK1700522

Style: Country Cottage
First Floor: 3,347 sq. ft.
Second Floor: 1,696 sq. ft.
Total: 5,043 sq. ft.
Bedrooms: 5
Bathrooms: 6½
Width: 120' - 0"
Depth: 99' - 11"
Foundation: Crawlspace

eplans.com

Gently flaring eaves and curved dormers contrast with the straight rooflines and angled gables on this attractive stone exterior. A breezeway connects the house to the three-car garage, above which an apartment offers living space for a mother-in-law or grown child. On the second floor of the main house you'll find three more bedroom suites, a sewing room, and a future exercise room. Downstairs, the foyer opens to the formal dining room and leads ahead to the grand room, elegant and inviting with its massive fireplace, built-ins, and French doors to the terrace. A large informal area features a second fireplace and includes a gathering room, a breakfast nook, and an island kitchen with a huge walk-in pantry. Amenities in the master suite include two walk-in closets, a corner garden tub, and dual vanities. A wet bar is shared with the nearby study, which boasts a third fireplace.

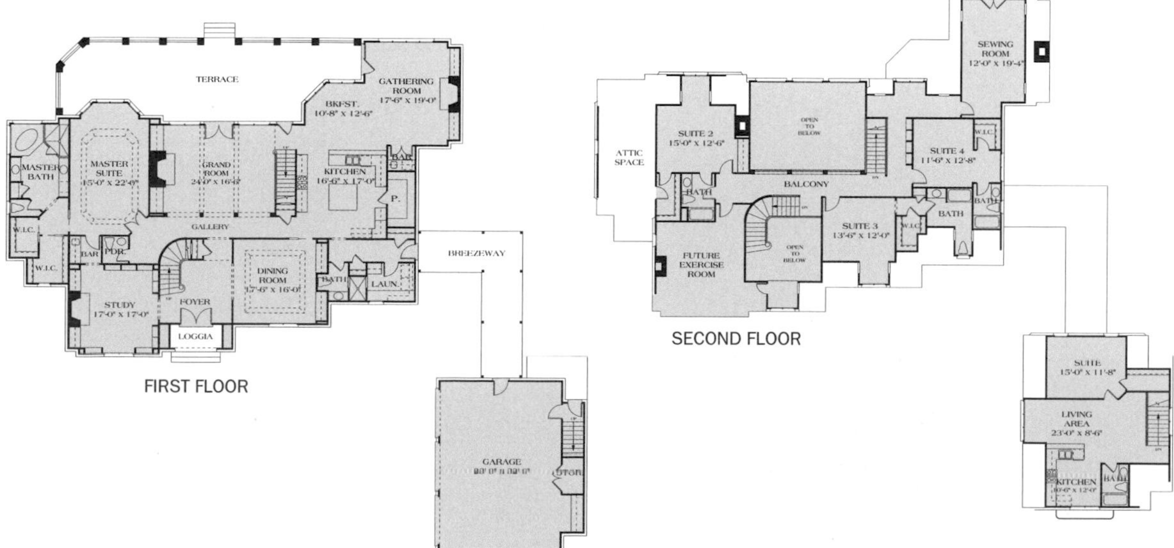

FIRST FLOOR

SECOND FLOOR

plan # HPK1700523

Style: Farmhouse
First Floor: 3,520 sq. ft.
Second Floor: 1,638 sq. ft.
Total: 5,158 sq. ft.
Bonus Space: 411 sq. ft.
Bedrooms: 5
Bathrooms: 4½
Width: 96' - 6"
Depth: 58' - 8"

eplans.com

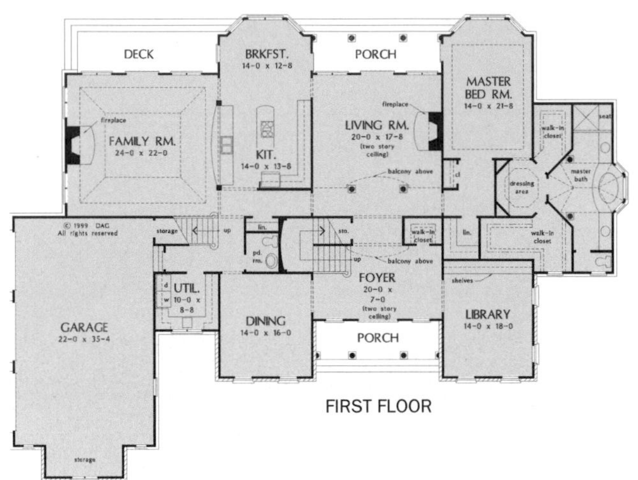

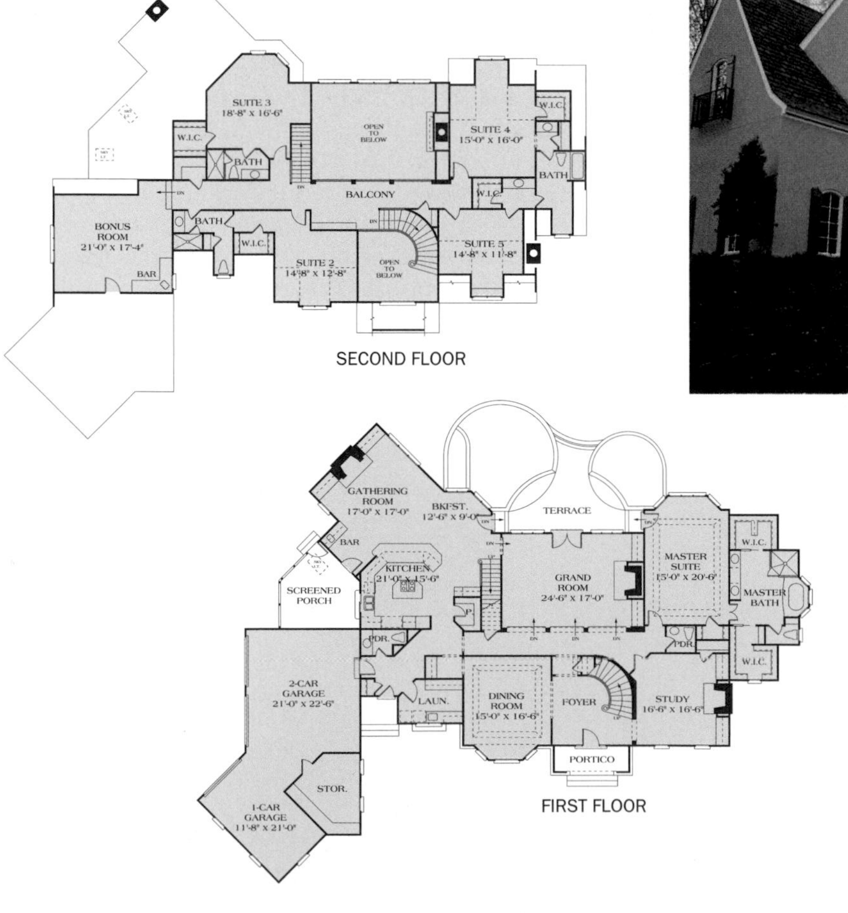

plan # HPK1700524

Style: Country Cottage
First Floor: 3,387 sq. ft.
Second Floor: 1,799 sq. ft.
Total: 5,186 sq. ft.
Bonus Space: 379 sq. ft.
Bedrooms: 5
Bathrooms: 4½ + ½
Width: 110' - 10"
Depth: 84' - 6"
Foundation: Crawlspace

eplans.com

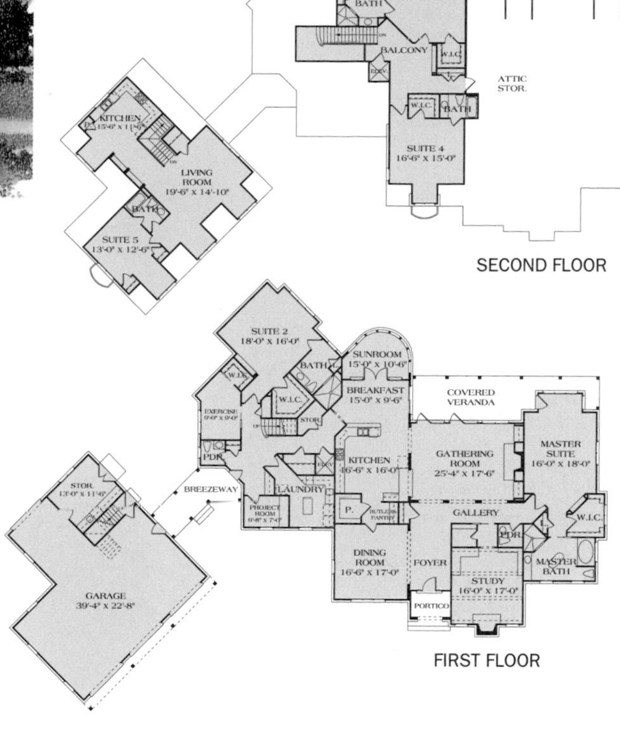

SECOND FLOOR

FIRST FLOOR

plan# HPK1700525

Style: Country Cottage
First Floor: 4,218 sq. ft.
Second Floor: 1,208 sq. ft.
Total: 5,426 sq. ft.
Bedrooms: 5
Bathrooms: 5½ + ½
Width: 138' - 0"
Depth: 98' - 6"
Foundation: Crawlspace

eplans.com

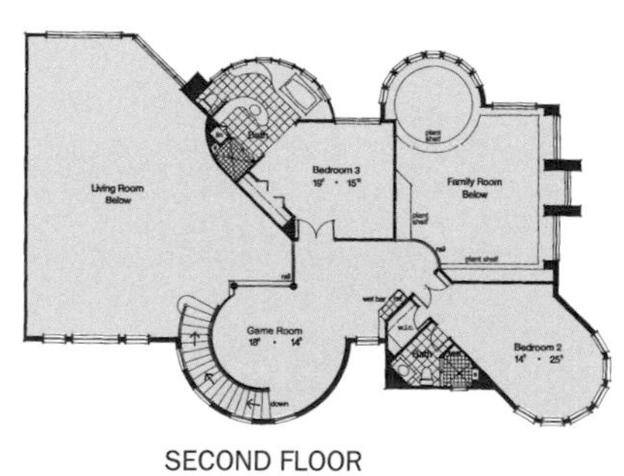

SECOND FLOOR

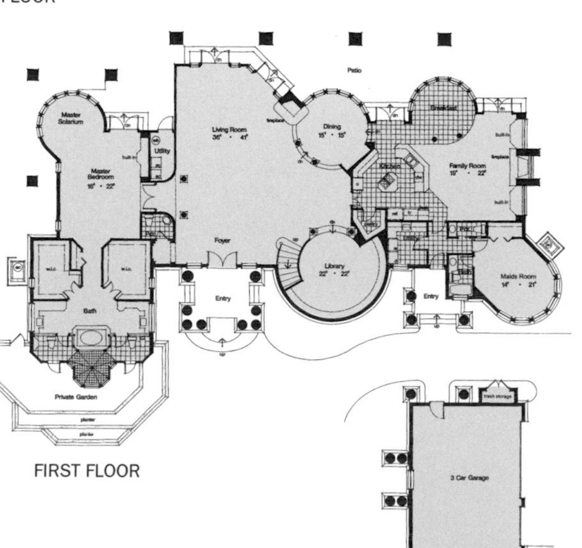

FIRST FLOOR

plan# HPK1700526

Style: Mediterranean
First Floor: 4,284 sq. ft.
Second Floor: 1,319 sq. ft.
Total: 5,603 sq. ft.
Bedrooms: 4
Bathrooms: 4½ + ½
Width: 109' - 4"
Depth: 73' - 2"
Foundation: Slab

eplans.com

REAR EXTERIOR

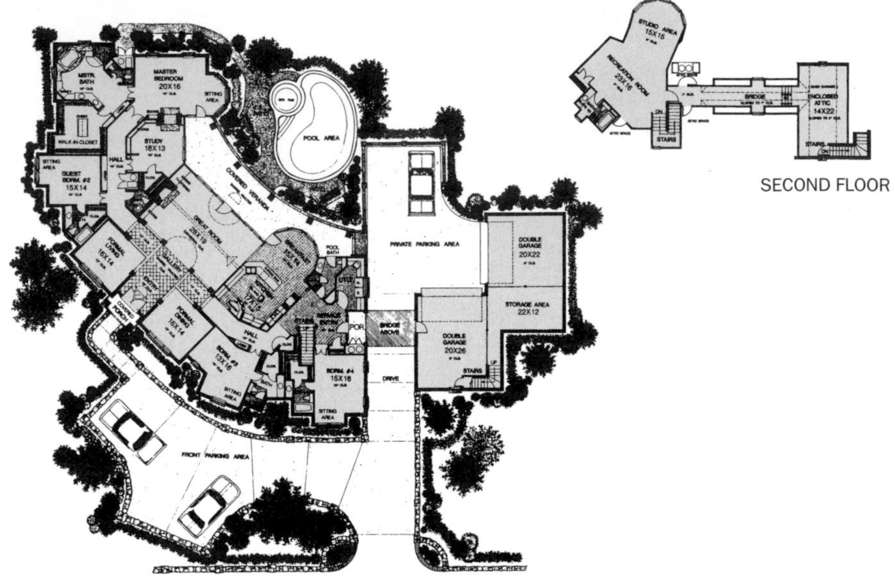

SECOND FLOOR

FIRST FLOOR

plan # HPK1700527

Style: French

First Floor: 5,152 sq. ft.

Second Floor: 726 sq. ft.

Total: 5,878 sq. ft.

Bedrooms: 4

Bathrooms: 5½

Width: 146' - 7"

Depth: 106' - 7"

Foundation: Slab

eplans.com

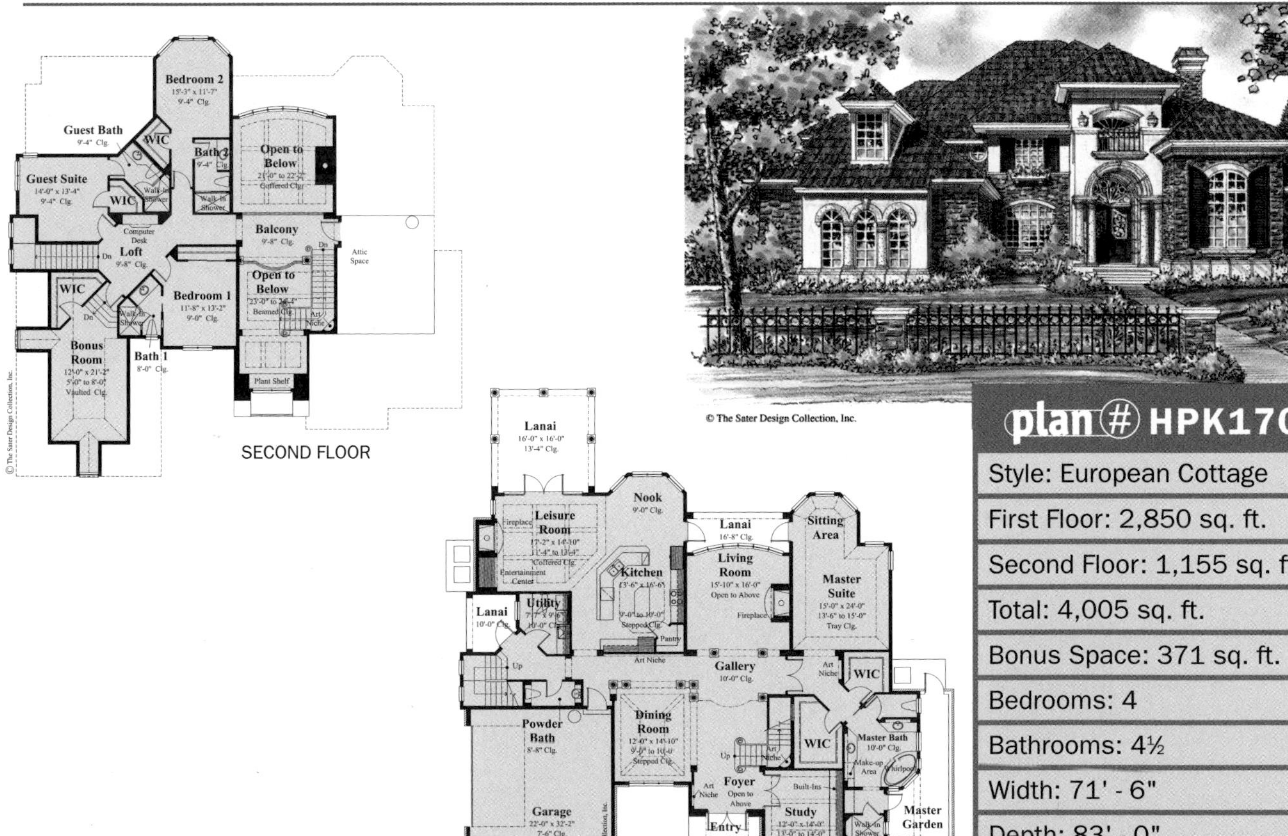

SECOND FLOOR

© The Sater Design Collection, Inc.

FIRST FLOOR

plan # HPK1700528

Style: European Cottage

First Floor: 2,850 sq. ft.

Second Floor: 1,155 sq. ft.

Total: 4,005 sq. ft.

Bonus Space: 371 sq. ft.

Bedrooms: 4

Bathrooms: 4½

Width: 71' - 6"

Depth: 83' - 0"

Foundation: Slab

eplans.com

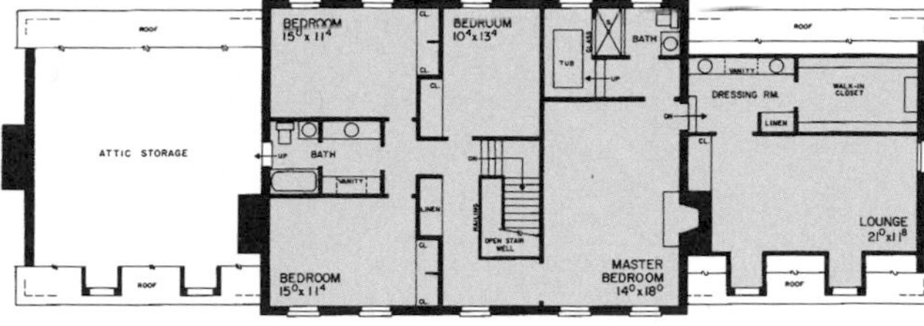

SECOND FLOOR

plan# HPK1700529

Style: Georgian
First Floor: 2,126 sq. ft.
Second Floor: 1,882 sq. ft.
Total: 4,008 sq. ft.
Bedrooms: 4
Bathrooms: 2½
Width: 92' - 0"
Depth: 64' - 4"
Foundation: Unfinished Basement

eplans.com

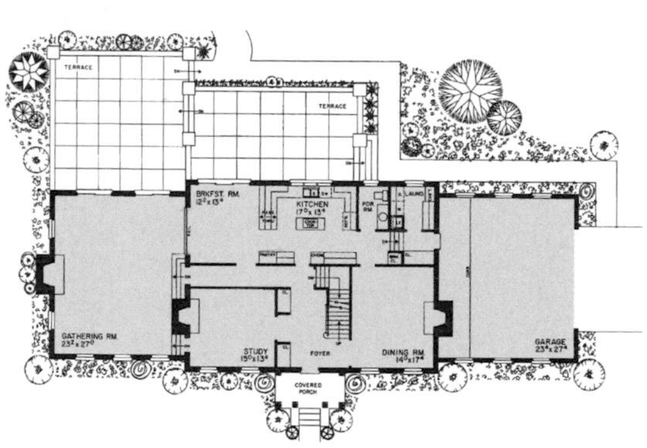

FIRST FLOOR

SECOND FLOOR

FIRST FLOOR

plan# HPK1700530

Style: French
First Floor: 2,608 sq. ft.
Second Floor: 1,432 sq. ft.
Total: 4,040 sq. ft.
Bedrooms: 4
Bathrooms: 3½
Width: 89' - 10"
Depth: 63' - 8"
Foundation: Crawlspace, Slab

eplans.com

SECOND FLOOR

FIRST FLOOR

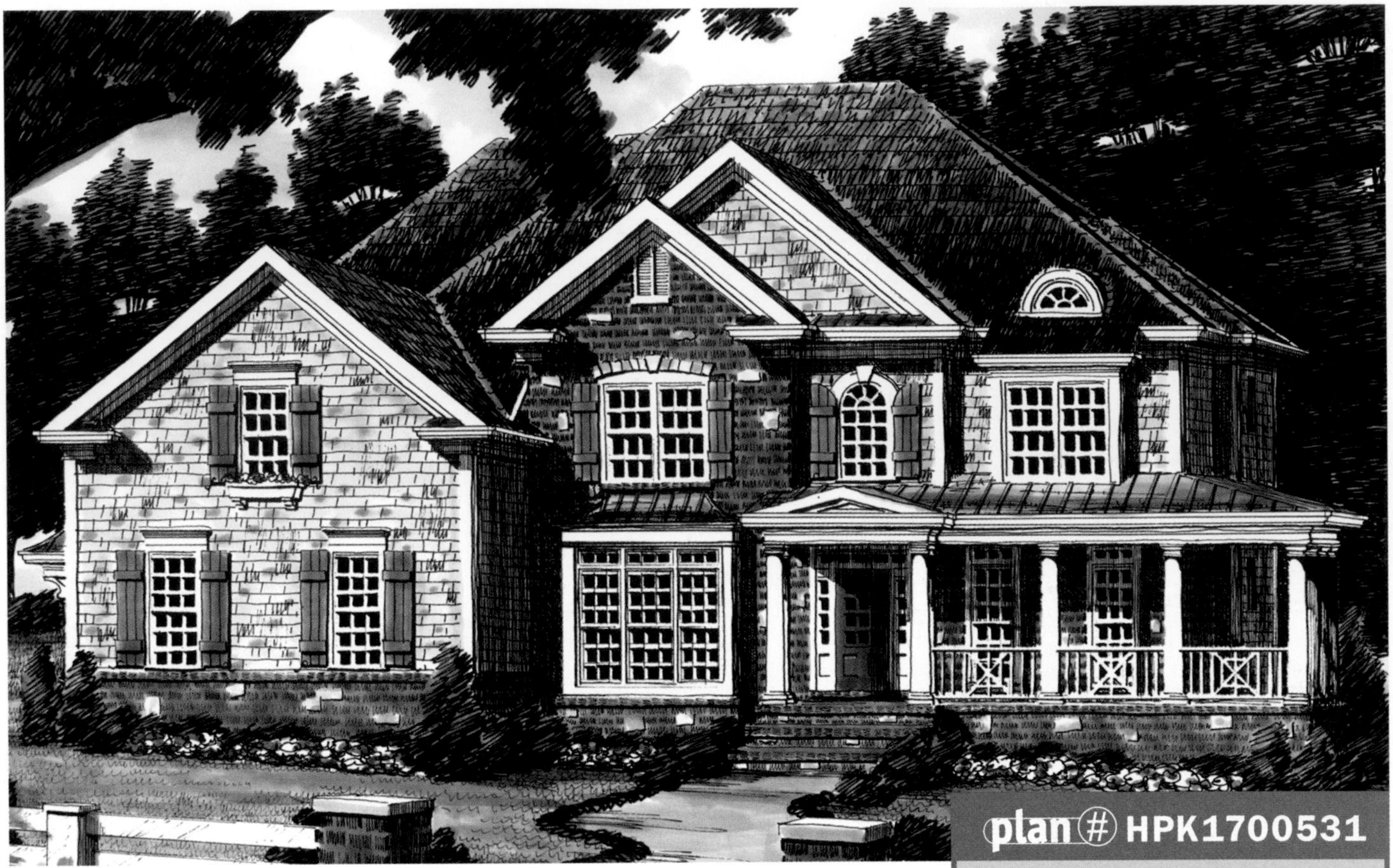

plan# HPK1700531

Style: Farmhouse
First Floor: 1,999 sq. ft.
Second Floor: 2,046 sq. ft.
Total: 4,045 sq. ft.
Bedrooms: 5
Bathrooms: 4 ½
Width: 66' - 4"
Depth: 64' - 0"
Foundation: Unfinished Walkout Basement, Crawlspace

eplans.com

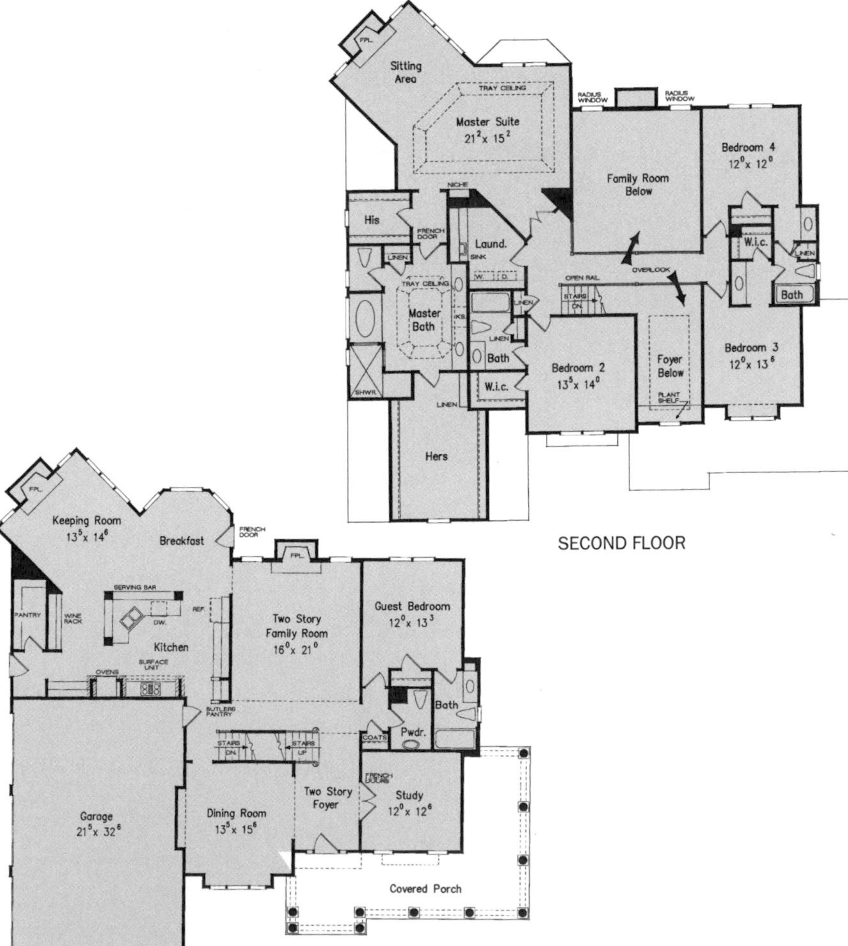

This luxury farmhouse design is reserved for the hardworking homeowner who seeks a relaxing retreat. A front covered porch that wraps around the side adds a country accent to the exterior. Inside, a study and formal dining room flank the two-story foyer. A guest suite is placed to the right of the two-story family room, warmed by a fireplace. The kitchen is open to the nook and casual keeping room. A three-car garage is located nearby. Upstairs, the master suite features a hearth-warmed sitting room, private bath, and two large walk-in closets.

plan# HPK1700532

Style: French
First Floor: 2,814 sq. ft.
Second Floor: 1,231 sq. ft.
Total: 4,045 sq. ft.
Bedrooms: 5
Bathrooms: 3½
Width: 98' - 0"
Depth: 45' - 10"
Foundation: Slab, Unfinished Basement

eplans.com

This very formal Georgian home was designed to be admired, but also to be lived in. It features handsome formal areas in a living room and formal dining room, but also an oversized family room with a focal fireplace. The master suite sits on the first floor, as is popluar with most homeowners today. Besides its wealth of amenities, it is located near a cozy study. Don't miss the private patio and sitting area with glass in the master bedroom. Upstairs, there are four family bedrooms with great closet space. A three-car garage contains space for a golf cart and a work bench.

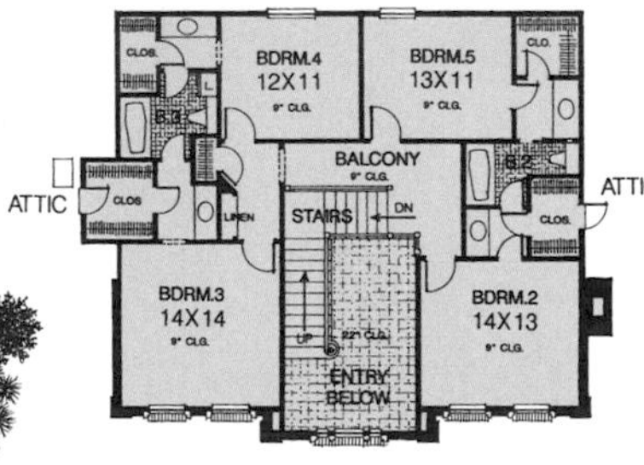

SECOND FLOOR

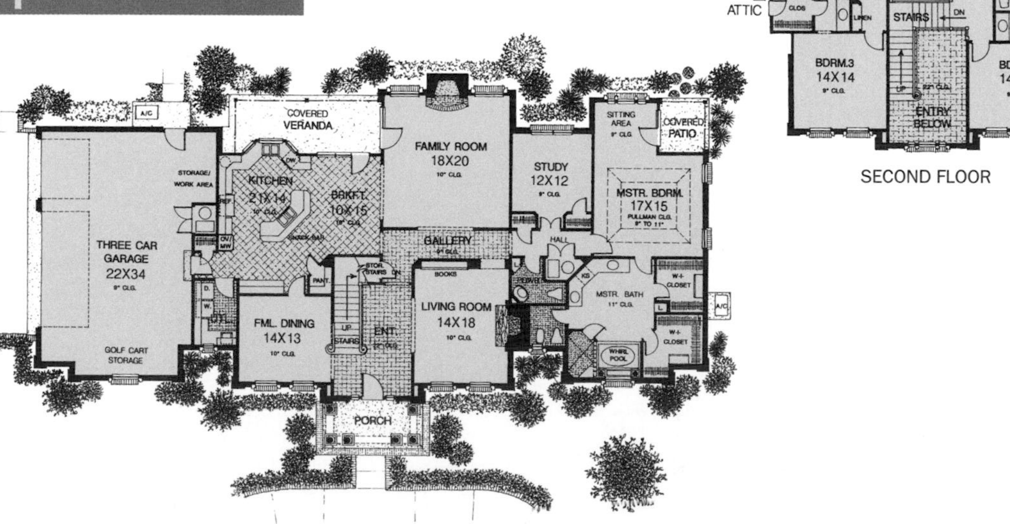

FIRST FLOOR

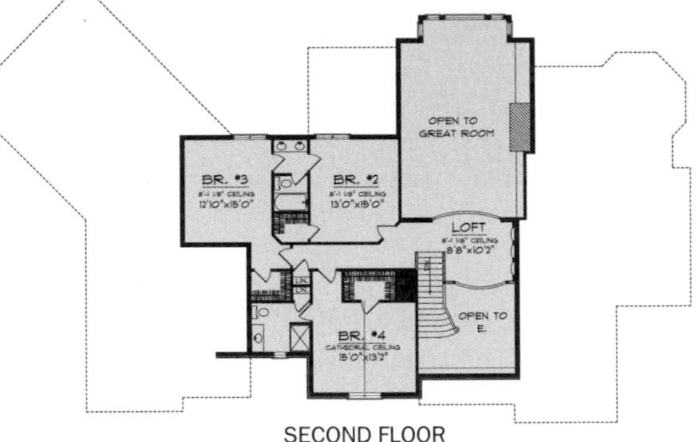

SECOND FLOOR

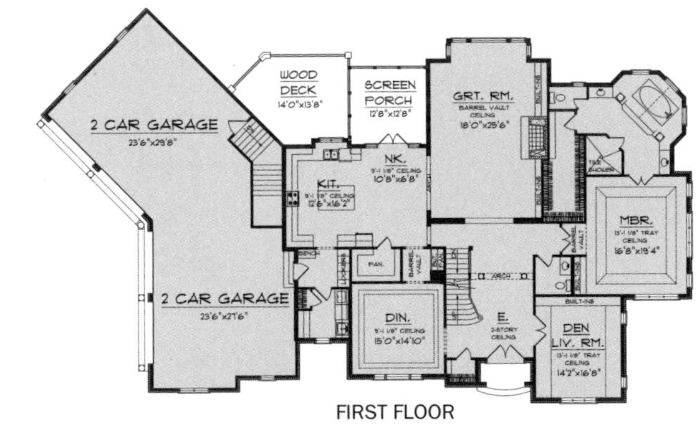

FIRST FLOOR

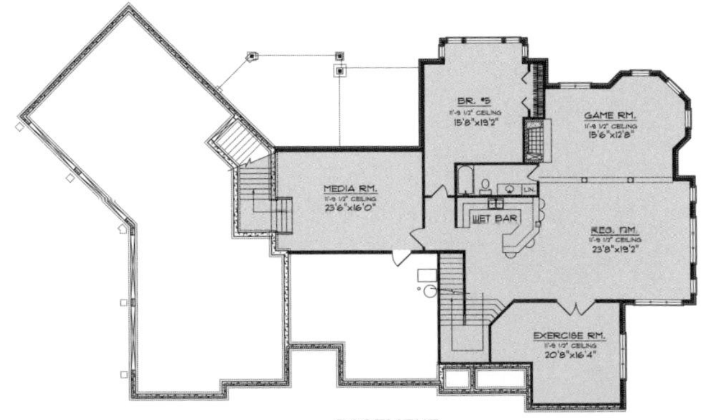

BASEMENT

plan# HPK1700533

Style: Traditional

First Floor: 2,896 sq. ft.

Second Floor: 1,154 sq. ft.

Total: 4,050 sq. ft.

Bedrooms: 4

Bathrooms: 3½

Width: 106' - 8"

Depth: 59' - 4"

Foundation: Unfinished Basement

eplans.com

This stunning French Country two-story will impress you with its unique character and substantial square footage. This home offers four bedrooms, a four-car garage, and 4,050 square feet of living space. You will be astonished by the layout and will enjoy the comfort of a fireplace great room. You will adore the barrell vaulted ceiling in the great room. You will love the way the kitchen/nook opens to the great room. From the nook you can open double doors to the screen porch. The master bedroom features a tray ceiling and double doors to the master bathroom with a large walk-in closet. On the second floor there are three bedrooms, two bathrooms, and a loft.

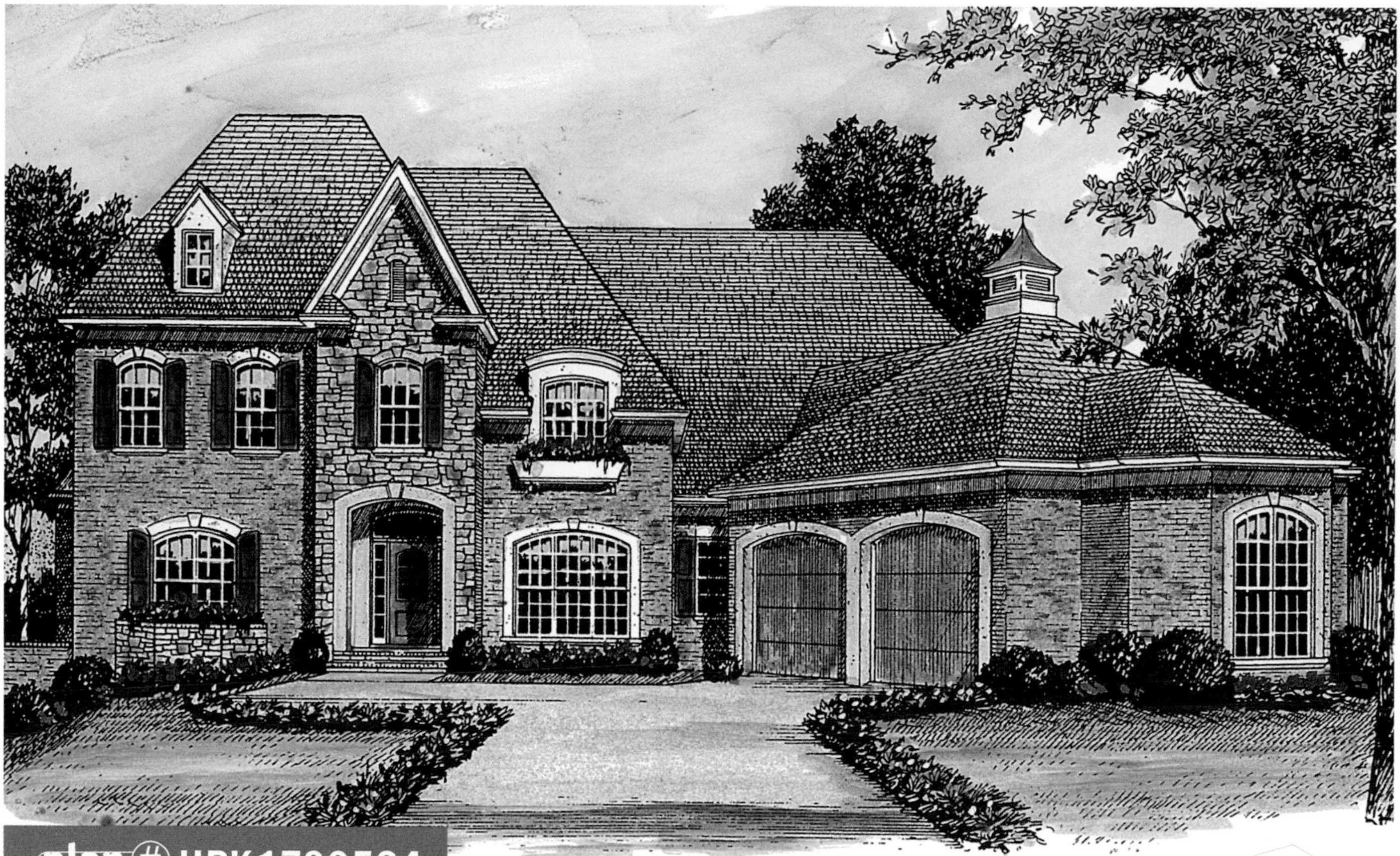

plan# HPK1700534

Style: French Country
First Floor: 2,291 sq. ft.
Second Floor: 1,796 sq. ft.
Total: 4,087 sq. ft.
Bonus Space: 1,633 sq. ft.
Bedrooms: 4
Bathrooms: 3½
Width: 74' - 1"
Depth: 88' - 10"
Foundation: Unfinished Walkout Basement

eplans.com

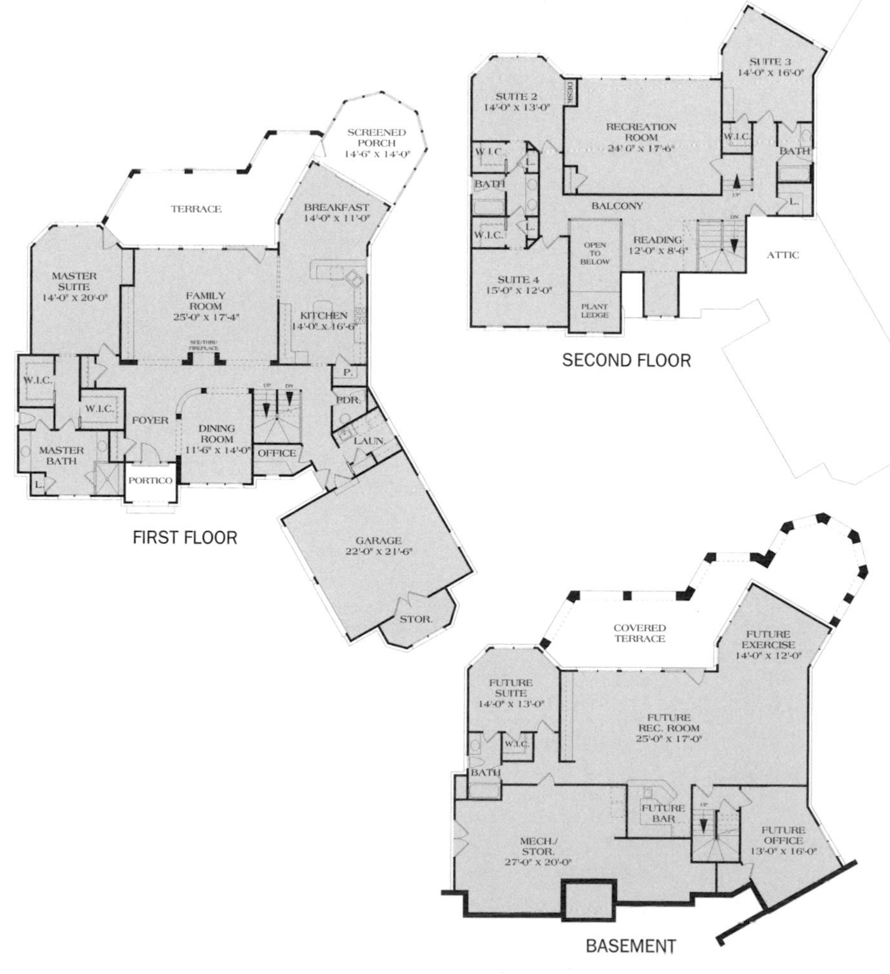

Three floors of living come with this plan, with a fully appointed basement of future space included. The main floor includes a terrace and screened porch, dining room, kitchen with breakfast area, and a master suite, all situated around an inviting family room. A small office and a laundry are located off of the garage. Three more bedrooms with two baths, a separate reading room, and a recreation room are found upstairs. A built-in plant ledge and upper balcony provide extra decor.

SECOND FLOOR

FIRST FLOOR

BASEMENT

PHOTO COURTESY OF: GARRELL ASSOCIATES, INC.

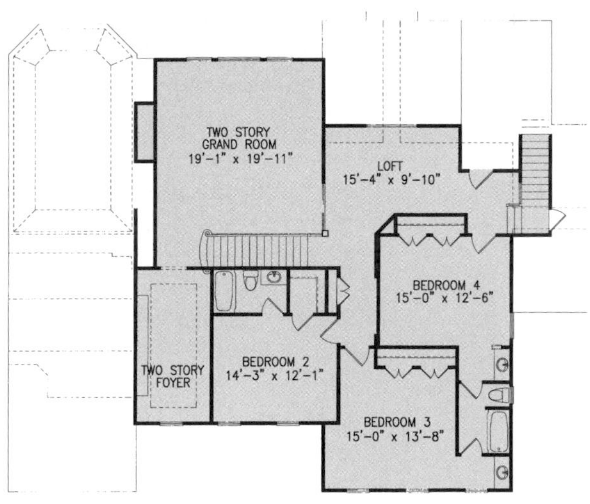

SECOND FLOOR

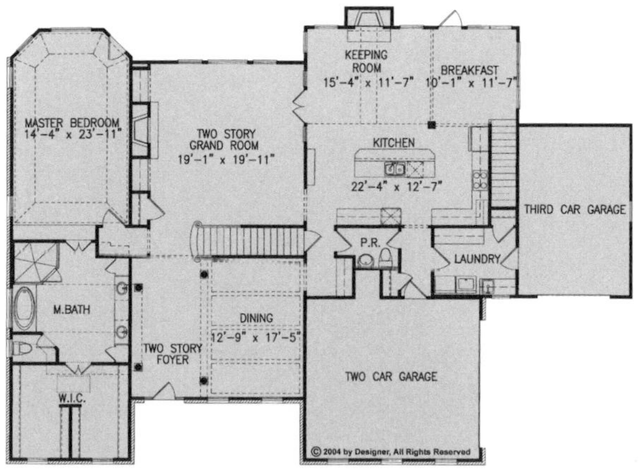

FIRST FLOOR

plan # HPK1700535

Style: Federal

First Floor: 2,950 sq. ft.

Second Floor: 1,138 sq. ft.

Total: 4,088 sq. ft.

Bedrooms: 4

Bathrooms: 3½

Width: 77' - 0"

Depth: 56' - 0"

Foundation: Unfinished Basement

eplans.com

Steeped in Early American flair, this four-bedroom home impresses from the first glance. Inside, the master suite occupies the entire left side of the first floor. To the right, the gourmet kitchen is nestled between the warmth emanating from fireplaces in both the grand and keeping rooms. Upstairs, bedroom 2 annexes a private, full bath. Bedrooms 3 and 4 share a Jack-and-Jill bath. The loft area is ideal for a family computer. A double garage and a separate single garage complete this plan.

plan# HPK1700536

Style: European Cottage
First Floor: 2,995 sq. ft.
Second Floor: 1,102 sq. ft.
Total: 4,097 sq. ft.
Bedrooms: 4
Bathrooms: 3½
Width: 120' - 6"
Depth: 58' - 8"
Foundation: Slab

eplans.com

This enchanted chateau sings of refined European luxury. A formal dining room and study flank the entry. The master bedroom is a sumptuous retreat with a bayed sitting area, pampering bath, and two walk-in closets. A massive stone fireplace warms the great room. Casual areas include the kitchen, breakfast, and recreation rooms. Three additional bedrooms are located upstairs.

SECOND FLOOR

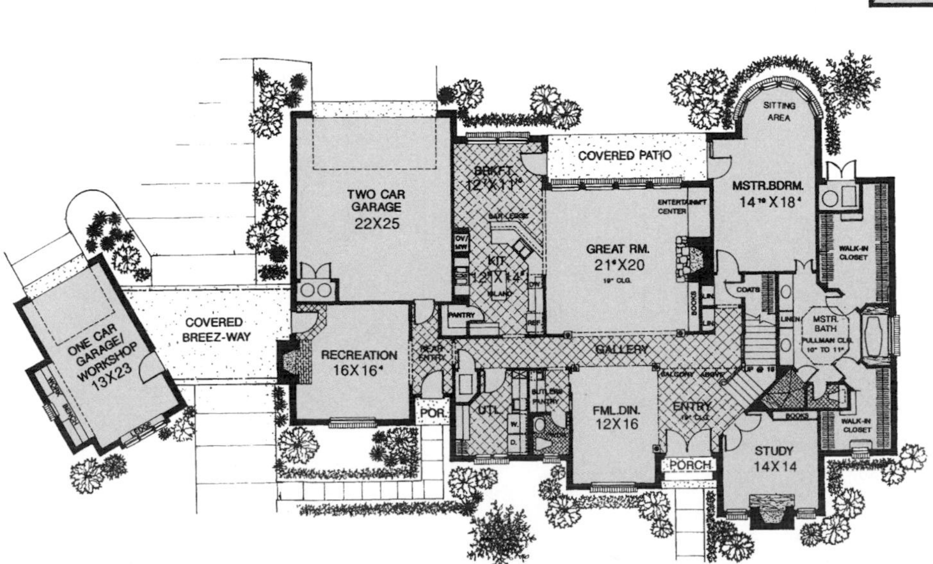

FIRST FLOOR

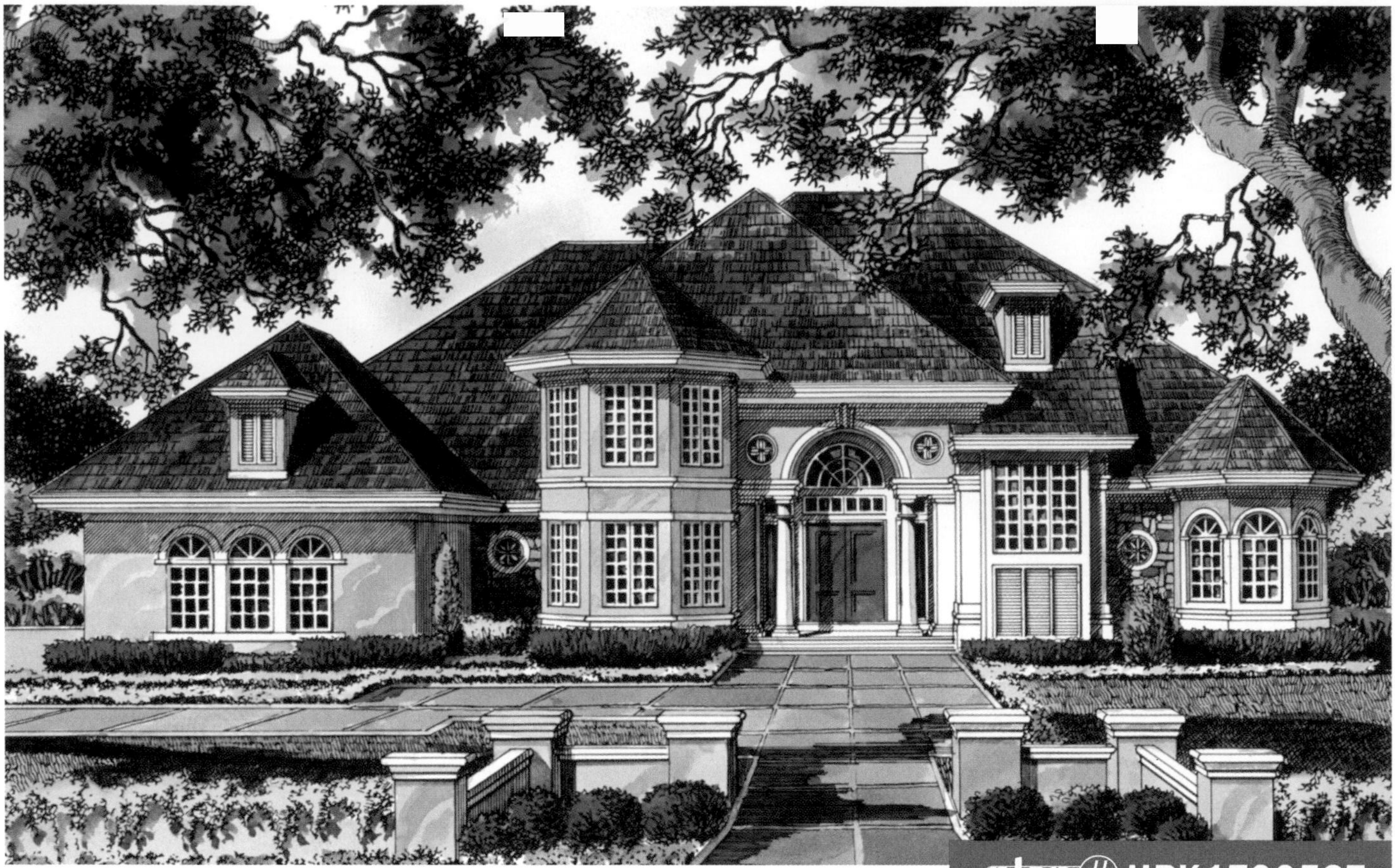

plan# HPK1700537

Style: Traditional	
First Floor: 3,027 sq. ft.	
Second Floor: 1,079 sq. ft.	
Total: 4,106 sq. ft.	
Bedrooms: 4	
Bathrooms: 3½	
Width: 87' - 4"	
Depth: 80' - 4"	
Foundation: Unfinished Basement	

eplans.com

SECOND FLOOR

FIRST FLOOR

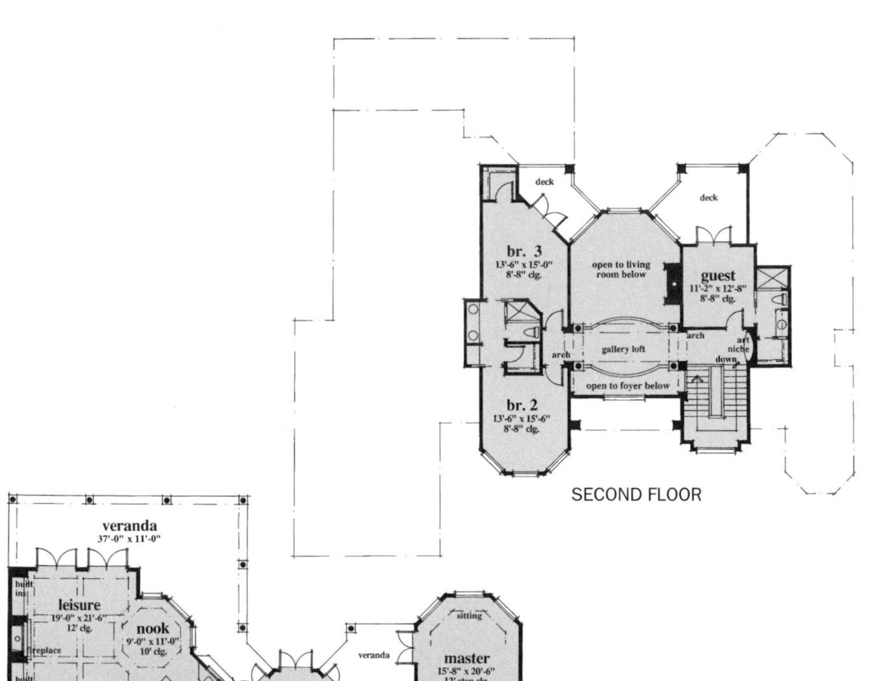

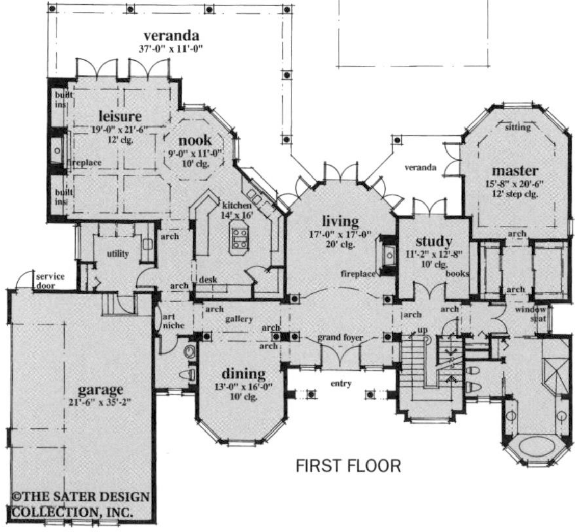

The inside of this design is just as majestic as the outside. The grand foyer opens to a two-story living room with a fireplace and magnificent views. Dining in the bayed formal dining room will be a memorable experience. A well-designed kitchen is near a sunny nook and a leisure room with a fireplace and outdoor access. The master wing includes a separate study and an elegant private bath. The second level features a guest suite with its own bath and deck, two family bedrooms (Bedroom 3 also has its own deck), and a gallery loft with views to the living room below.

plan# HPK1700538

Style: Craftsman

First Floor: 2,218 sq. ft.

Second Floor: 1,919 sq. ft.

Total: 4,137 sq. ft.

Bedrooms: 4

Bathrooms: 4

Width: 87' - 0"

Depth: 58' - 4"

Foundation: Crawlspace

eplans.com

A charming broken gable highlights the facade of this cottage design. The interior layout is perfect for empty nesters who love to entertain, or as a second home near the lake. Decorative columns show off the dining and gathering rooms, dressing up this more formal space. The gourmet kitchen has plenty of room for two or more chefs, and is well-suited for leisurely conversation. The breakfast room enjoys a sunny bank of windows and access to the screened-in porch. The guest room would make a perfect den or home office. Relax in the first-floor master suite outfitted with porch access, twin walk-in closets, and a superb bath. For guests and family, the second level has two suites, an office—or bedroom—bonus room, library, and home theater.

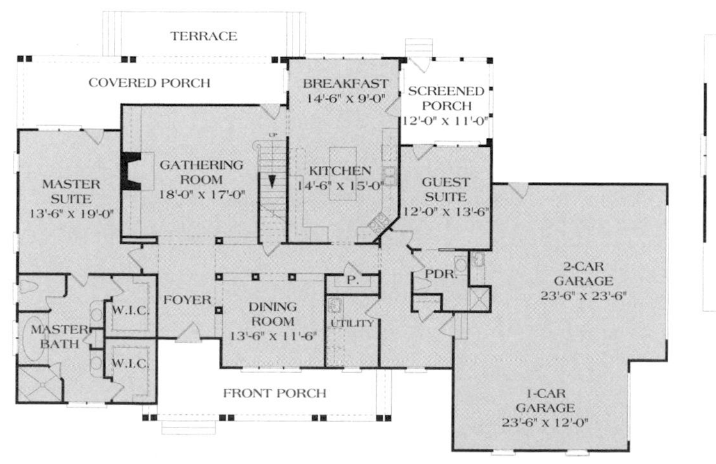

FIRST FLOOR

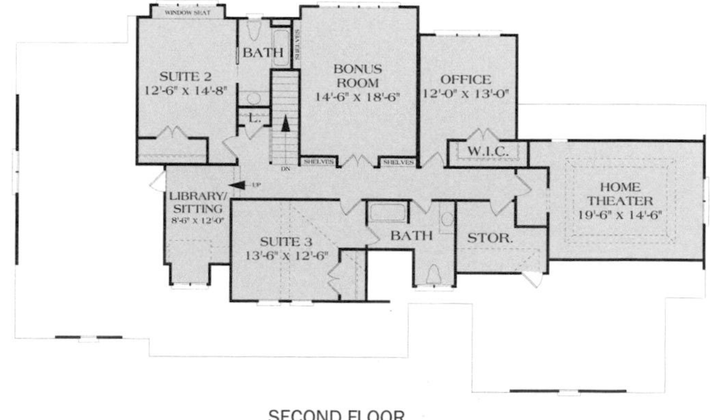

SECOND FLOOR

plan# HPK1700539

Style: Contemporary
First Floor: 2,489 sq. ft.
Second Floor: 1,650 sq. ft.
Total: 4,139 sq. ft.
Bonus Space: 366 sq. ft.
Bedrooms: 4
Bathrooms: 3 ½
Width: 72' - 8"
Depth: 77' - 0"

eplans.com

This captivating luxury home puts a contemporary spin on Old World style. Stucco provides a wonderful complement to multiple arched windows on the exterior; inside, natural light streams into the two-story entry. Just ahead, the living room is graced with a rear window bay and a warming fireplace. The professional-grade kitchen is ready to serve the elegant dining room and bright breakfast nook, both set in bays. A built-in entertainment center in the family room gives the space a definite focus. The right wing is devoted to the master suite: a bayed window lets in the light, as the dazzling bath soothes with a whirlpool tub and room-size walk-in closet. Follow the U-shaped staircase to a mid-level study; three grand bedrooms, a lofty game room, and a sun deck complete the plan.

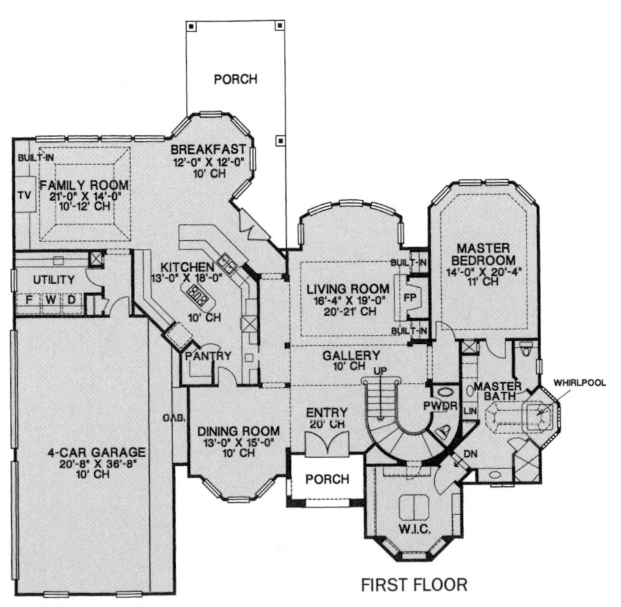

FIRST FLOOR

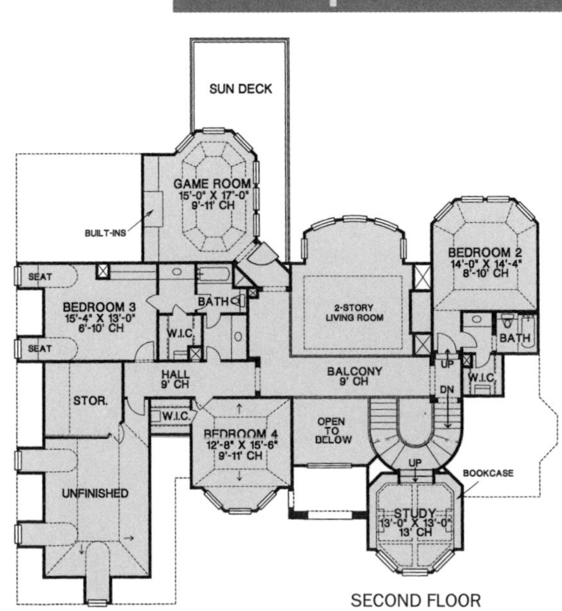

SECOND FLOOR

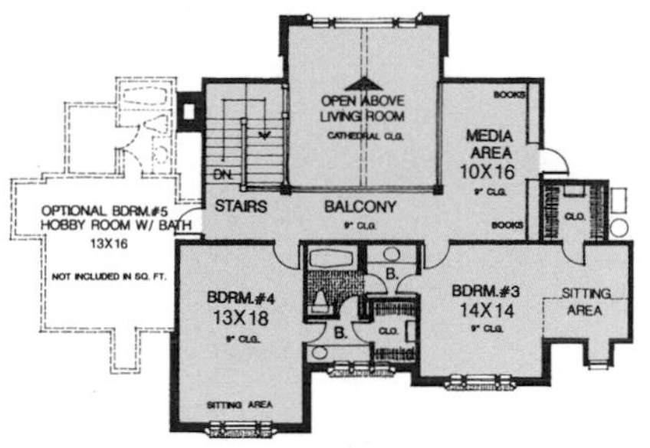

SECOND FLOOR

plan# HPK1700540

Style: French

First Floor: 3,168 sq. ft.

Second Floor: 998 sq. ft.

Total: 4,166 sq. ft.

Bonus Space: 210 sq. ft.

Bedrooms: 4

Bathrooms: 3½

Width: 90' - 0"

Depth: 63' - 5"

Foundation: Slab, Unfinished Basement, Crawlspace

eplans.com

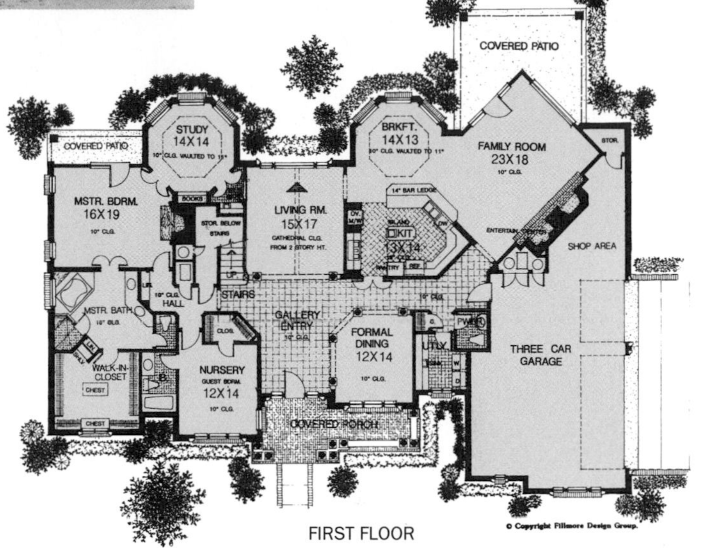

FIRST FLOOR

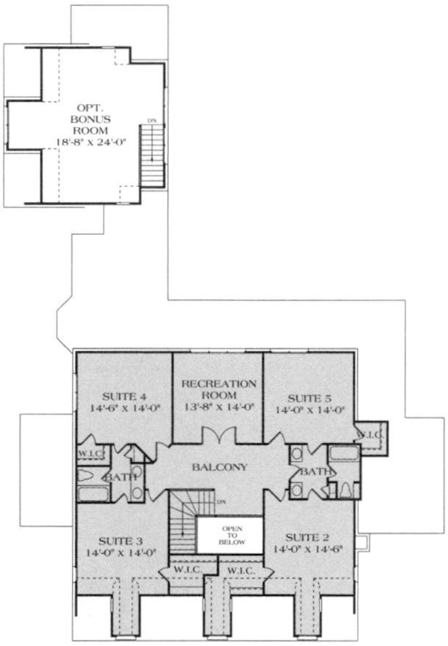

SECOND FLOOR

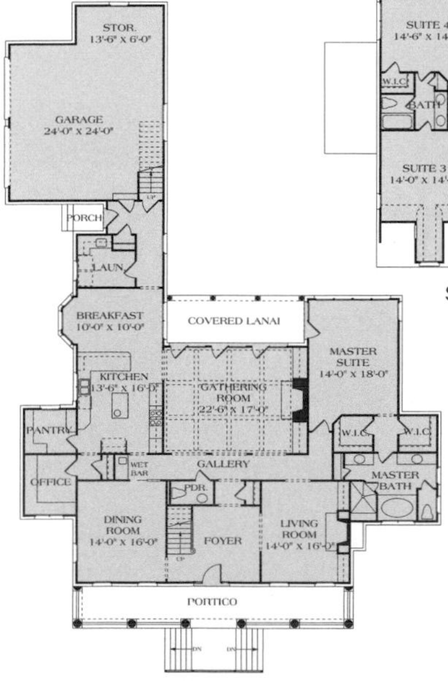

FIRST FLOOR

plan# HPK1700541

Style: Traditional

First Floor: 2,521 sq. ft.

Second Floor: 1,655 sq. ft.

Total: 4,176 sq. ft.

Bonus Space: 498 sq. ft.

Bedrooms: 5

Bathrooms: 3½

Width: 68' - 7"

Depth: 98' - 8"

Foundation: Crawlspace

eplans.com

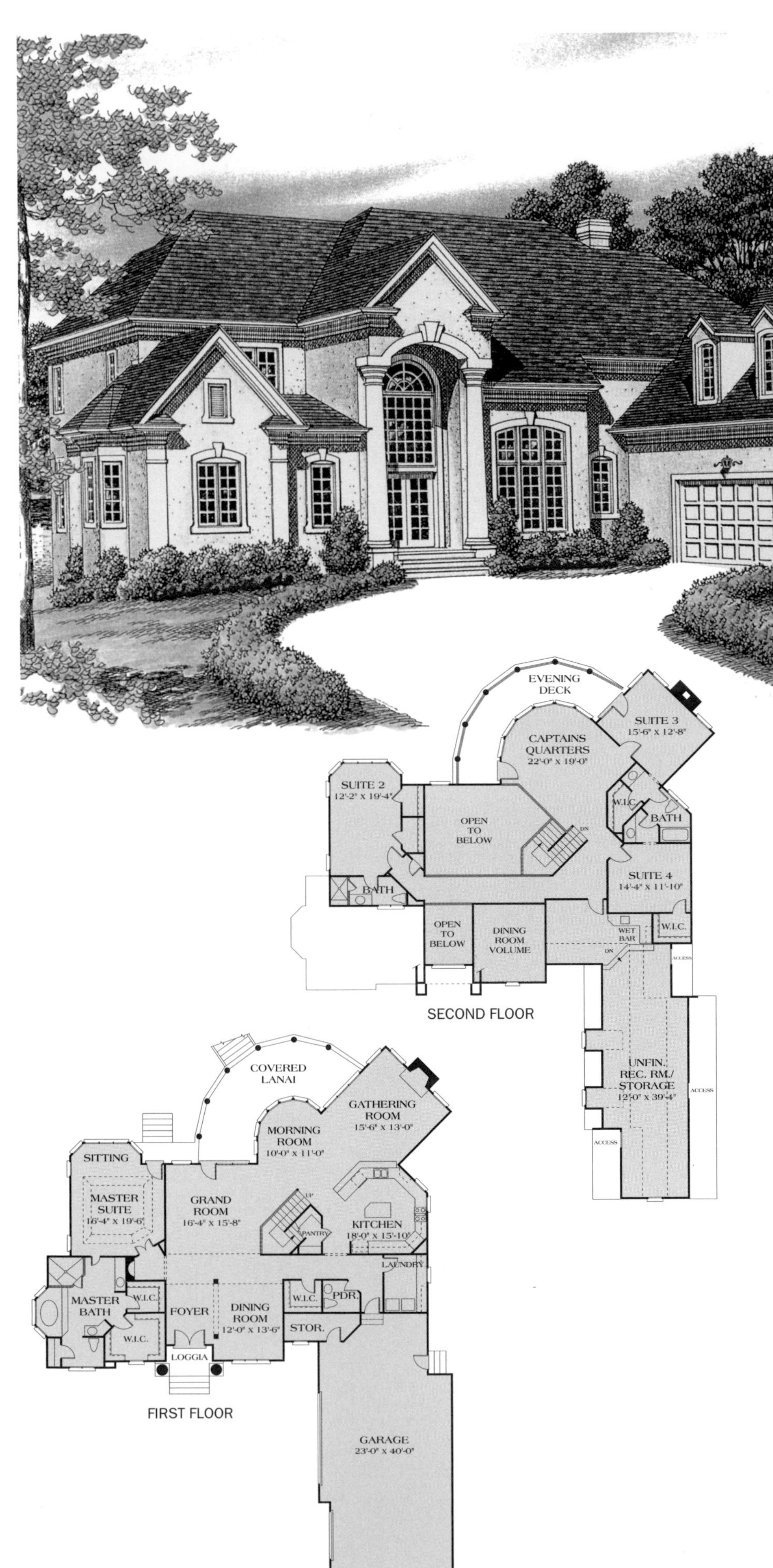

plan # HPK1700542

Style: Transitional
First Floor: 2,547 sq. ft.
Second Floor: 1,637 sq. ft.
Total: 4,184 sq. ft.
Bonus Space: 802 sq. ft.
Bedrooms: 4
Bathrooms: 3 ½
Width: 74' - 0"
Depth: 95' - 6"
Foundation: Crawlspace

eplans.com

Double columns flank a raised loggia that leads to a beautiful two-story foyer. Flanking this elegance to the right is a formal dining room. Straight ahead, under a balcony and defined by yet more pillars, is the spacious grand room. A bow-windowed morning room and a gathering room feature a full view of the rear lanai and beyond. The master bedroom suite is lavish with its amenities, which include a bayed sitting area, direct access to the rear terrace, a walk-in closet, and a sumptuous bath.

plan# HPK1700543

Style: Craftsman
First Floor: 2,979 sq. ft.
Second Floor: 1,209 sq. ft.
Total: 4,188 sq. ft.
Bedrooms: 3
Bathrooms: 3 ½
Width: 101' - 8"
Depth: 78' - 5"
Foundation: Crawlspace

eplans.com

A charming stone facade, a steeply-pitched roofline with abundant dormers, a columned porch, and a cute corner lot attached garage with spire single out this exterior for special attention. The master suite sits at the front of the house, to the right of the floor plan off of the main foyer. It holds two enormous walk-in closets and a private sitting area with terrific bayed windows. The family room and access to the covered terrace are opposite the foyer at the end of the floor, with a screened porch immediately adjacent. An ample breakfast, kitchen, and pantry area are situated to the left of the family room. Two bedrooms with private baths and walk-in closets, attic space, and a library await upstairs.

REAR EXTERIOR

SECOND FLOOR

FIRST FLOOR

plan# HPK1700544

Style: Mediterranean
First Floor: 2,926 sq. ft.
Second Floor: 1,268 sq. ft.
Total: 4,194 sq. ft.
Bonus Space: 353 sq. ft.
Bedrooms: 4
Bathrooms: 4 ½
Width: 75' - 0"
Depth: 85' - 4"
Foundation: Slab

eplans.com

This magnificent Mediterranean-style home is full of the charms that make entertaining gracious and family life comfortable. From the elegant covered entry, pass into the foyer or, through separate French doors, into the den on the right and the formal dining room on the left. A superb kitchen, sunlit breakfast nook, and family room flow together, creating a relaxed unit. Splendor awaits in the master suite with its gracefully curved bedchamber, huge walk-in wardrobes, and luxuriant bath. On the opposite side of the house, a guest bedroom enjoys a full bath. Two more bedrooms share a bath on the second level, and additional space is available for another bedroom and bath. The rear covered patio can be entered from the living room, the master suite, or the breakfast nook. Three vehicles will easily fit into the side-loading garage.

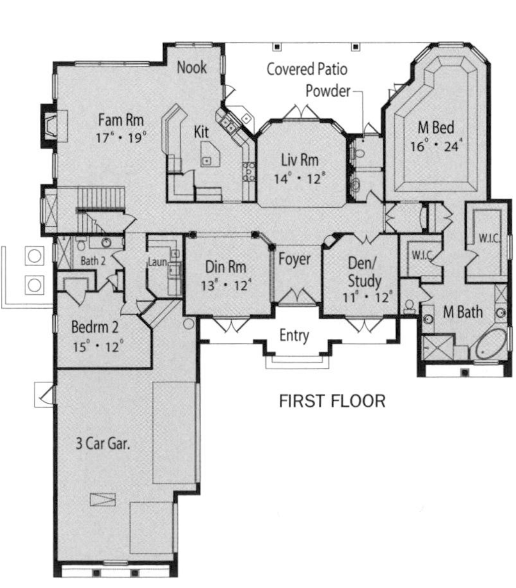

FIRST FLOOR

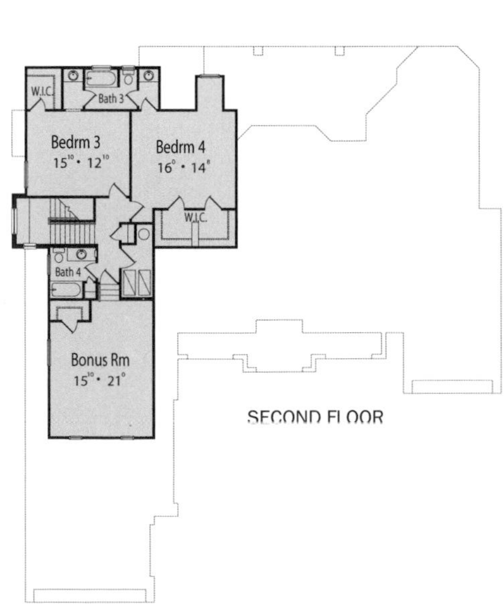

SECOND FLOOR

plan# HPK1700545

Style: European Cottage
First Floor: 2,207 sq. ft.
Second Floor: 1,993 sq. ft.
Total: 4,200 sq. ft.
Bedrooms: 4
Bathrooms: 3½
Width: 74' - 6"
Depth: 46' - 0"
Foundation: Unfinished Basement

eplans.com

Spindle railings and multipane archtop windows distinguish this brick home from others on the block. At the top of the circular front steps, the double doors open to a vestibule with a coat closet. Go through another set of double doors to the main hall, which accesses all the first-floor rooms and a stately staircase to the second floor. The first floor offers a living room with a corner fireplace, an office, a family room that provides a second fireplace, a kitchen with a breakfast area, a powder room, a laundry room, and a formal dining room. The second floor includes a master suite with a private bath, two family bedrooms that share a bath, and a fourth bedroom with a private bath.

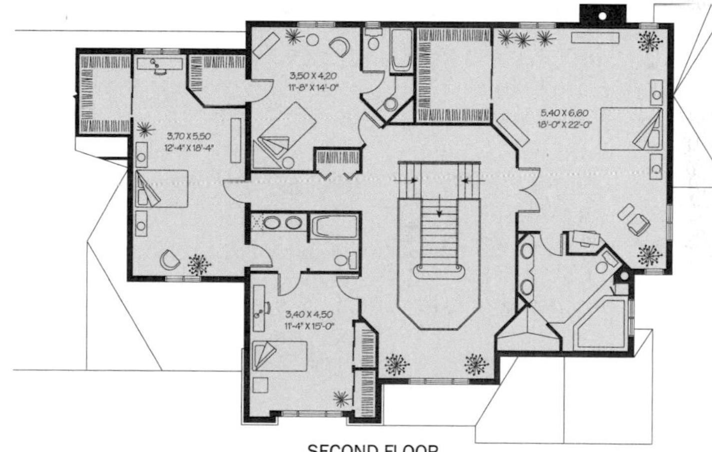

SECOND FLOOR

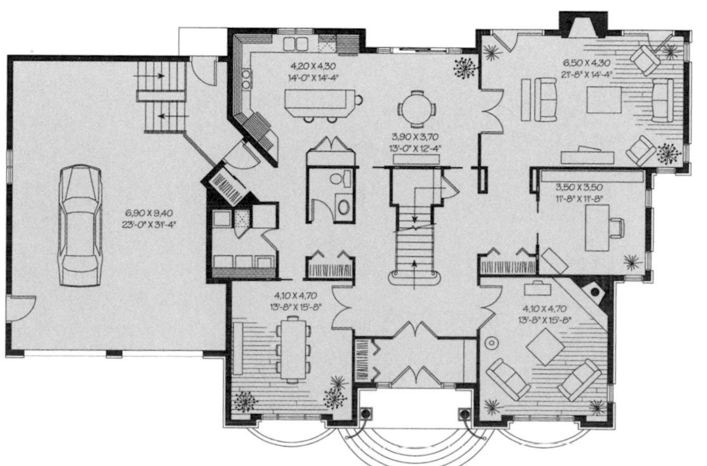

FIRST FLOOR

This two-story farmhouse has much to offer, with the most exciting feature being the opulent master suite, which takes up almost the entire width of the upper level. French doors access the large master bedroom, featuring a coffered ceiling. Steps lead to a separate sitting room with a fireplace and sun-filled bay window. His and Hers walk-in closets lead the way to a vaulted private bath with separate vanities and a lavish whirlpool tub. On the first floor, an island kitchen and a bayed breakfast room flow into a two-story family room with a raised-hearth fireplace, built-in shelves, and French-door access to the rear yard.

plan# HPK1700546

- Style: Plantation
- First Floor: 2,113 sq. ft.
- Second Floor: 2,098 sq. ft.
- Total: 4,211 sq. ft.
- Bonus Space: 76 sq. ft.
- Bedrooms: 5
- Bathrooms: 4½
- Width: 68' - 6"
- Depth: 53' - 0"
- Foundation: Slab, Unfinished Walkout Basement, Crawlspace

eplans.com

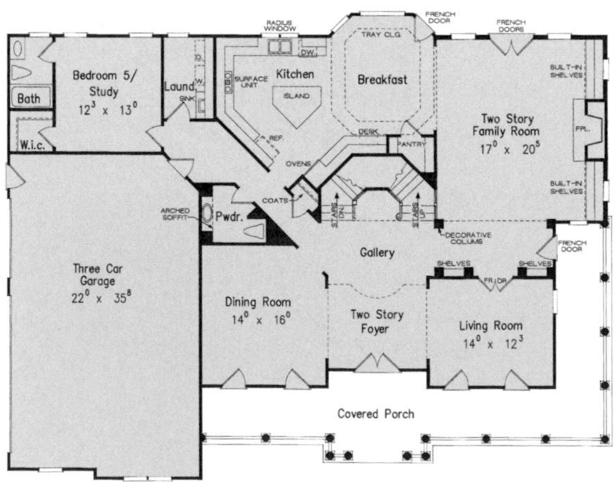

FIRST FLOOR

SECOND FLOOR

plan# HPK1700547

Style: Contemporary
First Floor: 2,688 sq. ft.
Second Floor: 1,540 sq. ft.
Total: 4,228 sq. ft.
Bedrooms: 4
Bathrooms: 3½
Width: 84' - 3"
Depth: 80' - 1"

eplans.com

This home's facade eschews frou-frou in favor of refined elegance. Enter through a set of stately columns to a gracious foyer, opening to a formal dining room on the left and enjoying a view of the gorgeous spiral staircase to the right. Straight ahead, behold the stunning hearth-warmed living room, which boasts a curved wall of windows looking out to the rear. The right side of the first floor is taken up by a sumptous master retreat—make the study an extension of the bedroom if you wish! Adjacent to the spacious kitchen on the left is the media room, ready to become the most popular spot in the house. It features a built-in media wall, access to its own porch, plenty of room for seating, and a serving-bar counter to the kitchen—perfect for movie-time snacking! Three bedrooms and two baths share the second floor with a game room, which has a second built-in media wall—ideal for a "kids-only" theater!

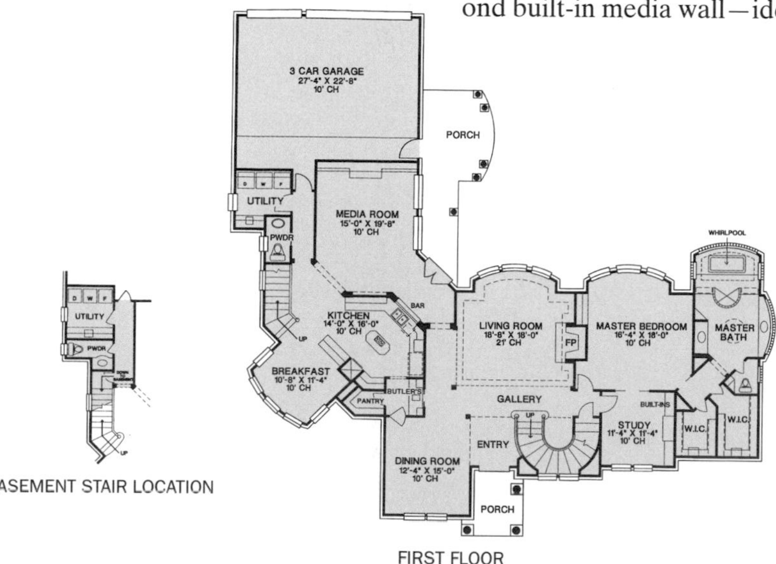

BASEMENT STAIR LOCATION

FIRST FLOOR

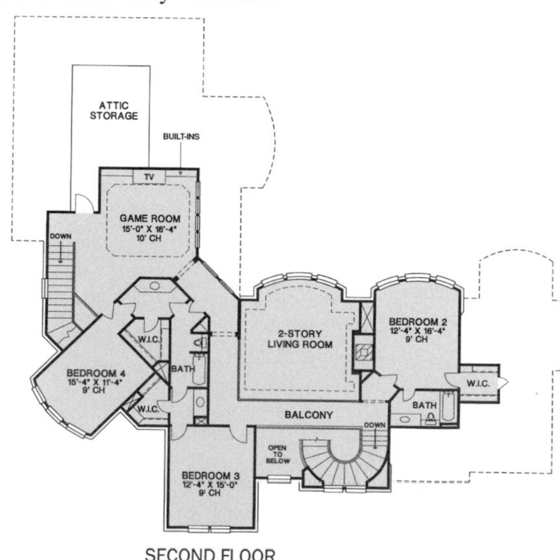

SECOND FLOOR

plan# HPK1700548

Style: European Cottage

First Floor: 2,950 sq. ft.

Second Floor: 1,278 sq. ft.

Total: 4,228 sq. ft.

Bedrooms: 4

Bathrooms: 4½

Width: 91' - 8"

Depth: 71' - 10"

Foundation: Crawlspace, Slab, Unfinished Basement

eplans.com

An elegant European manor with family appeal, this beautiful four-bedroom plan will be a joy to own for generations to come. The two-story foyer presents a dramatic curved staircase that leads to two bedroom suites and a game room. Continue to the great room, full of natural light and warmed by a cozy hearth. A unique shape in the kitchen maximizes counter space and offers easy access to the breakfast nook and a butler's pantry to the dining room. A nearby bedroom is perfect as a guest suite or live-in help's quarters. The master suite is located for privacy, exquisite with a sitting bay and a lavish bath that features a prominent step-up tub. The plan is completed by a three-car garage and two-car porte cochere.

3 CAR GARAGE
UTIL 11-4 X 13-0 10 FT CLG
PAN
COVERED PORCH
BREAKFAST ROOM 17-0 X 11-0 10 FT CLG
GREAT ROOM 18-6 X 18-0 10 FT CLG
FP
SITTING AREA 10-0 X 3-6
MASTER BEDROOM 17-0 X 14-6 10 FT CLG
MASTER BATH 15-4 X 12-0 10 FT CLG
FRIENDS ENTRY
PORCH
KITCHEN 17-0 X 12-8 10 FT CLG
PWDR
PORTE-COCHERE
BATH 2
BUTLERS PANTRY
STUDY 13-0 X 11-8 10 FT CLG
BEDROOM 2 13-6 X 11-0 10 FT CLG
DINING ROOM 13-0 X 16-0 10 FT CLG
FOYER 10-6 X 21-6 2 STORY CLG
PORCH

FIRST FLOOR

GAME ROOM 18-6 X 15-0 9 FT CLG
OPEN TO GREAT ROOM BELOW
ATTIC ACCESS
BALCONY
BATH 3
BATH 4
ATTIC ACCESS
BEDROOM 3 13-0 X 14-4 9 FT CLG
OPEN TO FOYER BELOW
BEDROOM 4 13-0 X 12-4 9 FT CLG

SECOND FLOOR

plan# HPK1700549

Style: Georgian

First Floor: 2,255 sq. ft.

Second Floor: 1,976 sq. ft.

Total: 4,231 sq. ft.

Bedrooms: 5

Bathrooms: 4

Width: 71' - 0"

Depth: 67' - 7"

Foundation: Unfinished Walkout Basement

eplans.com

BEDROOM 2
12'-9" x 10'-1"
TWO STORY GREAT ROOM
MASTER BEDROOM
21'-0" x 17'-9"
SITTING AREA
W.I.C.
BATH
GALLERY
UP.
DN.
W.I.C.
BEDROOM 3
12'-9" x 11'-1"
TWO STORY FOYER
BEDROOM #4
12'-6" x 14'-3"
BATH
M. BATH
HIS
HERS
12'-0" x 9'-1"
EXERCISE RM.
20'-5" x 6'-7"

SECOND FLOOR

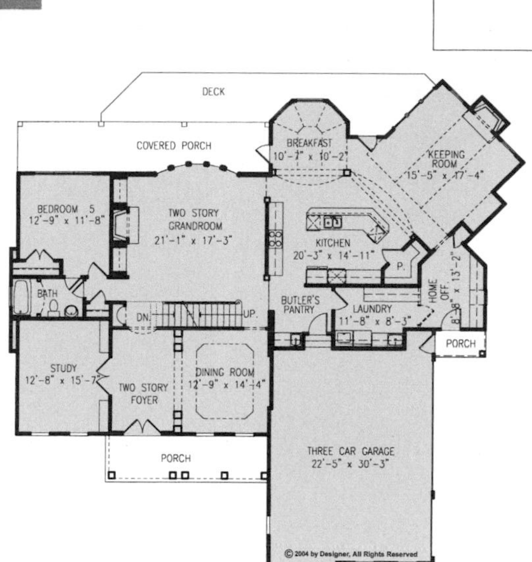

FIRST FLOOR

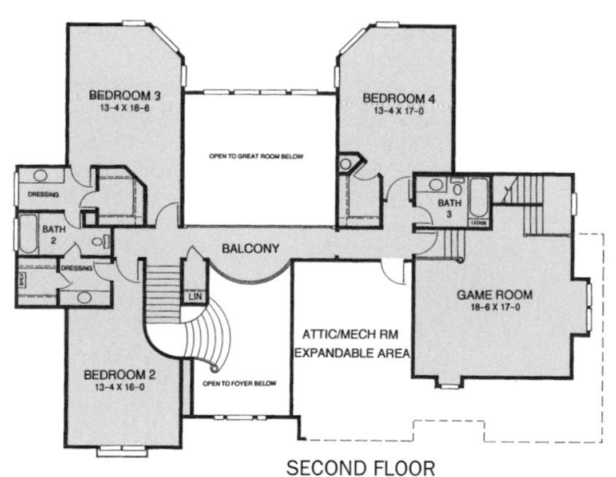

SECOND FLOOR

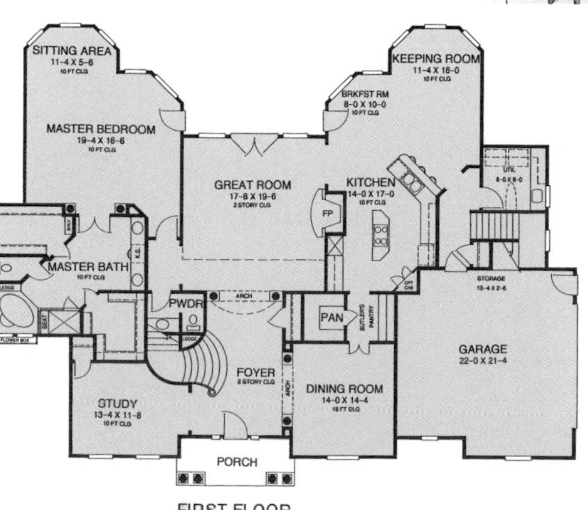

FIRST FLOOR

plan# HPK1700550

Style: Norman

First Floor: 2,639 sq. ft.

Second Floor: 1,625 sq. ft.

Total: 4,264 sq. ft.

Bedrooms: 4

Bathrooms: 3½

Width: 73' - 8"

Depth: 58' - 6"

Foundation: Slab, Crawlspace, Unfinished Basement

eplans.com

PHOTO COURTESY OF GARRELL ASSOCIATES, INC.

plan# HPK1700551

Style: Federal
First Floor: 2,139 sq. ft.
Second Floor: 2,147 sq. ft.
Total: 4,286 sq. ft.
Bedrooms: 4
Bathrooms: 3½ + ½
Width: 62' - 0"
Depth: 63' - 6"
Foundation: Unfinished Walkout Basement

eplans.com

The exterior of this home speaks volumes on its appeal, but once inside, the distinctive layout has the last word. Traditionally formal spaces blend with a more modern, open design to increase the livability of the home. This is best exemplified with the flow from the grand room to the kitchen/breakfast nook, and into the family room. This functionality is ideal for family interaction or entertaining. The second floor houses the master suite, a grand retreat for the homeowners—adorned with a private sitting area, tray ceilings, and an expansive walk-in closet.

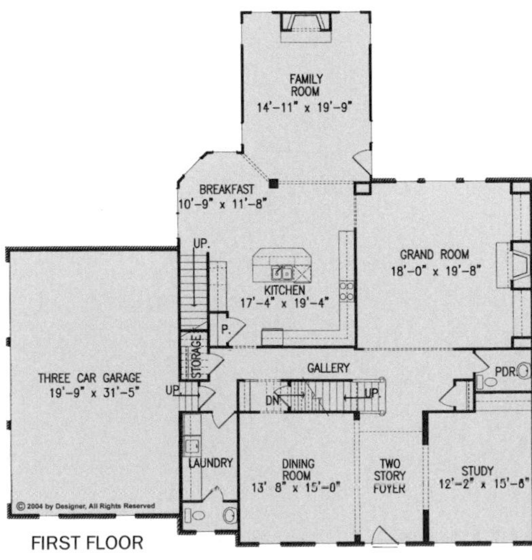

FIRST FLOOR

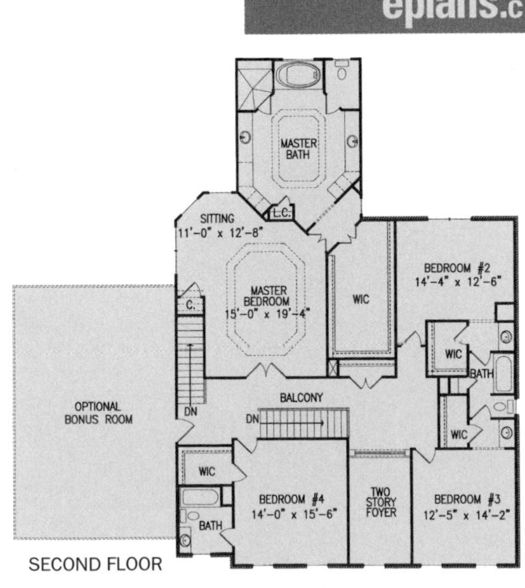

SECOND FLOOR

plan# HPK1700552

Style: Mediterranean
First Floor: 3,633 sq. ft.
Second Floor: 695 sq. ft.
Total: 4,328 sq. ft.
Bedrooms: 5
Bathrooms: 5½
Width: 115' - 7"
Depth: 109' - 8"
Foundation: Slab

eplans.com

Arched windows and a dramatic portico with scrolled columns are gracefully featured in this Mediterranean design. The foyer is just as expressive, with more scrolled columns and soft curves to match the arched doorway. Mosaic tiles on the floor and steps bring touches of color and polish to earth-toned surfaces. The master suite and bath with patio are to the right of the plan; the guest rooms are to the left, near the family room and kitchen. A spacious lanai, here enclosed by a greenhouse, features a pool and spa lined with trees and other botanicals. Notice the wet bar, ready with cool drinks for visitors to this unexpected sanctuary.

REAR EXTERIOR

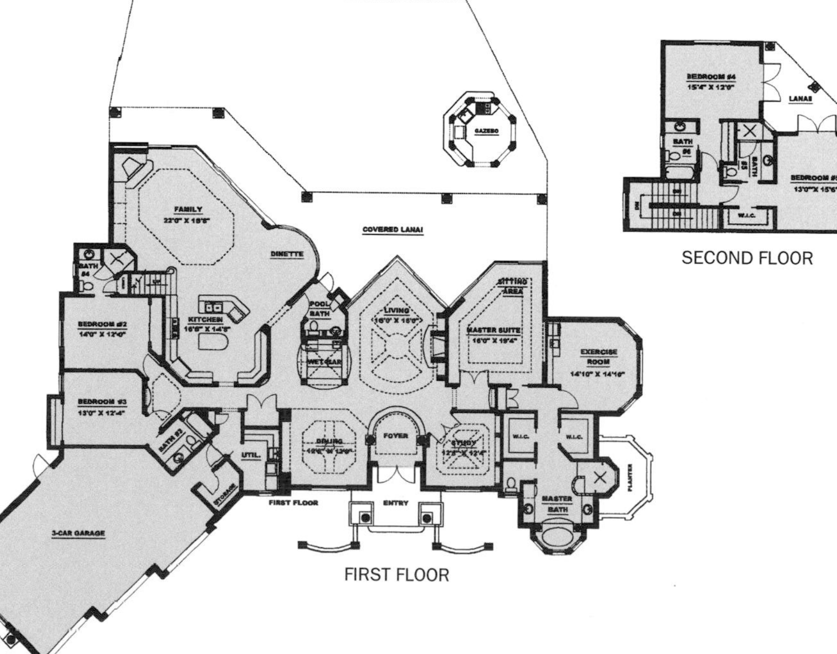

FIRST FLOOR

SECOND FLOOR

plan# HPK1700553

Style: French Country
First Floor: 2,734 sq. ft.
Second Floor: 1,605 sq. ft.
Total: 4,339 sq. ft.
Bonus Space: 391 sq. ft.
Bedrooms: 4
Bathrooms: 4½
Width: 88' - 0"
Depth: 92' - 8"
Foundation: Finished Walkout Basement

eplans.com

Attractive stone, curved dormers, and varied rooflines give this fine European manor a graceful dose of class. Inside, the foyer introduces a formal dining room defined by columns and a spacious gathering room with a fireplace. The nearby kitchen features a walk-in pantry, beam ceiling, adjacent breakfast nook, and a screened porch. The first-floor master suite features two walk-in closets, a lavish bath, a corner fireplace, and a sitting room with access to the rear veranda. Upstairs, three suites offer walk-in closets and surround a study loft. On the lower level, a huge recreation room awaits to entertain with a bar, a fireplace, and outdoor access. A secluded office provides a private entrance—perfect for a home business.

REAR EXTERIOR

SCREENED PORCH 13'-0" x 17'-0"
VERANDA
BREAKFAST 14'-0" x 8'-0"
SITTING 13'-0" x 8'-0"
KITCHEN 17'-6" x 19'-0"
GATHERING ROOM 24'-0" x 18'-0"
MASTER SUITE 19'-6" x 13'-0"
LAUN.
GALLERY
HIS
HERS
MUD RM.
OFFICE
PDR.
DINING ROOM 12'-0" x 13'-6"
FOYER
MASTER BATH
PORCH
STOR.
GARAGE 23'-0" x 22'-4"

FIRST FLOOR

SUITE 3 17'-2" x 17'-0"
BATH
W.I.C.
OPEN TO BELOW
BALCONY
W.I.C.
STUDY LOFT 8'-10" x 11'-0"
DRESS.
SUITE 2 12'-6" x 14'-2"
OPEN TO BELOW
BATH
BATH
SUITE 4 / BONUS RM 16'-2" x 23'-0"

SECOND FLOOR

COVERED VERANDA
COVERED VERANDA
OFFICE 12'-0" x 11'-6"
EXERCISE ROOM 13'-0" x 13'-2"
BATH
RECREATION ROOM 32'-0" x 23'-0"
GARAGE 20'-0" x 23'-6"
BAR 10'-0" x 10'-6"
STOR. 10'-10" x 13'-0"
WINE
MECH./STOR.

BASEMENT

plan# HPK1700554
Style: Craftsman
First Floor: 2,533 sq. ft.
Second Floor: 1,820 sq. ft.
Total: 4,353 sq. ft.
Bonus Space: 507 sq. ft.
Bedrooms: 4
Bathrooms: 3½
Width: 85' - 10"
Depth: 81' - 6"
Foundation: Crawlspace
eplans.com

Take advantage of views on a hilly lot with this raised-foundation design. Craftsman touches outfit this home in rustic character, but the floor plan keeps living spaces entirely modern. Four columns define the foyer and introduce the large gathering room. This space enjoys three sets of French doors, essentially opening the room to the outside. This open floor plan works magic in the kitchen, which serves up an island, pantry, and planning desk. A screened porch sits just off the spacious dining room. The first-floor master suite offers a place to relax. Three family suites, an open study nook, and bonus space creates room for everyone.

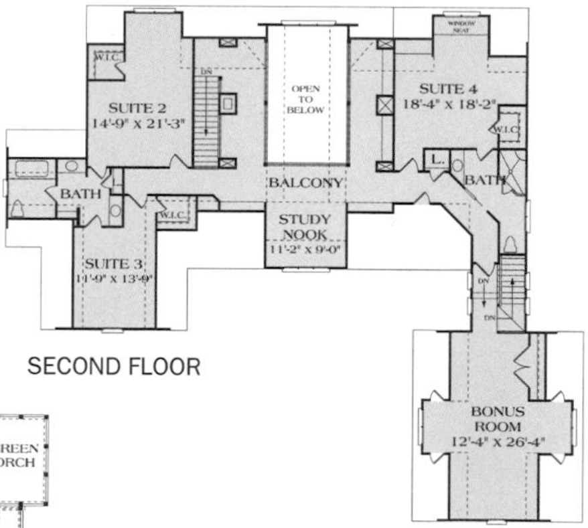

SUITE 2 14'-9" x 21'-3"
OPEN TO BELOW
SUITE 4 18'-4" x 18'-2"
BATH
W.I.C.
BALCONY
STUDY NOOK 11'-2" x 9'-0"
BATH
SUITE 3 14'-9" x 13'-9"
BONUS ROOM 12'-4" x 26'-4"

SECOND FLOOR

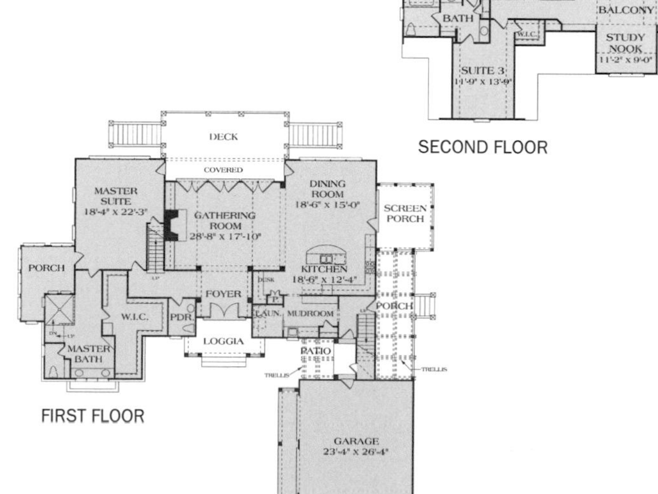

FIRST FLOOR

REAR EXTERIOR

SMART TIP

The two-story vaulted foyer shown here is a good example of an eye-catching room that isn't just another pretty space. The two closets flanking the door can become one of the home's most effective wards against clutter. Let the closets work as a one-stop drop zone for your keys, wallets, umbrellas, pet leashes, and outer garments. Installing an outlet will let you plug in cell phones and PDAs in one place. More than just an organization space, a well-adapted utility closet can let you mentally adjust to entering and leaving the home.

plan # HPK1700555
Style: Norman
First Floor: 3,056 sq. ft.
Second Floor: 1,307 sq. ft.
Total: 4,363 sq. ft.
Bonus Space: 692 sq. ft.
Bedrooms: 4
Bathrooms: 4½
Width: 94' - 4"
Depth: 79' - 2"
Foundation: Crawlspace, Basement
eplans.com

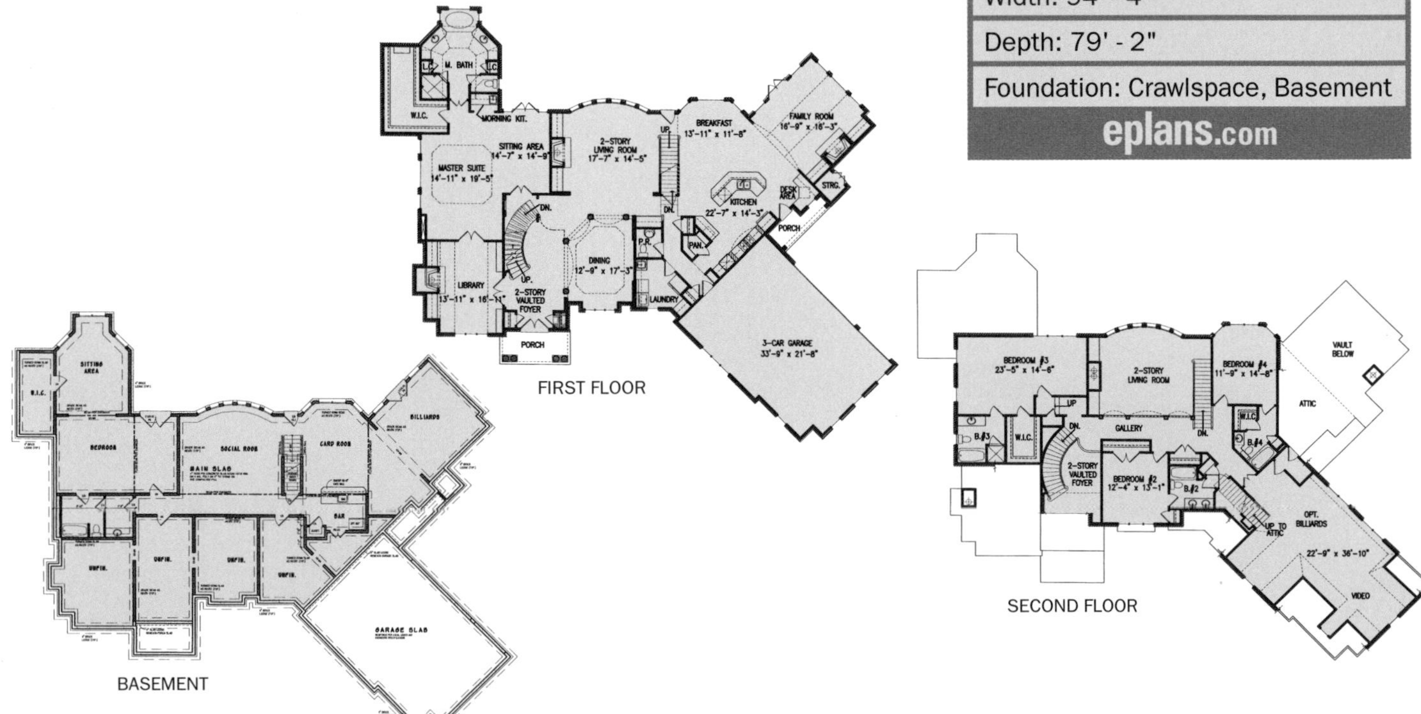

plan# HPK1700556

Style: French
First Floor: 2,899 sq. ft.
Second Floor: 1,472 sq. ft.
Total: 4,371 sq. ft.
Bedrooms: 4
Bathrooms: 3½ + ½
Width: 69' - 4"
Depth: 76' - 8"
Foundation: Slab

eplans.com

Finished with French Country adornments, this estate home is comfortable in just about any setting. Main living areas are sunk down just a bit from the entry foyer, providing them with soaring ceilings and sweeping views. The family room features a focal fireplace. A columned entry gains access to thc master suite where separate sitting and sleeping areas are defined by a three-sided fireplace. There are three bedrooms upstairs; one has a private bath. The sunken media room on this level includes storage space. Note the second half-bath under the staircase landing.

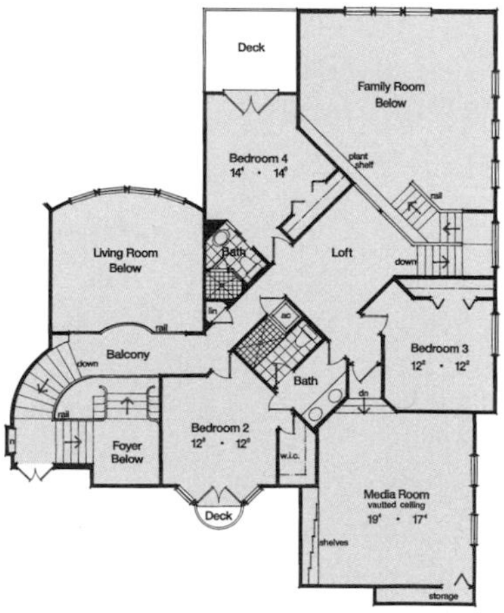

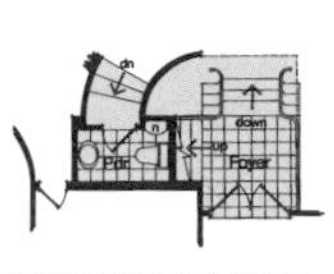

OPTIONAL LAYOUT

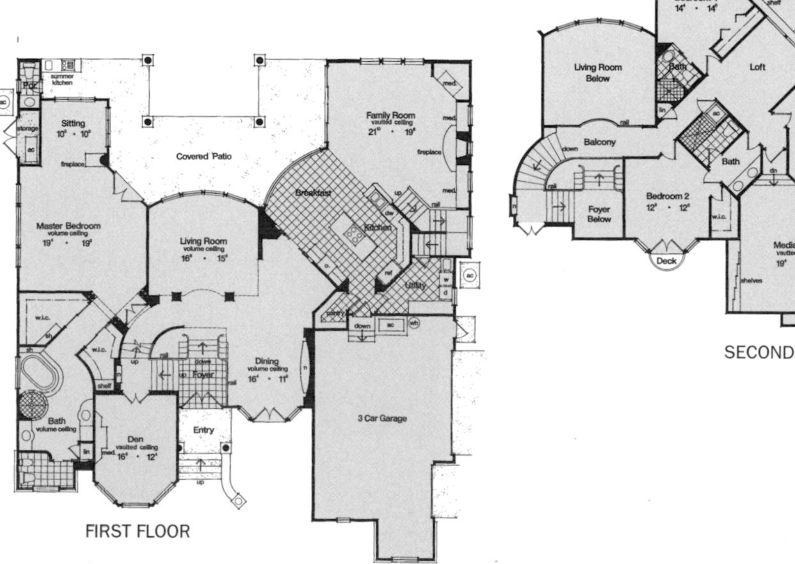

FIRST FLOOR

SECOND FLOOR

PHOTO COURTESY OF GARRELL ASSOCIATES, INC.

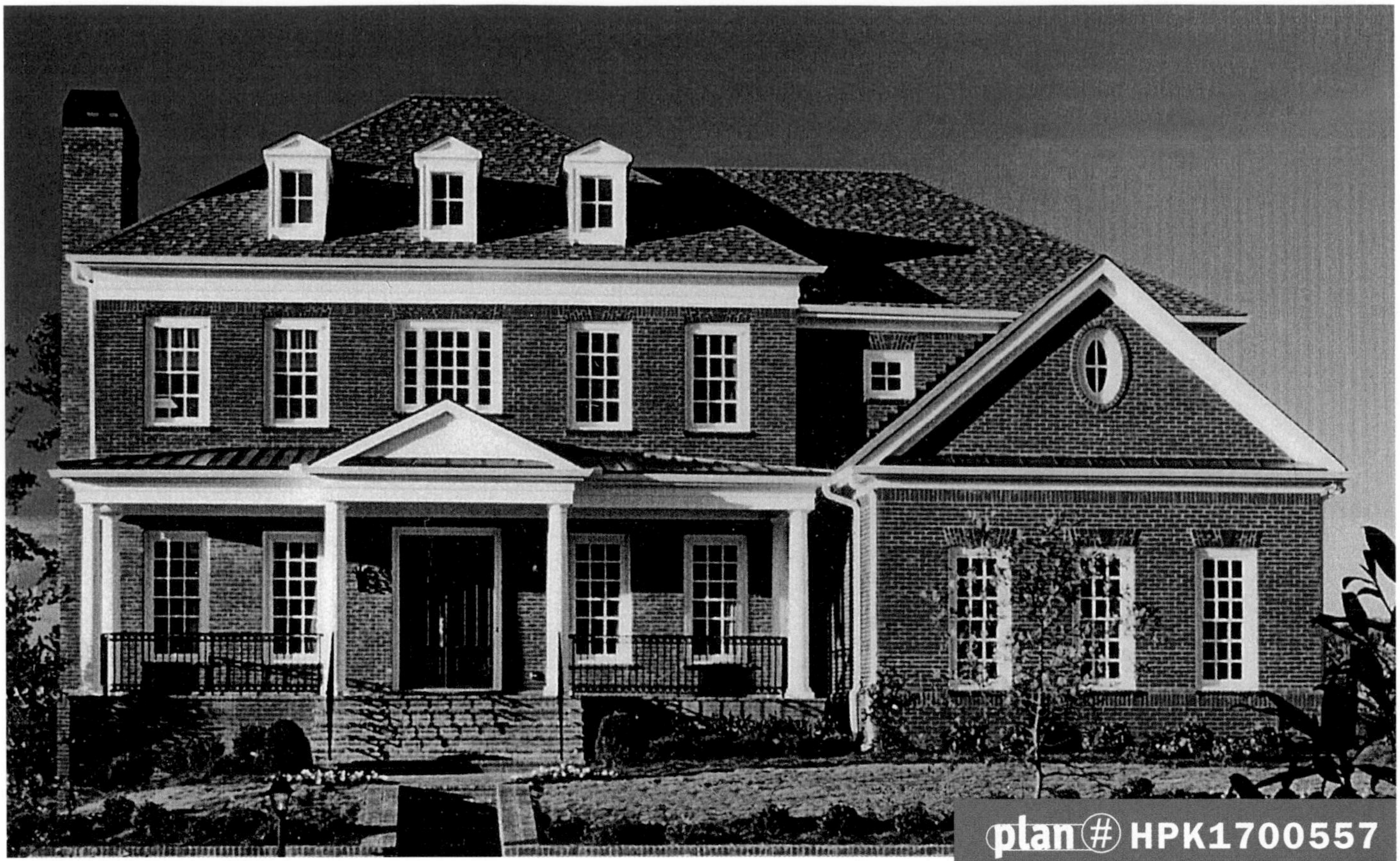

plan # HPK1700557

Style: Georgian

First Floor: 2,756 sq. ft.

Second Floor: 1,631 sq. ft.

Total: 4,387 sq. ft.

Bedrooms: 4

Bathrooms: 4½

Width: 66' - 2"

Depth: 75' - 0"

Foundation: Unfinished Walkout Basement

eplans.com

A Georgian flavor permeates this exterior, with an abundance of multipaned windows and three dormers along the roof. A pleasingly wide porch is centered by a triangular pediment, leading to a long foyer. An elegant banquet hall is open to the right, with a library to the left, past double doors. A curving staircase unwinds just next to the library. A V-shaped gallery anchors the grand room, at the end of which one accesses the covered terrace, through French doors. The upper level confers views to the banquet hall, grand room, and foyer below.

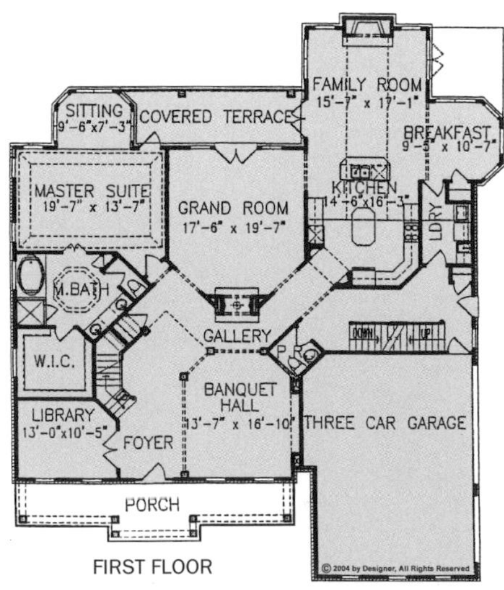

FIRST FLOOR

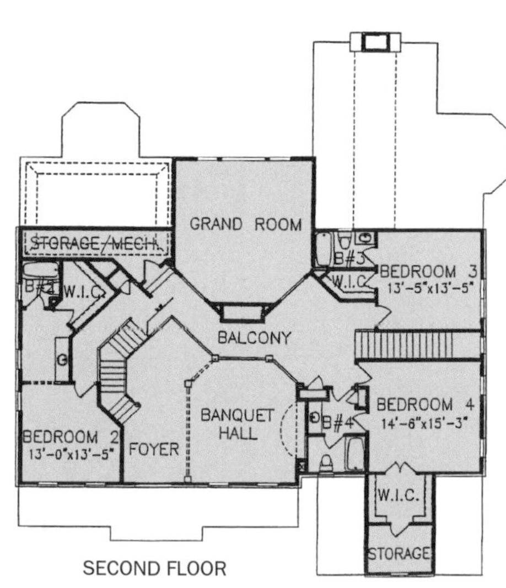

SECOND FLOOR

plan# HPK1700558

Style: Norman
First Floor: 3,121 sq. ft.
Second Floor: 1,278 sq. ft.
Total: 4,399 sq. ft.
Bedrooms: 4
Bathrooms: 3½ + ½
Width: 86' - 7"
Depth: 81' - 4"
Foundation: Basement

eplans.com

A brick/stone facade creates the solid exterior of this French Country design. Insidc, a library in the front is warmed by a fireplace, but the heart of the house is found in a large, open great room with a second fireplace. The spacious gourmet kitchen enjoys warmth from the grand room to the left and a third fireplace in the adjoining family room on the right. Access to a rear covered porch and deck/patio can be gained from the family room. There are three bedrooms upstairs and a bonus room/optional fifth bedroom. Each bedroom boasts a walk-in closet and convenient access to a full bath.

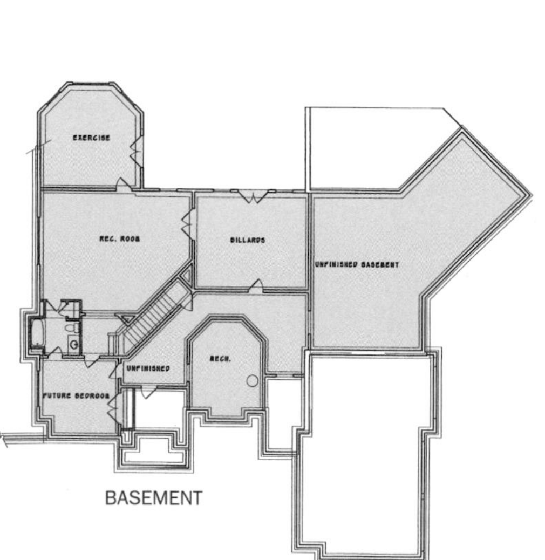

BASEMENT

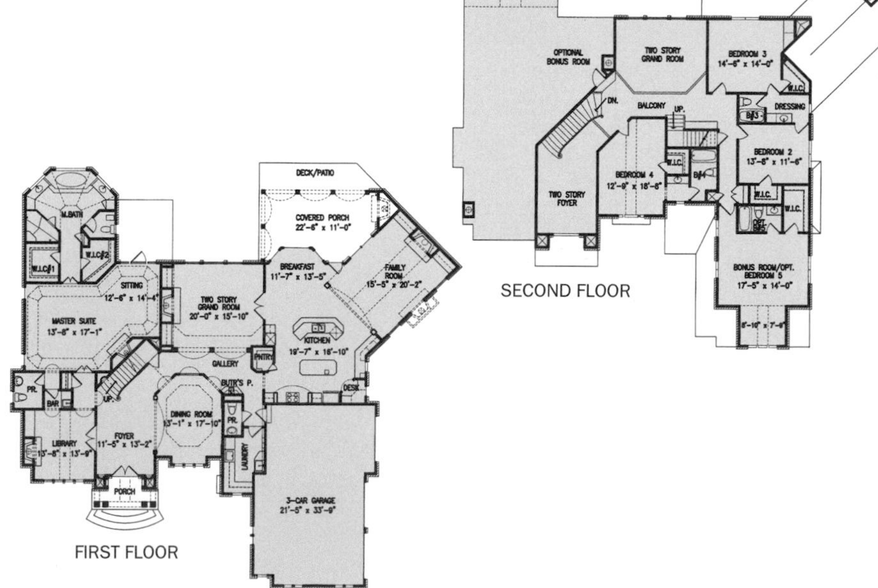

FIRST FLOOR

SECOND FLOOR

plan# HPK1700559

Style: Farmhouse

First Floor: 2,090 sq. ft.

Second Floor: 2,317 sq. ft.

Total: 4,407 sq. ft.

Bedrooms: 5

Bathrooms: 4½

Width: 71' - 4"

Depth: 62' - 8"

Foundation: Unfinished Walkout Basement

eplans.com

A bevy of windows lends a wealth of natural light to this Colonial design. Inside, a fireplace in the expansive great room warms the adjoining breakfast nook and island kitchen. A side covered porch is accessed from this area. A guest suite completes this level. Upstairs, the master bedroom features a see-through fireplace that also warms the adjacent sitting area. A walk through the amenity-filled master bath leads to an enormous walk-in closet. A third bedroom boasts a full bath and the fourth and fifth bedrooms share a hall bath, complete with separate vanities. The three-car garage is the finishing touch on this plan.

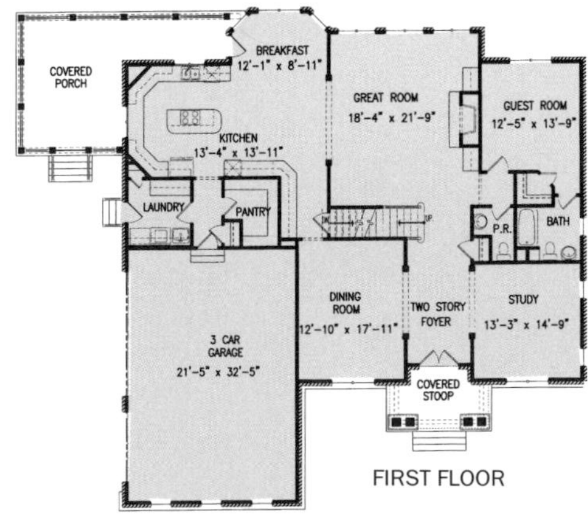

FIRST FLOOR

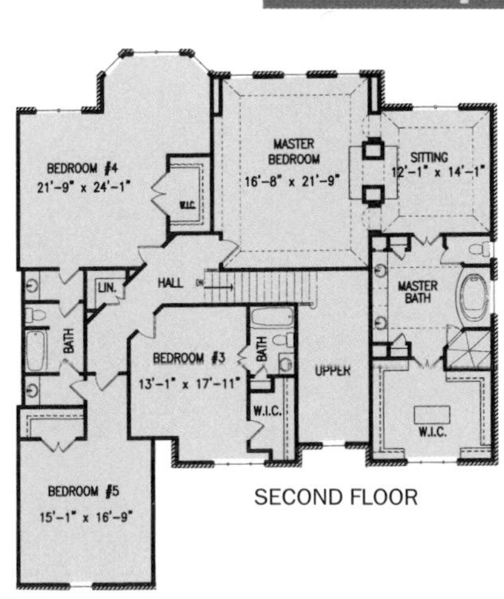

SECOND FLOOR

plan# HPK1700560

Style: Farmhouse
First Floor: 3,566 sq. ft.
Second Floor: 864 sq. ft.
Total: 4,430 sq. ft.
Bedrooms: 4
Bathrooms: 4½
Width: 127' - 9"
Depth: 75' - 8"
Foundation: Finished Basement

eplans.com

Arch-topped windows, graceful details, and a stunning stucco facade give this manor plenty of appeal. Inside, the foyer is flanked by a cozy drawing room and the formal dining room. Entertaining will be a breeze with the huge keeping room near the efficient kitchen, and the grand room; both rooms havc fireplaces and access to the covered rear terrace. A guest suite provides privacy for visitors. The lavish master suite features a walk-in closet, deluxe bath, covered balcony, and fireplace. Upstairs, two amenity-filled suites are separated by a balcony. The basement level of the home expands its livability greatly, with a spacious exercise room (complete with a full bath), a summer kitchen, a gathering room (includes a fireplace and bar), and a suite for future needs. Note the studio apartment over the main garage.

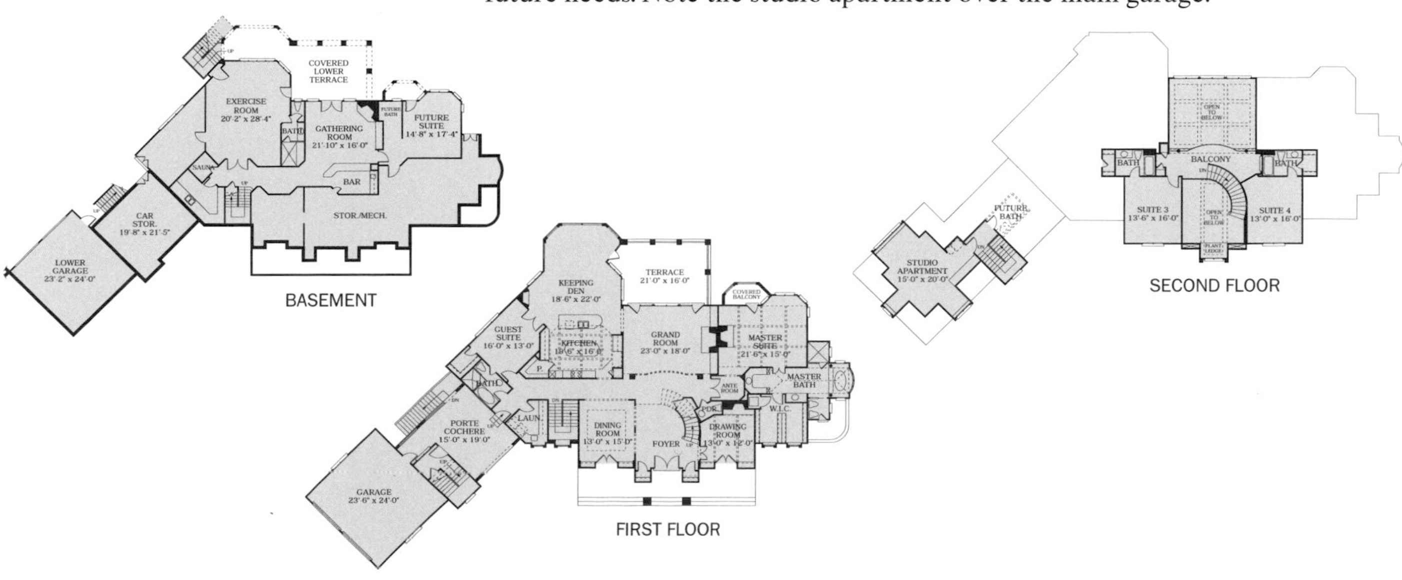

BASEMENT

FIRST FLOOR

SECOND FLOOR

plan# HPK1700561

Style: Tidewater

First Floor: 3,179 sq. ft.

Second Floor: 1,265 sq. ft.

Total: 4,444 sq. ft.

Bonus Space: 626 sq. ft.

Bedrooms: 4

Bathrooms: 4½

Width: 81' - 8"

Depth: 75' - 10"

Foundation: Unfinished Walkout Basement

eplans.com

Three dormers and a columned covered porch welcome visitors to this country dream home. The right side of the bottom floor is dominated by the master bedroom, which includes an optional private entry to the adjacent study. Fireplaces in the family room and keeping room warm the adjoining kitchen and breakfast nook. The rear screened porch and terrace are conveniently accessed from this area. Upstairs, an unfinished bonus room offers space for future expansion. Three family bedrooms, each with a full bath, complete the second floor.

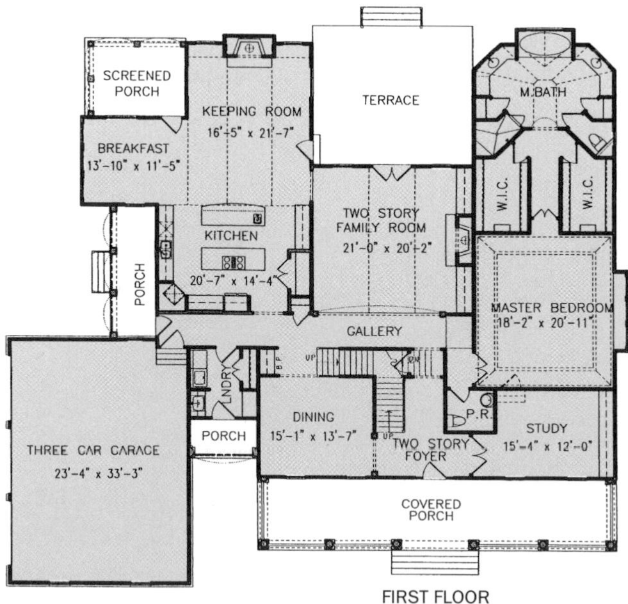

FIRST FLOOR

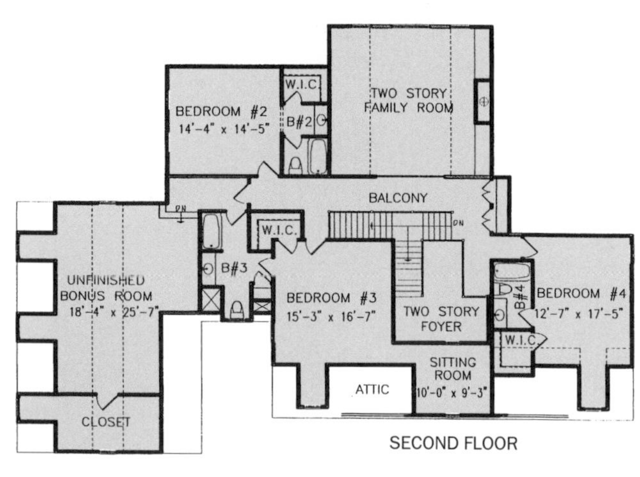

SECOND FLOOR

plan# HPK1700562

Style: Italianate
First Floor: 3,240 sq. ft.
Second Floor: 1,215 sq. ft.
Total: 4,455 sq. ft.
Bedrooms: 4
Bathrooms: 3½
Width: 65' - 0"
Depth: 99' - 0"
Foundation: Slab

eplans.com

A pleasing Old-World Spanish design conjures stylish California and Florida neighborhoods of the 1930s. Magnificent ceiling details can be found in the foyer, study, master suite, and dining room. A modern open kitchen features a large island and a smaller central island that creates plenty of space and work room for the family. The family and eating nook are open to the kitchen and offer views of the covered patio, which features a mini-kitchen and pool bath. Three family bedrooms—two upstairs—a loft, and a media room provide room for guests and family privacy.

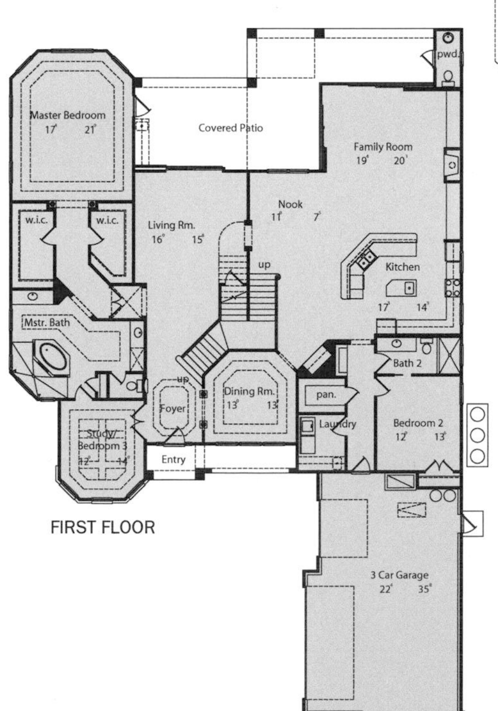

FIRST FLOOR

SECOND FLOOR

PHOTO PROVIDED BY FRANK BETZ ASSOCIATES, INC.

plan# HPK1700563

Style: Farmhouse

First Floor: 2,092 sq. ft.

Second Floor: 2,372 sq. ft.

Total: 4,464 sq. ft.

Bedrooms: 5

Bathrooms: 4½

Width: 75' - 5"

Depth: 64' - 0"

Foundation: Unfinished Walkout Basement, Crawlspace

eplans.com

A country-style wraparound porch provides a cheerful welcome to this distinguished traditional design. The kitchen boasts a serving bar and a walk-in pantry, as well as a butler's pantry. A first-floor bedroom with a walk-in closet can double as a study. The master suite, with a sitting area, vaulted bath and access to a private covered porch, dominates the second floor. Three additional bedrooms all offer tray ceilings and walk-in closets. A large playroom completes the plan.

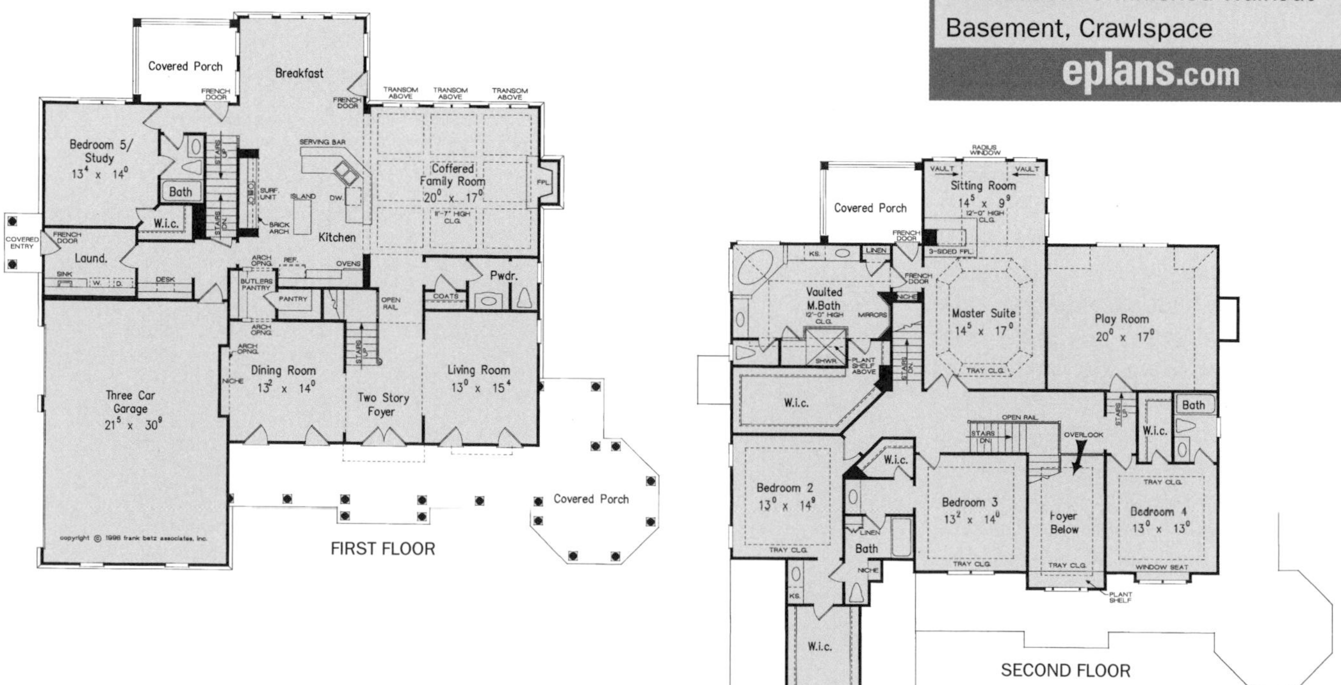

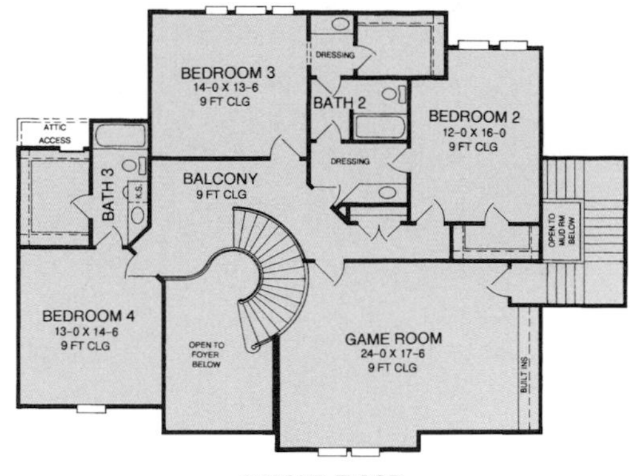

SECOND FLOOR

plan# HPK1700564

- Style: European Cottage
- First Floor: 3,033 sq. ft.
- Second Floor: 1,545 sq. ft.
- Total: 4,578 sq. ft.
- Bedrooms: 4
- Bathrooms: 3½ + ½
- Width: 91' - 6"
- Depth: 63' - 8"
- Foundation: Crawlspace, Slab, Unfinished Basement

eplans.com

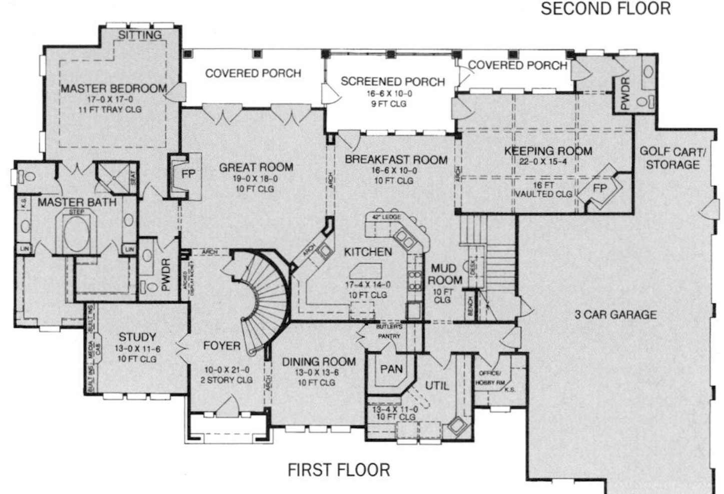

FIRST FLOOR

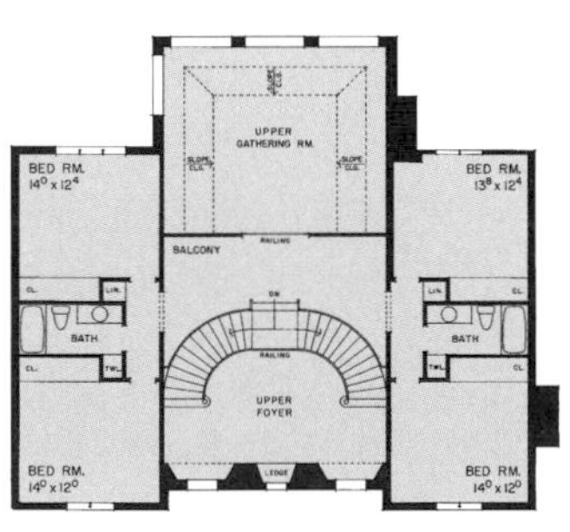

SECOND FLOOR

plan# HPK1700565

- Style: Mediterranean
- First Floor: 3,350 sq. ft.
- Second Floor: 1,298 sq. ft.
- Total: 4,648 sq. ft.
- Bedrooms: 5
- Bathrooms: 3½ + ½
- Width: 97' - 0"
- Depth: 74' - 4"
- Foundation: Unfinished Basement

eplans.com

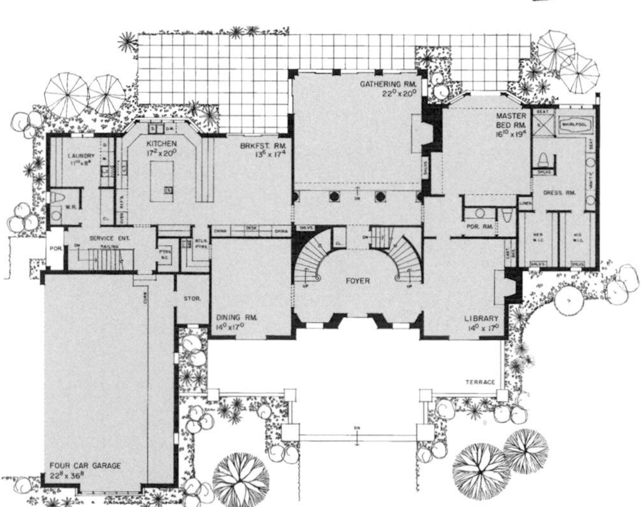

FIRST FLOOR

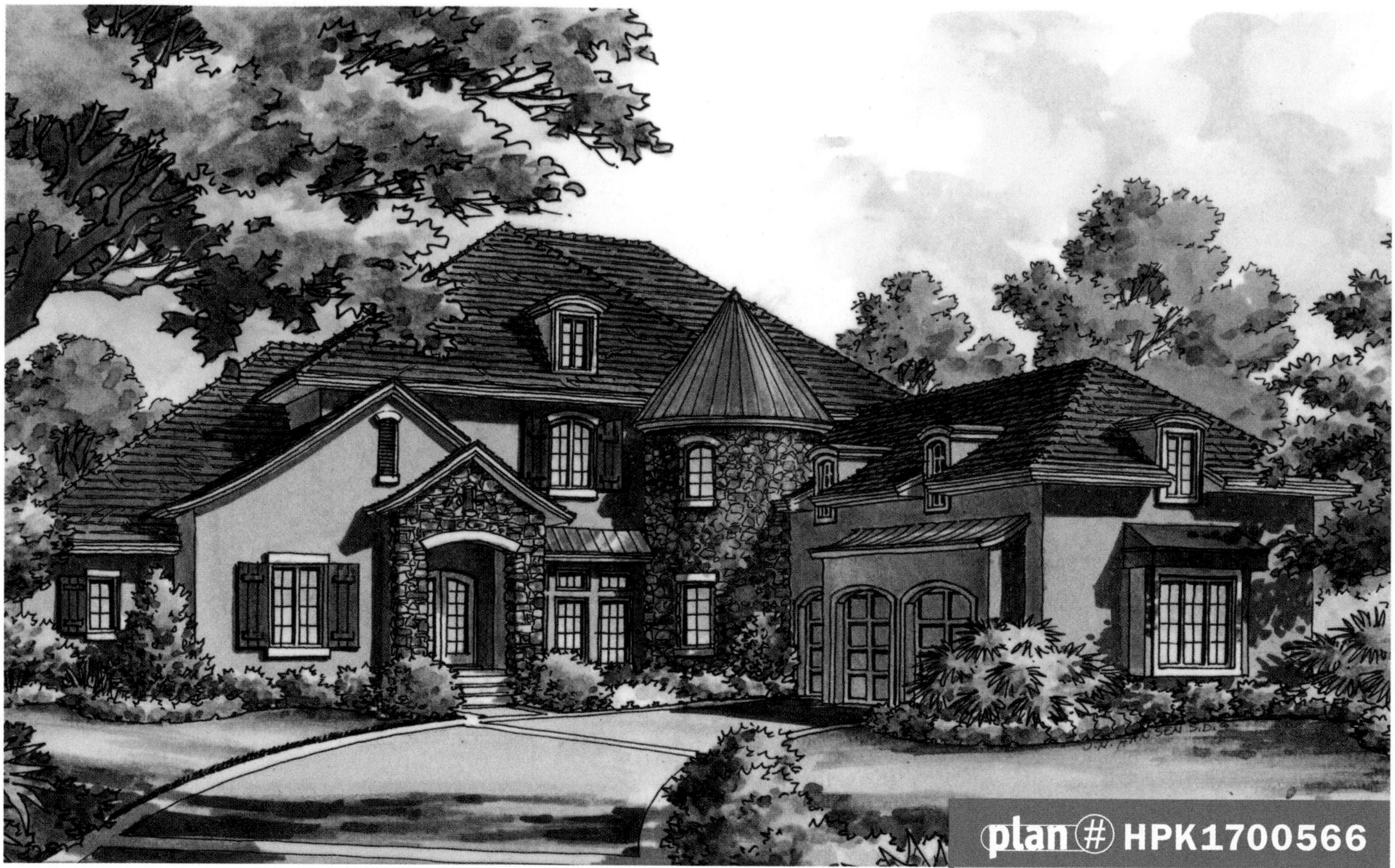

plan# HPK1700566

Style: European Cottage

First Floor: 3,526 sq. ft.

Second Floor: 1,143 sq. ft.

Total: 4,669 sq. ft.

Bedrooms: 4

Bathrooms: 4

Width: 84' - 2"

Depth: 109' - 1"

Foundation: Slab

eplans.com

Stone and stucco combine with a great many windows to create a beguiling facade for this expansive European design. Some interestingly angled rooms, such as the rounded laundry room housed in a turret and the angled family room, make for great decorating options. Two bedrooms—the master suite included, occupying the entire left wing—are housed on the first level. Central to this floor are the living and dining rooms, kitchen, and nook. Don't miss the library as well. Upstairs are three more bedrooms—check out the sitting area off bedroom three—and two more bedrooms. Plenty of bonus space allows for future renovations.

FIRST FLOOR

SECOND FLOOR

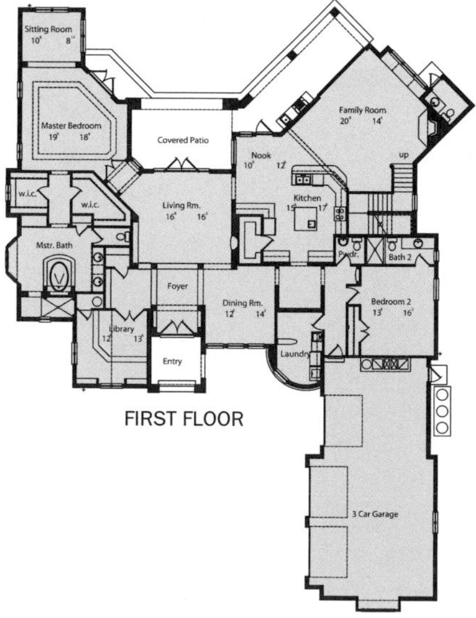

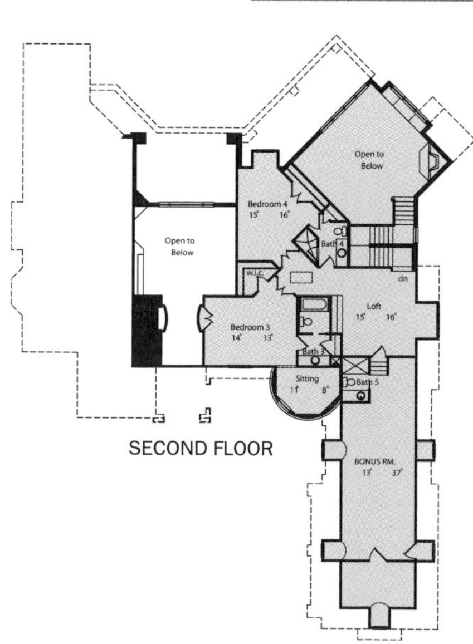

plan # HPK1700567

Style: French

First Floor: 2,559 sq. ft.

Second Floor: 2,140 sq. ft.

Total: 4,699 sq. ft.

Bedrooms: 5

Bathrooms: 4

Width: 80' - 0"

Depth: 67' - 0"

Foundation: Unfinished Basement

eplans.com

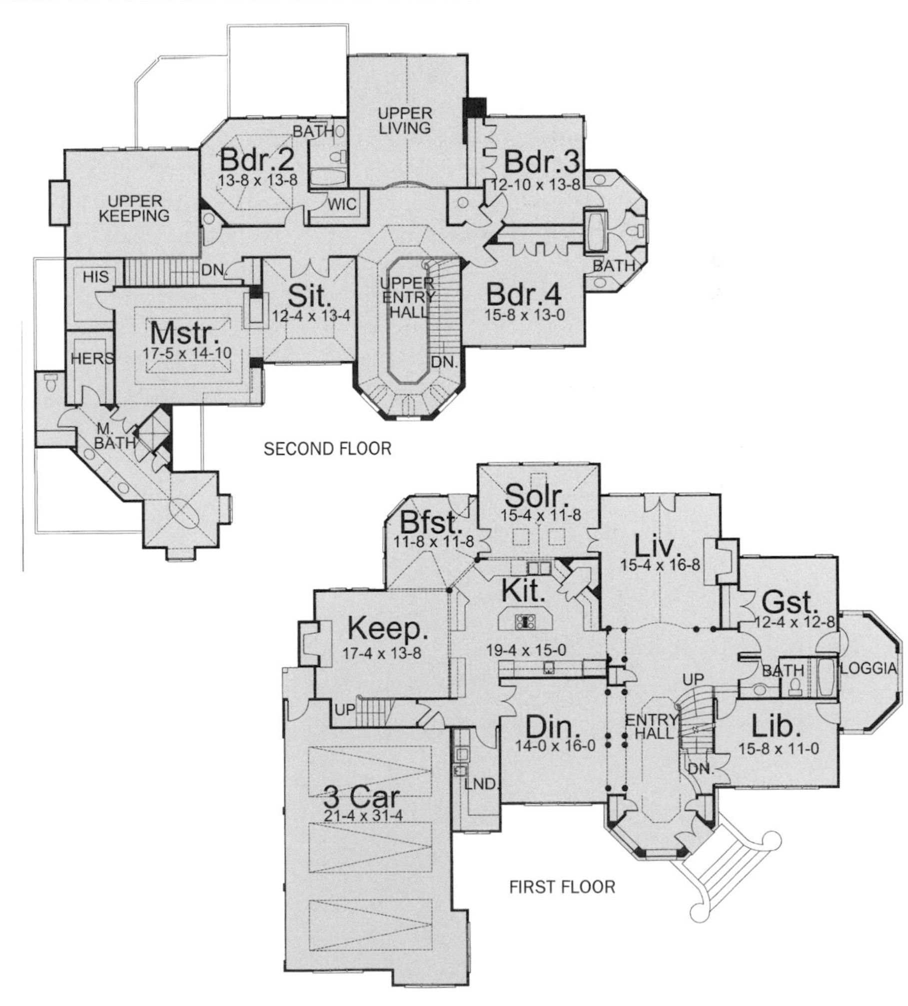

Accommodate your life's diverse pattern of formal occasions and casual times with this spacious home. The exterior of this estate presents a palatial bearing, while the interior is both comfortable and elegant. Formal areas are graced with amenities to make entertaining easy. Casual areas are kept intimate, but no less large. The solarium serves both with skylights and terrace access. Guests will appreciate a private guest room and a bath with loggia access on the first floor. Family bedrooms and the master suite are upstairs. Note the gracious ceiling treatments in the master bedroom, its sitting room, and Bedroom 2.

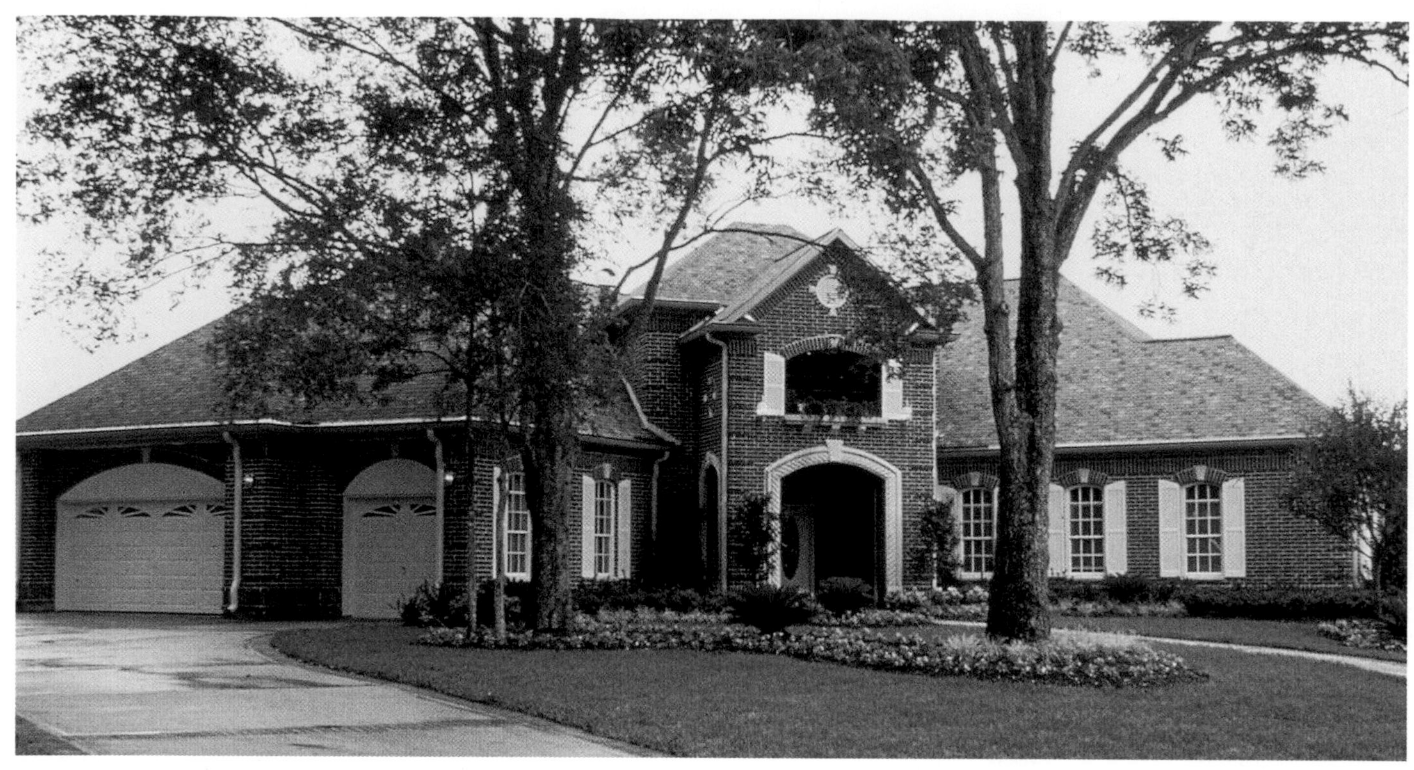

This elegant home combines a traditional exterior with a contemporary interior and provides a delightful setting for both entertaining and individual solitude. A living room and bay-windowed dining room provide an open area for formal entertaining, which can spill outside to the entertainment terrace or to the nearby gathering room with its dramatic fireplace. On the opposite side of the house, French doors make it possible for the study/guest room to be closed off from the rest of the first floor. The master suite is also a private retreat, offering a fireplace as well as an abundance of natural light, and a bath designed to pamper. The entire family will enjoy the second-floor media loft from which a balcony overlooks the two-story gathering room below.

plan # HPK1700568

Style: Traditional
First Floor: 3,297 sq. ft.
Second Floor: 1,453 sq. ft.
Total: 4,750 sq. ft.
Bedrooms: 5
Bathrooms: 4 ½
Width: 80' - 10"
Depth: 85' - 6"
Foundation: Slab

eplans.com

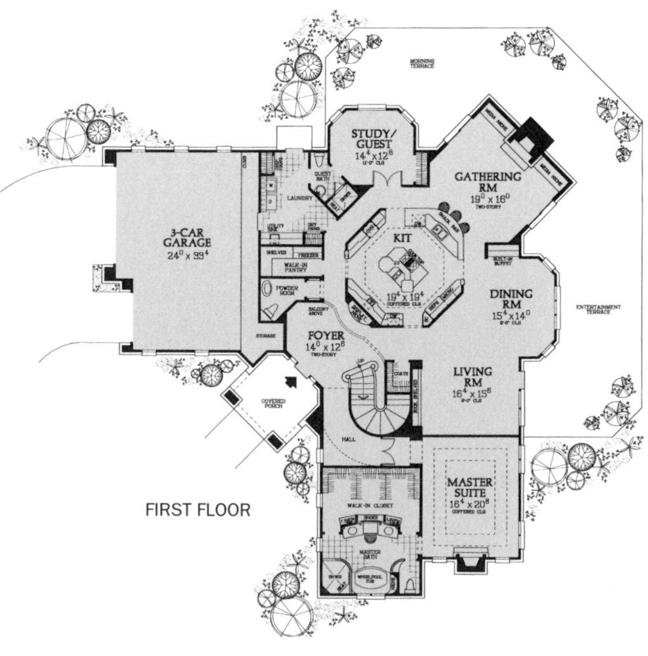

FIRST FLOOR

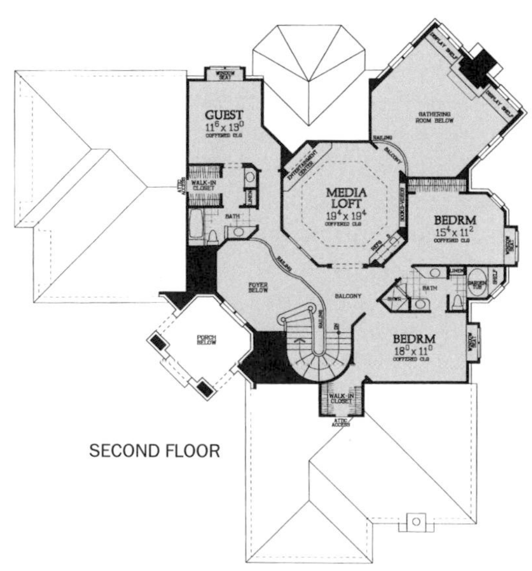

SECOND FLOOR

plan # HPK1700569
Style: Traditional
First Floor: 3,546 sq. ft.
Second Floor: 1,213 sq. ft.
Total: 4,759 sq. ft.
Bedrooms: 4
Bathrooms: 3½
Width: 96' - 0"
Depth: 83' - 0"
Foundation: Unfinished Basement
eplans.com

This grand home offers an elegant, welcoming residence with a Mediterranean flair. Beyond the grand foyer, the spacious living room provides views of the rear grounds and opens to the veranda and rear yard through three pairs of French doors. An arched galley hall leads past the formal dining room to the family areas. Here, an ample gourmet kitchen easily serves the nook and the leisure room. The master wing includes a study or home office. Upstairs, each of three secondary bedrooms features a walk-in closet, and two bedrooms offer private balconies.

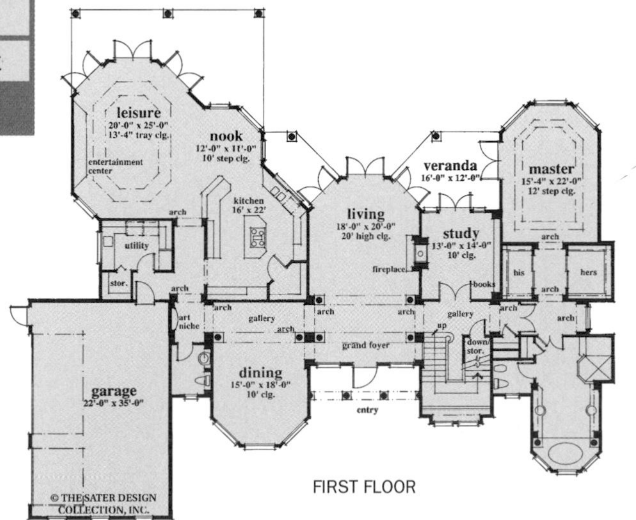

FIRST FLOOR

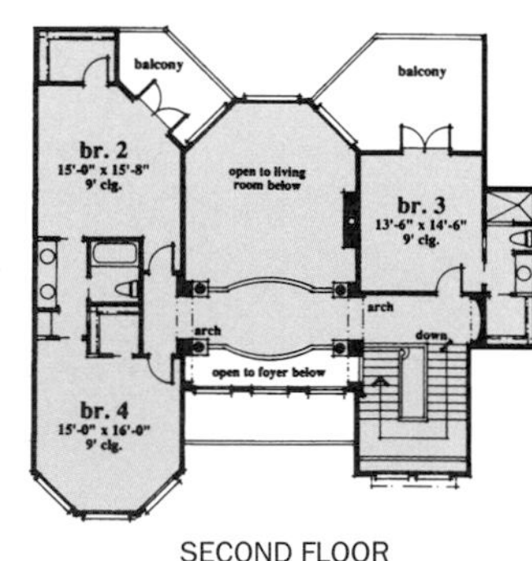

SECOND FLOOR

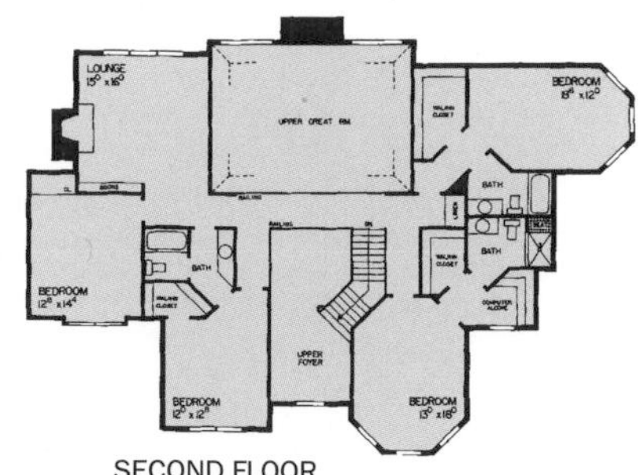

SECOND FLOOR

plan# HPK1700570

Style: Victorian

First Floor: 2,995 sq. ft.

Second Floor: 1,831 sq. ft.

Total: 4,826 sq. ft.

Bedrooms: 5

Bathrooms: 4 ½ + ½

Width: 95' - 0"

Depth: 99' - 3"

Foundation: Unfinished Basement

eplans.com

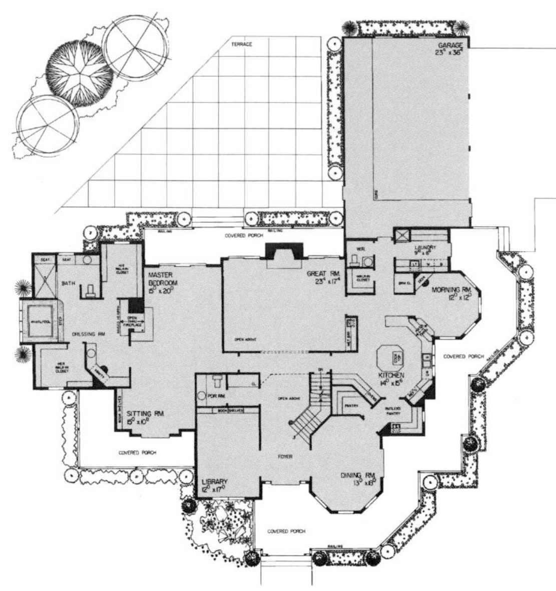

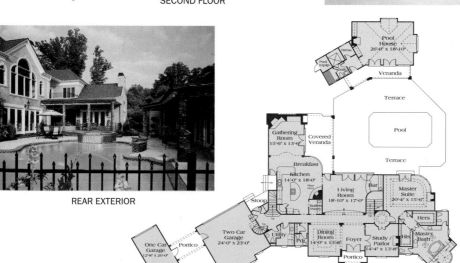

FIRST FLOOR

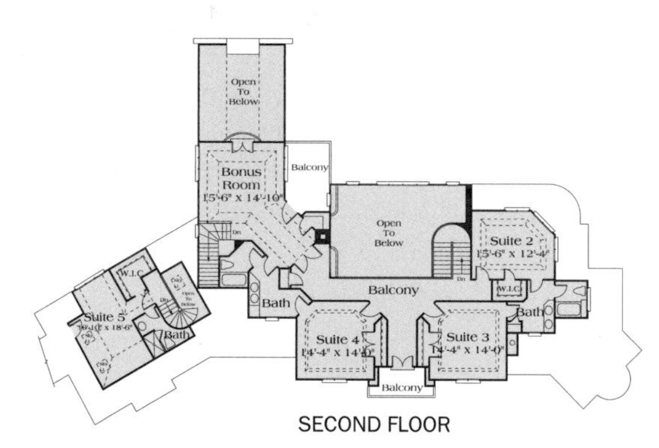

SECOND FLOOR

REAR EXTERIOR

FIRST FLOOR

plan# HPK1700571

Style: Mediterranean

First Floor: 3,307 sq. ft.

Second Floor: 1,642 sq. ft.

Total: 4,949 sq. ft.

Bonus Space: 373 sq. ft.

Bedrooms: 5

Bathrooms: 4 ½ + ½

Width: 143' - 3"

Depth: 71' - 2"

Foundation: Crawlspace

eplans.com

plan # HPK1700572

Style: Tidewater

First Floor: 2,642 sq. ft.

Second Floor: 2,479 sq. ft.

Total: 5,121 sq. ft.

Bonus Space: 339 sq. ft.

Bedrooms: 4

Bathrooms: 5½

Width: 76' - 0"

Depth: 51' - 0"

Foundation: Unfinished Walkout Basement

eplans.com

A wealth of windows lends abundant natural light to this classic Colonial design. Once inside, the kitchen immediately impresses with a U-shaped serving bar accessible to the grand room and the butler's pantry. The breakfast area/sunroom offers a bayed view of the backyard and access to a rear deck. The kitchen area is flanked by the grand room on the right and the keeping room on the left. A home office and a library/guest suite complete the first floor. Upstairs, the immense master suite, complete with a sitting room, His and Hers walk-in closets, a roomy bath, and an optional exercise room, is the main attraction. Three additional family bedrooms with full baths, an optional TV room, and a convenient second-floor laundry room complete this plan.

SECOND FLOOR

FIRST FLOOR

plan# HPK1700573

- Style: French
- First Floor: 3,703 sq. ft.
- Second Floor: 1,427 sq. ft.
- Total: 5,130 sq. ft.
- Bonus Space: 1,399 sq. ft.
- Bedrooms: 4
- Bathrooms: 3½ + ½
- Width: 125' - 2"
- Depth: 58' - 10"
- Foundation: Walkout Basement

eplans.com

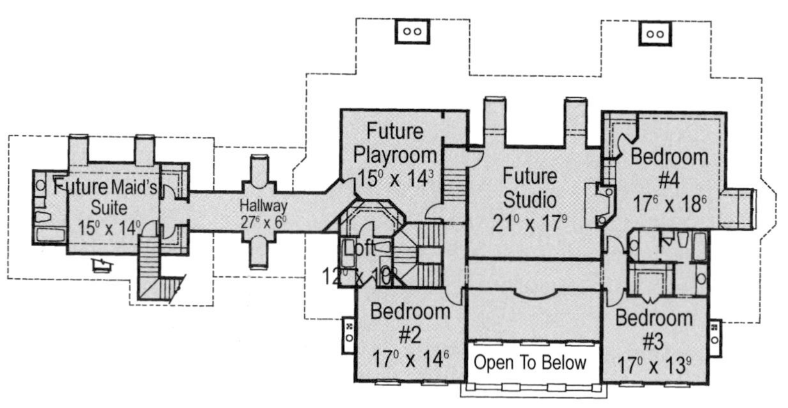

SECOND FLOOR

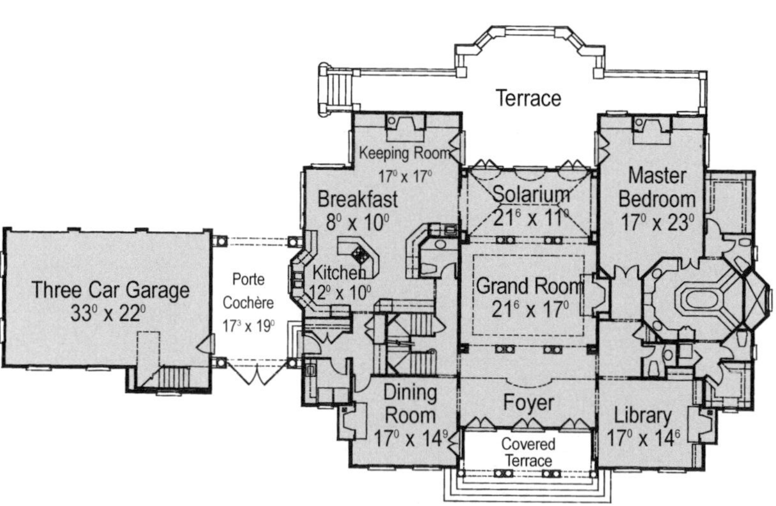

FIRST FLOOR

This magnificent estate is detailed with exterior charm: a porte cochere connecting the detached garage to the house, a covered terrace, and oval windows. The first floor consists of a lavish master suite, a cozy library with a fireplace, a grand room/solarium combination, and an elegant formal dining room with another fireplace. Three bedrooms dominate the second floor—each features a walk-in closet. For the kids, there is a playroom, and up another flight of stairs is a room for future expansion into a deluxe studio with a fireplace. Over the three-car garage there is space for a future mother-in-law or maid's suite.

plan# HPK1700574

Style: French

First Floor: 3,058 sq. ft.

Second Floor: 2,076 sq. ft.

Total: 5,134 sq. ft.

Bedrooms: 4

Bathrooms: 4½

Width: 79' - 6"

Depth: 73' - 10"

Foundation: Slab, Unfinished Basement, Crawlspace

eplans.com

SECOND FLOOR

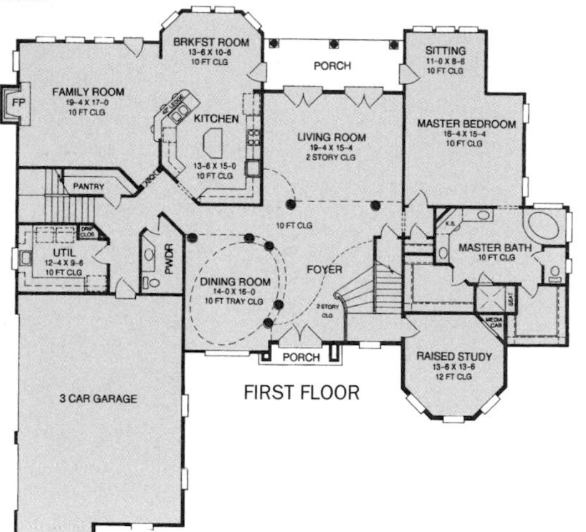

FIRST FLOOR

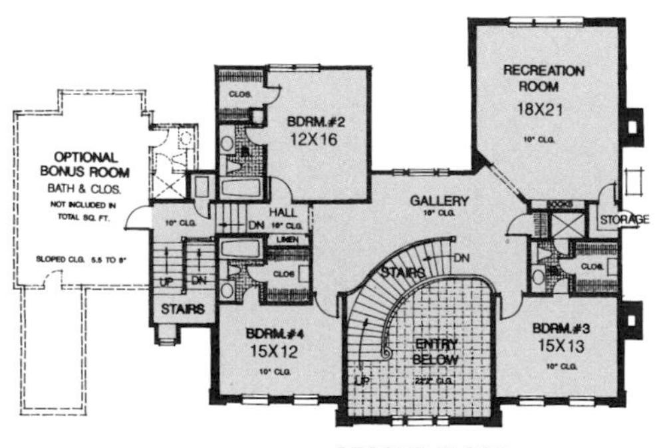

SECOND FLOOR

plan# HPK1700575

Style: Georgian

First Floor: 3,599 sq. ft.

Second Floor: 1,621 sq. ft.

Total: 5,220 sq. ft.

Bonus Space: 537 sq. ft.

Bedrooms: 4

Bathrooms: 5½

Width: 108' - 10"

Depth: 53' - 10"

Foundation: Slab, Unfinished Basement

eplans.com

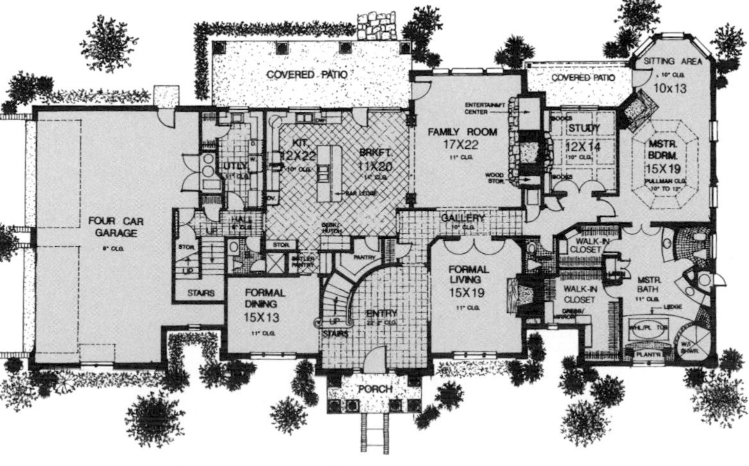

FIRST FLOOR

plan# HPK1700576

Style: Mediterranean

First Floor: 3,568 sq. ft.

Second Floor: 1,667 sq. ft.

Total: 5,235 sq. ft.

Bedrooms: 4

Bathrooms: 3½

Width: 86' - 8"

Depth: 79' - 0"

Foundation: Walkout Basement

eplans.com

The ornamental stucco detailing on this home creates an Old World charm. The two-story foyer with a sweeping curved stair opens to the large formal dining room and study. The two-story great room overlooks the rear patio. A large kitchen with an island workstation opens to an octagonal-shaped breakfast room and the family room. The master suite, offering convenient access to the study, is complete with a fireplace, two walk-in closets, and a bath with twin vanities and a separate shower and tub. A staircase located off the family room provides additional access to the three second-floor bedrooms that each offer walk-in closets and plenty of storage.

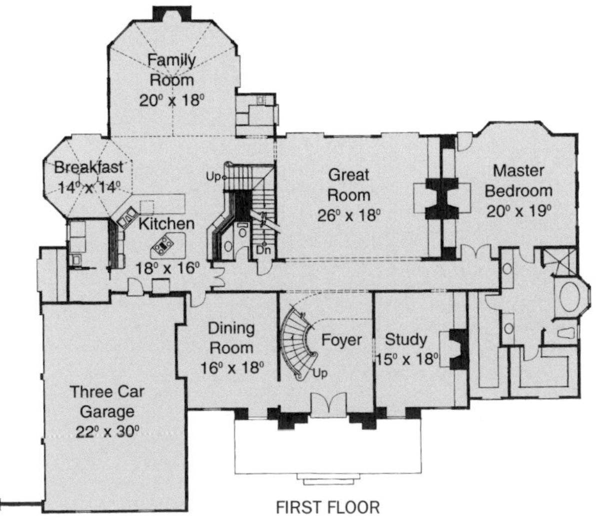

FIRST FLOOR

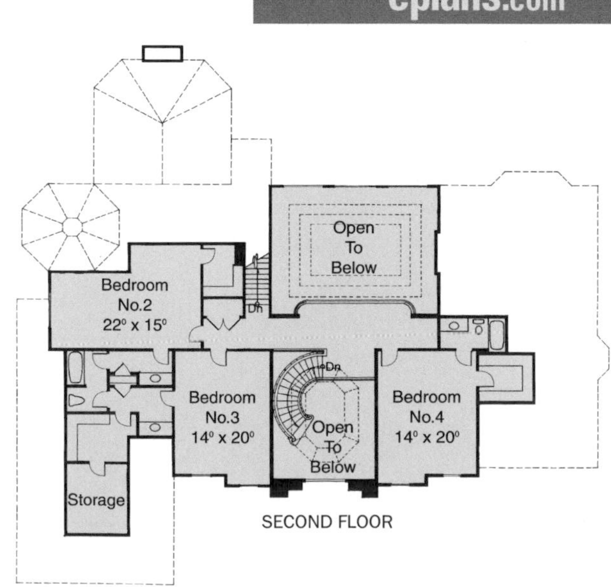

SECOND FLOOR

plan# HPK1700577

Style: French
First Floor: 3,745 sq. ft.
Second Floor: 1,643 sq. ft.
Total: 5,388 sq. ft.
Bonus Space: 510 sq. ft.
Bedrooms: 5
Bathrooms: 4½ + ½
Width: 100' - 0"
Depth: 70' - 1"
Foundation: Slab, Unfinished Basement, Crawlspace

eplans.com

Steep rooflines and plenty of windows create a sophisticated aura around this home. Columns support the balconies above as well as the entry below. An angled family room featuring a fireplace is great for rest and relaxation. Snacks and sunlight are just around the corner with the nearby breakfast room and island kitchen. A ribbon of windows in the living room makes for an open feel. A bay-windowed study/library has two sets of French doors—one to the living room and one to the master suite. The master bedroom offers a bath with dual vanities and a spacious walk-in closet. Three family bedrooms are located on the upper level with a recreation/media room and an optional bonus room.

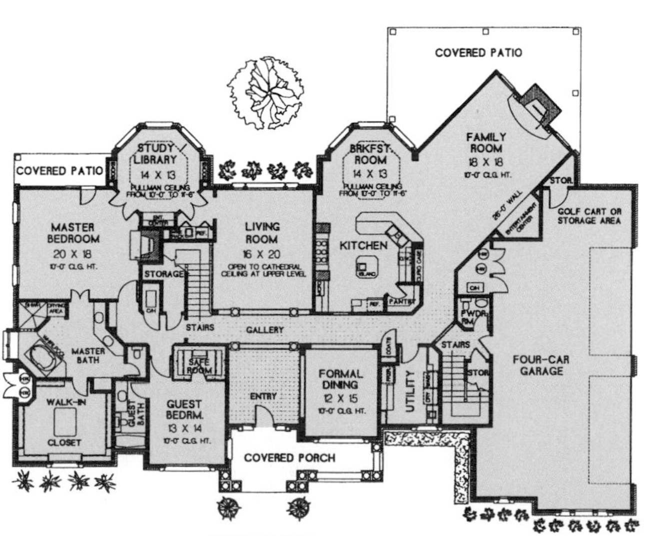

FIRST FLOOR

SECOND FLOOR

plan# HPK1700578

Style: Plantation
First Floor: 2,732 sq. ft.
Second Floor: 2,734 sq. ft.
Total: 5,466 sq. ft.
Bedrooms: 5
Bathrooms: 5½ + ½
Width: 85' - 0"
Depth: 85' - 6"
Foundation: Crawlspace, Slab, Unfinished Walkout Basement

eplans.com

A wraparound covered porch adds plenty of outdoor space to this already impressive home. Built-in cabinets flank the fireplace in the grand room; a fireplace also warms the hearth room. The gourmet kitchen includes an island counter, large walk-in pantry, and serving bar. A secluded home office, with a separate entrance nearby, provides a quiet work place. A front parlor provides even more room for entertaining or relaxing. The master suite dominates the second floor, offering a spacious sitting area with an elegant tray ceiling, a dressing area, and a luxurious bath with two walk-in closets, double vanities, and a raised garden tub. The second floor is also home to an enormous exercise room and three additional bedrooms.

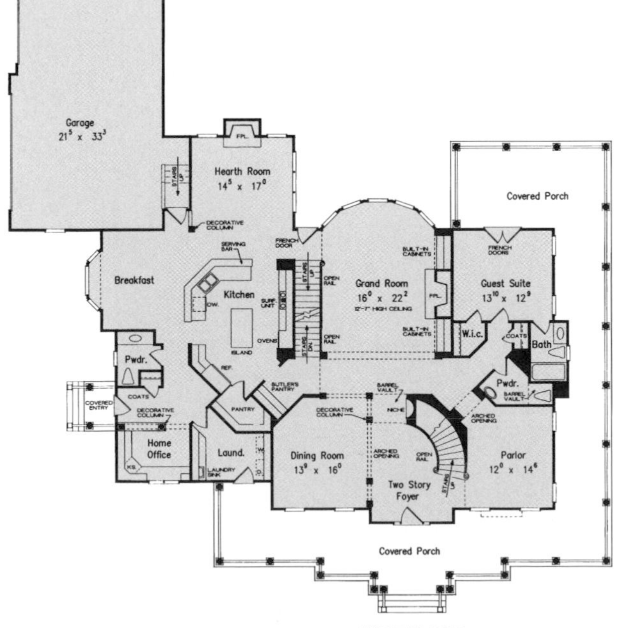

FIRST FLOOR

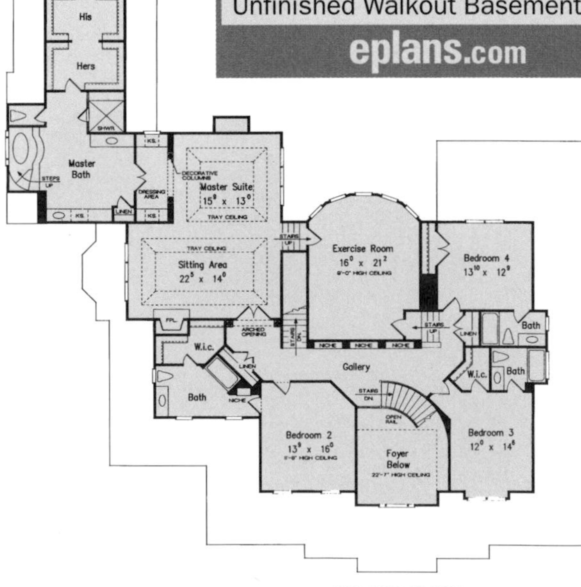

SECOND FLOOR

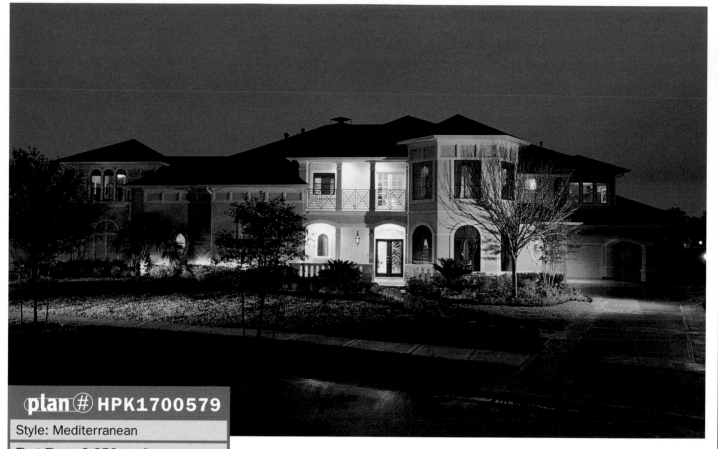

plan# HPK1700579

Style: Mediterranean
First Floor: 2,856 sq. ft.
Second Floor: 2,662 sq. ft.
Total: 5,518 sq. ft.
Bedrooms: 4
Bathrooms: 4½
Width: 115' - 4"
Depth: 53' - 4"
Foundation: Slab

eplans.com

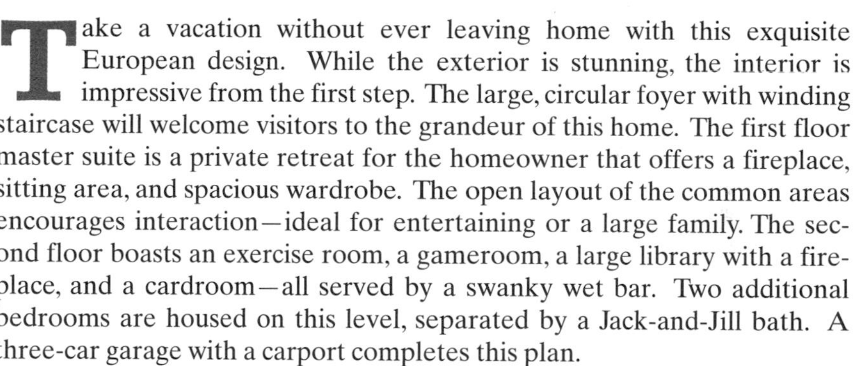

Take a vacation without ever leaving home with this exquisite European design. While the exterior is stunning, the interior is impressive from the first step. The large, circular foyer with winding staircase will welcome visitors to the grandeur of this home. The first floor master suite is a private retreat for the homeowner that offers a fireplace, sitting area, and spacious wardrobe. The open layout of the common areas encourages interaction—ideal for entertaining or a large family. The second floor boasts an exercise room, a gameroom, a large library with a fireplace, and a cardroom—all served by a swanky wet bar. Two additional bedrooms are housed on this level, separated by a Jack-and-Jill bath. A three-car garage with a carport completes this plan.

REAR EXTERIOR

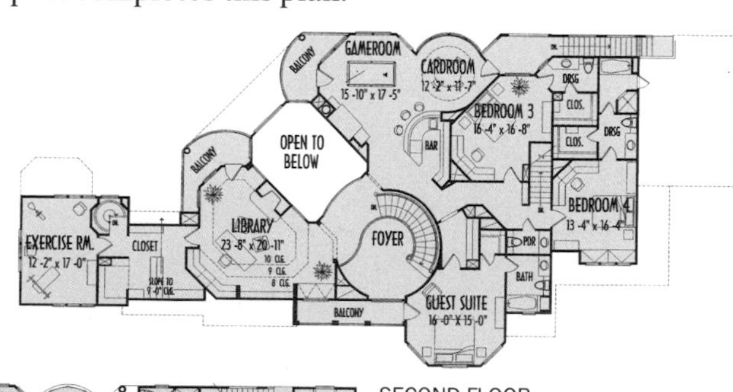

SECOND FLOOR

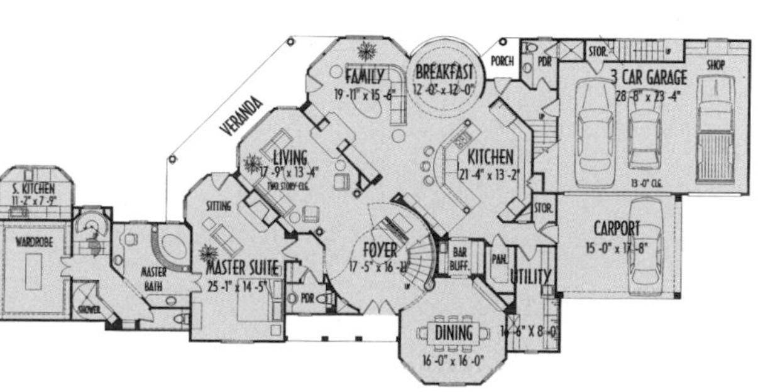

FIRST FLOOR

plan# HPK1700580

Style: Italianate

First Floor: 3,465 sq. ft.

Second Floor: 2,118 sq. ft.

Total: 5,583 sq. ft.

Bonus Space: 454 sq. ft.

Bedrooms: 5

Bathrooms: 6½

Width: 101' - 4"

Depth: 86' - 0"

Foundation: Slab

eplans.com

Arch-topped windows and doorways, a tiled roof, and window terraces are inspiring features of this Spanish-style home. Sunlight bathes the interior through plentiful windows and French doors in every room. Two complete levels of living; the first floor for casual and formal entertaining and the second floor for private living and recreation. The first-floor master suite is a work of spectacular comfort and seclusion. A gorgeous master bath includes a compartmented commode and bidet, garden tub, shower enclosure, dual-sink vanity, a private courtyard view, and two walk-in closets. Above the twin two-car garages, future guest or staff quarters are available.

plan# HPK1700581

Style: Mediterranean
First Floor: 3,060 sq. ft.
Second Floor: 2,530 sq. ft.
Total: 5,590 sq. ft.
Bedrooms: 5
Bathrooms: 5½
Width: 81' - 4"
Depth: 80' - 2"
Foundation: Finished Walkout Basement

eplans.com

A distinctively Mediterranean feel is found in this plan. A fully appointed basement provides three floors of living. A main floor gallery connects the master suite, foyer, dining and living rooms, and kitchen. The upper floor contains an attic, library, sitting room, and a nanny suite, along with three bedrooms with private baths and walk-in closets. The basement hosts a game room with separate billiards room, guest suite, covered terrace, game room with bar, and home theater.

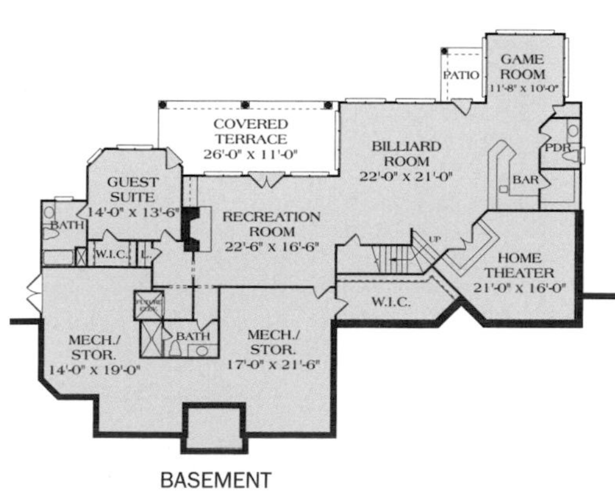

BASEMENT

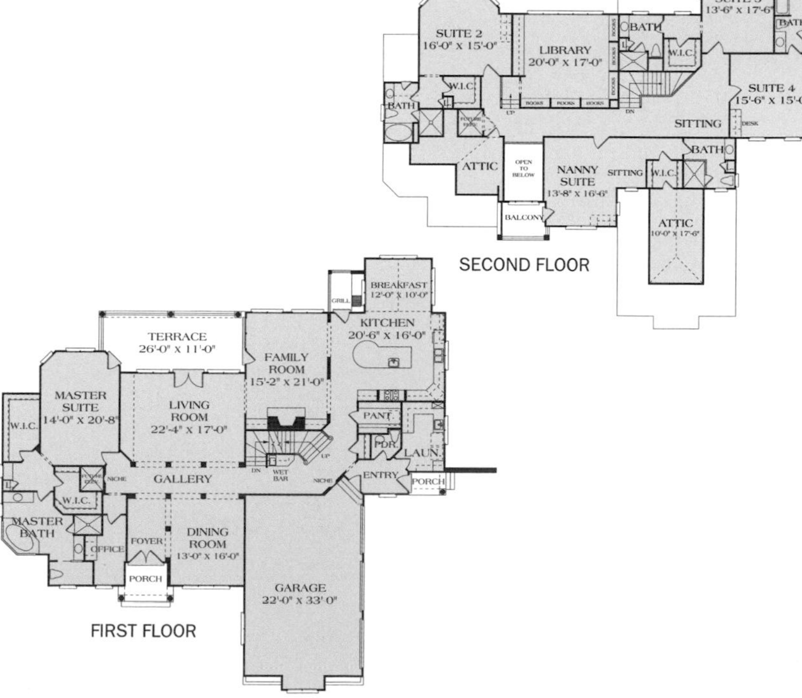

SECOND FLOOR

FIRST FLOOR

plan# HPK1700582

Style: Tidewater
First Floor: 2,902 sq. ft.
Second Floor: 2,791 sq. ft.
Total: 5,693 sq. ft.
Bedrooms: 5
Bathrooms: 5½
Width: 72' - 10"
Depth: 67' - 6"
Foundation: Unfinished Walkout Basement

eplans.com

SECOND FLOOR

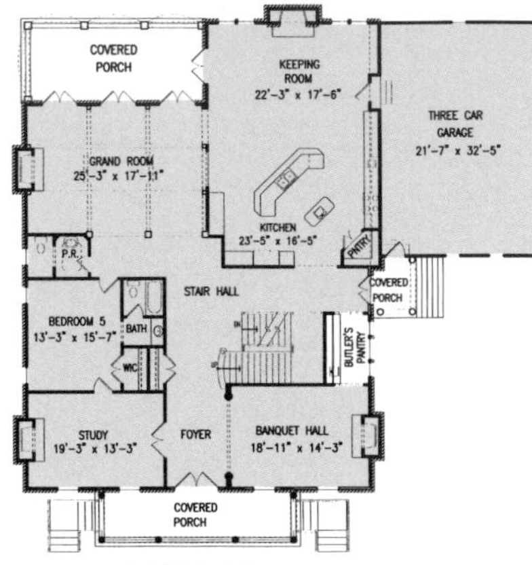

FIRST FLOOR

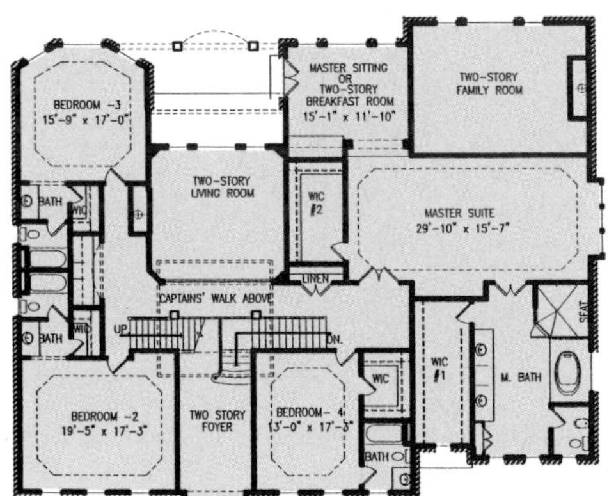

SECOND FLOOR

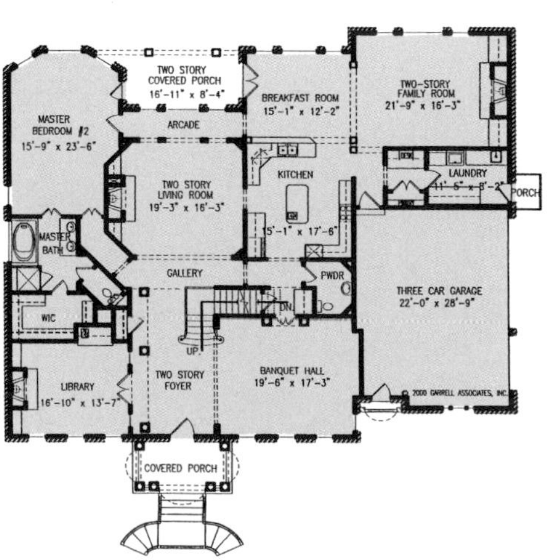

FIRST FLOOR

plan# HPK1700583

Style: Italianate
First Floor: 3,156 sq. ft.
Second Floor: 2,557 sq. ft.
Total: 5,713 sq. ft.
Bedrooms: 5
Bathrooms: 5½
Width: 71' - 0"
Depth: 58' - 8"
Foundation: Unfinished Basement

eplans.com

plan# HPK1700584

Style: Tidewater
First Floor: 2,891 sq. ft.
Second Floor: 2,825 sq. ft.
Total: 5,716 sq. ft.
Bedrooms: 5
Bathrooms: 5½
Width: 69' - 0"
Depth: 61' - 6"
Foundation: Unfinished Walkout Basement

eplans.com

Columned porches on both levels create a stately appearance for this Colonial beauty. Inside, a mini master bedroom can serve as a luxurious guest suite. The open design of the kitchen and family room coupled with the adjacent two-story veranda make for easy family interaction. Upstairs, the master suite offers a massive, amenity-filled retreat, complete with a sitting area, huge wardrobe, and roomy master bath. Three additional family bedrooms each boast a full bath. A sitting area and a reading room complete this floor.

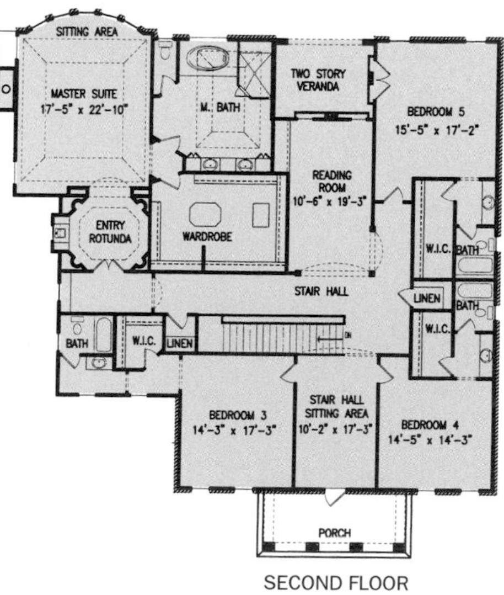

SECOND FLOOR

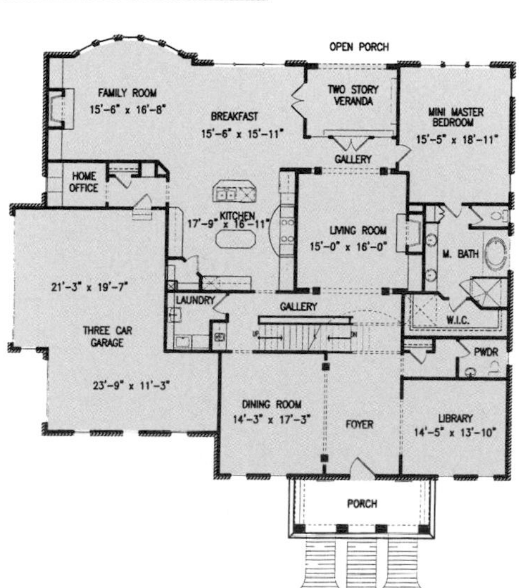

FIRST FLOOR

plan# HPK1700585

Style: Contemporary

First Floor: 4,257 sq. ft.

Second Floor: 1,468 sq. ft.

Total: 5,725 sq. ft.

Bedrooms: 5

Bathrooms: 4

Width: 91' - 0"

Depth: 100' - 8"

Foundation: Slab

eplans.com

This home is classically Mediterranean, with its stucco facade, sprawling layout, and expansive rear view from within. Bedrooms have been split to the far sides of the first floor with three on the left—sharing a full bath, but with the pool bath nearby as well—and the master suite occuping the right wing. Living areas are clustered in the center, making gathering family and friends together for any occasion a breeze. A guest suite and game room are the attractions on the second level, along with a spacious loft area.

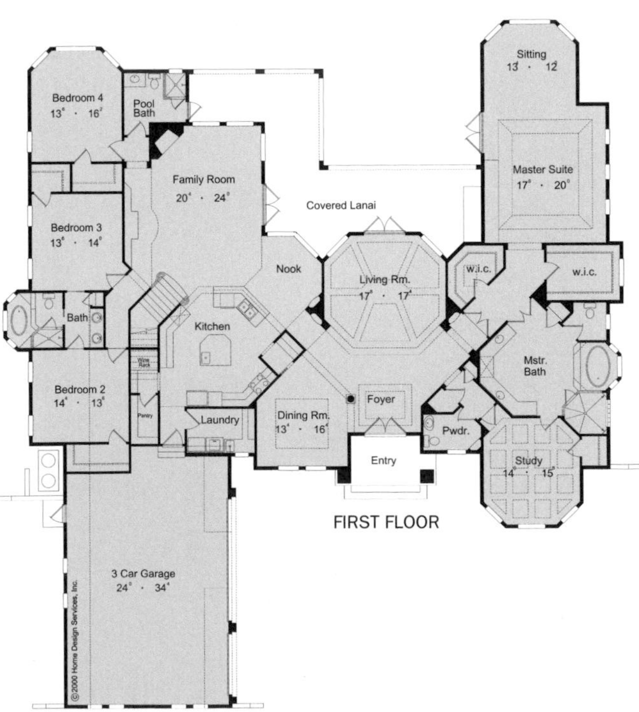

FIRST FLOOR

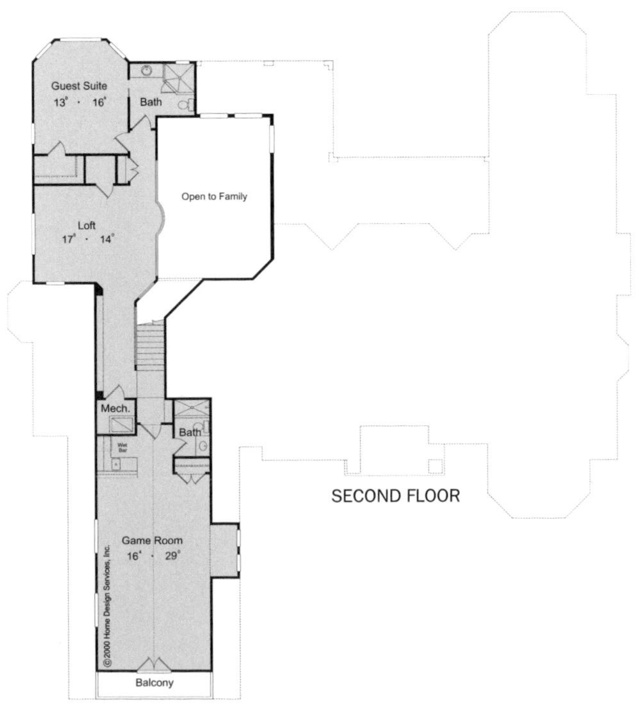

SECOND FLOOR

plan # HPK1700586

Style: Mediterranean
First Floor: 4,385 sq. ft.
Second Floor: 1,431 sq. ft.
Total: 5,816 sq. ft.
Bedrooms: 5
Bathrooms: 6
Width: 88' - 0"
Depth: 110' - 1"
Foundation: Slab

eplans.com

Low rooflines and grand arches lend a Mediterranean flavor to this contemporary estate. Lovely glass-paneled doors lead to an open interior defined by decorative columns, stone arches, and solid coffered ceilings. A formal living room boasts a fireplace and amazing views. Leisure space invites casual gatherings and allows the family to kick off their shoes and relax. A favorite feature, the outdoor kitchen encourages dining alfresco. A secluded master suite rambles across the right wing and includes a quiet study with a vintage high-beam ceiling, a sitting area, splendid bath, and access to the veranda.

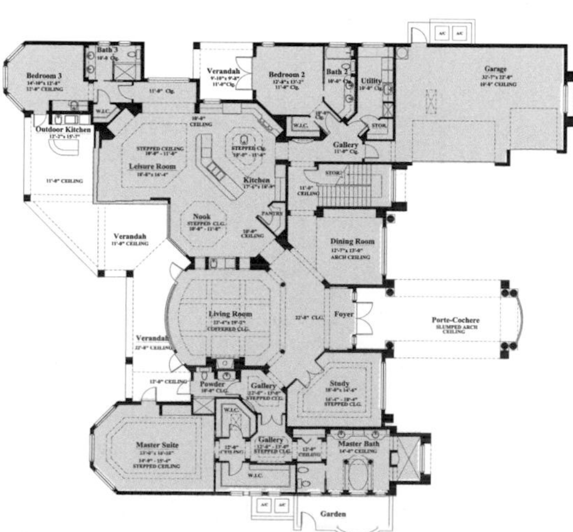

FIRST FLOOR

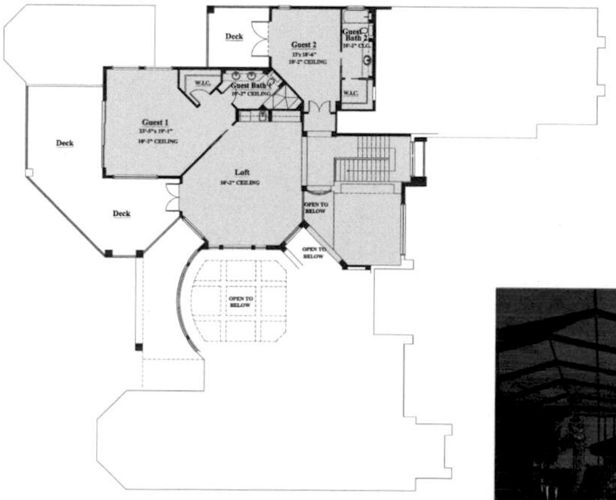

SECOND FLOOR

REAR EXTERIOR

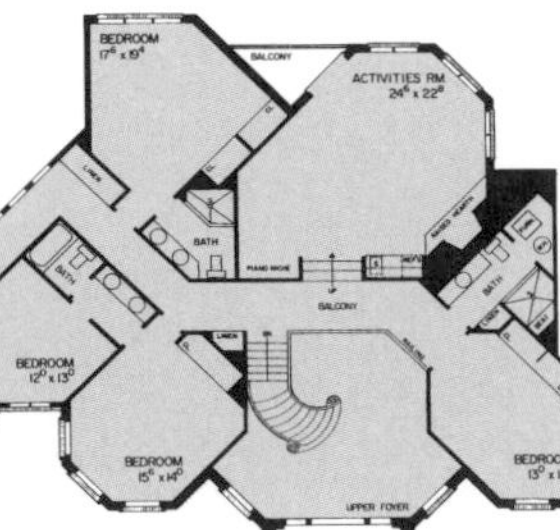

REAR EXTERIOR

SECOND FLOOR

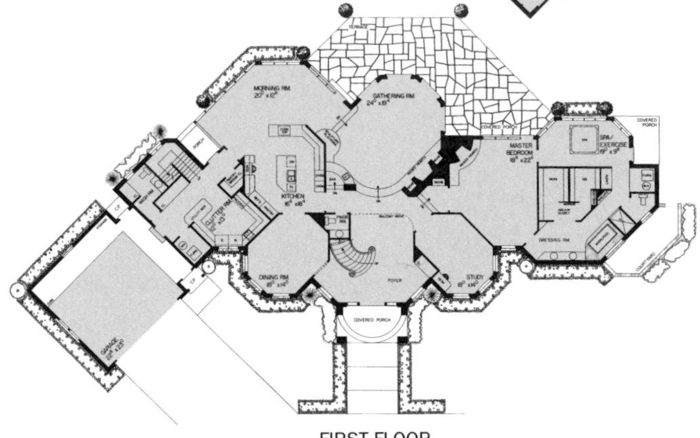

FIRST FLOOR

plan# HPK1700587

Style: Norman
First Floor: 3,736 sq. ft.
Second Floor: 2,264 sq. ft.
Total: 6,000 sq. ft.
Bedrooms: 5
Bathrooms: 5½ + ½
Width: 133' - 4"
Depth: 65' - 5"
Foundation: Slab

eplans.com

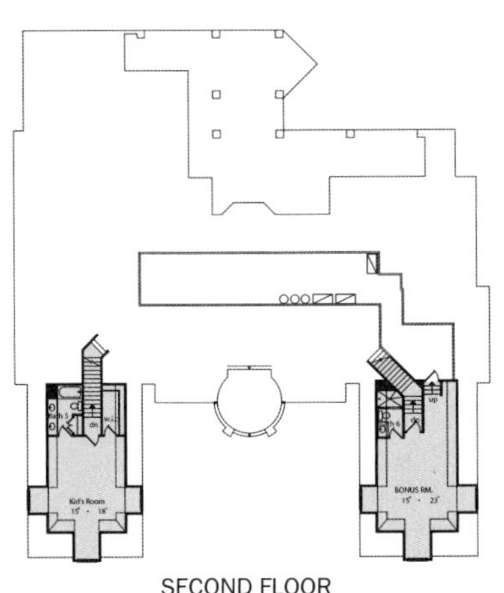

SECOND FLOOR

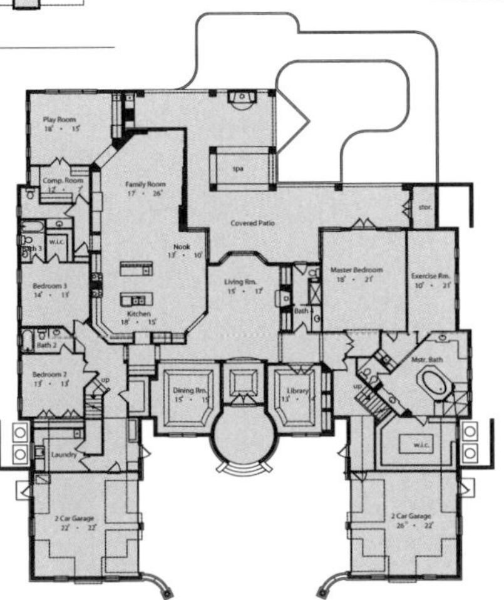

FIRST FLOOR

plan# HPK1700588

Style: French
First Floor: 5,204 sq. ft.
Second Floor: 1,055 sq. ft.
Total: 6,259 sq. ft.
Bedrooms: 3
Bathrooms: 5½
Width: 95' - 0"
Depth: 103' - 10"
Foundation: Slab

eplans.com

© The Sater Design Collection, Inc.

plan# HPK1700589

Style: Mediterranean
First Floor: 4,760 sq. ft.
Second Floor: 1,552 sq. ft.
Total: 6,312 sq. ft.
Bedrooms: 5
Bathrooms: 6½
Width: 98' - 0"
Depth: 103' - 8"
Foundation: Slab

eplans.com

This home features a spectacular blend of arch-top windows, French doors, and balusters. An impressive informal leisure room has a 16-foot tray ceiling, an entertainment center, and a grand ale bar. The large gourmet kitchen is well appointed and easily serves the nook and formal dining room. The master suite has a large bedroom and a bayed sitting area. His and Hers vanities and walk-in closets and a curved glass-block shower are highlights in the bath. The staircase leads to the deluxe secondary guest suites, two of which have observation decks to the rear and their own full baths.

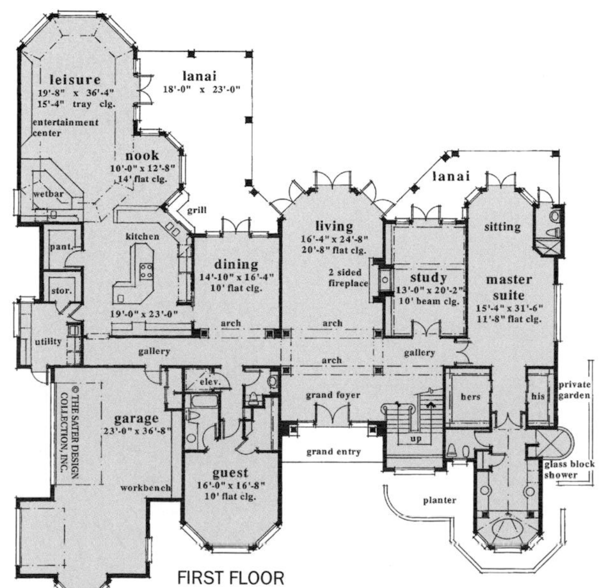

FIRST FLOOR

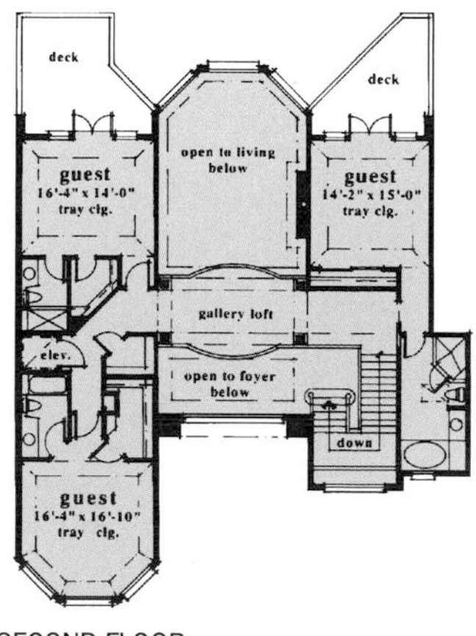

SECOND FLOOR

VANTAGE POINT PHOTOGRAPHY, INC.

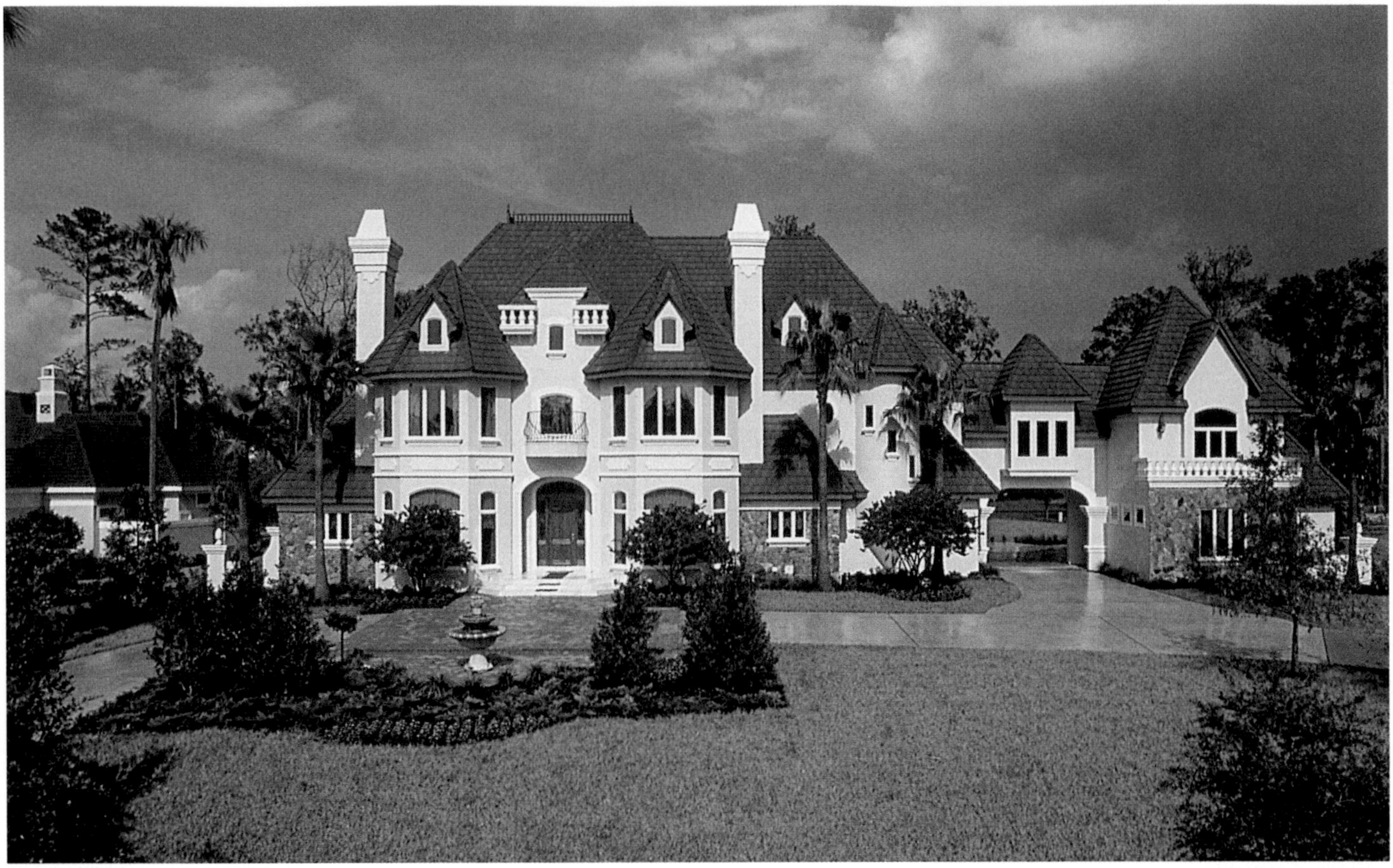

An oversized front entry beckons your attention to the wonderful amenities inside this home: a raised marble vestibule with a circular stair; a formal library and dining hall with views to the veranda and pool beyond; and a family gathering hall, open to the kitchen and connected to the outdoor grill. The master suite is embellished with a nature garden, His and Hers wardrobes, a fireplace, and an elegant bath. The second floor offers more living space: a media presentation room and game room. Each of the family bedrooms features a private bath—one suite is reached via a bridge over the porte cochere.

plan# HPK1700590
Style: French
First Floor: 3,874 sq. ft.
Second Floor: 2,588 sq. ft.
Total: 6,462 sq. ft.
Bedrooms: 4
Bathrooms: 5½ + ½
Width: 146' - 8"
Depth: 84' - 4"
Foundation: Slab
eplans.com

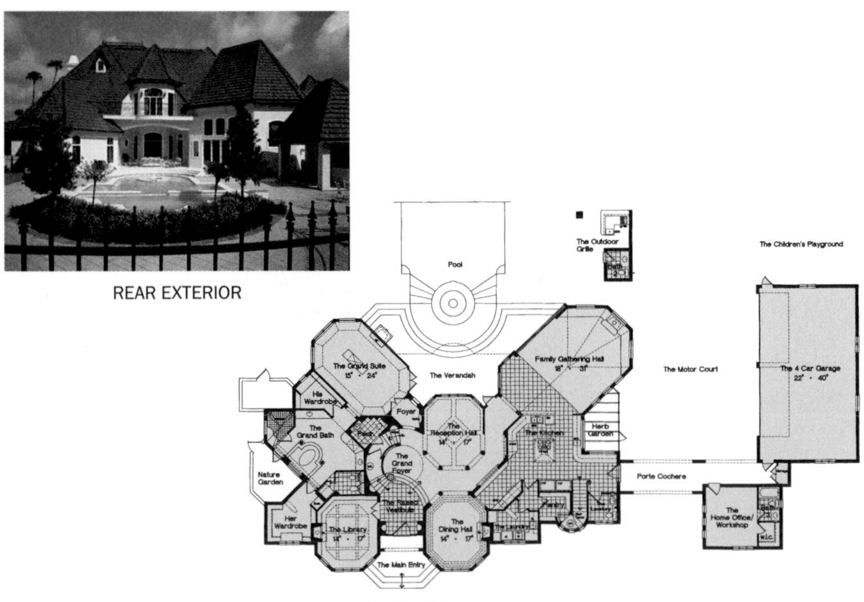

REAR EXTERIOR

FIRST FLOOR

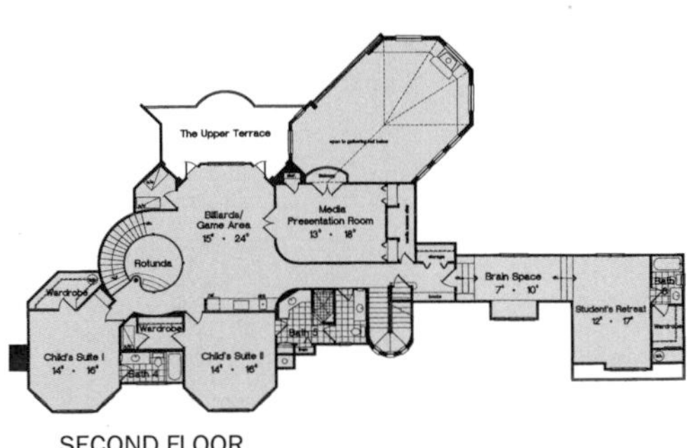

SECOND FLOOR

plan# HPK1700591

Style: French
First Floor: 4,463 sq. ft.
Second Floor: 2,507 sq. ft.
Total: 6,970 sq. ft.
Bedrooms: 5
Bathrooms: 5½
Width: 131' - 0"
Depth: 73' - 0"
Foundation: Unfinished Basement

eplans.com

Soaring ceiling heights allow full walls of glass for gorgeous views within this estate home. The grand salon, library, and foyer all have two-story ceilings that expand on their already expansive areas. More intimate in ambience, the keeping room and attached morning room are designed for casual gatherings—and found near the kitchen for convenience. The kitchen features a curved work counter, a walk-in pantry, and a built-in desk. Sharing a through-fireplace with the grand salon, the formal library is tucked away beyond gathering spaces. Sitting-room space complements the master suite where you will also find an exquisite bath and His and Hers walk-in closets. Twin staircases lead to four staterooms upstairs—each has a private bath.

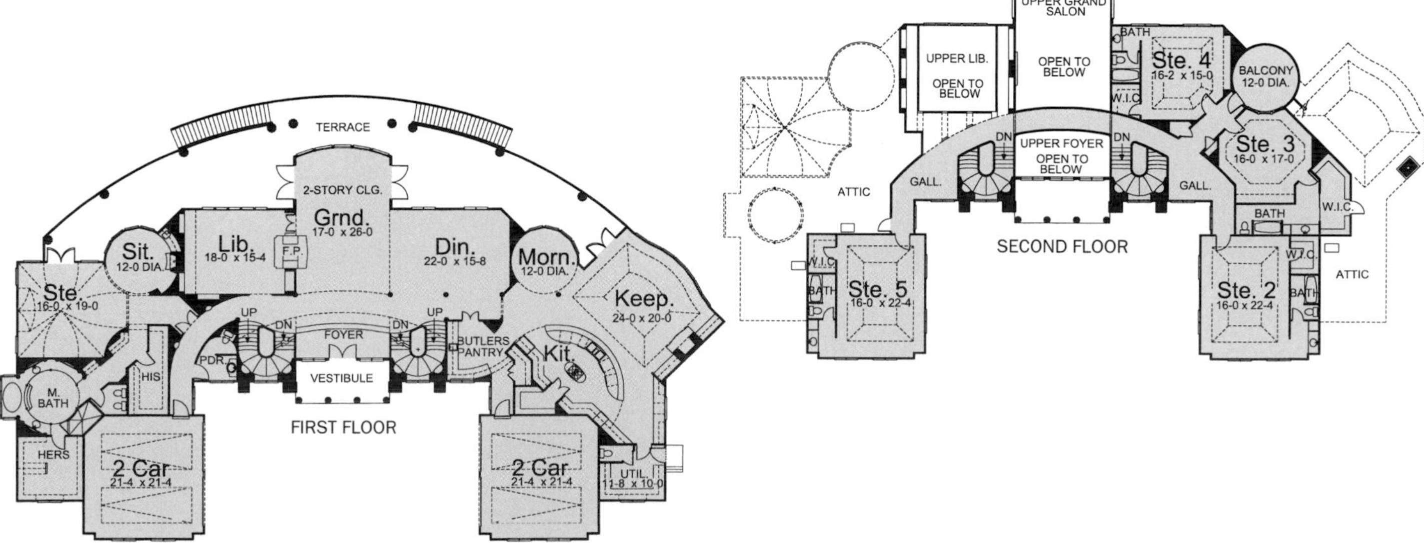

PHOTO COURTESY OF LIVING CONCEPTS

plan# HPK1700592

Style: European Cottage
First Floor: 2,620 sq. ft.
Second Floor: 2,001 sq. ft.
Third Floor: 684 sq. ft.
Total: 5,305 sq. ft.
Bedrooms: 4
Bathrooms: 5½ + ½
Width: 67' - 0"
Depth: 103' - 8"
Foundation: Crawlspace

eplans.com

With unique angles, brick detailing, and double chimneys, this home is as sophisticated as it is comfortable. The foyer enters into a refined gallery, which runs past a dining room complete with French doors opening to the front covered porch. The gallery also passes the grand room, which boasts a fireplace and three sets of French doors to the rear covered veranda. On the right, the master retreat provides its own private fireplace and access to the veranda. The kitchen and breakfast area is situated on the left side of the plan. Follow the steps up and an abundance of rooms will greet you. The recreation room directly accesses a small covered veranda. Two additional family suites flank the rec room, and each accesses a full bath. An apartment—perfect for renters or parents—and an office complete this floor.

REAR EXTERIOR

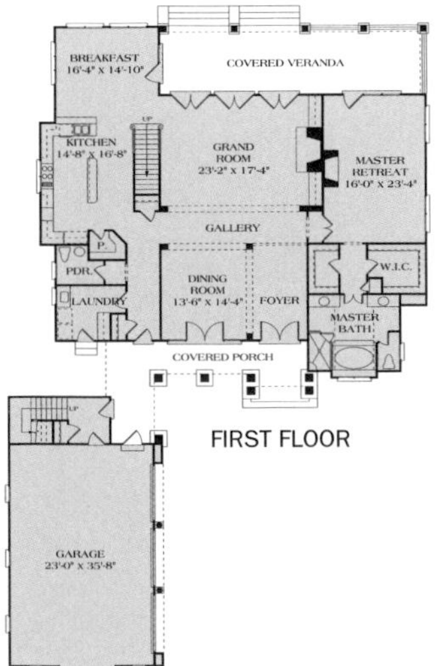

FIRST FLOOR

SECOND FLOOR

THIRD FLOOR

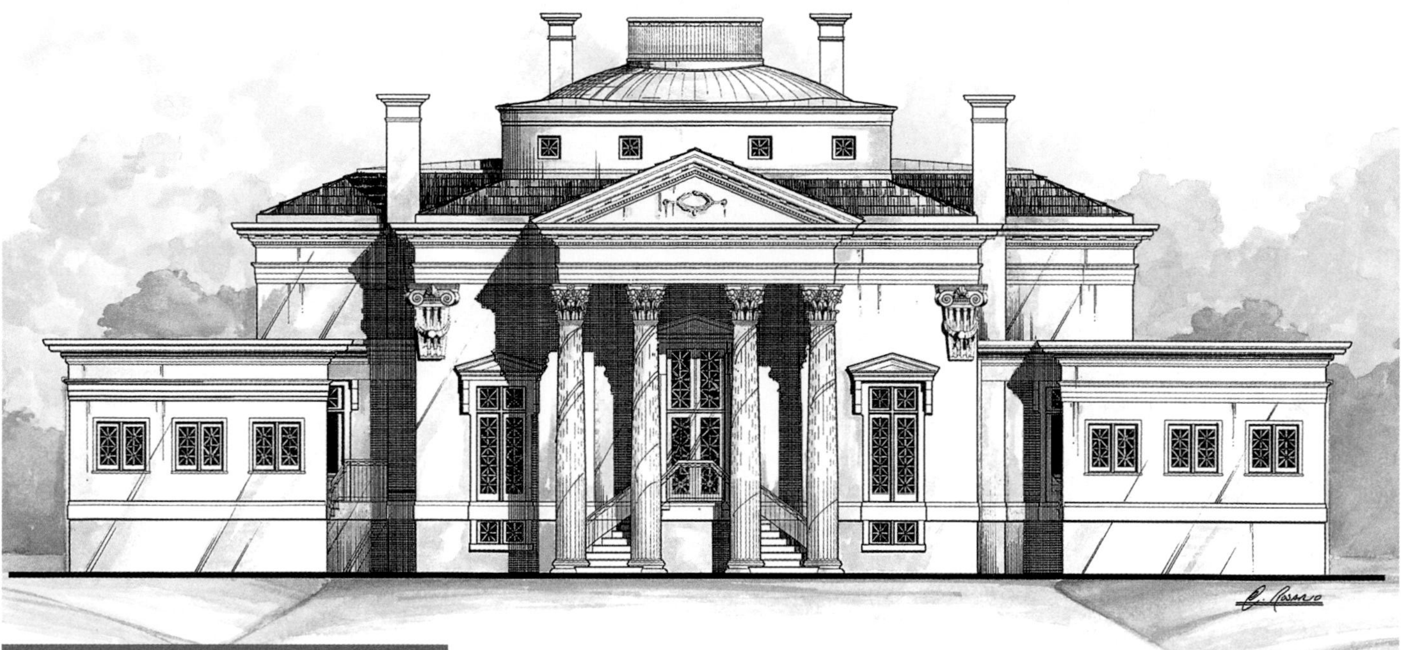

plan# HPK1700593

Style: Mediterranean
First Floor: 3,340 sq. ft.
Second Floor: 1,540 sq. ft.
Third Floor: 850 sq. ft.
Total: 5,730 sq. ft.
Bedrooms: 3
Bathrooms: 4½
Width: 106' - 0"
Depth: 82' - 0"
Foundation: Finished Basement

eplans.com

DESIGN NOTE

This three-story design, measuring in at over 5,700 square feet, is for those looking to spare no expense when it comes to style and comfort. Not only impressive for its size, a home of this stature will feature the best in materials, upgrades, and design. Every room is an attempt to deliver a home that deeply satisfies. The cost-conscious method of building interior walls at right angles with as few corners as possible is abandoned for layouts that favor eye-catching forms and gorgeously detailed ceilings. The master suite attains the highest comforts of the modern home; the baths are spacious and exquisitely detailed. In short, here's a home to fulfill the most grand of dreams.

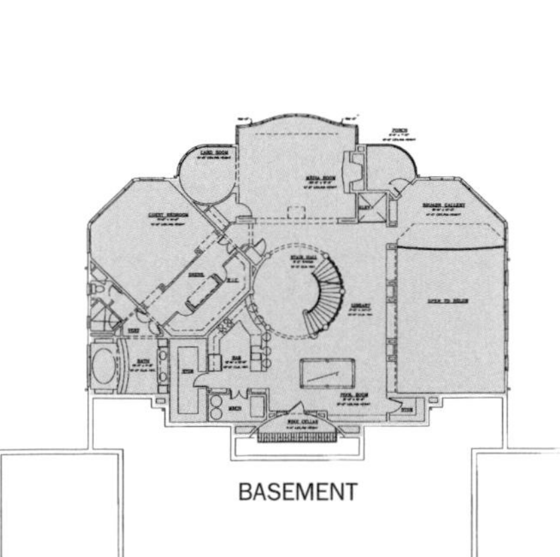

BASEMENT

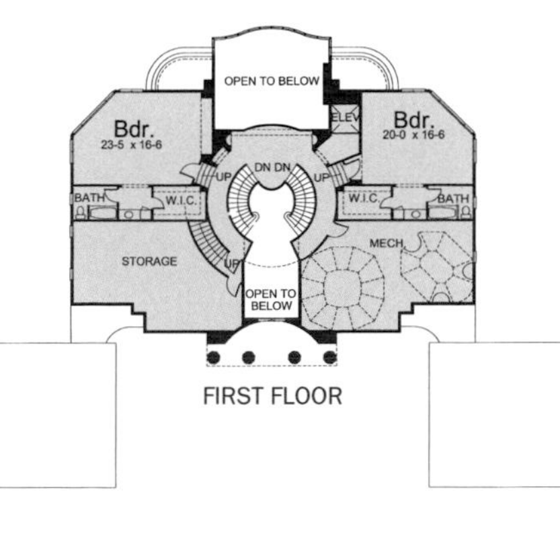

FIRST FLOOR

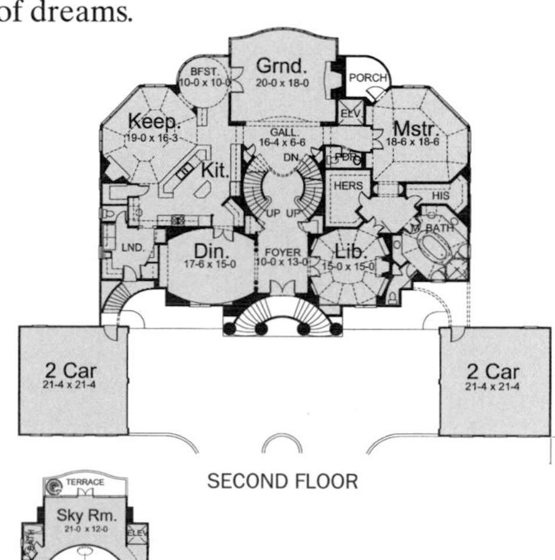

SECOND FLOOR

TERRACE
Sky Rm.
21-0 x 12-0
DOME ABOVE
OPEN TO BELOW
GALLERY

THIRD FLOOR

PHOTO COURTESY OF EXPOSURES UNLIMITED RON & DONNA KOLB. BUILT BY SANNEMAN HOMES

Stone accents provide warmth and character to the exterior of this home. An arched entry leads to the interior, where elegant window styles and dramatic ceiling treatments create an impressive showplace. The gourmet kitchen and breakfast room offer a spacious area for chores and family gatherings, and provide a striking view through the great room to the fireplace. An extravagant master suite and a library with built-in shelves round out the main level. On the lower level, two additional bedrooms, a media room, a billiards room, and an exercise room complete the home.

plan # HPK1700594
Style: European Cottage
Main Level: 2,582 sq. ft.
Lower Level: 1,746 sq. ft.
Total: 4,328 sq. ft.
Bedrooms: 3
Bathrooms: 3½
Width: 70' - 8"
Depth: 64' - 0"
Foundation: Finished Basement
eplans.com

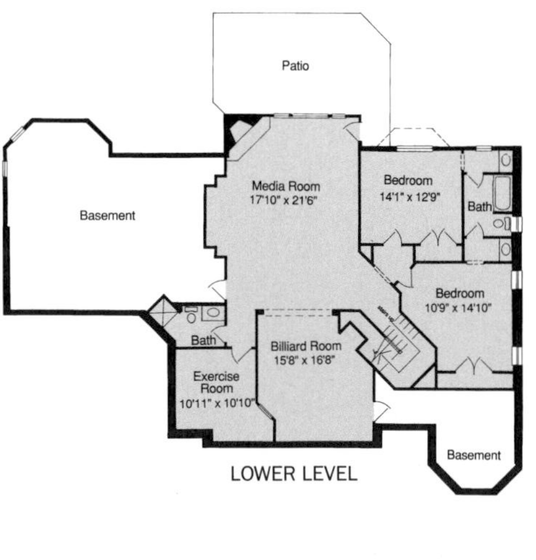

LOWER LEVEL

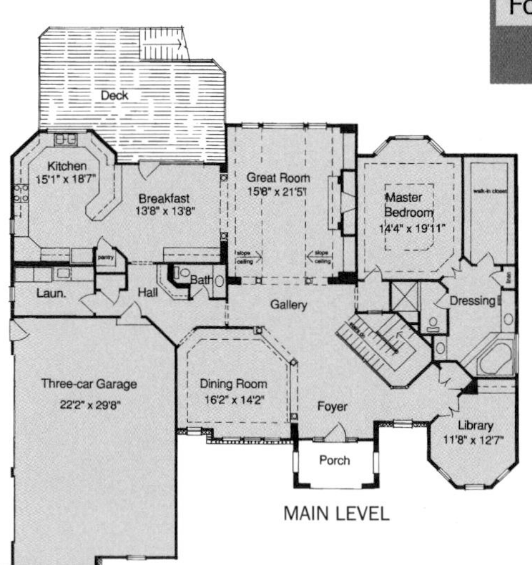

MAIN LEVEL

REAR EXTERIOR

plan# HPK1700595

Style: Country Cottage
Main Level: 2,932 sq. ft.
Lower Level: 1,556 sq. ft.
Total: 4,488 sq. ft.
Bedrooms: 3
Bathrooms: 3½ + ½
Width: 114' - 0"
Depth: 83' - 0"
Foundation: Unfinished Walkout Basement

eplans.com

With a shingle and stone facade and rustic Craftsman touches, this country home will fit perfectly on a hill or mountainside. Designed to take advangtage of a glorious rear view, it both blends in with and celebrates its natural surroundings. The heart of the home is the enormous chimney with fireplaces on three sides including the master bedroom, the family room, and the covered terrace. Inside, massive trusses stretch above the kitchen and family room. These spaces connect seamlessly with the dining room. A decadent master suite resides on the main level, complete with two walk-in closets, a luxurious bath, and access to the covered terrace.

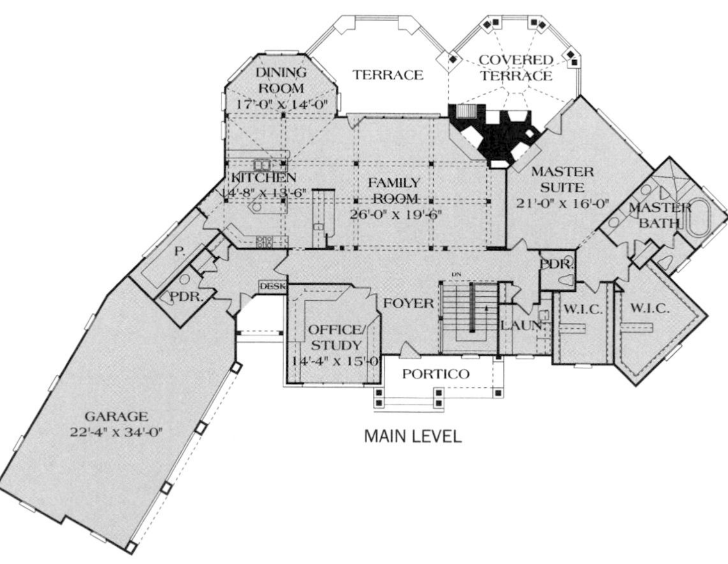

MAIN LEVEL

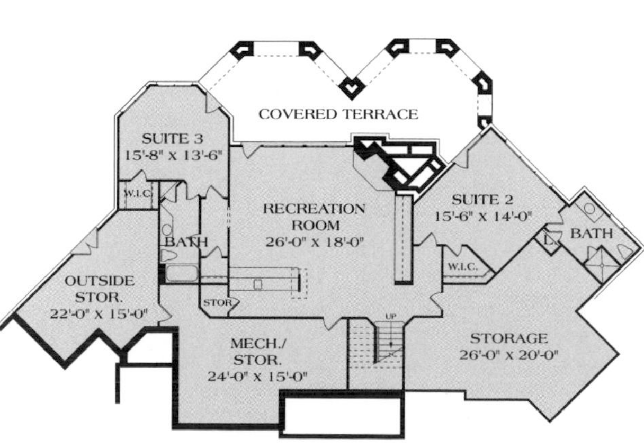

LOWER LEVEL

EXPOSURES UNLIMITED, RON & DONNA KOLB

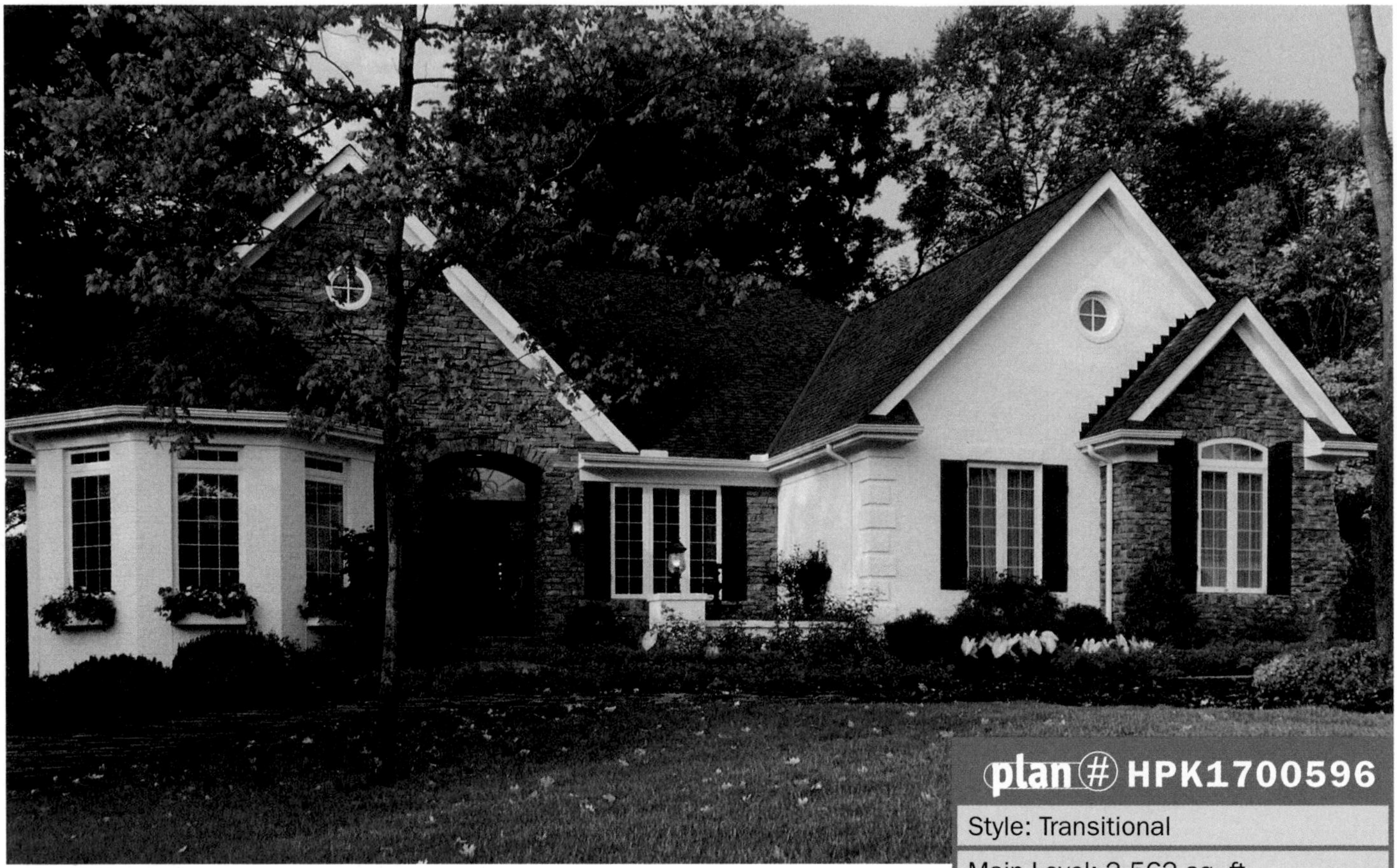

plan# HPK1700596

Style: Transitional

Main Level: 2,562 sq. ft.

Lower Level: 1,955 sq. ft.

Total: 4,517 sq. ft.

Bedrooms: 3

Bathrooms: 2½ + ½

Width: 75' - 8"

Depth: 70' - 6"

Foundation: Finished Walkout Basement

eplans.com

A brick and stone exterior with a tower and recessed entry creates a strong, solid look to this enchanting home. The large foyer introduces the great room with beamed ceiling and tall windows for a rear view. The dining room is defined by columns and topped with a coffered ceiling. Complementing the kitchen is a convenient walk-in pantry and center island with seating. An extra-large hearth room with gas fireplace and access to the rear deck provides a comfortable family gathering place. The master bedroom with sloped ceiling and a spacious dressing area offers a relaxing retreat. Split stairs located for family convenience introduce the spectacular lower level with a wine room, exercise room, wet bar, and two additional bedrooms.

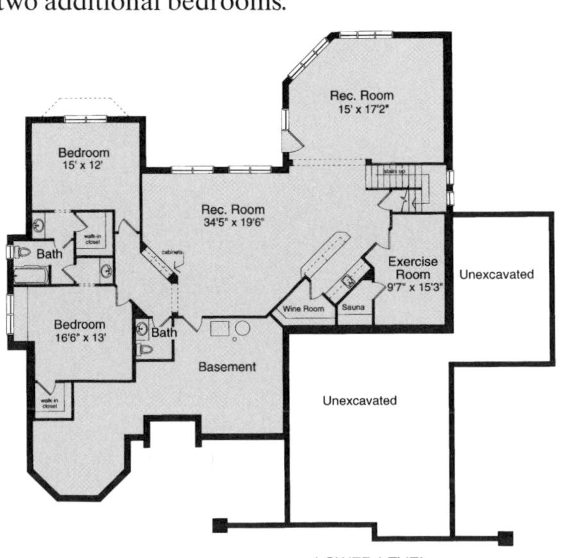

LOWER LEVEL

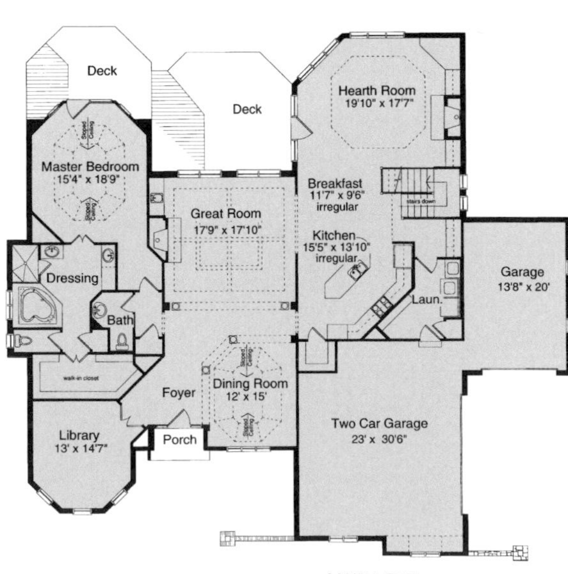

MAIN LEVEL

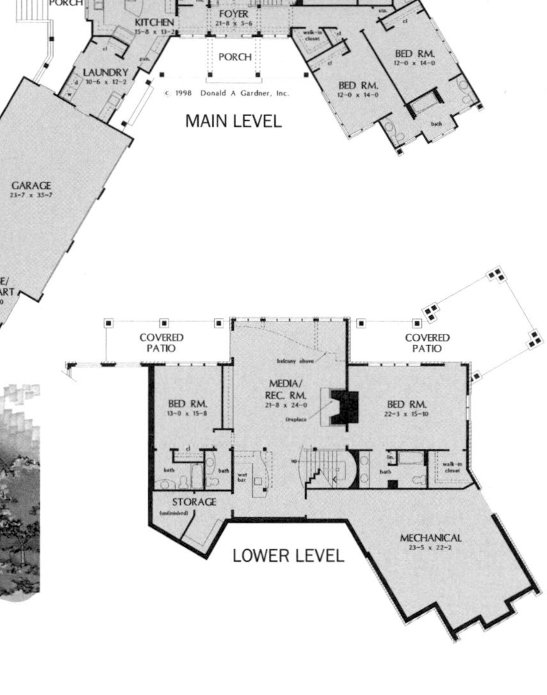

plan# HPK1700597

Style: Craftsman

Main Level: 3,040 sq. ft.

Lower Level: 1,736 sq. ft.

Total: 4,776 sq. ft.

Bedrooms: 5

Bathrooms: 4½ + ½

Width: 106' - 5"

Depth: 104' - 2"

eplans.com

REAR EXTERIOR

REAR EXTERIOR

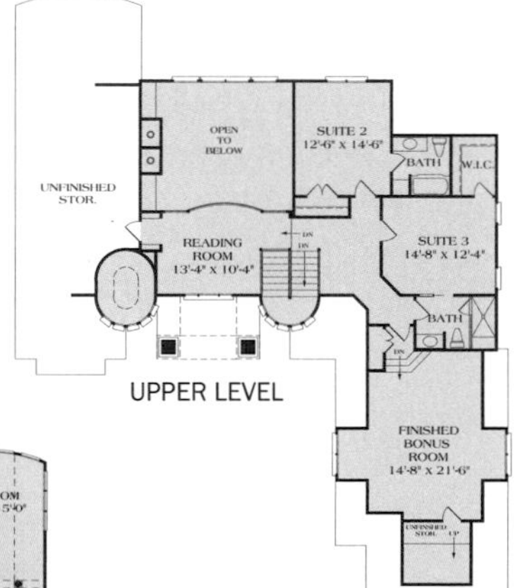

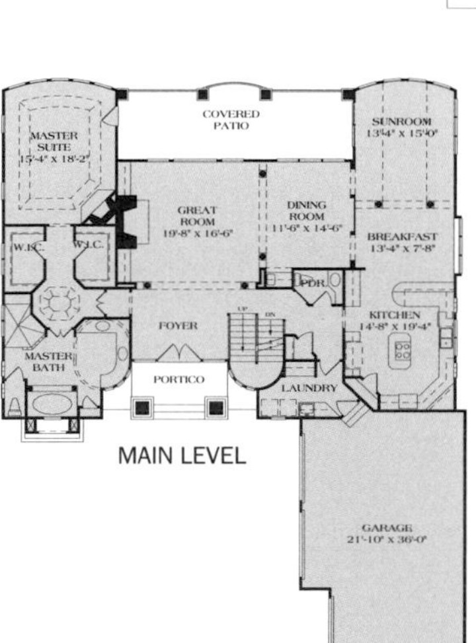

plan# HPK1700598

Style: Mediterranean

Main Level: 2,391 sq. ft.

Upper Level: 922 sq. ft.

Lower Level: 1,964 sq. ft.

Total: 5,277 sq. ft.

Bonus Space: 400 sq. ft.

Bedrooms: 4

Bathrooms: 4½

Width: 63' - 10"

Depth: 85' - 6"

Foundation: Finished Walkout Basement

eplans.com

plan# HPK1700599

Style: French Country
Main Level: 1,805 sq. ft.
Upper Level: 2,098 sq. ft.
Lower Level: 1,393 sq. ft.
Total: 5,296 sq. ft.
Bedrooms: 5
Bathrooms: 4½
Width: 62' - 2"
Depth: 54' - 0"
Foundation: Finished Walkout Basement

eplans.com

Three levels of European-style living include all the perks of a modern, amenity-filled home. The first floor combines both formal spaces—dining room and study—and family spaces (family room, breakfast nook, and island kitchen). Each room is showered in natural light from banks of windows. The second level houses three family suites, a spacious study loft, and a magnificent master suite. The lower level focuses on entertainment and games. A huge home theater enjoys a wet bar for snacks and covered-lanai access. A large recreation room would make a great billiards hall. An additional guest suite and full bath complete this level.

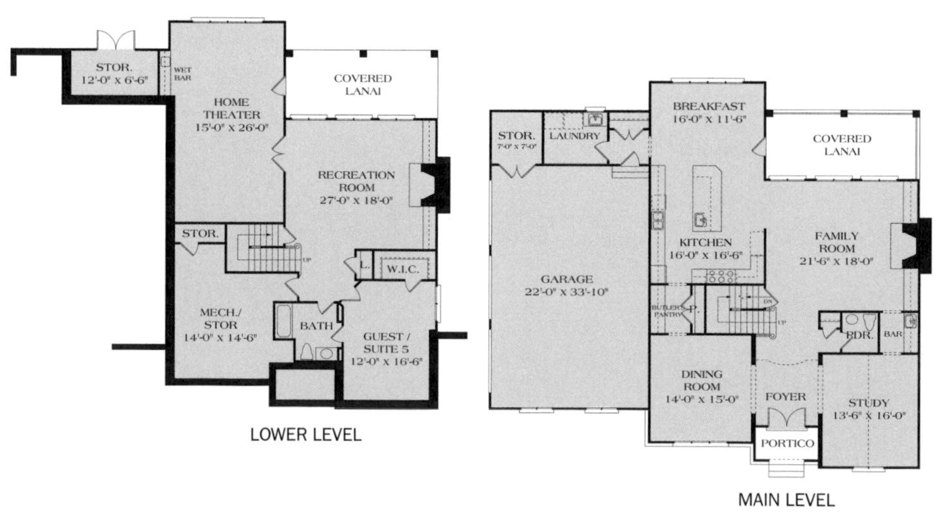

LOWER LEVEL

MAIN LEVEL

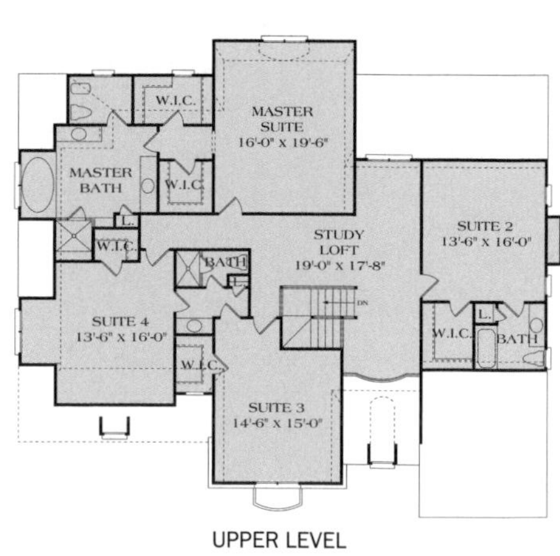

UPPER LEVEL

plan# HPK1700600

Style: French Country
Main Level: 2,981 sq. ft.
Upper Level: 1,017 sq. ft.
Lower Level: 1,471 sq. ft.
Total: 5,469 sq. ft.
Bedrooms: 4
Bathrooms: 4½ + ½
Width: 79' - 4"
Depth: 91' - 0"
Foundation: Finished Walkout Basement

eplans.com

Majestic through and through, this stately home enjoys a stone exterior inspired by classical French architecture. In the center of the main floor, the conservatory and elegant formal dining room reign. The massive country kitchen flows easily into the family room and the casual eating area. It also enjoys a butler's pantry leading to the dining room and a walk-in pantry. An exercise room and resplendent bath are found in the master suite, also on this level. Two more suites with private baths share a sitting room upstairs. The finished basement includes another bedroom suite, a recreation room, office, storage, and a book niche. Additional room is available for setting up a workshop.

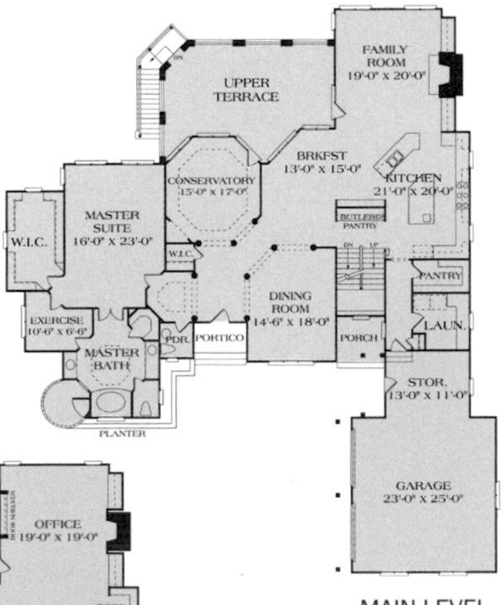

REAR EXTERIOR

MAIN LEVEL

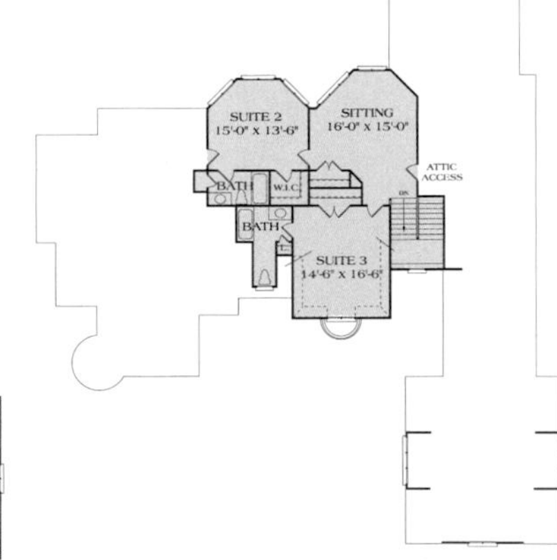

UPPER LEVEL

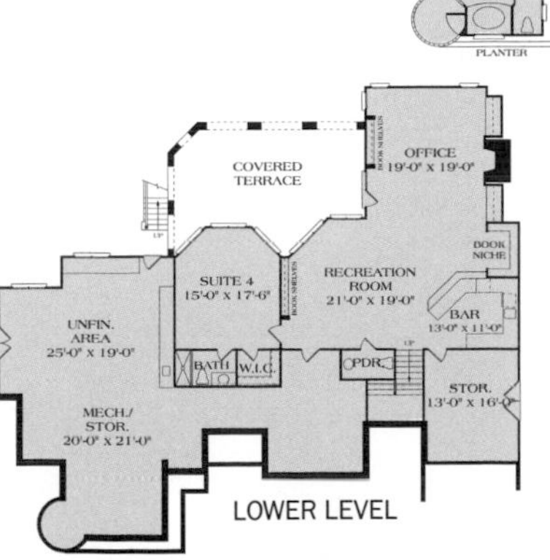

LOWER LEVEL

Turn Your Dream Home Into A Reality

ARTS & CRAFTS HOME PLANS
1-931131-26-0

$14.95 (128 PAGES)
This title showcases 85 home plans in the Craftsman, Prairie and Bungalow styles.

WATERFRONT HOMES
1-931131-28-7

$10.95 (208 PAGES)
A collection of gorgeous homes for those who dream of life on the water's edge—this title features open floor plans with expansive views.

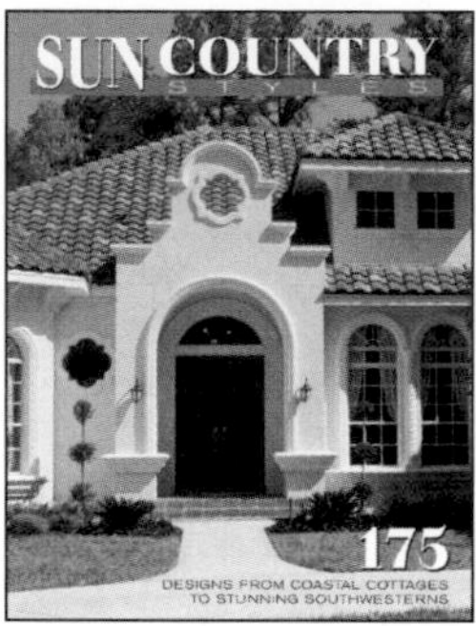

SUN COUNTRY STYLES
1-931131-14-7

$9.95 (192 PAGES)
175 designs from Coastal Cottages to stunning Southwesterns.

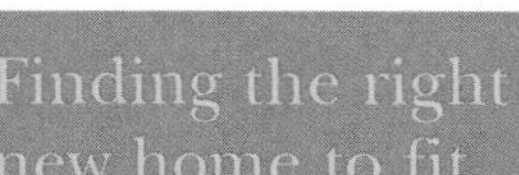

- Your style
- Your budget
- Your life

...has never been easier.

Our spring collection offers distinctive design coupled with plans to match every wallet. If you are looking to build your new home, look to HomePlanners first.

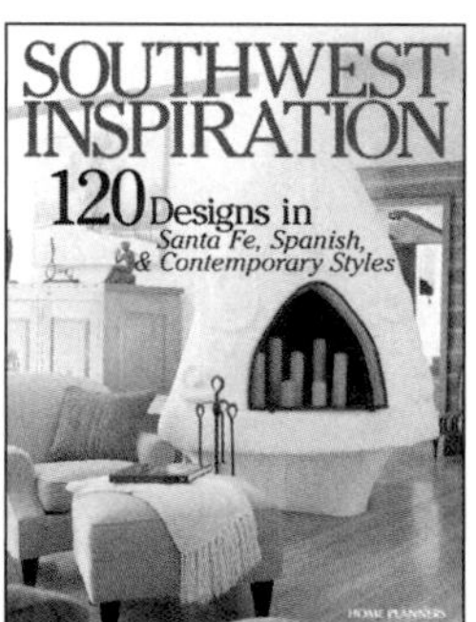

SOUTHWEST INSPIRATION
1-931131-19-8

$14.95 (192 PAGES)
This title features 120 designs in Santa Fe, Spanish and Contemporary styles.

MEDITERRANEAN INSPIRATION
1-931131-09-0

$14.95 (192 PAGES)
Bring home the timeless beauty of the Mediterranean with the gorgeous plans featured in this popular title.

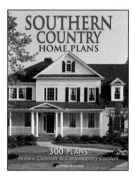

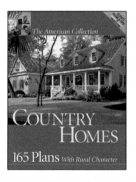

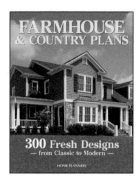

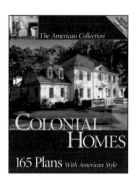

hanley wood

SELECTION, CONVENIENCE, SERVICE!

With more than 50 years of experience in the industry and millions of blueprints sold, Hanley Wood is a trusted source of high-quality, high-value pre-drawn home plans.

Using pre-drawn home plans is a **reliable, cost-effective way** to build your dream home, and our vast selection of plans is second-to-none. The nation's finest designers craft these plans that builders know they can trust. Meanwhile, our friendly, knowledgeable customer service representatives can help you every step of the way.

WHAT YOU'LL GET WITH YOUR ORDER

The contents of each designer's blueprint package is unique, but all contain detailed, high-quality working drawings. You can expect to find the following standard elements in most sets of plans:

1. FRONT PERSPECTIVE

This artist's sketch of the exterior of the house gives you an idea of how the house will look when built and landscaped.

2. FOUNDATION AND BASEMENT PLANS

This sheet shows the foundation layout including concrete walls, footings, pads, posts, beams, and bearing walls, and foundation notes. If the home features a basement, the first-floor framing details may also be included on this plan. If your plan features slab construction rather than a basement, the plan shows footings and details for a monolithic slab. This page, or another in the set, may include a sample plot plan for locating your house on a building site. Additional sheets focus on foundation cross-sections and other details.

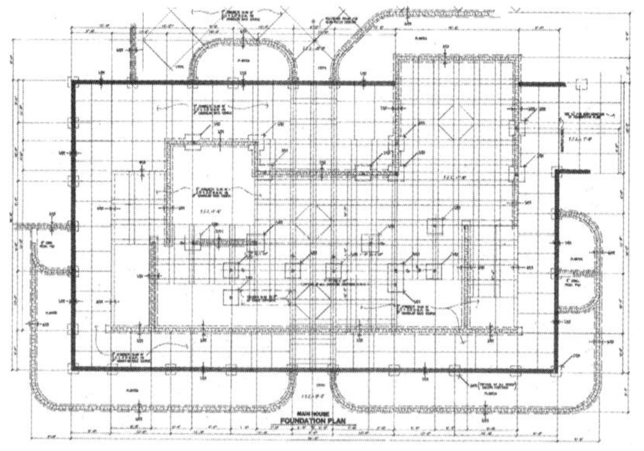

3. DETAILED FLOOR PLANS

These plans show the layout of each floor of the house. Rooms and interior spaces are carefully dimensioned, doors and windows located, and keys are given for cross-section details provided elsewhere in the plans.

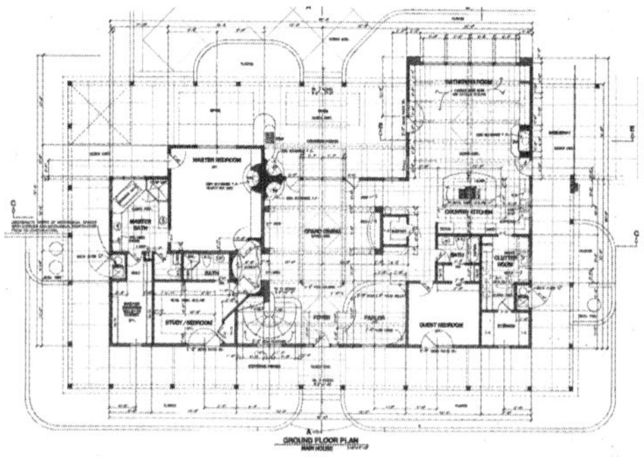

4. HOUSE AND DETAIL CROSS-SECTIONS

Large-scale views show sections or cutaways of the foundation, interior walls, exterior walls, floors, stairways, and roof details. Additional cross-sections may show important changes in floor, ceiling, or roof heights, or the relationship of one level to another. These sections show exactly how the various parts of the house fit together and are extremely valuable during construction. Additional sheets may include enlarged wall, floor, and roof construction details.

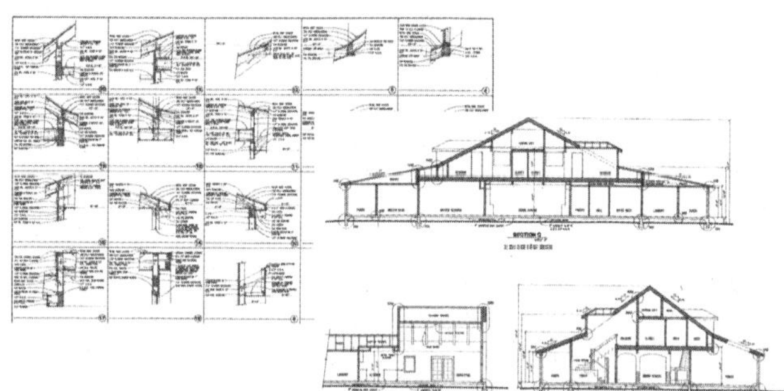

5. ROOF AND FLOOR STRUCTURAL SUPPORTS

The roof and floor framing plans provide detail for these crucial elements of your home. Each includes floor joist, ceiling joist, rafter and roof joist size, spacing, direction, span, and specifications. Beam and window headers, along with necessary details for framing connections, stairways, skylights, or dormers are also included.

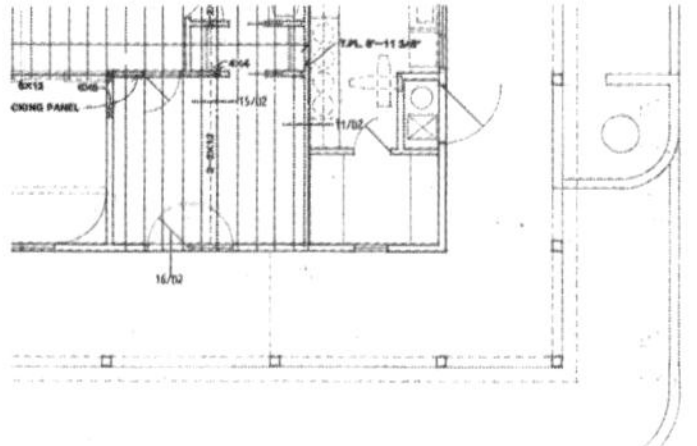

6. ELECTRICAL PLAN

The electrical plan offers a detailed outline of all wiring for your home, with notes for all lighting, outlets, switches, and circuits. A layout is provided for each level, as well as basements, garages, or other structures.

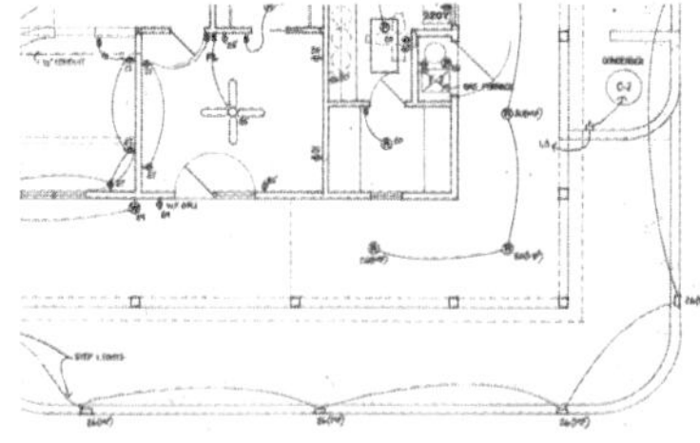

7. EXTERIOR ELEVATIONS

In addition to the front exterior, your blueprint set will include drawings of the rear and sides of your house as well. These drawings give notes on exterior materials and finishes. Particular attention is given to cornice detail, brick and stone accents, or other finish items that make your home unique.

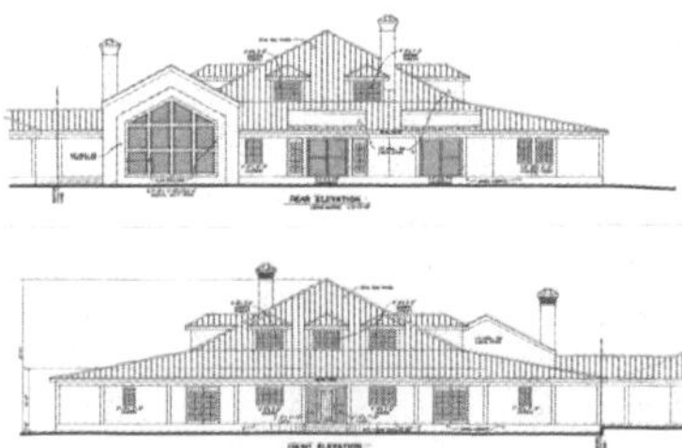

BEFORE YOU CALL

You are making a terrific decision to use a pre-drawn house plan—it is one you can make with confidence, knowing that your blueprints are crafted by national-award-winning certified residential designers and architects, and trusted by builders.

Once you've selected the plan you want—or even if you have questions along the way—our experienced customer service representatives are available 24 hours a day, seven days a week to help you navigate the home-building process. To help them provide you with even better service, please consider the following questions before you call:

■ Have you chosen or purchased your lot?
If so, please review the building setback requirements of your local building authority before you call. You don't need to have a lot before ordering plans, but if you own land already, please have the width and depth dimensions handy when you call.

■ Have you chosen a builder?
Involving your builder in the plan selection and evaluation process may be beneficial. Luckily, builders know they can have confidence with pre-drawn plans because they've been designed for livability, functionality, and typically are builder-proven at successful home sites across the country.

■ Do you need a construction loan?
Construction loans are unique because they involve determining the value of something that is not yet constructed. Several lenders offer convenient contstruction-to-permanent loans. It is important to choose a good lending partner—one who will help guide you through the application and appraisal process. Most will even help you evaluate your contractor to ensure reliability and credit worthiness. Our partnership with IndyMac Bank, a nationwide leader in construction loans, can help you save on your loan, if needed.

■ How many sets of plans do you need?
Building a home can typically require a number of sets of blueprints—one for yourself, two or three for the builder and subcontractors, two for the local building department, and one or more for your lender. For this reason, we offer 5- and 8-set plan packages, but your best value is the Reproducible Plan Package. Reproducible plans are accompanied by a license to make modifications and typically up to 12 duplicates of the plan so you have enough copies of the plan for everyone involved in the financing and construction of your home.

■ Do you want to make any changes to the plan?
We understand that it is difficult to find blueprints for a home that will meet all of your needs. That is why Hanley Wood is glad to offer plan Customization Services. We will work with you to design the modifications you'd like to see and to adjust your blueprint plans accordingly—anything from changing the foundation; adding square footage, redesigning baths, kitchens, or bedrooms; or most other modifications. This simple, cost-effective service saves you from hiring an outside architect to make alterations. Modifications may only be made to Reproducible Plan Packages that include the license to modify.

■ Do you have to make any changes to meet local building codes?
While all of our plans are drawn to meet national building codes at the time they were created, many areas required that plans be stamped by a local engineer to certify that they meet local building codes. Building codes are updated frequently and can vary by state, county, city, or municipality. Contact your local building inspection department, office of planning and zoning, or department of permits to determine how your local codes will affect your construction project. The best way to assure that you can make changes to your plan, if necessary, is to purchase a Reproducible Plan Package.

■ Has everyone—from family members to contractors—been involved in selecting the plan?
Building a new home is an exciting process, and using pre-drawn plans is a great way to realize your dreams. Make sure that everyone involved has had an opportunity to review the plan you've selected. While Hanley Wood is the only plans provider with an exchange policy, it's best to be sure all parties agree on your selection before you buy.

CALL TOLL-FREE 1-800-521-6797

Source Key
HPK17

hanley wood

DREAM HOME SOLUTIONS

CUSTOMIZE YOUR PLAN – HANLEY WOOD CUSTOMIZATION SERVICES

Creating custom home plans has never been easier and more directly accessible. Using state-of-the-art technology and top-performing architectural expertise, Hanley Wood delivers on a long-standing customer commitment to provide world-class home-plans and customization services. Our valued customers—professional home builders and individual home owners—appreciate the convenience and accessibility of this interactive, consultative service.

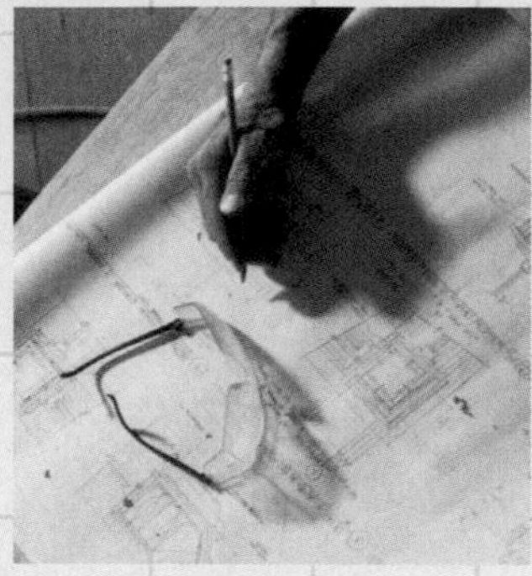

With the Hanley Wood Customization Service you can:

- Save valuable time by avoiding drawn-out and frequently repetitive face-to-face design meetings
- Communicate design and home-plan changes faster and more efficiently
- Speed-up project turn-around time
- Build on a budget without sacrificing quality
- Transform master home plans to suit your design needs and unique personal style

All of our design options and prices are impressively affordable. A detailed quote is available for a $50 consultation fee. Plan modification is an interactive service. Our skilled team of designers will guide you through the customization process from start to finish making recommendations, offering ideas, and determining the feasibility of your changes. This level of service is offered to ensure the final modified plan meets your expectations. If you use our service the $50 fee will be applied to the cost of the modifications.

You may purchase the customization consultation before or after purchasing a plan. In either case, it is necessary to purchase the Reproducible Plan Package and complete the accompanying license to modify the plan before we can begin customization.

Customization Consultation $50

TOOLS TO WORK WITH YOUR BUILDER

Two Reverse Options For Your Convenience – Mirror and Right-Reading Reverse (as available)

Mirror reverse plans simply flip the design 180 degrees—keep in mind, the text will also be flipped. For a minimal fee you can have one or all of your plans shipped mirror reverse, although we recommend having at least one regular set handy. Right-reading reverse plans show the design flipped 180 degrees but the text reads normally. When you choose this option, we ship each set of purchased blueprints in this format.

Mirror Reverse Fee (indicate the number of sets when ordering) . . $55
Right Reading Reverse Fee (all sets are reversed) $175

A Shopping List Exclusively for Your Home – Materials List

A customized Materials List helps you plan and estimate the cost of your new home, outlining the quantity, type, and size of materials needed to build your house (with the exception of mechanical system items). Included are framing lumber, windows and doors, kitchen and bath cabinetry, rough and finished hardware, and much more.

Materials List . . . .$75 each
Additional Materials Lists . . . .$20 each
(at original time of purchase only)

Plan Your Home-Building Process – Specification Outline

Work with your builder on this step-by-step chronicle of 166 stages or items crucial to the building process. It provides a comprehensive review of the construction process and helps you choose materials.

Specification Outline . . . .$10 each

Get Accurate Cost Estimates for Your Home – Quote One® Cost Reports

The Summary Cost Report, the first element in the Quote One® package, breaks down the cost of your home into various categories based on building materials, labor, and installation, and includes three grades of construction: Budget, Standard, and Custom. Make even more informed decisions about your project with the second element of our package, the Material Cost Report. The material and installation cost is shown for each of more than 1,000 line items provided in the standard-grade Materials List, which is included with this tool. Additional space is included for estimates from contractors and subcontractors, such as for mechanical materials, which are not included in our packages.

Quote One® Summary Cost Report $35
Quote One® Detailed Material Cost Report $140*
***Detailed material cost report includes the Materials List**

Learn the Basics of Building – Electrical, Pluming, Mechanical, Construction Detail Sheets

If you want to know more about building techniques—and deal more confidently with your subcontractors—we offer four useful detail sheets. These sheets provide non-plan-specific general information, but are excellent tools that will add to your understanding of Plumbing Details, Electrical Details, Construction Details, and Mechanical Details.

Electrical Detail Sheet $14.95
Plumbing Detail Sheet $14.95
Mechanical Detail Sheet $14.95
Construction Detail Sheet $14.95

SUPER VALUE SETS:
Buy any 2: $26.95; Buy any 3: $34.95; Buy All 4: $39.95

Best Value

GETTY IMAGES (2)

MAKE YOUR HOME TECH-READY – HOME AUTOMATION UPGRADE

Building a new home provides a unique opportunity to wire it with a plan for future needs. A Home Automation-Ready (HA-Ready) home contains the wiring substructure of tomorrow's connected home. It means that every room—from the front porch to the backyard, and from the attic to the basement—is wired for security, lighting, telecommunications, climate control, home computer networking, whole-house audio, home theater, shade control, video surveillance, entry access control, and yes, video gaming electronic solutions.

Along with the conveniences HA-Ready homes provide, they also have a higher resale value. The Consumer Electronics Association (CEA), in conjunction with the Custom Electronic Design and Installation Association (CEDIA), have developed a TechHome™ Rating system that quantifies the value of HA-Ready homes. The rating system is gaining widespread recognition in the real estate industry.

Developed by CEDIA-certified installers, our Home Automation Upgrade package includes everything you need to work with an installer during the construction of your home. It provides a short explanation of the various subsystems, a wiring floor plan for each level of your home, a detailed materials list with estimated costs, and a list of CEDIA-certified installers in your local area.

Home Automation Upgrade $250

GET YOUR HOME PLANS PAID FOR!

IndyMac Bank, in partnership with Hanley Wood, will reimburse you up to $600 toward the cost of your home plans simply by financing the construction of your new home with IndyMac Bank Home Construction Lending.

IndyMac's construction and permanent loan is a one-time close loan, meaning that one application—and one set of closing fees—provides all the financing you need.

Apply today at www.indymacbank.com, call toll free at 1-866-237-3478, or ask a Hanley Wood customer service representative for details.

DESIGN YOUR HOME – INTERIOR AND EXTERIOR FINISHING TOUCHES

Be Your Own Interior Designer! – Home Furniture Planner

Effectively plan the space in your home using our Hands-On Home Furniture Planner. It's fun and easy—no more moving heavy pieces of furniture to see how the room will go together. The kit includes reusable peel-and-stick furniture templates that fit on a 12"x18" laminated layout board—enough space to lay out every room in your house.

Home Furniture Planning Kit $15.95

Enjoy the Outdoors! – Deck Plans

Many of our homes have a corresponding deck plan, sold separately, which includes a Deck Plan Frontal Sheet, Deck Framing and Floor Plans, Deck Elevations, and a Deck Materials List. A Standard Deck Details Package, also available, provides all the how-to information necessary for building any deck. Get both the Deck Plan and the Standard Deck Details Package for one low price in our Complete Deck Building Package. See the price tier chart below and call for deck plan availability.

Deck Details (only) $14.95
Deck Building Package . . . . Plan price + $14.95

Create a Professionally Designed Landscape – Landscape Plans

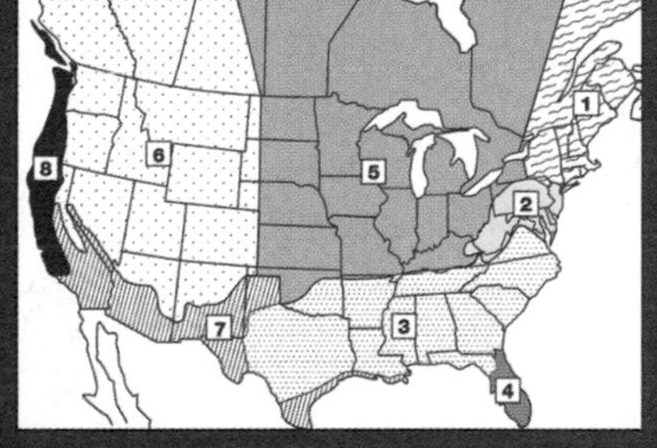

Many of our homes have a front-yard Landscape Plan that is complementary in design to the house plan. These comprehensive Landscape Blueprint Packages include a Frontal Sheet, Plan View, Regionalized Plant & Materials List, a sheet on Planting and Maintaining Your Landscape, Zone Maps, and a Plant Size and Description Guide. Each set of blueprints is a full 18" x 24" with clear, complete instructions in easy-to-read type. Our Landscape Plans are available with a Plant & Materials List adapted by horticultural experts to eight regions of the country. Please specify your region when ordering your plan—see region map below. Call for more information about landscape plan availability and applicable regions.

LANDSCAPE & DECK PRICE SCHEDULE

PRICE TIERS	1-SET STUDY PACKAGE	5-SET BUILDING PACKAGE	8-SET BUILDING PACKAGE	1-SET REPRODUCIBLE*
P1	$25	$55	$95	$145
P2	$45	$75	$115	$165
P3	$75	$105	$145	$195
P4	$105	$135	$175	$225
P5	$145	$175	$215	$275
P6	$185	$215	$255	$315

PRICES SUBJECT TO CHANGE

* REQUIRES A FAX NUMBER

TERMS & CONDITIONS

OUR 90-DAY EXCHANGE POLICY

BUY WITH CONFIDENCE!

Hanley Wood is committed to ensuring your satisfaction with your blueprint order, which is why we offer a 90-day exchange policy. With the exception of Reproducible Plan Package orders, we will exchange your entire first order for an equal or greater number of blueprints from our plan collection within 90 days of the original order. The entire content of your original order must be returned before an exchange will be processed. Please call our customer service department at 1-888-690-1116 for your return authorization number and shipping instructions. If the returned blueprints look used, redlined, or copied, we will not honor your exchange. Fees for exchanging your blueprints are as follows: 20% of the amount of the original order, plus the difference in cost if exchanging for a design in a higher price bracket or less the difference in cost if exchanging for a design in a lower price bracket. (Because they can be copied, Reproducible blueprints are not exchangeable or refundable.) Please call for current postage and handling prices. Shipping and handling charges are not refundable.

ARCHITECTURAL AND ENGINEERING SEALS

Some cities and states now require that a licensed architect or engineer review and "seal" a blueprint, or officially approve it, prior to construction. Prior to application for a building permit or the start of actual construction, we strongly advise that you consult your local building official who can tell you if such a review is required.

LOCAL BUILDING CODES AND ZONING REQUIREMENTS

Each plan was designed to meet or exceed the requirements of a nationally recognized model building code in effect at the time and place the plan was drawn. Typically plans designed after the year 2000 conform to the International Residential Building Code (IRC 2000 or 2003). The IRC is comprised of portions of the three major codes below. Plans drawn before 2000 conform to one of the three recognized building codes in effect at the time: Building Officials and Code Administrators (BOCA) International, Inc.; the Southern Building Code Congress International, (SBCCI) Inc.; the International Conference of Building Officials (ICBO); or the Council of American Building Officials (CABO).

Because of the great differences in geography and climate throughout the United States and Canada, each state, county, and municipality has its own building codes, zone requirements, ordinances, and building regulations. Your plan may need to be modified to comply with local requirements. In addition, you may need to obtain permits or inspections from local governments before and in the course of construction. We authorize the use of the blueprints on the express condition that you consult a local licensed architect or engineer of your choice prior to beginning construction and strictly comply with all local building codes, zoning requirements, and other applicable laws, regulations, ordinances, and requirements. Notice: Plans for homes to be built in Nevada must be redrawn by a Nevada-registered professional. Consult your local building official for more information on this subject.

TERMS AND CONDITIONS

These designs are protected under the terms of United States Copyright Law and may not be copied or reproduced in any way, by any means, unless you have purchased a Reproducible Plan Package and signed the accompanying license to modify and copy the plan, which clearly indicates your right to modify, copy, or reproduce. We authorize the use of your chosen design as an aid in the construction of ONE (1) single- or multifamily home only. You may not use this design to build a second dwelling or multiple dwellings without purchasing another blueprint or blueprints or paying additional design fees. Multi-use fees vary by designer—please call one of experienced sales representatives for a quote.

DISCLAIMER

The designers we work with have put substantial care and effort into the creation of their blueprints. However, because we cannot provide on-site consultation, supervision, and control over actual construction, and because of the great variance in local building requirements, building practices, and soil, seismic, weather, and other conditions, WE MAKE NO WARRANTY OF ANY KIND, EXPRESS OR IMPLIED, WITH RESPECT TO THE CONTENT OR USE OF THE BLUEPRINTS, INCLUDING BUT NOT LIMITED TO ANY WARRANTY OF MERCHANTABILITY OR OF FITNESS FOR A PARTICULAR PURPOSE. ITEMS, PRICES, TERMS, AND CONDITIONS ARE SUBJECT TO CHANGE WITHOUT NOTICE.

IMPORTANT COPYRIGHT NOTICE

From the Council of Publishing Home Designers

Blueprints for residential construction (or working drawings, as they are often called in the industry) are copyrighted intellectual property, protected under the terms of the United States Copyright Law and, therefore, cannot be copied legally for use in building. The following are some guidelines to help you get what you need to build your home, without violating copyright law:

1. HOME PLANS ARE COPYRIGHTED

Just like books, movies, and songs, home plans receive protection under the federal copyright laws. The copyright laws prevent anyone, other than the copyright owner, from reproducing, modifying, or reusing the plans or design without permission of the copyright owner.

2. DO NOT COPY DESIGNS OR FLOOR PLANS FROM ANY PUBLICATION, ELECTRONIC MEDIA, OR EXISTING HOME

It is illegal to copy, change, or redraw home designs found in a plan book, CDROM or on the Internet. The right to modify plans is one of the exclusive rights of copyright. It is also illegal to copy or redraw a constructed home that is protected by copyright, even if you have never seen the plans for the home. If you find a plan or home that you like, you must purchase a set of plans from an authorized source. The plans may not be lent, given away, or sold by the purchaser.

3. DO NOT USE PLANS TO BUILD MORE THAN ONE HOUSE

The original purchaser of house plans is typically licensed to build a single home from the plans. Building more than one home from the plans without permission is an infringement of the home designer's copyright. The purchase of a multiple-set package of plans is for the construction of a single home only. The purchase of additional sets of plans does not grant the right to construct more than one home.

4. HOUSE PLANS IN THE FORM OF BLUEPRINTS OR BLACKLINES CANNOT BE COPIED OR REPRODUCED

Plans, blueprints, or blacklines, unless they are reproducibles, cannot be copied or reproduced without prior written consent of the copyright owner. Copy shops and blueprinters are prohibited from making copies of these plans without the copyright release letter you receive with reproducible plans.

5. HOUSE PLANS IN THE FORM OF BLUEPRINTS OR BLACKLINES CANNOT BE REDRAWN

Plans cannot be modified or redrawn without first obtaining the copyright owner's permission. With your purchase of plans, you are licensed to make nonstructural changes by "red-lining" the purchased plans. If you need to make structural changes or need to redraw the plans for any reason, you must purchase a reproducible set of plans (see topic 6) which includes a license to modify the plans. Blueprints do not come with a license to make structural changes or to redraw the plans. You may not reuse or sell the modified design.

6. REPRODUCIBILE HOME PLANS

Reproducible plans (for example sepias, mylars, CAD files, electronic files, and vellums) come with a license to make modifications to the plans. Once modified, the plans can be taken to a local copy shop or blueprinter to make up to 10 or 12 copies of the plans to use in the construction of a single home. Only one home can be constructed from any single purchased set of reproducible plans either in original form or as modified. The license to modify and copy must be completed and returned before the plan will be shipped.

7. MODIFIED DESIGNS CANNOT BE REUSED

Even if you are licensed to make modifications to a copyrighted design, the modified design is not free from the original designer's copyright. The sale or reuse of the modified design is prohibited. Also, be aware that any modification to plans relieves the original designer from liability for design defects and voids all warranties expressed or implied.

8. WHO IS RESPONSIBLE FOR COPYRIGHT INFRINGEMENT?

Any party who participates in a copyright violation may be responsible including the purchaser, designers, architects, engineers, drafters, homeowners, builders, contractors, sub-contractors, copy shops, blueprinters, developers, and real estate agencies. It does not matter whether or not the individual knows that a violation is being committed. Ignorance of the law is not a valid defense.

9. PLEASE RESPECT HOME DESIGN COPYRIGHTS

In the event of any suspected violation of a copyright, or if there is any uncertainty about the plans purchased, the publisher, architect, designer, or the Council of Publishing Home Designers (www.cphd.org) should be contacted before proceeding. Awards are sometimes offered for information about home design copyright infringement.

10. PENALTIES FOR INFRINGEMENT

Penalties for violating a copyright may be severe. The responsible parties are required to pay actual damages caused by the infringement (which may be substantial), plus any profits made by the infringer commissions to include all profits from the sale of any home built from an infringing design. The copyright law also allows for the recovery of statutory damages, which may be as high as $150,000 for each infringement. Finally, the infringer may be required to pay legal fees which often exceed the damages.

BLUEPRINT PRICE SCHEDULE

PRICE TIERS	1-SET STUDY PACKAGE	5-SET BUILDING PACKAGE	8-SET BUILDING PACKAGE	1-SET REPRODUCIBLE*
A1	$450	$500	$555	$675
A2	$490	$545	$595	$735
A3	$540	$605	$665	$820
A4	$590	$660	$725	$895
C1	$640	$715	$775	$950
C2	$690	$760	$820	$1025
C3	$735	$810	$875	$1100
C4	$785	$860	$925	$1175
L1	$895	$990	$1075	$1335
L2	$970	$1065	$1150	$1455
L3	$1075	$1175	$1270	$1600
L4	$1185	$1295	$1385	$1775
SQ1				.40/SQ. FT.
SQ3				.55/SQ. FT.
SQ5				.80/SQ. FT.

PRICES SUBJECT TO CHANGE

* REQUIRES A FAX NUMBER

PRICES & OPTIONS

PLAN #	PRICE TIER	PAGE	MATERIALS LIST	QUOTE ONE®	DECK	DECK PRICE	LANDSCAPE	LANDSCAPE PRICE	REGIONS
HPK1700001	A1	18	Y						
HPK1700002	A2	19							
HPK1700003	A4	20							
HPK1700004	A2	21							
HPK1700005	A3	22	Y	Y			OLA091	P3	12345678
HPK1700006	A2	23	Y						
HPK1700007	A2	24							
HPK1700008	A2	24	Y						
HPK1700009	A4	25							
HPK1700010	A4	26							
HPK1700011	A4	27							
HPK1700012	A2	28	Y						
HPK1700013	A3	28	Y	Y	ODA025	P3	OLA085	P3	12345678
HPK1700014	A2	29	Y						
HPK1700015	A2	30							
HPK1700016	A2	30							
HPK1700017	A2	31							
HPK1700018	A2	32	Y						
HPK1700019	A2	33							
HPK1700020	A2	34							
HPK1700021	A2	34	Y						
HPK1700022	A1	35	Y						
HPK1700023	A4	36							
HPK1700024	A2	37							
HPK1700025	A4	37	Y						
HPK1700026	A4	38							
HPK1700027	A3	39	Y	Y			OLA001	P3	123568
HPK1700028	A2	40	Y						
HPK1700029	A2	41	Y						
HPK1700030	A4	42							
HPK1700031	A4	42							
HPK1700032	A4	43							
HPK1700033	A2	44							
HPK1700034	A4	45	Y						
HPK1700035	A2	46	Y						
HPK1700036	A2	46	Y						

PRICES & OPTIONS

PLAN #	PRICE TIER	PAGE	MATERIALS LIST	QUOTE ONE®	DECK	DECK PRICE	LANDSCAPE	LANDSCAPE PRICE	REGIONS
HPK1700037	A2	47	Y						
HPK1700038	A2	48							
HPK1700039	A4	48	Y						
HPK1700040	A4	49							
HPK1700041	A2	50							
HPK1700042	A3	50							
HPK1700043	A2	51							
HPK1700044	A2	52	Y						
HPK1700045	A4	53							
HPK1700046	A4	54							
HPK1700047	A4	54	Y				OLA012	P3	12345678
HPK1700048	A4	55	Y						
HPK1700049	A2	56							
HPK1700050	A2	56							
HPK1700051	A2	57	Y						
HPK1700052	A4	58	Y						
HPK1700053	A2	58	Y						
HPK1700054	A3	59	Y	Y	ODA016	P2			
HPK1700055	A4	60	Y						
HPK1700056	A2	60	Y						
HPK1700057	A2	61	Y						
HPK1700058	A4	62							
HPK1700060	A3	63							
HPK1700059	A2	64	Y						
HPK1700061	A4	65							
HPK1700062	A2	66	Y						
HPK1700063	A1	66							
HPK1700064	A3	67	Y						
HPK1700065	A2	68	Y						
HPK1700066	A3	69	Y						
HPK1700067	C4	70	Y						
HPK1700068	A2	71	Y						
HPK1700069	A2	72	Y						
HPK1700070	P6	73							
HPK1700071	A2	74	Y						
HPK1700072	A2	74	Y						

PRICES & OPTIONS

PLAN #	PRICE TIER	PAGE	MATERIALS LIST	QUOTE ONE®	DECK	DECK PRICE	LANDSCAPE	LANDSCAPE PRICE	REGIONS
HPK1700073	A4	75	Y						
HPK1700074	A2	76	Y						
HPK1700075	C4	77	Y						
HPK1700076	A2	78	Y						
HPK1700077	A4	78							
HPK1700078	A4	79	Y						
HPK1700079	A2	80	Y						
HPK1700080	A4	81							
HPK1700081	A2	82	Y						
HPK1700082	A3	84	Y						
HPK1700083	C1	85	Y						
HPK1700084	A4	86	Y						
HPK1700085	A3	87	Y						
HPK1700086	C1	88							
HPK1700087	A3	88	Y						
HPK1700088	A3	89	Y						
HPK1700089	A3	90	Y						
HPK1700090	A3	90	Y						
HPK1700091	A3	91	Y						
HPK1700092	C1	92	Y						
HPK1700093	A3	92							
HPK1700094	A3	93	Y						
HPK1700095	C1	94							
HPK1700096	C1	95	Y	Y					
HPK1700097	C1	96							
HPK1700098	C1	96							
HPK1700099	A3	97							
HPK1700100	A3	98							
HPK1700101	C1	98							
HPK1700102	C1	99							
HPK1700103	A3	100							
HPK1700104	C1	100	Y						
HPK1700105	A4	101	Y		ODA013	P2	OLA001	P3	123568
HPK1700106	C1	102							
HPK1700107	A4	103	Y						
HPK1700108	A3	104	Y						
HPK1700109	C1	104	Y						
HPK1700110	A3	105							
HPK1700111	C1	106	Y						
HPK1700112	C1	106	Y						
HPK1700113	C1	107	Y						
HPK1700114	C1	108	Y						
HPK1700115	A3	109	Y						
HPK1700116	A3	110							
HPK1700117	A3	110							
HPK1700118	C1	111							
HPK1700119	C1	112							
HPK1700120	A4	113	Y	Y					
HPK1700121	A3	114							
HPK1700122	A3	115							
HPK1700123	C2	116							
HPK1700124	C1	116	Y	Y					
HPK1700125	A4	117	Y						
HPK1700126	A4	118							
HPK1700601	A3	119	Y						
HPK1700127	A3	120							
HPK1700128	C1	121							
HPK1700129	A3	122	Y						
HPK1700130	A3	122	Y						
HPK1700131	C1	123	Y						
HPK1700132	C1	124	Y						
HPK1700133	C1	125	Y						
HPK1700134	A3	126							
HPK1700135	A2	127	Y						
HPK1700136	C1	128							
HPK1700137	A3	129	Y						
HPK1700138	A3	130	Y						

PRICES & OPTIONS

PLAN #	PRICE TIER	PAGE	MATERIALS LIST	QUOTE ONE®	DECK	DECK PRICE	LANDSCAPE	LANDSCAPE PRICE	REGIONS
HPK1700139	A4	131							
HPK1700140	A3	132	Y						
HPK1700141	A4	132	Y	Y	ODA012	P3	OLA083	P3	12345678
HPK1700142	A3	133							
HPK1700143	A3	134							
HPK1700144	A3	134	Y						
HPK1700145	A3	135	Y						
HPK1700146	C1	136	Y						
HPK1700147	A3	137	Y						
HPK1700148	A3	138	Y						
HPK1700149	C1	138							
HPK1700150	C1	139	Y						
HPK1700151	A4	140	Y						
HPK1700152	A4	140							
HPK1700153	C1	141							
HPK1700154	C1	142							
HPK1700155	C1	142							
HPK1700156	C1	143							
HPK1700157	C1	144							
HPK1700158	C1	145	Y						
HPK1700159	A4	146							
HPK1700160	A3	146							
HPK1700161	A3	147	Y						
HPK1700162	C1	148	Y						
HPK1700163	C1	149							
HPK1700164	C1	150							
HPK1700165	A3	151	Y						
HPK1700166	A3	152							
HPK1700167	C1	153							
HPK1700168	A3	154	Y						
HPK1700169	C1	155	Y						
HPK1700170	C1	156	Y						
HPK1700171	A4	158							
HPK1700172	A4	159							
HPK1700173	C1	159	Y	Y					
HPK1700174	A4	160	Y						
HPK1700175	C2	160							
HPK1700176	A4	161	Y				OLA010	P3	1234568
HPK1700177	A4	161							
HPK1700178	C2	162							
HPK1700179	C1	163	Y	Y	ODA006	P2	OLA021	P3	123568
HPK1700180	A4	164							
HPK1700181	C1	165	Y	Y			OLA037	P4	347
HPK1700182	C1	165	Y		ODA012	P3	OLA010	P3	1234568
HPK1700183	C2	166							
HPK1700184	A4	166							
HPK1700185	C1	167	Y	Y					
HPK1700186	C2	167	Y	Y					
HPK1700187	A4	168							
HPK1700188	C1	168							
HPK1700189	C2	169	Y	Y					
HPK1700190	A4	170							
HPK1700191	C2	171							
HPK1700192	SQ1	172	Y	Y			OLA038	P3	7
HPK1700193	C1	172							
HPK1700194	C2	173							
HPK1700195	A4	174	Y						
HPK1700196	C2	175							
HPK1700197	A4	176							
HPK1700198	C1	177							
HPK1700199	A4	178	Y						
HPK1700200	C2	179							
HPK1700201	C1	180	Y	Y			OLA014	P4	12345678
HPK1700202	A4	180							
HPK1700203	C2	181							
HPK1700204	A4	181							
HPK1700205	C2	182							

PRICES & OPTIONS

PLAN #	PRICE TIER	PAGE	MATERIALS LIST	QUOTE ONE®	DECK	DECK PRICE	LANDSCAPE	LANDSCAPE PRICE	REGIONS
HPK1700206	C2	183							
HPK1700207	C2	184							
HPK1700208	C1	185	Y						
HPK1700209	C1	186	Y						
HPK1700210	C2	187	Y						
HPK1700211	C1	188	Y	Y					
HPK1700212	C1	188	Y						
HPK1700213	A4	189							
HPK1700214	SQ3	190							
HPK1700215	C2	191	Y						
HPK1700216	A4	191	Y						
HPK1700217	C2	192							
HPK1700218	A4	193	Y						
HPK1700219	A4	193	Y						
HPK1700220	C1	194							
HPK1700221	C2	195							
HPK1700222	A4	196							
HPK1700223	C2	197							
HPK1700224	A4	198	Y						
HPK1700225	A4	199							
HPK1700226	C2	200							
HPK1700227	C2	201							
HPK1700228	A4	202	Y						
HPK1700229	C2	203							
HPK1700230	C1	204	Y						
HPK1700231	C2	205							
HPK1700232	C2	206							
HPK1700233	C1	207	Y						
HPK1700234	A4	208							
HPK1700235	C2	209	Y	Y					
HPK1700236	A4	210	Y						
HPK1700237	C2	210	Y						
HPK1700238	C2	211							
HPK1700239	C2	212							
HPK1700240	C2	213							
HPK1700241	C2	213							
HPK1700242	C2	214	Y						
HPK1700243	C2	215							
HPK1700244	C2	216							
HPK1700245	SQ1	216	Y						
HPK1700246	A4	217	Y						
HPK1700247	A4	218							
HPK1700248	A4	219							
HPK1700249	C2	220							
HPK1700250	C2	221							
HPK1700251	C2	222							
HPK1700252	C2	223	Y						
HPK1700253	C2	224							
HPK1700254	C1	225	Y	Y			OLA025	P3	123568
HPK1700255	C2	226							
HPK1700256	A4	227							
HPK1700257	A4	228							
HPK1700258	A4	229							
HPK1700259	A4	230							
HPK1700260	SQ1	232	Y						
HPK1700261	C1	233							
HPK1700262	C3	233	Y						
HPK1700263	C3	234	Y						
HPK1700264	C2	234							
HPK1700265	C3	235	Y						
HPK1700266	C3	235							
HPK1700267	C2	236							
HPK1700268	C3	237							
HPK1700269	C3	238	Y				OLA004	P3	123568
HPK1700270	SQ1	239	Y						
HPK1700271	C3	240							
HPK1700272	C3	241	Y						

PRICES & OPTIONS

PLAN #	PRICE TIER	PAGE	MATERIALS LIST	QUOTE ONE®	DECK	DECK PRICE	LANDSCAPE	LANDSCAPE PRICE	REGIONS
HPK1700273	C2	241	Y				OLA015	P4	123568
HPK1700274	C3	242							
HPK1700275	C3	243							
HPK1700276	C2	244	Y	Y			OLA007	P4	1234568
HPK1700277	C1	244	Y						
HPK1700278	C2	245							
HPK1700279	C3	246							
HPK1700280	C3	247							
HPK1700281	C1	248	Y						
HPK1700282	C3	249							
HPK1700283	C2	250							
HPK1700284	SQ3	251	Y						
HPK1700285	C3	252							
HPK1700286	C3	253	Y	Y					
HPK1700287	C2	253	Y	Y	ODA012	P3	OLA024	P4	123568
HPK1700288	C1	254							
HPK1700289	C3	255							
HPK1700290	C3	256							
HPK1700291	C1	257	Y						
HPK1700292	C3	258							
HPK1700293	C3	259							
HPK1700294	C3	260							
HPK1700295	C3	261							
HPK1700296	C3	262	Y						
HPK1700297	C1	262							
HPK1700298	C1	263							
HPK1700299	C3	263	Y						
HPK1700300	C1	264							
HPK1700301	C1	265	Y						
HPK1700302	C3	266							
HPK1700303	C2	267	Y						
HPK1700304	C1	268	Y						
HPK1700305	C2	269	Y						
HPK1700306	C3	270							
HPK1700307	C1	271	Y						
HPK1700308	C1	272							
HPK1700309	C1	273	Y						
HPK1700310	C1	274	Y						
HPK1700311	C3	275							
HPK1700312	C1	276	Y						
HPK1700313	C2	277	Y						
HPK1700314	C3	278							
HPK1700315	C3	279							
HPK1700316	C1	280							
HPK1700317	C3	281	Y						
HPK1700318	C2	282							
HPK1700319	C1	283							
HPK1700320	C1	284	Y				OLA091	P3	12345678
HPK1700321	C3	284	Y						
HPK1700322	C3	285							
HPK1700323	C1	285	Y						
HPK1700324	C3	286							
HPK1700325	C1	287							
HPK1700326	C1	288							
HPK1700327	C1	288							
HPK1700328	C3	289							
HPK1700329	C1	289	Y						
HPK1700330	C1	290							
HPK1700331	C3	291							
HPK1700332	C2	292							
HPK1700333	C3	293							
HPK1700334	C1	294							
HPK1700335	C1	294							
HPK1700336	SQ1	295	Y	Y					
HPK1700337	C2	295							
HPK1700338	C2	296							
HPK1700339	C3	296							

PRICES & OPTIONS

PLAN #	PRICE TIER	PAGE	MATERIALS LIST	QUOTE ONE®	DECK	DECK PRICE	LANDSCAPE	LANDSCAPE PRICE	REGIONS
HPK1700340	C2	297							
HPK1700341	C3	298							
HPK1700342	C4	298							
HPK1700343	C3	299	Y						
HPK1700344	C3	299	Y						
HPK1700345	C3	300	Y						
HPK1700346	C3	302							
HPK1700347	C4	303							
HPK1700348	C2	304							
HPK1700349	C3	304	Y	Y			OLA037	P4	347
HPK1700350	C3	305	Y	Y			OLA038	P3	7
HPK1700351	C2	306							
HPK1700352	C3	306							
HPK1700353	C4	307							
HPK1700354	C3	308	Y	Y			OLA036	P4	12356
HPK1700355	SQ3	309	Y						
HPK1700356	C4	310							
HPK1700357	SQ1	310							
HPK1700358	SQ1	311							
HPK1700359	C4	312							
HPK1700360	C2	312							
HPK1700361	C4	313							
HPK1700362	C2	314							
HPK1700363	C3	315	Y	Y	ODA007	P3	OLA018	P3	12345678
HPK1700364	C2	316							
HPK1700365	C2	317							
HPK1700366	C2	318	Y						
HPK1700367	C4	318							
HPK1700368	C4	319							
HPK1700369	C2	320							
HPK1700370	C4	320							
HPK1700371	C3	321	Y						
HPK1700372	C4	322	Y						
HPK1700373	C4	322							
HPK1700374	C2	323							
HPK1700375	C3	324							
HPK1700376	C2	324							
HPK1700377	C4	325							
HPK1700378	L1	326							
HPK1700379	C4	326							
HPK1700380	C2	327							
HPK1700381	C2	328							
HPK1700382	C4	328							
HPK1700383	C4	329							
HPK1700384	SQ1	330	Y	Y					
HPK1700385	C4	330							
HPK1700386	C2	331							
HPK1700387	C4	332							
HPK1700388	C3	332	Y	Y			OLA038	P3	7
HPK1700389	SQ1	333							
HPK1700390	C2	334							
HPK1700391	C2	335							
HPK1700392	C4	336							
HPK1700393	SQ1	336	Y						
HPK1700394	C3	337							
HPK1700395	SQ1	338	Y	Y					
HPK1700396	C4	338							
HPK1700397	SQ3	339							
HPK1700398	C4	340							
HPK1700399	C4	341	Y						
HPK1700400	C4	342							
HPK1700401	C2	343	Y						
HPK1700402	C2	344							
HPK1700403	C2	345							
HPK1700404	C2	346							
HPK1700405	C4	347							
HPK1700406	C4	348							
HPK1700407	C4	349							
HPK1700408	C2	350	Y	Y			OLA008	P4	1234568
HPK1700409	C4	351							
HPK1700410	C2	352							
HPK1700411	C2	353							
HPK1700412	C4	354	Y						
HPK1700413	C4	355							
HPK1700414	C3	356							
HPK1700415	C2	357	Y	Y			OLA038	P3	7
HPK1700416	C3	358							
HPK1700417	C2	359							
HPK1700418	C2	360							
HPK1700419	C3	360							
HPK1700420	C4	361							
HPK1700421	C3	362	Y	Y			OLA024	P4	123568
HPK1700422	SQ1	363							
HPK1700423	C2	364							
HPK1700424	C4	365							
HPK1700425	C2	366							
HPK1700433	C2	366	Y						
HPK1700434	C2	367	Y				OLA004	P3	123568
HPK1700426	C4	368							
HPK1700427	C2	369							
HPK1700428	SQ1	370					OLA010	P3	1234568
HPK1700429	C1	371							
HPK1700430	C2	372	Y						
HPK1700431	A3	373							
HPK1700432	SQ1	374	Y	Y					
HPK1700435	C3	376							
HPK1700436	SQ1	377	Y						
HPK1700437	C4	378	Y						
HPK1700438	C4	378							
HPK1700439	SQ1	379							
HPK1700440	C3	380	Y						
HPK1700441	SQ1	380							
HPK1700442	L1	381	Y						
HPK1700443	C3	382							
HPK1700444	SQ1	382							
HPK1700445	SQ1	383							
HPK1700446	SQ1	384	Y	Y					
HPK1700447	SQ3	384							
HPK1700448	C3	385							
HPK1700449	C3	386	Y						
HPK1700450	C3	386							
HPK1700451	C3	387							
HPK1700452	C3	388							
HPK1700453	C3	388	Y						
HPK1700454	SQ1	389							
HPK1700455	L1	390							
HPK1700456	C3	390							
HPK1700457	SQ1	391	Y	Y					
HPK1700458	C3	392							
HPK1700459	L1	392	Y						
HPK1700460	SQ1	393	Y						
HPK1700461	SQ1	394							
HPK1700462	C4	394	Y	Y	ODA005	P3	OLA013	P4	12345678
HPK1700463	C3	395							
HPK1700464	SQ1	396	Y						
HPK1700465	SQ1	396							
HPK1700466	L1	397							
HPK1700467	C4	398							
HPK1700468	C3	398							
HPK1700469	C3	399	Y						
HPK1700470	L1	400							
HPK1700471	SQ1	400							
HPK1700472	C3	401					OLA017	P3	123568
HPK1700473	C3	402							

PRICES & OPTIONS

PLAN #	PRICE TIER	PAGE	MATERIALS LIST	QUOTE ONE®	DECK	DECK PRICE	LANDSCAPE	LANDSCAPE PRICE	REGIONS
HPK1700474	C3	402	Y	Y	ODA016	P2	OLA006	P3	123568
HPK1700475	SQ1	403	Y						
HPK1700476	SQ1	404							
HPK1700477	C3	404							
HPK1700478	C3	405							
HPK1700479	C3	406							
HPK1700480	C4	407							
HPK1700481	L1	408							
HPK1700482	C3	408							
HPK1700483	C3	409					OLA001	P3	123568
HPK1700484	L1	410	Y	Y	ODA011	P2	OLA003	P3	123568
HPK1700485	C3	410							
HPK1700486	L1	411							
HPK1700487	C3	412							
HPK1700488	SQ1	413	Y						
HPK1700489	C3	414					OLA008	P4	1234568
HPK1700490	C3	415	Y						
HPK1700491	L1	416							
HPK1700492	C3	416	Y						
HPK1700493	L1	417							
HPK1700494	C4	418							
HPK1700495	C3	419	Y						
HPK1700496	SQ1	420							
HPK1700497	SQ1	420							
HPK1700498	C3	421	Y						
HPK1700499	L1	422							
HPK1700500	L1	423							
HPK1700501	C3	424							
HPK1700502	SQ1	425							
HPK1700503	C3	426							
HPK1700504	SQ1	427							
HPK1700505	L1	428							
HPK1700506	L1	429							
HPK1700507	SQ1	430							
HPK1700508	L1	431	Y						
HPK1700509	SQ1	432							
HPK1700510	C3	433							
HPK1700511	C3	434	Y	Y			OLA024	P4	123568
HPK1700512	SQ1	435	Y						
HPK1700513	L1	436							
HPK1700514	C4	438	Y						
HPK1700515	A4	439							
HPK1700516	SQ1	440							
HPK1700517	L1	441	Y	Y			OLA037	P4	347
HPK1700518	L2	441							
HPK1700519	C4	442							
HPK1700520	L2	443							
HPK1700521	SQ3	444	Y						
HPK1700522	L1	445							
HPK1700523	L4	446	Y						
HPK1700524	SQ1	446	Y						
HPK1700525	L2	447							
HPK1700526	SQ1	447							
HPK1700527	SQ1	448							
HPK1700528	SQ1	448							
HPK1700529	L1	449	Y	Y	ODA002	P2	OLA015	P4	123568
HPK1700530	C4	449	Y						
HPK1700531	L2	450							
HPK1700532	SQ1	451							
HPK1700533	C4	452							
HPK1700534	L2	453							
HPK1700535	C4	454							
HPK1700536	SQ1	455							
HPK1700537	SQ1	456	Y						
HPK1700538	L2	457							
HPK1700539	L2	458							
HPK1700540	C4	459							
HPK1700541	L2	459							
HPK1700542	L2	460	Y						
HPK1700543	L2	461							
HPK1700544	C4	462							
HPK1700545	C4	463	Y						
HPK1700546	SQ3	464							
HPK1700547	SQ3	465							
HPK1700548	C4	466							
HPK1700549	C4	467							
HPK1700550	L1	467					OLA008	P4	1234568
HPK1700551	C4	468							
HPK1700552	SQ1	469							
HPK1700553	L2	470	Y						
HPK1700554	L2	471							
HPK1700555	SQ3	472							
HPK1700556	SQ1	473	Y						
HPK1700557	C4	474							
HPK1700558	SQ1	475							
HPK1700559	C4	476							
HPK1700560	L2	477							
HPK1700561	C4	478							
HPK1700562	C4	479							
HPK1700563	SQ3	480							
HPK1700564	C4	481	Y						
HPK1700565	L1	481	Y	Y					
HPK1700566	C4	482							
HPK1700567	SQ1	483							
HPK1700568	L1	484	Y	Y					
HPK1700569	SQ1	485	Y						
HPK1700570	C4	486	Y	Y	ODA012	P3	OLA024	P4	123568
HPK1700571	SQ1	486	Y						
HPK1700572	L1	487							
HPK1700573	SQ1	488	Y						
HPK1700574	L1	489	Y						
HPK1700575	SQ1	489							
HPK1700576	SQ1	490							
HPK1700577	SQ1	491							
HPK1700578	SQ3	492							
HPK1700579	SQ1	493							
HPK1700580	L2	494							
HPK1700581	L3	495							
HPK1700582	L1	496							
HPK1700583	L1	496							
HPK1700584	L1	497							
HPK1700585	L2	498							
HPK1700586	SQ3	499	Y						
HPK1700587	SQ1	500	Y	Y			OLA028	P4	12345678
HPK1700588	L2	500							
HPK1700589	SQ1	501	Y	Y			OLA008	P4	1234568
HPK1700590	SQ1	502	Y						
HPK1700591	L2	503							
HPK1700592	L2	504							
HPK1700593	L1	505							
HPK1700594	C4	506	Y						
HPK1700595	L2	507							
HPK1700596	C4	508	Y						
HPK1700597	SQ1	509	Y						
HPK1700598	SQ1	509	Y						
HPK1700599	L1	510							
HPK1700600	L3	511							

STYLE & SQUARE FOOTAGE

PLAN #	PAGE	SQUARE FOOTAGE
CONTEMPORARY		
HPK1700067	70	1148
HPK1700012	28	1292
HPK1700035	46	1405
HPK1700075	77	1480
HPK1700060	63	1484
HPK1700078	79	1484
HPK1700051	57	1495
HPK1700129	122	1659
HPK1700092	92	1680
HPK1700228	202	2037
HPK1700185	167	2133
HPK1700192	172	2226
HPK1700193	172	2237
HPK1700242	214	2265
HPK1700198	177	2293
HPK1700202	180	2376
HPK1700203	181	2387
HPK1700252	223	2393
HPK1700208	185	2412
HPK1700325	287	2768
HPK1700329	289	2807
HPK1700332	292	2880
HPK1700275	243	2907
HPK1700363	315	3082
HPK1700387	332	3124
HPK1700394	337	3200
HPK1700355	309	3312
HPK1700432	374	3443
HPK1700436	377	3556
HPK1700479	406	3689
HPK1700462	394	3715
HPK1700507	430	3970
HPK1700539	458	4139
HPK1700547	465	4228
HPK1700585	498	5725

PLAN #	PAGE	SQUARE FOOTAGE
COUNTRY		
HPK1700001	18	972
HPK1700064	67	992
HPK1700002	19	996
HPK1700065	68	1073
HPK1700003	20	1080
HPK1700004	21	1092
HPK1700005	22	1118
HPK1700066	69	1148
HPK1700010	26	1232
HPK1700011	27	1288
HPK1700013	28	1295
HPK1700015	30	1298
HPK1700016	30	1299
HPK1700054	59	1309
HPK1700080	81	1320
HPK1700055	60	1338
HPK1700017	31	1344
HPK1700019	33	1360
HPK1700056	60	1365
HPK1700021	34	1370
HPK1700023	36	1373
HPK1700027	39	1389
HPK1700028	40	1390
HPK1700036	46	1408
HPK1700037	47	1416
HPK1700039	48	1426
HPK1700040	49	1429
HPK1700043	51	1455
HPK1700044	52	1467
HPK1700058	62	1467
HPK1700073	75	1470
HPK1700046	54	1477

STYLE & SQUARE FOOTAGE

PLAN #	PAGE	SQUARE FOOTAGE
HPK1700074	76	1479
HPK1700050	56	1492
HPK1700053	58	1498
HPK1700126	118	1508
HPK1700167	153	1509
HPK1700083	85	1517
HPK1700085	87	1580
HPK1700086	88	1583
HPK1700601	119	1583
HPK1700137	129	1584
HPK1700138	130	1597
HPK1700139	131	1606
HPK1700128	121	1658
HPK1700141	132	1669
HPK1700131	123	1684
HPK1700093	92	1688
HPK1700144	134	1737
HPK1700098	96	1749
HPK1700145	135	1753
HPK1700102	99	1792
HPK1700104	100	1827
HPK1700105	101	1830
HPK1700106	102	1832
HPK1700148	138	1838
HPK1700149	138	1844
HPK1700150	139	1853
HPK1700153	141	1862
HPK1700109	104	1864
HPK1700154	142	1866
HPK1700110	105	1869
HPK1700155	142	1871
HPK1700151	140	1875
HPK1700111	106	1879
HPK1700156	143	1879
HPK1700112	106	1882
HPK1700115	109	1895
HPK1700157	144	1928
HPK1700119	112	1933
HPK1700162	148	1936
HPK1700160	146	1952
HPK1700133	125	1968
HPK1700123	116	1973
HPK1700164	150	1995
HPK1700177	161	2061
HPK1700178	162	2072
HPK1700179	163	2076
HPK1700180	164	2086
HPK1700215	191	2086
HPK1700182	165	2090
HPK1700183	166	2096
HPK1700230	204	2103
HPK1700217	192	2115
HPK1700220	194	2139
HPK1700232	206	2146
HPK1700189	169	2170
HPK1700190	170	2172
HPK1700237	210	2183
HPK1700239	212	2215
HPK1700221	195	2246
HPK1700195	174	2267
HPK1700222	196	2272
HPK1700243	215	2275
HPK1700244	216	2276
HPK1700200	179	2322
HPK1700245	216	2324
HPK1700248	219	2335
HPK1700223	197	2338
HPK1700250	221	2350
HPK1700251	222	2351
HPK1700204	181	2387
HPK1700206	183	2400

STYLE & SQUARE FOOTAGE

PLAN #	PAGE	SQUARE FOOTAGE
HPK1700207	184	2403
HPK1700225	199	2438
HPK1700210	187	2454
HPK1700256	227	2476
HPK1700214	190	2491
HPK1700279	246	2500
HPK1700296	262	2506
HPK1700299	263	2511
HPK1700301	265	2518
HPK1700302	266	2530
HPK1700303	267	2558
HPK1700281	248	2562
HPK1700282	249	2568
HPK1700305	269	2594
HPK1700283	250	2619
HPK1700311	275	2631
HPK1700312	276	2633
HPK1700285	252	2644
HPK1700286	253	2658
HPK1700287	253	2658
HPK1700314	278	2684
HPK1700316	280	2695
HPK1700321	284	2756
HPK1700322	285	2757
HPK1700324	286	2762
HPK1700326	288	2772
HPK1700268	237	2777
HPK1700291	257	2797
HPK1700292	258	2806
HPK1700331	291	2842
HPK1700293	259	2884
HPK1700333	293	2889
HPK1700294	260	2910
HPK1700336	295	2935
HPK1700276	244	2946
HPK1700339	296	2953
HPK1700341	298	2989
HPK1700342	298	2990
HPK1700374	323	3006
HPK1700360	312	3042
HPK1700347	303	3074
HPK1700380	327	3078
HPK1700382	328	3096
HPK1700383	329	3098
HPK1700365	317	3102
HPK1700385	330	3112
HPK1700386	331	3121
HPK1700389	333	3139
HPK1700391	335	3195
HPK1700393	336	3200
HPK1700397	339	3219
HPK1700398	340	3220
HPK1700399	341	3224
HPK1700401	343	3245
HPK1700403	345	3253
HPK1700404	346	3260
HPK1700352	306	3270
HPK1700353	307	3271
HPK1700368	319	3285
HPK1700414	356	3320
HPK1700370	320	3411
HPK1700421	362	3434
HPK1700428	370	3435
HPK1700371	321	3439
HPK1700468	398	3570
HPK1700469	399	3574
HPK1700470	400	3585
HPK1700438	378	3589
HPK1700471	400	3590
HPK1700456	390	3593
HPK1700455	390	3618

STYLE & SQUARE FOOTAGE

PLAN #	PAGE	SQUARE FOOTAGE
HPK1700440	380	3623
HPK1700511	434	3722
HPK1700481	408	3728
HPK1700442	381	3743
HPK1700443	382	3766
HPK1700486	411	3775
HPK1700493	417	3855
HPK1700494	418	3855
HPK1700448	385	3886
HPK1700503	426	3923
HPK1700505	428	3946
HPK1700510	433	3990
HPK1700514	438	4038
HPK1700531	450	4045
HPK1700517	441	4116
HPK1700546	464	4211
HPK1700518	441	4227
HPK1700559	476	4407
HPK1700560	477	4430
HPK1700561	478	4444
HPK1700562	479	4455
HPK1700563	480	4464
HPK1700595	507	4488
HPK1700520	443	4554
HPK1700521	444	4652
HPK1700570	486	4826
HPK1700522	445	5043
HPK1700572	487	5121
HPK1700523	446	5158
HPK1700524	446	5186
HPK1700578	492	5466
HPK1700580	494	5583
HPK1700582	496	5693
HPK1700583	496	5713
HPK1700584	497	5716

EARLY AMERICAN		
HPK1700069	72	1246
HPK1700026	38	1383
HPK1700072	74	1468
HPK1700076	78	1480
HPK1700077	78	1482
HPK1700101	98	1768
HPK1700166	152	1788
HPK1700125	117	1997
HPK1700227	201	2023
HPK1700216	191	2101
HPK1700191	171	2191
HPK1700238	211	2214
HPK1700240	213	2225
HPK1700241	213	2227
HPK1700253	224	2396
HPK1700255	226	2426
HPK1700257	228	2482
HPK1700298	263	2508
HPK1700306	270	2594
HPK1700266	235	2639
HPK1700315	279	2685
HPK1700328	289	2784
HPK1700290	256	2797
HPK1700274	242	2869
HPK1700334	294	2898
HPK1700373	322	3001
HPK1700375	324	3021
HPK1700381	328	3093
HPK1700384	330	3104
HPK1700367	318	3201
HPK1700395	338	3202
HPK1700406	348	3284
HPK1700416	358	3335

STYLE & SQUARE FOOTAGE

PLAN #	PAGE	SQUARE FOOTAGE
HPK1700417	359	3397
HPK1700425	366	3442
HPK1700484	410	3754
HPK1700487	412	3777
HPK1700506	429	3946
HPK1700529	449	4008
HPK1700532	451	4045
HPK1700535	454	4088
HPK1700549	467	4231
HPK1700551	468	4286
HPK1700557	474	4387
HPK1700575	489	5220
HPK1700593	505	5730

EUROPEAN		
HPK1700170	156	996
HPK1700033	44	1399
HPK1700061	65	1491
HPK1700088	89	1595
HPK1700089	90	1612
HPK1700143	134	1727
HPK1700122	115	1964
HPK1700134	126	1991
HPK1700172	159	2007
HPK1700186	167	2150
HPK1700187	168	2163
HPK1700188	168	2168
HPK1700194	173	2259
HPK1700197	176	2288
HPK1700205	182	2388
HPK1700254	225	2403
HPK1700280	247	2508
HPK1700261	233	2530
HPK1700304	268	2586
HPK1700264	234	2590
HPK1700308	272	2605
HPK1700267	236	2696
HPK1700318	282	2710
HPK1700323	285	2759
HPK1700270	239	2816
HPK1700271	240	2816
HPK1700273	241	2831
HPK1700330	290	2831
HPK1700295	261	2957
HPK1700344	299	2976
HPK1700359	312	3024
HPK1700346	302	3032
HPK1700377	325	3038
HPK1700378	326	3046
HPK1700379	326	3051
HPK1700361	313	3053
HPK1700362	314	3064
HPK1700366	318	3155
HPK1700390	334	3168
HPK1700396	338	3215
HPK1700405	347	3281
HPK1700408	350	3298
HPK1700409	351	3304
HPK1700410	352	3304
HPK1700411	353	3317
HPK1700357	310	3398
HPK1700418	360	3408
HPK1700358	311	3424
HPK1700419	360	3430
HPK1700420	361	3434
HPK1700422	363	3435
HPK1700434	367	3472
HPK1700427	369	3489
HPK1700435	376	3504
HPK1700450	386	3531

STYLE & SQUARE FOOTAGE

PLAN #	PAGE	SQUARE FOOTAGE
HPK1700437	378	3556
HPK1700452	388	3565
HPK1700472	401	3595
HPK1700474	402	3645
HPK1700475	403	3667
HPK1700476	404	3680
HPK1700478	405	3683
HPK1700461	394	3690
HPK1700480	407	3705
HPK1700441	380	3723
HPK1700482	408	3732
HPK1700483	409	3736
HPK1700485	410	3769
HPK1700488	413	3793
HPK1700489	414	3825
HPK1700490	415	3841
HPK1700491	416	3843
HPK1700447	384	3877
HPK1700496	420	3878
HPK1700497	420	3886
HPK1700498	421	3889
HPK1700500	423	3901
HPK1700501	424	3904
HPK1700502	425	3912
HPK1700508	431	3977
HPK1700528	448	4005
HPK1700530	449	4040
HPK1700534	453	4087
HPK1700536	455	4097
HPK1700537	456	4106
HPK1700540	459	4166
HPK1700544	462	4194
HPK1700545	463	4200
HPK1700548	466	4228
HPK1700550	467	4264
HPK1700552	469	4328
HPK1700594	506	4328
HPK1700553	470	4339
HPK1700555	472	4363
HPK1700556	473	4371
HPK1700558	475	4399
HPK1700519	442	4478
HPK1700564	481	4578
HPK1700565	481	4648
HPK1700566	482	4669
HPK1700567	483	4699
HPK1700571	486	4949
HPK1700573	488	5130
HPK1700574	489	5134
HPK1700576	490	5235
HPK1700598	509	5277
HPK1700599	510	5296
HPK1700592	504	5305
HPK1700577	491	5388
HPK1700525	447	5426
HPK1700600	511	5469
HPK1700579	493	5518
HPK1700581	495	5590
HPK1700526	447	5603
HPK1700586	499	5816
HPK1700527	448	5878
HPK1700587	500	6000
HPK1700588	500	6259
HPK1700589	501	6312
HPK1700590	502	6462
HPK1700591	503	6970

SOUTHWESTERN		
HPK1700014	29	1298
HPK1700113	107	1883

STYLE & SQUARE FOOTAGE	PLAN #	PAGE	SQUARE FOOTAGE
	HPK1700114	108	1895
	HPK1700120	113	1934
	HPK1700219	193	2132
	HPK1700201	180	2350
	HPK1700320	284	2739
	HPK1700349	304	3144
	HPK1700356	310	3343
TRADITIONAL			
	HPK1700081	82	669
	HPK1700063	66	945
	HPK1700006	23	1140
	HPK1700008	24	1195
	HPK1700009	25	1204
	HPK1700070	73	1267
	HPK1700018	32	1360
	HPK1700020	34	1360
	HPK1700022	35	1370
	HPK1700024	37	1376
	HPK1700025	37	1377
	HPK1700029	41	1392
	HPK1700030	42	1393
	HPK1700031	42	1393
	HPK1700038	48	1417
	HPK1700079	80	1430
	HPK1700041	50	1444
	HPK1700042	50	1452
	HPK1700057	61	1466
	HPK1700045	53	1472
	HPK1700059	64	1485
	HPK1700048	55	1488
	HPK1700049	56	1488
	HPK1700345	300	1493
	HPK1700052	58	1498
	HPK1700135	127	1500
	HPK1700082	84	1501
	HPK1700136	128	1505
	HPK1700169	155	1632
	HPK1700140	132	1637
	HPK1700090	90	1643
	HPK1700091	91	1675
	HPK1700142	133	1704
	HPK1700094	93	1721
	HPK1700095	94	1724
	HPK1700096	95	1733
	HPK1700097	96	1746
	HPK1700099	97	1755
	HPK1700100	98	1759
	HPK1700146	136	1797
	HPK1700103	100	1812
	HPK1700147	137	1814
	HPK1700107	103	1836
	HPK1700108	104	1850
	HPK1700084	86	1869
	HPK1700132	124	1884
	HPK1700116	110	1895
	HPK1700118	111	1932
	HPK1700158	145	1940
	HPK1700159	146	1948
	HPK1700161	147	1958
	HPK1700163	149	1974
	HPK1700124	116	1977
	HPK1700168	154	1978
	HPK1700171	158	2003
	HPK1700174	160	2018
	HPK1700176	161	2034
	HPK1700184	166	2097
	HPK1700229	203	2100
	HPK1700218	193	2127
	HPK1700231	205	2139

STYLE & SQUARE FOOTAGE	PLAN #	PAGE	SQUARE FOOTAGE
	HPK1700233	207	2163
	HPK1700234	208	2163
	HPK1700235	209	2175
	HPK1700236	210	2182
	HPK1700196	175	2275
	HPK1700199	178	2311
	HPK1700246	217	2328
	HPK1700247	218	2335
	HPK1700249	220	2345
	HPK1700224	198	2428
	HPK1700226	200	2444
	HPK1700209	186	2452
	HPK1700211	188	2456
	HPK1700212	188	2483
	HPK1700213	189	2489
	HPK1700258	229	2498
	HPK1700259	230	2499
	HPK1700297	262	2508
	HPK1700300	264	2514
	HPK1700260	232	2517
	HPK1700262	233	2544
	HPK1700263	234	2586
	HPK1700307	271	2605
	HPK1700309	273	2606
	HPK1700310	274	2613
	HPK1700265	235	2625
	HPK1700313	277	2638
	HPK1700284	251	2639
	HPK1700288	254	2691
	HPK1700317	281	2705
	HPK1700289	255	2739
	HPK1700327	288	2773
	HPK1700343	299	2815
	HPK1700272	241	2818
	HPK1700335	294	2901
	HPK1700337	295	2949
	HPK1700338	296	2949
	HPK1700340	297	2954
	HPK1700278	245	2990
	HPK1700376	324	3033
	HPK1700429	371	3079
	HPK1700348	304	3084
	HPK1700364	316	3095
	HPK1700392	336	3197
	HPK1700402	344	3246
	HPK1700430	372	3246
	HPK1700354	308	3278
	HPK1700369	320	3305
	HPK1700412	354	3320
	HPK1700413	355	3320
	HPK1700431	373	3320
	HPK1700423	364	3436
	HPK1700372	322	3440
	HPK1700424	365	3440
	HPK1700433	366	3457
	HPK1700426	368	3479
	HPK1700449	386	3501
	HPK1700466	397	3505
	HPK1700467	398	3512
	HPK1700451	387	3538
	HPK1700513	436	3545
	HPK1700453	388	3568
	HPK1700454	389	3586
	HPK1700439	379	3615
	HPK1700457	391	3623
	HPK1700473	402	3633
	HPK1700458	392	3644
	HPK1700459	392	3681
	HPK1700477	404	3681
	HPK1700460	393	3689
	HPK1700463	395	3765

STYLE & SQUARE FOOTAGE	PLAN #	PAGE	SQUARE FOOTAGE
	HPK1700444	382	3818
	HPK1700492	416	3850
	HPK1700495	419	3863
	HPK1700464	396	3904
	HPK1700465	396	3921
	HPK1700504	427	3936
	HPK1700509	432	3980
	HPK1700512	435	3985
	HPK1700533	452	4050
	HPK1700538	457	4137
	HPK1700541	459	4176
	HPK1700543	461	4188
	HPK1700554	471	4353
	HPK1700515	439	4658
	HPK1700568	484	4750
	HPK1700569	485	4759
	HPK1700597	509	4776
TRANSITIONAL			
	HPK1700007	24	1151
	HPK1700032	43	1395
	HPK1700087	88	1593
	HPK1700152	140	1859
	HPK1700165	151	1999
	HPK1700319	283	2737
	HPK1700277	244	2962
	HPK1700400	342	3239
	HPK1700407	349	3293
	HPK1700445	383	3828
	HPK1700499	422	3900
	HPK1700516	440	4096
	HPK1700542	460	4184
	HPK1700596	508	4517
VACATION			
	HPK1700068	71	1176
	HPK1700071	74	1286
	HPK1700034	45	1404
	HPK1700047	54	1487
	HPK1700062	66	1498
	HPK1700127	120	1650
	HPK1700130	122	1670
	HPK1700117	110	1899
	HPK1700121	114	1950
	HPK1700173	159	2015
	HPK1700175	160	2019
	HPK1700181	165	2086
	HPK1700269	238	2794
	HPK1700388	332	3136
	HPK1700350	305	3163
	HPK1700351	306	3231
	HPK1700415	357	3328
	HPK1700446	384	3838